GIFTS

GIFTS

A STUDY IN COMPARATIVE LAW

RICHARD HYLAND

OXFORD
UNIVERSITY PRESS

OXFORD
UNIVERSITY PRESS

Oxford University Press, Inc., publishes works that further Oxford University's objective of excellence in research, scholarship, and education.

Oxford   New York
Auckland   Cape Town   Dar es Salaam   Hong Kong   Karachi   Kuala Lumpur   Madrid   Melbourne
Mexico City   Nairobi   New Delhi   Shanghai   Taipei   Toronto

With offices in
Argentina   Austria   Brazil   Chile   Czech Republic   France   Greece   Guatemala   Hungary   Italy
Japan   Poland   Portugal   Singapore   South Korea   Switzerland   Thailand   Turkey   Ukraine
Vietnam

Library of Congress Cataloging-in-Publication Data
Hyland, Richard, 1949–
   Gifts: a study in comparative law / Richard Hyland.
      p. cm.
   Includes bibliographical references and index.
   ISBN-13: 978-0-19-534336-6 (alk. paper)
   1. Gifts—Law and legislation. 2. Conflict of
   laws—Gifts. I. Title.
   K898.H95 2009
   340.9'4—dc22   2008003518

1 2 3 4 5 6 7 8 9
Printed in the United States of America on acid-free paper

Man Ray, *Le cadeau* (The Gift)
(c. 1958, replica of the 1921 original)

for António Hespanha, Detlef Leenen, Dennis Patterson, and Pablo Salvador Coderch, my friends in the law, this foreign country

As soon as [Dylan] Thomas learned that my informant was
—like most of us—a professor of comparative literature,
he asked: "What do you compare it with?"

—Harry Levin
"Comparing the Literature"

CONTENTS

ACKNOWLEDGMENTS

I began writing this book twenty years ago to repay the debt I owe to three of my teachers. It took somewhat longer than expected, and it is now a little late. Two of them, unfortunately, are no longer alive to receive it.

Peter Schlechtriem asked me to write this book the day I told him I had found a job teaching law. There were no congratulations, just this request. Studying with him had already convinced me that the only way to think about the law was comparatively. I was pleased with myself to receive a commission from one of the world's leading comparativists on my first day on the job. Only now do I understand what he was thinking. If he had waited, even a little, I would have figured out how much work it takes to write even a few decent pages in the law, and I would never have accepted. He wanted someone to write a book like this, and he surely also thought it would do me a lot of good—it would straighten out my misconceptions—if I were to write it. Because he thought the project was important, we argued about my ideas every time we met. With his extraordinary generosity, particularly toward foreigners, he cited an earlier draft of this book in some of his last writings, though, irritatingly, only on points about which I myself remain uncertain and for which he could find no other source. If he were still around, and I am so sorry he is not, there is no doubt he would disagree with most of what I have written. He would explain what was wrong with it in a couple of startlingly insightful sentences. I would not know how to respond, and there would be a few awkward moments of silence. Then he would remember there was a wine fair going on in some small town near Freiburg. He would smile and say we really should take a drive over there and open a bottle together.

Many years before that, in my first year in law school, I had Fritz Kessler for contracts. As we sat around talking after one of his classes, he told us he had been to a meeting of Restatement advisers, and he had expressed his view that American law should abolish the consideration doctrine. After that comment, he told us, they had decided not to invite him back. I could not understand why they would reject Fritz Kessler, the kindest and best human being I have ever met. By the time his course ended, I had decided what I would do with my life. I wanted to be like him. I am a contracts professor because he was a contracts professor. If I could get away with it, I would speak English with his incomprehensible German accent. Actually, I can imitate it a little. Whenever the occasion arises, I cannot resist speaking to my students of *ze g-rrr-eat Holmes.*

A year or so after I finished my American law degree, I applied to a graduate program in private law in Paris. Michelle Gobert was directing the program at the time. I still cannot figure out why she accepted my application. I know she is intrigued by foreign students, and I was probably one of the first Americans to apply. She surely did not realize that I had never seen the French Civil Code before she walked into the first meeting of her seminar carrying a brand-new copy of the latest Dalloz edition. The room quieted instantly. She looked us over for a long minute without speaking. I do not think anyone feels entirely comfortable in Mme Gobert's presence. She has an air about her of royalty, or of a terribly distinguished French actress. She did not welcome us or chat about administrative matters. She does not enjoy small talk. Instead, she asked simply: *L'article 2 du Code civil, qu'est-ce qu'il dit?* Article 2 of the Civil Code, what does it say?

My classmates were some of the best private law students in France. This was a question to which they knew the answer. One of them explained that article 2 provides for the nonretroactivity of the law. Mme Gobert looked at the student without smiling. Then she repeated the question. *L'article 2 du Code civil, qu'est-ce qu'il dit?* A different student mentioned Paul Roubier's suggestion that a new law may be applied to *les situations juridiques en cours*, legal affairs that are already in process. Again she repeated the question. *L'article 2 du Code civil, qu'est-ce qu'il dit?* Another student tried, and then another, each new voice attempting yet a more refined statement of the concepts involved. After each comment, she responded in the same way. It was my first French law class, so I did not know what to think. It seemed like a Zen-like version of the Socratic method. The French students were terrified. This was material they thought they knew, and yet they could not guess what was on her mind. Finally, one of the students had the presence of mind simply to read the code provision aloud. Mme Gobert's eyes lit up. *Mais bien sûr!* she responded. *C'est ça qu'il dit!* But of *course!* That's what it says!

It is always hard to understand why students take what they do from a particular class. Yet I know that the spirit behind that question—the indomitable passion for precision in the law, which is all the more intoxicating because it is impossible to achieve—set the standard I have aspired to attain on every page of this book.

The Max Planck Institute for Comparative and International Private Law in Hamburg generously made it possible for me to spend two summers in the institute's library collecting materials. Ulrich Drobnig, formerly one of the institute's directors, has constantly encouraged me. He provided research grants, read the entire manuscript, and, with his erudition and fine eye for detail, pointed out numerous errors. He also taught me how to cite a mass of foreign material in a consistent manner. Werner Lorenz kindly examined an early draft. Jürgen Basedow and Reinhard Zimmermann helped make it possible for me to publish this work with Oxford, as did Peter Gruss, president of the Max Planck Society.

Roger Dennis and Ray Solomon at the Rutgers Law School in Camden gave me support in every way they could think of and have shown the kind of patience that I did not know was compatible with law school deanship. Debbie Carr, my secretary, is the best in the business.

My friends at the Rutgers Law School Library in Camden have a magical ability to locate sources in foreign languages from small shreds of bibliographical information. I am grateful to all of them—David Batista, Hays Butler, Gloria Chao, Lucy Cox, Anne Dalesandro, Cathy Fleming, Eric Gilson, John Joergensen, Mary McGovern, and Lori Rowland. I am also grateful to Kent McKeever, Sabrina Sondhi, and their colleagues at the Arthur Diamond Library at Columbia Law School and the librarians of Biddle Library at the University of Pennsylvania Law School. This book would not have been possible if their priceless collections had not been just a walk or a train ride away. Laurent Mayali, director of the Robbins Collection in Berkeley and Sigrid Amedick at the Max Planck Institute in Frankfurt generously located rare sources for me. I am also grateful to interlibrary loan librarians all over the country who have been willing to pull rare books from their collections, pack them up, and send them to someone they have never met and whose research they know nothing about.

This project would never have made it past the mountain of photocopies without Jim Morgan's help. He developed a filing system for the boxes of photocopies and spent a year filing the sources in such a way that I have always been able to find them. He has also helped by repeatedly asking when this book was finally going to be published. Over the past fifteen years, dozens of other Rutgers students have worked tirelessly on this book as research assistants. Todd Fox, Jason Cohen, and Brian Bailey were among them. I am lucky that so many gifted students pass through my life at Rutgers. I enjoy working with them immensely, but I now have to admit that it never occurred to me to keep track of who exactly was involved in which of my projects. I am grateful to them all, and embarrassed that I have found no way to discover all their names in order to list them here.

Jeremy Thompson and Sarah Wahlberg helped me translate some of the Latin texts. Annette Beier, Miriam Nabinger, and Ole Böger updated references to the German commentaries. Annette also showed me the kind of hospitality in Heidelberg I always dream of being able to show to others. I think I owe Miriam a letter of recommendation.

A few lawyers, judges, and scholars have been kind enough to review some of what I have written about their legal systems or fields of scholarship. They have all added to the accuracy of the descriptions, though, it goes without saying, the errors that remain are my own. I am grateful to Tracy Andrews, Peter Bogaert, Allain Caillé, Rohit De, Pablo De Doncker, Volker Drecktrah, Georges Durry, Mel Eisenberg, Jay Feinman, Michael Furmston, Antonio Gambaro, Jacques Godbout, Carlos Gómez, Andrew Halpin, Carsten Jungmann, John Langbein, Franziska Leonhardt, Michael Moody, Craig Oren, Alex Pospisil, Rebecca Probert, Sonia Ramos, Anna Riberti, and Martin Schmidt-Kessel. I also benefited greatly from suggestions made by fellow participants in the Fourth Works-in-Progress

Workshop, sponsored jointly by the American Society of Comparative Law and Princeton's Law and Public Policy Program.

I am grateful to my editors and production team at Oxford—Larry Selby, Chris Collins, Isel Pizarro, Diem Bloom, Manojkumar Lakshmanan, and Jaimee Biggins. My copyeditor, Shea Spindler, has a wonderful eye for detail. Two anonymous reviewers read the first chapters and made important suggestions that led to a complete revision of the text.

António Hespanha, Detlef Leenen, Dennis Patterson, and Pablo Salvador Coderch have taught me that friendship is an art form. I have spent much of my adult life regretting that I will never be able to find an appropriate way to reciprocate their gestures of friendship, large and small—from saving my life (literally) to causing me rare moments of bliss. Even after having studied generosity for twenty years, I still cannot understand how they are able to do their own very important work and yet always find time for their friends. I wish I could do that.

Dave King, William Logan, and Legs McNeil are more than, closer than, friends. Though they almost certainly will never read a word of this book, they inspire pretty much everything I write.

To Sharka, Rivka, Lorenzo, Toman, and Libuše—all my love.

PREFACE

I have discerning friends who read widely in the natural and social sciences and the humanities but who would never read a book about the law. I have never understood why this is. Of course, many law books are uninspiring, but so are many other books. For some reason, the law seems inherently uninteresting. But why are questions of unconscionability, good faith purchase, and apparent agency necessarily less rewarding than the diet of the Nambikwara?

The problem is even worse than it seems. Even lawyers do not read law books. They consult them, read a couple of pages that might be relevant to the brief they are writing, but they do not take law books home with them. Yet more strangely, this also applies to law professors, especially in the United States. We keep up with the articles in our field, but it is rare for us to sit down with a book about the law and read it through. After teaching for a few years, most of us have developed a personal theory about how the law works. No amount of discussion or case law can convince us that our theories might be wrong. And so most law books, like most talks at the faculty seminar, either tell us something we already know or else they seem to get it very wrong.

This goes even for the classic books of the common-law tradition. There are maybe two dozen books that might legitimately make the claim to be included in the list of the common law's ten great books. Whichever books one puts on that list, it is extremely unlikely that more than a handful of the members of the law-teaching profession has read all ten of them from beginning to end. My guess is that it is less than that, which in any other field would be absurd. It is therefore clear that, now that my parents are no longer alive, no one will ever read this book through from cover to cover. It might be said of it what Byron once said of the work of Southey—Robert Southey, then poet laureate of England. It will be read long after Homer is forgotten. But only then.

Nonetheless, someone might eventually run across the book in a library and open it, if only to see why so many pages have been devoted to a topic as obscure as the law governing the giving of gifts. It therefore might be useful to explain for whom the book was written. I have had four different readers in mind.

The first is the lawyer or scholar, in the United States or abroad, who practices or writes in the various fields that touch on gift law, including the law of trusts and estates—successions law as it is known to the civilians—and the laws of contract and restitution. A surprising number of cases in these fields now involve gifts that have contacts with more than one jurisdiction. A detailed guide to how gifts are treated in the major common- and civil law systems may therefore prove useful. Though the number of legal systems considered here is limited, this survey manages to include many of the ideas that are discussed in modern legal systems. One problem, of course, as with all books about positive law, is that it will already be out of date by the time it is released. Laws are revised; case law evolves. But this area of the law is complex, and the revisions, which now seem to have become frequent, are often designed to eliminate the problems created by a previous generation's choices. This book discusses the foundational issues in the field in a way that may make it easier to understand the new developments.

Second, the book may interest those who write and teach in the field of comparative law, as well as those who have wondered how, or why, laws should be compared. For reasons that, upon reflection, are obvious and that I have tried to explain elsewhere,[1] broad-based comparative studies are rare, in any field of the law. In fact, this may be the first wide-ranging, detailed comparative study of the law governing the giving of gifts ever attempted, at any time in any language.[2] Because many of the sources are difficult to find, I have done my best to pack this book full of information—rules, principles, exceptions, and case holdings, history, policy, and doctrinal justifications. My goal has been to provide data to those who think about the differences between the civil and the common laws, data that can be used to support their theories and criticize the theories of others, whatever those theories happen to be. I too have a theory about these differences, but I have done my best not to make it a part of this book.

Third, I have written this book for those who are engaged in comparative work in fields of study other than the law. As will become clear in chapter 2, the methodological difficulties in comparative law have not been settled. It surprised me, though of course it should not have, to discover that the confusion seems to

---

1. Hyland (2007) 1139–1151.

2. I have encountered nothing similar in English, French, German, Italian, or Spanish. John Dawson's brilliant book, discussed at length below, is a different enterprise. Moreover, no scholar who writes in any of these languages has, to my knowledge, cited to such a study in another language.

Nonetheless I am haunted by a memory. The library where I was working was about to close for the evening. Because I wanted to leave town the next morning, I was rushing to finish my photocopying. The last of the volumes I had gathered was written in a language I do not speak. It might have been Romanian, or maybe Polish. It was a thick book, and, as I remember it, a book written in the 1950s, printed on the acidic paper used at the time for European law books. I could read the title and enough of the table of contents to recognize it as a detailed comparative study of the law of gifts in the major legal systems.

I had five minutes to decide what to do with the book. I now realize I should have photocopied the title page, the copyright page, and the table of contents and filed them away. But I was tired and not thinking clearly. I already had more material than I would ever be able to read. And I knew I would never read an entire book in a language I do not speak. So I left the book on the table next to the copier. I have never run across it again. I have also never seen it cited. I would now give a lot for that book. But I am no longer sure the book is actually a memory, and not simply a dream.

be present whenever comparison is attempted in any field.³ The method that is used here—or, since *method* is much too serious a word for the intuition that lies at the base of this book, I will just call it a thought—is borrowed from discussion about comparison in the social sciences. I hope that, by presenting gift law from the point of view of other disciplines, I help to include the law in the interdisciplinary conversation about the practice and purpose of comparison.

Finally, I have written this book for those who think about gift giving from the perspective of the humanities and the social sciences. The gift has created an extraordinary interdisciplinary conversation, one of the most exciting in all of the human sciences. During the course of these discussions, some scholars occasionally make forays into the law, either into current law or into the long history of the law of gifts. The difficulty is that few nonlawyers have direct access either to the relevant legal norms or to the justifications that are offered to support them. The reason is that it takes an entire academic career—to this I can testify—to learn enough law to be able to make sense of the cases and legal scholarship on these questions. In many legal systems, principal among them the common law, gift law includes, or relies on, some of the most arcane conceptual structures elaborated in any legal system. As a practical matter, it is impossible for any nonlawyer to read and understand the original sources of gift law. Some of the questions are so complex that I now wonder whether even a career studying this material is sufficient preparation for the task.

I have decided that it would not really assist nonjurists to present this material without using legal concepts. As a result, I use legal concepts from the private law to explain the legal concepts involved in gift law. That may make this book seem difficult, but it is not. To the contrary, it offers a means for nonlawyers from any country to acquire a basic common-law legal vocabulary, much as law students do during their first year of law school. Because I have tried to translate the foreign legal concepts, all that is needed is a willingness to look up a few words in an English dictionary. For this purpose I recommend an unabridged dictionary rather than the legal dictionaries, which, in the languages I know, are inadequate and misleading.

Graz, in the garden of Gasthaus Meinhart
June 2008

---

3. "The most serious sign of the precarious state of our study [of comparative literature] is the fact that it has not been able to establish a distinct subject matter and a specific methodology." Wellek 282. "[A] *methodology* of comparative political analysis does not really exist." Lijphart 682 (emphasis in original).

1. THE CONTEXT OF GIFT LAW

1. *Prohibition.* The French revolutionaries abhorred gift giving. And the gifts they most detested were those that parents were in the habit of giving to their children. As soon as the occasion presented itself, the National Convention prohibited those gifts. It forbade them all, absolutely and without exception. Because this book explores why the legal mind so often concludes that gift giving is a danger to society, it seems reasonable at the outset to ask how the revolutionaries justified their position.

2. *Absolute control.* Gratuitous transfers had played a role in French family life for a thousand years. Though laws and customs varied greatly by region and period, at the end of the *ancien régime* primogeniture generally governed descent among the nobility. The eldest son took the château and at least half of the family's real estate.[1] Succession rights among commoners were complex. Both rich and poor peasants in the Mediterranean south followed the Roman law tradition that allowed the father to chose his heir (*coutume de préciput*).[2] The father's goal was to avoid fragmenting his estate. He gave his property to his heir and left his other children with a scanty inheritance.[3] To pass his property to his favorite son, the father used three traditional forms of gratuitous transfer (*libéralité*)—the *inter vivos* gift (a gift completed while the donor is alive), the last will and testament, and the contractual designation of a principal heir (*institution contractuelle*)—and excused his heir from having to return the property to the executor of the father's estate (*dispense de rapport*).[4] As Le Roy Ladurie explained, gifts were the instruments the father used to reach beyond his grave to impose inequality and to guarantee that his property would remain intact.[5]

To the revolutionaries, the family father was a despot, an absolute monarch within his small realm who tolerated no disobedience.[6] Yet even despots cannot escape the consequences of their actions. By privileging one of his offspring, the

---

1. Traer 42; Ourliac and Malafosse 401–406.
2. Le Roy Ladurie 61–65.
3. Id. 62.
4. Yver 155–226.
5. Le Roy Ladurie 63.
6. Traer 41.

father left his daughters and his other sons at the mercy of the heir.[7] The selection so often turned sibling against sibling that many fathers kept their choice a secret so they might die in peace. When Chancellor d'Aguesseau, the creator of modern civilian gift law, first proposed the Ordinance of 1731, the regional *parlements* were outraged at its publicity provisions. If the father could not keep his choice confidential, he would be pulled into the rancor that his choice often generated.[8]

3. *Reform.* As soon as the Bastille fell, pamphleteers and petitioners began to rage against the unequal inheritance rules that seemed to be responsible for favoritism, feudalism, and geographic particularism.[9] The petitions argued that only an end to gift giving could restore equality within the family, permit love within households, and end the tyranny of the strong over the weak.[10] Political clubs formed to press for a more egalitarian system.

The revolutionaries immediately took up the cause and dismantled the successions law of the ancien régime piece by piece.[11] They passed many statutes and decrees, all with the same goal: to institute absolute equality among heirs of the same degree. In 1790, the National Assembly abolished primogeniture.[12] In a hushed moment in April 1791, Talleyrand read to the Assembly a speech Mirabeau had dictated as he was dying.[13] The marquess argued that it violated the laws of nature and the principle of equality to permit parents to leave unequal shares to their children. He proposed that parents be permitted to make gratuitous transfers of only one tenth of their estates. The remainder was to be divided equally among heirs of the same degree. Robespierre rose to second the critique.[14] The Assembly voted to require intestate estates to be divided equally among the testator's children, regardless of gender or birth order.[15]

---

7. Once the heir was chosen every other member of the household was marked in the eyes of village society on a subtle scale of deference and respect. Monteil likened the nominated heirs of the bourgeois families of Rodez to petty kings with the cadets acting as subjects .... [E]ach rural collectivity possessed an invisible superstructure of biological and emotional obligations as well. The constraints of kinship and household position were tenacious and allowed little freedom of manoeuvre. Jones (1985) 101.

8. Regnault 594; Lagarde 25–26.

9. Desan 145, 167.

10. Id. 171.

11. Traer 158.

12. Decree of 15 Mar. 1790 art. 11. Most remaining feudal privileges were abolished by the Decree of 13 Apr. 1791.

13. Mirabeau, "Discours sur l'égalité des partages dans les successions en ligne directe" (2 Apr. 1791), in 24 Mavidal and Laurent 510–515.

14. Discussion contribution (5 Apr. 1791), in id. 562–564.

15. Decree of 8 Apr. 1791 art. 1.

The reforms grew more egalitarian as the revolution became more radical.[16] In 1793, little more than a month after the Convention voted to execute Louis XVI, the deputies attacked the remaining vestiges of paternal power. France was at war with most of Europe. Prices were rising, the sansculottes were rioting, and counterrevolutionaries were active everywhere. Parents who favored the old regime had discovered that they could prevent their children from participating in the revolution by threatening them with disinheritance.[17] The Convention decided to prevent its enemies from using successions law as a weapon. It decreed that children should inherit equally and charged a committee to present a draft.[18] Pénières again raised the issue two days later and asked that a committee consider how to prevent disinheritance.[19] The root of the problem, in Mailhe's view, was the right to make a will. He proposed that it be abolished and asked that the matter be referred to committee. Gensonné made clear that if anything was to be done it had to be done quickly. Once it became known that the Convention was considering abolishing testamentary succession, the revolution's opponents would make alternative arrangements and the chance for change would be lost for a generation. Lamarque suggested that there was no need to abolish the right to make a will. The Convention could prohibit legacies in direct line while permitting bequests to collateral relatives. Buzot thought that any concessions would benefit the enemy. A parent could simulate a sale to a relative, who would then leave the property to the parent's chosen heir. Mailhe explained that, by the same reasoning, inter vivos gifts and the contractual designation of an heir should be abolished as well. Prieur de la Marne trumped all the others by demanding that the prohibitions operate retroactively to the fall of the Bastille. "Without that, you sacrifice the younger descendents who are devoted to the Revolution; you endorse the hatred fathers have for their patriotic children."[20] Duroy rose with a point of order. To avoid excesses resulting from momentary enthusiasm, the Convention had agreed not to enact legislation of general interest without a committee report. The others disagreed, and the vote was taken. The Convention prohibited transfers in direct line, though, for the moment, it decided not to make the prohibition retroactive. On 7 March 1793, in one of the most extraordinary of history's forgotten acts, the French legislature prohibited parents from making gratuitous transfers to their children.[21]

---

16. For a history of these reforms, see Desan 141–177.

17. Pénières, Discussion contribution (7 Mar. 1793), in 59 Mavidal and Laurent 680.

18. Decree of 5 Mar. 1793.

19. The debate cannot have lasted more than an hour. For the discussion, see 59 Mavidal and Laurent 680–683. The debate is summarized in Desan 148; 5 Duvergier 185; Carette (1843) 220–221.

20. Discussion contribution (7 Mar. 1793), in 59 Mavidal and Laurent 682.

21. "The National Convention decrees that the power to make gratuitous transfers to direct descendants, whether mortis causa, inter vivos, or by contractual gift, is abolished;

Over the next several months, as the Convention lost its taste for compromise, the prohibitions escalated. The next to go were inter vivos gifts given by parents to the prejudice of their children, whether to collateral relatives or strangers. All such gifts were invalidated back to the fall of the Bastille.[22] At the same time, the Convention voided all gifts given by collateral relatives to the prejudice of their presumptive heirs, whether to other collateral relatives or to strangers. These gifts were also retroactively invalidated back to the beginning of the revolution.[23] Retroactivity had an extraordinary reach, since heirs could receive inheritances only if they returned gifts received prior to 14 July 1789.[24] Two months later, a new decree voided all inter vivos gifts. The prohibition was made retroactive to include gifts given during the four and a half years since the fall of the Bastille.[25] Théophile Berlier, one of the decree's drafters, took the floor to explain that, because the provision restated the law of nature, it should not be considered retroactive.

> The reign of nature and reason was born on 14 July 1789. It was still feeble at the time. It is true that it rose to its true stature only later, but that was the moment it began. You have not legislated with retroactivity. Instead you have simply tied the effects to their cause. You have proclaimed that property acquired gratuitously since that great event must be distributed according to the rules that you have prescribed with regard to those who nature designated to receive them, and you have removed the obstacles that might result from contrary provisions emanating either from human beings or from the law.[26]

4. *Hérault de Séchelles*. For those who lived through those events, equality was more than a theoretical demand. The revolutionary prohibitions caused property to be seized from privileged donees and distributed to neglected heirs. For some legislators, personal and ideological interests merged. The life of Marie-Jean

---

and, as a result, that all descendants will have an equal right in the division of the property of their ascendants." Decree of 7 Mar. 1793.

22. Decree of 5 Brumaire II art. 12. Gifts to impoverished servants were maintained. Decree of 5 Frimaire II art. 1.

23. Decree of 5 Brumaire II art. 13.

24. Id. arts. 8–9; Decree of 17 Nivôse II art. 8 par. 1.

25. Decree of 17 Nivôse II art. 1 par. 1. There were numerous exceptions. For example, if the donee, at the time of the gift, had assets not exceeding 10,000 pounds (*livres*), a gift not exceeding that sum was valid. Id. art. 34. Gifts given in marriage settlements were also maintained, as were gifts given by a donor who died without relatives. Id. arts. 15, 32. The provisions of the Decree of 5 Brumaire were abrogated. Id. art. 61. Bequests (and presumably gifts) to charitable organizations were not excepted from retroactive effect. Decree of 22 Ventôse II no. 5.

26. Berlier, "Rapport d'un nouveau travail sur les donations et successions" (22 Ventôse II [12 Mar. 1794]), in 86 Mavidal and Laurent 388 no. 76

Hérault de Séchelles is exemplary. He seems to have been instrumental in lobbying for retroactivity.[27]

Hérault came from a distinguished family of the *noblesse de robe*. His great-grandfather had served as Louis XIV's finance minister and had given his name to the Seychelles archipelago. Hérault was first cousin to the Duchess of Polignac, a confidant of Marie Antoinette, who had him appointed advocate general of the Parlement of Paris while he was still eighteen. Despite his noble lineage, fully documented back to 1390, Hérault joined the revolution and was present at the storming the Bastille.[28] In December 1789 he was among the first judges appointed by the revolution. He proclaimed his zeal for the defense of freedom in his acceptance address.[29] His older judicial colleagues were offended by his comments and reported them to his grandmother. There was a heated discussion. Hérault refused to back down, broke with his family, and was disinherited. Once he was elected to the Legislative Assembly his ideas moved further to the left. He twice chaired the Convention. He was the sole author of the Declaration of the Rights of Man and of the Citizen of 1793 and the principal drafter of the Constitution of Year I (1793).[30] For close to a year, he served on the Committee of Public Safety.

A report has survived of a prerevolutionary moment that may have convinced Hérault of the dangers of gift giving. Just a few years before the revolution, Hérault, as a young magistrate, argued a gift case before the Châtelet court. The case involved a deceased donor who had made three gifts to the poor of the parish of St. Sulpice but had left nothing to his poor relatives. Hérault convinced the court to invalidate the gifts because they had not been completed using the required forms. Dominique Joseph Garat, editor of the *Journal de Paris*, jotted down Hérault's argument and described the scene in a detailed news report.[31] One phrase in the piece seems to have come directly from Hérault's plaidoyer, namely his view that, though the gifts demonstrated a laudable humanitarian sentiment, only an unenlightened mind would make gifts in those circumstances—the gifts had been dictated *par un sentiment d'humanité peu éclairée*.[32]

Less than a decade later, Hérault, then at the summit of power, miraculously found himself in a position to prohibit such unenlightened transfers. As he did, it must have seemed unjust that his zeal for liberty had left him impecunious,

---

27. Merlin de Douai, Discussion contribution, National Convention (5 Floréal III [24 Apr. 1795]), in Panckoucke and Thuau-Grandville no. 219 at 890 (9 Floréal III [28 Apr. 1795]). Merlin's comments are summarized in Carette (1843) 325–326 note 2.

28. Anchel.

29. Dard 135; Bernier 57.

30. Dard 225–226.

31. Garat 903–904; Dard 6–7.

32. Schama discusses Garat's article in his history of the French Revolution. Unfortunately, his reading of it and his report of the incident are inaccurate. Cf. Schama 162–163.

and even more unjust that equality in inheritance had been achieved only a short time after he had been disinherited. As Merlin de Douai later explained, Hérault stood to gain 80,000 pounds (*livres*) of annual income if equality among heirs was made retroactive to the fall of the Bastille.

During the discussion of the successions provisions of the draft Civil Code, the poet Fabre d'Églantine, one of Hérault's close friends, proposed making equality among heirs retroactive. Merlin de Douai and Cambacérès opposed retroactivity. They argued that it violated the prohibition against retroactive legislation contained in article 14 of the Declaration of the Rights of Man. The proponents of retroactivity responded that article 14 applied only to the criminal law. Private law norms could be given retroactive effect all the way back to the Flood. Ramel, one of the delegates, saw that Merlin was perplexed. He leaned over and explained that the idea had come from Hérault, who had drafted the Declaration of the Rights of Man with retroactivity in mind.[33] Several orators had criticized the retroactivity provision in the Declaration for its limitation to penal matters, but Hérault had insisted and his draft had passed.

The retroactive prohibition of gift giving was also approved, and the legislative committee was asked to draft appropriate legislation. Merlin and Cambacérès, who were on the committee, refused to work on a measure with which they so strongly disagreed.[34] They eventually charged Berlier with the task because he had been out of the country during the debates. He too adamantly refused and even tried to resign to avoid the task.

Once the decree was drafted and approved, the Convention was deluged with petitions from outraged peasants demanding that it be rescinded.[35] During the debate on those petitions, Merlin rose to explain the circumstances that had led Hérault to suggest retroactivity. Merlin favored prohibiting parental gifts and agreed that heirs should take equally, but he thought the retroactivity provision was excessive. His proposal that it be suspended was passed. Moreover, article 14 of the Declaration of the Rights of Man was subsequently revised to prohibit retroactive legislation in the civil law as well, a prohibition that still survives (CC art. 2).

Hérault de Séchelles was not present at that debate and never had the chance to defend himself against the conflict-of-interest charge. He had been linked with Danton, convicted of complicity with the émigrés, and guillotined a year

---

33. In 1796 Bonneville also suggested that Hérault was responsible for the retroactivity legislation. Émile Dard, Hérault's principal biographer, noted that he could not confirm that claim from the debate transcripts. Dard 136 note 1. As one of the Convention's presiding officers, however, Hérault would not have needed to make the proposal himself.

34. The lawyers in the Convention knew that d'Aguesseau had not given retroactive effect to the Ordinance of 1731. Ordinance art. 47.

35. Traer 163.

earlier, together with Danton and Fabre d'Églantine. That was just three months after the Decree of 17 Nivôse that made his fortune.

5. *Retraction.* The retroactivity provision was suspended and ultimately retracted.[36] During the deliberations on the Civil Code, Tronchet described retroactivity as "the abuse of an overheated imagination by a brilliant metaphysical theory, the destruction of all parental authority, an unjust equality."[37] It took decades for French jurists to unravel the legal chaos that retroactivity and its subsequent abrogation created.[38] In 1800, the Directory removed the mandate of equality and validated gifts and wills, provided they were done in the required formalities and did not exceed the disposable share.[39]

6. *Legacy.* It now seems extraordinary that a legislature once contemplated prohibiting parents from giving gifts to their children, a practice that has been engaged in at all times and in all places. It is stranger still that those lawmakers actually acted on their idea. The explanation for their measures seems obvious. The revolutionaries looked at gift giving through the eyes of disadvantaged siblings and focused on the role that gift giving played in the oppressive structure they were seeking to overthrow. The decrees were an aberration, a moment of excess in excited times.

Yet the history of gift law suggests that the actual explanation is more complex. Gift giving and Western law have been in conflict from the beginning. Since the first gift legislation, the *lex Cincia* of the Roman Republic, jurists have seen in gift giving a danger to family and society.[40] Though the revolutionary prohibition was eventually lifted and gifts permitted in France, a distrust of gift giving has often haunted the law. Distrust was the policy foundation for d'Aguesseau's eighteenth-century formulation of the law of gifts, the substance of which passed into the French Civil Code and ultimately into the laws of Europe and most of the civilian world. And there the suspicion about gift giving survives to this

---

36. Decree of 5 Floréal III; Decree of 9 Fructidor III; Carette (1843) 326 note 2 *in fine.*
37. Tronchet, Discussion contribution (21 Pluviôse XI [10 Feb. 1803]), in 12 Fenet 305.
38. For the attempts to manage the effects of abrogation, see Decree of 3 Vendémiaire IV; Law of 18 Pluviôse V.
39. Law of 4 Germinal VIII arts. 1, 3.
40. In the evaluation of legal acts (*Rechtsgeschäfte*) the total freedom of individual will should be considered the rule. Roman law instituted exceptions to the rule only in those rare cases that seemed to present a particular danger that the freedom might be abused. Examples include ... the limitations on gift giving, and its complete prohibition between spouses, since precisely in the case of the gift, cool self-interest can more easily take advantage of good-natured, unsuspecting carelessness than it can in other types of transactions.
Savigny (1841) 5 note d.

day, together with its constant companion, "the eternally mistreated figure of the gift."[41] It thus seems more accurate to see in the revolutionary decrees the moment in which a long-standing hostility to gift giving surfaced in pure form.

A. NOTIONS OF THE GIFT

7. *Customary norms*. The giving of gifts, perhaps more than any other field governed by the private law, is already structured by customary norms before it becomes a legal institution. Because gift giving did not develop in mutual interaction with the law, it operates with relative autonomy. Extra-legal norms and enforcement mechanisms are usually sufficient. The social understanding that competes with much of modern gift law is the insight that quite a lot occurs in society that is not, and should not be, governed by the law.

For example, the marriage ritual is almost everywhere an occasion for gift giving. The customs include fabulously intricate gift exchange in the Gujjar villages of northern India,[42] different kinds of monetary gifts offered at the traditional Jewish wedding,[43] as well as, at the minimalist extreme, the single, unreciprocated gift, usually of housewares, that a guest must bring to a wedding in the United States, or, according to some specialists, send within the year.[44] Much of the time gifts must be reciprocated, which means a return gift must be given in a value closely, but not exactly, equivalent to the opening gift.[45] Such obligations, though socially binding and usually respected, are not imposed by the legal sources. In fact, many of these norms are not written at all. Instead, they operate at such a subliminal level that we may be surprised to learn that rules are involved. In Middletown (Muncie, Indiana), the giving of Christmas gifts follows a uniform pattern, yet the participants seem to be unaware they are

---

41. García García 899.

42. Raheja 118–147.

43. Zelizer 88–89.

44. Bride's Book of Etiquette 275. Radcliffe-Brown's description of wedding gifts among the Andaman Islanders seems to describe our own customs as well. "At marriage the giving is one-sided, no return being expected, for it is an expression not of personal friendship on the part of the givers, but of the general social good-will and approval. It is for this reason that it is the duty of everybody who is present to make some gift to the newly-married pair." Radcliffe-Brown (1948) 238.

45. Schwartz 6. "Returning 'tit for tat' transforms the relation into an economic one and expresses a refusal to play the role of grateful recipient. This offense represents a desire to end the relationship or at least define it on an impersonal, non-sentimental level." Id.

following rules.[46] Perhaps most curiously of all, these rules are often not enforced. They have no explicit form, no institutional backing, and little moral sanction.

The social practice that seems most closely to resemble these aspects of gift giving is language. Gifts are actions that convey meaning.[47] Theodore Caplow concluded that every culture has a *language of prestation* to express the nature of interpersonal relationships, particularly on special occasions, just as verbal language conveys meaning in other ways.[48] The language of gift giving, Caplow suggested, is learned in early childhood and becomes assimilated to the personality as it is used with increasing assurance and understanding. Like linguistic rules, the norms governing gift giving are enforced among native speakers without being promulgated, often without a conscious understanding that the speakers are following rules. The sanction for violating the rules is the inability to communicate.

Legislation attempting to dictate language use generally proves to be ill-advised.[49] Even the spelling rules promulgated by academies, dictionaries, and grammar books are usually unable to alter actual practice.[50] If gift giving is indeed a form of language, the law, in its encounter with it, faces a unique challenge. In attempting to govern the giving of gifts, the law undertakes a mission somewhat like wrestling with Proteus—the kind of task at which generally only epic heroes have been successful.

8. *Encounter with the law.* A number of consequences flow from the primarily extra-legal character of gift giving, particularly because, in the West, the world of the law and the world of the gift inhabit such different environments. Private law is formulated for the market-related activities about which it is chiefly concerned.

---

46. Although we infer from the uniformities observed in Middletown's Christmas gift giving that, somewhere in the culture, there must be statements to which the observed behavior is a response, the crucial point is that we cannot find those statements in any explicit form. Indeed, they are not recognized by participants in the system. In effect, the rules of the game are unfamiliar to the players, even though they can be observed to play meticulously by the rules.

Caplow 1317.

47. Camerer S182. "Gift exchange, in effect, is a language that employs objects instead of words as its lexical elements." Caplow 1320.

48. Caplow id.

49. "It is beyond doubt that people will learn a new language when they perceive the economic and social advantages of doing so. And if they do not want to change to a new language, legal measures are not going to do any good .... [E]ven in situations in which people do want to acquire the new language, we find that attempts to impose it officially invariably backfire." Nunberg 121, 122 (examining numerous examples).

50. "[M]ost attempts at reform of French spelling in the last two centuries have drawn protests, and many well-meaning attempts have failed .... [T]he *Académie* did not ultimately succeed in standardizing spelling because its own members refused to abide by its rules." Schiffman 118, 298 note 78.

It has often proven incapable of grasping the fundamentally different social dynamic that governs gift giving. From the point of view of the quid pro quo that defines the law's prototypical transactions, giving something away for nothing is an inexplicable event. Whoever engages in it is either incompetent or misguided—and in need of legal protection. The law and its concepts are often designed to domesticate this dangerous world. When it cannot be domesticated, the law often attempts to limit its reach. In other words, Western gift law is a critique of gift giving. It offers the perspective of individual self-interest on activities structured by social custom.

As a first consequence, the law attempts to restrict gift giving. The law's primary goal, when it confronts this realm, is often to protect citizens from the urge to give away their property. Protection is thought to be necessary because gift giving is not based on rational self-interest to the same extent as is exchange in the marketplace. For example, the appropriate limit for gifts to relatives or to charities is not clearly established, and some legal systems are concerned that donors might easily become prodigal. Moreover, it is thought that heirs and family are victimized when the donor decides to give away the clan's wealth. The survival of the family as an institution seems to depend on confining gift giving within narrow limits.

The second consequence is the confusion gift giving creates in the law. Legal systems generally have no choice but to employ traditional private law concepts to structure the law of gifts. Unfortunately, concepts from the language of exchange are unable to describe the world of the gift. In some cases, the concepts applied in gift law cannot even be defined. They are frequently incoherent, even when examined in the terms of the legal system that created them. A further difficulty arises from the fact that judges themselves inhabit both the world of the marketplace and the world of the gift. Despite the law's protective aspirations, the case reports show that judges are constantly attempting to validate gift transfers they consider meaningful, even though those transfers would be void under the letter of the law. These case-specific judgments have transformed gift law into a maze of rules and exceptions that, in the end, conceal the courts' impromptu efforts to reconcile the law with the strikingly different world it seeks to govern. In any case, because gift law comes to gift giving with its own agenda, the legal notion of the gift coincides even less with ordinary language than is the case with other concepts in private law.

9. *Everyday notion.* In daily usage, various transactions are spoken of as gifts. These include the presents given to friends and close relatives on special occasions, transfers within the family to reduce taxes or as an advancement of inheritance, surprises between spouses, incentives given to good customers and productive members of the sales force, awards made to employees upon retirement, and donations to charity.

Particularly in civilian jurisdictions, however, these transactions are not all subject to the law of gifts to the same extent. For example, gifts of modest value—sometimes known as customary gifts—are often excluded from the scope of gift law. Due to their business context, incentives to customers and sales representatives are in some systems also not considered gifts. Gifts between spouses are commonly governed by an elaborate set of exceptions to the general rules. In some systems, special provision is made for remunerative gifts, which may include gifts given to employees upon retirement.

10. *Legal notion.* Gift law governs the enforceability and legal consequences of certain gratuitous transactions. Though legal conceptions of the gift vary considerably from one legal system to another, gift law focuses chiefly on those gratuitous transactions subject to the private law that, from the point of view of exchange and the marketplace, provide grounds for concern. These generally include larger gifts made between family members or given to charitable institutions.

As discussed in detail below, the most adequate notion of the gift for comparative law purposes involves the transfer of an interest that occurs in conjunction with four additional elements. First, the transfer is gratuitous, a characteristic that is often inferred either from the absence of a quid pro quo or from the fact that the donor acted without being obligated to do so. Second, certain subjective factors are present, usually either donative intent or the parties' agreement about the gratuitous character of the transaction. Third, the transaction takes place inter vivos, which distinguishes gifts from transfers made under a will. Finally, the object of the transfer involves rights, particularly property rights, rather than services or other types of advantage.

When these elements coincide, a number of consequences often ensue. The capacity requirements for both making and, surprisingly, even for receiving a gift are often more restrictive than those imposed on parties to nongratuitous transactions. Promises held to be gift promises are less likely to be judicially enforced than those that are part of a bargain. When it comes to making the gift transfer, some systems mandate complex form requirements. If they are lacking, the gift is usually held to be void. Some legal systems reduce the warranty obligations of the donor and, in certain circumstances, impose an obligation on the part of the donee to provide the donor with support. Furthermore, a gift may be revocable, even after it has been fully executed.

11. *Characterizations.* In a comparative perspective, the field of gift law has received a variety of systematic placements. In the common law, because executory gift promises are generally not enforceable at law, gifts are considered an aspect of property law, namely a transfer of title without consideration. The enforceability of gift promises is governed by equity. The legal systems derived from the French Civil Code tend to consider the gift and the last will and testament together as the two forms of gratuitous transfer (*libéralité*). Germanic legal systems, together with most recent civilian codifications, characterize the gift—not merely the accepted gift promise, but also the gift transfer itself—as

a contract, for which particular rules are elaborated in the special part of contract law. These differing characterizations are examined in detail below.[51]

12. *Complexity*. It would be irresponsible not to emphasize at the outset that the law that governs gift giving is one of the most complicated fields in the private law, and that is true in most of the legal systems examined here. As the extent of the complexity becomes clear, it is a perfectly understandable reaction, at least it was mine, to close the books and wonder why so much law has been created to govern something so essentially simple.[52] After the initial frustration wears off, the complexity becomes interesting, and then, finally, meaningful. As mentioned above, the complexity is symptomatic rather than coincidental. Gift law is always intervening in the ongoing social practice of gift giving. The complexity is due chiefly to the difficulty of defining and preventing those gifts that a legal system considers dangerous while at the same time allowing gift giving to continue.

Gift law has always been complex. Despite all the research, we know little of the content and purpose of the first Western gift law, the *lex Cincia*, the Roman law that governed gift giving for half a millennium. The difficulty arises partially because the *lex Cincia* survives today only in excerpts and fragments. The fact remains that we are unable even to make an educated guess as to exactly what it provided, which gifts were covered, which were excepted, and whether it provided a cause of action (*actio*) or merely a defense (*exceptio*). From the beginning modern gift law has been confused as well. Modern American legal scholarship, even as we first glimpse it—in the first sentence of the first article of the first issue of the first American law review—is already complaining about the befuddling complexity of the law of gifts.[53]

B. APPROACHES TO GIFT GIVING

13. *Total social phenomena*. Marcel Mauss's short work *Essai sur le don*, translated into English as *The Gift*, has inspired much of the modern thinking about gift giving. In his essay, Mauss suggested that institutions such as gift exchange and

---

51. Infra nos. 1314–1352.

52. The desire, however, of power and influence, of esteem among men, of winning a friend or propitiating an enemy,—all these are among the active principles of our being; gratitude, too, the love of family, friendship, and that wider affection for humanity which prompts the generous possessor of goods to impart of his abundance to those who have not. Hence no artificial system of laws is needed, no social polish, to give easy play to machinery whose motive power lies deep in the human heart.
2 Schouler § 55 at 60–61.

53. Comment (1852) 1. The article discusses the *donatio mortis causa*. The sentence is quoted infra no. 972.

potlatch in primitive and archaic society are *total social phenomena* because they involve numerous social institutions, including religion, the law, morality, politics, the family, economics, and aesthetics.[54] Such phenomena cannot adequately be described from the point of view of any one discipline.[55]

Mauss's intuition about the all-encompassing nature of gift giving in premodern society applies with equal force to gift giving in contemporary culture. All that is needed to be convinced of this is to glance at the tables of contents of the scholarly journals. A debate about the nature of gift giving is thriving in all the disciplines that deal with human thought and society. A discussion so wide-ranging is difficult to summarize, especially within the confines of a study such as this one. Nonetheless, basic concepts from that discussion provide the context for any comparative discussion of the law of gifts. Chief among them is the peculiar difficulty of reconciling the individual and the social aspects of gift giving, the moment of freedom and the moment of obligation.

14. *Individual and society.* Virtually all human activity involves both the exercise of individual will and the formative influence of social structure and tradition. For most of human history, these two elements did not seem to conflict to the extent they do today. How else are we to understand the decision of Socrates, that arch-individualist, to accept a judgment of death that he considered unjust? Modern culture formulates this relationship as an opposition. We think of life in terms of the proper allocation of time and energy between what we owe to others and what we owe to ourselves.

Parents become aware of how the individual and society conflict when the time comes to read fairy tales to their children. *Once upon a time* and *They lived happily ever after* magically transport us to other times and places, or, to be more accurate, to the place from which the tradition announces some of its most cherished wisdom. According to Bettelheim, children benefit from hearing these tales at a young age.[56] Yet much about these tales obviously points in the wrong direction, particularly the overt gender bias. Women appear as witches or villains; or they seem vain, idle, or foolish; or they passively wait to be brought back to consciousness by a prince's kiss.[57] Yet if we want to read fairy tales to our children, we have no choice. These are the stories the tradition offers. We can comment on them (though Bettelheim discourages that), place them in context, and provide our own interpretations, but, whatever we do, we are constantly negotiating with the tradition. Fairy tales cannot be created to order. Paul Veyne asked whether the Greeks believed in their myths.[58] The question turns out to

---

54. Mauss (1990) 3, 79.
55. Hyde xv.
56. Bettelheim 3–19.
57. Tatar 94–119.
58. Veyne.

be misconceived. The Greeks believed in their myths when they were useful; they ignored them when they were not. Whichever tack they took, they had no choice but to come to terms with the specific myths they inherited.

The opposition between individual and collective is inherent even in the market, though, since market theory has largely been left to economics, the social constitution of the market is usually forgotten. It is true that residents in industrial societies are offered a wide selection of commodities and a seemingly endless choice of toothpastes and cell phones (and cell phone plans), but the market does not provide a way for an individual to purchase decent public transportation, universal health care, or good public education. The limits to the market's offerings are elements of the social constitution of the market, which is reflected in the market's mirror in the law, the law of contract.

One of the goals of both social science and the humanities has been to examine the relationship between our individual and social selves. One of the reasons for all the scholarly fuss about gift giving today is that it encapsulates this relationship in a bewitching and indecipherable unity of opposites and contradictions. Gift giving is about the Other; it involves self-sacrifice; it is dedicated to the pursuit of altruistic goals. Yet it is also about self-promotion, fame, and advancement. Gifts help create and maintain friendships and love affairs, gifts are cherished symbols of affection, but they may also produce ruthless competition and provide a means to humiliate an opponent. In gift giving, the relationship between individual act and social practice becomes mysteriously complex. One way to investigate how individual agency operates within societal forms is to explore the riddle of the gift.

1. Anthropology

15. *Marcel Mauss.* Ethnographers have found much to criticize in Mauss's methodology. He never engaged in fieldwork, never experienced what Malinowski called the imponderabilia of actual life,[59] but instead gathered data from epic literature, travel diaries, and field reports.[60] His work on gifts has also been criticized for comparing a single, particular aspect of widely varying cultures in the attempt to discover a universal constant of human life, a method that some have argued assumes an unchanging and homogenous human nature.[61]

Nonetheless, Mauss's essay on the gift was one of the founding moments of cultural anthropology.

What happened in that essay, for the first time in the history of ethnological thinking, was that ... the social ceased to belong to the domain of pure quality—anecdote, curiosity, material for moralizing description or for

---

59. Malinowski 18.
60. Reinhardt 102–103.
61. Silber (2000) 116.

scholarly comparison—and became a system, among whose parts connections, equivalences, and interdependent aspects can be discovered.[62]

In fact, Mauss attempted to create new relationships between sociology, biology, psychology, history, linguistics, and psychoanalysis and, in the space thereby created, provide a new role for the study of the total human being, *l'homme total, l'homme tout entier.*[63] The total human being is the living organism in which the psychological and social meet, a being it is possible to study as a complex whole. In his work on the gift, Mauss followed Durkheim in exploring the efficacy of the social context as it manifests itself in the socialized behavior of the individual.[64]

Anthropologists today are still deeply involved in the controversies Mauss initiated. Many of their contributions have been based on a particular reading of Mauss's text, and the belief that he had uncovered a universal element of human society, a basic human principle, namely that human beings are engaged in multiple social relationships involving the reciprocal giving and receiving of gifts.[65] Moreover, these gifts are paradoxical. Though they seem to be the product of individual will and initiative, they are in fact compulsory as a matter of social custom.[66]

Mauss's understanding of the gift was partly inspired by ethnographic studies of gift giving in non-European societies. As a result, anthropologists have examined a wide variety of cultures to ascertain whether Mauss's conception of the gift might represent something of a universal across all types of societies and whether, in the end, there is any difference between the way gifts are given in premodern societies and the way they are given in our own.[67] As Mauss wrote, "It is possible to extend these observations to our own societies. A considerable part of our morality and our lives themselves are still permeated with this same atmosphere of the gift, where obligation and liberty intermingle."[68] In fact, there seems to be a considerable amount of empirical evidence to support the claim that the obligations involved in gift exchange continue to govern modern society as well.[69] Davis has calculated that the proportion of goods circulating as gifts among the West African Hausa people is not significantly different from the proportion in modern societies.[70]

---

62. Lévi-Strauss (1987) 38.
63. Karsenti 73.
64. Id. 78.
65. Geary 129.
66. Mauss (1990) 13.
67. Geary 131.
68. Mauss (1990) 65.
69. "[T]here are some hard data to back up the didactic point, that we are as much obliged by rules of reciprocity as primitive peoples are." Davis (1972) 409.
70. Id. 419–421.

In other words, implicit in the anthropological approach is the idea that gift giving is practiced in all societies, though not always generalized throughout society and with different functions according to the circumstances.[71] Of course, theories that rely on transhistorical and trans-social universals are always risky. Human beings are social by nature and cannot confront an otherwise changing world while remaining essentially unchanged. Nonetheless, to anyone convinced that reality is a constantly changing social construction, there is something eerie about the way gift giving often serves as the initial interface between radically different cultures. As Michael Harbsmeier has noted, the initial interaction between the Old and the New Worlds took the form of reciprocal gift giving, which both sides conducted with subtlety and nuance.[72] Once it became apparent that the New World's inhabitants understood the practice of gift giving, the Europeans shamelessly took advantage of the custom, exploiting their fears and good will to gain friendship, trust, and dominion. Yet without some commonality in their understanding of the institution, none of these strategies could have succeeded.[73] These historical examples illustrate the difficulty of coming to any firm conclusion about the relationship of similarity and difference among human cultures.

a. Clan-based Societies

16. *Kula.* In some societies, gifts form part of a social network that has taken on a life of its own. In the Trobriand Islands, for example, Malinowski encountered a society in which life revolved around a pair of gift-giving cycles known as the *kula.*[74] Twice a year, villagers undertook long canoe voyages to exchange gifts with partner villages. One of the kula partners offered *soulava*, long necklaces made of red shell, while the other presented white shell bracelets known as *mwali*. Some time after receiving their gifts, donees became donors. Soulava passed through the ring of islands in a clockwise direction, while the mwali moved in the opposite direction. Malinowski concluded that kula did not involve barter or exchange. It was rather a case of mutual gift. The giving of gifts in Melanesian society was not a market transaction but rather a concatenation of obligations arranged into chains of mutual prestations, with the give-and-take

---

71. "For gift-exchange is not only the significant form in which archaic societies reproduce themselves; giving and taking are also the elementary activities through which sociability became rich in evolutionary chances, and upon which any community-building process still rests." Berking 31.

72. Harbsmeier 390–410.

73. See Reinhardt 123–129 for an analysis of the initial gift exchange between Columbus and the inhabitants of Guanahani, the still unidentified island where Columbus first made landfall. For a description of the gift exchange between Bougainville and the natives of Tahiti, as well as Lapérouse's exchanges with the residents of Easter Island, see Greene.

74. Malinowski (1964) 81–104.

extending over generations.[75] For the Trobriand Islanders, market phenomena were secondary to the main purpose of their lives, which was the giving and receiving of gifts.[76]

Anthropologists have occasionally romanticized the kula as an expression of generalized altruism. Subsequent fieldwork, however, has revealed that the kula was actually a form of agonistic gift exchange, by which donors competed with each other for prestige and rank.[77] The Trobriand Islanders were obsessed with gift exchange because it provided a mechanism for choosing their social leaders.

17. *Potlatch.* The potlatch among the First Nations of the American Northwest involved the giving away of enormous quantities of goods. It took place during ritual celebrations held on important social occasions that often involved dancing and feasting.[78] Like the kula, the potlatch did not involve altruistic giving. Among the Kwakwaka'wakw (formerly known as the Kwakiutl), potlatch was rather a continuation of warfare by other means.[79] Potlatches were planned like military campaigns. The participants were occasionally humiliated to the point of committing suicide.[80]

18. *Contemporary analogues.* Analogous behavior seems to be observable in contemporary society as well. Lévi-Strauss, who was fascinated with how modern society incorporates many of the practices of primitive cultures, argued that the American exchange of Christmas gifts, practiced by different social classes with religious fervor, resembles a gigantic potlatch, implicating millions of individuals and causing permanent disequilibrium in the family budget.[81] Thorsten Veblen understood conspicuous consumption as competition by means of expensive gifts.[82] Until recently, middle- and upper-class wives were modern society's principal ceremonial consumers of goods. The reputation of the head of household, Veblen argued, depended on showering her with unnecessary and extravagant gifts. As women have entered the workplace, that role has gradually passed to children and in some cases to pets.[83]

---

75. Malinowski (1989) 67.

76. Malinowski (1964) 100–101. For a more exchange-oriented understanding of the kula, see Strathern.

77. Weiner 131–148. For a critique of the understanding of gift giving as altruism, see Schroeder 851–859.

78. For a description of a Kwakwaka'wakw potlatch, see Halliday 18–88, particularly 73–88. Halliday was a photographer and, from 1906 to 1932, the Indian agent for what was then known as the Kwakiutl Agency.

79. Codere 118–125.

80. Id. 122–123.

81. Lévi-Strauss (1969) 56.

82. Veblen 83–85; Schwartz 2–3.

83. "Sure, the hotelier and real estate magnate Leona Helmsley left $12 million in her will to her dog, Trouble. But that, it turns out, is nothing much compared with what other

b. To Give, to Receive, and to Reciprocate

19. *Chains of gifts.* In clan-based societies, a gift is not principally the transfer of an object from one individual to another. Its more important role is to create and maintain long-term relationships among social groups. This is often the role of gift giving in contemporary society as well. For example, the extraordinary culture of gift giving among the Japanese seems to have its origin in rituals devoted to group solidarity.[84]

As Mauss suggested, gift giving does not function as a series of discrete transactions. Instead, each transfer creates a debt, which in turn must be reciprocated. The fact that reciprocation takes place over time, and thus requires the parties to cultivate a relationship, distinguishes the gift from the exchange, which, paradigmatically, is reciprocated immediately and thus does not require, or even encourage, a continuing bond. To refuse to reciprocate a gift means to deny the relationship. Primitive and archaic societies are constituted by a culture of gift giving that consists of the obligations to give, to receive, and to reciprocate.[85] Mauss was particularly interested in discovering the rules of primitive law or self-interest that require a gift to be reciprocated. He speculated that some power might reside in the gift that causes the donee to feel obligated to offer a gift in exchange.[86]

In attempting to answer this question, Mauss noted that some informants in the ethnographic literature seemed to suggest a metaphysical basis for reciprocity—namely that a spirit residing in the gift wished to return to its home.[87] Mauss suggested that reciprocity may be due to the belief that something of the owner continues to reside in the gift object even after the transfer. There seems to be evidence, for example, that the ancient Scandinavians believed that objects acquired their owners' personal characteristics. In fact, the word *nautr* in Old Icelandic referred both to the donor and to the gift the donor bestowed.[88] In our own day, books donated to libraries, particularly by important figures, often are furnished with bookplates so that subsequent readers may know of the books'

---

dogs may receive from the charitable trust of Mrs. Helmsley, who died last August." Strom 1.

84. In traditional Japanese society gifts of food or drink, such as rice or sake, were offered to gods and other supernatural beings. The gods returned the gifts so that human beings might share the food and receive divine power. As a result, commensalism became an essential characteristic of Japanese social groups, and the sharing of community power became anchored in an extremely ritualized practice of giving and reciprocating gifts. Befu 447–451.

85. Mauss (1990) 13.

86. Id. 3.

87. Id. 11–12.

88. Gurevich 136; Pétursdóttir 61.

provenance.[89] Nonetheless, scholars have quarreled over the interpretation of the ethnographic reports Mauss relied on,[90] and it is now agreed that, whatever its basis, the phenomenon of reciprocity is considerably more complex.[91] In fact the phenomenon of reciprocity reaches beyond gift giving to include all gratuitous action. Once I ask a favor of someone, it is very difficult to refuse when that person asks a favor of me.

Mauss's major contribution was his decision to group apparently dissimilar activities from widely diverse cultures—phenomena as disparate as the birthday present and the potlatch—under the single concept of the gift.[92] After discovering that gifts must usually be reciprocated, Mauss might simply have characterized gifts as a type of exchange and assimilated them to market behavior. Instead Mauss recognized that these diverse phenomena share a fundamental similarity: they are all instances in which individual action, whatever the individual's motivation, plays a constitutive role in the creation of social relations. Moreover, by insisting on the contradictory notion of gift exchange, he shifted the focus from modern, developed society to preliterate cultures, thereby making clear that societies involving commodity exchange are not necessarily more advanced than those without it. By identifying a commonality in all human culture, he reduced the sense of distance and difference between developed and developing societies and shifted the focus from economics to total social interaction, thereby including all aspects of human life in the analysis.

c. Social Reproduction

20. *Marginalization of gift law.* Given that Mauss's essay and the discussion he provoked occupy a central role in cultural anthropology, it may seem odd that none of these texts play any role in the admittedly rare doctrinal discussions about how best to structure the law of gifts. The law's ignorance of the anthropological debate on these questions, however, is more than coincidence. The refusal to allocate a constitutive social function to gift giving is a premise on which both developed society and modern law are based.[93] A market-oriented legal system carefully distinguishes among the different exchange-oriented contracts and correspondingly marginalizes gift law. Western legal codifications arose from the rejection of the gift economy and the identification of the private law with the market. For this reason, an understanding of the modern law of gifts requires

---

89. Marais 326.
90. Sahlins (1972) 149–168.
91. Godelier 10–107; Wiener 44–65.
92. Reinhardt 120.
93. "Naturally gift giving has no significant economic meaning for economic life." Kieckebusch 285.

a brief comparison of our contemporary conception of gift giving with the understanding present in clan-based societies.[94]

21. *A reproductive role.* In *Ancient Society*, Lewis Morgan drew on the anthropological data available at the time to present a vision of society as a reproductive
mechanism. In the societies he discussed, kinship and land tenure were both
needed for social reproduction—the one essential for creating offspring, the
other providing the basis for cultivation.[95] Building on Morgan's contribution,
Mauss argued that clan-based societies are not essentially subsistence economies, even though they do not produce principally for exchange. Instead, the
transfer of things serves as a vehicle for the creation and maintenance of social
relationships. In fact, exchange, as we know it, is impossible in clan-based societies. These cultures often do not know private property, and thus no individual
has a right to alienate anything. Mauss considered gifts to represent transfers of
inalienable objects between persons who are mutually dependent. Because the
things are inalienable, they are loaned rather than sold. Throughout their useful
life they maintain a bond with all the persons through whose hands they pass.
An individual's goal, in such a society is not to maximize profit but rather to
acquire as many gift-debtors as possible, partially to be confident of assistance in
case of emergency.

22. *Creation of hierarchy.* In such societies, gift giving also participates in the
maintenance of social hierarchy. The giving of a gift promotes both solidarity
and dominion. Donees become indebted to their donors and to some extent
dependent, at least as long as the gifts have not been reciprocated.[96] In certain
circumstances, the inequality created by the gift can create and maintain a social
system of dependency. In the Icelandic sagas, important personages insisted on
taking property by purchase rather than gift in order to avoid the dependency
relationship.[97] Those who control sufficient wealth to be prolific in gift giving
establish their superiority and place both donees and less magnanimous donors
in a subordinate position. Individuals in these societies strive to accumulate
wealth, not so they can retain it but rather so they might have more to give away.

In *The Elementary Structures of Kinship*, Claude Lévi-Strauss suggests that
women, particularly nubile women, represent the supreme gift.[98] Since the

---

94. For a brief summary of the classical anthropological discussion, see Gregory
15–24.

95. Morgan's underlying vision was rooted in an understanding of social reproduction,
though the concept did not become explicitly available until it was formulated by Marx.
Morgan himself spoke in terms of *social organization*, by which he meant interpersonal
relationships, and *political organization* or the allocation of land. Morgan 62.

96. Godelier 12.

97. Gurevich 130–131.

98. Lévi-Strauss (1969) 65. For a feminist critique of the anthropological tradition that
runs from Malinowski to Lévi-Strauss, see Weiner 1–19.

incest taboo prohibits marriage within certain relationships, marriage is the system whereby one consanguineous group gives away its sisters in order to receive wives. Because such exchanges take place only once every generation, the giving of things helps to preserve the relationships necessary to enable clans to obtain brides.[99]

d. Comparative Notes

23. *Paradoxes.* What anthropologists have discovered about gift giving is paradoxical in the extreme. On the one hand, gift exchange seems to be something close to a universal practice in human societies and is in most situations governed by the three Maussian obligations—to give, to receive, and to reciprocate. Gift giving creates chains of giving through time and maintains broad networks of relationships. On the other hand, no institution serves as many different, and conflicting, roles as does gift exchange. At one extreme it creates pathways of good will and serves as a physical embodiment of the sentiments of love and affection, while, at the other, it imposes crushing obligations and symbolizes relationships of domination and dependence.

Another paradox has to do with the relationship between gift and exchange. Gifts are one-sided actions; they are the prototypical unilateral act, the transfer of property without a quid pro quo. Yet gifts must be reciprocated. The mandatory quality of the countergift is just as integral to the nature of the gift as its unilateral quality.[100] No one has yet developed the conceptual vocabulary to describe this seeming contradiction. "It is especially difficult to describe the reciprocal relationship involved in gift giving by means of a terminology based on the conception of the gift as a unilateral transfer."[101]

Everyone who has received a gift has felt the urge to restore the balance, *sich revanchieren*, to take revenge, as is said in German. The coincidence in time of gift and countergift, together with the mandatory equivalence in their value, are in some societies so marked that the transaction is easily mistaken for an exchange. In fact, gift and exchange can resemble each other so closely that the gift may appear to be nothing but a market transaction. The ultimate paradox is that, at that moment, the gift, this universal feature of social interaction, vanishes into mirage, chimera, and illusion.[102]

---

99. Gregory 90.

100. "But there is also the legal side, a system of mutual obligations which forces the fisherman to repay whenever he has received a gift from his inland partner, and vice versa. Neither partner can refuse, neither may stint in his return gift, neither should delay." Malinowski (1989) 22.

101. Pappenheim 80.

102. If the gift and the counter-gift are unequal, then there's a winner and a loser, and possibly exploitation and trickery. If, on the other hand, they are the same, then there's apparently no difference between the gift and a rational, self-interested

24. *Unexplained.* In other words, the most interesting features of gift giving remain unexplained. The most obvious conundrum is the virtually incomprehensible intermingling of freedom and obligation. Essential to the practice is the shared belief that gift giving is an act of the donor's free will. If the donee senses that the donor feels compelled, the transaction fails in its purpose.[103] And yet everyone knows that gifts are not freely given, that social custom prescribes complex rules concerning gift giving behavior, and that most gifts are anything but optional. The obligation is so strong that it is extremely difficult to waive. No matter what the host says, a savvy guest will always bring a bottle of wine or a bouquet of flowers, and a *no presents* line on a birthday invitation has little effect. No one has managed to articulate this paradoxical relationship between gratuitousness, on the one hand, and social obligation, on the other.

25. *Inevitable failure.* The anthropological discussion makes clear that, when a legal system seeks to regulate gift giving, it sets for itself an impossible task. The gift is the ultimate shape-shifter, one about which we understand next to nothing. So little is understood about gift exchange that the law cannot possibly get it right.

For this reason, a comparative study of gift law cannot focus on determining the optimal approach. All it can hope to do is demonstrate which of the manifold aspects of gift giving each legal system chooses to privilege as it promulgates its rules. The way each system chooses to order gift giving, and especially the extent to which it favors or restricts the process, speaks to that system's understanding of gratuitous action and its vision of social relationship.

2. History

26. *Contemporary approach.* Some historians have used the pattern of the three Maussian gift obligations as an organizational schema by which to understand gift giving in the different historical periods.[104] More contemporary historians, however, refuse to consider Mauss's system as a pure form of universal social activity with shared meanings and preestablished harmony.[105] Gifts are seen instead as modeling devices, as a family name for a range of forms that can be honored in their breach or even mixed and matched according to the particular

---

mercantile exchange. In short, either the gift results from uncharitable motives and is therefore illegitimate or it is non-existent, illusory.
Godbout and Caillé 5.

103. No equivalence exists between what the donee has done and what is given. No obligation is imposed which the donee must fulfill. The donee's thanks are but the ghost of a reciprocal bond. That the gift should operate coercively is indeed repugnant and painful to the donor, destructive of the liberality that is intended.
Noonan 695.

104. "Twenty years ago I showed that gift-giving in the Homeric poems is consistent, I might even say absolutely consistent, with the analysis made by Mauss." Finley 145.

105. Algazi 12.

meaning a social actor wishes to convey.[106] In fact, historians have begun to conceive of gift giving not in terms of any type of fixed structure but instead as "contested constructions of social transactions," of meanings negotiated between social actors.[107]

27. *Modern philanthropy.* In several nuanced studies, the historian Ilana Silber has argued that gift giving is not as uniform as Mauss suggested. Troubled by the essentializing nature of the Maussian vision, she has suggested, for example, that the obligation to reciprocate is not universal,[108] a fact many have noted.[109] It is lacking, for example, in modern philanthropy. She believes that this difference suggests that many of the other institutions that Mauss grouped together under the category of the gift might also best be examined as separate institutions.[110]

An anthropologist might respond that modern philanthropy displays traditional traits of competitive giving. Major donors continue to seek recognition, which can be provided only by other major donors, in the form of memberships, awards, and publicity. Moreover, the donor continues to be identified with the gift object. One of the incentives for major donations is that they permit the donor to be memorialized by naming a school, a hospital facility, a scholarship, or an academic chair. Reciprocity too is present. The opening gift is the wealth that society has bestowed on the donor. Those engaged in philanthropy often speak of it as a way to "give something back" to the community.[111]

The methodological issue historians confront is whether it is useful to remove modern philanthropy from the ambit of the broad concept of the gift, or whether it represents instead a particular variation. However this issue is resolved, it remains clear that the structure of gift giving is intimately related to the context of the gift—the power relations between the parties, the social hierarchies, the requirements of social reproduction. As Algazi has pointed out, the particular contribution of the historian to this discussion is to historicize the various theoretical concepts of the gift, to demonstrate that they are embedded in particular historical conjunctures, and to evaluate their meaning in different historical contexts.[112] "[I]f historians of pre-modern Europe are to contribute fruitfully to

---

106. Id. 15.

107. Id. 10.

108. Silber (2000) 118–119. She speaks of "the possibility of a new, non-monolithic approach, more intent to start mapping out a diverse range of gift-processes (e.g. ideologically reciprocal vs. non-reciprocal) than to keep searching for the latter's 'essential', or ubiquitous features." Id. 119.

109. Marais 305.

110. Silber (1998) 146–147. Silber argues that modern charitable giving is indirect and impersonal in the sense that it is a gift made to strangers. It creates no personal bond and no expectation of a return gift.

111. See Shore.

112. Algazi 20.

the ongoing dialogue with sociology and anthropology, then their contribution could hardly consist in subsuming their findings under fixed, general models. Rather, it must provide precise reconstructions of the variety, richness, and internal contradictions of European traditions."

a. Classical Antiquity

28. *No general concept.* There was no general concept of gift in classical antiquity.[113] Both Greek and Latin distinguished various types of gifts, and, in both, the meaning of gift giving was wider than the concept we use today. Brief moments of this complex topic are particularly relevant here.

i. The Homeric Epics

29. *Wide latitude of meaning.* The Homeric word for gift—δῶρον—also referred to many transactions that are unrelated to our current understanding of the concept.

> [T]he word "gift" was a cover-all for a great variety of actions and transactions which later became differentiated and acquired their own appellations. There were payments for services rendered, desired or anticipated; what we would call fees, rewards, prizes, and sometimes bribes .... Then there were taxes and other dues to lords and kings, amends with a penal overtone ... and even ordinary loans—and again the Homeric word is always "gift."[114]

There were also the celebrated *xenia*, guest-friendship gifts, which "extended the rights and duties proper to kinship and close comradeship beyond the *demos* to foreigners."[115] Each type of gift required reciprocity. "It may be stated as a flat rule of both primitive and archaic society that no one ever gave anything, whether goods or services or honours, without proper recompense, real or wishful, immediate or years away, to himself or to his kin. The act of giving was, therefore, in an essential sense always the first half of a reciprocal action, the other half of which was a counter-gift."[116]

30. *Competitive giving.* Gift giving in Homeric society generally constituted a public declaration of status, with superiors giving to create obligations in others and to cause their dominion to be recognized, while inferiors gave to foster favor and goodwill. Competitive giving occurred when relative status was uncertain.[117] The lavishness of some of the competitive giving had the same goals as a potlatch, namely to elevate the donor's prestige and to place the donee under heavy obligation. The *Iliad* recounts two paradigmatic examples of competitive

---

113. Wagner-Hasel (2003) 167.
114. Finley 66; see also Donlan 3–4.
115. Donlan 6; see also Wagner-Hasel (2000) 79–130.
116. Finley 64.
117. Donlan 6.

giving—the extravagant gifts Agamemnon offered to Achilles, which included seven well-peopled cities, and the equally lavish gifts given by Achilles for Patroclus's funeral.[118]

ii. Aristotle

31. *Right giving.* A passage in the *Ethics* suggests that Aristotle already understood the paradoxical nature of gift giving. He mentions that giving is the province of the free human being, of the gentleman (ἐλευθέριος), and yet every aspect of giving is socially determined. "Free human beings will give for the sake of beauty. They will give properly (ὀρθῶς), to those to whom it is necessary to give, as much as and when required, and in all other respects according to what is proper."[119]

iii. The Roman Vision

32. *Dona and munera.* Classical Latin distinguishes two types of gifts, *dona* and *munera.*[120] The *munus* was the more specific category. Though delimitation is difficult, it seems to have included those gifts that, for whatever purpose, were considered socially, and later legally, obligatory, including both customary gifts given in appropriate amounts on the occasion of special events and festivals; gifts given as recompense for professional services that, in the Roman view, were to be performed without compensation; and also the games, feasts, and public construction required to maintain the prestige of those in positions of power. *Donum*, the more general category, included the vast range of giving, and more specifically designated the spontaneous gift designed to begin a new relationship.

Gift giving was a central part of late Roman aristocratic life.[121] To begin with, because there was little trade and the wealthy lived largely off the produce of their own estates, gift giving permitted them to obtain otherwise unavailable luxuries. Gifts often consisted of edible delicacies, rare books (all books were rare), exotic animals, and sacred relics, such as keys made from the chains of St. Peter. Second, Roman citizens aspired to glory, which could be attained not only by military greatness and political success, but also by impressive charitable contributions.[122] Large donations, particularly to beautify the city, were necessary to please the plebs and garner public support.[123] Constantine instituted the practice of making significant gifts to soldiers and veterans, particularly of land complete with cattle and seed, as a means to retain their loyalty, and also endowed

---

118. *Iliad* bk. 9 lines 121–156 (Agamemnon), bk. 23 lines 29–34, 168–176, 257–270 (Achilles); Donlan 2.

119. *Nicomachean Ethics* 1120a, bk. 4 sec. 1 lines 12–13.

120. Michel nos. 787–814; Archi (1964) 935; Ascoli (1894) 175 note 2.

121. Wood 301–304.

122. Byrne 1045.

123. Id. 1050.

churches with land and precious ritual objects.[124] Roman emperors were expected to be especially generous, yet they were not to be profligate or squander the state's resources.[125] Nonetheless, the extravagance of certain public practices, particularly during the republic, calls to mind a potlatch.[126] At the end of the empire, political office had become so identified with great giving that public service often bankrupted the officials.[127] Finding the proper path between miserliness and prodigality required considerable wisdom.

33. *Latin literature.* Despite the centrality of gift giving to Roman political life, the Romans remained suspicious because they thought gifts lacked the rationality of exchange.[128] It was not until the Christian period that gift giving came to be seen as a laudable expression of generosity. Thus, during the classical period Roman writers expressed a guarded view. As Zimmermann explains, the Roman *bonus vir* did not squander his assets. Instead he did his best to preserve them for himself and his *familia*.[129] Cicero reminded his son that, though it was important to give to the poor, gifts should be given in moderation. Many had squandered their wealth by indiscriminate giving—Cicero may have had Julius Caesar in mind—and the impoverishment that can result can lead to crime. Cicero was particularly opposed to gift expenditures designed to win public approbation, including public banquets, the distribution of meat to the people, gladiatorial shows, games, and combat with wild beasts.[130]

Some writers focused instead on the dangers gift giving poses to donees, an insight taught by an episode in the Trojan War. In the *Aeneid*, as the Trojans gathered around the wooden horse, Laocoon warned them of the danger—*Timeo Danaos et dona ferentis*, I fear the Greeks, even when they are bearing gifts.[131] Martial conveyed the same idea in his *Epigrams*. "I abhor the crafty and cursed trickery of presents; gifts are like hooks; for who does not know that the greedy sea bream is deceived by the fly he has gorged: Every time he gives nothing to a rich friend, O Quintianus, a poor man is generous."[132]

34. *Lex Cincia.* The stoicism of the Roman vision is evident in the republican *lex Cincia de donis et muneribus*, a *plebiscitum* passed in 204 B.C. during the tribunate of M. Cincius Alimentus. For five hundred years it seems to have been the only Roman law governing gift giving. One of its provisions prohibited payment to lawyers who argued cases, either in the form of fees or as gifts. The remainder

---

124. Dupont 315, 318, 320–321.
125. Wood 310.
126. Michel nos. 835–836.
127. Byrne 1058.
128. D'Ors § 120.
129. Zimmermann 482.
130. Cicero, *De officiis* bk. 2 secs. 15–17 nos. 54–64.
131. *Aeneid* bk. 2 line 49.
132. Bk. 5 no. 18 lines 6–10. Translation from 1 Martial 309.

seems to have regulated gift giving more generally. The restrictions concerning gift giving have not survived intact and can only be surmised. They seem to have limited the amount that could be given as a gift and may have required gifts to be made with certain formalities. Savigny concluded that the lex Cincia prohibited gifts of greater than a stated (but now unknown) value (*ultra modum legitimum*), unless made by *mancipatio, in iure cessio*, or delivery.[133] The fact that the amount of the *modus* remains uncertain makes it difficult to establish the purpose of the norms. Ascoli thought that the value of the modus could not have been very high.[134] In contrast, Savigny argued that it was designed to assure sufficient reflection before larger amounts were gifted.[135] Others have suggested that the law was designed to address large gifts given to politicians by rich families.[136]

It seems that the law was later altered to apply only between certain categories of individuals (*personae non exceptae*). Relatives to the fifth degree seem to have been excepted, as were family members who were dependents (*in potestate*) of

---

133. Savigny (1850) 332. Savigny's essay was originally published in 1818, a few years before the discovery and eventual publication of the *Fragmenta vaticana*, which provide additional information about the lex Cincia. Savigny argued that the amount stated in the law was 20,000 *sestertii*. Savigny (1850) 353–357.

Mancipatio and *in iure cessio* were two early Roman forms for transferring title. Nicholas 62–64. Neither survived into the law of Justinian.

The mancipatio required the presence of five witnesses and the *libripens*, who held a pair of bronze scales. For a gift, the donee, while holding the gift object in one hand and a piece of bronze in the other, recited specified words, struck the scales with the piece of bronze, and then gave the bronze to the donor. All participants had to be Roman citizens. Mancipatio was used only for the conveyance of free persons *in postestate*, slaves, and property known as *res mancipi*, such as beasts of burden, Roman land, and praedial servitudes, including rights of way. Nicholas 105–106.

In iure cessio was applicable to any type of property but, in practice, was used chiefly for the creation of *iura in re aliena*, which included various types of servitudes. For a gift, the donee held the gift object before the magistrate and recited the opening words of the *vindicatio* action, which were identical to the initial clause of the mancipatio. The donor did not assert a competing claim, and the object was adjudged to the donee.

Delivery (*traditio*) was a form of conveyance accepted by Justinian. Nicholas 117–118. The extent of rights transferred depended on the reason for the transfer (*iusta causa*). In principle, traditio was accomplished by the acquisition of possession in terms of both intent and physical control (*animo et corpore*). In most cases, at least a minimum of physical transfer was required. For the case of immovables and bulky movables, *traditio longa manu* permitted transfer by visual designation, a type of symbolic delivery. When the property was already in the possession of the transferee, *traditio brevi manu* did not require a renewed transfer.

134. Ascoli (1894) 182–183.

135. Savigny (1850) 334–335.

136. Byrne 1101. Baltrusch argued that the lex Cincia prohibited gift giving principally in order to prevent jurists from showing undue preference for their richer clients and to require them to respect their fiduciary obligations (*fides*). Baltrusch 63–69.

those excepted.[137] The catalog of permitted gift relationships was large enough to include all those generally considered members of the ancient family.[138] The thought may have been that family members would not be able to exert improper pressure on the paterfamilias. Ulpian called the lex Cincia a *lex imperfecta*. Though his meaning is uncertain, it seems that, though the described gifts were prohibited, the law provided no remedy to recover the property if the gifts were made.[139] In other words, they were not void.[140] The prohibition was perhaps interpreted as a defense (*exceptio*), which permitted the donor to revoke the gift at any time before it was perfected.[141] The effect may have been to make it impossible for the donee to require the donor to perform an unexecuted gift. In the late classic period, the donor's failure to revoke an executed gift demonstrated enduring intent (*perseverantia voluntatis*), which prevented the heirs from revoking— *morte Cincia removetur*.[142]

The arresting fact is that the concept of the gift, *donatio*, was probably unknown to Roman law before the lex Cincia.[143] In other words, the law first recognized the gift in order to prohibit it.[144]

b. The Middle Ages

35. *An aspect of feudal society.* Gift giving so dominated the thoughts of medieval thinkers that Bracton considered the gift to be "the most celebrated and famous of the *causae acquisitionis*."[145] Yet there was no single medieval discourse of the gift, no common cultural code of gift giving, and no single model according to which all gifts behaved.[146] Nonetheless, the medieval practices of gift giving, when compared to a system of commodity exchange, revealed several differences. It created and preserved social relationships and encouraged solidarity and community. Yet it also created and maintained long-term social hierarchies. Gift giving was for both reasons a constitutive element of feudalism.

---

137. Ascoli (1894) 222–223; Savigny (1850) 341–345; Girard 989–994; Ourliac and Malafosse 455–456; Zimmermann 482–484. Dawson speculated that the classical Roman jurists did not support the limitations because they made no mention of them in their surviving writings. There also seems to be little evidence that repentant donors took advantage of the law. Dawson (1980) 19–20.

138. Archi (1964) 932.

139. Id. 940–942.

140. 2 Windscheid § 367 note 7 at 558.

141. Biondi nos. 4, 8; Michel nos. 464–466.

142. "The Cincia prohibitions are removed at death." Archi (1964) 944–945; Ascoli (1894) 193–195.

143. Archi (1964) 931.

144. Michel no. 466.

145. 2 Bracton 49.

146. Algazi 20–21.

It is difficult to estimate the extent to which gifts were generally exchanged among the bulk of the population. Altruistic gifts, gifts based on pure affection, seem to have been rare in the early Middle Ages. In fact, there is remarkably little evidence of personal gift giving at all.[147] This may have been because, in the absence of extensive commodity transactions, exchanges of all types were limited.

i. Germanic Custom

36. *Hierarchy.* Gift giving experienced a distinct evolution among the Germanic tribes.[148] Gifts apparently were not part of original Germanic legal thought.[149] Based on two passages from Tacitus,[150] Scovazzi has argued that gifts developed from the unilateral transfers that followers made to demonstrate their loyalty to their leaders. Tacitus mentioned silver vessels, cattle, and grain. Though the subordinates sought their leaders' benevolence, the superiors obligated themselves to nothing by accepting the gifts. Later, the leaders began to give gifts to their lieutenants, including arms, rings, and armbands. These gifts, though running in the opposite direction, were also designed to reinforce the hierarchy. Hierarchy, however, contradicted the ancient Germanic custom of equality of right. In fact, the acceptance of a unilateral gift was considered a vile act of servitude. For example, those migrating from Norway to Iceland at the end of the ninth century refused to accept gifts of land from earlier settlers in order to emphasize their independence.[151]

Scovazzi argued that the hierarchical relationships established by unilateral gift giving produced a reaction. In both literary and legal texts, a countergift gradually emerged as a condition to making the opening gift irrevocable. Gifts were eventually structured as bilateral transactions that were not perfected until receipt of the countergift. This would explain the compensatory payment celebrated in Lombard law (*Launegild* or *Lohngeld*), the countergift required of the donee at acceptance.[152] The requirement of a counterprestation graduated from

---

147. Curta 697.
148. The following is drawn largely from Scovazzi.
149. Bellomo 955.
150. *Germania* chaps. 5, 15.
151. Scovazzi 253–255.
152. On reciprocal gifts (*De launegild*). If a man gives his property to someone else and afterwards he who made the gift seeks a reciprocal gift in return, then he who received [the gift] or his heirs—if he cannot swear that [a return gift] had been provided—shall return [the gift] singlefold (*ferquido*), that is, in the same amount as it was on the day it was given. But if he does so swear, he shall be absolved. Edictus Rothari art. 175 in Drew 83, original in Beyerle 46. See also art. 184 in Drew 86, Beyerle 49; Liutprandi Leges art. 73 in Drew 175, Beyerle 133–134. See generally Pappenheim.

a moral to a legal obligation over time.[153] Similarly, the morning gift (*Morgengabe*) was the wife's counterpart to the husband's marriage gift.

Drew, on the other hand, derives the Launegild from the centrality of the family bond in Germanic custom.[154] To preserve property within the family, Lombard law essentially forbade individual alienation of family property.[155] Gifts were prohibited unless, by countergift, similar value was returned to the family's holdings. Drew speculated that the rigorous prohibition of gift giving was present in early Germanic law, and that, by the time of Rothair's Edict, the law required a symbolic return rather than a return of equivalent value. In many Lombard gift acts the return gift consisted of a relatively worthless trinket.[156] Pappenheim, however, points out that return gifts of great value are also documented.[157] The lack of a countergift did not void the gift but rather permitted the donor or the donor's heirs to recover either the gift or something of equivalent value.[158] A gift to the church was valid without a return gift.[159]

The Lombards did not recognize the concept of the gift until they converted to Christianity and private property became more widespread.[160] Even then, Lombard law permitted the revocation of gifts upon the birth of a child or for the donee's ingratitude. It was assumed that the donor would not have made the gift if such events had been foreseen.

ii. Official Gifts

37. *Great value.* Throughout the early Middle Ages, the sources document a lively exchange of gifts among kings, popes, bishops, and abbots.[161] These gifts were an element of political and diplomatic strategy.[162] They sometimes flowed from the more to the less powerful as a means to create relations of dominion. These were gifts of great value that served to overwhelm the recipients and put them lastingly in the donor's debt.[163] Gifts included spices, perfumes, horses, precious books, fabrics woven with gold, and handcrafted objects in gold and silver. The donor often expected—and even requested—a return gift. The gifts—*munera*,

---

153. Scovazzi 257–258.

154. Drew 245 note 46.

155. Bellomo 956, citing Edictus Rothari art. 172.

156. Gino Gorla suggested that the Lombard return gift represented a formality and demonstrates that either a form or a sufficient cause is generally needed to make gratuitous transfers irrevocable and gift promises enforceable. 1 Gorla 30.

157. Pappenheim 37–38.

158. Id. 49.

159. Bellomo 956.

160. Id.

161. Kulischer 89.

162. Hannig 153.

163. Curta 698.

dona, xenia, benedictiones—came either from the donor's possessions or manufacture or had to be obtained.[164] The gifts were often exchanged at festive meals (*convivium et munera*), which were essential for the conclusion of peace treaties, together with the brotherly kiss and a shared visit to Mass.[165]

Gifts in the early Middle Ages also served as a substitute for war, a means to achieve goals that had been unsuccessfully sought in battle—a continuation of warfare by different means.[166] Weaker lords were known to offer presents and hostages to stronger armies about to attack them. The offerings prevented the attack, averted destruction, and achieved peace, often through submission to the overlordship of the stronger party.[167] These gifts were not simply a form of spoils but instead were praised throughout the period as a resourceful application of the *ars donandi*.[168] Agonistic gift giving was also a constant feature of medieval power relations.[169]

In addition, gifts were used to constitute public authority after the demise of the Roman Empire. With the decline of the Roman administration, the primary means of creating reciprocal duties passed to the system of gift exchange.[170] Public authority in the early Middle Ages consisted of a constellation of personal alliances created primarily by the giving of gifts.[171] The powerful used gifts to recruit retainers, to obtain secret information, and to entice others to engage in criminal acts. Retainers, on the other hand, used gifts to obtain favors and appointments from their lords.[172] As with gifts given between rulers, these gifts too were usually exchanged at elaborate feasts, and the feasts themselves were considered a form of gift.[173]

38. *Bribes and taxes.* There seems to have been a floating boundary between bribes and *instrumental gifts*. Both were used to assure the stability of power relations. In fact, the reciprocal quality of the gift encouraged fluidity in this regard. Gifts seem to have been given without condition, yet every donee knew that something was expected in return. Gifts were therefore used both to express gratitude for services rendered and to encourage prestations that otherwise would not have been forthcoming.[174] Throughout most of the Middle Ages,

---

164. Kulischer 89.
165. Hannig 153; Grøbech 56.
166. Curta 693.
167. Id. 693 note 123.
168. Hannig 149–150.
169. Id. 155.
170. Hannig 156–157.
171. Curta 677.
172. Curta 685–686.
173. Id. 692 note 118.
174. Valentin Groebner has used the Germanic *miet* to explore the characterization difficulty. Groebner 229–232.

feudal taxes and tributes were made to rulers in the form of gifts (*dona*), for which protection and other services were given in return.[175]

39. *Schenkbücher.* From the fourteenth century, Swiss and German cities maintained specially designed gift catalogues (*Schenkbücher*), listing donations to princes, diplomats, messengers, and meritorious citizens.[176] Gift giving was considered the city officials' most important duty. They were charged with making gifts that redounded to the city's honor and profit. *Schenken*, in both medieval and modern German, means both to give a present and to pour a liquid. Most municipal gifts involved alcohol. Gifts of wine (*Schenkwein*), given in specially designed jugs to prominent visitors and meritorious citizens, constituted a public proclamation of the bond. The quantity and quality of the wine corresponded to the rank of the visitor.[177]

40. *New Year's gifts.* Hirschbiegel has documented the astonishing evolution of New Year's gifts, from the Roman *strenae* to the late medieval *étrennes*.[178] The practice was so widespread and so extravagant that both Roman writers and the church tried to limit or forbid it. On the first of each year until the French Revolution, gifts were exchanged at festive banquets in noble residences. This courtly gift culture was based on reciprocal prodigality and agonistic waste. Only those with the means to participate in the system could vie for power. The king's control of taxation made him the mightiest and most prodigal giver of gifts. He occupied the center of the system.[179] Especially among the French and Burgundian nobility, the presents consisted of fabulously intricate works of art.[180] Hirschbiegel's catalog of rare and exquisite gifts—from tableware, goblets, artisan jewelry, and paternosters, almost all of it of gold and silver and studded with diamonds, pearls, and other precious stones, to horses and tooled saddles—reveals perhaps better than any summary the extraordinary role that gift giving must have played in the constitution of social relations.[181]

---

175. Hannig 152.
176. Groebner 223–224.
177. Id. 224–226.
178. Hirschbiegel 37–69.
179. Id. 17.
180. In 1393, for example, Jean, Duke of Berry, gave Charles VI an image of St. George standing on a dragon. Two diamonds were encrusted at the sides of the saint's helmet visor, a pearl on the flat surface, a large ruby and a pearl on the hilt of the sword, and pearls at either end of the cross. The image also contained a large cut ruby and four other cabochon rubies. Id. 370 no. 547.
181. The catalog includes over 1,800 objects given as aristocratic New Year's gifts between 1381 and 1422. Id. 314–514.

iii. Religious Gifts

41. *To the church.* Gift giving served a religious function as well. The medieval aristocracy was bound by long-standing gift relationships with church institutions, particularly the monasteries. Between the ninth and twelfth centuries, "donations to monasteries constituted a phenomenon of such massive proportions that it has been referred to as 'the most powerful current animating the economic life of the time.'"[182] The gift of large land holdings to the church formed the institution of *laudatio parentum*, gifts by which a family, to obtain a spiritual blessing, authorized a land transfer to a Christian saint and to the religious community the saint protected.[183] The church thereby acquired dominion over vast tracts of land, a wealth that was immobilized and served as the economic foundation for the church's struggles against secular authority.

42. *To Brahmans.* The Catholic Church was not the only religious institution that regularly received gifts from the faithful. Brahman priests in India were required by caste rules to maintain independence from employment. They therefore accepted compensation for performance of their priestly functions only in the form of gifts (*dakshina*).[184] Gifts that were not forthcoming could be compelled. Because of their magical powers, Brahmans could take revenge by means of curses or deliberate mistakes in the prescribed rituals. During certain periods the gifts consisted of extensive land grants or agricultural rents to be received in perpetuity. According to Brahmanic theory, Brahmans alone were permitted to receive gifts of land.

c. The Early Modern Period

43. *The Mortmain Act.* The intimate connection between gifts and feudal power caused the political institution of gift giving to fall into disrepute at the beginning of the early modern period. Distrust of ecclesiastical charity became so widespread in England that, in 1736, Parliament passed the Mortmain Act to protect a testator's family from disinheritance.[185] As stated in the act's preamble,

> [G]ifts or alienations of lands, Tenements or Hereditaments, in *Mortmain*, are prohibited or restrained by *Magna Charta*, and divers other wholesome Laws, as prejudicial to and against the common Utility; nevertheless this publick Mischief has of late greatly increased by many large and improvident Alienations or Dispositions made by languishing or dying Persons, or by

---

182. Silber (1995) 210, quoting Duby 174.
183. White 19–39.
184. Bendix 161–162.
185. Jones (1969) 109–113.

other Persons, to uses called *Charitable Uses*, to take Place after their Deaths, to the Dishersion of their lawful Heirs.[186]

44. *The Ordinance of 1731.* As Voltaire famously noted, France under the ancien régime was governed by so many different legal customs, 144 by his count, that travelers changed laws almost as often as they changed post-horses. "[W]hat's true in the Faubourg Montmartre becomes false at the Abbaye St.-Denis. May God have pity on us!"[187] With the goal of unifying the customs and creating a single code of laws, Henri François d'Aguesseau, chancellor to Louis XV, promulgated a number of private law decrees, including the Ordinance of 1731,[188] the direct ancestor of modern French codification and the central document in the history of the civilian law of gifts.[189] His confidence that unification could be achieved was probably due to his admiration for the treatise of his teacher and friend Jean Domat and his studious consultation of the work of Joseph Bretonnier, who had brilliantly attempted to reconcile and restate French law.[190] Yet little is known about how d'Aguesseau chose one customary solution over another. Two likely influences were his mercantilist economic views and his Jansenist convictions. As a mercantilist, he believed that, in a well-run state, wealth should be concentrated in the hands of those who would use it productively and thereby provide tax revenues.[191] Transactions outside of the market may thus have seemed especially suspicious. D'Aguesseau's strict Jansenist morality caused him to disfavor speculative ventures, including card games, the stock market, and banking.[192] In order to assure that a contract was not scandalous or contrary

---

186. Mortmain Act of 1736 sec. 1. The Magna Charta of Henry III already prohibited gifts into mortmain. Ch. 36. In 1279 and 1290, Parliament again prohibited gifts to religious or other institutions that would increase mortmain. Statute of Mortmain of 1279 sec. 2; Statute of Westminster (*Quia emptores*) of 1290 ch. 3. The crown was concerned because feudal dues and other incidents could not be extracted from property held in mortmain. Raban 3–4. A system of royal licenses soon emerged and the church found ways to use them to advantage. Though effort and expense was involved, the church's freedom of action was not greatly impaired. Id. 23, 26.

187. "Customs—Usages," in 8 Voltaire 48–49 (translation revised).

188. Ordinance concerning gifts of 1731.

189. 1 Regnault 50–57.

190. For d'Aguesseau's legislative activity, see Monnier 280–368. For his relationship with Domat, id. 316–326. For his reading of Bretonnier, id. 328–332. Bretonnier's *Receuil* was first published in 1718. For Bretonnier's views on the difficulty of unifying French customary law, see Bretonnier lxxxvij–lxxxviij. Bretonnier noted that Aristide (d'Aguesseau's pen name) first suggested to him the project of his *Receuil*. In Bretonnier's view, d'Aguesseau was a Hebrew prophet sent from God who brought to the task of legislation profound scholarship, long experience, and a passion for justice. Id. lxxxix–xc.

191. Bayart 99–100. For an analysis of d'Aguesseau's mercantilist views, see Harsin 213–226.

192. Carbonnier (1953) 40–41; see also Storez 551–565.

to social mores, he thought it necessary to examine its cause. Because d'Aguesseau believed that gift giving was more susceptible to duress and undue influence than were market transactions, he decided to subject the practice to stricter legal control.

d. The Market Economy

45. *Common-law evolution.* The evolution of the common law was based on different concerns, particularly the difficult task of reorienting the writ system away from its focus on land tenure and toward actions relevant to resolving disputes arising in the marketplace. Because gift giving was an activity associated more with feudalism than with entrepreneurship, the later forms of action generally ignored the giving of gifts. Equity, the other major component of modern common law, regulated gift giving only in situations of marked unfairness. As a result, gifts in common-law countries have long been governed largely by extra-legal norms.

46. *Economic liberalism.* In the mid-nineteenth century, the limited intervention of the common law in gift giving was reinterpreted from the perspective of economic liberalism. Oliver Wendell Holmes, a leading architect of American law, narrowly interpreted the scope of contract law to preserve as much scope as possible for the self-regulated activity of the individual subject.[193] Holmes therefore sought to restrict the intervention of the courts to situations in which there was a quid pro quo.[194] Implicit in his vision was the idea that individuals should be permitted to decide for themselves whether to perform gratuitous promises.

47. *Development of the market economy.* As the market economy developed, legal concepts were reformulated from a market perspective.[195] "[C]ommon law doctrines create incentives for people to channel their transactions through the market."[196] Because gift giving, even when mutual, does not involve a bargain, the law considered it an anomaly, a unilateral transaction in which a donor, for no good economic reason, gives something away. Gift giving represented an unproductive exchange, an idiosyncratic whim that, if too often repeated, leads to destitution.

> A gratuitous transfer (*l'acte à titre gratuit*) is, in all senses, the *exception*. It is even, economically speaking, an absurd act, one that, from many points of view, poses serious risks. In fact, one of the typical forms of the gratuitous transfer, the gift, often serves ends completely different from those that

---

193. For the canonic but controversial discussion of the limitations Holmes sought to impose on American contract law, see Gilmore (1974) 14–61.

194. "[I]t is the essence of a consideration, that, by the terms of the agreement, it is given and accepted as the motive or inducement of the promise." Holmes 230.

195. Horowitz 160–210; Gilmore (1974).

196. Posner (2007) 249.

constitute its essence: the intention to give, to gratify. The pure and true *animus donandi* certainly should not be entirely proscribed—if only not to encourage a too pessimistic conception of humanity—but it is permissible to say that an act, at least inter vivos, that is inspired solely by the desire to gratify, is *rare*.[197]

48. *Emancipation.* The gift became the quintessential nonmarket transaction. As the eighteenth century Enlightenment campaigned for individual freedom, it recognized that, in the feudal version of the gift economy, an individual lived under long-term dependencies that were impossible to sunder, whereas, under a system of commodity exchange, individuals are free to enter and exit from relationships as they choose. In his *Solitary Walker*, Rousseau captured the potential tyranny of the gift economy, a tyranny all the more powerful because it is willed by neither participant.[198] Because the market was able to break apart the web of dependency that characterized feudalism, it became the Enlightenment's ally in the quest for human freedom. Whereas the gift signified dependence, exchange meant freedom.[199] In this process, the virtues of rationality and freedom became identified with commodity transactions, whereas gift giving was

---

197. 8 De Page no. 2 (emphasis in original).
198. I know that there is a kind of contract, indeed the most sacred of contracts, between the benefactor and the recipient; together they form a kind of society, which is more closely knit than the society which unites men in general, and if the recipient tacitly promises his gratitude, the benefactor likewise commits himself to continue showing the same kindness as long as the recipient remains worthy of it, and to repeat his acts of charity whenever he is asked and is capable of doing so. These are not explicit conditions, but they are the natural consequences of the relationship which has just come into being. A person who refuses a gratuitous favour the first time it is asked of him gives the person he refuses no grounds for complaint, but anyone who in a similar situation refuses the same person the same favour which he had previously granted, frustrates a hope which his behaviour has authorized; he disappoints and belies an expectation which he himself has brought into being. This refusal is felt as being harsher and more unjust than the former, but nevertheless it is the product of an independence which is dear to our hearts and cannot be relinquished without dificulty. Rousseau 97–98 (Sixth Walk).
199. The market makes free. The economy based on exchange is a system of freedom. The obligational relationship and exchange are born and evolve in free societies .... The economy based on the gift, and thus on the values that rest on the unilateral gratuitous act, is an economy deprived of the perspective of freedom, it is a society that maintains the ties of personal dependence. Both feudal society and Roman civilization found in the client relationship the reason and the cause of personal relations based on the concession of favors, of benefits, of privileges of which the donor is the sole dispenser because titulary of a personal power over other subjects. Mazzoni 705.

understood to result from an irrational impulse, derived either from emotions of affection, from the desire for dependence, or from excessive religiosity.[200] Schroeder's masterly Hegelian-Lacanian reading of the gift transaction makes clear that, to German idealism, the gift compared unfavorably to contract as a means to promote mutual recognition and freedom.[201] By the end of the nineteenth century gift giving had acquired a negative valence. Donors were those who sacrificed their families in quest of elusive goals such as divine grace or posthumous recognition.[202]

"Gift-exchange ... has been fractured, leaving gifts opposed to exchange, persons opposed to things and interest to disinterest. The ideology of a disinterested gift emerges in parallel with an ideology of a purely interested exchange."[203] The sphere of commodity exchange became gendered as male, whereas communal and personalized labors that could not as easily be commodified because they have neither beginning nor end, such as the bearing and raising of children, keeping house, and managing affective relationships, were relegated to the women's sphere.[204]

e. Comparative Notes

49. *Response to particular circumstances.* Historians have shown how gift giving has responded to the historically existing aspects of different societies. The goals of the historian are also appropriate for this comparative study. The goal here is to explore how gift norms dialogue with other aspects of a society's culture and

---

200. Here had I time I could inveigh with warmth against those base, those wicked women, who calmly play their arts and false deluding charms against our strength and prudence, and act the harlots with their husbands! Nay, she is worse than whore, who impiously profanes and prostitutes the sacred rites of love to vile ignoble ends, that first excites to passion and invites to joys with seeming ardour, then racks our fondness for no other purpose than to extort a gift, while full of guile in counterfeited transports she watches for the moment when men can least deny.

Mandeville 100.

For a modern statement of the idea, see Eisenberg (1997) 847: "[T]he world of contract is a market world, largely driven by relatively impersonal considerations and focused on commodities and prices .... In contrast, much of the world of gift is driven by affective considerations like love, affection, friendship, gratitude, and comradeship."

201. Gift, in contrast, is not merely the failure to achieve perfect mutuality and equality in practice, it is one-sided and hierarchical by its very nature. Consequently, insofar as the modern rule of law in the constitutional state is based on an ideal of equality and autonomy, there is an inherent logic in the law's privileging of contractual relations and suspicion of gift.

Schroeder 903. See also id. 870–873.

202. Marais 289–292.

203. Parry 458.

204. Margolis 13; Di Leonardo.

history and contribute to a particular social understanding of the role of gift giving. Comparative law participates by revealing essential differences in legal conception and doctrinal construction, even among otherwise similar legal orders. Because, as the historians remind us, these conceptions change over time, this comparative study also examines the evolution of this give-and-take between gift norms and social practice.

3. Economics

50. *Direct challenge.* Gift giving provides economics with a direct challenge. Economists seek to explain human behavior in terms of rational, self-interested action. One of the fundamental premises of most economic models is that individuals are principally actuated by self-interest.[205] Economists are aware that the premise is not realistic. Human beings act from many motivations. Yet the assumption helps to show the contribution egoistic behavior can make to the general good.[206] Economists often conclude that a decentralized market guided by price signals in which actors are motivated by self-interest is superior to the alternatives.

51. *Self-interest and gift giving.* The problem for the economist is that much of gift giving does not seem to fit the mold of self-interested action. A donor parts with something and gets nothing in exchange. Because economics is concerned with the role of self-seeking action and because much contemporary gift giving appears to be based on altruistic motives, it might be expected that economics would leave gift giving to one side. But that is not what has happened. Instead, economists have challenged themselves to explain the gift economy in terms of self-interested action. In much of the literature, the goal is to explain why a rational person would engage in gift giving. "Why would 'economic man' ever make a promise without receiving in exchange something of value from the promisee ... ?"[207] In other words, the challenge to economics is to explain the practice of gift giving based on a conceptual structure that, at least at first glance, seems foreign to the gift relationship.

52. *Inadequacy.* Inadequacy is a typical problem. The question is why gifts are often made in kind rather than in cash.[208] Because economic theory suggests that money is the perfect gift,[209] both donor and donee should prefer a gift of cash to a gift in kind. With a gift of cash, the donor avoids the time-consuming quest for the perfect gift, while the donee can choose among all the riches of the

---

205. "Each individual or family generally is assumed to have a utility function that depends directly on the goods and services it consumes." Becker 1065; see also Sen 317.
   206. Sen 321.
   207. Posner (1977) 411–412.
   208. Ven (2000) 3.
   209. Solnick and Hemenway 1303.

market. Nonetheless, as everyone knows, and as empirical research seems to confirm, though money is frequently gifted,[210] a cash gift is often improper.[211] This fact creates what Waldfogel has called *the deadweight of gift giving*. His research among Yale undergraduates has shown that the inadequacy of Christmas gifts creates a deadweight loss of between a tenth and a third of the value of the gifts.[212] In other words, donors and donees are obviously not attempting to maximize utility in a traditional economic sense.

a. Proposed Explanations

53. *Various issues.* Three discussions in the economics literature are relevant to this study, namely those seeking to explain why rational donors give gifts, why gift giving survives in a fully commodified economy, and why gift promises are made.

i. Donor Motivation

54. *Numerous theories.* Economists have proposed numerous constructions to reconcile the giving of gifts with the assumption that rational individuals maximize utility. Unfortunately, no theory consistent with the rational action model is able to explain all of the conduct typically associated with gift giving.

(A) ALTRUISM

55. *Pure altruism.* The simplest explanation for gift giving is that donors are altruistic. In economics terms, the donor's own preferences include optimizing the donee's utility.[213] Though intuitively apt, the pure altruism thesis fails to explain some aspects of gift giving. For example, it is inconsistent with the fact that gifts are often not given in cash. The cash gift would provide the greatest increase in donee utility.[214] Pure altruism also cannot explain why charities publicize the names of their donors, or why large gifts are broadly communicated and publicly celebrated.[215]

56. *Warm-glow altruism.* To solve these problems, some economists suggest that altruism is not pure. Donors also think of themselves when they give. They give because they have developed a personal taste for giving, they "experience a 'warm glow' from having 'done their bit.'"[216] Donors derive utility from helping others

---

210. Zelizer 85–91.
211. "The look of horror and disbelief on many subjects' faces when asked to imagine giving money to the person they had chosen was perhaps the best indication of their general reluctance to use it as a gift." Webley and Wilson 99.
212. Waldfogel (1993) 1328. See also Waldfogel (1996).
213. Ven (2000) 4–5; Posner (1977) 412; Becker.
214. Ven (2002) 478.
215. Posner (1997) 574.
216. Andreoni 1448.

to become more satisfied, and particularly from their own contributions.[217] Thus, their goal is not just to improve the donee's situation but also to experience the pleasure that assisting others provides.[218]

From a noneconomist's point of view, the warm-glow thesis seems accurate. Its problem is on a different level. To begin with, it explains nothing. No formula is needed to reach the conclusion that donors give away property because it gives them pleasure. More importantly, including donative pleasure in the definition of self-interest creates a tautology.[219] It is circular to suggest that individuals seek to maximize utility and then to define utility as whatever they happen to be seeking to maximize.

(B) SOCIAL RELATIONSHIPS

57. *Symbolic utility.* The symbolic utility thesis is based on the understanding that reciprocal gift exchange, by producing mutual sympathy and recognition, yields the self-respect that comes from having gained the respect of others.[220] In contrast to substantive utility, which involves material advantage, symbolic utility provides what is needed to affirm the psychological advantage of mutual bonds.[221] The thesis is that donors give because they enjoy the relationships that gift giving produces. Gift exchange persists alongside the market economy because, though the market provides higher substantive utility, it cannot provide symbolic utility. Once again, the explanation seems accurate. Yet once again it is tautological. Once utility is redefined to include the noneconomic benefits of mutual respect, there is no need for economic analysis.

58. *Social approval.* The social approval thesis is based on the theory that individuals have two basic goals: economic gain and social acceptance. The thesis suggests that gifts are given to increase the donor's social approval rating.[222] Empirical research suggests that donors are more generous when their gifts are publicized. Other research confirms that individuals have a taste for social status and approval.[223] For example, it appears that charitable gifts are rarely made

---

217. Arrow 348.
218. I finally provided a *dénouement* by buying the apples from the little girl and letting her share them out among the little boys. Then I had one of the sweetest sights that the human heart can enjoy, that of seeing joy and youthful innocence all around me, for the spectators too had a part in the emotion that met their eyes, and I, who shared in this joy at so little cost to myself, had the added pleasure of feeling that I was the author of it."
Rousseau 146 (Ninth Walk).
219. Sen 322.
220. Ven (2000) 5–7.
221. Klundert and Ven 4.
222. Ven (2000) 7–8.
223. Ven (2002) 465.

anonymously.[224] The suggestion is that the desire for social approval is as important as the need for consumption goods. "[P]eople not only want to be admired, but also want to be admired more than others."[225] Status attaches to those with great wealth. But wealth itself is not usually observable. The wealthy obtain status by doing what only the wealthy can do, which is to live on a grand scale.[226] Status can be gained by consumption, but it is also can be gained by giving gifts.

Social approval is difficult to obtain in the market because the market, in its pure form, is an anonymous institution. Moreover, a certain type of social approval is incompatible with the market. Though universities solicit donations, they would refuse to sell naming rights to the highest bidder. The sale would diminish the reputation of both parties to the transaction. A charitable donation, on the other hand, even in an equivalent amount, confirms that the university is worthy and that the donor is a patron of culture. "In a phrase, people value reputations for generosity, ingenuity, and fair-mindedness; but if one could purchase such reputations, then they would cease to exist."[227] In the social approval model, two factors influence the amount of the gift. The first is the correlation between value and the magnitude of social approval. Social approval increases with the value of the gift. The second is the fact that concern about status differs among individuals. As a result, some individuals give more than others.

The social approval thesis integrates gift giving into the framework of rational action by redefining utility to include the goal of social approval. Because social approval is not available in the market but can be obtained by making gifts, especially charitable donations, individuals who seek approval act rationally when they give gifts. The difficulty with the thesis becomes apparent when we ask why social approval cannot be obtained in the market. It seems obvious that social approval is produced by participating in activities that benefit society, often by sacrificing time, money, and energy that otherwise might be devoted to self-serving activity. A charitable donation, therefore, represents a renunciation of personal interest to achieve a social benefit. But the assumption of the rational self-interest model has always been that rational individuals prefer their private interests to social benefit. The social approval thesis has simply redefined self-interest in such a way that it accords with the type of action individuals tend to engage in. The thesis thus fails to integrate gift giving into the model of rational self-interest. Moreover, the thesis fails to explain some aspects of gift exchange, such as anonymous giving.

---

224. Posner (1997) 574 note 17.
225. Ven (2002) 468.
226. Posner (1997) 575.
227. Id. 574.

(C) MARKET RELATIONS

59. *Trading partners.* Another thesis explains gift giving as a market mechanism with a signaling function. Buyers and sellers can use gift giving as a means to locate trustworthy trading partners.[228] Eric Posner points out that some nonlegal mechanism such as trust must be present to account fully for those contracts, known as relational contracts, in which the contract's value depends on the parties' ability to rely on each other over time.[229] Relational contractors seek trustworthy partners. The argument is that gift giving provides a reliable signal of trustworthiness. Those who sincerely intend to enter into long-term relationships can afford to make significant gifts, whereas those who are focused on short-term gains cannot.[230]

The thesis correctly recognizes that gift giving can create and maintain a relationship of sympathy and mutual respect. It then suggests that this characteristic of gift giving can have subsidiary benefits in the market. However, this thesis explains little about the vast field of gift giving beyond market relations. It also does not attempt to explain anonymous giving.[231]

(D) COMMITMENT

60. *Unexplained.* Amartya Sen grasps more of the practice of gift giving, but at the cost of abandoning much of the model of rational self-interest. Sen distinguishes between two motivations for giving assistance to others: sympathy and commitment.[232] Donors who contribute to homeless shelters because it pains them to think of the plight of the homeless give out of sympathy. When they give because they wish to improve the living conditions of the homeless, they give out of commitment. Sympathy is a type of egoism, a variety of self-interest. Commitment is not. Someone who gives out of commitment chooses to use resources to improve society at the price of a diminution in the donor's own personal welfare. As Sen notes, much economic theory assumes that properly informed individuals will choose to maximize personal utility. Economic theory has no place for a distinction between personal choice and personal welfare.

In other words, the basic quality of much modern gift giving, the choice to improve another's welfare with no equivalent compensation, cannot be explained by the economic model of the rational actor. As Sen points out, human beings do

---

228. Ven (2000) 12–16.

229. Posner (1997) 578.

230. Id. 579–580.

231. In its sociological version, signaling theory becomes an attempt to understand how meaning can be conveyed when gift giving is assumed as a social convention. See Camerer. By using this conventional background, sociological analysis is able to explain many features of inadequate giving. However, this method is not available to economic analysis, which is attempting to explain the convention itself.

232. Sen 326.

not spend every waking moment maximizing personal gain.[233] Many of us go out of our way to help complete strangers. We do this based on what Sen calls social conditioning. Our lived relationship to the world is largely a result of the context produced by socialization. Economics does not address the role of social custom and tradition. When this context is ignored, gift giving seems irrational. "The *purely* economic man is indeed close to being a social moron. Economic theory has been much preoccupied with this rational fool decked in the glory of his *one* all-purpose preference ordering. To make room for the different concepts related to his behavior we need a more elaborate structure."[234]

The challenge is to understand the rationality of the socially aware human being who is both actor and acted upon, who has volition and agency but at the same time acts within social forms that represent an internalization of social custom. We do not always maximize utility, we occasionally give gifts, and yet we have no doubt that our choices are rational. It seems imprudent to settle for a theory that models anything less than the whole of our being, especially if the part that is left out is so fulfilling.

ii. Gift and the Market

61. *Allocation of goods.* Kenneth Arrow suggested that economists who investigate the gift economy suffer from a particular blindness. Contrary to standard economic models, the allocation of goods and services in modern society does not take place entirely by exchange.[235] This is true not only for intangibles like respect, love, and status, but also, for example, for such critical items as the blood supply. Philanthropy has always been an essential part of economic systems. Public goods, ranging from roads and street lighting to foreign aid, education, and cultural offerings, have grown dramatically as a share of the domestic economy.[236] Personal services are donated both to the local Little League and to the political system. The redistribution of wealth through the tax system also does not take place through the market.

Arrow agrees with Eric Posner's observation, mentioned above, that non-economic virtues such as truthfulness are essential to the economic system. "Virtually every commercial transaction has within itself an element of trust ...."[237] In Arrow's words, the categorical imperative and the price system are complements. As a result, even the overwhelming commodification of modern society will not cause the gift economy to vanish.[238]

---

233. Id. 331–332.
234. Id. 336 (emphasis in original).
235. Arrow 344.
236. Sen 330.
237. Arrow 357.
238. For the fear that the gift economy is on the way out, see Klundert and Ven 20–21.

62. *Production value.* Yet even Arrow fails to grasp the true economic importance of gift giving in modern society. Despite the frequently expressed view that gift giving is a sterile, useless activity, a relatively large proportion of modern economies is devoted to producing gifts. Davis calculates that about 4 percent of consumer expenditure in the UK is the result of donor purchases.[239] The value of manufacturers' sales of commodities used for gifts exceeds sales by the shipbuilding and marine engine industry and approaches the total sales from coal mining. "In this sense gifts are five times more important in the economy than all nuts and bolts and screws; forty-five times more than cement; eighty-six times more than glue. In short, the apparently small percentages conceal really quite important magnitudes."[240] Davis included only new purchases in his calculations, what we call presents. He did not include the value of existing property, both real and personal, that is gifted every day.

63. *Redistributional effects.* Gifts also play an important role in redistributing wealth to those in whose hands the gift property has a higher utility. Redistribution may have a positive effect on aggregate demand[241] and may enhance the utilities of both donor and donee.[242]

iii. Gift Promises

64. *Deferred giving.* Economic analysis encounters unexpected difficulty in explaining the familiar institution of the gift promise. Economists seek to understand why donors sometimes wish to defer gift giving, why they prefer to make a promise rather than an immediate transfer, and why they announce their intentions in advance. They also consider whether gift promises should be legally enforceable and the consequences that would result if donors were bound to their promises.

(A) ECONOMIC ANALYSIS

65. *Reasons to defer.* Shavell suggests three reasons why donors may wish to defer their gifts.[243] Donors may not have sufficient assets when the promise is made, they may be able to attain a higher return on principal than their donees, or they may wish to keep their options open in light of possible contingencies, such as unforeseen economic difficulties, new investment opportunities, or the donee's ingratitude.

66. *Reasons to announce.* Richard Posner suggests that donors benefit by announcing their intentions in advance. The promise increases the likelihood

---

239. Davis (1972) 412.
240. Id.
241. Eisenberg (1979) 4.
242. Hochman and Rodgers 543.
243. Shavell 402.

that the gift will be made in the future, which in turn increases the present value of the gift and therefore the donor's own utility.[244] Because there are no costs to a gift promise, the promise itself increases net social welfare. Goetz and Scott suggest that the importance of a promise is that it provides information about the future.[245] The promise will give the donee greater confidence that the gift will be made and will encourage the donee's beneficial reliance.[246]

67. *Reasons to be bound.* Shavell suggests that donors generally do not wish to be bound to their gift promises.[247] However, some donors may prefer enforceability to distinguish themselves from those who seek to entice the donee to rely but do not in fact intend to make the promised gift. In that situation, the binding gift promise improves the welfare of both donor and donee. On the other hand, Kull argues that enforcing gratuitous promises benefits donors by permitting them to arrange their affairs in a secure manner. If gift promises are not binding, donors can attain their goals only through more cumbersome arrangements, such as a trust.[248]

68. *Effects of a binding promise.* Shavell concludes that the effects of a binding gift promise are not always positive. If gift promises were binding, donors who fear financial setbacks may reduce the number of promises they make, and therefore perhaps also the number of gifts. Posner's premise is that gift promises should only be enforced when the net gain from enforcement exceeds the enforcement cost. He concludes that the case for enforcement is stronger when the promised transfer is larger.[249]

Goetz and Scott provide a subtle economic analysis of the incentive structure surrounding the gift promise. They believe that the goal of enforcing promises is to maximize what they call the net beneficial reliance derived from promise making.[250] That can be achieved by increasing the donee's confidence in performance without overly reducing the total number of promises. Goetz and Scott reject the award of expectation damages because they believe it would overdeter promise making.[251] They also reject reliance damages because courts do not have a cost-effective means to make the subtle judgments required to make a proper damage award.[252] Goetz and Scott conclude that the parties themselves, by adjusting their actions to take account of any perceived uncertainty of performance,

---

244. Posner (1977) 412.

245. Goetz and Scott 1267.

246. Id. 1276–1283. For a critical analysis of this rigorous but difficult article, see Fellows (1988).

247. Shavell 419–421.

248. Kull 59–64.

249. Posner (1977) 414–415, 420, 426.

250. Goetz and Scott 1321.

251. Id. 1287.

252. Id. 1290–1291, 1309.

can more accurately maximize beneficial reliance than can the courts. In sum, the extra-legal sanctions available to the promisee together with the adjustments both parties can make to accommodate contingencies provide a satisfactory substitute for legal enforcement.

(B) DIFFICULTIES

69. *Practical problem.* The practical problem the gift promise presents is how the law should react when the donee relies on a gift promise that the promisor later decides not to perform. Economists have therefore tried to determine the situations in which social welfare is increased by enforcing a gift promise. In some circumstances they would compensate the donee for detrimental reliance. Significantly, economic analysis has not yet been able to distinguish the two different cases that frequently arise.

70. *Change of heart.* The first case involves the donor's change of heart. Donors may change their minds after making a promise, but not principally, as the economists assume, due to unforeseen financial reversals. Sometimes the relationship between the parties changes. If, given the relationship, the promise was socially proper when it was made, and if that relationship continues, it seems likely that the gift will be completed. If, however, the donee and the donor have drifted apart, if the donee has been ungrateful or in some other way has disappointed the donor, the gift may no longer be appropriate. Goetz and Scott suggest that the parties might agree in advance to the consequences of a change in circumstances. The two scholars also recognize, however, that a donative promise is fragile and that it is likely to be difficult to spell out the consequences of the donee's ingratitude.[253]

When the results of economic analysis are examined from the point of view of social practice, the economists' questions—the potential economic gain from the promise and the economic loss from reliance—seem to be of secondary importance. The economic perspective does not take account of the subtle interpersonal context of the relationship between the parties, which is the essence of the gift relationship. When that relationship changes, money damages may not be appropriate, even in the face of significant detrimental reliance.

71. *The executor's refusal.* In the common law, suits to enforce gift promises are usually brought against the donor's estate.[254] It is not the donor who recants the promise but the donor's executor, and not because the donor has decided against the gift, but rather because the executor is prohibited from making transfers that are not legally required. If the donor maintained the promise until death,

---

253. Id. 1304–1305.
254. Kull 45–46.

there seems to be no reason not to enforce the full expectation value of the promise.[255]

In other words, depending on the circumstances, it may not be appropriate to award damages even in the case of reliance, or it may be proper to award expectation damages even without reliance.[256] The economic approach has not yet focused on this central distinction.

b. Comparative Notes

72. *Much is ignored.* Economists' assumptions exclude much that is essential about gift giving. The problem is not just that their motivation theses do not form a comprehensive theory.[257] The problem is rather that the theses have little explanatory force. Economics is unable to grasp that gift giving is both a voluntary act and an element of social practice.[258] The obvious question is whether the same is true of the law.

The inadequacy problem serves well as an example. As discussed above, economic analysis attempts to reconcile the theoretical postulate that cash would be the best gift with the fact that gifts are often given in kind. The difficulty, it turns out, is with the formulation of the problem. As a moment's reflection makes clear, cash given as a gift is not a universal equivalent. Zelizer has pointed out that the donee who receives a check as a birthday present is not free to spend it on just anything.[259] The check cannot be cashed for groceries or used to pay a gambling debt. Instead, the gifting of money transfers the difficult choice of an appropriate gift from the donor to the donee. Since the thank-you note must mention how the money was spent, the donee who receives cash has the task of finding a gift that is suitable to the relationship. In this regard, gift certificates, though they restrict the donee's freedom of choice, help the donee understand the type of gift the donor had in mind. In other words, much of economic analysis of gift giving has been devoted to resolving a puzzle that does not exist.

---

255. "In all the cases just mentioned, however, the promisor died solvent without a change of heart. Whether the promisee would have been allowed to recover against the wishes of the promisor, or to take his place in line with creditors, is sheer conjecture." Gordley (1995) 579.

256. "[T]he presumptive unenforceability rule makes sense for a renounced promise and makes no sense for an unrepudiated promise." Fellows (1988) 28.

257. "As it stands, no single theory can explain everything." Ven (2002) 479.

258. "Probably the main explanation for the neglect of social interactions by economists is neither analytical intractability nor a preoccupation with more important concepts, but excessive attention to formal developments during the last 70 years. As a consequence, even concepts considered to be important by earlier economists, such as social interactions, have been shunted aside." Becker 1091.

259. Zelizer 111.

i. Relationships as Externalities

73. *Essential to the market.* For economics, moral sensibility is an externality. The market relies on mutual trust, yet economics is unable to grasp the gift relationship that creates and maintains this trust. It is symptomatic that Waldfogel, as he calculated what appeared to him to be the deadweight loss of Christmas giving, instructed his Yale undergraduates to ignore any "sentimental value"[260] when estimating the value of the gifts they received. Other investigators have determined that a gift's sentimental value is significant.[261] Many respondents ascribe a value to the gifts they receive that exceeds their cost.[262] In other words, when all factors are included, gifts actually create value.

Because the relational context is so crucial to the gift relationship, a comparative study must find a way to take account of it. The difficulty, of course, is that legal norms, like the economists' model, often do not explicitly consider the relationship between the parties. Yet the courts consider these subtleties. In this field, the path to the heart of the matter leads through an analysis of the facts of individual cases.

ii. Subeconomies

74. *Differing contexts.* Both economics and the law focus on the market economy. Yet the reproduction of a modern society, even economic reproduction, depends on numerous subeconomies. Each of those subeconomies functions according to its own logic and rules. Davis distinguishes four:[263] the market, governed by commercial and labor law; the redistributive economy of taxation and state expenditure; the family economy, governed by family law and the expectations of family life; and finally the gift economy, governed by the Maussian obligations and the law of gifts.

As Davis noted, even this enumeration ignores much of economic life. No picture of modern transactions is complete without an account of other economies as well: the patronage economy, the expenses of turning out the vote and lobbying for the pork; the vice economy, including drug traffic, illegal gambling, and prostitution, practices often governed by their own norms, such as the code of silence (*omertà*); the war economy, which causes the destruction of lives and capital for symbolic and material goals and which is partially subject to international law; the legal economy, including transactions between lawyers and clients as well as agreements and exchanges between opposing counsel, including sub-subeconomies, such as the forensic economy and agreements and exchanges with the police and plea bargains; and the volunteer economy, which involves

---

260. Waldfogel (1993) 1331.
261. Solnick and Hemenway 1301. For Waldfogel's response, see Waldfogel (1996).
262. Solnick and Hemenway 1300.
263. Davis (1972) 408.

services rendered for the public good and which are excluded from the gift economy because no transfer of rights is involved.

Given the numerous economies required for social reproduction, it is obvious that rules developed for the relatively narrow practice of market exchange cannot possibly govern all of these fields. And it becomes clear that the motivational analysis that applies to rational actors in the marketplace does not always describe rational action in other contexts. A comparative study of the law should examine how the law interacts with the rules native to the domains it governs.

iii. Market Blindness

75. *Grasping the essential.* The failings of economic analysis mirror similar failings in the law. The same presuppositions and the same blindnesses are present in both. Sometimes the law discourages gift giving because, from the point of view of the rational, self-interested actor, it is absurd to give something away without getting something in return. Economists reformulate gift giving to reconcile it with the self-interested actor. But the unsatisfying results of their efforts suggest instead that the economics of the marketplace are irreconcilable with the gift economy. We live in (at least) two different and somewhat incompatible worlds. We experience the incompatibility at certain moments, such as when we are stumped about the proper present for a boss or a secretary, but we generally do not conceptualize the problem.

To grasp the relationship between these different spheres, it is useful to analyze the role that social custom and practice play and the obligations they impose from beyond the law. In other words, this study can succeed only to the extent that it abandons Western law's self-understanding as the predominant source of social norms. Extra-legal norms are not always an enemy to be besieged and vanquished. In the end, both economics and the law should expand the concept of the rational actor. A legal system is dysfunctional if it understands rationality only in terms of market-oriented behavior and then protects against or prohibits everything else.

4. Philosophy and Sociology

76. *Meaning and paradox.* Philosophy and sociology seek the meaning contained within the paradoxes that constitute the social practice of gift giving. As discussed above, gifts must be given freely, and yet, at the same time, they are obligatory. The giving of a gift is experienced as a discrete, individual act, yet it necessarily participates in a chain of repeated events. The gift cannot be seen as a quid pro quo without destroying its gratuitous character, yet gift giving always involves the obligation to reciprocate. Gifts establish and confirm relationships, they express gratitude, they do favors for friends; and yet they establish hierarchy, they annoy, they embarrass, and they dominate. In no other social institution are such conflicting meanings encoded and conveyed, often at the same time.

Among the gift-related questions that philosophers and sociologists seek to answer, two are particularly relevant here: first, whether any coherent meaning can be found in the practice of gift giving, and, second, whether gift theory can play a role in social reform.

a. The "Pure" Gift

77. *Contract and gift.* As the gratuitous transaction surrendered its central role in societal reproduction to the marketplace, it was retooled to fit the needs of the private sphere and individual conscience.[264] This is what Helmut Berking has called the transition from *Gabe* to *Geschenk*, from social gift to individual present.[265] As Eisenberg has explained, we live today in two worlds, in a *world of contract* and a *world of gift*.[266] Whereas market exchange augments public wealth, the gift is considered a *sterile transaction*.[267] Yet its economic infertility has been its boon. The gift is now *pure*. It is the product of individual whim, an act done without obligation. In this modern conception, the gift has been reconciled with individual freedom by eliminating its connection to dependency and promoting its role as a direct expression of individual altruism.[268] The selflessness of the gift provides a counterpoint to the market economy, which can leave conscience to one side and focus without reserve on the pursuit of self-interest.

78. *Spheres of influence.* Gift giving has now been relegated to particular spheres, including the intimacy of friends and family. Individuals who have developed a sensitivity for gift giving can use gifts to maintain relationships at the desired level or to advance them toward greater intimacy.[269] In the private sphere, gifts given during familiar rites of passage—presents for birthdays and holidays, weddings, anniversaries, graduations, and baby showers, gifts given to the host or hostess at dinner parties, and those placed under the pillow by the tooth fairy—operate to create and maintain relationships, though of course they may also serve as a mechanism of hierarchy and control. Santa Claus, that most industrious of gift givers, retains the ability to withhold gifts to assure good behavior. And he is all the more unapproachable since his gifts cannot be reciprocated.[270]

---

264. Godelier 207.
265. Berking 3.
266. Eisenberg (1997) 823 passim.
267. Bufnoir 487, quoted in Fuller (1941) 815.
268. Carrier (1990) 20–21; see also Emerson.
269. "What makes gift selection an elaborate and difficult task, however, is that gifts not only reflect social ties but can redefine them. Giving an overly personal gift to a mere acquaintance, a much too expensive gift to a fiancée, or an impersonal gift to one's mother confuses, annoys, or offends by implying or forcing a mistaken definition of the social relation." Zelizer 78–79.
270. Schwartz 4.

A particularly developed example of the role gift giving plays in maintaining close personal relationships is found in the German institution of the godparent (*Taufpate*), who, in exchange for honorary status in the family, has been expected, in certain regions and in certain periods, to make prescribed presents at specific moments in the child's life. The godparent purchases the clothing worn to baptism (*Taufkleid*), is responsible for the baptismal certificate (*Patenbrief*), and inserts the baptismal medal (*Patentaler*) into the baptismal cushion (*Taufkissen*). At Christmas the godparent makes a gift of a new piece of clothing, at New Year's a pretzel, at Easter a specific number of eggs, at the beginning of the school year a backpack, at confirmation a watch or a chain, and at marriage a meaningful monetary gift.[271] In the Austrian region of Gmunden, it was long customary for the godparent (*Goden*), shortly after the child's birth, to bring chicken soup as a gift (*Weigert*). The soup was always contained in a special bowl (*Godenschale*) that was custom-decorated with a picture of the child's name saint and was accompanied with a distinctive lid, saucer-shaped and fitted with three short feet to support it when it was turned upside down.

79. *Modern philanthropy.* Another role of the pure gift is the modern practice of public charity. The monotheist religions, which systematically ethicize social behavior, have developed a particularly extensive culture of disinterested giving.[272] Virtually everyone in modern society, at one time or another, is involved in either the giving or the receiving of charity. Media reports of natural catastrophes and social cataclysms in distant parts of the world have globalized this activity. The vast majority of these gifts represent only a small portion of any individual's wealth, though charity also functions on a vaster scale, namely in the elite world of charitable giving that occupies much of the lives of the wealthy, involving charitable board meetings and gala balls.

Of course, it would be naïve to suppose that considerations of self-interest and obligation play no role in private gift giving and philanthropy. Gifts given to secretaries, letter carriers, apartment house door personnel, and even occasional romantic partners may partially represent compensation and are in any case obligatory. In the realm of public charity, large corporations often make donations based on a rational calculation of potential profit. Individual donors able to make significant gifts use their charitable giving to compete for seats on charity boards, to establish social rank and prestige, and to affix their names to buildings, grants, and prizes. At times it may even be difficult to determine whether the contribution represents a charitable donation or the purchase price for

---

271. "Thus these are gifts the child can, under normal circumstances, take for granted, to which it has a customary right and which in turn involve a certain reciprocity, including the invitation of the godparent to all family celebrations." Weber-Kellermann 5–6.

272. Parry 467–469.

naming rights.[273] In other words, even in modern society, as Mauss noted about preliterate societies,[274] giving is almost always based on a combination of motives, some altruistic, others self-interested.

80. *The impossibility of the pure gift.* The construct of the pure gift is of course artificial. Jacques Derrida has deconstructed this modern conception and demonstrated that it is literally impossible. Even in the rare cases in which a gift is not reciprocated, the donee responds with gratitude, which constitutes a symbolic equivalent that testifies to dependency, while the donor cannot help but experience self-satisfaction and superiority for having made the gift.[275]

Pierre Bourdieu has argued that gift giving is designed to accumulate symbolic capital and has little if anything to do with pure gratuitousness.

[A]s the gift economy has tended to shrink to an island in the ocean of the equivalent-exchange economy, its meaning has changed .... Within an economic universe based on the opposition between passion and interest ... the gift loses its real meaning as an act situated beyond the opposition between constraint and freedom ... and becomes a simple rational investment strategy directed toward the accumulation of social capital, with institutions such as public relations and company gifts, or a kind of ethical feat that is impossible to achieve because it is measured against the ideal of the true gift, understood as a perfectly gratuitous and gracious act performed without obligation or expectation, without reason or goal, for nothing.[276]

Yet the attempts to eliminate the altruistic aspect of gift giving are ultimately unsatisfying. It is tempting, and much too easy, to construct theories of the gift as an activity that is completely determined by social norms. In the modern gift,

---

273. Ron Perelman of Revlon recently made a $20 million gift to the University of Pennsylvania. In exchange, he received the right to rename the building formerly known as Logan Hall. See Lipson. Naming rights carry a price tag. The Penn Web site lists naming opportunities for the Quad renovations, including archways ($500,000 each), bosses ("non-spouting gargoyles," $25,000 each), college houses ($15 million each), courtyards ($2.5 million each), fitness centers ($100,000 each), music practice rooms ($50,000 each), and seminar rooms ($150,000 each). See http://www.alumni.upenn.edu/collegehouses/quad/semi.html.

Buildings are not all that can be named. Penn State sports boosters can attach their names to positions on sports teams ($300,000 each). The USC pep squad Song Girls can be sponsored ($1,900 each). Las Vegas sells the naming rights to monorail stations ($2 to $4 million each). Sun City, Arizona, has proposed to allow individuals to name streets after themselves (price undetermined). See Lipson.

274. Mauss (1990) 3.

275. Derrida (1992) 1–33. For a discussion of the Heideggerian context of Derrida's conception of gift giving, see Reinhardt 97–131. See also Marion 74–79.

276. Bourdieu (1997) 235–236. For a more developed statement, see Bourdieu (1990) 98–134.

there usually remains an irreducible element of individual generosity. The challenge the gift poses to social theory is to find a way to integrate these conflicting aspects of gift giving.

b. A Social Alternative

81. *The advantages of the gift economy.* Though the conception of the gift as pure gratuity ignores much that is fundamental about gift giving, the vision it implies has stimulated some of the most creative thinking in the social sciences. As the profit motive comes under increasing criticism and is charged with being one of the principal causes of contemporary social problems—from the unequal distribution of wealth to the AIDS epidemic and global warming—the idea of pure gratuity has inspired social scientists to conceive of a society in which human beings enter into relationships directly and no longer exclusively through commodity exchange, a society in which the transfer of things is designed principally to constitute and preserve ongoing relationships. In the view of these thinkers, a society inspired by the gift economy would reject the profit motive as the major spur to human action and would thereby eliminate the need for unsustainable economic growth.

Mauss believed society would be improved if a strong dose of gift were mixed back into commodity exchange. "These concepts of law and economics that it pleases us to contrast: liberty and obligation; liberality, generosity, and luxury, as against savings, interest, and utility—it would be good to put them into the melting pot once more."[277] The French legal scholar Louis Josserand understood that gift and commodity exchange point toward two different futures.

> Depending on whether a human community prefers gratuitous transfers or exchanges based on a quid pro quo, it will follow different drives with divergent impulses and channel them in opposite directions. Communities take pleasure either in business or in mutual assistance. They are ruled either by a spirit of competition or by the spirit of charity and public good, the *affectio societatis.* Like Hercules, every society has before it two paths ....[278]

Godelier has concluded that "[g]ift-giving has become the bearer of a utopia (a utopia which can be projected into the past as well as into the future)."[279]

Even when gift giving is considered solely in terms of altruistic social behavior, it remains uncertain how it might assist in achieving a better society. "[D]oes the Maussian 'model' ... offer the ideal image of what our society *ought to be like* if its members were to convert, so to speak, to an ethics of the gift which has been lost and has receded into the misty past? Or does it merely provide a phenomenology of unveiling which describes the way our society *in fact operates*

---

277. Mauss (1990) 73.
278. Josserand 135–136.
279. Godelier 208.

without our being aware of it?"[280] As Christian Arnsperger points out, Mauss held both views simultaneously, believing both that our society functions unawares along the lines of the gift economy and that, by becoming aware of this societal bedrock, we increase our reciprocal generosity and rescue society from the disadvantageous social relations that increasingly obscure its essence.[281]

82. *Anti-utilitarian thought.* Despite the difficulties, the anti-utilitarian thought that the gift economy has inspired serves as a reminder that altruism is fundamental both to our private lives and to the public sphere.[282] Giving something back is a large part of what the good life is about. Much of what we value in society is what we do for one another without compensation.[283] Both scientific discoveries and works of art now seem more closely to resemble gifts than they do commodities.[284] Within the family, of course, relations are not generally mediated by commodity exchange. The same is true of relationships between friends, colleagues, and neighbors. Even in the workplace, many aspire to offer to their customers, their clients, and their employers something more than they receive in compensation. An active network of relationships outside the framework of the market is essential to life in contemporary society, and those relationships are nourished by gratuitous acts—making time to give advice to a friend, helping strangers, showing team spirit, donating blood, making charitable contributions, volunteering, giving life, and even, when necessary, agreeing to risk one's life for one's country.

When seen in this light, utilitarian exchange in the marketplace is a subsidiary activity designed to create the material conditions necessary for more rewarding forms of human interaction. What Malinowski was able to say of the Trobriand Islanders might just as accurately be said of developed society—the gift is primary while the market is merely a secondary phenomenon.[285]

c. Comparative Notes

83. *Deviationist doctrine.* Anti-utilitarian thought has proved so productive in the social sciences that it might be asked whether it could help to restructure the private law as well. Roberto Unger suggested that two sets of norms compete for the heart of American contract law.[286] The dominant norms require strict compliance with contractual terms to satisfy the market's need for certainty, whereas

---

280. Arnsperger 71 (emphasis in original).
281. Id. 72.
282. Godbout and Caillé. See also the work of M.A.U.S.S. (*Mouvement Anti-Utilitariste dans les Sciences Sociales*), particularly two symposium issues of the group's periodical. Symposium 1991; Symposium 1991a.
283. Godbout and Caillé 3–20.
284. Hyde 273–282; Godbout and Caillé 82–87.
285. Godbout and Caillé 14–15.
286. Unger 57–90.

the subordinate view favors more leniency and a focus on the specific circumstances of each contract. Unger has suggested that it might promote social reform to rethink contract doctrine from the point of view of the subordinate vision.

84. *Dual views.* Gift law also offers competing visions. The dominant view insists on compliance with required formalities. It invalidates any gift, however reasonable and clearly intended, that does not comply. The subordinate vision gives greater weight to donative intent and to the gift's reasonableness in the circumstances. As discussed below, American law now seems to have abandoned delivery as the criterion for a valid gift of chattels and relies instead on proof of donative intent.[287] French law has long provided an array of exceptions to the code's rigorous formalities[288] and may eventually embark on significant *de-formalization*.[289]

85. *Subordinate vision and social reform.* Can this subordinate vision contribute to social reform? The subordinate view favors altruism and gratuitous transfers. Yet altruism may not always be appropriate. The donor may make a disproportionately large gift on impulse, and there is no guarantee that any gift will be made for a socially useful purpose. In fact, the roles of the dominant and subordinate doctrines seem reversed in the context of gift giving. The more rigorous formalities provide greater protection for those who rely on the family's resources.

Nonetheless, most would agree that society benefits from selfless activity. Charitable giving, indeed, gratuitous activity of all types, deserves to be encouraged and facilitated. The challenge for gift law is to discover how to facilitate the transfer of wealth to good causes while protecting those who rely on the donor against the donor's arbitrary whim and fraudulent claims of gift by purported donees. The law that governs anatomical gifts, discussed below, provides a helpful framework.[290] If gift law were able to create mechanisms to facilitate selfless activity, they might be worth generalizing throughout the private law.

5. The Approach of Death

86. *Constant companion.* A gift is the transfer of rights between living human beings. The passing of property at death is left to the will. Yet the division of labor is not simple. Death is the gift's constant companion. The symbiosis between death and the gift raises important metaphysical issues.

a. In Contemplation of Death

87. *Focus on mortality.* Many gifts, and often the most important gifts, are given in contemplation of death. Organ donations are obvious examples. Individuals often

---

287. Infra no. 887.
288. Infra nos. 779–842.
289. Montredon.
290. Infra nos. 1005–1024.

decide to become organ donors when they put their material affairs in order by drafting a will. Even when a living donor makes an organ donation, it is virtually always a sacrifice designed to save a loved one from death. The *donatio mortis causa* involves gifts made expressly in contemplation of death, at a moment when the donor is confronting a life-threatening operation or a dangerous trip. Life insurance policies, which may be gifts to the beneficiaries, also represent attempts to solve the financial problems that arise when thinking about death. For centuries donors made gifts so that Mass would be recited for the departed and prayers offered to reduce the time the dead would spend in purgatory.[291] Gifts were also made for the care of the family burial site. Painters offer their works to museums so their names will survive their deaths.

The gift's relationship to death is not limited to these special cases. Mortality may be the most significant facilitator of gift giving. Some gifts represent advancements of inheritance. Others epitomize the simple desire to experience while alive the situation that will prevail after the donor's death, to see how the children will live in the house after the donor has passed. Much charitable giving is triggered by the lure of a plaque or a building bearing the donor's name. In all of these cases, the gift seems to offer, in a limited way, a triumph over inevitable biological limitations.

Even the normal gifts of daily life are a tribute offered to death. Presents are given at moments of life transition—at birthdays, confirmations, graduations, engagements, weddings, and anniversaries. Each of those occasions marks a step along life's path, but each also signifies another stride toward the grave. Gifts, presents, make their contribution by turning attention back to the present. They assist in avoiding a confrontation with the fear of death that may arise on these occasions.

Finally, most of the conflict about gifts takes place after the donor's death.[292] Often the extent of the donor's bounty, and the objects of the donor's affection, are usually not revealed until the donor has passed. At that moment, families may feud and break apart. Greed triumphs. Close relatives vow never to speak with one another again. Suits are brought to avoid the transfers on the basis of undue influence, incompetence, or fraud; by proving a violation of the disposable share; or by preventing the execution of a gift promise. In some cases, gift giving provokes as much pain as death.

b. Metaphysical Issues

88. *Rarely discussed.* Perhaps the most curious fact about the intimate relationship between gift and death is that the relationship is never discussed. In the literature about gift giving, the law included, only rare sentences acknowledge

---

291. Marais 319–336.
292. Kull 45–46.

the connection.[293] Why is there such a reluctance to talk about this relationship? Is it simply a Heideggerian fleeing in the face of death (*Flucht vor dem Tode*)?[294]

89. *Constant obsession.* While no one talks about the relationship, many are obsessed with the opportunities the gift provides. Most of us will vanish without a trace. Once the generation that follows ours has passed on, we almost all will have been forgotten. A century further on, only the rarest of our names will survive. Only the most famous are able to escape absolute oblivion. The fact that gift giving is universal, that it is encountered at all times in all cultures, may have something to do with the fact that death, the fascination with death, and the efforts to grasp the metaphysical meaning of bodily death are all universal elements of the human condition.

90. *Socially acceptable.* Gift giving is the socially acceptable vehicle by which we consider the meaning of life and death and attempt to come to terms with the inevitability of our own end. Though thinking about death in this manner is a kind of fleeing, the gift provides a rare mechanism to grapple with a fact that is too painful for most of us to bear. Gift giving turns a metaphysical dilemma into a question of exchange. The social practice of gift giving expresses the hope that death can be transcended by making the right gifts in the right amounts to the right people. In the end a quid pro quo may be built into gift giving, not an exchange cognizable in the marketplace, but a spiritual bargain, a deal cut with mortality.

c. Comparative Notes

91. *Protective aspirations.* When gift giving is examined from the point of view of its ties with death, the law's protective aspirations gain credibility. The problem is not just that donors may be tempted to ignore their families and give excessively to their favorite charities. The real problem is that the gift offers a Faustian bargain. A donor might come to believe that it is possible to defeat death. There is no limit to what some would pay for that privilege.

92. *Civil law.* Romanic civilian systems attempt to protect donors from themselves. They constrain gift giving by limiting the capacity to make gifts, imposing rigorous formalities, permitting gifts to be revoked, and requiring collation (*rapport*), which means that all gifts exceeding the donor's disposable share must

---

293. "In nearly all gifts apart from weddings, Christmas and birthdays, the thought of death is a factor." Havighurst 149. "And yet for many donors, the gift is a method to combat anonymity. The gift seeks to stop the march of time that consigns all human beings to oblivion. It reveals 'the anguish of disappearance and the obsession with the trace.'" Marais 318 (quoting oral comments of Alain Corbin). One of Derrida's works approaches this relationship but then passes by without examining it. Cf. Derrida (1995); Kemp.

294. Heidegger § 51.

be returned to the estate at the donor's death.[295] The most rigorous protections are found in legal systems rooted in countries with a predominantly Catholic culture, a culture that is, to judge only by its art, fascinated by and somewhat terrified of death. It was suggested above that these protective regimes may have evolved through the efforts of the secular state to restrict the power and resources of the church. But it is also possible that these protective regimes are anchored in the complex relationship these cultures have with death.

93. *Common law.* The common law, in contrast, seems much less concerned with the danger that donors may overextend themselves. Formalities are easier to avoid in the common law and forced heirship more limited. The common law may be rooted in a more secular culture. On the other hand, the common law may also be unwilling to acknowledge as clearly as do some civilians the temptations that death presents. The common-law of gifts may simply represent an unacknowledged flight from the human condition.

94. *The task of comparative law.* These metaphysical concerns complicate the task of comparative law. They render more difficult any attempt to determine the best structure and content for gift law. The only way of reducing the abstractions to a manageable level is to ask whether individuals should be protected from these weighty concerns by state regulation or whether, instead, individuals can be trusted to resolve these issues for themselves. Though individuals may indeed be tempted to engage in excessive gift giving in their attempts to overcome death, the law, particularly the sometimes incoherent law that governs gift giving, may not be well suited to determining the appropriate limits.

6. Art

95. *A relationship, not an object.* Artists remind us of the one essential aspect of the gift that is stated almost nowhere. The gift is a relationship, not a physical object.[296]

a. The Gift as Itself

96. *Two examples.* Much remains to be written about the representation of the gift and gift giving in literature, music, and the visual arts.[297] There is only enough room here to mention two works that signal the type of insight about gift

---

295. "Collation, or the return of property to a succession, is the means by which the law seeks to assure the equal distribution of the ancestor's property among the direct descendants." *Successions of Webre,* 172 So.2d 285, 289 (La. 1965). Dawson provides the best description in English of the mechanisms civilian gift law employs to protect the heirs. See Dawson (1980).

296. "Gifts evince a semantic surplus that by far exceeds their material quality." Reinhardt 129.

297. For an exquisite study of this type, see Starobinski. See also Miller.

giving that the arts can achieve: O. Henry's short story "The Gift of the Magi" and Man Ray's readymade *The Gift*.

i. O. Henry

97. *The story.* "The Gift of the Magi," first published in 1906, is probably O. Henry's most well-known short story.[298] Jim and Della are married and live in a furnished flat they rent by the week. It is Christmas Eve and Della has no present for her husband. As she looks at herself in the glass, she is reminded of her most valuable asset, wavy auburn hair that reaches down to below her knees. She decides to sell her hair. With the proceeds she purchases the perfect watch chain for the watch Jim inherited from his father and grandfather. Jim comes home tired. He stares at Della without speaking. She explains what she has done. He hands her a set of tortoise shell combs she had once admired in a Broadway shop window. She shows him the watch chain. He sold the watch to buy the combs. They are wise, O. Henry tells us, because they have sacrificed their dearest possessions for each other.

98. *Futile sacrifice.* The story points to another of the paradoxes of gift giving. The greatest gift entails the greatest sacrifice. It is irrelevant that the sacrifice is futile. In fact, if either gift had retained its use value, it would still make a nice present, but not a great story. The essence of the gift relationship is sacrifice, and the depth of the sacrifice reveals the relationship. A surrender of something of great value may be a great gift even if it offers no material benefit.

As perplexing as this insight may seem, it accounts for the otherwise incomprehensible acts described in the ethnographical reports, the gifts of meaningless objects, such as those exchanged in the Melanesian kula, or the destruction of valuables in the potlatch. Gift giving distinguishes itself from commodity exchange perhaps most starkly in this. Commodities are meaningless if they are useless, whereas uselessness can endow a gift with meaning. A gift is not a use value. Certain utilitarian wares, such as a washing machine, can almost never be given as a gift, while nearly useless objects, such as a badly framed and to others unappealing photograph, may speak better than words.

ii. Man Ray

99. *Readymade.* In *The Gift*, Man Ray may have created the most successful visual representation of the gift paradoxes.[299] The small work consists of what would now be considered an old-fashioned flat iron resting on its base. From the back it seems it might be picked up and put to use, but a view from the front makes clear that the iron will never be used. Fourteen tacks are glued in a row

---

298. Henry (1953).

299. See Frontispiece. The photograph is of a later reproduction. For the story of how the work was created, see Baldwin 89–93.

down the center of the iron's working surface, the sharp tips pointing out.[300] The composer Erik Satie helped Man Ray create the object, his first Dadaist creation, just before Ray's first solo show opened in Paris in 1921. Man Ray photographed the object and then offered it as a present to the poet Philippe Soupault, the gallery owner. By the end of the day, the object had disappeared.

100. *Transfer and transformation.* To art historians, *The Gift* is the decontextualization of a flatiron. The fourteen tacks prevent functionality. They strip away the iron's former reality to reveal its *Sachlichkeit*, its quality as an object. With its familiar context removed and its connection to material culture eliminated, it becomes suitable for presentation in an art gallery.[301] The object becomes a fresh and expressive entity once it is free to reveal its identity as a thing.

By labeling the object *The Gift*, Man Ray decontextualized the flatiron in a different way as well. An object is transformed when it is transferred as a gift. Its usefulness becomes a secondary, sometimes even an irrelevant characteristic. Whether useful or not, the gift symbolizes the relationship in which it is given. Potlatch goods, a thousand Hudson Bay blankets, for example, were not given for their use value. They were bestowed instead to increase the host's prestige.[302] Even today, gifts are often characterized by their redundancy, by the fact that they do not actually make the recipient better off.[303] Yet the redundancy is the least of it. Man Ray's object reminds us that an object transferred as a gift may grow fangs. A gift cannot be discarded. Even when the relationship and the setting change, a place must still be found for the object. Man Ray's *Gift* symbolizes the social conventions that many seek to escape.

At the same time Man Ray's readymade is a work of art, a piece so striking it was stolen the day it was made, an object of such importance that photographs of it, even images of a later replica, are stored in museum vaults. Like Man Ray's object, a gift is a use value that cannot be used, an object to cherish and yet fear, a necessary redundancy.

b. Comparative Notes

101. *Need for regulation.* The uncanny desire to sacrifice what is most valuable, so cleanly imagined in O. Henry's short story, makes the case for those legal systems that seek to restrict gift giving. We feel fear when we approach the edge of a tall building, not because we might fall, but because we might jump. That is the argument for guardrails—and gift laws. The question comparative law must

---

300. The original had fourteen tacks, though they are apparently easily dislodged. See Baldwin 90 and illustration at 91.

301. Foster 245.

302. Barnett 351–352; Snyder 151–152.

303. Cheal 12–13; Curta 672.

explore is whether there are circumstances in which individuals need the law to protect them because they cannot protect themselves.

Man Ray's *Gift* portrays something of the mind-set with which some legal systems have approached the regulation of gift giving. The gift is a common social institution, as old as society itself and one that testifies to enduring elements of the human condition. From that perspective, the law has little to do. Gift law gains its special calling only in those situations in which gift giving seems ominous.

2. METHODOLOGY

102. *Controversial.* Because methodological questions are so controversial in comparative law, it is probably wise for every inquiry to begin by explaining its goals. An explanation is particularly useful here because gift law is in many ways unique.

A. COMPARATIVE LAW FUNCTIONALISM

103. *Common methodology.* Since the birth of modern comparative law in Paris in 1900, comparativists have focused much of their effort on debating how legal systems should be compared. Over the last several decades, however, despite a multitude of competing theories, many wide-ranging comparative studies have tended to follow one version or another of a much-discussed methodology. This method has been called functionalism,[1] a name that is seriously misleading, but which is convenient, for the moment, to retain. The method was developed by the students of Ernst Rabel during the 1930s, elaborated by Konrad Zweigert beginning in 1960, and ultimately presented in a provocative manner by Zweigert and Kötz in a short chapter in their important treatise.[2] One way to introduce the different methodology used in this study is to explore the incoherencies of comparative law functionalism.

The incoherencies, however, are not the end of the problem. It turns out that comparative law functionalism is not functionalism at all. Durkheim and other proponents of functionalist social science would have dismissed it out of hand. The problem is the confusion that reigns in comparative law between a subjective and an objective understanding of the central concept of function. Comparative law is not social science—it probably is not science at all—but it at least aspires to be a scholarly undertaking. It is therefore useful for comparativists to strive for the self-critical distance needed to avoid confusions that have long since been described and transcended in neighboring fields.

---

1. "There is general agreement about the basic methodological principle of comparative law. The basic methodological principle of comparative law is that of functionality." Mäntysaari 8.

2. Zweigert and Kötz 32–47. For a detailed analysis of the evolution of functionalism in modern comparative law, see Michaels. For related methodological suggestions in anthropology contemporary with Zweigert and Kötz, see Goldschmidt.

1. Tertium Comparationis

104. *Fundamental dilemma.* At the core of functionalist methodology is a particular approach to what has been presented as the fundamental dilemma of comparative law, namely the transition from description to comparison. Comparative law has always strived to provide accurate knowledge of foreign legal systems. Once the different systems are accurately described, it becomes immediately clear that, at least on their surface, they vary dramatically. Nonetheless, comparative law has always assumed that the different systems share important commonalities.[3] This assumption translates into one of the principal methodological questions of contemporary comparative law: how to descend from surface difference to the similarities that are assumed to be concealed beneath. Once the common features have been uncovered, a new goal emerges: to discover the role of law in modern society.[4]

105. *Common characteristics.* It was received wisdom in 1950s social science that comparison must begin by distinguishing between features common to all societies and those unique to each one. The thought was that the common characteristics, *nonculture-bound units* or *invariant points of reference*, once isolated, would anchor the comparative method.[5] It was assumed that two phenomena could be compared only in terms of the characteristics they share. Despite popular wisdom, apples can be compared to oranges in many ways—their culinary use, how long they hang on the limb before they drop from the tree, or the way they are represented in the European visual arts. Since the perspective chosen determines the understanding produced, the critical question for comparative law is how to establish the perspective from which different legal systems should be compared.

106. *Law and social problems.* Zweigert and Kötz made what at the time was a provocative suggestion. As their basis of comparison, they did not choose one of the law's internal characteristics, a feature that might be assumed to exist in all legal systems. Instead, they based comparison on the relationship they felt must exist between the law and society.[6] The two scholars argued that different legal systems are comparable because all legal norms are designed to fulfill a social function. Laws should be compared in terms of how they resolve the social problems they confront.[7]

---

3. Mincke 320.

4. "The comparative method achieves fundamental importance only when it ceases to compare from the perspective of difference and focuses instead on commonality, for only then do we stand before a method for the general exploration of essence (*einer Methode genereller Wesensforschung*)." Mincke 320, quoting Rothacker 100.

5. Sjoberg 1–2.

6. Mincke 322–323.

7. Zweigert and Kötz 34. See also Mincke 323–324.

107. *What the courts do.* A second aspect of the functionalist system is an equally daring insight, drawn this time from legal realism, about how to ascertain the solution a legal system provides to a particular real-world problem. Every legal system is constructed as a hierarchy of norms. In code systems, for example, the statute is generally considered superior to case law.[8] Nonetheless, law is often compared as applied.[9] This is also required by the functionalist method. Functionalism is not interested in rules as such. It focuses instead on the solutions legal systems provide to practical problems. Those solutions appear only in the practical results of dispute resolution.[10] Functionalism thus abandons normative hierarchy and focuses instead on court decisions as the practical interface between the law and the extra-legal world. In other words, the tertium comparationis chosen by modern comparative law is the effective judicial response to common practical problems.[11] In their comparative studies, the world's leading comparativists have often adopted this approach.[12]

2. Common Problems

108. *Assumed similar.* The functionalist method assumes that societies governed by modern legal systems face common problems, and that these societies are similar enough for comparable situations to be arise frequently. "[T]he legal system of every society faces essentially the same problems ...."[13] Zweigert and Kötz state this assumption as a third element of their methodology, an assumption that, they believe, is obvious to everyone. They may have borrowed this aspect of their theory from functionalism in the social sciences. Radcliffe-Brown and Malinowski had been publishing similar ideas over the previous decades.[14]

---

8. 2 Constantinesco nos. 62–66.

9. "The comparativist must determine the actual practical application of the legal rules." Mäntysaari 9.

10. "[A]t the end of the [nineteenth] century, jurists realized that they could only provide an exact description of a legal norm if they took into account the official interpretation of the courts, the only one that counts on a practical level." 1 Mazeaud (-Chabas) no. 99.

11. For the history of the tertium comparationis in comparative law, see 2 Constantinesco nos. 9, 25.

12. Direct comparison at the level of doctrine is out of the question, as the doctrines diverge very widely. A focus or basis for comparison can be found in the functional problems that the doctrine to be studied handles and resolves, in whole or in part, for its own legal system. Comparative analysis focuses on these problems, locating them in the systems under investigation and explaining the rules and principles through which they are handled and the practical results achieved.
Von Mehren 1010.

13. Zweigert and Kötz 34.

14. Any social system, to survive, must conform to certain conditions. If we can define adequately one of these universal conditions, *i.e.* one to which all human societies must conform, we have a sociological law. Thereupon if it can be shown that a

Both Zweigert and Kötz and the social science functionalists employ the notions of common problems and necessary conditions to explain social structure.[15]

"[T]he legal system of every society faces essentially the same problems ...." In a moment it will be useful to consider the remainder of that sentence, but for now it is worth conceding that the proposition seems plausible. Those who travel frequently learn to recognize the activities engaged in by individuals in other developed societies, even without special training in foreign languages or area studies. On most long-distance flights anywhere in the world, the flight attendants show us how to strap ourselves in, they ask what we would like to drink, and they bring us our meal. On arrival, we fill out a disembarkation form, show our passports to the uniformed officers in the glass booths, then stand around the carousel and wait for our luggage. Taxis are lined up outside the terminal, though perhaps they are not all painted yellow, or at least not the same yellow we are used to. At our hotel, we again show our passport, give an imprint of our credit card, and let the bellhop take our luggage up the service elevator. We take a nap between freshly pressed sheets, then go down and ask the concierge for a restaurant recommendation. As we wander through the unfamiliar streets, we recognize which establishments are bookstores, which are cafés, and which are elegant boutiques. We make a mental note about where we will be able to buy a pen and a notebook in the morning, we get a map of the public transit system, and we try our debit card in the ATM machine on the corner. We can easily find our sea legs in another contemporary culture. The small differences are even more intriguing because there are so few of them, and they seem threatened with extinction.

In the dispute about the functionalist method in comparative law, this element of the methodology has caused almost no one to think twice. Yet the obviousness of the proposition only serves to conceal the fact that it is wrong. By exploring this point in more detail, as will be done a little further on, it will be possible to discover why an alternative approach to comparing legal systems is necessary.

---

particular institution in a particular society is the means by which that society conforms to the law, *i.e.* to the necessary condition, we may speak of this as the "sociological origin" of the institution. Thus an institution may be said to have its general *raison d'être* (sociological origin) and its particular *raison d'être* (historical origin). The first is for the sociologist or social anthropologist to discover by the comparative method.
Radcliffe-Brown (1935b) 297. Functionalism became the dominant theoretical perspective in American sociology during the late 1940s and 1950s. It dominated the field into the 1960s. Turner and Maryanski 114–115. Talcott Parsons's book *The Social System* was published in 1951.

15. Turner and Maryanski 113.

3. Praesumptio Similitudinis

109. *Presumption of similarity.* The final element of comparative law functionalism is its most famous, or infamous, aspect. Every comparativist recognizes that the legal discussions in different systems do not coincide. In some systems, certain questions serve as the focus for legal norms, scholarly discussion, and case decisions, whereas in other systems these questions are rarely asked and the answer almost impossible to find. For Zweigert and Kötz, this is mere appearance. If real-world problems must be solved in one system, those same problems must be solved in the others as well. If we find no relevant provision where we expect it in the code, we will certainly find a norm somewhere else, or a case decision. Zweigert and Kötz hypothesize, therefore, not only that legal systems in developed societies all confront the same practical social problems, but also that they will resolve those problems in a similar manner, though they may employ different doctrinal constructions. That is how the sentence quoted above concludes. "The proposition rests on what every comparatist learns, namely that the legal system of every society faces essentially the same problems, and solves these problems by quite different means though very often with similar results."

Zweigert and Kötz call their thesis the *praesumptio similitudinis*, the presumption of similarity.[16] They consider it a basic rule of comparative law. "[D]ifferent legal systems give the same or very similar solutions, even as to detail, to the same problems of life, despite the great differences in their historical development, conceptual structure, and style of operation."[17] To do comparative law, we must shift our focus away from legal concepts. "[T]he solutions we find in the different jurisdictions must be cut loose from their conceptual context and stripped of their national doctrinal overtones so that they may be seen purely in the light of their function, as an attempt to satisfy a particular legal need."[18] The rule also operates as a method to check the accuracy of the results.

> [C]omparatists can rest content if their researches through all the relevant material lead to the conclusion that the systems they had compared reach the same or similar practical results, but if they find that there are great differences or indeed diametrically opposite results, they should be warned and go back to check again whether the terms in which they posed their original question were indeed purely functional, and whether they have spread the net of their researches quite wide enough.[19]

---

16. Zweigert and Kötz 40. The Latin phrase is invented. I have found it in no classical source. In classical Latin, *praesumptio* usually means *presumption* in the sense of audacity. It would be better Latin to speak of a *conjectura similitudinis*.

17. Id. 39.

18. Id. 44. See also Kötz (1990) 209–210.

19. Zweigert and Kötz 40. I have slightly revised the translation.

110. *Universal legal language.* The final goal of comparative law functionalism involves an aspiration that may seem utopian, but which could be realized if enough comparativists uncover the functional foundation of enough institutions in enough legal systems. That goal is the discovery of a universal legal language, a conceptual scheme capable of comprehending all of the world's existing legal orders.[20] In other words, because the problems of modern societies are universal and because the role of the law is to solve those problems, the actual workings of the law will become clear as local doctrinal idiosyncrasies are discarded. Once all systems have been examined and a language universal enough to describe them has been developed, the essence of law in human society finally will have been understood. At that moment, functionalism will reveal itself as the scaffolding necessary for the construction of the pure legal language needed to portray the essence of the seemingly diverse institutions we know as the law.[21]

111. *Significant achievement.* In a world in which national legal training induces jurists to remain loyal to their native legal conceptions and convinces them to suspect ideas that arrive from abroad, the international scholarly agreement that comparative law functionalism has forged represents an astonishing achievement. Among other things, it permitted the world's leading comparative scholars to collaborate on an international encyclopedia that describes the private law of the world, an effort that reconnected legal systems after the Second World War.[22]

4. State of the Discussion

112. *Difference theory.* It is odd that it took so long for anyone to object to the functionalist vision. A critique was developed during the 1980s and 1990s.[23] One group of opponents, the difference theorists, criticized the focus on similarity and argued that there may be no level on which the differences between legal systems disappear.[24] Difference theory suggests that legal systems should be

---

20. "The ideal would be reached when, in the end, a language was found capable of portraying every legal order. This would be a universal language of legal science. It would contain as basic elements all of the building blocks out of which the law is put together." Mincke 327–328.
21. In the activity of comparative description we glimpse a field in which legal science is fully autonomous and self-reliant .... The language elaborated by means of comparison ... is the basic language of legal science, one that alone is capable of portraying the legal material in its complete differentiation. It is formed exclusively from the material of the legal orders and reveals the building blocks out of which legal orders are composed.
Id. 328.
22. See International Association of Legal Science.
23. See, e.g., Frankenberg; Legrand; Hyland (1996) 187–192.
24. Hyland (1996) 193–197.

understood in their social context as expressions of an internally conflictual national culture, much in the way we understand literature, historiography, and philosophy.

113. *Moderation and tolerance.* As the debate progressed over the past decade, it produced a tolerance for diverse methodological approaches and efforts at reconciling the competing positions.[25] To begin with, functionalism now exists in a number of different versions.[26] Functionalists have reduced their claims and emphasized that the methodology is appropriate only when comparing legal systems in similar societies, and then only in fields not subject to strong moral or religious influence. Hein Kötz has also suggested that some of the most interesting differences are found in legal styles, techniques, and value judgments, aspects of the law that functionalism has traditionally ignored.[27] Difference theory has also been moderated to focus both on similarity and on difference in balanced proportions.[28] The consensus today is that no single methodology is appropriate for all comparative investigations. Instead, a new methodology will probably have to be developed for each project.

B. CRITIQUE

114. *Problems remain.* Despite the relative consensus, fundamental difficulties remain. The first is the frequent assumption that all developed societies confront the same problems. The second is the common belief that the law is essentially a mechanism to solve problems posed in the extra-legal world.

1. The Same Problems

115. *As confronted by the law.* One aspect of functionalist method continues as an assumption of many contemporary comparative methodologies. It is functionalism's third element, the seemingly innocent assumption that developed societies all face the same problems. This view has long since been rejected in the social sciences, even by functionalists. The social problems that functionalism believes the law is designed to address, the issues of practical life, are already shaped by history, culture, religion, and language—as well as by the legal tradition—before they become legal problems. A legal system can only confront the problems as they present themselves, and the actual problems differ dramatically from one society to the next.

---

25. For a contemporary synthesis, see Husa.
26. Michaels distinguishes at least seven. Michaels 344–363.
27. Kötz 505.
28. Dannemann 406.

116. *Basic needs.* The deceptively simple example of the basic human need for food serves as an illustration. Everyone, every day, in every society has to eat. If there are universals across all times and civilizations, the daily meal has to be one of them. Comparative law functionalism operates with problems at this level of abstraction. However, no society, and no legal system, ever confronts food-related problems in this generic form.[29] If our need for food meant simply that we are required to introduce into our bodies the particular quantity of nutrients necessary to stoke the human machine, we would sit down at the next restaurant and order the first item on the menu. But that is not what happens.

If I am hungry and I find myself in front of a McDonald's, even if I am very hungry, I do not go in. I do not eat at McDonald's. Usually when I get hungry, I am looking for something specific. If I am in a city I do not know well, I look in a guidebook, or I simply walk down the street and examine the menus or look through the windows until I find the type of food I feel like eating. Though I am usually happy to have pancakes for breakfast and salad for lunch, I do not eat salad for breakfast or pancakes for lunch (though if I have not eaten for a couple of days, of course, I would eat whatever is put in front of me). I have been brought up to know what counts as breakfast and what counts as lunch, and I am powerless to change that. Though I know there is nothing logical or natural about it, I also know that, at this point in my life, it is much more than a preference. It is a part of who I am.

If food were just about fuel, there would be no eating disorders—no obesity, anorexia, or bulimia. We would eat what we need and then stop. There would also be no three-star French restaurants. No one would keep kosher, or fast during Ramadan, or be a vegetarian or fruitarian, or refuse to eat vegetables that grow at night or underground. Food would not be shipped from one continent to another, with all of the consequences, both foreseen and unexpected. The British craze for tea developed the teahouse, the tea break, and the art of porcelain. It also set the stage for the Boston Tea Party and thereby forged the unity of the colonies and the American Revolution.[30] In addition, it caused the British to begin importing opium into China, which not only provoked the Opium Wars but, through the destruction of the Chinese economy and the humiliation caused

---

29. Nowhere and never will man, however primitive, feed on the fruits of his environment. He always selects and rejects, produces and prepares. He does not depend on the physiological rhythm of hunger and satiety alone; his digestive processes are timed and trained by the daily routine of his tribe, nation, or class .... The raw material of individual physiology is found everywhere refashioned by cultural and social determinism. The group has molded the individual in matters of taste, of tribal taboos, of the nutritive and symbolic value of food, as well as in the manners and modes of commensalism.
Malinowski (1939) 943–944.
  30. Labaree.

by the treaty ports, also contributed significantly to the Chinese Revolution.[31] No issue, when conceived as a universal, is concrete enough to provide a basis for comparison.[32]

117. *Specific desires.* Another way to put the same point is that there is often no difference between the function and the means used to fulfill it. We do not first feel hungry, experience the need to consume a foodstuff, and then pick up whatever we find in front of us, whether sushi, or pizza, or a chocolate chip cookie. Instead we generally have an urge for some specific range of foods. All too often we decide to eat when we are not hungry and could easily do without the additional calories. Our generalized animal hunger and our specific desires are not even analytically separable. It is not meaningful to say that our craving for the cookie is just the form by which we seek nourishment for the body, because a chocolate chip cookie provides no nourishment at all. Due to its composition of white sugar, white flour, and fat, it is instead a slow-acting poison.

118. *Chocolate connections.* The example of chocolate illustrates how the consumption of a particular foodstuff is intimately connected to the rest of national and global culture. The European elite was enthralled with the chocolate they met as a rare and expensive import from the New World. After several centuries, the sweet rich taste has now become an element of popular culture, indeed a national addiction.[33] Chocolate leads a double life. As a product of highly skilled artisans, it serves as an elegant consumable, while it is also mass-produced as an element of the sugar culture. In this second form it contributes to obesity and type 2 diabetes, and thereby implicates questions of public education, medical care, and the federal budget. Chocolate is also a commodity for which free trade is sought by some and fair trade by others. It therefore raises difficult questions involving the international economic order, the International Monetary Fund, the World Bank, the future of the bottom billion, globalization, and the antiglobalization protestors. When the law addresses chocolate, these are some of the challenges to which it must respond. Chocolate is not just a food. It is a part of the intricate web of modern culture.

---

31. Moxham 64–70.

32. Ralf Michaels, in his recent survey of functionalist methodologies, suggests that the universality of basic problems might be understood in a constructive rather than an empirical sense. Though the problems are not actually universals, they may be perceived as such. These constructed universals would serve as the *tertium comparationis*. Michaels 368–369. The problem with this suggestion is that whatever universals there may be in the abstract, whether constructed or empirical, do not present themselves to the various legal systems as such. They present themselves, and must be solved, in their specificity.

33. For the history of the consumption of chocolate in Europe and the United States, see Coe and Coe.

119. *Abstraction necessary.* Nonetheless, no comparison is possible without abstraction.[34] Comparison always requires putting some contextual aspects to one side. Yet comparison is meaningless if the evaluation is stripped of all situational context. In the field of history, comparativists start from the maxim "as little abstraction as necessary, as much concretion and contextual relationship as possible."[35] This is what Clifford Geertz meant when he wrote that "the comparative study of law cannot be a matter of reducing concrete differences to abstract commonalities ... it cannot be a matter of locating identical phenomena masquerading under different names."[36] The goal rather is to lift living organisms from their support systems, examine them briefly as their hearts continue to beat, and then, delicately, return them to their homes.

120. *Society specific.* A comparison of legal approaches to human food consumption should consider eating as an element of widely varying cultural situations. In other words, it would accept it in the multilayered form in which it presents itself to the law. Readers of the Hart and Sacks materials are familiar with the complex social, historical, and political factors that must be taken into account when the law attempts to organize something as basic as American commerce in fresh fruits and vegetables.[37] Legal process theory taught that rich contextual knowledge is essential to an understanding of the law. It is all too easy to forget that the circumstances prevailing at other times and places were very different. The problems the law faced in sixteenth century France, for example, were not those we face today. At the time, a villager might have been accused of witchcraft for giving a neighbor a loaf of bread or a wheel of cheese that the recipient feared was hexed or poisoned. A major social issue was the perceived excesses of dinner parties. Charles IX issued an edict mandating that no dinner, not even a wedding banquet, could include more than three courses (the entrée, either meat or

---

34. "Phenomena cannot be compared with one another in their complex totality, as complete individualities, but always only in certain aspects. Comparison implies selection, abstraction, and separation from context." Haupt and Kocka 23.

35. Id. 23–24.

36. Geertz (1983c) 215–216. At about the same time that Zweigert was formulating comparative law functionalism, Geertz was writing the definitive critique of what Geertz called the "stratigraphic" conception, the view on which Zweigert's method is based.

> In this conception, man is a composite of "levels," each superimposed upon those beneath it and underpinning those above it .... Strip off the motley forms of culture and one finds the structural and functional regularities of social organization. Peel off these in turn and one finds the underlying psychological factors—"basic needs" or what-have-you—that support and make them possible. Peel off psychological factors and one is left with the biological foundations—anatomical, physiological, neurological—of the whole edifice of human life.

Geertz (1973c) 37.

37. Hart and Sacks 10–68.

fish, and finally cheese and dessert), each course could have no more than six dishes, and only one kind of meat would be allowed on each plate.[38]

In a celebrated article, Malinowski noted that a digging stick might be used not only for digging but also, in identical form and in the same or different cultures, as a punting pole, a walking staff, or a rudimentary weapon. "[I]n each of these specific uses the stick is embedded in a different cultural context; that is, put to different uses, surrounded with different ideas, given a different cultural value and as a rule designated by a different name. In each case it forms an integral part of a different system of standardized human activities. In brief, it fulfils a different function."[39] In other words, even the classical theorists of functionalism in the social sciences recognized that comparison focuses not on universals but rather on the way the element fulfills a social need within a specific cultural context.[40] "The direct motive for human actions is couched in cultural terms and conforms to a cultural pattern."[41]

What is true of tools is also true of legal norms. It makes no sense to tear them out of context in order to compare them. As Peter Winch has observed, the relation between ideas and their context is an internal one. "The idea gets its sense from the role it plays in the system. It is nonsensical to take several systems of ideas, find an element in each which can be expressed in the same verbal form, and then claim to have discovered an idea which is common to all the systems."[42] In other words, if the comparison of laws is possible at all, it can only occur by examining the norms as elements of particular social and cultural contexts.

---

38. Davis (2000) 35–36; Edict of 1563.

39. Malinowski (1937) 625.

40. "The true comparative method consists of the comparison, not of one isolated custom of one society with a similar custom of another, but of the whole system of institutions, customs and beliefs of one society with that of another. In a word, what we need to compare is not institutions but social systems or types." Radcliffe-Brown (1948) 230.

41. Malinowski (1937) 629.

[I]t is clear that in every human society each impulse is remolded by tradition. It appears still in its dynamic form as a drive, but a drive modified, shaped, and determined by tradition .... In the case of breathing ... [i]t is a well-known fact that even in European cultures, the emphasis on fresh air as against level of temperature is not identical in England, Germany, Italy and Russia. Another complication in this simple impulse of air intake to fill the lungs with oxygen is due to the fact that the organs of breathing are also, to a large extent, organs of speech. A compromise, an adjustment of deep breathing to performances in public oratory, the recital of magical formulae, and singing, constitutes another domain in which cultural breathing differs from the mere physiological act.

Malinowski (1944) 85–86.

42. Winch 100–101.

2. A Problem-Solving Activity

121. *A more basic assumption.* The assumption that the law confronts similar problems all over the developed world is in turn based on another, even more basic assumption, one that seems so obvious that it is never stated. The idea is that the law is primarily a problem-solving activity, that laws have the principal effect of solving, or attempting to solve, difficulties encountered by the extra-legal world.

Functionalist methodologies conceive of the law as in some way separate from the society it is designed to structure. They see society as a house in need of repair. We are the general contractors; the legal norms are our tools. The social problems come first. Legal norms are crafted to solve the problems.

But very often the law does not work that way. The norm comes first, and only then is a particular functionality ascribed to it. That function, however, is an imaginary attribution of an acceptable purpose, our attempt to justify our normative structure on rational grounds. The deeper problem with current functionalist methodologies is that they depend on a theory about the origin and function of legal norms that contradicts what we know about how the law works.

If the law were functional in the way legal functionalists assume, it would demonstrate two characteristics. First, we would know the purpose for which our legal norms are promulgated. Second, we would be able to determine the social consequences of applying the norms. Yet neither characteristic describes the legal systems examined here.

a. The Purpose of a Norm

122. *Interplay of factors.* A legal norm comes into existence through the interplay of a series of factors so complex that no social scientist will ever be able to disentangle them. That is the sense of the old adage about legislation and sausage making. Our laws arise from historical custom, linguistic idiosyncrasies, the dominant religious ethic, the particular form of government, currently accepted philosophical truths, perceived social needs, and the obvious fact that certain groups and individuals benefit from these laws and would not benefit from others. It is usually possible to ascribe some rational purpose both to the laws and to the holdings in the various cases. But that purpose is not something inherent in the rules.

123. *Statutory interpretation.* This is not a radical claim. To the contrary, it represents an important position in American statutory interpretation. Lon Fuller's understanding is the dominant view. A statute cannot be applied until the purpose the statute was designed to achieve has been ascertained.[43] The attempt to discover that purpose often begins by asking about the goals the legislator had in

---

43. Fuller (1958) 661–669.

mind when the statute was promulgated. But as Max Radin made clear long since, "[T]he law maker, *der Gesetzgeber, le législateur*, does not exist."[44] Moreover, Radin noted, nothing is gained by assuming that the members of the legislative body are the subjects of the process. "A legislature certainly has no intention whatever in connection with words which some two or three men drafted, which a considerable number rejected, and in regard to which many of the approving majority might have had, and often demonstrably did have, different ideas and beliefs." Radin concluded that the intention of the legislature is "undiscoverable in any real sense."

Moreover, even if we were somehow able to discover the legislature's precise purpose, that purpose would not bind those charged with interpreting the norm.[45] Once the statute is promulgated, its words become tools that the administration and the courts use to perform their functions. Judges determine the purposes for themselves. But how do judges do that? As best they can, Radin answered. "That this is pure subjectivism and therefore an unfortunate situation is beside the point. It is hard to see how subjectivism can be avoided or how the personality of the judge can be made to count for nothing in his decision on statutory interpretation as on everything else."[46]

Well over a century ago, Holmes explained that the law develops by continually reformulating the purposes ascribed to legal norms.[47] As society changes, the wording of the norms can remain largely unchanged because judges are continually recognizing new social policies and ascribing them to the old rules. In other words, the *purpose* of a legal institution is something we add to the norm, not something inherent within it.

This understanding also has a distinguished civilian pedigree. The Italian Constitutional Court, as it invalidated the prohibition of gifts between spouses, recognized that norms may outlast their purposes, sometimes by as long as two millennia.[48] The origins of the rule were unclear, even to the Roman jurists. Nonetheless, because it was the law, the Roman scholars immediately set about trying to find a purpose for it. They were not troubled by the fact that the justifications were not only insufficient but also inconsistent with each other. Medieval and modern scholars respected the rule because it was Roman, but they had as little idea as the Romans about what it was designed to accomplish. Even after the discovery of the *Fragmenta vaticana* revealed that the Romans may once have permitted gifts between spouses, and despite the fact that both Italian courts and

44. Radin 870.
45. Id. 871.
46. Id. 881.
47. Holmes 5–33.
48. C. Cost. 27 June 1973 no. 91, *Foro it.* 1973 I 2014 note A. C. Jemolo. For the prohibition of gifts between spouses in Roman and Italian law, see infra nos. 541–545, 549–550.

legal scholars argued that the prohibition was irrational and should be abolished, it was retained in the twentieth-century redrafting of the Italian Civil Code out of respect for the tradition. Despite the general belief that the prohibition served no purpose, the Italian legislature never abrogated it, and the courts continued to apply the rule according to its terms. In the end it was invalidated, not by any civil law authority but by the Constitutional Court.

124. *Negotiorum gestio.* Another example might serve to make clear how little the survival of the norms owes to the purposes we ascribe to them. The civilian legal institution of *negotiorum gestio*, the management of the affairs of another, demonstrates how hard it is to ascertain purpose in the law. Until relatively recent times, a surprising number of suits in different legal systems sought to recover the expenses incurred in rescuing lumber that had been washed away by rising water. In American law, this question arises under the heading of restitution for benefits conferred without request. In the leading American case, the court refused recovery.[49] American law generally does not reward volunteers for their efforts, even in emergencies, unless they are health-care professionals.[50] An older English case indicated that payment may be required but doubted the wisdom of granting it.[51] "[P]erhaps it is better for the public that these voluntary acts of benevolence from one man to another, which are charities and moral duties, but not legal duties, should depend altogether for their reward upon the moral duty of gratitude."[52] In contrast, one German case granted recovery.[53] In other civilian jurisdictions, the plaintiff might also be able to recover in this situation.[54]

What is the social problem that these different rules are designed to solve? The comparativists who have explored this field have generally not posed this

---

49. *Glen v. Savage,* 13 P. 442 (Or. 1887).

50. The law will never permit a friendly act, or such as was intended to be an act of kindness or benevolence, to be afterwards converted into a pecuniary demand. It would be doing violence to some of the kindest and best effusions of the heart to suffer them afterwards to be perverted by sordid avarice. Whatever differences may arise afterwards among men, let those meritorious and generous acts remain lasting monuments of the good offices, intended in the days of good neighborhood and friendship; and let no after-circumstances ever tarnish or obliterate them from the recollection of the parties.

Id., 13 P. at 448.

51. *Nicholson v Chapman* (1793) 2 H Bl 254, 259, 126 ER 536, 539.

52. Id., 126 ER at 539. *Nicholson* has subsequently been read to stand for the proposition that recovery is available only if the owner requested the rescue. *Aitchison v Lohre* (1879) 4 HL 755, 760 (Lord Blackburn J).

53. OLG Königsberg 29 Apr. 1938, 15 *Höchstrichterliche Rechtsprechung* 485, as summarized in Dawson (1961) 1077. See generally German CC §§ 677–687 (*Geschäftsführung ohne Auftrag*).

54. See French CC arts. 1372–1374 (*gestion d'affaires*); Italian CC arts. 2028–2032 (*gestione de affari*); Spanish CC arts. 1888–1894 (*gestión de negocios ajenos*).

question.[55] Yet it is a particularly intriguing issue, because, in these cases, the contents of the norm will rarely influence anyone's behavior. Few individuals, besides contracts professors, are aware of the rule. Most rescuing is done from humanitarian motives, and, in an emergency, no one asks whether expenses can be recovered. A legal system can either provide compensation or not, but little else depends on the decision. Whatever issue the law is confronting is a question of its own making.

Questions of this type provide us the opportunity to elaborate the vision that is implicit in our legal system. When it comes to negotiorum gestio, a common lawyer might argue that letting the defendant decide whether to compensate the Good Samaritan provides an opportunity for the development of moral subjectivity. A civilian, on the other hand, might believe that the law should require reimbursement for those who do good deeds, both because it is the right thing to do and because it might encourage others to perform in the same way. The civilian institution has its origins in Roman law,[56] while the common law has refused to recognize it. No one today really knows why the two systems approach this question in such different ways. Whatever purposes we ascribe to the various approaches are products of our own creativity.

b. A Norm's Consequences

125. *Knowledge of consequences.* The lack of ascertainable purpose, however, is only part of the problem. The notion of function implies not only a recognized purpose but also ascertainable consequences. A norm can be considered functional only if we know both why it was promulgated and what its effects are likely to be. Yet, as Radin already noted, there can be no accuracy in predicting the consequences of a particular interpretation of a statute.[57] In fact, total shock at the unexpected consequences of our own actions must be one of the truly universal human experiences. We are often surprised by what our actions yield. Everyone has a story about some lucky misfortune, like missing the train to an important interview only to meet the love of one's life while asking about the schedule. The problem is even worse in comparative law because, when comparativists examine the function of a legal institution, they do not engage in sociological study. In the best case, they imagine what seem to them the likely

---

55. See Dawson (1961) 1075–1086 (discussing *negotiorum gestio* in the context of the preservation of another's property), 1227–1228 (indicating briefly at the end of his study that the question is one of morality); Lorenzen. But see Sheehan 262–266.

56. Justinian suggested that negotiorum gestio was derived from convenience, "to prevent the entire neglect of the affairs of absent persons, who may be forced to depart in haste, without having entrusted the management to anyone, and certainly no one would pay any attention to their affairs, unless the expenses that might arise could be recovered by action." Inst. 3, 27, 1, in Sandars 386. See generally Zimmermann 433–450.

57. Radin 878.

consequences. Less justifiably, they sometimes identify the consequences of applying the norms with their own desires. But those human foibles are not the real problem. Even scientific study would not help. The literature in decision theory makes clear that human beings have remarkably little ability to predict the future, and especially the consequences of current action.[58]

126. *Role of the law.* In fact, it is difficult to determine the role legal institutions play in society. For example, does compensation in the context of negotiorum gestio increase the likelihood of humanitarian activity? There are no studies, but even the studies would be beside the point. If a study were to determine that societies that provide compensation behave more charitably, the causal element would still be lacking. Individuals who live in those societies might, for other reasons, be more eager to do good deeds. Their charitable frame of mind might be responsible both for humanitarian action and for its reflection in the law. How exactly is anyone to know? Even in fields in which scholars have devoted considerable attention to the social consequences of legal institutions, the results remain uncertain. For example, it is difficult to predict which reforms of the penal code would more successfully deter crime.

One standard criticism of social science functionalism is that it operates an illegitimate teleology. The criticism applies as well to the functionalism used in comparative law. First, a social need is assumed. Then that social need is used to explain the structures that are thought to meet that need. "[U]nless one can document the historical processes—usually some combination of chance, intent, design, and luck—by which a particular requisite-failing situation led to the requisite-fulfilling end state, the explanation will be an illegitimate teleology."[59]

3. Gifts and Promises

127. *A great book.* Despite its limitations, functionalist methodology has produced a great law book, though perhaps only one. Oddly, it is also the only other broad comparative study of the law of gifts. It is John Dawson's magnificent—and magnificently flawed—*Gifts and Promises.* Dawson delivered these Storrs lectures at Yale Law School in 1978. Though he was seventy-eight when he published them two years later, he had somehow managed to retain his astonishing mastery of the great systems of the private law. The four lectures, one each on gift law in Rome, France, and Germany, together with a concluding lecture on the common law's consideration doctrine, demonstrate a monstrous erudition, unprecedented insight into the spirit of foreign legal systems, an uncanny ability to find intriguing cases, and Dawson's trademark ability to sense in judicial opinions the vectors of social policy that determine the outcome. Dawson was arguably the best legal comparativist the United States has produced. His book,

---

58. Lempert, Popper, and Bankes 25.
59. Turner and Maryanski 117.

together with André Tiraqueau's wide-ranging summa, Biondo Biondi's Romanist-inspired treatise, and Gino Gorla's comparative law meditation, are the only indisputably great books ever written about the law of gifts.

a. Harvard Meets Yale

128. *Legal realism.* Yet Dawson's book is flawed, flawed precisely because he adhered with such conviction to functionalist methodology. Dawson was a legal realist, a legal scholar who was convinced of "the overriding need for skepticism, the need to read everything not only along but between and behind the lines."[60] The cases were best read, as he put it, "as efforts—even though assumed to be honest efforts—to describe the action the judge was about to take in the most favorable light." Dawson believed that it was simply a delusion to think that the case holdings "could be fitted together ... into a coherent system of law."[61] He was instead convinced, to borrow from Holmes, that the decisions owe less to syllogism than they do to the felt necessities of the time, prevailing moral and political theories, intuitions of public policy, and even personal prejudice.[62] Dawson did not believe he had understood a case until he could articulate the force field in which the judge was operating and the purposes that the judge was seeking to achieve. And because, at the time, legal realism seemed to be the law's version of functionalism,[63] Dawson assumed that the functionalist method would be realism's *pendant* in comparative law.

Dawson's goal, in his Yale lectures, was to impart the synthesis that he had finally achieved in his thinking about the consideration doctrine. In a way, the consideration doctrine and realism were made for each other. The doctrine provides the quintessential example of an inflexible rule with no recognizable social benefit that often must be circumvented if justice is to be done. In other words, the consideration doctrine demonstrates that, as Llewellyn liked to put it, judges, not rules, decide cases. Even today, realist-inspired contracts professors continue to demonstrate all that is wrong with that doctrine. Corbin went everyone one better by basing one of the most famous treatises in American law on the claim that there never was any such thing as the consideration doctrine.[64]

---

60. Dawson (1983) 407.
61. Id. 408, 407.
62. Holmes 5, 31–32.
63. Kallen 525.
64. Immense effort has been made to discover the "origin" of the concept of consideration .... The present writer believes that there never was any specific and definite "origin" to be discovered, that no particular definition can (or ever could) be described as the only "correct" one, and that there has never been a simple and uniform "doctrine" by which enforceability can be deductively determined.
Corbin (1952) § 109. Llewellyn, Corbin's best student, was of the same view. "Consideration" is not in any meaningful sense *a* topic. The term ... relates to no unified body of states or problems of fact.

129. *The Death of Contract.* No one has ever attacked the consideration doctrine with the insight and subversive glee that Grant Gilmore brought to the task. Eight years before Dawson's Yale lectures, Grant Gilmore trumped all previous efforts with the four witty, sarcastic, in fact totally outrageous lectures he delivered at Ohio State and that he called *The Death of Contract.*[65] He argued that the entire law of contract, and in particular the consideration doctrine, had been cobbled together by Harvard law professors, and that the whole crazy scheme had never really existed outside the lecture halls of Harvard Law School.[66] Around the same time, Kessler and Gilmore, both Yale law professors, were reminding the readers of their contracts casebook that the civil law, "the common law's great rival," has no consideration doctrine. They went on to suggest that the German Civil Code is superior to the common law because it enforces gratuitous promises as long as certain formal requirements are met.[67] During an advisors' meeting for the Restatement (Second) of Contracts, Kessler went so far as to suggest that the consideration doctrine should be abolished.[68] That was, of course, an affront both to the consideration doctrine and to American contract law, but it was also an affront to Harvard. Dawson felt that someone should respond.

Though Dawson too was a realist, he had always understood the calling of the contracts professor to be a serious matter. The problem was not just that the story Gilmore told was totally made up. The problem was that Gilmore was making fun of the entire law-teaching profession. The time had come for a call to order. However, very few were worthy of Gilmore's steel. Dawson had proudly taught at Harvard for close to twenty years, and, though he had by then retired from the law school, he remained Harvard's great contracts scholar. He also had the sense of balance and propriety that comes to those who spend long years at the pinnacle of their profession. Dawson was the heir to Langdell, Holmes, and Williston. The task of resisting the Yale attack obviously fell to him. Yet Dawson also knew that it would be a supreme challenge. His lectures would be compared

---

There is instead an historically collected agglomeration of states of fact—like pebbles in pudding-stone—held together by the sole tie of being allegedly covered by "the same" legal doctrine. But the legal doctrines concerned are not "the same"; they are not a single body.

Llewellyn (1941) 778 (emphasis in original).

65. Gilmore (1974).

66. "It seems perfectly clear that Holmes was, quite consciously, proposing revolutionary doctrine and was not in the least interested in stating or restating the common law as it was." Id. 20.

67. Kessler and Gilmore 205.

68. "If one reflects on the complex of problems and solutions that are collected under the term 'consideration,' the thought cannot be dismissed out of hand that the entire doctrine is now outdated .... Isn't it time to establish as the fundamental rule the principle that promises are binding and for exceptions to that rule, such as the doctrine of unconscionability, to be rigorously elaborated?" Kessler (1954) 276.

not only to Gilmore's Ohio State lectures, which were already on their way to achieving cult status,[69] but also to Gilmore's own recently published Storrs lectures, in which Gilmore had continued to make fun of the Harvard law faculty.[70] As John Dawson stepped onto the stage at the Yale Law School, the turf of Corbin, Kessler, and Gilmore, he surely felt the electric anticipation that precedes every playing of the Harvard-Yale game.[71]

b. For Consideration

130. *Gratuitous promises.* Dawson opened his lectures with an explicit challenge to Gilmore's suggestion that consideration, and contract, have outlived their usefulness.[72] Dawson argued instead that the consideration doctrine has generally served us well, that its central idea is healthy, and that it would be easy to curtail its excesses. He also suggested that, in the end, civilians do not live in a world so different from our own. Even in civilian jurisdictions few gratuitous promises are enforced.

As he finished his introduction, however, something went dreadfully wrong. Dawson's erudition took over, and his lectures struck out on their own. Certainly no one in the audience was prepared for that rugged—yet extraordinary—march through two millennia of obscure sources and complex rules that govern gifts and successions in civilian jurisdictions. Even today it is hard to understand why Dawson believed that such an anabasis was needed to demonstrate the relatively

---

69. Even before Dawson began to speak, the book reviewers had devoted more than 150 pages to Gilmore's short book. Danzig 1125. For more on the book's success, see Hillman.

70. "Christopher Columbus Langdell, who in 1870 became the first dean of the Harvard Law School ... seems to have been an essentially stupid man who, early in his life, hit on one great idea to which, thereafter, he clung with all the tenacity of genius." Gilmore (1977) 42. "So, what was a judge who took the stare decisis business seriously—as many did—supposed to do when it turned out that the precedents in his state were, according to the learned gentlemen from Cambridge, wrong?" Id. 70.

The editors of the *Harvard Law Review* were not amused.

[Gilmore's] *The Ages of American Law* does not pretend to be a work of rigorous scholarship. It is basically a straightforward account of two hundred years of American law, seen from a particular point of view. Gilmore's book is also a repository of legal lore, but its intriguing descriptions of personalities and events are, unfortunately, occasionally marred by petty and perhaps groundless irrelevancies. One wonders, for instance, what purpose is served by asserting that "Langdell was an essentially stupid man" (p. 42), or by portraying Holmes' writing of *The Common Law* as motivated by personal vanity (p. 51).

Book Note 907.

71. "Indeed Professor Twining suggests, by implication, that Legal Realism was, so to say, a play-off for the Ivy League championship, with the combined faculties of the Columbia and Yale Law Schools taking the field against Harvard." Gilmore (1977) 78.

72. Dawson (1980) 3 and note 1.

simple proposition that the consideration doctrine might still play a useful role in the common law.

For four days Dawson did not flinch. He slogged relentlessly forward through his erudite demonstration that the civil law experiences endless and needless difficulties solely because it lacks an equivalent to our consideration doctrine. He believed that he had thereby proved that there would be only minimal benefit to rendering gratuitous promises enforceable in the common law. As he put it in his peroration, any difficulties the consideration doctrine causes are of our own making. They can be eliminated by a purposeful construction of our rules. There is no need to borrow anything from Europe.[73]

c. Inconsistencies

131. *Out of print.* Yale won that game. It was not even close. Gilmore's lectures, now out in a second paperback edition, have been the focus of at least one symposium[74] and continue to be read by first-year contracts students around the country. Dawson's book, on the other hand, never made it into paperback and is long out of print. Aside from a handful of kind reviews,[75] the book remains both undigested and indigestible. If it is read at all today, it is for its discussion of the consideration doctrine, except for the few who find themselves desperate for information in English about the intricacies of European successions law at the turn of the twentieth century.

132. *Flaws.* As a realist, Dawson was convinced that a case does not reveal its secrets until the discussion turns to the purpose the decision is designed to achieve. Dawson was the grand master of this method. A lifetime of shrewd analysis, of continually asking why the courts responded to the fact situations as they did, permitted him otherwise unobtainable insights into the workings of the common law. But the purposive method failed him in his comparative work.

The fundamental flaw of *Gifts and Promises* is its suggestion that a simple purpose is at work in the legal norms governing gift giving in civilian jurisdictions. Dawson believed that he had been able to reduce the multifarious web and texture of this elusive field to a single rationale. By postulating that every legal system has the same problems to solve, he failed to address the cultural component of the comparative puzzle. That is why he felt no qualms about condemning any law that seemed unable to achieve the purpose he ascribed to it. As a result,

---

73. "This survey leads me to only one conclusion: that our disadvantages, the main sources of our own discontent, are those of our own creation, are not found elsewhere and cannot be removed by borrowings from Europe. But this very fact, that they are strictly our own, offers the hopeful prospect that we should be able to eliminate them and set our own house in order." Dawson (1980) 230.

74. Symposium (1995).

75. See, e.g., Baade.

Dawson had no compunction about finding fault with the decisions. That may be a progressive attitude when an American law professor writes about American cases, but, when transferred to comparative work, it evidences a certain lack of sensitivity.

133. *Negotiorum gestio.* Dawson's earlier analysis of the German law of negotiorum gestio provides an example of his method. Despite his unequaled mastery of the cases, Dawson had a tin ear for cultural context. He seems never to have asked himself whether one country might have a need for an institution while another might not. He judged everything from the point of view of his office in Langdell Hall. And so he condemned.

> In important respects we are already well in advance of Germany and Switzerland in traveling along this road .... I should disclose my own conviction that the extreme extensions of liability found in the German decisions are unacceptable .... I have given reasons for believing that the transfer to life-rescue cases of rules of tort liability has produced, especially in Germany, indefensible injustice and gross distortion of *gestio* doctrines.[76]

The German doctrines he challenged may or may not be misguided, but some analysis of why such a doctrinally sophisticated system as German law considers those rules to be proper would be a useful prelude to total rejection.

134. *Law of gifts.* Dawson followed a similar procrustean method in his work on the law of gifts, and it led him to similar petulance. He was irritated that civilian judges seemed intent on concealing the purpose of their decisions from him.[77] Moreover, the creatures he found roaming through the civilian landscape seemed to him so strange that no amount of study could render them sympathetic.[78] "It is hard to believe that in a mature legal system which otherwise disclaims the use of voodoo, courts, authors, and other spokesmen for the regime accept this use of transparent pretense as fully justified because notarization would otherwise be needed."[79]

But there was an even more decisive difficulty. Dawson believed that he had discovered the purposes behind the decisions. In France, for example, he found two such purposes. First, he believed that the courts conspired with donors to

---

76. Dawson (1961) 836, 1114, 1129.
77. "One must look to the authors for explanations of the *don manuel*, since here as elsewhere the high court keeps its own secrets well .... The high court judges give no clue to their own motives in opening up this avenue, but enough good reasons can be surmised so that no one seems to worry that it is not authorized, indeed is forbidden, by the Code." Dawson (1980) 72, 74.
78. "The other invention [the disguised gift], however, can only be described as bizarre." Dawson (1980) 74.
79. Dawson (1980) 120.

eviscerate the gift law formalities established by the Civil Code.[80] However, Dawson also noted that, while the courts liberally created exceptions to the form requirements, they continued to subject all gifts to the limitations imposed by French successions law. Dawson therefore concluded that gift law was structured to respect what he considered the wrongheaded restrictions French law places on gratuitous transfers. Though these limitations are familiar to civilian jurists, they are very different from what is established in the common law. A brief review of the basic principles may therefore be useful in the context of this study.

French law allocates a part of the decedent's estate (*réserve*) for distribution to specified close relatives, the residuary heirs (*héritiers réservataires*; CC art. 912). Only the remainder, the disposable share (*quotité disponible*), is available for gratuitous transfers, whether inter vivos or by will. When the estate is opened, the reserve is calculated as a specified fraction of the property the decedent left at death, including any bequests made in the will, together with the value of all of the decedent's inter vivos gifts (CC. art. 922). When gratuitous transfers exceed the disposable share, the bequests are first eliminated, and then gifts are recalled for collation (sometimes called *hotchpot* in English) (*réduction* and *rapport*; CC art. 923). The last gift is first recalled. Donees who have received a gift subject to collation must either indemnify the residuary heirs or return the gift (CC arts. 924, 924-1). The value of property that the decedent alienated during life by onerous transfer, such as by sale, is not included in the reserve, since it is assumed that the decedent received equivalent value. Dawson believed that French gift law was designed to respect the role of the family in the transmission of property from one generation to the next.

135. *Inconsistencies.* There are two principal problems with Dawson's thesis. First, it makes no sense. If the courts are attempting to protect families from improvident gift giving, why do they create exceptions to the form requirements that are so broad as to permit virtually all gifts to be made without documentary evidence? The system rewards deception, which is cheaper and just as effective.

Second, Dawson was wrong on his facts. He believed that, though the French system opens broad exceptions to the form requirements, it subjects all gifts to the rules that protect the hereditary reserve. Yet that vision fails to explain much of the French law of gifts. To take the disguised gift as an example, Dawson's theory fails to explain why there is no penalty when a disguised gift exceeds the disposable share. The gift is simply reduced to the maximum allowable.[81]

---

80. "Most of the confusion and disarray that have already been described can be traced to a single, overriding impulse in the courts: to open wide the avenues of escape from the Code's requirements of notarization." Dawson (1980) 119.

81. "This means that the fraud against the rights of the residuary heirs receives no penalty, since the reduction penalizes only the surpassing of the disposable share and not the fraud, for which the normal sanction would be to render the gratuitous transfer

Dawson's theory also fails to explain the case law, which provides wide discretion to the trial courts to decide whether the donor tacitly dispensed the disguised gift from collation, a dispensation that, aside from manual gifts, must otherwise be made expressly and by notarial act.[82]

The main difficulties with Dawson's approach reveal themselves once his two premises are compared. He was convinced that French successions rules are irrational, and yet he postulated that the law pursued those irrational goals by rational means. There are punctual moments when history seems to work in just that way. Yet there is something contradictory about assuming that generations of French jurists insisted simultaneously on extremes of rationality and irrationality in the same norms.[83]

The constructions Dawson observed become less strange when the methodology is relaxed and the holdings need not all be explainable by reference to an abstract judicial purpose. Once it becomes clear that the law does not have its own way with things, that it not only acts but also is acted upon, that vectors point in many different directions, then the contradictory nature of the system makes some sense. What gift law needs is a comparative methodology that is open to more than purposive action.

4. Functionalism and the Law of Gifts

136. *Two problems*. When compared to neighboring areas of the law—the law of sales, for example—gift law creates particularly daunting problems for functionalist comparison. A functionalist study of sales laws can begin from agreement about the purpose of commodity exchange in the marketplace. The study would focus exclusively on the functionality of the law, perhaps by asking which norms reduce transaction costs and contribute to fairness and efficiency in exchange. A functional approach to gift law faces an additional hurdle. It must first determine the purpose of gift giving before it can evaluate how the law might best regulate it.

---

totally void." Blaise 104; see also Claude-Étienne Delvincourt, note to Civ. 31 May 1813, S. 1812–1814 I 362.

82. CC arts. 843 par. 1, 919 par. 2; Souleau no. 375; Blaise 100–102.

83. There is one additional problem with Dawson's work, which is worth mentioning only because few of his readers will have sufficient access to the sources to evaluate Dawson's argument independently. Dawson frequently cited to case law developments, that, though accurately presented, had long since ceased to be the law, even at the time Dawson was writing. That is an entirely excusable defect. It is impossible to ensure the timeliness of all statements in such an ambitious study. Yet the cases seem somewhat less objectionable once it becomes clear that the legal system concerned had, on its own, already acknowledged and corrected many of the difficulties Dawson so trenchantly observed.

a. The Purpose of the Gift

137. *Wide range.* The first problem is acute. As discussed above, social scientists have ascribed a wide range of purposes to the gift.[84] In certain circumstances, gift giving creates solidarity and smoothes the path for future interaction. In other situations, it maintains relationships of domination and may actually create enmity. In other words, gift giving has no unique function. It fills different roles at different times in different societies.

Even in a particular context, it is difficult to determine the precise functionality of the gift. For example, what is the function of the tribal leader's extravagant distribution of wealth known as the potlatch? Is it a means to reciprocate previously received gifts? Is it the method by which a family establishes a claim to power? Is it a weapon to crush a rival with future obligations? Or is it all of these? Or none of them? When the time came for Lévi-Strauss to explain the purpose of the institution, he found these three purposes in the ethnographic literature and lumped them together without further comment.[85] Or is the purpose of the potlatch, as Georges Bataille suggested, to provide a mechanism for squandering excess energy and profit that must be spent?[86] We do not know. Upon closer investigation, as Michael Orans has demonstrated, even the most promising functionalist explanations turn out to be speculative. There is no evidence to support them. They produce the appearance of explanation without providing one.[87]

What is the purpose of mutual gifts of bracelets and necklaces? Why do the Trobriand Islanders engage in the kula? What is the function of passing pieces of dysfunctional jewelry from hand to hand over generations? Our effort to understand these activities is the tribute we pay to our fellow human beings. But no one, after hearing the explanations, would seriously claim that we have understood them.

b. The Function of Gift Law

138. *Different approaches.* Law is a social practice that attempts to govern other social practices. To compare the functionality of different gift norms, we have to understand both the purposes gift law attempts to achieve and its success in regulating that behavior. Gift law varies greatly from system to system. Gift promises are enforceable in some systems but not in others. In some systems the validity of a gift depends on carrying out a complicated set of formalities. In others there is no special form requirement. Yet no one has studied the relative

---

84. Supra nos. 19, 21–22, 26–27, 37–40.

85. Lévi-Strauss (1969) 53.

86. "[I]f the excess cannot be completely absorbed in its growth, it must necessarily be lost without profit; it must be spent, willingly or not, gloriously or catastrophically." Bataille 21. For Bataille's discussion of the potlatch, see id. 67–77.

87. Orans 326.

effectiveness of these different norms. In fact, there is little agreement about the purposes these norms are designed to achieve. For example, until recently French law automatically revoked all prior gifts upon the birth of the donor's first child.[88] No French scholar has managed to explain the purpose or consequences of that surprising norm. Until we have at least some idea of the aims and effects of these norms, no functionalist approach is possible.

139. *No greater risks.* Moreover, the giving of gifts is not itself a problem that demands a legal solution. There are risks in all human activity. A donor might make an impulsive gift that later turns out to be extravagant or misguided. A swindler might con a gift. A scoundrel might grab something valuable from the room of a dying acquaintance and claim that a gift had been made. But the risks are no greater than those that arise in other fields of private law, no greater, for example, than the risk of making a disastrous investment on a stock tip, or falling prey to a scam artist, or having a check stolen and forged. The law generally recognizes that most of these problems can be reduced to a mere social nuisance by proper education. It thus prefers to grant individuals the opportunity they need to develop as moral subjects. In other words, the giving of gifts does not pose problems different in degree or kind from those encountered throughout the private law. If the law finds in gift giving a problem to solve, the law has conjured that problem from its own premises and has not discovered anything objectively related to the practice itself.

c. Potlatch as Paradigm

140. *Obstruction and avoidance.* A study of gift law must confront what, unexpectedly, turn out to be the field's two dominant features. First, in many systems the law demonstrates a profound distaste for gift giving and generally does what it can to obstruct it. Yet the law is singularly inept at creating roadblocks, which produces the field's second fundamental feature. Those subject to these legal restrictions have developed numerous techniques to avoid them. The potlatch provides a paradigmatic example of both themes.

i. Nature of the Potlatch

141. *Linchpin of the social system.* The potlatch was—and, to some extent, still is—practiced by the First Nations on and around Vancouver Island in the Canadian West, and even more broadly throughout the region, on both sides of the Canadian border. In its heyday, the potlatch involved a tribal chief's large-scale distribution of commodities to each member of an invited tribe according to rank and debt obligation. The objects of bounty were everyday items, such as Hudson's Bay blankets, though, because they were distributed in vast quantities,

---

88. Infra nos. 1215–1294.

the symbolism of the gift overshadowed its use value.[89] The ceremony some-times included the destruction of valuable property such as canoes and ritual coppers. The entire community was involved. Because a successful potlatch required more resources than any individual chief possessed, the chief borrowed from other members of the tribe and called in debts, together with the usual 100 percent interest. Sometimes children were mortgaged for potlatch debts.

Potlatches generally took place at nodal moments in tribal life, chiefly during rites of passage, such as when young men received new names and, even more importantly, in the context of marriage.[90] Due to differences in kinship structure and leadership succession, aspects varied from tribe to tribe, including the nature and timing of the festivities, the identity of the invited guests, and the type and quantity of goods distributed. The Kwakwaka'wakw celebrated frequent pot-latches, whereas the Tlingit potlatched principally during funerals. Potlatching, however, was much more than a series of isolated events. Each distribution was a moment in an endless cycle. The term *potlatch* refers to this cycle of accumulation and distribution, together with the obligations and culture that grew up around it.[91]

The potlatch was actually the linchpin of a complex social system, a focus for the other subsystems of tribal culture.[92] For the Kwakwaka'wakw, that included the structure of kinship and lineage (*numaym*), political office and succession to the status of chief, the religious societies, performance arts, beliefs regarding ancestry, supernatural spirits, and mythology, as well as the life cycle and rites of passage.[93] For example, succession to a position of rank was valid only if accom-panied by a ceremony involving the large-scale distribution of goods. If the dis-tribution did not take place, the chief lost prestige and the succession could fail.[94] Because the Kwakwaka'wakw did not keep written records, the potlatch provided publicity and witnesses. Business too was frequently settled at potlatch gather-ings. The witnesses always received gifts.[95]

ii. Potlatch and the Law

142. *Outlawed.* The potlatch has proven crucially important to generations of social theorists. Mauss derived the three gift obligations from his reading of Malinowski's study of the Melanesian kula and Franz Boas's ethnographic

---

89. Codere 64.

90. For the structural role of the potlatch in tribal society, see Rosman and Rubel (1971) 34–68 (Tlingit), 128–175 (Kwakwaka'wakw); Rosman and Rubel (1972).

91. Codere 63.

92. Piddocke 258.

93. Rosman and Rubel (1971) 157.

94. Id. 201.

95. Halliday 5.

reports of the potlatch. Even today the kula and the potlatch remain the quintessential examples of clan-based gift exchange.

What rarely is mentioned, however, and what both Boas and Mauss were far too courteous to insist upon, is the fact that, already, before either began to write, the potlatch had been outlawed. In 1884 the Canadian Indian Act was amended to prohibit participation both in the potlatch and in specified tribal dances.[96] Five years later, the judge in the first attempted prosecution released the defendant after suggesting that, because the elements of the offense were not enumerated, the statute could not be enforced.[97] In 1895 the Indian Act was therefore again amended to define the prohibited conduct.[98] A number of Kwakwaka'wakw Indians served two-month prison sentences for potlatching because no other penalty was provided.[99] Thus, as Boas sat for days on end in a heroic display of participant observation, jotting down every detail of the epic potlatches of 1895, he was actually recording evidence of criminal activity.[100] A few years later George Hunt, Boas's principal informant and translator, was tried for potlatching.[101]

---

96. Every Indian or other person who engages in or assists in celebrating the Indian festival known as the "Potlatch" or in the Indian dance known as the "Tamanawas" is guilty of a misdemeanor, and shall be liable to imprisonment for the term of not more than six nor less than two months in any gaol or other place of confinement; and any Indian or other person who encourages, either directly or indirectly, an Indian or Indians to get up such a festival or dance, or to celebrate the same, or who shall assist in the celebration of same is guilty of a like offense, and shall be liable to the same punishment.

S.C. 1884 chap. 27 sec. 3, in Venne 93, codified, R.S.C. 1886 chap. 43 sec. 114, in Venne 157, repealed, S.C. 1894 chap. 35 sec. 6. For the history of the prohibition and ultimate repeal, see Cole and Chaikin.

97. Cole and Chaikin 35–36 (unreported case).

98. With regards to the potlatch, the prohibition covered anyone who "engages in, or assists in celebrating or encourages either directly or indirectly another to celebrate, any Indian festival, dance or other ceremony of which the giving away or paying or giving back of money, goods, or articles of any sort forms a part, or is a feature, whether such gift of money, goods or articles takes place before, at, or after the celebration of the same." S.C. 1895 chap. 35 sec. 6, codified R.S.C. chap. 43 sec. 6, in Venne 158. See Harring 268–269.

The relevant provision of the Indian Act was again amended in 1906 to eliminate the need for a grand jury indictment and instead to allow for "summary conviction" by the Indian agents. R.S.C. 1906 chap. 81 sec. 149, as amended by S.C. 1918 chap. 26 sec. 7, in Venne 229.

99. For a brief history of the potlatch prohibition, see Halliday 188–189.

100. For Boas's account of potlatches during the Kwakwaka'wakw Winter Ceremonial in November 1895, see Boas (1966) 179–241.

101. Cole and Chaikin 73–75. Hunt was eventually acquitted.

(A) THE PURPOSE OF THE PROHIBITION

143. *Practical problems.* In the context of a discussion of functionalism, it is useful to ask what the Canadian government hoped to achieve by suppressing the potlatch and the tribal dances. The government's Indian agents attributed numerous problems to those practices. They believed the devotion to potlatching and dancing caused tribal chieftains to die without resources. They also assumed that Native women worked as prostitutes in Victoria because their men were in debt from purchasing potlatch goods. The long break for the winter potlatches meant that no money was earned, and Native children were kept from school from December through April.[102] The sanitary conditions at the large gatherings were thought to be unsatisfactory. The blankets exchanged at the ceremonies, which were dragged through the dirt and accumulated filth, spread tuberculosis. Pneumonia was highest at the end of the potlatch season, as was infant mortality.[103] During the potlatch, young Kwakwaka'wakw women were sold as wives, redeemed, and then resold. Though spousal purchases accumulated prestige for both parties, women often did not find a final mate until the fourth exchange.[104]

William Halliday, the Kwakwaka'wakw Indian agent, made the following case for the prohibition.

[The potlatch] was looked upon by the natives themselves as a sort of banking system whereby they loaned out their property to others at ruinous rates of interest, as the recipient of the bounty might be called on at any time for the full amount of the gift with accrued interest often of two hundred per cent. Gradually the privilege of giving began to be abused and distorted until it resembled a huge octopus, which held all customs and habits of the Indians in its embrace. It was a particularly wasteful and destructive custom, and created ill-feeling, jealousy, and in most cases great poverty, and it was only after having considered the matter from every angle, and for a long time, that the Government of Canada passed the statute forbidding it ....[105]

The political problem was that the potlatch provided an obstacle to assimilation. The Indian agents believed that the First Nations would never become Canadians as long as they insisted on stopping work for long periods in the winter to dance and to give away their belongings. The Indian Department officials believed that the only way to domesticate the Native peoples was to destroy their ceremonial life.[106] It is worth noting that the Kwakwaka'wakw have always

---

102. Halliday 11.
103. Id. 7–8.
104. Cole and Chaikin 76–83.
105. Halliday 4.
106. Indian Department officials were only partially aware of the place of ceremony in native life, but they did understand that it was at the heart of tribal culture. This

had some difficulty finding an appreciative audience. Even Ruth Benedict, who, as a student of Franz Boas, was passionately committed to cultural egalitarianism, could not resist calling the potlatch *an obsession* and Kwakwaka'wakw behavior *megalomaniac paranoid*.[107]

(B) THE CONDITION OF THE KWAKWAKA'WAKW

144. *High living standard*. The prohibition focused particularly on the potlatch among the Kwakwaka'wakw, so it might be imagined that they were particularly destitute. But that was not the case. The Kwakwaka'wakw had one of the highest standards of living of any Indian group in North America.[108] They were among the best fed and best housed, extremely wealthy in tools, and highly skilled as artists and artisans.[109] Moreover, through the first three decades of the twentieth century, their per capita earnings more than quadrupled, and the value of their real and personal property increased more than sixfold.[110] They were able and industrious and usually managed to produce a large storable surplus. It was only their nonceremonial dress, made of fur and woven cedar bark, that may have made a poor impression.

The Kwakwaka'wakw also adjusted productively to the new economy and competed successfully with settlers from Europe and Asia. After the Hudson's Bay Company opened its trading post at Fort Rupert, the Kwakwaka'wakw abandoned their long tradition of warfare, which they practiced with particular ferocity,[111] and devoted their time instead to underselling Hudson's Bay and making a handsome profit. Ironically, as trade increased and new wealth flowed into Kwakwaka'wakw society, the potlatch flourished.[112] Profit intensified status rivalry and the frequency and volume of the potlatch, which, as a result, became the predominant Kwakwaka'wakw institution and a substitute for war.[113]

---

culture was to be broken. It not only symbolized values primitive and un-Christian, considered inappropriate in a modern Canada, but was a direct threat to Canadian domination of the Indian tribes and to an assimilationist Indian policy. The Indian agents could never understand the complexity of what went on in Indian ceremonies, but it bound the people and tribes together in a unique world.
Harring 268.

107. Benedict 193, 222.
108. Codere 4, 18–19.
109. Despite abundance in historical times, the earlier Kwakwaka'wakw may have known hard times and occasionally suffered from famine. Orans 315; Piddocke 248–249, 253–254.
110. Codere 43–49.
111. For the history of warfare among the Kwakwaka'wakw, see Codere 98–117.
112. Codere 118–129.
113. Piddocke 245.

Kwakwaka'wakw health suffered as settlement increased, but that was largely through diseases transmitted from the settlers.[114]

The real problem was that the Canadians and the Kwakwaka'wakw did not share the same worldview. The Kwakwaka'wakw spent their lives doing the one thing that the government could not abide. The Northwest Indians—about this there was never a doubt—really had fun. And as long as they were having fun, there was no chance they would abandon their traditional lifestyle and become church-going Canadians.[115] At least that was how Halliday explained the problem in 1910.[116] It is revealing that a subsequent enactment prohibited Indians from wasting their time in pool halls.[117]

(C) EFFECTIVENESS OF THE PROHIBITION

145. *Totally ineffective.* The potlatch also provides an example of the second theme involved here, which is that the prohibition proved unsuccessful. The Northwest tribes disregarded the prohibition. They continued to perform potlatches in venues so far removed that the police could not reach them. When the police did manage to make arrests, the Indians liberated their prisoners in hand-to-hand combat.[118] The police were more successful at Dan Cranmer's potlatch in the Mamalilikulla tribal settlement on Village Island, near Alert Bay, in December 1921. Almost fifty of the three hundred participating villagers were convicted for attending. Twenty were imprisoned. The rest received suspended sentences in

---

114. Codere 51–56.

115. It is very hard to try and stop us; the White man gives feasts to his friends and goes to theatres; we have only our "potlatchs" and dances for amusement; we work for our money and like to spend it as we please, in gathering our friends together and giving them food to eat, and when we give blankets or money, we dance and sing and all are good friends together; now whenever we travel we find friends; the "potlatch" does that.

Nootka response to the government critique of the potlatch, quoted in Cole and Chaikin 26.

116. The chief reason for want of progress is the apathy of the Indians themselves. They do not realize that they have sunk into a rut, and only an active effort on their own part can pull them out of it. They make their living very easily, that is so far as the actual necessities are concerned. Fish in one form or another is the chief article of diet, and the waters of the coast teem with fish. Then their ideas of the ideal and that of the whites do not at all correspond. Their chief aim is to go through life easily and get all the fun and glory they can out of it. The glory comes from giving a potlatch, the fun in doing nothing as often as possible. The only hope of improvement is through the education of the young.

William Halliday, in Canada, Annual Report of Indian Affairs (1910) at 238, quoted in Codere 12.

117. R.S.C. 1927 chap. 98 sec. 140A, as amended by S.C. 1930 chap. 25 sec. 16, in Venne 300.

118. Cole and Chaikin 68.

return for their agreement to surrender their potlatch paraphernalia. Perhaps as many as 750 pieces of ceremonial regalia were confiscated.[119] Some of the items were sold to the Museum of the American Indian in New York. Those left over were shipped to what became the National Museum of Man in Ottawa. From there, some of the objects were transferred to the Royal Ontario Museum and into the private collection of Duncan Scott, superintendent-general of Indian Affairs.

The Natives soon found legal loopholes that permitted them to continue to potlatch. By means of something like negotiable warehouse receipts, the Kwakwaka'wakw potlatched with the expropriated coppers that were displayed at the time in the ethnological museums.[120] Camouflage was also successful. The potlatch had always been part of the Winter Ceremonial. It was adjusted to coincide with Christmas, and each gift was individually wrapped as a present. Because the Kwakwaka'wakw refused to inform on fellow tribe members, prosecutions eventually ceased.[121]

It now seems that the prohibition actually intensified the potlatch, at least among the Kwakwaka'wakw. The law turned the potlatch into a symbol of resistance to the government. The rebellious backlash helped to perpetuate the institution.[122] Relentless civil disobedience finally caused the prohibition to be lifted in 1951.[123] During the 1970s the potlatch experienced a rebirth and again became a primary symbol of Indian identity.[124] The ritual objects confiscated in 1922 were returned in 1979 to community societies that now exhibit the items on Vancouver Island. A recent study of the returned pieces suggests that they were painted and sculpted in an unusually crude manner. Specialists now speculate they had been manufactured specifically for the purpose of surrender to the authorities.[125]

In 2002, the Kwakwaka'wakw and other First Nations in British Columbia filed a claim with the Canadian Indian Claims Commission, alleging that the prohibition of the potlatch and the enforcement of the prohibition, particularly on Village Island, violated Canada's fiduciary obligations to the Indian tribes.[126]

---

119. Carpenter 64; Loo; Cole and Chaikin 119–124.
120. Codere 88.
121. Cole and Chaikin 143–144.
122. Id. 61, 175.
123. S.C. 1951 chap. 29 sec. 123 par. 2, in Venne 353.
124. Cole and Chaikin 172–173.
125. Carpenter 68; Cole and Chaikin 173.
126. The claim was submitted as a special claim and then placed in abeyance at the claimants' request. U'mista Cultural Centre [Prohibition of the potlatch], Indian Claims Commission, www.indianclaims.ca/claimsmap/umista_1-en.asp (10 Feb. 2008).

d. Comparative Notes

146. *Difficulties with functionalism.* The law governing the giving of gifts seems to be an area in which it is particularly inadvisable to ask questions from a functionalist point of view. Nothing seems to make much sense once the conversation turns to the purpose and effectiveness of these norms.

5. The Ambiguity of Function

147. *Emic and etic.* Perhaps the most serious difficulty with comparative law functionalism is the ambiguity at the core of its central concepts, *function* and *purpose.* The problem does not arise in the natural sciences. When biologists explain that the function or purpose of the heart is to circulate the blood supply, it is understood that they are referring to the heart's objective contribution to the functioning of the body. In the human sciences, however, function and purpose can be conceived either objectively or subjectively, from the point of view of either an outsider or an insider, from either the *etic* or the *emic* perspective.[127]

For example, when an anthropologist asks about the purpose or function of the Hopi rain dance, the answer depends on the perspective from which the purpose is judged. Hopi tribe members might say that they dance to convince the gods to send abundant rainfall. An outside observer might instead decide that the rain dance functions to reinforce group identity and ensure social cohesion. Sociologist Robert Merton, referring to this example, distinguished between a social institution's manifest or purported function, the conscious motivation of those involved, and its latent function or objective consequence.[128] The distinction had long been made by ethnologists.[129]

148. *Focus on the objective.* Rigorous functionalists in the social sciences focus on the objective side of this dichotomy, for they believe that "the real animus of

---

127. "If behavioral events are described in terms of categories and relationships that arise from the observer's strategic criteria of similarity, difference, and significance, they are etic; if they are described in terms of criteria elicited from an informant, they are emic." Harris 340.

128. Merton 114, 118–119.

129. An example is Radcliffe-Brown's analysis of the function of dance among the Andamanese. "If an Andaman Islander is asked why he dances," Radcliffe-Brown noted from an emic perspective, "he gives an answer that amounts to saying that he does so because he enjoys it." Radcliffe-Brown (1948) 247. After describing the dance in detail, Radcliffe-Brown reached a conclusion about its social function. "In this way the dance produces a condition in which the unity, harmony and concord of the community are at a maximum, and in which they are intensely felt by every member. It is to produce this condition, I would maintain, that is the primary social function of the dance." Id. 252. In this setting, the individual dancer's perspective is not only accurate but actually essential to the dance's social function.

functionalism lies in the conception of function without purpose."[130] Functionalist social scientists are interested in the contribution institutions make to society as an ongoing system, independently of what the participants believe about those institutions. As Durkheim put it, "The determining cause of a social fact must be sought among antecedent social facts and not among the states of the individual consciousness."[131] Functionalists understand participants' beliefs as yet further components of the system, components that in turn need to be explained.[132] Moreover, there are often numerous etic theories. For example, economists and Canadian politicians considered the potlatch to be wasteful foolishness, whereas anthropologists saw in it a mechanism for maintaining social structure.[133]

Functionalists often have difficulty maintaining the proper focus. The language difficulty is fundamental. Language of purpose is taken from ordinary discourse and bent to serve objective analysis.[134] Moreover, it is easy to make the honest mistake of accepting the informant's subjective view as the ultimate basis of explanation.[135] The temptation is less serious when the manifest purpose of an activity, such as the Hopi rain dance, is to achieve a goal that natural science suggests cannot be achieved. But when the goal seems plausible, even experienced observers are less likely to ask about the institution's latent functions.[136] "Throughout anthropological literature there is confusion between cultural needs, which find their expression in vast schemes or aspects of social constitution, and conscious motivation, which exists as a psychological fact in the mind of an individual member of a society."[137]

Yet the distinction between the etic and the emic are crucial if functionalism is to succeed. The functionalist social scientist must "distinguish carefully between what the actor has in mind and what the social causes and consequences of his action may be, to keep separate always the point of view of the actor and the point of view of the observer. To the extent he cherishes certain goals or puts

130. Kallen 524.
131. Durkheim 134 (the sentence is in italics in the original).
132. Such a reason as is produced by this process of rationalisation [among the Andamans] is rarely if ever identical with the psychological cause of the action that it justifies, yet it will nearly always help us in our search for the cause. At any rate the reason given as explaining an action is so intimately connected with the action itself that we cannot regard any hypothesis as to the meaning of a custom as being satisfactory unless it explains not only the custom but also the reasons that the natives give for following it.
Radcliffe-Brown (1948) 235.
133. Radcliffe-Brown (1940) 8.
134. "Such words as 'function,' 'disfunction,' 'latent,' 'needs' are treacherous for the same reason that they are handy." Davis (1959) 763.
135. Davis (1959) 765.
136. Merton 119.
137. Malinowski (1937) 629.

his analysis in terms of them and thus adopts the role of an actor, he loses the sociological level of analysis."[138]

149. *The etic in law.* A functionalist social scientist would carefully distinguish two facets of a legal system. The investigator would ask, first, about the goals that those who promulgate the norms seek to achieve—legislative intent and the policy reasons behind a judicial decision. The functionalist asks this question not because the answer will explain a norm's function, but rather to gather further data for functional analysis. A functionalist might ask, for example, how judges and legislators came to believe that the institution works as intended, much as one would ask a Hopi kachina dancer why the dancer believes that the dance actually might bring rain. However, when exploring the role legal norms play in a given social system, a functionalist would look exclusively at how those norms function. As Radcliffe-Brown noted, the method that is convenient for lawyers in their professional studies is not satisfactory for a social scientist, who must examine the role played by the law in maintaining a certain social structure.[139]

150. *Comparative law.* Modern comparative law, in contrast, has never experienced these difficulties. For the century of its existence, it has remained unaware of this distinction. Comparative law functionalists generally do not ask whether legal institutions might have objective functions that differ from the goals the lawmakers intend to achieve. In fact, many comparative lawyers, like many other legal scholars, assume that an institution's objective function corresponds to the goals those who create the norms are seeking to achieve.

151. *Purposivism.* For this reason, what is known as functionalism in comparative law is in fact not functionalism at all. It might more accurately be described as *purposivism.* It investigates how the institutions created by the various legal systems fulfill their articulated purposes. Purposivism does not distinguish between the emic and the etic. It assumes, as does the law itself, that human institutions fulfill the purposes their creators ascribe to them and that, as social purposes change, society purposefully alters its institutions to meet its evolving goals.

Purposivism has nothing to do with functionalism in the social sciences. In fact, social scientists have repeatedly explained that the method is not social science at all. Instead, a functionalist social scientist might suggest that comparative law purposivism demonstrates such a lack of self-knowledge, such a fascinating incongruity in an age of postmodern navel gazing, that it itself would require explanation.

152. *Law meets gift.* In the field of gift law, purposivism attempts to justify the legal restrictions imposed on donative activity. It seeks to explain why gift giving

138. Davis (1959) 765.
139. Radcliffe-Brown (1940) 8–9.

represents a problem for which a legal solution is needed. The assumption is that human beings, through their legislators, are able to structure social life as they see fit. In other words, purposivism understands gift law as another element of the traditional story that the law tells about itself.

Yet a moment's reflection makes clear that the law's perspective on gift giving has to be wrong. The world has many problems, but surely altruism is not such a major nuisance that it deserves the degree of attention it has received in the law of gifts. Many would conclude that favoring altruism might even represent the beginning of a solution. It is at this point that the emic perspective of comparative law reveals itself to be inadequate. Even a traditional purposivist might be surprised and begin to ask whether gift norms might serve some function other than the one legislative intent ascribes to them.

153. *Objective function.* When examined objectively, gift law does help resolve a problem, though it is not a problem gift giving presents to society. It is rather a difficulty gift giving poses to the law, for the gift threatens the law's conception of itself. The three Maussian gift obligations, despite the bewildering array of functions they appear to fulfill in different societies, seem to represent a basic pattern of human interaction, one that escapes legislative control. It might therefore be argued that, in contrast, the law's restriction of gift giving is designed to reinforce the conception of the individual that provides the foundation for modern law, the marketplace, and microeconomics. The foundation of all those activities is the rational actor who maximizes utility by increasing profit and reducing expense.

The law correctly recognizes that gift giving is subject to a different dynamic. The gift is an autonomous institution that no legal system can domesticate. This much was clear to the Canadian government when it prohibited the potlatch. Legal systems usually integrate such institutions into society by recharacterizing them as legal concepts. But gift giving to some extent refuses to be subsumed under traditional legal categories. And it suffers the consequences. Modern legal systems tend to prohibit what they cannot integrate.[140]

154. *Inferiority.* Gift giving offers a glimpse of a different world, one that serves as a reminder of the artificiality and, in a sense, inferiority of legal norms.

---

140. As Halliday indicated, Canadian potlatch legislation was actually designed to eradicate Indian culture.

A very large percentage of the Indians to-day are not of pure Indian blood, but have a large admixture of white blood, and, as one can imagine, it is not the better class of white men who have thus degraded themselves by intermingling with the Indian women, so that the result morally is not so great as the result physically. However, it will hasten the time when the Indians as such will be no more, but will be absorbed into the white race, and will help to carry the burden that so far has been borne by the white man for his benefit.

Halliday 226–227.

The norms that actually govern the giving of gifts are customary. They are almost universally followed, even though they are not sanctioned by the state. The simple existence of these customary norms threatens the foundation of the law, because it makes clear that society is structured by norms that do not depend on legal enforcement. It raises the question of how many customary norms would be followed irrespective of legal sanction, and the further question of whether society would really degenerate into a war of all against all in the absence of Leviathan. If the law that governs the giving of gifts proves to be largely unnecessary, it might well be asked just how much of the rest of the law is superfluous as well.

In other words, in its encounter with gift giving, aspects of the law reveal themselves to be guarantors of the conceptual foundation of life in the market. In the encounter between these two elemental social forces—the law and the giving of gifts—gift giving seems relatively harmless when compared to the extraordinary scope of the limitations imposed on it in many legal systems. If a legal system tends to prohibit what it cannot understand, the limits of legal understanding are obviously of great consequence to society. It is therefore useful to note those moments when legal norms seem to adopt the point of view of the market.

At this point, the methodological and the substantive preoccupations of this comparative study meet. Actually, they do not just meet. Eerily, they fuse. Gift giving challenges the law in the same way that it challenges the story legal scholarship tells about the law. There is thus no way to explore the interaction between the law and the giving of gifts without questioning the understanding that much of modern Western law has of itself.

C. AN INTERPRETIVE APPROACH

155. *Alternative to purposivism.* This study departs from the tenets of purposivism. It takes instead an interpretive approach to the comparative examination of the law of gifts. The hope is that this approach makes it possible both to avoid the difficulties of the traditional method and to discover something of the meaning of the law that governs the giving of gifts.

1. Social Science Functionalism and Comparative Law

156. *Functionalism in the social sciences.* Once it becomes clear that social science functionalism differs dramatically from comparative law purposivism, it might be asked whether an authentic functionalism might provide a workable method for comparative law research. It turns out, however, that functionalism, as it has evolved, has abandoned its rigorous goals and now provides little more than a useful intuition.

a. Critique of Functionalism

157. *Constant critique.* Functionalist methodology arose implicitly in the course of a number of influential ethnographic studies conducted at the beginning of the

twentieth century. Though the method was not formulated systematically, the ideas, often discussed in short articles, were fully developed by the 1930s.[141] From the beginning, functionalism was the object of criticism, sometimes even invective.[142] The critique of functionalism has generated many of the more recent social science methodologies. In fact, the university course on social science methodology frequently begins by rehearsing the failings of the functionalist method.[143]

Functionalism has been criticized for failing to take account of history, change, and conflict, as well as for a conservative, perhaps even reactionary, bias.[144] Functionalism has been described as the social science methodology that corresponds to the machine age, "with its impersonal automatic engines in continuous action; the tremendous acceleration of the tempo of life by the industrial establishment; the adoption of 'efficiency,' 'service,' 'progress' and the like as measures of value in the community."[145] More importantly, it has been argued that, even once an institution's functionality is fully described, nothing is thereby explained. Functionalists and neofunctionalists have in turn defended the method.[146] There is no reason to rehearse this dispute here because, in the end, very little is at stake. The functionalist method has long since been reformulated to remove the sting of most of these criticisms, but only at the price of becoming a commonsense, heuristic device that yields little in terms of methodological focus.

b. Merton's Reformulation

158. *Three postulates.* In his seminal article on functionalist methodology, Robert Merton summarized the three fundamental axioms of the functionalist method, and then, after demonstrating their defects, he reformulated the method as a heuristic tool.[147] An examination of these axioms, together with their Mertonian reformulations, makes clear how little is left of functionalism as a discrete method.

In Merton's view, functionalism postulates, first, that society is a functional unity. Each societal element is integrated into the total structure with enough

---

141. See Radcliffe-Brown (1935a); Malinowski (1939). Somewhat later, Radcliffe-Brown famously declared that the functional school never existed. It was "a myth invented by Professor Malinowski." Radcliffe-Brown (1940) 1.

142. For a more or less contemporary critique, see Gregg and Williams. For a response, see Radcliffe-Brown (1949).

143. "There is one theoretical approach that every undergraduate in the social sciences is quickly taught to dismiss: 'functionalism.'" Mills 326.

144. "If what the Western world has now in the way of institutions is 'functioning, active, efficient' the outlook is dim indeed." Gregg and Williams 602.

145. Kallen 524.

146. For citations to the principal critiques, defenses, and compromise proposals, see Camic 693.

147. Merton 79–91.

harmony and consistency to prevent irresolvable conflict. Second, functionalism assumes universal functionality. Every social custom, material object, and idea fulfills a social function. Finally, functionalism presupposes that all institutions are indispensable. Every social institution is functionally necessary for the society of which it is a part.[148]

159. *Doubts.* It took Merton only a couple of pages to demonstrate that these postulates are mistaken. Even from a commonsense perspective they seem rigid and excessive. Yet it is important to recall why orthodox functionalists, even if only implicitly, adopted these postulates for their ethnographic studies, and it is even more important to make clear the consequences of rejecting them, as we will be forced to do. These three postulates provide the necessary deductive framework for rigorous functionalist analysis. As long as it can be assumed that societies function as systemic wholes and that each of their elements fulfills an indispensable function, social scientists are justified in assuming that, when they encounter a social institution, no matter how odd it may seem, that institution plays some useful role. If any of the postulates does not obtain, rigorous functionalist analysis becomes impossible.

Difficulties already surface in biology. We know that certain elements of the body serve no useful purpose. Examples include nipples on male mammals and, to borrow an example from Holmes, the cat clavicle. As far as the social sciences are concerned, there is no way to prove or disprove the functionalist postulates. In the end, some will believe them, others will not. The buttons on the sleeve of a man's suit jacket provide a good example. Whether they serve a function, such as maintaining a connection to tradition, or are a simple atavism is a question of judgment and preference—or a question of the definition of the term *function*.

In the end, it does not matter. Once it becomes clear that we cannot be certain whether any particular social institution actually has a function, then functionalism is demoted to a heuristic suggestion.[149] It stands today for the proposition that we should try to find functions for the social institutions we investigate. As Kingsley Davis explained in a now-classic essay, functionalism, properly understood, simply restates the fundamental goal of all social science, namely to

---

148. Because the views of the functionalists continued to evolve in response to criticism, Merton chose to delineate the view of an ideal functionalist. For example, although Radcliffe-Brown maintained his view that a social system is a functional unity, Radcliffe-Brown (1935a) 397, he retracted his belief in the functionality of every custom. Early in his career, he argued that "Every custom and belief of a primitive society plays some determinate part in the social life of the community, just as every organ of a living body plays some part in the general life of the organism." Radcliffe-Brown (1948). (Radcliffe-Brown began work on the book in 1908–1909, but it was not published until 1922.) Some years later he rejected the idea as a "dogmatic assertion" and decided instead that it was enough to assume that every institution *may* have a function. Radcliffe-Brown (1935a) 399.

149. Turner and Maryanski 119–120.

understand how society works, and therefore to reflect on how different social institutions function.[150]

160. *From observation to explanation.* The goal of functionalism is explanation. Every attempt at explanation must make a difficult transition from description of the data to more general statements that link the data in causal relationships. Though functionalism encourages a playful speculation about the roles social institutions may fulfill in society, it offers no suggestion on how to move from description to explanation; neither does it tell us how to distinguish explanations that are useful from those that are not. *Les guides rouges* and *les trois macarons*, the Michelin restaurant guides with their three stars, may serve the function of making restaurant choice more convenient and informed; of maintaining French dominance in the culinary arts; of promoting Michelin brand tires; of generating celebrity status for chefs; of diverting attention from serious social problems by reaffirming our collective fascination with talent, ambition, and fame; of contributing to restaurant segregation in terms of wealth and class status; or they may serve none of these functions. Functionalism provides no insight into how any suggestion can be considered more accurate than any other. Yet to the extent a scholarly undertaking strives for explanation, criteria have to be available.

c. Functionalism and Comparison

161. *Incompatible with comparison.* Functionalism has generally proven to be incompatible with comparison. In anthropology, for example, the triumph of the functionalism of Malinowski and Margaret Mead led to the decline of the comparative method.[151] Malinowski believed that general laws of social and cultural practice could be elaborated from the functional observation of a single tribe.[152] In the end, functionalists rely, as Boas put it, quoting Bastian, "on the appalling monotony of the fundamental ideas of mankind all over the globe."[153]

Once anthropologists became convinced that the correct functional analysis of any individual society uncovers general principles of social organization, the comparative method proved unnecessary. In fact, the elimination of difference transformed anthropology into a matter of public interest. General laws of social development were obviously more interesting than the curious customs and beliefs of strange peoples. "The fact that many fundamental features of culture are universal, or at least occur in many isolated places, interpreted by the assumption that the same features must always have developed from the same causes, leads to the conclusion that there is one grand system according to which mankind has developed everywhere; that all the occurring variations are no more

---

150. Davis (1959).
151. Ackerknecht 117.
152. Id. 122–123.
153. Boas (1896) 901.

than minor details in this grand uniform evolution."[154] In the context of comparative law, Zweigert and Kötz, following the same path, supplemented their functionalist method with the presumption that the practical effect of the norms is everywhere the same. Yet if culture, including legal culture, is everywhere the same, it is difficult to understand why anyone would engage in comparative studies.

2. Imagined Worlds

162. *Purpose and purposivism.* "Many a gallant knight has gone forth to do battle with the functional dragon," Martin Orans has written, "only to see him slip away and continue his mischief."[155] The problem has always been that it is remarkably difficult to find something coherent to put in its place.

a. Purpose in Law

163. *Fundamental fact.* The place to begin, perhaps, is to delineate those aspects of purposivist methodology that can be retained. Whatever the problems with the purposivism often involved in the contemporary study of comparative law, it remains our purposivism. It has been a regular feature of the past century of comparative law scholarship. The central concept of purposivism—the attribution of purpose to the norms—accurately reflects a main preoccupation of every legal system. There is no reason to abandon it merely because it has been abused. The attribution of purpose to the norms remains a fundamental fact of the law, and there is much to be learned from focusing our attention on it—not as a solution, but rather as an element of the law that deserves study.

The principal problem with purposivism is that it accepts that the meaning and function of the norms are those proposed by the jurists who create and interpret them. For this reason, the point of view of the jurist has only rarely become the object of comparative study. Yet the purposes legal actors seek to advance are largely imaginary. Jurists construct for themselves a world—sometimes the world as they would like it to be and sometimes as they fear that it is—they imagine the impact they would like to have on that world, and then they create, apply, and interpret the norms so they might have the intended effect.

When examined in this way, it becomes clear that the work of the law is to draw from the imagination.[156] Legislators imagine the society they are called on to regulate based on the information gathered through legislative hearings and expert reports. They *read* these facts from the particular perspective they bring to

---

154. Id. 904.

155. Orans 312.

156. "[T]he 'law' side of things is not a bounded set of norms, rules, principles, values, or whatever from which jural responses to distilled events can be drawn, but part of a distinctive manner of imagining the real." Geertz (1983c) 173.

their position. Their observation, most observation, is prestructured by theory.[157] So the world for which they design their regulations is a fictional construct. One lawmaker might believe that our world is threatened by illegal drugs, radical activists, same-sex couples, undocumented workers, and terrorists, whereas another will see a world threatened by global warming, multinational corporations, world hunger, and the AIDS epidemic. One will see a world that rewards hard work, whereas another will see a world in which ruling elites monopolize power and reduce everyone else to a position of subservience. Every legislative enactment implies a view of the world. Legislation is therefore an act of the imagination.

Judges are engaged in a similar process. Before deciding their cases, many judges try to determine, often by simple intuition and personal experience, how the decision in the case will affect society, the consequences it will have for those who are not at the moment before the court. They might hope to encourage safety and reduce accidents, or they might instead feel it more important to give social actors the widest reasonable range of conduct. In either case, their decisions are based on their vision of the world and on the role they imagine that their decisions will play in it.

In their opening and closing arguments, common law trial lawyers contend that their clients have acted appropriately while their opponents have erred. Every law review article implies a vision of what the world is like and how the law should be organized to function within it. In the American law school classroom, we present these worlds to our students. Many of those involved in creating these worlds engage in no empirical observation or other fact-finding. Most of the time, these constructions are based on elements gleaned from legal training and extra-legal belief.

b. The Proper Role of Purpose

164. *The influence of cultural factors.* The vision legal actors have of the world is accessible through the statements they make about the purpose of the norms. When unpacked, the purposes carry with them a vision both of the world and of the role of the law. In other words, purpose is the key to understanding the law, provided it is held up to the light and examined as the object of study.

Purpose serves another salutary function as well, which is to bring into focus the role of cultural factors in the law. The law as an official enterprise does its best to conceal the role of background assumptions. It attempts to justify the norms in terms of objective social necessity. Legal realism drew attention to the fact that judges do not simply apply legal norms but instead evaluate all of the facts and circumstances. But even realism is restrictive, for it suggests that facts and circumstances can be objectively evaluated. The law, however, is enmeshed in the web of cultural understanding of which it is a part. The notion

---

157. "[N]ormal science ... [is] a strenuous and devoted attempt to force nature into the conceptual boxes supplied by professional education." Kuhn 5.

of purpose—actually the law's competing purposes—provides access to the role of culture in legal decision making.

165. *Vanishing the law.* There is one final disadvantage in the way purposivism deals with the purposes it discovers in the norms. It manages the remarkable and entertaining feat of making the law disappear. (Some might argue that is not a disadvantage.) What I mean is that purposivists do away with the law as the object of study. Purposivism sees the law as a tool to achieve the law's purposes, as the instrument social volition employs to achieve change. Once the law is conceived as a simple instrument, it disappears into the wings. It is hard to imagine a bridge engineer who would take the bridge for granted and focus instead on the development it has facilitated across the river. Yet that is what comparativists have often done. The fundamental flaw of purposivism is that it is not interested in the law. From the purposivist perspective, the norms themselves are expendable. The law is transparent, obvious, unimportant. Only the law's purposes and effects are worth studying.

3. From Explanation to Interpretation

166. *Internal relation.* There is no doubt that the goals and purposes as legal actors envision them must play a role in comparative law. The law is what Max Weber has described as *meaningful action*, human behavior inspired by a subjective sense of meaning.[158] It would be impossible to make sense of most social relations without taking into account the ideas that inspire them.[159] What we compare, therefore, when we compare legal systems, includes not only statutes and case holdings but also the reasoning that explains those results, the explanations provided by legal actors about what the norms are designed to accomplish. "[T]he social relations between men and the ideas which men's actions embody are really the same thing considered from different points of view."[160] In other words, there is an internal relation between the law and its justifications.

The problem with purposivism is not that it considers purposes, but rather that it assumes that a norm's social function coincides with the purposes legal actors ascribe to it. We can avoid this problem by understanding both the norms and their purposes as elements of a wider cultural framework. There is nothing new to this. Common-law scholars have long understood the law in this way.

What is needed, however, is a justification for this broad approach, a reason to consider the law not only as a normative force but also as a cultural manifestation, both as an intervention in social life and as an expression of the culture in

---

158. 1 Weber 4. For Winch's interpretation of this Weberian concept, see Winch 42–48.

159. Winch 22.

160. Id. 113.

which it is embedded. The elements of such a theory have long been in place. Little more is needed here than to enumerate them.

a. The Nature of Law in Comparative Law

167. *Where to find the law.* To begin with, to the extent we focus on purpose, we place adjudication at the center of legal theory. The task of determining the purpose of the norms is, in large part, entrusted to the courts. As indicated above, courts in many jurisdictions apply norms not merely by interpreting the text of the law but also, and principally, by making a judgment about how society should be structured.[161] Comparativists have generally agreed that the norms to be compared are not those found in the statute books but are rather the norms that result from the case holdings. Thus, when a comparativist speaks of the law, what is often meant is the law as applied. Such an understanding of the decisions requires an investigation of the social context of the norms and the goals the judges believe they are pursuing. For these purposes, the internal resources of the law—the statutes, the case precedents, and the like—are insufficient to constitute a field of study.

168. *No logical deduction.* In this perspective, then, the case holdings do not represent logical deductions from preexisting principles. In other words, from one typical comparative point of view, the norms do not preexist the dispute. Instead, these comparativists study how judges use their understanding of the law and the facts to formulate holdings that are appropriate to the cases. Judges often consider the appropriate role of the courts, the proper respect for precedent and tradition, the extent to which the law should coincide with social custom, the equities of the case in light of the applicable criteria of value, the evolving needs of society, and the kind of society that the judge would prefer. As a result, judicial decisions cannot be said to be true or false. A judicial decision, in H. L. A. Hart's insightful phrase, is *ascriptive* rather than *descriptive*: it ascribes to the parties responsibility for the actions they have taken.[162]

b. Reading the Law

169. *A coherent pattern.* One challenge for comparative law is to make sense of the countless acts of individual judges as they decide disputes, create legal norms, and, by doing so, intervene in social reality. The goal is to find a coherent pattern in the mass of decisions. Paul Ricoeur has suggested that intentional social activity, whether the writing of fiction or the creation of legal norms, can be understood

---

161. As regards the common law, this is a relatively uncontroversial proposition. I believe that it also applies to adjudication in the civil law. Many civilians would contest this. Though there is no room here for a theoretical proof, much of this book is devoted to demonstrating that civilian court decisions, at least in the field of gift law, cannot be explained solely by reference to the codes.

162. Hart 171, 182.

by recourse to the techniques of interpretation that are usually applied to the understanding of texts.[163] The paradigm of reading treats society like a text, which means as a holistic process. Moreover, the text is plurivocal. When taken as a whole, it permits different readings and constructions. Though authorial intent, both the intent of the novelist and the intent of the judge, may be taken into account, it does not determine the meaning of the text.[164] Intent is simply an additional datum that may be used in the interpretation process.

In this perspective, the goal of comparative law would be to interpret the meaning of the text that is constituted by the multitude of judicial decisions. To grasp this pattern, we are justified in taking into account all of the law's elements. The text in question is not any actual legal text. It consists rather of all the elements of the life of the law. This includes judicial opinions and statutes, scholarly articles and perspectives, efforts at law reform, the practitioner's point of view, and the customs and practices of those whose behavior the law seeks to regulate. These elements, when taken together, can be read as a collective—though often internally inconsistent—expression of a particular vision of the role of the law in society. In sum, comparative law considers the law—including the myriad statements made by legislators, judges, and scholars about the purposes and meaning of the norms—as a collective fabric of justification.

170. *Focus on the law.* The benefit of the interpretive method, when compared to purposivism, is that it refocuses attention on the law. For this study of the law of gifts, for example, it recommends that we think of gift law in the context of the world that jurists imagine for its operation, the purposes gift norms are designed to achieve, and the effects these norms are imagined to have. There is no need to consider beforehand the extent to which that world is real or whether the norms have any particular effect or function.

c. Law as an Element of Culture

171. *Meaning embodied in symbols.* The final step in elaborating an interpretive method for comparative law is to grasp a particular legal system as an expressive element of a larger cultural context. Clifford Geertz has similarly suggested that the rituals and activities of clan-based societies may best be understood as elements of a cultural whole, each one symbolizing a web of signification. Culture thus understood is "an historically transmitted pattern of meanings embodied in symbols."[165]

---

163. Ricoeur.

164. Id. 549.

165. Geertz (1973d) 89. "The culture of a people is an ensemble of texts, themselves ensembles, which the anthropologist strains to read over the shoulders of those to whom they properly belong." Geertz (1973b) 452.

172. *Benefits and pitfalls.* Geertz's work provides a useful example of both the benefits and the pitfalls of the interpretive method. Geertz's goal was to explore meaning rather than provide explanation.[166] Of course, other anthropologists, including some functionalists, have occasionally looked at culture in this way,[167] but Geertz relied on it to the exclusion of all else. If comparative law were to follow this tradition, it would seek to decipher and explicate the symbolic web in which legal norms are embedded.[168]

To develop this idea further, it is useful to examine the methodological contribution of Geertz's celebrated essay on the Balinese cockfight, together with the scholarly criticism his essay has generated. It turns out that comparative law is uniquely able to avoid the difficulties Geertz's critics have found in his work.

i. The Interpretive Method

173. *Thick description.* Geertz described his ethnographic method as *thick description*. For purposes of a comparative study of the law of gifts, the idea is easily summarized. The method abandons the project of attempting to determine the function gift law plays in society. Gift norms are therefore not to be explained in causal terms as necessary responses to imperative social needs. The question shifts instead to the symbolic significance of the norms. Their symbolic meaning can be elicited only when the norms are described in their full contextual richness. The goal is to understand what a particular legal system's gift norms indicate about that culture's vision of the role of the law in the giving of gifts. In other words, the question is not what the norms do but rather what they mean.

174. *Neither emic nor etic.* Geertz applied this interpretive method in his essay on the deeper meaning of the Balinese cockfight.[169] Geertz did not try to understand the cockfight from the point of view of a Balinese villager. Geertz's perspective was neither emic nor etic. He formulated concepts unavailable to the Balinese themselves that allowed him to explore what the cockfight symbolizes to the Balinese and how it relates to other manifestations of Balinese culture.

---

166. Geertz (1973e) 5.

167. This Yin-Yang philosophy of ancient China is the systematic elaboration of the principle that can be used to define the social structure of moieties in Australian tribes, for the structure of moieties is ... one of a unity of opposing groups, in the double sense that the two groups are friendly opponents, and that they are represented as being in some sense opposites, in the way in which eagle hawk and crow or black and white are opposites.
Radcliffe-Brown (1951) 21.

168. Schneider 810.

169. Geertz (1973b).

175. *Symbol creation.* For Geertz, the cockfight was a symbol of the *deep play* he believed is at work in Balinese society.[170] The cockfight is essentially an opportunity for gambling, but the stakes are so irrationally high that the principal participants constantly run the risk of financial ruin. To explain the rapture with which Balinese men participate in this activity despite these risks, Geertz suggested that the cocks represent both their owners and their owners' clans and thereby provide a mechanism by which social tensions are displayed. In other words, the Balinese fascination with cockfighting is due to the way it displays fundamental passions in Balinese society that are normally hidden from view and thereby both symbolizes and comments on status difference and hierarchy.[171] The cockfight is "a Balinese reading of Balinese experience, a story they tell themselves about themselves."[172] They tell themselves that they exist as Balinese on two levels, on the level of external calm and collective solidarity and on a deeper level that involves a desperate striving after status. The constant repetition of the event provides the Balinese with a means to experience personally and ever anew this significant aspect of their culture.

ii. The Challenge

176. *Not objective.* Geertz's method has often been challenged.[173] One frequent criticism is that Geertz relied so heavily on his imagination that there is nothing objective about his construction.[174] Geertz manages to make sense of puzzling phenomena by weaving them into a broader fabric, but, because it is not a fabric woven by the natives themselves, there is no way to judge whether the interpretation is valid.[175] When the Balinese engage in the cockfight, for example, they do not do so with the purpose of communicating, whether consciously or otherwise. It is Geertz who conceived of the event as a text. He configured the cockfight, a nonlinguistic cultural event, as textual, as communication open to interpretation, and then hypothesized that the text encodes information that reveals the deepest nature of Balinese sensibility.[176] But there is no way to know whether the cockfight expresses a symbolic principle of Balinese life or rather whether it masks an inconvenient social reality.[177] In other words, Geertz's use of the textual approach is purely speculative. In the words of Mark Schneider,

---

170. For an interpretation of Geertz's text, see Schneider 814–820.

171. Geertz (1973b) 443–444; Roseberry 1018.

172. Geertz (1973b) 448.

173. For brief surveys of the critique and citations to the principal critical literature, see Sewell 35–37; Swidler 301; Schneider 836 note 4.

174. Schneider 811.

175. Shankman 263.

176. Schneider 825.

177. Shankman 268.

one of Geertz's most insightful critics, Balinese culture became a text for Geertz without ever having been one for the Balinese.[178]

William Roseberry, another critic of Geertz's work, takes seriously the metaphor of the text. He notes that Geertz's interpretive method sees culture as an art form but neglects the process of its creation.[179] The fact that culture is created means that some members of society have more influence than others over the statement it makes. To understand a text means first to ask who is doing the writing. Symbols, like literary texts, can transcend context and authorial intent, yet, as Borges taught, it meant one thing to write *Quijote* at the height of the *Siglo de Oro* and something very different for Pierre Menard to produce it in the 1930s.

177. *Challenge.* Geertz's work thus presents more of a challenge than a solution. Geertz relied so heavily on the assumption that the phenomena under investigation represent an organic whole that he could not avoid attributing to all such phenomena "an integrity and profundity normally reserved for art, for those intentionally symbolic phenomena that are commonly seen as 'wholes' or 'totalities.'"[180] The real meaning of Geertz's work, as Schneider has perceptively explained, is to challenge us to recognize those cultural efforts that seek to impose meaning on human existence while preserving our understanding that culture is an inconsistent pattern of diverse, and at times mundane, phenomena that often cannot reasonably be construed to produce insight.

d. Comparative Notes

178. *Inscribed meaning.* The goal of the textual approach, as Robert Darnton has explained, is to grasp "the meaning inscribed by contemporaries in whatever survives of their vision of the world."[181] As far as this comparative study is concerned, the immediate goal is to read the gift law of each legal system as a meaningful whole. Gift norms are examined in the context of the purposes a system's jurists imagine for them, the world as those jurists understand it, and the effects the norms are believed to produce. Of course, the gift law of any society forms an integral part of the private law, of the entire legal system, and, beyond that, of the rest of each society's culture. Unfortunately, it is not possible to pursue all these connections in the limited space accorded to a study such as this one.

179. *Speculation risk.* Due to the law's methodological lag, the criticism of Geertz's work, namely the speculative nature of his interpretations, has not yet found its way into the law. As a result, legal scholars commonly explain aspects of a legal system as expressive of a particular vision, even when the legal sources

---

178. Schneider 812.
179. Roseberry 1022.
180. Schneider 826.
181. Darnton 5.

themselves make no mention of those ideas. Due to its unsystematic nature, the common law is particularly susceptible to this type of interpretation. For example, Richard Posner argues that the common law of gifts follows notions of efficiency, even though the common-law courts almost never mention efficiency or related concepts.[182] Beginning from a different vision, James Gordley believes that the Aristotelian principle of equality best explains modern American gift law.[183]

180. *Close contact with the sources.* One way to avoid speculation is for the investigation to remain in close contact with contemporary sources. To the extent the study references the pronouncements made by the participants themselves, the meaning that emerges is less likely to be speculative.

The object of cultural study is not to be found in an informant's unspoken subjectivity but is rather what is publicly available as symbols[184]—the inscription in writing, the fixation of meaning.[185] In this regard, modern law provides a more hospitable field for the application of the interpretive method than do the clan-based cultures studied by anthropologists. In comparative law, the raw material is easily available. In modern legal systems, the purposes the norms are thought to achieve are publicly announced. When the legislature fails to state its goals, the courts attribute purposes and elaborate the social policies that serve as the foundation for their decisions. Legal scholars put the norms into context, fit them into a system, and describe how the system is supposed to operate. In this interpretive effort, legal scholarship appears as one the law's voices and not merely as a secondhand report about something that is happening elsewhere. Therefore, there is no reason to keep it at a distance, as is suggested by the traditional comparative methods.[186] The law's resources also include pleadings, motions, depositions, and letters of counsel. Jury deliberations and legal advice are shielded by confidentiality, but they nonetheless often find their way into print. Practitioners are constantly making reform suggestions. Geertz himself noted that the comparative study of law should focus on the various mechanisms

---

182. "I do not argue that economic analysis can explain every rule and outcome, but only that it gives structure to, and suggests a fundamental economic motivation for, the general legal approach in this area." Posner (1977) 424.

183. Gordley (1995) 548. "A thesis of this Article is that the 16th century jurists [of the Spanish natural law school] had the best explanation of the way American law enforces [donative] promises." Id. 570.

184. Swidler 299.

185. Geertz (1983a) 31.

186. "The comparativist may not rely without scrutiny on the opinions of the domestic scholars. Domestic scholarship sometimes fails to recognize essential elements. At times the authors remain imprisoned in their own theories and tend to defend them at any price." Mäntysaari 10. See also 2 Constantinesco no. 60.

available for the creative interpretation of the law.[187] This study of gift law treats the different voices in each system as a single text.[188] Though gift law is frequently incoherent and internally contradictory, there is implicit agreement on the basics of the discussion, which is what I take to be the meaning of the law.

181. *Attention to detail.* Due to the critical importance of the sources, comparative studies require ceaseless attention to detail. A comparative study that paints with a broad brush provides the reader with no means to gauge the accuracy of the account. The efforts made in this study to adhere closely to all variety of texts yields what, in most contexts, would rightly be considered an excessive number of references at the bottom of the page. The goal is simply to ensure that interpretation remains faithful to the meaning of the law of gifts in contemporary society.

182. *Traditional in the law.* It is worth emphasizing that the law has long been familiar with the interpretive method. In *The Death of Contract*, for example, Gilmore examined the consideration doctrine as a symbol of the Holmesian conception of contract. Gilmore examined the world as Holmes imagined it, the purposes Holmes imagined for his rules, and the vision that emerges from the doctrine when read as a text. Gilmore attempted, as Geertz did, to demonstrate how we are suspended in webs of significance that we ourselves have spun.[189] Gilmore showed that a particular vision of law generates an ethos that both makes that particular worldview seem true and that, at the same time, makes the ethos seem realistic, given that we believe we live in a world of that kind.[190]

183. *The goal here.* This study is not concerned with whether gift norms achieve their stated purposes. The goal is rather to grasp the symbolic significance of the gift for the legal imagination. A number of difficulties arise when attempting to operationalize this project. The first concerns the choice of standpoint. In Geertz's view, laws should be compared by examining one system through the lens of another.[191] This method is not helpful for gift law, since none of the

---

187. "[T]his imaginative, or constructive, or interpretive power ... upon which the comparative study of law ... should, in my view, train its attention ... is there—in the method and manner of conceiving decision situations so that settled rules can be applied to decide them (as well, of course, of conceiving the rules), in what I have been calling legal sensibility." Geertz (1983c) 215.

188. In a similar manner, Lynn Hunt, in his study of the French Revolution, treated the utterances of the various revolutionary politicians as constituting a single text. Hunt (1984) 25. As Hunt later explained, the method can be justified only if it succeeds. Hunt (1989) 17.

189. Geertz (1973e) 5.

190. Swidler 299.

191. "[A] comparative approach to law becomes an attempt ... to formulate the presuppositions, the preoccupations, and the frames of action characteristic of one sort of legal sensibility in terms of those characteristic of another." Geertz (1983c) 218.

approaches can be termed neutral. The minimalist German system may appeal to some more than the baroque system elaborated in the French Civil Code, but to choose one over the other would mean disregarding some legitimate concerns from the outset. The arcane and amorphous constructions employed in the common law are particularly ill-suited as a baseline. Nonetheless, the gravitational pull of the common law has been so strong that I have constantly fought against the temptation to present all systems from its point of view, and my efforts have not always been successful. Another difficulty is the bias the law itself brings to the regulation of gift giving. I have tried to resolve these difficulties by constantly shifting the standpoint. At times the focus is on the discussion about a given topic in a particular system and its relationship to the system's premises. At other times it seemed helpful to isolate each system's distinctive voice. In some cases I step outside the law and examine the legal approach from the perspective of social practice.

These difficulties converge when the time comes to choose a conceptual framework for the presentation. I have tried to maintain analytic distance by using concepts that do not coincide with those of any one legal system. Yet there seems to be no way to divide up the subject matter without prejudicing the analysis. Each system tells a story about gift giving, and each story has the feel of an organic whole. There are common elements to the stories, but when they are teased apart and compared, the rhythm of each individual tale is lost. Lévi-Strauss teaches that there is only one solution to this problem. In *Tristes tropiques* and his *Mythologies* cycle, he pieced aspects of different cultures together and created from them a larger narrative, an enduring mythos. On a much more modest scale, that has also been the goal here.

184. *Substance and method.* Here again substance coincides with method. The functionalist and the interpretive methods are each adopted to different understandings of social life, and therefore different aspects of the law. The functionalist method claims to offer a rigorous method for explaining social phenomena. An explanation is considered valid if it uncovers human rationality as the principal motor behind the maze of cultural phenomena. Rational purpose is often understood in terms of utility maximization.[192] Comparative law purposivism follows the functionalists along this path.

On the other hand, theories of gift giving from Mauss forward have argued that the most meaningful aspects of social interaction do not maximize individual utility in an economic sense. Those who accept theories such as Mauss's have little alternative but to adopt a method that focuses on meaning rather than utility.

---

192. "The individual who makes up functionalist society might have stepped from any economics text. He is a rational creature and (under whatever social system) ceaselessly pursues his own self-interest, scrupulously avoiding pain and seeking pleasure." Gregg and Williams 596.

Balinese gambling, the distribution of piles of blankets at a Kwakwaka'wakw potlatch, Mother Teresa's work in Calcutta, Dan Ellsberg's decision to publish the *Pentagon Papers*, the decision to write fiction that will never make money and probably will not even be published, all of this is irrational when judged from the standpoint of utility maximization, and yet these remain examples of the most meaningful gestures found in human culture.

185. *This study.* This study examines how major Western legal systems imagine goals for themselves, how they develop and apply their concepts, and how they use their thoughts about gift giving as a means to discover their own premises and convictions. The giving of gifts provides a challenge to the law. Based on that challenge different legal systems imagine different worlds of meaning. The purpose of this study is to explore these different worlds.

4. A Maussian Inquiry by Other Means

186. *Law and custom.* "All law generally arises from the lap of custom, and the relationship between law and custom is most clearly revealed in the gift."[193] That is how Jacob Grimm began his celebrated exploration of the terminology of giving and gifting. Yet when studied comparatively, the law of gifts suggests exactly the opposite. Instead of following the customary structure of gift exchange, gift law subjects it to critique.

The goal of gift law varies from system to system. At one extreme, certain civilian systems—such as those those in France and Italy where the church has been especially powerful—have largely sought to displace customary norms, particularly those related to how the gift is made. In their original conception, these gift laws validated few gifts given by customary means. They required instead that virtually all gifts be made by notarial act. At the other extreme, German law conceives of the gift as a contract. With the exception of the gift promise, it generally imposes only those formalities otherwise required by contract law. The common law has created a sui generis system based in principle on delivery, more out of a desire to avoid proof problems than from hostility to the gift.[194] All of these systems invalidate at least some gifts that custom would consider valid. No system has adopted a legal framework that favors gift giving; none has formulated concepts useful to facilitating the gift as it arises in social practice.

187. *Gift overwhelms law.* This study focuses on the conceptual structure of gift law. Concepts from market-based transactions have often been pressed into service to regulate gift giving. These concepts are used because the private law has

193. Grimm 173.

194. "In the history of the common law it would be hard to find any evidence of suspicion or hostility directed toward gifts, either gifts in general or those of some particular form or type." Dawson (1980) 223.

no others. Yet the law often finds itself bending these concepts, sometimes to the point of creating total conceptual confusion, as it tries to integrate the giving of gifts into the structure of the private law. Legal concepts with a relatively clear meaning in other areas become distorted beyond recognition when applied to the law of gifts. Indeed, some systems are unable to offer a workable definition for many of their basic gift law concepts. Gift laws are occasionally incoherent, even when examined within the framework of their own conceptual structures. These distortions arise because, in the field of gift giving, social practice refuses to conform to the categories the law seeks to impose.[195] When gift giving and the law confront each other, it is not gift giving that submits, but rather the law.

A useful example of the difficulties is the tip, the virtually universal custom of offering gratuities to service employees. As Zelizer has pointed out, the tip straddles a number of the law's definitional boundaries.[196] It is not quite a payment for services (since payment is made to the employer), not quite a bribe (though the $20 to the *maître d'* may lead to faster seating), not quite charity (though the waitstaff includes starving artists), and yet not quite a gift (employees receive it with a sense of entitlement). Tipping is generally excluded from the definition of the gift and the intrusive regime of gift law, yet it is difficult to explain why.

188. *Lessons from the difficulties.* These doctrinal difficulties provide insight into the interaction between state authority and social practice in the creation of legal norms. The norms that govern gift giving result from an encounter between promulgated rules and deeply felt views about gift giving. Social custom is able to subvert the norms by convincing courts to apply the norms in a way that respects social practice.

189. *Tribute to Mauss.* The difficulty that many legal systems experience when confronting the practice of gift exchange seems to validate Mauss's hypothesis. Mauss argued that gift exchange is one of the bedrock structures of human societies. It is therefore consistent with his theory that gift giving would survive undaunted by the law's attempts to restrict it. In fact, gift giving continues to thrive. This comparative study is therefore intended as a tribute to, and a continuation by other means of, the work done by Malinowski, Mauss, and contemporary gift theorists. This study seeks to demonstrate that, despite its efforts over the past two millennia, the law has been unable to tame the social practice of giving, receiving, and reciprocating.

Yet this study remains a study of the law. It does not explain the law by reference to extra-legal causes. The point is rather to determine the effect that the

---

195. "The gift is an event that brings disorder into clear and defined relationships, such as those modeled on the bond of obligation. As a result, the gift is something of an intruder, the Other, like the stranger who causes disagreement, who perturbs relations based on balance and equality, 'the ungrateful guest.'" Mazzoni 701.

196. Zelizer 95.

confrontation with gift giving has had on modern Western legal systems. By following the evolution of gift norms, we track the fears that gift giving provokes in the different legal systems, how those fears create norms, and how gift giving has managed to circumvent the prohibitions.

190. *Community and self-interest.* Enlightenment philosophy separated self-interest and community into different spheres of social action. In civil society, individuals follow self-interest and seek what is personally best for themselves and their families, whereas as members of political society they act in the best interests of the community. Western law has tended to follow this same division. The private law is constructed to optimize the pursuit of self-interest, whereas public law facilitates political action devoted to achieving social goals.

Gift giving does not fit within that structure. It represents instead an island of social custom in the sea of the self-interested private law. Yet there is nothing necessary about its isolation. If the concepts of the private law were altered to accommodate the giving of gifts, the law might be more able to encourage altruism. The pursuit of self-interest that dominates contemporary society can move society forward, but, when insufficiently restrained, it can destroy community and lead to a culture of selfishness. If the gift were accepted as contract's equal, it might help alleviate the imbalance. Mauss devoted attention to the gift specifically to stir altruism back into the mix of civil society, to find a way to integrate self-interest with selfless action.[197]

5. Constituting the Field of Study

191. *Three questions.* A comparative study pursued by the interpretive method must make choices without recourse to function as a *tertium comparationis.* Three questions arise. They involve the identity of the relevant norms in each legal system, the choice of legal systems to be compared, and the topics on which to focus.

a. The Relevant Norms

192. *No functional definition.* The first question is how to recognize the norms in each jurisdiction that are relevant to gift giving. This study follows the obvious path. Gifts are given everywhere. The norms discussed here are those that attempt to regulate the giving of gifts. This is not a functionalist choice. No attempt has been made to locate parallel situations in the different legal systems. Instead, the criterion has been simple, arguably even superficial, and almost exclusively linguistic. In each legal system studied here, there is a discrete body

---

197. "There must be more good faith, more sensitivity, more generosity in contracts dealing with the hiring of services, the letting of houses, the sale of vital foodstuffs. And it will indeed be necessary to find a way to limit the rewards of speculation and interest." Mauss (1990) 69.

of law that is labeled with a cognate of the English term *gift*. In civilian systems, for example, this law was to some extent derived from the Roman law concept of *donatio*, though in each of these jurisdictions the local legal tradition has reworked the principles found in the Digest. The norms of gift law examined here are those that each system has gathered into its law of gifts. This approach follows that of Mauss, who did not select for his study those social activities that fulfilled a common function but rather gathered the very different institutions that involve a particular type of gratuitous transfer.

193. *Analogy.* This focus is analogous to the choice that might be made in a study of comparative literature. Take, for example, a study of novels that relate to the Second World War. The study would take the novel as it finds it in each domestic literature and select those longer works of fiction, however different they may be, that match the criteria of time and place. In American literature, the choice might involve *Tales from the South Pacific, A Bell for Adano, From Here to Eternity, The Naked and the Dead, The Caine Mutiny, Catch-22,* and *Gravity's Rainbow.* These books occupy such different places in American literature that it is surprising to find them all in the same sentence. Moreover, none of them is really the equivalent of *The Flanders Road* or *The Bridge over the River Kwai* in French letters, *And Where Were You, Adam?* or *Tin Drum* in German culture, or *Caught, Look Down in Mercy,* and *From the City, From the Plough* in English literature. Nonetheless, we would want to include them all in the study.

As with the choice of novels, so with this study's choice of norms. There is no concern about functional equivalents. To begin with, many transactions colloquially called *gifts* are not included in the legal notion of gift in many of these systems. As noted above, civilian jurisdictions tend to exclude from the definition most customary gifts, gifts to employees or customers, and a number of other transfers that everyone refers to as gifts. The civil law excludes these common transactions in order to free them from the restrictive regime of gift law, including the rules of capacity, the form requirements, and the collation and revocation that apply to gifts that satisfy the legal definition. The common law of gifts has a different peculiarity: it governs chiefly transfers of personal property. The conveyancing of real property is by deed, for which no consideration is required. In other words, this study takes the different domestic institutions of gift law as it finds them, with whatever limitations each system has imposed on itself. The focus is on the institution that each legal system calls its gift law, whatever it has chosen to include within its scope.

194. *Doctrinal categories.* This study also explores doctrinal categories as it finds them. The principal goal is to examine what happens in the law as the law encounters the social practice of gift giving. In other words, this study is not concerned with how the law has affected the giving of gifts. It focuses instead on how gift giving has affected the law. In the course of this encounter, new legal concepts are formed and others are borrowed from neighboring fields. These

concepts are different, or used differently, in each legal system. It thus seems unwise to attempt to explain all the cases in terms of a single set of concepts. That was the method that Dawson was hoping to apply. For example, he was convinced that most anomalous civilian decisions in the field of gift law could be understood in terms of justifiable reliance.[198] But the goal of this study is not to decide how the cases should come out or what characterization would produce the most socially acceptable results. It is instead to watch the law as it reacts to the challenges gift giving presents. The focus, in other words, is not on gift giving, a topic explored by social scientists, but rather on the law.

195. *Indeterminacy.* This study is concerned with the vast tapestry of norms that make up the law of gifts in the common and civil laws. Yet, as a practical matter, these norms do not exist. The rules of gift law do not offer statements of principle sufficiently authoritative to dictate the case results. In the legal systems involved here, gift law norms can be, have been, and will continue to be molded to the shape of the controversy before the court. The courts' appreciation of the facts and the circumstances of the cases shape their decisions. The rules are called into service to provide legal justification. This seems to be true both in the civil and in the common laws. This is what is meant by the widely recognized flexibility that the courts exercise in this area of the law, what has been described as "the indeterminacy of the rules regarding gifts."[199]

---

198. "There was one old French word, *estoppel*, that the court might have mentioned, but this has dropped out of the modern French vocabulary and in French sources, so far as I know, there is no other word that can be used to describe harmful and foreseeable reliance. So in the emperor's case, 'onerosity' had to carry the load." Dawson (1980) 90 (emphasis in original).

199. Kreitner 1935. "Over the course of the century, attempts to evaluate doctrine through a close reading of case law have revealed that the rules emerge riddled with exceptions that threaten to swallow the rules themselves. Moreover, even when the rules themselves are left unchallenged, they leave judges wide latitude to decide cases according to an ad hoc sense of justice and propriety." Id. 1945.

> In numerous cases, therefore, the validity of an attempted disposition is dependent on its being classified as inter vivos rather than testamentary. The doctrinal test supposed to determine this choice is extremely flexible and can be manipulated almost at will by the courts. It is stated in terms of the time at which an "interest" is intended to pass to the transferee .... But the postulated "interest" is entirely abstract in character. It has no necessary relationship to the physical possession or economic enjoyment of the property, since a right to future possession and enjoyment may be, and frequently is, held to be a present interest .... [T]he test is not per se determinative in the more marginal cases. It has achieved respectability as the verbal clothing of the result; but the compelling precedent will be the actual decision on similar facts, not judicial reiteration of this vague and abstract criterion.

Gulliver and Tilson 18.

An additional problem is that the parties often do not structure their transactions to comply with the law's requirements. As even a fleeting examination of the material contained in this book makes clear, no nonlawyer can really be expected to understand what those rules provide. At virtually every point in virtually every system discussed here, there are majority and minority views among the scholars. Often the courts follow neither. There is no predictability because the conceptual structure does not fit and the equities are often pointing away from the results the norms prescribe. Many cases are rooted in their particular facts and seem to be cases of first impression. Most individuals who give gifts are attempting to conform not to the law but rather to the dictates of social custom.[200] Because the law does not mirror that custom—in many legal systems the law operates as a radical critique of it—it is not by following their intuitions that, in this field, the parties would end up abiding by the law.[201]

In other words, the focus on doctrinal distinctions should not be misunderstood to suggest that the judges actually respect them. This study focuses on rules for a different reason, or for several different reasons. These rules, together with their scholarly elaboration and justification and the commentaries provided by the courts, provide access to the vision that each particular legal system has of gift giving. They express an attitude, a belief. It seems fair, for this purpose, to take the norms at face value. Those who promulgate and interpret these norms say something with them, and what they are saying is the subject of this book. The norms also provide a convenient mechanism by which to compare the visions contained in the different legal systems. Thus, the emphasis in this study on the norms that govern the giving of gifts is not meant to suggest that these norms necessarily determine, or even influence, the judicial decisions. In other words, the focus on the norms of gift law is not meant to suggest that these norms actually govern the giving of gifts at all.

b. The Convenient Legal Systems

196. *Families of legal systems.* Comparative law traditionally divides the legal systems of the world into families.[202] The underlying assumption is that legal systems share a great many characteristics with their relatives. Once the families are properly delineated, it is said to be most profitable to compare the most characteristic representatives of each of the families. Legal systems that are

---

200. "[I]f most people shaped their conduct really with reference to the law and to their legal rights, for any serious fraction of their time, rather than with reference to the patterns of action, the patterns of thought, the standards of judgment which they inhale as the social atmosphere they breathe, then life in our society would become unlivable." Llewellyn (2008) 17.

201. Kreitner 1945–1946; Leslie 619–620.

202. David and Brierley; Glenn.

derivative, in the sense that they have borrowed their private law from more advanced legal orders, need not be taken into account. Zweigert and Kötz note:

> Mature legal systems are often adopted or extensively imitated by others; as long as these other so-called "affiliated" legal systems maintain the style of the parent system, they usually do not possess to the same degree that blend of originality and balanced maturity in solving problems which characterizes the "significant" legal system. While they are at this stage of development, the comparatist may ignore the affiliate and concentrate on the parent system .... The legal systems of Spain and Portugal ... do not often call for or justify very intensive investigation.[203]

i. Family Difficulties

197. *No easy division*. Nonetheless, the law of gifts does not divide easily along family lines. In many questions, the major variations are within families and not between them. On some questions German law, a civilian system, is closer to the common law than it is to other civilian systems such as French law. On other questions French law is closer to the common law, and German or Italian law lie farther afield.[204]

It should come as no surprise that legal systems derived from the same historical source differ dramatically from each other both in norm content and in interpretive method. This is a common phenomenon in cultural history. Every institution is influenced both by diachronic considerations, such as historical origins, and by synchronic factors, such as interaction with other elements of the same cultural constellation. To take a purposely exotic example, though both Chinese and Vietnamese metaphysical conceptions are derived from the basic Yin-Yang paradigm, the two cultures construct the system in radically different ways. While the Chinese construction is analytic and metaphysical, Vietnamese thinking is synthetic and dialectic. As a result, the Chinese Eight Diagrams more closely resemble the workings of the four elements in pre-Socratic Greek metaphysics than they do the corresponding Five Principles of Vietnamese culture.[205]

This East Asian example may make it easier to understand why French and German gift law, though both are ultimately derived from Roman law, might differ from one another. The borrowings from Roman law occurred at different times and in the course of different historical processes. Even more important, the Roman borrowings were integrated into the different circumstances of French civilization and German culture. Until its recent postmodern turn,

---

203. Zweigert and Kötz 41.
204. For a review of the difficulties involved in classifying legal systems, see 3 Constantinesco nos. 248–261.
205. Trần Ngọc Thêm 194–195.

French thought has generally been based on an Enlightenment confidence in the power and benefit of human reason, whereas German culture has tended to emphasize the nonrational factors that determine human action. It is actually an interesting coincidence when laws based on these different visions coincide. If the notion of *families* of legal systems is ever to have a use value, a way will have to be found to take into account not only the historical origins but also the differing cultural contexts.

For these reasons, the praesumptio similitudinis does not really obtain. As far as gift law is concerned, the practical results, the case decisions, vary dramatically from one legal system to the next.[206] Moreover, each system has developed its own series of debates. Some legal systems explore certain issues in surprising depth, while others ignore those questions entirely. On many topics, the most productive suggestions and intriguing ideas come from what are considered derivative legal systems. For example, Spanish law, contrary to the suggestion of Zweigert and Kötz, has produced some of the most interesting reflections on the law related to gift giving.

ii. A Pragmatic Choice

198. *Easy access.* No comparative study can examine all of the world's legal systems. This study is limited to gift law in a handful of modern Western legal systems. It focuses pragmatically on those legal systems that use a language this investigator speaks and, for the civilian systems, those he has had occasion to be trained in and for which ample material is available in American law libraries. For the common law, this study examines principally England, India, and the United States.[207]

199. *Civil law.* Because gift law is largely a creation of the civil law, a broad sampling of civilian systems proves useful. The civilian systems discussed include Germany, Italy, and Spain, together with the French tradition, which here includes both France and Belgium. Some reference is made to the law of the Spanish regions, which have some legislative competence in gift law.

200. *Indian law.* The law of gifts in India, though partially derived from British enactments in the fields of contract and property, has other sources as well. Both the Hindu and the Muslim legal systems have traditional rules governing gifts. In 1772, British Governor-General Warren Hastings declared that the traditional

---

206. And this remains the case even if the praesumptio is understood in the extremely lax manner proposed by Michaels, namely that all responses to the same problem constitute functional equivalents. Michaels 369–372. Aside from all other difficulties, it remains impossible to understand to which problem the law of gifts is actually the solution.

207. Because Louisiana maintains its civilian heritage with regard to gift law, it is not considered here a common-law jurisdiction.

rules were to be respected.[208] A few years later, Hastings's declaration was enacted into law.[209] Legal historians suggest that Hastings was following the practice of the Moguls, who allowed non-Muslim subjects to follow their customary laws. However, unlike the Moguls, who let the communities administer their own laws, these religious laws were administered and interpreted by the British courts. In 1882, the governor-general's legislative council enacted the Transfer of Property Act, which governs property-law questions in India, Pakistan, and Bangladesh. Although much of Hindu law has been abrogated since the passing of the Transfer of Property Act, the Muslim law of gifts remains in force.[210] Thus, some questions of Indian gift law require reference to Islamic jurisprudence and therefore provide brief glimpses of a different legal perspective.

201. *"American law."* With regard to the law of the United States, an apology is in order. It is common among jurists in the United States to refer to our system as "American law." This will offend some of those who live in other countries in the Western Hemisphere and who, rightly, consider themselves to be Americans. They might also point out, again rightly, that there is no America-wide law of gifts. There is no way to resolve this difficulty here, because, in the context of a book published in the United States, "United States law" is uncolloquial and might be misunderstood to refer to United States federal law.

There is another problem with the term. Gift law is almost exclusively state law in the United States. Little of it is uniform throughout the country. In this study, *American law* refers to the generally accepted elements of the American common-law tradition, as discussed in frequently cited cases, Restatements, uniform laws, model acts and rules, and the leading treatises.

iii. Legal Sources

202. *Fewer cases.* The scope of the study determines the choice of sources. A comparative study narrowly focused on a particular issue and limited to two legal systems must work, as the German historians say, *quellennah,* from the original sources. That means that close attention must be paid to the case decisions. A wide-ranging study such as this one, however, attempts instead to capture general propositions. For this reason it relies largely on commentaries

---

208. Fyzee 49.

209. "[T]heir Inheritance and Succession to Lands, Rents, and Goods, and all Matters of Contract and Dealing between Party and Party, shall be determined, in the Case of *Mahomedans,* by the Laws and Usages of *Mahomedans,* and in the Case of *Gentûs,* by the Laws and Usages of *Gentûs;* and where only one of the Parties shall be a *Mahomedan* or *Gentû,* by the Laws and Usages of the Defendant." East India Company Act sec. 17 (emphasis in original). Hastings's regulations were replaced in 1793 by the Cornwallis Code, which similarly preserved native law and usage. Adam 25.

210. Indian Transfer of Property Act § 129; *Karam Ilahi v. Sharf-ud-din,* AIR 1916 All 351.

and treatises.[211] The approach is borrowed from Arthur von Mehren's study of the consideration doctrine.

> The common-law lawyer will not find in this article the detailed and exhaustive discussion, to which he is accustomed, of the facts and results of individual cases. Such analysis is not necessary nor particularly appropriate in a comparative study of doctrine. The problem is to understand the general frames of reference and techniques of analysis through which the several systems discussed approach various problems. The central concern is not to examine critically the handling of particular fact situations, drawing out all possible implications.[212]

203. *Precedent.* One aspect of case authority in the common law may confuse jurists trained in other systems. I am referring to the age of the precedent cited. This is a subtle question that I have never seen addressed in print, and I cannot be certain I have it exactly right. Civil lawyers rely on precedent too. In fact, they are more careful about their precedent than we are. The notes following the case reports in many civilian jurisdictions reveal exemplary focus to the facts of the case, the chosen legal construction, and the justice of the decision. Civilian treatises cite cases for every point, sometimes including string citations that most common-law scholars would avoid.

One difference concerning precedent may be the age of the cited authority. Civilians prefer recent case law. It is relatively rare for a civilian treatise to cite cases more than fifty years old as authority for current law. A case report from the nineteenth century is generally cited only if it established a fundamental principle, or by way of historical contrast to current law. Civilians may feel that the interaction of judicial decision, scholarly critique, and code reform produces real progress in the law. The older cases must seem to them like out-of-date physics textbooks.

In contrast, everyone in the common law knows that there is nothing scientific about what we do. Though very recent cases are powerful, very old cases are sometimes even more powerful. There is no prejudice in the common law against cases a century old, or two centuries. Even in a brief I would not hesitate to cite Lord Mansfield on any relevant point of law. Cases decided in the seventeenth century are particularly exquisite, and important. The older cases would have especially pleased Blackstone, because they demonstrate not only that the principle in issue has always been the law but also that it is likely to remain the law. In other words, the older cases provide some shelter from the storm that is the common law.

---

211. "The greater the number of comparative cases that are included, the smaller the possibility of working from the original sources and the greater the reliance on secondary literature." Haupt and Kocka 22.

212. Von Mehren 1010.

The cases cited here were chosen to satisfy both civilian and common-law instincts, no matter which legal system is under discussion. I have cited older cases when they state a rule with particular clarity. To satisfy the civilian jurist, I have also cited the most recent authority I could find. On many questions, however, common-law principles seem to be so well established that no recent authority has been located. I have often asked my research assistants to update the cites, and they usually come back empty-handed.

With minor alterations, I have cited to case reports in the form traditional in the jurisdiction concerned. I recognize that, for those unfamiliar with a particular system, the citations are incomprehensible. Yet most cases are cited to reporters readily available in any standard comparative law collection. The Cardiff Index to Legal Abbreviations, available on-line, provides a key to the abbreviations.[213]

204. *Doctrine.* Civilian systems have a convenient name to designate scholarly opinion (*doctrine, Lehre*). In this study, scholarly opinion is understood as "the opinions formulated by law professors, but also, more broadly, as the constellation of reflections engaged in by jurists who attempt to think the law, not only as it is but as it should be."[214] Though scholarly opinion is not today a primary source of law as it was in the classical days of Rome, civilians still respect scholarly opinion as an important secondary source of law.[215] Scholarly writing plays a different role in the common law. Common-law scholars are generally less persuasive to the courts. They often take advantage of the situation by exploring more theoretical issues. The careful, systematic work that is the staple of an academic career in the civil law is a relatively neglected aspect of common-law scholarship.

Scholarly opinion is especially important to this study because, in many jurisdictions, it is the principal source of systematic analysis and policy reasoning. Scholars are responsible for generating consensus about the purpose of the norms. For this reason, this study takes scholarly opinion more seriously than is conventionally the case in comparative studies. In fact, this is really a study of doctrine.

In some legal systems, doctrinal debates take on a life of their own and create a discussion that far transcends disagreements on technical issues. One enjoyable example is the constant rivalry between Biondi and Torrente in the Italian discussion. They are the Hillel and Shammai of gift law, taking opposing positions on almost every issue. If their differences were systematized, two competing visions would emerge, not merely of gift law, but of the law in general, its relationship to history and morality, and the proper role of the individual in society.

---

213. http://www.legalabbrevs.cardiff.ac.uk/index.jsp.

214. Barrière 143.

215. Statute and custom are direct sources. Practice, doctrine, and case law are sources of interpretation. 1 Mazeaud (-Chabas) 112; 1 Ghestin no. 227.

Another remarkable discussion takes place in the French tradition between the treatise named after the renowned French scholars Planiol and Ripert and the two more personal treatises written by the great Belgian scholars Laurent and De Page. The French scholars strain to find justifications for seemingly irrational institutions, while the Belgians are constantly frustrated by what they perceive as dysfunctional and illogical provisions. Those who enjoy precision and an unflinching willingness to confront inconsistency may find the work of Jacques Flour especially rewarding.

Each of the theorists, even each of the articles, expresses a personal vision. The most remarkable fact about the law of gifts, which itself may be the most remarkable field in the private law, is that, over so many centuries, so many amazing minds have dedicated so much time to resolving the intractable puzzles the field presents. Most fields in the private law, in their modern construction, are relatively recent. The law of gifts has posed more or less the same questions from the beginning. One of the opportunities this field offers is to watch as some of the greatest legal minds in the West over the past two thousand years repeatedly confront the same problems and attempt to provide them with definitive solutions. Nonetheless the debates continue.

205. *Translations.* Unless otherwise indicated, all translations from works cited to foreign language editions are my own. When I had to choose, I decided to convey meaning rather than style. Since this is law and not literature, it is not always the case that the author's formulations are the best vessel for the author's thought. For many passages, a more literal translation would be incomprehensible to anyone who does not also speak the source language. As a result, I have not hesitated to divide long sentences, change tense, employ colloquial formulations, and generally slice through the verbiage to reveal the insight.

I have also tried to find English approximations for the concepts used in civilian legal systems. It is a truism, but it is also painfully true, that there are no equivalents. A legal concept is not just a word. It is an element of a theoretical construction. A vast theoretical vision is contained, the world in a grain of sand, in each concept. Nonetheless, some terms can be brought over into English more easily, and others are so bound into their cultural context that a long explanation would be necessary. I recognize that my efforts have had mixed success, and so I have placed the original concept in parentheses following my translation. Instead of trying to solve the well-known difficulty of translation, I have instead hoped to evade it by discussing at some length what the foreign concepts mean to the jurists who use them, "displaying the logic of their ways of putting [things] in the locutions of ours."[216]

---

216. Geertz (1983b) 10. "Interpretive explanation ... trains its attention on what institutions, actions, images, utterances, events, customs, all the usual objects of social-scientific interest, mean to those whose institutions, actions, customs, and so on they are." Geertz (1983a) 22.

206. *Close of research.* It has proved impossible to keep all information valid to a uniform date. Research necessarily takes time, and, while the cases and commentaries in one jurisdiction are being located and examined, the legislatures and the courts are busy in the others changing the law. Attempts were made to update statements about basic gift law propositions into early 2007. It goes without saying, however, that cases and some legislation may have altered the situation in some respects with regard to the description offered here. And of course there are many changes that I have simply, and inexcusably, missed. As a logistical matter, it has also proven impossible to take into account the most recent production of monographs and articles in the various jurisdictions examined here.

c. Selected Topics

207. *Principal questions.* This study examines the private law governing the giving and revoking of gifts. It therefore does not discuss the important practical topics related to estate and gift taxation. It also does not cover related institutions of the private law such as the law of successions. Furthermore, this study ignores consumer protection law[217] and questions about gifts that arise in more remote fields such as labor law.[218]

More importantly, this investigation does not examine all facets of gift law. This study focuses on those gift law institutions, such as capacity, form, and revocation, that most clearly reveal the attitude of each legal system toward the giving of gifts. To permit a somewhat extended presentation of the doctrinal discussions, other topics have been omitted. Questions traditionally discussed in the law of gifts that are not, or not fully, examined here include validity, obligations of the donor and the donee, conditions (including revocation for failure of a condition), avoidance, rights of third parties, the return of gifts at the end of an engagement and after the dissolution of marriage,[219] changed circumstance, and the special rules governing particular varieties of gifts, such as remunerative gifts, gifts with an obligation (*donatio sub modo*), gifts in a marriage settlement (*contrat de mariage*), and gifts mixed with an exchange contract (*negotium mixtum cum donatione*).[220]

---

217. For the prohibition of gifts used in sales promotion, see the Dutch Free Gifts Restriction Act, discussed in *Oosthoek's Uitgeversmaatschappij BV*, Case 286/81, [1983] 3 C.M.L.R. 428 (E.C.J.).

218. For a discussion of whether a Christmas bonus should be characterized as a gift or as compensation for purposes of the duty to bargain under the Wagner Act, see *Niles-Bement-Pond Co.*, 97 N.L.R.B. 165 (1951).

219. The return of gifts at the end of an engagement and after dissolution of marriage is discussed in Schwenzer secs. 67–74. For the return of engagement gifts in American law, see Glassman, Frazier, Tushnet, White. For English law see Law Reform (Miscellaneous Provisions) Act of 1970 sec. 3.

220. For the gift with an obligation and the mixed gift in French and German law, see Dawson (1980) 102–113, 165–185. For the mixed gift, see also Von Mehren 1031–1033.

3. THE LEGAL CONCEPT OF THE GIFT

208. *No systematic definition.* In the rich tapestry offered by the gift laws of the world, one of the few commonalities lies in the striking and confusing fact that a systematic definition of *gift* is hard to find. Instead of a definition, some codes enumerate the requirements for executing a valid gift, defining the gift not by its constituent elements but rather in terms of the formalities required for its execution. The assumption seems to be that what constitutes a gift is both so difficult to resolve into elements and yet so obvious that a proper definition is not needed. The rudimentary definitions that are provided are perhaps also a nod to the fact that gift (unlike contract) is not constituted by the law but merely regulated by it, and that the law must take the gift as it finds it.

A. A LEGAL DEFINITION

209. *Realist approach.* A comparative study of gift law must begin by attempting to define the concept. The difficulty is that the definition cannot easily be separated from its regime and effects. Legal characterizations are often made with one eye to the potential consequences. In fact, there is a productive tension between the definition and the effects of a legal institution. In many systems, notions of social policy restrict the legal definition of the gift so that fewer transactions are subject to the dramatic legal consequences. Because the substance of the definition seems to be determined by the results, a legal realist might begin the discussion with the legal consequences of characterizing a transaction as a gift.

Unfortunately, the realist approach also leaves something to be desired. It suggests that doctrinal categories are arbitrary, or at least irrelevant. Yet the definitions are not infinitely malleable. They are the meaningful result of the vision a particular legal system has of gift giving. The legal consequences must often be structured to accommodate those fact situations that will most likely be characterized as gifts.

210. *Equilibrium.* This study assumes that, in the legal systems studied here, the definition and legal consequences are in equilibrium, both with regard to each other and with regard to the vision of gift giving that informs them both. Doctrinal differences are neither irrelevant nor merely idiosyncratic. They point rather to distinct conceptualizations. Gift concepts are related to history, to legal development, and to even more fundamental questions, such as ideas about the proper

relationship between law and custom. In fact, the notion of gift varies so fundamentally that it is tempting to follow Judge Frank's suggestion and give it a different name in each system—*gift* in one, *gaft* in another, and *geft* in a third.[1]

1. Terminology

211. *Verb and noun.* In Continental languages, the legal term for *gift* actually designates *gift giving* and is generally derived from the verb for making a gift: *donare* → *donatio*; *schenken* → *Schenkung*; *darovat* → *darování*. A different word denotes the gift object—*donum, Geschenk, dar* (or *dárek*).[2] English, usually rich in vocabulary, has two words to signify the gift object—gift and present—but no convenient noun to name the act of giving a gift (the Latinate *donation* being reserved for a gift to a charitable organization) and no convenient verb to express the action involved. The absence actually reveals a truth, namely that legal norms in the Anglo-American tradition generally do not intervene in the act of gift giving but rather focus on whether a transaction constitutes an executed gift. Nonetheless, because this study is largely devoted to the civilian legal tradition, some flexibility is needed, and expressions like *gift giving, to gift, gifted,* and the like are used here in a way that is hardly colloquial.

2. Purpose of the Definition

212. *Difference with anthropology.* If the law were to follow the anthropological literature, the legal definition of the gift would rely neither on an absence of obligation nor on a lack of equivalence. Instead, it might define the gift as the transfer of an object in the context of a relationship that implies obligations to give, to receive, and to reciprocate.[3]

The anthropological definition, however, would not serve the law's purposes. When defining the gift, a legal system has two concerns that differ from those of the anthropologist. First, it seeks to grasp the real-world institution of gift giving in terms of the system's conceptual structure. This translation assures that gift giving will appear in a different light in the law. The difficulty arises partially because private law concepts evolved to regulate exchange in the marketplace. For example, most contemporary legal systems understand gift giving as a contract. Yet for most nonjurists a gift is not a contract. In fact, many might define a gift as a transfer that is not contractual. Contracts deal with market transactions whereas gift giving takes place outside of the market. Contracts create legally enforceable obligations whereas gift giving is not legally required.

---

1. *Commissioner of Internal Revenue v. Beck*, 129 F.2d 243, 246 (2nd Cir. 1942) (Frank, J.).
2. For the Indo-European origins of the words related to gift and giving, see Benveniste 53–83. In the Germanic languages, the word *Gift* may mean both *gift* and *poison*. For the assimilation of the two ideas, see Mauss (1997).
3. Supra no. 19.

Contracts usually result from bargains, whereas what is bargained for is not a gift. The use of concepts from the private law guarantees distortion.

A legal system's second concern is to specify the extent to which it should intervene in the social pattern of gift giving. Once an activity is legally characterized as a gift, a number of consequences ensue. For one, not everyone who can enter into a contract can make, or even receive, a gift. Moreover, the transaction is generally void unless the gift is made in the proper form. Furthermore, what the law characterizes as a gift is subject to collation and may be revocable. The purpose of the definition § is to provide a means to identify cases in which these consequences are appropriate. This function cannot be fulfilled by a reference to the traditional characteristics of gift exchange.

213. *Two sets of criteria.* In place of a definition, many codifications enumerate the requirements and legal effect of a valid gift disposition. This strategy coincides with the definition of a contract as a concurrence of legally relevant acts—offer, acceptance, and consideration, to use a common-law example. Though the strategy is widely accepted, it is defective. The defect is due to the fact that the law's role in gift giving differs from its role in contractual bargains. If a transaction meets the requirements of a legal contract, it is judicially enforceable. Yet even if it does not, the parties are still free to perform. In the case of a gift, however, the failure to meet the legal requirements often means that the gift is void. The parties are not free to perform. If they nonetheless make the transfer, the property can be recovered by any interested party. In other words, the law's definition of *gift* has higher stakes than its definition of *contract*.

3. Comparative Survey

214. *Definitional elements.* Many elements are used to define gift giving in the private law. Each legal system uses a slightly different combination.

215. *Germanic definitions.* To Savigny, a gift transfer involved three elements. It must take place inter vivos, it must enrich the donee at the donor's expense, and the donor must intend a gratuitous transfer.[4] In his comparative study of gift law for Schlegelberger's *Handwörterbuch*, Wolfgang Siebert elaborated on Savigny's definition. He distinguished three principal characteristics. First, there must be a disposition (*Zuwendung*) that both enriches the donee's patrimony and impoverishes that of the donor. Second, the disposition must be gratuitous (*unentgeltlich*). Third, the donee must accept the disposition and its gratuitous character.[5] Siebert's definition closely corresponds to what are still considered the essential elements of a gift in German law.[6] Other systems influenced by German law adopt similar elements. Swiss law defines the gift as an inter vivos

---

4. Savigny (1841) 4.
5. Siebert 144–146.
6. Jauernig (-Mansel) § 516 nos. 1–2.

disposition that enriches the donee from the donor's patrimony without a quid pro quo (CO § 239 par. 1). In Greek law, the gift is the transfer of a patrimonial object, if it is agreed that the transfer is to take place without a quid pro quo (CC art. 496). In Austrian law, a gift is a thing ceded (*überlassen*) gratuitously (CC § 938).

216. *Other Western European systems.* The statutory language varies, however, even among Continental codifications. In the Code Napoleon, a gift was defined as an inter vivos act by which a donor is immediately and irrevocably divested of the gift object in favor of a donee who accepts (CC arts. 893–894). In Spain, the gift is an act of generosity (*liberalidad*; CC art. 618).[7] Under the former Dutch Code, a gift was defined as an inter vivos agreement (*overeenkomst*) by which the donor is irrevocably divested of something.[8] In Italy, a gift is defined as a contract by which the donor, in a spirit of generosity (*per spirito di liberalità*), enriches the donee, either by disposing of a right or by assuming an obligation (CC art. 769)[9]

217. *Central and Eastern Europe.* Some Central and Eastern European legal systems define the gift in terms of obligation. The Hungarian Code defines the gift contract as an act by which the donor assumes the obligation to grant a gratuitous property benefit to the donee.[10] The Polish Civil Code states that, by the gift contract, the donor becomes obligated to a gratuitous performance (*bezplatnego swiadczenia*) for the benefit of the donee (CC art. 888 § 1). The Czechoslovak Civil Code defined the gift contract to include both a gratuitous transfer and a gratuitous promise.[11] Earlier law from these countries added additional qualifications. Former Latvian law defined the gift as a juridical act by which the donor, out of generosity and without a quid pro quo, disposes of a patrimonial object.[12] The civil code of the former kingdom of Albania specified that the gift must be made from a spontaneous feeling of generosity.[13] An earlier draft of the Hungarian Civil Code specified that, to qualify as a gift, the disposition must be made in the absence of an obligation.[14]

218. *Latin America.* Additional elements appear in Latin America. In Argentina, a gift transfer must be voluntary (CC art. 1789). In Brazilian law, a gift transfer

---

7. Diez-Picazo and Gullón 335.

8. Dutch CC art. 1703 par. 1 (1838). For the definition in the current Dutch Civil Code, see art. 7:175 par. 1.

9. For a definitional history of gift in Italian law, see Piccinini.

10. Hungarian CC § 579 par. 1 (1959/1977).

11. Czechoslovakian CC § 383 (1955). The same is true of the 2008 draft of a Civil Code for the Czech Republic. See § 1783 par. 1.

12. CC § 4464 (1928).

13. Albanian CC art. 1483 (1939).

14. Hungarian Draft CC § 1448 (1928).

may include either a good or an advantage (CC art. 538). Ecuadorian law specifies that a gift may involve only a portion of the donor's property (CC art. 1429).

219. *Additional elements.* Beyond the limits of Continental Europe and Latin America, yet other ideas are at work. In Lebanon the donor may gift the donor's entire estate,[15] a provision that was recently added to the French Civil Code as well.[16] The Syrian Civil Code specifies that the gift object must belong to the donor (CC art. 454). The American Restatement (Third) of Property considers a gift to be a transfer of an ownership interest to the donee without consideration and with donative intent.[17] The Islamic concept of *hiba*, which is somewhat narrower than the English term *gift*, is defined as the immediate and unqualified transfer of the corpus of the property without possibility of return.[18] Israeli gift law follows the same model.[19] The Indian Transfer of Property Act permits a gift to be made of both movables and immovables, as long as the movables exist at the time of the gift.[20]

220. *No definition.* Substantive variation is not the only disparity. Some civil codes regulate gift giving but provide only a rudimentary definition of the concept, or sometimes none at all.[21] Other civil codes, though otherwise providing a comprehensive regulation of the private law, do not govern gift giving, thereby leaving it to customary norms.[22]

4. Need for Precision

221. *Similarities.* In sum, the statutory definitions reveal no universal agreement. There are differences not only in detail but also in conceptual structure. Yet they all seem to refer to the same real-world institution. In fact, a jurist from one jurisdiction might read several of these definitions and conclude that they are pretty much the same, by which is usually meant that they seem but a variation of the definition found in that jurist's own legal system. Thus Siebert, writing in the *Handwörterbuch*, concluded that the elements of the German definition were universally accepted.[23]

222. *Elements of dispute.* This is a field, however, in which precision is useful. A definitional element adds more than descriptive detail. It establishes limits,

---

15. Lebanese COC art. 504 (1973).
16. CC art. 893 par. 1 (2006).
17. Restatement (Third) of Property (Wills and Other Donative Transfers) § 6.1 par. a.
18. Fyzee 218.
19. Gift Law sec. 1 par. a.
20. Indian Transfer of Property Act § 122 (1882).
21. CZECHOSLOVAKIA: CC §§ 407–409 (1964); JAPAN: CC arts. 549–554; NEPAL: Legal Code.
22. Former Belgian Congo CC (1934); Burundi CC (1970).
23. Siebert 144.

creates the subject of dispute, and may require additional proof from those who wish to invalidate a transaction and those who are asking the court to approve it. Each element inspires debate in the scholarly literature and adds factors for judicial interpretation. Because an element in a legal definition may decide which of two claimants gains title to property, even minute differences are meaningful.

5. Elements for a Comparative Study

223. *For present purposes.* No particular legal definition is objectively proper for a comparative study. No element in any of the codified definitions is universal. For example gifts do not always involve a transfer. They also do not always involve a tangible object or enrich the donee at the donor's expense. The usefulness of the definition depends on the goals of the study.

a. Four Grounds for Concern

224. *Outside the marketplace.* The gift regime has generally been applied to those gratuitous transfers that take place outside the self-interested realm of market exchange. Unfortunately, no legal system has formulated that thought as its legal definition. Because this comparative study attempts to explore this aspect of gift law, it is useful to tailor the definition to the model transaction that raises suspicion and provokes legal systems to impose a protective regime. Four factors are involved.

The first element is *gratuitousness.* Gratuitousness is variously defined in terms of a lack of quid pro quo or consideration, the absence of an obligation on the part of the donor, or the presence of liberality or generosity. The second element involves certain *subjective factors,* generally either donative intent on the part of the donor or an agreement between the parties that the transaction is gratuitous. A third factor is the *inter vivos* nature of the transaction. If the transfer is made during the donor's lifetime, the donor parts with resources that might be useful in the future. The final factor imposes limitations on the *gift object.* This is the most difficult element to define. In most cases, the object of the transaction involves a transfer of wealth, particularly some type of property right. Gift law generally does not govern services. In some cases, however, such as the release of a debt, there can be a gift without the transfer of a gift object.

225. *To mitigate risk.* To sum up, many legal systems express a particular concern about a transaction in which, during the donor's lifetime, the donor intentionally enriches the donee without compensation. This is the concept of the gift that has been adopted for this comparative study.[24] When these four elements coincide, the law seeks to mitigate the risks the transaction is thought to pose to society.

---

24. Perozzi's definitional essay reached a similar conclusion. "[T]he gift involves the production, intentionally without cause [donative intent], by means of a patrimonial act [gift object] among the living [inter vivos], and by diminution of the patrimony of the

THE LEGAL CONCEPT OF THE GIFT 133

That perception of risk and those mitigation mechanisms are the objects of this study.

Why is this combination of factors so troubling? In general modern legal systems do not fear for their citizens. Though they impose duties and proscribe conduct, they do not generally require citizens to come in for consultation before initiating a course of conduct, even if the conduct creates risk. Western law permits individuals to buy stock, smoke cigarettes, drink alcohol, and make love, all without prior consultation. Legal norms encourage human beings to engage in their own rational calculus of cost and benefit, no matter how destructive the result might be. Though individuals may have to pay for the harm they cause, they are not cautioned in advance. The law's fear is reserved for activities that fail to conform to the common Western conception of rationality. Beyond that domain, it knows, its writ does not run.

Gift giving is one of these activities. Regardless what the anthropologists might suggest, there is more to the gift than grudging compliance with social custom. Gifts, as Merlin de Douai explained, are often based on the passions, "the most formidable opponents of human freedom."[25] They substitute an uncontrolled will for the reflective reason that should preside over human activity. Yet not all passions are dangerous. The law can negotiate with many of them. But there is one—love—that will have its way, with or without the law.

> Among the passions that agitate and trouble so often the human heart there is none as imperious as love. This passion exercises a tyrannical empire, and the first of its fatal effects is to alter the senses and destroy reason. In effect, everything beside the object of affection disappears in the eyes of the person who is subject to its power. The human being in love is impervious to the voice of reason. Caught in this delirium those in love disobey their most sacred obligations in order to pursue the irresistable impulse that attracts them.[26]

Merlin drew the inevitable conclusion. Modern legal systems tend to distrust gifts given out of love. "The law, which watches over the happiness of its citizens, does not hesitate to annul gifts made between persons caught in the chains of passion."[27]

The law fears passion because it cannot control it. And the passion it fears most is love. The intricate legal constructions that this study explores are thus often the result of legal efforts to suppress the feared excesses of love. There is no way to prove this thesis. But it was the view of Philippe-Antoine

---

donor, of an augmentation of the donee's patrimony [gratuitousness]." Perozzi 550–551. (I have indicated in brackets the elements related the the definition chosen here.)

25. 5 Merlin (1825) *Concubinage* 331.

26. Id.

27. Id. Merlin was specifically concerned with gifts given between unmarried cohabitants. See infra no. 559.

Merlin de Douai, revolutionary, proponent of the death of Louis Capet, drafter of an early gift law project for the French Civil Code, Minister of Justice, member of the Council of Ancients, member of the Directory, member of the *Académie française*, Grand Officer of the Legion of Honor, and one of the shrewdest jurists who ever lived.

b. The Point of View of the Notary

226. *Operational focus.* Notaries, the civilian specialists in gift law, do not conceive of the gift in this manner. They rarely think about the definitional elements. The notary's view follows the codes, which are written for those who intend to make a gift. When a client asks how to give away property, the notary focuses on the validity requirements. Most legal systems require special forms, such as a notarial act or completed delivery. The notary also offers advice concerning the risks involved and mentions the possibility of financial reversal and the competing claims of the donor's family. The notary then structures the transaction to ensure that the object is proper, that the transfer is completed inter vivos, and that nothing impairs irrevocability.

The scholars often adopt this perspective. Though in most fields of the law the discussion usually begins with a definition, neither in the common nor the civil law do discussions of gift law typically begin by defining the reach of the institution. The view is understandable. Since gratuitous transfers are generally void if not made in proper form, a gift might be thought of as a transfer done using gift formalities. Any transfer not completed in those forms is not a gift. Yet there are two problems with this approach. First, there is the logical flaw. The form requirements do not apply unless the transaction is characterized as a gift. More importantly, the approach assumes that the legal and customary understandings of the gift coincide, a view that permits the social practice of gift giving to disappear. Though this study generally tracks the scholarly discussion in the different systems, on this point it departs from the tradition. The legal concept of the gift is understood here as a construction fabricated for each legal system's purposes and from its premises.

c. Comparative Notes

227. *A different focus.* It is useful to remember that the gift law regime conflicts not only with social custom but often also with the parties' wishes. This is another difference between gift and contract. The case law in this field concerns chiefly transactions concluded either in ignorance of the law's protective mechanisms or as attempts to avoid them. In a great many of these cases, the law prohibits a transaction that both parties intended and desired. Gift law turns the private law notion of party autonomy on its head. Gift law favors a transaction when it excludes it. It is thus critical to remember, though it is also easy to forget, that the law facilitates a transaction when gift law's rigorous regime does not apply.

B. THE FOUR FACTORS

227a. *Definitional elements.* The remainder of this chapter discusses the four definitional elements of the gift. The requirements required for a valid gift disposition are examined below.[28]

1. Gratuitousness

228. *No adequate definition.* One of the features that most clearly distinguishes the modern gift transaction from most other transactions governed by the private law is its gratuitousness. Though the concept is intuitively simple—the donor gives something away and receives nothing in exchange—legal systems are rarely able to define the idea clearly. There are several reasons for the difficulty. To begin with, the consequences often weigh heavily on the definition. The characterization question is often raised for the first time post hoc, at the moment when a court is asked to invalidate a transaction that proceeded without the requisite formalities. In these circumstances, the validity of the transaction depends on whether it is characterized as gratuitous or whether, following civilian usage, it may be considered *onerous*. Fairness considerations thus influence the determination. Another reason for the difficulty is that, from a theoretical point of view, the notion of gratuitousness represents the boundary between market-oriented transactions and transactions designed to fulfill other sorts of needs and goals. Because, as Mauss taught, transactions frequently involve both types of motivation, the line proves difficult to draw. Due to the complexity of the problem, it is often resolved by reference to flexible concepts from the law of contracts, such as the consideration doctrine or the notion of natural obligation.

229. *Roman law.* Surprisingly, classical Roman law did not consider the donatio gratuitous. Gratuitousness was a characteristic of certain legal acts, such as the loan for use (*commodatum*) and the bailment for safekeeping (*depositum*). The donatio, however, was not a legal act. It was simply a *causa* for a transfer.[29] When evaluating whether the cause was gratuitous, the Roman jurists seem to have asked whether there was a correlation between the gift and a counterperformance. If there was a willed correlation, the transfer was *ob causam* and could not be a gift.[30]

a. The Common Law

230. *Without consideration.* In the common law, as Blackstone noted, gifts are always gratuitous.[31] As an Indian commentator has written, "A gift is essentially

---

28. Infra nos. 728–992.
29. Michel nos. 468–469.
30. Archi (1964) 932.
31. 2 Blackstone 440.

a gratuitous transfer."[32] At least on one level, gratuitousness in the common law is easy to define. It involves a transaction without a valid legal consideration. "In fact, if there be a consideration the transaction is no longer a gift, but a contract."[33] This is the unanimous view of the statutes,[34] the case law,[35] and the commentators.[36] The Restatement (Third) of Property adds that gratuitousness requires not only that the transfer take place without consideration, but also that it not be done in satisfaction of a legal obligation, including any obligation imposed by court judgment or a legal duty of support.[37]

The consideration doctrine is the central concept in the common law of contract formation. Simply stated, it provides that no promise is enforceable at law without a quid pro quo. The consideration doctrine thus serves to distinguish legally enforceable promises from all other promises, including those enforceable in equity and those left to the moral discretion of the promisor.[38] The basic idea of the consideration doctrine is that a promise is enforceable only if it is part of a bargain.[39] A promised performance, or the performance itself, is consideration for another promise or performance if the two were bargained for and given in exchange for each other. Anything short of a bargain—such as the desire to reciprocate natural love and affection—does not constitute consideration and therefore does not permit the promise to be enforced at law.[40]

The consideration doctrine received scholarly recognition during the last third of the nineteenth century as a means to distinguish enforceable bargains from unenforceable gift promises.[41] The precise nature of the requirement had been the subject of constant dispute since the days of Lord Mansfield.[42] Some authors doubt that the courts ever recognized the consideration doctrine at all.[43]

---

32. Gour § 122 no. 6.

33. Thornton § 4.

34. "A gift is a transfer of personal property, made voluntarily and without consideration." California CC § 1146. "Gift is the transfer of certain ... property made voluntarily and without consideration." Indian Transfer of Property Act § 122.

35. *Gray v. Barton*, 55 N.Y. 68, 72 (1873).

36. "It is essential to the legal idea of a gift that there should be an absence of consideration." Graves 871. "To the voluntary transfer of a thing without consideration, the term 'gift,' which in our law corresponds with the *donatio* of the civil law, is commonly applied." 2 Schouler § 54.

37. Restatement (Third) of Property (Wills and Other Donative Transfers) § 6.1 comments d and e.

38. Hyland (2004) 71–73.

39. Restatement (Second) of Contracts § 71.

40. Gour § 122 no. 6.

41. Kreitner 1897.

42. "I take it, that the ancient notion about the want of consideration was for the sake of evidence only." *Pillans and Rose v van Mierop and Hopkins* (1765) 3 Burr 1663, 97 ER 1035 (KB) (Lord Mansfield J).

43. Corbin (1952) § 109; Gilmore (1974) 21–77.

Unfortunately, the consideration doctrine, even when freed from historical encrustations and understood in contemporary fashion as bargain theory, does not provide a flawless guide for defining gratuitousness.[44] This is because consideration is often found for promises that, in both the common and the civil laws, would generally be considered to be gifts. Consideration is deemed to be present because justice nonetheless demands enforcement.

There are principally three types of cases in which the courts find consideration to be present, even in the context of gift promises. These circumstances are generally referred to under the headings of adequate consideration, conditional promises, and moral consideration.

i. Adequate Consideration

231. *Equivalence.* Unless there is evidence of unconscionability, bad faith, or fraud, common-law courts generally do not review a bargain to ensure that the consideration is adequate—that, in some objective sense, it is of equivalent value.[45] However, there is a long-standing disagreement between English and American law about whether the law may entirely disregard the adequacy question. In English law, a nominal consideration is sufficient to make a promise enforceable, whereas in American law it is not.

(A) ENGLAND

232. *Nominal consideration.* English courts do not examine the adequacy of consideration. An early case held that it was adequate consideration for a promise to pay £50 that the recipient agreed to come to claim the money.[46] A more recent case suggests that a consumer's return of wrappers from chocolate bars would be consideration for the promise to deliver gramophone records, even though the wrappers were worthless and the seller intended to discard them.[47] "[A] contracting party can stipulate for what consideration he chooses. A peppercorn does not cease to be good consideration if it is established that the promisee does not like pepper and will throw away the corn."[48] English scholars conclude that

---

44. "What then is the purpose of the continued existence of the [consideration] doctrine? It cannot be to distinguish between onerous and gratuitous agreements because adequacy of consideration is wholly immaterial, and some promises which are technically held to be supported by consideration are, in fact, nothing more or less than purely gratuitous promises." Law Revision Committee no. 20 at 14–15.

45. ENGLAND: Anson (2002) 987; 1 Chitty par. 3-014; Treitel par. 3-013; UNITED STATES: *Parker v. Dodge*, 98 S.W.3d 297, 301–302 (Tex. App. 2003).

46. *Gilbert v Ruddeard* (1608) 3 Dy 272b, 73 ER 606 note 32 case 5.

47. *Chappell & Co Ltd v Nestlé Co Ltd* [1960] AC 87. "If the delivery of the wrappers formed part of the consideration it could, presumably, have formed the whole of the consideration, so that a promise to deliver records for wrappers alone would have been binding." Treitel par. 3-032. See also 1 Chitty par. 3-016.

48. *Chappell & Co Ltd* id. 114 (Lord Somervell J).

a nominal consideration is sufficient to make a promise binding, such as £1 for a valuable property or a peppercorn for a substantial sum of money.[49]

The enforceability of promises supported only by nominal consideration is usually justified as a logical consequence of the adequacy doctrine.[50] Atiyah, however, has pointed out that the two doctrines might easily be distinguished.[51] Adequate consideration is bargained for; nominal consideration is a sham. Whether or not logically required, the doctrine of nominal consideration permits evasion of the consideration doctrine. A gift promise is binding if clothed in nominal consideration. "Where an agreement is legally binding on the ground that it is supported by nominal consideration, the doctrine of consideration does not serve its main purpose, of distinguishing between gratuitous and onerous promises."[52]

(B) UNITED STATES

233. *Pretense.* In American law, a mere pretense of bargain does not suffice. Nominal consideration is no consideration.[53] The courts and commentators have had difficulty drawing a clear line between a small but sufficient consideration, which indicates that a bargain was concluded, and nominal consideration, which would mean that, legally, the promise is gratuitous.[54] The problem arises because courts enforce certain promises, even when no bargain is involved. Some courts permit nonfinancial considerations, such as the friendship relationship between the parties, to provide the required consideration.[55] In one case, the donor promised he would bequeath a home to his daughter-in-law so she would continue to live near him.[56] Though the donor left the property to a third party in his will, the court held that the daughter-in-law's willingness to stay, together with the close personal bond between the two, was adequate consideration to render the donor's promise enforceable.[57] A court may also decide that a transaction is part bargain and part gift. The element of bargain then furnishes consideration for the entire

---

49. 1 Chitty par. 3-018.

50. "To equate 'nominal' with 'inadequate' or even 'grossly inadequate' consideration would embark the law on inquiries which I cannot think were ever intended by Parliament." *Midland Bank & Trustee Co Ltd v Green* [1981] AC 513, 532 (Lord Wilberforce J).

51. Atiyah 194.

52. 1 Chitty par. 3-019; see also Treitel par. 3-014.

53. *Parker v. Dodge*, 98 S.W.3d 297, 301–302 (Tex. App. 2003).

54. Compare Page § 646 with 2 Corbin (1995) § 5.17.

55. *Ornbaun v. Main*, 17 Cal.Rptr. 631, 634 (Cal. App. 1961).

56. *Poporato v. Devincenzi*, 68 Cal.Rptr. 210 (Cal. App. 1968).

57. When testing the adequacy of consideration, "the court may consider 'such factors as the relationship of the parties, their friendship, love, affection, and regard for each other, and the object to be obtained by the contract.'" Id. 214.

transaction.[58] As a result, some transactions that are intended to be gratuitous are found to satisfy the consideration doctrine.

ii. Conditional Promises

234. *Difficult distinction.* A second difficulty arises when a condition is added to an otherwise gratuitous promise. A school example involves the case in which A promises B $100 if B goes to college.[59] A's statement may constitute an offer to enter into a unilateral contract, or it might be a conditional gift promise.[60] Which it is depends on whether "the circumstances give B reason to know that A is not undertaking to pay B to go to college but is promising a gratuity."[61] As Williston wrote, it is difficult in some situations to determine whether the suggested contingency is a request for an exchange or a condition attached to a gratuitous promise.[62] "[T]he distinction between bargain and gift may be a fine one, depending on the motives manifested by the parties."[63]

In English law conditions can be interpreted as promises. The promisee's satisfaction of the condition may constitute consideration if the promisee's action reasonably can be regarded as having been requested.[64] In one case, a father bought a house subject to a mortgage.[65] He allowed his son and daughter-in-law to live in the house and told them that, if they paid the mortgage installments, the house would be theirs when the mortgage was satisfied. Though the couple did not promise to pay the installments, the court held that a unilateral contract had been formed and could be enforced against the donor's personal representative.

iii. Moral Obligation

235. *Moral consideration.* Common-law courts sometimes enforce promises lacking consideration if they fulfill a moral obligation. In *Webb v. McGowin*, a celebrated case, a worker heroically diverted a large block of wood that, if allowed to continue its fall, might have killed his employer.[66] The worker was disabled for life. The employer promised him a small biweekly pension, which was paid regularly until the employer's death. The employer's executor refused to make further payments. The court held that the executor was contractually bound by the promise. In the court's view, because the employer received the contemplated

---

58. Restatement (Second) of Contracts § 71 comment c.
59. Id. § 24 illus. 2.
60. Id. § 24 comm. b.
61. Id. § 24 illus. 2.
62. 3 Williston § 7:18 at 415.
63. Restatement (Second) of Contracts § 71 comment c.
64. Treitel par. 3-011.
65. *Errington v Errington and Woods* [1952] 1 KB 290 (CA).
66. *Webb v. McGowin*, 168 So. 196 (Ala. App), aff'd, 168 So. 199 (Ala. 1936).

material benefit, his moral obligation to the employee was sufficient consideration to support the promise.[67] Because it is well settled that past consideration is no consideration—there must be an actual exchange and not a retroactive remuneration—the consideration seems to have been the employee's implicit agreement to release the employer from his moral debt. Yet there is certainly a gratuitous element to the transaction. In some civilian jurisdictions, a case such as *Webb* might be considered either the fulfillment of a natural obligation or a remunerative gift. In the American common law, however, it must be swept up into contract if it is to be enforced.

236. *Difficulties.* Two problems arise when the notion of moral obligation is used to distinguish gratuitous from nongratuitous transfers. First, moral obligation is not universally accepted as consideration.[68] More importantly, there is no standard definition of moral obligation. "Whether a moral obligation exists in a particular situation is primarily a question of policy and ethics rather than one of law."[69] Great leeway exists to determine whether a particular promise or transfer is gratuitous. "[I]n nearly all circumstances where a promise is made there is some moral aspect of the situation which provides the motivation for making the promise even if it is to make an outright gift."[70] In cases like *Webb*, the feeling of justice may outweigh the need for clear definitions.[71]

b. France and Belgium

237. *Objective and subjective elements.* Though the French Civil Code does not expressly state that a gift must be gratuitous,[72] gratuitousness operates indirectly in French law as a distinguishing characteristic of a gift. French doctrine distinguishes three types of legal acts—those that are onerous (*actes à titre onéreux*), those that are gratuitous (*actes à titre gratuit*), and those that are valid without regard to whether they are onerous or gratuitous.[73] Gratuitous acts include

---

67. Id. 168 So. at 198.

68. *Davis v. Davis*, 2007 WL 2409845 *2 (Mass. App. Div. 2007); *Manwill v. Oyler*, 361 P.2d 177, 178 (Utah 1961).

69. *Koike v. Board of Water Supply*, 352 P.2d 835, 840 (Haw. 1960) (the case involved the power of the state legislature).

70. *Manwill v. Oyler*, 361 P.2d 177, 178 (Utah 1961).

71. "The questions involved in this case are not free from doubt, and perhaps the strict letter of the rule, as stated by judges, though not always in accord, would bar a recovery by plaintiff, but following the principle announced by Chief Justice Marshall ... [namely] 'I do not think that law ought to be separated from justice, where it is at most doubtful,' I concur in the conclusions reached by the court." *Webb v. McGowin*, 168 So. at 199 (Samford, J., concurring).

72. Cf. CC art. 894.

73. Transactions that are valid regardless of whether they are onerous or gratuitous include the loan for use (*prêt à usage* or *commodatum*) and the deposit (*dépôt*) as well as the power of attorney (*mandat*). 5 Planiol and Ripert no. 9.

gratuitous transfers (*libéralités*), which in turn include both gifts and wills. A lack of gratuitousness thus excludes a transaction from the domain of gift law.

Gratuitous acts are characterized by both an objective and a subjective element.[74] The objective element, gratuitousness, is examined here, whereas the subjective element, donative intent (*intention libérale*), is discussed below.[75]

238. *Lack of equivalence.* The French Civil Code does not define gratuitousness. To define the term, some writers refer to the definition of the charitable contract (*contrat de bienfaisance*)—a contract "in which one of the parties promises a purely gratuitous advantage to the other" (CC art. 1105). Unfortunately, as many have noted, the definition is tautological.

Other authors make indirect use of a code provision that distinguishes between two types of onerous contracts—commutative and aleatory—in terms of their shared characteristic, namely that "each of the parties agrees to give or to do something that is regarded as the equivalent of what is given or to be done by the other party" (CC art. 1104). An act in which one of the parties does not receive an equivalent may thus be considered gratuitous.[76] Following this view, Planiol and Ripert defined gratuitousness as a "voluntary lack of equivalence between the reciprocal obligations of the parties," or "the voluntary creation of an obligation without a counterpart."[77] Other authors have defined gratuitousness as "the fact that the donor receives nothing in exchange for what is given," or "gives without receiving a counterpart."[78] In general, French scholars and courts tend to define gratuitousness in terms of an absence of equivalence.[79]

239. *Gift with an obligation.* When gratuitousness is defined in terms of equivalence, a gift in which the donee assumes obligations (*donation avec charges* or *donatio sub modo*) presents characterization problems.[80] If the obligations are in

---

74. Beudant et al. 11; 6 Planiol and Ripert no. 39.

75. Infra nos. 257–273.

76. Champeaux 1–2. "To make a gratuitous disposition means transferring property to another without receiving anything in its place. To make an *onerous* transfer means to receive the equivalent, or something that is deemed the equivalent, of what is given." 1 Delvincourt 703 note 2 to page 228 (emphasis in original).

77. 5 Planiol and Ripert no. 9.

78. Flour and Souleau no. 1; see also 8 De Page no. 2.

79. "A contract is commutative when each party undertakes to give or do something that is regarded as the equivalent of what is given to or done for that party ...." Civ.¹ 10 June 1986, *Bull. civ.* I no. 159; Dawson (1980) 83–102.

80. Dawson (1980) 102–109. French law distinguishes between a gift with an obligation (*donation avec charges*) and a conditional gift (*donation conditionelle*). Only the gift with an obligation raises the question of gratuitousness. In many cases these two types of gift are difficult to distinguish. The distinction is important because the regimes differ. If the gift imposes an obligation, the donor can sue to enforce it. A simple condition, however, is left to the donee's discretion. Scholars tend to consider matters affecting property, such as the promise to maintain a school, to be obligations. Matters affecting personal

the interest of the donor or a third party, the gift is gratuitous only if the value of the condition does not exceed the value of the gift. Otherwise, gratuitousness is thought to be absent.[81] A typical case involves a gift of real property coupled with the donee's obligation to pay the donor a life annuity (*rente viagère*).

If the obligations are in the *donee's* interest, such as the requirement that the gift funds be used for a study trip or to print the donee's dissertation, the transfer is generally characterized as a gift, even if the donee will need additional funds to complete the project.[82] The transfer also is considered a gift if the donee's obligation is in the parties' joint interest. When the donee is an association or other legal person, the transfer is gratuitous if the obligation is within the association's defined purposes. Otherwise, it is onerous.[83]

240. *Natural obligation.* French law also experiences difficulty in distinguishing between a gift and the execution of a natural obligation (*obligation naturelle*). A natural obligation cannot be legally enforced, though, if it is voluntarily executed, the payment is not subject to restitution. The concept of the natural obligation is mentioned[84] but not defined in the Civil Code. There is considerable disagreement concerning which debts actually constitute natural obligations. The traditional doctrine tended to consider natural obligations to be authentic but imperfect civil obligations.[85] According to this view, a natural obligation arises either when a civil obligation loses its sanction (as by prescription) or, due to a missing element, fails to arise completely (as with a promise made by a party without capacity). The performance of any civil obligation, even a natural obligation that cannot be legally compelled, constitutes payment of a debt. Payment of a debt implies a quid pro quo and thus is never characterized as a gift.

Unfortunately, when the payment of a natural obligation is distinguished from a gift in this manner, a major difficulty arises.[86] The party who receives payment of an unenforceable obligation certainly receives something for nothing. There is a lack of equivalence that appears to amount to gratuitousness. For this reason, Laurent, author of a classic Belgian treatise, concluded that the execution of a natural obligation is *always* a gift. However, he argued that imperfect civil obligations, such as debts barred by the statute of limitations or incurred by a party without capacity, were not natural obligations. They were rather debts

---

relations, such as the donee's promise not to remarry, cannot be specifically enforced and are considered conditions. Malaurie and Aynès no. 364; Grimaldi nos. 1192–1195; Flour and Souleau no. 140; Terré and Lequette nos. 321, 324.

81. Malaurie and Aynès no. 363; Grimaldi nos. 1001 note 9, 1197; Flour and Souleau no. 143.

82. Flour and Souleau no. 148.

83. Id. no. 149; Grimaldi no. 1200.

84. CC art. 1235 par. 2.

85. Dupeyroux 326–329.

86. 5 Planiol and Ripert nos. 980–981.

subject to novation.[87] Modern French doctrine has chosen a different tack. French scholars today argue that it is not a lack of gratuitousness but rather a lack of donative intent that distinguishes the execution of a natural obligation from a gift. This view is discussed below.[88]

241. *The dowry.* The dowry (*dot*) seems to disprove all the theories. It is treated in some respects like a gift and in others like a natural obligation.[89] At least at one time, parents were believed to have an obligation to provide a dowry for their children. Since that obligation was not legally enforceable (CC art. 204), it was considered a natural obligation.[90] French law has decided that the parents' constitution of a dowry is exempt from gift formalities though substantive rules, such as those relating to collation and revocation, continue to apply.

Planiol and Ripert considered the bifurcated solution to be "an artificial mental construction." It does not convincingly reconcile the gratuitousness requirement with the presence of a natural obligation.[91] De Page, author of the leading Belgian treatise, suggested that the double characterization is based on social policy. It is a "technical expedient" to save dowries constituted by those of modest income who are not able to afford gift formalities, which generally require the presence of a notary.[92] De Page also suggested that the case opinions are misleading.[93] The judges recognize that the dowry is the economic foundation for the new household. They characterize the dowry as an onerous act to protect it from creditors and prevent rescission under fraudulent conveyance law.

c. Spain

242. *Equivalence.* For there to be a gift in Spanish law, the donor must transfer the object gratuitously (*gratuitamente*; CC art. 618). The concept of gratuitousness is generally defined in terms of equivalence. "A contract is gratuitous if it supposes a simple benefit without counter performance for one party and

---

87. 12 Laurent nos. 355–356.

88. Infra nos. 262–266.

89. 8 Planiol and Ripert no. 113.

90. 8 Planiol and Ripert nos. 114 to 115-2; 8 De Page no. 4. One case decided that the parental duty to create a dowry is a natural obligation. The creation of the dowry is thus onerous and is not subject to gift formalities. Poitiers 26 Apr. 1923, D.P. 1923 II 121 note René Savatier. According to another case, however, as long as the child is not impecunious, a gift in contemplation of the child's marriage does not represent the fulfillment of a natural or moral obligation and is therefore gratuitous. Paris 22 Dec. 1924, *Gaz. Pal.* 1925 I 272.

91. 8 Planiol and Ripert no. 117-4; Gobert 87–121.

92. 8 De Page no. 403 par. B.

93. "[T]he reasons that inspire the judges are not those that are inscribed in the reasoning of the opinions." Id. no. 118.

a diminution in patrimony without economic compensation for the other: something is given in exchange for nothing."[94]

d. Italy

243. *Different definitions.* In the Italian discussion several different definitions of gratuitousness have emerged.

i. Lack of Equivalence

244. *Subjective intent.* One position follows the French tradition and defines gratuitousness in terms of a lack of equivalence. According to this view, a transaction is gratuitous when it is not onerous, and it is onerous when the parties intend for the performances to be equivalent.[95] Even the parties' subjective evaluation may be considered. However, if the parties' subjective intent differs so dramatically from an objective valuation that equivalence could not seriously have been intended, the transaction is considered to be partly onerous and partly gratuitous (*negotium mixtum cum donatione*).

This definition of gratuitousness eliminates the difficulties that typically arise when the concept is defined in terms of a simple lack of equivalence, issues such as how to characterize a transaction in which the parties err about the value of the rights involved. Unfortunately, however, it only postpones the difficulties by defining the concept in terms of donative intent. In this conception, gratuitousness ceases to form a separate requirement for a valid gift.[96]

ii. The Typical Gift

245. *Usual characteristics.* Biondo Biondi, one of the leading Italian authorities, attempted to resolve the definitional difficulty by suggesting that the terms *gratuitous* and *onerous* refer not to the act or transaction itself, but rather to the manner by which title is passed or acquired.[97] Individual transactions may or may not produce equivalence, depending on the circumstances. If, in a sales transaction, for example, the goods turn out to be worthless, then the buyer has paid something for nothing and equivalence is lacking. Similarly, if a gift proves to be worth nothing or even turns out to be a liability, then the donee has not received the something for nothing that gratuitousness would seem to require. According to Biondi, the question should instead be posed in terms of what is typical for the kind of transaction involved. In a sale, the price is generally equivalent to the value of the goods, whereas in a gift, the donee receives a right

---

94. Paz-Ares Rodríguez (-Guardiola) art. 1274 no. VI at 484; see also id. (-Albaladejo García) art. 618 no. IV at 1574.

95. Balbi 13–14.

96. Torrente (2006) 223.

97. Biondi no. 30.

without surrendering an equivalent. Gratuitousness and onerousness are then to be determined in accordance with the usual characteristics of such transactions.

By specifying that the inherent nature of the gift transaction is that rights are to pass without equivalent, this approach avoids the conceptual difficulties that arise when a transaction does not turn out as intended. Unfortunately, however, this position provides no assistance in determining whether any individual transaction is or is not a gift.

iii. Freedom from Compulsion

246. *No preexisting duty.* Casulli arrived at his definition of gratuitousness by means of the Roman law contrast between *liberalitas* and *necessitas*.[98] Roman law, influenced by Stoic philosophy, understood liberality or generosity as a freedom that cannot coexist with compulsion. Those in need rarely can afford to be generous.[99] The gratuitousness essential for a gift cannot exist in the context of any sort of compulsion, whether physical or moral. Any transaction designed to satisfy a preexisting moral or social duty is compelled.[100] Because the obligor is not fully free, the payment of an obligation, even a natural obligation, is not a gift.[101] There is one exception. From all moral and social duties, the legislator has excepted only one from the ambit of the natural obligation, namely the debt of gratitude. According to the Italian Code, payment of a debt of gratitude amounts to a remunerative gift (*donazione rimuneratoria;* CC art. 770 par. 1), which generally follows the normal gift regime.[102]

This focus on the social and moral context of the transaction avoids the difficult questions of actual equivalence and relies, instead, on whether the transferor would have been morally or socially free to refuse the transfer. Unfortunately, this perspective raises even greater problems than it solves. First, as Mauss noted long since, gifts are often given in the context of relationships that render them morally or socially obligatory.[103] Casulli's approach operates with a conception of freedom that cannot be reconciled with the conventional experience of gift

---

98. Casulli (1964) no. 2 at 968–969.

99. *[C]um nemo in necessitatibus liberalis exsistat.* D. 34, 4, 18 (Modestinus).

100. Rescigno (-Carnevali) 490; Oppo no. 49 at 228.

101. "There must not exist a legal obligation, which means an obligation derived directly from the law or originating from a previous transaction. Moreover, there must not even exist an obligation that, even though not legal, the law nonetheless considers relevant and to which are attached legal effects." Cass. 3 June 1980 no. 3621, *Giur. it.* 1981 I 1101 at 1108.

102. "[T]he donor [of a remunerative gift] is bound neither by a legal obligation nor in fulfillment of a moral duty or social custom. As a consequence the transfer can in no case be considered to involve compensation." Cass. 14 Feb. 1997 no. 1411, *Rep. Foro it.* 1997 *Donazione* no. 10. See Rescigno (-Carnevali) 491. The remunerative gift is not subject to revocation for ingratitude or birth of a child. Infra nos. 1165, 1204, 1275.

103. Supra nos. 19, 21.

giving, namely the paradox that the gift is freely given, even though it is socially obligatory. Second, a requirement phrased in terms of spontaneity, freedom, and lack of compulsion seems to restate the subjective requirement, discussed below, of *animus donandi*.

iv. Sacrifice

247. *Common themes.* Angeloni has suggested that sacrifice is the essence of a gratuitous transaction. The execution of an onerous transaction requires sacrifice of both parties. In contrast, only one party makes the sacrifice when the transaction is gratuitous.[104] More recently, Capozzi has rephrased the idea, suggesting a stepwise gradation of gratuitousness.[105] In certain types of gratuitous transfer (*liberalità*), the patrimonial advantage obtained by one party is not compensated by a corresponding sacrifice on the part of the other. The loan for use (*commodatum*) and the loan for consumption without interest (*mutuum*) are gratuitous in this sense. In the case of the gift, another variety of gratuitous transfer, the specific quality of the gratuitousness is that the transfer not only enriches the donee but also impoverishes the donor.[106] Unfortunately, these definitions do little more than restate the notion of gratuitousness, namely that one party gives something away without receiving a quid pro quo. They provide no criteria for determining when gratuitousness is present.

A frequently cited case provides an example of the difficulties. A gift of land and money was made subject to the condition that the donee, a town, would construct an agricultural school on the property and name the school after the donor's deceased son.[107] Gift formalities were not completed, and the donor sought to recover the property. The town argued that the transaction involved an exchange and not a gift. The Cassation Court concluded that the transfer was gratuitous because the donee was enriched without providing a quid pro quo. The Court explained that the naming of the school did not diminish the town's patrimony and provided no economic benefit to the donor. The reasoning seems confused. First, though the naming of the school would not have diminished the town's patrimony, surely the school's construction would have done so. More importantly, there seems to be no reason why a transaction must be considered gratuitous merely because one of the parties seeks noneconomic benefit. Otherwise a portrait painter could never conclude an enforceable contract.[108]

---

104. Angeloni 29–30.

105. Capozzi no. 329 par. a.

106. Capozzi nos. 331 par. a, 332 par. b. This was also Savigny's position. See Savigny (1841) § 142 at 4.

107. Cass. 18 Dec. 1975 no. 4153 (en banc), *Giur. it.* 1976 I 1913.

108. Related issues concerning cause are discussed below. Infra no. 278.

e. Germany

248. *Narrowly defined.* The German concept of gratuitousness (*Unentgeltlichkeit*) is distinctive because it does not involve a lack of equivalence. The concept is quite restricted.The parties must also agree that the transfer is to be gratuitous, a requirement that is discussed below.[109]

249. *No reliance on equivalence.* The German law principle of private autonomy permits parties to contract for an exchange of unequal performances. As a result, gratuitousness cannot be defined in terms of a lack of equivalence.[110] Gratuitousness is only one possible explanation for a lack of equivalence. There may be a subjective disagreement about value, a simple mistake, a mistaken expectation that other factors would compensate for the disequilibrium, or the parties may involve family or friends.[111] German law does not characterize a transaction as gratuitous even when the parties' belief in the equivalence of the counterparts is unreasonable or irrational. In the view of German scholars, the parties to such a transaction do not need the protection of gift formalities. The parties can always investigate value questions before entering into the transaction. If there is a mistake, inequality sometimes provides grounds for avoidance.[112] Gift law formalities are devoted chiefly to protecting the interests of third parties, such as relatives entitled to a compulsory share.

250. *Connection between performances.* The German concept of gratuitousness depends instead on a subjective connection between two performances. If two performances are linked in the minds of one or both of the parties or if a transfer is intended to extinguish an obligation, the transaction is not gratuitous.[113] Thus, Savigny argued that, because the performance of a gift promise represents the fulfillment of an obligation, it is not itself gratuitous.[114]

Any one of three linkages prevents the transaction from being gratuitous.[115] The first linkage is in terms of a bargain, the synallagmatic bond typical of bilateral contracts. The second linkage is established by a condition, including unilateral legal acts such as the offer of a reward. Finally, a transaction is not gratuitous if there is a causal link between the two performances. A causal connection is

---

109. Infra nos. 283–285.

110 . RG 29 Oct. 1934, JW 1935, 275 at 276 note Leo Raape; Staudinger (Wimmer-Leonhardt) § 516 no. 37; MünchKomm-BGB (-Kollhosser) § 516 no. 26; Dawson (1980) 151–165.

111 . MünchKomm-BGB (-Kollhosser) § 516 no. 26.

112 . Id. § 516 no. 27.

113 . RG 17 Jan. 1902, RGZ 50, 134; MünchKomm-BGB (-Kollhosser) § 516 no. 16; Staudinger (-Wimmer-Leonhardt) § 516 no. 33.

114. Savigny (1841) 57. German law today holds that performance of a gift promise remains gratuitous, though it is itself not a gift. Infra nos. 661, 715.

115 . MünchKomm-BGB (-Kollhosser) § 516 no. 17–27.

somewhat more tenuous than a condition and not always easily distinguished from it. In cases of causal connection, the donee's performance does not operate as a condition to the donor's duty to perform, but rather serves as the basis of the bargain (*Geschäftsgrundlage*). For example, a husband transfers property to his estranged wife to persuade her to return to him, or the donor transfers property to the donee to encourage the donee to lend money to a third party. Such transactions are not gratuitous even if patrimonial rights are not involved, as when a husband seeks to persuade his wife to accept divorce.

The code expressly excludes from gift law the endowment (*Ausstattung*) that parents give to their children in consideration of marriage or to make them independent or otherwise to assist their economic endeavors, even when the transfer is not obligatory, except to the extent that the endowment is excessive in the circumstances (CC § 1624 par. 1).

251. *Natural obligation.* German law attempts to avoid the difficult issues that arise in relation to the natural obligation (*unvollkommene Verbindlichkeit*) by deciding simply that payments to satisfy a natural obligation are not gratuitous.[116] German scholars reason that payment of a natural obligation cannot be a gift because, under restitution law, "what is performed on that basis may be retained by the recipient as the payment of a debt."[117] Theoretically, of course, this is no answer at all. The question is not whether a natural obligation provides a legal basis (*Rechtsgrund*) for retaining payment—in many legal systems these obligations provide a *causa adquirendi*—but rather how a natural obligation may be considered to be a debt if it is not enforceable.

252. *Consequences.* The German law definition of gratuitousness is purposely restrictive. It excludes from the category of gifts any transfer that is designed to encourage another to act or that is designed to extinguish a debt, even if the debt is unenforceable. By narrowing the concept of gratuitousness, German law limits the application of gift law, and the reach of its gift-promise formalities, to purely one-sided transactions.

2. The Subjective Element

253. *Two types.* The second defining characteristic of a gift involves a subjective element, either donative intent or an agreement between the parties that the transaction will be gratuitous. In the common law, donative intent is, with delivery, one of the gift's two essential elements. As discussed below, civilian systems,

---

116 . Id. § 516 no. 16; Savigny (1841) 57.

117 . MünchKomm-BGB (-Kollhosser) § 516 no. 16. "In exchange for the receipt of this payment, the *naturalis obligatio* is discharged. Though it provides no cause of action, a natural obligation is nonetheless a patrimonial advantage [for the obligee], since a debtor with a proper legal attitude will satisfy this obligation even in the absence of legal compulsion." Savigny (1841) 57.

in contrast to the common law, characterize the gift as a contract.[118] In those jurisdictions, the general part of contract law usually validates a transaction only if the parties reach agreement on all essential elements. Some civilian jurisdictions specifically provide that the parties must agree that the transaction is to be gratuitous. In other civilian jurisdictions, legal acts must have a cause. The cause provides a legal basis for enforcing a transaction and serves as a guide to its characterization. In a synallagmatic contract, the cause is the quid pro quo. The notion of cause has been expanded to include donative intent (*animus donandi*). In those systems, the subjective issue is whether the donor had the subjective intent to make a gratuitous transfer.

254. *Justinian.* Justinian defined the gift principally in terms of animus donandi, the desire to perform an unselfish act of liberality in the absence of egoistic motives.[119] This represented a shift in focus. The Roman law definition had previously centered on gratuitousness, which Ulpian seemed to understand as the willed lack of equivalence. Gratuitousness had also been understood as the simultaneous enrichment of the donee and impoverishment of the donor (*locupletatio/depauperatio*). Justinian was not seeking to replace gratuitousness with an element more appreciative of the power of human will.[120] The problem was rather that the Byzantine jurists were aware of the characterization difficulties that arise when the gift is defined chiefly in terms of enrichment and impoverishment. They sought a definitional characteristic that would accommodate a greater variety of gifts. Once they settled on animus donandi, they had to define it. One of their chief criteria was whether the transfer takes place *spontaneously*, in other words *without legal compulsion* (*nullo iure cogente*).[121]

255. *Defining donative intent.* Donative intent has proved especially difficult to define. In legal systems in which cause is an issue, the competing doctrines differ widely in approach. One common element involves the judicial search for the donor's reasons for giving the gift. Yet, as Kreitner has explained in a well-documented article, placing the gift within the *economy of reasons* misconstrues

---

118. Infra nos. 1315–1340.
119. The Digest's chapter on gifts (*De donationibus*) opens by defining the gift in terms of the donor's motive.

> A person makes a gift with the intent that the property will immediately pass to the recipient and will, under no other circumstances, revert to the donor, and does this with no other motive (*causam*) than to display the donor's liberality and munificence (*et propter nullam aliam causam facit, quam ut liberalitatem et munificentiam exerceat*). This is properly called a gift.

D. 39, 5, 1 pr. See Zimmermann 496–497. The passage is generally considered interpolated from *et propter* to *exerceat*.
120. Archi (1964) 934. Ulpian's position can be inferred. See D. 39, 5, 19, 6.
121. Archi (1964) 935.

the gift's essential nature.[122] Many of the reasons for giving gifts, such as family bonds, charitable impulses, and the desire to reciprocate a prior kindness or to establish friendly relations, are usually not as clearly articulated as may be the case with an investment. Only rarely are the benefits of a gift explicitly weighed against its cost. We tend to rely rather on custom, on our feelings, and on a sense of our better selves. Because the motivation for gift giving remains unarticulated, we generally attribute the gift impulse to vague conceptions like gratitude and generosity. Yet a finding of donative intent may often depend on whether it is possible to create a convincing narrative about the donor's motivations.[123] If a gratuitous transfer is made without identifiable reasons, the courts are inclined to believe either that no gift was intended or that the donor was incompetent.

256. *Mutual dependency.* The elements of the legal notion of the gift are intended to operate together to exclude from the definition two types of transfers—those that, in common understanding, do not constitute gifts, and those for which the protection of the gift law regime is inappropriate. Those legal systems that construe one of the elements more narrowly tend to conceive another more expansively.

Gratuitousness and donative intent present an example of mutual dependency. In practice they are concerned with many of the same facts. The difference is that gratuitousness is examined from the objective point of view whereas donative intent is viewed subjectively. For this reason, donative intent tends to become more important as a limiting factor in legal systems, such as the French,

---

122. Kreitner 1925.

123. An American example may help to make clear the extent to which a finding of donative intent often depends on whether it is possible to discover a rational basis for the gift. See *In re Clark's Estate*, 39 N.Y.S. 722, 729–730 (Sur. Ct. 1896).

Ms. Richardson, the donee, had worked as the donor's housekeeper for twenty years. Her annual salary was $500. After the donor's death, cash and securities equal to $60,000 (over $1 million in today's dollars) were found in her possession. Nearly all of it came into her possession after the donor reached the age of eighty. Some time after the donor had reached that birthday, he accidentally fell while out walking, and $6,000 in cash that had been concealed in his hat was scattered on the ground. It was argued that he was incompetent and that there was no evidence of a gift to the donee.

The court was left to choose between several possible narratives, including incompetence, undue influence, fraud, and an executed gift. The court reached the latter result, based on the following reasoning.

> It appears that Mrs. Richardson had been his faithful housekeeper for almost a quarter of a century, taking charge of his elegant home, in which he was accustomed to entertain quite largely; and she was, no doubt, his confidential adviser in business matters, as she seems to be possessed of financial skill and ability scarcely less marked than that of her benefactor. It is easy to see how Dr. Clark might well have desired to reward her in a sum far exceeding simple compensation for services.

in which gratuitousness is defined broadly to include the simple lack of equivalence. Although donative intent constitutes an essential definitional element in some jurisdictions, it is considered unnecessary in others.

a. France and Belgium

257. *Cause.* In French law, the gift is considered a contract and, at least in theory, its formation is governed by the general principles of contract law.[124] Those principles require a valid cause (CC art. 1108).[125] The subjective element, donative intent (*intention libérale*), serves as the cause of the gift transaction.[126] Nonetheless, a few French authors have argued that neither cause nor donative intent are relevant to gift law.[127] De Page has contended that "[i]t was wrong to attempt at all costs to transpose the notion of cause, as it appears in the context of onerous acts, into a domain that is *essentially different*, namely gratuitous acts."[128] Cause is best understood as the essential reason that justifies both the legal act and its judicial recognition and enforcement.[129] For onerous acts, each party performs in order to receive the quid pro quo. De Page calls that a fundamental principle of human commerce. When examined from this point of view, the gift has no cause. As is frequently noted in the Italian discussion, the gift is *uncaused* or *acausal*.[130] Marcel Planiol, one of the leading critics of the notion of cause, believed that the gift is sufficiently defined by the notion of gratuitousness. Any recourse to subjective factors is surplusage.

> Whether a contract is gratuitous or onerous is determined solely by examining the relationship between the parties. It depends on whether the obligations they have undertaken are mutual. If each gives something to the other or undertakes an obligation as a counterpart of what is received, the act is onerous. This characterization is clear and easy to recognize .... If mutuality is lacking—that is, if one of the parties gives or does something while receiving nothing in return—the act is gratuitous.[131]

---

124. Nonetheless, there are numerous differences. See infra nos. 1331–1333. For differences relating to defects in consent (*vices de consentement*), see 5 Planiol and Ripert nos. 182–192.

125. 5 Planiol and Ripert no. 313.

126. Flour and Souleau nos. 40–42; see also Hamel.

127. Dawson believed that the notion of cause fulfilled "no meaningful functions at all .... In the gallery of ideas that have helped to liberate thought it therefore deserves a small corner located out in a distant wing." Dawson 114.

128. 8 De Page no. 250 (emphasis in original).

129. Id. no. 35.

130. Perozzi 544; infra no. 275.

131. Planiol, note to Nîmes 22 Jan. 1890, D.P. 1891 II 113.

In direct contrast to Planiol, Paul Esmein suggested that donative intent alone is sufficient to characterize a transfer as a gift, without recourse to the notion of gratuitousness.[132]

The majority view is that both gratuitousness and donative intent are essential to the legal notion of the gift. Neither element alone sufficiently delimits the institution. For example, the mere fact that an act is gratuitous, in the sense that equivalent value is not received, does not mean that the transaction is necessarily a gift. "The seller who sells property below market price is impoverished to the buyer's benefit. The insured who pays fire insurance premiums on property that does not perish by fire is impoverished to the carrier's profit. Yet neither the seller nor the insured has made a gift. The material element [gratuitousness] is present; what is missing is the element of intent."[133] The courts hold that there is a gift only if there is a showing of donative intent.[134] The simple lack of equivalence is not sufficient.[135]

i. The Classical View

258. *Abstract conception.* The nature of donative intent is subject to considerable controversy in French law.[136] The principal issue is whether the notion of cause should be understood abstractly or concretely. The classical authors—including Pothier, Aubry and Rau, Baudry-Lacantinerie, and Huc—construed the concept abstractly. They modeled the cause required for a gratuitous act on the notion of cause in synallagmatic contracts. In the context of a bargain, the parties' motives—the reasons they enter into the bargain—are irrelevant to the cause. The cause is rather the quid pro quo. Following this model, the classical authors held that cause in a gift transaction is the abstract intent to transfer property without receiving an equivalent.

The classical conception yields two problematic consequences. First, because the classical conception ignores the individual donor's particular motives, the cause of a gift can never be illicit. If it is concealed, it can never vitiate a gift. On the other hand, if the illicit motives are announced as a condition, a code provision specific to gratuitous transfers invalidates the condition but preserves the gift (CC art. 900). Illicit cause in the law of gifts would then differ from the principles that govern the remainder of French contract law. Second, the classical notion of cause seems to merge with the notion of consent. The desire to enter into a gratuitous transaction serves both as consent and as cause. The construction abrogates the code's requirement of two separate elements (CC art. 1108).[137]

---

132. Esmein 465–471.
133. Flour and Souleau no. 40.
134. Civ.¹ 1 June 1977, *Bull. civ.* I no. 259.
135. Civ.¹ 14 Feb. 1989, *Bull. civ.* I no. 79.
136. 8 De Page nos. 249–252.
137. 2 Mazeaud (-Chabas) no. 264.

Grimaldi, who defends the classical conception, responds that consent and cause are distinguishable. The intent to enter into a gratuitous transaction usually precedes the exchange of consent.[138]

ii. The Modern View

259. *Doctrinal view.* Partially to solve these problems, modern doctrine in the French tradition has tended to abandon the abstract conception of cause in the gift law context. Contemporary authors find cause not in the simple intent to give without receiving an equivalent, but rather in the motives that provoke the gift. Not all motives are taken into account. The notion of cause looks only to the main motive (*la cause impulsive et déterminante*).[139]

Though this view resolves the difficulties of the classical conception—once the reasons that motivated the gift can be examined, the cause may be found to be illicit[140]—this view too has been criticized.[141] It is often impossible to isolate a principal motive behind a gift. Moreover, the modern conception seems to contradict the well-accepted principle that gift and self-interest are not incompatible. A transaction may be considered a gift even if the donor's chief motive is an expectation of profit or the desire to cause harm. Some donors give with the hope of eliciting even greater favors in return, whereas others make gift transfers out of disdain for their families. In both cases, even if the nongratuitous motives predominate, the transaction remains a gift.[142] Some authors argue that only rarely does anyone do anything that does not provide personal benefit. The pleasure donors seek is their own.[143] Because of these difficulties, some contemporary authors recommend returning to the abstract conception of cause.[144]

260. *Case law.* The case law makes use of both the abstract and the concrete conceptions of donative intent. The abstract conception is used to distinguish gifts from onerous transactions. Donative intent here means the intent to make

---

138. Grimaldi no. 1006.

139. 8 De Page no. 35.

140. Id. no. 249 par. B.

141. Flour and Souleau no. 41.

142. Some *coutumes* in the ancien régime voided gifts made with the principal purpose of causing prejudice to the heirs. 1 Ricard no. 619 (referring to the Custom of Brittany art. 199).

143. "If someone gives, it is always due to some moral interest; without it, the gift would not be made. The interest consists, at a minimum, in the intimate satisfaction that a generous act provides—in this joy that moralists claim is the most pure—the joy at the pleasure given to others." Flour and Souleau no. 44. In this context, Grimaldi invokes Pascal, "Nothing is as close to charity as greed, and nothing is as remote." Grimaldi no. 1006 note 56, quoting Pascal, *Pensées* sec. 10 no. 663.

144. Grimaldi no. 1006; Flour and Souleau no. 42; Vincent Brémond, note to Civ.² 28 Nov. 2002, D. 2003, 1871.

a transfer without receiving an equivalent.[145] This animus donandi exceeds the normal contractual notion of consent because the donor must have the intent to make a sacrifice (*volonté du sacrifice*). Mere knowledge that a quid pro quo is lacking is not sufficient to characterize the transaction as a gift.

The cases draw subtle distinctions when the transfer responds to a sense of obligation. The donor's sense that the transfer fulfills a moral duty is not sufficient to prevent the transaction from being characterized as a gift. However, the intent to compensate the donee for exceptional services is enough to negate donative intent. Two recent cases illustrate the distinction.

The first concerned the alleged tax liability of the Jehovah's Witnesses for a large number of small gifts they had received. The gifts amounted to FF 250,000,000.[146] The group argued that the small contributions were not gifts because they were made in fulfillment of a natural obligation of Christian generosity. The donors' goal was to receive moral satisfaction from the contributions. Applying the abstract notion of cause, the court held that intentional economic sacrifice was a sufficient gift cause. The concrete motives, including the moral conviction that a natural obligation was involved, were not sufficient to characterize the transfers as onerous. Only the existence of a genuine material counterpart would have indicated that the contributions were not gifts.

In the second case, the French tax authority sought gift tax due on two checks, totaling more than a million French francs, that the donor delivered to the donee a few months before the donor's death.[147] The donor intended to compensate the donee for services of exceptional quality performed over a long period. The appellate court held that the existence of a counterpart prevented the transaction from being gratuitous. The Cassation Court rejected the reasoning based on a lack of gratuitousness. The appellate court had not inquired whether the two performances were of equivalent value. Yet the high court affirmed, holding that the existence of the counterpart negated the existence of donative intent.

When the gift is challenged for a false or illicit cause, however, the courts engage in a subjective or concrete appreciation of motives. If the gift is avoided on these grounds, it is avoided as a gift.[148]

iii. Conceptual Difficulties

261. *Problematic questions.* The notion of donative intent distinguishes gifts from onerous transactions. The delimitation is especially difficult in two cases.

---

145. 5 Planiol and Ripert no. 320.

146. Trib. gr. inst. Nanterre 4 July 2000, *Rép. not. Defrén.* 2002 art. 37454 at 3 obs. Nathalie Peterka.

147. Com. 19 Dec. 2006, *Bull. civ.* IV no. 260, *Rev. trim. dr. civ.* 2007, 603 obs. Michel Grimaldi.

148. 5 Planiol and Ripert no. 320.

The first involves the payment of a natural obligation. The second concerns the proper characterization of a gift that benefits the donor.

(A) PAYMENT OF A NATURAL OBLIGATION

262. *Duty of conscience.* As discussed above, classical doctrine considers the execution of a natural obligation to be equivalent to the payment of a debt.[149] Because payment of a debt is not gratuitous, it can never be a gift. In the modern conception, however, gift and natural obligation are no longer mutually exclusive.[150] French writers generally no longer conceive of the natural obligation as a civil obligation that has failed to ripen completely or that has lost its sanction. Instead, the natural obligation is thought of as a duty of conscience to be recognized and performed.[151] The performance of a duty of conscience may be characterized as a gift. Modern French doctrine has tended to use donative intent as the criterion for determining which payments of a natural obligation should be characterized as gifts. The discussion is varied and complex. The summary here is greatly simplified.

263. *Compensation and generosity.* According to Georges Ripert, one of the leading authorities, the distinction depends on the nature of the moral duty involved.[152] Current doctrine seems to follow Ripert in distinguishing between a duty of compensation (*devoir de justice*) and a duty of generosity (*devoir de charité*).[153] If a transfer is made under a duty of compensation—such as the payment of a debt on which the statute of limitations has run—the act constitutes payment. If, on the other hand, the transfer is dictated by a duty of generosity—such as the constitution of a dowry by the young person's parents or providing assistance to a collateral relative—the transaction is a gift.[154]

264. *Distinctions.* Several distinctions remain to be made. The first is the basic task of identifying those moral duties that create natural obligations. "Though there has been a progressive assimilation of natural obligation and moral duty, the two do not completely coincide Only those moral duties are transformed into natural obligations that, at a certain time, are determined by the legislature

---

149. Supra no. 240.

150. Some contemporary authors in the French tradition continue to insist on the incompatibility of the two concepts. See 4 Mazeaud (-Leveneur and Mazeaud-Leveneur) no. 1325; 8 De Page no. 402 par. A.

151. "[T]here is a natural obligation when the law attaches certain legal effects to the fulfillment of a moral duty." Ripert (1949) no. 192. Flour and Souleau nos. 46–48.

152. Ripert (1949) nos. 194–202.

153. Id. no. 199; 5 Planiol and Ripert no. 319; Flour and Souleau no. 47.

154. As indicated below, the same distinctions arise with regard to the enforceability of gift promises. Promises to perform a natural duty of compensation may be enforceable, whereas promises to perform a natural duty of charity are gratuitous and therefore void. See infra no. 676.

or the courts to conform completely to general social interest and to be fully recognized by common opinion."[155] The case law today derives natural obligations from the duty not to harm others, the duty of gratitude, the duty of assistance, the duty to pay gaming debts and other illicit obligations, and the duty to perform obligations that are unenforceable because they have not been completed in the proper form.[156]

A second difficulty is the distinction between the duty of compensation and the duty of generosity. The problem arises, as Dean Ripert noted, because virtually every gift represents the satisfaction of a duty of conscience.[157] However, some duties are more precise; others are more general. Some are owed to a specific individual for a specific reason; others represent a more general sense of social obligation. In some, the debtor feels a debt-like obligation; in others, the debtor feels simply that it is the right thing to do. An obligation sufficiently precise and strict is a duty of justice. Its satisfaction constitutes payment. A transfer made simply because it is the right thing to do is a gift. Finally, if the transfer represents a simple humanitarian gesture, it does not fulfill any obligation at all.[158]

265. *Unresolved.* The continuing discussion is complex and has not reached consensus. "In sum, it is apparent that the question of the existence of a natural obligation to give remains rather confused and that no theory finds decisive support in the case law."[159] Even Dean Ripert, whose theory seems to have prevailed, admitted that the courts take advantage of the doctrine's flexibility to validate transactions they believe should be enforced. "In many cases there seems to be no reason to speak of a natural obligation, but when the courts wish to avoid finding a gift but also are unable to locate a legal duty, they say, in order to make donative intent disappear, that there has been fulfillment of a natural obligation."[160] Ghestin has suggested that the flexibility may be a benefit in this area, because the courts can more easily accommodate the needs of individual cases. "The recourse to natural obligation permits the courts, under the cover of this fluid concept, to deform the institutions of positive law, particularly the notion and regime of gratuitous transfers, as required by practical considerations."[161]

266. *Comparative notes.* Donative intent plays a critical role in French law in distinguishing a gift from neighboring transactions. The distinction between

---

155. 7 Planiol and Ripert no. 982.
156. Id. nos. 985–990. Dean Ripert seems to have been the first to enumerate these duties. Ripert (1949) nos. 195–202.
157. Ripert (1949) no. 202.
158. Id. nos. 199, 202.
159. 1 Ghestin no. 689 at 670.
160. Ripert (1949) no. 202.
161. 1 Ghestin no. 689 at 668.

donative intent and the intent to fulfill a natural obligation is a central aspect of this delimitation. Gifts are often given in the context of interpersonal relationships that, over time, have generated different types of obligations. Gift law must therefore find a method to distinguish those transactions that can be left to customary norms from those for which a protective regime is required. The distinction matters. Gifts are absolutely void if not completed in the required formalities, while a natural obligation can be satisfied without form. Gifts are subject to capacity limitations and collation and revocation, whereas the satisfaction of a natural obligation often is not. If the boundary between gift and natural obligation is imprecise, it means that, in practice, French law has not managed to define the legal institution of the gift.

(B) INTENT TO BENEFIT THE DONOR

267. *Conditional gifts.* When a gift is made to benefit the donor, characterization problems arise that are difficult in every system. These are usually conditional gifts or gifts coupled with an obligation.[162] As discussed above, French law uses the abstract conception of cause to distinguish a gift from an onerous transaction.[163] It is sufficient cause for a gift that the donor intends to become poorer without receiving a counterpart. However, these gifts satisfy some interest of the donor. Can the transaction be a gift if the donor receives a counterpart?

268. *Moral and material interest.* French law distinguishes between two types of benefit that donors may intend to gain from their gifts. The first is material, the second moral. In a traditional hypothetical, a donor donates real estate to a township to permit the construction of a church. If the donor makes the gift to increase the value of the donor's contiguous property, the donor is satisfying a material interest.[164] If, on the other hand, the donor is feeling charitable, the interest is moral.

269. *Earlier case law.* Both the school hypotheticals and the cases frequently involve either a gift to a charitable institution or what is known as an offer of collaboration (*offre de concours*).[165] The case law is difficult to interpret and has evolved with the years.[166] It seems that the courts initially held that any intended interest on the part of the donor, whether material or moral, rendered the

---

162. Flour and Souleau nos. 43–45.

163. Supra no. 260.

164. Civ. 19 July 1894, D.P. 1895 I 125.

165. The offer of collaboration (*offre de concours*) involves a gift made to permit a public entity to complete public works that will ultimately benefit the donor.

166. Flour and Souleau nos. 44–45; Grimaldi no. 1007 (explaining the case law evolution) and notes 68–70 (collecting cases). Dawson provides a critical assessment of the older case law. See Dawson (1980) 83–96.

act onerous.[167] In a celebrated case, the donor gave funds to replace a church bell tower. It was to be restored exactly as he remembered it during his youth, *telle qu'il la rêvait dans les vagues réminiscences de son jeune âge.* The court found that the gift was designed to satisfy the donor's caprice, fantasy, and vanity. He therefore received the equivalent of what he had promised. As a result, the act was onerous.[168] Apparently, this and similar decisions were chiefly concerned with whether the transactions should be exempted from gift law formalities, it being understood that they would remain subject to the substantive rules pertaining to collation and reduction.[169] As a result, whenever the donor specified the use for which the funds were to be used, the gift became an onerous act.

270. *More recent case law.* Subsequent French case law at first accepted the doctrinal suggestion that material and moral interests should be distinguished. In the earlier of the more recent cases, the courts held that the act was onerous if the interest was material, while it was a gift if the interest was merely moral. Then, in a new phase, the courts held that both types of interest were compatible with gift giving, provided a specific condition was not mentioned in the documentation.[170] The most recent case law now seems to have returned to the original conception. As *favor donationis*, the courts once again hold that any interest, whether material or moral, renders the transfer onerous.[171] However, there is no agreement as to the legal effect. Some authors suggest that a transfer that

---

167. Considering that a contract does not necessarily cease to be onerous and become an act of pure liberality merely because one of the parties does not receive a material advantage capable of expression in monetary terms;—That, on the contrary, it is a certain principle that one of the two obligations that make up the synallagmatic contract can have for cause a purely moral interest, even though its object, the cause of the agreed counterpart, is of an exclusively pecuniary interest;—That it is for this reason that the interest that a person might attach to the execution of a natural obligation, to the accomplishing of a duty of pure conscience, or even, according to certain decisions ... to the simple satisfaction of vanity or self esteem (*amour-propre*) or to greater convenience in performing acts of piety may constitute a sufficient cause for a commutative contract."
Trib. Langres 15 March 1900, D. 1900 II 422 at 424.
168. Req. 24 April 1863, D. 1863 I 402, S. 1863 I 362.
169. 5 Planiol and Ripert no. 315.
170. Flour and Souleau no. 45.
171. "[H]aving found that Pierre de Bausset, fulfilling the wishes of his uncle, attempted, by his contribution, to receive moral and religious satisfaction from 'having given support to the free school of Boigny,' the Court of Appeal decided as a question of fact (*souveraine-ment*) that this benefit excluded donative intent." Civ.[1] 1 Mar. 1988, *Bull. civ.* I no. 52, J.C.P. 1989 II 21373 note Martine Béhar-Touchais, *Rev. trim. dr. civ.* 1988, 800 obs. Jean Patarin; Grimaldi no. 1007.

responds to the donor's moral interest should not be exempt from collation and reduction.[172]

Not all the scholars agree that a gift cannot be made in the donor's interest. As Martine Béhar-Touchais has written, "This reasoning fails to satisfy at least this commentator, who, leaving aside for the moment whether the decision is justified on a technical level, believes that it would be difficult to explain to a person in the street that religious or moral interest is enough to disqualify an act as a gift."[173] The excessively subjective conception of the notion of cause, she argues, is, in effect, "a device to destroy (*à faire sauter*) the law governing liberalities."[174] The problem seems especially difficult when gifts are made to charitable or religious associations, because all such gifts are designed to fulfill some religious or moral purpose.[175] Mme Béhar-Touchais fails to mention, however, that a person in the street might reconsider once the focus shifts to the practical consequence, namely that these charitable transfers are facilitated if they are not considered gifts.

iv. Tipping

271. *Civil obligation.* The tensions among the various theories of cause become apparent by examining the controversy about whether a tip (*pourboire*) should be considered a gift.[176] The analysis begins by asking whether tipping satisfies the customer's civil obligation to the employee. If it does, it cannot be a gift. Though tipping is a customary practice, French doctrine believes that, because it cannot be judicially compelled, it does not represent a civil obligation. Nor does tipping fulfill a natural obligation of compensation, since restaurant, hotel, and taxi charges generally include a service component. Because the tip does not constitute payment of a civil obligation, some scholars argue that it fits within the legal definition of a gift. Moreover, because tipping might be said to satisfy a duty of generosity, donative intent is arguably present. The difficulty, however, is that duties of generosity are most frequently found in the family context. A second theory considers the tip to be a remunerative gift, a reward for services rendered.

If tipping is characterized as a gift, the rigorous gift law formalities of French law would usually not pose a problem. Tips are generally given by manual transfer, and the *don manuel* is valid in French law as an exception to the form requirements.[177] The problem concerns rather the legal effects. Tips would then be subject to collation and reduction. French doctrine generally argues that tips are

---

172. 5 Planiol and Ripert no. 315 *in fine.*
173. Martine Béhar-Touchais, note to Civ.[1] 1 Mar. 1988, J.C.P. 1989 II 21373 no. 1.
174. Id. no. 6.
175. One effect of these holdings was to circumvent the restrictions on the capacity of associations to receive gifts. For those limitations, see infra nos. 503–519.
176. 5 Planiol and Ripert no. 317.
177. Infra nos. 780–797.

not gifts to avoid this result.[178] According to a third theory, a tip satisfies the donor's moral or material interest. The donor receives moral satisfaction from the tip and may seek to assure good service in the future. As mentioned above, if tipping satisfies any of the donor's interests, the tip may be excluded from gift law, at least for purposes of gift formalities.

However, though the satisfaction of the donor's moral or material interest allows the transfer to be onerous for the purpose of form, the transfer might remain a gift for other purposes. It is precisely the other consequences that French law has sought to avoid. To achieve the desired result, French law has become creative. Tipping is now said not to be a gift because a tip represents only a small portion of the donor's patrimony. The donor does not become noticeably poorer as a result of the tip. Moreover, the employee does not consider the tip to be a gift but looks on it rather as a salary component, as compensation for services rendered. And of course tips are taxed as salary. In other words, there is no agreement on its gratuitous character. Moreover, as a practical matter, it would be impossible to apply the full force of substantive gift law to tipping. "The heavy regime governing liberalities is not designed to apply to the small presents that a person distributes, in the course of a lifetime, to family members or strangers."[179]

272. *Maussian view.* From the point of view of the Maussian obligations to give, to receive, and to reciprocate, tipping makes sense. Even when the employee's salary amply compensates the employee for the service (which is not always the case), many employees seek to offer something more. Some employees may be seeking a larger tip, but others may simply wish to offer more than they receive in compensation. In the Maussian scheme, this excess must be reciprocated. For the same reason, even professionals may occasionally receive a transfer that resembles a tip. When medical doctors provide personalized care that significantly exceeds their obligations to the health insurance carrier, their patients may send elaborate holiday baskets in an attempt to reciprocate.

273. *Comparative notes.* As the example of the tip demonstrates, it is difficult to grasp the relationship between giving and reciprocating in the categories available to French law. These categories are designed to determine which gratuitous transfers should be subject to the protection afforded by the gift regime. The traditional concept of cause as used in contract law is not able to draw the proper distinctions. In the end, both the case law and the scholars ignore traditional legal constructions and rely instead on a commonsense view of the societal customs appropriate in the circumstances.

---

178. 5 Planiol and Ripert no. 317; Flour and Souleau no. 33.
179. Flour and Souleau id.

b. Italy

274. *Cause*. The Italian Civil Code expressly characterizes the gift as a contract (CC art. 769). Since a valid cause is a prerequisite for an enforceable contract (CC art. 1325 no. 2), it also serves as a definitional element for the gift. The code also expressly requires animus donandi (*spirito di liberalità*; CC art. 769).[180] Animus donandi is therefore generally considered the cause of the gift.[181] Animus donandi is defined in case law and doctrine as the donor's intent to make a gratuitous transfer without being obligated to do so, even by a natural obligation.[182]

i. Relevance

275. *No cause*. Respected Italian comparativists deny that the gift has a cause.[183] In their view, it is the absence of cause that explains gift law's strict form requirements.[184] Biondo Biondi questioned whether cause serves any function in the typical gift transaction. He noted that cause was retained in the 1942 Civil Code, partly out of respect for the tradition, but "chiefly because a Fascist Code, inspired by the regime of solidarity, could not ignore the notion [of cause] without neglecting its view that a contract should have socially useful content."[185] In some of the most lucid pages ever devoted to the topic, Biondi explained that the notion of cause, when applied to the gift transaction, does not offer a logically coherent unity but rather presents inconsistent layers of law and doctrine as they have piled up over the course of history.[186]

In the typical gift transaction, Biondi argued, cause serves none of the functions that are traditionally ascribed to it. For example, it does not prevent the enforcement of illicit contracts. Those contracts are invalidated instead based on statutory or judicial prohibition. Of course, if a transaction lacks animus donandi, it is not a gift, but that conclusion is derived from the statutory definition of gift in Italian law rather than from the notion of cause. Biondi concluded that the typical gift transaction does not contain a cause that could in any way be isolated from its other elements. The cause of the gift is the gift itself.[187]

---

180. Cass. 10 Jan. 1973 no. 37, *Rep. Foro it.* 1973 *Registro (imposta di)* no. 185.

181. Cian and Trabucchi art. 769 no. 2.

182. Id.

183. [I]n exchange contracts, the cause is part of the contract's content. This makes clear why, outside contract, cause is not mentioned—and it would make no sense to mention it!—and why cause is irrelevant to the nature of the gift. It also makes clear that it took some effort to insert generous motive into the notion of cause, a subjective 'cause,' so that gratuitous transfers might be said to have a cause.

1 Sacco 637.

184. 1 Gorla 196, 316.

185. *Relazione al Re* no. 79, in 4 Pandolfelli et al. 171.

186. Biondi nos. 134–140.

187. Id. no. 138 at 425–426.

Should we perhaps wait for a jurist of genius who, like a new Messiah, will finally inform us what cause means for contracts and for gift law in particular? The wait would be in vain. Our positive law, particularly in the matter of contracts and gifts, is the result of a centuries-old stratification in which rationality is so tightly interwoven with chance, tradition with progress, precision with confusion, that it is extremely difficult, if not impossible, to create a doctrinal construction that conforms to our positive law.[188]

ii. Conflicting Conceptions

276. *Divergent views.* Among those who maintain that a cause is required for a valid gift, the nature of the requirement has inspired widely divergent views. The authors almost universally reject the French doctrinal view that the donor's principal motive might serve as the cause. In general, the donor's motives are irrelevant, except in the case of remunerative or customary gifts.[189] To avoid the subjectivist French doctrinal conception, the Italian authors have produced numerous theories.

277. *Abstract conception.* The abstract conception, also called the objective theory, seems to be the prevailing view. It considers the cause of the gift to be the willed enrichment of the donee at the donor's expense,[190] or the willed enrichment of the patrimony of another without receipt of a counterpart.[191] The difficulty with this understanding is that it duplicates the requirement of consent.[192] Balbi considers the cause to be the psychological representation that is present in the minds of each of the parties to the gift transaction. This representation or conception precedes the volitional act and, to some extent, can be said to cause it.[193] In Torrente's view, the gift's cause is its goal or purpose (*scopo*).[194] When considered objectively, the purpose of the transaction is to enrich the donee, a goal that distinguishes the gift from other gratuitous transactions. When the purpose is instead considered from the parties' subjective point of view, it is animus donandi, the intent to make a patrimonial attribution without a quid pro quo.[195]

278. *Case law.* The case law seems to follow Torrente and combine the objective and the subjective theories. It considers the cause to be the coincidence of two

---

188. Id. no. 138.
189. Id. The donor's personal motives, including affection, charity, vanity, and the like, are relevant to the Italian notion of cause when questions of voidability arise, such as mistake with regard to motive (CC art. 787) or illegal motive (art. 788).
190. Capozzi nos. 330 par. a, 332 par. b.
191. Cian and Trabucchi art. 769 no. 2.
192. Balbi 16.
193. Id.
194. Torrente (2006) 212.
195. Id. 221–222.

factors. The first is the economic-social function of the typical gift, enrichment of the donee and impoverishment of the donor. The second is animus donandi, the purpose of making a gratuitous transfer freely and spontaneously and without being bound to do so.[196] In difficult cases, however, the conception proves unhelpful. In a case discussed above, a donor gave land and funding to a town, subject to the proviso that the town construct an agricultural school on the property and name it after the donor's deceased son.[197] The Cassation Court held that the transaction was a gift. Yet from the perspective of the dual nature of cause, it is difficult to understand how the donor can be said to have intended to enrich the donee without receiving a benefit in return.[198]

iii. Atypical Liberalities

279. *Liberalities beyond gift law.* As Biondi also noted, cause provides a means to characterize what Italian law considers *atypical* liberalities *(liberalità atipiche),* namely those that result in a gratuitous transfer outside the domain of gift law. These liberalities are made by acts that can produce either gratuitous or nongratuitous transfers, such as a third-party beneficiary contract or the construction of a building on another's property. Because atypical liberalities have economic results similar to gifts, they are governed by some substantive elements of gift law (CC art. 809). Atypical liberalities are distinguished from nongratuitous uses of the same institutions by their cause, which, like the direct gift, includes the donee's enrichment as an objective factor and animus donandi as the subjective element.[199]

(A) TYPES

280. *Several categories.* Atypical liberalities can be divided into several categories. A first group involves gifts usually given on the occasion of services rendered or otherwise in conformity with custom. These are usually called customary gifts *(liberalità d'uso).* For reasons discussed just below, the code excludes customary gifts from the domain of gift law (CC art. 770 par. 2). A second group resembles in practice what French jurists call the indirect gift, a concept also used to

---

196. Cass. 3 June 1980 no. 3621, *Giur. it.* 1981 I 1101 at 1108–1109.

197. Cass. 18 Dec. 1975 no. 4153 (en banc), *Giur. it.* 1976 I 1913; supra no. 247.

198. The Court's answer to the question was circular. Id. at 1915–1916. The Court conceded that the donor's principal motive was the moral benefit of seeing a school named after her son, but noted that the transfer would lack donative intent only if the parties' performances were connected as part of a bargain. The Court concluded that there could be no bargain because the donor had chosen to make the transfer in the form of a gift. The problem with the reasoning is that legal characterization is usually considered a question of law and is not generally left to the parties.

199. Biondi no. 139.

describe them in Italian law (*donazione indiretta*).[200] These include transactions that differ from the gift but that result in the same type of enrichment.[201] For some authors, the category of indirect gifts also includes the gift mixed with an exchange contract (*negotium mixtum cum donatione*).

(B) CUSTOMARY GIFTS

281. *Theories.* As mentioned above, the Italian Code excludes certain gratuitous transfers from the domain of gift law. These include both gifts given in conformity to custom (*conformità agli usi*) and gifts usually given on the occasion of services rendered (*servizi resi*; art. 770 par. 2). Customary gifts include most common presents, from depositing spare change in collection boxes and giving tips to servers to bestowing significant wedding presents.[202] A typical gift on the occasion of services rendered is the present given to a doctor who provides particularly attentive care.[203]

Numerous theories have been proposed to explain why these transfers are not considered gifts. Some authors argue that gratuitousness is lacking because these gifts are not given freely but instead are intended to satisfy a customary obligation.[204] However, as the leading case points out, usages are not usually equivalent to social obligations.[205] Though it may be customary to make payments on certain occasions, such as a tip to servers or bellhops, individuals remain free to follow or reject the practice. Custom can suggest but not require these payments.[206] A failure to perform is not sanctioned, not even socially. Since rules of custom are not binding, the transfer remains gratuitous. Others contend that the transferor's intent to conform to custom negates donative intent, since the transferor does not intend to enrich the transferee at the transferor's expense but seeks rather to follow the rules prescribed by custom.[207]

For Torrente, in contrast, the difference between gift and customary gift is not found in their elements. Both are spontaneous acts and neither fulfills a legally recognized obligation. The difference lies rather in their differing social roles. A gift transfer generally concerns only the donor and the donee. A customary gift, on the other hand, has a more profound social impact. The customary gift is designed to improve social relations, to make life in society more cordial and

---

200. Id. no. 294. For the manner of making a customary gift in Italian law, see infra nos. 763–766. For the indirect gift, see infra nos. 344, 767. For indirect gifts in French law, see infra nos. 827–843.

201. Rescigno (-Carnevali) 498.

202. Biondi no. 244.

203. Capozzi no. 332 par. d.

204. Torrente (2006) 105, referring to the positions of Fulvio Maroi and Francesco Messineo.

205. Cass. 3 June 1980 no. 3621, *Giur. it.* 1981 I 1101 at 1110.

206. Biondi no. 245.

207. Torrente (2006) 106, referring to the view of Antonio D'Angelo.

affectionate.[208] Gifts given on the occasion of services rendered also satisfy the important social goal of assuring appropriate compensation. The distinction is not caused by a missing element, such as donative intent. Instead, customary giving is exempted from the gift regime in order to encourage it.

Biondi argued that there is no theoretical basis to distinguish gift and customary gift. The distinction is purely practical. Customary gifts are a staple of social life. They are by definition socially acceptable and pose little risk to the donor. It would make no sense to subject them to the elaborate regime of gift law.[209]

There is difficulty distinguishing between gifts made for purposes of special remuneration, which are subject to gift formalities, and customary gifts on the occasion of services rendered, which are not. The leading case distinguishes the two on the basis of the presence or absence of animus donandi, present in the remunerative gift and absent in the customary gift.[210] The following factors usually imply animus donandi: the gift is given freely and spontaneously, proportionality is lacking between the value of the service rendered and the value of the transfer, and there is no relevant usage. When these factors are present the gift is remunerative and not customary.

iv. Natural Obligation

282. *Never a gift.* In Italian law, the execution of a natural obligation (*obbligazione naturale*) is never a gift.[211] The satisfaction of an obligation is considered incompatible with the required spontaneity. A transfer is a gift only if made *nullo iure cogente.*[212] Italian law has had difficulty defining the notion of natural obligation.

According to the dominant view, followed in part by the case law, natural obligations are based on socially recognized moral duties.[213] These are duties that have been respected consistently enough over a long period that they are felt to be ethically binding. A breach would generally be considered improper. When these duties are performed, the transfer is not spontaneous, and therefore not a gift.[214] This view seems to be consistent with the language of the code, which implicitly refers to the fulfillment of a natural obligation (without using the

---

208. Torrente (2006) 109–110.

209. Biondi no. 245 at 755.

210. Cass. 5 Apr. 1975 no. 1218, *Giur. it.* 1975 I 1984 at 1987 note M. Grossi.

211. Torrente and Schlesinger § 235. For an analysis and critique of the competing Italian theories on the relation between gift and natural obligation, see 1 Gorla § 11; Oppo.

212. Cass. 3 June 1980 no. 3621, *Giur. it.* 1981 I 1101 at 1108.

213. Torrente (2006) 229; Balbi 64.

214. "[T]he fact that the natural obligation is not legally binding (*la non vincolatività per l'ordinamento giuridico*) does not prevent the donor from believing that a duty is owed to the donee and that the gift satisfies that duty .... This belief negates all necessary freedom and spontaneity with regard to the patrimonial attribution and thereby precludes a gratuitous transfer, which is incompatible with the belief that one is acting in fulfillment

phrase) in terms of "what has been transferred spontaneously in performance of moral or social duties" (CC art. 2034 par. 1). Numerous particular duties have been recognized in the case law, including the performance of a contract that is void due to a form defect, providing maintenance to a needy relative or to children born out of wedlock, payment for services rendered without fee, reimbursement for harm caused, payment of interest earned but not contracted for, payment of a debt discharged in bankruptcy, and the confirmation or execution of a void gift or bequest.[215]

It remains difficult to distinguish between remunerative gifts, which must be made by notarial act (CC art. 770) and the satisfaction of a natural obligation, for which no form is specified.[216] The Italian discussion distinguishes the duty of gratitude from the remaining social and moral duties. If the gift is motivated by gratitude for a specific service rendered, it is a remunerative gift and subject to the form requirements. If, on the other hand, the intent is to fulfill a general moral or social duty, a natural obligation is involved and the transfer is not a gift.[217] In other words, a gift is remunerative only if it is given spontaneously with the intent to enrich the donee and in the belief that it fulfills no obligation, whether legal, moral, or social, and is not compelled by legal or moral norms. Because the duty of gratitude is believed to have less intensity and create less of a sense of obligation, a transfer made in satisfaction of that duty may be a gift.

Nonetheless, as Richter has pointed out, the boundary between the remunerative gift and the fulfillment of a natural obligation remains conceptually unclear. He speaks of the

> difficult distinction ... given the rather fluid if not totally uncertain boundary between the two institutions, such that some have doubted whether there is any difference between the two, observing that the two figures in the end coincide and overlap to the point that their substantial identity actually permits the characterization, in the majority of cases, of the same facts as either the fulfillment of a natural obligation or as a remunerative gift.[218]

Yet this is the line in Italian law between animus donandi and onerous transaction, between gift and nongift.

In the Italian understanding, if a transfer fulfills a socially recognized moral duty, the law leaves the parties as it finds them. The obligation is not legally

---

of an obligation." Cass. 3 June 1980 no. 3621, *Giur. it.* 1981 I 1101 at 1108, *Giust. civ.* 1980 I 2138 at 2141 note Maria Costanza.

215. Torrente (2006) 237–248.

216. As noted in the Italian discussion, remuneration of past services is also a moral and social duty. Some authors have therefore questioned why it is treated differently from the performance of a natural obligation. Moscati no. 6.

217. Capozzi no. 348 pars. f, h.

218. Richter 153.

enforceable, and the law will not coerce performance. Yet these transfers remain valid despite the absence of form. If the obligation is satisfied, the law will not provide restitution (CC art. 2034). In contrast, Italian law considers gifts to rest on individual moral choices that do not correspond to social obligations.[219] When purely individual conscience is at work, public policy is thought to mandate the protective regime of the notarial act and the corresponding penalty of nullity. Yet the contrast between gift and performance of a natural obligation is not easy to maintain. Both are dictated by the demands of social morality, and both leave room for individual discretion. The decision to make payment on an unenforceable obligation is an act of individual conscience that differs little from gift giving. In its effort to distinguish the fulfillment of a natural obligation from a gift, Italian law raises a question that it does not answer, namely why the duty of gratitude, as recognized in the Maussian obligations, should not be considered a socially sanctioned moral duty. If it were, then most gifts would not be subject to the form requirements.

c. Germany

283. *Agreement.* As the subjective element, the German Civil Code requires an agreement about the gratuitous character of the transaction (CC § 516 par. 1). The agreement may be implied.[220] The requirement is justified by the general principle that parties cannot be compelled to give or receive gifts against their will.[221] In one case, one party rendered services gratuitously, while the recipient later promised to pay for them. The payment was held not to be gratuitous.[222] Similarly, when the transferor considers the transfer to be gratuitous but the recipient considers the transfer to be compensation, the transfer is not a gift.[223] The result depends on the goals and intent of the parties at the moment the contract was concluded.[224]

At the turn of the previous century, a German scholar suggested that agreement on the gratuitous nature of the transaction is the gift's only essential characteristic.[225] Nonetheless, the suggestion that agreement is required for a valid gift has been challenged by scholars who believe that a unilateral declaration should suffice.[226] All agree that donative intent is not required.[227] Because

---

219. Moscati no. 6 at 370–371.

220. Palandt (-Weidenkaff) § 516 nos. 6, 11.

221. MünchKomm-BGB (-Kollhosser) § 516 no. 9.

222. RG 22 Nov. 1909, RGZ 72, 188; Dawson (1980) 158–159.

223. Staudinger (-Wimmer-Leonhardt) § 516 no. 42; Dawson (1980) 159.

224. RG 22 Feb. 1940, RGZ 163, 257 at 259–260.

225. Burckhard 145.

226. Heck § 94 par. 3 lit. a.

227. The provisions on contract formation in the German Civil Code do not expressly require proof of a valid cause. Though the code has not completely abandoned the notion

German law defines gratuitousness as the absence of mutuality of obligation, a separate requirement of animus donandi is thought to be unnecessary.

284. *Motive.* The donor's extra-contractual motives are not relevant. Whether the donor acts altruistically or egoistically does not affect the characterization. If the transfer constitutes payment of a natural obligation, it is not a gift. Objectively, as discussed above, the payment of a natural obligation is not gratuitous because the transfer and the obligation are linked. Moreover, subjective agreement about gratuitousness is also lacking. On the other hand, if the transfer is intended as the performance of a moral or customary duty, the (often implicit) agreement about gratuitousness will suffice to make it a gift.[228] However, as Dawson correctly pointed out, donative intent comes in through the back door, because the decision often turns on whether the donor felt a sense of obligation in making the transfer.[229]

285. *Tipping.* Despite assurances by the German doctrine to the contrary, animus donandi is used occasionally when characterization difficulties arise. One such case involves the tip (*Trinkgeld*) and other payments made for services rendered. German law employs several theories to avoid imposing the gift law regime on such payments. To begin with, many tips are considered customary gifts (*Anstandsschenkungen*). Customary gifts are those that the donor must give to avoid the loss in respect and reputation that a breach of the customs of a particular milieu would entail (CC § 534).[230] Because tips are generally made by manual transfer, they pose no formation difficulty, and the code expressly exempts them from the rules governing revocation.[231]

Jhering suggested that the legal concept of the tip has little practical consequence.[232] Nonetheless, a problem arises in distinguishing tips considered gifts from those understood as compensation. Some tips, such as those given to furniture movers, represent additional compensation for especially competent performance. The boundary between the two institutions is "admittedly fluid."[233] German law asks whether the donor intended the payment to be compensation (*Entlohnung*) or a bonus (*Belohnung*). To resolve the matter, German law turns to the subjective criteria it normally eschews and closely examines the transferor's intent. "In the case of 'compensation,' the transferor is of the belief that the

---

of cause, it tends to replace it, where needed, with a form requirement. See MünchKomm-BGB (-Thode) § 305 nos. 16–22.

228. Staudinger (-Wimmer-Leonhardt) § 516 no. 42.

229. Dawson (1980) 162; RG 30 Sept. 1929, RGZ 125, 380 at 383–384.

230. Staudinger (-Wimmer-Leonhardt) § 534 no. 9.

231. CC § 534. Restitutionary actions are also unavailable when the tip corresponds to custom. CC § 814.

232. Jhering 9.

233. Staudinger (-Wimmer-Leonhardt) § 534 no. 10.

transferee's performance is worth a (higher) wage .... In the case of a 'bonus,' the transferor wishes ... to show gratitude for ... the high quality of an (already compensated) contractual performance."[234] The distinction developed in German law closely parallels the use of principal motive in the modern French doctrinal conception.

d. Spain

286. *Mixed approach.* Spanish law has adopted some of the different approaches found in other legal systems. Spanish case law requires both agreement as to the gratuitous nature of the transaction as well as animus donandi.[235] The special agreement requirement seems to have been borrowed from German law, and German authors are cited in support.[236] Animus donandi is defined abstractly as the intent to provide a benefit without receiving a counterpart. The donor's motives are not taken into account. The distinguished treatise writers Diez-Picazo and Gullón, however, have concluded that, once agreement is reached on the gratuitous nature of the transaction, animus donandi is superfluous.[237]

e. The Common Law

287. *Mutual consent not required.* The common law does not characterize the gift as a contract. Mutual consent is therefore not an essential element. What is required is donative intent—the donor must intend to make a gift.[238] When a transfer is made with donative intent, Bracton explained, title passes even though the donee may think of the transaction as a loan.[239]

288. *United States.* In American law, donative intent must be clear and unmistakable.[240] Donative intent, however, is only one aspect of the intent required for a valid gift. The donor must also intend the gift to operate immediately. Donative intent is examined here, while the intent to make an immediate transfer is considered below with the gift disposition.[241]

The courts look to all the facts and circumstances to determine whether donative intent is present. The wording of a written gift instrument is therefore not conclusive.[242] In particular, the traditional recitation in such instruments that

---

234. MünchKomm-BGB (-Kollhosser) § 516 no. 22.

235. STS Civ. 7 Dec. 1948, 24 *Juris. civ.* no. 62; Paz-Ares Rodríguez (-Albaladejo García) art. 618 no. IV.

236. 2 Lacruz Berdejo no. 501 par. d, citing Larenz.

237. Diez-Picazo and Gullón 336.

238. *Midland Ins. Co. v. Friedgood,* 577 F.Supp. 1407, 1412 (S.D.N.Y. 1984).

239. 2 Bracton 63.

240. *McLean v. McLean,* 374 S.E.2d 376, 381 (N.C. 1988); 38 Am.Jur.2d Gifts § 18; 38A C.J.S. Gifts § 15.

241. Infra no. 856.

242. *Callwood v. Cruse,* 2006 WL 1120646 (V.I. Super.)

the transfer was in exchange for "other good and valuable consideration" does not generally preclude a finding of donative intent.[243] Some courts hold that donative intent is present only if the facts and circumstances are consistent with no other explanation.[244]

Donative intent does not depend on the donor's motives.[245] Animus donandi is not negated by the fact that the donor was seeking to place property beyond the reach of creditors,[246] to disinherit a spouse,[247] or to avoid taxes.[248] In some circumstances, compliance with applicable statutory transfer provisions, such as those for the creation of a joint tenancy in stock, makes a prima facie case for the presence of donative intent.[249] Compliance with the provisions of the Uniform Transfers to Minors Act[250] also provides prima facie evidence of donative intent.[251] When the transfer is made in circumstances that usually accompany a gift, such as from a parent to a child, some courts presume that such the transfer was made with donative intent.[252]

289. *England and the Commonwealth.* Courts in England and the Commonwealth countries follow rules similar to those found in the United States. Some courts speak in terms of the donor's intent,[253] whereas others note that the donor had "perfect knowledge of the nature and effect of the transaction."[254] Donative intent is not negated by the fact that the donee's intent does not coincide with the donor's, such as when the donee considers the transaction to be a loan and intends to return the property.[255]

290. *India.* The Indian Transfer of Property Act defines a gift as a transfer "made voluntarily and without consideration" (§ 122 par. 1). Though the act does not require separate proof of donative intent, Indian commentators sometimes imply such a requirement by noting that the burden of proof on the issue of voluntariness lies with the party who is attempting to prove the gift.[256] Donative intent is particularly important because Indian courts strictly interpret the words

243. *Ellinwood v. Estate of Lyons,* 731 S.W.2d 23, 28 (Mo. App. 1987).
244. *Kuebler v. Kuebler,* 131 So.2d 211, 218 (Fla. App. 1961).
245. 38 Am.Jur.2d Gifts § 18; 38A C.J.S. Gifts § 15.
246. *Ingersoll v. Ingersoll,* 502 P.2d 598 (Or. 1972).
247. *Estate of Barnhart,* 574 P.2d 500, 503 (Colo. 1978) (en banc).
248. *Brown v. Brown,* 479 A.2d 573, 577 note 2 (Pa. Super. 1984).
249. *In re Pokorney's Estate,* 236 N.E.2d 396, 397 (Ill. App. 1968).
250. See infra nos. 895–896.
251. *Gordon v. Gordon,* 419 N.Y.S.2d 684, 688 (App. Div. 1979).
252. *In re Marriage of Blunda,* 702 N.E.2d 993, 1001 (Ill. App. 1998).
253. *Spooner v. Webb* (1951) 3 W.W.R. (n.s.) 490, 493 (Sask. App.).
254. ENGLAND: *Howard v Fingall* (1853) 22 LTR (os) 12, 1 WLR 515, 516; CANADA: *Kinsela v. Pask* [1913] 12 D.L.R. 522, 526 (Ont. H.C.).
255. 20 Halsbury part 1 sub Gifts no. 1.
256. Gour § 122 no. 24.

of a gift against the donor. Indian scholars quote Coke on Littleton to this effect. "It is a maxime in law, that every man's grant shall be taken by construction of law most forcible against himselfe."[257] Obligations created by love and affection are not considered legal obligations and therefore do not preclude a finding that a gift was intended.[258]

In Islamic law a gift depends on the donor's manifestation of the wish to make a gift. This element has been interpreted to require donative intent. When donative intent is lacking, there is no gift.[259]

3. An Inter Vivos Transfer

291. *Life and death.* All modern legal systems distinguish between gratuitous transfers that take place during the donor's lifetime and those that take effect at the donor's death. If the other conditions have been met, transfers of the first type constitute gifts and are said to operate inter vivos. Transfers of the second type are considered testamentary and are valid only if completed in testamentary formalities. For the gifts discussed in this study, an inter vivos transfer is, in general, an essential element.

292. *Definitional difficulties.* Though experience suggests that the distinction between life and death is absolute, the law has frequently attempted to blur the distinction. To begin with, some legal systems extend the notion of inter vivos gifts to include transfers that take effect at the donor's death. The common-law institution of the *donatio mortis causa* combines elements of inter vivos gift with testamentary transfer. These gifts are discussed below.

In the opposite direction, some legal systems apply successions law rather than gift law to transfers made during the donor's last days. In some French customs during the ancien régime, gifts were void if made during the donor's final illness or within a certain number of days of death.[260] The provisions were justified in two ways. First, these were thought to be gifts only in appearance. Donative intent is present only if the donor intends to lose a benefit, yet when gifts are given in the last days of life, the donor "seems to surrender property but does so only in appearance, since the property in any case can no longer be retained."[261] Second, such gifts are made under conditions that encourage undue influence. They should therefore be done in will formalities. While d'Aguesseau was drafting the Ordinance of 1731, he received petitions from the Romanist-inspired south to include this provision in the ordinance. D'Aguesseau declined.

---

257. Coke (1809) 183a–183b, quoted by Gour id. Coke was commenting on Littleton's similar statement: *Quaelibet concessio fortissimè contra donatorem interpretanda est.*

258. Gour § 122 nos. 5–6.

259. Fyzee 218.

260. Customs of Paris art. 277, in 3 Dumoulin (1691) 32; D'Aguesseau, Letter no. 284 of 13 May 1730, in 9 d'Aguesseau 341 at 342.

261. D'Aguesseau id.

A late draft of the French Civil Code provided that gifts not accepted during the donor's life or those made within six days of the donor's death were valid only as testamentary bequests.[262] The provision was rejected, this time because the donee, by delaying acceptance until after the donor's death, could use the provision to evade any conditions the donor may have attached to the gift.[263]

In 1736, the English Parliament provided that no gift was valid unless fully executed twelve months before the donor's death and recorded within six months of execution.[264] The goal was to inhibit donors from leaving their possessions to the church in the hope of receiving eternal salvation. Gifts to Oxford or Cambridge, or to the established public schools, were exempted.

a. France and Belgium

293. *Gifts and wills.* French law recognizes two types of gratuitous transfer: inter vivos gifts and last wills and testaments (CC art. 893). If the gratuitous transfer occurs during the donor's lifetime, it must be done in the formalities required by the law of gifts and must be irrevocable.[265] Any transfer that is to take place after the donor's death is valid only if done in the form of a will. Due to the differing form requirements, French case law carefully specifies the criteria for determining when a disposition operates inter vivos. French law does not recognize the validity of intermediate types of gratuitous transfer. Thus a donatio mortis causa, a gift that is executed while the donor is alive but remains revocable until the donor's death, is not valid in French law.[266]

294. *Distinction based on irrevocability.* One of the principal substantive differences between the gift and the will is that, in principle, a gift is irrevocable, whereas a will is revocable until the testator's death.[267] During the Middle Ages, the French law maxim *Donner et retenir ne vaut* (To give and retain is not valid) had the effect of postponing the validity of a gift until the moment possession was actually transferred.[268] The Civil Code abandoned the criterion of transfer of possession (*tradition*), and substituted for it a test of irrevocability. If the gift

---

262. Art. 46 (12 Ventôse XI [3 Mar. 1803]), in 12 Fenet 355.

263. Portalis, Discussion contribution (12 Ventôse XI [3 Mar. 1803]), in 12 Fenet 366. See also Cambacérès, Discussion contribution, id. 369; arts. 53–54 (3 Germinal XI [24 Mar. 1803]), in 12 Fenet 423; arts. 53–54, in "Communication officieuse à la Section de législation du Tribunat" (10 Germinal XI [31 Mar. 1803]), in 12 Fenet 452.

264. Mortmain Act of 1736 secs. 1, 3.

265. For the formalities required by French gift law, see infra nos. 770–778.

266. Bufnoir 502. Delvincourt, one of the Code's early commentators, approved the mortis causa gift on the grounds that immediate transfer of possession was equivalent to good faith purchase. 1 Delvincourt 751 note 6 to page 238.

267. Compare CC arts. 894 and 895. For the principle of irrevocability in French gift law, see infra nos. 1074–1096.

268. 8 De Page no. 548 par. B.

becomes irrevocable before the donor's death, it is considered to take place inter vivos, regardless of when the actual transfer of possession occurs. On the other hand, if the donor retains the right to reclaim the gift, even if possession is in the donee, the transfer is void.[269] Thus, in determining whether a gift operates inter vivos, the courts look to whether the donor had the intent to make an irrevocable disposition. The purported gift is not irrevocable if, at the time the transfer is made, the donor intends to retain the right to recover the gift in case of need.[270] The requirement of an inter vivos transfer, being a rule of substance rather than of form, also applies to disguised gifts.[271]

295. *Si praemoriar conditions.* For French law, the most difficult cases seem to be those involving gifts made under the condition that the donee survive the donor *(si praemoriar).* In principle, such a gift is valid if concluded inter vivos, even if possession is not to be transferred until after the donor's death and despite the presence of a condition subsequent that would restore the gift to the donor should the donee die first.[272] In an early but still much cited case, three monetary gifts were made to donees in their marriage settlements.[273] Each of the gifts was collectible only after the deaths of the respective donors. Two gifts were secured by a mortgage for the donees' benefit, of which one provided for the payment of interest, while the third gift provided for neither security nor interest. Two of the gifts stipulated that the funds would revert to the donors if the donees predeceased them. The lower court held that the two gifts secured by mortgages had operated a complete disposition, while the third remained at the mercy of the donors' continued good fortune. If the donors declared bankruptcy, the donees' interest would effectively terminate. The Cassation Court reversed as to the third gift, holding that the gift became irrevocable when the donee accepted its terms. In a similar vein, a check transferred to the donee while the donor is alive constitutes a valid inter vivos gift, even if the check is not paid until after the donor's death.[274]

b. Italy

296. *Revocability not a factor.* Italian law also considers the gift to be an inter vivos act. The gift is considered a bilateral contract that generally operates with immediate effect. It is distinguished from transfers made under a will, which are

---

269. 7 Aubry and Rau (1875) no. 699.

270. Req. 14 May 1900, D.P. 1900 I 358.

271. Civ. 22 Mar. 1848, D.P. 1848 I 94. For the disguised gift in French law, see infra nos. 798–826.

272. 8 De Page no. 374 par. B.

273. Civ. 28 Jan. 1839, D. 1839 I 74.

274. Aix 12 Mar. 1987, D.P. 1988 J 167 note Beignier. For gift by check in French law, see infra nos. 788–793.

said to operate *causa mortis* and which are unilateral and take effect at death.[275] The criteria used to delimit the two domains differs from those used in French law. The Italian doctrine considers revocability to be an unsatisfactory test for determining whether an act is completed inter vivos.[276] The Italian doctrine is reluctant to use revocability as the test because the Italian Code expressly permits donors to reserve the right to dispose, even after the gift has been executed, of a particular object included in the gift (art. 790). This provision reversed the rule in the previous Italian Civil Code, which, following the French model, voided, for lack of irrevocability, gifts with regard to which the donor had reserved the right to dispose.[277]

297. *Two types of transactions.* Andrea Torrente, author of a principal Italian treatise, suggested that the distinction should instead be based on the fact that the cause differs in the two types of transactions. In both the testament and the Roman law institution of the donatio mortis causa, the donor's death is the cause or determining factor in the transfer.[278] Italian law does not generally validate mortis causa gifts.[279] When, on the contrary, the donor's death operates merely as a temporal element specifying the moment of the transfer, the act should be considered to operate inter vivos.[280] Death is considered to represent a mere temporal moment when gifts are fully concluded while the donor is alive, with only the transfer of possession to take place at the donor's death.[281]

The same principles may be used to evaluate transfers made under a si praemoriar condition. If such a condition is intended, it is not invalidated by a provision that causes the gift to revert to the donor's patrimony if the donee (or the donee, together with the donee's issue) predeceases the donor (CC art. 791–792). If the donor dies first, the transfer takes effect retroactive to the moment of the gift, which allows it to operate inter vivos.[282] In some cases the condition is meant as a condition precedent. The donee is to have nothing but an expectancy as long as the donor is alive. Transfers of this type should be considered to operate mortis causa. If irrevocable, they fail, because they are generally thought to violate the essential revocability of the mortis causa transfer. Nonetheless, Torrente believed that, under certain circumstances, such transfers should be valid.[283]

---

275. Torrente (2006) 387–388.
276. Id. 395.
277. Italian CC art. 1069 (1865); French CC art. 946; Cian and Trabucchi art. 790 note.
278. For the donatio mortis causa, see infra nos. 314–315.
279. Casulli (1964a) no. 1.
280. Torrente (2006) 394–399.
281. Casulli (1964a) no. 2.
282. Id.
283. Torrente (2006) 397.

c. Spain

298. *Broad definition.* The Spanish Civil Code appears to characterize both those transfers that produce their effects at the donor's death and those that take effect inter vivos as gifts (CC arts. 620–621). The first are said to be governed by the rules for the last will and testament, whereas the second are considered to be contracts. Despite the code's wording, the majority view is that only transfers that take place inter vivos are gifts.[284] A transaction is considered to operate inter vivos when it produces any effect during the donor's lifetime, including the simple creation of an obligation on the part of the donor.[285] Spanish law thus characterizes all of the following as inter vivos gifts: the immediate transfer of title to the gift object; transfer of title with possession remaining in the donor until the donor's death; and transfers subject to a condition subsequent, as long as the donor does not retain the right to revoke and as long as the condition does not suggest that no immediate transfer is actually contemplated.[286]

The Catalonian Civil Code now permits gifts in contemplation of death (*por causa de muerte*). The gifts are not binding on the donor even if accepted.[287] Si praemoriar gifts are treated like gifts causa mortis.[288] Causa mortis gifts do not seem to be limited to movables and may be made by public act.[289] Delivery is not required. In fact, if the property is not delivered before the donor's death, the donee may then take possession.[290]

d. Germany

299. *Si praemoriar conditions.* The German Code provides that a gift promise subject to the condition that the donor dies before the donee (*si praemoriar*), is generally subject to successions law (CC § 2301 par. 1). However, if the gift is executed by effective transfer, the transfer is governed by gift law (§ 2301 par. 2). The distinction does not depend, as it does in French law, on whether the gift becomes irrevocable before the donor's death. Under German law, a gift may represent an inter vivos transfer even if the donor expressly reserves the right to revoke.[291] The distinction is also not related to whether the si praemoriar condition is considered a condition precedent or a condition subsequent. As a condition precedent, it does not subject the transfer to successions law as long as all

---

284. Paz-Ares Rodríguez (-Albaladejo García) arts. 620–621 nos. II and III.
285. Id. no. IV.
286. Id.
287. Catalonian CC art. 432-1 par. 1 (2009), enacted by the Law of 10 July 2008 art. 1.
288. Catalonian CC art. 432-1 par. 2.
289. Id. art. 432-3 par. 1 sent. 2.
290. Id. art. 432-4 par. 2.
291. MünchKomm-BGB (-Musielak) § 2301 no. 22; see also infra no. 1106.

gift law requirements have been met.[292] The distinction generally depends simply on whether there has been an effective transfer of title.

i. Interest Analysis

300. *Concerned with order.* German law does not seek to protect the parties as rigorously as do some Romanic systems. Instead, German law is concerned with order. "Nonetheless, difficulties continue to arise ... when it comes to making order out of the multifarious variety of real life transactions among the living that are somehow related to the event of death."[293] The problem for German law is not to discourage gifts but rather to subject each transaction to appropriate rules. Some criterion is thus needed to distinguish between cases that should be governed by gift law and those for which successions law is more appropriate.

To solve this problem, German scholars have interpreted Roman law from the point of view of interest analysis. As the Roman jurists put it, a transfer is testamentary when the donor prefers to keep the property rather than transfer it to the donee, but at the same time prefers the donee to the donor's heirs.[294] According to Philipp Heck, the element of sacrifice characterizes the gift and is lacking in the testamentary transfer.[295] The donor gives something away, whereas the testator gives away only that which death would take in any case. The fact that the rights of the estate's creditors are preferred to those of the legatee is related to the absence of sacrifice on the testator's part.

ii. Si Praemoriar Conditions

301. *Execution.* Gift promises made under a si praemoriar condition are governed by successions law. However, if the donor "executes the gift by transfer of the gift object," the transfer is governed by gift law (CC § 2301 par. 2). According to the legislative history, the issue is whether the donor's patrimony has actually been diminished.[296] The gift has been executed when the diminution affects the donor's own patrimony and not merely that of the heirs.[297] As a practical matter, this criterion corresponds to that used in the common law to define a valid mortis causa gift.[298] In deciding when a transfer is sufficiently complete, the policy issue is whether the donor should be granted control over transfers relating to death or whether contractual freedom should be restricted to assure compliance with

---

292. Id. § 2301 no. 21.

293. Id. § 2301 no. 3.

294. *Et in summa mortis causa donatio est, cum magis se quis velit habere quam eum cui donatur, magisque eum cui donat quam heredem suum.* Inst. 2, 7, 1; see also D. 39, 6, 1 pr.; infra no. 315.

295. Heck § 95 par. 2.

296. 5 Motive 352.

297. MünchKomm-BGB (-Musielak) § 2301 no. 19.

298. Infra no. 964–969.

testamentary formalities.[299] The policy difficulties have nourished a considerable debate among German scholars, who as a result have produced a finely honed but extremely complex set of rules.

302. *Two poles.* At the extremes, the matter presents no difficulty. On the one hand, unconditional gifts made inter vivos, if made in the required forms, are binding, even if transfer of possession is delayed until the donor's death. If the donee predeceases the donor, the donee's claim descends to the donee's heirs. The mere existence of the contract claim is enough for the gift to operate inter vivos.[300] At the other extreme, gifts made under a si praemoriar condition and that are in no way executed before the donor's death are considered to be testamentary.[301]

Difficulties arise when a gift is subject to a si praemoriar condition and is, to some extent, executed before the donor's death. Such transactions are considered to operate inter vivos if title has passed. Problems arise when the donor has done what is necessary or has asked a third party to do so but dies before the transfer is complete. In this context, the transfer is inter vivos when the donee has obtained an enforceable expectancy or contingent right (*Anwartschaftsrecht*).[302] Such an expectancy increases the donee's patrimony and diminishes that of the donor. The transfer is not inter vivos unless the donee can enforce the right without any additional action by the donor. The donor's subjective understanding that everything necessary has been accomplished is insufficient.

iii. The Donor's Death

303. *Not determinative.* Additional problems arise when, before death, the donor has performed all actions necessary to create an expectancy in the donee, yet the donor's declarations do not reach the donee and are not accepted until after the donor's death.[303] Because, in this case, the donee does not receive an enforceable expectancy before the donor's death, the transaction would seem not to operate inter vivos. However, German law on contract formation, contrary to that of many other jurisdictions, provides that offers to contract and other declarations of intent do not expire and may be accepted, even after the offeror's death.[304] German law applies this rule when determining whether a gift has been sufficiently executed to constitute an inter vivos transfer. According to the dominant view, the nature of the gift should not depend on whether the donor happens to die before the donor's declaration of intent is communicated to and accepted by

---

299. MünchKomm-BGB (-Musielak) § 2301 no. 3.

300. Id. § 2301 no. 4.

301. Jauernig (-Stürner) § 2301 nos. 4 and 9.

302. MünchKomm-BGB (-Musielak) § 2301 no. 19.

303. Id. § 2301 no. 23.

304. German CC §§ 130 par. 2, 153.

the donee. An exception is made when the donor actually intended the communication to reach the donee after the donor's death.

304. *Agency.* When execution is to be completed by the donor's agent,[305] German law distinguishes two cases. If the agent is employed as a messenger, the general rules apply. The donee may accept a declaration of intent received after the donor's death, provided the donor did not intend for the communication to occur postmortem.[306]

If the donor has created a power of attorney (*Vollmacht*), the agent may, even after the donor's death, make declarations and perform other acts on the donor's behalf.[307] The creation of the power of attorney is not itself equivalent to execution. The gift is not executed until the agent performs as requested. Though the gift object enters the estate at the donor's death, the agent may complete the gift, provided the donor did not direct the agent to postpone action until after the donor died. However, the heirs may revoke the power of attorney. The gift is executed only if the necessary acts are completed before the power is revoked.[308]

305. *Release.* Despite the extensive German law on these questions, both the doctrine and the courts, when determining whether a transaction is designed to create rights while the donor is alive, examine all the facts and circumstances.[309] The release of a debt is a good example. If a donor-holder returns a promissory note to the maker so that it will be destroyed, the courts may consider the release to be executed. However, if the donor indicates that the debt is to be forgiven at the donor's death, there is either a mortis causa gift promise or an executed gift, depending on the circumstances.[310]

306. *Third-party beneficiaries.* Savings accounts for the benefit of third parties are frequently created subject to a si praemoriar condition. These and some other third-party beneficiary contracts raise a difficult characterization issue.[311] If the contract with the bank is valid, the surviving beneficiary's rights vest at the donor's death.[312] However, the donee may retain the proceeds only on the basis of a legal cause, such as a gift contract.[313] The problem is that the gift contract is not formed until after the donor's death. The German high court nonetheless

305. MünchKomm-BGB (-Musielak) § 2301 no. 24.
306. RG 28 Oct. 1913, RGZ 83, 223 (*Bonifazius–Fall*).
307. German CC §§ 168 sent. 1, 672.
308. MünchKomm-BGB (-Musielak) § 2301 no. 24.
309. Id. § 2301 no. 28.
310. Id. no. 30.
311. Id. nos. 32–36.
312. German CC § 331 par. 1; MünchKomm-BGB (-Gottwald) § 331 no. 2.
313. German law distinguishes the underlying deposit contract from the gift relationship. MünchKomm-BGB (-Gottwald) § 328 nos. 25–29.

applies gift law to the donor-donee relationship.[314] Some scholars criticize the result because it permits an essentially testamentary transfer without the protection of will formalities.[315]

307. *Negotiable instruments.* In contrast to French law but in line with common-law principles, the drawer's delivery of a check to the payee does not complete a gift. Execution occurs only upon payment by the bank. Thus, if the donor deposits a negotiable instrument with instructions that it is to be transferred to the donee at the donor's death, the instrument becomes part of the donor's estate and, theoretically, should be governed by successions law. The German high court, however, has decided that, upon the donor's death, the donee-beneficiary has a claim for specific performance against the bank.[316]

e. The Common Law

308. *Fully executed.* In American law, a gift generally operates inter vivos only if it is fully executed during the lifetime of the parties. It is fully executed only if no other act or contingency, such as the donor's death, must occur before it takes effect.[317] Delivery, to the extent required,[318] must take place before the donor's death.[319] The donatio mortis causa, an exception to some of these rules, is nonetheless considered a valid inter vivos transfer.

i. Particular Examples

309. *Interest must pass before death.* Any transfer that is not to take effect until the donor's death is testamentary and ineffective as an inter vivos gift.[320] For example, transfer by means of a joint bank account is testamentary if the depositor intends to retain access to the account while alive and for the donee to make withdrawals only at the donor's death.[321] However, if a present interest is transferred, the gift is valid even if enjoyment or use is postponed.[322] Thus, the transfer of a deed to real property may constitute a valid gift even if the donor retains a life estate.[323] The test is whether some present interest is meant to pass at the

---

314. BGH 26 Nov. 2003, NJW 2004, 767 at 768.

315. MünchKomm-BGB (-Musielak) § 2301 nos. 34–36.

316. BGH 29 Jan. 1964, BGHZ 41, 95 at 96; MünchKomm-BGB (-Musielak) § 2301 no. 42.

317. 38 Am.Jur.2d Gifts § 7.

318. For the requirement of delivery of chattels in the common law, see infra nos. 865–888.

319. 38A C.J.S. Gifts § 27.

320. *Norman v. Norman*, 169 N.E.2d 414, 419 (Ind. App. 1960); Brown § 7.4.

321. *McGillivray v. First Nat'l Bank*, 217 N.W. 150 (N.D. 1927); Havighurst 152. For joint bank accounts in the common law, see infra nos. 941–948.

322. *Neuschafer v. McHale*, 709 P.2d 734, 739 (Or. App. 1985).

323. *Abercrombie v. Andrew College*, 438 F.Supp. 243, 268 (S.D.N.Y. 2006).

time of the gift. As far as chattels are concerned, one court has held that a gift is valid even if the donor reserves a life estate and the donee does not obtain possession until after the donor's death.[324] However, if the donor intends to retain the full property interest until death, the purported gift is illusory, and the gift fails.[325] Thus, when the donor delivered a certificate of deposit to her mother indicating that it was for her mother when the donor died, the transfer failed as an inter vivos gift and could be validated only if will formalities were met.[326] Moreover, if any condition is deemed a condition precedent, the purported gift is in futuro, not inter vivos.[327]

310. *Negotiable instruments.* When the donor is the maker or drawer of a negotiable instrument, the common law follows principles similar to those in German law. The gift of the instrument is complete only when paid. It fails if not paid before the donor's death.[328] Timing questions affecting the gift of a negotiable instrument are examined below.[329]

311. *Representation.* When the donor's agent fails to complete delivery before the donor's death, whatever had been accomplished is revoked and there is no gift. Thus, when the donor authorized his agent to transfer real property but the donor died before the agent executed and delivered the deed, the power of attorney was revoked at the donor's death, and the gift failed.[330] If, however, the third party is acting as the *donee's* agent, the transfer of possession to the agent executes an inter vivos gift.[331] The presumption, however, is that the third party acts for the donor.[332]

312. *Loans.* When a loan agreement provides that any balance remaining unpaid at the donor's death is forgiven, some courts decide that the donor has not parted with dominion and control, because, if the donor lives long enough, the debt may be completely repaid.[333] Other courts uphold the transaction, not as a gift but as a valid contractual condition.[334]

---

324. *Gruen v. Gruen*, 505 N.Y.S.2d 849 (N.Y. 1986); infra no. 887.
325. *Estate of Barnhart*, 574 P.2d 500, 503 (Colo. 1978) (en banc).
326. *Cain v Moon* [1896] 2 QB 283.
327. Brown § 7.13.
328. *Sucher v. Nabenkoegl*, 141 N.E.2d 648 (Ill. App. 1957); *Estate of Wood*, 108 Cal.Rptr. 522, 531 (Cal. App. 1973).
329. Infra nos. 354, 906–911.
330. *Pocius v. Fleck*, 150 N.E.2d 106, 111 (Ill. 1958).
331. *Estate of Wilson*, 206 N.Y.S.2d 323, 327–328 (Sur. Ct. 1960).
332. *Pocius v. Fleck*, 150 N.E.2d 106, 111 (Ill. 1958).
333. *Estate of Gardner*, 162 N.E.2d 579, 583–584 (Ohio Probate Ct. 1959).
334. *Walston v. Twiford*, 105 S.E.2d 62, 65 (N.C. 1958).

313. *India.* The registered instrument Indian law requires for gifts of immovable property, which may also be used to gift movable property, need not be registered during the donor's lifetime, though it is not enforceable until registered.[335]

ii. Donatio Mortis Causa

314. *In contemplation of death.* The mortis causa gift, also known as a gift in contemplation of death or a deathbed gift, is a gift of personalty made in expectation of the donor's imminent death, such as might be anticipated before major surgery, an impending battle, or a dangerous trip. The gift is valid if the donor does not revoke the gift and dies as anticipated and if the donee survives the donor. If those requirements are not met, the donee must return the property.[336]

315. *History.* A passage in the *Odyssey* makes clear that the donatio mortis causa was already recognized at the time of Homer.[337] In Roman law, the donatio mortis causa appeared relatively late, probably in the first or second century B.C. Though Blackstone supposed that the Romans adopted the institution from the Greeks,[338] Romanists today believe that there was never more than a generic relationship between the two institutions.[339] Mortis causa gifts, like other gifts in classical Roman law, were made without special formality in the mode appropriate for the property concerned. Justinian imposed as an additional requirement the presence of five witnesses.[340] In a celebrated definition in the *Institutes*, Tribonian explained that donors making a mortis causa gift prefer themselves to their donees but their donees to their heirs.[341] Due to the similarity between mortis causa gifts and testamentary bequests, the Romans accorded a subsidiary function to the deathbed gift. The glossators also noted the similarity and disagreed about whether the mortis causa gift should be considered a gift or a

---

335. Mulla sec. 123 note entitled "Whether donor may revoke gift after delivery of deed and before registration."

336. Restatement (Third) of Property (Wills and Other Donative Transfers) § 6.2 comment zz and Reporter's notes 22–26; 2 Blackstone 514. See generally 2 Schouler (1896) §§ 133–195; Graves 882–894.

337. Then wise Telemachus answered him: "Peiraeus, we know not how these matters will end up. If the proud suitors shall secretly slay me in the palace and divide among themselves all my father's property, then I would rather have you yourself keep and enjoy these things then let any of these men have them. But if I am able to find a way to bring death to the suitors, please bring the gifts back to me and I will be grateful to you."
Odyssey bk. 17 lines 77–83.

338. 2 Blackstone 514 and note m. For the Roman law rules, see D. 39, 6. For a brief discussion in English of the Roman principles governing the donatio mortis causa, see Comment (1852) 6–8.

339. Amelotti no. 1.

340. C. 8, 56, 4; Amelotti no. 2.

341. Inst. 2, 7, 1. Latin text quoted supra no. 300.

testamentary bequest.[342] The common law borrowed the institution from the Romans. Apparently, the mortis causa gift did not appear in the case reports prior to the eighteenth century. The doctrine was probably designed to validate deathbed gifts after the Statute of Frauds restricted the availability of the nuncupative will.[343] One court suggested that the donatio mortis causa was particularly useful before will formalities were generally understood.[344]

316. *Exception to gifts and wills.* Under normal principles, the mortis causa gift does not qualify as a gift. The gift remains revocable until the donor's death and delivery is subject to a condition precedent. When will formalities are not present, it cannot be validated as a will. It is thus an exception to both sets of norms. The requirements for and regime of the donatio mortis causa are examined below.[345]

4. The Gift Object

317. *Dual functions.* The final definitional element concerns the type of rights that may be given by gift. This element of the definition serves principally to distinguish gifts from other gratuitous transactions. In civilian parlance, a gift generally involves an obligation to give (*dare, donner*), which means the gratuitous transfer or creation of a patrimonial right. A gratuitous performance of services involves the obligation to do (*fare, faire*) and is generally not considered a gift. As Gino Gorla explained, modern civil law is much more concerned about the obligation to give. Transactions involving the obligation to give are generally valid only in the presence of an objective cause, such as a quid pro quo. When transactions involving the transfer of property are gratuitous, they are validated only in the presence of a rigorous formality, such as a notarial act.[346] On the other hand, when the transaction involves the obligation to do, such as to perform a service, all that is required is a reasonable cause. In many cases that means simply that the transaction must be reasonable in light of all of the facts and circumstances.[347]

---

342. Bellomo 963.

343. Schouler (1886) 447–448; Rundell 646–647 and note 26.

344. "This doctrine of donatio causa mortis was borrowed from the Roman civil law by our English ancestors. There was much greater need for such a law at the time it was incorporated into the civil law and into the English law than there is now. Learning was not so general, nor the facilities for making wills so great, then as now." *Newman v. Bost,* 29 S.E. 848, 848 (N.C. 1898).

345. Infra nos. 963–971.

346. 1 Gorla 82–83.

347. Id. 174–179. Gorla argued that the gift is uncaused. As a result, it can be validated only on the basis of its form. As Piccinini has pointed out, however, the fact that an agreement for the gratuitous rendering of services may be validated without compliance with form requirements seems to contradict Gorla's thesis. Piccinini 193. Gorla responded to

As a practical matter, the exclusion of a particular type of property from gift law may produce two different consequences. In some cases, the exclusion operates to facilitate the transfer. Such transfers may be made without formalities and are not subject to capacity limitations, collation, or revocation. In French law, the creation of a security interest generally does not constitute a gift from the debtor to the creditor.[348] As a result, no notarial act is required. In other cases, however, the exclusion means that the particular type of property may not be the subject of an inter vivos gratuitous transfer. In French and Italian law, the attempted gift of future property is generally void.[349] These questions are complex. In most systems, even the general principles cannot be stated succinctly. In addition, a variety of particular issues have proven especially difficult.

a. General Definition

318. *Middle Ages.* The medieval masters of the notarial arts created long catalogs of permitted gift objects for the benefit of local notaries. These included all things movable and immovable, corporeal and incorporeal, individual or universal, as well as various types of rights.[350]

i. France and Belgium

319. *Patrimonial rights.* The question is which of the rights that make up an individual's patrimony can be transferred by gift. The issue has generated significant conflict in French and Belgian doctrine. Patrimony is an outgrowth of the concept of legal personality. An individual's patrimony is a universality that encompasses all of that individual's rights, present and future, that can be economically valued and transferred for compensation.[351] An individual's rights to name, honor, and personal integrity are not included in the concept of patrimony. Patrimony includes essentially two types of rights—property rights (*droits réels*) and rights that arise as a result of legal obligations on the part of others (*droits personnels* or *droits de créance*).[352] The traditional doctrinal view is that gifts are limited to property rights—transmissions of patrimonial property (*biens patrimoniaux*),[353] including ownership rights (*droits réels*) of both movable and

---

this difficulty by suggesting that the law correctly considers the agreement to perform services without compensation inherently less dangerous than a gift. 1 Gorla 86.

348. Infra nos. 325–326.

349. Infra nos. 359–367.

350. Bellomo 965.

351. 1 Carbonnier (1980) no. 42; 1 Ghestin no. 205. For a critique of the concept of patrimony, see Hiez.

352. *Droit de créance* is a concept for which no equivalent exists in English. It might be translated as *contract rights* because that term is sometimes used, at least in American law, as a shorthand for rights arising from tort, restitution, and contract.

353. 5 Planiol and Ripert no. 9.

immovable property, together with the various limited interests (*démembrements*), such as usufructs and easements.[354]

The French Civil Code specifically prohibits gifts of certain patrimonial rights, such as future property (*biens à venir*; CC art. 943), which, as discussed below, includes property not yet owned by the donor but to which title may in the future be acquired.[355] The difficulty is to determine which remaining property and contract rights may validly be made the object of a gift.

(A) GIFTS OF MODEST VALUE

320. *Customary gifts.* The French Civil Code expressly exempts customary gifts (*présents d'usage*) from collation (art. 852).[356] On the basis of this provision, the courts have turned the customary gift into an institution, exempting it as well from the revocations applicable to the marriage settlement (art. 1088) and to gifts between spouses (art. 1096).[357] Customary gifts are gratuitous transfers given on certain occasions, including births, baptisms, marriages, and anniversaries, that both conform to a particular usage and are of a value appropriate to the circumstances.[358] For characterization purposes, their value is determined at the date of the gift. The extent of the donor's resources must be taken into account (art. 852 par. 2).[359] In a celebrated case, the Cassation Court considered the resources of the donor, the actor Sacha Guitry, and held that a diamond bracelet worth six million French francs was a customary gift.[360] However, family jewels of great value, even when given according to usage, are generally not considered customary gifts.[361]

321. *Modest gifts.* In addition, some authors suggest that gifts of minimal value (*dons modiques*), even when they do not qualify as customary gifts, should also be

---

354. The definition of *libéralité* in the French Civil Code was modified in 2006 to include "rights." The intent was to make clear that a usufruct or the right to collect fruits may be included in a gratuitous transfer. CC art. 893 par. 1 (2006); Forgeard et al. (2007) no. 256 at 132.

355. Infra nos. 360–362.

356. André Breton, note to Civ.[1] 23 Mar. 1983, D. 1984, 81 at 82 (collecting authorities). Art. 1083 also permits a donor who has made a gift by contractual designation (*institution contractuelle*) to dispose of modest sums, for remuneratory or other purposes. 5 Planiol and Ripert no. 322.

357. Jean Bernard de Saint Affrique, note to Civ.[1] 10 May 1995, *Rép. not. Defrén.* 1996 art. 36422 at 1285.

358. Flour and Souleau no. 34.

359. Civ.[1] 10 May 1995, *Rép. not. Defrén.* 1996 art. 36422 note Jean Bernard de Saint Affrique.

360. Civ.[1] 30 Dec. 1952, D. 1953, 161; J.C.P. 1953 II 7475 note Mihura.

361. Civ.[1] 20 June 1961, D. 1961, 641 note René Savatier (*affaire de la Rochefoucauld*).

excluded from the domain of gift law.[362] The purpose would be to benefit charitable associations that receive large numbers of small donations. Modicity would generally be determined relative to the donor's wealth. The burden of proof would be on the party seeking a dispensation from the form requirements, generally the donee. The problem is that it would be almost impossible for charitable associations to satisfy the burden. As a result, it has been suggested that all small gifts made for charitable purposes, such as those made during the weekly collection, should be excluded from the domain of gift law. As some scholars have noted, such gifts were exempted from the rules requiring administrative authorization for gifts to charities that prevailed prior to 2005.[363] The courts consider the charitable motive and have exempted some charitable gifts from the form requirements.[364]

(B) FRUITS AND INCOME

322. *Profit.* The concept of *fruits and income* (*fruits et revenus*) signifies the profit derived from property. The typical case involves the gift of a usufruct in income-producing property, in other words, the gift of the revenue stream. It remains unresolved whether a transfer of fruits should be considered a gift.[365] If the profits are minimal, it is agreed that modicity should validate the gift.[366]

Two articles in the Civil Code, though not directly relevant, seem to suggest that the transfer of fruits and income does not qualify as a gift object (arts. 856, 928). The two provisions provide that, when property is recovered by the estate under successions law, fruits need only be returned from the moment of the decedent's death. Based on these provisions, some scholars have argued that fruits do not represent a patrimonial benefit. The donor would have spent the money in any case (*lautius vixisset*, the donor would have lived more grandly) and therefore would not be impoverished, and the donee would probably have spent the money as it was received and would therefore not be enriched.[367]

323. *Early case law.* The matter was resolved at the beginning of the last century.[368] Over eighteen years, a father had allowed his son to manage and retain the profit from two of the father's properties. At the father's death, the notary asked the son to return the profit to the estate. The Cassation Court indicated that the norms exempting fruits from return under successions law were

---

362. Nathalie Peterka, obs. to Trib. gr. inst. Nanterre 4 July 2000, *Rép. not. Defrén.* 2002 art. 37454 at 10–13.

363. Law of 23 July 1987 art. 16, modifying Law of 1 July 1901 art. 6 par. 1; infra no. 507.

364. 5 Planiol and Ripert no. 322.

365. Dawson (1980) 60–66.

366. Malaurie and Aynès no. 360.

367. 5 Planiol and Ripert no. 323.

368. Civ.¹ 27 Nov. 1917, S. 1917 I 105 note Charles Lyon-Caen.

presumed to represent the donor's intent. No donor would have intended that, at the moment of the donor's death, the donee would be required to return not only the gift property but also the profit derived from it. Most donees would have spent the income.[369] The Court held that the same reasoning should apply when the gift is limited to the income stream. Moreover, the Court concluded that fruits do not really satisfy the material element of the definition of gift in French law. "[T]he fruits thus given do not diminish the donor's patrimony, since he might well have spent them, and do not augment the donee's patrimony, since they were paid year by year and might have been spent as they were collected." The unmistakable conclusion was that the granting of a revenue stream does not constitute a gift.

324. *More recent cases.* More recent case law and scholarship suggest that a revenue stream, unless the amounts involved are modest, may constitute a valid gift object. In one case, for example, children were allowed to live for fifteen years on property owned by their parents without making rental payments. The Cassation Court decided that the children had received a gift of revenue.[370] The question is whether a gratuitous bailment should be characterized as a gift. The issue is controversial in both French and German law.[371]

(C) SECURITY

325. *Mortgages and security interests.* The creation or transfer of accessory property rights, such as mortgages and security interests, may constitute gifts. A pledge (*gage*) or mortgage (*hypothèque*) created gratuitously by a third party may constitute a gift (to the creditor).[372] The gift is realized upon execution.[373] However, there is no gift if the donor provides security for a debt the donor owes to the donee. The creation of that interest does not diminish the donor's patrimony.[374]

326. *Personal guarantees.* Payment under a personal guarantee (*caution*) may sometimes be a gift. If the guarantor's intent, when making payment, is to make

369. Charles Lyon-Caen, note to id. at 105; 6 Aubry and Rau (1875) § 631 at 633–636.

370. Civ.¹ 14 Jan. 1997, D. 1997, 607 note Véronique Barabé-Bouchard; see Malaurie and Aynès no. 360; CC art. 893 par. 1 (2006) (revised to include "rights").

371. Véronique Barabé-Bouchard, note to id. at 609; for the German law discussion, see infra no. 336.

372. 5 Planiol and Ripert no. 417.

373. 8 De Page no. 418.

374. As far as property rights are concerned, it is generally agreed, though sometimes subject to discussion, that [a gratuitous transfer] can involve only a principal property right. The creation of a security interest, an accessory property right, does not cause the owner of the collateral to lose any element of patrimony. In the patrimony of the creditor who profits from it, the security interest also does not represent an asset.
Flour and Souleau no. 32.

a gift to the debtor, the code considers it to be the gratuitous payment of the debt of another (CC art. 1236) and valid as a gift to the debtor.[375] A further question is whether the payment may sometimes constitute a gift to the creditor. Under normal circumstances, the guarantee of an existing obligation is not a gift to the creditor,[376] even when the guarantor pays, because the guarantor has an action over against the debtor.[377] If the guarantor abandons recourse against the debtor, however, or for other reasons cannot collect (and if the guarantee was made with animus donandi), French doctrine suggests that the guarantee constitutes a conditional gift to the creditor,[378] which is executed when the guarantor makes payment. In a nineteenth-century case, the donor promised his wife an annuity.[379] The donor's parents guaranteed the gift. The resources of the donor's estate were insufficient, and the wife sought payment from her mother-in-law. The court held that the guarantee represented a gift to the creditor-wife. De Page argued that a guarantee can never constitute a gift to the creditor.[380]

(D) RIGHTS

327. *Transfer and release.* Rights that preexist the gift may be gifted by transfer or release. The gift of a debt, even one subject to litigation, was already permitted under the ancien régime.[381] Today, the authors seem to agree that the release of a debt (*remise de dette*) or the assignment (*cession de créance*) or renunciation (*renonciation*) of a right may constitute a gift, even those authors, curiously, who insist that only property rights may be given as a gift.[382]

328. *Creation.* Under certain circumstances, the creation of a right for the donee's benefit may also operate a valid gift. For example, a gift may be made by the conclusion of a third-party beneficiary contract (*stipulation pour autrui*) for the donee's benefit (CC art. 1121).[383] An example is the death benefit from a life insurance policy.[384] The gift object is the beneficiary's right to enforce the promise

---

375. 5 Planiol and Ripert no. 414. The gift is considered indirect and therefore escapes the French law form requirements. For the indirect gift, see infra nos. 827–843.

376. *"There is no such thing as a gift of credit."* Flour and Souleau no. 31 (emphasis in original).

377. 5 Planiol and Ripert no. 263 note 1 at 361 and no. 417; see CC arts. 2028–2029 (guarantor's recourse against the debtor).

378. 5 Planiol and Ripert no. 417.

379. Civ. 12. Aug. 1872, D.P. 1873 I 15 (with a critical note). See also 12 Laurent no. 172; 1 Baudry-Lacantinerie no. 847.

380. 8 De Page no. 418.

381. Bretonnier 128.

382. 5 Planiol and Ripert nos. 416, 419–420; 8 De Page no. 416.

383. 8 De Page nos. 503, 397.

384. Ins. Code art. L132-9 no. 1 par. 4, The proceeds are not subject to collation. Id. art. L132-13 par. 1. See 5 Planiol and Ripert no. 325. The purchase of a life insurance policy is a gift only if the purchase was made with donative intent. Donative intent is usually lacking

against the carrier. A donor may also make a gift of an obligation by creating a debt payable directly to the donee. The gift is valid if the right is immediately transferred, even if it is not due until the donor's death.[385] This is the case even though French law generally refuses to enforce gift promises.[386]

329. *Acknowledgment.* The acknowledgment of a debt (*reconnaissance de dette*) is typically considered a means to interrupt the running of the prescription period.[387] An acknowledgment operates a novation of the debt, thereby extending shorter prescription periods for up to thirty years.[388] Legal scholars universally agree that such an acknowledgment may also constitute a valid gift.[389] Because of its novative implications, one might imagine that French law would consider the acknowledgment of an existing debt to constitute a valid gift object. That issue, however, is apparently not discussed.

Instead, both the cases and the authors validate as a gift the acknowledgment of a debt that did *not* previously exist. They reason from the situation in which "it must be supposed that there was no debt, and that the act that establishes or acknowledges it is a sham."[390] In these circumstances, the acknowledgment is considered a gift, either indirect or disguised. Though the absence of the requisite formalities makes a simple gift promise void, simulation, as discussed below, renders the acknowledgment of a debt valid as a disguised gift.[391]

(E) JUSTIFICATIONS

330. *Only patrimonial rights.* An accurate summary of the state of French law on this question is difficult. A gift in French law generally may be made only of patrimonial rights.[392] With possible exceptions, some of which are controversial in the literature, a gift may involve the transfer of either a property right or a contract right. The transfer of the obligation to perform a service or to provide lodging, nourishment, or maintenance, because they are obligations to do (*obligations de faire*), is not considered a gift.[393] Loans made without interest or loans to be repaid according to the debtor's ability are also not considered gifts.[394]

---

in policies payable to the survivor and purchased by married couples for estate-planning purposes or in policies purchased to fulfill support obligations. See Coron and Lucet.

385. Civ. 30 Nov. 1937, S. 1938 I 241 note René Morel.

386. 5 Planiol and Ripert no. 382; 8 De Page no. 369; infra nos. 674–676.

387. 7 Planiol and Ripert nos. 1364–1367.

388. 2 Planiol nos. 672–676.

389. 5 Planiol and Ripert no. 413; 8 De Page no. 413; Malaurie and Aynès no. 411.

390. 8 De Page no. 413 par. A.

391. Infra nos. 802–803.

392. 4 Mazeaud (-Leveneur and Mazeaud-Leveneur) no. 1492; Flour and Souleau no. 32.

393. 8 De Page no. 419.

394. When made among family members, such *soft* loans often function as gifts. Brault 1428.

In the French legal tradition, the limitation of the legal concept of the gift to patrimonial rights is justified as an attempt to coordinate the notion of gift giving with the legal regime that governs the gift. French doctrine admits that a service may provide enrichment equivalent to a property transfer. In the case of services, however, there is no corresponding diminution of the donor's patrimony. Of course, services performed may always be valued in money, but the legal rules concerning gratuitous transfers are designed to prevent the voluntary diminution of the donor's patrimony.[395] "All of the rules specific to liberalities are precisely and *solely* designed to prevent the voluntary reduction of a person's patrimony, of 'property,' of *capital;* they aim only at that."[396] In the French tradition, the discussion about whether to include a particular type of right within the scope of gift law tends to turn on whether a voluntary transfer of that right represents a risk to the donor's wealth.

ii. Germany

331. *Broad concept.* The Germanic legal tradition follows a movement contrary to that of French law. French law begins its reflection regarding the nature of the gift object with a core concept of property rights and then expands it to include some contract rights. German law, on the contrary, begins with a broad conception of the gift object and tailors the definition by gradual reduction. There is a gift when the donee's enrichment comes from the donor's patrimony (CC § 516 par. 1). There are therefore two questions. The first is to determine whether the donee's patrimony is increased. The second, which provides the basis for limiting the reach of gift law, asks whether the advantage results from a diminution in the donor's patrimony.

(A) INCREASE TO THE DONEE'S PATRIMONY

332. *Any patrimonial advantage.* The basic principle is that any patrimonial advantage (*Vermögensvorteil*)—any increase in the donee's assets or decrease in the donee's liabilities—can be the object of gift giving.[397] Property and contract rights are included, as are the release of a debt, a waiver of rights, the permission to proceed with the occupation of property (*Aneignungsgestattung*), and the discharge of a debtor by the donor's assumption of the debt (*befreiende Schuldübernahme*).[398] Payment of a debt that the donee owes to a third party may also be a gift,[399] as may the donor's purchase of property in the donee's name.[400] If the price differs from the property value, the gift, for purposes of collation or

---

395. 5 Planiol and Ripert no. 9.
396. 8 De Page no. 13 par. B (emphasis in original).
397. Jauernig (-Mansel) § 516 no. 5.
398. Id.
399. RG 19 June 1941, RGZ 167, 199; Dawson (1980) 147.
400. RG 19 Dec. 1927, JW 1928, 894 at 895 note Paul Oertmann; Dawson (1980) 147.

revocation, consists in the smaller of the two amounts. Both impoverishment and enrichment are necessary for a gift.[401] Other objects of gift giving include an agreement not to sue (*pacto de non petendo*) and the release or reduction of a security interest. As in French law, the debtor's creation of a security interest for the debtor's own debt is never a gift, even when the debt is otherwise uncollectible.[402] The creation of a security interest to secure the debt of a third party can be a gift.[403] It is a gift to the creditor when it adds an asset to the creditor's patrimony, as with the guarantee of an otherwise uncollectible debt. The gift is to the debtor when the donor renounces recourse.[404]

The patrimonial advantage to the donee must be substantive and not merely formal.[405] Thus, the transfer of property to a trustee does not turn the trustee into a donee, nor does the transfer of money to an intermediary.[406] It is also not a gift when money is given so that it can be loaned back to the transferor. The definition of the donee's enrichment is even broader than the one found in the German law of restitution. The restitutionary concept of enrichment requires a subjective element, namely that the enrichment result from a purposeful increase in the defendant's patrimony.[407] In the law of gifts, on the contrary, the test is purely objective. A gift can result from purely selfish activity, as when an employer creates a fund for widows and orphans to ensure employee loyalty.[408]

(B) DIMINUTION OF THE DONOR'S PATRIMONY

333. *Reduction in value.* Beginning from a broad conception of donee enrichment, German law refines the concept of the gift object by requiring that the gift also diminish the donor's patrimony. The current value of the donor's patrimony must be reduced. "The donor must become poorer."[409] This aspect of the definition excludes ideal or immaterial property, such as a poetry reading or a music concert.[410] The same principle excludes loans without interest and the

---

401. Dawson (1980) 147.

402. MünchKomm-BGB (-Kollhosser) § 516 no. 9; Dawson (1980) 148–149; Savigny (1841) 55; Schütz 453.

403. Schütz noted that it is often unhelpful to characterize the creation of a security interest as a gift, since gift tax must then be paid, usually at the highest rate, which greatly increases credit costs. Schütz 454.

404. Schütz id. In Savigny's view, a personal guarantee of the debt of a third party is never a gift to the creditor, even when the debtor is insolvent, because the debt was already an asset in the creditor's patrimony. Savigny (1841) 54–55.

405. MünchKomm-BGB (-Kollhosser) § 516 no. 10.

406. The rule is different when the recipient is a charitable organization.

407. Jauernig (-Stadler) § 812 no. 4.

408. Staudinger (-Wimmer-Leonhardt) § 516 no. 41.

409. MünchKomm-BGB (-Kollhosser) § 516 no. 3.

410. Id. no. 2; Staudinger (-Wimmer-Leonhardt) § 516 no. 19.

permission to use property without the payment of rent.[411] Services of all kinds are also excluded, as is the rejection of an inheritance (for the benefit of another heir) or a creditor's intentional failure to allow a condition precedent to occur.[412]

334. *Intent to charge.* In general, services, interest-free loans, and gratuitous bailments are not considered gifts. However, the rule changes when the service-provider, creditor, or lessor would normally have charged for the benefit. In that context, the case law considers the gift to be the release of the obligation to pay compensation rather than the performance of the service, the making of the loan, or the transfer of possession. Savigny, for example, considered providing rent-free living space to be a gift because living space is usually leased when not in use.[413] He also believed that a gratuitous storage (*depositum*) or agency (*mandatum*) in some cases might be a gift, namely when the *solvens* would otherwise have charged for the service.[414] On the other hand, for Savigny, an interest-free loan would not be a gift because many people keep cash on hand.[415] In a leading case, two considerations convinced the German Supreme Court to hold that a father's labor in renovating his son's house did not constitute a gift. First, the retired father would not otherwise have been gainfully employed. Second, the parties had agreed that the services would be rendered without compensation. Because no claim for compensation arose, none could be released.[416]

335. *Statutory exclusions.* The Civil Code specifically excludes three transactions from gift law, chiefly because they do not impoverish the donor (CC § 517). The first is the benefit that accrues to one party when another refuses to make a patrimonial acquisition. Examples include one party's rejection of an offer to contract that can then be accepted by another, the refusal to ratify a transaction concluded by an agent without authority, and failing to assert a right to avoid a contract.[417] The second exclusion is the renunciation of rights that have not fully matured, such as contingent rights. The classical definition of contingent rights included the expectancy (*Anwartschaftsrecht*), which would mean it could not be a potential gift object. However, the case law now includes some expectancies in current patrimony. As a result, some authors suggest that this provision

---

411. Staudinger (-Wimmer-Leonhardt) § 516 no. 7.

412. Savigny (1841) 29, 31.

413. "Living without charge in the building of another is considered a gift" (*In aedibus alienis habitare gratis, donatio videtur*). Savigny (1841) 32–33 and note b, quoting D. 39, 5, 9 (Pomponius).

414. Savigny id. 35.

415. Id. 37–39.

416. BGH 1 July 1987, NJW 1987, 2816.

417. MünchKomm-BGB (-Kollhosser) § 517 no. 2.

should be revised.[418] Finally, the renunciation of an inheritance or bequest is also excluded from gift law. This provision has also been criticized.[419]

(C) JUSTIFICATION

336. *Clear distinctions.* In German law, the exclusion from gift law of services, loans, and rent-free possession is not chiefly designed to confine the protective regime of gift law to cases in which the donor is actually impoverished. In fact, a significant minority of the authors, at times well supported by the case law, proposes to apply gift law protections, including form requirements and measures for the protection of creditors, to these transactions as well.[420]

Rather the goal seems to be to elaborate clear distinctions between the neighboring private law institutions. German law attempts to create a seamless web of legal norms, without overlap and without gaps. Because German law conceives of the gift as a contract, gift law can be expanded up to the boundary with, but not beyond, adjacent contractual institutions. A distinguished voice in the German discussion has suggested that gift law, and especially its form requirements and other protective provisions, should apply when the service rendered, the amount of interest saved on the loan, or the free rent exceeds a certain value.[421] The dominant view has rejected the suggestion because "it would blur the boundary between gifts and other gratuitous contracts to a degree that would no longer be compatible with legal certainty."[422] The case law makes clear that a particular transaction cannot be subsumed under more than one of the nominate contracts. Thus, providing rent-free living space can be either a gift, which was the former view, or a gratuitous bailment (*Leihe* [*commodatum*]), the current view, but not both.[423]

iii. Italy

337. *Differing degrees of regulation.* Italian law, borrowing from both French and German law, has created a different understanding of the limits of the gift object and a different vision of the purpose of gift law. Italian law combines the French law goal of confining gift law's protective measures with the German law interest in clear delimitation. The result is an attempt to provide a range of legal regulation for the different transactions that involve the giving of gifts.

---

418. Id. no. 3.
419. Id. no. 4.
420. Id. § 516 nos. 4–5.
421. Heck § 94 par. 6.
422. MünchKomm-BGB (-Kollhosser) § 516 no. 5.
423. BGH 11 Dec. 1981, BGHZ 82, 354 at 356–358; Slapnicar; Nehlsen-von Stryk.

(A) GENUS AND SPECIES

338. *Gratuitous acts.* In Italy, as in France, the broad category of gratuitous acts (*atti a titolo gratuito*) includes all transactions in which the benefit received is not counterbalanced by a corresponding sacrifice[424] or in which the parties intended a nonequivalent exchange.[425] Gratuitous acts thus include loans without interest, unpaid agencies and other services, and gratuitous bailments. The category of gratuitous transfer (*liberalità*) is reserved for those gratuitous acts that permit the donee, at the donor's expense, to acquire patrimonial rights that are, or are closely related to, property rights. The last will and testament is governed exclusively by the rules relating to successions and therefore is not considered a gratuitous transfer.

339. *Typical liberality.* The gift does not exhaust the category of gratuitous transfers. The gift is considered the *typical* liberality and is specially regulated as a named contract. The concept of liberality also includes other transactions that, though they do not meet the definition of the gift in all respects, nonetheless "produce, or are designed to produce, an economic effect of equivalent content."[426] What is typical about the gift is that it achieves its result directly, without employing other legal institutions. The indirect means of achieving the same end—what in other civilian systems are known as indirect gifts—are considered in Italian law to be nongift liberalities and thus are governed by less rigorously protective norms. These are known both as *atypical liberalities* (*liberalità atipiche*) and as *indirect gifts* (*donazioni indirette*).[427] Because the concept of gift is used exclusively for the prototypical form of gratuitous transaction, the term is even more restrictive than in other systems.

(B) TYPES OF GIFT

340. *Tripartite division.* The Italian Code defines the gift as an enrichment that occurs by means of a disposition or the assumption of an obligation (CC art. 769). The Italian doctrine includes within this definition three types of giving. The three are often named for the tripartite division in the Roman law of gifts, namely *in dando*, *in obligando*, and *in liberando*.[428]

341. *In dando.* The first category, *in dando*, refers to the obligation to give, to transfer rights in property. The basic transaction involves the creation or transfer of a property right or the assignment of a contract right that already exists in the donor's patrimony (*donazione reale traslativa*).[429] Virtually any property right will

---

424. Rescigno (-Carnevali) 488.
425. Balbi 13.
426. Carnevali (1989) no. 1.1.
427. Casulli (1964) no. 10. See supra nos. 279–281.
428. Capozzi no. 330 par. a; Archi (1964) 938.
429. Cian and Trabucchi art. 769 no. IV par. 1.

do, including an undivided joint interest, a usufruct, the underlying rights to property, whether or not burdened by usufruct (*nuda proprietà*; CC art. 796), a right to use or habitation, an easement, a right to surface construction (*diritto di superficie*), and intellectual property rights.[430] A gift may also involve the *creation* of a property right (*donazione reale constitutiva*), such as a usufruct or easment. Also considered gifts are transfers of negotiable instruments, stock certificates, and a definite collection of personal property (*universalità di mobili*).[431] A gift may be validly structured as periodic deliveries (art. 772). Unless otherwise stated, the deliveries terminate on the donor's death.[432]

The gift of an inheritance is expressly mentioned in the code (arts. 477, 1547 par. 2). The prevailing view seems to be that the object of the gift is not a *universitas iuris* but rather the individual rights contained in the inheritance. As a result, the transfer of the inheritance does not convey the status of heir, which the donor retains, together with liability for the estate's debts. Capozzi suggests that it is preferable to consider the gift to be of the totality of the property, so that the donee becomes jointly liable for the debts.[433] The gift of a business or a going concern is also proper.[434]

The creation of a guarantee or security interest is not a gift.[435] At the moment the suretyship arises, there is neither impoverishment nor enrichment.[436] However, there may be an indirect gift if the surety is obliged to pay and renounces the claim against the debtor. Services may not be the object of a gift. The refusal to be compensated for a service is considered an *omissio adquirendi* rather than a transfer. Giving free medical or legal advice or an uncompensated lesson or lecture are not gifts.[437] Omissions are also not generally gifts—agreeing not to construct a wall, abstaining from a public auction, failing to exercise

---

430. Balbi 41–44. Scholars generally exclude from the category of gift objects the gratuitous creation or transfer of an *emphyteusis*, the long-term lease of real property with the obligation to make improvements (*enfiteusi;* CC arts. 957–977). The creation is not a gift because the obligation to make improvements serves as its cause. The transfer of an existing emphyteusis without compensation is not a gift because the transferee will have to make lease payments and improvements. If the transferee is exempted from the obligation to pay rent, the transfer is considered a simple gift of real property. Capozzi no. 333 par. a.

431. Rescigno (-Carnevali) 524–525. CC art. 771 par. 2 recognizes that a collection of personal property, defined as a group of things that belong to the same person and have a common purpose (*destinazione unitaria;* CC art. 816), may be the object of a gift. A typical example is a library or a stamp collection.

432. Such gifts do not violate the prohibition against gifts of future property. Infra no. 366.

433. Capozzi no. 333 par. c.

434. Id. no. 333 par. d.

435. Carnevali (1989) no. 1.1; Ascoli (1935) 138; Torrente (2006) 267–268.

436. Capozzi no. 334 par. d.

437. Balbi 37–38.

a right of redemption. An unretributed use, such as enjoying another's hospitality for a meal or lodging, is also not a gift.

342. *In obligando.* The second variety of gift is the assumption of an obligation toward the donee (*donazione obbligatoria*).[438] The code expressly includes the gift of an obligation in the definition of the gift (CC art. 769). The effect is to enrich the donee's patrimony with a contract right against the donor.[439] According to the traditional view, not all obligations may become the object of a gift. Gifts may include obligations to give (*dare*) but not obligations to perform an act (*facere*). In other words, a gift may be made by assuming an obligation only when the obligation, when performed, causes the donee to acquire a property right. The agreement to perform a service is not a gift. The limitation is thought to follow from the definition. A gift enriches the donee and impoverishes the donor. Rendering a service is not thought to impoverish the donor.[440]

Biondi argued that a gift may consist in the donor's assumption of an obligation to perform—or not to perform—an act.[441] Modern authors have adopted this view. It is thought that any limitation on gifts of an obligation would contradict the broad language of the code.[442] For definitional purposes, the donor's impoverishment may be found in the absence of a quid pro quo. Moreover, in some cases, such as the work of actors and actresses, a gratuitous performance would represent a legal impoverishment.

343. *In liberando.* The final type of gift, recognized though much disputed, is the release of a debt or the waiver of a right, whether specifically with respect to the donee (*remissione*) or *erga omnes* (*rinuncia*). The two types of release are known collectively as the *donazione liberatoria*. All types of rights may be waived, both contract rights and limited property rights.[443] Though the majority view admits that a release may be a valid gift,[444] some authors disagree. Both the code and the doctrinal conception of a gift require a disposition, yet a release does not dispose of any right. Moreover, a gift is a contract while a release is considered a unilateral act. Acceptance of a release does not form a contract and is legally irrelevant. According to this view, the release should be an indirect gift.[445]

---

438. The gift of an obligation closely resembles the Roman *donatio in obligando*, which was executed by *stipulatio*. Archi (1964) 937. For the stipulatio, see infra no. 646.

439. Capozzi no. 346 at 815.

440. Id. Capozzi also suggests that the limitation avoids difficult valuation problems that would arise at collation or revocation. Id. no. 334 par. e.

441. Biondi nos. 126–127.

442. Capozzi no. 346 at 815–816.

443. Id. no. 347 at 819.

444. Id. at 818–819.

445. Id. at 818; Balbi 107–111.

Cataudella, however, has argued that the debtor's statutory right to reject the release (CC art. 1236) introduces a contractual moment into the transaction.[446] Though the simple release is a unilateral act, when it is done gratuitously, agreement, even if implicit, is required. Agreement is needed to give legal effect to the act by ensuring that the release will not be rejected. Moreover, though a simple release is purely abdicative, a gratuitous release also has an attributive function. The principal practical concern of the debate is whether to subject a gratuitous release to gift formalities.

(c) ATYPICAL LIBERALITIES

344. *Indirect gifts.* Beyond the three basic types of gift giving, Italian law identifies other transactions that, though they gratuitously enrich the donee and reduce the donor's patrimony, do so by indirection, usually by means of other contractual institutions. The Italian Civil Code provides that these other forms of liberality, though not governed by all of gift law, are subject to various gift law provisions, including those relating to collation (*collazione*) and revocation (CC arts. 737, 809).[447] "Indirect gifts, better known as atypical liberalities, include all those acts or even simple activities that, with intentional generosity (*liberalità*), achieve the same *result* (enrichment of the donee and corresponding impoverishment of the donor) as do typical gifts."[448]

Thus, in Italian law, the liberality is considered a purpose or goal (*uno scopo*) that can be realized in various ways, with the gift being only the most typical.[449] Atypical liberalities are recognized by their economic content and specifically by whether they produce, directly or indirectly, an economic effect equivalent to a gift transaction.[450] Examples of indirect gifts include sowing seed or constructing with one's own materials on the property of another, a third-party beneficiary contract, a partition of joint property intentionally benefiting one of the joint owners, a failure to interrupt the term for adverse possession, or registration in the donee's name of property purchased by the donor.[451] When, in the context of an indirect gift, the amount of the donee's enrichment does not equal the diminution of the donor's patrimony, the value of the gift object is the value surrendered by the donor,[452] though Carnevali has suggested that the valuation method should depend on the legal question that is being asked.[453]

---

446. Cataudella 763–765.
447. Carnevali (1989) no. 9.1.
448. Cian and Trabucchi art. 809 no. I (emphasis in original). See supra nos. 279–281.
449. Carnevali (1974) 216; Rescigno (-Carnevali) 486.
450. Carnevali (1974) id.; Rescigno (-Carnevali) id.
451. Cian and Trabucchi art. 809 no. I.
452. Id. no. III.
453. Rescigno (-Carnevali) at 605–607.

iv. Spain

345. *Three coequal types.* In Spanish law as well, any patrimonial right may become the object of a gift. The Civil Code defines the gift, in terms similar to those used in the French Civil Code, as an act of generosity (*liberalidad*) by which the donor gratuitously disposes of a thing for the benefit of the donee, who accepts it (art. 618). Spanish doctrine notes that this definition seems to imply that only property that can be immediately transferred may be the object of a gift. However, the scholars have broadened this understanding considerably. Instead of beginning with a core understanding of the gift object as a property right and then acknowledging a penumbra of other possible gift objects, Spanish law recognizes three coequal types of gifts. These include a gift of property rights (*donación real*), a gift of contract rights (*donación obligacional*), and a gift by release or waiver (*donación liberatoria*).[454]

346. *Owed by the donor.* In some of the most sensible pages in the long history of reflection about the giving of gifts, the Spanish doctrine has carefully demonstrated the role played by each of the three varieties of gift object.[455] In particular, the authors expressly acknowledge that the creation of an obligation may constitute a gift. If a donor may validly give 1,000 Euros as a gift, there is no reason why the donor should not be able to enter into a gift contract to transfer the funds at a later date. In the first case, personalty is transferred from one patrimony to another. In the second, the gift consists in creating in the donee the legal right to demand the transfer. Both are important forms of gift giving in the real world. Spanish legal thinking believes that the principle of party autonomy requires that the law acknowledge and accept transactions of both types.[456]

v. The Common Law

347. *All property.* The general rule in the common law is that all property may be transferred by gift. However, it does not seem possible to make what in the Romanic systems is known as a gift of an obligation. In other words, a donor may not become bound to make a payment or to transfer property in the future. Particular difficulties arise with regard to gifts of rights, often referred to as *choses in action,*[457] particularly incorporeal rights.

---

454. Paz-Ares Rodríguez (-Albaladejo García) art. 618 note VI.

455. Id. note III; 2 Lacruz Berdejo no. 499.

456. Diez-Picazo and Gullón 337.

457. A *chose in action* is a right to bring suit to recover chattels, money, or a debt. The various choses in action have little in common beside the characteristic that they are not currently subject to physical possession. (The term is sometimes contrasted with *chose in possession.*) Examples include debts, stocks, bonds, shares, negotiable instruments, contract and tort claims, and the heir's interest in the estate, as well as rights not immediately available for recovery, such as a debt due in the future. 6 Halsbury sub Choses in Action no. 1 and note 2; 2 Blackstone 396–397.

(A) ENGLAND

348. *Limited exceptions.* In English law, all property—real and personal, corporeal and incorporeal—may generally be the object (in English, it is usually referred to as the *subject*) of a gift.[458] Exceptions include attributes that are inalienable by nature, such as honorary titles and other dignities, and any property made inalienable by law,[459] including real estate granted for distinguished service.[460] An advowson (the right of presentation to a vacant ecclesiastical benefit), which is considered a *chattel real* because it is often appendant to the neighboring manor, may be the object of a gift if the statutory requirements are observed.[461] As far as personalty is concerned, English law permits only an absolute interest to be given by inter vivos gift.[462] The personal property that can be given by gift object is otherwise restricted only by the well-known limitations to property rights. For example, because the right must be ascertainable, an unreclaimed wild animal cannot be the object of a gift.

349. *Choses in action.* Choses in action are generally gifted by assignment. The history of assignments, particularly gratuitous assignments, has long been contested and remains obscure.[463] In the oldest common law, choses in action, expectancies, possibilities, and the like were not assignable. Coke believed that assignment would multiply suits and subvert justice.[464] The suspicion that assignment is a form of champerty or maintenance lasted into the twentieth century.[465] As a result, assignment was considered against public policy and possibly illegal,[466] and the law courts refused to enforce an assignee's rights. By the seventeenth century, however, equity recognized assignments of choses in action, at least when they were supported by consideration.[467] Before the Judicature Act (1873), a gratuitous transfer of a chose in action was generally accomplished by a declaration of trust,[468] though a mortis causa gift of a specialty

---

458. 20 Halsbury part 1 sub Gifts no. 23.

459. Id.

460. Though the fee may not be gifted, a gift of rents and profits is permitted. Id.

461. Id. no. 22.

462. Id. no. 23. A limited interest in chattels can be conveyed by trust.

463. See infra nos. 899–901.

464. "[T]he great wisdom and policy of the sages and founders of our law [has] provided, that no possibility, right, title, nor thing in action, shall be granted or assigned to strangers, for that would be the occasion of multiplying of contentions and suits, of great oppression of the people ... and the subversion of the due and equal execution of justice." *Lampet's Case* (1613) 10 Co Rep 46b, 48a, 77 ER 994, 997. See also 2 Blackstone 442.

465. *Fitzroy v Cave* [1905] 2 KB 364; Bridge 146.

466. 3 Pomeroy § 1270.

467. Rundell 643; Mechem (1925) 10; 2 Blackstone 442.

468. Anson (1901).

could be made by delivery.[469] The Judicature Act expressly permitted assignments and did not require consideration.[470]

Today, all choses in action that may be assigned may generally be transferred by gift.[471] Problems arise concerning a mere expectancy, particularly the expectation of succession to property. The difficulty is that, because there is no forced share in the common law and wills are revocable, the extent of the successory interest becomes verifiable only upon the decedent's death. As a result, such expectancies can generally not be given by gift.[472] Mere possibilities may also not be given, unless coupled with an interest. The possibility itself then becomes a present interest. When the interest is in land, it is alienable by deed and therefore may become the object of a gift transfer.[473]

(B) INDIA

350. *Life estate.* Earlier decisions of the Indian high courts deemed a life interest in an Islamic hiba to be a gift coupled with a condition. Any conditions attached to a hiba are void, while the gift remains valid. The modern trend, however, is to uphold the life interest.[474]

(C) UNITED STATES

351. *Broad definition.* In American law as well, the general rule is that every type of property, as long as it is property in being, may be the object of a gift.[475] This includes property real and personal, legal and equitable, corporeal and incorporeal, reversionary interests, remainders, and interests vested and contingent. Some state statutes appear to limit the object of a gift to personal property.[476] This is because, in these statutes, the gift of real property is called a grant. The case law applies the same principles to gifts of real property.[477] Thus, the transfer of a joint interest in property, including real property[478] and the title to a cooperative apartment,[479] may also pass by gift. A partnership interest is considered

---

469. Thornton § 267.

470. Supreme Court of Judicature Act of 1873 sec. 25 par. 6, now in Law of Property Act of 1925 sec. 136 par. 1. See infra nos. 899–901.

471. 20 Halsbury part 1 sub Gifts no. 24.

472. Nonetheless, the assignment of an expectancy, if supported by consideration, seems to be enforceable in equity as a contract. *Tailby v Official Receiver* (1888) 13 AC 523 (HL).

473. 20 Halsbury part 1 sub Gifts no. 24.

474. Fyzee 221.

475. 38A C.J.S. Gifts § 29. For future interests, see infra nos. 374–375.

476. "A gift is a transfer of personal property, made voluntarily, and without consideration." California CC § 1146.

477. *Kinsell v. Thomas,* 124 P. 220, 222 (Cal. App. 1912) ("a gift of real estate").

478. *Estate of Lee v. Graber,* 462 P.2d 492, 494 (Colo. 1969).

479. *Will of Katz,* 539 N.Y.S.2d 659 (Sur. Ct. 1989).

personal property and may be gifted by way of assignment.[480] Public property, of course, generally cannot be given by gift.[481]

352. *Expectancies.* Mere expectancies are too contingent to be the object of a gift. Some courts hold that the designation of a beneficiary in a life insurance policy constitutes a gift, subject to the contingencies that the insured might cancel without notice and that the assignee must survive the insured.[482] Other courts hold that the designation is a mere expectancy.[483] It has also been held that the right to repudiate a contract cannot be the object of a gift.[484]

353. *Services.* Interestingly, research has revealed no explicit American discussion, either in the cases or in the treatises, about whether the gratuitous performance of services or other gratuitous acts may be considered a gift. The problem is resolved indirectly in American law, for delivery is a requisite of an effective gift.[485] Delivery is generally not thought to encompass the performance of services.

(1) Choses in action

354. *Assignment.* The early American authorities held that choses in action, because they could not be assigned, could not constitute the object of a gift transaction.[486] Assignments were eventually recognized by statute.[487] However, a distinction arose between law and equity. In order not to burden the obligor with multiple suits, law did not recognize partial assignments.[488] Equity was able to recognize such assignments because it could compel the presence of all necessary parties.[489] Today, a partial assignment transfers an equitable interest in the chose.[490] If the chose is existing, it may be transferred gratuitously.[491]

---

480. *Estate of Schreiber*, 227 N.W.2d 917 (Wisc. 1975).

481. California Const. art. 16 par. 6.

482. *Givens v. Girard Life Ins. Co.*, 480 S.W.2d 421, 424 (Tex. Civ. App. 1972); Restatement (Third) of Property (Wills and Other Donative Transfers) § 7.1 comment c and illus. 3 (2003).

483. *Mutual Benefit Life Ins. Co. v. Clark*, 254 P. 306 (Cal. App. 1927).

484. *Armitage v. Widoe*, 36 Mich. 124, 129 (1877).

485. For the general requirement of delivery in American law, see infra nos. 865–888.

486. *Cowen v. First Nat'l Bank of Brownsville*, 63 S.W. 532, 534, rehearing denied, 64 S.W. 778 (Tex. 1901).

487. 3 Pomeroy § 1273.

488. *Mandeville v. Welch*, 5 Wheat. 277, 288–289 (U.S. 1820) (Story, J.).

489. *Richardson v. White*, 44 N.E. 1072, 1073 (Mass. 1896) (Holmes, J.); Dickinson 2–3.

490. Dickinson 10.

491. Id. 13–14.

The general rule today is that choses in action may be assigned at law without consideration, though some states consider an assignment unsupported by consideration to be ineffective. Most choses in action may be transferred by gift if they are of the type that survives the deaths of the assignor and the obligor, such as most contract and many tort claims.[492] The insured may make a gift of the insurance policy to the beneficiary.[493] More personal claims are not assignable. These include tort claims related to injuries to person or character and certain contract claims, such as the breach of a promise to marry and service contracts for which personal performance is of the essence.[494] Assignments that would violate public policy are not permitted, such as transfers of honorary rewards paid by the government for past or future services.[495]

Bonds, mortgages, and books of account may all be assigned.[496] Promissory notes and other negotiable instruments of which the donor is payee or endorsee may also be transferred by gift and are effective upon delivery. The same is true of a cashier's check.[497] However, when the donor is drawer of the check, only payment of the instrument executes the gift.[498] A promissory note of which the donor is maker represents a simple promise and therefore the gift is executed not on transfer but upon payment.[499] A pecuniary legatee may make a gift of the equitable interest in the estate by gratuitous assignment.[500] Some states permit gifts of parol choses in action (those not evidenced by a writing) to be made by deed.[501]

(2) Renunciation

355. *Release and waiver.* Gifts may also be made by relinquishment, release, or waiver. For example, the holder may validly discharge the obligation to pay a negotiable instrument without consideration.[502] A renunciation of rights made

---

492. *Grover v. Grover*, 24 Pick. 261 (Mass. 1837); 38A C.J.S. Gifts § 30. Common-law courts refer to the gift of a chose in action as an assignment. See, e.g., *Speelman v. Pascal*, 222 N.Y.S.2d 324, 326 (N.Y. 1961) ("gift ... by way of assignment").

493. *Mutual Life Ins. Co. v. Franck*, 50 P.2d 480, 484 (Cal. App. 1935). For the gift of a life insurance policy in American law, see infra nos. 918–921.

494. 3 Pomeroy § 1275.

495. Id.

496. 38A C.J.S. Gifts §§ 45, 54.

497. *Malloy v. Smith*, 290 A.2d 486, 488 (Md. App. 1972).

498. *Estate of Bolton*, 444 N.W.2d 482 (Iowa 1989); *Simmons v. Cincinnati Sav. Soc.*, 31 Ohio St. 457, 461 (Ohio 1877); see 38A C.J.S. Gifts § 56; supra no. 310; infra no. 909.

499. *Blanchard v. Williamson*, 70 Ill. 647 (Ill. 1873).

500. *Chase Nat'l Bank v. Sayles*, 11 F.2d 948, 953 (1st Cir. 1926).

501. *Driscoll v. Driscoll*, 77 P. 471 (Cal. 1904); Rundell 655 editor's note.

502. UCC § 3-604 par. a.

with the intent to benefit another may be a gift.[503] The waiver of the power to change the beneficiary of an insurance policy may constitute the object of a gift.[504] A gift may also consist in allowing the statute of limitations to run on a debt.[505]

(3) Tipping

356. *Consideration.* The question of whether tips constitute gifts has rarely been litigated. In what may be considered the leading case, an en banc panel of the Washington Supreme Court held that tips are not gifts because the services rendered constitute adequate consideration.[506] The court relied on the "well established custom, tradition, practice and standard" that restaurant customers must pay for their service in the form of a tip, as well as the fact that both employers and employees consider tips to be compensation.

Similarly, for purposes of calculating the amount of worker's compensation benefits, tips constitute wages and not gifts.[507] The applicable statutes typically define wages as the money rate of compensation under the contract received from the employer. Nonetheless, the courts characterize tips as wages. The employee, with the employer's knowledge and consent, furnishes a service that compels the customer to pay a tip, "and if the tip is not paid the service is so grudgingly and unsatisfactorily given that the person served is willing to pay it the next time."[508] Tips represent the portion of the employee's wages that is to be paid by the customer.

b. Particular Types of Property

357. *Vigorous debate.* Three specific categories of property are often specially regulated by gift law: future property, property belonging to another, and the totality of the donor's property. Gifts of organs and other parts of the human body are governed by special norms.

i. Future Property

358. *Prodigality.* In jurisdictions in which gift law is designed to protect the donor, some gifts of future property are prohibited. The purpose seems to be to prevent

---

503. *Del Giorgio v. Powers,* 81 P.2d 1006, 1014 (Cal. App. 1938).

504. *Mahoney v. Crocker,* 136 P.2d 810, 814 (Cal. App. 1943).

505. Restatement (Third) of Property (Wills and Other Donative Transfers) § 6.1 comment k.

506. *City of Bellevue v. State,* 600 P.2d 1268, 1270 (Wash. 1979) (en banc). The court also held that, since tipping is required by custom, donative intent was also lacking.

507. UNITED STATES: *Sloat v. Rochester Taxicab Co.,* 163 N.Y.S. 904 (App. Div. 1917); ENGLAND: *Penn v Spiers & Pond Ltd* [1908] 1 KB 766.

508. *Sloat v. Rochester Taxicab Co.,* id. 904.

donors from falling prey to the temptation of making gifts of property they do not yet possess.

(A) FRANCE AND BELGIUM

359. *Two problems.* In French law, future things (*choses futures*) generally may be the object of an obligation (CC art. 1130). However, adjustment has been necessary to accommodate the principle to gift law. Pothier already noted the two problems.[509] First, French law defines a gift as the immediate transfer of a property interest (CC art. 894). Things not yet in existence are generally not transferable. The second problem involves the special principle of irrevocability in French gift law.[510] If gifts of future things were permitted, a donor might circumvent special irrevocability by making a gift of property not yet in existence and later refusing to make or acquire the property.[511]

(1) Prohibition

360. *Limited prohibition.* The French Civil Code has reconciled the competing principles by prohibiting gifts of those future things that it denominates future property (*les biens à venir*; art. 943). The prohibition strikes only that property in which the donor has no interest at the moment of the gift, such as property the donor merely hopes or intends to acquire.[512] Property may be given by gift as long as the donor has a current right to it, even if the thing does not exist at the time of the gift.[513] For example, an approaching harvest, interest to come due on a debt, and dividends to be declared may all be the object of gift giving. Property that the donor holds under a condition is also part of the donor's patrimony and can be transferred by gift.

361. *Successive usufructs.* There has been some dispute about whether the creation of successive usufructs transfers present or future property. A donor may gift the underlying property (*nue-propriété*), while reserving an initial usufruct and creating a second usufruct for the benefit of a third party. Because the third party often begins possession only at the donor's death, some scholars argue that the second usufruct is future property. The Cassation Court holds that the second usufruct is present property. It passes immediately to the donee, with only the enjoyment being postponed to the death of the first usufructuary.[514]

362. *Determination in the future.* French law has extended the prohibition to include property that is future in that it is determinable only at a future date,

---

509. 8 Pothier, *Donations* no. 80.
510. Infra nos. 1075–1096.
511. 8 Pothier, *Donations* no. 80.
512. 8 De Page no. 237 par. B.
513. Id. no. 237 par. C.
514. Civ.¹ 21 Oct. 1997, J.C.P. 1997 II 22969 note Isabelle Harel-Dutirou.

such as a gift of the personalty that the donor will possess at death. However, the prohibition is narrowly construed, and many similar transactions continue to be valid. For example, the gift is valid if the gift property is identified at the moment of the gift (*corps certain*) and is immediately gifted, even if possession is not to be transferred until the donor's death.[515] If the gift object is no longer in the donor's patrimony at death, the donee has a claim for damages. If the property is fungible, such as a sum of money, the gift is valid if the donor's intention was immediately to create a debt in the donee's favor, even though payment could not be demanded before the donor's death.

(2) Exceptions

363. *Between spouses.* There are a number of exceptions. These include gifts of future property between spouses during marriage, which, as explained below, are valid, though to some extent revocable,[516] and gifts by the spouses themselves or others in the marriage settlement (*contrat de mariage*).[517] As between spouses, gifts of future property generally involve the transfer by one spouse to the other of part or all of the property the donor will leave at death. In other words, it is an inter vivos transfer concerning a decedent's estate that does not yet exist.[518] The authors and the case law validate such a gift, even though it represents a radical departure from normal principles and even though it is not authorized by any code provision.

364. *Present and future property.* One further exception is known somewhat misleadingly as the gift of present and future property (*biens présents et à venir*).[519] These gifts, which are valid if made in the marriage settlement, are alternative rather than cumulative. The donee receives the option of taking either the donor's property at the time of the donor's death or, in the alternative, the donor's property at the moment the gift was made. The donee who chooses the gift of future property is also liable for the debts the donor owes at death, while the choice of present property subjects the donee only to the debts due at the moment the gift is made. The choice of present property is available only if a statement of the debts and charges the donor owed at the moment of the gift is attached to the gift document. The choice of future property allows the donee to recover the gratuitous transfers the donor made subsequent to making the gift, whereas the choice of present property allows recovery of any transfers, whether or not

---

515. 5 Planiol and Ripert no. 442; Civ. 30 Nov. 1937, D.H. 1938, 19.
516. CC arts. 947, 1096 par. 1 (2005); see infra nos. 1301–1303.
517. CC arts. 1093, 1082.
518. Véron 99.
519. CC arts. 1084–1085, 1093; Flour and Souleau nos. 431–435.

for consideration, of the property that belonged to the donor at the moment of the gift.[520]

(3) Sanction

365. *Absolutely void.* In French law, the gift of future property is absolutely void,[521] even if the donor subsequently acquires the property. Even the donor can invoke the nullity. Usually the entire gift is void, but, if divisible, the gift of any present property remains valid. To explain why gifts of future property are absolutely void and, in particular, why the gift is not validated by the donor's acquisition of the property, De Page suggested that the sanction of absolute nullity "is, in the end, consistent with the goal pursued by the statute when it requires irrevocability: to discourage gifts because, societally, it is important to prevent them."[522]

(B) ITALY

366. *Extensive prohibition.* The Italian Civil Code provides that gifts may include only the donor's present property (*beni presenti*; art. 771 par. 1). Any gift of future property is void, except in the case of fruits not yet separated from the tree.[523] The prohibition is even more extensive than in French law. A gift of fruits may include only those natural fruits already in existence at the moment the gift is made.[524] Civil fruits seem to be exempt from the prohibition. A minority of the authors argue that the prohibition should not apply to the gift of an obligation.[525] A gift involving periodic performances is not prohibited. Such performances are deemed to represent the legal consequence of the original gift.

367. *Justification.* Italian law generally permits future things (*cose future*) to be the object of obligations (CC art. 1348). Because Italian law expressly characterizes the gift transfer as a contract (CC art. 769), it should be possible to give future property as a gift. The traditional explanation for the prohibition was that permitting gifts of future property would make the gift revocable. Today, some authors assimilate the rule to the prohibition of successoral pacts (CC art. 458). The dominant view is that the prohibition of gifts of future property is justified by the legislative goal of restraining prodigality.[526] As one Italian writer explains, the rule is justified by "the disfavor with which the legal order regards gratuitous transfers and the goal of applying a brake to hasty liberalities."[527]

---

520. For the difficulties that arise when the donee recovers property long after the donor has sold it, see Civ.¹ 22 Feb. 2000, *Rev. trim. dr. civ.* 2000, 378 obs. Jean Patarin. This type of gift has fallen into desuetude. Grimaldi no. 1640.

521. 8 De Page no. 553.

522. Id.

523. Id. art. 771 par. 1 sent. 2.

524. Cendon art. 771 note.

525. Biondi no. 123.

526. Capozzi no. 334 par. a.

527. Rescigno (-Carnevali) 526.

(C) SPAIN

368. *General rule.* The Spanish Civil Code also prohibits gifts of future property (*bienes futuros*), which it defines as property over which the donor does not have the power to dispose at the moment of the gift (art. 635). As the authors have noted, this provision would limit gifts to property that actually exists, is in the donor's patrimony at the time of the gift, and over which the donor has the power to dispose gratuitously.[528] The prohibition seems to be required by the conception of the *donación real* as an immediate transfer of property rights. It seems irrelevant to the *donación obligacional*.[529] The gift of an obligation cannot be considered a gift of future property because, at the moment the gift is made, there is no attempt to transfer property.[530] Yet if obligations regarding rights not currently in the donor's possession may be gifted, the prohibition against gifts of future property loses much of its importance.

369. *Interpretation.* Manuel Albaladejo García resolved the issue in a tour de force of statutory interpretation.[531] In light of the fact that gifts of an obligation are an important part of daily life, he argued that subjecting them to the prohibition of gifts of future property satisfies no legitimate need of the legal order and does not comport with a reasoned understanding of the notion of party autonomy. Albaladejo García proposed an interpretation of the provisions that respects both the letter of the code and the customary desire to promise a gift that is to be executed in the future. The two provisions at issue are the prohibition of gifts of future property (CC art. 635) and the provision that authorizes a gift of all or part of the donor's present property, provided that the donor reserves sufficient wealth for the donor's own maintenance (CC art. 634). Taken together, Albaladejo García argued, the two provisions signify that a donor may not gift everything that the donor has or will ever own. Because the code prohibits a gift of *"the* future property" (los *bienes futuros*), the text does not mean to exclude all future property from gift giving. What the code prohibits, Albaladejo García argued, is a gift of *all* future property.

(D) GERMANY

370. *No prohibition.* Future things (*noch nicht existente Sachen*) may become objects of obligations in German law.[532] Thus, any patrimonial advantage may be given as a gift, including a contractual right to claim property at a later date.[533]

---

528. Paz-Ares Rodríguez (-Albaladejo García) art. 635 no. I.

529. Diez-Picazo and Gullón 339.

530. 2 Lacruz Berdejo no. 503.

531. Paz-Ares Rodríguez (-Albaladejo García) art. 635 no. I.

532. Jauernig (-Berger) § 433 no. 12.

533. Jauernig (-Mansel) § 516 no. 5.

(E) THE COMMON LAW

371. *Rigid rule and flexible interpretation.* At the end of the day, the common law permits most common gifts of future property. This result is achieved by tempering a relatively rigid legal rule with the flexibility and creativity of equity.

(1) General rule

372. *Things in being.* In the common law, a gift is generally valid only if the donee receives a present interest in the gift property.[534] An interest that is only to take effect in the future is invalid—for example, the gift of the personal property that the donor will possess at death.[535] Thus, the general rule is that personalty may be the subject matter of a valid gift only if it is *in esse* at the time the gift is made.[536] Some American courts hold that future profits or the increase in property may be the object of a gift, but other courts hold otherwise because such property is not in esse. The rule is the same in trust law. "The mere fact that one hopes or expects to acquire property in the future is not an interest in property and thus cannot be held in trust."[537] An assignment of future property may operate as a contract to assign the property when it comes into existence or into the donor's possession, but the contract is enforceable only if supported by consideration, even if the assignment is done by deed.[538]

373. *India.* Indian law defines the gift as "the transfer of certain existing movable or immovable property."[539] Gifts of future property are expressly made void.[540] Thus, though the gift of a right of management is valid, the gift of the future revenue of a village is void.[541]

Islamic law requires a gift to be executed by physical delivery. A gift is valid only if the object is in actual existence at the time of the gift. A gift cannot be made of anything to be produced in the future, even if the donor is in possession of the necessary means of production. A gift of the fruit to be produced this year from the donor's palm tree is void, as is the gift of an annuity from future income produced by identified property. A declaration purporting to transfer property by way of hiba at a future time is also void.[542]

---

534. Brown § 7.12.
535. *Estate of Salzwedel*, 177 N.W. 586 (Wisc. 1920).
536. 38 Am.Jur.2d Gifts § 39.
537. 2 Scott and Ascher § 10.10.
538. 6 Halsbury sub Choses in Action no. 36.
539. Transfer of Property Act sec. 122.
540. Id. sec. 124.
541. Mulla sec. 122 no. 4. The cases cited were actually decided under religious law (Hindu and Mohammedan) rather than the Transfer of Property Act, but the result would be the same under the latter.
542. Fyzee 221.

(2) Future interests

374. *Flexibility.* Despite the restrictive general rule, the common law retains sufficient flexibility to permit many of the gifts of future property that are valid in civilian jurisdictions. There is no difficulty when real property is concerned, because future interests in real estate are regularly transferable in common-law jurisdictions.[543] As to personalty, the most common judicial expedient is to interpret the transaction as the present gift of a future interest, a current right to the future enjoyment of property.[544] In determining the validity of a gift of a stock certificate, for example, one court indicated that "[t]he test is whether the maker intended the instrument to have no effect until after the maker's death, or whether he intended it to pass some present interest."[545] Another common example of a valid gift of a future interest involves the deposit of funds in a bank to the credit of a donee, the donor to receive interest on the funds until the donor's death.[546]

375. *Choses in action.* Economically important gifts of future property often involve choses in action—bank accounts, notes evidencing debts, bonds, shares of stock, ordinary debts, and even rights that have not, at the time of the gift, sufficiently matured to be enforced by action. In some cases, these may be future property. Though the donor may have a legitimate expectation of payment, at the time of the gift the donor may not have an enforceable interest.

Equity is able to transfer these rights to the donee when they mature. In a leading case, the donor had been granted the exclusive right to produce a musical and a motion picture, both later known as "My Fair Lady," from George Bernard Shaw's play *Pygmalion.*[547] Before either the musical or the movie was commissioned, the donor, by letter, gave a "present" of specified percentages of the donor's prospective profit. The court held that the letter represented a valid assignment of a right to the royalties. "[W]hile there was not at the time of the assignment any presently enforceable or even existing chose in action but merely a possibility ... of such which the parties expected to ripen into reality and which did afterwards ripen into reality ... the assignment created an equitable title which the courts would enforce."[548] In other words, equity is able to solve technical timing problems by holding the effect of the transaction in abeyance until the moment is ripe.

---

543. Thompson §§ 23.06, 30.03 par. b.
544. Brown § 7.12.
545. *Innes v. Potter*, 153 N.W. 604, 606 (Minn. 1915).
546. *Candee v. Connecticut River Sav. Bank*, 71 A. 551 (Conn. 1908); infra nos. 936–938.
547. *Speelman v. Pascal*, 222 N.Y.S.2d 324 (N.Y. 1961).
548. Id. 327, referring to the holding in *Field v. City of New York*, 6 N.Y. 179 (1852).

ii. The Property of Another

376. *Different interpretations.* It is often difficult to understand the intent of the donor who makes a gift of property that belongs to someone else. Several interpretations are possible. The gift might be based on a mistake. It might indicate the donor's intent, or promise, to acquire the property. Or it might indicate the transfer of as much title as the donor has. Different legal systems interpret this type of gift differently. As a result, some permit it, while others prohibit it.

(A) FRANCE AND BELGIUM

377. *Prohibited.* The French Code does not expressly mention the gift of the property of another (*chose d'autrui*), though it does prohibit other transactions involving such property.[549] For example, the code declares all bequests of the property of another to be void, whether or not the testator was aware that the object belonged to another (CC art. 1021). The case law, however, severely restricts the operation of this statutory prohibition. If the testator was not mistaken about the ownership of the property, such a bequest may impose on the heir the obligation to purchase the property and transfer it to the legatee.[550]

It might therefore be expected that the French courts would follow the same permissive interpretation with regard to gift law. If the donor is mistaken, the gift would be void. Otherwise, the donor may be presumed to assume an enforceable obligation to acquire the property and transfer it to the donee. Instead, however, in what appears to be the only reported case, a Belgian court held that the gift of the property of another is void.[551] The nullity is justified by the fact that the gift of the property of another is properly understood as a means of gifting future property, namely "property which the donor intends to acquire but in which the donor has as yet no right."[552] De Page suggests that the nullity is also jusified by the nature of the gift in French law. The gift is not a promise to transfer title but is that transfer itself. Since title is immediately transfered upon conclusion of the gift act (art. 938), the gift is meaningless if title is not already in the donor.[553]

(B) ITALY

378. *Majority view.* The Italian Code does not expressly prohibit the gift of the property of another (*cose altrui*). A majority of the scholars follow the French law view. The gift is void and is not validated by the donor's subsequent acquisition

---

549. CC arts. 1021 (bequest), 1599 (sale), 1704 (exchange).
550. 5 Planiol and Ripert no. 604; 8 De Page nos. 242–245.
551. Liège 29 May 1869, *Pas.* 1870 II 404. See 8 De Page nos. 239–241.
552. 5 Planiol and Ripert no. 439.
553. 8 De Page no. 586.

of the property.[554] Nonetheless, the issue remains controversial.[555] As with the gift of future property, the doctrine senses the risk of prodigality. Accordingly, some authors argue that the gift of the property of another is equivalent to the gift of future property. Because, in both cases, the property does not, or does not yet, belong to the donor, both types of gift would contradict the code's definition of the gift, which permits only the gift of a right actually belonging to the donor (art. 769).[556] Moreover, if the donor is aware that the property belongs to another but does not disclose the fact, the gift is void due to a lack of donative intent. If the donor is not aware of the fact, the gift fails because the transaction does not impoverish the donor.[557]

379. *Minority view.* A minority argues that the gift is valid as an obligational gift and requires the donor to acquire the property for the donee's benefit.[558] These authors suggest that the code implicitly permits gifts of the property of another by providing a warranty for the case in which proper title is not conveyed (CC art. 797). Moreover, in contrast to French law, the Italian Code in some cases expressly permits both the sale (CC art. 1479 par. 1) and the bequest (CC art. 651) of the property of another. If gift law followed the rules applicable to bequests, the gift would be valid if the donor was aware that the property belonged to another and void if the donor was misinformed.[559] Biondi argued that gift law should follow the provision concerning the sale of another's property (CC art. 1478). Title should pass to the donee when acquired by the donor.[560] Moreover, under the code's good faith purchase rules, the donee's possession in good faith of movables, in conjunction with suitable title, would validate the acquisition as a purchase *a non domino* (CC art. 1153). Some scholars suggest that the gift of the property of another constitutes a legitimate title for such purposes.[561]

The Cassation Court also seems to be split on the question. In one case, the first section of the Court assimilated the gift of the property of another to the gift of future property and invalidated the gift.[562] In another recent decision, the

---

554. Rescigno (-Carnevali) 527–528; Torrente 497; Capozzi no. 334 par. b.
555. Rescigno (-Carnevali) id.
556. Biondi no. 112.
557. Massimo d'Auria, note to Cass. 5 Feb. 2001 no. 1596, *Giur. it.* 2001, 1595 at 1598 no. 7.
558. Rescigno (-Carnevali) 528 note 19; Biondi no. 123.
559. Biondi no. 112 at 348–349.
560. Id. at 349.
561. Id. at 349–350; Rescigno (-Carnevali) 528.
562. Cass. 18 Dec. 1996 no. 1131, *Rep. Foro it.* 1997 *Contratti della p.a.* no. 437. In 1936 the town of Agrigento agreed to transfer to the province of Agrigento a piece of property that it did not own but agreed to expropriate. The province agreed to construct baracks for the Fascist militia. The ministry of finance was to make payment to the province. The Court characterized the transaction as an invalid gift of future property.

Court's second section held that the gift of the property of another is not void.[563] The Court agreed with the scholars who argue that the gift of property that exists at the time of the gift and belongs to a third party cannot be analogized to the gift of future property. Instead, when the donor, in the gift act, expressly undertakes to acquire property not at the moment in the donor's patrimony, it operates as the gift of an obligation.[564]

(C) SPAIN

380. *Valid.* Spanish legal scholars would validate the gift of another's property. A donor should be permitted to make a gift of the obligation (*donación obligacional*) to acquire property.[565] However, if the donor intends to make an immediate transfer of rights in another's property, the Spanish courts hold that the gift is void.[566]

(D) GERMANY AND AUSTRIA

381. *Permitted.* The German Civil Code permits gift promises concerning property that the donor must first acquire (*den er erst erwerben sollte*; § 523 para. 2). The Austrian Code permits the gift of another's property (*eine fremde Sache*), provided the donee is aware of the circumstances (CC § 945). Austrian case law also enforces a gift promise concerning the property of another.[567]

(E) THE COMMON LAW

382. *Historical.* Bracton considered the gift of another's property (*res aliena*) to be binding between donor and donee, though invalid as against the true owner.[568] Fleta argued that a gift of another's property cannot be valid because, if not delivered, it might be revoked.[569] In Hindu law, the unauthorized gift of joint family property by an individual coparcener is considered either void ab initio or voidable by the other coparceners. In either case it may be recovered from the donee.[570]

---

563. Cass. 5 Feb. 2001 no. 1596, *Giur. it.* 2001, 1595 note Massimo D'Auria.

564. The holding conflicts with the traditional view that the gift of an obligation may involve only the obligation to give (*dare*) and not the obligation to do (*facere*). See supra no. 342.

565. 2 Lacruz Berdejo no. 503.

566. STS Civ. 12 Nov. 1964, RJ 5080.

567. OGH 24 Apr. 1906, Glaser/Unger (n.f.) no. 3400.

568. 2 Bracton 49, 56–57, 101–104.

569. Fleta bk. 3 ch. 3 at 5.

570. Derrett nos. 463–465. See *D. Nagaratnamba v. K. Ramayya*, AIR (50) 1963 AP 177, 181, [1962] 2 An WR 169. However, the father or managing member has the right to gift the property for pious purposes. Id.

(1) General rule

383. Generally ineffective. In the common law, the gift of another's property is generally ineffective,[571] especially if the donor intends to transfer rights by delivery. The same rule applies to the creation of a trust.[572] In an American case, a donor attempted to gift an automobile that was titled in the name of his sister.[573] The court held the gift to be ineffective. An English court has held that the lessee under an automobile lease-purchase agreement could not make a gift of the automobile to his wife, even though the residual payment at the end of the lease was nominal.[574] Moreover, the good faith purchase rules do not apply to donees. "[C]onsequently a valid gift can only be made by a person whose title to the subject matter admits of a disposition by gift."[575] It therefore goes without saying, though it has actually been decided, that a gift of the proceeds of a theft is void.[576] The courts are more accommodating when there is no attempt to deliver possession. Despite the wording of the gift, the donor may be held to have conveyed whatever title the donor had. For example, the gift of the contents of an apartment was held to be subject to the sublease granted by the donor.[577] The Restatement (Third) provides that, when the donor purports to transfer a greater interest than the donor has, the donee receives whatever the donor had the power to transfer.[578]

(2) Particular issues

384. Assignments. Even in the American jurisdictions that permit assignments of future rights, the assignment of the rights of another is void.[579] "One cannot legally give or assign a chose in possession or a chose in action unless he had some legal or equitable interest to give or assign. And it follows that a person is not a donee or assignee of property unless the concomitant donor or assignor

---

571. Restatement (Second) of Property (Donative Transfers) § 32.2 comment a.

572. ENGLAND: 48 Halsbury sub Trusts no. 654; UNITED STATES: 1 Scott and Ascher § 4.4.3. The purported creation of a trust in property that the settlor hopes to acquire is considered a promise to create a trust. It is unenforceable without consideration. 2 Scott and Ascher § 10.10.

573. *Marlin v. Merrill*, 156 S.W.2d 814, 821 (Tenn. App. 1941) (on petition for rehearing); Restatement (Third) of Property (Wills and Other Donative Transfers) § 6.1 comment c.

574. *Spellman v Spellman* [1961] 2 All ER 498 (CA); 20 Halsbury part 1 sub Gifts no. 1 note 3, no. 5 note 10.

575. Crossley Vaines 299.

576. CANADA: *R. v. Percival and McDougall* (1971) 16 D.L.R.3d 561, 564–566 (B.C.).

577. *Estate of Goodwin*, 185 N.Y.S. 461 (Sur. Ct. 1920).

578. Restatement (Third) of Property (Wills and Other Donative Transfers) §§ 6.1 comment c and illus. 1, 6.2 comment v.

579. 38A C.J.S. Gifts § 29.

has some interest in property which can be the subject matter of a gift or assignment."[580]

385. *Not considered a promise.* The common law does not interpret the gift of the property of another as a promise to procure the property and transfer it to the donee. In the common law, promises are generally not binding without consideration. Equity also seems not to give effect to gifts of the property of another. When chattels to be afterward acquired are involved in a sale, equity transfers the beneficial interest to the vendee as soon as the vendor acquires them.[581] However, the same rule does not apply to gifts or trusts because a gift takes effect only with the transfer of legal title.[582] Indian scholars argue that the prohibition against gifts of future property prevents equity from enforcing an implied promise to acquire and transfer the property even if the donor subsequently does acquire it.[583]

American case law refuses to require the donor to acquire the property, even when the donor has expressly promised to do so. In one case, a father deeded real property to his daughter and promised in the deed to pay off encumbrances on the property as they came due. The father failed to pay, and the property was sold at foreclosure. The court held that the donor's estate was not liable in damages. "If [property] is incumbered, the donor gives only what he has to give. He cannot give the interest of a third party in the property. However clear may be the intention of the donor to pay the incumbrances and thus give the entire property, he can accomplish this only by actually paying them."[584]

iii. All of the Donor's Property

386. *Medieval commentators.* Medieval commentators questioned whether a gift could be made of all of the donor's property, regardless of whether it involved merely present property or both present and future property.[585] The views ranged, on the one hand, from Martino Silimani, who denied the validity of such a gift even if it involved only present property, to Paolo di Castro, who considered that the inclusion of future property vitiated the entire transaction. Bartolus validated gifts of all present and future property, but only as far as the present property was concerned.

387. *Ancien régime.* Scholars under the French ancien régime were concerned with whether the donee of a universal inter vivos gift would be liable for any debts the donor contracted after the gift was made. The risk was that the donor

---

580. *Smith v. Barrick*, 85 N.E.2d 101, 103 (Ohio 1949) (quoting from the opinion of the court of appeals in the same case).
581. *Block v. Shaw*, 95 S.W. 806, 807 (Ark. 1906).
582. *In re Cohn*, 176 N.Y.S. 225 (App. Div. 1919); 1 Scott and Ascher § 4.4.3.
583. Mulla sec. 124 note (first paragraph)
584. *Fischer v. Union Trust Co.*, 101 N.W. 852, 855 (Mich. 1904).
585. Bellomo 965.

might in practice revoke the gift by incurring debts in the amount of the gift. The authors did not reach consensus.[586] D'Aguesseau believed that the gift of all of the donor's present and future property was "a kind of insane act" (*une espèce d'acte de folie*).[587]

(A) SPAIN AND LATIN AMERICA

388. *Spain.* Spanish law provides that a gift may include "all of the present property of the donor, or a portion of it, provided that the donor reserves, either as owner or usufructuary, what is necessary to live on in a manner corresponding to the donor's circumstances" (CC art. 634). If the donor does not provide sufficiently for future needs, some Spanish scholars argue that the gift is void as to the portion the donor requires.[588] Others would consider the gift to be valid, subject to the donor's right to recover (or refuse to deliver) what the donor needs for maintenance.[589] Because, in either case, the validity of the gift does not depend on whether the donor has reserved enough to live on, no statement about the matter is required when the gift is made, nor is any proof required that the donor's needs will be met.[590] The purpose of the rule is to provide not merely for the donor, but also for the donor's dependents.[591] The Spanish Code does not explicitly provide an action for the donor to recover necessaries. As a result, the period within which suit may be brought remains uncertain.[592]

389. *Argentina.* The Argentinean Civil Code generally follows the Spanish model (CC art. 1800 sent. 2). However, to avoid fraud on creditors, it specifies that creditors must be paid.[593] To some Argentinean authors, the reserve required to meet the donor's needs seems to infringe on the owner's right to dispose freely of property. The problem is resolved by noting that no rational person would wish to become a mendicant. If the donor parts with all property without reserving enough to live on, the act can be assumed involuntary and therefore void.[594] It follows from this reasoning that the reserve of necessaries is a condition for the validity of the gift.[595] For Argentinean scholars, therefore, a gift of all of the

---

586. 1 Louet 566–569.

587. D'Aguesseau, Letter no. 290 of 25 June 1731, in 9 d'Aguesseau 360 at 363.

588. Diez-Picazo and Gullón at 340.

589. 2 Lacruz Berdejo no. 503 lit. a. For the donor's right to revoke in case of impoverishment, see infra no. 1205.

590. Paz-Ares Rodríguez (-Albaladejo García) art. 634 no. II; Dir. gen. Registros 17 Apr. 1907, *Juris. civ.* 1907 no. 24.

591. Paz-Ares Rodríguez (-Albaladejo García) art. 634 no. I.

592. Id. art. 634 no. V.

593. Llerena art. 1800 no. 7.

594. Id. art. 1800 no. 3.

595. Id.

donor's property is valid only if the gift instrument reserves a usufruct or equivalent resources.[596]

390. *Chile.* The Chilean Civil Code resolves the problem in a different manner. Even without a reserve, a gift of all property is not void. However, the donor may, at any time, require the donee to provide the donor with the property necessary for maintenance, either from the property that was the object of the gift or from the donee's other property (CC art. 1408).

(B) GERMANY

391. *Present patrimony.* In German law, though any contract for the alienation of a party's future patrimony is void, a party may alienate that party's entire present patrimony or any portion of it (CC § 311b pars. 2-3).[597] Thus, a gift of the donor's entire property is valid under German law.[598] Until 1999 the donee of an entire patrimony was liable to the donor's creditors up to the value of the property and rights received.[599] Should the donor prove unable to secure necessaries, including what is needed by those to whom the donor owes a duty of support, the donor may recover the gift from the donee or the amount required for the support (CC § 528 par. 1).[600] The same principles apply to the gift of an inheritance (CC § 2385).

(C) ITALY

392. *Distinctions.* A universal gift of the donor's property (*donazione universale*), both present and future, is not permitted in Italian law.[601] A gift of the future property involved would in any case be invalid.[602] There is disagreement about whether the gift of all or a portion of the donor's present property may be considered a legal universality.[603] The majority view seems to be that the gift of the donor's current patrimony is analyzed as a gift of the individual rights that compose it and is valid as long as the individual rights are valued in the gift act.[604] Such a gift does not include rights to possession, guarantees, or security

---

596. Id. art. 1800 no. 5.

597. Staudinger (-Wimmer-Leonhardt) § 516 no. 22.

598. Jauernig (-Stadler) § 311 nos. 55 ff.

599. CC § 419 was abrogated as of 1 Jan. 1999.

600. See infra nos. 1202–1203.

601. Biondi no. 288. Such a disposition would be considered testamentary.

602. Supra no. 366.

603. Compare Biondi no. 288 ("shows some characteristics of universality") with Capozzi no. 334 par. c (not a universality). See Torrente (2006) 508–509.

604. Balbi 43; Capozzi id.

interests.[605] Though the donee is not generally liable for the donor's debts, the agreement or the circumstances may indicate otherwise.[606]

(D) THE COMMON LAW

393. *India.* Indian law also recognizes a gift of all of a donor's property.[607] A universal donee becomes personally liable for the donor's debts to the extent of the gift. This rule is derived from the provision in Hindu law that governs the transfer of property when an individual retires from the world to become an ascetic.[608] The provision is designed for the protection of creditors and does not apply if the donor retains any portion of the patrimony, except when the part retained is either insignificant or for the donor's maintenance.[609] Islamic law also permits an inter vivos gift of all of the donor's property, even though testamentary dispositions are limited to one-third of the net estate.[610]

394. *England.* English law does not generally recognize the category of universal donee, and English scholars do not discuss the possibility of a gift of the donor's entire property. However, English trust law permits a settlor to transfer the entire estate into trust.[611]

395. *United States.* American law recognizes the gift of an inheritance.[612] However, partially because American law does not recognize the concept of patrimony, donors do not seem to make inter vivos gifts of all of their property. In some American jurisdictions, a gift of all of the donor's personalty was considered to violate the Wills Act,[613] though this type of gift is now generally accepted.[614] A gift of all of the donor's property may be made by trust. The income is usually reserved to the settlor during the settlor's life, with the remainder going to other

---

605. At the moment security interests are created, the donee is not enriched and the donor is not impoverished. Carnevali (1989) no. 1.1; Ascoli (1935) 138; Torrente (2006) 267–268.

606. Biondi no. 291.

607. Indian Transfer of Property Act sec. 128.

608. Mulla sec. 128 note "Universal donee."

609. Id. sec. 128 note "Subject to the provisions of sec. 127."

610. Fyzee 217.

611. Thomas and Hudson no. 3.05.

612. *Jones v. Causey,* 206 N.W.2d 534 (Mich. App. 1973). The case involved the gratuitous assignment of an heir's interest in an inheritance after the decedent's death.

613. *Headley v. Kirby,* 18 Pa. 326 (1852), overruled by *In re Elliott's Estate,* 167 A. 289, 292 (Pa. 1933).

614. *Thomas' Adm'r v. Lewis,* 15 S.E. 389, 398 (Va. 1892).

beneficiaries.[615] Such trusts are not considered testamentary,[616] though they may be subject to challenge for undue influence.[617]

iv. Gifts from the Body

396. *Typically inalienable.* The human body has generally been considered inalienable for purposes of the private law.[618] However, though elements of the human body are not available for market transactions,[619] they may be given gratuitously. The *jātakas*, Indian stories of the Buddha's previous lives, already mentioned gifts from the body. A king scratched out his eyes and gave them to a blind man, or a prince threw himself from a cliff to feed a starving tigress.[620] Today, bodily organs, eyes, tissue, blood, and semen may generally be donated for therapeutic purposes.[621] In the legal systems examined here, the requirements for making the gift of an organ do not coincide with those for making a gift of property. The different procedures for making gifts from the body are considered below.[622]

---

615. *In re Coyle's Estate*, 104 N.Y.S.2d 260 (Sur. Ct. 1951).

616. *In re Ford's Estate*, 108 N.Y.S.2d 122 (App. Div. 1951).

617. *Olson v. Harshman*, 668 P.2d 147 (Kan. 1983).

618. ENGLAND: Human Organ Transplants Act of 1989; FRANCE: CC art. 16-1 par. 3, arts. 16-2 to 16-3, 16-5 to 16-6; ITALY: CC art. 5.

619. The sale of human organs is generally considered a criminal offense. FRANCE: Penal C art. 511-2; GERMANY: Law of 5 Nov. 1997 (TPG) §§ 17–18; INDIA: Transplantation of Human Organs Act sec. 19; ITALY: Law of 1 Apr. 1999 art. 22 par. 3; UNITED KINGDOM: Human Tissue Act sec. 32 par. 1; UNITED STATES: National Organ Transplant Act, 42 U.S.C. 274e; Uniform Anatomical Gift Act § 16 par. a.

620. Ohnuma 323.

621. Godbout and Caillé 87–91; Titmuss.

622. Infra nos. 993–1024.

4. GIFT CAPACITY

397. *Medieval law.* The medieval paterfamilias held title to all family property. Only he had *potestas alienandi* and with it the general capacity to make a gift.[1] Children and servants lacked the capacity to give, as did prodigals, the insane, monks, converted Christians, heretics, those convicted of lese majesty, and wards without consent of their tutors. On the other hand, virtually everyone had the capacity to receive a gift, whether they were present or absent, known or unknown, though in some jurisdictions unemancipated children could not receive gifts from their parents, except weaponry, certain usufructs, and necessaries. Gifts were permitted between fiancés in contemplation of marriage, though gifts between spouses were prohibited.

398. *Today.* Today the principle is everywhere the same. "All persons may give and receive ... by inter vivos gift ... except those the law declares lacking in capacity" (French CC art. 902). The question of gift capacity involves the exceptions to this general principle. The required capacity is generally that necessary to dispose of property (Italian CC art. 774 par. 1), though in some jurisdictions it is the capacity to make a will (French CC art. 901).[2] The principle of general gift capacity competes with the law's interest in protecting individuals from their desire to give and their eagerness to receive. Some protection is achieved by requiring forms for the validity of the gift. Yet even rigorous formality is considered insufficient. Additional protection is achieved by restricting those who may give and receive by gratuitous transfer. Capacity rules prohibit many of those otherwise capable of concluding contracts and transferring property from making and receiving gifts. In some jurisdictions, gift capacity differs so markedly from both contractual and testamentary capacity that it is best understood as a separate regime.

399. *Types of incapacity.* The restrictions can be classified in several ways. Some incapacities are absolute. They prohibit the person involved from giving to or receiving from anyone. Relative incapacities, on the other hand, prohibit gifts between individuals in certain relationships. Other distinctions concern the representation requirement. Some individuals may not engage in gift activity even if represented (*incapacité de jouissance*), while others may give or receive a gift

---

1. Bellomo 964–965.
2. In common-law jurisdictions, the capacity to create an irrevocable trust generally follows gift capacity. 1 Scott and Ascher § 3.2.

with a representative or with the required approvals (*incapacité d'exercise*). For a comparative presentation, the fundamental distinction is between the restrictions related to the capacity to give and those related to the capacity to receive.

The systematic placement of the rules relating to gift capacity varies. In some codes they are found among the general rules establishing legal capacity. In others they are included in the special rules governing gifts. The diversity in placement is suggestive. Gift capacity represents a series of exceptions to the general rules, but it is also an expression of a legal system's understanding of gift giving.

A. THE CAPACITY TO GIVE

400. *Wide variety.* Legal systems vary widely in the types of restrictions they place on gift giving and the individuals on whom they are imposed. With regard to organ donations, the capacity to make the gift is so closely related to the means of expressing consent that capacity questions are examined below in conjunction with the manner of disposition.[3]

1. Minors

401. *Principle.* All legal systems place some restriction on the ability of minors—*infants*, as they are known in the common law—to make gratuitous transfers. In most systems, unemancipated minors do not generally have the capacity to make a valid gift, though their guardians may make customary gifts on their behalf.[4] One author has suggested that the basis for the rule is not the minor's lack of capacity. Rather, because a minor's gift is generally invalid even if approved, the principle is that a minor's property is not alienable by gift.[5]

402. *Exceptions.* A minor is often permitted to gift property purchased from money the minor earned or from funds specially received for the purpose.[6] Emancipated minors may also make certain gifts on their own behalf.[7] Moreover, with proper authorization, a minor may make gifts to a future spouse in the marriage settlement.[8] It is thought inappropriate to allow a minor to marry without

---

3. Infra nos. 993–1024.

4. 8 De Page no. 109; 1 Planiol and Ripert nos. 277, 588.

5. 2 Lacruz Berdejo no. 502 lit. a.

6. SPAIN: CC art. 164 par. 3; FRANCE: CC art. 387; 5 Planiol and Ripert no. 198 note 1; GERMANY: CC § 110 (*Taschengeldparagraph*).

7. SPAIN: CC art. 321; FRANCE: CC art. 481; ITALY: CC art. 394 par. 1 (only customary gifts (*liberalità d'uso*); Cian and Trabucchi art. 394 no. II par. 1; UNITED STATES: Restatement (Third) of Property (Wills and Other Donative Transfers) § 8.2 comment i.

8. FRANCE: CC art. 1095; ITALY: CC arts. 774 par. 1 sent. 2, 165; Torrente (2006) 407–410.

having the opportunity to make those gifts that normally accompany marriage—*habilis ad nuptias, habilis ad nuptiarum consequentias*. Nonetheless, despite the code provision, one Italian author has argued that minors should not be permitted to make gifts in a marriage settlement when gift giving is otherwise prohibited to them.[9] After the wedding, the minor generally loses the capacity to make gifts, even to the minor's own spouse.[10] In the common law as well, minors generally lack the capacity to give a gift. Nonetheless, because a minor's gift is voidable and not void, the minor may ratify the gift upon coming of age.[11]

403. *Gifts by the guardian.* In Roman law, tutors were permitted to make gifts from the minor's patrimony only for the *solemnia munera*, gifts given annually on special occasions or holidays.[12] Bracton noted that a minor cannot consent to a gift, even with the approval of the tutor.[13]

In Spanish law, the guardian (*tutor*) may make gifts on the minor's behalf with judicial authorization.[14] However, as one Spanish author has suggested, the gift transaction is inherently *intuitu personae*. The donor personally assesses the needs and merits of the donee, together with the donor's affection, financial capabilities, and family obligations. It seems inappropriate to delegate the appreciation of these factors.[15]

In France, Germany, and Italy, unemancipated minors lack the capacity to make a gift, even if represented.[16] The prohibition is justified on the grounds that "a liberality is a serious and economically abnormal act that ... requires more discernment than one involving a quid pro quo."[17] In German law, exceptions are made for gifts that fulfill a moral duty or are required by custom.[18]

In the common law, the guardian may make gifts on the minor's behalf when authorized by the court.[19] In one case, a minor had won a large personal injury award but was likely to die from the injuries in the near future. The court authorized the guardian to make annual gifts of $10,000 to each of the minor's four siblings to minimize estate taxes.[20]

---

9. Biondi no. 76.

10. 5 Planiol and Ripert no. 198 and note 1.

11. UNITED STATES: Restatement (Third) of Property (Wills and Other Donative Transfers) § 8.2 par. b and comment d; ENGLAND: 20 Halsbury part 1 sub Gifts no. 12.

12. Michel no. 796.

13. 2 Bracton 52.

14. Spanish CC art. 272 par. 9.

15. 2 Lacruz Berdejo no. 502 lit. a.

16. French CC arts. 903–904; German CC §§ 1641, 1804; Italian CC art. 777 par. 1.

17. 8 De Page no. 105.

18. German CC §§ 1641 sent. 2, 1804 sent. 2.

19. INDIA: Mulla sec. 122 note 2; UNITED STATES: Restatement (Second) of Property (Donative Transfers) § 34.4 par. 2 (1992).

20. *Petition of Daly*, 536 N.Y.S.2d 393 (Sur. Ct. 1988).

2. Adult Incompetents

404. *Of sound mind.* The law almost everywhere provides that donative capacity is present only when the donor is of sound mind (*sain d'esprit*; French CC art. 901).[21] At English common law, gifts made by *idiots* or by those considered *lunatics so found* were absolutely void, even if made during a lucid interval. That vocabulary is no longer in use. English law in Bracton's day also did not permit gifts to be made by the totally deaf, true mutes, or confined lepers.[22] In some codes, the size of the gift suggested a lack of capacity. For example, under the Prussian General Law, whenever a gift involved more than half the donor's property, the judge was required to examine whether the donor was a prodigal who should be placed under guardianship.[23] The role of gift law is to provide the flexibility needed for adults who are otherwise incompetent to give gifts in appropriate circumstances.

a. General Principle

405. *Common law.* English law provides that those who have been committed to the Court of Protection due to mental disorder lack the capacity to make a gift.[24] In American law, donors generally have the capacity to make a gift only if they understand the extent of their property, the natural object of their bounty, the nature of the disposition, and the effect the gift may have on their future financial security.[25]

Though this is easily stated, the proof difficulties are often intractable. It is often impossible to separate the capacity question from all of the facts and circumstances of the transaction. The fact that a donor may be old, sick, or absent-minded is not enough to prohibit the gift. To determine capacity, the courts tend to look instead at the facts surrounding the gift. If the gift seems reasonable, the courts are likely to conclude that the donor was competent. If the gift is difficult to explain, the court may reach the opposite conclusion. In other words, the capacity to make a gift may depend on the gift the donor is attempting to make.[26]

---

21. French scholars have noted that CC art. 901 duplicates CC art. 489, which applies to all legal acts. Grimaldi no. 1048. Moreover the provision is more closely related to the protection of consent than it is to capacity. Beaubrun 1440. For Bracton, the donor had to be "in possession of oneself and of good memory" (*compos sui et bonae memoriae*). 2 Bracton 61.

22. 2 Bracton 52.

23. Gen. Law pt. 1. tit. 11 § 1111.

24. 20 Halsbury part 1 sub Gifts no. 13.

25. Restatement (Third) of Property (Wills and Other Donative Transfers) § 8.1; *Estate of Clements*, 505 N.E.2d 7, 9 (Ill. App. 1987); *Estate of Brown*, 722 S.W.2d 345 (Mo. App. 1987).

26. But what shall be said of unreasonableness and the unnatural character of the gift? True, one who *is* competent may make an unreasonable, and even an utterly unnatural, disposition of his property. But that is so only *if* he is competent.

406. *Civil law.* The German Civil Code denies donative capacity to adults who suffer from long-term mental disturbance (§ 104 par. 2). French law offers legal protection to adults who, due to an alteration of personal faculties, are unable to protect their own interests. Those who, due to prodigality, intemperance, or laziness, risk becoming needy or unable to fulfill their family obligations are similarly protected (CC art. 488).[27]

In Italian law, a gift can be invalidated if the donor, for whatever reason and however transitorily, lacked the capacity to understand or intend (*d'intendere o di volere*) at the moment the gift was made (art. 775 par. 1). The provision differs from the corresponding rule governing contract capacity, which permits rescission only if the contract causes the party serious harm (art. 428 par. 1). According to Capozzi, prejudice is presumed in the case of a gift, and, in contrast to contract law, there is no reason to protect the other party.[28] Furthermore, contracts, like most legal acts, can be avoided only if made after the declaration of incompetency or the appointment of the guardian, while gifts can be avoided if made any time after the initiation of incompetency proceedings.[29]

b. Gifts by the Ward

407. *Generally prohibited.* French and Italian law provide that gifts made by adults under guardianship (*tutelle*) are generally void,[30] even if the incompetent is momentarily lucid.[31] There are, however, exceptions. In France and Italy, the adult ward, with approvals, may make gifts to a future spouse in the marriage settlement.[32] In Italy, the ward may also make gifts, with assistance, to descendants on the occasion of their marriage (CC art. 777 par. 2). In German law, those for whom a caretaker has been appointed maintain the capacity to give unless they are ruled incompetent by a substantive evaluation of their ability to

---

But, when the question is whether he is competent, then the fact that he deals with his property in an unnatural manner will, when added to such testimony as has been adverted to, warrant a jury in finding that the party was incapable of transacting business and of disposing of his property. An unnatural and unreasonable disposition of property may be shown as bearing on the issue of mental condition.

Richmond v. First Nat'l Bank, 179 N.W. 59, 61 (Iowa 1920) (emphasis in original).

27. As of 1 Jan. 2009, protection will be provided to those who are unable to protect their interests due to a medically diagnosed alteration of either mental or bodily functions sufficient to prevent the expression of will. No special protection will be provided to those afflicted with prodigality. Law of 5 Mar. 2007 art. 7 (amending CC art. 425). The elimination of protection for prodigals has been criticized. See Malaurie (2007) 568–569.

28. Capozzi no. 359 at 856.

29. Id. no. 335 par. a.

30. French CC art. 502; Italian CC art. 774 par. 1.

31. Flour and Souleau no. 288.

32. French CC art. 1399, together with arts. 506, 407; Flour and Souleau no. 288; Italian CC art. 774 par. 1, together with art. 166.

make a free determination of will.[33] In American law, if, despite a lack of contractual capacity, the donor remains a "person of adequate mentality"—for example, if the incapacity is due to physical rather than mental disability—the incompetent retains the power to make gifts.[34] English courts have enforced gifts made after a declaration of incompetency on the grounds that the gifts discharged what the patient, when competent, considered to be a moral obligation.[35] In both German and American law, a moment of lucidity restores legal capacity for as long as the moment lasts.[36]

c. Gifts by the Representative

408. *Generally prohibited.* In Italian law, as in most systems, the incompetent's representatives generally lack the power to make gifts for their wards (Italian CC art. 777 par. 1). This is due to the personal nature and "the absence of objective utility" of gift giving.[37] Here too there are exceptions. In France, the guardian (*tuteur*), when authorized by the family council, may make gifts to the ward's spouse or, as an advancement, for the benefit of the heirs (CC art. 505). Those adults with lesser incapacities who are subject to a regime of supervision (*curatelle*; CC art. 508) may give gifts with the assistance of their supervisors (*curateur*; CC art. 513 par. 2). In German law, the caretaker may consent to a gift if it is of modest value and required by custom or tradition.[38]

In some American states, a legal guardian is permitted to make gifts of the ward's property only to donees who are members of the ward's family or to likely heirs.[39] In some states, the statutes are even more specific. One state permits gifts only to close relations who have cared for the ward for a specified period. The gifts may be distributed only upon the ward's death.[40]

d. Role of the Courts

409. *Limited approval.* The Spanish Civil Code provides that a guardian may only make a gratuitous transfer of an incompetent's property with judicial authorization.[41] In Italian law, the courts may review gifts made even while the donor was competent. For example, a spendthrift's gift may be voided if made within the six months preceding the declaration of disability (CC art. 776 par. 2). In German

---

33. MünchKomm-BGB (-Schwab) § 1896 no. 131.

34. *In re Spindle*, 733 P.2d 388, 390–391 (Okla. 1986).

35. 20 Halsbury part 1 sub Gifts no. 13; *In re Whitaker* (1889) 42 Ch D 119 (CA).

36. GERMANY: Jauernig (-Jauernig) § 104 no. 3 lit. b; UNITED STATES: Restatement (Third) of Property (Wills and Other Donative Transfers) § 8.1 comment m.

37. Capozzi no. 359 at 857.

38. German CC § 1908i par. 2, together with § 1804 sent. 2, MünchKomm-BGB (-Schwab) § 1908i no. 44.

39. FLORIDA: Fla. Stats. Ann. § 744.441 par. 17.

40. ILLINOIS: Ill. Rev. Stat. ch. 755 act 5 § 11a–18.1.

41. Spanish CC art. 272 par. 9.

law, the caretaker, with the court's approval, may make a gratuitous transfer as an endowment for the ward's children (*Ausstattung*; CC § 1908). French law permits a judge, with the advice of the treating physician, to provide the ward with the capacity to make certain gifts (CC art. 501).

In England, a court may authorize gifts made by those suffering from a "mental disorder"[42] to members of the incompetent's family or to those for whom the incompetent might have provided if not for the mental disorder.[43] In the United States, a court may authorize a guardian to make gifts that are reasonable from the point of view of taxation or estate planning,[44] provided the amount remaining in the estate is sufficient for the ward's support and there is no evidence that the ward would not have made the gift.[45] Furthermore, if the ward previously provided support to an individual and promised that the support would continue, the donee may petition the court to authorize continued payments.[46]

e. Durable Power of Attorney

410. *Loss of capacity.* A final facility for adult incompetents is a durable power of attorney (*Vollmacht*). Where available, a durable power is valid only if the principal had legal capacity at the moment it was granted. Once validly issued, it generally remains valid, even if the principal subsequently becomes incompetent.[47] The durable power of attorney may authorize inter vivos donative transfers. The common law achieves similar results by means of a funded revocable trust. The trustee may be authorized to determine whether the settlor has become incompetent and, thereafter, to make gifts to family members when desirable from the standpoint of tax or estate planning.[48] There is considerable dispute in German law regarding whether the agent may freely make gifts or whether, once the principal loses capacity, the limitations otherwise imposed on guardians should apply.[49]

---

42. Mental Health Act of 1983 sec. 1 par. 2.

43. Id. sec. 95 par. 2 lit. d.

44. Restatement (Third) of Property (Wills and Other Donative Transfers) § 8.1 comment k; supra no. 408.

45. Restatement (Second) of Property (Donative Transfers) § 34.5 illus. 4; *In re Christiansen*, 56 Cal.Rptr. 505, 525 (Cal. App. 1967).

46. Restatement (Second) of Property (Donative Transfers) § 34.5 illus. 5; INDIANA: Ind. Code Ann. § 29-3-9-4 (Burns 2000); *In re Brice*, 8 N.W.2d 576 (Iowa 1943).

47. GERMANY: CC §§ 168 sent. 1, 672, 675; Staudinger (-Schilken) § 168 no. 23; CCProc. § 86; UNITED STATES: Restatement (Third) of Property (Wills and Other Donative Transfers) § 8.1 comment l; see Uniform Power of Attorney Act sec. 104; Uniform Durable Power of Attorney Act §§ 1–2; Uniform Probate Code § 5-502.

48. Restatement (Second) of Property (Donative Transfers) § 34.5 comment d.

49. MünchKomm-BGB (-Schwab) § 1896 no. 243.

3. Civil Death

411. *Elements*. In Roman law, legal personhood (*caput*) resulted from the coincidence of three elements—freedom from bondage, citizenship, and family membership.[50] Upon the loss of any one of the three, the individual suffered some form of civil death (*capitis diminutio*). Those convicted of felonies lost all patrimonial rights and therefore could make no gifts.[51]

a. France and Belgium

412. *History*. Under the French ancien régime, those who entered religious life were thought to die to the world. For the law, they suffered civil death (*mort civile*).[52] Moreover, until the middle of the nineteenth century, civil death was also the lot of felons sentenced to death, to forced labor in perpetuity, or to deportation. Though they were still alive, they were dead in the eyes of the law and prohibited from making gifts.[53] During the revolution, the Convention banished the émigrés in perpetuity, punished them with civil death, and confiscated their property.[54] Any gift or other liberality made by an émigré after 1 July 1789 was void.[55]

After the revolution, the restrictions on those taking religious vows were gradually lifted. The Constituent Assembly granted to members of religious communities who left their institutions the right to make gifts of the personal property and real estate they had acquired since entering secular life.[56] Under the Restoration, members of female religious communities were allowed to make gifts to their communities or its members, but only up to the value of a quarter of their property, unless the gift was to a direct descendant or the amount of the gift was less than FF 10,000.[57]

413. *Remnants*. Though civil death was abolished in France in 1854, two gift-related remnants of the doctrine survived until 1994. First, those condemned to life sentences were declared permanently incompetent to make or receive gifts. The courts were permitted to make exceptions on a case-by-case basis, though a prisoner was not permitted to dispose of property at the institution where the sentence was being served.[58] Second, those serving sentences involving infamy

---

50. Girard 201, 204.
51. 1 De Page no. 107. In the French tradition this type of incapacity is known as an incapacity of enjoyment (*incapacité de jouissance*).
52. 1 Planiol nos. 372–374.
53. C Nap. art. 25 par. 3.
54. Decree of 28 Mar. 1793 art. 1.
55. Id. art. 38.
56. Decree of 19 Mar. 1790 art. 2.
57. Law of 24 May 1825 art. 5.
58. French Penal C former art. 36; 3 Planiol nos. 2904–2905.

(*une peine afflictive infamante*) were placed under legal guardianship (*interdiction légale*) and thereby lost the capacity to make gifts to the same extent as adult incompetents.[59] The felon's lack of donative capacity was criticized. The felon's spouse and children were primarily affected because the felon could not transfer the family's patrimony to them.[60] Neither provision was included in the Penal Code of 1994.[61]

414. *Belgium.* Civil death was abolished by the Belgian Constitution in 1831.[62] Until 2004, however, Belgian law continued to place felons under legal guardianship, which deprived them of the capacity to give and receive gifts.[63] Those provisions have now been abrogated.[64]

b. The Common Law

415. *History.* In the early common law, a person convicted of a capital offense was considered *attaint*.[65] The principal incidents of attainder were forfeiture, corruption of blood, and extinction of civil rights. The felon's land was forfeited to the king, and, by corruption of blood, the felon was prevented from transmitting by inheritance. Bracton indicated that a felony conviction thus had wide-ranging effects on gift giving. A conviction retroactively voided any gifts the felon made after committing the crime.[66] Gifts made before the felony was committed remained valid. If the donor died before trial, the gifts remained good, since death extinguished the punishment.[67] An accused who fled before trial could be outlawed (*utlagatus*), which caused the outlaw's property to be forfeited to the crown and voided gifts made subsequent to the crime.[68] Moreover, because prisoners were not considered masters of their affairs, no prisoner could make a valid gift.[69] A father may also have been prohibited from making gifts if his eldest son committed a felony.[70]

---

59. French Penal C former art. 29; 3 Planiol no. 2906.

60. 5 Planiol and Ripert no. 210.

61. These two forms of punishment are now regarded as abrogated. 1 Pradel nos. 624–626.

62. Belgian Const. art. 13 (now in art. 18).

63. Belgian Penal C arts. 21–24 (2004); Law of 31 May 1888 art. 7; 1 De Page nos. 107, 109.

64. Law of 22 Nov. 2004 art. 2.

65. *Avery v. Everett*, 18 N.E. 148, 150–153 (N.Y. 1888) (discussing the early common-law practice).

66. 2 Bracton 366; see also Fleta bk. 3 ch. 3 at 6. Bracton indicated that English law in this respect corresponded to Roman law, citing D. 39, 5, 15 (Marcian).

67. 2 Bracton 367.

68. Id. 352, 361, 363.

69. Id. 66.

70. Id. 99–100 (doubtful passage; *addicione*).

Blackstone noted that forfeiture prevented the traitor from taking advantage of the social privilege of transferring property to others.[71] Yet it seems that even in Blackstone's day, the strict consequences of civil death applied only to those who entered religion, abjured, or were banished from the realm.[72] Forfeiture did not occur by operation of law. If the king did not exercise his rights, the felon apparently retained the right to convey property and may have been able to convey by gift.

416. *United States.* In the United States, in the absence of statute, a felon's property was not forfeited and the felon's civil rights were not suspended.[73] For example, civil death was not an incident of a felony conviction in New York before 1799 when the state enacted a civil death statute.[74] However, as late as the end of the nineteenth century, some state statutes declared that life convicts were civilly dead (*civiliter mortuus*) and lacked power to manage or possess property.[75] The rights of a felon sentenced to a term of years, however, were merely suspended while the sentence was served.[76] It seems that even a life sentence did not generally work a forfeiture, though in a few states the felon's property was distributed to the heirs.[77] Apparently, only two states prevented prisoners from conveying title to property.[78] Other states permitted convicted felons to convey to the same extent as if they were not confined.[79]

417. *Forfeiture abolished.* Forfeiture has long since been abolished as an incident of punishment.[80] Common-law jurisdictions now generally guarantee to felons the right to convey both real and personal property.[81]

4. Married Women

418. *Common law.* At common law, an unmarried woman enjoyed essentially the same legal rights as a man.[82] Once she married, however, she lost these rights by

---

71. 2 Blackstone 499.

72. 1 Blackstone 128–129; *Platner v. Sherwood*, 6 Johns.Ch. 118 (N.Y. 1822) (Kent, J.); *Avery v. Everett*, 18 N.E. 148, 150–153 (N.Y. 1888).

73. Note (1939) 913.

74. *Platner v. Sherwood*, 6 Johns.Ch. 118 (N.Y. 1822).

75. "He became civilly dead in the law, and the law ceased to know or to take any notice of him. He no longer possessed any rights growing out of organized society, or depending upon and given by the law. As to all such rights he was in law dead and buried." *Avery v. Everett*, 18 N.E. 148, 155 (N.Y. 1888) (Earl, J., dissenting).

76. *Estate of Nerac*, 35 Cal. 392 (Cal. 1868).

77. Note (1939) 914 and note 16 (collecting statutes).

78. Id. 914 and note 14. The two states were Missouri and Rhode Island.

79. *Estate of Nerac*, 35 Cal. 392 (Cal. 1868).

80. Fellows (1986) 538 note 147, 540.

81. California Penal C § 2601 par. a.

82. Lord 27. I follow Lord's account.

virtue of the doctrine of *coverture*. She became one person with her husband, in whom the couple's legal existence was vested.[83] The husband controlled the wife's real property and its income but could not dispose of it without her consent. Her personal property was vested in the husband and could be disposed of at his pleasure. In general, married women therefore lacked the ability to make gifts. Eventually, marriage settlements and trusts provided the wife with separate property and mitigated these harsh consequences. In 1935, English law was reformed to permit married women to have the same rights over their property as were enjoyed by unmarried women.[84]

419. *France and Belgium.* Under the Code Napoleon, a married woman could not make inter vivos gifts without her husband's assistance or special consent (arts. 905, 217). If the husband refused, the wife could request authorization from the court (art. 219).[85] Reforms passed in France between 1938 and 1942 granted married women full legal capacity, including the capacity to make gifts.[86] The corresponding Belgian provisions were revised in 1976.[87]

5. Marital Property

420. *Individual spouses.* Some legal systems limit the ability of individual spouses to make gratuitous transfers of marital property, or even of their separate property. Though these restrictions do not technically concern legal capacity—they apply to spouses who otherwise have full capacity—they are relevant here because they limit the power of individuals to make gifts of property in which they have an interest.

a. France

421. *Community property.* In French law until 1985, the husband administered the community property.[88] Under the ancien régime, the husband's exclusive control raised the concern that the husband might fraudulently deprive his wife of her share.[89] As a result, the Code Napoleon prevented the husband from making gifts of certain types of community property, including immovables, movables burdened with a usufruct for the husband's benefit, and a universality

---

83. Id.; 1 Blackstone 430.
84. Law Reform (Married Women and Tortfeasors Act) of 1935 sec. 2.
85. 8 Planiol and Ripert no. 560.
86. Law of 18 Feb. 1938 art. 1 (modifying CC art. 215). The effect of the reform was to establish the principle that married women had full civil capacity, including the capacity to make and accept gifts. Marcel Nast, note to Law of 18 Feb. 1938, D. 1939 IV 1 at 6 col. 1.
87. Law of 14 July 1976 art. 1, modifying CC art. 212 par. 3.
88. French CC former art. 1421, abrogated by Law of 23 Dec. 1985 art. 13.
89. 8 Planiol and Ripert no. 518.

of movables.[90] There was an irrebuttable presumption of fraud with regard to the prohibited gifts.[91] However, the husband was permitted to make gifts of the community's movables.[92] In 1942, the code was revised to prohibit the husband from making any gifts of community property without his wife's consent.[93] The scholars suggested that the revision corresponded to evolving mores. Husband and wife were thought to share the right to dispose of community property.[94] In 1985, the code was again revised to grant each spouse the right to administer and dispose of community property (CC art. 1421). Spouses were prohibited from individually making gifts of community property.[95] However, a spouse who exercises a profession may make a gift from his or her own profits and salaries, once the obligations to the community are satisfied (CC art. 223).

b. Other Civilian Jurisdictions

422. *Joint consent.* In German law, if spouses adopt the community property regime (*Gütergemeinschaft*), the spouse who administers the community property cannot dispose by gift of community assets without the other's consent (CC § 1425 par. 1). Exceptions are made for gifts required by custom or tradition (CC § 1425 par. 2). Spanish[96] and Italian law[97] have similar provisions. Under the Italian Civil Code, if the transaction benefits the family and the spouses fail to agree, a court may authorize the disposition (art. 181).

c. The Common Law

423. *Separate property.* There is no community property regime under English law. Neither spouse has the right to dispose of the other's separate property.[98] The majority of American states are separate property jurisdictions. At common law, the husband was not restricted in making gifts of his property during his lifetime.[99] That remains the rule in some states.[100] However, many states now provide that, during coverture, the husband's real estate is subject to an inchoate right of dower in the wife. As a result, the wife must consent to or join in any transfer.[101]

---

90. C Nap. art. 1422 par. 1.
91. 8 Planiol and Ripert no. 518.
92. C Nap. art. 1422 par. 2.
93. CC art. 1422 (1942).
94. 8 Planiol and Ripert no. 524.
95. French CC art. 1422; see also Belgian CC art. 1419.
96. Spanish CC arts. 1322 par. 2, 1378.
97. Italian CC art. 180 par. 2; Cian and Trabucchi art. 180 no. III par. 1.
98. Bromley and Lowe 563–566.
99. *Hirschfield v. Ralston*, 66 N.Y.S.2d 59, 61 (Sup. Ct. 1946).
100. *Moedy v. Moedy*, 276 P.2d 563 (Colo. 1954) (en banc); *Sorrells v. Sorrells*, 134 S.E. 767 (Ga. 1926).
101. McClanahan § 2:25.

424. *Community property.* In the nine community property states in the United States [102] and in the Commonwealth of Puerto Rico, neither spouse has the right to make a gift of the community's real property without the other's consent.[103] As for personal property, it seems no state requires the owner to obtain permission from the nonowning spouse before making a gift,[104] though some courts protect the dependent spouse by doctrines of *illusory transfer* or *fraud on the wife's rights.*[105]

6. Government Entities

425. *The issue.* Constitutional and statutory provisions often prohibit governments from making gifts of public funds. The Constitution of the State of New York, for example, provides that the state's funds are not to be gifted to a private corporation or association or to a private undertaking.[106] Exceptions are made to permit the legislature to provide care and support of the needy and for other public purposes.[107]

In Italian law, the question has produced an extensive discussion. Italian scholars ask whether government entities have the capacity or power to make gifts to individuals. The answer turns on the resolution of a previous question, namely whether the capacity of public bodies to make gifts is subject to private or public law.[108] The issue is whether gifts by public entities should be governed by private law concepts or whether public law categories, such as the pursuit of public welfare, are more appropriate. Despite the energy and complexity of the discussion, Italian legal scholars have not reached consensus, and doctrine and case law continue to diverge.

a. Private Law

426. *Capacity.* The former Italian Civil Code provided that a party without the capacity to make a will also lacked the capacity to make a gift.[109] Because legal persons, whether public or private, cannot make wills, some authors concluded that they also cannot make gifts. A preliminary draft of the current Civil Code provided that legal persons have the capacity to make gifts as long as the gift

---

102. Arizona, California, Idaho, Louisiana, Nevada, New Mexico, Texas, Washington, and Wisconsin.

103. McClanahan § 7:14.

104. Id. § 2:25.

105. Id. note 8. See LeFevre.

106. Art. 7 sec. 8 par. 1. See *State v. Upstate Storage, Inc.*, 535 N.Y.S.2d 246, 248 (App. Div. 1988).

107. New York Const. art. 7 sec. 8 par. 2.

108. Biondi no. 80; Torrente (2006) 411–419.

109. Italian CC art. 1052 (1865).

conforms both to the entity's nature and purpose as well as to custom.[110] However, because the final draft characterized the gift as a contract, a provision devoted to the capacity of public entities was thought to be superfluous.[111] The provision was therefore eliminated. As a result, the Italian Civil Code does not expressly resolve the issue, and even those who suggest that private law should govern the question do not agree.

Some authors suggest that the question is governed by the general principle that all persons are presumed to have the capacity to make a gift unless the law specifies otherwise.[112] Public entities usually have full legal capacity, and the Civil Code contains no restriction. Moreover, gifts seem to be inspired by ideals consistent with the obvious purpose of governmental entities.[113] Because there is no problem with capacity, these authors contend that a gift by a public entity is valid even if the gift violates the entity's governing norms. The remedy would be a tort action against the individuals involved for misuse of resources. The courts hold that public entities have the capacity to make gifts[114] and permit gifts within the scope of an entity's charter and goals, as idealistically conceived.[115]

427. *Contrary view.* Some scholars take the contrary view.[116] They reason from the indisputable fact that the Civil Code does not prohibit a public entity from making a will. Nonetheless, no one would suggest that a public entity has testamentary capacity. Moreover, it has long been the rule in Italian law that animus donandi must emanate from a particular human will. For that reason the code prohibits an agent from making gifts on behalf of the principal. Because legal persons cannot be said to have an actual will, the idea of gift giving is incompatible with their nature.

b. Public Law

428. *Public goals.* Those who suggest that public law should govern the question point out that the state's transfer of its alienable property is governed by public law. Private law applies only in the absence of other norms (CC art. 828 par. 1). According to the dominant view, state property may be validly disposed of, with or without a quid pro quo, only pursuant to legislative or administrative

---

110. Progetto preliminare art. 400, in 2 *Lavori* 492.

111. Relazione Guardasigilli al progetto definitivo no. 235, in 2 Pandolfelli et al. art. 325 at 372.

112. See Torrente (2006) 411–413, summarizing the position of those who favor the application of private law to the question.

113. Capozzi no. 335 par. e.

114. Cass. 18 Dec. 1996 no. 11311, *Rep. Foro it.* 1997 *Contratti della p.a.* no. 437.

115. Cass. 22 Jan. 1953 no. 157, *Foro it.* 1954 I 716; Cass. 17 Nov. 1953 no. 3540, *Rep. Foro it.* 1953 *Donazione* no. 21; Cass. 18 Feb. 1955 no. 470, *Foro it.* 1955 I 471.

116. See, e.g., Biondi no. 80 at 210–212.

directive.[117] Such a transfer is never gratuitous, even if made without compensation. It is rather mandated by law to achieve public goals. The state's goals do not include the gratuitous enrichment of particular individuals. The state seeks rather to provide assistance to the needy and to reward the deserving. Moreover, no Italian legislation authorizes public entities to make gifts.[118] Thus, transfers made by government entities are subject to public and not private law. Furthermore, the bulk of gift law formalities and other restrictions do not apply to transfers made by the state. Because the state and other public entities do not actually give gifts, the question of their donative capacity does not arise.[119] Some cases hold that gratuitous transfers by public entities, when based on appropriate public goals, are made without donative intent and therefore are not considered gifts.[120]

c. Administrative Practice

429. *Remunerative gifts.* Continuous administrative practice permits government entities to make gifts—they would be called remunerative gifts—to individuals, such as scientists and artists, who have rendered service to the nation. Legal scholars who favor the application of public law in this context suggest that these are not gifts in the sense of the private law, since the administration is not motivated by animus donandi but is rather carrying out a public charge. The entities may have discretion as to amounts and beneficiaries, but their actions are mandated by law or institutional charter. These entities may make actual gifts only if they are of modest value.[121]

7. Business Associations

430. *Historical suspicion.* Although modern law grants corporations many of the powers of natural persons, corporate gift giving has historically been regarded with suspicion. Gift giving seems to contradict the purpose for which these entities are formed, namely to pursue profit-making activities for the benefit of their shareholders. Nonetheless, recent legislation in many jurisdictions has extended donative capacity to business associations.

a. Italy

431. *Corporate purpose.* No provision in the Italian Civil Code prohibits business associations from making gifts. Exclusions, however, need not be expressly stated.[122] The authors attempt to resolve the matter by asking whether gift giving

---

117. Trib. Catanzaro 7 July 1959, *Giur. it.* 1960 I (2) 98 note Biondi at 102.

118. Torrente (2006) 416–417.

119. Biondi no. 80 at 220.

120. Cass. 10 Jan. 1973 no. 37, *Rep. Foro it.* 1973 *Registro (imposta di)* nos. 630–631.

121. Biondi no. 80 at 213–221. The extent of the entity's resources may be considered for purposes of calculating the permissible extent of the gift.

122. Id. no. 80 at 221–223; Torrente (2006) 419–420.

conforms to a corporation's purpose. Because the pursuit of profit is the main purpose of a stock corporation (CC art. 2247), gift giving seems to exceed its function and power.[123] Yet some gratuitous transfers are clearly permitted. A business entity may reward its employees, gratify faithful customers, and offer free samples to prospective clients. These transfers are not considered gifts in Italian law. The courts generally presume that a corporation's gratuitous transfers are made for business purposes and therefore lack the animus donandi required of a gift.[124] More broadly, the case law recognizes that business associations have the general capacity to make gifts of all kinds.[125] The only question is the justification.[126]

432. *Debate.* Biondi argued that transfers based on the business entity's self-interest fall outside the scope of the law of gifts, "since the disposition, even though it constitutes an enrichment, is not made with the donative intent (*spirito di liberalità*) that is essential to gift giving. In fact, if the transfer is actually gratuitous, it falls outside the scope of the entity's economic purpose."[127]

Torrente, in contrast, contended that a gratuitous transfer does not cease to be a gift merely because its long-term goal is to retain or increase the client base or employee morale.[128] It is precisely because these acts constitute gifts that their validity depends on their relationship to the company's goals. Torrente also suggested that the courts should not construe corporate purpose too narrowly. Gifts to disaster victims and contributions to religious festivals should be permitted if those gifts may attract public interest and goodwill.[129] When a corporation makes a humanitarian gesture, the approval of all associates or shareholders should be required.

b. Germany

433. *Public corporations.* In German law, corporate capacity for charitable giving depends on the type of corporation involved. The board of directors of a large public corporation (*Aktiengesellschaft* [AG]) is required to use business judgment

---

123. Capozzi no. 335 par. d.

124. "[I]t is a serious legal error to confuse donative intent (*spirito di liberalità*) with a gratuitous but economically not disinterested transaction and to attempt to deduce automatically from the simple absence of a legally enforceable quid pro quo the fact that the act is absolutely useless to the party involved." Cass. 14 Sept. 1976 no. 3150, *Giur. it.* 1977 I 1998 at 2004.

125. Rescigno (-Carnevali) 508–509.

126. The drafters of the Civil Code of 1942 suggested that the controversy had been resolved in practice because business entities had long participated in gift giving. Relazione della Commissione Reale 96, in 2 Pandolfelli et al. art. 325 at 372.

127. Biondi no. 80 at 222.

128. Torrente (2006) 422–423.

129. Id. 423–424.

when balancing the relevant interests, including those of shareholders, employees, and the public.[130] According to the dominant scholarly view, the board may authorize contributions for scientific, artistic, and cultural purposes, to benefit victims of accidents and natural catastrophes, and to promote athletic associations.[131] Because corporations are not required to remain politically neutral, the majority also approves contributions to political parties, though this view has been contested.[132] Charitable contributions are not considered extraordinary measures (*Maßnahmen von herausragender Bedeutung*) and therefore do not require shareholder approval.[133]

Nonetheless, corporate contributions are limited in both quality and quantity. The contributions must suit the corporate purpose and must be appropriate given trade custom, the corporation's financial condition, and the purpose to be promoted. Contributions may not be illegal or involve directors in a conflict of interest.[134] If the limitations are not respected, the board violates its duties, and the contribution conflicts with the shareholders' interest in maximizing profit.[135]

434. *Limited liability companies.* Directors of a limited liability company (*Gesellschaft mit beschränkter Haftung* [GmbH]) are bound to follow shareholder instructions.[136] As a result, GmbH shareholders have more control over corporate contributions. The directors may not make contributions that exceed or contradict the shareholders' presumed intent. This limitation is particularly important with regard to political contributions. As a result, the question of GmbH charitable contributions remains controversial. The dominant view seems to be that, when appropriately restricted, such contributions are permissible.[137]

c. The Common Law

435. *Evolution.* American law originally followed the English restrictions on corporate gift giving. However, American model laws drafted over the past several decades now facilitate corporate charitable giving.

i. England

436. *Incidental.* In English law, the validity of a corporate gift depends upon whether the transfer is reasonably incidental to the company's business. In a leading case, the court enjoined a proposed gift of corporate assets, even though it had been approved by a majority of the shareholders, on the grounds that the

---

130. Corp. L [AktG] § 76 par. 1; Hüffer § 76 nos. 10 ff.
131. MünchKomm-AktG (-Hefermehl and Spindler) § 76 no. 72.
132. Kölner Komm. (-Mertens) § 76 no. 35.
133. Hüffer § 76 no. 14 (collecting sources).
134. MünchKomm-AktG (-Hefermehl and Spindler) § 93 no. 31; Fleischer.
135. Corp. L [AktG] § 174 par. 1; Kessler (1995) 126.
136. Limited Liab. Corp. L [GmbHG] § 37; Kind 572.
137. Kommentar zum GmbH-Gesetz (-Haas) § 43 nos. 66, 83.

payments had no reasonable prospect of benefiting the company.[138] In the absence of an express provision in the company's memorandum of association, this seems to be the English rule,[139] though the courts have occasionally been lenient when considering the connection between the business purpose and the challenged gift.[140]

ii. United States

437. *Ultra vires*. American common law followed English precedent. If the corporation was not established for charitable purposes, a gift of its property was held to be *ultra vires*.[141] The early cases strictly construed the purposes enumerated in the charter of incorporation and did not make use of the doctrine of incidental powers to justify transfers.[142] Already before the turn of the twentieth century, however, gratuitous transfers were sustained if they would result in a direct and proximate benefit to the corporation.[143] Beginning in the 1920s, the cases interpreted the concept of benefit broadly. Some courts even accepted charitable giving as a legitimate use of corporate resources. A railroad was permitted to give passes and reduced rates to ministers and others engaged in charitable work.[144] In 1935, Congress granted a tax deduction for corporate charitable contributions.[145] Modern courts have acknowledged the great accumulation of wealth in corporate form and recognize that corporations have both private and social responsibilities.[146]

438. *Model acts*. The case law developments have now been superseded by statute in all fifty states.[147] Many state laws follow one of the model business corporation acts developed over the last half century. The Model Business Corporation Act of 1971 provides that corporations shall have the power "To make donations for the public welfare or for charitable, scientific or educational purposes."[148] It also provides that corporations may contribute in aid of governmental policy.[149] The Revised Model Act of 1984 contains a nonexclusive enumeration of corporate powers, including three provisions concerning the giving of gifts. A corporation

---

138. *Hutton v West Cork Railway* [1883] 23 Ch D 654.
139. Parkinson 271–281.
140. *Evans v Brunner Mond and Co Ltd* [1921] 1 Ch 359.
141. 6A Fletcher on Corporations § 2938 (cases collected in note 2).
142. *Davis v. Old Colony R.R.*, 131 Mass. 258 (1881).
143. *Whetstone v. Ottawa Univ.*, 13 Kan. 320 (1874).
144. *State ex rel. Sorenson v. C.B. and Q. R.R.*, 199 N.W. 534 (Neb. 1924).
145. Revenue Act of 1935 § 23 par. r (allowing a corporation to deduct charitable contributions to the extent of 5 percent of its income).
146. *A.P. Smith Mfg. Co. v. Barlow*, 98 A.2d 581 (N.J. 1953).
147. 6A Fletcher on Corporations § 2939 (statutes referenced in note 1).
148. § 4 par. m; see also Delaware Gen. Corp. L § 122 par. 9.
149. § 4 par. n.

may make donations for public welfare and for charitable, scientific, or educational purposes; it may transact any lawful business that will aid governmental policy; and it may make any donations that further the corporations' business and affairs.[150] The most recent restatement of the law in this field, the Principles of Corporate Governance of 1994, provides that corporations may devote "a reasonable amount of resources to public welfare, humanitarian, educational, and philanthropic purposes."[151] As far as federal law is concerned, national banks are expressly authorized to contribute to local community funds or other institutions conducive to public welfare, provided the bank's board considers the contributions to be in the bank's interest.[152]

439. *Limitations.* In contemporary American understanding, corporate giving may be justified by both social and economic considerations.

> The modern corporation by its nature creates interdependencies with a variety of groups with whom the corporation has a legitimate concern, such as employees, customers, suppliers, and members of the communities in which the corporation operates. The long-term profitability of the corporation generally depends on meeting the fair expectations of such groups. Short-term profits may properly be subordinated to recognition that responsible maintenance of these interdependencies is likely to contribute to long-term corporate profit and shareholder gain.[153]

Nonetheless, corporate activity related to social concern is limited by considerations of reasonableness. Relevant factors include the level of charitable support provided by comparable enterprises and the strength of the connection between the gift and corporate business activity.[154] As a practical matter, corporate charitable contributions are in practice limited by the rules in the Internal Revenue Code relating to the deductibility of corporate contributions.[155] The shareholders, however, if unanimous, may probably specify limits to the corporation's profit-making objective and permit charitable activity in excess of what is deductible.[156]

8. Gifts from the Body

440. *Cross-reference.* The capacity questions raised by gifts from the body are considered below in the context of the gift disposition.[157]

---

150. Rev. Model Bus. Corp. Act § 3.02 pars. 13–15.
151. § 2.01 par. b no. 3.
152. 12 U.S.C.A. § 24 par. Eighth.
153. Principles of Corporate Governance § 2.01 comment f.
154. Id. § 2.01 comment i; see generally Symposium (1997).
155. 6A Fletcher on Corporations § 2939.
156. Principles of Corporate Governance § 2.01 Reporter's note 6 at 73.
157. Infra nos. 993–1024.

B. THE CAPACITY TO RECEIVE

441. *Concerns.* Many legal systems limit the ability of certain persons to receive gifts. In civilian systems, the limitations raise some of the most complex questions in gift law. There are three principal concerns. First, capacity to receive is denied to individuals or entities that do not exist, or are not determinable, at the moment the gift is made.[158] Second, capacity is denied to implement protective or penal policies. Finally, gifts are prohibited within specified relationships.

1. Uncertainty Concerns

442. *Personae incertae.* Some modern legal systems withhold the capacity to receive when the donee's identity is in doubt. The prohibition originated in the Roman law of successions, which invalidated bequests to persons whom the testator could not specifically identify at the moment the testament was made.[159] Today, the uncertainty prohibition involves two types of donees. The first group includes those who are not, or are not yet, considered legally to exist, such as unborn children, legal persons without legal capacity, and nonpersons, like animals. The second group includes donees who exist but are not sufficiently identified, either because, as a matter of fact, they are indeterminate, such as a charitable gift to *the poor*, or because a third party has been asked to designate the donee.

a. Unborn Children

443. *Roman law.* The Roman lawyers thought it unfair for successoral rights to depend on the moment of a child's birth. They therefore permitted a paterfamilias to leave property in his will to a child who had been conceived but was yet unborn (*nasciturus*). Gifts were governed by other rules, largely because gifts were usually made by formal act (*mancipatio, traditio,* or *stipulatio*) which required the parties to be present. Because Roman law was also reluctant to recognize agency relationships, unborn children were not permitted to receive gifts. The postglossators permitted the nasciturus to receive by constructing gift giving in analogy to wills.

i. France and Belgium

444. *Actual acceptance.* During the ancien régime, gifts were often made, particularly at marriage, to a couple's unborn children, whether or not they had been conceived.[160] The notary was said to represent the donee. The Ordinance of

---

158. The question is whether a gift to a donee who is uncertain is valid. That is a capacity question only in a broad and untechnical sense. The discussion is included here following the universal practice of those legal systems in which the issue arises.

159. 5 Planiol and Ripert no. 171.

160. Id. no. 167 at 235 note 1.

Villers-Cotterêts (1539) put an end to the practice by providing that such gifts would take effect only upon the donee's actual acceptance in the presence of the donor and the notary and only after registration (art. 133). D'Aguesseau adopted the same provision in the Ordinance of 1731 (art. 5).

(A) PRINCIPLE

445. *Nasciturus.* The French Civil Code provides that an unborn child has the capacity to receive a gift, provided that the child has been conceived at the moment the gift is made and that the child is subsequently born viable (CC art. 906). The code provision is thought to follow from the maxim *Infans conceptus iam pro nato habetur quoties de commodis eius agitur.*[161] Despite the provision's terms, French scholars today believe that it is not a rule of capacity. Instead, the limitation follows logically from the legal principle that there can be no right without a rightholder.[162] Moreover, because minors below the age of discernment do not have legal capacity to conclude contracts, the assistance of the unborn child's legal guardian would in any case be necessary.[163]

446. *Concepturus.* In contrast, a gift may not validly be made to a child not yet conceived at the time of the gift (*concepturus*),[164] and such gifts are not validated by the child's subsequent conception and birth. Furthermore, though conditions typically have retroactive effect in French law, this incapacity cannot be eluded by use of conditional language, such as *si nascatur.*

(B) EXCEPTIONS

447. *Marriage settlement.* There are a number of exceptions to the incapacity of the *concepturus.*[165] The first involves the gift of future property in a marriage settlement, which is also known as a contractual designation (*institution contractuelle*) because it employs a contract to select an heir.[166] Relatives—typically the parents—may make irrevocable gifts to one or both fiancés in the marriage settlement and may include as additional donees the children to be born of the marriage (CC art. 1082 par. 1). The gift disposes of future property (an exception in this regard as well), namely part or all of the donor's patrimony at death. If the donor survives the donee, the donee's children are presumed to be the intended beneficiaries (CC art. 1082 par. 2). Only children born of the particular marriage may take under the designation. There has been some controversy about whether

---

161. "A conceived child is considered to have been born whenever it benefits the child."

162. Flour and Souleau no. 293.

163. Infra nos. 498–499.

164. 5 Planiol and Ripert no. 168; 8 De Page no. 124.

165. 5 Planiol and Ripert nos. 169–170; 8 De Page no. 126; Flour and Souleau nos. 294–295.

166. 5 Planiol and Ripert no. 767.

the designation may omit the fiancés and make a transfer directly to the unborn children.[167]

448. *Entailment.* The remaining exceptions involve gifts made by means of intermediaries. The first involves entailment (*substitution fidéicommissaire*). The donor requests the donee to retain the gifted property and convey it at the donor's death to a designated third party.[168] Entailment was practiced in Rome by conveyance to a fiduciary. Under the ancien régime, property could be entailed over several generations, even in perpetuity, to conserve wealth within the family, a rule that particularly benefited the nobility. Entailment was gradually restricted by royal decree and finally prohibited during the revolution.[169] The Civil Code codified the prohibition (CC art. 896), together with a number of exceptions (CC arts. 1048–1074). In particular, parents may give property to their children under the condition that the children transfer the property to the grandchildren, including both grandchildren already born and to those yet to be born (*aux enfants nés et à naître*), a phrase which, in French law, includes children not yet conceived.[170] Entailment may restrict property to only one degree—to nieces and nephews or to grandchildren.

449. *Indirect transfer.* Another exception involves indirect transfers, which may be achieved either by a gift coupled with an obligation (*donation avec charges*) or by an indirect gift (*donation indirecte*).[171] For example, a donor may couple a gift to an intermediary with the obligation to transfer a portion of it to the ultimate donee.[172] Doctrinally, this type of gift escapes the prohibition against gifts to children not yet conceived because no attempt is made to transfer property directly to a nonexistent person. Instead, an obligation is created in the donee to convey the property further. Though the distinction is a fine one, French scholars argue that it satisfies the principal purpose of the prohibition, which is to reduce the danger that property might become inalienable. The gift is void, however, if it conceals a prohibited entailment, as would be the case, for example, if the obligation absorbed the totality of the gift.

450. *Third-party beneficiaries.* The final exception involves third-party beneficiary contracts. The French discussion has focused almost exclusively on life insurance policies. During the nineteenth century, the case law tended to void a policy's beneficiary designation to the extent the beneficiaries were children not conceived at the moment the designation was made. In 1930 French insurance

---

167. Id. no. 773.

168. Id. nos. 282–284; Brissaud § 513.

169. Decree of 14 Nov. 1792 art. 1.

170. Flour and Aubert no. 467.

171. Indirect gifts are examined below. See infra nos. 827–843.

172. 5 Planiol and Ripert no. 170; 8 De Page nos. 126, 131–135 bis; Flour and Souleau no. 294.

law was revised to permit such designations.[173] The justification resembles the one employed to validate gifts coupled with an obligation. In both cases, an obligation is created in an existing party (the insurance carrier), and no attempt is made to transfer property rights directly to the unborn. Nonetheless, the policy's beneficiary immediately acquires the right to enforce the contract.

ii. Spain

451. *Nasciturus.* The Spanish Civil Code provides that a gift may be made to a nasciturus and that it may be accepted by the child's legal representative (CC art. 627).[174] Because the donee does not yet exist, Spanish legal scholars view this not as a case of agency but rather as a means to protect the rights of the unborn child. The gift object remains in the donor's patrimony until the child is born, at which point the gift operates retroactively to the moment it was made. Thus, if the donor dies before the child is born, the gift remains valid.

452. *Concepturus.* The majority view in Spanish law is that a gift may not be made to a child not yet conceived.[175] Two reasons have been advanced. The first is an *a contrario* argument from the code provision that expressly permits gifts to children conceived but yet unborn. A second reason is derived from the contractual nature of the gift. No unconceived being has the ability to accept a gift, even through a representative.

A minority of the scholars, however, argue that there is no legal impediment to making a gift to a concepturus.[176] The contractual nature of the gift does not logically require that the donee have gift capacity at the moment of the gift. There is no reason to impose a requirement of immediate acceptance. In successions law the will is valid when made, even without the legatee's acceptance.

iii. Italy

453. *Broad capacity.* Italian law generally validates gratuitous transfers made to unborn children, whether or not they have been conceived when the gift is made. A child not yet conceived is specifically permitted to inherit (CC art. 643 par. 1) and receive gifts (CC art. 784).[177] A gift to a concepturus, however, is valid only if the child is identified as to its parent or parents (CC art. 784 par. 1). Thus, a gift may not be made to the child of a child yet unconceived.[178]

---

173. Ins. C art. L132-8 par. 3 (derived from the Law of 13 July 1930 art. 63).

174. Paz-Ares Rodríguez (-Albaladejo García) art. 627 no. II.

175. Id. art. 627 no. III.

176. Díez Pastor.

177. The gift provision is found in the chapter of the Civil Code concerning the form and effect of the gift transaction rather than in the chapter governing gift capacity.

178. Biondi no. 86.

(A) ACCEPTANCE

454. *Parental representation.* Gifts made to unborn children may be accepted in conformity with the rules governing the representation of minors and the administration of their property (CC art. 784 par. 2). However, the representatives, usually the parents (CC art. 320 par. 1), may accept gifts for unborn children only with authorization from the guardianship judge, unless the matter is urgent or the gift is of obvious benefit to the child (CC art. 320 par. 3). If the parents are unable or unwilling to accept the gift, the court may name a special guardian (CC art. 321). Capozzi concludes that the gift contract is perfected at the moment the child's representative accepts, which usually precedes the child's birth, and therefore is a case of anticipated consent (*negozio a consenso anticipato*).[179] A prenuptial gift made to the children to be born from a particular marriage is perfected without acceptance but takes effect only if the couple is married (CC art. 785 par. 1). Gifts to unborn children remain in effect, even if the marriage is later annulled or invalidated, to the extent the parties to the marriage were in good faith (*matrimonio putativo*).[180]

(B) PASSING OF TITLE

455. *Upon birth.* When the gift is made, the donor irrevocably loses the power to dispose of the gift object, yet it is not clear when the unborn child receives title. Because the gift contract is generally perfected upon acceptance, some argue that, at least as to a nasciturus, title passes upon acceptance by the representative.[181] Others believe that, as regards both the nasciturus and the concepturus, title passes only upon the donee's birth.[182] Yet the child's birth may not properly be considered a condition in Italian law. A conditional right always has a rightholder, which the nasciturus cannot be.[183]

To the extent title does not pass immediately, the scholars conclude that it is temporarily suspended when the gift is made.[184] During the pendency of the gift, unless otherwise agreed, the property is managed by the donor or the donor's heirs.[185] At the donee's birth, the child's parents assume management responsibility.

456. *Right to dispose.* There is also disagreement concerning whether prospective parents, before conception, may dispose of a gift made to a concepturus.[186]

---

179. Capozzi no. 337 par. b.
180. CC arts. 785 par. 3, 128.
181. Torrente (2006) 453.
182. Biondi no. 88; Rescigno (-Carnevali) 512; Capozzi no. 337 par. d.
183. Biondi id.
184. Id.
185. CC arts. 784 par. 3, 1179; Capozzi no. 337 par. 3. The construction resembles the common law construction of a trust declared for the benefit of the nasciturus.
186. Biondi no. 88.

The courts hold that the parents may, with court approval, dispose of the property of their unborn children, including the property of a concepturus.[187] The scholars disagree. Though parents may dispose of their children's property, gifts to an unborn child are in suspension and have not yet entered the child's patrimony. The parents' authority is limited to accepting the gift. If, nonetheless, the parents dispose of the property, they do so *a non domino*. The transaction is confirmed by the child's birth.

The attribution of fruits depends on when the child was conceived. If, at the moment the gift is made, the donee has been conceived, then fruits maturing prior to birth are reserved for the donee. If the donee is a concepturus, fruits remain with the donor.[188] Biondi has constructed from these rules the general principle that the child's birth has retroactive effect to the moment of the acceptance for a nasciturus, while only to the moment of birth for a concepturus.[189]

(C) JUSTIFICATION

457. *Meeting of the minds.* The giving of gifts to unborn children, and particularly to children yet unconceived, "presents dogmatic difficulties that the doctrine has attempted to overcome at the cost of true logical somersaults and verbal virtuosities."[190] The question is how there can be a meeting of the minds with a child in the womb or, even more problematically, with a child who has not yet been conceived.

Numerous solutions have been proposed. As mentioned above, some authors suggest that the unborn child's parents accept the gift as the child's agents. The difficulty with the agency theory is that it presupposes the existence of a legal subject as principal. In response, it has been suggested that the Civil Code anticipates legal personality for unborn children. The code, however, explicitly provides that legal personality begins at birth (CC art. 1). Some derive the parents' right from the legal fiction that the unborn exist and thus have rights. However, the fiction seems not to explain the statutory provision, because, in the more difficult case of the concepturus, the code does not adopt that fiction. Title passes and the fruits are reserved only upon the child's birth.[191]

Pratis suggested that the parents, though not agents, have been designated to protect the rights of the unborn during the period before birth.[192] However, the

---

187. Cass. 8 Sept. 1952 no. 2864, *Foro it.* 1953 I 299, *Giur. compl. Cass. civ.* 1953 II no. 631 at 71 note Carlos Maria Pratis; Cass. 28 Nov. 1927, *Rep. Foro it.* 1927 *Patria potestà* no. 2.

188. CC art. 784 par. 3 sents. 2–3.

189. Biondi no. 89.

190. Id. no. 84.

191. Torrente (2006) 194.

192. Carlos Maria Pratis, note to Cass. 8 Sept. 1952 no. 2864, *Giur. compl. Cass. civ.* 1953 II no. 631 at 73.

protection of rights, in these circumstances, must be limited to conserving those rights during gestation. Moreover, because the rightholder does not yet exist, the expectancy created by the gift has no subject. It is therefore impossible to speak of a valid alienation. To avoid the difficulties involved when gifts to the unborn are considered bilateral contracts, some Italian authors consider these gifts to be enforceable unilateral acts.[193] That solution also proves to be unhelpful, however, because a unilateral act, in Italian law, takes effect only when the beneficiary becomes aware of it (CC art. 1334).

iv. Germany

458. *No direct gifts to the unborn.* In Germany unborn children do not generally have legal capacity.[194] Nonetheless, gifts to unborn children are permitted when they result from a third-party beneficiary contract (CC § 331 par. 2). The promisee may request the promisor to make delivery to the donee-beneficiary. In such a case, an unborn child does not immediately acquire the right to enforce the promise. Instead, the unborn child, whether or not conceived, usually is deemed to have an irrevocable expectancy (*unwiderrufliche Anwartschaft*) that matures upon birth.[195] Weick argues that a nasciturus should have the capacity to accept a gift or a gift promise directly through the agency of the unborn's representatives.[196]

v. The Common Law

459. *Contingent remainder.* In most jurisdictions, an infant *en ventre sa mere* is *in esse* from the moment of conception. As long as the child is born alive, it may take any estate. Gifts to unborns are typically delivered in trust to the child's guardian. Possible future children may receive not only an equitable interest[197] but, in some circumstances, a legal one as well. For example, a gift "To A for life and then to A's children" is, in the United States, generally considered to create a legal contingent remainder in A's unborn children, including those as yet unconceived.[198] A conveyance by deed of a present interest in real property to a person not yet in existence is inoperative to transfer the legal estate but is valid between the grantor and the grantee in equity.[199]

460. *Theoretical difficulty.* During the 1930s, the Restatement of Property recognized the theoretical difficulty involved in allowing an unborn child to receive an

---

193. Manendi 373–377.
194. Staudinger (-Weick) § 1 nos. 10–11.
195. Palandt (-Grüneberg) § 331 no. 6; Staudinger (-Jagmann) § 331 nos. 24–25.
196. Staudinger (-Wieck) § 1 no. 16.
197. 42 Am.Jur.2d Infants § 4.
198. Thompson § 23.13 par. a; *Miller v. Brown*, 109 S.E.2d 741 (Ga. 1959).
199. 23 Am.Jur.2d Deeds § 21.

interest in property. It concluded that no future interest arises until after the child's birth.[200] Several states enacted legislation restricting the creation of an interest in unborn children.[201] Those statutes have now generally been repealed. Moreover, trusts for the benefit of after-born children, whether or not the children have been conceived, are frequently made and unquestionably valid.[202]

Whether a gift to the unborn (or even unconceived) child is made at law or in equity, it creates not a mere expectancy but rather an enforceable interest.[203] Legal scholars have had difficulty specifying where the interest abides during the interval between the creation of the interest and the moment it either vests or fails. At early common law, the authors suggested that title was *in nubibus* or *in gremio legis*. Others argue that it remains in the grantor until the contingency is resolved.[204] Yet others suggest that, while the contingency is pending, either title or the conveyance remains in abeyance.[205]

b. Legal Persons without Legal Capacity

461. *Two difficulties.* Groups and entities may lack legal personality for two reasons. First, they may not be of a type the law recognizes. Second, their creation may not comply with the required formalities. The question arises whether entities may receive gifts if they are not—or not yet—recognized as legal persons. The limitations encountered by unrecognized entities is examined here, while those that apply to legally constituted associations are examined below.[206]

i. France and Belgium

462. *Retroactive effect.* In French law, entities that lack legal personality also lack the capacity to receive gifts.[207] If the entity is formed or legally recognized subsequent to the making of the gift, French case law is split. Some scholars suggest that the gift is valid but subject to the implied condition that the entity later be legally recognized.[208] The French statute governing the establishment of municipalities contains a provision to this effect.[209] This is also the position of the administrative courts. The civil courts, however, refuse retroactive effect.

---

200. Restatement of Property (Future Interests) § 153 comment a.
201. California CC former §§ 774, 777 (1872), repealed 1959.
202. Restatement (Third) of Trusts § 44 comment c.
203. 2 Scott and Ascher § 12.1.1.
204. Id.; Megarry and Wade 1177.
205. Thompson § 23.12 par. a.
206. Infra nos. 502–528.
207. 8 De Page no. 124; 5 Planiol and Ripert no. 865.
208. 5 Planiol and Ripert no. 866.
209. Law of 5 Apr. 1884 art. 111 par. 3, as modified by Law of 4–6 Feb. 1901 art. 3.

463. *Indirect gifts.* Nonetheless, unrecognized or even nonexistent entities may benefit from indirect gifts in French law.[210] Such gifts are made to an existing person, who accepts it together with the obligation to transfer the gift to the entity once it is formed or recognized. This type of gift seems to be employed chiefly for the creation of foundations. Once the entity is established, it acquires the right to sue the intermediary to perform the obligation. In Belgian law, on the contrary, gifts to unrecognized entities seem to be prohibited even as indirect gifts. Belgian law applies to these gifts the prohibition of gifts to those without capacity, which are invalid even when made through an intermediary (*personne interposée*; CC art. 911 par. 1).[211]

ii. Italy

464. *Irrevocable offer.* Until 1997, the Italian Code provided that gifts to unrecognized entities were without effect unless, within a year of the donor's offer to make the gift, the donor received notice of the entity's application for administrative authorization.[212] Once the donor was notified, the offer became irrevocable. If the entity was not recognized within a year of the application, the offer lapsed.[213] A gift to such an entity was perfected only when the entity was recognized and the entity's acceptance was authorized.[214] These restrictions seemed to be required by fairness considerations. Legal persons were only permitted to accept gifts after administrative authorization. It would have been illogical for associations to have greater privileges before recognition. Moreover, the authorization requirement would have been unenforceable unless only recognized entities were permitted to receive gifts.[215] Nonetheless, unrecognized entities were able to accept gifts of modest value, as well as customary and indirect gifts, without recognition or administrative authorization.

465. *Abrogation.* The provisions in Italian law permitting legal persons, associations, and foundations to accept gifts only after authorization have now been abrogated.[216] The restrictions on unrecognized entities have also been abrogated.[217] Their capacity no longer differs from that of recognized legal persons.[218]

---

210. 5 Planiol and Ripert no. 867.
211. 8 De Page no. 124. For the principles governing the interposition of third parties in French and Belgian law, see infra nos. 633–638.
212. CC former art. 786.
213. CC former arts. 786 par. 1 and 782 par. 4.
214. For gifts to recognized entities in Italian law, see infra nos. 520–524.
215. Cendon art. 786.
216. Law of 15 May 1997 art. 13, as modified by Law of 22 June 2000 art. 1 par. 1.
217. Id.; Rescigno (-Carnevali) 515.
218. Capozzi no. 336 par. d.

iii. Other Civilian Systems

466. *Spain.* Spanish law does not permit unrecognized entities to receive gifts. Rules from successions law, which provide that associations or corporations that are not authorized may not take by inheritance (CC art. 745 no. 2), are applied by analogy.[219]

467. *Germany.* German law does not specifically address the capacity of unrecognized entities to receive gifts. Associations and partnerships have no legal personality and therefore are not able to receive gifts before the conclusion of the memorandum of association or the partnership agreement (*Gesellschaftsvertrag*).[220] That is not the case with corporations. Though neither the public corporation (*Aktiengesellschaft* [AG]) nor the limited liability company (*Gesellschaft mit beschränkter Haftung* [GmbH]) exists *as such* before registration,[221] preliminary forms of both types of entities are generally recognized.[222] From the moment the articles of incorporation (*Satzung*) are approved and the founder accepts the shares,[223] the entity forms a type of jointly held company (*Gesamthandgesellschaft eigener Art*) that has the ability to own property and receive gifts.[224] Even before this moment, the pre-formation company (*Vorgründungsgesellschaft*) may exist as an association or partnership and, as long as it is externally recognizable (*Außengesellschaft*), it may receive gifts.

There is no consensus on the gift capacity of the pre-formation foundation (*Stiftung*).[225] Some authors believe that the fully formed foundation continues the existence of the preliminary entity. However, the majority suggests that the foundation has no recognizable existence before formation is complete.

iv. The Common Law

468. *Executory devise.* In American law, a corporation generally does not come into existence until incorporation. It therefore is incapable of accepting the transfer of property or even of constituting an agent to do so.[226] Nonetheless, one

---

219. Paz-Ares Rodríguez (-Albaladejo García) art. 625 no. III.

220. Schmidt 295–296. This principle applies to the association (*BGB-Gesellschaft*), the general partnership (*offene Handelsgesellschaft*), and the limited partnership (*Kommanditgesellschaft*).

221. Corp. L [AktG] § 41 par. 1 sent. 1; Limited Liab. Corp. L [GmbHG] § 11 par. 1.

222. Hüffer § 41 no. 2 (*Vor-AG* and *Vor-GmbH*).

223. Corp. L [AktG] §§ 23, 29.

224. BGH 18 Jan. 2000, BGHZ 143, 314 at 319; BGH 16 Mar. 1992, BGHZ 117, 323 at 326–327; Hüffer § 41 no. 2; Lutter and Bayer § 11 nos. 4–5. The one-person public corporation does not have existence as a preliminary entity.

225. MünchKomm-BGB (-Reuter) §§ 80–81 nos. 62–66.

226. 1A Fletcher on Corporations § 205.

court has held such a gift to be valid as "an executory devise."[227] The gift was made to a corporation that was to be created with the purpose of accepting and administering the gift. The quoted term means only that the gift was somehow valid, even though incomplete.

469. *Corporate promoters.* In the typical case, corporate promoters, who are neither the corporation itself nor its agents, receive gifts on the corporation's behalf. Because they are bound to the corporation by fiduciary duty, they are obligated to complete any gift transfer once the corporation is formed.[228] Once incorporated, the corporation may gain the benefits of any preincorporation transfer made to the promoters by adopting the transaction.

470. *England.* English law does not seem to restrict the right of future corporate entities to receive gifts.[229] The Companies Act of 1985 provides that contracts may be made by or on behalf of a company even before it has been formed (sec. 36C par. 1). Subject to contrary agreement, the transaction has the effect of binding the person purporting to act for the company, who is personally liable.[230]

471. *India.* In Indian law, gifts may not be made to unregistered societies.[231]

c. Nonpersons

472. *Some exceptions.* Typically only human beings may hold legal rights. Thus gifts may not be made to inanimate objects. A trust for the benefit of an inanimate object is also invalid. A court has invalidated a trust created for the purpose of keeping the settlor's clock in working order.[232] The common justification is that there is no beneficiary to enforce the rights. In some circumstances, however, gifts given to nonpersons may be valid.

i. The Dead

473. *No capacity.* A corpse cannot receive property. If the donee dies before the gift has been executed, the gift lapses. A coffin or shroud given to a person after death remains the property of the donor, even if the decedent is interred in it.[233] In some cases, the donee's personal representative may take advantage of a presumption that the donee was alive when the gift was made.[234]

---

227. *Watkins v. Bigelow*, 100 N.W. 1104, 1109 (Minn. 1904).
228. 1A Fletcher on Corporations § 192.10.
229. For pre-incorporation matters, see generally Palmer pars. 3.001–3.006.
230. For a sales transaction, see *Braymist Ltd & Ors v Wise Finance Co Ltd* [2002] BCC 514 (CA).
231. Mulla sec. 122 no. 3.
232. *Kelly v. Nichols*, 21 A. 906, 908 (R.I. 1891).
233. *Haynes's Case* (1614) 12 Co R 113, 77 ER 1389.
234. Crossley Vaines 300.

ii. Gods and Idols

474. *Debutter-property.* In modern Hindu law, an idol may be a juristic person.[235] The idol may own property and file suit. Property may be dedicated to an idol, even without the interposition of trustees. The property belongs to the idol in perpetuity, even though no acceptance has been made on the idol's behalf. However, when idols receive real estate above a certain value, the transfers are not complete until registered.[236] A valid dedication requires a renunciation of property in favor of a god with the intent for the property or its income to benefit the particular deity. The god must also be represented by a properly consecrated idol with a particular name in a particular shrine or holy place.[237]

The Anglo-Indian name for the idol's property is *debutter-property*, a name derived from the Hindu word for property dedicated to a deity (*devottaram*), which in turn is related to the Hindu word for deity (*devata*). The dedication must be absolute to create debutter-property, a complete divesting of the donor's interest. The dedication may not be illusory, in the sense that it is actually designed to benefit the donor's relatives or nominees. On the other hand, care of the idol need not absorb the bulk, or even a substantial portion, of the income, which may instead be used for other purposes approved by the manager.[238] Indian law provides tax benefits for this type of donation.

iii. Animals

475. *Common law.* Scholars argue that animals have moral rights[239] and even that they should enjoy legal personhood.[240] Only rarely, though, have courts recognized these rights.[241] The law, therefore, has not generally permitted gifts to be given to animals, either directly or as trust beneficiaries.[242] However, the same result can be achieved by making a gift of the animal together with a sum of money, with the proviso that if the animal is neglected the money shall revert to

---

235. Keith.

236. Derrett no. 782.

237. Id. no. 783.

238. Id. no. 785–787. The idol's needs are generally modest. "In the case of family idols the cost of their worship in clothes and ornaments, and daily *puja* by a Brahman, could be (and still is) very small. The idol's food consists in the savour of food cooked for the family and placed before it. Its bath requires hardly any expenditure." Id. no. 787.

239. Regan 266–329.

240. Bryant 258–295.

241. "The statute relating to animals is based on 'the theory, unknown to the common law, that animals have rights which, like those of human beings, are to be protected. A horse, under its master's hands, stands in a relation to the master analogous to that of a child to a parent.'" *State v. Karstendiek*, 22 So. 845, 847 (La. 1897), quoting Bishop § 1101.

242. *In re McNeill's Estate*, 41 Cal.Rptr. 139, 141 (Cal. App. 1965).

the donor's heirs.[243] Another method involves an honorary trust, which, though not enforceable, permits the trustee, if willing, to carry out the trust's purposes and permits the court to refuse to decree a resulting trust for the benefit of the settlor's heirs.[244] Today, the common law of trusts in some American states permits gifts for the benefit of animals. The general rule in England is that an animal may not be the beneficiary of a trust, though trusts for the maintenance of particular animals have sometimes been enforced.[245] The law on these questions generally concerns trusts established by testamentary bequest. However, the same principles should apply to the creation of inter vivos trusts.

476. *Fiduciary relationship.* Trusts for the benefit of animals raise two difficult questions. The first arises from the fact that the declaration of trust creates a fiduciary relationship between trustee and beneficiary.[246] If an animal is the beneficiary, there is no one to enforce the fiduciary obligation. Nonetheless, bequests in trust for the care of animals have long been valid.[247] They are often justified not as gifts to the animals but rather as charitable gifts for educational purposes, namely for the improvement of human beings by suppressing cruelty to animals.[248] The courts are generally lenient with the wording and validate the gifts despite some uncertainty as to the beneficiaries. For example, one court has enforced a bequest "for the purpose of founding and supporting a Cattery, to be situated in or near Ansonia, for the care of homeless animals and boarders."[249]

477. *Pet trusts.* Second, trusts are typically measured by the life of a human being and terminate on the beneficiary's death. Some courts have therefore held that a trust created for the purpose of caring for a specific animal is invalid.[250] To solve this problem, many states now permit *pet trusts*.[251] The Uniform Probate Code

---

243. Bogert and Bogert § 165 at 161.

244. ENGLAND: *In re Dean* [1889] LR 41 Ch D 552; UNITED STATES: *Phillips v. Estate of Holzmann*, 740 So.2d 1 (Fla. App. 1998); Restatement (Third) of Trusts § 47; Bogert and Bogert § 166; Bogert and Bogert (-Hess) § 166.

245. *Pettingall v Pettingall* (1842) 11 LJ Ch 176; 48 Halsbury sub Trusts no. 507 notes 3 and 7 (collecting cases).

246. 1 Scott and Ascher § 2.1.5.

247. I give and bequeath to the Colorado State Board of Child and Animal Protection ... requesting it to use the same in perpetuity, in affording relief to hungry, thirsty, abused and neglected cattle, horses, dogs and cats in Denver .... I request that three (3) iron drinking fountains for animals be erected in downtown Denver, the City of Denver having been niggardly and selfish in that respect; I especially request that my dog Shep (if living) be given every care and a good home during his life and a decent burial upon his passing.
In re Forrester's Estate, 279 P. 721, 722 (Colo. 1929).

248. *Re Wedgewood* [1915] 1 Ch 113.

249. *Shannon v. Eno*, 179 A. 479, 480 (Conn. 1935).

250. *In re Mills' Estate*, 111 N.Y.S.2d 622 (Sur. Ct. 1952).

251. Bogert and Bogert § 165; Bogert and Bogert (-Hess) § 165 (collecting statutes).

has also adopted a validating provision.[252] Pet trusts may be created inter vivos. Under the Texas statute, for example, trusts may be declared for the purpose of caring for an animal that is alive during the settlor's lifetime.[253] An individual is appointed to represent the animal's interests. The trust terminates on the death of the animal. The trust fails if the pet is not sufficiently identified.[254]

Trusts for the benefit of animals are becoming increasingly common. A New York court was asked to treat five chimpanzees as persons so they might protect their interests as income and principal beneficiaries of a trust.[255] More recently, it was announced that Leona Helmsley left $12 million to her dog Trouble. Trouble's trust provided detailed instructions for her care.[256] Helmsley also left nearly $8 billion to a charitable trust with the purpose of providing for the care of dogs. The bequest created one of the largest foundations in the United States. "A network of lawyers and animal activists has orchestrated these changes, largely without opposition, in order to whittle down the legal distinctions between human beings and animals."[257]

d. Indeterminacy

478. *Individualization.* Some legal systems, particularly French and Belgian law, permit gratuitous transfers only to donees who are designated with sufficient definiteness. The scholars unanimously accept the rule, even though it is required by no text in the Civil Code.[258] The donee is sufficiently determined only if, on the date the gift is to take effect, the donee has been individualized. Indeterminacy can be of two types. The first involves a factual difficulty—it is not possible to determine which donee was intended. The second concerns indefiniteness intentionally created by the donor. As De Page has indicated, these questions are particularly complex and even obscure.[259] Moreover, though the same principles

---

252. Unif. Prob. C § 2-907 par. b.

253. Prop. C § 112.037 (V.T.C.A.).

254. *Hahn v. Estate of Stange,* 2008 WL 372467 (Tex. App.).

255. *Matter of Fouts,* 677 N.Y.S.2d 699 (Sur. Ct. 1998). For a similar case, see *Sarah v. Primarily Primates, Inc.,* 255 S.W.3d 132 (Tex. App. 2008).

256. Trouble's guardian estimated that the dog's annual security costs would be $100,000, her grooming costs $8,000, food costs $1,200, and veterinary care up to $18,000. Toobin 41.

257. Id. 38.

258. Indeterminacy concerns the question of whether there is any donee at all. It therefore exceeds the scope of the notion of capacity. Nonetheless, the issue is traditionally discussed in the context of CC art. 906 as a question of the capacity to receive. The issue arises only in the context of gratuitous transfers. This capacity restriction is typically justified as a consequence of the nature of the gift transfer. Since the nature of the gift is to transfer patrimonial rights, the transfer cannot take place unless the donee is sufficiently determined. See 8 De Page no. 123 pars. B, E.

259. De Page no. 123.

apply in theory to all gratuitous transfers, most of the cases and scholarly hypotheticals involve testamentary bequests. Given the formalities required for a valid gift, situations involving indeterminate donees are rare.

i. Lack of Specificity

479. *France and Belgium.* An example of the first type is a gift *to the poor (aux pauvres).*[260] Because the poor certainly exist and should be able to receive charitable assistance, some authors argue, "it would be absurd to prohibit gratuitous transfers made to the poor merely because the determination of the actual beneficiaries may, in certain cases, require discretion on the part of those charged with distributing the funds."[261]

Today, a gift to the poor is valid if the specific category of poor that was meant can be determined. Valid specifications include "to the choir boys of the cathedral," "for the creation of a school," or "to provide for the burial of the indigent." If the donor did not specify, the courts attempt to attribute the gift to the intended group. If the gift is given to the poor through the intermediary of a religious or secular entity, the courts redirect the gift to the local social services office. The monopoly this office exercises has apparently inhibited gifts to the poor in France.[262]

480. *Common law.* There is disagreement in the common law about whether a charitable trust may be valid if the beneficiaries are uncertain. It seems to be settled in England and in many American states that both gifts and trusts may be made on charitable uses for the benefit of uncertain groups such as *the poor* of a certain district or *the children* of a certain town.[263] Yet the language may not be so general and vague as to leave both the beneficiaries and the purposes of the trust completely to the judgment of the trustees or the court.[264] Other states hold that the beneficiary of a trust must either be identified with certainty or be capable of being rendered certain. In those states, a gift in trust "for the worthy poor of the city of St. Paul" is "so uncertain, changeable, and indeterminate" that the trust is void.[265]

ii. Powers of Appointment

481. *Intended.* A second, very different type of indeterminacy is purposefully sought. The issue arises most often when the donor, granting a power of appointment *(faculté d'élire)*, asks a third party to designate the donee.[266] This type of

---

260. 5 Planiol and Ripert nos. 889–897.
261. Id. no. 889.
262. Id. no. 896.
263. 3 Pomeroy §§ 1019, 1022, 1025.
264. Id. § 1019.
265. *Watkins v. Bigelow,* 100 N.W. 1104, 1108 (Minn. 1904).
266. 8 De Page no. 129; 5 Planiol and Ripert nos. 599–601.

indeterminacy arises in French law when the gift is to be given "to two children born out of wedlock between the ages of ten and twelve, a boy and a girl, from the foster home of the province of Gers, as selected by the mother superior of the Condom hospital,"[267] or "according to the donor's wishes, as communicated orally," or "in the manner agreed upon."

Roman law, which prohibited legacies to *personae incertae*, nonetheless recognized powers of appointment, provided the beneficiaries were clearly determined—*incertus ex certis personis*. Powers of appointment were permitted under the French ancien régime, though they were voided if the group of potential beneficiaries was too large. In order to prevent the family father from reaching beyond the grave to intimidate his children, the revolution prohibited granting a power of appointment to the testator's surviving spouse.[268] Powers of appointment were later prohibited when conferred on any party.[269] Today, any liberality made by a power of appointment is void.

In Italian law, the power to choose the donee or determine the gift object may not be delegated (CC art. 778 par. 1). However, an agent may choose the donee from among those the donor has designated, from those who belong to a particular category, or from the legal persons the donor has indicated (art. 778 par. 2).[270]

482. *Justification.* In French law, property must, at every moment, have an owner. Because the third party, upon the granting of the power of appointment, acquires no immediate interest in property, an interlude occurs during which title is suspended. Because the problem is merely technical, French law permits donors to achieve a similar result by other means. Though the interposition of third parties is generally prohibited when the goal is to make gifts to those without capacity, the prohibition does not apply to gifts coupled with an obligation.[271]

Belgian law, on the other hand, justifies the prohibition on policy grounds. If enforceable, the power of appointment would permit the donor to evade restrictions on the capacity to receive.[272] The courts determine whether gifts are being used to that effect.[273] A gift coupled with an obligation is valid only if the portion of the gift to be designated by the third party does not absorb the quasitotality of

---

267. Agen 25 Nov. 1861, D. 1862 II 34, S. 1862 II 17, on appeal, Civ. 12 Aug. 1863, D. 1863 I 356, S. 1863 I 446.

268. Decree of 17 Nivôse an II art. 23.

269. 5 Planiol and Ripert no. 600.

270. Capozzi no. 335 par. c. The donor may also permit the agent to select the gift object from among several indicated possibilities or within the value the donor has established. CC art. 778 par. 3.

271. 5 Planiol and Ripert nos. 172, 600. See supra no. 449. For the interposition of third parties, see infra nos. 633–638.

272. 8 De Page no. 129.

273. Id. no. 134.

the gift.[274] However, the focus on policy grounds makes it possible to validate a third-party beneficiary contract to an undetermined beneficiary, even when the gift amounts to the entire benefit of the contract, provided the contract is not used to circumvent capacity restrictions.[275]

2. Social Policy Concerns

483. *Public interest.* Gift capacity may be limited for policy reasons as well. At times in the past, for example, it has been thought to violate public policy for felons and foreigners to receive gifts. The gift capacity of both minors and the deaf is restricted to ensure that they receive necessary assistance. The capacity of legal persons to receive has been limited in order to permit public officials to evaluate whether the gift is appropriate.

a. Civil Death

i. France and Belgium

484. *Preventing mortmain.* As discussed above, under the French ancien régime, monks and nuns admitted to religious orders, as well as certain felons, suffered civil death (*mort civile*).[276] One consequence was the loss of the right to receive a gift.[277] The rule was thought necessary to prevent large fortunes from accumulating in religious institutions where they became subject to the dead hand (*mainmorte*).[278]

(A) MEMBERS OF RELIGIOUS COMMUNITIES

485. *Revolution.* The Constituent Assembly refused to permit members who left their religious communities to receive gifts, other than pensions of lifetime annuities.[279] Jean-Baptiste Treilhard, president of the Assembly and a future drafter of the Civil Code, justified the rule as a means to avoid troubling the families' preexisting patrimonial arrangements. Monks and nuns now have the capacity to receive gifts, even if they have taken vows of poverty. Under Belgian law, members of religious orders may receive gifts as individuals (*ut singuli*). However, if the gift is meant for an unrecognized entity, such as the order itself, the gift may represent an invalid interposition of an intermediary.

(B) FELONS

486. *No restriction.* The Code Napoleon provided that felons punished by civil death could receive only gifts of necessaries (art. 25 par. 3). Though civil death

---

274. Id. no. 131. See supra no. 449.
275. Id. no. 136.
276. Supra nos. 411–412.
277. 5 Planiol and Ripert no. 196 at 285 note 1; 8 De Page nos. 124 par. 2 lit. E, 185.
278. Carette 14 note 1.
279. Decree of 20 Feb. 1790.

was abolished in 1854, the same rule continued to apply to life prisoners until 1994.[280] The doctrine found the restriction to be of questionable value.[281] It was of uncertain effectiveness as a deterrent and, because its principal effect was on the felon's relatives, it contravened the principle of personal responsibility. The French Penal Code, adopted in 1994, does not restrict the right of felons to receive gifts.[282]

ii. The Common Law

487. *History.* As indicated above, a number of American states punished felons sentenced to life imprisonment with civil death.[283] Civil death worked "a deprivation of all rights whose exercise or enjoyment depends upon some provision of positive law."[284] The right to receive by inheritance was thought to be a right existing only by virtue of law. Thus, in some states, when civil death was declared, that right was forfeited as an element of punishment.[285] In other states, however, civil death did not mean that the felon could not inherit.[286] No cases have been found concerning the right to receive by gift.

488. *Today.* In the United States, a felon, even if serving a life sentence, may generally receive by gift.[287]

b. Foreigners

i. France and Belgium

489. *Right of escheat.* During most of the ancien régime, foreigners (*aubains*) were in principle prohibited from taking or transmitting by inheritance.[288] Any property a foreigner left on French soil at death passed to the king by virtue of the royal *right of escheat* (*droit d'aubaine*). The right of escheat did not affect the capacity of foreigners to make or receive inter vivos gifts. Though the right of escheat was provided with an apocryphal Roman law heritage during the Renaissance, the rule probably originated in German customary law. The mercantilists later justified the rule as a means to prohibit French property from enriching other countries.[289]

---

280. French Penal C former art. 36 par. 1.
281. 5 Planiol and Ripert no. 218.
282. From the fact that this form of supplementary punishment is not mentioned in the new penal code, scholars conclude that it was abrogated. 1 Pradel nos. 624–626.
283. Supra no. 416.
284. *In re Donnelly's Estate*, 58 P. 61 (Cal. 1899).
285. Id.
286. *Avery v. Everett*, 18 N.E. 148 (N.Y. 1888).
287. *In re Johnson*, 56 N.Y.S.2d 568, 570 (Sur. Ct. 1945).
288. Sahlins (2004) 5; 4 Planiol and Ripert no. 35.
289. Sahlins (2004) 33, 45, 237.

490. *Reciprocal rights.* The rule was tempered with regard to certain foreigners, including professionals, city residents, and citizens of countries with which France had settled the question by treaty.[290] Enlightenment thinkers, particularly Montesquieu, considered the institution barbaric.[291] During the last twenty years of the ancien régime, largely on account of Physiocratic ideas about the importance of international commerce, the right of escheat was slowly dismantled.[292] Commercial treaties with over sixty countries included reciprocal inheritance rights. The right of escheat was not abolished outright because it was feared that unilateral abrogation would not be reciprocated.

491. *Abolition.* The right of escheat was abolished by the Constituent Assembly as a remnant of the feudal regime.[293] All foreigners were subsequently granted the right to transmit and to receive by inheritance.[294] After war broke out with Europe, however, foreigners were suspected of being enemies, traitors, and spies.[295] The Decree of 17 Nivôse Year II restricted the right to inherit to citizens of states with which France was not at war.[296] Except for England, no other country had followed the French example of unilateral abolition.[297] This was especially galling because it provided advantages to nationals of Prussia and the Ottoman Empire, countries with which France had no treaty on the matter and which fought against France during the Revolutionary and Napoleonic Wars.

492. *Civil Code.* To remedy the problem, the Code Napoleon reimposed a reciprocity requirement on the capacity of nonresident foreigners, regarding both their general enjoyment of civil rights (arts. 11, 13) and specifically their capacity to receive gratuitous transfers, including gifts (arts. 726, 912). As a result, nonresident foreigners had whatever capacity was granted by treaty. The right of escheat was not reinstated. Those who supported unilateral abolition argued that reciprocity would impose on French courts the impossible task of determining exactly what rights were accorded French citizens abroad. Unilateral abolition would also require France to follow foreign law, which, in the case of Spain, for example, would grant greater rights to foreigners than to French citizens.

---

290. Id. 171.

291. Id. 240–241.

292. Id. 13, 225.

293. Decree of 6 Aug. 1790 Preamble and art. 1. The abolition itself did not give foreigners the right to inherit from their *French* relatives. It merely permitted them to inherit the property that their *foreign* relatives left on French soil. 1 Duvergier 272 note 1.

294. Decree of 8 Apr. 1791 art. 3.

295. Sahlins (2004) 283.

296. Decree of 17 Nivôse II art. 59.

297. Sahlins (2004) 295–296.

493. *Abrogated.* These capacity limitations were abrogated in 1819 in France[298] and in 1865 in Belgium.[299]

ii. England

494. *British ships.* In England, an alien may receive gifts of all types of property except title to, or a share in, a British ship.[300]

iii. United States

495. *Inheritance.* Some American states permitted nonresident aliens to receive by inheritance only when there was reciprocity with the nonresident's country of residence.[301] The original purpose of the legislation seems to have been to prevent decedents' estates from benefiting the governments of states at war with the United States.[302] The reciprocity requirement was variously interpreted. Some states required only that the foreign inheritance law meet certain minimum standards and not discriminate against U.S. citizens,[303] while other state laws were more restrictive.[304] Apparently these laws did not restrict the capacity to receive inter vivos gifts. They have now generally been repealed.

c. The Deaf

496. *France.* Though the deaf (*sourd-muet*) do not lack the capacity to receive a gift in French law, the code prescribes how they may accept. Those who are able to write may accept in writing or through an agent (CC art. 936 par. 1). Otherwise, the gift is accepted by the donee's guardian (CC art. 936 par. 2). There is no agreement as to the rule's justification.[305] Some authors contend that it protects the deaf against burdensome gifts. These authors suggest that acceptance should always involve the guardian. It has been objected, however, that, if

---

298. Law of 14 July 1819 art. 1; 4 Planiol and Ripert no. 36.

299. Law of 27 Apr. 1865 art. 3.

300. 20 Halsbury part 1 sub Gifts no. 19. Aliens, who are not allowed to own a British ship, are also prohibited from disposing of one by gift. Id. no. 7.

301. CALIFORNIA: Prob. C former § 259 (repealed in 1974); OREGON: O.R.S. § 111.070 (repealed 1969), disapproved by *Zschernig v. Miller*, 389 U.S. 429, 88 S.Ct. 664 (1968).

302. Because the foreign governments guilty of these practices constitute a direct threat to the Government of the United States, it is immediately necessary that the property and money of citizens dying in this country should remain in this country and not be sent to such foreign countries to be used for the purposes of waging a war that eventually may be directed against the Government of the United States.

California Prob. C former § 259 Enabling Clause, quoted in *Crowley v. Allen*, 52 F.Supp. 850, 853 (D. Cal. 1943), rev'd sub nom. *Allen v. Markham*, 147 F.2d 136 (9th Cir. 1945), rev'd, 326 U.S. 490, 66 S.Ct. 296 (1946).

303. *In re Larkin's Estate*, 416 P.2d 473 (Cal. 1966).

304. *In re Krachler's Estate*, 263 P.2d 769 (Or. 1953).

305. 5 Planiol and Ripert no. 227; 8 De Page no. 180.

the restrictions were imposed for protective reasons, the *giving* of gifts should also be limited. But it is not. Others argue that the rules favor the deaf by providing them with additional means to accept. This justification too has been contested. Though the Civil Code requires that gifts be accepted expressly, an acceptance is sufficient if it is indicated to the notary and noted in the act. Presumably, the deaf can communicate acceptance by signing. In any case, the rules apply only when gift acceptance is made by formal act. Other gifts may be accepted without supervision.

d. Minors

497. *Prescribed form.* In no legal system examined here do minors lack the capacity to receive a gift. However, a form is often prescribed for acceptance to guarantee the opportunity for consultation.[306] These acceptance requirements sometimes impose formalities more involved than those required in synallagmatic transactions.

i. France and Belgium

498. *Representative.* In French law, the guardian of an unemancipated minor may accept a gift that imposes no obligation on the donee. Authorization by the family council is not required.[307] The child's father or mother also may accept gifts to the child without authorization (CC art. 935 par. 2). Moreover, each of the child's ancestors is given an independent right to accept, even while the child's parents are alive. If the gift is coupled with an obligation, acceptance usually requires authorization.[308]

499. *Ancestors' right.* There is considerable dispute concerning the ancestors' right to accept on the minor's behalf.[309] The provision was adopted from the Ordinance of 1731 (art. 7). During the code deliberations, Berlier suggested that the situation contemplated by the rule would rarely arise, and therefore the provision needlessly disrespects parents.[310] Tronchet responded that the matter was important because the father might be absent, might detest the child, or, as a potential heir, might have a conflict of interest.[311] Cambacérès resolved the dispute by pointing out that the code should attempt to maximize the minor's opportunities.[312]

The code's language would permit any of the child's ancestors, without authorization, to accept any gifts, including gifts imposing obligations on the

---

306. 8 De Page no. 138.
307. CC arts. 935 par. 1, 463.
308. Flour and Souleau no. 297.
309. 5 Planiol and Ripert nos. 221–222; 8 De Page nos. 139, 141.
310. Berlier, Discussion contribution (12 Ventôse XI [3 Mar. 1803]), in 12 Fenet 356.
311. Tronchet, Discussion contribution, id.
312. Cambacérès, Discussion contribution, id. 358.

donee, no matter how onerous (CC art. 935 par. 2).[313] Some authors argue that such gifts should be accepted only by the guardian and only after authorization by the family council.[314] Delvincourt argued that grandparents should not be permitted to trump a parent's refusal, since a father may have good reasons for preventing his child from receiving a gift.[315] Others suggest that the ancestors' powers are not merely concurrent with those of the tutor, but trump them. If the ancestors refuse the gift, the guardian is not authorized to accept it.[316] The justification is that the ancestors may be more aware of the gift's provenance. Others, following Cambacérès, argue that, because the purpose of the rule is to render acceptance as likely as possible, a refusal should never trump an acceptance.[317]

No ancestor may accept a gift that the same ancestor has given to the minor. When a gift is given jointly by the child's parents, the father accepts the mother's share, while the mother accepts the father's gift.[318] Before married women had the capacity to give gifts, the father not only accepted the mother's gift for the child but also intervened as husband to authorize the mother to make the gift.[319]

ii. The Common Law

500. *England.* In Bracton's day, minors could receive gifts only with the tutor's authority.[320] Today in English law, a minor is generally capable of receiving gifts of any property other than legal estates in land, unless it would clearly be to the child's prejudice to do so.[321] Gifts vest in the child immediately. The child's acceptance is voidable during minority or upon the child's coming of age.[322] Before 1997 the gift of a legal estate in land vested equitable title in the child and obligated the donor to execute a vesting deed and trust instrument and to hold the land in trust for the child. Since 1997 the conveyance operates as a declaration that the land is held in trust for the minor. If the conveyance is to both a minor and an adult, the conveyance vests the land in the adult to hold in trust for the minor.[323]

---

313. 8 De Page no. 141.

314. 5 Planiol and Ripert no. 222.

315. "Might not a father, for example, have a significant interest in preventing his daughter from receiving a gift from a particular person? Which authority has the right, in this case, to usurp his rights and to assist, perhaps, in a seduction that the father has a duty to prevent?" 1 Delvincourt 756 note 4 to page 240.

316. 8 De Page no. 141.

317. 5 Planiol and Ripert no. 222.

318. Id.

319. Id. no. 310 note 3; supra no. 419.

320. 2 Bracton 54.

321. 20 Halsbury part 1 sub Gifts no. 19; 5 Halsbury part 3 sub Children and Young Persons no. 39.

322. 5 Halsbury part 3 id. no. 41. Once avoided, the gift is considered void ab initio and revests in the donor.

323. Id. no. 31.

501. *United States.* In American law, every person, including a minor, has the capacity to receive a beneficial gift. Uniform acts adopted in virtually all American states now facilitate gifts to minors, including minors without legally-appointed guardians.[324] The child's acceptance is presumed, or, as some courts remark, the law accepts the gift for the child.[325] If the gift is not in the child's interest, the law will repudiate it, even if the child has accepted it.

e. Legal Persons

502. *Authorization.* Several legal systems restrict the capacity to receive of legally recognized associations and corporations. Often a governmental authorization is required. The restriction is justified by the need to police the activities of these entities, to ensure that they pursue only the goals for which they were chartered, and to prevent them from removing too large a segment of society's capital from the marketplace.

i. France

503. *Freedom of association.* D'Aguesseau permitted associations in the public interest to receive gifts without authorization (Ordinance art. 8). During the course of the eighteenth century, however, letters patent and other types of authorization were required before certain associations, both secular and religious, could receive gifts.[326] The French revolutionaries greatly increased the required authorizations. They opposed freedom of association because they thought associations might encourage resistance to the new order. Until the beginning of the twentieth century, the right to form associations of any type was severely limited in France.[327] In 1901 the Third Republic permitted citizens to associate freely without prior authorization.[328] However, only associations in the public interest (*associations reconnues d'utilité publique*) were given the capacity to receive gifts. There has been considerable evolution over the past century. In particular, the requirement that associations could not receive gifts without administrative approval was radically altered in 2005 to permit gifts unless the administration objects.

504. *Two restrictions.* Today, French law places two restrictions on the ability of legal persons to accept gifts. First, some recognized legal entities are not

---

324. 38 Am.Jur.2d Gifts § 15. For the Uniform Transfers to Minors Act and its predecessors, see infra nos. 895–896.

325. *Hillary Holding Corp. v. Brooklyn Jockey Club,* 88 N.Y.S.2d 198, 203 (Sup. Ct. 1949); *Youngblood v. Hoeffle,* 201 S.W. 1057, 1057 (Tex. Civ. App. 1918).

326. Antoine Bergier, Notes et additions, in 1 Ricard 152–160.

327. Georges Daublon and Dominique Randoux, obs. to Order no. 856 of 28 July 2005, *Rép. not. Defrén.* 2006 art. 38302 at 3–5.

328. Law of 1 July 1901 art. 2.

permitted to receive any gifts, or they may accept only specified types of gifts. Second, gifts to some legal persons, gifts long subject to governmental authorization, are now valid unless the government objects.

(A) RESTRICTIONS

505. *Evolution.* Restrictions on gifts to certain types of associations were slowly relaxed. To circumvent the remaining restrictions, the courts occasionally recharacterized gifts as contributions, which are not subject to the same requirements.

(1) Gifts to Associations

506. *Business associations.* Over the years, legal persons have been increasingly permitted to receive gifts. Public entities have the basic capacity to receive gifts, as do the French state, the departments, and the municipalities.[329] The remaining limitations concern legal persons established under the private law. It was long debated whether business entities governed by the civil law (*sociétés civiles*) as well as those that are organized under the commercial law (*sociétés commerciales*), such as corporations, have the capacity to receive gifts.[330] Some authors argued that, because the goal of commercial entities is to make a profit, the receipt of gratuitous transfers would be ultra vires. The capacity of stock companies to receive gifts is now accepted, especially because, unlike some other types of legal persons, business companies are unlikely to accumulate a significant mortmain.

507. *Benevolent associations.* Associations in the public interest may receive gifts. However, any real property that is not necessary to the association's activities, with the exception of woods and forests, must be sold.[331] These associations may not accept gifts of any property in which the donor attempts to reserve a life estate (*usufruit*).[332] Associations devoted to charitable purposes may also receive gifts, subject to administrative approval, as described below.[333] Officially recognized associations that are neither declared to be in the public interest nor exclusively devoted to charitable purposes may only receive manual gifts and gifts from foundations.[334]

(2) Recharacterization

508. *Contributions.* The courts have occasionally circumvented the prohibitions and complex authorization requirements by recharacterizing gifts to benevolent

---

329. 5 Planiol and Ripert no. 872.
330. Id. no. 873.
331. Law of 1 July 1901 art. 11 pars. 1–2.
332. Id. art. 11 par. 3.
333. Id. art. 6 par. 2. See infra nos. 511–512.
334. Id. art. 6 par. 1, modified by Law of 23 July 1987 art. 16.

associations as contributions (*apports*).[335] Contributions are not subject to the prohibitions and are valid without authorization. Earlier scholars suggested that transfers could be considered contributions only if they were made at the time the association was created. This definition proved unhelpful because it made it impossible for associations to increase their capital.[336] More recently, transfers have been considered contributions if the *solvens* maintains some control.

509. *Explanations.* Gény suggested that a contribution is not an actual transfer of title but is rather a temporary allocation (*affectation*) of the property to the association's purposes. The case law, however, has decided otherwise. Others argue that a contribution differs from a gift in that it is revocable. This theory also seems to fail because the association has the right to alienate the property and thereby deprive the contributor of the reversion. A third theory suggests that a contribution cannot be a gift because the contributor benefits personally from the transaction. Yet this theory too fails because a quid pro quo is often absent.

510. *Trust analogy.* Martine Béhar-Touchais invokes a rare French doctrine that resembles the common-law trust (*fiducie-gestion*) to explain the distinction. She suggests that the contribution is intended as a gift to the beneficiaries of the association's activities rather than to the association itself. In common-law terms, the contributor transfers the property to the association to hold in trust for the beneficiaries. The transfer is always onerous with regard to the association (*fiduciaire*) and potentially so to the settlor (*fiduciant*), depending on whether the settlor benefits from the transaction. Because (to continue the trust analogy) the association receives legal title, it has the right to alienate the property. And because the transaction is not a gift, the association's incapacity does not invalidate the contribution. One case seems to validate this explanation. The court held that a transfer of real property to a cultural association with the purpose of ensuring the existence of a private school constituted a contribution rather than a gift.[337]

(B) REQUIRED AUTHORIZATIONS

511. *Broad interpretation.* Until 2005 governmental authorization was required before some entities could accept a gift. The Civil Code requires authorization only for gifts made for the benefit of retirement homes (*hospices*), a municipality's poor (*communes*), or foundations (*établissements d'utilité publique*) (CC arts. 910, 937). The requirement was extended to include all legal persons

---

335. Martine Béhar-Touchais, note to Civ.¹ 1 Mar. 1988, J.C.P. 1989 II 21373 nos. 9–16.

336. Jean Honorat, obs. to Civ.¹ 1 Mar. 1988, *Rép. not. Defrén.* 1988 art. 34373 no. 6 at 1403.

337. Civ.¹ 1 Mar. 1988, J.C.P. 1989 II 21373.

(*personnes morales*),[338] with the significant exceptions of business entities (whether governed by the civil or the commercial law), labor and professional unions, and, under certain circumstances, French departments and municipalities and other public entities.[339]

(1) Procedure

512. *Complex.* The procedure for obtaining the required authorization was extremely complex, a "veritable obstacle course," even for gifts of small value.[340] The administrative authorities conducted an investigation to ensure that the association intended to pursue beneficial social purposes. When the association's purposes involved scientific research, approvals were also required from the ministry in charge of the particular type of research, and if the field involved medicine, from the Ministry of Health. If the donor's family challenged the gift during probate, the matter was referred to the Conseil d'Etat.[341]

The authorization requirement was fundamental, "an organic principle."[342] In all cases, authorization had to occur before acceptance. A prior acceptance was invalid and had to be repeated.[343] However, French and Belgian law generally permitted a provisional acceptance to bind the donor until it was decided whether authorization would be forthcoming.[344] If the gift included rights in real property that could be subject to mortgage (*susceptibles d'hypothèque*), Belgian law required recordation of the gift act, of the provisional acceptance, of the notification of the provisional acceptance to the donor, and of the definitive notification.[345] Provisional acceptance prevented the donor from revoking and prevented the offer from lapsing upon the donor's incapacity or death. Nonetheless, the gift contract was not formed until the authorization was given and acceptance was made as required by the code.[346]

Pending authorization, transfer of title was suspended.[347] When the gift was authorized, the property was transferred with retroactive effect. During the intervening period, the property was considered to have left the donor's patrimony,

---

338. 5 Planiol and Ripert no. 882; 8 De Page no. 148.

339. Law of 4 Feb. 1901 arts. 2 and 4.

340. Clotilde Pézerat-Santoni, obs. to C.E. 8 Nov. 2000 (en banc), *Rép. not. Defrén.* 2001 art. 37364 at 688–689.

341. Id.

342. 8 De Page no. 146.

343. Id.

344. BELGIUM: Law of 12 July 1931; 7 De Page no. 981; 8 De Page no. 155. FRANCE: Law of 4–6 Feb. 1901 art. 8; 5 Planiol and Ripert no. 885.

345. BELGIUM: 7 De Page no. 981; Law of 19 Dec. 1864 art. 47 par. 3.

346. For the acceptance requirement in French and Belgian law, see infra nos. 1035–1038.

347. Georges Daublon and Dominique Randoux, obs. to Order of 28 July 2005, *Rép. not. Defrén.* 2006 art. 38302 at 4.

but it had not yet entered that of the donee. During that time, the association was only permitted to take conservatory measures. Due to the long delays, both the associations and the notaries argued for reform.

(2) Justifications

513. *Dead hand.* There were several justifications for the authorization requirement.[348] The first was to prevent the abuse of the dead hand *(mainmorte)* and to avoid excessive accumulation of property by entities, such as the church, that maintain property in perpetuity. The problem is thought to arise both when an excessive quantity of society's wealth is removed from circulation as well as when there is a possibility that the wealth may be put to subversive use. As a result, the government refused authorization if the gift would render the entity's patrimony excessive or if the gift would not be useful to accomplish the entity's purposes.

514. *Specialization.* The authorization requirement was also designed to enforce the principle of specialization, which encourages state-chartered entities to pursue only the goals specified in their charters.[349] The principle is not rooted in any code provision or statute. Moreover, gifts that violated the specialization principle were sometimes permitted.[350] If the obligations attached to the gift did not fall within the entity's purpose, for example, the entity might nonetheless receive authorization under the condition that the obligations be delegated to the proper institution. Thus, a municipality was permitted to accept gifts coupled with an obligation of religious charity, provided a religious association fulfilled the charitable mission.

The administration also resorted to a substitution of beneficiaries.[351] If the donee, by virtue of its enumerated purposes, was incompetent to perform the obligations attached to the gift, another entity could be authorized to accept in the donee's stead. If substitution was found to be inappropriate, the gift failed.

515. *Protecting the heirs.* When the heirs challenged a gift, the purpose of administrative review, though not stated in the legal texts, seemed to be to assure that the heirs received a proper level of support.[352] The administrative authorities were permitted to negotiate with the association to reduce the amount. "The spirit of generosity is a beautiful thing, but it would be inadmissible for it to be used, consciously or unconsciously, to the prejudice of heirs who may be poor or needy. The interest of the family deserves as much protection as does that

---

348. 8 De Page no. 147.
349. 5 Planiol and Ripert no. 878.
350. Flour and Souleau no. 356.
351. Id.
352. Clotilde Pézerat-Santoni, obs. to C.E. 8 Nov. 2000 (en banc), *Rép. not. Defrén.* 2001 art. 37364 at 690.

of society."³⁵³ Pézerat-Santoni argued that extensive administrative review disregarded the decedent's wishes. She suggested that the donor's intent should trump administrative rationales and that the extent of administrative power should be reduced.³⁵⁴

(3) Formalities

516. *Complex.* Under the Code Napoleon, authorization required a governmental order (*arrêté du Gouvernement*; art. 910). The provision was revised in 1816 to require a royal edict (*ordonnance royale*). Authorization subsequently was granted by decree.

The system was complex. Public establishments organized by the state, other than retirement homes and hospitals, could accept or refuse gifts, provided they were made without charge or condition and did not involve an encumbrance to real property.³⁵⁵ Gifts coupled with obligations, in contrast, as well as those to which the donor's family objected, required authorization by the Conseil d'État.³⁵⁶ Gifts to foundations or to religious associations in lesser amounts were authorized by order of the departmental prefect and in larger amounts by the Conseil d'État and the minister of the interior.³⁵⁷ Gifts to associations organized for purposes of public welfare and scientific research were authorized by the departmental prefect after review of a detailed application.³⁵⁸ Such associations could receive gifts only if their charters required them to provide annual reports to the minister of the interior.³⁵⁹ Gifts to convents required authorization from the head of state.³⁶⁰ Pézerat-Santoni noted that the extreme complexity of the authorization requirements undeniably manifested "the great distrust that pertains with regard to private actors who claim to have some type of benevolent intention with regard to their fellows."³⁶¹

In Belgium, state universities, other establishments of higher learning, and the National Orchestra can accept gratuitous transfers of personal property without authorization, provided that their value does not exceed a prescribed amount and that the gifts are not coupled with an obligation.³⁶² Special rules apply to

---

353. 8 De Page no. 147 at 214.

354. Clotilde Pézerat-Santoni, obs. to C.E. 8 Nov. 2000 (en banc), *Rép. not. Defrén.* 2001 art. 37364 at 691–692.

355. C State Prop. [Domaine de l'État] art. L15 par. 1; Dementhon no. 1580.

356. C State Prop. arts. L15 pars. 2 and 19; Dementhon no. 1573.

357. Decree of 13 June 1966 art. 1.

358. Id. arts. 3–4.

359. Id. art. 4.

360. Law of 24 May 1825 art. 4, as modified by Law of 30 May 1941 art. 1.

361. Clotilde Pézerat-Santoni, obs. to C.E. 8 Nov. 2000 (en banc), *Rép. not. Defrén.* 2001 art. 37364 at 686, 688.

362. 8 De Page no. 148.

gifts made to parish churches, cathedrals, seminaries, convents, and municipal associations.[363]

517. *Manual gifts.* Throughout the nineteenth and the early twentieth centuries, especially in Belgian law, there was controversy about whether a manual gift might be accepted without authorization.[364] Some authors argued that, because authorization is a form requirement, the manual gift is exempt. Both the courts and the scholars, however, generally held that authorization is a question of legal capacity and therefore applies to all gifts. The practical difficulty was the timing. Manual gifts would be difficult to accept if authorization must always precede acceptance. The question was initially resolved by providing that authorization need not precede acceptance. Eventually provisional acceptance was permitted. Exceptions were also made for the small donations that religious groups and charitable organizations receive through collection urns placed in public places. Gifts of modest value (*dons modiques*) also did not require authorization.[365]

(4) Nature of the Incapacity

518. *Different views.* Difficulty arose concerning the type of incapacity involved.[366] Some authors suggested that it was an absolute prohibition (*incapacité de jouissance*), relieved only by the authorization. Others argued that it was rather an incapacity requiring assistance (*incapacité d'exercice*), with the necessary supervision provided by the government. Another view was that legal persons were fully competent to receive gifts, the authorization being simply a condition precedent imposed by governmental regulation. A consensus eventually developed that, though legal persons were competent to receive gifts, the government was required to play a special role in balancing the competing interests.[367]

(5) Reform

519. *Abolition.* In 2002 the French authorization process was streamlined. In 2005 the authorization requirement was abolished altogether.[368] Now all associations may accept gifts without authorization, subject to two exceptions. First, organizations considered a threat to fundamental freedoms remain subject to authorization requirements.[369] Second, the administration retains the right to oppose any gifts that are inappropriate for the association's purpose. For example, the administration is probably permitted to object to gifts of real estate that

---

363. Id. no. 149 at 216–217 note 4.
364. Id. no. 156; 5 Planiol and Ripert no. 886.
365. Id.
366. 8 De Page no. 151.
367. Id.
368. Decree of 2 April 2002; Order of 28 July 2005.
369. The organizations concerned are those that can be dissolved under the Law of 12 June 2001.

exceed the needs of associations in the public interest. The commentators have expressed the hope that the administration will restrict its intervention to what is strictly necessary.[370]

ii. Italy

520. *Authorization requirement.* Italian scholars once doubted whether corporations organized under commercial law had the capacity to perform the essentially civil law act of accepting a gift.[371] When the distinction between civil and commercial acts was abrogated, that capacity was no longer in doubt. Until 1997, however, legal persons (*persone giuridiche*) other than corporations could not accept gifts, other than those of modest value, without prior authorization.[372] Because the Civil Code did not distinguish between public and private legal persons, some authors argued that the authorization requirement extended to both.[373] Others believed that the capacity of public entities to accept gifts was sufficiently regulated by administrative law.[374]

(A) PURPOSE AND NATURE

521. *Social interest.* Some scholars suggested that authorization provided legal persons with the capacity to receive a gift. This view was criticized, however, on the grounds that legal capacity is a general issue, whereas authorization concerned a specific gift.[375] The majority view seems to have been that authorization was a limitation imposed in the social interest, to prevent the accumulation of noncirculating wealth and to discourage tax evasion.[376]

522. *Condition.* Italian law treated the authorization as a *condictio iuris.* That characterization, however, produced difficulties. Normally, conditions, once fulfilled, are given retroactive effect. Some authors, however, suggested that the text of the code expressly rendered invalid an acceptance that had not been preceded by a proper authorization.[377] Prior authorization was expressly required for ecclesiastical entities.[378] Those who doubted the wisdom of the authorization

---

370. Georges Daublon and Dominique Randoux, obs. to Order of 28 July 2005, *Rép. not. Defrén.* 2006 art. 38302 at 5.

371. Torrente (2006) 466.

372. CC former art. 17. For the specifics of the authorization process, see Rescigno (-Carnevali) 513–514.

373. Biondi no. 67.

374. Cendon art. 17 no. 2; cf. CC art. 11.

375. Torrente (1956) no. 157.

376. Id.

377. Id.

378. Law of 27 May 1929 arts. 9–11.

requirement suggested that a subsequent authorization should validate a prior acceptance.[379]

(B) CRITIQUE

523. *Mistrust of legal persons.* The traditional policy justifications were disputed. Ecclesiastical entities seemed to pose the risk of mortmain, but the concern did not seem equally relevant to all legal persons.[380] Moreover, if the simple accumulation of wealth was the worry, the resources of certain families and even of certain physical persons posed the same risk. Authorization was also justified as a means to protect the heirs against the donor's prodigality. Yet this justification too seemed inadequate, especially because no text required the government to solicit the views of the heirs prior to authorization. The authorization requirement was also not required to protect the prospective donee. Legal persons were already subject to state supervision.[381]

Biondi concluded that the authorization requirement had been instituted out of a thinly veiled political jealousy of the church and was expanded for similar reasons. The requirement was incorporated into the current Civil Code "as an element of the spirit of the Fascist regime, which sought to subject to state control all human activity that may in any way touch the goals pursued by the State. The political nature of authorization is undeniable. The State has manifested its distrust for certain entities, since refusing authorization ... in practice prevents entities from increasing their patrimony by gratuitous transfer."[382]

524. *Abrogation.* These authorization requirements were abrogated in 1997.[383]

iii. Other Civilian Systems

525. *Spain.* The Spanish Civil Code provides that gifts may be accepted by all those the law does not specifically render incompetent (art. 625). As a result, legal persons generally have the capacity to receive gifts.[384]

526. *Germany.* German law does not seem to limit the gifts that may be received by legal persons nor require authorization before such gifts may be accepted. For example, contributions made to charitable organizations, whether of an initial endowment or an increase in capital, are often characterized as gifts.[385]

---

379. Biondi nos. 67–68.
380. Id. no. 67.
381. Id. no. 67 at 171–172.
382. Id. 172.
383. Law of 15 May 1997 art. 13, as modified by Law of 22 June 2000 art. 1 par. 1.
384. Paz-Ares Rodríguez (-Albaladejo García) art. 625 no. III.
385. MünchKomm-BGB (-Kollhoser) § 516 nos. 94–97.

iv. Common Law

527. *England.* During the Middle Ages, it was possible in principle to make a gift of land to a corporation.[386] However, feudal emoluments were not forthcoming from corporate bodies. It was therefore thought to be contrary to the nature of the feudal system for corporations to hold large quantities of land. As discussed above, the Mortmain Acts did not prohibit these transfers, but they did permit the lord to recover the land or to extract a fee.[387] Eventually, the lord gained rights to restrict and to license corporate land holdings. Those rights eventually passed to the crown. The restrictions, which applied to both private and charitable corporations, were eliminated in 1960.[388]

The Mortmain Act of 1736 provided restrictions on the transfer of land and personal property for charitable uses. The transfer was valid only if done by deed in the presence of two or more witnesses at least a year before the death of the grantor and recorded with the Chancery Court within six months of the grant.[389] In 1891 such transfers were permitted to the extent required for the actual operation of the charity.[390] The law of mortmain was repealed in 1960.[391]

528. *United States.* A few American states continue to restrict the amount and type of property that can be held by charitable trusts and corporations, particularly those with religious purposes.[392] Public entities such as municipalities may receive gifts.[393] In many American states, as mentioned above, constitutional *no gift* clauses prohibit the government from making gifts to private corporations or associations.[394]

3. Protected Relationships

529. *Undue influence.* The law often prohibits individuals from giving gifts to those with whom they maintain a special relationship. These incapacities are generally based on a presumption of duress or undue influence. If the elements of those traditional defenses are proven, the gifts would be avoidable under the

---

386. 5 Scott and Ascher § 37.2.6.1.

387. Supra no. 43.

388. Charities Act of 1960 sec. 38.

389. Mortmain Act of 1736 sec. 1.

390. Mortmain and Charitable Uses Act of 1891 sec. 8.

391. Charities Act of 1960 sec. 38.

392. 5 Scott and Ascher § 37.2.6.4. West Virginia permits the trustees of an individual church to hold no more than ten acres of land in a city and sixty acres outside the city limits. West Virginia C § 35-1-8.

393. IOWA: I.C.A. § 565.6; *Keokuk & Hamilton Bridge, Inc. v. C.I.R.*, 180 F.2d 58 (8th Cir. 1950).

394. See, e.g., New York Const. art. 7 sec. 8 par. 1; supra no. 425.

rules protecting consent.[395] The difficulty is that gifts are often challenged only after the donor's death, and often by those who have little knowledge of the surrounding circumstances. To avoid proof problems, many legal systems create what amount to irrebuttable presumptions of defective consent. Logically, each of these prohibitions is correlated with an equivalent incapacity to make the gift. If the guardian is incompetent to receive a gift from the ward, the ward must also lack the capacity to make a gift to the guardian.[396] Nonetheless, these questions are traditionally examined from the point of view of the capacity to receive. A final set of prohibitions involves conflicts of interest.

a. Parent and Illegitimate Child

530. *Now abrogated.* The common law generally permitted parents to give gifts to their children born out of wedlock.[397] However, restrictions were common in the Romanic legal systems. Those long-standing provisions have now been abrogated. They were generally held to violate the equality principle contained in modern constitutions and human rights conventions.

i. France and Belgium

531. *Successoral share.* As discussed below, the ancien régime did not directly prohibit extramarital cohabitation and also did not invalidate gifts between cohabitants. It sought to control the practice in a different way, by restricting the successoral share of any children born of the union.[398] The Code Napoleon continued this policy. It provided that illegitimate children (*enfants naturels*) lacked the capacity to receive gifts from their natural parents beyond the reduced share accorded by successions law.[399] Children born of adulterous or incestuous relationships could receive no gifts because they had no successoral rights. The code

---

395. The scope of this study does not cover questions of invalidity, such as the requirements for alleging undue influence in the gift context.

396. Flour and Souleau no. 300.

397. *Clifton v Goodbun* (1868) LR 6 Eq 278. Gifts to unborn or future illegitimate children were void as *contra bonos mores*. *Occleston v Fullalove* (1873–1874) LR 9 Ch App 147, 154–155. Some older statutes permitted the legitimate family to avoid gifts to illegitimate children to the extent they exceeded a specified portion of the estate. *White v. White*, 48 S.E.2d 189, 190–191 (S.C. 1948). The right to avoid the gift expired at the death of the legitimate wife and could not be exercised by her executor. *Taylor v. McRa*, 3 Rich.Eq. 96, 24 S.C.Eq. 96 (S.C. App. Eq. 1850). Distinctions regarding the capacity to receive gratuitous transfers based on the legitimacy of the transferee have now generally been held unconstitutional. *Trimble v. Gordon*, 430 U.S. 762, 97 S.Ct. 1459 (1977); *In re Estate of Mercer*, 342 S.E.2d 591 (S.C. 1986).

398. Barrière 145–146. For the capacity of cohabitants, see infra nos. 558–568.

399. C Nap. art. 908, together with arts. 756–761.

provided them with basic support (*alimens*), which represented the fulfillment of the parents' natural obligation rather than a gift.[400]

(A) REGIME

532. *Protect the family.* The illegitimate child's inability to receive was not a question of legal capacity. It did not protect the child's interests. The restriction was rather designed to discourage adultery and protect the interests of the spouse and the legitimate family. As a result gifts to illegitimate children were absolutely void. The action in avoidance was open for thirty years and could be brought by anyone with an interest. When the relationship was adulterous, proof problems arose because the Code Napoleon did not permit the acknowledgement of the child of an adulterous relationship (art. 335). The courts therefore permitted avoidance if the gift act itself provided clear evidence of the adultery. The case law eventually permitted gifts to these children from the unmarried parent.[401] In 1972 the capacity of illegitimate children to receive gifts was restored. Children born out of wedlock now have the capacity to receive gifts from their parents.[402] The only remnant of the former rule, discussed just below, concerned children of adulterous relationships.

(B) CHILDREN OF ADULTEROUS RELATIONSHIPS

533. *Protect succession.* Until 2001 the former rule continued in force with regard to the incapacity of children of an adulterous relationship. As indicated above, such children could not receive from the adulterous parent any amount that exceeded the child's successoral share.[403] The restriction applied to indirect, disguised, and manual gifts, though not to customary gifts.[404] However, after 1972 the incapacity was no longer considered a question of public policy. Only members of the legitimate family could challenge the gift, and only after the donor's death.[405] As a result, the legitimate heir could ratify the gift.[406] Moreover, the gift took effect except to the extent it was reduced by collation.[407] The restriction was justified as a means to enforce the limitations to the child's successoral

---

400. C Nap. arts. 908, 762–764; Viatte 828.

401. Civ. ass. plén. 23 June 1967, D. 1967, 525 concl. Lindon, note Philippe Malaurie; Viatte id.

402. Flour and Souleau no. 301; cf. CC art. 908-2.

403. CC former art. 908 par. 1, together with former arts. 759–760. The remainder of the share of the child born out of wedlock was allocated to the children of the legitimate family.

404. 8 De Page nos. 161, 408.

405. CC former art. 908 par. 2; Viate 828.

406. Paris 23 Oct. 2000, *Rép. not. Defrén.* 2002 art. 37600 no. 60 at 1165 obs. Jacques Massip.

407. Viatte 828–829.

rights, which might easily be evaded if inter vivos gifts were freely permitted.[408] Nonetheless, as the scholars pointed out, the rule was easily circumvented. Children of adulterous relationships could receive from other relatives, including, for example, from their grandparents,[409] even if they were ancestors of the adulterous parent.[410] However, such gifts would often be voidable due to the rules relating to the interposition of intermediaries.[411]

534. *Critique.* The incapacity of children of adulterous relationships was criticized. Scholars argued that it violated the legal principle that requires equal treatment of children regardless of descent, a principle found in the French Civil Code, the European Convention on Human Rights, and the United Nations Convention on the Rights of the Child.[412]

535. *The Mazurek case.* In 1991 Claude Mazurek, who had been born of an adulterous relationship, sued in France alleging discrimination. The lower courts held that the inequality of treatment was not designed to discriminate against or punish the child but was rather intended to protect the rights of the spouse and the legitimate children. The Cassation Court rejected his appeal, holding that questions of gift and inheritance law were unrelated to the respect for private and family life guaranteed by the various conventions.[413] The European Court of Human Rights accepted the case and held that the French code provisions violated the European Convention. In the Court's view, the means employed were disproportionate to the goal sought to be attained.[414]

536. *Abrogation.* The exception has now been abrogated. French and Belgian law permit children of adulterous relationships to receive gifts to the same extent as other children.[415]

ii. Italy

537. *Incestuous and adulterous relationships.* As promulgated in 1942, the Italian Civil Code invalidated any gift made by a parent to certain children born out of wedlock.[416] The prohibition covered gifts to children of incestuous relationships,

---

408. 8 De Page no. 161.

409. Flour and Souleau no. 304; 5 Planiol and Ripert no. 231.

410. 8 De Page no. 166.

411. For the principles relating to the interposition of third parties in French and Belgian law, see infra nos. 633–638.

412. Forgeard et al. (2002) no. 68.

413. Civ.¹ 25 June 1996, *Rép. not. Defrén.* 1997 art. 36516 no. 7 obs. J. Massip.

414. *Mazurek v. France*, no. 34406/97, 1 Feb. 2000, E.C.H.R. 2000-II at 1, (2006) 42 E.H.R.R. 9 at 170.

415. BELGIUM: Law of 31 Mar. 1987 arts. 72, 75; FRANCE: Law of 3 Dec. 2001 art. 16. See Forgeard et al. (2002) no. 69.

416. CC art. 780 par. 1 (1942).

except as to a parent who was unaware of the impediment.[417] It also covered gifts to children of adulterous relationships, who could generally not receive gifts from the parent who was otherwise married.[418] However, the effect of the incapacity was limited due to restrictions imposed on the establishment of paternity.[419]

538. *Justification*. The incapacity was justified by a constitutional provision that protected children born out of wedlock only to the extent "compatible with the rights of the members of the legitimate family."[420] Due to the conflicting interests, the incapacity was not complete. Gifts were permitted if given in contemplation of the child's marriage or to assist the child in undertaking a career, provided the gift corresponded to the donor's economic and social situation.[421] Customary gifts, which are not considered gifts in Italian law, were also permitted.

539. *Abrogation*. The incapacity of illegitimate children to receive gifts from their parents was abrogated by the Italian family law reforms of 1975.[422]

b. Between Spouses

540. *From prohibition to revocability*. The Roman law prohibition on gift giving between spouses was adopted, sometimes in the late classical form of free revocability, in many modern civil codes. The prohibition has now been abolished almost everywhere, though in some circumstances gifts between spouses remain revocable. The incapacity resulting from the prohibition is examined here, while the nature of the revocability and its consequences are discussed below.[423]

i. Roman Law

541. *Prohibition*. In the Roman Republic there would have been little need for rules relating to gifts between spouses. Most marriages took place *cum manu*, which meant that the wife's property was assimilated to the dowry and became part of the patrimony of her husband or of her husband's paterfamilias.[424] To the extent such gifts were made, they may have been valid as one of the rare exceptions to the prohibitions of the lex Cincia.[425] By the end of the Republic, however, *sine manu* marriages had become more common, as had the frequency of repudiation.[426]

---

417. Id. art. 251 (1942).
418. Id. art. 252 (1942).
419. Id. art. 269 (1942).
420. Italian Const. art. 30 par. 3.
421. CC art. 780 par. 2 (1942).
422. Law of 19 May 1975 art. 205.
423. Infra nos. 1295–1313.
424. Ourliac and Malafosse 175, 223.
425. Biondi no. 323. For the lex Cincia see supra no. 34.
426. Ourliac and Malafosse 456.

542. *Dona and munera.* For reasons that remain unclear, gifts between spouses were prohibited. The prohibition originated in, or was incorporated into, the *lex Iulia et Papia Poppea,* which dates from the reign of Augustus.[427] A distinction was made between normal gifts (*dona*) and gifts given annually at festivals or on other special occasions (*munera*).[428] Dona were prohibited among spouses. Appropriate munera were permitted, while excessive munera (*munus immodicum*) were prohibited.[429] Thus, except for small gifts given on special occasions or for personal use, all gifts between husband and wife were void by operation of law. If possession was transferred, the property could be summarily repossessed.[430] Because the prohibition was absolute, Roman jurists restricted the definition of the gift to include only transfers that diminished the donor's patrimony while enriching that of the donee (*depauperatio-locupletatio*).[431] Moreover, there were many exceptions.[432] Spouses were permitted to make gifts, usually from wife to husband, to assist in career advancement. Furthermore, any gift that remained with the donee at the donor's death was presumed valid.

543. *Purpose.* The prohibition may originally have been designed to prevent spouses from eluding the restrictions on their inability to succeed each other. That justification must have seemed insufficient because Roman jurists soon suggested a series of other policy considerations.[433] They argued that the prohibition prevented spouses from impoverishing themselves on account of their mutual affection,[434] maintained their ability to educate their children, prevented a husband's reluctance to part with his property from destroying the marriage, and prevented one spouse, by *venale concordium,* from using gifts to prolong a marriage that the other wished to end. As subsequent commentators have pointed out, none of the justifications was convincing, even when considered from the point of view of the Roman jurists.

---

427. Biondi no. 323. Watson and Corbett accept instead Ulpian's statement that the prohibition derived from custom and originated in the late republic. Watson 229–230; Corbett 114–115. For the passage from Ulpian, see infra no. 543.

428. Michel no. 799. For the distinction see supra no. 32.

429. Michel no. 797.

430. Dawson (1980) 14–15. Gifts given in consideration of marriage, however, were permitted. See Bellomo 964.

431. Corbett 115; Dawson (1980) 15–16.

432. Corbett concluded that the exceptions were so numerous that there was little left of the prohibition. Corbett 117.

433. See generally Zimmermann 484–490.

434. "The custom among us is that gifts between husband and wife are invalid. The purpose is to prevent husband and wife from impoverishing themselves when, on account of their love for one another, they make unreasonable gifts out of excessive indulgence." D. 24, 1, 1 (Ulpian). See Kaser § 79 par. 3 no. 1; Archi (1964) 942–943.

544. *Post-classical law.* The prohibition became increasingly unpopular and was eventually attenuated.[435] By 206 AD only the donor had standing to invoke the prohibition. Upon the donor's death, if the gift remained unchallenged, it was considered a valid mortis causa transfer. In other words, the donor's *perseverantia voluntatis* validated at death a gift that had been absolutely void during the donor's lifetime.[436] The prohibition gradually disappeared in the West, though it continued under the Eastern Empire. It was received into continental Europe from the Digest and became part of the *ius commune*.[437]

545. *Unintended benefit.* The principle beneficiaries of the Roman prohibition of gifts between spouses have been the generations of Roman Law scholars since the Renaissance. Much of what is known today both about the Roman law of marriage and about the Roman law of gifts is due to the Roman jurists' *responsa* concerning the prohibition. In each case the jurists were required to decide, first, whether the couple was married, and, second, whether the transfer met the definition of a gift.

ii. France and Belgium

546. *Ancien régime.* In the Romanist-influenced *droit écrit* of the ancien régime, gifts between spouses were revocable. They became final only if the donor died without revoking them.[438] Some of the *coutumes* permitted only mutual gifts and gifts mortis causa. In the northern regions gifts between spouses were generally held to be void.[439] Because, at the time, a wife was not considered part of her husband's family and did not inherit from him, the goal of the prohibition seems to have been to prevent property from passing between unrelated families. Successions law was based on lineage. The customary maxim was *paterna paternis, materna maternis*—the father's property was to descend to the father's kin and the mother's to the mother's. The marriage bed, as Le Roy Ladurie wrote, was simply a piece of furniture.[440] The customs smiled on children, not on love. "If transfers between spouses, whether direct or indirect, were not prohibited, conjugal love would become venal, and much property would pass into other families .... [I]t would often come to pass that, in order to purchase peace, the more virtuous, the more peaceful, of the two would lose out."[441]

The only exception seems to have concerned mutual gifts, which were permitted only with regard to movables and community property and only if no children had been born of the marriage. The gift had the effect of granting a usufruct

---

435. Zimmermann 490.
436. Archi (1964) 945–946.
437. Id.
438. Ourliac and Malafosse 466, 513.
439. Id. 513; 5 Planiol and Ripert no. 753.
440. Le Roy Ladurie 56, 58.
441. 2 Bourjon art. 282 no. III.

to the surviving spouse. Gifts between spouses in a second marriage were subject to even greater suspicion. In the north, some customary norms required the
consent of the children from the first marriage. In 1560 wives were prohibited
from making a gift of their property to their second husbands.[442]

547. *Civil Code.* The revolution removed the restrictions on gifts between
spouses.[443] Under the Civil Code, gifts between spouses are generally valid, though,
until 2005, all such gifts were revocable until the donor's death.[444] In this way
the code followed Domat, for whom the purpose of the prohibition was limited
to preventing donors from suffering the gift's consequences during their lifetimes. If the gift remained unrevoked at the donor's death, there was no reason
not to validate it.[445] Due to the code's principle of free revocability, some French
authors suggested that gifts between spouses resulted in a causa mortis transfer.[446] Yet the courts have continued to hold that such gifts operate inter vivos.
The gift immediately transferred title to property existing and determined at the
time the gift was made.[447] As an exception to general gift principles, spouses
may also validly make gifts of future property to each other (CC art. 947). Because
gifts of future property are transferred only at the donor's death, a stronger argument can be made that this type of gift should be characterized as a testamentary
transfer.[448]

For gifts of present property, the general rules of gift capacity apply.[449] Minors
are automatically emancipated upon marriage and therefore may give and receive
to the extent their status permits (CC art. 476). Gifts of future property pose
greater difficulty. Josserand took the position that they too are governed by the
general rules of gift capacity. Even though the actual transfer is postponed until
the donor's death, the form, substance, and effects of the gift are all governed by
gift law.[450] The courts, apparently assuming that, in practice, a gift of future
property between spouses has the same effect as a bequest, have permitted gifts

442. Ourliac and Malafosse 466.
443. Decree of 17 Nivôse II arts. 13–14. For an earlier version, see Decree of 5 Brumaire
II art. 2.
444. French CC former art. 1096 par. 1, abrogated by Law of 26 May 2004 art. 21 par.
1; see infra nos. 1296–1300. Moreover, as discussed below, while indirect gifts were considered valid under CC art. 1099 par. 1, disguised gifts and gifts by interposition were void
under CC art. 1099 par. 2. The provision concerning disguised gifts and interposition was
also abrogated by the Law of 26 May 2004. See infra no. 826.
445. 1 Domat no. 915.
446. 5 Planiol and Ripert no. 754.
447. Flour and Souleau no. 448.
448. Id. no. 449.
449. Id. no. 450.
450. Josserand (1930).

of future property by a spouse who lacked the capacity to make a gift but who met the less stringent requirements permitting testation.[451]

548. *Recent reforms.* Since 2005 gifts between spouses of present property are irrevocable. Gifts of future property remain revocable.[452] In Belgian law the reforms of 1981 made all gifts between spouses irrevocable.[453]

iii. Italy

549. *Traditional view.* Italian law traditionally prohibited gifts between spouses,[454] as did the Civil Code of 1865, which invalidated them even if disguised as an onerous transactions.[455] The original project for the current code made gifts between spouses revocable. A later draft made them voidable. As ultimately promulgated, gifts between spouses were again prohibited. As a concession to practicality, life insurance policies purchased by one spouse for the benefit of the other were held to be valid, not as an exception to the prohibition but rather because, as the fulfillment of the spousal obligation of mutual assistance, the benefit was not considered a gift.[456]

The prohibition was based on the belief that an egotistical, utilitarian calculation might otherwise replace mutual affection as the basis for the spousal relationship. Moreover, because spouses share possessions while married and are permitted to favor each other in their wills, the prohibition was thought to have little effect.[457] Italian scholars concluded, virtually unanimously, that the justifications were incoherent and unconvincing, especially because, unlike French customary law, the prohibition applied only to inter vivos gifts and not to testamentary transfers.[458]

550. *Unconstitutional.* In 1973 the Italian Constitutional Court held that the prohibition of gifts between spouses was unconstitutional.[459] At the time, gifts were permitted between couples in a putative marriage, between cohabitants of all types, and between fiancés up to the moment they took their vows, relationships in which the dangers that allegedly justified the prohibition were arguably

---

451. Civ. 20 Feb. 1929, D.P. 1929 I 104; Flour and Souleau no. 450.

452. French CC art. 1096 (2005).

453. Belgian CC 1096. The former art. 1096 was abrogated by Law of 14 May 1981 art. 29.

454. Torrente (2006) 470.

455. CC arts. 1054–1055 (1865).

456. Cass. 27 Mar. 1939 no. 965, *Giur. it.* 1939 I 1122; Torrente (1956) no. 160 at 389.

457. Torrente (2006) 471.

458. Id.; Biondi no. 325.

459. C. Cost. 27 June 1973 no. 91, *Foro it.* 1973 I 2014 note A. C. Jemolo; Torrente (2006) 471–472.

present to an even greater degree. The prohibition thus lacked "any rational purpose."

iv. Spain

551. *Prohibition.* The Spanish Civil Code originally prohibited gifts made between spouses during marriage.[460] The only exception involved presents of modest value given on occasions of family rejoicing.[461] The justification followed Roman law:

> The principal motivation for the prohibition must be seen in the special situation created between spouses during marriage, in their intimate and constant relationship, which leaves the weaker of the two at the mercy of the will of the stronger, whichever one that may be, compelling the weaker spouse, sometimes by flattery and abuse of tenderness, sometimes by threats, by fear, or by force, to cede a larger or smaller portion of that spouse's property, consummating an iniquitous despoliation and encouraging impulses arising from evil passion and marriages celebrated solely for the prospect of gain.[462]

Some Spanish regional laws did not prohibit gifts between spouses. "Aragon law never succumbed to the fears of other untrusting legislators who prohibited gifts and contracts between spouses and who permitted them only when agreement was reached before marriage."[463]

552. *Abrogation.* The prohibition was abrogated in 1981.[464] Spanish law now expressly provides that husbands and wives may transfer between themselves any property and may conclude any type of contract (CC art. 1323). "The old prejudices concerning the danger of undue influence by one spouse on the will of the other and the presumption of fraudulent intent with regard to third parties ... revealed themselves to be without basis."[465]

v. Germany

553. *Valid.* Gifts between spouses were generally prohibited in Germany before the promulgation of the German Civil Code.[466] Today German law considers gratuitous transfers between spouses to partake of the life of the spousal community. They are generally not characterized as gifts. Particular purchases involving unequal financial contributions are also not considered gifts.[467] Gifts between spouses, however, are not unknown. The spouses may agree to a

---

460. CC former art. 1334 par. 1.
461. Id. par. 2.
462. Manresa y Navarro art. 1334 at 307.
463. ARAGON: Law of 12 Feb. 2003 Preamble.
464. Law of 13 May 1981 art. 3.
465. Paz-Ares Rodríguez (-Herrero García) art. 1323 no. I.
466. Zimmermann 490.
467. BGH 24 Mar. 1983, BGHZ 87, 145 at 146.

gratuitous transfer of property belonging to one of the spouses. Such agreements are governed by the general principles of gift law.[468]

vi. The Common Law

554. *De jure valid.* At common law a gift from a husband to his wife was void.[469] As Fleta explained, it was feared that the gifts would be made from lust or would impoverish the husband.[470] Moreover the gift was also void if done by interposition of a third party.[471] Because husband and wife were understood as a legal unit, the wife, for her part, could neither own nor transfer property.[472] An exception was made for gifts to the wife's dower.[473] Today the de jure validity of inter-spousal gifts is undoubted,[474] though in some American states such transactions are deemed to create a fiduciary relationship.[475] The special (class 2A) presumption of undue influence in English law does not apply between husband and wife.[476]

555. *Practical difficulties.* Nonetheless, such gifts confront two de facto limitations. First such gifts must be established by evidence "beyond suspicion,"[477] which creates considerable proof problems.[478] Gifts between spouses are distinguished from gifts of separate property that a spouse may make to the marital estate. When a spouse, using separate funds, purchases property in both names in joint tenancy, a gift is presumed. In many American states, the presumption can be rebutted only by clear and convincing evidence of an alternative purpose.[479]

A second difficulty arises from the classification of spousal property as either separate or marital. The donor's intent governs the characterization, but it is

---

468. MünchKomm-BGB (-Kollhosser) § 516 no. 68. Should the marital property regime terminate other than by the death of one of the spouses, any inter vivos transfers between the spouses that do not qualify as customary gifts are considered accrued gain (*Zugewinn*) for purposes of the final property settlement. CC §§ 1372, 1380.

469. 2 Bracton 54; *Kitchen v. Bedford*, 80 U.S. 413 (1871).

470. Fleta bk. 3. ch. 3 at 6.

471. Id.

472. 41 Am.Jur.2d Husband and Wife § 2.

473. Fleta bk. 3. ch. 3 at 6–7.

474. ENGLAND: 20 Halsbury part 1 sub Gifts no. 5; UNITED STATES: 41 C.J.S. Husband and Wife § 101.

475. 43 Okl. Stats. Ann. §204 (West 2001).

476. *Nat'l Westminster Bank Plc v Morgan* [1985] AC 686, 703 (HL); Treitel par. 10-016.

477. *Walter v Hodge* [1818] 2 Swans 92, 36 ER 549 (Ch D).

478. *Winner v. Winner*, 370 So.2d 845 (Fla. App. 1979).

479. *Bartlett v. Bartlett*, 144 P.3d 173, 177 (Okl. Civ. App. 2006). The courts disagree about whether a transfer intended for estate-planning purposes or to avoid probate or taxes constitutes a gift. Id. 181–182.

usually not expressed. In the absence of expressed intent, American cases seem to follow one of three theories.[480] According to the first, gifts given on the assumption that the marital relationship will continue are rescinded in case of divorce. The property then regains the status it had prior to the gift. A second set of cases holds that such gifts are made with no reservation and should be treated as the donee's separate property.[481] The American Law Institute suggests that the better rule would treat interspousal gifts as marital property because that is the character of all property that cannot otherwise be established.[482] Under both the first and the third theories, in the absence of expressed intent, these gifts would rarely cause the donee to acquire the gift as separate property. [483]

c. Between Cohabitants

556. *Cohabitation*. In the countries examined here, it has become common for two individuals to live together in an enduring intimate relationship, on a part-time or full-time basis, without the legal sanction of marriage. Some jurisdictions now legally recognize these relationships. Recent reforms of the French Civil Code define cohabitation (*concubinage*) as a union of two individuals, whether of the same or of different gender, who live as a couple in a stable and continuous relationship (art. 515-8).[484] California recognizes domestic partnership of same-sex couples and of couples that include a senior citizen.[485] Despite this recent legal recognition, cohabitation is in some places considered immoral, as it is almost everywhere when one of the cohabitants is otherwise legally married. To prevent donors from giving gifts in the heat of passion and to protect the interests of the donor's family, some jurisdictions have restricted gifts between cohabitants. Though cohabitants do not generally lack the capacity to receive, the restrictions are examined here because they express the law's concern with gift giving in this context.

557. *Roman law*. As discussed above, late classical Roman law prohibited gifts between spouses.[486] Gifts to lovers or concubines however were valid.[487]

---

480. Principles of the Law of Family Dissolution: Analysis and Recommendations § 4.03 comment b at 651–652.

481. 41 C.J.S. Husband and Wife § 102.

482. See, e.g., *McArthur v. McArthur*, 353 S.E.2d 486 (Ga. 1987).

483. These issues arise chiefly during divorce. Property settlements in that context typically involve factors beyond those discussed here.

484. For French law, see Huet-Weiller.

485. California Family C § 297.

486. Supra nos. 541–545.

487. "Neither honorable nor dishonorable gifts are prohibited if they are made out of affection. Honorable are gifts to well-deserving friends and relations, dishonorable are those made to prostitutes." D. 39, 5, 5 (Ulpian). Michel no. 472. See also D. 39, 5, 31 pr. (Papinian).

Since the donatio was not considered a legal act, it was not subject to public policy restrictions. Constantine prohibited gifts by high personages to female cohabitants. It is not clear whether the prohibition was generalized. Subsequent emperors relaxed the restrictions.[488]

i. France and Belgium

558. *Ancien régime.* Planiol and Ripert suggested that, under the ancien régime, gifts between cohabitants were void—*don de concubin à concubin ne vaut.*[489] An ordinance from the time of Louis XIII generalized the prohibition of gifts between cohabitants present in many customary laws.[490] Two justifications were offered. The first was the desire not to favor an extramarital affair at the expense of the legitimate spouse. The second was to prevent gifts dictated by passion.[491]

In actuality, however, gifts between partners in adulterous cohabitation (*concubinage adultérin*) were distinguished from those made between unmarried individuals living together (*simple concubinage*). For some authors, since adulterous cohabitation was a crime, all gifts associated with it should be void.[492] Nonetheless, the Custom of Poitou permitted gift giving among cohabitants, even those engaged in adultery.[493] Some authors validated gifts between simple cohabitants, while others believed that they too should be void. Ricard argued that the law could not prohibit gifts between spouses while at the same time approving gifts between cohabitants.[494] In one case, the cohabitants decided to legitimate their relationship. The groom gave gifts to his bride in their marriage settlement. The heirs challenged the settlement after the husband's death. The court invalidated the gifts on the ground that gifts between cohabitants were void.[495] Not all the cases were that strict. In general the case law validated small gifts that

---

488. Dupont 311–313.

489. 5 Planiol and Ripert no. 196; 3 Planiol no. 2943 *bis.*

490. Ordinance of 1629 art. 132; Barrière 144–145. For a list of the *coutumes* that invalidated gifts between cohabitants, see 1 Louet 481–482.

491. Barrière 146.

492. 1 Louet 482; 1 Ricard 96–97 nos. 403–406 note s.

493. Chambre des Enquestes 5 Apr. 1599, 1 Louet 481.

494. "The law assumes that there is reason to fear that, due to the reciprocal affection they owe to each other, two persons united in matrimony may not be able to moderate their gifts. How then can it be believed that those who are embarked on the same subject of love and who are caused to persevere because their fire augments every day may better be able to retain their freedom? The empire of their passion does not even permit them to recognize the turpitude of their conduct." 1 Ricard no. 410.

495. Grand'Chambre of Paris 16 Mar. 1663, 1 Ricard no. 415. "The case law especially limits the capacity of those who lived together as cohabitants before legitimating their union." 5 Merlin (1825) *Concubinage* 331.

could be considered support payments (*aliments*), even between adulterous cohabitants.[496]

(A) IMMORAL CAUSE

559. *Civil Code.* Though the Project for the Civil Code from Year VIII prohibited gifts between cohabitants who were living together in a public manner (*dans un concubinage notoire*),[497] the prohibition was rejected in the final draft. The code does not prohibit gifts between cohabitants, even in adulterous relationships, nor does it limit their capacity to receive. *Les concubins se passent de la loi, la loi se désintéresse d'eux*, Napoleon is reported to have said.[498] The drafters felt that the courts should avoid "inquiries that might be both unjust and odious."[499] In one early decision, for example, a man made a formal gift to the woman with whom he had lived publicly in an adulterous relationship and who bore his son. The court refused to enforce the gift, but not because of the adulterous relationship. Instead, the gift to the woman was thought to represent a gift by interposition to the child, who lacked the capacity to receive.[500]

Soon after the promulgation of the code, some commentators suggested that the code's silence on the question should not be taken as approval.[501] Delvincourt, for example, conceded that the case law validated gifts between cohabitants but suggested that constructions were available to void them.[502] First, several appeals courts had voided promissory notes given between cohabitants for illicit cause.[503] Delvincourt argued that it was illogical to validate gifts that so clearly violated principles of good morals when the same transfers, when concluded as a loan, would be void.[504] Moreover, if the female cohabitant gave birth from an adulterous relationship, gifts to the child beyond support payments would be void, as would be gifts to the mother as a prohibited interposition.[505] Delvincourt argued

---

496. Barrière 145; 1 Ricard nos. 407, 417.

497. Tit. 9 art. 11, in 2 Fenet 275.

498. "Cohabitants are not interested in the law; the law does not concern itself with them." I have found no written source for Napoleon's comment, though it is often quoted. See De Schutter and Weyembergh 465. The Code Napoleon mentioned cohabitation only once, in a provision permitting the wife to request divorce on grounds of adultery if the husband brought the cohabitant into the family home. Art. 230.

499. Treilhard, "Présentation au Corps législatif et Exposé des motifs," (19 Germinal XI [9 Apr. 1803]), in 12 Fenet 141. See 5 Merlin (1825) *Concubinage* 335.

500. Bordeaux 15 Feb. 1807, Devilleneuve and Gilbert, *Donation déguisée* no. 27.

501. The debate is summarized in Barrière 151–158.

502. 1 Delvincourt 722–723 note 9 to page 231.

503. Besançon 25 Mar. 1808, in 5 Merlin (1825) *Concubinage* 341; Grenoble Jan. 1812, in 5 Merlin (1825) id.

504. 1 Delvincourt 723 note 9 to page 231

505. The gifts were void under C Nap. arts. 762, 908, provisions that have since been abrogated. For the prohibition of gifts by interposition, see infra nos. 633–635.

that it would be unreasonable to prohibit gifts to the female cohabitant if she had a child but permit them if she did not. He speculated that such a distinction might even lead to infanticide.[506] It would also be absurd to think that the legislator intended to punish the child while encouraging the crime that led to the birth. Despite serious misgivings about these gifts, Merlin de Douai reached the opposite conclusion. He followed the majority of appellate courts that validated gifts between cohabitants based on the principle that everyone has gift capacity unless the law declares otherwise.[507]

560. *Judicial interpretation.* During the course of the nineteenth century, as cohabitation spread from the upper strata to the working classes, traditional marriage attracted fewer adherents and seemed to enter a crisis.[508] Midway through the nineteenth century, the French Cassation Court adopted the view of the commentators and decided that gifts between cohabitants could be avoided if based on an illicit cause.[509] In French and Belgian law, as discussed above, a challenge based on an illegal or immoral cause focuses on the gift's principal motive.[510] As a result, the Court distinguished two situations. Gifts designed to initiate or maintain the cohabitation were considered immoral and could be avoided. Such transfers ceased to be gifts and were considered payment for immoral services, a *pretium stupri*.[511] On the other hand, gifts made to terminate the relationship were considered payment of a natural obligation if made to provide financial security for the other partner and were held to be valid.[512] The same principles applied to adulterous cohabitation.

The traditional Belgian rule was that cohabitants had the capacity to give gifts to each other. The scope of the exception for illicit cause has varied over the years. In 1903 the Cassation Court seemed to suggest that gifts between cohabitants would be voided only if the gift "had no other cause but the desire to pay wages

---

506. "Indeed, since the female cohabitant lacks the capacity to receive when she has children from the relationship and since the absence of children restores her capacity, is it not obvious that [permitting these gifts] is an open invitation to crime, that it will drive her to destroy the unfortunate fruit of her shameful union, either before or after birth, or at least to abandon it to public charity while preventing anyone from learning of the situation." 1 Delvincourt 723.

507. 5 Merlin (1825) *Concubinage* 334. Merlin's article demonstrates the remarkable loyalty the Code Napoleon inspired in jurists of the time. Merlin himself believed that cohabitation was "a debauchery contrary to the purity of religion and good morals ... a blind passion that offends social custom." Id. 331. And yet he refused to interpret the Code to conform to his beliefs. It was sufficient for him that the Code's drafters had considered the prohibition of gifts between cohabitants and had rejected it. Id. 334–335.

508. Barrière 158–159.

509. Ascencio 251–252 (citing cases). The avoidance was based on CC arts. 1131, 1133.

510. Supra no. 260.

511. 3 Planiol no. 2943 *bis*.

512. Flour and Souleau no. 331; 5 Planiol and Ripert no. 266; 8 De Page nos. 84, 256.

for immoral commerce and to assure its continuation."[513] Moreover, gifts with the sole purpose of indemnifying the woman after the termination of the relationship were generally validated as the fulfillment of a natural obligation.[514]

In the middle of the twentieth century, the Court prevented one cohabitant from recovering for the wrongful death of the other. It held that cohabitation was "an illict and immoral situation of fact contrary to the rules of positive civil law that govern the organization of the family."[515] As a result of this new view, the Court vastly extended the role of illicit cause. Gifts between cohabitants were thenceforth void if any of the donor's principal motives included the intent to initiate, maintain, or remunerate the cohabitation relationship.[516]

The leading case reversed a trial judge who had found that the cause would be immoral only if the gift was intended to pay for sexual pleasures or to purchase the donee's silence.[517] The trial court had validated the gift after finding that several of the donor's motives were legitimate. First the couple was bound by sincere affection. Second the donor wished to compensate the donee for long years of quality service as his secretary. Finally he wished to alleviate the harm caused by the fact that, due to the relationship, the donee's marriage had ended in divorce. The Cassation Court rejected the trial court's findings and held that if any of the donor's principal motives were designed to solidify the cohabitation relationship, the gift was void.

Since, in principle, cohabitants had the capacity to receive, their gifts should have benefited from a presumption of validity. The scholars disagreed. They concluded that a cohabitation relationship involving sexual relations created instead a presumption of immoral cause.[518] To defeat the presumption, it was not enough for the donee to demonstrate that the donor felt actual affection or was liable for services rendered.[519] Instead the donee had to prove either that the gift facilitated the termination of the relationship, that it compensated for material or moral harm, or that it was payment for legitimate services rendered.[520] The decisions were often more severe when the cohabitation involved adultery, which was a crime at the time.[521] In one case, the court validated the gift after it became clear that the cohabitants had not engaged in sexual relations at all.[522] Gifts based on

513. Civ.[1] 14 May 1903, *Pas.* 1903 I 216 at 217.
514. 8 De Page no. 84 at 140 note 1 (collecting cases).
515. Civ.[2] 21 Apr. 1958, *Pas.* 1958 I 921.
516. De Page (1992) 167.
517. Civ.[1] 13 Nov. 1953, *Pas.* 1954 I 190 note R. H.
518. Nicole Jeanmart, note to Bruxelles 7 Dec. 1976, *Rev. not. belge* 1977, 300 at 309.
519. De Page (1992) 168.
520. Nicole Jeanmart, note to Bruxelles 7 Dec. 1976, *Rev. not. belge* 1977, 300 at 310. The note contains a detailed analysis of the factors that contributed to validating and invalidating gifts between cohabitants under the former regime.
521. Id. 305, 315.
522. Civ.[1] 5 Feb. 1970, *Pas.* 1970 I 484 note W.G.

an illicit cause remained invalid even if the cohabitants were subsequently married.[523] Cohabitation even vitiated agreements with third parties. In one case, the donor's son promised the donor to make weekly payments, after the donor's death, to the donor's cohabitant. The Cassation Court invalidated the agreement for providing remuneration for past sexual relations.[524]

(B) JUDICIAL REVERSAL

561. *Overruled.* In February 1999, the French Cassation Court overruled its previous holdings and held that a gratuitous transfer designed to maintain cohabitation, even if adulterous, does not violate good morals and therefore cannot be avoided for immoral cause.[525] Though decided in the context of a testamentary bequest, there was no doubt that the same principle applied to gifts.[526] Thus, until the 2005 reforms, gifts between legally married spouses, though valid, were revocable until the donor's death, whereas gifts between cohabitants, even those in adulterous relationships, were binding and irrevocable.

The high court thereby unleashed what has become the most passionate controversy in modern French gift law. The authors were the first to rebel. They argued that gratuitous transfers made in the course of an adulterous relationship violated the spousal obligation of fidelity (CC art. 212). The motivation for the gift was therefore not merely immoral but actually illegal. Some scholars urged the lower courts to disregard the high court decision.[527]

562. *L'affaire Galopin.* In 2004, in the case that became known as *l'affaire Muriel Galopin*, the lower courts did just that. The case involved a testator who, at the age of ninety-five, feared that his mistress, who was thirty-one, would abandon him. For fifteen years, largely for financial gain, she served both as his secretary and as his mistress. Three months before his death, in order to retain her services, he added a codicil to his will making her his residual beneficiary. The testator's wife of eighty-two years was thereby disinherited. Both the trial court and the prestigious Paris Appeals Court held that the transfer was based on an immoral cause and therefore void. The Cassation Court reversed and returned the case to the Paris Court of Appeal. In formal session, at which French judges wear red ceremonial robes, the Paris court maintained its original ruling. The Cassation Court, meeting en banc, attempted to close the controversy by insisting

---

523. Brussels 17 June 1939, *Pas.* 1941 III 27; 8 De Page no. 84 at 140 note 1.

524. Civ.¹ 19 Jan. 1968, *Pas.* 1968 I 640 note W. G.

525. Civ.¹ 3 Feb. 1999, *Bull. civ.* I no. 43, D. 1999, 267 argument X. Savatier and note J.-P. Lagalde-O'Sughrue, *Rép. not. Defrén.* 1999 art. 36998 no. 30 at 680 obs. J. Massip, *Rép. not. Defrén.* art. 37008 no. 37 at 738 obs. D. Mazeaud.

526. Gérard Champenois, obs. to Civ.¹ 3 Feb. 1999, *Rép. not. Defrén.* 1999 art. 37017 no. 62 at 814, 820.

527. Id.; Véronique Mikalef-Toudic, obs. to Civ. ass. plén. 29 Oct. 2004, *Rép. not. Defrén.* 2005 art. 38183 at 1045, 1046 (citing sources).

on its ruling, holding broadly that a gratuitous transfer made in the course of an adulterous relationship does not violate good morals.[528]

Thus, under current law, gifts between cohabitants are not voidable for immoral cause, regardless of whether the relationship is homosexual or heterosexual, whether adulterous or not, or whether intended to maintain the relationship or to terminate it, though gifts made in the course of an incestuous relationship may still be voidable. The justification is that it proved virtually impossible for the trial courts to determine the donor's principal motives, especially because the donor was often deceased when the issue arose.

563. *Belgium.* In Belgium, judicial reversal occurred already in 1977.[529] The decision did not change the general principle. A gift continued to be void for illicit cause if the donor's principal motives included the intent to initiate, maintain, or remunerate sexual relations. However, the Cassation Court approved a lower court decision that shifted the burden of proof.[530] A gift would no longer be avoided on mere proof of cohabitation. Cohabitation, as such, was no longer immoral. Those challenging the gift would have to prove that the donor's motive was to encourage the cohabitation relation. Yet the case law remained uncertain. Some appellate courts continued to presume immorality from the fact of cohabitation, particularly when adultery was involved.[531] Others insisted that the burden was on the party challenging the transfer, particularly when the cohabitation was not adulterous.[532]

(C) LEGISLATIVE REFORM

564. *Civil union.* In the 1990s, the French National Assembly began considering legal recognition for nonmarital unions, particularly for same-sex couples.[533] In November 1999, the Civil Solidarity Pact (CSP; *Pacte civil de solidarité* or *Pacs*) was introduced into the Civil Code.[534] The CSP is a type of union midway between the formality of marriage and the informality of cohabitation.[535] The parties may

---

528. Civ. ass. plén. 29 Oct. 2004, *Bull. civ.* ass. plén. no. 12, *Rép. not. Defrén.* 2004 art. 38073 no. 105 at 1732 obs. Rémy Libchaber, *Rép. not. Defrén.* 2005 art. 38096 at 234 obs. Stéphane Piedelièvre.

529. Civ.[1] 23 June 1977, *Pas.* 1977 I 1083; De Page (1992) 168–173; de Schutter and Weyembergh 465.

530. Other appellate courts had prepared the terrain. See Bruxelles 7 Dec. 1976, *Rev. not. belge* 1977, 300 note Nicole Jeanmart.

531. Liège 19 May 1982, *Rev. not. belge* 1985, 275 note F. Delobbe (testamentary bequest).

532. Anvers 5 Jan. 1987, *Rev. not. belge* 1988, 247. For a summary of the grounds that prevented a gift from being considered immoral, see De Page (1992) 171–172.

533. Borrillo 476–484.

534. Law of 15 Nov. 1999, adding CC arts. 515-1 to 515-8.

535. Borrillo 484.

agree on their property regime (CC art. 515-5-1) and are jointly and severally liable for common living expenses (CC art. 515-4 par. 2).[536]

The legislation does not regulate gifts between CSP partners. Three choices seemed to be available. Gifts between partners might be avoidable for illicit cause, as had long been the case for gifts between cohabitants; the gifts might be permitted but freely revocable, as were gifts between spouses; or they might be subject to normal gift rules. The scholars have decided that gifts between CSP partners are subject to the normal regime of French gift law.[537] The pact itself, however, is not a marriage settlement. Gifts must be concluded outside the pact in the normal forms. Indirect gifts are permitted, such as the naming of one of the partners as the beneficiary of a life insurance policy.[538]

565. *Legal recognition.* The new provisions recognized cohabitation (*concubinage*) and defined it as a de facto union (*union de fait*), characterized by a stable and continuing life in common between two persons, of the same or different genders, who live together as a couple (CC art. 515-8).

566. *Belgium.* In 1987 the Belgian penal provisions that made adultery a crime were abrogated.[539] The Belgian Cassation Court immediately took advantage of the reform. In two bold decisions, the Court permitted cohabitants, even adulterous cohabitants, to recover for the wrongful death of their companions.[540] Though adultery remained a civil wrong, the only sanction was divorce. In other words, it could be asserted by no one but the adulterer's spouse. In 1998 Belgium established statutory cohabitation (*cohabitation légale*). The new institution legitimated extra-marital relationships and permitted cohabitants to arrange their financial affairs.[541] The legal effects are similar to those of the French CSP.[542] It now seems that gifts between cohabitants are once again valid in Belgium, as they were a century ago,[543] unless they represent a simple exchange for sexual services. Philippe De Page concludes that the courts base the decision on the

---

536. Tracol 73–76.

537. "In a certain way, the CSP legitimates these gifts." Le Guidec 135–136.

538. Id. 136–138.

539. Law of 20 May 1987.

540. Civ.[2] 1 Feb. 1989, *Pas.* 1989 I 582 concl. R. Declercq (*aud. plén.*); Civ.[1] 15 Feb. 1990, *Pas.* 1990 I 694. Recommending the opposite result, Advocate General Declercq argued that, since adultery remained an important public policy concern (*ordre public*), both third parties and even the court should be able to assert it.

541. Law of 23 Nov. 1998.

542. De Schutter and Weyembergh 466.

543. "[I]t should be noted today that the idea that cohabitation is immoral must be included in the catalogues of legal archeology and with it the theory that the immorality of cohabitation invalidates gratuitous transfers by the mere fact that the transfers were, or might have been, chiefly inspired by a sexual relationship." De Page (1992) 178.

preponderant motive, the actual basis of the gift.[544] Courts will continue to invalidate gifts that essentially constitute the purchase of sexual favors. Relevant considerations include the short duration of the relationship, a quick succession of significant gifts, and a multiplicty of partners.[545]

(D) CRITIQUE

567. *Resistance.* The authors have refused to accept the high court's decision. Philippe Malaurie, the dean of French civil law scholars, argues that the immorality involved in *l'affaire Galopin* was so patent as to be scandalous. In his view, the sanction of nullity was appropriate both for the bequest and for the employment contract, which expressly provided that the secretary was to serve as a mistress. Though morals have evolved, a woman should not be permitted to debase herself by selling her body.[546] Véronique Mikalef-Toudic argues that the decision challenges the authority of the Civil Code. The validation of gifts given in violation of the spousal obligation of fidelity abrogates an essential feature of marriage.[547]

568. *Comparative notes.* In a comparative perspective, the change of course in the French case law is striking. The French legal system is generally devoted to reducing the social role of gift giving. Because, in the context of an adulterous relationship, gift giving is often one of the mechanisms by which the relationship survives, these gifts would seem to be particularly suspect. Yet French law has recognized that it cannot prohibit these gifts. In other words, French law no longer prohibits one of the rare instances of gift giving that not only has been unanimously condemned as immoral but that sometimes produces unconscionable deprivation for the donor's legitimate family.

ii. Italy

569. *Formalities.* In Italian law, transfers between cohabitants (*conviventes more uxorio*) are now generally valid. Two issues had to be overcome.

The first concerns the required formalities. As discussed below, Italian law generally validates only those gifts made by public act.[548] If movables are involved, they must be individually enumerated. Cohabitants who wish to avoid publicity do not comply with these formalities. Instead they make gifts of money and

---

544. De Page (1992) 173–174.

545. "[I]n sum, a collection of indices that demonstrate that the sexual relation is the predominant element, that it is not serving its natural purpose but that it is pursued in a context of pressure that one cohabitant utilizes to gain material advantages." De Page (1992) 175.

546. Malaurie (2006) 38.

547. Véronique Mikalef-Toudic, obs. to Civ. ass. plén. 29 Oct. 2004, *Rép. not. Defrén.* 2005 art. 38183 at 1045, 1048–1049.

548. Infra nos. 754–755.

movables by simple delivery and gifts of real property by simulating a sales contract.[549] If transfers between cohabitants were considered to be gifts, they would often be void.[550]

The solution to this problem experienced a significant evolution during the 1940s and 1950s.[551] The courts first held that the transfer remained a gift unless it constituted performance of a legal obligation.[552] Donees, usually women, challenged this view. They argued that donative intent was lacking. The transfers were generally intended to compensate for the prejudice caused when the man terminated the relationship. The courts responded that not every prejudice arising from an illicit act creates a legal duty of compensation. Seduction, even based on deception, generally does not create legally cognizable harm, nor does the termination of a long-term cohabitation relationship.[553] The moral duty was lacking because, except when the seduction is based on deception, the woman has consented—*volenti non fit iniuria*. Any payment was based on *pietas* rather than moral duty.

However, the courts assisted the donees by recharacterizing the transfers. Except for gifts that significantly reduced the donor's patrimony,[554] they would henceforth be considered remunerative gifts.[555] As discussed below, remunerative gifts are generally not subject to revocation on the basis of ingratitude or the birth of a child.[556] However, the problem with form remained, since remunerative gifts must be completed by notarial act (art. 770 par. 1). Eventually, this theory permitted the validation of even those gifts that did not comply with the form requirements. Since the remunerative gift is designed to compensate for services rendered, the transfer is only a gift to the extent it exceeds the value of the services. Thus, when the value of the services rendered exceeds the value of the remuneration, the transfer is valid without formalities.[557]

Throughout the period, scholars continued to argue that these transfers represented the fulfillment of a natural obligation.[558] The performance of a natural obligation is never a gift in Italian law.[559] The final step in the case law evolution

---

549. Carlo Brusco, note to Cass. 15 Jan. 1969 no. 60, *Foro it.* 1969 I 1511 at 1511.

550. Infra no. 761.

551. The case law evolution is described in Cass. 15 Jan. 1969 no. 60, *Foro it.* 1969 I 1511 at 1516–1517.

552. Cass. 28 Apr. 1942 no. 1107, *Rep. Foro it.* 1942 *Donazione* no. 16.

553. Cass. 7 Oct. 1954 no. 3389, *Foro it.* 1955 I 847; Cendon art. 770 no. 2.

554. Cass. 12 Oct. 1955 no. 3046, *Rep. Foro it.* 1955 *Donazione* nos. 23–24.

555. Cendon art. 770 no. 2; Cass. 17 July 1948 no. 1147, *Foro it.* 1949 I 951.

556. Infra nos. 1165, 1275.

557. Cendon art. 770 no. 2; Cass. 13 Dec. 1954 no. 4448, *Rep. Foro it.* 1954 *Donazione* no. 45; Cass. 24 Apr. 1957 no. 1398, *Rep. Foro it.* 1957 *Donazione* nos. 4–6.

558. For an overview of the discussion, see Moscati no. 6 note 154 at 372.

559. Supra no. 282.

was the judicial adoption of this view.[560] Though the courts did not wish to prolong what were at the time considered immoral relationships, especially in light
of the legal *favor matrimonii*, and therefore did not wish to penalize termination,
the courts nonetheless held that persistance in cohabitation created a moral duty
to provide for the woman's future if the relationship was terminated. The courts
recognized that an inquiry focused on the elements of the remunerative gift did
not confront the principal issue, which was the harm caused to the weaker
cohabitant, most often the woman. In some cases, the relationship was terminated after years of mutual affection and support that greatly resembled marriage, and yet the woman received none of the traditional benefits.[561] When the
woman was induced to remain on the basis of false representations, she not only
suffered moral and social prejudice but was never able to achieve a stable economic situation.[562] Though the economic loss is not the only, or in some cases
even the principal harm, the courts held that it is a moral duty, and therefore
a natural obligation, to remedy whatever economic harm is caused.

570. *Illicit cause.* The second difficulty in validating gifts between cohabitants
involved what some considered to be the illicit motive. A rule special to gift law
voids a gift if the donor's sole motive in making the gift is illicit and if that motive
is apparent from the gift act (CC art. 788). A related provision, similar to French
law, voids any contract with an illicit cause, which means a cause that violates
an imperative norm, public policy, or accepted custom (CC arts. 1343, 1418).

Italian law had relatively little difficulty overcoming this limitation. In the
1940s, Giorgio Oppo, arguing that these transfers satisfy a natural obligation,
suggested resolving the question of illicit cause by distinguishing the morality of
the *obligation* from the morality of the *act* that gives rise to the obligation.[563]
Cohabitation, he conceded, was immoral, but there was nothing immoral about
the duty to compensate for the harm caused by termination. Natural obligations
often arise when an immoral act has produced negative consequences that
morality demands should be repaired.[564] The Italian courts early decided to avoid
these transfers only if the donor's exclusive motivation is to procure sexual favors

---

560. Cass. 17 Jan. 1958 no. 84, *Foro it.* 1959 I 470; Cass. 25 Jan. 1960 no. 68, *Foro it.*
1961 I 2017. As Richter has pointed out, the evolution was abrupt. Richter 153. Within the
space of three years, the Cassation Court, presided over by the same judge, first held that
gifts between cohabitants cannot represent the performance of a legal or natural obligation, Cass. 7 Oct. 1954 no. 3389, *Giur. it.* 1955 I (1) 872, and then reversed itself in 1958.

561. "[I]t cannot be denied that an extra-marital relationship, when it exceeds the limits
of a transitory caprice, normally creates in the woman an expectation of economic stability
such as to induce her to renounce other opportunities available for a permanent arrangement." Cass. 17 Jan. 1958 no. 84, *Foro it.* 1959 I 470 at 471.

562. Cass. 15 Jan. 1969 no. 60, *Foro it.* 1969 I 1511 at 1518.

563. Oppo no. 50 at 238–239.

564. Id. no. 51 at 241.

and only if the motivation is unequivocally apparent from the gift act.[565] The courts generally hold that cohabitation involves a complex sense of caring and familial assistance that cannot be reduced to a purely sexual relationship.[566]

571. *Now generally valid.* Today transfers between cohabitants, often now called a *de facto family* (*famiglia di fatto*) are generally valid.[567] When the transfers are made during cohabitation[568] or are made to compensate one of the parties for the economic harm caused by termination, the transfers may satisfy a natural obligation,[569] even when made from the woman to the man.[570] Some authors derive the obligation from the duty of solidarity found in the Italian Constitution, which they interpret to prohibit the abandonment of a partner to indigence and illness.[571] The transfer performs a natural obligation if it is intended to satisfy a moral or social duty. It is instead a gift if it is intended to enrich the donee[572] or if there is no prejudice requiring compensation.[573] When the transfer constitutes the fulfillment of a natural obligation, it is not a gift and is not subject to gift formalities. It is also not voidable as a result of the donor's illicit motive. However, if the parties are merely involved in a sentimental or affective relationship and are not cohabiting *more uxorio*, the transfer does not satisfy a natural obligation and will generally be valid only if it satisfies the requirements for a valid gift.[574] Moreover, if the transfer is intended as payment for sexual services, it violates good morals and is therefore void—not due to an illicit motive but rather due to an illicit cause (CC arts. 1343, 1418).

iii. Spain

572. *Immoral cause.* On the basis of a code provision that renders void any contract concluded with an illicit cause (CC art. 1275), Spanish courts traditionally invalidated gifts designed to maintain or terminate a relationship between cohabitants (*convientes more uxorio*).[575]

573. *Valid.* Today gifts between cohabitants are valid in Spanish law and are subject to the normal gift law regime.[576] The older cases were overruled in 1994 in a

---

565. Cass. 4 May 1957 no. 1514, *Rep. Foro it.* 1957 *Donazione* no. 33; Cass. 18 Oct. 1955 no. 3264, *Rep. Giur. it.* 1955 *Donazione* no. 36.
566. Cass. 17 July 1948 no. 1147, *Foro it.* 1949 I 951.
567. Torrente (2006) 641–642. See Richter.
568. Roma 13 May 1995, *Rep. Foro it.* 1995 *Obbligazioni in genere* no. 78.
569. Cass. 20 Jan. 1989 no. 285, *Rep. Foro it.* 1989 *Obbligazioni in genere* no. 23.
570. Cass. 26 Jan. 1980 no. 651, *Rep. Foro it.* 1980 *Indebito* no. 6.
571. Italian Cost. Art. 2; Richter 151–152.
572. Cass. 15 Jan. 1969 no. 60, *Foro it.* 1969 I 1511 at 1519.
573. Cagliari 29 July 1988 no. 6481, *Rep. Foro it.* 1988 *Donazione* no. 9.
574. Terni 2 July 1997, *Rep. Foro it.* 1998 *Obbligazioni in genere* no. 65.
575. STS Civ. 17 Oct. 1959, RJ 3679; STS Civ. 5 Oct. 1957, RJ 2853.
576. Álvarez Lata 43.

case involving a couple living in a long-term relationship.[577] The Spanish high court held that the constitutional protection of family life does not discriminate according to type of family.[578] Gifts given solely as compensation for a sexual relationship are still considered void. Lacruz Berdejo contends that gifts made between partners in an adulterous relationship may also be void.[579] Some Spanish regions have enacted laws recognizing the status of the more uxorio relationship.[580]

iv. Germany

574. *Evolution.* Until 1968 German courts generally invalidated testamentary bequests between parties engaged in adulterous sexual relations (*Geliebte-Testament*), regardless whether the bequests actually served to maintain the relationship. The bequests were invalidated for the simple reason that they arose in the course of an immoral liaison.[581] The bequest was invalid even if the legatee did not learn of the bequest during the testator's lifetime. The bequests were usually validated only as compensation for services rendered or care provided. Nonetheless, occasional older decisions characterized some transfers as onerous to achieve equitable results.[582] Between 1968 and 1973 the courts changed course and validated gratuitous transfers as long as they were not principally intended to initiate, encourage, or reward sexual favors.[583] The courts shifted the focus away from the sexual relationship to concentrate on the circumstances surrounding the transaction.[584] Gratuitous transfers made in long-term relationships were generally considered to be based on factors other than the continuation of the sexual relationship.[585] The courts examined all of the facts and circumstances, including the transaction's potential effect on third parties, particularly children.

---

577. STS Civ. 18 Nov. 1994, RJ 8777.

578. Spanish Const. art. 39 par. 1.

579. 4 Lacruz Berdejo no. 213.

580. Martín Casals 55.

581. "The basis for the case law discussed above is that sexual relations between unmarried persons are considered to be immoral (*sittenwidrig*), not to speak of those between an unmarried man and a married woman .... Marriage is not simply a matter for the spouses. It is an institution that is also, and to a large extent, created and supported in the public interest. Without it, a polity of culture and law, as conceived in the Basic Law, would be unthinkable." BGH 26 Feb. 1968, JZ 1968, 466 at 468. For a critical view, contemporary with the decision, see Müller-Freienfels.

582. Lorenz 554–556.

583. D. Olzen, note to BGH 12 Jan. 1984, JR 1984, 413.

584. "[T]he determination of whether, and to what extent, sexual relations outside of marriage violate good morals lies on a fundamentally different level from the judgment about the corresponding transaction, which ... concerns exclusively the sphere of material goods." BGH 31 Mar. 1970, BGHZ 53, 369 at 377.

585. BGH 29 June 1973, NJW 1973, 1645.

575. *During cohabitation.* German law now recognizes freedom of contract between cohabitants and permits them to make both bequests and inter vivos gifts.[586] The gifts are not considered improper, even when the partners are otherwise married. They are also no longer void merely because the parties engage in extramarital or even adulterous sexual relations.[587] The law now favors gifts to the weaker partner with the goal of reducing the financial risk of the relationship.[588] Gifts given between cohabitants in long-term relationships now benefit from a presumption that they are based on valid motives. However, any transfer that constitutes payment for sexual services violates good morals and is void (CC § 138 par. 1).[589] The test is whether the gift's purpose is exclusively to reward or encourage sexual relations.[590] If other motives are involved, the courts determine validity by examining all the facts and circumstances, including the effects of the gift on third parties, including legitimate spouses.[591]

576. *Termination.* Due to the general German law principle of changed circumstances (*Störung der Geschäftsgrundlage*; CC § 313), courts may be reluctant to characterize transfers between cohabitants as gifts.[592] Gifts given under the assumption that the relationship will continue must be returned upon termination.[593] The courts consider it to be of the nature of such relationships that there is no expectation the law will intervene to return any transfers. A restitutionary action may however be available for gifts that greatly exceed what is usual.

v. The Common Law

577. *Traditional view.* Gifts between cohabitants have generally been permitted in the common law. Fleta considered gifts made to concubines and their children (*concubine et pueris suis*) to be valid.[594]

(A) ENGLAND

578. *Generally valid.* Gifts given to assist a former cohabitant have always been valid in England. A gift, or a promise to pay money, to a former cohabitant is not contrary to public policy.[595] In fact, the man was thought to have a moral duty to provide for his female cohabitant.[596] Though in an oft-cited case a court refused

---

586. MünchKomm-BGB (-Kollhosser) § 516 no. 84.
587. BGH 12 Jan. 1984, JR 1984, 412 note D. Olzen.
588. MünchKomm-BGB (-Kollhosser) § 516 no. 84.
589. OLG Schleswig 13 May 2004, NJW 2005, 225.
590. Staudinger (-Wimmer-Leonhardt) § 516 no. 54.
591. BGH 12 Jan. 1984, JR 1984, 412 note D. Olzen.
592. MünchKomm-BGB (-Kollhosser) § 516 no. 86
593. Id. no. 85.
594. Fleta bk. 3 ch. 4 at 7.
595. Treitel no. 11-039.
596. *Soar v Foster* (1858) 4 K & J 152, 161, 70 ER 64, 67.

to validate a promise to pay an annuity made in consideration of past cohabitation, the court did not suggest the promise was immoral. The problem was rather a lack of consideration.[597] Gifts of assistance given during current cohabitation, such as a trust that one party establishes for the benefit of the other, have also generally been validated.[598]

Nonetheless, it was sometimes argued that gifts intended to secure the continuance of cohabitation were illegal. English law has now abandoned virtually all restriction on the gifts that may be given between cohabitants. "The traditional common law approach to immoral contracts no longer applies to persons who live together in a common household as husband and wife without being married."[599] The High Court confirmed that it is not contrary to public policy when agreements on property relationships are reached by adults who intend to cohabit or are currently cohabiting, even if the effect is to encourage unlawful sexual relations. As Justice Hart indicated, "I accept also that this may be so whatever is planned to take place in the bedroom, provided that the criminal law is not infringed."[600] The gifts remain valid even though they are given to initiate a cohabitation involving a sexual relationship that may violate public policy.[601] The Civil Partnership Act in 2004 implicitly confirms that gifts between cohabitants are valid.[602] The invalidity of gifts between cohabitants now seems confined chiefly to meretricious relationships.[603]

579. *Resulting trust.* In one respect English gift law continues to prefer marriage to cohabitation. A resulting trust arises when one party purchases property in the name of the other or in their joint names and the two parties stand in no relation to one another. The person in whose name the property is purchased must hold the property for the benefit of the party who advanced the funds.[604] When the transfer is from parent to child, spouse to spouse, or even fiance to fiancee, the resulting trust is overcome by a presumption of advancement. The purchase then operates as a gift.[605] In contrast to American law, however, the

---

597. *Beaumont v Reeve* [1846] 8 QB 483, 115 ER 958.

598. "The policy of the law (and, therefore, of this and every other Court in the realm) is, no doubt, opposed to all immorality and to all unlawful cohabitation; but the equitable doctrines applicable to such cases do not depend upon, and do not vary with, the species or degree of immorality in each particular case." *Ayerst v Jenkins* (1873) LR 16 Eq 275, 282.

599. Treitel no. 11-040.

600. *Sutton v Mishcon de Reya* [2003] EWHC 3166 (Ch), [2004] 1 FLR 837 no. 22. See also Probert.

601. *Sutton v Mishcon de Reya*, id. nos. 33, 37.

602. Civil Partnership Act of 2004 sec. 74 par. 5. The Act also permits civil partners to make each other beneficiaries of life insurance policies. Id. sec. 70.

603. Treitel nos. 11-038, 11-040.

604. Infra nos. 990–991.

605. *Rider v Kidder* (1805) 10 Ves Jun 360, 32 ER 884.

presumption does not arise in English law in the case of a transfer from one cohabitant to the other, even in the case of a void marriage.[606] As a result the donee must prove donative intent.[607]

(B) INDIA

580. *Good consideration.* Some Indian high courts hold that, while past cohabitation is good consideration for a transfer, future consideration is not. A transfer of property as compensation for past cohabitation is therefore valid. "[T]hough a contract to enter into the relationship of protector and mistress is undoubtedly immoral, unenforceable and void, yet a contract to compensate a mistress for what she has lost on account of past association and so long as that loss shall continue, cannot be regarded as immoral."[608] However, when a manager of a coparcenary transfers real estate for that purpose, it is void.[609]

(C) UNITED STATES

581. *No restriction.* Some early American statutes and cases prohibited gifts to adulterous cohabitants to the extent they exceeded a specified portion of the estate.[610] The prohibitions were later retracted, though the legitimate spouse was still permitted to avoid such gifts.[611] Today American law does not in principle restrict gift giving between cohabitants. To the contrary, courts sometimes seem especially willing to find that transfers in this context were gifts. In one case, the cohabitants had pooled their money and purchased an engagement ring. When they separated without marrying, the court validated the purchase as a gift.[612] Moreover, cohabitants sometimes benefit from presumptions that generally apply to the donor's spouse and family. When property is transferred to one person and the purchase price is paid by another, the general rule is that a resulting trust arises in favor of the person who pays the purchase price.[613] However, if the transferee is a spouse, descendant, "or other natural object of the bounty" of the payor, the resulting trust does not arise and the transaction is presumed to

---

606. *In re A Policy No. 6402 of the Scottish Equitable Life Assurance Society* [1902] 1 Ch 282; *Soar v Foster* (1858) 4 K & J 152, 70 ER 64. For American law, see infra no. 581.

607. For a case in which the donee carried the burden, see *Paul v Constance* [1977] 1 WLR 527 (adulterous cohabitation).

608. *D. Nagaratnamba v. K. Ramayya*, AIR (50) 1963 AP 177, 182, [1962] 2 An WR 169.

609. Id. AIR (50) 1963 AP at 181; Derrett no. 464.

610. *Hull v. Hull*, 2 Strob.Eq. 174, 21 S.C.Eq. 174 (S.C.App.Eq. 1848).

611. *White v. White*, 48 S.E.2d 189, 190–191 (S.C. 1948). The applicable statute, S.C. Code Ann. § 21-7-480 (1976), was held to violate equal protection. *In re Estate of Mercer*, 342 S.E.2d 591 (S.C. 1986).

612. *Kohler v. Flynn*, 493 N.W.2d 647 (N.D. 1992).

613. Restatement (Third) of Trusts § 9 par. 1; see infra nos. 990–991.

be a gift.[614] Many of the older cases hold that a purchase in the name of a mistress is presumed to be a resulting trust rather than a gift.[615] "One cannot escape the feeling that in these cases the court was not attempting to ascertain the intention of the payor but was moved by reluctance to permit the woman to keep property because of a rather vague conception of public policy."[616] The more recent Restatement (Third), however, provides that the presumption of gift applies when the donor and donee "have cohabited for a significant period of time."[617] The burden is on the donor to rebut the presumption.[618]

582. *Public policy.* The older cases were willing to validate gratuitous transfers that served at least partially as compensation for prior adulterous cohabitation, as long as they did not serve to induce future cohabitation. The courts reasoned that "the illicit connection was an evil already past and done and the public had no interest to defeat" it.[619] Even transfers made solely as consideration for future sexual relations were not void. Instead, the courts refused to intervene to enforce, revoke, or rescind them. The courts left the parties where they found them.[620] More recently, the cases acknowledge the dramatic evolution that has taken place in social mores and are reluctant to infer that transfers between cohabitants are exclusively designed to induce sexual favors.[621]

d. Guardian and Ward

583. *Narrow interpretation.* In many legal systems, a guardian lacks the capacity to receive a gift from the ward. In general, these prohibitions are interpreted narrowly and are not extended by analogy. As a result, situations with an equivalent or superior potential for abuse escape legal control.[622]

584. *France.* The Ordinance of Villers-Cotterêts invalidated gifts by wards to their tutors or guardians (art. 131). Today under French law, minors, even after attaining the age of sixteen, may not give gifts to their tutors until the guardianship accounts have been settled (CC art. 907). A relative of the minor who has served as guardian is excepted.[623]

---

614. Id. § 9 par. 2 and comment a.
615. 5 Scott and Fratcher § 442 at 184–185.
616. Id. at 185.
617. Restatement (Third) of Trusts § 9 comment b.
618. *Rakhman v. Zusstone,* 957 S.W.2d 241 (Ky. 1997).
619. *Brown v. Kinsey,* 81 N.C. 245 (1879).
620. *Baker v. Couch,* 221 P. 1089, 1090 (Colo. 1924).
621. *Salzman v. Bachrach,* 996 P.2d 1263, 1267–1269 (Colo. 2000).
622. Flour and Souleau 196.
623. "[T]he law should presume filial piety rather than undue influence or the improper use of authority." Bigot de Préameneu, "Présentation au Corps législatif, et Exposé des motifs" (2 Floréal XI [22 Apr. 1803]), in 12 Fenet 520.

The prohibition is justified by a presumption of undue influence. The case law applies the prohibition to gifts made to any of those who, because they manage the minor's property, have the opportunity to exert undue pressure on the ward, including a coguardian and a guardian in fact.[624] However, because capacity restrictions are narrowly interpreted, the prohibition is not extended by analogy to similar situations, such as to a surrogate guardian or guardian *ad litem* or to a parent who acts as legal administrator. In the past, the incapacity has not applied to the guardian of an adult incompetent.[625] However, beginning in 2009 the code provides that guardians of adult incompetents may not receive gifts from their wards.[626] The exceptions are those relating to the physician's incapacity to receive, described below.

585. *Italy.* In Italian law, any contractual transaction—including a gift—between a guardian and an incompetent ward that is concluded before the guardianship accounts are approved is voidable at the option of the ward or the ward's heirs or assigns (CC art. 388). In addition, a more specific provision renders void any gift from the ward to a former guardian or acting guardian (*tutore* or *protutore*) if the gift was made before the guardianship accounts were approved or the statute of limitations ran on the accounting action (CC art. 779 par. 1).[627] The rules relating to the interposition of third parties expressly apply to this incapacity.[628] The scholars suggest that the prohibition does not apply when the ward has a lessor degree of incapacity requiring only a curator.[629]

586. *Spain.* Spanish law also prohibits a guardian from receiving gifts from the ward or the ward's assigns before the guardian's administration has been definitively approved (CC art. 221 no. 1). The inclusion of the ward's assigns is due to a fear of simulation related to interposition. The scholars criticize the inclusion of the assigns because they may have no relationship to the guardian.[630]

587. *Germany.* In German law the guardian is prohibited from making gifts of the ward's property, except customary presents (CC § 1804). Therefore no gift can be made to the guardian during the guardianship. German law does not regulate gifts given after guardianship has ended.

---

624. 5 Planiol and Ripert no. 235.

625. Flour and Souleau no. 307 note 51.

626. French CC art. 909 par. 2 (in force 1 Jan. 2009), Law of 5 March 2007 art. 9.

627. Biondi has suggested that this second provision "was legislatively reenacted by force of inertia, even though no convincing justification for it has been or could be offered." Biondi no. 95. The general voidability of contracts between guardian and ward, together with the doctrine of undue influence, already provide sufficient protection.

628. CC arts. 779 par. 2, 599. For the rules relating to the interposition of third parties in Italian law, see infra no. 639.

629. Capozzi no. 359 at 857.

630. Paz-Ares Rodríguez (-Hualde Sanchez) art. 221 no. II par. 2.

588. *Common law*. American law on this question varies. Many American courts hold that the guardian lacks capacity during guardianship to receive a gift from the ward.[631] However, some state statutes specifically permit the courts to authorize gifts to guardians who are prospective heirs.[632] Other courts rely on a presumption against validity rather than an absolute incapacity, especially when the guardian and the ward are related. One court held that, if the ward is otherwise competent, a guardian related to the ward may receive the gift.[633] In order to overcome the strong presumption against validity, the guardian must show, by clear and convincing evidence, that the relationship did not influence the transaction, that the ward was aware of the circumstances, and that the guardian was in good faith. The presumption of invalidity continues beyond termination and "extends as long as the relationship of influence by the guardian and dependence by the ward continues to exist."[634] A few courts presume that a ward's gift to the guardian was procured by fraud. The guardian is permitted to offer proof to the contrary.[635]

In English law, the relationship of guardian and ward is one of the special (class 2A) relationships of trust and confidence. The law maintains an irrebuttable presumption that the guardian had influence over the ward.[636] If the ward demonstrates that the gift "calls for explanation," then a rebuttable presumption arises that the gift was procured by undue influence.

e. Physician and Patient

589. *Potential for abuse*. Due to the potential for undue influence, some legal systems prohibit doctors, under certain circumstances, from receiving gifts from their patients. The incapacity is justified by the need to place the medical profession above suspicion.[637]

i. France and Belgium

590. *History*. In French law, the physician's incapacity to receive is justified by an irrebuttable presumption of undue influence (CC art. 909). These rules are a product of a rare case law elaboration under the ancien régime. Incapacity rules are traditionally interpreted narrowly.[638]

---

631. *Webster and Moorefield, P.A. v. City National Bank*, 453 So.2d 441, 443 (Fla. App. 1984).

632. Indiana C Ann. § 29-3-9-4 (Burns 2000).

633. *In re Spindle*, 733 P.2d 388 (Okla. 1986).

634. Id. 389.

635. *Laufert v. Wegner*, 62 N.W.2d 758, 763 (Iowa 1954).

636. *Hylton v Hylton* (1754) 2 Ves Sen 548, 28 ER 349; Treitel par. 10-016.

637. 5 Planiol and Ripert no. 237.

638. 8 Pothier, *Donations* no. 40; 8 De Page no. 171 at 252 note 1. The incapacity of physicians is apparently first found in the *Arrêtés* of Guillaume de Lamoignon (1702). See Paris 8 Mar. 1867, D. 1867 II 145 at 147 concl. de Vallée.

(A) REQUIRED ELEMENTS

591. *Four conditions.* The physician's incapacity arises if four conditions are met.[639]

592. *Medical doctors and pharmacists.* First, the incapacity generally applies only to medical doctors and pharmacists,[640] though it has also been applied to quacks and to those who practice medicine illegally.[641] Subsequent legislation applies similar incapacities to those who provide psychiatric services,[642] as well as to physical persons who own, administer, or are employed by homes for minors, the aged, the ill, or the poor, and halfway houses,[643] and to those who, for profit, care for the aged or for handicapped adults in their homes.[644]

The traditional incapacity did not apply to health workers who were not, or who did not pretend to be, physicians. Nurses and doctors' aids were exempt. Due to the rigor with which the rule was interpreted, interns still in training and midwives, both of whom often serve as treating physicians, were also excepted, unless they actually assumed treatment responsibility, in which case they could be counted among those who practice medicine illegally.[645] Beginning in 2009, the incapacity has been extended to include all members of the medical and pharmacy professions as well as medical auxiliaries.[646]

593. *Treatment.* Second, the donee must have *treated* the donor. The case law of the ancien régime included pharmacists in the prohibition because, at the time, they treated patients and prescribed medication.[647] Today, pharmacists rarely satisfy the treatment requirement. French case law has vacillated concerning the extent to which a consulting physician lacks capacity under this provision.

594. *Illness.* Third, the incapacity applies only to gifts given during the course of the illness the physician has treated. The case law has construed the notion of illness to include an accident, as well as a remission between two periods

---

639. Flour and Souleau no. 308.

640. The code also mentions surgical doctors and public health officials, but those titles have since been abolished.

641. Civ.[1] 10 Oct. 1978, *Bull. civ.* I no. 296, J.C.P. 1980 II 19341 note Dagot; Trib. gr. inst. Seine 5 Dec. 1963, *Gaz. Pal.* 1964 I 164, *Rev. trim. dr. civ.* 1964, 590 obs. René Savatier.

642. CC art. 1125-1 (1968) prohibits all property transfers from patient to provider, whether or not gratuitous, unless judicially authorized.

643. Id.; C Family and Soc. Services art. 209 bis (1977), replaced by C Soc. Action and the Family art. L331-4 (2000).

644. Law of 10 July 1989 art. 13, codified in C Soc. Action and the Family art. L443-6.

645. 5 Planiol and Ripert no. 239.

646. CC art. 909 (in force 1 Jan. 2009), Law of 5 March 2007 art. 9.

647. "Communication officieuse à la Section de législation du Tribunat" (10 Germinal XI [31 Mar. 1803]), in 12 Fenet 443.

of treatment.[648] Only the physician who treats the donor for the fatal disease lacks the capacity to receive. In one case, the physician who treated the donor's rheumatism during the final illness was held competent to receive a gift.[649]

595. *Death.* Finally, the incapacity applies only if the donor dies from the illness during the course of which the gift was made. Some scholars suggest that this final requirement is too narrow. Undue influence may have been exerted even if the donor survives the illness. Several authors favor a broad interpretation of the causation requirement, especially in the case of chronic illness.[650] However, if the donor dies from an accident or a disease unrelated to the illness treated by the donee, the incapacity does not apply, unless the treatment differs from that required by the fatal disease only because the physician erred in the diagnosis.[651] Because the incapacity is designed to protect the consent of a person who is about to die, it seems the incapacity should not apply if the gift was made while the disease was latent.[652]

(B) EXCEPTIONS

596. *Two situations.* Even when all four requirements have been satisfied, the physician, in two situations, maintains the capacity to receive.

597. *Remunerative gift.* The first is the case of a remunerative gift intended to compensate the physician for services rendered (CC art. 909 par. 2 no. 1).[653] In general, such a gift is valid only if it is proportional both to the value of the services and to the donor's resources. The literature suggests the additional requirement that the services must not have been previously remunerated.

598. *Close relatives.* Second, a patient may make gifts to physicians who are close relatives—within four degrees of separation (CC art. 909 par. 2 no. 2). It is thought that the close relationship negates the presumption of undue influence. However, the exception does not apply if the decedent has direct descendants, unless the physician is among them. Otherwise, French scholars suggest, the gift would be suspicious. Though the exception applies by its terms only to wills,

---

648. Civ. 22 Oct. 1940, *Gaz. Pal.* 1940 II 192 (concerning a testamentary bequest). CC art. 909 par. 1 expressly applies the same principles to gift law.

649. Civ.¹ 1 July 2003, D. 2003, 2404 concl. J. Sainte-Rose, *Rép. not. Defrén.* 2004 art. 37853 at 31 obs. Nathalie Peterka.

650. Flour and Souleau no. 308.

651. 8 De Page no. 173.

652. Nathalie Peterka, obs. to Civ.¹ 1 July 2003, *Rép. not. Defrén.* 2004 art. 37853 at 37.

653. "We did not want to deprive the patient of the satisfaction of demonstrating gratitude, provided the gift is proportional to the patient's resources and the services provided." Bigot de Préameneu, Thibaudeau, and Duchâtel, "Présentation au Corps législatif, et Exposé des motifs," in 12 Fenet 520.

the doctrine extends it to gifts as well.[654] Though, in general, the exception does not extend to relatives by affinity, it has been decided that the spouse who cares for the other spouse should not thereby lose the capacity to receive.[655] However, if the physician marries the donor during the course of the donor's final illness, the scholars argue that the exception should no longer apply,[656] while the case law permits such gifts unless there is proof of undue influence.[657]

ii. The Common Law

599. *England.* In English law, the doctor-patient relationship is one of the special (class 2A) relationships of presumed trust and confidence that give rise to an irrebutable presumption of influence.[658]

600. *United States.* The American principle is that nothing in the confidential relation between medical advisor and patient need interfere with the patient's gift.[659] A court of equity, however, is permitted to infer from the circumstances of the gift, particularly if the donor was ill and no third parties were present, that the gift was procured by undue influence.[660] Whenever a donor in a state of infirmity makes a gift to a person in a relationship of trust and confidence, the gift is presumptively void. The donee has the burden of establishing that the transaction was fair and untainted by undue influence.[661]

American courts have avoided gifts to doctors in circumstances that would not fit within the relatively narrow French law prohibition. In one case the gift was made a year before the patient's death at a moment when the patient was not yet suffering from the fatal illness.[662] American courts have also avoided gifts on this basis even when made to a hospice volunteer rather than to a practicing physician.[663] Once the existence of the confidential relationship is established, the medical professional bears the burden of proving the fairness of the transaction.

---

654. 8 De Page no. 176 note 5.

655. Civ. 22 Aug. 1822, S. 1823 I 100; Trib. civ. Dax 25 May 1899, D.P. 1899 II 357.

656. 5 Planiol and Ripert no. 241 at 333 note 2; 8 De Page no. 173.

657. Req. 11 Jan. 1820, *J. Pal.* 1819–20, 689, 5 *Rép. gén.* 1791–1846, *Dispositions à titre gratuit* no. 438 (Paris 1846).

658. Crossley Vaines 291; *Dent v Bennett* (1839) 4 My & Cr 269, 41 ER 105; Treitel par. 10-016. See supra no. 588 for the effect of this presumption. In *Dent*, the civil law restrictions regarding doctor and patient were raised during the course of the argument. Lord Chancellor Cottenham noted that he did not wish to restrict the doctrine of undue influence by limiting it to certain relationships. Id. 4 My & Cr at 276–277, 41 ER at 108.

659. 2 Schouler (1896) § 60 at 70 note 2.

660. Id.

661. *Madden v. Rhodes,* 626 So.2d 608, 619 (Miss. 1993); *Ostertag v. Donovan,* 331 P.2d 355 (N.M. 1958); *Hall v. Knappenberger,* 11 S.W. 239 (Mo. 1889).

662. *Ostertag v. Donovan,* 331 P.2d 355 (N.M. 1958).

663. *Madden v. Rhodes,* 626 So.2d 608 (Miss. 1993).

In this way voidability due to undue influence has a practical result similar to an incapacity.

f. Priest and Penitent

601. *Final illness.* Some jurisdictions provide that the clergy lacks the capacity to receive gifts from those to whom they minister during a final illness.

i. France and Belgium

602. *Comfort and assistance.* The code applies the rules regarding physician incapacity to the clergy (CC art. 909 par. 3). A member of the clergy lacks the capacity to receive a gift made during the donor's final illness if the donee provided religious comfort and assistance to the donor during that period. Like the rules relating to physicians, the clergy's incapacity resulted from case law development,[664] and the same exceptions apply mutatis mutandis. The treatment of the soul is assimilated to treatment of the body. The two situations seem to present equivalent opportunities for undue influence.[665]

There is little case law about who qualifies as a member of the clergy for these purposes.[666] Scholars agree that those who lead ephemeral cults should be included because of the influence they may exercise over their followers. The prohibition is also thought to apply to those who fraudulently hold themselves out as ministers. Leaders of societies proclaiming atheism or free thought, because they do not profess a religion, are not subject to this incapacity. It is difficult to determine the religious equivalent to treatment. For priests, the administration of the sacraments, especially confession, is an important factor. However, a priest does not lose capacity merely by administering the last rites.

ii. Spain

603. *Possible application.* Under Spanish law, no testamentary disposition may be made during a last illness to the priest who received the testator's confession, or to any of the priest's relatives to the fourth degree, or to the priest's church, chapter, community, or institute (CC art. 752). Gifts of modest value are excepted.[667] Spanish scholars have suggested that the same prohibition should apply to inter vivos gifts.[668] Moreover, when the minister is permitted to take a spouse, it is thought that the spouse should suffer the same incapacity.[669] The prohibition

---

664. 5 Planiol and Ripert no. 242. Pothier justified the incapacity by the great influence a minister may sometimes exercise over a congregant. 8 Pothier, *Donations* no. 38 par. 7.

665. Flour and Souleau no. 310.

666. 5 Planiol and Ripert no. 243.

667. Paz Ares Rodríguez (-Díaz Alabart) art. 752 no. I par. 1.

668. Paz-Ares Rodríguez (-Albaladejo García) art. 625 no. III.

669. Paz Ares Rodríguez (-Díaz Alabart) art. 752 no. II par. 2.

would apply only to religions that have a rite similar to confession.[670] The provision also applies to self-proclaimed priests who hear confession, even if they are not actually members of the clergy. The Spanish Supreme Court seems to interpret this provision as a rebuttable presumption, permitting proof that the donor was not subjected to undue influence.[671]

iii. The Common Law

604. *Undue influence.* In the United States, ministers are generally permitted to receive personal gifts from their parishioners, as well as gifts for religious and charitable purposes.[672] However, a court of equity may infer undue influence from the circumstances surrounding the gift.[673] English law irrebuttably presumes influence when a member of a religious community makes a gift to the minister.[674] In one case, a woman became a professed member of a religious sisterhood, the rules of which required her to give up her property, either to her relatives, to the poor, or to the sisterhood itself. The rules also required obedience to the order's superior as if to the voice of God and prohibited advice from external sources.[675] When the woman left the sisterhood some years later, she attempted to recover the gifts of money and stock she had made to the order. The court held there was a presumption of influence, even though all of the money had been devoted to charity.

g. Lawyer and Client

605. *Lex Cincia.* The lex Cincia prohibited payment *ob causam orandam*, which included any fees or gifts paid by clients to the lawyers who represented them.[676] Tacitus justified the prohibition by the notorious venality of lawyers, who apparently were not averse to receiving fees from opposing parties.[677]

i. Civilian Systems

606. *Ancien régime.* During the ancien régime, some argued that lawyers, who often exercise influence equivalent to physicians and members of the clergy, should be prohibited from receiving gifts from their clients.[678] The suggestion

---

670. Id. art. 752 no. III par. 1.

671. Id. par. 3.

672. 2 Schouler (1896) § 60 at 70 note 2.

673. Id.; *Klaber v. Unity School of Christianity*, 51 S.W.2d 30 (Mo. 1932).

674. Crossley Vaines 291; Treitel par. 10-016. See supra no. 588 for the effect of this presumption.

675. *Allcard v Skinner* (1887) LR 36 Ch D 145 (CA). Recovery was denied on the basis of laches.

676. Savigny (1850) 317.

677. "Nor was any public good as subject to venality as the perfidy of lawyers." Tacitus, *Annals* bk. 11 par. 5. See also Pliny, *Letters* bk. 5 no. 4.

678. 8 Pothier, *Donations* no. 39.

was rejected. "[T]he noblesse of their profession should suffice to remove from them any suspicion of conflict of interest."[679] Moreover, during the final stages of a last illness, the lawyer's influence usually yields to that of the physician and the minister.

607. *France and Belgium.* In French and Belgium law today, lawyers do not lack the capacity to receive gifts from their clients. It also seems that no other direct restrictions apply. Instead, lawyers decide whether gifts are appropriate by considering their duty of independence, which requires them to avoid the influence that may arise from personal interest.[680] Beginning in 2009, receivers (*mandataires judiciaires*) may not receive gifts from those whose interests they represent.[681] The exceptions relating to the physician's incapacity apply.

608. *Germany.* German law also does not specifically restrict the capacity of lawyers to receive gifts from their clients. Instead, lawyers decide whether to accept gifts based on their duty to protect their professional independence and objectivity and to avoid conflict of interest.[682]

609. *Other civilian systems.* In Italian law, if the notary, the notary's relatives, or any necessary witness or interpreter receives a gift in the notarial act, the gift is void.[683] A similar prohibition in Spanish law applies both to the notary who receives the gift act and to the notary's spouse and the notary's relatives within four degrees of consanguinity and two degrees of affinity.[684] Studies suggest that charitable bequests are frequently made to institutions with which the notary who concludes the act maintains an affiliation.[685]

ii. The Common Law

610. *England.* English law presumes influence when a client gives a gift to a solicitor.[686] The presumption is not irrebuttable, though it is not sufficiently rebutted by the fact that the client employed separate counsel to obtain advice concerning the gift. The presumption continues as long as the solicitor-client relationship continues[687] and even thereafter as long as the influence lasts.[688]

---

679. Id.
680. Council of Bars par. 2.1.1.
681. CC art. 909 par. 2 (in force 1 Jan. 2009), Law of 5 March 2007 art. 9.
682. Law of 1 Aug. 1959 (BRAO) § 43a pars. 1, 3–4.
683. Torrente (2006) 474; Law of 16 Feb. 1913 arts. 28 no. 3, 50 par. 2, 58 nos. 3–4.
684. Paz-Ares Rodríguez (-Albaladejo García) art. 625 no. III, referring to Law of 28 May 1862 arts. 22, 27–28.
685. Marais 332.
686. Crossley Vaines 291.
687. *Wright v Carter* [1903] 1 Ch 27.
688. Treitel par. 10-016.

611. *United States.* In American law, the validity of gifts made by clients to their lawyers are governed by complex rules involving considerations of professional responsibility and presumptions of undue influence. The scope of the relevant rules far exceeds the problem of the deathbed gift.

612. *Legal ethics.* As a matter of legal ethics, the bar associations have long advised lawyers to exercise extreme caution when accepting gifts from clients.

> A lawyer should not suggest to his client that a gift be made to himself or for his benefit. If a lawyer accepts a gift from his client, he is peculiarly susceptible to the charge that he unduly influenced or overreached the client. If a client voluntarily offers to make a gift to his lawyer, the lawyer may accept the gift, but before doing so, he should urge that his client secure disinterested advice from an independent, competent person who is cognizant of all the circumstances.[689]

American courts have been highly suspicious of gifts made by clients to their lawyers. "For over 100 years our courts have made it clear that a transaction between a lawyer and his client will be regarded with suspicion and that it will be presumptively void, subject to proof by the lawyer, usually through disinterested persons, that the transaction was fair and fully intended by the client."[690] The disciplinary rules that govern lawyers in American jurisdictions provide that a lawyer shall not prepare an instrument in which the lawyer or a specified close relative of the lawyer—parent, child, sibling, or spouse—receives a substantial gift from a client, unless the client is related to the donee.[691]

613. *Two prohibitions.* The applicable rules, in their most recent version, synthesize ethical considerations and case precedents into two prohibitions.[692] First, a lawyer may generally not prepare an instrument effecting a gift from the client to the lawyer unless the client is a relative or friend and the gift is not disproportionate to those given to other donees. Second, a lawyer may not accept a gift from a client unless the benefit to the lawyer is insubstantial, the lawyer is a natural object of the client's generosity, or the client has been encouraged to seek, or has received, independent advice before making the gift. The prohibition is not absolute, largely because it is thought that a client may actually be motivated by a genuine feeling of gratitude toward the lawyer. The client's wishes should be respected, though overreaching must be prevented.[693]

---

689. ABA Model Code of Professional Responsibility, Ethical Consideration 5-5.
690. *Radin v. Opperman*, 407 N.Y.S.2d 303, 304–05 (App. Div. 1978).
691. ABA Model Rules of Professional Conduct Rule no. 1.8 par. c.
692. Restatement (Third) of the Law Governing Lawyers § 127.
693. Id. comment b.

h. Conflicts of Interest

614. *Public decisions.* When the law prohibits gifts in the context of the special relationships discussed above, it is usually concerned with the risk of undue influence. One of the parties might use a position of dominance to cajole a gift the donor feels unable to refuse. Other relationships pose a different concern, namely the risk of conflict of interest. These generally involve gifts given to public employees. The risk is that the gift might cause the official to pursue a course of action that is not in society's best interest.

In some situations, of course, such gifts can result in charges of bribery and corruption.[694] Even short of bribery, a gift may have a detrimental effect on public decision making. In numerous situations, the law intervenes to limit or prohibit gifts when the risks seem excessive or when there is an appearance of impropriety. A number of these capacity restrictions exist in every jurisdiction examined here. An extensive survey would exceed the scope of this study. The limited discussion here is intended only as a brief reminder of the complexity of the issues involved.

i. Judge and Litigant

615. *Medieval exhortation.* Throughout history, judges have been cautioned against accepting gifts from the parties before them. In the early Middle Ages, provisions appeared in the capitularies requiring judges, counts, and vicars to reject gifts that might interfere with doing justice—*ut propter iustitiam pervertendam munera non accipiant.*[695] At the time, however, the distinction between public and private was undeveloped. Moreover, official salaries were not always sufficient to permit judges to support themselves. As a result, the provisions in the capitularies are perhaps best understood as paraenetical exhortations.[696] It seems to have been assumed that a just decision would be forthcoming despite, or perhaps because of, gratuitous transfers. It was not the receipt of gifts as such that was prohibited but rather a decision made on that basis. The actual prohibition of gifts to judges came only with the rise of modern judicial administration.

(A) CIVILIAN SYSTEMS

616. *France.* The French Code of Civil Procedure provides that judges may be compelled to recuse themselves if they or their spouses receive a gift from a litigant.[697]

---

694. For a detailed history of the practice of bribery and of the governmental attempts to suppress it, see Noonan.

695. "Let [officials and vicars] not accept gifts that might pervert justice." Ansegius bk. 4 par. 62 at 655. See also id. bk. 1 par. 60 at 461, bk. 2 par. 6 at 527; Curta 690.

696. Hannig 160–161.

697. CCProc. art. 341 par. 2.

617. *Spain.* Under the Spanish Penal Code, judges are prohibited from soliciting or accepting gifts that are intended to influence the judges to commit a crime in the course of their judicial service. They are also prohibited from soliciting or accepting gifts that are intended to, and do, provoke them to commit an injustice.[698]

618. *Germany.* In German law, both federal and state judges require approval before accepting presents or rewards related to their judicial duties.[699] Beginning in 2009, no provincial official may, for themselves or third persons, request or accept rewards, gifts, or other advantages related to their office, even after their employment has ended.[700] Anything received in violation of this prohibition can be confiscated. Moreover, a judge who requests or accepts a gift based on a past or future decision is subject to criminal punishment.[701] Gifts that violate any of these rules,[702] or the criminal law, are void.[703]

(B) UNITED STATES

619. *Variation.* In American law, the legislatures and the judicial authorities have specified situations in which judges may and may not receive gifts from lawyers and litigants. The rules vary widely.

(1) General

620. *Prohibitions.* Illinois specifically prohibits lawyers from making gifts to judges.[704] This prohibition is interpreted as a restriction on the judiciary's capacity to receive the gift.[705] In California, judges are prohibited from accepting gifts from any single source in any calendar year with a value exceeding $250.[706] The provision excepts certain defined payments, advances and reimbursements for travel. It also exempts wedding gifts and gifts given on birthdays and similar occasions. The value limit is adjusted every two years to take account of inflation. Judges may not accept honoraria—defined to include payments made in consideration of speeches, articles, or attendance at meetings. Gifts are defined to exclude gratuitous transfers from the judge's close relatives, including the judge's spouse,

---

698. Spanish Penal C arts. 419–427.

699. Law of 19 April 1972 (*Deutsches Richtergesetz*) § 46, together with Law of 31 Mar. 1999 (BBG) § 70 (federal judges); Law of 19 April 1972 § 71, together with Law of 1 July 1957 (BRRG) § 43 (provincial judges).

700. Law of 17 June 2008 (BeamtStG) § 42.

701. Penal C §§ 331 par. 2, 332 par. 2, 333 par. 2, 334 par. 2.

702. Staudinger (-Sack) § 134 no. 213.

703. MünchKomm-BGB (-Mayer-Maly and Armbrüster) § 134 no. 59.

704. Illinois C Prof. Resp. Disciplinary Rule no. 7-110 par. a.

705. *In re Corboy*, 528 N.E.2d 694, 701 (Ill. 1988).

706. California CCProc. § 170.9.

children, parents, grandparents, grandchildren, siblings, in-laws, nephews, nieces, uncles, first cousins, and their spouses.

(2) Judicial Ethics

621. *Detailed restrictions.* The California Code of Judicial Ethics provides more detailed restrictions.[707] It prohibits judges and their families from receiving any gifts from parties who may appear before the judge as well as gifts other than those in enumerated categories, which include research materials provided by publishers, reimbursements for travel in the service of law reform, benefits received due to the profession of a family member, ordinary social hospitality, traditional gifts on special occasions, and fellowships awarded on the same basis as to other applicants.

In Pennsylvania, the rules of judicial ethics once prohibited judges from accepting gifts from litigants, prospective litigants, or the lawyers who practice before them.[708] The rule was modified in light of the belief that occasions may arise in which such gifts would be proper.[709] The Pennsylvania courts have now decided that judges may not accept any gift that the judge knew or should have known was offered to influence the performance of the judge's judicial responsibilities.[710] The rule is designed to avoid the appearance of impropriety. In general, gifts are proper if there is a relationship between the donor and the donee, such that the judge can establish that the gift was given only in connection with the relationship and that the circumstances surrounding the gift would not lead the donor to believe that it would be possible to exert improper influence over the judge.[711]

ii. Government Official and Citizen

622. *Prohibitions.* Many legal systems prohibit politicians and other government officials from receiving gifts in prescribed amounts from those who have business before them. Some systems prohibit gifts of any kind.

(A) HISTORICAL PROHIBITIONS

623. *Roman law.* The capacity restrictions on Roman provincial magistrates were particularly strict. "It is contained in a proclamation that, to prevent bribes, no provincial magistrate may receive any gift except for food and drink, not to exceed an amount that can be consumed within a few days."[712] Other restrictions applied

---

707. California Canons of Judicial Ethics 4D pars. 5–6 (2005); see also Illinois C Judicial Conduct Rule no. 65 par. C no. 4.
708. Canons of Judicial Ethics 32 (1965).
709. *In re Cunningham*, 538 A.2d 473, 481 (Pa. 1988).
710. Id. 479.
711. *In re Braig*, 554 A.2d 493, 498 (Pa. 1989).
712. D. 1, 18, 18 (Modestinus); see also 8 Pothier, *Donations* no. 34; Michel no. 792.

to proconsuls. The Digest quoted an epistle from Emperor Antonius, which relied on an ancient Greek proverb to the effect that not all gifts should be accepted, nor at all times, nor from all persons, for it is impolite to accept gifts from no one, but, on the other hand, it is most despicable and avaricious to accept without distinction everything one is offered.[713]

624. *Medieval France.* In 1320 Philip the Tall prohibited bailiffs and seneschals, while in office, together with their spouses, parents, and companions, from receiving gifts from those residing in their provinces, except for food and drink not exceeding a weekly revenue of ten Parisian sous.[714]

625. *Medieval Germany.* The historiography of German public administration (*Beamtentum*) has undergone considerable evolution. Sociological studies at the turn of the last century suggested that modern administration begins at the moment when strict limits are imposed on gifts to public officials.[715] Groebner, however, in a fascinating study, emphasizes that gift giving played an important role as an instrument of patronage and client relationship.[716] Gifts to public officials were permitted, but permission had to be obtained on each occasion. In other words, gifts were carefully enacted to render social relations public and visible.[717] Only gifts secretly given (*miet*) were forbidden. "From this perspective, the rise of early modern state administration is literally based on gift-giving, even if not always of a voluntary nature."[718]

(B) UNITED STATES

626. *Complexity.* The gift capacity of American politicians and other government employees is subject to a bewildering array of limitations. The limitations have generally arisen as part of the post-Watergate suspicion of those involved in public life. The restrictions are found in numerous sources. They often conflict and are frequently revised.

627. *Federal law.* The Constitution prohibits government officials from accepting "any present, Emolument, Office, or Title, of any kind whatever, from any King, Prince, or foreign State" without the consent of Congress.[719] Restrictions in federal law vary depending on the official's position. By statute, no member, officer, or employee of the U.S. Senate, or their spouses or dependents, may knowingly accept, directly or indirectly, any gifts in any calendar year aggregating to more than $250, unless, in an unusual case, a waiver is granted by the

---

713. D. 1, 16, 6, 3 (Ulpian).
714. 8 Pothier, *Donations* no. 34.
715. Groebner 221, referring to Schmoller and Weber.
716. Id. 230.
717. Id. 237.
718. Id. 221.
719. U.S. Const. art. 1 sec. 9 cl. 8.

Senate's Select Committee on Ethics.[720] The capacity restrictions are contained in a half dozen highly complex, overlapping, and partially conflicting statutes.[721] The risk posed to federal employees by the uncertain scope of the various rules has been likened to "building a bridge halfway across a crocodile-infested river and posting road signs inviting motorists to cross."[722]

628. *State law.* State law often restricts the capacity of state officers to receive gifts. Kansas prohibits lobbyists from making gifts exceeding a value of $40 to any state officer, employee, or candidate for state office if the principal purpose of the gift is to influence the performance of official duties.[723]

iii. Miscellaneous Provisions

629. *Examples from American law.* Two further American examples suggest the variety of statutory provisions enacted to prevent conflicts of interest.

630. *Student athletes.* To prevent fans from encouraging athletes to join their favorite intercollegiate team, Michigan has imposed restrictions on gift giving.[724] Gifts or services may not be given to current or prospective student athletes or their families if those gifts have the effect of preventing an athlete from qualifying for play under institutional rules. These rules usually prohibit amateur athletes from receiving compensation for their athletic activities. However, a student athlete may receive gifts from the universities and from the athlete's immediate family.

631. *Pharmaceutical companies.* The American medical profession has expressed concern that decisions relating to patient care are compromised by gifts pharmaceutical companies give to physicians. It has been proposed that those gifts be regulated.[725]

4. Interposition of Third Parties

632. *Evasion prohibited.* Though simulated transactions are generally valid as between the parties,[726] they are void if their purpose is to circumvent a legal prohibition. Several Civil Codes specifically prohibit attempts to evade capacity restrictions. The concern is that the donee may accept a gift, either actually or only in appearance, while agreeing to reconvey it to a third party who lacks the capacity to receive it. A gift made with the goal of circumventing capacity

---

720. 2 U.S.C.A. § 31-2 par. a.

721. See generally Zinman 165–195.

722. Id. 191.

723. Kansas Stats. Ann. § 46–271.

724. Student Athletes and the Receipt of Money Act of 1988, Mich. Stats. Ann. § 600.2968.

725. Brennan et al.

726. See e.g., French CC art. 1321.

restrictions is void. The problem is that these maneuvers are difficult to discover. To block the likely means of evasion, some civilian jurisdictions conclusively presume that gifts given to close relatives of a person who lacks the capacity to receive the gift are intended as simulation and are therefore void. The common law does not recognize legal presumptions of interposition. As scholars have frequently pointed out, these exorbitant capacity restrictions frequently inhibit innocent gifts.

a. France and Belgium

633. *Generalized prohibition.* In French law, any gift made in an attempt to circumvent capacity restrictions is void, regardless whether the attempt takes the form of disguising the gift as a synallagmatic transaction or of interposing an intermediary (CC art. 911 par. 1). The principle applies to all gifts, including disguised, indirect, and manual gifts,[727] and concerns all limitations on the capacity to receive.[728] The prohibition against interposition has recently been extended to include gifts made using a legal person, such as a real estate trust, as the intermediary.[729] The party seeking to avoid the gift has the burden of proof.[730] A gift made through attempted deception is void, even if, had the gift been made directly to the incompetent, it would have been valid to the extent of the donee's successoral share.[731]

634. *Difficult distinction.* It is important to distinguish between gifts by interposition and gifts coupled with an obligation (*donation avec charges*). The former are void while the latter are valid.[732] Yet it is almost impossible to draw a clear boundary between the two institutions, especially because gifts coupled with an obligation often involve the interposition of an intermediary. A gift is coupled with an obligation, and therefore permissible, when the donee is obligated, at a later date, to transfer the property to persons, such as indeterminate or future persons, who, at the moment the gift is made, lack the capacity to receive it. The distinction is now considered a question of fact regarding the intent of the parties.

i. Presumptions

635. *Close relatives.* Interposition is difficult to discover and prove because the facts are easily concealed from those who have an interest in challenging the gift. To prevent deception, French law presumes that gifts made to specified close

---

727. 5 Planiol and Ripert no. 174 bis.
728. 8 De Page no. 223.
729. CC art. 911 par. 1 (2007); Forgeard et al. (2007) no. 257 at 132 note 7.
730 8 De Page no. 225; 5 Planiol and Ripert no. 176.
731. 5 Planiol and Ripert no. 174 bis.
732. Id. no. 175. See supra no. 449.

relatives of those who lack the capacity to receive are intended for the incompetents. All such gifts are therefore void (CC art. 911 par. 2). The relationships specified in the code include the incompetent's spouse, father, and mother, together with children and other descendants. Because capacity limitations are strictly construed, gifts to others, such as to the incompetent's fiancé or a cohabiting partner, are not subject to the presumptions, though such gifts would be void if an interposition were proven.[733] The Belgian Civil Code was amended in 1998 to include the incompetent's cohabitant within the irrebuttable presumption.[734]

Though a fraudulent interposition generally voids any gift, regardless of the type of incapacity involved, the presumptions are more narrowly applied. They concern only the lack of the capacity to receive that is due to a protected relationship (*incapacité relative de recevoir à titre gratuit*).[735] Recent legislation regarding protected relationships has incorporated similar presumptions.[736] Gifts that seek to evade other types of incapacity—such as that of unemancipated minors—are not subject to the presumptions.[737] Until 2007 the presumptions were deemed to be irrebuttable, as they remain in Belgium. French law now admits proof that the gift was not designed to circumvent the prohibitions.[738]

ii. Between Spouses

636. *Special presumptions.* Until 2002 a special set of interposition presumptions applied to gifts between spouses.[739] First, gifts given by one spouse to one or more of the children born to the other spouse during a previous marriage were presumed to be gifts to the other spouse and therefore void. The same presumption applied to gifts one spouse gave to a relative of the other spouse (such as the other spouse's parent) of whom the other spouse was the presumptive heir at the moment of the gift, even if that other spouse did not survive the donee. The scholars agreed that, without these presumptions, the revocability of gifts between spouses could easily have been circumvented. Though, in principle, presumptions relating to fraud are restrictively applied, the case law extended these presumptions to include gifts made to the other spouse's adopted children and to children born out of wedlock.[740]

---

733. Flour and Souleau no. 324. For the validity of gifts between cohabitants, see supra nos. 558–568.

734. Belgian CC art. 911 par. 2, amended by Law of 23 Nov. 1998 art. 3.

735. 5 Planiol and Ripert no. 256.

736. CC art. 1125-1 par. 2; C Family and Soc. Assist. art. 209 bis par. 2 (1977) (referencing French CC art. 911), replaced by C Soc. Action and the Family art. L331-4 (2000).

737. Flour and Souleau no. 326.

738. CC art. 911 par. 2 (2007); Forgeard et al. 2007 no. 257 at 132.

739. CC former art. 1100.

740. Flour and Souleau no. 469.

637. *Radical extension of incapacity.* Because the presumptions were irrebuttable, they effectively imposed an incapacity to receive on the relatives of those who lacked the capacity to receive the type of gift involved. "[W]henever an individual is subject to an incapacity to receive, that person's parents, descendants, and spouse suffer the consequences."[741] A father who was not permitted to make a gift to the child born of his adulterous relationship could also not make a gift to the child's mother. Moreover, though the gift given to the child would only have been void to the extent it exceeded the child's successoral share, gifts to one of the intermediaries enumerated in the code were completely void.

Some scholars argued that the effect was excessive. Others claimed that, without the presumptions, the incapacities would be easily circumvented. These authors believed that the relatives enumerated in the code have such affection for the incompetent that they would often facilitate the deception. More broadly speaking, gifts to any of the listed relatives would often benefit the incompetent in some way.[742]

638. *Abrogation.* French law abrogated these presumptions in 2002.[743] Effective in 2005, gifts between spouses by interposition are no longer void in France.[744] The prohibition against gifts between spouses by interposition continues to apply under the Belgian Civil Code.

b. Other Romanic Systems

639. *Italy.* In Italian law, interposition has generally been discussed in the context of the incapacities to receive by will.[745] In the context of gift law, the concept is applied to the guardian's incapacity to receive gifts from the ward.[746] Italian law recognizes two varieties of interposition—fictitious and real—and both are prohibited when used by the ward to make a gift to the guardian.[747] Fictitious interposition (*interposizione fittizia*), in which a transaction is simulated with one party (*persona interposta*) while, with the agreement of all parties, it is concluded with a person not mentioned (*interponente*), is of little relevance in the gift context. If the simulation is discovered, the interposition disappears, and the transaction is evaluated with regard to the actual donee. If the donee lacks the capacity to receive, the transaction would be void.

---

741. Id. no. 325.
742. 8 De Page no. 227.
743. Law of 4 Mar. 2002 art. 10.
744. Law of 26 May 2004 art. 23 par. 1 no. 2, abrogating CC art. 1099 par. 2.
745. CC art. 599 par. 1. The prohibition of interposition in testamentary bequests to children born out of wedlock was declared unconstitutional. C. Cost. 28 Dec. 1970 no. 205, *Foro it.* 1971 I 1.
746. CC arts. 779 par. 2, 599 par. 2. See supra no. 585.
747. Torrente (2006) 473; Biondi no. 100.

Real interposition (*interposizione reale*) involves the combination of two or more actual transactions in which the donor actually transfers to a donee, who, with the understanding of those involved, agrees to convey to a third party.[748] Outside the context of guardian and ward, the transaction is generally valid if concluded in the form required of gifts, usually the *atto pubblico*,[749] though it is void if the interposition is intended to violate public policy, regardless of the identity of the intermediary. Irrevocable presumptions of interposition apply when a ward makes gifts to the guardian's parents, descendants, and spouse, even if they are named jointly as donees (CC art. 599 par. 2).

Some Italian scholars argue that the legal presumption is too onerous. As in French law, it renders any of the guardian's relatives incompetent to receive a gift from the ward during the proscribed period, even if the guardian is related to the ward and many of the ward's family members thereby suffer the incapacity.[750] These authors suggest that a rebuttable presumption would suffice.

640. *Spain.* In Spanish law, any gift made to a person who lacks the capacity to receive it is void, whether made by disguise or by interposition (CC art. 628).

C. COMPARATIVE NOTES

641. *Purpose and vision.* The intended purpose of the gift law capacity restrictions is to protect the weak, the subordinate, and the dependent. The capacity rules are worth studying for an additional reason as well. They express some discomfort with the Maussian obligations—the customary practice of giving, receiving, and reciprocating.

1. Protective Policies

642. *Varying goals.* Capacity restrictions are of different types. Some incapacities protect those, such as minors and an adult incompetents, who are unable to make an informed decision. Other incapacities protect the weaker party in certain special relationships. They prevent one spouse from taking advantage of the other, a guardian from extracting a gift, a doctor from requesting additional compensation. The capacity restrictions and authorization requirements that some gift laws long applied to associations were justified by the desire to limit mortmain and prevent the accumulation of power.

---

748. Real interposition resembles the gift coupled with an obligation in French law. Supra no. 449.

749. Cass. 14 Mar. 2006 no. 5457, *Mass. Foro it.* 2006, 455; Cass. 15 Jan. 2003 no. 502, *Mass. Foro it.* 2003, 58. For gift formalities in Italian law, see infra nos. 754–768.

750. Biondi no. 101.

2. The Maussian Obligations

643. *Compassion.* Capacity restrictions within protected relationships also suggest the continued vitality of the Maussian obligations. The protected relationships generally have a similar structure. One of the parties, the party the law considers to be stronger or dominant, provides a service to the other. The service is often rendered with compassion, at times with a devotion that rises to affection and even love. The services are fashioned to the individual context. The doctor, the guardian, the minister, or, in the traditional marriage, the wife make a considerable emotional investment and a particularly meaningful contribution to the life of the recipient of the services, the party the law considers weak or subordinate. The excess above what is required by contract or custom yields a gratuitous benefit. It more closely resembles a gift than a market transaction. Mauss taught that gratuitous benefits must be reciprocated.

644. *Duty to reciprocate.* Doctors, guardians, and ministers are paid for their services. The traditional spouse is also taken care of. Yet the service provider is not compensated for the excess. The fee or family support does not satisfy the obligation to reciprocate. This was especially true in the traditional marriage. The wife spent much of her day serving her husband but, in contrast to professionals, she was not paid for her commitment. The need to reciprocate is felt strongly in all these relationships. The beneficiaries experience an overwhelming need to restore the balance. Yet the services cannot be repaid in kind. The patient has no way to heal the physician. Gratitude is usually expressed in the form of a gift.

645. *The law's response.* Some legal systems evaluate these gifts from the standpoint of their perceived protective mission. In their attempt to prevent the exercise of undue influence, they restrict or prohibit many of these gifts. The recipients nonetheless feel compelled to reciprocate. Extreme measures are then necessary. The rules prohibiting interposition provide a clear example. They testify to the ingenuity that donors employ to circumvent the capacity restrictions. The legal presumption that close relatives are willing to assist in evading the law speaks powerfully to the socially recognized duty to reciprocate. Little in the ethnographic literature testifies as eloquently to the power of the Maussian obligations as do the exorbitant restrictions some legal systems have imposed on the gift capacity of those involved in protected relationships.

5. THE GIFT PROMISE

A. INTRODUCTION

646. *Nudum pactum.* In classical Roman law, an informal promise without a cause (*nudum pactum*), was generally not enforced, except by way of defense.[1] Because the Roman *stipulatio* did not require proof of a counterperformance, it was available as a form for making gratuitous promises.[2] In 530 Justinian made informal gift promises binding.[3] His purpose was apparently to favor pious giving.[4] By then the formerly rigorous stipulatio had become little more than an informal agreement *inter praesentes.*[5] Nonetheless, Gino Gorla doubted whether a system as formalistic as Roman gift law ever actually enforced informal gift promises without additional proof.[6]

647. *Canon law.* Though the work of Aquinas is not entirely consistent on the question, some passages in the *Summa* suggest that a broken promise amounts to a lie.[7] Some medieval jurists therefore contended that informal gratuitous promises should be enforced.[8] Others argued that enforcement should not

---

1. "But when no cause exists, no obligation is incurred by the agreement. Therefore, a naked agreement (*nuda pactio*) gives rise not to an obligation but to a defense (*exceptionem*)." D. 2, 14, 7, 4 (Ulpian). See Lévy 93–94.

2. The *stipulatio* was used as a formal means of creating a binding promise. It consisted in an exchange of questions and answers using formal words: "Do you promise (*spondesne*)?" "I promise (*spondeo*)." Nicholas 159–160, 193. In the classical period, different questions could be posed. There were several requirements: the parties had to be present throughout; the question and answer were to be made orally; the answer had to correspond exactly to the question and follow it immediately. No witnesses were needed. See Zimmermann 480–481; Lévy 121–122, 130–132.

3. Zimmermann 495.

4. C. 8, 53, 35, 5 *in fine.*

5. Lévy 119–120.

6. 1 Gorla 21.

7. "If he does not do what he promises, then it would appear that, when he changes his mind, he acts in bad faith." Aquinas, *Summa Theologiae* 2a-2ae quest. 110 *de mendacio* art. 3 arg. 5.

8. "An action may be based on a naked pact." ([E]*x pacto nudo datur actio.*) Henricus de Segusio, *De pactis* ch. 1 no. 1 at 177. For the enforceability of gift promises in canon law and the law of early modern Europe, see Gordley (1997) sec. 28; Dawson (1980) 27.

be automatic.[9] Aquinas also recognized that ecclesiastic doctrine on the question need not coincide with temporal law.[10] Nonetheless, the canonist critique of Roman formalism initiated a debate about the enforcement of gift promises, and particularly whether the law should prefer caution or party autonomy. The controversy continues into contemporary law.

1. Variety of Positions

648. *Within families.* Legal systems offer varying answers to the question of whether gift promises should be judicially enforced. The two principal legal families—the civil law and the common law— wrestle with different concerns, yet within each family the solutions diverge, particularly the extent to which gift promises are actually enforced. Moreover, because the case holdings are deeply embedded in the context of the justifications, distinctions based on the practical results are more misleading than meaningful. Civilian systems choose either to respect party autonomy or to maintain doctrinal consistency. In contrast, the common law debates whether to respect form or protect detrimental reliance.

649. *No common vocabulary.* Furthermore, even when translation difficulties are put to one side, there is no common conceptual framework. The recommended approach in such cases is to abstract from the doctrinal differences and focus on practical events in the real world. In this matter, however, even that suggestion proves unhelpful. For example, if gifts were structured like synallagmatic contracts, the gift promise might be considered an offer. When accepted by the donee, it would form a contract and create an obligation requiring the donor to perform. Transfer of title and possession would constitute performance of the contract.

Yet that is not how it works in any system. Concepts from the law of onerous contracts receive new meanings in the field of gratuitous transactions. The civil law characterizes the gift as a contract. That contract is formed not when the donee accepts a *gift promise*, but rather when the donee accepts the *gift*. In Romanic jurisdictions, this occurs by acceptance of the formal gift act, often in the presence of a notary. That act is the gift—both the gift contract and, at the

---

9. See Gordley (1995) 553. The original force of the medieval maxim *Donner et retenir ne vaut* suggests that gift promises were not binding until performance. Lévy 120. The evolution of the meaning of the maxim is discussed below. See infra nos. 1075–1080.

10. But human legal institutions do not enforce a simple promise (*promissio simplex*) made between individuals, which is a position that seems to be based on the mutability of human will .... According to the demands of honesty, however, everyone is bound by a promise made to another as an obligation of natural law. But to be bound by a civil obligation to someone on the basis of a promise, other conditions must be met.

Aquinas, *Summa Theologiae* 2a-2ae quest. 88 art. 3 arg. 1 ad 1.

same time, its performance. With the exception of the manual gift of movables, the transfer of possession is neither required nor effective in making a gift.[11] Transfer of possession assures only that the property reaches the hands of its rightful owner. The making of a gift in the Romanic systems is not, and conceptually cannot be, the performance of a preexisting obligation created by the gift promise. Otherwise, the essential gratuitousness of the gift would be lost.

2. Irreconcilable Differences

650. *Misunderstanding.* Common lawyers have considerable difficulty grasping the civilian conceptual structure and, in particular, just what it is that civilians mean when they say that a gift is a contract. Mel Eisenberg, one of the common law's most distinguished contracts scholars, examined the civilian gift act and saw in it not the performance of a contract but rather a binding gift promise.[12] From the perspective of French law, this view is mistaken. As discussed below, gift promises are generally not enforceable in French law. Yet from the point of view of an American jurist, Eisenberg's description captures the essence of the event. The formal gift act involves no quid pro quo. Thus, for a common lawyer, its binding character is due entirely to its form. When the gift act is completed, the donor does not hand anything over to the donee.[13] A common lawyer might well understand the meaning of the formal act to be the creation of the obligation to transfer possession. From the perspective of the common law, delivery, the actual transfer of possession, is the gift. Delivery might mean either actual delivery or some form of constructive delivery, the delivery of something, such as a deed, that represents the object. The common-law view since Glanvill has been that a purported gift, without delivery, remains a naked promise.[14] An American jurist thus understands the notarial act as the form that makes the gift

---

11. "The gift duly accepted is perfected by the simple consent of the parties; and title to the gifted objects is transferred to the donee without any need for delivery (*tradition*)." French CC art. 938.

12. "Under French law a donative promise is normally enforceable to its full extent only if it is executed in writing before two notaries, or a notary and two witnesses, and formally accepted by the promisee, or is cast in the form known as disguised donation." Eisenberg (1979) 12. Kull and Shavell are of the same view. See Kull 58 note 64; Shavell 420.

13. The confusion is exacerbated by the fact that, in French law, title, even to real property, passes upon conclusion of the contract (*solo consensu*). No external act or formality is required. See French CC art. 938. "The obligation to deliver the property is perfected by the simple consent of the contracting parties." CC art. 1138 par. 1.

14. If seisin follows the gift, the land will remain forever with the donee and his heirs, if it was given to them heritably; however, if no seisin follows such a gift, then after the donor's death nothing can be claimed in reliance on such a gift against the will of the heir, because, according to the interpretation customary in the realm, it is deemed to be a naked promise (*nuda promissio*) rather than a true gift. Glanvill bk. 7 sec. 1 at 69–70.

promise binding. The inevitable conclusion, and the difficulty of comparative law, is that jurists are often confined to the Kuhnian paradigm of their own systems. The concepts of any one system are not translatable into those of another.

3. Enforceable Gift Promises

651. *Two issues.* In those civilian systems that enforce gift promises, such as German law, the promise fulfills a different function. It serves as a mechanism for generating the obligation to enter into the gift contract. In those jurisdictions that permit such promises to become binding, two questions arise. The first is the question of form. The second is whether the promise must be accepted before it can become binding.

652. *Formalities.* Some factor beyond the promise itself, usually a specified form, must accompany a gift promise to render it enforceable. German law, which requires no special formality for a valid gift, specifies a form for the gift promise. Even civilian jurisdictions that generally do not enforce gift promises permit a donor to become bound to an obligation similar to a gift promise if gift formalities are employed. In the common law, gift promises are valid in an array of circumstances involving either a formality or detrimental reliance.

653. *Acceptance.* The civil and common laws disagree about the importance of acceptance. In the civil law, contractual obligations are generally enforceable only when a contract has been formed, and formation generally requires mutual assent. Unilateral declarations are rarely accorded binding force without acceptance.[15] Those civilian jurisdictions that give legal effect to a gift promise or a similar institution all require acceptance. In those cases in which the common law enforces a promise without consideration, enforcement is not contingent on the donee's acceptance. The English deed and the American doctrine of promissory estoppel are typical examples.[16]

4. Terminology

654. *No existing concept.* It might be expected that at least one legal system would have produced a legal concept to designate the contract formed by the acceptance of a gift promise. Unfortunately none exists, at least none in general use. To solve the problem, Kollhosser, a German author, has created his own vocabulary.

> [This provision] assumes the existence of a unilaterally obligatory contract (*einseitig verpflichtenden Vertrag*), which arises when the donee accepts the

---

15. An example of a binding unilateral declaration is the offer of a reward (*Auslobung*) in German law. CC § 657.

16. Infra nos. 689, 707.

donor's gift promise (=offer). Often the entire gift contract is called a "gift promise." In order to avoid misunderstanding, it is useful ... to call the variety of gift contract that is immediately performed ... a "manual gift" (*Handschenkung*) and the gift contract that is based on the gift promise and that is yet to be performed ... a "promissory gift" (*Versprechensschenkung*).[17]

Because there is no precedent for any of these terms in English, something more colloquial might be appropriate. The agreement that is produced by the acceptance of the gift promise is called here a "gift promise contract."

5. Why Systems Differ

655. *Promoting human freedom.* The civil and the common laws sometimes discuss the question of the enforceable gift promise as an aspect of the larger topic of the law's role in promoting human freedom. When they differ, it is often about how freedom is best advanced.

656. *Civilian systems.* Some civilian scholars argue that enforcing gift promises provides social and moral benefits. To enforce a promise means to acknowledge its obligational force, which respects *pacta sunt servanda*, a fundamental principle of social relations.[18] Moreover, the enforcement of gift promises empowers citizens to create binding obligations, which increases their freedom and accords them the respect they deserve as the authors of the rules that bind them. On this basis, Gerhard Kegel suggested that the scope of gift law should be narrowed to permit greater enforceability of gift promises. The law of obligations, he noted, properly tends to the relaxation of required forms.[19]

Yet civilian jurists must carefully articulate these benefits with the civil law's other principles and policies. Gorla argued that respect for the donor's will is never the issue, since the enforceability question arises only when the donor has had a change of heart. Whenever a gift promise is enforced, unless the donor has died or become incompetent, it is over the donor's objection.[20] The real question is whether a court should enforce what the donor has willed in the past. At a minimum, it would seem, the law should ensure that the donor is sufficiently warned. For this reason, gift promises are rarely enforced without a formality that provides an opportunity for reflection and counsel. Moreover, because no quid pro quo is involved, proof is a greater concern than it is in bargain transactions. Civilian systems that enforce gift promises generally do so only based on solid evidence, which is another reason to require a formality.

---

17. MünchKomm-BGB (-Kollhosser) § 518 no. 2.
18. For a history of the maxim, see Hyland (1994).
19. Gerhard Kegel, note to BGH 3 Apr. 1952, JZ 1952, 657. See also Lorenz 547.
20. 1 Gorla 79–80.

657. *Common law.* According to the Holmesian vision, it is precisely because gift promises are morally binding that the law should not enforce them. When the law enforces a moral obligation, the particularly moral aspect of the obligation vanishes.[21] Enforcing gift promises would suppress the affective relationship at its root and highlight instead the commodity nature of the gift.[22] In addition, common law courts have always been jealous of their jurisdiction. Since the days of the writ system, they have been reluctant to intervene in daily affairs unless the law has felt itself summoned. The central task in most common law cases is not to determine what is just but is rather to decide the proper role of the law in the situation. The common law has usually decided that the harm caused by the breach of a gratuitous promise is not fundamental enough to warrant its involvement.[23] As in the civil law, however, the principle requires some modification as it encounters practical realities. There are moments when the refusal to enforce a gift promise would provoke as serious an injustice as might a breach of contract. When the common law intervenes, it does so not so much to enforce the promise as to prevent injustice.[24]

Despite the common-law principle that gift promises are not enforceable at law, a number of contemporary common-law scholars have suggested that gift promises should be enforced, even without proof of reliance. Baron argues that the common law's refusal to enforce gift promises marginalizes the institution of gift giving and makes it appear that gift promises are uncommon, unimportant, and unworthy. As long as only promises related to market transactions are

---

21. Eisenberg (1997) 847–852.

22. Id. 848.

23. When one receives a naked promise, and such promise is broken, he is no worse off than he was. He gave nothing for it, he has lost nothing by it, and on its breach he has suffered no damage cognizable by courts. No benefit accrued to him who made the promise, nor did any injury flow to him who received it. Such promises are not made within the scope of transactions intended to confer rights enforceable at law. They are lightly made, dictated by generosity, curtesy, or impulse, often by ruinous prodigality. To enforce them by a judgment in favor of those who gave nothing therefor would often bring such imperfect obligations into competition with the absolute duties to wife and children, or into competition with debts for property actually received, and make the law an instrument by which a man could be forced to be generous before he was just.
Davis & Co. v. Morgan, 43 S.E. 732, 733 (Ga. 1903).

24. Classical doctrine suggested that, even in the absence of consideration, courts should enforce some promises based on the promisee's detrimental reliance. Several authors have suggested that, in these *reliance cases*, the courts are more concerned about the seriousness of the promisor's commitment than they are about the harm that would result to the promisee absent enforcement. For a survey of the discussion, see Feinman; see also Gordley (1995) 579–582.

enforced, commodities will continue to appear superior to family bonds, friend-ship, and other forms of personal satisfaction.[25] From a different perspective, Richard Posner has argued that binding the donor to the gift promise would increase the present value of the promise and therefore the utility of both donor and donee.[26]

6. Constructions

658. *Conceptually unsatisfying.* Systems that enforce gift promises use a variety of legal constructions. None of them is entirely satisfying. American courts some-times manufacture consideration and turn the promise into an enforceable bar-gain. Equity enforces promises when they have been relied on, but only unpredictably. English law relies on the inconsequential formality of the seal and the subterfuge of nominal consideration. Some Romanic systems refuse to enforce gift promises but validate obligational gifts, which are nearly identical. German law respects only the formality of the notarial act, which tends to defeat some gift promises that were actually intended and made.[27]

As Gino Gorla noted, even when gift promises are enforced, the fundamental differences between the common and civil law systems remain. In the civil law, they are enforced as gifts, following the standard gift law regime, including capacity restrictions and the possibilities of collation and revocation. In the common law, in contrast, gift promises, when enforced, are enforced as con-tracts and are subjected to the same regime as onerous contracts.[28]

At the same time, as Gorla has also made clear, the two systems do not, in practice, differ dramatically.[29] As a general matter, no system enforces informal gift promises without more. In each system, gift promises are (once again, as a practical matter) enforced when supported either by a form demonstrating the intent to be bound, whether a notarial act or consideration, or what Gorla calls sufficient cause, namely a very good reason, whether a vague sense of a quid pro

---

25. Baron 188–189, 197.
26. Posner (1977) 411–413.
27. The classification problem is, however, ordinarily approached indirectly through a doctrinal analysis based in the common law on consideration and in French and German law on the concept of gift (*donation, Schenkung*). Consequently, the ulti-mate policy issue is not directly faced. At the same time, a tendency exists to use artificial reasoning, with consequent intellectual discomfort, in applying doctrinal propositions to these situations. The result, judging from the experience of the French, German, and common law, is frequently a malaise often combined with unpredictability.
Von Mehren 1033 (referring to promises in the context of natural obligations).
28. 1 Gorla 465 and note 3.
29. Id. 463.

quo, detrimental reliance, or a deeply felt family or social obligation. The irresistible temptation to construct the two systems as polar opposites is therefore misleading.[30] It is usually not the case that an embarrassing absence in one system is met by a fruitful plenitude in the next. No system is the other's Other.

659. *Questions examined.* The enforcement of the gift promise raises three questions: the circumstances that render a gift promise enforceable, the consequences and effects of an enforceable promise, and, finally, the defenses available to the promisor.

B. CIRCUMSTANCES PERMITTING ENFORCEMENT

660. *Limited enforcement.* In no legal system examined here are gift promises enforced to the same extent as are promises that are part of a bargain.

1. Germany

661. *Basic rule.* In German law, a promise to make a gift is judicially enforceable if the form requirements have been met and the promise has been accepted (CC § 518 par. 1).[31] The gift promise contract is a unilateral obligational contractual undertaking (*einseitig verpflichtender Schuldvertrag*).[32] The gift lies in the creation of the obligation. The subsequent execution of the gift, though itself the performance of an obligation and therefore not a gift, is nonetheless considered to be gratuitous.[33]

a. Required Form

662. *Notarial act.* Enforceability requires documentation of the promise by a notary (*notarielle Beurkundung*; CC § 518 par. 1). The same form is also required for two related acts, namely a gratuitous unilateral promise to repay a debt and the acknowledgment of a debt.[34] The notarized promise must contain all elements necessary to bind the donor to a gift contract, with the exception of the agreement concerning gratuitousness, which can be proved by parol evidence.[35] Subsidiary duties of the donor or any burdens imposed on the donee must also be mentioned. A modification increasing the donor's duties must also be notarized, while if the donor's obligations are diminished oral modification is sufficient. Notarial form is generally required for all gift promises, including

---

30. Gorla concluded that each system tends to see its desiderata fulfilled in the other. Id. § 37.

31. MünchKomm-BGB (-Kollhosser) § 518 no. 2.

32. Larenz § 47 par. I.

33. Id.; infra no. 715.

34. Infra no. 665.

35. MünchKomm-BGB (-Kollhosser)§ 518 nos. 4–5.

remunerative and customary gifts, regardless of their value.[36] Notarization is required even for those gift promise contracts in which the parties simulate a quid pro quo, as when the donor signs a sham IOU or falsely states in a sales receipt that the price has been paid.[37] The granting of free participation in an association (*Gesellschaft bürgerlichen Rechts*), or a participation at the cost of other members, may in some cases be considered a gift promise subject to form requirements.[38]

663. *Acceptance.* A gift promise is not binding in German law until it is accepted. Because the form requirement is designed to protect the donor, no special formalities are required for acceptance, though other form requirements, such as those affecting transfers of real property, may apply.[39]

b. Particular Situations

664. *Third-party beneficiary contracts.* Gifts made in the context of third-party beneficiary contracts are generally exceptions to the notarization requirement.[40] For example, once an insurance policy is concluded, the necessary gift contract between donor and beneficiary does not require notarial form. The issuance of the policy satisfies the donor's duties because a claim immediately arises in the beneficiary.[41] If the gift contract is concluded first, the issuance of the policy cures any absence of notarial form (CC § 518 par. 2). Some third-party beneficiary contracts provide that the property will be transferred at the donor's death, as when a bank agrees to transfer the funds in the donor's account to the donee when the donor dies. Both the courts and a majority of the authors agree that generally no form is needed between donor and donee.[42]

665. *Unilateral promises and acknowledgment of a debt.* German gift law imposes the gift promise form requirements on two types of promise to perform a unilateral act when they are made gratuitously—the unilateral promise to pay (*Schuldversprechen*) and the acknowledgment of a debt (*Schuldanerkenntnis*).[43] The two institutions are distinguished by the wording—as examples, "I promise to pay" in the first case, "IOU" in the second—and are governed by separate code provisions (CC § 780, 781). Their legal consequences are essentially the same.[44]

---

36. Staudinger (-Wimmer-Leonhardt) § 518 no. 7.
37. Heck § 93 par. 2 lit. e.
38. MünchKomm-BGB (-Ulmer) § 705 nos. 42–48.
39. Staudinger (-Wimmer-Leonhardt) § 518 no. 5.
40. MünchKomm-BGB (-Kollhosser) § 518 nos. 6–7; Staudinger (-Wimmer-Leonhardt) § 518 no. 10.
41. As noted above, the object of the gift promise is the creation of an obligation, in this case the beneficiary's action against the promisor. Supra no. 661.
42. BGH 9 Nov. 1966, NJW 1967, 101 at 102. See supra no. 306.
43. CC § 518 par. 1 sent. 2.
44. Palandt (-Sprau) § 780 no. 1.

Because the two institutions may be used to make a a gift promise, the Civil Code provides that, when made gratuitously, they must be documented by a notary. The justification for requiring the involvement of a notary is as follows. As discussed below, the execution of a gift promise cures some defects in notarial form.[45] For example, if a donor were to promise, without complying with the required formalities, to acknowledge a debt, the subsequent acknowledgment might be assumed to constitute execution of the promise and thereby cure the form defect.[46] Because acknowledgments of this type are only valid if in writing, the execution would provide some protection to the donor. Yet the donor would not have received cautionary advice from a notary and would not have made an actual sacrifice sufficient to serve as an equivalent warning.

666. *Negotiable instruments.* As far as negotiable instruments are concerned, gift promise formalities are required only if the donor is intended to pay.[47] When a third party is primarily liable, such as when the donor is payee or endorsee, the paper may be gifted without a notarial act, even if, by the transfer, the donor becomes secondarily liable as endorser. However, if the donor is principally liable, a gratuitous transfer is considered a gift promise and is valid only if made in proper form. Such a gift is not considered complete until the instrument is paid. Thus, both the drawee's gratuitous acceptance of a draft and the gift of a check by the drawer to the payee must be done by notarial act.[48]

As a practical matter, notarization is rarely an issue for a check because payment cures the form defect (CC § 518 par. 2). Moreover, drafts are subject to good faith purchase rules, and thus, in many cases, transfer cures the lack of form.[49]

c. Purpose

667. *Cautionary function.* The principal purpose of the form requirement is to caution the donor against overly hasty commitment.[50] In the typical gift transaction, which is valid only if immediately executed, the donor is aware of the sacrifice involved and is therefore not thought to require this protection. "However, those who promise a gratuitous transfer only for the future may not clearly enough recognize the impending sacrifice and must, according to the view of the legislator, be protected from themselves."[51] The form requirement is also designed to provide proof of the promise and to prevent the evasion of the

---

45. CC § 518 par. 2; infra nos. 711–715.
46. MünchKomm-BGB (-Kollhosser) § 518 no. 8.
47. Id. nos. 10, 29; Staudinger (-Wimmer-Leonhardt) § 518 no. 15.
48. RG 16 June 1909, RGZ 71, 289 at 291.
49. Staudinger (-Wimmer-Leonhardt) § 518 no. 15; MünchKomm-BGB (-Kollhosser) § 518 no. 10.
50. MünchKomm-BGB (-Kollhosser) § 518 no. 1.
51. Id.

formalities required by successions law. However, because these last two goals could equally be met by a simple writing, the cautionary function is presumed to be the primary purpose of notarization.[52]

d. Reliance

668. *Good faith.* Exceptions are occasionally made to the rigorous form requirements based on the doctrine of good faith.[53] Dawson suggested that, when informal gift promises are enforced in German law, it is typically after a finding of justifiable reliance. Some scholars have recommended that the courts apply the doctrine of promissory estoppel even though the code does not mention it and even though the form requirement for gift promises would seem to preclude it.[54] The Roman law maxim *venire contra factum proprium* is thought to provide a civilian basis for the doctrine. Yet the courts have refused to accept the idea. When a contract is unenforceable due to a form defect, German law generally grants reliance damages but not specific performance.[55] Dawson speculated that the doctrine has been rejected because German courts are entrusted with the responsibility of protecting the heirs and therefore may not enforce gift promises as freely as do American courts.[56]

2. Italy

669. *Unenforceable.* A preliminary contract is generally valid in Italian law if it is completed in the form prescribed for the final contract (CC art. 1351). On that basis, a minority of Italian scholars argue that the gift promise contract should be valid, provided that the promise is made and accepted by public act.[57] The majority view, however, is that the promise is not enforceable, even if accepted.[58] If the promise were valid, the gift could be specifically enforced, which would contradict the essential spontaneity of the gift.[59] However, alternative forms are available to achieve the same goal.

---

52. Id.

53. CC § 242; BGH 16 Feb. 1954, BGHZ 12, 286 at 298–304; Dawson (1980) 187–188.

54. Zweigert (1964) 354. See also Grundmann 475-479.

55. BGH 29 Jan. 1965, NJW 1965, 812 (home sale). On the basis of a preliminary contract, the seller constructed a house for the buyer. The buyer paid the price and moved in. Years later, the seller sought to avoid the contract on the grounds that the required formal contract was never concluded. Though the court granted considerable reliance damages on the basis of *culpa in contrahendo*, it rescinded the contract and required the buyer to move out. In the common law, the contract would most likely have been enforced based on part performance or detrimental reliance.

56. Dawson (1980) 190, 228.

57. Biondi no. 318.

58. Torrente (2006) 294. The gift promise is "radically void." Cass. 18 Dec. 1975 no. 4153 (en banc), *Giur. it.* 1976 I 1913 at 1917.

59. Cass. 18 Dec. 1975 no. 4153 (en banc) id.

a. Alternatives

670. *Preliminary contract.* The courts and a majority of the scholars agree that there can be no binding preliminary agreement to make a gift.[60] Such an agreement would be the equivalent of a binding gift promise. The concern is that a binding preliminary contract would eliminate the donor's spontaneity, the animus donandi. For those who support the abstract conception of cause, which holds that gift cause consists merely in the will to enrich the donee without receiving a quid pro quo, spontaneity is not required, and there would be no obstacle to a binding preliminary contract.[61] Other scholars suggest that the preliminary contract should be considered the actual gift, with the subsequent gift act constituting the execution. This view has been criticized on the grounds that it would impose on the donor an obligation to do (*facere*), which cannot be the object of a valid gift.[62]

671. *Gift of an obligation.* The Italian Civil Code specifically provides that a gift may consist in the donor's assumption of an obligation toward the donee (art. 769).[63] Thus, what German and American law considers a gift promise is characterized in Italian law as a gift. "Whoever intends to make a gratuitous promise in favor of another does not use an ordinary contract ... but rather the typical gift contract."[64] Like all gifts, except those of modest value, the gift of an obligation is valid only if done in the form of an *atto pubblico*.[65] In other words, a donor may become bound to a promise to make a gratuitous transfer by completing the same formalities that are generally required for the actual giving of the gift.

672. *Other equivalents.* Moreover, as both Gorla and Torrente have noted, transactions with superior risks escape the formality requirement entirely. "The gift of the obligation to transfer 100,000 [lire] ... must be done by public act, while the promise to loan 100,000,000 lire for five years without interest (which, given a 5 percent interest rate, involves the cumulative loss of 25,000,000 lire, as well as the possibility that the loan may not be repaid) may be made orally (questions of proof aside)."[66]

---

60. Capozzi no. 352.
61. For the abstract conception, see supra no. 277.
62. In Italian law, as noted above, a gift may involve only the creation of an obligation to transfer a property right (*dare*), as opposed to an obligation requiring the performance of an act (*facere*). See supra no. 342.
63. Supra no. 342.
64. Biondi no. 123.
65. For the form requirements in Italian law, see infra nos. 754–760.
66. Torrente (2006) 293. Since all gratuitous promises pose a risk to the donor, whether or not they are technically gift promises, Gorla has suggested that they all should be treated similarly. Either none should be valid without the formality or no formality should be required at all. 1 Gorla 86–87 note 3.

Palazzo has argued that, even if the gift promise is unenforceable, the donor should be liable in damages when the donee, in reliance on the promise, has foregone other advantages.[67] This suggestion resembles the common-law notion of promissory estoppel.[68] The courts have not adopted the suggestion. In one case, the donor promised to gift land and money to a town if the town constructed an agricultural school on the property and named it after the donor's deceased son.[69] After construction began, the donor sued to recover the property based on the absence of the necessary formalities. The court required the town to return the unimproved portion of the property and to pay for the remainder at market value.

Finally, Italian law enforces some promises to perform a natural obligation. Since the satisfaction of a natural obligation is never a gift in Italian law,[70] some promises that in other systems would be considered gift promises are enforced by this means.[71]

b. Justifications

673. *Technical problems.* The literature offers two justifications for the refusal to enforce gift promises. Neither justification is substantive.[72] The justifications are instead based on the technical problems that would arise if the gift promise were enforceable. First, the obligation created by a preliminary contract in Italian law—and that would be the nature of the gift promise contract—is to perform an act (*facere*). The object of a gift, however, can only be the transfer of property (*dare*).[73] Yet even based on the premises of Italian law, it is unclear why the preliminary contract to make a gift should be binding only if it results in a transfer

---

67. Palazzo art. 782 no. 4 at 216.
68. Infra nos. 686, 692, 707–708.
69. Cass. 18 Dec. 1975 no. 4153 (en banc), *Giur. it.* 1976 I 1913; supra nos. 247, 278.
70. Supra no. 282.
71. As Gorla indicated, though a natural obligation is sufficient grounds to allow the *accipiens* to retain payment, it is not always sufficient to allow a court to enforce an informal promise to perform the obligation.

> [T]o see whether a duty is sufficient not only for payment but also for the promise often depends on the *intensity* with which the duty is felt by social conscience and also often on the complex circumstances of each concrete case, in the sense that the judge may not believe that the duty is of sufficient intensity to justify enforcing an informal promise. To search for a precise measure, in a matter that by nature is so elastic and delicate, is to hope for too much.

1 Gorla 133 (emphasis in original).

72. Italian law has no difficulty binding the donor to a gratuitously created obligation. For that purpose, the obligational gift is available.
73. Torrente (2006) 294. See supra no. 342.

obligation. Gratuitous contracts requiring performance of an act are generally enforceable in Italian law.[74]

The principal justification is that, if the gift promise were binding, the execution of the gift would constitute the performance of an obligation. That would mean that the gift would no longer be gratuitous.[75] The problem appears to the Italian scholars to be especially serious because, in the Italian system, the obligation to conclude a contract can be specifically enforced (CC art. 2932). This conceptual problem does not arise with regard to the gift of an obligation (*donazione obligatoria*). In that case, the gift is not the performance of the obligation but rather the donor's assumption of the duty.[76]

3. France and Belgium

674. *No case authority.* In the French tradition, the promise to perform a formal contract (*contrat solennel*), a contract that must be done by notarial act, is generally binding if made in that same form.[77] Because the gift is one of the Civil Code's four solemn contracts, it might be thought that the gift promise contract would be binding if completed using gift formalities. Yet there seem to be no cases in French or Belgian law enforcing a gift promise contract. In Belgian law, the gift promise is void.[78] Because the solemnities required for a valid gift disposition are designed to protect the donor's will, it is thought that the donor should be free to retract until the gift has been completed. In Belgian law, a parent's promise to constitute a dowry is enforceable as an exception.[79]

a. Alternatives

675. *Equivalent results.* Unlike Italian and Spanish law, French law does not recognize the gift of an obligation. Thus, French law does not generally permit donors to bind themselves to make a gratuitous transfer in the future. However, French law can achieve an equivalent result. The acknowledgment of a debt (*reconnaissance de dette*), when no cause is mentioned, is valid as an indirect gift.[80] The typical purpose of the acknowledgment is to restart the running of the limitations period.[81] However, if the debt never existed, the acknowledgment has the effect of a binding promise to pay.[82]

---

74. For example, the *commodatum*. See CC art. 1803.
75. Torrente (2006) 294–295; Cass. 14 July 1950 no. 1916, *Foro it.* 1951 I 316. German law has decided that gratuitousness is not lost in this situation. See infra no. 715.
76. Biondi no. 123.
77. 2 Ghestin no. 325.
78. "It is absolutely certain that the promise to make a gift is *void*." 8 De Page no. 369 (emphasis in original).
79. Id. nos. 369, 403.
80. 5 Planiol and Ripert no. 413.
81. CC art. 2248.
82. 8 De Page no. 413.

Moreover, as noted above, a current gift of a sum of money is valid in French law, even if the transfer is reserved for a later date—even if the later date is the donor's death.[83] The gift is valid if the donor intended to create a present debt in favor of the donee, even though payment could not be required immediately. If the gift object is no longer in the donor's patrimony at death, the donee has a claim for damages. The present gifting of money with the transfer to take place in the future closely resembles the operation of an enforceable gift promise. This gift promise would be valid only if completed by notarial act.

b. Natural Obligations

676. *Promise valid.* Dawson shrewdly observed that the rules relating to natural obligations sometimes permit French law to enforce what in other legal systems are considered gift promises.[84] As discussed above, transfers intended as payment of some natural obligations are considered to lack donative intent. The promise to make such a payment would therefore not qualify as a gift promise.[85]

The current French view is more guarded. As discussed above, contemporary doctrine holds that a transfer intended to fulfill a natural obligation of compensation (as opposed to a natural obligation of justice) is not a gift. An example is the payment of a debt on which the statute of limitations has run.[86] Because the promise to make such a payment lacks donative intent, the promise may be enforced under French contract law, which does not have the consideration doctrine. A promise to make a payment, once accepted, creates a valid contract.[87] In fact, when the promise is to perform a natural obligation, the promise is binding even without acceptance.[88]

c. Comparative Notes

677. *Additional complexity.* The distinction between different types of natural obligations adds a layer of complexity to the comparative law question of whether gift promises are enforceable in French law. In a recent case, a husband used his separate funds to purchase real estate in the name of both spouses. He argued that the purchase constituted a gift and that he could therefore revoke his wife's interest when she proved ungrateful. The Paris Court of Appeal held that, because the wife had contributed to the family's success by abandoning her

---

83. 5 Planiol and Ripert no. 442; supra no. 362.

84. Dawson (1980) 101.

85. Supra nos. 262–266.

86. Id.

87. 7 Planiol and Ripert no. 993. Dean Carbonnier considered the accepted promise to be a bilateral act (because both parties have manifested assent) but a unilateral contract (because only one party assumes obligations). 4 Carbonnier (1980) 40.

88. 7 Planiol and Ripert no. 994.

career and taking care of the home and the children, the purchase in their joint names constituted the performance of a natural obligation. Donative intent was therefore lacking.[89] It would seem, therefore, that, in the same circumstances, a husband's promise to title the property in both names, once accepted, would also be enforceable, even though it would resemble a gift promise.

In a similar vein, the French courts hold that transfers for remuneration of services previously rendered, if not disproportionate in amount, are not subject to the form requirements because they lack donative intent.[90] Once again, the promise to make such transfers should therefore be enforceable under general contracts principles.

It should be emphasized that, though methods are available in French law to create the equivalent of an enforceable gift promise, neither the courts nor the scholars discuss these institutions in these terms.[91]

4. Spain

678. *No doctrinal difficulty.* In Spanish law, the gift is a solemn contract. A donor who informally promises to make a gift is not obligated to make the transfer.[92] In fact, the promise is void.[93] Nonetheless, gift promises can be enforceable. When a gift promise is made and accepted, the resulting contract is considered the gift of an obligation, with the formalities and effects governed by the law of gifts.[94] The Spanish Civil Code recognizes contracts in which only one of the parties undertakes an obligation (CC art. 1254). It also recognizes generosity as a sufficient cause (CC art. 1274). Freedom of contract would therefore permit the gift promise contract, and the Spanish authors see no reason for the law to prohibit it.[95] The form requirements are those for an obligational gift.[96] One court has enforced a signed gratuitous promise, made and accepted by simple writings, to pay a large sum of money in the future.[97]

---

89. Paris 20 Jan. 1998, D. 1998, 309 note Ibrahim Najjar. The court purported to apply Lebanese law, but, as pointed out in the note, the decision was based on French legal principles.

90. Req. 12 Mar. 1918, S. 1921 I 70; Malaurie and Aynès no. 358.

91. Dawson nonetheless concluded that French law enforces gift promises. "There have been statements made in English that countries governed by 'the civil law' will freely enforce all promises, including promises of gift. For France such a statement has become almost true." Dawson (1980) 226. A review of the case law and the scholarly discussion, however, suggests that Dawson's claim was made principally for effect.

92. Infra nos. 844–853.

93. Paz-Ares Rodríguez (-Albaladejo García) arts. 632–633 no. I.

94. Diez-Picazo and Gullón 337; Paz-Ares Rodríguez (-Albaladejo García) art. 618 no. III.

95. Paz-Ares Rodríguez (-Albaladejo García) id.; Spanish CC art. 1255.

96. Infra no. 850.

97. STS Civ. 6 Apr. 1979, RJ 1273.

5. The Common Law

679. *Theoretically unenforceable.* In common-law jurisdictions, gift promises are not enforceable at law. Bracton made clear that no action could arise from what he called a nude promise (*ex nuda promissione*).[98] As Blackstone wrote, "A consideration of some sort or other is so absolutely necessary to the forming of a contract, that a *nudum pactum*, or agreement to do or pay anything on one side, without any compensation on the other, is totally void in law; and a man cannot be compelled to perform it."[99]

Nonetheless, every common-law jurisdiction enforces promises that, in other jurisdictions, would be considered gift promises. Some of these promises are enforced under statutory or equitable exceptions to the consideration doctrine. In other cases, the courts discover consideration, and thus a synallagma, in transactions that civilians would characterize as conditional gifts. This is a much vexed topic. The law in this field has resisted systematization, perhaps to ensure that the courts have the flexibility necessary to do justice among the parties. Only the general lines of the discussion can be summarized here.

a. India

680. *Consideration generally required.* Under Indian contract law, an agreement made without consideration is generally void.[100] The oft-stated justification for enforcing only those promises supported by consideration is that gratuitous promises are often made without due deliberation. Nonetheless, the Indian Contract Act codifies a number of exceptions.[101]

i. Exceptions

681. *Natural love and affection.* First, a promise unsupported by consideration is valid if it is based on love and affection between parties standing in near relation to one another. Such promises must be expressed in writing and registered under the law regarding the registration of documents.[102] For these purposes, the law does not insist on a blood relationship. A near relation includes spouses, siblings, parents, and children, as well as the relation between Mohammedans and their in-laws. Whether the parties are near relations is a question of fact.[103] Gift promises have been held to be unenforceable when the documents reveal the lack of love and affection, such as when a husband promises a gift to his wife on the condition that she not communicate with or bother him.[104]

---

98. 2 Bracton 64.
99. 2 Blackstone 445.
100. Indian Contract Act § 25.
101. Id.
102. Id. § 25 par. 1.
103. Sanjiva Row § 25 no. 8.
104. *Mr I v. Mr G*, AIR (1926) Nagpur 501, 503, 98 IC 217 (HC).

682. *Remuneration.* Second, a promise without consideration is binding if made, in whole or in part, to compensate the donee for a service voluntarily performed or for having performed the donor's duty.[105] Two issues arise. First, some scholars argue that the service is voluntarily performed only if it is done without the donor's request, and perhaps even without the donor's knowledge. The case law, however, is to the contrary. In one case, the donee performed a *loilena* ceremony for the donor in exchange for a promise of compensation that may have been too uncertain to enforce. The court validated a more specific subsequent promise despite the fact that the donor had requested the donee's performance.[106] Second, some courts enforce an adult's promise to compensate services rendered when the donor was a minor.[107] Others do not.[108]

683. *Debt on which the statute has run.* Third, a promise to pay a debt barred by the statute of limitations is binding if made in writing and signed by the person to be charged or by that person's agent.[109] The promise is enforceable even if the promisor was not aware that the debt was barred.[110] The promisor need not be the obligor. Thus, the promise to pay the time-barred debt of a third party is enforceable. Because the promise must also be express, the promise to pay that common-law jurisdictions generally imply from the acknowledgment of a debt is not enforceable in Indian law without consideration.

684. *Inadequate consideration.* Finally, a promise freely given is not void merely because the consideration is inadequate, though inadequacy is relevant in determining whether consent was free. If A promises to sell a horse worth Rs. 1,000 for a price of Rs. 10, the promise, if freely given, is binding if accepted, despite the inadequacy of the consideration.[111] In some civilian systems, such a promise would be considered a promise to make a disguised gift.

685. *Debt discharged in bankruptcy.* Indian law has rejected an exception available in American law, according to which the promise to pay a debt discharged in bankruptcy is valid.[112]

---

105. Indian Contract Act § 25 par. 2.

106. *Nanhi Saheba v. Deputy Commissioner* (1950) All LJ 168 (HC); Sanjiva Row § 25 no. 9.

107. *Vannathi Valappil Janaki and Others v. Puthiya Purayil Paru and Others,* 2004 AIR 1257 (SC).

108. See 1 Ramachandran § 25 no. 4.

109. Indian Contract Law § 25 par. 3.

110. Sanjiva Row § 25 no. 10.

111. Indian Contract Act § 25 expl. 2 and illus. f.

112. *Naoraji v. Kazi Sidick,* ILR 20 Bombay 636, 642 (1896). For American law, see Restatement (Second) of Contracts § 83.

ii. Promissory Estoppel

686. *Discussion.* Some Indian scholars suggest that a gratuitous promise may be enforced on the basis of promissory estoppel.[113] Other authors argue that estoppel should be used only as a defense. They suggest that the doctrine is relevant when a promisor, without consideration, has promised to abandon rights under an existing contract.[114] Some Indian courts have enforced charitable subscriptions on the basis of promissory estoppel. "[S]uch promises become enforceable as soon as any definite step is taken in furtherance of the object and on the faith of the promise."[115] This use of reliance as a substitute for consideration is based on American law.[116]

iii. Promises under Seal

687. *Rejected.* In England, as discussed just below, consideration is unnecessary for a promise made under seal. The seal is said to import consideration. Indian law has not adopted this rule.

b. England

688. *Incomplete gift.* In English law, a gift promise is one variety of *incomplete gift.* It can be revoked at any time. "Where a gift rests merely in promise, whether written or verbal, or in unfulfilled intention, it is incomplete and imperfect, and the court will not compel the intending donor, or those claiming under him, to complete and perfect it."[117] It is not legally improper for donors to change their minds before the gift is complete. The purpose of the rule is to guarantee a *locus poenitentiae.*

i. Deed

689. *Writing under seal.* In medieval England, at a time of widespread illiteracy, the seal took the place of the signature as a means of authenticating a writing.[118]

---

113. Sanjiva Row § 25 no. 3 lit. a.

114. 1 Patra 131 (1966).

115. *Nair Service Society v. Kunjukrishna Pillai,* AIR 1964 Kerala 265 (HC) (relying on *Allegheny College v. Nat'l Chatauqua County Bank,* 159 N.E. 173 (N.Y. 1927) (Cardozo, J.)); see also Nair 65–66.

116. Restatement (Second) of Contracts § 90 par. 2; infra no. 708. Charitable subscriptions are enforced today in many American jurisdictions even without proof of reliance.

117. 20 Halsbury part 1 sub Gifts no. 67.

118. "The seal, a gentleman's privilege in France, soon fell into decadence, while in England, due to an historical process proper to the English spirit, which tends to imitate the gentleman and to consider everyone a gentleman, the seal spread from the nobility to the common people and is still valid today." 1 Gorla 445.

For the difference between a sealed writing in the common law and the civilian form requirements, see 1 Gorla § 34, particularly 447–449. In Gorla's view, the common law deed resembles the Roman stipulatio, since both validate promises and transactions

Coke defined a seal as requiring an impression upon wax.[119] The sealing of a document was at the time a striking procedure, involving the dripping of hot sealing wax onto a document and impressing it with the family crest or other individual mark.[120] In the mid-sixteenth century, when questions of consideration began to arise, the courts continued to enforce promises under seal. They held that a seal "imports consideration," which was understood to mean that a promise contained in a sealed document was valid even without consideration.[121] Today gift promises are enforceable in English law if made in a deed, which is a writing made under seal.[122] A deed becomes operative upon delivery, whether or not the promisee has accepted or even knows of the promise, though of course the donee has the right to disclaim.[123]

Because the seal today represents an inconsequential formality, some jurists have argued that a signed document should have the same effect.[124] In 1937 the Law Revision Committee recommended that an agreement without consideration should be valid, even absent a seal, as long as it is in writing and the parties intend it to be legally binding.[125] There was a wave of criticism, and the consideration doctrine prevailed. None of the committee's recommendations became law.[126]

ii. Nominal Consideration

690. *Any consideration.* Though informal gift promises are unenforceable, anyone who knows the secret handshake can achieve an equivalent result. The trick is nominal consideration. As mentioned above, the common law does not examine the adequacy of consideration.[127] There is no requirement that the

---

regardless of content, whereas forms in the modern civil law validate only those transactions with the proper cause.

119. "A seal is impressed wax, since wax without an impression is not a seal." (*[S]igillum est cera impressa, quia cera sine impressione non est sigillum.*) Coke (1797) 169.

120. Plucknett 612; 1 Restatement (Second) of Contracts, Introductory Note 255.

121. Plucknett 634.

122. Bridge 93; 9 Halsbury sub Contract no. 617 par. 1.

123. *Xenos v Wickham* (1867) LR 2 HL 296, 312 (Blackburn J); see also Stern 682.

124. One theory advanced for the distinction is that there is some solemnity attaching to the sealing and delivery of a deed. Whatever truth there may have been in this view in medieval times, or in the days of Lord Coke, a seal nowadays is very much in the nature of a legal fiction. The seal is no longer a wax impression of a man's crest or coat of arms; it is usually no more than an adhesive wafer attached by the law stationer when the document is engrossed. It is the party's signature, and not his seal, which in fact authenticates the document.
"Memorandum by Mr. Justice Goddard as to Contracts Under Seal," in Law Revision Committee 35.

125. Law Revision Committee no. 29 at 18–19.

126. Stern 679.

127. Supra no. 231.

contractual performances must be of equivalent value.[128] English law draws the not entirely logical conclusion that any consideration at all is adequate, even if purely nominal.[129] A promise is therefore binding if exchanged for a promise to pay a peppercorn.[130] The doctrine of nominal consideration, despite appearances, does not, in the mind of English jurists, violate the principle that gratuitous promises are unenforceable. Only *informal* gift promises are unenforceable. Nominal consideration is thought to provide an equivalent form. "[T]he deliberate use of a nominal consideration can be regarded as a form to make a gratuitous promise binding."[131]

691. *Flexibility rejected.* In the late eighteenth century, Lord Mansfield suggested that consideration should be interpreted not as a requirement but rather as evidence that the promise had been made.[132] His suggestion was rejected. Despite the flexibility permitted by nominal consideration, a valid consideration is needed. Thus, the fact that a gift is promised based on long acquaintance or great familiarity is not in English law sufficient to make the promise binding.[133]

iii. Promissory Estoppel

692. *Defense.* In the *High Trees* case, Lord Denning held that a court may estop a promisor from suing for breach of a promise when there has been reliance.[134] In that case, the lessor, without receiving consideration, reduced the contractual rent on demised premises due to the difficulty of subleasing during the war. Lord Denning indicated that, if the lessor had attempted to recover the pre-reduction rent, promissory estoppel would have been a valid defense to the lessor's action. Under this principle, promissory estoppel may be used to defend a donee's rights under a gratuitous release, waiver, or renunciation of rights.[135] In some situations, promissory estoppel may have the effect of suspending, rather than extinguishing, the debt.[136] On the other hand, it has also been held that promissory estoppel does not represent an affirmative cause of action in English law.[137] It may therefore not serve to require performance of gratuitous promise.

---

128. 1 Chitty par. 3-014.
129. Supra no. 232.
130. 1 Chitty par. 3-018.
131. Id. par. 3-019.
132. Von Mehren 1035.
133. *Sharington v Strotton* (1765) 1 Plowd 298, 302, 75 ER 454, 460.
134. *Central London Property Trust Ltd v High Trees House Ltd* [1947] KB 130, 134–135; *Lyle-Miller v A Lewis and Co (Westminster) Ltd* [1956] 1 All ER 247, 250–251 (CA).
135. *Smith v Lawson* (1998) 75 P & CR 466 (CA); Anson (2002) 112–118.
136. Jaconelli 434 and note 5.
137. *Combe v Combe* [1951] 2 KB 215; Crossley Vaines 317–318.

There are exceptions. Charitable subscriptions are enforceable when the donee has relied.[138] Moreover, the related doctrine of proprietary estoppel protects those who reasonably rely on the belief that they will receive property rights from another in situations in which the denial of those rights would be unconscionable.[139] The principal cases involve improvements made to specific property, but the doctrine involves any reliance on the transfer of rights. For example, one court enforced a promise to make a testamentary bequest when enforcement seemed necessary to prevent serious injustice.[140]

c. United States

693. *Unenforceable at law.* In American law, the traditional rule is that a promise is binding only if supported by consideration.[141] The principal effect of the consideration doctrine, at least in theory, is to make gift promises unenforceable at law. In a classic article, Lon Fuller argued that the consideration doctrine fulfills a critical role in distinguishing between promises that the law should enforce and those that it should not. In Fuller's view, gratuitous promises should not be enforced because, in the absence of the donee's reliance, they are socially and economically unimportant. Posner also suggests that gift giving is not as socially valuable as commercial contracting and therefore not as deserving of legal protection.[142] Moreover, Fuller argued, there is often no reliable evidence of a gratuitous promise, no means to protect against unconsidered promising, and no reliable indication that the donor intended to be legally bound.[143]

i. Debate

694. *For enforceability.* It is difficult to determine the extent to which gift promises are enforced in American law. After reviewing the case law, Andrew Kull concluded that courts no longer regard the absence of consideration as grounds to deny the enforceability of a promise. "[I]f the case law is scrutinized for outcomes rather than for judicial statements, an unequivocal promise of a gift, seriously intended, should probably be seen as presumptively enforceable rather than the contrary."[144]

---

138. *In re Soames* (1897) 13 TLR 439 (Ch); 20 Halsbury part 1 sub Gifts no. 69.

139. Anson (2002) 120–121.

140. "Mr Gillett and his wife devoted the best years of their lives to working for Mr Holt and his company, showing loyalty and devotion to his business interests, his social life and his personal wishes, on the strength of clear and repeated assurances of testamentary benefits .... I would find it startling if the law did not give a remedy in such circumstances." *Gillett v Holt* [2000] Ch 210 (CA) (proprietary estoppel) (includes a detailed discussion of the case law); Gray and Gray no. 7.24 *in fine*.

141. *Dugan v. First Nat'l Bank*, 606 P.2d 1009, 1017 (Kan. 1980).

142. Posner (1997) 567.

143. Fuller (1941) 799–801, 815.

144. Kull 40, 43–45.

Moreover, for almost a century, some American legal scholars have argued that gift promises supported by sufficient proof should be enforceable. That was the position of Samuel Williston, then the nation's leading contracts scholar, when the question arose during the 1925 meeting of the National Conference of Commissioners of Uniform State Laws.[145] One commissioner considered it unseemly that a promise exchanged for a minimal monetary obligation may be legally binding, while a carefully considered and deeply felt promise to make a gift is unenforceable.[146] Others, however, vehemently disagreed.[147]

The disagreement continues today. On the one hand, Kull argues that the principle of party autonomy strongly suggests that gratuitous promises should be judicially enforceable.[148] "[A] person who makes a serious gratuitous promise of a magnitude that will later justify litigation is particularly unlikely to do so except as a matter of conscious choice."[149] Eisenberg, on the other hand, suggests that informal gift promises frequently arise when the promissor is motivated by emotion.[150] These promises therefore suffer from a problem akin to lack of capacity. Eric Posner would deny enforcement for indefiniteness. When a promise is part of a bargain, there is usually sufficient definiteness to enforce the promise. Gift promises, however, should not be enforced without a thorough knowledge of all of the facts and circumstances, information that is often difficult, and costly, to obtain in the context of gratuitous promises.[151]

Mary Louise Fellows argues that the two typical enforcement situations each raises conceptually different issues.[152] The first involves promises the donor repudiates. If gift law is interpreted consistently with trust law, these promises

---

145. "Mr. WILLISTON: ... It is something, it seems to me, that a person ought to be able to do, if he wishes to do it,—to create a legal obligation to make a gift. Why not?... I don't see why a man should not be able to make himself liable if he wishes to do so." National Conference (1925) 194.

146. "If you give a dollar you may support the most enormous obligation, but no matter how great may be the moral duty to do a thing, no matter how solemnly you promise, unless a paltry dollar is paid, all these moral obligations are of no account .... We have no method by which the contract may be made binding, or an obligation can be made binding unless you pass over a pitiable little sum of money." Rose, Discussion conribution, in National Conference (1925) 200.

147. "Mr. BEERS: ... [I]t would seem that it is so sweeping, so broad, it makes such radical changes, that any little incidental good it may do is very much overbalanced by the dangers which it opens up. I, personally, am very much opposed to it." National Conference (1925) 195.

148. Kull 49, 51.

149. Id. 63.

150. Eisenberg (1979) 5.

151. Posner (1997) 604–609.

152. Fellows (1988).

should not be enforced. In the law of trusts, the equivalent institution of the self-declared trust, examined below, is today generally held to be revocable, unless the declaration provides otherwise.[153] Because the self-declared trust and the donative promise fill a similar function, they should be similarly interpreted. The second situation involves unrepudiated promises. They should be enforceable against the donor's executor. In trust law, if the donor dies without revoking the trust, the beneficiary may enforce it. The common law's unwillingness to enforce unrepudiated gift promises against the donor's executor thus contradicts trust law principles.[154] The inconsistency is particularly evident when the donor has performed the promise until death. In one case the donor granted a pension to the donee, which was paid until the donor's death. Thereafter the executor argued that further payment was barred by the consideration doctrine. The court enforced the promise.[155] Despite the scholarly discussion, the consideration doctrine, at least theoretically, continues to prevent the enforceability of gift promises, subject only to limited exceptions.

ii. Exceptions

695. *Law and equity.* Law and equity do not enforce gift promises to the same extent. Nonetheless, as von Mehren has noted, neither law nor equity provides the American cases with a satisfying conceptual structure.[156] The courts oscillate between a mechanical application of the consideration doctrine and an imprecise use of equitable factors. The doctrinal categories obscure the reasoning rather than facilitate it. In particular, they divert attention from the principal issue, which is whether in a particular case the functions of the consideration doctrine have been fulfilled by alternative means.

(A) AT LAW

696. *Two situations.* Donative promises are enforced at law in two situations. First, in certain American jurisdictions, the use of a designated formality makes a promise binding, even in the absence of consideration. Second, transactions that would be considered gift promises in other legal systems are occasionally enforced in American courts as synallagmatic contracts.

(1) Special Formalities

697. *Several forms.* Several American jurisdictions enforce gift promises made using a designated formality. There are several possible forms.

---

153. Id. 35; see infra no. 958.
154. Id. 36.
155. *Webb v. McGowin*, 168 So. 196 (Ala. App. 1935), aff'd 168 So. 199 (Ala. 1936). The case is discussed supra no. 235 and infra no. 705.
156. Von Mehren 1035.

[a] Promises under Seal

698. *Most prevalent formality.* In some states, gift promises are enforceable at law if made under seal.[157] In English law, as mentioned above, the seal is conclusively presumed to import consideration. It appears that some American states initially adopted this English rule, whereas others considered the presumption to be rebuttable.[158] Today the only thing uniform about the seal is the uncertainty that surrounds it. Due to doubt about the seal's effect, its meaning has been altered in some way by statute in almost every American state.[159] As a result, it is difficult to summarize the general requirements for the enforcement of a gift promise under seal in the United States.[160] Close to half the states have abolished the distinction between sealed and unsealed instruments.[161] In some of these states, the abolition has meant that even promises contained in informal writings benefit from a rebuttable presumption of consideration.[162]

699. *Restatement.* The Restatement (Second) of Contracts provides that, in the absence of a statute, a promise under seal is binding upon delivery. The promisor and promisee must be named in the document or must be so described as to be capable of identification.[163] Delivery may be accomplished by transferring the document containing the sealed promise either into escrow or conditionally or unconditionally to the promisee.[164] The promise is binding upon delivery, whether or not the promisee has accepted it or is even aware of it.[165] Within a reasonable time after the promisee learns of the promise, the promisee may render it inoperative by disclaimer.[166]

---

157. *Trustees of Jesse Parker Williams Hospital v. Nisbet*, 7 S.E.2d 737 (Ga. 1940).

158. Eisenberg (1979) 8–9 note 20. Even when the statute specifies a rebuttable presumption, some courts refuse to look behind the seal. Those courts would enforce purely donative promises. See *Cochran v. Taylor*, 7 N.E.2d 89, 91 (N.Y. 1937); *Aller v. Aller*, 11 Vroom 446 (N.J. 1878). This demonstrates "[t]he plentiful resistance of the courts against the abrogation of the binding force of the seal." Kessler (1964) 272.

159. See, e.g., California CC § 1629; 1 Restatement (Second) of Contracts, Statutory Note 255–259.

160. For the status of the seal in the various states, see 1 Restatement (Second) of Contracts, Introductory Note 255–259. The seal has the almost universal effect of extending the statute of limitations. In those states that recognize the seal, the statute of limitations for suit on a document under seal is generally twenty years, instead of the four to six years typically applicable to a promise contained in an informal writing. See 42 Pennsylvania C.S.A. § 5529 par. b.

161. See, e.g., *Foster v. J.W. Champlin & Co.*, 29 Tex. 22 (1867).

162. *Driscoll v. Driscoll*, 77 P. 471 (Cal. 1904).

163. Restatement (Second) of Contracts § 95 par. 1.

164. Id. § 101 and illus. 1; see also id. §§ 102–03.

165. Id. § 104 par. 1.

166. Id. § 104 par. 2.

700. *What constitutes a seal.* The nature of the seal formality has eroded over the years. Where it is effective, it now often can be met by a simple printed form. The Restatement (Second) defines a seal as any manifestation in tangible and conventional form of an intent to seal a document, including a piece of wax, a wafer affixed to the document, or an impression made on the paper, as well as a written or printed seal, or simply a word, scrawl, or other sign.[167] A dash or wavy line after a signature is enforceable as a seal if the document recites that it is under seal.[168]

701. *Objections.* Many have objected to enforcing promises merely because they are under seal.[169] Promisors may not be aware of the effect of licking a seal and placing it after their signatures. Moreover, it is not difficult for the promisee to add an unauthorized seal after delivery. Promises under seal have occasioned much litigation, both to determine whether a particular mark is a seal and to ascertain whether the presumption of consideration has been overcome. On the other hand, Richard Posner argues that the seal eliminates the major administrative costs associated with the enforcement of unilateral promises. Its abolition "is therefore a mysterious development from the standpoint of efficiency."[170]

[b] Written Instruments

702. *Informal writings.* In two jurisdictions, a promise is enforceable if contained in a written document, even in the absence of both seal and consideration.[171] The Model Written Obligations Act, adopted only in Pennsylvania,[172] also makes enforceable a gratuitous promise made in writing, if the writing expressly states that the donor intends to be legally bound.[173] The purpose of the Model Act was to replace the seal with a modern substitute, namely a clear statement that the promisor intends to be legally bound.[174] The act has been criticized for providing even less protection to promisors than did the seal. The seal was usually affixed by the promisor, while the recital of the intent to be bound might easily be buried in the boilerplate by the promisee.[175]

---

167. Id. § 96.
168. Id. § 96 illus. 2–3. See *Appeal of Hacker*, 15 A. 500 (Pa. 1888). In *Hacker*, a written dash of between one-sixteenth and one-eighth inch in length following the signature was held to be a seal.
169. Williston, Discussion contribution, in National Conference (1925) 197.
170. Posner (1977) 419-420.
171. Mississippi C Ann. § 75-19-3. New Mexico has adopted a similar rule, but the writing merely creates a rebuttable presumption of consideration, which is destroyed if lack of consideration is apparent from the face of the instrument. New Mexico Stat. Ann. § 38-7-2; *Burt v. Horn*, 641 P.2d 546 (N.M. App. 1982).
172. 33 Pennsylvania Stat. Ann. § 6–8.
173. Model Written Obligations Act (1925).
174. Williston, Discussion contribution, in National Conference (1925) 196.
175. Note (1929) 208.

Lloyd has proposed a more nuanced solution.[176] First, forms should be made available for those knowledgeable about the law. For example, the seal should be restored to its common law rigor. A gratuitous promise should be enforced if contained in a deed sealed by a wax impression, and, in order to prevent the other party from subsequently affixing a seal, if it includes the promisor's holograph recitation that the document is sealed. When the promisor knows the legal effect of the seal and uses it deliberately, no further proof of intent should be required. Second, those without advanced legal knowledge must also be permitted to make enforceable promises. Until other informal devices are developed, a promise in writing should be sufficient if the courts establish that the promisor intended to create a legal obligation.

[c] Sham Transactions

703. *Scholarly support.* Goetz and Scott have argued that a promise made in the form of a sham transaction should be legally enforceable.[177] They suggest that a sham transaction is functionally as reliable as a seal. Both serve to encourage deliberation, preserve evidence, and confirm the promisor's intention. The case law, however, has not followed the suggestion.

(2) Recharacterization

704. *Implied bargain.* American courts have occasionally recharacterized gratuitous promises as bargains in order to enforce them as contracts.[178] In one case, the grantor intended to make a gift of land to his sister.[179] The two executed a land sale contract stating a price of $ 1,100. It was orally agreed that the price would not be paid. The contract remained executory on both sides. Nonetheless, the grantor subsequently endorsed the contract with a receipt for full payment. The court granted specific performance. It found that the land sale contract was supported by the stated consideration. The receipt functioned as a valid release of the debt.[180] However, as Roscoe Pound commented, a court probably would not enforce such a contract if the result would be to require the donee to pay the sales price.[181]

---

176. Lloyd 32–36.
177. Goetz and Scott 1303 and note 98. For the related view of Dean Ripert, see infra no. 810.
178. "[W]hen [the courts] get to gratuitous promises, really gratuitous promises, which they wish to enforce, they hunt around and find something which they treat as consideration *pro hac vice*, though it is really not an agreed exchange." Williston, Discussion contribution, in National Conference (1925) 198.
179. *Ferry v. Stephens*, 21 Sickels 321 (N.Y. 1876).
180. For the gratuitous release of a debt in the United States, see infra no. 927.
181. Pound 672.

In perhaps the most celebrated case of this kind, a liberal arts college sued to enforce the unpaid balance of a charitable subscription.[182] In a masterpiece of American judicial construction, Justice Cardozo reinterpreted a simple gift promise as a contract. Because the college had accepted the donor's initial installment, Justice Cardozo implied a return promise by the college to name a scholarship after the donor. He then implied a counterpromise from the donor to provide full funding for the scholarship. As discussed below, such cases no longer require judicial acrobatics. Charitable subscriptions today are often enforceable in the absence of both consideration and reliance.[183]

American courts also occasionally reinterpret the condition in a conditional gift promise as bargained-for consideration. In a case frequently used for classroom hypotheticals, an uncle promised his nephew $5,000 if the nephew abstained from drinking, smoking, swearing, and playing cards and billiards for money before he reached the age of twenty-one.[184] Though many legal systems would interpret this promise as a conditional gift promise, the American court enforced it as a contractual bargain.[185] One court has even interpreted a simple promise as a completed gift, despite the absence of delivery.[186]

705. *Moral consideration.* In another well-known case, an employee became disabled for life as a consequence of preventing a falling wood block from striking his employer.[187] The employer subsequently promised to pay the employee a small, biweekly stipend. There was no consideration for the promise. The employee's actions had not been bargained for, and, in the common law, *past consideration* is thought to be no consideration. Nonetheless, the court enforced the promise against the employer's executor and justified its decision with "an opinion that demonstrates, by its incoherence, the sheer inadequacy of available doctrine to explain an inevitable result."[188]

---

182. *Allegheny College v. Nat'l Chautauqua County Bank,* 159 N.E. 173 (N.Y. 1927) (Cardozo, J.).

183. Infra no. 708.

184. *Hamer v. Sidway,* 27 N.E. 256 (N.Y. 1891).

185. "[In the common law,] the gift coupled with an obligation (*donazione con un onere*), which is not a mere nominal consideration, is validated as a bargain, which means it is absorbed into the generic or atypical conception of contract, whatever the character or value of the obligation and whatever the parties' principal or secondary 'causa.'" 1 Gorla 443.

186. *Faith Lutheran Retirement Home v. Veis,* 473 P.2d 503 (1970), together with the interpretation of the case in Eisenberg (1979) 3 note 5. The case is also discussed infra no. 893.

187. *Webb v. McGowin,* 168 So. 196 (Ala. App. 1935), aff'd 168 So. 199 (Ala. 1936); see also *Slayton v. Slayton,* 315 So.2d 588 (Ala. Civ. App. 1975). *Webb* is also discussed above. See supra no. 235.

188. Kull 43.

The case has subsequently been interpreted to stand for the proposition that, in limited circumstances, fulfillment of a moral obligation may constitute consideration. Lord Mansfield made the same suggestion a century and a half earlier.[189] The Restatement (Second) has adopted a limited version of the doctrine. A promise made in recognition of a benefit previously received by the promisor from the promisee is binding to the extent necessary to prevent injustice.[190] In other legal systems, the promise would be characterized as a promise to make a remunerative gift or to satisfy a natural obligation.

(B) IN EQUITY

706. *Two situations.* Equity enforces donative promises in two ways. First, it protects the donee's detrimental reliance by means of the doctrine of promissory estoppel. Second, the self-declared trust of a future interest provides a close equivalent to an enforceable gift promise.

(1) Promissory Estoppel

707. *Detrimental reliance.* When an American court enforces a gift promise, it generally relies on the equitable doctrine of promissory estoppel. The doctrine has been approved by the Restatement (Second) and has been adopted in most American jurisdictions. This doctrine provides that promises made without consideration may be enforced to the extent the promisee has detrimentally relied.[191] A promise that the promisor should reasonably expect to induce action or forbearance on the part of the promisee or a third person, and that does induce such action or forbearance, is binding if enforcement of the promise is necessary to prevent injustice.[192] Because the promisee's action or forbearance is not bargained for, there is no consideration. Nonetheless, reliance on the gratuitous promise forms a contract and renders the promise enforceable. In a frequently cited case, a father put his son in possession of land and orally promised to convey it to him as a gift.[193] The son paid taxes on the land and made significant improvements. Though the land was never conveyed, the court enforced the promise after the father's death, despite the absence of both consideration and a writing.[194]

---

189. *Hawkes v Saunders* (1782) 1 Cowper 289, 290, 98 ER 1091 (Mansfield J). For the English debate on Lord Mansfield's suggestion, see Teeven 76–103.

190. Restatement (Second) of Contracts § 86.

191. Id. § 90.

192. Id. § 90 par. 1. See generally Eisenberg (1979), who criticizes the provision for, among other things, wrongly focusing attention on the expectations of the promisor rather than on the promisee's reliance. Id. 32.

193. *Seavey v. Drake*, 62 N.H. 393 (1882).

194. Though the statute of frauds generally requires a writing for the conveyance of land, part performance—here, entry into possession and the making of improvements—operated as an exception. Id. The Restatement (Second) of Contracts reconceptualizes the

In a more recent case, a husband made a gift of a car to his wife.[195] The car was paid for partially from the husband's separate funds and partially from a bank loan on which both parties were liable. Following the parties' divorce, the court divided the transaction into two parts. It distinguished, first, a perfected gift of the equity in the car and, second, the husband's promise to pay the balance due. The promise was held to be binding based on the wife's reliance, which was her agreement to cosign on the note.

The Restatement (Second) suggests that enforcement generally should be limited to avoiding injustice.[196] Courts should therefore consider awarding damages sufficient to return the promisee to the *status quo ante* (the reliance interest) rather than enforce the full extent of the promise (the expectation interest).[197] In the context of gift promises, consequential damages are rarely recovered.[198] Civilian systems generally would not enforce these promises without the requisite formality. The justification and legal construction of promissory estoppel are matters of controversy in American law.[199] For example, it seems that courts only rarely limit recovery to the promisee's reliance interest. They enforce the promise fully or not at all.[200] Some promisees recover without proving reliance, while those who demonstrate reliance do not always recover.[201] As a result, Feinman has suggested that current doctrine is unable to offer a coherent explanation of the cases.[202] Feinman believes that the courts may be focusing on the parties' relationship, as theorized by relational contract theory, but he does not explore the idea in the context of donative promises.[203]

708. *Charitable subscriptions.* Promises to contribute to charitable institutions and marriage settlements are often enforceable today even in the absence of reliance.[204] Under the original version of the Restatement, the enforcement of

---

part performance exception as a type of detrimental reliance. Restatement (Second) § 129, together with comment a and illus. 4 (based on *Seavey v. Drake*). In a remarkable article, Pound indicated several additional conceptualizations that would justify enforcing promises in these circumstances. See Pound 674–675.

195. *Newmeyer v. Newmeyer*, 140 A.2d 892, 895 (Md. 1958).
196. Restatement (Second) of Contracts § 90 comment b.
197. Id. § 90 comment d. The reliance interest is often difficult to calculate, as is demonstrated by a hypothetical Eisenberg proposed. If Uncle promises Nephew an amount to purchase a new car and then retracts after the car is purchased, can Nephew recover the promised amount or only the loss that would result from the car's resale? See Eisenberg (1979) 26.
198. Restatement (Second) of Contracts § 90 comment d.
199. Gordley (1995) 559–570 (citing to the relevant scholarly literature).
200. Yorio and Thel 136.
201. Id. 151.
202. Feinman.
203. Feinman 311–315. For relational contract theory, see MacNeil and Campbell.
204. *Salsbury v. Northwestern Bell Telephone Co.*, 221 N.W.2d 609, 612–613 (Iowa 1974); Restatement (Second) of Contracts § 90 par. 2.

charitable subscriptions was justified by a finding that the charity or the other donors relied on the promise. Such promises are now enforced as a matter of social policy, especially in a country, such as the United States, that allocates to private charities much of the burden of public assistance and support of the arts.[205]

(2) Self-Declared Trust

709. *Future interest.* The irrevocable gift into trust of a future interest has effects that closely resemble those of an enforceable gift promise.[206] As discussed below, a donor in possession of property may declare a trust in the donee's favor.[207] No delivery is required. The declaration is valid regardless whether the donee accepts or even knows of the trust. Though the declaration of trust must be presently operative, the present grant of a future beneficial interest is valid, even if the donor is to retain lifelong enjoyment of the property.[208] The settlor may make the trust irrevocable.

C. GIFT PROMISE FORMALITIES AND THE EXECUTED GIFT

710. *Defective promise and execution.* When a gift promise made without the required formalities is subsequently executed, some jurisdictions provide that the subsequent gift disposition is valid, whereas others hold that it is void.

1. Germany

711. *Execution cures defects.* The German Civil Code provides that the execution of the promised gift cures (*heilt*) formal defects in the promise (§ 518 par. 2). Execution cures only formal defects and only those related to the formalities required of an enforceable gift promise. If the promise is defective for other reasons—if it fails to comply with other form requirements, violates public policy, or is voidable on other grounds—the subsequent transfer does not defeat the donor's restitution action.[209]

a. Intent and Execution

712. *Voluntary.* The subsequent gift disposition is valid only if it is freely made (*freiwillige Vollziehung*).[210] A gift transfer is not freely made when it results from a setoff or an execution of judgment. A voluntary act by the donor is required.[211]

---

205. Eisenberg (1979) 4 note 8.
206. Fellows (1988) 35–36.
207. Infra no. 955.
208. Brown § 7.21 at 148.
209. Staudinger (-Wimmer-Leonhardt) § 518 no. 25.
210. Id. § 518 no. 22.
211. MünchKomm-BGB (-Kollhosser) § 518 no. 11.

713. *Performance.* Cure of the defective formalities results from performance (*Bewirkung*) of the promise. For a majority of the German authors, performance is judged in terms of the donor's act (*Leistungshandlung*).[212] The donor must have done everything that the donor is required to do to complete the transfer.[213] For a minority, the defect is cured only if the gift disposition is successful.[214] The minority argument is that the defective promise can be cured only by a valid manual gift, which takes effect only when the transfer is complete.[215]

b. Timing

714. *When execution occurs.* There is considerable controversy about when a transfer is sufficiently executed.[216] Though there are few practical differences between the two prevailing theories, one important disparity involves the case in which the donor, before death, attempts but does not complete performance. A school example, derived from an actual case, involves the acknowledgment of a debt or an IOU (*Schuldschein*) upon which the donor-creditor had written: "This debt is canceled at my death."[217] The question is whether a release that is intended to operate in the future is void in the absence of gift promise formalities. Under the majority view, depending on the specific circumstances, it might be validated as a fully executed manual gift of a release subject to a condition precedent. The minority view would consider it void as an unexecuted promise of a future release.[218]

c. Gratuitousness

715. *Cause.* As noted above, a disposition made pursuant to a valid gift promise is gratuitous, though it is not itself a gift.[219] When the gift promise is validly made, the cause of the promise passes into the subsequent disposition. Theoretical issues arise, however, when the gift promise is defective in form. An invalid gift promise cannot pass a valid cause to the ensuing transfer. A transfer is not

---

212. Jauernig (-Mansel) § 518 nos. 3 and 6.

213. Staudinger (-Wimmer-Leonhardt) § 518 no. 19.

214. MünchKomm-BGB (-Kollhosser) § 518 nos. 12 ff.; Alternativkommentar § 518 no. 3.

215. MünchKomm-BGB (-Kollhosser) § 518 no. 14.

216. The discussion focuses on two types of cases: payments made into bank accounts titled in the donee's name and the gift of a partnership. See MünchKomm-BGB (-Kollhosser) § 518 nos. 25–35; Staudinger (-Wimmer-Leonhardt) § 518 nos. 36 ff.

217. RG 11 Feb. 1908, *Warneyer* 1908 no. 302, *Das Recht* 1908 no. 1165 at 195; see also RG 17 Jan. 1903, RGZ 53, 294 at 296. See infra no. 752.

218. MünchKomm-BGB (-Kollhosser) § 518 no. 24; id. (-Musielak) § 2301 no. 30. If the acknowledgment is considered a promise, it would not necessarily be testamentary. See supra no. 305.

219. Supra no. 661.

thought to be gratuitous if the transferor mistakenly believes that the obligation is valid.[220]

As indicated above, gratuitousness, in German law, is judged subjectively. If the donor believes that the transfer in question is made in fulfillment of an obligation, the transfer is not gratuitous.[221] It might therefore be argued that a transfer made pursuant to a gift promise that is defective in form is not gratuitous,[222] and that the property should be recoverable in restitution. An exception would be made only if the transfer is itself gratuitous, which would be the case, for example, if the donor decides to proceed with the gift though fully aware that there is no obligation to do so.[223]

According to the legislative history, however, the code's gift promise provision bars the restitutionary claim when the donor mistakenly makes the transfer *solvendi causa* (§ 518 par. 2). Thus, despite the provision's wording, the defective gift promise is not technically cured by performance. It is more accurate to say that subsequent execution of the gift is valid despite irregularities in the form of the promise.[224]

2. Other Civilian Systems

716. *Italy*. Gift promises are unenforceable in Italian law. As a result, a gift made in performance of the promise is also generally void.[225] One exception involves a negotiable instrument given as evidence of a gift of an obligation to transfer money. Because the transfer of the instrument is meant to reinforce the obligation rather than perform it, a subsequent gratuitous payment of the instrument is not void.[226] Moreover, when a gift is independent of the promise, in the sense that the donor is not attempting to fulfill an obligation, the gift may also be valid.

717. *France*. In French law, the donor is permitted to retract at any moment before the gift is consummated. Gift promises are therefore not enforced.[227] Once the gift is actually executed, however, there seems to be no reason not to respect it. Research has revealed no case or doctrinal discussion about whether the gift is valid if the donor believed that the gift promise created an enforceable obligation. However, the French tradition would not necessarily invalidate the gift based on the donor's erroneous belief. French law defines gratuitousness in

---

220. RG 6 July 1922, RGZ 105, 246 at 248; Staudinger (-Wimmer-Leonhardt) § 516 no. 42.
221. Supra no. 250.
222. Staudinger (-Wimmer-Leonhardt) § 518 no. 22.
223. MünchKomm-BGB (-Kollhosser) § 518 no. 14.
224. Staudinger (-Wimmer-Leonhardt) § 518 no. 17.
225. Torrente (2006) 294–295.
226. Id. 295
227. 8 De Page no. 369.

terms of a simple lack of equivalence, which, in such a case, continues to be present.[228]

718. *Spain.* If an obligational gift made orally is subsequently executed in proper form, the scholars suggest that only an excess of formalism would invalidate the gift.[229]

3. The Common Law

719. *Consideration.* In the common law, a gift executed pursuant to a gift promise is valid, even if the gift promise would have been unenforceable. The consideration doctrine serves only to prevent the enforcement of unexecuted promises. If donative intent is present, the lack of consideration is unavailable as a defense to a completed transfer.

D. DEFENSES AND OTHER LIMITATIONS

720. *Chiefly German law.* The problem of defenses to liability arises only in those jurisdictions that enforce gift promises. As discussed above, German law is the only system studied here that enforces simple gift promises. Other systems recognize legal structures, such as the gift of an obligation, that may produce equivalent results. As discussed below, Spanish law permits revocation of an executed gift in situations that are related to the donor's impoverishment.[230] In the common law, gift promises are enforced as such only in equity, which is able to take account of all of the facts and circumstances of the transaction.

1. Germany and Switzerland

721. *Impoverishment.* The German and Swiss Civil Codes permit a donor who has made an otherwise enforceable gift promise to withhold execution if performance would cause the donor to risk impoverishment.[231] The provision was derived from the Roman law institution of *beneficium competentiae*, which seems to have been inspired by Christian notions of charity. With various modifications, it was received into customary German law.[232]

a. Changed Circumstances

722. *Timing.* Today, the rule is understood as a case of changed circumstances (*Wegfall der Geschäftsgrundlage*)[233] and is related conceptually to the revocation of

---

228. Supra no. 238.
229. Paz-Ares Rodríguez (-Albaladejo García) arts. 632–633 no. III.
230. Infra no. 1205.
231. German CC § 519; Swiss CO art. 250 par. 1 no. 2.
232. Biondi no. 180.
233. Jauernig (-Mansel) § 519 no. 1.

a gift on the grounds of the donor's impoverishment.[234] In neither case may the donor renounce the right in advance. The defense obtains regardless of whether the threat to the donor's subsistence arises before or after the gift promise is made.[235] However, the defense is available only so long as the gift has not been executed. Thereafter, the donor may revoke, but the conditions of the revocation action are somewhat more restrictive.

b. Defense and Revocation

723. *Two distinctions.* Two features of the defense of impoverishment distinguish it from revocation based on the same grounds. First, the defense is available to donors who risk impoverishment due to their own foolishness,[236] whereas a donor may revoke only if the deterioration in the donor's financial condition is not due to the donor's gross negligence or intentional act.[237] Second, while revocation is premised on actual impoverishment, the defense is based on the mere risk. The defense is available as soon as it becomes clear that, should the gift be executed, the donor would no longer be able to sustain the donor's lifestyle or to satisfy the donor's legal obligations to others. The defense may be invoked not merely when there is a risk to basic necessities but also when the situation may deteriorate beyond what is appropriate in the circumstances (*angemessener Unterhalt*). The donor's assets and liabilities are compared, and, if the risk is confirmed, the donee's claim for breach will be rejected, though the action may be brought again if the donor's circumstances improve.[238] The defense is personal to the donor and may not be asserted either by the donor's guarantors or by those with whom the donor is jointly and severally liable.[239]

724. *Several gift promises.* Should the donor have promised gifts to several donees and then, because of a contretemps, become unable to complete them, the promises first accepted are to be preferred to those accepted subsequently (CC § 519 par. 2). If the donor mistakenly fails to respect the code's priority rules, some authors suggest that the donor may still use the defense of necessity against an earlier claim. As noted above, the code protects donors against their own negligence. Only the fraudulent donor is not protected.[240]

---

234. Infra nos. 1202–1203.
235. Staudinger (-Wimmer-Leonhardt) § 519 no. 10.
236. MünchKomm-BGB (-Kollhosser) § 519 no. 3.
237. German CC § 529 par. 1; see infra no. 1202.
238. MünchKomm-BGB (-Kollhosser) § 519 nos. 2, 4.
239. Id. § 519 no. 5.
240. Id. § 519 no. 6; but see references in Staudinger (-Wimmer-Leonhardt) § 519 no. 22.

2. Other Legal Systems

725. *Italy.* The preliminary project for the Italian Civil Code authorized the courts to excuse a donor's performance "when the donor's economic conditions, arising subsequent to the gift, are modified without the donor's fault, such that execution would become excessively onerous."[241] The provision was initially praised but ultimately rejected. It was thought that it was inconsistent with the binding nature of contractual liability.

726. *France and Belgium.* Gift promises are not generally enforceable in the French tradition. In the different context of the obligation to deliver the property after conclusion of the gift act, Domat suggested that there should be no obligation to perform if performance would impoverish the donor. "For it would be unjust for his generosity to become an occasion for inhumane treatment by his donee."[242] Domat's suggestion has not been adopted.

727. *United States.* When an American court characterizes a gift promise as an enforceable contract, contractual notions of impossibility, impracticability, and frustration of purpose should be available as defenses. Several American authors have suggested that changed circumstances should be taken into account when suit is brought to enforce a gift promise. Those circumstances might include the promisee's ingratitude, the promisor's improvidence, and even the birth of children.[243] Kessler argued that the recognition of the defense of changed circumstance would meet most of the objections to the enforceability of gift promises.[244] There seems to be no relevant case law.

241. Draft art. 420; Biondi no. 180.
242. 1 Domat no. 939 (translation slightly revised).
243. Farnsworth (1995) 376–377; Eisenberg (1979) 5–6; Steele 187.
244. Kessler (1954) 277.

6. MAKING THE GIFT

728. *Formal requirements.* When the four definitional elements of the gift are united in a transaction, the law expresses its concern by prescribing the form the transaction must take. Some systems dictate a form both for the donor's disposition and for the donee's acceptance. If the prescribed formalities are not present, the transaction is generally void. That means the courts will not require the donor to deliver the property. In some legal systems it also means that the donor cannot voluntarily complete the gift by delivery. Unless the donee has acquired title by good faith purchase, anyone with an interest can avoid the transaction and recover the property for the donor.

A. INTRODUCTION

729. *Why required.* The insistence on formalities in a field based on donative intent may at first seem puzzling. It might seem that the law should simply facilitate the realization of the donor's wishes.[1] Yet the strict form requirements frequently defeat that intent. The question is why a legal system would intervene in this way. As Baron has asked in an insightful article, "The ultimate question is why *any* donative transfer should be invalidated on purely formal grounds."[2]

1. Justifications

730. *Several answers.* There are several standard answers.[3] A first set of answers concerns the need to protect the donor from impulsiveness, misinterpretation, and pressure. It is often suggested that, without required forms, emotion might

---

1. One fundamental proposition is that, under a legal system recognizing the individualistic institution of private property and granting to the owner the power to determine his successors in ownership, the general philosophy of the courts should favor giving effect to an intentional exercise of that power. This is commonplace enough, but it needs constant emphasis, for it may be obscured or neglected in inordinate preoccupation with detail or dialectic.
Gulliver and Tilson 2.
2. Baron 159 note 7 *in fine* (emphasis in original).
3. Id. 159–160. Gulliver and Tilson discuss three functions form might play in the gift disposition: the ritual function (a ceremonial act impresses the donor with the consequences of the action); the evidentiary function (the act provides necessary evidence to the

prevent donors from focusing on the consequences of the gift. Forms requiring the participation of a notary are also thought necessary to deter fraud, mistake, and undue influence. A second group of answers focuses on the societal benefit. Formalities provide reliable evidence of donative intent and therefore decrease litigation and other administrative costs. The forms also document the terms of the gift, providing evidence that protects both the donee and the heirs. Documentation seems especially important in a field such as gift law in which disputes frequently arise only after the donor's death.[4]

731. *Not well adapted.* The commentators have long noted that the formal requirements found in some systems are not well adapted to these purposes. It is highly unlikely that so many donors are unaware of the consequences of making a gift that it is worth invalidating all informal gift transfers to guarantee this protection. As far as fraud, mistake, and undue influence are concerned, the corresponding affirmative defenses are generally considered adequate in other areas of the law, and there is no reason to think these problems arise preferentially in gift giving. While the notarial act provides reliable evidence of the gift's terms, nullity seems a somewhat excessive sanction. If more evidence is needed, the court can hold a hearing. If the donee is unable to prove the gift, that would be time enough to decide against enforcing the transaction. As for litigation, the required formalities provoke at least as many lawsuits as they prevent. In all the legal systems examined here, disappointed donees are constantly seeking to fit the gift into one of the frequent exceptions to the form requirements. So many disputes already find their way to the courts that it is difficult to imagine that litigation would increase if formalities were no longer required.[5] There is the additional problem that gift law is so intricate and its rules so counterintuitive that individuals who seek to obey the law are often unable to do so.[6] As a result, many scholars argue that the form requirements should only be enforced when their absence has failed to protect against one of the designated risks.[7]

732. *Unjustifiable assumptions.* Baron has also pointed out that the functional justifications for the form requirements make unjustifiable assumptions about the human condition. They assume that individuals are by nature not only

---

court); and the protective function (the act protects the donor against undue influence). Gulliver and Tilson 3–5.

4. Gulliver and Tilson 4 note 4.

5. "A very brief examination of the authorities is sufficient to convince one that recent years have witnessed a large increase, both in the number of litigated gifts, and in the value of the property involved." Mechem (1926–1927) 341 note 5.

6. "First, people still litigate the [gift] occurrences a great deal; second, people continue to behave in ways that bring them into conflict with the rules as stated. This is at least some indication that for the people who end up litigating these cases, the rules and the cases more generally have little incentive effect." Kreitner 1908.

7. Gulliver and Tilson 17.

imprudent and careless but also dishonest, selfish, and grasping.[8] Oddly, these assumptions directly contradict contract law's confidence in individuals as rational actors. If the problem is that a small number of individuals who engage in gift transactions display these negative qualities, there is no reason to construe the form requirements so inflexibly. Baron's point is that there is no evidence to support the functional justification of the form requirements. The main purpose of these requirements may simply be to express the law's discomfort with gift giving.

2. Types of Formalities

733. *Delivery.* Once it is agreed that the gift disposition should be subject to formal requirements, it must be decided which forms should be required. Philip Mechem, the common law's most insightful student of gift transfer mechanisms, contended that the law should choose forms the parties will consider normal in the circumstances.[9] From his pragmatic American perspective, the proper form is delivery. Mechem was not alone. Cujas too thought that delivery is the natural mode of gift disposition.[10] When the gift is a chattel, delivery involves what Mechem called *tradition,* the manual handing over of the gift object.[11] In the case of real property and intangibles, delivery would involve the handing over of a deed or of some other document evidencing the right.

Mechem's suggestion serves as a reminder that, when regulating gift giving, the law does not write on a clean slate. As the cases demonstrate, much gift giving takes place without concern for legal norms. In a field largely constituted by custom and social practice, it might seem that the law should borrow preexisting forms "to frame rules which will fit with a minimum of friction into the mechanism of ordinary life."[12] Everyone understands that, under normal circumstances, a gift is made by transfer of possession. As Mechem put it, it is difficult to believe that the donor actually gave a gift if, at the end of the day, the gift is still in the donor's pocket.[13]

734. *Representational form.* The civil law has tended to adopt a different perspective. It shifts the focus away from the social custom of gift giving toward the gift's festive, representational side. Gift giving is both a traditional practice and yet

---

8. Baron 168–172.

9. Mechem (1926–1927) 346.

10. "The gift, when done by mancipatio is the legal means of acquiring title, while gift by delivery is the natural mode (*naturalis modus*)." 9 Cujas, *Recitationes solemnes* ad tit. 3 lex 20 *Traditionibus, & usucapionibus* at 104C.

11. Mechem (1926–1927) 346 and note 18a.

12. Id. 365.

13. Id. 346–347.

also something quite extraordinary, an unusual event in which otherwise self-interested individuals decide, often out of quite noble motives, to give away wealth or property they have worked hard to acquire. The civil law seeks to provide a form that is sufficiently ceremonial to represent the most generous gift. In most civilian systems, smaller gifts and presents are either exempted entirely from form requirements or accomplished by simple delivery.

735. *Ritual.* In Romanic systems, the prescribed forms involve an elaborate ritual. Actors playing prescribed roles must all come together at the same time. The details of the act and the conversation are recorded, both for the disposition and for the acceptance. These formalities are in addition to any forms required to create an enforceable gift promise. The forms discussed in this chapter are those required for the simple transfer of title. The decline of formal requirements that increasingly structures the law of obligations in many legal systems encounters resistance in the field of gifts.

3. Constant Difficulty

736. *Technical problems.* Insurmountable technical problems arise when a legislature seeks to impose forms on gift giving. From the point of view of the private law, there is little conceptual unity to the practice other than the sense of concern it may provoke. As a result, two thousand years of legislation have left some legal systems with an historical accumulation of rules, exceptions, and exceptions to exceptions that must frequently be corrected by additional and highly subtle variations. This may be the truth in Archi's claim that "the gift represents a typical specimen of the absurdity that results when there is dissociation between law and historical experience."[14] The form requirements for the donor's disposition are discussed first, followed by those relevant to the donee's acceptance, and finally the requirements for perfection and renunciation.

B. THE DISPOSITION

1. Roman, Medieval, and Early Modern Law

737. *No specified form.* Until the Byzantine period, the execution of a gift required no special form.[15] Gifts were made in the mode appropriate for the transfer of the particular type of property involved. When the gift involved an object, transfer was made by traditio, mancipatio, in iure cessio, or *usucapio*, which made the gift

---

14. Archi (1964) 931.
15. Ourliac and Malafosse 455.

binding among persons not excepted under the lex Cincia.[16] Receivables were transferred by delegation or mandate. The release of a debt was accomplished by a procedure such as the *acceptilatio*.[17] The gift was generally not valid until the transfer was complete.[18] When the gift involved an entire patrimony, transfer was required for each element. It seems that the donor could revoke at any time before the donee acquired dominion. The gift thus differed from the sales contract, which was perfected by agreement without need for transfer or execution.[19]

By the beginning of the third century AD, the lex Cincia was no longer fully in force. To some extent its prohibitions were replaced by a registration requirement.[20] The fact that generally accepted forms were not available for gratuitous transfers created what has been called a legal crisis, particularly in the newly Romanized areas unaccustomed to the complexities of Roman gift law.[21]

738. *Constantine's reform*. Constantine responded by making a radical break with tradition. Some time after 319 he abrogated the lex Cincia.[22] In his constitution of 323, he reconceived the gift as a bilateral act that was to be immediately executed and that instantly transferred title.[23] The donatio was thereby transformed from the cause for a great many transactions to a specific mode of transfer of title.[24] Constantine also promulgated a single set of formalities for all gift transfers.[25] It seems that every gift had to be given before witnesses drawn from the neighborhood (*advocata vicinitate*). The required writing named the donor,

---

16. For traditio, mancipatio, and in iure cessio, see supra no. 34. *Usucapio* was similar to the common law institution of adverse possession. It cured defects both in the mode of conveyance and in the transferor's title. Nicholas 122–123, 128. There were several requirements: conveyance by means of a transaction with a good cause (*ex iusta causa*); of property capable of ownership and that had never been stolen or taken by force; and uninterrupted possession of the property in good faith for the required period. The periods laid down in the Twelve Tables were very short. By the time of Justinian, movables could be usucapted in three years, and land in twenty or thirty, depending on the location of the property.

17. *Acceptilatio* was an oral form for releasing a debt. Nicholas 198–199. The debtor asked the creditor whether satisfaction had been received. The creditor replied that it had. By the classical period, the creditor's statement was sufficient even if fictitious.

18. Lévy 97–101. Lévy noted that the texts often do not specify whether it was title or merely possession that had to be transferred. Id. 97 note 13.

19. Lévy 102–103.

20. Ourliac and Malafosse 456–457.

21. Archi (1964) 947–949.

22. By 326 it was no longer in force. Lévy 108 note 60.

23. Constantine promulgated approximately twenty constitutions related to gifts, the majority before 324. The fundamental reform is found in *Fragmenta vaticana* no. 249. For a discussion of the date of the constitution, see Dupont 293–294.

24. Zimmermann 492; Archi (1958) 391–392.

25. Dupont 298.

designated the gift object, and confirmed the donor's title.[26] Traditio remained essential. Movables were to be handed over before the witnesses.[27] Real estate was delivered when the donor ceremoniously walked away from the property.[28] Acceptance was also indispensable, as was registration (*insinuatio*). Registration took place before the governor, or, in his absence, a magistrate. The registration had to note that the formalities had been complied with.[29] Constantine seems to have borrowed these formalities from those required in public law for imperial gifts.[30] Failure to comply with any of the requirements meant invalidity.[31] The reforms do not require animus donandi or even mention it, but the formalities were so extensive that intent could be presumed.

Constantine stated that he designed the protective regime to avoid complex legal proceedings and particularly to prevent dispositions by nonowners. He may have imposed the publicity requirements to facilitate tax collection.[32] Since his reforms impose significant restrictions on gift giving, they were probably not motivated by Christian charity. Yet Constantine did favor certain types of gifts, especially those from children to their parents.[33] Children were encouraged to demonstrate filial piety by offering to their fathers a third of the property they acquired upon emancipation. Filial piety was also encouraged by the rule revoking emancipation if the child proved ungrateful.[34] Whatever Constantine's grounds may have been, his new regime ensured that donors were protected and that gifts were publicized.

739. *Resistance.* Subsequent constitutions provide evidence of deep resistance to the Constantinian reforms, particularly by practitioners and scholars who approved the growing respect for the donor's will.[35] Later emperors eventually

---

26. Zimmermann 492–493; Michel no. 480. One scholar has suggested that the edict was in the nature of instructions to a public officer rather than a formal constitution. Because the magistrate took notes of the parties' declarations, a writing may not actually have been required. Moreover, the rules may have been advisory rather than binding. See Comment (1852) 4–5.

27. Witnesses were apparently required in order to prevent false claims of gifts of land. Lévy 112.

28. Dupont 300.

29. Apparently only gifts made to a minor female on the day of her wedding could be made without registration. Dupont 305.

30. Dupont 303.

31. Michel no. 480. Exceptions were made for certain gifts in the family context. Lévy 111–112.

32. Archi (1964) 948. Dupont found no evidence to this effect. Dupont 302–303.

33. Dupont 308–310.

34. Infra no. 1118.

35. Archi (1964) 949–950.

dispensed with witnesses and validated gifts if they were drawn up by a notary and signed by the donor, or if they were registered.[36]

740. *Justinian.* In 528 Justinian began yet another epoch in the law of gifts.[37] In contrast to Constantine, his legislation favored gifts. The Byzantine jurists understood the gift to be perfected *nudo consensu* and structured it on the model of sales law.[38] Neither writing nor traditio was required. Registration was needed only for gifts exceeding a value of 300 (later 500) solidi. Other gifts followed the normal requirements for conveyance of title.

741. *Early Middle Ages.* By the early Middle Ages, municipal authorities had largely ceased to function and registration became impossible. There is an account of a donor from the beginning of the ninth century who attempted to register his gift but could find no one to receive it.[39] The rebirth of law in the West, together with the rapid growth of the notarial profession, resuscitated the possibility of form. The twelfth century author of the *Summa tricensis* indicated that a gift could be made by stipulatio, by traditio, or by writing.[40] If the gift exceeded 500 solidi, it also required insinuatio. The author of the *Summa* also suggested that even gifts in a lesser amount that were done in a writing should publicly state the names of the parties and should not be done in a secret, sly, or private manner (*nec occulte seu subodole uel priuatim*).

742. *Villers-Cotterêts.* By the sixteenth century, registration requirements varied according to custom.[41] The Ordinance of Villers-Cotterêts of 1539, in which Francis I instituted recordation for births and deaths and required all notarial acts to be written in French, also required gifts to be registered (art. 132).[42] However, despite the clear text of the ordinance and its successors, registration was required not for validity but only to protect against challenges by third parties.[43]

---

36. C. 8, 53 [54], 29 (Theodosius and Valentinian); 8, 53 [54], 31 (Zeno); Comment (1852) 5; Lévy 112–113. Witnesses were thought to be superfluous if there was a public record of the gift.

37. Archi (1964) 952; Comment (1852) 5; Lévy 113–115.

38. Archi (1958) 424.

39. Ourliac and Malafosse 464.

40. *Summa trecensis* C. 8, 49, no. 4 *De donationibus, in Irnerius* fol. 307; Bellomo 958. See also Placentinus C. 8, 57 *De donationibus* (fol. 416).

41. Regnault 271–307; Ourliac and Malafosse 464–465. For the formalities required in medieval and early modern Europe, see also Gordley (1997) sec. 24.

42. "We desire that all gifts ... be recorded and registered (*insinuées et enregistrées*) in our courts in the ordinary jurisdictions proper for the parties. Otherwise they will be considered void and will only take effect from the date of said registration." Ordinance of 1539 art. 132. Gifts given in the donee's absence were valid only if subsequently accepted in the presence of the donor and the notary and registered. Id. art. 133.

43. Regnault 330–331. For the similar provisions in the unpublished Edict of 1549 and the Ordinance of Moulins of 1566 art. 58, see Regnault 269–271.

As a result, Cujas, who sought a return to Roman law, was able to claim that, as between the parties, gifts were concluded by simple agreement.[44]

743. *Ordinance of 1731.* Following the dominant view in the *parlements*, d'Aguesseau's Ordinance of 1731 imposed a uniform formality for the validity of all gifts, even between the parties. Any gift not made before a notary was void (art. 1). The formalities mandated by local law, custom, and usage continued in force and were also to be satisfied (art. 2). Though the Ordinance did not explicitly except manual gifts from the formality requirement, d'Aguesseau's correspondence made clear that he would validate them without notarial act.[45] Since the requirement of a notarial act passed from the Ordinance directly into the Civil Code and thence into the laws of Romanic civilian systems, it is unfortunate we understand so little about d'Aguesseau's reasoning. D'Aguesseau's substantive justification was that the required form would prevent surprise and fraud. He also explained the provision as an attempt to unify the law of the various *coutumes*.[46] In addition, D'Aguesseau may have been influenced by the ideas of his teacher, Jean Domat, who taught that a notarial act was necessary to prevent revocation.[47]

The Ordinance also required most gifts to be registered. There were several exceptions, including gifts of movables with a value of less than 1,000 *livres* that had been fully executed and some gifts made in a marriage settlement (arts. 19–22). Registration involved the transcription of the entire gift act "without any omissions" into a special register in the offices of the royal administration (arts. 23–24). If the gift was registered within four months of its making, registration was retroactive to the date of the gift. A subsequent registration was effective ex nunc.[48] In contrast to the legal tradition since Constantine, registration became a general and uniform condition of validity. If the gift was not registered, or if it was registered after the donor's death, it was void and could be challenged by anyone with an interest, except the donor (art. 27). Any clause in which the donor agreed to pay damages if the gift was not registered was invalid. The registration requirement was thought to prevent fraud against creditors.[49] The church, the primary beneficiary of inter vivos gifts, objected to registration because it was reluctant to reveal to the king the extent of its receipts.[50]

---

44. "Today the gift is concluded by simple agreement (*nudo consensu*) like the sale." 8 Cujas, *Recitationes solemnes* ad tit. 7 bk. 44 lex 10 *Naturales obligationes* at 339B.

45. See infra no. 795.

46. "Réponses," in Regnault 611; Preamble, Ordinance of 1731, 343–344; supra no. 44.

47. 1 Domat no. 909.

48. 8 Pothier, *Donations* nos. 108–112.

49. Bretonnier 101.

50. Lagarde 26 note 6.

744. *Prussia.* Under the Prussian General Law of 1794, only gifts concluded before a court were fully effective.[51] A gift concluded before a notary or judicial officer (*Justizcommissar*) had the effect of a preliminary agreement (*Punctation*) and was without the force of gifts concluded judicially.[52] For example, if the gift was made before a notary, the donee could not sue for specific performance. Manual gifts of movables were validated by actual manual delivery (*wirkliche Naturalübergabe*). Gifts of immovables were executed by delivering a writing.[53]

745. *Today.* Today, in order to transfer title to gift property, some systems require both a formal gift act and, in addition, a written inventory. This chapter concludes with a discussion of the more relaxed mechanisms used to make a gift of organs and other body parts.

2. Germany

746. *Minimalist approach.* German law requires no independent formality to execute a gift. Whatever means are sufficient to accomplish the immediate transfer of rights in the type of property involved are also generally sufficient to make a gift. The disposition (*Zuwendung*) is simply the process of effectuating the patrimonial displacement (*Vermögensverschiebung*) that characterizes the type of property involved in the gift.[54] For the purposes of comparative study, German law represents a minimalist approach, the zero degree of gift formality. The fact that the transaction is a gift has no impact on the required form.

747. *Abstraction principle.* The German law principle of abstraction (*Abstraktionsprinzip*) distinguishes two separate contracts in the gift transaction. There is, first, an obligational contract (*schuldrechtlicher Vertrag*), an agreement as to the gratuitous nature of the transaction (CC § 516 par. 1). This provides agreement concerning the transaction's causal basis (*Rechtsgrundabrede*).[55] The second agreement is the real contract (*dinglicher Vertrag*). The real contract provides the agreement required in German law for all transfers of property, whether real or personal (CC §§ 873 par. 1, 929).

a. Types of Gift

748. *Normal conveyance.* Because German gift law has not created specific gift formalities, the gift disposition may take various legal forms. In most cases, it is accomplished by means of a legal transaction (*Rechtsgeschäft*), but it can also take place by means of other acts or omissions. Frequent transactional forms of gift disposition include the creation of new property rights or the transfer of existing

---

51. Gen. Law pt. 1 tit. 11 § 1063.
52. Id. §§ 1067, 1069.
53. Id. §§ 1064–1066, 1068.
54. Staudinger (-Wimmer-Leonhardt) § 516 nos. 17 ff.
55. Infra no. 1350.

rights. The form of the conveyance is the same, whether the transfer is a sale or a gift.

749. *Real property.* A gift of real property requires an agreement (*Auflassung*) before a notary or other proper authority together with recordation in the land title records (*Eintragung*).[56] No documentation is necessary,[57] but, if there is no notarial writing, the transfer is generally not binding between the parties until the transfer is recorded (CC § 873 par. 2).

750. *Movables.* For movables as well, a gratuitous transfer is made in the same manner as an onerous transfer, by agreement and delivery (*Einigung und Übergabe*; CC § 929). Generally, the donor must completely relinquish possession. In some cases transfers to third parties meet the delivery requirement, though the question is controversial.[58] As for negotiable instruments, the general rule is that instruments payable to bearer (*Inhaberpapiere*) are transferred by delivery, whereas order paper (*Orderpapiere*) is transferred either by endorsement and agreement or by assignment. Special form requirements are imposed only if the donor is principally liable on the paper.[59] Contract rights may be transferred gratuitously by assignment (*Abtretung*; CC § 398). An obligation may be gratuitously extinguished by release (*Erlaß*; CC § 397 par. 1) or assumed (*Schuldübernahme*; CC § 414) as a gift. Gift law requires notarial form only for transactions considered gift promises.[60]

751. *Nontransactional gifts.* A gift may also be given in nontransactional form. The donor may purposefully permit a prescription period to elapse or abandon a security interest.[61] The gratuitous construction of a house on the property of another is also a form of nontransactional gift. The transfer occurs at the moment when, under the doctrine of combination or fixtures (*Verbindung*), the law recognizes the land owner's rights in the improvements. No form is needed.

b. Timing

752. *Present transfer.* Rights enforceable against third parties may be gifted by assignment, provided words of present transfer are used. If the language contains nothing more than a promise to assign in the future, the promise, considered a gift promise, is void unless done in notarial form.[62] Similarly, a release

---

56. CC §§ 873 par. 1, 925 par. 1.

57. BGH 7 July 1983, NJW 1983, 2933; Jauernig (-Jauernig) § 925 no. 4 par. b no. 12.

58. Jauernig (-Jauernig) § 929 nos. 3 and 8 ff.

59. Baumbach and Hefermehl, *Wechselgesetz* art. 11 no. 1, art. 14 nos. 1–2; id. *Scheckgesetz* art. 14 nos. 1–5; Zöllner § 14 par. 1. See supra no. 666.

60. MünchKomm-BGB (-Schlüter) §§ 398 no. 33 (assignment), 397 no. 2 (release); RG 17 Jan. 1903, RGZ 53, 294 at 296 (release); MünchKomm-BGB (-Möschel) § 414 no. 2 (assumption of a debt). See supra nos. 665–666.

61. Staudinger (-Wimmer-Leonhardt) § 516 no. 27.

62. Dawson (1980) 146.

must take immediate effect to be valid as a gift. If the language instead suggests a promise of a future release, it is valid only if made in gift promise formalities.[63] When a creditor endorses a promissory note with the language "This note becomes void on my death," there is disagreement about whether the creditor has made a presently effective release or a gift promise that is valid only if made before a notary.[64]

c. Disguised Gifts

753. *Valid*. Due to the minimalist requirements for making a gift in German law, the disguised gift has not evolved, as it has in some Romanic systems, as an exception to the form requirements. Nonetheless, disguised gifts are used in German law, often to avoid obligations under tax or successions law.[65] Transactions intended as gifts are concluded in the form of a sale or a remuneration for services. The goods or the services either do not exist or are of only minimal value. The transfer is governed by the normal rules concerning sham transactions (*Scheingeschäfte*; CC § 117). The sham transaction is void, and gift law applies. The gift or gift promise is valid if the required formalities are present. In some cases the disguise is employed in the opposite direction, with the gift concealing an onerous transaction.

It may be difficult to decide whether the transaction is a sham. Because there is no consideration doctrine in German law, the parties are free to ignore market value. The courts tend to rely on the parties' subjective understanding.[66] The parties' actual intent prevails over the transactional form. However, if the parties' position has no objective foundation, the courts may decide that the transfer is gratuitous.

3. Italy

754. *Formalism*. Italian law occupies the other end of the spectrum. For all but modest gifts, Italian law requires a formalistic ritual known as the public act (*atto pubblico*).[67] Moreover, any movables involved in the gift must be specifically enumerated. There are few exceptions.

a. The Basic Rule

i. Public Act

755. *Notary*. In most contexts, public acts may be drafted either by a notary or by a number of public officials (CC art. 2699). In the case of a gift, however, the act

---

63. RG 2 Nov. 1910, JW 1911, 37.

64. RG 11 Feb. 1908, *Warneyer* 1908 no. 302, *Das Recht* 1908 no. 1165 at 195. See supra no. 714.

65. Staudinger (-Wimmer-Leonhardt) § 516 no. 57.

66. Id. § 516 no. 58.

67. Italian CC art. 782 par. 1 sent. 1.

may be completed only in the presence of a notary.[68] Usually both the donor and the donee are present.[69] The notary reads the document aloud. What the parties discuss is duly noted. The notary is required to warn the donor of the consequences of the gift. The donor must sign in the presence of two witnesses, who also must sign. The parties may not dispense with the presence of the witnesses.[70] If these formalities are not complied with—if, for example, the witnesses are not present—the gift is void and may not later be confirmed.[71] In contrast to French law, the formalities are required even when the gift transaction is disguised as onerous.[72] Moreover, the only acceptable proof of the gift is the public act itself, unless the act has been lost without the donee's fault.[73]

Gifts of specialties (*titoli nominativi*), such as shares of stock and negotiable instruments, require compliance with both gift formalities and the forms otherwise necessary for an effective transfer of the paper. Stock must sometimes be registered and reissued. Commercial paper must be endorsed (CC arts. 2022–2023).[74] The extraordinary result is that an aunt cannot make a gift to her nephew of a check for more than a modest sum in Italy without completing a public act, which involves consulting a notary, drafting several documents, and, of course, paying the applicable fees.

756. *Confirmation.* Italian law does not permit void contracts to be confirmed (*conferma*; CC art. 1423). Nonetheless a void gift may be confirmed by the heirs. The gift is confirmed if it is executed after the grounds for the nullity have become known (CC art. 799). The provision is not extended by analogy. In particular, the donor is not permitted to confirm the gift. The donor's only option to correct a defective gift is to redo the gift in the proper form. It is then effective ex nunc.[75]

757. *Justifications.* There are two traditional justifications for the elaborate form requirements. First, the donor should be encouraged to reflect before completing the gift. The goal is "to assure the maximum possible soul-searching with regard to an act that results in the reduction of the donor's patrimony (which is why the gift is considered with disfavor by the legal order)."[76] Second, due to the

---

68. Rescigno (-Carnevali) 538. If the gift is given abroad, it may be done before the Italian consul.

69. Law of 16 Feb. 1913 arts. 47 ff.

70. CC arts. 1423, 799; Cass. 14 July 1950 no. 1916, *Foro it.* 1951 I 316.

71. Cass. 18 Dec. 1975 no. 4153, *Mass. Giur. it.* 1975, 1185.

72. Cass. 14 July 1950 no. 1916, *Foro it.* 1951 I 316; infra no. 768. For the disguised gift in French law, see infra nos. 798–826.

73. Cass. 15 Mar. 2006 no. 5786, *Mass. Foro it.* 2006, 475. The court held that the fact that the gift was mentioned in the donor's holographic will was not sufficient proof.

74. Capozzi no. 333 par. f.

75. Capozzi no. 360 at 859.

76. Cass. 15 Mar. 2006 no. 5786, *Mass. Foro it.* 2006, 475.

possibility of disputes, gifts require unassailable documentation.[77] These justifications are bolstered by reference to historical-comparative studies that demonstrate that agreement alone (*nudum pactum*) has never been sufficient to validate
a gift. Validity has always required both form and donative intent.[78]

ii. Enumeration of Movables

758. *Specific description.* A gift of movables is valid only if, in addition to the
public act, the movables are specifically described, either in the gift document or
in a separate writing signed by the donor, the donee, and the notary.[79] The enumeration must be drafted at the same time as the gift act. The gift is invalid if
reference is simply made to a previous enumeration or if the enumeration is
drafted later.[80] The exact value of the movables must also be stated. For purposes
of this requirement, movables include money and negotiable instruments of all
kinds, whether order or bearer paper.[81] The gift act is void if the objects are not
specifically enumerated.[82] However, the sanction strikes only those objects that
are not mentioned and valued.

759. *Varieties of movables.* There is disagreement about how the enumeration
requirement should be applied to the gift of a going business enterprise (*azienda*)
or the gift of a collection (*universalità di mobili*), such as a library, an art collection, or an inheritance. Some scholars argue that a description of the principal
items and an overall valuation should suffice. The interpretation respects both
the ordinary understanding of the nature of a collection and the statutory wording, which expressly provides that items that subsequently become part of the
collection also become part of the gift, unless the gift act provides otherwise
(CC art. 771 par. 2).[83] These scholars suggest that it should be possible to make
a gift of an inheritance without knowing its contents (*a scatola chiusa*). A business's concern value usually exceeds the worth of the company's individual
assets. Other scholars, together with several courts, hold that separate listing and
valuation are required.[84] Gifts of stock are not subject to the enumeration and
valuation requirement. Appurtenances (*pertinenze*) are similarly exempt.

760. *Justification.* The enumeration requirement is so unusual that the Italian
doctrine has sought additional justification. The reasons suggested include the
prevention of fraud against the donor's creditors and heirs and the goal of

---

77. Rescigno (-Carnevali) 539.
78. Id. 539–540, relying on 1 Gorla 159–161, 322–326.
79. CC art. 782 par. 1 sent. 2.
80. Cian and Trabucchi art. 782 no. 5.
81. Rescigno (-Carnevali) 524, 541.
82. Id. 541.
83. Capozzi no. 333 pars. c–d; Cian and Trabucchi art. 782 no. 5.
84. Cendon art. 782 no. 3 (collecting cases).

encouraging the donor to focus attention on each individual item included in the gift.[85]

b. Exceptions

761. *Limited exclusions.* As a practical matter, Italian law recognizes only three exceptions to the form requirements. First, gifts of modest value are excepted from gift formalities. Second, customary gifts and atypical liberalities, otherwise known as indirect gifts, are not characterized as gifts in Italian law and are therefore not subject to the form requirements. On the other hand, disguised gifts are valid only if done as a public act. There is also no general exception for manual gifts.

i. Gifts of Modest Value

762. *Sole exception.* The sole exception to the elaborate Italian form requirements is the gift of movables of modest value (*donazione di modico valore*). The modicity of the gift is judged objectively on the basis of an examination of all factors related to the donor's particular economic situation.[86] In one case, the lower court held that, given "the donor's solid economic situation," a gift of a necklace of emeralds and diamonds was modest. The Cassation Court reversed, holding that a more comprehensive examination of all of the facts and circumstances was required.[87] Modest gifts may include negotiable instruments.[88] The Civil Code provides that, upon delivery (*tradizione*), modest gifts are valid, even in the absence of a notarized public act (art. 783). Delivery must be actual and not symbolic. Attornment (*costituto possessorio*) is also insufficient.[89] Some change in possession is required, though if the donee is already in possession of the gift property, a *traditio brevi manu* has been held to suffice.[90]

ii. Customary Gifts

763. *Scope.* As discussed above, those gratuitous transfers typically given for services rendered or otherwise given in conformity to custom are not considered gifts in Italian law (CC art. 770 par. 2).[91] The exclusion covers not only presents normally given on holidays and special occasions but also tips for services rendered.

764. *Custom.* Customary gifts must conform to custom in all respects, including the relationship of the parties and the value of the gift. Some authors have

---

85. Rescigno (-Carnevali) 541.
86. Cass. 28 Feb. 1980 no. 1400, *Giur. it.* 1980 I 984 at 987.
87. Id.
88. Rescigno (-Carnevali) 547.
89. Id. 549 and note 55.
90. Cass. 24 Jan. 1979 no. 529, *Foro it.* 1979 I 2686 note Cuffaro.
91. See supra no. 281.

suggested that customary gifts must be of modest value and proportional to the donor's economic circumstances. One justification for excluding these gifts from the domain of gift law is that they do not cause any significant impoverishment.[92] Nonetheless, one court held that a gift of engagement rings in a value exceeding 100 million Italian lire (approximately US $ 100,000) was customary, given the wealth of the family and the family custom of making a substantial gift at the moment of engagement.[93] In any case, custom does not dictate which types of gift are permissible. That decision is left to the donor's discretion.

765. *Transfer.* A customary gift is valid only if executed. Some authors have suggested that a gift does not conform to custom unless it is immediately delivered.[94] Others suggest that customary gifts may also include both the transfer of future property[95] and the creation of an obligation. For example, it is common for parents to promise a graduation gift.[96]

766. *Regime.* Those rules of gift law that do not contradict the nature of the customary gift continue to apply.[97] Minors and adult incompetents generally have the capacity to make and receive customary gifts.

iii. Indirect Gifts

767. *Exclusion.* Atypical liberalities are gratuitous transactions that are not carried out in the legal form of a gift. They employ instead a legal transaction that typically has a purpose distinct from gift giving. Such transfers are atypical liberalities if made with animus donandi.[98] Although they are often called indirect gifts, Italian law excludes them from the domain of gift law. They need not be done by public act.[99] They are valid if the requisites of the chosen legal form are fulfilled. Nonetheless, indirect gifts are subject to collation and revocation due to ingratitude and the birth of a child.[100]

Indirect gifts may take a variety of forms, including sowing, planting, and construction on another's property; the extinctive renunciation of a right; the discharge of a debt; the fulfillment of another's obligation; the judicial acknowledgment of a nonexistent debt; a confession of judgment; the failure to interrupt

---

92. Torrente (2006) 125.
93. Cass. 10 Dec. 1988 no. 6720, *Rep. Foro it.* 1988 *Donazione* no. 5.
94. Torrente (2006) 123–124.
95. Oppo no. 16 at 107–108.
96. Cendon art. 770 no. 4.
97. Id. no. 6.
98. Supra no. 279; Casulli (1964) no. 10 at 988.
99. Supra nos. 279–281; Cass. 16 Mar. 2004 no. 5333, *Mass. Giur. it.* 2004, 383.
100. Casulli (1964) no. 10 at 991. Casulli argues that indirect gifts should not be subject to revocation. If the transfer is made in a form other than the public act, the donor should be deemed to have assumed the risks of ingratitude and the subsequent birth of a child.

the running of a prescription period; a third-party beneficiary contract; or a *negotium mixtum cum donatione*.[101] The courts have extended the concept to include not merely the purchase of property in the name of another but also the gift of the purchase monies, provided the purpose is specified at the time of the transfer.[102] A transfer does not, however, constitute an indirect gift unless the cause is that of a nongift transaction. When the donor gratuitously agrees to assume the debt the donee owes to a third party, the gift is direct and not indirect and must be completed in the proper forms.[103]

Due to the great variety of forms that may be used for indirect gifts, some Italian authors argue that the indirect gift is not a coherent legal concept.[104] Casulli contends that direct and indirect gifts should receive the same treatment. In his view, their common features, namely donative intent and the corresponding gratuitous transfer of rights, is more important than the variation in the mechanisms used to achieve that goal.

iv. Disguised Gifts

768. *No substitute.* Disguised gifts, though not prohibited, are valid only if completed in the required gift formalities, including the two witnesses and the enumeration of movables. The form requirement applies whenever the actual substance of the contract is a gift.[105] The disguise does not provide a substitute for form as it does in French law.[106] Unlike other gifts that lack proper form, they may not be confirmed by the heirs.[107]

4. France and Belgium

769. *Rule and exception.* Between German law, which generally requires no special formalities for a valid gift disposition, and Italian law, which requires an elaborate procedure, a number of paths are possible. Perhaps the most well-known is the complex play of rule and exception in the French tradition, particularly in Belgian law. As a general rule, the French code, like the Italian code, provides that a gift disposition is valid only if accomplished by notarial act. Some have argued, however, that the three exceptions developed in the French case law have long since swallowed the rule.[108]

---

101. Casulli id.

102. Cass. 24 Feb. 2004 no. 3642, *Mass. Giur. it.* 2004, 233.

103. Cass. 30 Mar. 2006 no. 7507, *Mass. Foro it.* 2006, 2023. See also Cass. 12 July 2006 no. 15873, *Mass. Foro it.* 2006, 1390 (gift made in contemplation of marriage (*donazione obnuziale*) is not an indirect gift).

104. The discussion is summarized in Casulli (1964) no. 10 at 989–990.

105. Capozzi no. 332 par. d.

106. For the disguised gift in French law, see infra nos. 798–826.

107. Capozzi no. 360 at 860. See supra no. 756.

108. Montredon 6.

a. The Basic Rule

770. *History.* In the seventeenth century, some French courts, following Bartolus, enforced gifts made by simple writing and without registration.[109] The general view, however, seems to have required a notarial act, or at least the appearance before a notary.[110] The current form requirements originate in the Ordinance of 1731.[111] They were taken over, almost word for word, into the Code Napoleon.

i. Notarial Act

771. *Solemn contract.* French obligations law is consensualist. In principle, obligations arise from simple agreement. As a result, there are generally no form requirements in French contract law. The Civil Code prescribes a specific form (*contrat solennel*) for only four types of agreement. The gift is one of these.[112] These agreements are void unless the parties' consent is expressed in the form of a notarial act (*acte authentique*).[113] The form is thus required for validity (*solemnitatis causa*) and not simply as a matter of proof (*probationis causa*).[114] The act must be done before a notary, in the ordinary form of a contract, and the original (*minute*) must remain with the notary (CC art. 931). Until 1966, the gift was one of the rare notarial acts that required the presence of two notaries, or of one notary and two witnesses.[115] Today the presence of one notary without additional witnesses is sufficient.[116] The notary must read the document aloud in the donor's presence. Both the donor and the notary must sign.[117]

(A) LEGAL NATURE

772. *Substantive requirement.* Though the notarization requirement is included in a section of the code entitled "Of the Form of Inter Vivos Gifts," it is actually more than a rule of form. The gift only comes into existence is by virtue of the

---

109. Regnault 172–173.

110. Id. 173–184.

111. For the forms required by the Ordinance of 1731, see supra no. 743.

112. The others are the marriage settlement (*contrat de mariage*; now in art. 1394 par. 1), the creation of a mortgage (*constitution d'hypothèque*; art. 2416), and one type of contractual subrogation (*subrogation conventionnelle consentie par le débiteur*; art. 1250 no. 2).

113. 2 Ghestin nos. 321, 323.

114. 1 Delvincourt 748 note 1 to page 238.

115. Law of 25 Ventôse XI art. 9; Law of 21 June 1843 art. 2 par. 1; 5 Planiol and Ripert no. 347. The presence of the second notary, or of the two witnesses, was only required at the moment the act was read aloud and the parties signed. The gift act was also required to state that the notary, or the two witnesses, were present. Otherwise the act was void. Law of 21 June 1843 art. 2 par. 2.

116. Law of 28 Dec. 1966.

117. 5 Planiol and Ripert no. 350.

prescribed rules—*Forma dat esse rei.*[118] If any required element is missing—for example, if a co-donor fails to sign—the act is void.[119] Moreover, if the gift is void due to a formal defect—for example, if a witness fails to sign—the act must be redone. It cannot be resuscitated retroactively by correcting the defect (CC art. 1339).[120] Because gift formalities are considered to be matters of public policy (*ordre public*), the parties may not negotiate about them or agree to accept less than what the statute mandates.[121] Moreover, because gifts are invalid if the donor does not maintain donative intent throughout the notarization process, donors may cancel their own signatures at any time before the other signatures have been completed.[122] However, not all errors in the document render the gift void. For example, though the gift act should state that the document was read aloud, the gift is not void if that statement is omitted.[123]

(B) REGIME

773. *Absolutely void.* As long as the donor is alive, the nullity is absolute and can be invoked by any interested party, including the donor. The prescription period is thirty years.[124] The gift cannot be confirmed. Actual delivery, even with donative intent, does not cure the form defect and is not valid as a manual gift.[125] When a gift is void because of a form defect, the donor does not have to transfer title and may recover what has already been given—including fruits, if the donee was aware of the defect.[126] If the donor has transferred the property to a third party, the transfer is valid, while any transfer by the donee is void.[127] When the donor dies, successions laws permits the heirs to waive opposition to the gift (CC art. 1340). At that moment, the nullity becomes relative and is interpreted as a protection for the heirs.[128]

---

118. 8 De Page no. 435. In French law thinking, these formalities are required as a condition of the gift's existence. If they are missing, the gift is not simply void. It never existed. Bufnoir 492.

119. Civ.¹ 28 Nov. 1972, J.C.P. 1973 II 17461 note Dagot.

120. Civ.¹ 15 June 1962, *Gaz. Pal.* 1962 II 181.

121. Civ.¹ 12 June 1967, D. 1967, 584 note Breton; J.C.P. 1967 II 15225 note R.L.

122. Orléans 13 June 1838, D. *Jur. gén., Dispositions entre vifs* no. 1418.

123. 5 Planiol and Ripert no. 350.

124. Id. no. 351.

125. Richard Crône, obs. to Civ.¹ 23 Jan. 2001, *Rép. not. Defrén.* 2001 art. 37357 at 626–635. For the manual gift exception to French gift law formalities, see infra nos. 780–797.

126. 5 Planiol and Ripert no. 354.

127. Id.

128. Id. no. 352.

(C) JUSTIFICATIONS

774. *Early rationales.* As discussed above, D'Aguesseau indicated that he imposed the form requirement to prevent surprise and fraud. He may also have followed the thought of his teacher, Jean Domat, who suggested the notarial act as a means to prevent revocation.[129] Pothier was convinced by this reasoning. "The Ordinance required this precaution in order to prevent the donor from retaining the gift instrument, or delivering it to a third person, who would return it to the donor upon demand. The donor's power to cancel would violate the irrevocability required of inter vivos gifts."[130] Bigot de Préameneu, one of the code's drafters, accepted Pothier's explanation. "[I]t should not be within the power of either of the parties to cancel the gift by destroying the instrument (*acte*) by which it could be proved."[131]

These early justifications involve two thoughts that are both probably incorrect.[132] The first has to do with irrevocability. The principle of special irrevocability that governs French gift law has nothing to do with the disappearance of a document. Rather, it prevents terms from being inserted into the gift act that would permit rescission at the donor's discretion.[133] The second thought has to do with the original copy of the gift. If the notary were not involved, the original gift document would normally be remitted to the *donee* because the donor is the only party obligated. In most situations, the donor would not be able to destroy the document unilaterally.[134]

775. *Modern justifications.* Modern scholars offer other justifications. First, the notary's presence may protect the donor from undue influence. Second, the notary is able to draw the donor's attention to the family's competing interests. Finally, the notarized act provides indisputable proof of the gift for purposes of calculating the donor's disposable share.[135] Nonetheless, Planiol and Ripert were not convinced. In their view,

> [a]ll of these reasons are insufficient ... [T]he solemnity is illogical and inefficacious. It is illogical in the sense that there exist many other ways to ruin oneself and one's family and all just as dangerous as the gift. Individuals who would never rashly consent to a gift frequently enter into contractual bargains

---

129. 1 Domat no. 909. See supra no. 743.

130. 1 Pothier tit. 15 no. 28; see also 8 Pothier, *Donations* no. 130.

131. "Présentation au corps législatif et exposé des motifs," 12 Fenet 544.

132. 8 De Page no. 438 at 547 and note 5.

133. Infra nos. 1086–1087.

134. In Dumoulin's view, if the donor retained the original of the gift act, that in itself would violate the maxim *Donner et retenir ne vaut* (as originally interpreted), since the donor would not have surrendered possession. Customs of Paris art. 274 note, in 3 Dumoulin (1691) 27.

135. 5 Planiol and Ripert no. 342.

through which they are cheated by skillful crooks. The solemnity is also especially inefficacious. To play a useful role it would have to govern all gifts without exception. But that is radically impossible at a time when fortunes are made without difficulty, in an age of money, bearer instruments, and checks.[136]

(D) COMPARATIVE NOTES

776. *Clear message.* The one clear message of the French form requirement is that the drafters of the Civil Code did not approve of gift giving. A number of commentators have emphasized the fact. Delvincourt, writing shortly after the Code's promulgation while he was Dean of the Paris law faculty, explained the form requirement as an aspect of the law's suspicion of gift giving. "To justify this provision it is first necessary to note that, in our law, in contrast to Roman law, gratuitous transfers are not in general favored."[137] As Bufnoir put it, "[T]hese are acts that cause doubt about whether the donor's motives are always honorable."[138] De Page agreed.

> The truth is that, because the gift is an essentially *dangerous* act, as much for the individual as for the family, the law, without completely prohibiting it, has placed various obstacles in the road to its realization .... The goal is to make gifts as rare as possible. They have been rendered laborious and difficult by the complications imposed by the multiple rules relating *to form*, rules both arbitrary and conventional, which have no other justification than the goal mentioned here.[139]

The courts do not seem concerned about the danger. Over the past two centuries, as discussed below, they have carved out three generous exceptions. Today virtually any gift can be made without complying with the mandated formalities. The three exceptions are a concession to social custom. Gifts are permitted in the forms that conform to social practice. The survival on the books of a principle that has long since been hollowed out by exceptions demonstrates the conflict that exists between gift law and social practice. The curious persistence of two contradictory sets of rules can also not be ascribed to the traditional respect accorded the text of the code. Over the past decade, the French legislator has modified many of the provisions that govern gift law without ever revamping the form requirement.

---

136. Id.

137. 1 Delvincourt 749 note 1 to page 238.

138. Bufnoir 487.

139. 8 De Page no. 438 (emphasis in original); see also Dawson (1980) 224–25.

ii. Written Inventory

777. *Enumeration of movables.* The Italian law requirement of a written inventory is derived from French law. In French law, gifts of movables are valid only if they are accompanied by a written inventory (*état estimatif*), signed by both the donor and the donee (or the donee's representative), and annexed to the original gift act (CC art. 948). The inventory may be included either in the gift act or in a separate document. Because a form is not prescribed, the inventory may be made either by formal act or by signed writing (*acte sous seing privé*).[140] It must be contemporaneous with the gift, though the inventory itself need not be notarized.[141]

The inventory must both enumerate the movables and provide an estimate of their value. Generally, each gift item must be separately enumerated and valued, but collections and other items that belong together may be valued as a whole.[142] The inventory requirement applies to virtually all movables, whether corporeal or incorporeal, including contract rights. Specific liquid debts must be enumerated but not valued.[143] Though the written inventory is considered essential to the gift's validity, the requirement is interpreted less strictly than the requisites of the notarial act. An inventory previously established by the parties and referred to in the gift act is an acceptable equivalent, as are other writings that specify the property and its value.[144]

Without a written inventory, the gift is absolutely void while the donor is alive and void at the heirs' discretion after the donor's death.[145] The inventory is required even when the gift is accompanied by delivery, though in that case the gift may be valid as a manual gift, which is not subject to the form requirements.[146] Gifts of future property between spouses are also exempted because such property is generally not determinable on the date of the gift.[147]

778. *History and justification.* D'Aguesseau prescribed the inventory only for goods not delivered at the moment the gift is made.[148] The project of a Civil Code from Year VIII also excepted the case of immediate delivery,[149] but the exception was removed in the final text.[150] The requirement seems to be designed to ensure

---

140. Response of the minister of justice, *Rép. not. Defrén.* 2006 art. 38340 at 370.

141. 8 De Page no. 466.

142. 5 Planiol and Ripert no. 358; 8 De Page no. 470.

143. 5 Planiol and Ripert no. 356; 8 De Page id.

144. 5 Planiol and Ripert no. 357.

145. 8 De Page no. 477.

146. 5 Planiol and Ripert no. 356. For the manual gift in French law, see infra nos. 780–797. A late draft of the Code did not require a written inventory if there was delivery. Art. 52 (19 Ventôse XI [10 Mar. 1803]), in 12 Fenet 370, 373.

147. Véron 100.

148. Ordinance of 1731 art. 15.

149. Bk. 3 tit. 9 art. 41, in 2 Fenet 281.

150. 5 Planiol and Ripert no. 356.

irrevocability. Without an inventory, the donor might be tempted to substitute items of lesser value for the objects given, thereby partially revoking the gift.[151] However, because unwarranted revocation would be impossible for goods already delivered, supplementary justifications have been advanced. The inventory is also thought to be useful in cases in which the property must be returned to the heirs or in which the donor wishes to revoke.[152]

b. Exceptions

779. *Circumventing the formalities.* The code does not expressly permit exceptions to the solemnity principle. Moreover, exceptions would seem to be excluded by the fact that the formalities are said to be mandated by public policy and sanctioned by absolute nullity. Nonetheless, the scholars and the case law unanimously approve gift-giving mechanisms that circumvent the form requirements. In fact, the intricate web of exceptions is now so extensive that there is no kind of gift that cannot validly be made in a relatively simple alternative form. The three exceptions to the form requirements are the manual gift, the disguised gift, and the indirect gift. The bulk of the scholarly discussion and case law in the field of gift law involves attempts to produce a coherent understanding of these exceptions.

i. Manual Gifts

780. *Unanimous authority.* In general, a manual gift of movables (*don manuel*) is effective if there is actual delivery (*tradition*)—an effective hand-to-hand transfer—of the property.[153] "It requires, as its essential constitutive element, the delivery (*tradition*) of the gift object, *by which alone* it exists, and not by the gift contract which, nonetheless, is its foundation."[154] No writing is required. The transfer must be made for the independent purpose of making a manual gift (*à titre autonome et distinct*). Thus, delivery cannot cure a gift that is otherwise invalid as to form.[155] Though manual gifts are authorized by no provision in the Civil Code, there is no doubt they are valid.[156] D'Aguesseau and Pothier both approved them.[157] The parlements validated them before the promulgation of the Ordinance of 1731 and continued to accept them once the ordinance took

---

151. Bufnoir 492; 5 Planiol and Ripert no. 355; 8 De Page no. 467.

152. Bufnoir id.; 5 Planiol and Ripert id.; 8 De Page id.

153. "As far as the manual gift is concerned, it is possession, and it alone, that is equivalent to title." Req. 28 Oct. 1935, D.P. 1936 I 29 concl. Pilon.

154. 8 De Page no. 516 (emphasis in original). See 5 Planiol and Ripert no. 381; Dawson (1980) 70–74.

155. Richard Crône, obs. to Civ.¹ 23 Jan. 2001, *Rép. not. Defrén.* 2001 art. 37357 at 626–635.

156. For the history of the doctrine, see Peterka nos. 3–8.

157. D'Aguesseau, Letter no. 290 of 25 June 1731, in 9 d'Aguesseau 360 at 361; 8 Pothier, *Donations* no. 131 *in fine.*

effect.[158] The case law under the Civil Code has always approved them, the French legislator has recognized their existence in gift tax legislation, and, aside from a couple of case notes dating from the time of the July Monarchy,[159] the scholars have unanimously approved them,[160] though some have done so against their better judgment.[161]

(A) TYPES OF MOVABLES

781. *Corporeal movables.* In principle, corporeal movables, and only they, may be given by manual gift. Registered movables for which delivery is insufficient to transfer title—principally cars, ships, and aircraft—may not be the object of a manual gift. Under certain circumstances, the delivery of a work of art or a manuscript may transfer the author's intellectual property rights as well.[162]

(1) Incorporeal Rights

782. *Negotiable instruments.* Though incorporeal movables may not generally be transferred by manual gift,[163] the principle is attenuated when the rights are incorporated into documents, such as bearer paper, that are transferred by delivery.[164] The delivery of a check or other negotiable instrument, whether order or bearer paper, may constitute a manual gift, as may the transfer of stock certificates, even when they are electronic or otherwise noncertificated.[165]

783. *Critique.* Michel Dagot argues that, because the manual gift is an exception, it should be interpreted strictly and permitted only for chattels that are subject to actual delivery.[166] That means that both order paper and noncertificated (*dématérialisés*) stock certificates should not be transferable by manual gift. "These solutions do not conform to the spirit of French law, which normally requires a writing. Not only do the exceptions approve nonwritten forms, but, even worse, the mechanism expressly provided by the legislature is rejected.

---

158. Merlin (1820) *Donation* § 6 at 403; Lagarde 29. Merlin provides a summary of the case law under the Parlements as well as of the early case law under the Civil Code. Merlin id. 403–414.

159. Note to Req. 6 Feb. 1844, D.P. 1844 I 151; note to Bordeaux 4 May 1843, D.P. 1843 II 203.

160. See 8 De Page nos. 516 ff.; 5 Planiol and Ripert no. 381.

161. "[T]he manual gift is not a normal mode of gratuitous transfer but rather one that must be tolerated or, to put it another way, a disease that cannot be cured and that must be accepted." J.-E. Labbé, note to Paris 30 Dec. 1881, S. 1883 II 241.

162. 5 Planiol and Ripert no. 386.

163. 7 Aubry and Rau (1875) § 659.

164. 5 Planiol and Ripert no. 385.

165. Com. 19 May 1998, D. 1998, 551 note Didier Martin; Civ.[1] 27 Oct. 1993, *Bull. civ.* I no. 299.

166. Dagot (2000) 1472.

That provides grounds for reflection. The generalized validation of gifts that are not in writing contradicts the spirit of French law in a domain that is nonetheless extremely sensitive."[167]

784. *Bank transfers.* A bank transfer of funds (*virement de compte*), when gratuitous, was originally characterized as a manual gift.[168] One scholar explained that a bank transfer involves the required "concrete process of delivery."[169] However, many have noted that a transfer made by notation on a bank's books seems to depart markedly from the original justification for the manual gift.[170] When a manual gift is executed through the intermediary of a bank, Dean Carbonnier commented, "we dive into nonlaw (*non-droit*) to escape formalism."[171] Moreover, because a third party is involved in the transfer, it might more properly be characterized as an indirect gift.[172] The same is true for a gift of securities made by transfer on the company's books.[173] Under Belgian law, gifts made by bank transfer are considered indirect.[174]

(2) Partial Interests

785. *Side agreements.* Though once subject to discussion, it is now clear that a partial interest (*démembrement*) may be given by manual gift. The fact that the gift concerns only a usufruct (*usufruit*), for example, or the underlying property right (*nue-propriété*), may be established by a side agreement (*pacte adjoint*).[175] In both cases, the apparent delivery is deceptive because it suggests that full title has been transferred. The courts have solved the practical issues by validating the grant as stated in the side agreement.

These side agreements pose a problem for French law when they are not in the form of a notarial act.[176] Logic would seem to dictate that, where the delivery

---

167. Id. 1475.

168. Civ.[1] 12 July 1966, D. 1966, 614 note J. Mazeaud. More recently, French authors consider these to be indirect gifts. Infra no. 837.

169. Didier Martin, note to Com. 19 May 1998, D. 1998, 551 at 552.

170. Jean Patarin, obs. to Com. 19 May 1998, *Rev. trim. dr. civ.* 1999, 677–678.

171. Carbonnier (1983) 49.

172. Lagarde 32 note 27.

173. For the indirect gift in French law, see infra nos. 827–843.

174. "'Immaterial bank deposits (*monnaie scripturale*) cannot really be delivered. As a consequence, the conveyance that operates a transfer of these funds cannot be realized by means of a manual gift. There is no tangible personal property subject to delivery *animo donandi*.'" Bruxelles 25 Nov. 1991, *Pas.* 1991 II 209 at 212, quoting J. Delnoy, obs. to Mons 20 Nov. 1979, *Rev. crit. jur. belge* 1984, 206 at 214. These gifts fit within the narrow Belgian doctrine of indirect gifts since they result from third-party beneficiary contracts. Bruxelles 25 Nov. 1991, *Pas.* 1991 II 209 at 212. See infra no. 829.

175. 5 Planiol and Ripert no. 383; 8 De Page no. 535; Jean Patarin obs. to Civ.[1] 25 Feb. 1997, *Rev. trim. dr. civ.* 1998, 439 at 441–442.

176. Terré and Lequette no. 497.

does not speak for itself, a notarial act should be required.[177] D'Aguesseau seems
to have accepted the validity of manual gifts only to the extent they were not
accompanied by a writing. Joseph-Emile Labbé, a celebrated nineteenth century
commentator, suggested that the manual gift should be valid, while any accom-
panying agreement should be void.[178] However, the courts have accepted written
side agreements because they provide proof advantages for all concerned. The
decisions even permit a manual gift of a usufruct of a sum of money.[179] The
usufructuary may use the funds freely and keep the proceeds, and is only required
to return the principal at the end of the term.

Nonetheless, a theoretical issue remains.[180] The manual gift of a usufruct
cannot be considered the gift of a usufructuary interest separate from the underlying property right (*nue-propriété*). French law does not recognize the common-
law distinction between life estate and remainder. In French law, the donor of a
partial interest gives an intangible right rather than a property interest. In the
nineteenth century, it was noted that classical Roman law did not recognize
delivery as a means to transfer title to incorporeals.[181] Today in French law, in
contrast, incorporeal rights may be transferred by manual gift.[182]

(B) NATURE OF DELIVERY

(1) Transfer of Possession

786. *Good faith purchase.* The delivery must effectively transfer possession. The
early case law required possession with all the elements required for the good
faith purchase of movables—good faith, together with peaceable, public, and
nonequivocal possession under a claim of ownership.[183] Today, however, a defect
in possession means only that the donee must prove the manual gift and may not
rely on the presumption of title that usually accompanies possession.[184]

787. *Actual delivery.* The case law on the issue of delivery is not overly rigorous.
A *traditio brevi manu* suffices—if the goods are in the hands of the donee, an oral
declaration of gift is all that is needed. Attornment (*constitut possessoire*), however, does not make a valid manual gift. If the donor wishes to make a gift while

---

177. Frédéric Zenati, obs. to Civ.[1] 25 Feb. 1997, *Rev. trim. dr. civ.* 1999, 655 at 657.

178. J.-E. Labbé, note to Paris 30 Dec. 1881, S. 1883 II 241.

179. Civ.[1] 25 Feb. 1997, *Bull. civ.* I no. 70, *Rép. not. Defrén.* 1997 art. 36703 no. 176 at
1448 obs. Gérard Champenois, *Rev. trim. dr. civ.* 1998, 439 obs. Jean Patarin, *Rev. trim. dr.
civ.* 1999, 655 obs. Frédéric Zenati.

180. Frédéric Zenati, obs. to Civ.[1] 25 Feb. 1997, *Rev. trim. dr. civ.* 1999, 655 at
657–658.

181. "It is obvious that incorporeal movables (*incorporales res*) cannot be transferred by
delivery or adverse possession." D. 41, 1, 43, 1 (Gaius).

182. Frédéric Zenati, obs. to Civ.[1] 25 Feb. 1997, *Rev. trim. dr. civ.* 1999, 655 at 658.

183. These are the conditions for invoking CC arts. 1141, 2279.

184. 5 Planiol and Ripert no. 381.

retaining use of the goods, there has to be an actual delivery followed by a bailment back.

(2) Donor's Check

788. *Comparison.* As noted above, the delivery of a check may constitute a manual gift. French law on this question is more complex than the corresponding German and common-law rules. In the latter two legal orders, a check drawn by the donor and made payable to the donee operates a gift transfer only when it is finally paid by the bank. In French law, delivery of the check itself may, in some situations, function as a valid gift. There are two principles.

[a] Actual Delivery

789. *Actual and irrevocable.* First, the donor must make a valid manual gift, complete with actual and irrevocable delivery. If the drawer simply places the signed and completed check in a safe deposit box to which the payee does not have access or to which the parties have joint access, there is no gift. Even the donor's irrevocable order to a bailee in possession is not sufficient.[185] The gift is not effective until the intended donee takes possession.[186] Similarly, a transfer of funds into a joint account does not complete the manual gift. Such a transfer would permit the donor to revoke the transfer.[187]

[b] Available Funds

790. *Sufficient funds.* Second, the validity of the gift depends on whether there are sufficient funds in the drawer's account.

791. *Operates assignment.* In French law, in contrast to the common law, payment by check functions as an assignment of the drawer's funds (*provision*) that are in the drawee's possession.[188] If there are sufficient funds, the right to receive payment is immediately transferred to the payee. The gift is effective even before the bank has made payment.[189] Such a gift is valid even in cases in which the check is later wrongfully dishonored[190] or is not presented to the drawee bank until after the drawer's death.[191]

792. *Insufficient funds.* If, at the moment the check is issued, the account does not have funds sufficient to cover the check, the rules are complex. First, if the

---

185. Civ.¹ 27 Oct. 1993, *Bull. civ.* I no. 299.

186. Civ.¹ 3 Apr. 2002, *Rev. trim. dr. civ.* 2002, 554 obs. Jean Patarin, *Rép. not. Defrén.* 2003 no. 37649 no. 08 at 46–47 obs. Gérard Champenois.

187. Jean Patarin, obs. to Civ.¹ 30 March 1999, *Rev. trim. dr. civ.* 1999, 678. For the irrevocability requirement in French law, see infra nos. 1075–1096.

188. For a comparison of the two systems on this question, see Mitchell 241–243.

189. Jean Patarin, obs. to Civ.¹ 5 Feb. 2002, *Rev. trim. dr. civ.* 2002, 551.

190. Arrighi.

191. Civ.¹ 4 Nov. 1981, *Bull. civ.* I no. 327.

donor subsequently makes a covering deposit, delivery is retroactively deemed to operate a manual gift.[192] A check properly dishonored after the donor's death functions as a manual gift if the heirs voluntarily make payment.[193] As the authors have pointed out, this rule allows the donor to decide whether to provision the check, which seems to violate the special principle of irrevocability.[194]

In a recent case, a husband, just before he died, wrote a check as a gift to his wife for FF 250,000.[195] At the time, only FF 16,544 were on deposit in the account. The wife, invoking the normal principles of French negotiable instruments law, argued that, because delivery of the check operates as an assignment of the funds in the account, the check should be considered a manual gift of the funds then in the account. Though the court did not mention the issue, her argument presented serious practical problems. Because checks are processed around the clock, the actual amount available in a checking account varies from moment to moment and is relatively arbitrary. The Cassation Court avoided this difficulty by deciding that, if there are insufficient funds, delivery of the check does not operate a gift, even as to the funds then in the account.

793. *No suit on the check.* Finally, the donee/payee is not permitted to sue either the donor or the donor's heirs on the gifted instrument, even though such a cause of action would otherwise be available under negotiable instruments law. Though there is authority to the contrary,[196] the scholars suggest that such a suit would undercut the informal and spontaneous nature of the manual gift.[197]

(C) BURDEN OF PROOF

794. *En fait de meubles.* The powerful presumptions attached to the possession of chattels (*meubles corporels*) in French law gives the manual gift an especially wide reach. The maxim *En fait de meubles, la possession vaut titre*, the Civil Code's good faith purchase provision,[198] produces what is known as its *subsidiary* effect in the context of the manual gift. In this context, the maxim's effect is to reverse the

---

192. Gérard Champenois, obs. to Civ.¹ 5 Feb. 2002, *Rép. not. Defrén.* 2003 art. 37649 no. 07 at 43, 44. In the case of a special deposit, the result is likely to be similar in common-law systems as well. See 3 Pomeroy § 1280.

193. Boujeka.

194. For the special principle of irrevocability in French gift law, see infra nos. 1075–1096. The case decided on 5 Feb. 2002, as explained in the text, involved an attempted inter vivos gift between spouses. At the time, gifts between spouses were revocable in French law. The gift in that case was thus not subject to the special principle of irrevocability. For the revocability of gifts between spouses in French law, see infra nos. 1295–1313.

195. Civ.¹ 5 Feb. 2002, *Bull. civ.* I no. 39.

196. Paris 19 June 1963, D. 1964 Somm. 45.

197. Didier R. Martin, obs. to Civ.¹ 5 Feb. 2002, D. 2003, 344 at 345.

198. "In matters involving movables, possession is equivalent to title." CC art. 2279 par. 1; see 3 Carbonnier 331–332.

burden of proof on the requirements of a valid gift. Once the donee has established the elements of good faith possession, the party challenging the gift has the burden of demonstrating that no manual gift was made.[199]

When the Civil Code was promulgated, this proof presumption was not yet clearly distinguished from the principal function of the maxim, which is very different. It permits acquisition by good faith purchase from someone other than the owner (*a non domino*).[200] Due to the confusion, the code's early interpreters argued that, because possession is equivalent to title, a notarial act was not necessary for an executed gift of movables.[201] The presumption's more limited role in the context of gift law seems not to have been clearly understood until the end of the nineteenth century.[202] Even today, however, the exceptionally strong role that French law attributes to the possession of corporeal movables seems to operate as a background justification for the manual gift.[203]

(D) JUSTIFICATION

795. *D'Aguesseau.* The fact that French law permits a gift to be made by simple delivery "is so odd as to require an explanation."[204] In his official correspondence, d'Aguesseau made clear that the formalities did not apply to "the case of a gift that would be consummated without act (*sans acte*) by means of the actual delivery (*tradition réelle*) of a movable or of a modest sum."[205] D'Aguesseau's approval of the manual gift could not have been based on his understanding, or even his misunderstanding, of the maxim *En fait de meubles*. At the time the Ordinance was promulgated, the maxim was just beginning to develop in the practice of the Châtelet Court in Paris, and Bourjon had not yet formulated his celebrated phrase.[206] Instead, d'Aguesseau reasoned that the formalities apply only to *actes*, and a delivery is not an *acte*.[207] Jaubert, in his report to the Tribunate during the drafting of the Civil Code, made a similar remark.[208] Aubry and Rau were convinced by the reasoning.[209]

D'Aguesseau's argument has become less convincing over the years. Technically, he seems to have assumed that *acte* in the Ordinance should be understood to mean *written proof* (*instrumentum*) rather than *legal transaction*

---

199. Civ.[1] 19 Oct. 1983, *Bull. civ.* I no. 241; Civ.[1] 28 Apr. 1986, *Bull. civ.* I no. 130.
200. Lagarde 31.
201. 1 Delvincourt 750 note 3 to page 238; Bufnoir 495–498.
202. Req. 5 Dec. 1893, S. 1893 I 79, D. 1894 I 48; 3 Carbonnier 340.
203. Jean Patarin, obs. to Com. 19 May 1998, *Rev. trim. dr. civ.* 1999, 677.
204. 5 Planiol and Ripert no. 378.
205. D'Aguesseau, Letter no. 290 of 25 June 1731, in 9 d'Aguesseau 360 at 361.
206. Brissaud § 247 at 303–304; Bufnoir 498. The role of the maxim *En fait de meubles* in the gift law context is discussed just above. See no. 794.
207. Letter no. 290 of 25 June 1731, in 9 d'Aguesseau 360 at 361.
208. "Communication officielle" (9 Floréal XI [29 Apr. 1803]), 12 Fenet 598.
209. 7 Aubry and Rau (1875) § 659 note 13 at 80–81.

(*negotium*). If that were the case, however, then written proof of a gift would be unacceptable in court unless in notarized form, which is not the French rule.[210] If *acte* is understood as *negotium*, the manual gift is certainly an *acte* in that sense and thus would normally be prohibited by the formality requirement. Moreover, at the time of the Ordinance, wealth resided principally in landed property, which could never be transferred by manual gift. D'Aguesseau himself limited the value of the movables that could be transferred without registration (Ordinance art. 22).[211] Neither the code nor current case law, however, limits the value of manual gifts. Due to the importance of movable wealth in modern society, some authors have recommended capping the amount that may be transferred by manual gift and have favored other restrictions as well.[212]

796. *Code drafters*. Modern French authors assume that gift formalities were originally designed to govern all gifts. The manual gift must therefore be justified as an exception. Yet if gift giving always presents a risk that requires professional counsel, it is hard to see how the manual gift could ever be justified. A closer look at the legislative history suggests that the original purpose of requiring a notarial act was much narrower.

In the report that accompanied the proposed law that eventually imposed the special gift law formalities,[213] Philippe Dupin mentioned a critical respect in which gift giving frequently differs from exchange transactions. In an exchange, the property is almost always transferred immediately, or at least while both parties are still alive. The transfer serves as a means to ensure that some transaction was intended. Moreover, in case of dispute, both parties are usually alive to testify. A donor who makes a significant gift, however, usually reserves a usufruct. That means that the donor does not part with the property until death. Because the donor does not actually experience the loss of the property, it is important to ensure that the heirs' interests are impressed upon the donor. As a supplementary justification for the form requirement, Dupin noted that gifts are more frequently extracted by means of undue influence than are exchange transactions.

The manual gift, in contrast, generally operates an immediate transfer of the gift property. In this sense it is not as risky as a gift with reservation of a usufruct. The heirs will be disadvantaged by a manual gift, but the donor is aware of the fact. Moreover, if there is undue influence, the facts are fresh, and the parties are usually available to testify. In other words, the manual gift seems not to have been in the contemplation of the legislature when the formalities were imposed.

---

210. 5 Planiol and Ripert no. 379 and note 2 at 394.
211. Id. no. 378. The amount was 1,000 *livres*. See supra no. 743.
212. 8 De Page nos. 494, 517.
213. Carette and Devilleneuve 757–758 note 1.

797. *Today.* The manual gift is now considered an autonomous institution of customary origin. It functions independently, parallel with and not subordinate to the notarized act.[214] Some justify the institution by the fact that manual giving would continue even if prohibited.[215] For others, the manual gift exists beyond the reaches of what the law may regulate. It is located "at the very boundaries of law, is in fact almost 'nonlaw.'"[216] In the end, the manual gift today is considered not so much an exception to, as a critique of, the code's vision of the law's role in gift giving. "It would never be possible to eliminate [manual gifts], regardless of the force of the prohibition. Without doubt, the principle of solemnity as conceived in the Code is directly violated; but that proves only that the Code's conception, as far as solemnity is concerned, is false. It cannot pass the test of reality."[217]

ii. Disguised Gifts

798. *Simulation.* The disguised gift (*donation déguisé*) is a sham (*simulation*), a gift masquerading as an exchange. In a common example, the parties appear to conclude an act of sale but in fact agree either that the price will not be paid or that, if paid, it will be returned.[218] All acts that can be done for compensation may be used as disguised gifts. The *substantive* requirements are those of a valid gift. Both donor and donee must have donative capacity. There must be donative intent and a proper gift object. The *form* is that of the sham transaction. The form must be regular, and all formal conditions for its validity must be present.[219] Moreover, the donative nature of the transaction must not be apparent from the act.[220] Disguised gifts are undoubtedly valid today in French law.[221] However, as Blaise has described in an exquisite study, the institution has had a bumpy ride in the courts.[222]

(A) HISTORY

799. *Roman law.* Roman law validated some gifts that were disguised as sales. For example, a sale at a nominal price was valid.[223] In principle, a sale for which it was agreed that the price would not be paid was not considered a sale at all, and

---

214. 5 Planiol and Ripert no. 379.
215. 8 De Page no. 494.
216. Malaurie and Aynès 228.
217. 5 Planiol and Ripert no. 379.
218. Id. no. 493; Malaurie and Aynès no. 409.
219. 8 De Page no. 510; 5 Planiol and Ripert nos. 425, 425 bis.
220. 8 De Page no. 512 par. A; 5 Planiol and Ripert no. 425 bis.
221. 5 Planiol and Ripert no. 425 and note 1.
222. Blaise. See also Dawson (1980) 74–83. For a summary of the principal early cases, see Merlin (1820) *Donation* § 4 at 391–403.
223. D. 18, 1, 38 (Ulpian).

the transaction was ineffective.[224] However, because no action lay to recover the price, the transaction was effective as a gift if the donee received possession.[225]

800. *Ancien régime.* During the ancien régime, it seems that fathers disguised gifts to their chosen heirs to maintain privacy. Some argued that these disguised gifts represented a type of tacit gift (*donation tacite*) that was not subject to the form requirements of the Ordinance of 1731.[226] However, cases involving disguises seem rarely to have been litigated.

801. *The Revolution and after.* During the revolution, as discussed above, the Convention established absolute equality among children for the distribution of decedents' estates.[227] The peasantry opposed the change. When the Convention made the abolition retroactive to the fall of the Bastille, pandemonium broke out.[228] The result was what P. M. Jones has called "a long century of guerrilla warfare," pitting the ingenuity of the French peasantry against the code.[229] Disguised gifts were clandestine weapons used to sabotage egalitarianism. The battle raged throughout the nineteenth century.

Like the country itself, the early case law was split.[230] In a critical case decided in Year XI (1803), the Cassation Tribunal was at first evenly split on the question. After five judges were added and the case was reargued, there was a majority of one.[231] Two chambers of the French high court were unable to reconcile their positions,[232] so that, on successive days in Year XIII (1804), the two chambers issued conflicting judgments.[233] Courts that favored equality struck down disguised gifts once the sham was revealed. The gifts were held to be void even if the gift object was proper and the donee had the capacity to receive.[234] These courts held that gifts made without a notarial act were void and could be challenged by anyone with an interest.[235] Well into the nineteenth century, intermediate courts continued to invalidate disguised gifts.[236]

---

224. D. 18, 1, 36 (Ulpian); C. 4, 38, 3.

225. C. 4, 38, 9.

226. Civ. 6 Pluviôse XI [26 Jan. 1803], S. 1791–XII I 746 (pourvoi).

227. Decree of 8 Apr. 1791 art. 1. See supra no. 3.

228. Jones (1985) 101–104.

229. Id. 103.

230. For the history of the dispute, see Méau-Lautour nos. 11–14.

231. Civ. 6 Pluviôse XI [26 Jan. 1803], in S. 1791–XII I 746.

232. Blaise 91–98.

233. Compare Civ. 7 Frimaire XIII [28 Nov. 1804], S. XIII–1808 I 32 (disguised gifts valid) with Req. 8 Frimaire XIII [29 Nov. 1804], S. XIII–1808 I 33 (disguised gifts void).

234. Req. 24 Nov. 1808, S. XIII–1808 I 607.

235. Claude-Étienne Delvincourt, obs. to Civ. 31 May 1813, S. 1812–1814 I 362.

236. See, e.g., Civ. 20 Nov. 1826, S. 1825–1827 I 458 (reversing Orleans 29 Nov. 1822).

Other courts, together with a majority of the authors, validated disguised gifts.[237] Those courts that approved the institution relied on the fact that simulation does not provide grounds for invalidity in French law. Disguised gifts were valid if the parties had the requisite capacity and if the gift did not exceed the disposable share.[238] Jacques de Maleville, one of the Civil Code's drafters, presided over the court that finally resolved the question.[239] He had been trained in the tradition of the *droit écrit* and relied heavily on Roman law precedent. The decisive argument seems to have been the desire to prevent disappointed heirs from challenging all of a decedent's onerous transactions in the hope of uncovering a simulation.[240]

(B) DEFINING CHARACTERISTICS

802. *Form.* As for form, a disguised gift is valid only if it respects the form of the onerous transaction that it simulates.[241] If the chosen form is the acknowledgment of a debt (*reconnaissance de dette*), the writing must be signed by the debtor and, in the debtor's handwriting, state the amount of the debt in both words and numbers (CC art. 1326). It is surprising that validity is contingent on respect for this form. When the acknowledgment is not used to disguise a gift, these formalities are required only to the extent the document will be used as proof.[242]

803. *Complete sham.* The sham must be complete. The donative nature of the transaction must not be apparent either from the face of the writing or from the immediate circumstances. In one case, a mother acknowledged in her son's marriage contract that she owed him annual support in a fixed amount. The court held that the gratuitous nature of the transaction was evident from the face of the document. The transaction therefore could not be validated as a disguised gift.[243] Blaise concluded that the case law is inherently contradictory. On the one hand, the courts justify gift formalities as a means to protect against fraud, yet they require parties to a disguised gift to perfect the simulation, thereby rendering fraud all the more difficult to detect.[244]

804. *Belgium.* Early Belgian case law subordinated the validity of the disguised gift to three additional requirements. First, a disguised gift could not be used to

---

237. See, e.g., Liège 2 Germinal XI [23 Mar. 1803], S. 1791–XII II 124; Bruxelles 28 Floréal XII [18 May 1804], S. 1791–XII II 192; Civ. 20 Oct. 1812, S. 1812–1814 I 203; Nîmes 15 Mar. 1819, S. 1819–1821 II 43; Colmar 7 Aug. 1834, S. 1835 II 223; Req. 25 Feb. 1836, S. 1836 I 603.
238. Civ. 31 May 1813, S. 1812–1814 I 362.
239. Civ. 6 Pluviôse XI [26 Jan. 1803], S. 1791–XII I 746.
240. Blaise 95–96.
241. Malaurie and Aynès no. 411.
242. Id. See infra no. 835.
243. Paris 22 Dec. 1924, *Gaz. Pal.* 1925 I 272.
244. Blaise 114.

accomplish an otherwise prohibited transaction; second, it could not serve to circumvent the law; and third, it could not impair the rights of third parties.[245] Today Belgian writers consider these additional requirements superfluous. The substantive rules of gift law continue to apply and are sufficient to prevent illegality. Moreover, third parties have always been protected by the rule that simulated or sham transactions may not be enforced against them (CC art. 1321).

(C) EFFECTS AND BURDEN OF PROOF

805. *Effects.* Gift law, not the law of the simulated act, governs the substance of the transaction. In the case of a simulated sale, for example, the donor is not held to the warranty obligations of a true seller. Moreover, the general gift law regime of collation and revocation applies.[246] If the disguised gift exceeds the donor's disposable share, the gift is maintained, but the excess is subject to collation.[247]

806. *Burden of proof.* In numerous situations, transactions that appear to be onerous are challenged as gifts. The donor may wish to revoke or the donee may assert the donative nature of the transaction as a defense in a suit for the price.[248] The burden of proof is on the party who challenges the appearance. There is a special presumption for cases involving a transfer of property rights coupled with the reservation of a usufruct, a life annuity, or a loan for which the repayment is to be excused. There is an irrebuttable presumption in these cases that the transaction involves a disguised gift subject to collation and reduction (CC art. 918).

(D) DOCTRINAL DOUBTS

807. *Critique.* Disguised gifts are frequently used to avoid the operation of legal rules, such as the limitations on gift capacity, the limitations on the disposable share, or the high tax rate for gratuitous transfers between unrelated individuals.[249] Some authors are therefore reluctant to approve disguised giving.[250]

808. *Belgian doctrine.* Belgian authors have been especially unsympathetic to the institution. Toward the end of the last century, Laurent, at the time one of Belgium's leading civilists, launched a frontal attack. "[W]hen the simulated contract is not in earnest as a bargain, it is nothing but a gift; thus, a simulated sale is not a sale, because there is neither price nor consent: the seller no more wishes to sell than the buyer wishes to buy. And, similarly, there is no gift, since the solemn formalities without which a gift does not exist have not been observed.

245. 8 De Page no. 513.
246. Flour and Souleau no. III.
247. Civ. 22 Aug. 1810, S. 1809–1811 I 230; Civ. 6 June 1814, S. 1812–1814 I 577.
248. 5 Planiol and Ripert no. 426; 8 De Page no. 515; Flour and Souleau nos. 112–115.
249. Blaise 89–90.
250. 5 Planiol and Ripert no. 424.

What remains? The void."²⁵¹ Laurent admitted that technical arguments could be found to support the validity of disguised giving, but he also believed that the institution contradicts the most basic principles of law. "Let it be asked yet once again: Does it make any sense for an act to be void if the parties are truthful about the transaction yet valid if they camouflage it with a lie?"²⁵²

Modern Belgian scholarship is no less relentless. De Page noted that gift formalities are matters of public policy (*ordre public*). They are therefore not left to the will of the parties. Though sham transactions are generally valid, they are not valid when their purpose is to circumvent rules mandated by public policy. Based on fundamental legal principles, disguised gifts should be void.²⁵³

(E) JUSTIFICATIONS

809. *Equality and beyond.* Despite the initial hesitation in the case law, the original justification for validating disguised gifts is clear. The Convention prohibited gifts and testaments and mandated the equal distribution of decedents' estates. The revolutionary motto of equality seemed to require no less.²⁵⁴ The courts sought to prohibit attempts to circumvent these restrictions.²⁵⁵ Once the heroic phase of the revolution ended, the Civil Code abrogated the Decree of 17 Nivôse and permitted gifts and bequests that did not exceed the disposable share. With the rebirth of an aristocracy under the empire and yet again under the Restoration, the revolutionary conception of equality was abandoned. Because hierarchy had returned, there was no reason to prohibit disguised gifts.

During the course of the nineteenth century, however, disguised gifts acquired a different function. They were used to avoid the Civil Code's limitations on gift giving. As the contraventions increased, disguised gifts that violated the code's restrictions were avoided. The theory was that fraud should be sanctioned whenever it appeared—*fraus omnia corrumpit*. The harder question had to do with gifts that were disguised simply to avoid publicity. They did not violate any code provision other than the required formalities. Disguised gifts had by then been expressly validated by the Cassation Court. French scholars therefore tried to find a persuasive justification.

810. *Various theories.* Several arguments were presented.²⁵⁶ From the fact that two code provisions prohibited disguised gifts in particular circumstances,²⁵⁷

251. 12 Laurent no. 305.
252. Id. no. 306.
253. 8 De Page no. 493.
254. Supra no. 3.
255. Rouen 7 Fructidor X [25 Aug. 1802], S. 1791–XII II 94.
256. Flour and Souleau no. 104. Méau-Lautour provides a historical survey of the French doctrinal attempts to justify the disguised gift. Méau-Lautour nos. 15–24.
257. French CC former arts. 911, 1099 par. 2, abrogated by Law of 26 May 2004 art. 23.

some authors concluded that the institution was otherwise permitted. There was also an argument by analogy from a code provision that validates a disguised gift in a particular setting (CC art. 918). These exegetical arguments, however, were universally considered weak.[258]

More recently, scholars have relied on the principle that simulation never invalidates a transaction unless it effects a fraud. In other words, what can be done directly can also be done indirectly. The response is that a disguised gift always operates a fraud, at the very least on the form requirements.[259] Some French scholars thus agree with the Belgian writers that disguised gifts should be void.[260] These authors are concerned that, because disguised gifts often leave no trace, they significantly decrease the portion available for successoral distribution.[261] In reply, those supporting the disguised gift argue that *fraude à la loi* refers to the law's substantive requirements, such as capacity, and not to the forms the law employs to protect substantive rights.[262]

The justification most widely accepted today is Dean Ripert's clever suggestion that the disguise provides an adequate substitute for the formalities. The purpose of the notarial act is to ensure that donors give serious thought to the gift's consequences. The sham fulfills this purpose as successfully as do gift formalities because the careful construction of a sham requires determination.[263] It has been argued in response that, because protective form requirements are strictly enforced, there is no room for substitutes.[264] Ibrahim Najjar has suggested that the actual role of the disguised gift is to validate a social custom that cannot be suppressed. "The theory of substituted formalism is in reality a retrospective confirmation (*a posterioristique*) of the impossibility of correcting the 'deviations' and 'disagreeable' tendencies of daily practice. Given a positive law that is sometimes badly adapted to individual psychology, the scholars and courts have created for themselves a 'good conscience.'"[265]

---

258. Flour and Souleau no. 104; 4 Mazeaud (-Leveneur and Mazeaud-Leveneur) no. 1481.

259. Malaurie and Aynès no. 410.

260. 4 Mazeaud (-Leveneur and Mazeaud-Leveneur) no. 1481.

261. When the disguise remains undiscovered, a donee who has received a gift exceeding the disposable share in practice retains property for which the estate should be indemnified. Moreover, there is no penalty if the disguise is discovered. A disguised gift that exceeds the disposable share must be returned to the estate to the same extent as if the gift had been made by notarial act. The concern of those who disapprove of disguised gifts is that this exception to the form requirements rewards those who attempt to circumvent the distribution rules. For a brief explanation of the disposable share in French law, see supra no. 134.

262. Bufnoir 507–508.

263. 4 Ripert and Boulanger no. 3351.

264. Lagarde 35. For a critique of Dean Ripert's suggestion, see id. 34–41.

265. Ibrahim Najjar, note to Civ.¹ 29 May 1980, D. 1981, 273 at 276–277.

(F) CHARACTERIZATION DIFFICULTIES

811. *Two transactions.* Two types of disguised gifts pose particular interpretation difficulties, the gift disguised as a sale at a nominal price and the disguised gift between spouses.

(1) Sale at a Nominal Price

812. *Stated price.* In the typical case of a gift disguised as a sale, the stated price represents equivalent value. The transaction is gratuitous because the parties have agreed that the price will never be paid. A problem arises, however, when the stated price is nominal.

[a] Case Law

813. *Earlier view.* Nineteenth century courts offered two reasons for invalidating these transactions. The first was that the sham transaction was defective. Because a serious price is a condition for a valid sale, a purported sale at a nominal price would be invalid. As Pothier wrote, a sale for a trivial price is not a sale at all and should be subjected to the gift law solemnity.[266] Second, to ensure that the disguise fulfills its protective function, the veil must completely conceal the truth. However, if the stated price is nominal, the disguise is transparent and the gift should fail.[267] In one case, the sales price was stated as a life annuity markedly inferior to the property's revenue stream. The disguise was declared invalid.[268]

814. *Recent cases.* More recent cases validate this transaction. Moreover, the courts will not avoid the transaction on the grounds that the price was unconscionably low (*lésion*).[269] The theory is that a serious price is a substantive and not a formal requirement for a valid sale.[270] Gift law, not sales law, governs the substance of the transaction. Some authors have objected, however, that there is then no longer an appearance of a bargain sufficient to excuse the absence of form.[271]

---

266. 3 Pothier, *Vente* no. 19.

267. 10 Planiol and Ripert no. 41.

268. Req. 26 Apr. 1893, D. 1893 I 359; Dawson (1980) 111–113.

269. Civ.¹ 27 Oct. 1993, *Bull. civ.* I no. 300; Civ. 6 Mar. 1951, *Bull. civ.* I no. 83.

270. [T]he price is a substantive condition of the sale. In this case, the sale is only a form. The substantive elements of a sale are not required. The act is valid if the formal conditions of the simulated act are united with the substantive conditions of the gift .... [I]f the simulated act united both the formal and the substantive conditions of the onerous contract, it would not be a disguised gift but would be rather a valid onerous contract.

Trib. civ. Périgueux 1 June 1954, J.C.P. 1955 II 8536 note Jean-Charles Laurent, *Rev. trim. dr. civ.* 1955, 350 obs. René Savatier.

271. 5 Planiol and Ripert no. 425 bis; see also Dawson (1980) 74–83.

[b] Doctrinal Dispute

815. *Purpose of the institution.* In the end, this doctrinal dispute concerns the foundation of the disguised gift and particularly why it operates as an exception to the form requirements.

816. *Party autonomy.* Those who favor validating these transactions argue that the purpose of the disguise is merely to ensure that an actual transfer is intended. The courts should aim only to prevent fraud on the donor and prejudice to third parties.[272] In this view, the disguised gift exception is required by the principle of party autonomy (*volontarisme*) that lies at the core of French obligations law. In the disguised gift, the will of the parties triumphs over the impediments created by the form requirements. Once it is demonstrated that the parties actually intended a gift, the fact they have chosen a sales contract with a nominal price should not prevent the consummation of the transaction, at least as between the parties.[273] Because the parties to these transactions intend a gift and not a sale, the stated price will always be fictional. It makes no sense to insist on technicalities of form in the context of an exception to form requirements.

817. *Contrary view.* Other scholars argue that this demonstration proves too much. If party autonomy were the fundamental principle of French gift law, the code would not impose strict form requirements. Moreover, gifts that are clearly intended would be enforced. But neither is the case. Instead, the disguised gift is meant only as a narrow exception. René Savatier argued that the courts should not validate these transactions. If it is true that a sale at a nominal price may be enforced as a disguised gift, "the entire theory of disguised gifts seems to have been abandoned."[274] A gift may be made by simulation only if the simulation is persuasive. If a sale with a nominal price is an exception to the form requirement, then a gift could be given by a simple writing, as long as it was called a sale and some symbolic price is stated. The purpose of the exception is to impose a substantial enough risk that the parties will take it seriously. A real but fictional price presents the danger than the purported seller might demand that it be paid, or that third parties will consider it an actual sale. If the price is nominal, there is no risk sufficient to focus the parties' attention.

818. *Recent trend.* More recently, the courts have tended to validate these transactions as long as donative intent is proved.[275] As Ibrahim Najjar has pointed out in a brilliant note, these recent holdings turn the classic notion of the disguised gift

---

272. Jean-Charles Laurent, note to Trib. civ. Périgueux 1 June 1954, J.C.P. 1955 II 8536.

273. 10 Planiol and Ripert no. 41.

274. René Savatier, obs. to Trib. civ. Périgueux 1 June 1954 and Montpellier 8 Dec. 1954, *Rev. trim. dr. civ.* 1955, 350 at 351.

275. Civ.[1] 29 May 1980, D. 1981, 273 note Ibrahim Hajjar.

on its head.[276] Whereas previously the rigorous adherence to the form of the simulated transaction validated the gift despite the absence of gift formalities, now it is the proof of donative intent that validates a disguised gift despite the transparency of the simulation. This line of cases relies entirely on party autonomy and has abandoned the use of the disguise as a means to protect the donor's consent.[277] If even a transparent disguise, when supported by donative intent, is sufficient to render gift formalities unnecessary, the purpose of the disguise becomes unclear.

(2) Between Spouses

819. *Disguised gifts void.* Disguised gifts between spouses were void in Roman law.[278] During the ancien régime, as a passage in Molière suggests,[279] husbands made gifts to their wives in forms designed to avoid the restrictions imposed by law and custom. The French Civil Code declared any disguised gift between spouses to be void, but it did not invalidate indirect gifts (CC art. 1099 par. 2). The prohibition was designed to prevent fraudulent concealment and thereby protect the free revocability of gifts between spouses.[280] As noted below, French law has now abrogated the prohibition.

The invalidity of disguised gifts between spouses represented the only case in French civil law in which a transaction was void simply because it was simulated. Moreover, the case law extended the meaning of a disguised gift—solely in the context of gifts between spouses—to include transactions such as the purchase of property by one spouse in the name of the other (discussed below). However, a frequent type of gift between spouses—a life insurance policy purchased by

---

276. Id.

277. "[T]he substantive solution now appears to be a general principle of the law of simulation, a new attitude of the Cassation Court with regard to the distinctions and hypocrisies (there's no other word to describe them) of the prior solutions." Id. 276.

278. D. 18, 1, 38 par. 2 (Ulpian).

279. There are others whom you may consult with advantage on that point, and who have expedients for gently overriding the law, and for rendering effective that which is not allowed. These others know how to smooth over the difficulties of an affair and to find the means of eluding custom by some indirect advantage. Without that, what would become of us every day? ... What you can do? You can discreetly choose a friend of your wife, to whom you will give everything you own in due form by your will, and that friend will afterwards give it to your wife; or else you can sign a great many safe bonds in favour of various creditors who will lend their names to your wife, and in whose hands they will leave a declaration that what was done was only to serve her. You can also in your lifetime put in her hands ready money and bills which you can make payable to bearer.
Molière, *The Imaginary Invalid* act 1 scene 9.

280. Sauvage 1433. For the revocability of gifts between spouses, see infra nos. 1295–1313.

one spouse for the benefit of the other—has always been characterized as an indirect gift.

Gifts made in a contract creating a company (*contrat de société*) were statutorily excepted from the prohibition—for example, when one spouse overvalued the contribution of the other spouse.[281] The gift was not void, provided it was made by notarial act. The form was required in order not to impede revocation. These gifts remained revocable and subject to collation.

820. *Belgium.* Planiol suggested that indirect and disguised gifts, together with those given by interposition, should all be valid up to the disposable share between spouses. Gifts beyond that would be void.[282] Belgian law has followed this path.[283] Disguised gifts are valid between spouses, provided they do not take the form of a sales contract, which, under Belgian law, is generally prohibited between spouses (CC art. 1595). Both disguised and indirect gifts are valid, though subject to collation.[284]

[a] *Justification*

821. *Difficulty.* Scholars had great difficulty justifying the invalidity of disguised gifts between spouses.[285] A number of suggestions were made. First, it was argued that the invalidity protected the successoral reserve. Unfortunately, that reasoning could not justify voiding the gift when it did not exceed the donor's disposable share. It was also suggested that, by disguising the gift, the parties were attempting to circumvent what at the time was the essential revocability of these gifts. But this reasoning failed as well. Even if the disguised gift between spouses was valid, it would still be revocable upon proof of the simulation. It was also suggested that the simulation suggested undue influence. But there was no reason to think that undue influence was more likely with regard to a disguised gift than it would be if the gift were indirect or manual. Finally, it was argued that, because divorce occasionally results in conflict, transparency in marital property relations is especially important.[286] However, due to the reserve, all successoral matters easily become conflictual and would be served by transparency, and yet this reasoning had long been rejected as a sufficient foundation for voiding disguised gifts.

---

281. CC art. 1832-1 par. 2; Flour and Souleau no. 463. The provision remains in effect, despite the fact that disguised gifts between spouses are now valid. Sauvage speculates that the provision has been tacitly repealed. Sauvage 1433.

282. 3 Planiol no. 3252.

283. 8 De Page no. 762.

284. Id. no. 496.

285. Flour and Souleau no. 464.

286. Piedelièvre 2514.

Yet some justification for voiding disguised gifts between spouses was needed, for the courts were required to determine who had standing to bring the action.[287] If the rule's purpose was to protect the successoral reserve, the action should be given to the residuary heirs. If it was designed, instead, to ensure the revocability of gifts between spouses, the action should belong to the donor. If the principle represented a presumption of undue influence, it should belong to the donor, and, after the donor's death, to the heirs. The courts seemed to allow the donor and the residuary heirs to sue.

[b] Purchase in the Name of the Other Spouse

822. *Intriguing problem.* When spouses have chosen the marital property regime of separate property, one spouse occasionally acquires title to property that is paid for by the other. After the transaction is concluded, the spouse who supplied the funds may attempt to avoid it on the grounds that the transaction represented a disguised gift. In response, the donee would argue that the transfer was valid as payment for services rendered during marriage. Before the recent reforms, the legal characterization of this transaction represented one of the most intriguing problems in French gift law.[288]

823. *Compensation.* If one spouse has a cause of action against the other for services rendered during marriage,[289] the purchase of property by the other may represent the payment of a restitutionary debt rather than a gift. The action in restitution is based on a contribution to the marriage beyond traditional marital duties. This action is usually available only when one spouse, without remuneration, has collaborated in the other's business or has abandoned a career to care for the home and the family. No action lies if the contribution was intended to be gratuitous, but the courts seem to have established a presumption against donative intent in these situations.[290]

824. *Characterization.* If the transaction was characterized as a gift, two questions remained. First was the characterization problem. The case law tended to characterize this frequent transaction as a disguised gift, a characterization that, prior to 2005, rendered it void.[291] The proponents of this view pointed out that the purchase was indivisible from the gift. Yet that indivisibility is not sufficient in French law to create a disguised gift. Indivisible transactions are traditionally characterized as indirect gifts.[292] A disguised gift requires a simulation. The more recent cases characterize the transaction as a manual gift of funds, the

---

287. Flour and Souleau no. 465.
288. Id. no. 470.
289. Id. nos. 471–474.
290. Id. no. 475.
291. Id. nos. 479–482.
292. Id. no. 125.

amount of which depends on the value of the property. The transaction would become a disguised gift only if the origin of the funds was misstated with the intent of misleading heirs or creditors.[293]

825. *The gift object.* The second disputed question concerned the nature of the gift object. This question was important before the recent reforms because gifts between spouses were revocable until death. In a suit for revocation, the court was required to determine what the donee was obliged to return.[294] The courts long decided that the donee was obligated to repay the purchase price. However, when inflation became a factor in French life in the 1940s, the courts decided that the gift object was not the purchase price but rather the property itself. This rule privileged donors at the expense not only of donees, but also of those who held through the donee, including secured parties. In 1967, the legislature contradicted the case law evolution and provided that the gift consisted in the funds transferred and not the property (CC art. 1099-1). As a result, the gift was either a manual or indirect gift and therefore valid.[295] For purposes of restitution following revocation, the gift object was considered to be a monetary amount equivalent to the value of the property at the moment of revocation.

[c] Reform

826. *Abrogation.* The prohibition of disguised gifts between spouses was abrogated in France effective in 2005.[296] As mentioned above, though the prohibition remains in the Belgian Civil Code, the courts have long since considered disguised gifts between spouses to be valid, though subject to collation.[297]

iii. Indirect Gifts

827. *Independent legal act.* The indirect gift (*donation indirecte*)—the term is employed in the code itself[298]—is the third exception to the French Code's form requirements. A gift is indirect if accomplished without gift formalities by means of an independent legal act that is valid in itself. The gift is valid if the act is carried out as required by the other legal provisions that apply.[299] No additional requirements, such as delivery, are imposed. The indirect gift differs from the

---

293. Civ.[1] 26 Apr. 1984, *Bull. civ.* I no. 139, J.C.P. éd. N. 1985 II 26 note Rémy, *Rev. trim. dr. civ.* 1985, 199 obs. Jean Patarin.

294. Flour and Souleau nos. 476–478.

295. Dagot (1971).

296. Law of 26 May 2004 art. 23 par. 1 (abrogating CC art. 1099 par. 2).

297. 8 De Page no. 762 par. 2 *in fine*. See supra no. 820.

298. CC arts. 843, 1099.

299. 8 De Page no. 502.

disguised gift, discussed above, by the lack of simulation.[300] Like the other exceptions to the form requirements, the indirect gift remains subject to the substantive rules of gift law. For example, it is only valid if it is completed during the donor's lifetime.[301]

French case law and scholarship unanimously accept the validity of indirect gifts. Nonetheless, the institution remains surrounded by mystery. Despite two centuries of effort, it still has no workable definition. The indirect gift has become a residual category that includes those cases in which a gift is valid even though form, disguise, and manual delivery are lacking.[302] In Jean Boulanger's much celebrated formulation, "The notion of the indirect gift is one of those that, to use a formula that has become famous in philosophy, 'is posited by contradicting itself (*se posent en s'opposant*).'"[303]

(A) BELGIUM

828. *By nature gratuitous.* According to the Belgian view, an indirect gift may be made only by means of those institutions that are by nature gratuitous, in other words, those that yield a gratuitous transfer as a necessary part of their normal operation. There are four such institutions.[304] They provide useful examples of the operation of the indirect gift in both French and Belgian law.

829. *Third-party beneficiaries.* The Civil Code specifically provides that the third-party beneficiary contract (*stipulation pour autrui*) involving a donee beneficiary may be used to make a gift (art. 1121). The code specifies the example of the life annuity (*rente viagère*) and expressly exempts it from gift formalities (CC art. 1973 par. 2). In French law, the requisite formalities are governed by insurance law.[305]

---

300. 5 Planiol and Ripert no. 423; 8 De Page no. 500. For the disguised gift, see supra nos. 798–826.

301. Civ.¹ 17 Sept. 2003, D. 2003, 2986 obs. Marc Nicod.

302. "Under this denomination are collected all those gifts that the case law dispenses from the form requirements, other than manual and disguised gifts." 10 Aubry and Rau (-Esmein) (1954) § 659 note 8 at 522.

303. Jean Boulanger, note to Civ.¹ 27 May 1961, D. 1962, 657 at 660. Boulanger added that the notion of the indirect gift

> designates the totality of the procedures, or very diverse legal mechanisms (promise to pay without consideration, third-party beneficiary contract, transfer of order paper, release of a debt, etc.) by which a person, inspired by donative intent, transfers to another, who thereby becomes the donee, a gratuitous patrimonial advantage, without there being a need to adopt the form of a gift contract, since, once agreement has been reached, the utilization of the chosen procedure or mechanism, by its own force, makes it possible to achieve the desired result.

304. 8 De Page no. 501.

305. Ins. C arts. L132-1 ff.

830. *Release.* The second category is the release of a debt (*remise de dette*).[306] A release only rarely creates an indirect gift.[307] If the release is by means of a simulated receipt, the transaction is valid as a disguised gift.[308] If the creditor expressly releases the debtor, one case has held that the gift is indirect,[309] though Flour and Souleau argued that the gift is direct and must be accomplished in the usual forms.[310] A release becomes an indirect gift if the debt instrument is returned to the debtor. In that case the law presumes that payment has been made.

In a controversial pair of decisions, the Cassation Court also validated a loan that provided that the debt would be forgiven if the donor died before the gift was repaid. The court considered the gift indirect—a present gift of the debt subject to a si praemoriar condition subsequent.[311] Because the writing revealed donative intent, the gift theoretically should have been valid only if completed by notarial act. Marc Nicod suggests that the courts do not always penalize the parties for minor drafting errors.[312]

831. *Renunciation.* Provisions concerning the third category, the relinquishment of a right in favor of a particular person (*renonciation translative d'un droit*), are found throughout the code. They include the renunciation of a usufruct, of an inheritance, of a bequest, and of a mortgage.[313] The renunciation is an indirect gift only if it extinguishes the right (*renonciation abdicative*), such as the right to the inheritance or the usufruct. In contrast, if the right is transferred to third parties (*renonciation translative*), it is a direct gift subject to gift formalities.[314] In one case, François Truffaut renounced his right to royalties from his film

---

306. The release is governed by CC arts. 1282–1288.

307. Flour and Souleau no. 120.

308. For the French law regarding disguised gifts, see supra nos. 798–826.

309. Civ.[1] 21 Dec. 1960, *Bull. civ.* I no. 560. The official headnotes are misleading.

310. Flour and Souleau no. 120.

311. The Cassation Court twice reversed the courts of appeal. Civ.[1] 24 Feb. 1998, *Bull. civ.* I no. 79, D. 2000 Somm. 428 obs. Marc Nicod (*affaire Auriscote*); Civ.[1] 9 July 2003, discussed by Marc Nicod in obs. to Civ.[1] 17 Sept. 2003, D. 2003, 2986 at 2989. The characterization discussion is found in the notes by Marc Nicod. As discussed above, when similar cases arise in German law, the question is whether the donor's statement should be considered an executed release or a gift promise. The same practical question is involved in French law, namely whether the transfer must be done by notarial act. See supra nos. 714, 752.

312. Marc Nicod, obs. to Civ.[1] 17 Sept. 2003, D. 2003, 2986 at 2989 note 33. In French law, if an act is only relatively neutral, evidence in the writing of donative intent may exclude the transaction from the category of indirect gifts. See infra no. 834.

313. CC arts. 622 (usufruct), 784 (inheritance), 1043 (bequest), 2180 par. 2 (mortgage).

314. Jean Patarin, obs. to Versailles 20 Jan. 1987, *Rev. trim. dr. civ.* 1988, 802. Because the distinction between the two types of renunciation is not found in the code, some writers consider it arbitrary. 5 Planiol and Ripert no. 419 at 542.

Breathless to the benefit of one of the film companies involved in the production.[315] He later sued to annul the gift. The court held that the renunciation was a direct gift and therefore void for lack of gift formalities. The renunciation did not extinguish the right but only transferred it to a third party.

832. *Debt of another.* The final category involves the payment without recourse of the debt of another (*paiement pour autrui effectué sans recours*). A donor who pays for the education of the children of relatives makes an indirect gift.[316] The payment of another's debt is expressly permitted (CC art. 1236).

(B) FRANCE

833. *Broader definition.* In contrast, French law accepts not only the four Belgian categories but also characterizes as indirect gifts those transactions done gratuitously in the particular case but which, in other cases, may also be carried out for compensation.[317] The increased breadth of the concept makes delimitation difficult. "[I]t is a category about the content of which the authors are far from agreement, and concerning which the courts often employ an uncertain terminology."[318]

(1) Basic Notion

834. *Neutral act.* The central notion is the *neutral* or *abstract* act (*acte neutre* or *acte abstrait*)—neutral or abstract in the sense that the transaction concerned may be done either gratuitously or for compensation. When the transfer is made gratuitously, it is generally exempted from the form requirements.[319] There is a further distinction between acts that are *relatively neutral* and those that are *absolutely neutral*. Acts are relatively neutral if they produce valid indirect gifts only in cases in which the donative intent is not mentioned, whereas acts that are absolutely neutral are exempted from the form requirements even if donative intent is evident.

835. *Acknowledgment of a debt.* The acknowledgment of a debt (*reconnaissance de dette*) is relatively neutral. If the cause (donative intent) is not stated, the acknowledgment is an indirect gift and valid without gift formalities.[320] If a consideration

---

315. Versailles 20 Jan. 1987, D. 1988 Somm 207 obs. Claude Colombet, *Rev. trim. dr. civ.* 1988, 802 obs. Jean Patarin.

316. Req. 25 June 1872, D.P. 1874 I 16.

317. 5 Planiol and Ripert nos. 410–412.

318. Flour and Souleau no. 116.

319. 5 Planiol and Ripert no. 412.

320. Other form requirements may apply. See CC art. 1326. This is the *bon pour* formality Eisenberg discusses. Eisenberg (1979) 13 note 42.

is falsely stated, the gift is valid as a disguised gift.[321] If the donative intent is apparent, the gift must be completed by notarial act.[322]

836. *Other examples.* The payment of another's debt is absolutely neutral and valid without solemnities, even if donative intent is apparent.[323] An assignment cannot create an indirect gift. Should the documentation fail to mention the consideration, the donative nature would be apparent and the act would no longer be neutral.[324] A delegation of duties produces an indirect gift if the obligee thereby acquires a second obligor. The endorsement of a negotiable instrument or a stock certificate constitutes an indirect gift because no consideration need be stated.[325] The creation of security by a third party for the benefit of the creditor, either in the form of a personal guarantee, joint and several liability, a security interest, or a mortgage, constitutes an indirect gift if done without recourse.[326]

(2) Controversial Cases

837. *Bank transfers.* A bank transfer of funds (*virement de compte*), when gratuitous, is sometimes considered an indirect gift. The same is true for a gift of securities made by transfer on the company's books. Dagot has argued that these transfers are not acts of the parties at all but rather techniques employed by third parties.[327]

838. *Trust.* A trust created under American law may qualify as a neutral act. In one case, the settlor transferred stock to the trustee, reserving the profits for her lifetime, with the corpus to pass to her grandchildren at her death.[328] The French appellate court, noting that the settlor had reserved the right to revoke, held that, under French law, a revocable trust is testamentary and therefore void as a gift. The Cassation Court reversed. Because there was no doubt about donative intent and because the trust was properly created under American law, the transfer was an indirect gift that took effect at the settlor's death. Thierry Vignal criticized the decision in a perceptive note.[329] Under American law, the transfer remained

---

321. According to Belgian law, the gratuitous acknowledgment of a debt is always a disguised gift. A quid pro quo is absent, whether or not it is falsely stated in the act. 8 De Page no. 413 par. A at 523–524 note 6. See supra no. 802.

322. 5 Planiol and Ripert no. 413.

323. Id. no. 414.

324. Id. no. 416.

325. Id. no. 416 ter.

326. Id. no. 417. For the circumstances in which French law characterizes the creation of security as a gift, see supra nos. 325–326.

327. Dagot (2000) 1477–1478.

328. Civ.¹ 20 Feb. 1996, *Bull. civ.* I no. 93.

329. Thierry Vignal, obs. to Civ.¹ 20 Feb. 1996, *Rép. not. Defrén.* 1997 art. 36457 at 26–38. For the prohibition of gifts of future property in French law, see supra nos. 358–365.

revocable until the donor's death. French law generally considers revocable gifts to be invalid. Moreover, because donative intent was apparent, the transfer could not be an indirect gift, which is the only characterization that would validate it. Vignal concluded that the court reached a *functional* result in order to find a place for the American trust in French law.[330]

839. *Gifts to charity*. The case law appears to validate charitable subscriptions as indirect gifts *sui generis*.[331] Because only modest sums are generally involved, notarial form is impractical. If payment accompanies the promise, the gift would be valid as a manual gift. A pledge without payment would amount to a promise to make a manual gift, which would be void.[332] In deciding that such gifts are exempt from form requirements, the Cassation Court employs the same language that is often used to validate indirect gifts.[333]

840. *Reduced price*. Characterization is difficult when the consideration in an onerous transaction varies greatly from value, such as the sale or lease of property significantly below—or above—fair market value. Because there is a partial simulation of the price, some authors argue that the gift is disguised.[334] If the price is actually paid, others suggest that there is no simulation, and it is therefore indirect.[335] The more recent case law seems to follow the latter view.[336] If the price is too greatly reduced, Dagot argues the transaction should be avoidable for unconscionability (*lésion*).[337]

(c) JUSTIFICATIONS

841. *Expressly recognized*. Two code provisions expressly recognize indirect gifts.[338] Two others suggest that gifts may be made otherwise than by formal act,[339] though only the provision concerning life annuity contracts exempts the transaction from gift formalities. Because the institution is anchored in the code, it needs an explanation more than a justification. According to one theory, the code requires solemnity only for acts constituting a gift (*actes portant donation*). The transactions that result from an indirect gift are independent of the gift—a release, a life insurance policy, the relinquishment of a right. However, this justification has gained little support. It is thought to be purely exegetical, probably

---

330. Thierry Vignal, id. at 36.
331. 5 Planiol and Ripert no. 418.
332. Supra nos. 674, 789.
333. Civ. 5 Feb. 1923, D. 1923 I 20.
334. 4 Ripert and Boulanger no. 3342.
335. 5 Planiol and Ripert no. 421; Flour and Souleau no. 126.
336. Civ.¹ 16 July 1959, D. 1960, 185 note Savatier.
337. Dagot (2000) 1476.
338. CC arts. 843 (collation), 853 (same).
339. CC arts. 1121 (third-party beneficiary contract), 1973 (life annuity contract).

incorrect, and therefore "extraordinarily weak."[340] Another suggestion is that the indirect gift satisfies the form requirement by substitution.[341] The institution by which the indirect gift is carried out provides for sufficient reflection. Yet, as has been pointed out, this is not always the case.[342] It is unclear how a sale at a reduced price provides a substitute for the protection provided by the notarial act.[343]

842. *Reconceptualization*. Rémy Libchaber has recently made a brilliant, daring, and remarkably successful attempt to reconceptualize the distinction between direct and indirect gifts in French law.[344] One essential characteristic of the gift is the donee's enrichment at the donor's expense. In Libchaber's view, when the enrichment flows directly from the donor to the donee, the gift is direct. When the enrichment occurs in any other way, it is indirect.[345] A typical case involves a donee who needs family assistance in paying a debt. If the donee's relatives channel the necessary funds through the donee, the gift is direct. If, on the other hand, the family pays the money directly to the creditor, the gift is indirect (because the benefit to the donee/relative is indirect).

A gift can be indirect even without the participation of a third party. If a usufructuary unilaterally renounces the usufruct in order to consolidate title in the owner of the underlying property, the donee is enriched. Yet no patrimonial benefit has passed from the donor to the donee. The gift should be considered indirect whenever the donor does not transfer property directly to the donee.

843. *No consensus.* There is no accepted theory. Planiol and Ripert concluded that, as a practical matter, the law validates indirect gifts because it cannot prohibit them.[346] For De Page, the lesson of the indirect gift is that French gift law formalities are overly rigid.[347] On the other hand, Dagot rejects the institution. He suggests that indirect gifts serve chiefly illicit purposes, such as concealing gifts from the taxing authorities and residuary heirs.[348]

5. Spain

844. *Greater flexibility.* As in other aspects of gift law, Spanish law distinguishes itself by its flexibility. It has modified the rigorous Romanic tradition in a way that gives greater weight to the social custom of gift giving.

---

340. 5 Planiol and Ripert no. 411. See also 4 Mazeaud (-Leveneur and Mazeaud-Leveneur) no. 1472; Flour and Souleau no. 128.
341. Flour and Souleau no. 128.
342. Id.
343. Dagot (2000) 1477.
344. Libchaber.
345. Id. 1415–1416.
346. 5 Planiol and Ripert no. 411.
347. 8 De Page no. 492.
348. Dagot (2000) 1471–1472 note 3.

a. Basic Rule

845. *Coequal types.* As discussed above, Spanish law recognizes three coequal types of gift: the gift of property rights (*donación real*), the gift of contract rights (*donación obligacional*), and the gift by release or waiver (*donación liberatoria*).[349] The discussion concerning modes of disposition mirrors these distinctions.

i. Property Rights

846. *Less formalistic.* At least in principle, Spanish law is less formalistic than Italian or French law. It exempts gifts of movables from the requirement of a notarial act.

(A) REAL PROPERTY

847. *Notarial writing.* Following the Romanic tradition, the Spanish Civil Code expressly conditions the validity of a gift of real property on a notarial writing (*escritura pública*; CC art. 633 par. 1). The special enumeration required in French and Italian law for gifts of movables is, in Spanish law, required instead when the gift involves real property. Each piece of property involved in the gift must be separately listed in the notarial writing. The value of each personal obligation the donee assumes must also be stated.[350]

Because the notarial writing is required *ad solemnitatem*, a gift of real property is absolutely void without it.[351] As a consequence, neither party may require the other to complete the formality.[352] Thus, the treatment of the gift of immovables in Spanish law is an exception to two general principles in Spanish law—first, that contracts are effective regardless of their form (CC art. 1278), and, second, that once there is agreement, a party may be compelled to complete the required forms (CC art. 1279).

The solemn nature of the writing, however, refers only to the gift itself. If the donee's obligations are not mentioned, the donee is released from the charges, and the gift remains valid.[353] Moreover, the enumeration requirement applies only to the personal obligations the donee assumes. Mortgages and the like continue to burden the property whether or not included in the writing.

(B) MOVABLES

848. *Choice of form.* The Spanish Civil Code permits gifts of movables to be made either in writing or by oral agreement accompanied by delivery (CC art. 632).[354]

---

349. Paz-Ares Rodríguez (-Albaladejo García) art. 618 note VI; supra no. 345.
350. CC art. 633 par. 1.
351. STS Civ. 10 Sept. 2007, RJ 4980; STS Civ. 21 June 2007, RJ 5123; STS Civ. 5 June 2000, RJ 5094; Paz-Ares Rodríguez (-Albaladejo García) arts. 632–633 nos. IV, VI.
352. Paz-Ares Rodríguez (-Albaladejo García) id.
353. Id. arts. 632–633 no. IV.
354. Spanish law excludes customary gifts (*liberalidades de uso*) from collation but does not exempt them from the form requirements. CC arts. 1041 par. 1, 1378 sent. 2, 1423.

The writing may be a notarial act or a simple private contract. Because, in the absence of delivery, the writing is a condition of validity, Albaladejo García has asked whether the gift is valid if the writing is formalized only after agreement is reached.[355] Theoretically, a mere oral agreement to make a gift is void and cannot be resuscitated by a later writing. Albaladejo concludes, however, that, despite the logic of the code, such a typical transaction must be valid.

849. *Oral gift*. If the agreement to make a gift of movables is oral, delivery is of the essence of the transaction. In its absence, the gift is void. Actual delivery is generally required. An attornment with the donor in possession is not sufficient, though the *traditio brevi manu* is acceptable.[356] Albaladejo García argues that even those movables for which title may be transferred only by notation in a public register—cars, ships, and airplanes—may nonetheless be gifted by delivery. Presumably the donee could then require the donor to complete the registration.[357] In contrast, Lacruz Berdejo suggests that a manual gift may include only those movables that may be transferred by delivery.[358]

Characterization questions seem to be resolved in favor of validity. Thus, the gift of the purchase price for real property[359] and of the labor and materials necessary for improvements to the donee's real estate[360] both are considered gifts of movables rather than immovables.[361]

ii. Contract Rights and Releases

850. *No prescribed form*. Both the case law and the scholars permit gifts of an obligation and gifts of a release,[362] yet the code prescribes no form. Because, in Spanish law, the gift is a solemn contract—for validity, form is of the essence—the question arises as to the form required for gifts that do not involve the immediate transfer of a property right. Albaladejo García has suggested that all gifts, whether of property, of an obligation, or of a release, are essentially gifts of rights, and all rights are either movable or immovable.[363] By implication, the gift of an obligation or of a release should be made in the form required for the type of right involved. One court has enforced a signed gratuitous promise, made and accepted by simple writings, to pay a large sum of money in the future.[364]

---

355. Paz-Ares Rodríguez (-Albaladejo García) arts. 632–633 no. III.
356. Id. arts. 632–633 no. II.
357. Id.
358. 2 Lacruz Berdejo no. 504 at 136.
359. STS Civ. 29 Mar. 1954, *Juris. civ.* 1954 no. 50.
360. STS Civ. 3 May 1975, RJ 1990.
361. 2 Lacruz Berdejo no. 504 at 136.
362. Supra nos. 345–346.
363. Paz-Ares Rodríguez (-Albaladejo García) art. 632–633 no. I *in fine*; see also Spanish CC arts. 333–337 (classifying all property as either movable or immovable).
364. STS Civ. 6 Apr. 1979, RJ 1273.

b. Exceptions

851. *Different structure.* The relationship between rule and exception in Spanish law differs from the French paradigm. Because movables may be gifted by delivery, the manual gift is not an exception in Spanish law. Disguised gifts are generally invalid. The principal exception to the notarial act is the indirect gift.

i. Indirect Gifts

852. *Recognized exception.* After a long debate, the indirect gift (*donación indirecta*) now seems to be a recognized exception to gift law formalities.[365] Indirect gifts are defined as legal transactions other than the gift that achieve the typical result of the gift transaction, namely the donee's enrichment at the donor's expense, and are accompanied by agreement as to the gratuitous nature of the transaction.[366] Examples include the payment of another's debt (CC art. 1158) when the donor agrees not to seek reimbursement and a third-party beneficiary contract (CC art. 1257) involving a donee beneficiary. If an indirect gift complies with the requirements of the transaction employed as a means, it is valid even if gift formalities are lacking. Spanish law characterizes as an indirect gift the *negotium mixtum cum donatione.* An example is a sale in which the price is intentionally favorable to one of the parties.[367]

There is some disagreement, however, about the extent to which indirect gifts remain subject to gift law. Vallet de Goytisolo emphasized that the common result in all of these transactions is the giving of a gift. He contended that the gift law rules designed for the protection of the donor, third parties, and the social interest should apply.[368] Ortega Pardo focused instead on the transaction employed as a means. In his view, gratuitousness is only an extra-legal motive for the transaction. Because the gift motive is secondary, he argues that the cause and characteristics of the mediating transaction are determinative. Third parties and the social interest merit greater protection than the donor. Revocation should be permitted only to benefit a first child.[369]

ii. Disguised Gifts

853. *Generally void.* The gift disguised as a sale (*donación encubierta*) seems to be void in Spanish law, even if made in a notarial writing. Due to important differences in tax treatment between sales and gifts, these cases reach the Spanish high court in some number. Because the gift of personalty does not require a notarial writing, the question of the disguised gift concerns only gifts of immovables.

---

365. For a summary of the discussion about the indirect gift in Spanish and Italian law, see Ortega Pardo; Vallet de Goytisolo (1978a).

366. Vallet de Goytisolo (1978a) 295–296; Diez-Picazo and Gullón 356.

367. 2 Lacruz Berdejo no. 516; Diez-Picazo and Gullón 357.

368. Vallet de Goytisolo (1978a) 300; Diez-Picazo and Gullón id.

369. Ortega Pardo 943; 2 Lacruz Berdejo no. 515.

Some older cases considered disguised gifts of immovables to be valid as in French law, whereas others held the gift invalid in the absence of form.[370] As yet there is still no judicial consensus. According to what seems to be the majority of the more recent cases, no characterization validates the transaction.[371] The sales transaction is void because it is merely a simulation—there is no agreement to exchange property for a price.[372] Even if the sale is concluded in a notarial writing, the transaction is void as a gift because the writing does not indicate that a gift is intended.[373] Moreover, because the parties are seeking to conceal the gift—and perhaps also to avoid its legal consequences—the disguise is considered *fraudem legis* and is also for that reason void.[374]

Those courts that validate disguised gifts tend to do so principally in the context of remunerative gifts—gifts given as compensation for services previously rendered.[375] Although the case law is not uniform,[376] the remunerative gift now seems to serve as a de facto exception to the prohibition of disguised gifts. However, because the exception is not mentioned in the code, some authors argue that the courts should not facilitate this type of gift.[377] Thus, the distinction between indirect and disguised gifts has practical consequences for gifts of immovables. The first is permitted, whereas the second is void. It is a *negotium mixtum cum donatione*, and thus a permitted indirect gift, when property is sold at a low price. However, it would be considered a disguised gift and therefore prohibited if the property is sold for a peppercorn.[378]

6. The Common Law: Transfers at Law

854. *Property and trust.* In the common law, inter vivos gratuitous transfers can be made by means of two separate and very different institutions. The first is the law of property, which governs the transfer of title at law. The other is equity, which governs the creation and transfer of a beneficial interest. The distinction

---

370. The secondary literature does not present a unified view of the case law evolution. Compare Díaz Alabart 1102–1109 with de Castro 1011–1014 and Vallet de Goytisolo (1978b) 620–652.

371. See STS Civ. 1 Feb. 2002, RJ 2098 (citing cases on both sides of the dispute).

372. STS Civ. 20 June 2007, RJ 5574.

373. STS Civ. 26 Feb. 2007, RJ 1769. The dissent noted that the circumstances of that case seemed proper for an exception. The donor, a person knowledgeable about the law (*una persona culta y conocedora del derecho*), clearly intended to make a remunerative gift and entered into the transaction after a long consultation with the notary. The donee accepted in the same act.

374. STS Civ. 14 May 1966, RJ 2425.

375. 2 Lacruz Berdejo no. 504 at 139; STS Civ. 31 May 1982, RJ 2614.

376. STS Civ. 11 Jan. 2007, RJ 1502 (over a strong dissent).

377. Diez-Picazo and Gullón 341.

378. Diez-Picazo and Gullón 357 note 12.

between law and equity runs throughout the common law and has no real equivalent in civilian systems. The practical consequence for gift law is that gifts can generally be made either by performing those acts that, at law, amount to a conveyance or by performing those acts required in equity to transfer a beneficial interest. A typical example of a transfer of equitable title is the declaration of a trust.[379] The minimalism of the German system is also recognizable in the common law. Here too a gift is valid if it complies with the transfer requirements appropriate for the type of property concerned,[380] though the common law complicates matters by adding equitable doctrine, a preference for delivery, and the permissive use of a writing.

Gino Gorla, an astute student of the comparative law of gifts, concluded that the common law is less wary (*diffidente*) of gifts than is the civil law.

> In sum, both simple gifts and those coupled with an obligation are clothed in formalities much less burdensome than those required by the civil law. It is enough for there to be an act under seal (without the intervention of the notary, who is unknown in common law countries), a bargain, even if only nominal, reliance, or a trust, which is absolutely free in terms of form and also free in terms of the interpretation of the donor's intent.[381]

Gifts made at law are discussed here, whereas those made by means of equitable institutions are discussed in the next part.

a. Introduction

855. *Protection against fraud.* In general, common-law systems do not find it necessary to protect donors against ill-considered generosity. They are generally also not concerned with collation or revocation. Instead, a common law court's principal concern when evaluating gift transfers is "the perfectly reasonable desire ... to protect the property of the individual against ill-founded and fraudulent claims of gift."[382] As a practical matter, the most important factor in gift cases is the real-world sense of whether a gift was actually intended and made. Though ancient and exceedingly technical rules occasionally provide an obstacle, courts often do their best to effectuate the donor's intent. In fact, so much effort is devoted to doing justice in the particular circumstances that the rules seem more a problem to be overcome than the deciding factor in the result. For this reason, it is impossible to reconcile the various precedents found in the common law of gifts.

---

379. *Richards v Delbridge* [1874] LR 18 Eq 11, 14.

380. "The forms or means available in the common law for making a gift (which is not considered to be a nominate contract (*figura tipica*)) are the same forms and means available for making a disposition *in all contracts.*" 1 Gorla 443 (emphasis in original).

381. 1 Gorla 443.

382. Brown § 7.2 at 78.

856. *Immediate transfer.* One common element of all inter vivos gifts in the common law is the requirement that the donor intend for the gift to be immediately effective. The donor must intend to make a present transfer. An intent to give in the future does not suffice.[383] This aspect of intent is in addition to the requirement of donative intent examined above, which requires the donor to intend the transfer to be gratuitous.[384] Because gifts usually involve the transfer of title, either to the donee or to a trustee, the required intent is most often the intent to relinquish dominion over the gift object and to create it in another. However, some courts hold that it is sufficient for the donor to intend to transfer any current interest in the property. The New York high court has upheld a gift of personal property with the reservation of a life estate, which effectively amounts to the transfer of a nonpossessory remainder.[385]

Intent is considered entirely from a unilateral and subjective point of view.[386] Yet there is an important objective element. Donative intent may be manifested by acts or words or inferred from the relation of the parties and the surrounding facts and circumstances.[387] The courts attempt to make the best sense possible of the conflicting facts before them. For example, intent to make a present transfer has been inferred from the fact that the husband had a ring reset to his wife's size and then presented it to her as a gift, even though he later claimed that his wife was to have only temporary use of the ring.[388]

857. *Standard of proof.* Some American cases require a higher standard of proof in gift cases.[389] Courts that consider fraud to be a particular danger hold that "the evidence which proves the gift should be clear and convincing, strong and satisfactory."[390] Not all courts agree.[391]

858. *Real property and personalty.* The making of a gift in the common law is generally governed by the legal principles of conveyancing and the transfer of title together with equitable doctrines, principally the inter vivos trust.[392] However, due to a long-standing conceptual division in the common law, disposition issues vary depending on whether the gift involves real property or personalty.

---

383. 38 Am.Jur.2d Gifts §§ 17–18.

384. Supra nos. 287–290.

385. *Gruen v. Gruen,* 505 N.Y.S.2d 849 (N.Y. 1986); infra no. 887.

386. *Brown v. Brown,* 501 So.2d 24, 27 (Fla. App. 1986).

387. 38 Am.Jur.2d Gifts § 19.

388. *Sihler v. Sihler,* 376 So.2d 941 (Fla. App. 1979).

389. *Tilford v. Bank for Savings,* 52 N.Y.S. 142, 142–143 (App. Div. 1898).

390. *Devlin v. Greenwich Sav. Bank,* 26 N.E. 744, 744 (N.Y. 1891).

391. Kreitner 1915–1918.

392. For the principles governing the transfer to title to real property in American law, see Thompson ch. 94; for the creation of an inter vivos trust, see Restatement (Third) of Trusts §§ 20–26; see also Fratcher secs. 23–68.

The general requirement of a deed for gifting real property is relatively straightforward. The extravagant complexity of the field comes from its attempts to systematize and legalize the customary methods for making gifts of movables.

b. Real Property

i. England and the United States

859. *Deeds.* The Statute of Frauds, originally promulgated in England in 1677 and subsequently adopted in virtually all American states, provides that legal title to real property generally passes only when a deed has been properly executed and delivered to the grantee.[393] A deed is a signed instrument that describes the property to be conveyed. In some jurisdictions it must be made under seal.[394] The deed generally does not distinguish between gratuitous and nongratuitous conveyances. As Blackstone noted, some consideration is usually stated in every deed, even in gratuitous transfers.[395] Nonpossessory interests in land—easements, servitudes, life estates, and future interests—are generally also conveyed by deed.

860. *Delivery.* In England, the deed is not generally effective as a conveyance until it is delivered to the grantee. However, because gift law is concerned chiefly with preventing fraudulent claims of gift, delivery is considered complete when made to a third party for transfer to the donee. Though delivery is usually required in American law as well, there are exceptions. For example, recordation of the deed, though not necessary to perfect a gift of real property, may make the deed effective without delivery.[396] Moreover, delivery is not necessary when the circumstances make it superfluous. In one case, the donor purchased property in the donee's name and only later decided to gift the property to the donee. The court held that no deed was necessary. The gift was complete upon the donor's manifestation of donative intent.[397]

---

393. Statute of Frauds par. 3. For England, the deed requirement is now contained in the Law of Property Act sec. 52 par. 1. For the United States, see Thompson §§ 94.02 par. b no. 4, 94.06 par. g no. 1.

394. For more about writings under seal, see supra no. 689.

395. 2 Blackstone 440. If a consideration, regardless how minimal, is stated in the deed, some American courts may find that to be enough, in the context of other facts and circumstances, to indicate that no gift was intended. See *Wills v. Whitlock*, 139 S.W.3d 643, 655 (Mo. App. 2004).

396. Restatement (Third) of Property (Wills and Other Donative Transfers) § 6.3 comments d and e.

397. *Lewis v. Poduska*, 481 N.W.2d 898, 903 (Neb. 1992). The effect of the donor's gift was to release the claim for a resulting trust that generally permits the person supplying the funds, or that person's heirs, to recover the property.

ii. India

861. *Registered instrument.* Under Indian law, gifts of immovables may only be made by registered instrument, signed by or on behalf of the donor, and attested by at least two witnesses.[398] A gift disguised in the instrument as a sale is valid.[399]

862. *Islamic law.* Under Islamic law, in contrast, a writing is not essential to the validity of a gift. All gifts can be made by parol.[400] However, validity also requires both the donee's acceptance and the actual transfer of possession. The textbook example of an oral transfer of real property involves a declaration of gift made in the presence of a large gathering. Moreover, if the gift is made by formal instrument, the gift is not valid until the deed is registered and possession is transferred.[401]

c. Movables

863. *Different types.* In the common law, the validity of a gift of movables depends on the type of movable involved. The complexity of these rules is due largely to the historical process by which they arose. The common law first developed rules to govern the gifting of tangible personal property, known in the common law as *chattels*. Those rules generally require either delivery or a written deed of gift. The same rules were later extended to govern intangible personal property, often called *choses in action*. Yet, because a chose in action is nothing more than a right, it makes little sense to require delivery, even for a chose in action incorporated into a written instrument. The common law, however, "never a stickler for logical accuracy," uses the same terminology both for gifts of chattels and for gifts of choses in action.[402] As a result, the basic concept has lost any identifiable meaning. Though the basic principles are clear and repeated without variation from headnote to headnote, the notion of delivery has acquired so many disparate meanings that it often seems that each dispute is decided on its own facts.

i. Chattels

864. *Delivery primary.* In the common law, delivery is the primary means of making a gift of chattels, though the alternative of a formal, and sometimes even

---

398. Transfer of Property Act § 123 par. 1.
399. *D. Nagaratnamba v. K. Ramayya*, AIR (50) 1963 AP 177, 181, [1962] 2 An WR 169.
400. Fyzee 219.
401. Fyzee 219–220. In Fatimid law, which follows the Mālikī school, a gift is effective upon acceptance and delivery. There is no perfection requirement as there is in Hanafi law. Id. 218.
402. Mechem (1926–1927) 343 note 6a.

an informal, writing is also usually available.[403] Moreover, gift transfers have been effective in numerous situations when both delivery and a writing were lacking.

(A) DELIVERY

865. *Seisin.* In Germanic custom, the gift object possessed an almost magical ability to create bonds and merge fates, but the spirit residing in the gift could operate only if it actually reached the donee's hands. For example, the Germanic marriage began with the first hug but was not perfected until the husband's bridal gift (*Brautgabe*) was actually received.[404] Bracton explained the delivery requirement by reference to the concept of seisin, a complex idea that relates transfer to receipt of possession by the new owner. Because seisin can never lie vacant, the donor could not be divested of title until the donee received a livery of seisin. For that reason, Bracton explained, title passed concomitantly with possession.[405]

866. *No unanimity.* The delivery requirement is generally considered an indisputable feature of the common law of gifts. Yet some classic authors doubted whether delivery was sine qua non for a gift of chattels. Coke suggested that, though delivery was required in civilian jurisdictions, it was not essential in the common law.[406] For Blackstone, though delivery was the essential method by which gifts of chattels are made, title might also pass either by writing or by oral conveyance.[407]

867. *Consideration.* The delivery requirement does not seem to have become firmly established in England until the end of the nineteenth century.[408] The use of delivery as a gift formality arose at the same time the consideration doctrine was restructuring the law of contract. Kreitner argues that the two phenomena are related.[409] The consideration doctrine permitted contract law to enforce only

---

403. Under Indian law, a gratuitous transfer of movables may be made either by registered deed or by delivery. Transfer of Property Act § 123 par. 2. Nonetheless, the commentators note that delivery of possession is the usual mode of transfer. Mulla § 123 note "Mode of transfer—Movables." In the United States, the Restatement (Third) now also permits gifts of personalty either by delivery or written document. Restatement (Third) of Property (Wills and Other Donative Transfers) § 6.2.

404. Grønbech 59, 62–63.

405. 2 Bracton 124.

406. "In the civil law a gift of property is good without delivery but it is otherwise in our law." (*[L]e civil ley est que un done de biens nest bon sans tradition mes auterment est en nostre ley.*) *Wortes v Clifton* (1675) 1 Rol R 61, 81 ER 328 (quoting Justice Coke in *Futters case* (n.d.)).

407. 2 Blackstone 441.

408. *Cochrane v Moore* [1890] 25 QBD 57 (CA); Baron 161–162.

409. Kreitner 1929–1930.

those promises that were part of a bargain. It therefore became necessary to distinguish an unenforceable gift promise from an executed, and therefore valid, gift. The delivery requirement was pressed into service, eventually becoming a mantra that was constantly repeated in the opinions and treatises. As one might expect, however, the courts have always maintained flexibility.[410]

868. *Both traditional and modern.* The particular fervor with which the common law has insisted on the delivery requirement is thus due to the confluence of two distinct traditions. To begin with, the traditional common-law view, despite occasional dissenters, has always been that delivery is not simply evidence of intent but is rather the essence of the gift. In the absence of delivery, no matter how clear the donor's intent, no title passes and the gift fails.[411] The delivery requirement has seemed so obvious as to need no justification.[412] In one otherwise incomprehensible case, the donor, on his deathbed, asked his nurse to remove money from his wallet, which he kept under his pillow, and give it to the donor's wife as soon as she arrived. The donor died before the nurse was able to carry out his request. The court refused to enforce the gift because there had been no delivery.[413]

The consideration doctrine, by making gift promises unenforceable, supplied the second justification for the delivery requirement. In a system that lacks elaborate gift formalities, the easiest distinction between a gift promise and an executed gift is delivery. Once the two situations could easily be distinguished, judges in the Holmesian tradition left the enforcement of gift promises to social custom. Thus the delivery requirement represents both an *Ur*-element of medieval common law as well as an essential feature of market-based contract theory. It therefore provides a paradigmatic example of how the common law integrated the bourgeois perspective into its feudal framework.

869. *Nature of delivery.* Because delivery plays such a critical role in validating gifts of movables, it would make sense to define the concept in simple terms based on transfer of possession. Unfortunately, as Mechem has pointed out, such a definition is impossible for two reasons.[414] First, the courts frequently

---

410. "[T]here has probably been no time in the history of the law, certainly not since the time of Edward IV ... when ownership in a chattel might not under proper conditions be transferred without a deed or other instrument and without a delivery of the chattel as an essential element in the transfer of ownership." Stone 197.

411. ENGLAND: *Cochrane v Moore*, [1890] 25 QBD 57 (CA); 20 Halsbury part 1 sub Gifts no. 38; UNITED STATES: Brown § 7.2 at 79; *Shankle v. Spahr*, 93 S.E. 605 (Va. 1917).

412. "[A]fter all isn't the principle fundamental that if a man is going to make a gift he must do it; he must put his hand in his pocket and hand over what he intends to give?" Beers, Discussion contribution, National Conference (1925) 199.

413. *Wilcox v. Matteson*, 9 N.W. 814 (Wis. 1881).

414. Mechem (1926–1927) 341–342.

hold that gifts have been delivered even in the absence of any change in possession. Second, there is no uniform definition of the concept of possession. It is
defined differently based on the legal question raised and the type of property
involved. These conceptual difficulties led Mechem to suggest that the courts
should avoid "the insufferably difficult problem of possession" and should
decide the cases by asking instead whether the purposes the delivery requirement was designed to accomplish have been fulfilled.[415] In a series of thoughtful
articles written in the 1920s, Mechem suggested that the delivery requirement
had three purposes. First, the *wrench* of delivery reminds the donor of the significance of the act; second, delivery demonstrates the donor's unequivocal commitment to the transaction; and third, delivery provides prima facie evidence
that a gift has been made.[416]

870. *Delivery and intent.* The simple question to which the common law provides
no simple answer, or any real answer at all, is whether a gift that is clearly
intended can be validated without delivery. The first step in approaching this
question is to examine the basic elements of the delivery requirement for chattels. The discussion then turns to how cases are decided when delivery is, for
different reasons, ambiguous. Scholars have always been suspicious of the delivery requirement because it encourages courts to invalidate clearly intended
gifts.[417] In a remarkable evolution, it now seems that American courts, after considering the scholarly critique, have abrogated the delivery requirement *sub
silentio.*

(1) Basic Elements

871. *Difficult to define.* It proves to be almost impossible to specify in advance the
elements of a valid delivery. Moreover, exceptions are made when actual delivery
would prove superfluous. There is the additional problem that some courts do
not apply the standard delivery rules to gifts of registered chattels.

872. *Clear and unequivocal.* The English courts generally do not dilute the meaning of delivery in the context of the gift.[418] "The English law of the transfer of
property, dominated as it has always been by the doctrine of consideration, has

---

415. Id. 354–355.
416. Id. 348–349.
417. That the [delivery requirement] is psychologically unsound, if such expression be
permissible, is suggested by the persistence with which litigants, and even courts,
have attempted to evade it. Judges have found themselves between the Scylla of
enforcing patently fraudulent claims, and the Charybdis of doing intolerable hard-
ship by refusing to enforce attempts at gift, made in obvious good faith, but lacking, by reason of the donor's natural ignorance of the law, the technical requisite
of a delivery.
Mechem (1925) 9.
418. Bridge 94–95.

always been chary of the recognition of gifts."[419] Delivery therefore requires a clear and unequivocal transfer of possession. Words of gift will not substitute for an imprecise delivery.[420]

American law distinguishes a subjective and an objective element in delivery.[421] The subjective element is the donor's intent to transfer the gift to the donee. If that intent is absent, there is no delivery, even if the donee acquires possession.[422] The objective element requires that actual dominion and control over the property pass to the donee. If the donor retains the power to manage, use, or control the property, there is no delivery. However, once delivery has taken place, the donee may return the property to the donor—for safekeeping, for example, or as a loan—without negating the gift.[423]

873. *When superfluous.* Though delivery is said to be required, arbitrariness can be avoided only by introducing numerous exceptions.[424] One exception covers those situations in which actual delivery would be superfluous. The donee who is in possession of the chattel at the moment of the oral gift or who takes possession pursuant to a license granted by the donor is not required to perform the ritual act of returning the property to the donor to permit a new delivery.[425] Thus, words of gift to a bailee are probably effective without redelivery. Attornment is also an exception. The gift is effective without redelivery if the current bailee agrees to hold the chattel for the donee.[426]

874. *Registered chattels.* Registered chattels, such as automobiles, can be validly transferred only in accordance with statute. In the United States, such a transfer often involves written formalities and a certificate of title.[427] Many statutes hold that a sale is void if the statute's requirements are not met.[428] As a result, some American courts have held, as in French law, that simple delivery, in this context, is ineffective to execute a gift.[429] This holding is justified if the gift law delivery requirement is understood as adopting the rules that normally prevail for transfer of title. Under this view, when simple delivery is ineffective for

---

419. *In re Cole* [1964] Ch 175, 185.

420. Bridge 95.

421. Brown § 7.3 at 81–82.

422. *Liebe v. Battman*, 54 P. 179 (Or. 1898); *Whisnant v. Whisnant*, 928 P.2d 999, 1002 (Or. App. 1996).

423. Brown § 7.3; Mechem (1926–1927) 361–364; *Hudson v. Tucker*, 361 P.2d 878, 887–888 (Kan. 1961); *Grover v. Grover*, 24 Pick. 261 (Mass. 1837).

424. Mechem (1926–1927) 351.

425. UNITED STATES: Id. 364–374; ENGLAND: *In re Stoneham* [1919] 1 Ch 149; *Kilpin v Ratley* [1892] 1 QB 582.

426. Stone 198.

427. Brown § 7.3 at 84.

428. Texas Transportation C § 501.073.

429. *Varvaris v. Varvaris*, 124 N.W.2d 163 (Iowa 1963); supra no. 781.

the purposes of property law, it should be ineffective for gift law purposes as well.

However, some American courts hold that the statutory scheme for transfer of title does not apply to gratuitous transfers.[430] The failure to comply with property law formalities does not void the gift transaction between the parties.[431] These courts adopt a solution similar to the one developed in Spanish law. The Restatement (Third) has adopted this view, providing that simple delivery may suffice.[432] Nonetheless, the donor's failure to follow the procedure legally required for making the transfer may, in some cases, cast doubt on whether a gift was intended. If the donee carries the burden of proof on this question, the donee may require the donor to comply with any necessary formalities.

(2) Ambiguous Delivery

875. *Unclear intent.* In several circumstances, the transfer of possession is deemed too ambiguous to satisfy the delivery requirement. These situations involve transfers to intermediaries, constructive delivery, and shared possession.

[a] Intermediaries

876. *Agency principles.* The donor may make a valid gift by delivering the chattel to a third party as the donee's representative.[433] When the third party delivers to the donee, the gift is perfected by operation of the principles of agency law.[434] Difficult questions arise when the third party does not consummate the transaction or does not do so before the donor's death. If the third party is held to be the *donor's* agent, the gift remains executory. If the third party was the *donee's* agent, delivery to the third party completes the gift. When the donee is unaware of the gift, it seems difficult to consider the donee to be the principal. As a result, the intermediary is sometimes considered a trustee.[435] The decision is said to turn on the donor's intent, in light of all of the facts and circumstances.[436]

Yet, as Mechem has pointed out, in many cases the donor had no intent about the issue.[437] The courts therefore engage in presumptions based on the relationship among the parties, the donee's availability, and the time set for the donee to receive possession. Some American courts presume that the third party is the

---

430. *Allen v. Holloway*, 168 S.E.2d 196 (Ga. App. 1969).

431. *Truck Ins. Exchange v. Schuenemann*, 391 S.W.2d 130, 132 (Tex. Civ. App. 1965).

432. Restatement (Third) of Property (Wills and Other Donative Transfers) § 6.2 comment i; supra no. 849.

433. ENGLAND: 20 Halsbury part 1 sub Gifts no. 39; *Lucas v Lucas* (1738) West T Hard 456, 25 ER 1030 (LC); UNITED STATES: *Bump v. Pratt*, 32 N.Y.S. 538, 540 (Gen. Term 1895); Mechem (1926–1927) 586–601.

434. Brown § 7.4.

435. Mechem (1926–1927) 586.

436. Brown § 7.4.

437. Mechem (1926–1927) 588.

donor's agent.[438] Others adopt the opposite presumption.[439] If the donee was available to accept delivery, the donor who delivers to a third party is sometimes presumed to have wished to retain a *locus poenitentiae*.[440] The decisions are diverse and inconsistent.[441] "We think too much nicety may be exercised in determining who the third man exactly represents. If it be possible to do so, the law ought to be construed not too logically, but to meet the common transactions of our people in their homes."[442]

877. *Delivery at death*. It is common for a donor to ask a third party to retain the gift during the donor's lifetime and deliver it to the donee upon the donor's death. The common law generally considers such gifts to be valid—sometimes as the present gift of a future interest, in other cases as a declaration of trust—but only if there is actual delivery to the third party.[443] Mechem would distinguish between inter vivos and mortis causa gifts. If inter vivos, the gift would be invalid. The donor should be understood to retain title until death, at which point the transfer is testamentary. If the gift is mortis causa, the donor is permitted to retain the right to revoke, and the gift is valid.[444] The courts often choose a characterization that validates the gift.

878. *Bailee*. If the chattel is already bailed to the third party when the gift is made, expression of donative intent to the donee, without notice to the bailee, is usually not sufficient to make a gift.[445] Some agreement with the bailee is necessary to constitute attornment, but generally no further change of possession is required.[446] Nonetheless, if the goods are represented by a document of title or even a simple receipt, courts hold that, when the goods are not otherwise available for delivery, endorsement and delivery to the donee of the document successfully gifts the property, even without notice to the bailee.[447]

---

438. *Pocius v. Fleck*, 150 N.E.2d 106, 111 (Ill. 1958), *Barasch v. Barasch*, 628 N.E.2d 833, 836 (Ill. App. 1993).

439. *Kintzinger v. Millin*, 117 N.W.2d 68, 77 (Iowa 1962); *Bauer v. Sterling*, 696 N.W.2d 41 (Iowa 2005).

440. *Merchant v. German B. & L. Co.*, 24 Ohio C.D. 348 (Ohio App. 1913).

441. Mechem (1926–1927) 590.

442. *Sharpe v. Sharpe*, 90 S.E. 34, 36 (S.C. 1916).

443. Brown § 7.4.

444. Mechem (1926–1927) 596. For the mortis causa gift, see infra nos. 963–975.

445. *Gartside v. Pahlman*, 45 Mo. App. 160 (1891).

446. *Northern Trust Co. v. Swartz*, 141 N.E. 433 (Ill. 1923); Crossley Vaines 308; Brown § 7.7.

447. *Schmidt v. Pirie*, 211 Ill. App. 367 (1918). Mechem questioned how the gift could be complete without attornment on the part of the bailee unless the document involved is negotiable. Mechem (1926–1927) 606.

[b] Constructive Delivery

879. *Inconvenient or difficult.* When actual delivery is inconvenient or unreasonably difficult—because of its bulk, for example—delivery may take place constructively. In constructive delivery, the donor transfers to the donee the means of obtaining possession and control or, in some other indirect manner, transfers power and dominion rather than actual possession.[448] Goods stored in a warehouse or chest can be gifted by delivery of the key.[449] In several cases, a simple oral gift of such property, together with some exercise of dominion by the donee, has been held sufficient.[450]

880. *Two views.* "In no part of the [common] law of gifts is there greater uncertainty and confusion than in the matter of constructive delivery."[451] The difficulty is due to a dispute about the purpose of the doctrine of constructive delivery. If constructive delivery is considered a substitute for manual delivery, then it should not be judged effective until every reasonable step has been taken to render the transfer of possession complete. On the other hand, some cases hold that the purpose of constructive delivery is simply to confirm the donor's intent. In one case, a father recorded a brand in the name of his daughter and branded some of his cattle with her brand. Though the father retained control over the herd, the court found a valid constructive delivery.[452] The Restatement (Third) rejects the view that physical delivery, if possible, must always be completed for the gift to be valid.[453]

881. *Keys.* American law upholds constructive delivery by means of a key to a locked receptacle, such as a safe deposit box, whenever actual delivery of the contents is impractical or inconvenient.[454] A difficulty arises, however, when actual delivery is neither inconvenient nor difficult.[455] Common-law courts have long expressed the worry that permitting constructive delivery by means of keys encourages fraud. It is a simple matter to remove a key from the decedent's pocket and claim that a gift was made.[456] Some American courts uphold gifts by

---

448. Brown § 7.5.

449. *Ryall v Rowles* (1750) 1 Ves Sen 348, 362, 27 ER 1074, 1082 (LC).

450. *MacKenzie v. Steeves*, 167 P. 50 (Wash. 1917); Mechem (1926–1927) 358–360 (discussing cases).

451. Brown § 7.5.

452. *Hillebrant v. Brewer*, 6 Tex. 45 (1851).

453. Restatement (Third) of Property (Wills and Other Donative Transfers) § 6.2 comment c.

454. Brown § 7.5 ff.

455. Id.

456. *Keepers v. Fidelity Title and Deposit Co.*, 28 A. 585 (1894); *Scherer v. Hyland*, 380 A.2d 698 (N.J. 1977).

transfer of the key even when the inconvenience is not demonstrated.[457] Others do not.[458] Some judges require a qualified intent, namely a showing that, in addition to the intent to deliver the key, the donor also intended to deliver the particular contents of the box.[459]

Apparently no English court has decided whether the transfer of a key constitutes a valid inter vivos gift of the objects behind the lock.[460] Reasoning from parallel fields such as secured transactions, English writers suggest a distinction in this regard between the inter vivos gift by means of a key, which may pass title to goods too bulky to be conveniently subject to actual delivery, and the donatio mortis causa, for which delivery of the key may also constitute an effective gift of documents and jewelry.[461]

Problems also arise when the key alone does not permit the donee access to the property. Safe deposit custodians usually permit third parties access to the box only upon the owner's written authorization. An English decision suggests that the transfer of the key would not perfect a gift in such circumstances,[462] whereas American courts may consider the transfer of the key to constitute a valid gift.[463]

882. *Symbolic delivery.* Barlow suggests that English courts would probably not validate what is known as symbolic delivery—the transfer of a photograph as a substitute for an original painting. The symbol does not provide the donee with access to the property.[464] Yet English courts have on occasion respected symbolic delivery. Courts permit the delivery of a single chair to represent all of the furniture in a house[465] and the delivery of purchase receipts and other documentation to pass title to a church organ.[466] American courts do not generally distinguish between constructive and symbolic delivery. They will accept either type in the proper circumstances.[467]

[c] Shared Possession

883. *Unequivocal.* Delivery must be unequivocal. The transfer must leave no doubt that the donor intended to relinquish possession. Difficult cases arise

---

457. *Bynum v. Fidelity Bank,* 19 S.E.2d 121 (N.C. 1942).
458. *Keepers v. Fidelity Title & Deposit Co.,* 28 A. 585, 587 (N.J. Err. & App. 1894).
459. *Phipard v. Phipard,* 8 N.Y.S. 728, 731 (Gen. Term 1890) (Van Brunt, P. J., dissenting).
460. Barlow 394–395.
461. Crossley Vaines 307.
462. *In re Wasserberg* [1915] 1 Ch 195, 202–203; Barlow 398.
463. *Harrison v. Foley,* 206 F. 57, 58 (8th Cir.), cert. den. 231 U.S. 750 (1913).
464. Barlow 395.
465. *Lock v Heath* (1892) 8 TLR 295 (QB).
466. *Rawlinson v Mort* (1905) 93 LTR 555, 21 TLR 774 (KBD).
467. Kreitner 1911 note 94 *in fine.*

when the donor and the donee share possession after the gift is made, such as when they are members of the same household. In a much cited case, a husband brought his wife into the new family home, covered her eyes and then uncovered them, telling her to look at the furniture and other objects in the room, some of which she then handled, and indicating that the contents of the rooms thenceforth were hers. The couple and their children continued to share use and enjoyment of the furnishings. The property was insured in the husband's name. Upon a later suit by the husband's bankruptcy trustee, the court held that the situation was equivocal, there having been insufficient change of possession to constitute delivery.[468] Bridge rightly notes that the case demonstrates the extraordinary rigor of the English notion of delivery. "No allowance was made for the fact that her husband had brought her to the contents of the home, that these were too many and too bulky to deal with by physical handing over and that she had touched some of them on her first visit to the new home."[469] It remains unclear in English law what constitutes delivery when the donor and the donee live together.[470]

A particularly difficult case arises when parents order bulky property as a present for their child and then locate it in the family room. Many of the cases involve pianos. A Canadian case validated the gift on the grounds that the right of possession had been validly transferred.[471] One American court sustained the gift based on the parental relationship.[472] In another case, the piano remained in the parlor, and, after the instrument was destroyed by fire, the donor collected and kept the insurance money, even though he had always referred to the piano as belonging to the donee. The court invalidated the transfer.[473] As proof of delivery the courts accept a number of factors, including the donor's statements to the vendor,[474] the fact that the gift was delivered to the donee's room,[475] purchase in the donee's name,[476] and exclusive control in the donee.[477] The courts occasionally admit that they relax the delivery requirement in the presence of manifest donative intent.[478]

---

468. "[W]hen a husband watches his wife pick up a carpet, that does not indicate livery of seisin. It is an ordinary event in the common household consistent with continuing possession in the husband." *In re Cole* [1964] Ch 175, 181 (Pearson LJ).

469. Bridge 95.

470. Crossley Vaines 310.

471. *Tellier v. Dujardin*, 16 Man. L.R. 423 (Man. App. 1906), criticized in Brown § 7.9.

472. *Haynes v. Gwin*, 209 S.W. 67 (Ark. 1919).

473. *Newman v. Bost*, 29 S.E. 848 (N.C. 1898).

474. *Patchel v. Thompson's Estate*, 193 N.W. 852 (Mich. 1923).

475. Brown § 7.9.

476. *Wiley B. Allen Co. v. Edwards*, 154 P. 1066 (Cal. App. 1915).

477. *Pierson v. Heisey*, 19 Iowa 114 (1865).

478. "[The donee] was regarded in every respect by the [donor] as his child; and, while in the case of one's child the necessity of a delivery is not dispensed with in order to

884. *Common possession.* When the gift object is in the common physical possession of the donor and the donee, the courts have found no easy solution. If such gifts are recognized, it becomes difficult to establish the rights of individual family members and creates a temptation to defraud creditors. English law, and some American courts, generally do not recognize a gift in this situation. When delivery is effectuated by handing over a key, the donor's retention of a duplicate may prevent an effective delivery.[479] American courts are sometimes willing to receive evidence about how the parties treated the property after the purported gift.[480]

Gifts have been held valid when the donor placed the property in a receptacle (a trunk or the like) that belonged to the donee but to which the donor continued to have access.[481] Some of the cases finding sufficient delivery can be explained chiefly on the ground that the court believed that a gift was actually intended.[482]

Under Virginia law, if the donor and the donee reside together at the time of the transfer, possession at the place of their residence is not sufficient to perfect the gift. The provision expressly excepts personal property used exclusively by the donee.[483] The Restatement (Third) facilitates the finding of a valid gift when possession is shared.[484] Under the Restatement's view, delivery is effective if the donor notifies the donee that the property belongs to the donee, and both parties' actions are consistent with the donee's ownership.

(3) Significant Evolution

885. *Abandoned.* Over the past several decades, the doctrine of delivery seems to have experienced a profound evolution in American law. For all practical purposes, the concept no longer plays a role in the gifting of movables. The delivery requirement has slowly been abandoned by the state courts. Though this represents a dramatic development, it is important to remember that, from the

---

constitute a gift, the formal ceremony of a delivery is not absolutely necessary, but is sufficient if it appears that the donor intended an actual gift at the time, and evidenced his intention by some act which may be fairly construed into a delivery." *Wiley B. Allen Co. v. Edwards*, 154 P. 1066, 1066 (Cal. App. 1915).

479. UNITED STATES: *Bauernschmidt v. Bauernschmidt*, 54 A. 637, 643–644 (Md. App. 1903); ENGLAND: Crossley Vaines 307; Barlow 401–402.

480. *Fletcher v. Fletcher*, 55 Vt. 325 (1883); Brown § 7.9.

481. *Patterson v. Greensboro Loan and Trust Co.*, 72 S.E. 629 (N.C. 1911).

482. *Thomas v Times Book Co Ltd* [1966] 2 All ER 241. In *Thomas*, the donee, on the instructions of the donor, Dylan Thomas, searched for and found the lost original manuscript of *Under Milk Wood* on the donor's premises. The court held that the fact that the donee obtained possession with the donor's consent amounted to a sufficient delivery.

483. Virginia C Ann. § 55-3 (2007). The provision, frequently cited in the cases, was previously codified as § 2414.

484. Restatement (Third) of Property (Wills and Other Donative Transfers) § 6.2 comment e.

beginning, the delivery requirement was often interpreted with sufficient flexibility to validate gifts that were clearly intended. When the question of the validity of a gift of movables arises today in American law, attention seems to focus almost exclusively on proof of the donor's intent.

886. *Evolution.* Bracton believed that delivery was the essence of the gift.[485] He required no additional explanation for the rule. For him, there could be no donatio without traditio. For Maitland, in more analytic times, the essence of the gift was not the transfer of a *thing* but rather the transfer of a *right*.[486] At the end of the nineteenth century, the delivery requirement was reconceived as a means to achieve the public policy goal of preventing fraudulent claims of gift.[487] That justification too began to seem less obvious. Writing in the 1920s, Mechem found it necessary to specify the policies the delivery requirement was designed to achieve.[488] He conceded that other scholars believed that delivery constituted "an arbitrary and unnecessary formality."[489] "It is not to be doubted that the tendency of the law had been away from formalities and towards the policy of allowing intention to govern, or that such a tendency is a wise one." One problem with the delivery requirement was that a great many exceptions seemed necessary for it to function responsibly. Moreover, as Roscoe Pound pointed out, English equity courts throughout the nineteenth century permitted a clear indication of donative intent to pass title, even in the absence of delivery.[490] The fact that equity permits title to pass by simple declaration, as discussed below,[491] seemed to require increased flexibility in the law courts as well.

887. *Current law.* The evolution toward a virtually exclusive focus on donative intent now seems complete. As McGowan reads the cases, the delivery of chattels is no longer necessary for the execution of a gift in American law.[492] He reports that the last case in which the lack of delivery defeated a gift that was clearly intended was decided in 1966.[493] Though the courts insist that delivery is required, their practice is to manipulate the delivery concept to arrive at a result

---

485. Supra no. 865.

486. "I may have here and there a reader who can remember to have experienced in his own person what I take to be the history of the race, who can remember how it flashed across him as a truth, new though obvious, that the essence of a gift is a transfer of rights." Maitland (1886) 489. See also id. 490, 495.

487. Labatt 365.

488. Mechem (1926–1927) 348–349.

489. Id. 350.

490. Pound 674 and note 29 (collecting cases).

491. Infra no. 955.

492. McGowan. See Restatement (Third) of Property (Wills and Other Donative Transfers) § 6.2 comment yy.

493. Id. 360.

consistent with the donor's intent or, when a court believes enforcement might work a serious injustice, to deny validity.

An example of this trend involves a gift of a check made immediately prior to the donor's suicide.[494] The donor endorsed the check and placed it on the kitchen table, together with a note indicating her intent to make a gift of the check to her roommate. The court held that the purpose of the delivery requirement is evidentiary. In this case, the clear evidence of donative intent perfected the otherwise incomplete delivery. In another oft-cited case, the donor wished to retain a life estate in the gift painting, a work by Gustav Klimt, despite transferring the remainder interest to his son.[495] The court held that the donor's letters to the son affirming the gift constituted sufficient delivery, even though the painting never left the donor's apartment. The court thought little would be gained by requiring the donor to transfer the painting to the son and then receive redelivery. Mechem suggested that rulings such as these are required by "pragmatic considerations, i.e. ... the attempt to frame rules which will fit with a minimum of friction into the mechanism of ordinary life."[496] McGowan argued that the court disregarded the delivery requirement to validate a clearly intended gift.[497]

Some cases have gone farther, holding that a gift is complete when the donor directs the donee to take possession and, pursuant to the instructions, the donee does so.[498] The result has been criticized on the grounds that the donor has merely issued a verbal order and has not executed the gift.[499] One commentator contends there is no need for the donor to direct the donee to take possession. Words of present gift grant an implied license to the donee.[500] If taken far enough, this position would negate the delivery requirement. However, there is no valid gift until the donee follows the donor's instructions and takes possession.[501] When the donee does not obtain possession until after the donor's death, the gift fails.[502] If the property is in the possession of the donee, transfer of possession *brevi manu* is accomplished *per verba di praesenti*.[503]

888. *Justification.* The focus on intent permits the proper resolution of a number of cases for which there is no satisfactory construction of the delivery

---

494. *Scherer v. Hyland*, 380 A.2d 698 (N.J. 1977). See supra no. 909.

495. *Gruen v. Gruen*, 505 N.Y.S.2d 849 (N.Y. 1986).

496. Mechem (1926–1927) 365.

497. McGowan 375–376.

498. *Bragg v. Martenstein*, 143 P. 79 (Cal. App. 1914); *Penfield v. Thayer*, 2 E.D. Smith 305 (N.Y. Com. Pl. 1854); *Waite v. Grubbe*, 73 P. 206 (Or. 1903).

499. Mechem (1926–1927) 468.

500. Pollock 446.

501. Brown § 7.3 at 84.

502. *Tilton v. Mullen*, 137 N.E.2d 125 (Ohio App. 1956).

503. UNITED STATES: Brown § 7.8 (citing American cases); ENGLAND: *In re Stoneham* [1919] 1 Ch 149; *Kilpin v Ratley* [1892] 1 QB 582.

requirement. In a frequently cited case, a father purchased a pipe of port, had it bottled, gifted it to his infant son, and let it age in the family cellar.[504] From the time of the gift the wine was known in the family as the boy's port. With the exception of a few bottles that were opened and consumed, the bottles remained in the father's cellar. Two decades later the father was declared insolvent. The court held that the father's declared intent was insufficient to validate the gift. The court examined all of the facts and circumstances and concluded that the father intended to retain control until the boy came of age. Yet it is difficult to imagine what else the father might have done. The father announced to his family that the port belonged to the son. It was reasonable for the father to care for the property until the son came of age. The father might have included the property in his will, but that also would not have defeated the bankruptcy trustee. Moreover, as the wine aged, it would have been the father and not the son who would have enjoyed the pleasure of ownership.

In a case discussed above, a father, who owned a painting by Gustave Klimt, made a gift of it to his son but kept the painting in the family's living room until he died.[505] The father wanted to continue to enjoy the painting while he was alive, but he wanted his son to enjoy the status of ownership. In this case, the court respected the gift, even though none of the essentials for a typical gift delivery was present. If donative intent is proved, it now seems that the law will respect this type of transfer.

(B) BY WRITING

889. *Deeds.* To ensure the possibility of gift giving in situations in which delivery may be equivocal or otherwise difficult, the common law permits gifts of chattels to be made by "the little understood and seldom used medium of a deed."[506] A deed is an unequivocal statement, traditionally under seal, that the donor gives, or at a future date will give, certain property to the donee. Due to the "great deliberation used in making deeds," they are binding without inquiry into consideration.[507] The deed occupies a unique place in the common law. The doctrine of gift by deed is grounded in the special significance in the common law of a

---

504. *In re Ridgway* (1884–1885) LR 15 QBD 447, discussed infra no. 951.
505. *Gruen v. Gruen*, 505 N.Y.S.2d 849 (N.Y. 1986), discussed supra no. 887.
506. Brown § 7.5. For more about the writing under seal, see supra no. 689.
507. *Sharington v Strotton* (1765) 1 Plowd 298, 308, 75 ER 454, 470.
    For when a man passes a thing by deed, first there is the determination of the mind to do it, and upon that he causes it to be written, which is one part of deliberation, and afterwards he puts his seal to it, which is another part of deliberation, and lastly he delivers the writing as his deed, which is the consummation of his resolution; and by the delivery of the deed from him that makes it to him to whom it is made, he gives his assent to part with the thing contained in the deed to him to whom he delivers the deed, and this delivery is as a ceremony in law, signifying fully his good-will that the thing in the deed should pass from him to the other.
Id.

sealed instrument, which operates as an irrevocable and irrebuttable grant.[508] The role of the seal is not merely to validate the text of the document. The seal is rather the mystical essence of the document. The text is mere vesture.[509]

(1) India

890. *Registered deed.* In India, chattels may be gifted by registered deed, signed by or on behalf of the donor, and attested by at least two witnesses.[510]

(2) England

891. *Seal no longer required.* In England deeds were generally found only as incidents to a settlement of personal property, but they are now used extensively. Until 1989 a deed had to be executed under seal, which usually took the form of a red paper disc.[511] A seal is no longer required. Instead, the instrument must now plainly indicate that it is intended to be a deed. It must be signed in the presence of a witness who attests to the signature. It must also be delivered.[512] The delivery of the deed constitutes an effective gift, even without delivery of the chattel and without a declaration of trust. However, when possession remains with the donor, a gift of chattels is void as against the donor's creditors unless it is attested and registered under the Bills of Sale Act.[513]

(3) United States

892. *More problematic.* The deed of gift is significantly more problematic in the United States. As a general rule, a valid gift of chattels may be made by a sealed instrument, even though the property itself is not delivered.[514] The problem is that the seal, except when attached to corporate documents, has either passed out of use or been replaced by terms imprinted on store-bought documents, such as *(seal)* or *L.S.* Once the seal lost its distinctive character, it was abolished in many American jurisdictions.

[a] General Principles

893. *Unsealed instruments.* The abolition of the seal has not meant that chattels can no longer be gifted by writing. Though the precedent is "conflicting, ill considered, and often inconclusive,"[515] a majority of American courts seems to recognize the validity of gifts of chattels made by means of ordinary (unsealed)

---

508. Mechem (1926–1927) 569.
509. Id. 577.
510. Transfer of Property Act § 123 par. 2.
511. Bridge 96.
512. Law of Property (Miscellaneous Provisions) Act of 1989 sec. 1 pars. 2 lit. a and 3 lit. a.
513. Bills of Sale Act secs. 4, 8; 20 Halsbury part 1 sub Gifts no. 33; Crossley Vaines 310. It is unlikely that a gift would today be challenged under this statute. Bridge 99.
514. Brown § 7.10; Mechem (1926–1927) 569.
515. Brown id.

written instruments.[516] Yet the courts are still seeking a distinct formality to validate gratuitous transfers. Not every informal writing seems sufficient to validate a gift.[517] The Restatement (Third) now provides that all personalty may be gifted by means of a special informal instrument it calls an *inter vivos donative document*. Gifts so made are effective, even absent physical delivery of the property.[518] The writing must satisfy a number of requirements. It must be signed by the donor, it must identify the donor and the donee, it must describe the subject matter of the gift, and it must specify the nature of the interest given.[519] Personal letters or e-mails may be used.[520] Most courts hold that the gift is ineffective unless the writing is delivered. The Restatement (Third), however, provides that the document may be effective without delivery, as long as the donor acts in a way that demonstrates an intent to make a present transfer.[521]

A case involving a charitable gift to a retirement home may represent the outer limit of common-law permissiveness. The donor inserted into his contract with the donee the following sentences: "For the comfort, care, happiness I have while I am here be it short or long I wish to pay for these values the sum of $10,000.00 on demand. This may however be collectable against my estate if not demanded sooner, or paid by me."[522] The court enforced the gift on the grounds that the writing, though informal, sufficiently evidenced donative intent.[523] Yet though donative intent may have been present, the intent to make an immediate transfer was not.[524]

894. *Difficulties.* The possibility of making a gift of a chattel by means of a writing has created numerous difficulties. For example, the courts must now parse informal memoranda and correspondence to determine whether a gift was intended. Some courts have considered the fact that the gift object would have been impossible to deliver manually.[525] Other complex problems arise when, after delivery of the instrument, the donor retains possession and continues to exercise dominion over the property.[526]

---

516. *In re Cohn*, 176 N.Y.S. 225 (App. Div. 1919); Restatement (Second) of Property (Donative Transfers) § 32.2 and the Reporter's Note.

517. Mechem (1926–1927) 577.

518. Restatement (Third) of Property (Wills and Other Donative Transfers) § 6.2 comment p.

519. Id. § 6.2 comment q.

520. Id. § 6.2 illus. 19, 21.

521. Id. § 6.2 comment u.

522. *Faith Lutheran Retirement Home v. Veis*, 473 P.2d 503 (Mont. 1970).

523. Id. 505–506.

524. Temple.

525. *Lipson v. Evans*, 105 A. 312, 315–316 (Md. App. 1918) (not capable of delivery because subject to a pledge).

526. *Francoeur v. Beatty*, 151 P. 123 (Cal. 1915).

[b] Gifts to Minors

895. *UGMA.* Partially due to the difficulties caused by the requirement of un-equivocal delivery, virtually all American states have enacted one version or another of a uniform law designed to facilitate gifts to minors. The law creates a statutory form for a trust in which the gift property can be held for the benefit of the minor. The trust form is especially useful for gifts of money and securities. This legislation is considered here because its most recent version specifies the contents of a written instrument that may be used for gifting chattels.

The original version, the Uniform Gifts to Minors Act (UGMA), was enacted in 1956. It closely followed the Gifts of Securities to Minors Acts, which had been adopted in fourteen states.[527] The UGMA included gifts of money as well as secu-rities. It was revised in 1966. Some version of the UGMA was adopted in every American jurisdiction.

896. *UTMA.* Largely because of a series of nonuniform amendments, the UGMA was restated and revised in 1983 as the Uniform Transfers to Minors Act (UTMA). The UTMA has now been adopted in virtually all American jurisdic-tions.[528] It provides for the transfer of property to a custodian for the benefit of the minor. All types of property may be gifted under the act, whether real or personal, tangible or intangible. Property is classified into seven categories. A different method of effectuating the transfer is designated for each.[529] In gen-eral, property capable of registration or recordation may be gifted by appropriate recording in the custodian's name together with an indication that the property is being held for the designated minor. For property not usually registered or recorded, the transfer may be made by written instrument. In all cases, transfer of control of the property to the custodian is to occur as soon as practicable, though the gift is not invalid if the transfer does not occur.[530] Title vests immedi-ately in the minor, but control is in the custodian. Neither the minor nor the minor's legal representative may exercise dominion over the property.

ii. Choses in Action

897. *Assignment and trust.* Choses in action are traditionally gifted either by assignment, which is examined here, or by the creation of a trust, which is exam-ined with other equitable institutions below.[531] In general, gratuitous assign-ments are effective to transfer rights to all choses in action. However, the typical

---

527. See, e.g., California CC former §§ 1154–1164 (1955) (repealed 1959); Note (1956); Prefatory Note, Uniform Transfers to Minors Act 3–4.

528. For the table of adoptions, see Uniform Transfers to Minors Act 1–2.

529. Uniform Transfers to Minors Act § 9.

530. Id. §§ 9 par. c, 11 par. a no. 1.

531. Infra nos. 953–958. For the definition of *choses in action*, see supra no. 347.

written assignment is not the exclusive mechanism for making the transfer. Mercantile documents, such as negotiable instruments, were transferred under the law merchant by delivery. The common law has now accepted this practice as well. Though in many cases these transfers, if examined closely, would qualify as gratuitous assignments, they are generally thought of as being distinct. Other rules apply to the gratuitous transfer of funds deposited in bank accounts.

(A) GRATUITOUS ASSIGNMENTS

898. *Rights generally assignable.* Today, the general rule is that gratuitous assignments are effective to transfer rights to all choses in action. "If the thing given be a chose in action, the law requires an assignment, or some equivalent instrument, and the transfer must be actually executed."[532] In England an assignment is valid only if made in writing and only after notice is given to the obligor.[533] However, English equity permits assignments that fail to meet these rigorous requirements. In the United States, in contrast, an assignment can be made by a mere manifestation to another of the intent to make an immediate transfer of right. Unless otherwise provided by contract or statute, the assignment may be made either orally or in writing.[534] However, gratuitous assignments remain revocable unless one of three formalities is present: the execution and delivery of a traditional written assignment; the transfer of an instrument embodying the right; or, for rights not embodied in an instrument, the transfer of documentation necessary to enforce the claim.[535] In American law, equity intervenes chiefly to protect the assignee's reliance. These different mechanisms are the product of an extraordinarily complex historical development. Due to the intricate relation between legal and equitable assignment, they are examined together here. The remaining equitable mechanisms for accomplishing a gift transfer are discussed below.

(1) History

899. *Equitable assignments.* As discussed above, choses in action were originally not assignable at common law.[536] Principles of agency provided a means to circumvent the restriction.[537] If the obligee granted a power of attorney to a third party, the third party could sue the obligor in the obligee's name. If the obligor objected to the third party's suit, equity would grant the third party a bill in equity, but only if the power of attorney was supported by consideration. Due to the fear of maintenance, the only acceptable consideration was the satisfaction of an existing debt. Beginning in the seventeenth century, rights became

---

532. 2 Kent 355.
533. Law of Property Act of 1925 sec. 136 par. 1.
534. Restatement (Second) of Contracts § 324.
535. Id. § 332 par. 1.
536. Supra no. 349.
537. Rundell 643–645.

assignable in equity, though if unsupported by consideration, the assignment remained revocable. Assignment was generally effective if the donor did everything necessary, given the nature of the property, to transfer the right.[538] A distinction was made between legal choses in action, which were claims that could be brought at law, such as for payment of a debt, and equitable choses in action, which involved rights enforceable only in equity, such as an interest in a trust fund or legacy. Both were assignable in equity, though, as discussed below, the mechanisms differed. Though the assignee of an equitable chose could sue in the assignee's own name, the assignee of a legal chose was required to join the assignor to the suit.[539] Partial assignments were possible.

Gratuitous assignments were more limited. Though no consideration was necessary for assignment of an equitable chose, a celebrated dispute later arose concerning whether consideration was required for the assignment of a legal chose.[540] The problem arises because, with an equitable assignment, legal title remains in the assignor. Since the transfer is not complete, and equity does not aid a volunteer, it seems the transfer would be enforceable only if supported by consideration.[541] Jenks nonetheless argued that gratuitous assignments were enforceable in equity,[542] while Anson contended that consideration was generally required.[543] As a result of the uncertainty, choses in action were generally transferred by declaration of trust, an institution that is examined below.

900. *Legal assignments.* The Judicature Act of 1873 recognized the validity of assignments at law. Under a provision of the act that is still in force, a legal assignment is valid if it is made in a signed writing, if the assignment is absolute (not given as security for a debt), and if express notice is given to the obligor.[544] When those conditions are met, the right to the debt passes to the assignee and permits the assignee to grant a good discharge. The act does not require consideration. Gratuitous assignments are thus valid. The act has been held to apply both to legal and to equitable choses in action.[545]

901. *Equity after the Judicature Act.* Once assignment became possible at law, equitable assignment, having no further purpose, might have been expected

---

538. *Milroy v Lord* (1862) 4 De GF & J 264, 274, 45 ER 1185, 1189; Sykes 125.

539. Hall 101.

540. Sykes 125.

541. Keeton 12.

542. Jenks.

543. Anson (1901). Dicta in opinions of the equity courts suggest that, before 1873, a gratuitous equitable assignment not under seal was enforceable if the chose was equitable but required consideration if the chose was legal. Keeton 17; Costigan 334. The courts seem to have been more lenient with regard to gifts causa mortis. Williston (1930) 3.

544. Supreme Court of Judicature Act of 1873 sec. 25 par. 6, now in Law of Property Act of 1925 sec. 136 par. 1.

545. *Torkington v Magee* [1902] 2 KB 427; Bridge 154; Sykes 129.

to disappear. Instead, it flourished. In England, equity continues to offer an alternate method for the execution of many types of assignment.[546] Because no consideration is required for a legal assignment, it would seem obvious that, whatever had been the case before the Judicature Act, consideration would not now be required for an assignment in equity. Yet because a statutory form is now available, many judges suggest that an assignor cannot be said to have done everything necessary to accomplish the assignment unless the statutory requirements are met. Equity should therefore be available only if the assignment is supported by consideration.[547] Even today, some American courts hold that the equitable assignment of a chose in action is invalid without consideration,[548] though, when justice seems to require it, those jurisdictions find consideration in the natural love and affection between the parties or in motives of natural duty and prudence.[549]

(2) Written Assignment

902. *Writing required.* In England, the assignment provision in the Judicature Act is still in force. It provides that an absolute assignment in writing, signed by the assignor, of a debt or other legal chose in action is effective upon notice to the obligor.[550] Modern American law discusses the effectiveness of gratuitous assignments in terms of what is necessary to make the assignment irrevocable. The Restatement (Second) provides that a gratuitous assignment may be made irrevocable if carried out by written assignment, either signed or under seal.[551] State statutes have similar provisions.[552] The assignment remains revocable, however, until the deed or other writing is delivered or the assignee receives payment from, or judgment against, the obligor.[553]

903. *Tangible choses in action.* There is controversy about the best means to reconcile the law merchant with the common law. Under commercial law, negotiable instruments and documents of title are generally transferred by endorsement and delivery. In some jurisdictions, a written assignment is therefore not effective to transfer rights in mercantile specialties. These jurisdictions are concerned that a holder who retains possession may transfer good title to a good faith purchaser. However, some courts enforce a written assignment of an interest in

---

546. *Durham Bros v Robertson* [1898] 1 QB 765 (CA); Hall 100. Hall's short essay is the best current summary of the complex relationship between legal and equitable assignments. I rely heavily on it here.

547. Sykes 127.

548. *Bleitz v. Bryant Lumber Co.*, 194 P. 550 (Wash. 1920) (en banc).

549. *Sundstrom v. Sundstrom*, 129 P.2d 783, 788 (Wash. 1942) (en banc).

550. Law of Property Act sec. 136 par. 1.

551. Restatement (Second) of Contracts § 332 par. 1 lit. a.

552. New York General Obligations Law § 5-1107.

553. Restatement (Second) of Contracts § 332 par. 3.

a negotiable instrument even without delivery of the paper.[554] An informal written assignment, together with the endorsement of the receipt, has been upheld as sufficient to make a gift of bonds.[555] Though the American Uniform Commercial Code specifies that delivery is required to transfer shares of stock, the delivery of an informal written instrument is often validated as symbolic or constructive delivery, even without delivery of the shares.[556] When the savings passbook was the recognized symbol of the deposit, written assignments of funds in the account were apparently rare and probably were not effective against a bona fide purchaser who received the passbook.[557] In England, all legal obligations can be assigned by written assignment.

(3) Delivery of Tangible Choses in Action

904. *Rights embodied in writings.* In most modern legal systems, a right may be embodied (*verbrieft*) in a document for purposes of transfer and release. Writings that embody rights have been called *tangible choses in action.* Both the law and business custom treat these writings to some extent as chattels. They are considered to have intrinsic value and are more than mere evidence of intangible rights.[558] The extent to which the writing embodies the right depends on the type of writing involved. Writings range from negotiable instruments and stock certificates to insurance policies and savings account books. These documents generally must be presented when demanding payment or performance from the obligor. To that extent, possession constitutes control. The courts have therefore generally held that a gratuitous transfer of tangible choses may be made by simple delivery.[559] In general, gifts of rights embodied in an instrument are valid as long as either legal or equitable title is transferred to the donee.[560]

905. *Title, legal and equitable.* In general, legal title passes when all of the requirements specified by applicable law have been met. There may be formalities in addition to simple delivery. Negotiable instruments and bonds are transferred at law by negotiation, which means delivery of the paper after any necessary endorsement. As discussed below, legal title to stock certificates sometimes does not pass until the transfer is recorded on the corporate books and new shares are issued in the name of the transferee. Despite the legal rules, equitable title, the

---

554. *Thatcher v. Merriam,* 240 P.2d 266 (Utah 1952); Mechem (1925) 11 and note 20 (collecting cases).

555. *Goldsworthy v. Johnson,* 204 P. 505 (Nev. 1922).

556. Infra nos. 914–917; *Hill v. Warner, Berman & Spitz,* 484 A.2d 344, 350 (N.J. App. Div. 1984); *Kallop v. McAllister,* 678 A.2d 526 (Del. 1996); *In re Cohn,* 176 N.Y.S. 225 (App. Div. 1919); Curtis 901–902.

557. Havighurst 136–137.

558. Williston (1930) 5–6.

559. Id. 8–10.

560. *Ridden v. Thrall,* 26 N.E. 627, 628–629 (N.Y. 1891).

beneficial interest, can often be transferred by simple delivery. An equitable assignment vests only equitable title in the donee, which enables the donee to sue to realize the benefit of the transaction.[561]

Bonds, unendorsed bills and promissory notes, certificates of deposit, savings bank books, and insurance policies may all be transferred by delivery.[562] Other writings, such as nonnegotiable instruments and life insurance policies, are often treated in the regular course of business as evidence that the person in possession is entitled to receive performance. Rights embodied in this manner may also be gifted by delivery, though these rights are frequently transferred by written assignment.

[a] Negotiable Instruments

906. *Delivery and endorsement.* Negotiable instruments are generally transferred by negotiation, which requires delivery together with any necessary endorsement.[563] A gratuitous transfer may also be made by simple delivery, which, under the shelter principle, conveys to the donee whatever right the donor has to enforce the instrument.[564] The distinction between negotiation and simple transfer has few consequences when the instrument is given as a gift. In either case, the donee becomes a holder in due course only if the donor already has that status.

907. *Written assignment.* As noted above, there is some question whether a written gratuitous assignment is valid without delivery of the instrument.[565] Delivery was thought to be necessary because the right generally could not be enforced without the instrument. However, both English and American law now permit rights embodied in specialties to be enforced without producing the instrument.[566] As a result, some courts enforce the assignment of an interest in a negotiable instrument even in the absence of delivery.[567]

908. *Parol gifts.* It would seem obvious, both from the negotiation requirement in the law governing negotiable instruments and from the gift law delivery requirement, that a parol gift of a negotiable instrument without delivery would

---

561. Graves 877.

562. Bruton 852 notes 75–80 (collecting cases). As discussed above, some courts hold that embodied rights may also be transferred by written instrument. Supra no. 903.

563. UNITED STATES: UCC § 3-201; ENGLAND: Bill of Exchange Act of 1882 sec. 31 par. 3.

564. UNITED STATES: *Grover v. Grover*, 24 Pick. 261 (Mass. 1837); UCC § 3-203; ENGLAND: Bill of Exchange Act sec. 31 par. 4.

565. Brown § 8.2; *Davis v. Adel Banking Co.*, 334 S.E.2d 874 (Ga. App. 1985) (gift valid).

566. Other proof can be admitted if the absence of the original can be explained. UCC § 3-309.

567. *Thatcher v. Merriam*, 240 P.2d 266 (Utah 1952).

be invalid.[568] Nonetheless, when the facts call for it, courts validate even oral transfers. In one case, the donor paid off notes evidencing a debt that the donor's son owed to her sister. She then asked her sister to return the paper so she might present the notes to the son. The sister refused to return the notes and later sued on them as the donor's heir. The court narrated in detail the story of the faithful son who, with his wife, stayed up every night comforting his blind, feeble, and grateful mother. To prevent the sister from profiting from her recalcitrance, the court validated the purely oral gift. "To allow [the sister] thus to prevent the gift from taking effect, when the mother regarded the gift as complete, would be to exalt form above substance and to prostitute a rule of law to defeat the purpose for which it was intended."[569]

909. *Donor's own paper.* Different rules apply to negotiable instruments of which the donor is the maker or drawer. In the common law, as opposed to some civilian systems, a check or a draft does not of itself operate as an assignment of the funds on deposit with the drawee.[570] An equitable assignment is generally found only when the check is drawn for the exact amount remaining in the account or a special deposit is made to cover the check.[571] Except for those limited situations, the drawer's paper is considered merely an order or promise to pay. The gift is not executed until the instrument is accepted or paid.[572] The drawee's authority to pay is generally held to be withdrawn at the donor's death,[573] though there is case law to the contrary.[574] If the bank receives the check before the donor's death but refuses to pay because it improperly doubts the donor's signature, one court has held the gift to be complete.[575] If the signature is in fact doubtful, there is no gift, even if the check turns out to be good.[576] If the donee detrimentally relies on the donor's check, some courts permit recovery.[577]

---

568. *Lounsberry v. Boger,* 193 Ill.App. 384 (1915).

569. *Simmonds v. Simmonds' Adm'r,* 118 S.W. 304, 306 (Ky. App. 1909).

570. ENGLAND: *In re Swinburne* [1926] Ch 38 (CA); UNITED STATES: UCC § 3-408; 3 Pomeroy § 1284. In contrast, an assignment of a specific existing fund held by a depositary may constitute a valid assignment. 3 Pomeroy § 1280. In the French conception, the draft operates as an assignment of the funds in the drawee's possession. For a comparison of the two systems, see Mitchell 241–243. See supra nos. 788–793.

571. *McEwen v. Sterling State Bank,* 5 S.W.2d 702, 705 (Mo. App. 1928); Comment (1951) 1021.

572. *Burrows v. Burrows,* 137 N.E. 923 (Mass. 1922); *Simmons v. Cincinnati Sav. Soc.,* 31 Ohio St. 457, 461 (Ohio 1877).

573. UNITED STATES: *Felder v. Felder,* 32 S.E.2d 550 (Ga. App. 1944); ENGLAND: *Hewitt v Kaye* (1868) LR 6 Eq 198 (Ch).

574. AUSTRALIA: *Sinnamon v Hardgrave* (1890) 4 Queen's LJ 16.

575. *Bromley v Brunton* (1868) LR 6 Eq 275 (Ch).

576. *In re Swinburne* [1926] 1 Ch 38 (CA).

577. *Armstrong v. Armstrong,* 142 Ill.App. 507 (1908); Restatement (Second) of Contracts § 322 par. 4 and illus. 9.

The gift law rule that the donor's check is not effective as a gift until it is paid is a consequence of the commercial law principle of nonassignment, which is designed to prevent banks from becoming involved in litigation.[578] Legal systems, such as the French, that consider the check to be an assignment of funds are more willing to consider a check effective as a gift. As Havighurst has noted, the differing gift rules in this field are "almost entirely the result of the operation of the 'legal mind.'"[579]

910. *Certificates of deposit.* Delivery of a certificate of deposit as a gift, with or without endorsement, may constitute an equitable assignment of the funds it represents.[580] This may be the case even when the certificate states that it is not transferable. Equitable title results from delivery, whereas legal title passes by completing the formal transfer.[581]

911. *Bonds.* In England prior to 1873, it was unclear whether bonds—obligations under seal to pay a sum of money—could be transferred by gratuitous assignment, even when the signed assignment was delivered to the donee.[582] The Judicature Act permitted assignment. In American law, gifts of bonds generally follow rules similar to those that govern gifts of negotiable instruments.[583] Even if the method of transfer specified in the bond is not followed, the delivery is generally good as between donor and donee. The specified method is considered to operate for the obligor's protection.[584] However, U.S. savings bonds, by their terms, are nontransferable. They may be gifted only by surrender and re-issue in the donee's name.[585]

[b] Shares of Stock

[1] England

912. *Statutory formalities.* In general, choses in action created by statute may be transferred only by observing the statutory requirements, which often include

---

578. "These rules are indispensable to the safe transaction of commercial business. Any other rule would produce confusion, and involve banking institutions and all depositaries of moneys, in responsibilities to conflicting claimants, which, while producing great embarrassments, would serve no beneficial purpose." *Att'y Gen. v. Continental Life Ins. Co.*, 26 Sickels 325 (N.Y. 1877); see Comment (1951) 1010.

579. Havighurst 134.

580. ENGLAND: *In re Griffin* [1899] 1 Ch 408, noted in 12 *Harv. L. Rev.* 498–499 (1899); UNITED STATES: *Baskett v. Hassell*, 107 U.S. 602, 613–615, 2 S.Ct. 415 (1883).

581. Mechem (1925) 11.

582. Compare *Fortescue v Barnett* (1834) 3 My & K 34, 40 ER 14 (Ch) (assignment effective), with *Edwards v Jones* (1836) 1 My & Cr 226, 236–237, 40 ER 361, 365 (Ch) (assignment not effective); see Costigan 333–334.

583. Brown § 8.2.

584. Restatement (Third) of Property (Wills and Other Donative Transfers) § 6.2 comment h.

585. *U.S. v. Chandler*, 410 U.S. 257, 93 S.Ct. 880 (1973).

a writing.[586] In English law, special formalities are necessary for any transfer of the rights embodied in stock certificates, whether gratuitously or for consideration. Some shares of stock must be transferred by deed.[587] Others may only be registered if there is a proper written instrument of transfer.[588]

913. *Equity.* When transfers are subject to statutory formalities and those formalities are not observed, equity will generally not perfect an imperfect gift.[589] However, the equity courts will validate gifts when the donor has done everything that was necessary and possible for the donor to do.[590] If the donor executes a proper share transfer and delivers it to the donee, the donee has the right to sue for rectification of the share register.[591] Equity therefore holds that the beneficial interest has passed.[592] Even this rule is interpreted flexibly. In one case, the donor executed a stock transfer form, but her auditors did not deliver it before her death, either to the donee or to the company.[593] Legal title could not pass until the company registered the share transfer. Those challenging the transfer argued that equitable title could not have passed without delivery. The court upheld the gift as an equitable assignment. The gift was clearly intended, and, since the donee had been made a member of the company's board, it would have been unconscionable for the donor to recall the gift. The court balanced the need to permit donors to reconsider with the equivalent need to effectuate the donor's intent and prevent unconscionable conduct. Those equitable factors led to the conclusion that the donor had done enough. "Although equity will not aid a volunteer, it will not strive officiously to defeat a gift."[594]

[2] United States

914. *Traditional method.* In American law, the formal process of transferring shares has traditionally involved the surrender of the old certificate, transfer on the company's books, and issuance of a new certificate to the transferee.[595] The method has always been considered cumbersome. The courts, and eventually

---

586. Bridge 97; Mechem (1925) 12.
587. Companies Clauses Consolidation Act of 1845 sec. 14.
588. Companies Act of 1985 sec. 182 par. 1 lit. b; Stock Transfer Act of 1963 sec. 1; see 20 Halsbury part 1 sub Gifts no. 34.
589. *Milroy v Lord* (1862) 4 De GF & J 264, 45 ER 1185; 20 Halsbury part 1 sub Gifts no. 34.
590. "Before long, equity had tempered the wind to the shorn lamb (i e. the donee). It did so on more than one occasion and in more than one way." *Pennington v Waine* [2002] EWCA Civ 227, [2002] 1 WLR 2075 no. 54. For a critical view, see Oakley par. 5-034.
591. Companies Act of 1985 sec. 359.
592. *In re Rose* [1952] Ch 499.
593. *Pennington v Waine* [2002] EWCA Civ 227, [2002] 1 WLR 2075; Bridge 97–98.
594. *T Choithram Int'l SA v Pagarani* [2001] 1 WLR 1, 11, [2001] 2 All ER 492 (CA).
595. Mechem (1925) 12.

the legislator, validated gifts by hand-to-hand transfer, even when the company's share register had not been updated.[596]

915. *Delivery.* Today in American law, legal title to certificated securities generally passes by delivery.[597] Endorsement is often needed for the transferee to become a bona fide purchaser. However, because a donee does not give value, the donee acquires the status of a bona fide purchaser for value only under the shelter principle.[598] Uncertificated securities are generally transferred by registration.[599]

916. *Legal title.* Legal title remains in the donor until the donee is recognized by the corporation. However, most American jurisdictions regard the gift as conceptually different from the transfer of title. The two sets of rules have different purposes. The rules regarding the transfer of stock ownership are designed to protect the corporation and third parties. The rules governing the gift disposition are principally designed to protect the donor from fraudulent claims of gift. American law has integrated the two sets of rules in the following manner. Once a court is satisfied that a gift was intended and executed, the court will consider the transfer to operate an equitable assignment and require the donor to complete whatever additional formalities are required.[600]

917. *Substitutes for delivery.* American courts often find substitutes for delivery if they are satisfied that the donor intended to make the gift. Under the earlier Uniform Stock Transfer Act, an attempted transfer, as by assignment, without delivery of the shares was considered a promise to transfer, enforceable only if supported by consideration.[601] Today the delivery of an informal written instrument is often held to be a symbolic or constructive delivery that is sufficient to transfer title to the shares, even though the shares did not accompany the instrument.[602] One court held that the transfer of an ownership interest on the corporate books, even though insufficient to transfer title, operated as a valid gift when coupled with other acts that provided a tangible expression of donative intent.[603] Another court invalidated a gift made in a similar manner—by listing on the

---

596. Id.

597. UCC §§ 8-301 par. a and comment 1, 8-302, 8-307. *Purchaser* is defined in the code to include a donee. UCC § 1-201 par. b nos. 29–30.

598. Under the shelter principle, a transferee gains all rights that the transferor had, or had the power to transfer. UCC § 8-302 par. a.

599. UCC § 8-301 par. b.

600. *Hill v. Warner, Berman & Spitz,* 484 A.2d 344, 350 (N.J. App. Div. 1984); Graves 878.

601. Uniform Stock Transfer Act § 10; *Johnson v. Johnson,* 13 N.E.2d 788, 791 (Mass. 1938); Curtis.

602. *Hill v. Warner, Berman & Spitz,* 484 A.2d 344, 350 (N.J. App. Div. 1984); *Kallop v. McAllister,* 678 A.2d 526 (Del. 1996); *In re Cohn,* 176 N.Y.S. 225 (App. Div. 1919).

603. *Elyachar v. Gerel Corp.,* 583 F.Supp. 907 (S.D.N.Y. 1984). See also Mechem (1925) 24–26.

corporate books—when the donor retained all incidents of ownership, including the right to receive dividends and the right to transfer the stock.[604] As one court remarked, "While courts have overlooked the absence of a physical delivery in some cases, the donative intent of the donor in those cases was clearly established."[605]

When the gift is made by transferring individually held stock into a joint account, the courts seem willing to accept even less in terms of delivery. In one case, the donor wrote a letter to a stockbroker requesting the transfer. The court sustained the gift on the grounds that the letter represented symbolic or constructive delivery.[606] However, another court held that, when the donor's motive in having stock issued jointly was to avoid probate costs, the gift was invalid.[607]

[c] Life Insurance

918. *Beneficiary designation.* As noted above, the death benefit from a life insurance policy may constitute a gift to the beneficiary.[608] The beneficiary designation constitutes a present gift of a contract right to collect the proceeds at the insured's death.[609] Unlike most other gifts in the common law, the gift is valid despite being revocable. The owner of the policy may revoke simply by executing the change-of-beneficiary form.[610]

919. *Gift of the policy.* The owner of the policy may also make a gift of the policy, which involves a transfer of the principal rights arising out of the policy, including the right to borrow against the policy's cash value, the right to surrender the policy for cash, the right to change the beneficiary, and the right to select the settlement option.[611] Once the policy is effectively assigned, only the assignee has the right to change the beneficiary.

920. *England.* A life insurance policy in England may be assigned only by endorsement on the policy or by written instrument as prescribed by statute. The assignment is effective against the carrier upon notice.[612]

---

604. *Kelly v. Maxwell,* 628 S.W.2d 931 (Mo. App. 1982).

605. *Lichtenstein v. Eljohnan, Inc.,* 555 N.Y.S.2d 331, 332 (App. Div. 1990).

606. *Tanner v. Robinson,* 411 So.2d 240 (Fla. App. 1982).

607. *Blanchette v. Blanchette,* 287 N.E.2d 459 (Mass. 1972).

608. Supa no. 352.

609. Restatement (Third) of Property (Wills and Other Donative Transfers) § 7.1 comment c.

610. Id. § 7.1 illus. 3.

611. Jerry § 52B par. d no. 1.

612. Policies of Assurance Act of 1867 secs. 3, 5. A simple writing without notice to the carrier is ineffective as an assignment. *In re Hughes* (1888) 59 LTR 586.

921. *United States.* Some American courts hold that a written assignment is necessary to perfect the gift of a life insurance policy,[613] while others hold that, although not required, a written assignment successfully executes the gift.[614] In most jurisdictions, the gift of a life insurance policy is also valid upon simple delivery to the donee without written assignment[615] and even without notice to the issuer.[616] The gift of the policy may be valid despite the fact that the disposition does not follow the method of transfer required by the policy.[617] Most courts permit the insured to give the policy to anyone, even a donee without an insurable interest. The carrier's consent is necessary for the assignment, but compliance with the formalities stated in the policy is tantamount to consent.[618]

[d] Bank Passbooks

922. *Delivery of the passbook.* According to the older American cases, the simple delivery of a savings deposit passbook, even without assignment, constituted a valid gift of the monies in the account.[619] Because savings bank bylaws generally did not permit the withdrawal of funds without presentation of the passbook, delivery transferred dominion over the account. Any provisions in the savings passbook or bank regulations prohibiting the withdrawal of funds without either written orders or the depositor's power of attorney did not, for gift law purposes, prevent delivery from effectuating a valid gift.[620]

The rule continues in effect for the donatio mortis causa in England and in some American jurisdictions, even when, under some circumstances, the bank permits funds to be withdrawn without the passbook.[621] Some courts have distinguished savings accounts from checking and general deposit accounts, holding that accounts other than savings accounts may not be gifted by delivery of the passbook, even in the case of a mortis causa gift.[622] In one case, the donor

---

613. *Steele v. Gatlin*, 42 S.E. 253 (Ga. 1902); 38A C.J.S. Gifts § 54.

614. *Hurlbut v. Hurlbut*, 1 N.Y.S. 854 (Sup. Ct. 1888); 38 Am.Jur.2d Gifts § 43.

615. *Franklin Life Ins. Co. v. Falkingham*, 229 F.2d 300 (7th Cir. 1956); 38 Am.Jur.2d Gifts § 43.

616. *Miller v. Gulf Life Ins. Co.*, 12 So.2d 127 (Fla. 1943) (on rehearing); *Sundstrom v. Sundstrom*, 129 P.2d 783, 785 (Wash. 1942) (en banc).

617. *Clarke v. Edwards*, 74 So.2d 912 (Ala. 1954).

618. Jerry § 52B par. d no. 1.

619. *Basket v. Hassell*, 107 U.S. 602, 2 S. Ct. 415 (1899); *Pierce v. Boston Five Cents Savings Bank*, 129 Mass. 425 (1880); Brown § 8.3; Havighurst 133; see G. S. G., R. E. H.

620. *Brooks v. Mitchell*, 161 A. 261, 268–269 (Md. 1932); *Donovan v. Hibernia Savings and Loan Society*, 265 P. 995 (Cal. App. 1928); 38 Am.Jur.2d Gifts § 66.

621. ENGLAND: *Birch v Treasury Solicitor* [1951] 1 Ch 298 (CA); UNITED STATES: *Hileman v. Hulver*, 221 A.2d 693, 696 (Md. 1966); *Ridden v. Thrall*, 26 N.E. 627, 628–629 (N.Y. 1891).

622. Compare *Jones v. Weakley*, 12 So. 420, 421 (Ala. 1893) (distinguishing between savings and other accounts) with *McCoy's Adm'r v. McCoy*, 104 S.W. 1031, 1031–1032

delivered two passbooks and a written assignment at the same time to the same donee with the same intent. One passbook was for a savings account, the other for a checking account. The court upheld the former as a gift but not the latter.[623] The distinction was justified by the fact that the savings account, at least in times past, more often served to accumulate a small inheritance to be passed to the next generation.[624]

Today, however, in the age of the automated teller machine, even where the savings passbook still exists, mere delivery no longer conclusively perfects an inter vivos gift in most American jurisdictions, largely because delivery is no longer considered tantamount to surrender of dominion.[625] Instead, the gratuitous transfer of funds in savings accounts follows the general rules for gift transfers of choses in action, requiring either a valid assignment[626] or proof of surrender of dominion and control.[627] It may be difficult to determine whether the donor has completely surrendered control. In one case, the donor, in her last days, handed her bankbooks to the donees and said she wished them to have the accounts if she died.[628] Subsequently, the donor asked the donees to pay a contractor's bill from the bank accounts. The court had to decide whether the donor's

---

(Ky. App. 1907) (no distinction). See also Restatement (Second) of Contracts § 332 illus. 7; Havighurst 133.

Courts that relied on the distinction sometimes failed to appreciate the equities of the situation. In *Jones*, the donor, who suffered serious injuries from a railroad disaster from which he died two days later, made a mortis causa gift of his passbook to his nephew. In the presence of witnesses, the donor stated clearly that he wanted his nephew to have the money in the account. The court held that the gift would have been valid if the account had been in a savings bank, but, because it was in a bank of issue, discount, and deposit, the gift could not be enforced.

623. *Goodson v. Liles*, 96 So. 262 (Ala. 1923).

624. A savings bank is entirely different from a commercial bank in its foundation, its place in the social structure and in its methods of business. A savings bank is an institution for the accumulation of small sums, chiefly the savings of the poorer classes .... The chief problem of a savings bank is the safekeeping of the funds. The commercial bank is one which receives deposits, makes discounts and issues notes. They are lenders and borrowers. They may or may not pay interest on deposits subject to check .... There is another keen distinction between savings banks and commercial banks with reference to the pass book. In the savings institution, title to the account may be created by gift accompanied by delivery of the bank book .... When deposits are made in checking accounts in commercial banks, there is no thought that it is there as the poor man's will.

In re Wilkins' Will, 226 N.Y.S. 415, 425 (Sur. Ct. 1928).

625. *Kukanskis v. Jissasut*, 362 A.2d 898, 902 (Conn. 1975); *Greer v. Hampton*, 240 So.2d 253, 255–257 (Miss. 1970).

626. *Ray v. Leader Federal Savings & Loan Ass'n*, 292 S.W.2d 458 (Tenn. App. 1953).

627. *Kukanskis v. Jissasut*, 362 A.2d 898, 902 (Conn. 1975).

628. *Birch v Treasury Solicitor* [1951] 1 Ch 298, 305 (CA).

instructions were a partial revocation of the donatio mortis causa or instead an indication that the donor never surrendered complete control.

(4) Delivery of Documentary Evidence

923. *Required for enforcement.* As discussed above, a gift involving rights embodied in an instrument usually requires delivery of the instrument.[629] In American law, the rule has been expanded to permit a gift of intangible choses in action by the delivery of those writings essential to proving the debt.[630] That rule was also incorporated into the original Restatement,[631] and continues to govern the donatio mortis causa in English law.[632] In contrast, the delivery of mere evidence was formerly thought to be insufficient at law to support a gratuitous assignment.[633]

924. *Evidentiary writing.* The difficulty with the rule was that it proved virtually impossible to decide when the transfer of documents prevents the donor from pursuing the claim.[634] The Restatement (Second), following modern judicial opinion and the scholarly discussion, now accepts the transfer of an evidentiary writing as sufficient documentation to validate a gift.[635] The writings usually involve either written contracts or the creditor's account books. In the United States, the test is whether the writing is of a type customarily accepted as evidence of the right.[636] As discussed below, the release of a debt and the transfer of future expectancies present particular problems.

In one case, the donor submitted a draft to a bank for collection and received a collection receipt. The court validated a gift made by the endorsement and delivery of the receipt.[637] The gift of an account has been sustained when the donor gave the donee the account books.[638] Though account books constitute mere evidence of the indebtedness, certain equitable rights arise from proof of their correctness, and those rights may be transferred in this way.

---

629. *Ward v Turner* (1752) 2 Ves Sen 431, 28 ER 275 (Ch); Bruton 843.

630. *Cook v. Lum*, 26 A. 803, 804 (N.J. 1893).

631. Restatement of Contracts § 158 par. 1 lit. b.

632. *Moore v Darton* (1851) 4 De G & Sm 517, 64 ER 938 (Ch). See infra no. 967.

633. Restatement of Contracts § 158 illus. 2; *Ward v Turner* (1752) 2 Ves Sen 431, 28 ER 275 (Ch); Bruton 843.

634. "Nothing has been more confusing in the law of gifts than this question-begging and mind-befogging dominion concept ...." Bruton 857. See Brown § 8.4.

635. Restatement (Second) of Contracts § 332 par. 1 lit. b alt. 1 and comment d; *In re Huggins' Estate*, 53 A. 746, 749–750 (Pa. 1902); Bruton 839. For the argument against permitting choses in action to be gifted by the transfer of mere evidence, see Williston (1930).

636. Restatement (Second) of Contracts § 332 comment d.

637. *Cronin v. Chelsea Sav. Bank*, 87 N.E. 484 (Mass. 1909) (donatio mortis causa).

638. *Jones' Adm'r v. Moore*, 44 S.W. 126 (Ky. App. 1898).

In general, delivery of an evidentiary writing is governed by the same rules that govern the delivery of chattels.[639] Mere instructions to the debtor to pay the donee, whether written or oral, do not constitute a valid gift.[640] The situation may be different when the obligation is exclusively parol. When there is no documentation at all for the debt, the creditor's oral instructions to the debtor to pay the debt to the donee may constitute a valid gift of the credit. In that situation the donor has done everything possible to become divested of the right.[641]

925. *Difficulty.* Permitting gifts to be made by the transfer of evidentiary writings seems to violate the delivery requirement. As the Restatement (Second) recognizes, a gratuitous assignment requires both the manifestation of the intent for the immediate transfer of a right and a formality such as delivery.[642] Some authors consider the transfer of evidentiary documents to be too ambiguous to satisfy the delivery requirement.

> The holding of the courts, which sustain gifts effected in this manner, seem to rest on a more or less veiled abandonment of the requirement of delivery, and the substitution therefore of any act on the part of the donor, not a mere oral declaration of the gift by the donor to the donee, which may be accepted as a concrete manifestation of the executed intent of the donor to transfer dominion over the subject matter of the donation to the donee.[643]

[a] Release of a Debt

926. *England.* In the absence of consideration, the English rule is that a creditor may not forgive a debt at law, except one evidenced by a negotiable instrument, unless the release is done by deed.[644] As indicated above, however, a donee who has relied on the release may invoke the doctrine of promissory estoppel to defend against an action on the debt.[645]

927. *United States.* In American law, when the obligation is incorporated into the paper, the delivery, cancellation, or destruction, with donative intent, of a bond or a negotiable instrument operates as a valid release. Consideration is not required.[646] For other obligations, the traditional rule of contract law is that even a written release is ineffective unless it is under seal or supported by

---

639. Restatement (Second) of Contracts § 332 comment e.
640. 3 Pomeroy § 1282.
641. *Dinslage v. Stratman,* 180 N.W. 81 (Neb. 1920).
642. Restatement (Second) of Contracts §§ 324, 332.
643. Brown § 8.4 at 170.
644. *Strong v Bird* (1874) LR 18 Eq 315 (Rolls Ct); *Flowers Case* (1597) Noy 67, 74 ER 1035.
645. Supra no. 692.
646. UCC § 3-604 par. a.

consideration.[647] The courts seem to be concerned that the creditor's unthinking remark might be misinterpreted as a release.[648] The presence of a formality reduces the concern. For this reason, some modern courts seem willing to accept a gratuitous release if it is made in writing.[649] Moreover, some state statutes validate releases even in the absence of consideration.[650]

However, there is an alternative. The release of a debt may also be viewed as the gift of a chose in action—the debt—to the debtor. When so viewed, the courts have virtually unanimously agreed that the delivery of a release or satisfaction in writing constitutes a valid gift.[651] If the debt is evidenced by written documents, the gift may also be executed by transferring to the donee the evidence needed to prevent suit on the obligation.[652] If the debt is not evidenced by a writing, some courts hold that it may be released orally,[653] whereas others hold that a mere oral statement that the debt has been satisfied or excused is insufficient.[654]

[b] Future Interests

928. *Flexible interpretation.* The traditional learning is that a gift of a future interest in personal property is only effective if made either in writing or by delivery to a third party.[655] Often the third party is to retain the gift during the donor's lifetime and then, at the donor's death, deliver it to the donee. The donor may also reserve the benefit or fruits of the property during the donor's lifetime. The courts interpret the delivery requirement with flexibility. In one case, as discussed above, the court validated the gift of a remainder interest in a painting in which the donor retained a life estate, even though the donor never parted with possession.[656] The donor's letters provided clear evidence of donative intent. Moreover, because a remainder interest does not involve possession, the court found there would have been nothing to deliver.

(5) Equitable Assignment

929. *Merger of law and equity.* Most common-law jurisdictions have attempted to merge law and equity at least to some extent. Nonetheless, equitable notions survive in the law of gratuitous assignments. In English law, equity continues to

---

647. Brown § 8.5; Restatement of Contracts § 402.
648. Kessler (1954) 264. As Kessler noted, the cases rarely mention the policy justification for the rule.
649. *Gartin v. Taylor,* 577 N.W.2d 410, 413–414 (Iowa 1998).
650. New York General Obligations Law § 5-1103.
651. *Ferry v. Stephens,* 21 Sickels 321, 325–326 (N.Y. 1876); *Lamprey v. Lamprey,* 12 N.W. 514, 515 *in fine* (Minn. 1882).
652. *Gray v. Barton,* 55 N.Y. 68, 72–73 (1873).
653. *Guardian State Bank and Trust Co. v. Jacobson,* 369 N.W.2d 80 (Neb. 1985).
654. *Estate of Carr,* 473 N.Y.S.2d 179 (App. Div. 1984).
655. Brown §§ 7.4, 7.12.
656. *Gruen v. Gruen,* 505 N.Y.S.2d 849 (1986); supra no. 887.

offer separate mechanisms for gratuitous transfers of choses in action. In American law, legal and equitable assignments are not usually distinguished. Nonetheless, as discussed above, the courts resort to the language of equitable assignment to explain why a transfer is valid even though legal requirements have not been met. In American law, the principal use of equity in this field is to protect the assignee's reliance.

[a] England

930. *Form.* No particular words are required to make an effective assignment in equity other than a clear expression of intent to make a present transfer of the property.[657] The assignee must consent, but the debtor need not be informed. Consideration is not necessary. As discussed just below, a writing is not always required. The rights must be in existence. A future debt or expectancy cannot be transferred in this manner.

931. *Equitable choses.* When the debt to be assigned is equitable, four mechanisms are available for a gratuitous equitable assignment.[658] First, a donor can make a direct assignment to the donee. For the disposition of an existing equitable interest, a writing is required.[659] Second, donors can declare themselves trustees of their equitable choses for the benefit of their donees. If the equitable chose is based on a trust, this would create a trust upon a trust. No writing is needed for the declaration of trust. Third, a donor may assign the equitable chose to a trustee to hold for the donee, which once again may create a trust on a trust. For this disposition, a writing is required. Finally, the donor can direct existing trustees to hold the rights in trust for the donee. Here too a writing is required. These assignments take effect once the assignee agrees.

932. *Legal choses.* When a legal chose in action is involved, it has long been unclear whether the assignment is valid if not supported by consideration. In fact, such confusion has reigned that Megarry called for "a monograph to end all monographs on the subject," though he also conceded that order could emerge out of chaos only if a number of dicta and decisions were disapproved.[660] Halsbury has concluded that consideration is not required for the assignment of a legal chose.[661] However, if the assigned debt is to arise in the future, consideration is always required. As a result, a mere expectancy cannot be gifted in this way. If the debt is existing, no consideration is needed if the gift is complete.

---

657. Bridge 148.

658. Hall 103–104.

659. Law of Property Act of 1935 sec. 53 par. 1 lit. c.

660. Megarry 62. "Anyone examining the text-books on this subject might well feel convinced of its strong claim to inclusion in what an American contemporary calls 'The Department of Utter Confusion'." Id. 58.

661. 6 Halsbury sub Choses in Action no. 38.

Two mechanisms exist by which to complete the gift, contract and trust.[662] A contractual assignment requires consideration. In the eighteenth century, natural love and affection was accepted as a sufficient quid pro quo. Today, however, a legal consideration is required. There are three ways to make a gratuitous assignment of a legal chose by means of a trust. First, donors may declare themselves to hold as trustees for their donees. No writing is required and no specific language is needed, though conduct alone is usually not sufficient. Second, legal ownership may be transferred to the trustees. Finally, equity validates an assignment when the donor has done all that can be done to transfer ownership of the chose to the donee.[663]

933. *All that can be done.* Equity developed this last-named method to validate assignments of legal choses during the time, before the Judicature Act, when they were not assignable at law. This doctrine has not only survived the act's enactment but has been greatly expanded. Initially, it concerned only transfers made to the trustee. It now covers transfers made directly to the donee. Equity will uphold an assignment if the donor purports to make an absolute transfer to the donee and does everything permitted by the nature of the chose to complete the gift. Hall noted that the doctrine is slightly illogical because the donor cannot be said to have done everything possible to complete the gift until all of the requirements for a valid statutory assignment have been met.[664]

Today, the doctrine has even greater flexibility. In particular, the assignor is no longer required to have done everything necessary to effect the transfer. The cases seem to validate an assignment by deed even if the obligor has not been notified as the statute requires. In one case, the donor assigned a bank deposit by writing the words "Pay my son" on the back of the deposit receipt and handing it to the son with the words, "Here you are, my lad. This is yours."[665] The receipt stated expressly that it was not transferable. Nonetheless, the court held that the assignment was good, even though notice was not given to the bank until after the donor's death. An oral assignment is probably not effective under this rule.

There is no agreement as to the legal principle that explains this type of equitable assignment.[666] Because the transfer is gratuitous, it cannot be based in contract. It is therefore enforced as a type of trust. Yet there has been no express declaration. Hall suggested the theory of constructive trust. Once the donor has

---

662. Hall 105–106.

663. Id. 110–112.

664. Id. 111. "Whatever justification [for this rule] there may have been before the [Judicature] Act, it is difficult to see any for maintaining a doctrine which may justly be regarded as one of the more amorphous and less distinguished issue of Bad Law out of Hard Cases." Megarry 61.

665. *In re Griffin* [1899] 1 Ch 408.

666. Hall 115.

executed a written document, equity will require the donor to participate in the donee's lawsuit. The obligation that thereby arises in some way (vaguely) resembles the obligations that arise under a constructive trust.

[b] United States

934. *Reliance.* In American law, equity enforces gratuitous assignments to the extent necessary to protect reliance.[667]

(B) BANK DEPOSITS

935. *Disposition at death.* It is common in the United States for individuals to make use of bank accounts as a mechanism to dispose of assets at death. Account holders pursue a variety of goals, usually without legal advice. Some donors may have prejudices against wills, courts, and lawyers. Others may wish to avoid the expense of probate.[668] Yet others may seek to maintain confidentiality about the gift or the donor's relationship to the donee. In some cases donors wish to defeat the rights of a spouse. Often there is also a desire to escape inheritance tax. For all of these reasons, these accounts are often known as *the poor person's will.*

Because a depositor may have a variety of goals in opening a bank account, difficulties often arise at the depositor's death in determining ownership. Problems surface particularly with regard to accounts that have been opened in one of several forms: in the name of another, in trust for another, as a joint account, or as a payable-on-death account. In each of these situations, the survivor may argue that the depositor made a gift of the funds in the account. It is helpful to examine together the legal and equitable issues that arise in this context.

(1) Account in the Donee's Name

936. *Intent.* In the United States, one common means of making a gift of money is to open a bank account in the donee's name. However, because deposits in another's name may serve many purposes—including defeating collection actions and evading banking and tax laws[669]—a deposit in another party's name does not of itself constitute a gift.

937. *No uniformity.* The cases usually involve savings accounts. They are not uniform.[670] At first glance, it might seem that the deposit creates a third-party beneficiary contract in which the bank promises the depositor to hold the funds

---

667. Restatement (Second) of Contracts § 332 par. 4 and illus. 9; *Armstrong v. Armstrong,* 142 Ill.App. 507 (1908).

668. Havighurst 129. One witness explained the decedent's motivation as follows. "'He had made a will, and then he thought that would have to be administered on, so much red tape gone through; he decided to have them put into bank books,' and he destroyed his will." *Howard v. Dingley,* 118 A. 592, 593 (Me. 1922).

669. Brown § 8.6.

670. Tellier 539.

for the donee. But that is not the general view.[671] There are several reasons for this. First, it seems unwise to involve banks in disputes about the validity of a three-party transaction. Moreover, the depositor may intend to retain the right to withdraw funds from the account. For these reasons, something more is required before these accounts may be considered gifts.

Some courts hold that surrender of possession or control of the passbook is required for a valid gift.[672] Others hold that the donor's intention, as revealed by the circumstances, should prevail.[673] Yet other courts apply general principles, requiring both donative intent and delivery. When the donee is not informed of the deposit and donative intent remains unclear, either because the bankbook is not delivered or for other reasons, many courts hold that there has been no gift.[674] In fact, the donee's knowledge and acceptance is sometimes raised to an independent requirement.[675] On the other hand, when donative intent is clear, some courts hold that the passbook or certificate of deposit need not be delivered to the donee, and the donee need not even be apprised of the gift.[676]

938. *In a child's name.* The courts are more willing to find a gift when deposits are made in the name of infants, particularly when the depositors are their parents. A court has held that a nonnegotiable certificate of deposit that the donor purchased in the name of the minor donee constituted a valid gift at the moment of purchase, even though the certificate was never delivered to the donee.[677] The court relied on two factors. First, the donor listed himself on the certificate as the donee's agent. Second, it would make no sense to deliver such a document to a minor. The court characterized the transaction as a third-party beneficiary contract for the donee's benefit.

Gifts to infants require no formal acceptance. If the gift is beneficial, acceptance is presumed.[678] Therefore, deposits in the name of infants, once donative intent is demonstrated, are deemed immediately accepted. If funds are subsequently withdrawn from the account, the proceeds are held for the infant donee in constructive trust.[679]

---

671. Havighurst 137–138.
672. *Ruffalo v. Savage,* 31 N.W.2d 175 (Wis. 1948).
673. Brown § 8.6.
674. *Getchell v. Biddeford Sav. Bank,* 47 A. 895 (Maine 1900); *Carter v. State Mutual Federal Sav. and Loan Ass'n,* 498 So.2d 324, 327 (Miss. 1986); *Peters' Adm'r v. Peters,* 6 S.W.2d 499 (Ky. App. 1928).
675. Havighurst 139.
676. *Meriden Trust and Safe Deposit Co. v. Miller,* 90 A. 228 (Conn. 1914); *Kelly v. Huplits,* 157 A. 704 (Pa. Super. 1931).
677. *Holloway v. Wachovia Bank,* 423 S.E.2d 752 (N.C. 1992).
678. Supra nos. 500–501; infra no. 1058.
679. *Collins v. Collins' Adm'r,* 45 S.W.2d 811, 815 (Ky. App. 1931).

(2) In Trust for the Donee

939. *General rule.* The trust is so widely recognized as a valid means to make a gift of a bank deposit that it is best examined here rather than in the context of equity, where it belongs as a conceptual matter. Monies deposited in the donor's name as trustee for the donee create a valid gift by declaration of trust, provided donative intent is present.[680] Donative intent may be established by clear declaration either to the donee or to a third party or by surrender of the passbook or the equivalent to the donee. The difficult cases arise when the donor retains control of the account and does not inform the beneficiary. Under the Massachusetts rule, such a deposit standing alone does not prove a trust.[681]

940. *Totten trust.* The Totten trust is the product of an evolution in New York law. At the end of the nineteenth century, when the donor declared to hold the deposit for the donee, the New York courts sustained the gift. The theory was that even an uncommunicated declaration created a valid trust.[682] In a celebrated case, the New York high court refined its view and held that such a trust—now eponymously called a *Totten trust*—is merely tentative. It remains revocable at will during the donor's life. However, if the donor dies without disaffirming the trust, there is a presumption that an irrevocable trust was created.[683] New York continues to adhere to the doctrine, and many other jurisdictions have followed.[684]

Traditional doctrine would invalidate the trust.[685] An inter vivos trust is generally considered irrevocable unless a power of revocation is expressly reserved. As one commentator has suggested, the Totten trust "lacks logical symmetry."[686] It represents a gratuitous transfer of a chose in action that is valid not only without delivery or a written instrument, but even without acceptance by, or even notice to, the donee and, moreover, is revocable until the donor's death.

The New York high court disregarded the doctrinal difficulties. The institution it created in its famous dictum was designed to mirror the parties' expectations. When the deposit is made in the donor's name in trust for the donee, the court believed that the parties' would generally intend for the donor to be able to make withdrawals while alive and, to that extent, revoke the trust, while leaving to the beneficiary any amounts remaining in the account at the donor's death.

---

680. Brown § 8.7.

681. *Gerrish v. New Bedford Inst. for Savings*, 128 Mass. 159 (1880). The general rules governing gifts made by declaration of trust are examined below. See infra nos. 953–960.

682. *Martin v. Funk*, 75 N.Y. 134 (1878).

683. *In re Totten*, 71 N.E. 748, 752–753 (N.Y. 1904); Restatement (Third) of Trusts § 26.

684. See, e.g., California Prob. C §§ 80, 5404.

685. Gulliver and Tilson 32–39.

686. Brown § 8.7 at 179.

As a later court wrote, the Totten trust represents "another evidence of the attempt of the courts to conform the law to the customs of the community."[687] The Totten trust "seems affirmatively justified by its simplicity and utility for those not in the most affluent class."[688] In all of these ways, the Totten trust is a typical common law product, facilitating gratuitous transfers when donative intent seems clear and indulging the practice of gift giving as it takes place beyond the dictates of the law.

(3) Joint Account

941. *Right of survivorship.* Another common transaction in the United States is the deposit of funds in an account in the name of both the depositor and another person. The account can be either a checking or a savings account. The funds may be withdrawn by either party.[689] A deposit into such an account does not necessarily indicate a gift. The deposit may be chosen merely to facilitate access to the funds if one of the parties should become incapacitated. The contract with the bank usually indicates that those named on the joint account are joint tenants with a right of survivorship.

942. *Delivery.* A majority of courts apply the ordinary principles of gift law to resolve the situation, examining both delivery and donative intent.[690] As far as delivery is concerned, some courts hold that the execution of a signature card, which permits the donee to withdraw the funds at will, operates as constructive delivery. Those courts hold that the donor thereby has done everything necessary under the circumstances to put the donee in control of the property.[691] In contrast, many courts have held that the mere addition of a second name to a bank account does not constitute delivery.[692] Because the donor may withdraw the funds at will, there is neither a valid delivery of the passbook nor unequivocal control on the part of the donee.[693]

943. *Donative intent.* To determine donative intent, courts often focus on the intent of the depositor, the party who originally owned the funds.[694] In one group of American cases, the courts have inexplicably relied on an exclusively linguistic test, holding that there is a valid gift if the names of the parties on the account are joined by *and* but not if they are joined by *or*.[695]

---

687. *In re Reich's Estate*, 262 N.Y.S. 623, 626 (Sur. Ct. 1933).
688. Gulliver and Tilson 39.
689. Brown § 8.8.
690. Id.; Spivey 980.
691. *Estate of Walker*, 890 A.2d 216, 225–226 (D.C. App. 2006).
692. *Burns v. Nolette*, 144 A. 848, 850 (N.H. 1929).
693. *Wantuck v. U.S. Savings and Loan Ass'n*, 461 S.W.2d 692 (Mo. 1971) (en banc).
694. *Shaffer v. Lohr*, 287 A.2d 42, 46 (Md. App. 1972).
695. *Morristown Trust Co. v. Capstick*, 106 A. 391, 392 (N.J. Ch.), aff'd sub nom. *Morristown Trust Co. v. Safford*, 108 A. 926 (N.J. Err. & App. 1919).

944. *Revocability.* One standard feature of the joint account is that the donor may continue to withdraw funds. Most courts decide that the revocability this permits does not render the gift invalid. The only question is whether adding the donee's name to the account was intended as a gift.[696] In contrast, some courts hold that the fact that the donor still has the right to withdraw funds from the account negates the idea of a gift.[697]

945. *Better view.* It has been suggested that the better view would sustain the gift, subject to the condition subsequent of the donor's withdrawal of the funds.[698] "The donee's present right is complete. He can draw from the account as long as funds remain. That right is what was given to him. It might subsequently prove valueless if the donor withdrew the whole deposit. But, for what it was worth, it was a completed gift. No further act of the donor was required."[699] Therefore, some courts hold that deposits into a joint account are presumed to be a gift if the other party is the survivor.[700] Others, however, presume that a joint account, even with an express right of survivorship, is opened for the convenience of the depositor, so that the burden of proof is on the donee. Moreover, when the claim arises after the donor's death, the gift must be proven by clear and convincing evidence.[701]

946. *Third-party beneficiary.* Some courts and commentators would hold the donee to be a third-party beneficiary of the donor's contract with the bank. Any funds remaining at the donor's death would pass to the survivor, even though the donor retained the passbook and even though will formalities were not

---

696. The external form of the gift is the absolute conversion of the donor's property into a binding obligation of a third party, the performance of which according to its terms may upon certain contingencies benefit the donee. There is nothing, however, contingent about the gift. The gift is absolute. The right is vested beyond recall in the donee. It is a matter of no consequence that the right so vested may prove in the end to be of no pecuniary value.

Dunn v. Houghton, 51 A. 71, 77–78 (N.J. Ch. 1902).

697. The deposit in the names of Miss O'Neill and Mrs. Whalen was payable to the order of either, or the survivor. Miss O'Neill, having by this form of entry retained undoubted power to draw the money out of bank whenever she pleased, obviously did not devest herself of dominion over it. There was nothing to prevent her from checking out every cent of the fund immediately, or at any time, after the deposit in the two names had been made. If this be true,—and it cannot be questioned,—there was no perfected gift to Mrs. Whalen.

Whalen v. Milholland, 43 A. 45, 47 (Md. App. 1899).

698. Brown § 8.8.

699. *Burns v. Nolette*, 144 A. 848, 850 (N.H. 1929). See also *Commonwealth Trust Co. v. Du Montimer*, 183 S.W. 1137 (Mo. App. 1916).

700. *Dalia v. Lawrence*, 627 A.2d 392, 404 (Conn. 1993).

701. *Estate of Walker*, 890 A.2d 216, 222 (D.C. App. 2006).

completed.[702] The result is the same when the deposit is in the form of a certificate of deposit payable to the donee at the donor's death.[703]

947. *Statutory provisions.* Many states have enacted statutes governing joint bank accounts. The New York statute, for example, creates a rebuttable presumption that the parties' rights follow the form of the deposit.[704] Under the Mississippi statute, a joint account with right of survivorship creates a presumption of intent to vest ownership in the survivor.[705] The Restatement (Third) provides that, if the account has a survivorship or pay-on-death feature, the balance on hand at death passes outside probate to the survivor.[706]

The Uniform Nonprobate Transfers on Death Act, incorporated into the Uniform Probate Code, structures multiparty accounts to correspond to the parties' intentions. The Act thereby disqualifies some of these accounts as inter vivos transfers. However, sums on deposit in certain multiple-party accounts belong to the donor during the donor's lifetime and then, on the donor's death, pass outside probate to the survivor.[707]

948. *No successful characterization.* None of the common law's traditional characterizations accurately tracks the parties' expectations. Under common law gift principles, there can be no gift without perfected delivery and the transfer of unequivocal control to the donee. Under the law of joint tenancy, the tenant who withdraws funds is liable to the other for the value. Without testamentary formalities, the law of wills is inapplicable. The deposit does not constitute a trust,

---

702. *Perry v. Leveroni*, 147 N.E. 826 (Mass. 1925); Note (1924); Havighurst 145.

703. *Peoples Bank v. Baxter*, 298 S.W.2d 732 (Tenn. App. 1957). In *Baxter*, the dissent argued that, in a suit brought by the heirs, the donee should have to show a valid gift. Yet because the donor had intended to retain control until death, there was no inter vivos transfer. Id. 739–743.

704. New York Banking Law § 675. The great majority of American states permit the funds in a joint account to be paid to the survivor even if there is no survivorship provision. The relevant statutes are listed in Restatement (Third) of Property (Wills and Other Donative Transfers) § 7.1 Statutory Note 5 par. a at 104–110 (Tent. Draft no. 3, 2001).

705. Mississippi C Ann. § 81-5-63; *Madden v. Rhodes*, 626 So.2d 608, 616–617 (Miss. 1993).

706. Restatement (Third) of Property (Wills and Other Donative Transfers) § 7.1 comment f.

707. Unif. Prob. C §§ 6-211 to 6-212. During the donor's lifetime, the donor's interest in a multiple-party account is proportional to the donor's net contribution. § 6-211 par. b. Multiple-party accounts are defined in § 6-201 par. 7. If the account specifies that it is without a right of survivorship, the donor's interest descends at death as part of the donor's estate. § 6-212 par. c sent. 1. However, if the account contains a survivorship provision, or if nothing is stated about survivorship, then an account that is payable to one or more of two or more parties is considered a survivorship arrangement. § 6-212 par. a sent. 1. The same provisions are contained in the Uniform Multiple-Person Accounts Act §§ 11–12 (1989).

both because there is generally no such intent and because both parties' interests are treated as legal. Moreover, unless the depositor owes support to the other party, there is a presumption that a resulting trust is created for the benefit of the depositor's heirs.[708] In many cases, no third-party beneficiary contract is formed because the bank contract does not include a right of survivorship. Nor does the law of torts apply—no trust has been declared and fiduciary duties are not appropriate. "The difficulty the courts have had with joint accounts can be traced primarily to the insistence on forcing an essentially novel ownership arrangement into the mold of an existing set of legal principles."[709] And yet, despite the characterization difficulties, many believe that the deposit should yield a valid gift. "[O]n the whole, it is an arrangement that has come to be regarded by people of small means and little legal knowledge as a way of designating where their pittances shall go after their deaths without the cost and the trouble of legal advice. And it seems that the state might well relax the rigor of the Wills Acts to tolerate these 'poor men's wills.'"[710]

(4) Payable-on-death Accounts

949. *Valid in some states.* By opening a payable-on-death (POD) account, the donor instructs the bank to pay the funds to the donee at the donor's death.[711] Unlike the many other will substitutes in the common law, POD accounts are not generally upheld in the absence of will formalities. Because no present interest is conveyed, it is believed that the POD account "brushes uncomfortably close to a purely testamentary transfer" and therefore should require a more serious formality.[712]

Nonetheless, statutes in several states validate POD accounts as will substitutes.[713] Under the Illinois statute, the donor may change the donee at any time by written notice to the bank. The donor may also make deposits and withdrawals. No notices or consents are required. At the death of the last surviving donor, the account vests in the donee or donees who survive, otherwise in the donor's estate. Since the statute represents an exception to wills formalities, it is strictly construed.[714] One court refused to validate the gift when the only evidence was a POD notation typed on the bank ledger card some time after the account was opened. Because the circumstances surrounding the notation could not be

---

708. Note (1924) 243 and note 7.

709. Hines 531.

710. Note (1924) 245.

711. McGovern 7.

712. Hines 557.

713. See, e.g., California Prob. C §§ 5140, 5403; Illinois Trust and Payable on Death Accounts Act of 1991, amended by P.A. 92–285 § 5 of 2002, 205 ILCS 625/4.

714. *In re Waitkevich's Estate*, 323 N.E.2d 545, 549 (Ill. App. 1975).

explained, the required written agreement was missing.[715] United States savings bonds can also be purchased in POD form.[716]

The Uniform Nonprobate Transfers on Death Act, incorporated into the Uniform Probate Code, defines an account with a POD designation as an account payable to the donor or donors during life and to the donee or donees on the death of the donors. A trust account with the same structure is also considered a POD account.[717] The effect of such a designation is to permit the bank to pay sums on deposit to one of the donors, even if some are incapacitated or dead, to pay the sums to the donees upon proof of death of all donors, and to pay to the personal representative or heirs of the donor who survives all the others.[718]

950. *Justification.* What the public really wants, William Hines explained, is "a simple and reliable device for transferring funds from a decedent to a survivor without creating lifetime rights in the donee."[719] The POD account therefore satisfies an important social need. Moreover, these accounts are less ambiguous than simple joint accounts because they are unlikely to be misconstrued either as a present gift or as a convenience account.[720]

The donee obtains no interest until the donor's death. The transfer is testamentary and should theoretically be subject to wills formalities. The POD account also cannot be considered a form of donatio mortis causa. These accounts are usually opened when there is no imminent threat of death and when there would usually be sufficient time for the drafting of a will. Hines suggested reconciling the competing interests by requiring that the donor's signature be witnessed by a disinterested party. McGovern suggests that POD accounts should be upheld, even in the absence of a statute, because they are essentially life insurance policies, with the difference that the stakeholder is a bank rather than an insurance carrier.[721] In view of the widespread popular belief in the validity of all types of joint accounts as gift vehicles, McGovern argued that it would be improper to frustrate these expectations in the hope that the public would be made aware of the necessity of complying with the Wills Act.[722]

iii. Comparative Notes

951. *Protection against fraud.* Most legal systems seek to protect donors from fraudulent suits by those who purport to be donees. To reduce this risk, Romanic systems tend to respect a gift only if there is a notarized writing. The notarization

---

715. Id. 548.
716. *Franklin Washington Trust Co. v. Beltram*, 29 A.2d 854, 856 (N.J. Ch. 1943).
717. Unif. Prob. C § 6-201 par. 8. For the similar Totten trust, see supra no. 940.
718. Id. § 6-223.
719. Hines 557.
720. McGovern 39.
721. Id. 10.
722. Id. 13.

requirement secures an aspect of individual liberty because improper claims are much less likely to be made. The disadvantage is that it obstructs an equally important aspect of individual freedom, namely the ability to make a gift. If the rather cumbersome and expensive procedure is not followed, gifts that were intended—and, in an extra-legal sense, made—are declared void.

The common law and the Germanic systems rely on the normal methods for transfer of title as the primary method of gift disposition. Gifts of movables are therefore generally effectuated by delivery. This system follows the real world understanding of gift giving but is still unable to eliminate entirely the gap between daily life and the results the rules produce. Because the only protection against fraudulent claims is delivery, there is an unavoidable tendency to manipulate the concept to produce the right result. Courts may hold that the chattel was delivered when indicia of intent are present and find a lack of delivery when they are not. "In general, the efforts of courts to find delivery or its equivalent in those hard cases where the donor's intent to give is perfectly clear, have produced much of the difficulty and uncertainty in the modern law of gifts."[723] When courts are unwilling or unable to find a way around the delivery requirement, some gifts that actually were intended and made are declared inoperative.[724]

7. The Common Law: Equitable Doctrines

952. *Several mechanisms.* Equity moderates the relative rigidity of legal norms in several ways. Historically, one of equity's major contributions to gift law has been the equitable assignment, a doctrine that was examined together with the legal assignment above.[725] In addition, there are several specifically equitable means of making a gratuitous transfer. These include the declaration of trust, the donatio mortis causa, the doctrine of equitable estoppel, certain uses of the constructive trust, and finally the English law doctrine of merger of title.

a. Declaration of Trust

953. *Equitable title.* Traditionally, all property, including choses in action, can be transferred by the creation of a trust. A trust need not be supported by consideration.[726] A completed trust is thus enforceable even though its creation is

---

723. Brown § 7.2 at 79.

724. See *In re Ridgway* (1884–1885) LR 15 QBD 447, discussed supra no. 888. In *Ridgway*, an oft-cited case, a father purchased, bottled, and cellared a pipe (cask) of port for his son shortly after the boy's birth. Twenty years later, the gift was voided at the request of the trustee in the father's bankruptcy on the grounds that there had been no delivery. See also *Douglas v Douglas* (1869) 22 LTR 127 (CA). In *Douglas*, another celebrated case, the donor in Australia wrote to the donee, his brother in England, giving him their father's sword, then in possession of the donor's wife. The wife refused to part with the sword. The Court of Exchequer held there was no gift.

725. Supra nos. 929–934.

726. 1 Scott and Ascher § 3.3.1; 3 Pomeroy § 996.

gratuitous—or, to use the language of equity, even though it is purely *voluntary*.[727] The declaration of trust differs conceptually from the legal notion of the gift, though it often fulfills a similar societal function. A perfected gift involves the transfer to the donee of both legal and equitable title, the latter of which is known as the beneficial interest. That does not mean that the donee at law necessarily acquires immediate rights of enjoyment. Future interests may validly be gifted at law. A declaration of trust, on the other hand, transfers equitable title to the donee and reserves legal title to a trustee, who may be either the donor or a third party. A common use of the trust is to permit a transfer to the beneficiary of a life interest in the fruits while reserving the interest in the corpus for the benefit of another party. One of the differences between the two institutions is that a completed gift transfers title that will prevail against a subsequent good faith purchaser, whereas the trust beneficiary's equitable title will not.

954. *Charitable trusts.* There are numerous distinctions between private trusts, which are those in which a named trustee holds the legal estate for clearly identified or easily identifiable beneficiaries, and public or charitable trusts, which may be valid even though the trustees, the beneficiaries, and even the object may be largely uncertain.[728] They differ in the method of creation and operation and in the extent to which they are recognized in the different American states. These distinctions are beyond the scope of this study.

i. Creation of the Trust

955. *Three methods.* A valid and irrevocable gift by way of trust may be made chiefly in one of three ways.[729] First, the donor may transfer the property to a trustee by any usual method for conveying legal title.[730] The transfer of property into trust constitutes an enforceable gift to the beneficiary. Second, a donor who has an equitable interest may direct the trustee to hold the interest for the benefit of the donee. Finally, a donor in possession of property may declare a trust in favor of the donee. The validity of the declaration of trust is not contingent on delivery of the property.[731]

---

727. 3 Pomeroy § 997.

728.Oakley pars. 11-001 ff; 3 Pomeroy §§ 1019 ff; 5 Scott and Ascher §§ 37.1 ff.

729. ENGLAND: Crossley Vaines 311; UNITED STATES: 3 Pomeroy § 997; 1 Scott and Ascher § 3.1.4. Uniform legislation in the United States has created special forms for the declaration of trust to facilitate gratuitous transfers to minors, including those without legally appointed guardians. See supra nos. 501, 895–896.

730. Oakley pars. 4-005, 4-020 to 4-042; *Estate of Smith*, 22 A. 916 (Pa. 1891).

731. 48 Halsbury sub Trusts no. 645; 3 Pomeroy § 998. A writing, though not necessarily a deed, is required if real estate is involved. Oakley par. 5-019. In some American jurisdictions, a writing is also needed to create a trust in personalty. See infra nos. 959–960. For possible Roman law influence, see Labatt 371, referring to C. 8, 54 [53], 35, 5.

A trust will only be enforced if it is complete, which means that the settlor has done everything that is necessary, given the nature of the property, to complete the transfer.[732] Moreover, as indicated by the frequently quoted maxim, "Equity will not assist a volunteer," equity will not enforce transfers that the donor intended as a gift. "[A] trust will not freely be discovered in the ruins of a failed gift by delivery or a failed contract."[733] In other words, a gift intended to take effect by one mode will not be facilitated by reinterpreting it in another.[734] Though the principle is clear, the decisions are based on the subtle interpretation of extremely scanty real world evidence. On the basis of a few words the donor might have uttered in passing, the courts must decide whether the donor intended an immediate transfer (inter vivos gift), a transfer conditional on the donor's death (donatio mortis causa), or a transfer into trust to be held for the donee's benefit (declaration of trust).[735]

(A) PRESENT TRANSFER

956. *Manifestation of intent.* An express trust arises only when the settlor properly manifests an intent to create one.[736] Questions regarding intent are resolved by interpretation of all of the facts and circumstances of the individual cases.[737] The matter is complex. Only basic principles can be examined here.

Neither specific words nor a specific intent to create a trust is needed. The donor need not state expressly, "I declare myself trustee." Even the words *trust*

---

732. Oakley pars. 5-006 to 5-014; 3 Pomeroy § 997.

733. Bridge 101.

734. "[I]f the settlement is intended to be effectuated by one of the modes to which I have referred, the Court will not give effect to it by applying another of those modes. If it is intended to take effect by transfer, the Court will not hold the intended transfer to operate as a declaration of trust, for then every imperfect instrument would be made effectual by being converted into a perfect trust." *Milroy v Lord* (1862) 4 De GF & J 264, 274–275, 45 ER 1185, 1189–1190. The passage is frequently quoted.

735. It would rather seem to be that the husband, intending to make a gift to the wife, did it in an insufficient manner—it may be from ignorance of the law, he thinking that handing over the certificates to her was sufficient .... He seems to have considered that this would amount in itself to a gift to the wife; he did not suppose that he was becoming a trustee for the wife; he thought the thing was complete; but his being mistaken is not, in my judgment, a reason why a person who never meant to become a trustee should be made a trustee, and thereby to assume an office which he never supposed he held, and never meant to undertake the responsibilities of. He meant apparently to give her what in his mind was a worthless thing ... by handing over to her the certificates, the matter being intended to be complete so far as the gift was concerned, and he having no more to do with it. *Moore v Moore* (1874) LR 18 Eq 474, 482.

736. Oakley pars. 3-003 to 3-010; 1 Scott and Ascher § 4.1.

737. "Each case must therefore turn upon its own circumstances, and not a little upon the sentiments and prepossessions of individual judges." 3 Pomeroy § 1016.

and *trustee* are not essential. Yet there must be some equivalent declaration[738] that sufficiently expresses the terms of the trust.[739] A trust was held to have been validly declared when the donor (settlor) gave property to a friend and asked him, as a favor, to keep it and, if something were to happen to the donor, to deliver it to the donor's son.[740] A deposit in a joint bank account may be considered a trust for the benefit of one of the named parties if the account is opened in that form or if the settlor manifests that intent.[741] However, a mere promise or intent to create a trust is insufficient. As noted above, one of the most frequently repeated rules in the case opinions is that equity will not perfect an imperfect gift, which means that equity will not assist a putative donee to establish a trust.[742]

957. *Notice.* The declaration need not be communicated to the beneficiaries. In one case, a bondholder kept the bonds in the trust company's vaults in an envelope indicating that they were "held for" the owner's nephew. An entry in the account book attributed the bonds and credited the interest to the nephew. The court held that the declaration of trust was sufficient, though the settlor had informed no one of the trust during his lifetime.[743] In fact, if the settlor's outward acts sufficiently manifest intent, the trust can be created without any communication with anyone.[744] On the other hand, the manifestation of intent must be unequivocal. When a donor, upon being asked by his child's nurse whether he had brought anything for the baby, placed a check, payable to the donor, in the baby's hands and said, "I give this to baby for himself," and then took the check back and stored it away, the court held that there was neither an effective gift by delivery nor a valid declaration of trust.[745] As one commentator has indicated, the only difference between an unenforceable gift and a valid declaration of trust may be the donor's words.[746]

958. *Immediately operative.* The declaration of trust must be intended to be presently operative.[747] If the trust is to take effect in the future, it is executory and, if unsupported by consideration, unenforceable.[748] A declaration of trust that is

---

738. ENGLAND: *Richards v Delbridge* (1874) LR 18 Eq 11, 14; UNITED STATES: *Estate of Smith*, 22 A. 916, 917 (Pa. 1891); 3 Pomeroy § 1009.

739. 3 Pomeroy § 1009; Bridge 101.

740. *Malloy v. Smith*, 290 A.2d 486, 489–490 (Md. App. 1972).

741. *Shaffer v. Lohr*, 287 A.2d 42, 48 (Md. App. 1972).

742. Crossley Vaines 311; 3 Pomeroy § 1009.

743. *Smith's Estate*, 22 A. 916 (Pa. 1891).

744. 1 Scott and Ascher § 4.2.2.

745. *Jones v Lock* (1865) 1 Ch App 25 (LC). The gift failed because the check was in the donor's name and had not been endorsed over to the child. See Oakley par. 5-016.

746. Stoljar 242–243.

747. 1 Scott and Ascher § 4.4.

748. 48 Halsbury sub Trusts no. 654; *Kempf v. Kempf*, 179 N.W.2d 715 (Minn. 1970); 1 Scott and Ascher § 4.4; Restatement (Third) of Trusts § 13 comment a.

unenforceable for that reason must be distinguished from the valid present gift of a future beneficial interest to the donee, the donor to retain lifelong enjoyment of the property.[749] The settlor's reservation of the right to revoke does not invalidate the trust,[750] though a trust is generally irrevocable unless a power of revocation is expressly reserved.[751]

(B) WRITTEN INSTRUMENT

959. *Real property.* At early common law, trusts, whether of real or personal property, could be declared orally.[752] Since the enactment of the Statute of Frauds, however, the creation of a trust involving land must be "manifested and proved" by a writing signed by the party who declares the trust. Otherwise the trust is void.[753] The Statute of Frauds provision is essentially still in effect today in England.[754] English law interprets the provision to mean that the trust need not be declared in the deed of conveyance but may be created by separate informal instrument subsequent to the execution of the deed.[755] In many American states, however, a trust is valid only if declared in the deed or other conveyance.[756]

960. *Personalty.* A writing is not generally required to create an enforceable inter vivos trust in personalty.[757] English law generally requires no form for its creation, though a writing is required if the rights transferred are equitable.[758] A few American states require a writing to create an enforceable inter vivos trust in personalty.[759] In New York all inter vivos trusts must be created in writing. The trust must be executed and acknowledged by the settlor, and, unless the settlor is the sole trustee, it must also be executed by at least one trustee, either in the manner of a real estate deed being prepared for recording or in the presence of two witnesses, both of whom must sign.[760] Nonetheless, one New York court has validated a trust that lacked the settlor's signature.[761]

---

749. 1 Scott and Ascher § 4.4.1; Brown § 7.21; *Estate of Petraka,* 204 N.E.2d 1 (Ill. 1965).

750. Brown id.; *Appeal of Dickerson,* 8 A. 64 (Pa. 1887); Restatement (Third) of Trusts § 63.

751. 20 Halsbury part 1 sub Gifts no. 41.

752. 3 Pomeroy § 1006.

753. Statute of Frauds of 1677 sec. 7.

754. Law of Property Act of 1925 sec. 53 par. 1 lit. b.

755. 48 Halsbury sub Trusts no. 644; 1 Scott and Ascher § 6.2; 3 Pomeroy § 1006.

756. 1 Scott and Ascher § 6.2.1; Montana Stats. Ann. § 513.04.

757. Restatement (Third) of Trusts § 20.

758. Law of Property Act of 1925 sec. 53 par. 1 lit. c; 48 Halsbury sub Trusts no. 644.

759. *Beckwith v. Peterson,* 181 S.E.2d 51, 53 (Ga. 1971).

760. New York Estates, Powers and Trusts Law § 7-1.17 par. a.

761. *In re Marcus Trusts,* 769 N.Y.S.2d 56, 57–58 (App. Div. 2003).

ii. Comparative Notes

(A) CONTRAST WITH GIFTS AT LAW

961. *Inconsistency.* The partial inconsistency between the traditional requirements at law and the declaration of trust in equity has long been noted. The two institutions are similar for the transfer of real estate. A valid gift of real property at law requires the execution and delivery of a deed. Similarly, a trust of real property must be declared in writing and signed by the settlor.[762] As far as personalty is concerned, however, law has traditionally required delivery, a requirement the courts continue to enforce, except, perhaps, for a gift of chattels in American law. A trust of personalty, however, can generally be declared orally.[763] In other words, equitable title to personal property may pass by a gratuitous declaration of trust without delivery, deed, writing, notice to the donee, or acceptance.[764]

Many have asked why delivery is required in the one instance and not in the other.

> [I]t is surely nothing less than a glaring anomaly that any method of transferring a chattel should be valid without delivery, and a yet more extraordinary circumstance, if possible, that the method actually allowed to take effect without delivery is not fenced about with any safeguards which might serve as reasonably adequate substitutes for that formality.[765]

One factor may help explain the anomaly. The circumstances in which disputes are likely to arise will differ depending on whether the transfer is made by gift or by trust. Disputes about *gifts* often arise after the donor's death, when those who claim through the donor are deprived of the testimony needed to contradict the purported donee. The delivery requirement protects the donor's heirs and creditors against fraudulent claims of gift. When the existence of a *trust* is questioned, the principal concern is not the donee's fraud. It is rather the settlor's desire to defeat creditors. The question is then not whether the settlor intended to execute the transfer but rather the settlor's motives in doing so. The settlor's heirs and creditors are thus not as threatened by third-party fraud as are those of the donor. This reasoning may justify the reduced formalities applicable in equity, though it is not mentioned in the cases.

---

762. Law of Property Act of 1925 sec. 53 par. 1 lit. b.

763. ENGLAND: 20 Halsbury part 1 sub Gifts no. 41; *M'Fadden v Jenkyns* (1842) 1 Ph 153; UNITED STATES: Brown § 7.21; Restatement (Second) of Trusts § 24; *Agudas Chasidei Chabad v. Gourary,* 833 F.2d 431 (2d Cir. 1987). The creation of a trust of an equitable interest requires a writing in English law. *Oughtred v Inland Revenue Commissioners* [1960] AC 206 (HL).

764. Crossley Vaines 311.

765. Labatt 365–366.

Nonetheless, over the years the discrepancy has rankled the commentators. Many have predicted that the two institutions would eventually converge.

It must be admitted that the doctrine of the voluntary declaration of trust presents something of an anomaly in the law. Not only is it extremely difficult to apply in practice, the line between imperfect gifts and executory trusts on one hand, and perfected declarations on the other, being an exceedingly shadowy one, but all the safeguards against frauds, perjuries, and hasty and ill-considered gifts which the requirement of delivery is supposed to afford in the ordinary case, are entirely lacking in the oral voluntary declaration of trust. The doctrine is apt to degenerate into little more than a means of sustaining imperfect gifts in especially hard cases. On the other hand, it may well be that the trust doctrine is simply a step in the inevitable course of the law whereby the requirement of delivery based on the early concepts of seisin is giving way before the more modern liberal tendency which tends to disregard formalities and to determine all transactions according to the clearly expressed intent of the parties.[766]

As indicated above, the suggestion that the law's delivery requirement should be replaced by an exclusive focus on donative intent seems to have convinced the American courts when the gift involves chattels.[767]

(B) CONTRAST WITH THE CIVIL LAW

962. *Two traditions.* Two great traditions govern the gifting of chattels. In principle, French and Italian law require a written instrument though French law makes exception when the chattel is actually delivered. The common law and German law generally require delivery, but the common law also permits a chattel to be gifted by writing. It might seem that no system validates a gift unless the donor performs some positive act beyond uttering words of transfer. The declaration of trust, however, violates this apparent consensus. In many jurisdictions, a settlor, by simple oral declaration, may validly make a gift of the beneficial interest in a chattel. Moreover, the gradual disappearance of the delivery requirement in American law suggests that American gift law is in a phase of deformalization and may increasingly focus on donative intent.

b. Donatio Mortis Causa

963. *Equitable jurisdiction.* As discussed above, the common law has long enforced the donatio mortis causa, a gift of personal property made in contemplation of death. These gifts are valid even when will formalities are lacking.[768] Because a mortis causa gift is not testamentary and does not enter the decedent's

---

766. Brown § 7.21 at 150.
767. Supra no. 887.
768. Supra nos. 314–316.

estate, the law courts, and not the English ecclesiastical courts, originally took jurisdiction.[769] However, the free revocability of these gifts prevented the law courts from providing a helpful remedy. Equity therefore assumed nonexclusive jurisdiction, based not on an equitable right but rather on the inadequacy of the remedy at law. In America, gifts in contemplation of death have now been recognized by state statute.[770]

964. *Requirements.* Three requirements must be met. First, the gift must be made in contemplation of impending death, whether from physical disease or from some external cause, such as a hazardous journey or military service; second, the gift must be intended to become fully effective only upon the donor's death; and third, there must be delivery to the donee or the donee's representative.[771] In other words, a donatio mortis causa, like a gift inter vivos, must be completely executed. The difference is that the mortis causa gift is subject to divesting upon the occurrence of any one of a number of conditions subsequent. These include revocation, the donor's survival, the donee's failure to survive the donor, and the inability of the donor's estate to satisfy the donor's debts.[772]

965. *Personal property.* A gift mortis causa is limited to the donor's personal property.[773] In some jurisdictions, as noted above, a gift mortis causa of all of the donor's personalty was considered a violation of will formalities and was not permitted,[774] though this type of gift is now generally accepted.[775] Originally choses in action could not be given by mortis causa gift because they were not transferrable by delivery.[776] Today choses in action evidenced by a written instrument can generally be given by transfer of the documents showing ownership, though in England shares of stock may still not be gifted in this manner.[777] Land was thought inappropriate for a mortis causa gift. An oral gift of land was precluded by the statute of frauds. Moreover, the mere delivery of a deed would

---

769. 3 Pomeroy § 1151.

770. See, e.g., California Prob. C §§ 5701–5704.

771. ENGLAND: Gray and Gray no. 7.29; UNITED STATES: 3 Pomeroy § 1146. In some jurisdictions, the donor's suicide may constitute the sort of peril that will sustain a gift causa mortis. See *Scherer v. Hyland*, 380 A.2d 698, 702 (N.J. 1977).

772. *Basket v. Hassell*, 107 U.S. 602, 609–610, 2 S.Ct. 415 (1883).

773. Though, as explained in the text, this type of gift was originally confined to chattels, gifts mortis causa of choses in action later became possible. See *Chase v. Redding*, 13 Gray 418, 420 (Mass. 1859); *Brown v. Brown*, 18 Conn. 410 (Conn. 1847); 3 Pomeroy § 1148.

774. *Headley v. Kirby*, 18 Pa. 326 (1852), overruled by *In re Elliott's Estate*, 167 A. 289, 292 (Pa. 1933). See supra no. 395.

775. *Thomas' Adm'r v. Lewis*, 15 S.E. 389, 398 (Va. 1892).

776. Rundell 648.

777. *Moore v Moore* (1874) LR 18 Eq 474, 483; *In re Weston* [1902] LR 1 Ch 680; Rundell 649 note 35.

not deprive a donor in possession of the ability to create short tenancies in the property.

Nonetheless, in 1991 the English Court of Appeal upheld a donatio mortis causa of land.[778] It remains unclear whether the case established a new rule.[779] The new rule, if it exists, might be that the mortis causa gift affects the conscience of the donor's executor and therefore creates a constructive trust for the donee's benefit. The statute does not require land transfer formalities for the creation of a constructive trust.[780] For similar reasons, a mortis causa gift of a deed of mortgage may be made by simple delivery without violating the statute of frauds.[781]

i. Execution

966. *Delivery.* Delivery is an essential feature of a mortis causa gift. It must be complete and unequivocal during the donor's lifetime.[782] American courts impose the same delivery requirements on gifts inter vivos and gifts mortis causa,[783] though in New Hampshire the mortis causa gift is valid only if proved by two "indifferent" witnesses.[784] English equity, in contrast, which will not perfect an incomplete *inter vivos* gift, will require the donor's executor or administrator to do what is necessary to complete a gift *mortis causa*.[785] One further distinction between the two institutions involves the situation in which the donee is in possession at the moment of the gift. For a gift mortis causa, some courts hold that redelivery is required,[786] while others hold that it is not.[787] In one English case, the delivery of keys to a car was considered sufficient delivery, even though the donee already had a set and was in possession as bailee.[788]

967. *Choses in action.* For reasons now probably lost to history, the requirements for a valid mortis causa gift of a chose in action in English law differ from those

---

778. *Sen v Headley* [1991] Ch 425 (CA).

779. Gray and Gray no. 7.29.

780. Law of Property Act of 1925 sec. 53 par. 2; Gray and Gray no. 6.39. For the constructive trust, see Gray and Gray nos. 7.6 to 7.17.

781. *Duffield v Elwes* [1827] 1 Bligh (ns) 497, 541–543, 4 ER 959, 975–976 (Ch).

782. Graves 883; 3 Pomeroy § 1149.

783. *Schenker v. Moodhe*, 200 A. 727, 729 (Md. 1938).

784. New Hampshire Rev. Stat. § 551:17.

785. *In re Swinburne* [1926] Ch 38 (CA).

786. *Waugh v. Richardson*, 147 S.E. 17, 21–22 (W.Va. 1929); Graves 887; Mechem (1926–1927) 368–369.

787. ENGLAND: *Cain v Moon* [1896] 2 QB 283; UNITED STATES: *Caylor v. Caylor's Estate*, 52 N.E. 465, 468–469 (Ind. App. 1899) ("The law does not deal in trifles, nor require the doing of unnecessary things"); Mechem id. 370.

788. *Woodard v Woodard* [1995] 3 All ER 980 (CA).

for an inter vivos gift of the same rights.[789] When the gift is inter vivos, it generally must be made by assignment.[790] The transfer of a symbolic writing, is usually not sufficient.[791] English law favors the gift mortis causa by permitting it to be made by the simple delivery of documents essential to ownership of the right involved, even if the donor does not thereby completely part with control.[792] The flexibility may be due to the fact that a donatio mortis causa cannot be effective as an assignment since it is intended to be revocable.[793] Though the cases often appear contradictory,[794] English courts seem to favor mortis causa gifts by upholding delivery as long as the document that has been delivered shows ownership of the debt and includes its essential terms.[795] Delivery of a deed of mortgage operates a mortis causa gift of the debt,[796] as does delivery of an unendorsed promissory note payable to order,[797] or of a postal savings passbook,[798] but not of a simple passbook[799] or unendorsed stock certificates.[800] On the other hand, the delivery of mere evidence of the debt is insufficient at law to support a gratuitous assignment.[801] American law rejects the English law distinctions and applies the same principles to all gifts of choses in action, whether inter vivos or mortis causa.[802]

Under these rules, as Schouler pointed out, a dishonest friend or relative might enter the room of a dying individual, appropriate the box in which bank deposits, bonds, mortgage securities, and promissory notes are kept, and then, by claiming to be the beneficiary of a mortis causa gift, defeat the claims of the executor under the will.[803] Schouler suggested that such gifts should be valid only upon the testimony of three or more witnesses together with clear language of intent.

---

789. Bruton 843–848. Rundell suggested that the equity courts facilitated the donatio mortis causa in order to assist legatees whose bequests ran afoul of the newly enacted Statute of Frauds. Rundell 654.

790. *In re Patrick* [1891] 1 Ch 82; Bruton.

791. Supra no. 923.

792. *Moore v Darton* (1851) 4 De G & S 517, 520, 64 ER 938, 939; Bruton 846–847; Schouler (1886) 448.

793. Bridge 103.

794. "This review of the English cases shows that the English law of gifts is in considerable confusion." Bruton 851.

795. *Birch v Treasury Solicitor* [1951] 1 Ch 298, 311 (CA); Bruton 843–846.

796. *Duffield v Elwes* [1827] 1 Bligh (ns) 497, 4 ER 959 (Ch).

797. *Veal v Veal* (1859) 27 Beav 303, 54 ER 118.

798. *In re Weston* [1902] 1 Ch 680.

799. *M'Gonnell v Murray* (1869) Ir LT 568.

800. *Moore v Moore* (1874) LR 18 Eq 474.

801. *Ward v Turner* (1752) 2 Ves Sen 431, 28 ER 275 (Ch).

802. *Rosenberg v. Broy*, 12 Cal.Rptr. 103, 106 (Cal. App. 1961); supra no. 924.

803. Schouler (1886) 449.

968. *Writing.* A writing without delivery of the property is generally ineffective as a mortis causa gift.[804] In one case, the donor, just before entering surgery that she did not survive, wrote a note in which she sought to transfer some of her property to her husband and her daughter and asked another patient to tell the husband of the note. The court, over a strong dissent, held that the gift was void because some affirmative act of delivery is required.[805] "If we decided otherwise," the court wrote, "we should, in effect, be enabling persons to drive a coach and four through the Wills Act."[806]

969. *Release.* The donor may release a debt owing from the donee by either canceling or destroying the written evidence of the debt, by returning the evidence to the donee, or by delivering a receipt.[807] In contrast, when the donor is the debtor, transfer of a writing does not execute a valid gift to the creditor-donee but instead merely represents an executory promise to pay.

ii. Regime and Effects

970. *Regime.* The donor retains the right to revoke the mortis causa gift until death. The gift fails if the donor escapes the feared danger, though the donee need not prove that the donor died of the anticipated risk. Even if the donor dies from an unexpected cause, the gift is effective, provided the donor did not survive the anticipated peril.[808] The gift also fails if the donee predeceases the donor.[809] Because the donatio mortis causa is revocable at will, some scholars and courts suggest that, in contrast to the inter vivos gift, the donor's retaking of possession should be considered a revocation.[810]

971. *Title.* English law differs from the weight of American law on the effect of the deathbed gift.[811] According to the English rule, followed by some American courts, title does not vest in the donee until the donor's death, at which point a trust arises in the executor.[812] In contrast, many American courts hold that title must pass to the donee at the time of the gift. If it does not, the gift is said to be testamentary and therefore void. In a leading case, the donor endorsed a certificate of deposit with language providing that the donee was not to receive payment until after the donor's death. Because title could therefore not immediately

---

804. For cases upholding a gift mortis causa by deed, see Note (1926).

805. *Foster v. Reiss*, 112 A.2d 553, 559 (N.J. 1955).

806. Id. 560, quoting *In re Hughes* (1888) 59 LTR 586, 587.

807. 3 Pomeroy § 1148.

808. *Stevens v. Provident Inst. for Savings*, 115 N.E. 404 (Mass. 1917); Graves 883.

809. Graves 884.

810. *Delfs v. Yeager*, 31 Ohio C.D. 606 (Cir. Ct. 1906); Mechem (1926–1927) 362–363.

811. Comment (1852) 1.

812. ENGLAND: *Edwards v Jones* (1836) 1 My & Cr 226, 235, 40 ER 361, 365; *Duffield v. Elwes* [1827] 1 Blight (ns) 497, 543, 4 ER 959 (Ch); UNITED STATES: *Foster v. Reiss*, 112 A.2d 553, 556 (N.J. 1955); *Hatcher v. Buford*, 29 S.W. 641, 643 (Ark. 1895).

pass, the gift was considered void as testamentary.[813] At the same time, vesting is not absolute. If the gift is intended to be absolute, it is an inter vivos gift, even if the donor expires immediately afterward.

iii. Critique

972. *Regretted institution.* "The *donatio mortis causa* is one of those perplexed topics in the law which are at once the despair of judges, and the delight of law schools."[814] The despair is as present today as when this sentence was written a century and a half ago. As far as the delight is concerned, law schools have long since moved on to other pleasures. Many scholars and judges have regretted the donatio mortis causa. They believe not only that it provides an unwarranted exception to the Statute of Wills, but also, as a policy matter, that it opens the door to fraud and incites perjury.[815] As a result, this type of gift is often narrowly construed.[816] Deathbed gifts are respected only because they arise so frequently that injustice would often be done if they were not enforced.

iv. Justification

973. *Logic.* Logically, it seems that gratuitous transactions should divide nicely between those that take effect during the donor's lifetime and are therefore governed by the law of gifts and those that take effect at death and are governed instead by the law of successions. All systems examined here tend to divide transactions into those two categories. The French law tradition, because it recognizes no intermediary category, rejects the institution of the mortis causa gift. The common law accepts it only reluctantly.

---

813. *Basket v. Hassell*, 107 U.S. 602, 615, 2 S.Ct. 415 (1883); Graves 890–891. See also *Grace v. Klein*, 147 S.E.2d 288 (W.Va. 1966) (no gift mortis causa when the donor asked the bank to pay the donee at the donor's death).

814. Comment (1852) 1 (emphasis in original). This is the first sentence of the first article of the first issue of the first American law review.

815. [W]hen the effort to carry out a giver's intention has resulted in encouragement to a giver to leave his deliberate intention in lasting doubt, where legal consistency seems to require reluctant courts to uphold a nurse in sole attendance upon some foolish person in carrying off stock, bonds, and promissory notes with little more ado than floor-sweepings, or waste paper, utterly regardless of equal claims of kindred, and where one with opportunity of secret access to a dying person's effects or trusted with their custody, has strong inducement to perjury, it is no wonder that we find the reports full of judicial regrets that the gift *causâ mortis* was ever admitted into our law at all.
2 Schouler (1896) § 197. See *Thomas' Adm'r v. Lewis*, 15 S.E. 389, 405 (Va. 1892) (Lacy, J., dissenting); Graves 885.

816. "Of all legal rules, however, those that have grown up around the doctrine of donatio causa mortis should be the least subject to relaxation." *Parker v. Copland*, 64 A. 129, 131 (N.J. Err. & App. 1906).

974. *Practical perspective.* Yet life's emergencies sometimes do not respect the law's attempted distinction between the quick and the dead. There are many instances in which it is perfectly legitimate for the donor to retain some control while at the same time transferring the property to the donee. In these cases, it is irritatingly difficult to situate the transactions on one side or other of the line. An illustrative case involved a donor who was about to be deported to the concentration camps.[817] Though the case did not involve a mortis causa gift, the facts are instructive. The deportees were suddenly informed that they had but a few minutes to collect their belongings. Of course, they were hoping that they would return to reclaim their property. It therefore would have made no sense to part with it for good. A will might have been useful, but there was obviously no time for testamentary formalities, and any will drafted earlier may no longer have responded to the circumstances. The donatio mortis causa seems the perfect solution to the terrible dilemma. It is mystifying that some systems allow logic to trump practical necessity.

975. *Great importance.* A second aspect of the problem is that gifts that hover between life and death are often especially important to the parties. The donatio mortis causa may represent the donor's last legal act. From the point of view of the individuals involved, it makes little sense for the law to decide that, in order to maintain easy conceptual distinctions, these gifts may not be made, or that they may only be made in forms and by methods that are not readily available.

Many have emphasized the importance of respecting individual intent in the field of gift giving.[818] Yet few scholars or courts have recognized that, in these and other instances, the rigor of gift law occasionally prevents individuals from realizing their last wishes. The fact that few are troubled by this problem suggests once again that there may be some imbalance in the law's approach.

c. Equitable Estoppel

976. *Reliance.* Estoppel is an equitable doctrine that protects reasonable reliance by perfecting transactions that would be unenforceable at law.[819] Estoppel takes essentially two forms. The two do not have the same weight and effect in all common law jurisdictions. The first is equitable estoppel, the second promissory estoppel. Promissory estoppel was discussed above in the context of the gift promise.[820] Equitable estoppel is examined here.

---

817. The background situation is that reported in Civ.[1] 14 Dec. 1960, *Bull. civ.* I no. 545, discussed infra no. 1308. The case raised the issue of revocation. A mortis causa gift would be void under French law.

818. "A court absorbed in purely doctrinal arguments may lose sight of the important and desirable objective of sanctioning what the transferor wanted to do, even though it is convinced that he wanted to do it." Gulliver and Tilson 2.

819. Restatement (Second) of Contracts § 90 comment a.

820. Supra nos. 686, 692, 707–708.

977. *Elements.* Equitable estoppel is related to the civilian doctrine that prohibits *venire contra factum proprium.* It prevents a party from retracting words or deeds that were meant to be relied upon, and in fact were relied upon, to the other's detriment. If the donor, by act or word, attempts to give a gift, intending the donee to rely on the gift, and the donee does rely and would suffer loss if the gift were not valid, equity will enforce the gift even though it would not be enforced at law.[821]

A classic example involves the case of a father who placed his son in possession of a tract of the father's land and signed a memorandum indicating that he was giving the land to the son as a dwelling. The proper formalities were never executed. After the son, at his own expense and with his father's approval, built a residence on the land, the court held that the son was entitled to the conveyance of the whole estate in fee simple, and not simply to restitution or a life estate.[822] On virtually the same facts, Canadian courts also hold for the donee and the donee's heirs.[823]

d. Constructive Trust

978. *Unjust enrichment.* Equity may also complete a gratuitous transfer as a matter of restitution law when the donor, if allowed to retain the property, would be unjustly enriched. The equitable remedy involved is the constructive trust, which requires a party who is unjustly enriched to hold the property for the benefit of another.[824] Once the constructive trust is declared, equity may compel the transfer.

As a general rule, a donor is under no duty to complete an ineffective gift transfer.[825] In some situations, however, equity in some states makes an exception and requires the donor to transfer title.[826] The Restatement interprets these as cases involving a constructive trust.[827] The first situation involves the donee's reliance, a case that would also be enforced under the doctrine of equitable estoppel examined above. In this type of case, the donee has so changed position that

---

821. Gray and Gray no. 7.21.

822. *Dillwyn v Llewelyn* (1862) 4 De GF & J 517, 45 ER 1285 (CA).

823. CANADA: *Dagley v. Dagley* (1905) 38 N.S.Rep. 313 (Alta.); *Brogden v. Brogden* (1920) 53 D.L.R. 362, [1920] 2 W.W.R. 803 (S.C.). For a related American case decided on the basis of promissory estoppel, see *Seavey v. Drake*, 62 N.H. 393 (1882); supra no. 707.

824. Restatement of Restitution § 160. The use of the term *trust* in this context is "not altogether a felicitous one." Unlike an express trust, a manifestation of intent is not involved and no fiduciary relationship is created. See id. comment a. A constructive trust is perhaps best understood as one of the specific remedies in the field of restitution.

825. Restatement of Restitution § 164 comment a.

826. Id. § 164 pars. a and b.

827. Id. § 164 Reporter's Notes. The opinions do not mention the concept of constructive trust.

it would be inequitable not to require the donor to complete the gift.[828] In the second situation, the intended donee is a natural object of the donor's bounty, usually a close relative, such as a spouse or child, and the donor dies believing that the conveyance is effective.[829] However, equity will not intervene if completing the gift would be inequitable to the heirs or other third parties.[830]

979. *Expansion.* The doctrine has now been expanded to include charitable institutions. In a prominent case, the donor announced at a large luncheon given in her honor, a luncheon attended by many notables including the president of the State of Israel, that she was gifting her husband's scholarly library to Hebrew University.[831] The donor also signed a news release announcing the donation. She subsequently refused offers from third parties to purchase the library on the grounds that it no longer belonged to her. The donor cataloged and crated the library for shipment and corresponded with the university about the procedure for making delivery. Ultimately, however, she died before she was able to ship the library. Based on her public declarations, the trial court decided that she held the library in trust for the university.

The state supreme court vacated the decision and ordered a new trial. There could be no trust because she had made no declaration of trust and there was no other evidence of her intent to hold the property as a trustee. Moreover, because there was not even a beginning of delivery, there was also no inter vivos gift.

On remand, the trial court nonetheless enforced the gift, holding it valid on numerous grounds.[832] First, there had been a valid gift. The donor's delivery to the donee of a document that listed most of the books in the collection was sufficient to constitute constructive delivery of the library. "[W]here the purpose of formalities is being served, an excessive regard for formalism should not be allowed to defeat the ends of justice."[833] The court insisted that it had not abandoned the delivery requirement.[834] Second, the transfer was enforceable based on detrimental reliance. The university had relied on the gift by removing from its fund-raising solicitations a room that it dedicated to the gift collection.

---

828. *Seavey v. Drake*, 62 N.H. 393 (1882). The case was decided on the basis of promissory estoppel. See supra no. 707.

829. Compare *McCall v. McCall*, 3 Day 402 (Conn. 1809) (defective conveyance enforced) with *Shears v. Westover*, 68 N.W. 266, 267 (Mich. 1896) (no reformation).

830. *Powell v. Powell*, 27 Ga. 36 (1859).

831. *Hebrew University Ass'n v. Nye*, 169 A.2d 641 (Conn. 1961).

832. *Hebrew University Ass'n v. Nye*, 223 A.2d 397 (Conn. Super. Ct. 1966).

833. Id. 400.

834. "The court recognizes, in arriving at this result, that it is abrogating in some respects the requirement of delivery in a case involving an intended gift inter vivos. Obviously, it would be neither desirable nor wise to abrogate the requirement of delivery in any and all cases of intended inter vivos gifts, for to do so, even under the guise of enforcing equitable rights, might open the door to fraudulent claims." Id.

"The setting aside of a room in a university library is no small matter."[835] Finally, the court held that the gift could be enforced as a constructive trust, thereby extending the natural bounty rule to include gifts to charitable institutions. "Rules of law must, in the last analysis, serve the ends of justice or they are worthless. For a court of equity to permit the decedent's wishes to be doubly frustrated for no better reason than that the rules so provide makes no sense whatsoever."[836]

e. Merger of Title

980. *Executor.* In one additional, and somewhat limited, circumstance, English equity courts will enforce a gift that would be unenforceable at law. Under the doctrine of *Strong v Bird*, an imperfect gift is perfected if the donee becomes the donor's executor or administrator or if more than one individual is appointed, and the donee is among them.[837] The leading case involved the forgiveness of a debt. The donor lent money to the donee, whom she later appointed as her executor. Afterward, she orally forgave the debt.[838] The general English rule is that a debt can be forgiven only by deed or when supported by consideration.[839] The court held that the gift was valid because, upon appointment, legal and equitable title merged in the person of the donee. Equitable title passes to the donee upon the expression of the donor's intent to make the gift.[840] Legal title passes at the moment the donee becomes executor. The rule applies not only to the forgiveness of a debt but also to outright gifts.[841]

981. *Requirements.* The operation of the rule requires that the donor intend to make a present gift and not merely to give in the future. Moreover, donative intent must continue unchanged until the donor's death. If the evidence shows that, in the meantime, the donor had forgotten about the gift, the doctrine does not perfect the gift.[842] Because the rule does not operate until the donor's death, the precarious proof situation would seem to require an affirmative act to reflect or confirm donative intent. Yet it seems that the courts do not impose such a requirement.[843] Subsequent cases seem to have expanded the doctrine to include

---

835. Id.

836. Id. 401.

837. 20 Halsbury part 1 sub Gift no. 70.

838. *Strong v Bird* (1874) LR 18 Eq 315 (Rolls Ct). As Jaconelli has pointed out, the case could easily have been decided without announcing the famous rule for which the case stands. The donor actually made payment of the amount of the gift. See Jaconelli 433.

839. *Flowers Case* (1597) Noy 67, 74 ER 1035; Crossley Vaines 316; supra no. 926.

840. "[E]quity regards as done that which ought to be done." Crossley Vaines 312.

841. *In re Stewart* [1908] 2 Ch 251. The case involved an oral gift of bonds that were not delivered to the donee/executor until after the donor's death.

842. *In re Wale* [1956] 3 All ER 280 (Ch D); Jaconelli 432.

843. Jaconelli 439–440.

real as well as personal property.[844] The rule now also applies in favor of a donee who is appointed the donor's trustee. In general, the absence of a writing does not defeat the transfer.[845] The principle is also valid in Canada[846] and Ireland.[847]

982. *Justification.* The doctrine of merger of title is considered an exception to the principle that equity will not perfect an imperfect gift. "Yet, of all the exceptions to the application of that maxim, the rule in *Strong v Bird* is surely the strangest."[848] It is a gift that cannot take effect until the donor's death, and yet it is neither subject to wills formalities nor justifiable either by the exigencies of the situation (as is the donatio mortis causa), by the circumstances (such as that immediate transfer was not possible) or by any type of unjust enrichment. The doctrine is also not rooted in moral principle or common sense.

Maitland argued that the debtor's equity arising from the imperfect gift is "as good as" the equity of the donor's heirs.[849] Yet it is difficult to understand why the fact that the donee happens to become the donor's executor should alter the equities. Another justification is that it would be absurd for executors to sue themselves to collect the debt or recover the property.[850] Yet the doctrine also applies when the donee is only one of several executors.[851] The rule has also been defended as representing the donor's presumed intent.[852] Yet contrary proof is not permitted. Jaconelli concluded that each of the rationales advanced in support of the doctrine is defective. "This should not appear entirely surprising since the rule is at odds with the general law on the making of gifts."[853]

8. Comparative Notes

983. *From a civilian perspective.* For the sake of comparison, it is worthwhile to examine the common law of gifts from the standpoint of the three principal Romanic law exceptions to the writing requirement—the manual gift, the indirect gift, and the disguised gift. These terms are not employed in the common law. There is no universal writing requirement to which exceptions are needed.

---

844. Id. 442–443.

845. *Vandervell v IRC* [1967] 2 AC 291 (HL); *In re Vandervell's Trusts* (No. 2) [1974] Ch 269 at 308 (CA).

846. *In re Barnes* (1918), 42 O.L.R. 352, 14 Ont.W.N. 19 (H.C.).

847. *Estate of Wilson* [1933] Ir R 729.

848. Jaconelli 435. Jaconelli provides an excellent summary of the justification discussion, which I follow here.

849. Maitland (1949) 73 note 1 (continuation from 72).

850. AUSTRALIA: *Bone v Comm'r of Stamp Duties* (1974) 132 CLR 38, 53 (HC) (justifying the related rule that the debtor's appointment as the creditor's executor extinguishes the debt).

851. *In re Stewart* (1908) 2 Ch D 251.

852. Id.

853. Jaconelli 437.

Nonetheless, the comparison reveals that similar transactions are characterized differently in the different systems.

a. Manual Gifts

984. *Standard*. The manual gift, which in some Romanic systems constitutes a valid exception to the writing requirement, corresponds in the common law to the principal method of gifting chattels and some choses in action, which is accomplished by actual delivery, the written deed being less frequently used.

b. Disguised Gifts

985. *Mention of consideration*. Disguised gifts are transactions in which the parties agree to a gratuitous transfer and then clothe that transfer in the form of a bargain. As Blackstone noted, virtually all common law deeds or other written gift instruments, especially concerning real property, include a statement of consideration.

> [T]hese very seldom carry the outward appearance of a gift, however freely bestowed; being usually expressed to be made in consideration of blood, or natural affection, or of five or ten shillings nominally paid to the grantor; and in the case of leases, always receiving a rent though it be but a peppercorn: any of which considerations will, in the eye of the law, convert the gift, if executed, into a grant; if not executed, into a contract.[854]

986. *Nominal consideration*. In the common law, the principle is that the courts will not review the adequacy of consideration.[855] However, modern American law distinguishes between adequate and nominal consideration. In the absence of a bargain, the purported consideration is considered a sham and is deemed nominal. Nominal consideration, as the rule goes, is no consideration. In other words, a pretense of a bargain is not enough to convert a gift into a contract.[856]

In English law, however, even nominal consideration is sufficient to create an enforceable contract. By respecting the sham, English law enforces transactions that, in the civil law, would be construed as disguised gifts.[857] The rule is usually justified as a logical consequence of the adequacy doctrine. Atiyah, however, echoing Dean Ripert, suggests that promises based on nominal consideration demonstrate seriousness of purpose. "[A] promise for nominal consideration is

---

854. 2 Blackstone 440.

855. Supra nos. 231, 690.

856. Restatement (Second) of Contracts § 75 comment b illus. 4–5; Eisenberg (1979) 9–10.

857. The difference, however, as Gorla pointed out, is that, in English law, the parties are not involved in simulation. Nominal consideration is effective whether intended as a bargain or whether merely designed to signal the intent to be legally bound. 1 Gorla 409–410 note 10.

just about the clearest possible indication that the promisor intended his promise seriously and intended to give the promisee a legally enforceable right."[858]

987. *Enforceable promise.* In the common law the disguise is not needed to protect executed gifts. Gratuitous transfers, once completed, are not subject to challenge due to lack of consideration. Instead, the disguise may sometimes serve to make a gift promise enforceable. For example, the New York high court enforced an executory gift promise that took the form of what in the civil law would be a disguised gift.[859] Intending a gift, the parties concluded a land sale contract. They agreed orally that the price would not be paid. Though the contract was not performed by either party, the grantor later endorsed the contract with a receipt confirming that payment had been made. The grantor's performance was specifically enforced. The court held that the promise to convey title was supported by the promise to pay the price. The debt for the price was released by the endorsed receipt.

988. *No independent protection.* When a court examines a transaction to determine whether it involves a quid pro quo or a gift, it looks to all the facts and circumstances of the case. If the consideration is deemed a sham, the disguise is disregarded. The simulation provides no independent protection for the transaction. In such cases, the courts then ask whether the basic requirements for a valid gift are present. In one case, for example, a creditor gratuitously released the debtor by delivering a receipt indicating that the debt had been paid in full. The creditor later changed his mind and sued. The simulation did not help the debtor. The court concluded that the debt had been neither paid nor settled. Instead, the court examined only whether the donor had fully executed the gift.[860]

c. Indirect Gifts

989. *Usual.* A gift is indirect when, without recourse to simulation, a gratuitous transfer is accomplished by means of another legal institution. As discussed above, most of the common law of gifts is based on the indirect gift. A gift is valid as long as the formalities otherwise required have been completed. The gratuitous transfer of title to real property is accomplished in the form required for conveyancing. The gratuitous nature of the transaction does not add supplementary requirements. The declaration of trust follows the requirements of trust law. The third-party beneficiary contract is a well-accepted method of making a gratuitous transfer to a donee beneficiary.[861] A similar result may be achieved by the

---

858. Atiyah 194. For Ripert's view, see supra no. 810.
859. *Ferry v. Stephens*, 21 Sickels 321 (N.Y. 321), discussed supra no. 704.
860. *Gray v. Barton*, 55 N.Y. 68 (1873).
861. Restatement (Second) of Contracts § 302 par. 1 lit. b and comment c.

contractual institution of novation—for example, the substitution of the donee for the donor as the obligee.[862]

990. *Resulting trust.* One type of indirect gift, namely the purchase of property in another's name, has experienced a significant case law development in the common law of restitution. The legal construction depends on presumptions of equity and the resulting trust. When one person pays part or all of the price and title is conveyed in the name of another or in their joint names, the presumption is that there is no gift but rather a resulting trust for the benefit of the person who pays the price.[863] This basic principle, however, is subject to a system of exceptions and counterexceptions that makes this one of the most challenging aspects of the common law of gifts.

991. *Presumption rebutted.* The presumption that a gift is not intended can be rebutted—for example, by a wish expressed at the time of purchase. All the surrounding circumstances are taken into account.[864] The most common of the exceptions involves *advancement*—the purchase of property in the name of a spouse, a child, or an adopted child.[865] When the purchaser is a husband or father, the presumption is that a gift was intended.[866] This presumption extends to a grandfather in loco parentis after the father has died[867] and to certain other family relationships.[868] The presumption is not rebutted by the fact that the donor retains control over the property and the right to receive profits during the donor's lifetime, but it may be rebutted by other evidence, including facts that suggest there was no intent to benefit the person in whose name the property was acquired or that reveal conflicting statements or actions of the alleged donor[869] or a business relation between the parties.[870] Statements made substantially after the purchase are taken into account only if they are against interest. As a counterexception, no presumption arises when a mother purchases property in her child's name,[871] even though the mother is widowed or separated

---

862. Id. § 280 and illus. 5; Brown § 8.4; *Froude v. Fleischmann,* 164 N.Y.S. 1003 (App. Div. 1917).

863. ENGLAND: 20 Halsbury part 1 sub Gifts no. 42; Gray and Gray no. 7.3; UNITED STATES: 5 Scott and Fratcher § 440 at 137. Statutes in some American states have abolished the presumption for purchase-money resulting trusts of land, while in other states the presumption is expressly stated. 5 Scott and Fratcher §§ 440.2 to 440.3.

864. 20 Halsbury id. no. 43; Gray and Gray no. 7.4.

865. *Elliot v Elliot* (1677) 2 Chan Cas 231, 22 ER 922 (LC).

866. 20 Halsbury part 1 sub Gifts no. 45.

867. *Ebrand v Dancer* (1680) 2 Chan Cas 26, 22 ER 829 (LC).

868. *Currant v Jago* (1844) 1 Coll 261, 63 ER 410 (VC) (uncle and nephew).

869. Id.

870. *Garrett v Wilkinson* (1848) 2 De G & Sm 244, 64 ER 110.

871. *In re De Visme* (1863) 2 De G & Sm 17, 46 ER 280 (LC); 20 Halsbury part 1 sub Gifts no. 45.

from her husband. Little evidence is needed, however, to establish the gift, especially in the case of a mother in loco parentis.[872]

In American law, the presumption extends to purchases in the name of parties related to the purchaser by blood or marriage in such a way that the party taking title is a natural object of the purchaser's bounty.[873] The presumption of advancement arises for purchases by a husband in the name of his wife and of a father in the name of his children, including illegitimate and adopted children. However the presumption does not arise when a wife purchases property in her husband's name or a child in the name of his parents. The presumptions are an attempt to recognize situations in which it would be natural for the purchaser to make provision for the other party's advancement.[874] The presumptions of advancement can also be rebutted.[875]

In English law, the proceeds from a life insurance policy purchased by the insured for the benefit of an unrelated third person belong to the insured's estate, unless a trust has been declared for the third party.[876] However, when the policy is purchased for the benefit of a spouse or child, a trust is automatically established. A policy on a child's life taken out by a parent may be presumed to be for advancement, entitling the child's estate to the benefit,[877] though the presumption may also be rebutted.[878]

d. Difference of Approach

992. *Relative status.* One intriguing difference between the civil law exceptions and their role in the common law has to do with their relative status. The common law shows no preference for one or the other method of gift giving. The discussion focuses instead on whether the requirements have been met. In French law, in contrast, the exceptions to the form requirements, though broadly applied, seem to provoke dismay. The distinguished French jurist Michel Dagot argues that the stakes are high.

> French law concerning gifts without a formal act is, in a way, at a crossroads .... A choice must be made: either law American style, with the omnipresence of the judiciary, and of a judiciary that is heavy-handed and ruinous for many, or law French style, which prefers the prior constitution of proof and the prior definition of legal situations by an impartial authority.[879]

---

872. 20 Halsbury id.
873. 5 Scott and Fratcher § 442 and note 1 (collecting cases).
874. Id. at 182–183.
875. Id. § 443.
876. 20 Halsbury part 1 sub Gifts no. 47.
877. *In re Roberts* [1946] Ch 1.
878. *Worthington v Curtis* (1875) 1 Ch D 419 (CA).
879. Dagot (2000) 1482.

9. Gifts from the Body

993. *Typically inalienable.* The human body has generally been considered inalienable for purposes of the private law.[880] However, though elements of the human body are not available for market transactions, they may be given gratuitously. Today, bodily organs, eyes, tissue, blood, bone marrow, and cells, as well as gametes (eggs and semen) may generally be donated for therapeutic purposes.[881]

The law distinguishes between extractions from living donors, which may involve a kidney, a section of the liver, blood, or semen, and donations from deceased donors, which are known in American law as *anatomical gifts*. In all cases the gifts are gratuitous, both in the sense that no payment is permitted to the donor and none required of the donee, though the donor may be reimbursed for expenses. For this type of gift, questions of capacity are closely related to the means of expressing consent. Both questions are examined here.

In no system described below are transfers from the body governed by gift law. Gifts of organs and the like are always governed by specific statutes. These gifts are included in this study because they reveal, by contrast, the highly protective nature of the law governing material gifts. In many ways, gifts from the body are significantly more important and subject to greater risk than are gifts of worldly possessions, yet the law goes to extremes to facilitate them.

a. Gifts from Living Donors

994. *Close relatives.* Living donors may make gifts of nonregenerating organs for purposes of transplant. The principal difference among legal systems concerns the relationship required between donor and donee. In many countries, the law limits potential donees to the donor's close relatives.

i. France

995. *Capacity.* Under French law, organ donations from living persons are generally permitted only between a parent and a child.[882] A committee of experts may also authorize donations by other relatives and close friends, including brothers and sisters, children, grandparents, uncles and aunts, first cousins, stepparents, as well as those who have lived together with the donee for at least two years.[883] Minors and adult incompetents may not make living organ donations,[884] though, in cases of necessity, a minor or adult incompetent may

---

880. ENGLAND: Human Organ Transplants Act of 1989; FRANCE: CC art. 16-1 par. 3, arts. 16-2 to 16-3, 16-5 to 16-6; ITALY: CC art. 5.

881. See generally Godbout and Caillé 87–91; Titmuss.

882. Pub. Health C [Santé publique] art. L1231-1 par. 1.

883. Id. art. L1231-1 par. 2. Art. L1231-3 provides for the committee of experts.

884. Id. art. L1231-2.

make a donation of bone marrow to a close relative.[885] Donations of blood[886] and gametes[887] are permitted, though gifts of gametes from the same donor may not deliberately lead to the birth of more than ten children.

996. *Consent.* The donor's consent must be expressed before the president of the trial court of general jurisdiction or a designated magistrate. The role of the judge is to ensure that the donor has been informed of the risks and that the donor's consent is without defect. In emergencies, other means of expressing consent are accepted. Consent may be revoked at any time. French law prohibits compensation for organ donation[888] and requires that the names of donor and donee remain confidential.[889] Public solicitation of an organ donation in favor of a particular person is prohibited.[890]

ii. Belgium

997. *Capacity.* Under Belgian law, nonregenerating organs may be gifted only by those who are at least eighteen years of age. If the removal may have consequences for the donor, the gift is only permitted if the donee's life is in danger and organs from a dead donor would not be satisfactory.[891]

998. *Consent.* The gift requires the spouse's consent and, if the donor is not yet twenty-one, the consent of whoever must consent to the donor's marriage. If the loss of the organ does not normally have serious consequences, it may be made by a minor who has turned fifteen. Consent must be obtained from the minor, from the minor's spouse, and from whoever is normally required to consent to the minor's marriage.[892] In all cases consent must be stated in writing before an adult witness and signed and dated by the witness as well as by those whose consent is required.[893] Consent to any of these donations can be revoked. The physician who is to remove the organ must inform all concerned of the potential consequences and ensure that the donor makes the decision knowingly and from altruistic motives.[894]

---

885. Id. arts. L1241-3 par. 2, L1241-4 par. 1.
886. Id. arts. L1221-1 to L1221-13.
887. Id. arts. L1244-1 to L1244-9.
888. CC art. 16-1 par. 3, arts. 16-2 to 16-3, 16-5 to 16-6; Pub. Health C art. L1211-4.
889. CC art. 16-8; Pub. Health C art. L1211-5.
890. Pub. Health C art. L1211-3 par. 1.
891. Law of 13 June 1986 art. 6.
892. Id. arts. 5, 7.
893. Id. art. 8 par. 2. The consent is void unless specific information is included in the writing. See Order of 30 Oct. 1986 [*personnes vivantes*] art. 1.
894. Law of 13 June 1986 art. 9.

iii. Italy

999. *Before a magistrate.* Italian law permits the donation of a kidney between close relatives, or, if no close relative is available, from more distant relatives or unrelated persons.[895] The donor must manifest assent before a magistrate. The magistrate, after determining that the donor is aware of the consequences, must record the declaration in writing.[896] The donor may revoke at any time before the operation. In case of doubt, the court decides the propriety of the transplant. The donee must also consent, except in an emergency.[897] Any agreement concerning compensation is void.[898]

iv. Spain

1000. *Twenty-four-hour delay.* Under Spanish law, a living donor must expressly manifest consent in writing before a magistrate. The document must be signed by the donor and the physician who is to perform the operation as well as by any other participating doctors.[899] A twenty-four-hour delay is imposed from the moment the declaration of gift is signed. The donor may revoke at any time before the operation. The donee must remain anonymous.[900] No compensation is permitted.[901] The organ removal is permitted only if it does not put the donor's life at risk. It is not permitted if the donor has been influenced by economic, social, or psychological pressure.[902]

v. Germany

1001. *To save a life.* German law permits organs to be removed from living persons if done to save a life or to prevent a serious illness.[903] The prospective donor must be warned of the risks in the presence of any necessary specialists as well as of two physicians who will not intervene in the procedure. Nonregenerating organs may only be given to relatives of the first or second degree, spouses, life partners, fiancés, or other persons with whom the donor indisputably maintains a special personal relationship.[904] Consent may be revoked, either orally or

---

895. Law of 26 June 1967 art. 1.
896. Id. art. 2.
897. Id. art. 4.
898. Id. arts. 6–7.
899. Decree of 30 Dec. 1999 art. 9 par. 4.
900. Law of 27 Oct. 1979 art. 4.
901. Id. art. 2.
902. Decree of 30 Dec. 1999 art. 9 pars. 1–2.
903. Law of 5 Nov. 1997 (TPG) § 8; Staudinger (-Jickeli and Stieper) § 90 no. 21.
904. The limitation to specified donees has been criticized as unduly restricting *cross donations* required due to incompatibilities of blood groups. See Gutmann and Schroth 5–18.

in writing. Blood donations, as well as other types of bodily donations, are governed by other laws.[905]

vi. England

1002. *Detailed interviews.* Recently promulgated regulations under the Human Tissue Act provide that organ donations from living donors are permitted only after detailed interviews with the donor, the person giving consent, and the donee.[906] The matter can be referred to the Human Tissue Authority only by a registered medical practitioner. The authority must ensure that no reward has been promised and that consent has been obtained. It must also make certain that the consent is informed and without defect and that the donor is aware that consent may be revoked at any time before the operation. If the donor is a child or adult incompetent, or a paired or pooled donation is involved, then decisions must be made by at least three members of the authority. If regulatory requirements are met, sperm and egg donations are also permitted.[907]

vii. India

1003. *Near relatives.* Under Indian law, donors may consent to organ removal before death for therapeutic purposes.[908] However, live organs may generally be received only by a near relative.[909] If there is no special affection or attachment between the parties, the authorities must approve any organ removal from a living being.

viii. United States

1004. *State regulation.* Organ donations by living donors are strictly regulated by the states.[910] Gifts of semen[911] and blood[912] are generally recognized implicitly by statute and governed by similar rules. Patients may also make a gift for research purposes of diseased tissue removed during operative procedures.[913] In some states, the uniform law applicable to organs to be removed after death are applied

---

905. For blood donations, see Law of 1 July 1998 (TFG). For other relevant laws, see Nickel et al. § 1 nos. 1–12.
906. Human Tissue Regulations secs. 9–12.
907. Human Fertilisation and Embryology Act of 1990 sec. 27 par. 1, sec. 28 par. 2.
908. Transplantation of Human Organs Act sec. 3 par. 1.
909. Id. sec. 9.
910. See, e.g., California Health & Safety C §§ 1635–1641.1.
911. Uniform Parentage Act § 702 comment.
912. See, e.g. California Health & Safety C § 1635 par. c.
913. *Washington Univ. v. Catalona*, 490 F.3d 667 (8th Cir. 2007). The gift is permitted even though federal and state regulations define excised body tissue and blood as hazardous substances or infectious waste. Id. 676.

by analogy.[914] A particular concern has been whether to permit donors to exclude potential recipients based on the donee's race or religious affiliation.[915]

b. Anatomical Gifts

1005. *Two systems.* When the gift involves an organ to be removed from a decedent, there are two principal systems for ensuring the donor's consent.[916] Much of continental Europe applies a system of *presumed* consent (*Widerspruchslösung*). The presumed consent system considers every decedent to be a potential donor unless the individual explicitly objects. In contrast, the principle of *informed* consent (*Zustimmungslösung*) prevails in much of the common law as well as in Germany. Under this system, the extraction of organs from a decedent's body is permitted only with the donor's express consent, which is often recorded on a donor registration card. In both systems, the next of kin often is given the right to consent to organ removal from the decedent's body, as well as, in some cases, to contravene the donor's gift. Though the two systems produce similar rates of organ donation, one study has concluded that presumed intent legislation may encourage donation by making families more willing to consent.[917]

i. Presumed Consent

1006. *Relatives.* In a system of presumed consent, donors are presumed to have agreed to become organ donors at death unless they declare their refusal during their lifetimes. The principal differences among presumed intent jurisdictions relates to the role the relatives play after the donor's death. Some jurisdictions proceed to organ donation without consulting the relatives (*strikte Widerspruchslösung*), while others confer with relatives to determine whether the donor had objected (*erweiterte Widerspruchslösung*). A third type of law requires the relatives to be informed so that, in the absence of a donor declaration, they have the opportunity to object (*Informationslösung*).[918]

1007. *France.* Under French law, organs may be removed from the body of any decedent who does not make a refusal known while alive. The refusal, revocable at any time, may be made in any manner, including by notation in the national automated registry.[919] Treating physicians who are unaware of the deceased's wishes are required to solicit information from close relatives about whether the

914. *Moore v. Regents of University of California*, 793 P.2d 479, 501–502 (Cal. 1990). For the Uniform Anatomical Gift Act, see infra nos. 1018–1024.

915. Truog.

916. Abadie and Gay 600. For a comparison of organ transplant legislation in different countries, see id. 617–619; Nickel et al. *Einführung* nos. 8–11.

917. Abadie and Gay 608, 613.

918. For a definition of the terms, see Nickel et al. *Einführung* no. 8.

919. Pub. Health C art. L1232-1 pars. 1–2. For comments on the 1976 version of the French law on organ donation, see Grenouilleau.

deceased refused.[920] If the decedent is a minor or an adult incompetent, no organs may be removed without the consent of parents or guardian.[921]

1008. *Belgium.* Under Belgian law, organs may be taken from any Belgian citizen domiciled in Belgium who has not refused organ donation.[922] Organs may be taken from others only if they have expressed their consent. A person aged eighteen may express a refusal. A person under eighteen who is capable of expressing consent may also refuse, as may, as long as the minor is alive, the minor's parents or guardian.[923] The refusal may be expressed by means of the official form, signed, dated, and delivered to administrative authorities at the place of residence.[924] An individual may also express the affirmative wish to become an organ donor.[925] No organ may be removed if the individual has expressed a refusal in the mode provided by regulation or has, by any other means, communicated the refusal to the physician. If the donor has not expressly consented, a close relative may oppose the gift.[926] The identities of donor and donee must remain confidential.[927]

1009. *Italy.* Under Italian law, the Ministry of Health is required to urge all citizens to express their intention concerning whether they wish to become organ donors.[928] Citizens have ninety days from receipt of the ministry communication to respond with either a consent or a refusal. The declaration must be signed and dated[929] and can be modified at any time by means of another signed and dated writing.[930] Those who fail to make a declaration are considered to have consented. Organs may be taken from those who have expressly consented as well as from those who have been informed of their rights and have not declared. Those who have not been informed, however, are deemed not to be donors. Parents express consent for their children. In case of disagreement between parents, there can be no gift. No consent is possible for unborn children, for those who lack the capacity to consent, or for children under the care of social services.

Corneas may be removed from a decedent upon the consent of the spouse, the children, or the parents, unless the individual manifested a refusal in writing.[931]

---

920. Pub. Health C art. L1232-1 par. 3.

921. Id. art. L1231-2.

922. Law of 13 June 1986 art. 10 par. 1, as modified by the Program-law of 22 Dec. 2003 arts. 156–168, and by the Law of 25 Feb. 2007.

923. Law of 13 June 1986 art. 10 par. 2.

924. Order of 30 Oct. 1986 arts. 1–2.

925. Id. art. 4.

926. Law of 13 June 1986 art. 10 par. 4.

927. Id. art. 14.

928. Law of 1 Apr. 1999 arts. 4–5.

929. Decree of 8 Apr. 2000 art. 1 pars. 1–2.

930. Id. art. 3 par. 1.

931. Law of 12 Aug. 1993 art. 1.

Italian law prohibits the removal of gonads and of the brain, as well as the use of embryos for transplant purposes.[932]

1010. *Spain.* Spain has a significantly higher rate of organ donation than any other country. As a result, the *Spanish model* of organ procurement has been extensively studied.[933] Under Spanish law, organs may be taken from any decedent who has not left an express declaration of opposition.[934] Individuals may specify that their opposition refers to some or all organs.[935] The legal representative declares for minors. In the case of those who die during an accident, a judge determines whether a declaration of opposition has been made. Spanish law permits organ removal without family consent. Nonetheless, as a practical matter, the donation is not considered authorized without express family approval.[936] No compensation is permitted for organ donation.[937] Special laws govern gifts of tissue and blood and plasma.[938]

ii. Informed Consent

1011. *Expanded consent.* Both Germany and the common-law systems examined here have chosen an expanded version of informed consent (*erweiterte Zustimmungslösung*). Though organ donations are permitted only upon an affirmative expression of consent, the necessary approval may be given either by the donor or, after the donor's death, by others, particularly the deceased's relatives.

(A) GERMANY

1012. *Bodies.* Under German law, individuals may contractually provide that their bodies will go to science upon death.[939] Those responsible for the care of the deceased's body may make the gift only if it does not contradict the deceased's actual or presumed intent.[940]

1013. *Organs.* Organs, parts of organs, and tissue may be gifted from the body of a deceased person.[941] The drafters originally planned to adopt a presumed intent system. Partially due to concerns about constitutionality, however, the legislature

---

932. Law of 1 Apr. 1999 art. 3 pars. 3–4.
933. Abadie and Gay 606.
934. Law 27 Oct. 1979 art. 5 pars. 2–3.
935. Decree of 30 Dec. 1999 art. 10.
936. Abadie and Gay 602.
937. Decree of 30 Dec. 1999 art. 2 par. 1, art. 8.
938. Id. *Disposición final primera—Exclusiones* (citing to other applicable norms).
939. Staudinger (-Jickeli and Stieper) § 90 no. 34. The transaction is not technically constructed as a gift.
940. Id.
941. Law of 5 Nov. 1997 (TPG) § 1.

eventually chose an expanded version of informed consent.[942] Thus, in Germany, organs may be removed after death only if the donor has consented or if the deceased has not prohibited the gift and a close relative authorizes removal.[943] A minor can agree to organ donation at the age of sixteen. In fact, an organ donation made by a minor at any age is valid if it remains unrevoked when the minor turns sixteen.[944] The donor's consent or refusal is considered final. The next of kin has the right to be informed of an organ donation but may not revoke it. Some grounds that typically vitiate consent, such as mistake, do not render the organ donation invalid.[945]

Consent must be declared. The declaration is typically by means of a donor card, though there is no form requirement. The declaration is valid if made on a scrap of paper or even if only communicated orally.[946] Any discriminatory conditions in the organ gift are void.[947]

1014. *Expanded consent.* If no manifestation of intent by the donor can be located, information must be solicited from the next of kin regarding the deceased's intentions. If the next of kin is unaware of any statement by the deceased, that relative, after taking into account the deceased's probable intent (*mutmaßlicher Wille*), may consent to the gift.[948] In terms of next of kin, priority is given first to the spouse or life partner, and then, in order, to adult children, parents, adult siblings, and grandparents. Relatives have the right to decide only if they were in personal contact with the decedent during the two years prior to death. An adult who maintained a close personal relationship with the donor until the donor's death, such as a fiancé, has rights equivalent to the next of kin. If the decedent appointed a representative to make this decision, the agent takes the place of the next of kin. No form is required for the relative's declaration of gift, though it is usually made to the physician, who is required to record the conversation.[949] If the relative who has the right to make the gift makes no decision, no gift can

---

942. For an overview of the legislative history, see Schroth (-König) *Einleitung* nos. 3–6; Nickel et al. *Einführung* nos. 18–27. For a discussion of the constitutional questions, see Höfling and Rixen; Gutmann 4–10. A decision of the German Constitutional Court suggests that a presumed intent system would be constitutional, provided it guaranteed individuals the right to refuse. Schroth (-Schroth) § 4 nos. 4–5, referring to BVerfG 14 Oct. 1998, NJW 1999, 858.

943. Law of 5 Nov. 1997 (TPG) §§ 3–4; Staudinger (-Jickeli and Stieper) § 90 no. 36.

944. Schroth (-Schroth) § 3 no. 4.

945. Id. § 3 no. 10.

946. Id. § 3 no. 6.

947. Id. § 3 no. 11.

948. Law of 5 Nov. 1997 (TPG) § 4 par. 1; Schroth (-Schroth) § 4 nos. 11–34.

949. Schroth (-Schroth) § 4 no. 16.

be made.[950] Priority rules determine the rights of the relatives when some are not available or there is disagreement.[951]

1015. *Refusal.* Organ donation may also be refused. No form is required. The refusal is valid if jotted down on a piece of scrap paper or mentioned orally, though a refusal will not be inferred from the facts and circumstances.[952] A minor may declare a valid refusal at the age of fourteen.[953] Consent may also be revoked, but a revocation will not necessarily be interpreted as a refusal.[954]

(B) ENGLAND

1016. *Exception.* At common law, a dead body was not subject to ownership.[955] As a result, individuals were unable to issue binding instructions regarding the disposition of their bodies after death.[956] Still today, for public policy reasons, no one may dispose of a body by gift, even if it is one's own.[957] Nonetheless, English law permits individuals to consent to having their body parts used after death for a series of purposes, including transplants, public display, and research.[958] If the use is for public display or anatomical examination, consent must be made in writing and signed by the individual or signed at the individual's direction, in the presence of at least one witness. Consent is effective if made in a valid will.[959] When the donation is to be used for other purposes, appropriate consent includes the individual's own consent or refusal, expressed before death, the consent of a nominated representative,[960] and the consent of a *qualified person*. Qualified persons include a spouse, certain relatives, and friends of longstanding.[961] Consent from qualified persons must be obtained in the order of rank and is sufficient if one of the members of the rank consents. If a qualified person does not wish to make the decision or is unavailable or unable to do so, the decision passes to

---

950. Id. § 4 nos. 15, 40.

951. Law of 5 Nov. 1997 (TPG) § 4 par. 2; Schroth (-Schroth) § 4 nos. 41–50.

952. Schroth (-Schroth) § 3 no. 19.

953. Law of 5 Nov. 1997 (TPG) § 2 par. 2; Schroth (-Schroth) § 3 no. 20.

954. Schroth (-Schroth) § 3 no. 8.

955. ENGLAND: *Williams v Williams* (1881–1882) 20 Ch D 659, 662–665; *Foster v Dodd* (1867–1868) 3 QB 67, 77; UNITED STATES: *Meagher v. Driscoll*, 99 Mass. 281, 284 (1868); Bucklin 325–326.

956. *Williams v Williams* (1881–1882) 20 Ch D 659, 665.

957. 20 Halsbury part 1 sub Gifts no. 25.

958. Human Tissue Act of 2004 sec. 1 par. 1 lit. c. The purposes that require the donor's consent are listed in Schedule 1.

959. Id. sec. 3 pars. 3–5.

960. See id. sec. 4 for the requirements for nominated representatives.

961. Id. sec. 3 par. 6, together with sec. 27 par. 4.

a person of the following rank.[962] The rules with regard to consent regarding children are similar.[963]

(C) INDIA

1017. *Witnesses required.* Under Indian law, anyone eighteen years of age or older may agree to the removal of organs after death.[964] The authorization must be completed in writing and in the presence of at least two witnesses, at least one of whom must be a relative. If, before death, the individual neither granted such consent nor expressed objection, the person lawfully in possession of the dead body may authorize the gift, unless there is reason to believe that a near relative objects. Parents of a minor may consent after the minor's death.[965] In case of bodies unclaimed for forty-eight hours in a hospital or prison, organ donation may be authorized by the management of the institution, provided there is no reason to believe that a relative is likely to claim the body.[966]

(D) UNITED STATES

1018. *Uniform law.* Shortly after Dr. Christian Barnard's first successful heart transplant in 1967, uniform legislation was drafted for state adoption in the United States permitting organ donation. Anatomical gifts are now permitted in all American jurisdictions. The uniform law has recently been revised with the goal of increasing the number of organs available for transplant.[967] The number of individuals who now have the right to donate an organ from the donor, both before and after the donor's death, has been increased. The priority between these different individuals, together with their differing competencies in terms of authorization and revocation, creates a far more complex system than those adopted in other legal systems. The summary here can only suggest the basic principles.

(1) Consent

1019. *Donor designation.* American law attempts to respect the decedent's expressed preference. The system is thus known as *donor designation* or *first-person consent.* Nonetheless, during the donor's lifetime, the gift may be made not only by anyone old enough to apply for a driver's license, but also by a minor's parent or a donor's agent or guardian.[968]

---

962. Id. sec. 27 pars. 7–8.

963. Id. sec. 2.

964. Transplantation of Human Organs Act sec. 3 par. 2, together with sec. 2 par. f.

965. Id. sec. 3 par. 7.

966. Id. sec. 5.

967. The original version of the Uniform Anatomical Gift Act (1968) was adopted by all fifty states and the District of Columbia. The act was revised in 1987 and adopted by twenty-six states. The most recent revision was approved in 2006.

968. Uniform Anatomical Gift Act § 4 (2006).

1020. *Declaration.* A gift made before death must generally be declared in writing. The donor's authorization by statement or symbol on a driver's license or identification card is sufficient.[969] The statement or symbol represents an effective anatomical gift and not merely evidence of intent.[970] The gift may also be made by will, by a signed donor card, or by authorizing a statement to be included in a donor registry. If the donor is unable to sign, the document may be signed by another individual at the donor's direction, provided it is witnessed by at least two adults, at least one of whom is not a close relative, and who both have signed. The revocation or cancellation of the driver's license or identity card or the invalidation of the will containing the gift does not invalidate the organ donation. During terminal illness, the gift may also be made by any form of communication addressed to at least two adults, at least one of whom is not a close relative. The gift may be amended or revoked before the donor's death. A writing is generally required.[971] The document of gift need not be delivered during the donor's lifetime.[972] A statement of intent to be an organ donor does not result in the anatomical gift of the entire body, for which more specific language is required.[973]

1021. *By others.* An organ donation may also be made by others when the donor is at or near death, though of course it takes effect only if the donor dies.[974] The law establishes the priority of those authorized to make gifts from the decedent's body, including representatives who received the authority before the decedent's death, close relatives, the donor's guardian, a person who has the authority to dispose of the body, as well as any adult "who exhibited special care and concern for the decedent." Complex rules govern the numerous situations that may arise when one member of a class knows of an objection by another member of the same class or when some members of a class are not reasonably available for consultation. In contrast to prior law, coroners and medical examiners do not have authority to make organ donations from the bodies they examine.[975]

Gifts made by others in these circumstances may be made by a signed document of gift, by an electronic communication, as well as orally, provided the communication is immediately reduced to writing and signed by the individual receiving it.[976] Amendment and revocation may also take place orally.

1022. *Preclusive effect.* Despite the great need for organ donation, it seems that organs validly donated before death typically have not been removed until

---

969. Id. § 5.
970. Id. § 11 comment.
971. Id. § 6.
972. Id. § 13.
973. Id. Prefatory Note.
974. Id. § 9.
975. Id. § 22 and the comment.
976. Id. § 10.

consent has been obtained from the next of kin and it has been determined that no other close relative wished to object.[977] The latest version of the uniform law seeks to eliminate this practice. It emphasizes that an anatomical gift has preclusive effect. After the donor's death, no one may amend or revoke the gift.[978] If a person other than the donor has made an unrevoked gift, that also remains irrevocable.

(2) Refusal

1023. *Conclusive.* An individual's express refusal to make an organ donation is also binding.[979] The refusal may be made in a signed document, in a will, or, during a terminal illness, in any form of communication directed to at least two adults, at least one of whom is not a close relative. The refusal, in contrast to the gift, may generally be made only by the potential donor. It may be amended or revoked. The effect of a refusal, though not of a revocation, is to bar any other person from making an anatomical gift from the individual's body.

(3) Donees

1024. *Organizations.* The law specifies the permissible donees, which generally include hospitals, medical schools, organ procurement organizations, tissue and organ banks, and, in a rare case, the individual designated to receive the organ.[980] Express acceptance is not required, though a donee is prohibited from accepting if the gift is known to be invalid.[981] In most cases, because the donee's identity is unknown, donor and donee do not communicate before the donor's death.[982]

iii. Comparative Notes

1025. *Compelling need.* Legal systems respond to the compelling need for organ donation by facilitating gratuitous transfers of body parts for humanitarian purposes. The need seems to have increased with the years, and no system has been able to produce donations sufficient to satisfy the demand.[983] Thus, the expansive nature of the law governing anatomical gifts is understandable and appropriate. Nonetheless, from a technical point of view, it is worth mentioning that no legal system has successfully resolved the theoretical difficulties. Even more importantly, the ease of organ donation contrasts markedly with the protectionist regime that governs gifts of property.

---

977. Bucklin 324, 329, 337; Uniform Anatomical Gift Act § 8 comment (2006).
978. Uniform Anatomical Gift Act § 8 (2006).
979. Id. § 7.
980. Id. § 11.
981. Id. § 11 comment.
982. Id. § 13 comment.
983. Schroth (-König) Einleitung no. 1; Uniform Anatomical Gift Act, Prefatory Note (2006).

(A) THEORETICAL DIFFICULTIES

(1) Ownership

1026. *Property rights.* The first technical difficulty concerns the right to make a gift from the donor's body. It is everywhere assumed that only the owner can make a valid gift. It is also generally held that individuals have no property rights either in their own bodies or in the dead body of another.[984] Though American jurists occasionally mention the notion of property rights in this context,[985] the reference can only be metaphorical.[986] There is no conceptual basis in traditional notions of property to permit anyone to make a gift of a body or any of its elements.

German law bases organ transfer on a postmortem right of privacy (*postmortales Persönlichkeitsrecht*), which can be protected both by the individual and close relatives.[987] The rights involved are not considered property rights, and consent is not understood as a transactional declaration (*rechtsgeschäftliche Willenserklärung*).[988] The privacy concept properly names the concern. Yet it provides no conceptual justification for allowing anyone to make a gift of parts of a human body.

(2) Personal Right

1027. *Intuitu personae.* A second technical matter concerns the propriety of permitting the gift to be made by someone other than the individual whose body is concerned. (The law's vocabulary universally follows medical usage and considers the *donor* to be the dead body.) Even normal gifts of property are generally considered highly personal matters (*intuitu personae*). Thus, the law generally does not permit one person to make gifts for another. In German law, in fact, anatomical gifts are thought to express a highly personal decision (*höchstpersönliche Entscheidung des Organspenders*). Yet even in German law, third parties are permitted to make organ donations.

---

984. *State v. Powell*, 497 So.2d 1188, 1193 (Fla. 1986).

985. "Section 8(a) strips surviving family members of at least one stick in a bundle of property rights they might otherwise have under state law." Uniform Anatomical Gift Act § 8 comment (2006). See also *Brotherton v. Cleveland*, 923 F.2d 477, 478 (6th Cir. 1991) (dictum) ("we find that Deborah Brotherton has a protected property interest in her husband's corneas").

986. Most state courts that have confronted the issue term the interest in the remains of deceased relatives to be a *quasi-property right*. See *Brotherton v. Cleveland*, id., 923 F. 2d at 480 (collecting cases).

987. Schroth (-Schroth) § 3 no. 2; Nickel et al. § 3 no. 3, § 4 no. 3.

988. Schroth (-Schroth) § 3 no. 12.

(3) Protective Regime

1028. *No traditional protections.* Most surprisingly, those making anatomical gifts receive none of the protections accorded to donors of property.

1029. *Capacity.* To begin with, the restrictive capacity rules do not apply. When gifts of material possessions are at issue, unemancipated minors may not make gifts, other than customary presents, even with the assistance of their guardians. The minor's property, it has been said, is inalienable by gift.[989] Yet in most systems the law extends the right to make anatomical gifts to minors, even though (as is well understood) they might frequently be incapable of understanding the meaning of their decisions. In German law, minors are permitted to make these gifts at the age of sixteen. In the United States, a minor who is permitted to obtain a driver's license may make an anatomical gift. These minors are offered no particular guidance or assistance in reaching the decision.

1030. *Formation.* Moreover, none of the traditional gift formalities applies. Those civilian systems that require a notarial act for the gift of property impose no such requirement for anatomical gifts. Common law jurisdictions, which traditionally hold that no gift is valid without delivery, are willing to enforce anatomical gifts that cannot be delivered before the donor's death. In presumed intent jurisdictions, the gift is valid even if the donor has performed no affirmative act at all. Moreover, anatomical gifts are binding even though they are revocable until death, even in those systems that consider irrevocability to be an essential feature of a gift.

1031. *Consent.* The same jurisdictions that consider consent to be so crucial that a normal gift must be concluded before a notary are willing to presume consent for organ donation from the fact that no refusal was made before death, or in some cases from the mere fact that no such declaration could be found. Acceptance is also not subject to formalities and is always presumed. It also goes without saying that none of the usual grounds for revocation is available.

(B) INTERPRETING THE DIFFERENCES

1032. *Understandable flexibility.* The flexibility with which the various legal systems approach anatomical gifts is both appropriate and admirable. The social need is overwhelming and urgent. The law does what it can to facilitate these important transactions. Yet it remains surprising that the regime that governs anatomical gifts differs so dramatically from the law governing gifts of property. At first glance it seems inexplicable that so much protection has been erected around the gratuitous transfer of rights in material objects, even though they are often of limited monetary value, and yet the law accords no protection at all to gifts from a human body.

---

989. Supra no. 401.

1033. *Possible interpretation.* The differences are not due simply to tradition and historical inheritance. Over the past several decades, legislatures and courts have actively revised the law that applies both to gifts of property and to anatomical gifts. These provisions thus reflect current views. The differences are due rather to differing attitudes toward the two institutions. When gratuitous transactions are to be encouraged, the principles that universally govern organ donation demonstrate that those who draft the norms know how to favor them. The fact that gifts of material property are surrounded by such rigorous restrictions suggests that such gifts are often considered more dangerous and less valuable. *De lege ferenda* it might be worth examining whether the flexibility that prevails in the one field might be acceptable in the other.

C. ACCEPTANCE

1034. *Great variance.* In civilian systems, a gratuitous transfer is not complete until the donee accepts. However, requirements for a valid acceptance vary widely. In French law, a valid gift acceptance is far more involved than the acceptance of an offer to contract. In German law, gift acceptance is essentially governed by the rules of contractual acceptance. In the common law, gifts are generally perfected without acceptance.

1. France and Belgium

1035. *Substantive requirement.* In French law, acceptance is a substantive requirement for a valid gift (CC arts. 894, 932). Acceptance announced before the notary is recorded in the gift act.[990] A gift may also be accepted subsequently, at which point it must be done by notarial act and the notary must keep the original (*minute*) (CC art. 932). If the acceptance is irregular with regard to its form, such as when the donee attempts to accept orally or by means of a simple writing, the gift is absolutely void.[991] Gifts made by contract of marriage are an exception. Though they too must be accepted, the acceptance may be tacit, and they may not be attacked based on a lack of acceptance (CC art. 1087).

1036. *While both parties are alive.* In general, acceptance is permitted only while both parties are alive. Acceptance must occur while the donor has gift capacity and before any revocation.[992] Once the donee has died or lost capacity, the donee's heirs may not accept.[993] However, due to the direct right of action that

---

990. 5 Planiol and Ripert no. 360.
991. Id. nos. 373, 376.
992. 8 De Page no. 386.
993. Bufnoir 491.

arises when a third-party beneficiary contract is concluded, both the donee-beneficiary and the beneficiary's heirs may accept after the donor's death.[994]

a. Express Acceptance

1037. *Unique to gift law.* Acceptance must be *express* (CC art. 932 par. 1). This is a requirement unique to gift law and derives from the Ordinance of 1731. "Acceptance shall be express, and the judges shall take no cognizance of the circumstances of an alleged tacit or presumed acceptance, and this remains the case even if the donee was present during the notarial gift act, even if the donee signed the act, and even if the donee received possession of the property" (Ordinance art. 6). In other words, the donee's presence before the notary and signature on the gift act does not constitute an express acceptance. Moreover, surrounding circumstances, however clearly they suggest acceptance, do not replace an acceptance expressly stated.[995] As Delvincourt explained, the solemn nature of the gift means that nothing can be done by equivalent.[996] In practice, notaries add the words *who accepts* before the donee's signature, but it remains a question of fact whether the words used are sufficient.[997]

b. Notification

1038. *Dispute about form.* A gift is not effective with regard to the donor until the donor is notified of the acceptance (CC art. 932 par. 2). This requirement too is peculiar to gift law. If acceptance takes place in the original gift act, no further notification is necessary.[998] The form required for notification is a matter of dispute between French and Belgian jurists. The Civil Code does not specify.

French courts have decided that notification may occur by any means and is effective even if tacit or implied.[999] The matter is resolved by a factual inquiry about whether the donor actually learned of the acceptance.[1000] In one case, notification was presumed because the donor paid the gift annuity over several years.[1001] Belgian scholars argue that the French interpretation incorrectly focuses on the donor's knowledge and ignores the fact that *notification* is required.[1002] De Page suggested that the only method of notification consistent with solemn gift formalities is notification by bailiff's writ (*exploit d'huissier*).[1003] The Belgian

---

994. 8 De Page no. 388 bis.
995. Civ.¹ 3 Mar. 1998, *Bull. civ.* I no. 89, *Rev. trim. dr. civ.* 1998, 716 obs. Jean Patarin.
996. 1 Delvincourt 751 note 1 to page 239.
997. 5 Planiol and Ripert no. 361.
998. Id. no. 368.
999. Id. no. 369.
1000. Id. no. 368.
1001. Paris 31 July 1849, D. 1849 II 189, S. 1849 II 418.
1002. 8 De Page no. 455.
1003. Id.

courts have adopted an intermediate system that requires that notification be communicated by notarial act *(acte authentique)*.[1004]

c. Completion

1039. *Dispute.* Though there is no time limit for notification, there is disagreement about the effect of notification on the completion of the gift. French authors suggest that completion does not occur at the same moment for both donor and donee. A gift is complete as to the donee upon acceptance, while, for the donor, completion must await notification. Thus, the donee's death or incapacity after acceptance does not prevent notification, while the donor's death or incapacity before notification prevents completion. Moreover, even when the gift is concluded in a notarial act, the donor may revoke until learning of the acceptance.[1005] Belgian authors believe that it makes no sense to say that a gift transaction is completed as to one of the parties before it is completed as to both, especially when the one who is not yet bound, namely the donor, is the only one whose performance matters.[1006] The Belgian view is that the gift is not completed as to either party until notification. The death or incapacity of either the donor or the donee before that moment prevents the consummation of the gift.[1007]

1040. *Effects.* The donor's acts of disposition before notification—such as the creation of a security interest—are valid.[1008] Dispositions by the donee before notification are invalidated by the donor's revocation but otherwise remain valid.[1009]

d. Exceptions

1041. *Express acceptance not required.* Gifts excepted from the French law form requirements—manual, indirect, and disguised gifts—are also exempted from the technical requirements of gift acceptance.[1010] The donee generally must still accept, but the acceptance need not be express.[1011] Acceptance is especially important for the manual gift, which is perfected not by an exchange of consent but rather by the completion of what Bufnoir termed the special formality of transfer of possession.[1012]

1004. Gand 27 Feb. 1883, *Pas.* 1883 II 250.

1005. 5 Planiol and Ripert no. 370.

1006. 12 Laurent no. 264.

1007. 8 De Page no. 388.

1008. 5 Planiol and Ripert no. 371; 8 De Page no. 388.

1009. Req. 4 Mar. 1902, D. 1902 I 214, S. 1902 I 161 note Lyon-Caen.

1010. 8 De Page no. 449; 5 Planiol and Ripert nos. 420, 425 ter.

1011. Bufnoir suggested that the specific nature of the transaction should determine the type of acceptance required. Certain types of indirect gift, such as the refusal of a legacy *(renonciation à succession)*, might be considered unilateral. Bufnoir 505.

1012. Bufnoir 500.

It is generally accepted that donees who accept these gifts are not required to notify the donor.[1013] Dagot disagrees. He argues that, because acceptance is a substantive rather than a formal requirement, no gift takes effect without express acceptance and notification. The rule would also apply to gifts made by bank transfer and check.[1014] A life insurance policy, a typical indirect gift, should not be irrevocable until the beneficiary has accepted.[1015]

e. Justification

1042. *Protection.* The notification requirement protects a donor who, before learning of acceptance, changes plans and makes a different disposition of the property.[1016] Yet it is not clear why the protection is needed. In French law, when a contract is concluded at a distance, acceptance is effective upon dispatch.[1017] All offerors encounter this problem. It seems especially odd to provide extra protection for donors. Gifts, at least those without conditions, are usually accepted. Bufnoir found the requirement of express acceptance to be especially difficult to justify.[1018] De Page attributed gift acceptance rules to the "arbitrary and formalist law" that governs gratuitous transfers in the French system.[1019] "The Legislature considered the gift to be a dangerous act from several points of view .... It sowed a variety of obstacles in the way of its consummation."[1020] As for the requirement of express acceptance, "[T]here is *no* rational *basis* to the rule."[1021]

2. Italy

1043. *Need not be express.* Italian law generally follows French law with regard to gift acceptance. Acceptance must be accomplished in a notarial act, either in the gift act or subsequently (CC art. 782 par. 2). If the gift is accepted subsequently, the authors disagree about whether witnesses must be present at the notarial act.[1022] The case law seems to dispense with them.[1023] The Italian Civil Code of 1865 deleted the requirement of express acceptance.[1024] The current code has not

---

1013. 8 De Page no. 458.

1014. Dagot (2000) 1478–1479.

1015. Id. 1477. See also Coron and Lucet 692.

1016. 5 Planiol and Ripert no. 367; "Communication officieuse à la Section de législation du Tribunat" (10 Germinal XI [31 Mar. 1803]), in 12 Fenet 450; "Communication officielle au Tribunat" (3 Floréal XI [23 Apr. 1803]), in id. 596.

1017. Com. 7 Jan. 1981, *Bull. civ.* IV no. 14, *Rev. trim. dr. civ.* 1981, 849 obs. Chabas.

1018. Bufnoir 490.

1019. 8 De Page no. 391.

1020. Id.

1021. Id. no. 447 (emphasis in original).

1022. Compare Capozzi no. 332 par. a note 1481 and par. d (witnesses required) with Torrente 535–536 (witnesses not required).

1023. Cass. 6 Mar. 1943 no. 511, *Rep. Foro it.* 1943–1945 *Notaro* no. 14.

1024. CC art. 1057 par. 1 (1865).

restored it.[1025] Italian scholars insist that acceptance must be express in the sense that a tacit acceptance or one inferred from silence is insufficient,[1026] though an express statement of acceptance is also not required.[1027]

As in Belgian law, the gift is not perfected until the donor is notified.[1028] Some courts, followed by some scholars, hold that notification is meant in the technical sense it has in Italian procedural law,[1029] which requires notification to be carried out by a judicial official.[1030] Other courts, and other scholars, believe that the notification requirement means only that the donor must learn of the acceptance.[1031] The death of either party, or the incapacity of the donor before notification, prevents conclusion of the gift. A revocation posted before notification is valid.

1044. *Inconsistency.* The rules for gift acceptance are difficult to reconcile with the Italian Code's general principles. Nongift contracts that create obligations for only one party generally do not require acceptance.[1032] An offer to enter into such a contract is irrevocable as soon as the offeree learns of it. A contract is formed as long as the offeree does not reject the offer within a reasonable time.

1045. *Justification.* Torrente explained the rigorous gift law formalities as a means of achieving certainty amid inconstant emotions. "[G]ifts are tied to the play of sentiment, which is often more fickle than the equilibrium of interests on which, in general, other contracts are based. It is therefore important to fix with absolute certainty, in order to avoid the possibility of doubt, the precise moment at which the [gift] contract is completed."[1033]

3. Spain

1046. *More relaxed.* The Spanish rules governing gift acceptance are slightly more relaxed than the corresponding rules found in other Romanic systems. Nonetheless, acceptance is an essential feature of Spanish gift law. A gift produces no effect until it is accepted (CC art. 629). When movables are transferred

1025. CC art. 782 par. 2.

1026. Cendon art. 782 no. 4; Rescigno (-Carnevali) 543.

1027. Torrente (2006) 535; Cass. 16 Nov. 1981 no. 6057, *Rep. Foro it.* 1981 *Donazione* no. 5; Cass. 22 Oct. 1975 no. 3499, *Rep. Foro it.* 1975 *Donazione* no. 17.

1028. Cass. 14 July 1950 no. 1916, *Foro it.* 1951 I 316.

1029. Italian CCProc. art. 137.

1030. Torrente (2006) 536; Cass. 29 Nov. 1988 no. 6481, *Rep. Foro it.* 1988 *Donazione* no. 10.

1031. Cass. 24 Feb. 1960, *Giust. civ. Mass.* 1962, 2515.

1032. Italian CC art. 1333. Examples include two suretyship contracts (*fideiussione*, CC arts. 1936–1957, and *mandato di credito*, CC arts. 1958–1959), gratuitous agency (*mandato gratuito*; CC arts. 1703–1709), and a gratuitous bailment (*deposito non retribuito*; CC arts. 1766–1782).

1033. Torrente (2006) 538.

by manual gift, the code requires delivery but no other formalities. Tacit acceptance, it seems, is permissible.[1034] When movables are gifted by writing, acceptance is required in the same form (CC art. 632 par. 2). Acceptance of a gift of immovables must be by notarial act, either in the original gift act or separately (CC art. 633).[1035] Acceptance must occur during the donor's lifetime. If acceptance is by separate notarial act, the donor must be notified, and the fact of notification must be noted in both the gift act and the acceptance.[1036]

1047. *When effective.* Spanish thinking about the gift acceptance has been captivated by the coexistence, in the Spanish Civil Code, of two apparently irreconcilable provisions concerning the moment the gift becomes effective. According to one provision, a gift is perfected at the moment "the donor learns of the donee's acceptance" (CC art. 623). According to the other, "the gift does not bind the donor, nor produce any effect, except from the moment of acceptance" (CC art. 629).

Numerous attempts have been made to reconcile the two provisions or to demonstrate why one should be preferred to the other. The case law seems to hold that the gift has no efficacy until the donor learns of the acceptance.[1037] Some authors have reconciled the two provisions by distinguishing their sphere of application. Everyone agrees that gift acceptance is not effective until receipt. Therefore the principal distinction is between gifts accepted at the time the gift is made and those that are accepted thereafter.[1038] The second code provision would govern gifts of movables by delivery or gifts of immovables in which acceptance occurs in the original instrument. The first would apply to gifts of movables by writing or to gifts of immovables accepted in a separate instrument.[1039]

According to a more widely accepted view, one that finds support in the legislative history,[1040] the second provision renders the gift effective against third parties as of the moment of acceptance. In this view, the effect of the first provision is to declare that, despite acceptance, the donor may still revoke at any time before notification. In the language of the common law, the gift would be effective upon acceptance yet still subject to the condition subsequent of the donor's revocation before notification. One consequence is that the donor's death before notification would not invalidate the gift.[1041] Instead, because revocation could no longer take place, the gift would become irrevocable.

1034. CC art. 632; Albaladejo García art. 632 no. V.

1035. STS Civ. 3 Dec. 1988, RJ 9297.

1036. CC art. 633 par. 3.

1037. Paz-Ares Rodríguez (-Albaladejo García) art. 623 no. II.

1038. Casanovas i Mussons 1626–1627. Casanovas details the drafting history, which originated with the corresponding provisions of the French Civil Code.

1039. Diez-Picazo and Gullón 342–343.

1040. Lalaguna 275.

1041. Paz-Ares Rodríguez (-Albaladejo García) art. 623 no. IV.

This theory resembles the French view of the effect of acceptance and, as the Spanish scholars have pointed out, suffers from the same defects, particularly that it makes the gift effective as to the donee—who might begin to rely on it—but continues to permit the donor to revoke. As Gullón Ballesteros suggested, "[I]f the gift is complete, it is not revocable, and if it is revocable, that is an indication that, as yet, it has not been completed."[1042]

1048. *Unilateral disposition*. Rubio has reached the same result in a different manner. He conceives of the gift as a gratuitous unilateral act, a disposition of property from one patrimony to another.[1043] The role of acceptance in this construction is not to evidence a meeting of the minds, but rather to conclude the transfer. In this regard, the gift closely resembles transfers under a will. In both there is a unilateral disposition. In both a moment arrives after which revocation is no longer permitted. For the will, that moment is the testator's death. For the gift, it is notification of acceptance. The point of the two seemingly contradictory provisions would then be to indicate that the gratuitous transfer is effective upon acceptance, though revocable until notification. This view too has been criticized.[1044]

4. Germany

1049. *Mutual consent*. Acceptance is an essential feature of the gift in German law. As is constantly repeated, individuals may not be compelled to accept gifts against their wills.[1045] The acceptance requirement, and the need for mutual consent to which it testifies, is the principal reason German law characterizes the gift as a contract.[1046] In fact German legal scholars distinguish in the gift transaction two conceptually separate contracts. When they concur, the result in a completed gift. In addition to the transfer of title (*Verfügungsgeschäft*), German law requires an obligational contract (*schuldrechtliche Einigung*).[1047] This second contract consists of two elements—agreement regarding the transfer and agreement about the gratuitous character of the transaction.[1048]

1050. *Tacit acceptance possible*. In practice, these contractual transactions often occur at the same time. Acceptance is then often considered tacit.[1049] Acceptance was presumed in the following circumstances. The donor announced the intention to make a gift of real estate and the donee accompanied the donor

---

1042. 1 Gullón Ballesteros 76.
1043. Rubio 368–373.
1044. 2 Lacruz Berdejo no. 505 at 141 note 18 *in fine*.
1045. MünchKomm-BGB (-Kollhosser) § 516 no. 11; see also German CC § 333.
1046. Heck § 94 par. 3 lit. b. See infra no. 1337.
1047. MünchKomm-BGB (-Kollhosser) § 516 no. 11. See supra no. 747.
1048. Jauernig (-Mansel) § 516 no. 10.
1049. Id.

to the notary's office, where the necessary conveyancing formalities were completed.[1050]

1051. *Offer precedes acceptance.* Special rules apply when the gift disposition (*Zuwendung*), which is considered to constitute the offer, precedes acceptance.[1051] Outside the gift law context, this is the typical means of contract formation. In gift law, however, the exchange of consent in this manner brings into operation a number of exceptions to general contract principles. To begin with, the offeror in a nongift contract is usually bound only so long as is reasonably necessary for the offeree to respond.[1052] In contrast, the donor is bound by the offer of gift until the donee accepts or rejects.[1053] A special provision allows the donor to fix a reasonable time limit (*angemessene Frist*) within which the donee must respond (CC § 516 par. 2). There is no form requirement for fixing the time limit.[1054] Second, under the general rules of contract formation, silence does not constitute acceptance.[1055] In the case of an offer of gift, however, a donee who does not respond before the time limit has passed is deemed to have accepted (CC § 516 par. 2), even if the donee never learned of the time constraint.[1056] This type of acceptance is known in German law as a *fictitious declaration of will* (*fingierte Willenserklärung*) or *regulated silence* (*normiertes Schweigen*).[1057]

5. The Common Law

1052. *Acceptance presumed.* In common law systems, acceptance of a gift is generally presumed. The donee's intent is usually only relevant when there is an intent to disclaim (refuse) an executed gift.

a. India

1053. *Two schools.* There was once a divergence of views between two schools of Hindu law as to the necessity of gift acceptance. The *Dayabhaga* held that acceptance was not necessary, while *Mitakshara* held that it was.[1058] The statutory definition of the gift in Indian law now requires acceptance.[1059] The same provision

---

1050. RG 25 June 1925, RGZ III, 151.
1051. CC § 516 par. 2.
1052. Id. §§ 145, 147 par. 2.
1053. Staudinger (-Wimmer-Leonhardt) § 516 no. 192; MünchKomm-BGB (-Kollhosser) § 516 no. 44.
1054. Staudinger (-Wimmer-Leonhardt) id.
1055. Jauernig (-Jauernig) § 147 no. 4.
1056. Staudinger (-Wimmer-Leonhardt) § 516 no. 193.
1057. Jauernig (-Jauernig) vor § 116 no. 10.
1058. Mulla § 122 no. 6. The *Dayabhaga* is a twelfth-century treatise on the laws of inheritance followed in West Bengal and Assam until 1956. See Hindu Succession Act of 1956 sec. 4 par. a. The *Mitakshara*, another twelfth-century inheritance law treatise, is followed elsewhere in India.
1059. Transfer of Property Act § 122.

specifies that acceptance is valid only if made while both the donor and the donee are still alive and while the donor has gift capacity. The statute does not state that acceptance must be express. Islamic law also requires acceptance.[1060]

1054. *Inferred.* Whether a gift has been accepted is ascertained from the circumstances of the case.[1061] The amount of evidence needed to prove acceptance is slight. The courts are often willing to infer acceptance,[1062] for example, when the donee is aware of the gift and does not object.[1063] Acceptance may also be inferred from the donee's possession of the property, unless the donor and the donee share possession.[1064] Silence may be sufficient if the donee is aware of the gift and the gift is not subject to an obligation.[1065] Acceptance of tenanted property has been inferred from the donee's collection of rent.[1066] The mere fact that the donor delivered a deed of gift to the donee has been held to satisfy the acceptance requirement, provided that the deed is later stamped and registered as required by law.[1067] It is also possible to infer gift acceptance from acts performed prior to the execution of the deed.[1068] Nonetheless, the case law does not dispense with the requirement. A finding of acceptance is always required. Though the dedication to an idol of land for the construction of the idol's temple is valid without acceptance under Hindu law,[1069] the idol's lack of the capacity to accept[1070] makes it incomplete under Indian law without registration.

1055. *Effect of acceptance.* One effect of acceptance is to alleviate the effect of the strict formalities required for the gift disposition. When the donee has accepted the deed of gift by signature, only the donor may challenge the gift for lack of delivery.[1071] Another effect is interpretative. If two gifts, one of which is subject to an obligation, are made to the same person as part of the same transaction, acceptance operates acceptance of the whole.[1072] The donee cannot repudiate the

---

1060. Fyzee 218.

1061. *Lakshmi Amma Kalliyani Amma v. Kunji Pillai Amma Kutty Amma,* AIR (41) 1954 TC 348, 349, ILR (1953) TC 1121 (HC).

1062. Mulla § 122 no. 6.

1063. *Lingiah v. Sidamma,* 1 Karn LJ 34 (1982).

1064. *Bancha Bhol v. Saria Bewa,* AIR (60) 1973 Orissa 18, 21 (HC).

1065. *Narayani Bhanumathi v. Lelitha Bhai* (1973) Ker LT 961, 962, (1973) Ker LJ 354 (HC).

1066. *Kolandiyil Ammad v. Changaran,* AIR (50) 1963 Kerala 344 (HC).

1067. *Purna Chandra Chakrabarty v. Kalipada Roy* (1942) 201 IC 557, (1942) AC 386.

1068. *Julkanti Krishnamurthi v. Appalarajugari Venkata Ramanaiah* (1958) 2 Andh WR 343, 347, AIR (45) 1958 AP 213.

1069. Gour § 122 no. 38; *Bhupati Nath Smrititirtha v. Ram Lal Maitra* (1909) ILR 37 Cal 128, 141–142, 161 (FB). See supra no. 474.

1070. *Pallayya v. Ramavadhanulu,* (1903) 13 MLJR 364 (HC).

1071. *Tirath v. Manmohan Singh,* AIR 1981 Punjab 174.

1072. Gour § 122 no. 39.

portion coupled with the obligation and accept the remainder. The donee may accept one and disclaim the other only if the two gifts are distinct. Characterization depends on the donor's intent.

b. England

1056. *Presumed.* English law presumes acceptance. In fact the rule exceeds the technical limits of a presumption. It applies whether or not the donee has learned of the gift. The presumption can be overcome only by a finding that the donee disclaimed the gift. "It was settled as long ago as the time of Lord Coke that the acceptance of a gift by a donee is to be presumed until his dissent is signified, even though the donee is not aware of the gift."[1073] New Zealand courts apply the same principle.[1074] The rule suggests that the gift is complete upon a proper disposition. No acceptance is needed. "[W]here there is a transfer of property to a person, even though it carries with it some obligations which may be onerous, it vests the property in him at once before he knows of the transfer, subject to his right when informed of it to say, if he pleases, 'I will not take it.'"[1075]

1057. *Disclaimer.* As in other legal systems, English law does not compel anyone to accept a repugnant gift.[1076] Disclaimer may be made once the donee becomes aware of the gift. Once made, the disclaimer cannot be withdrawn.[1077] Because a disclaimer operates by way of avoidance and not by disposition, a disclaimer need not be in writing, even with respect to a gift that can only validly be made by writing.[1078]

c. United States

1058. *Acceptance presumed.* Though a gift, even a purely beneficial one, is not valid without acceptance in American law, acceptance is almost universally presumed.[1079] The gift takes immediate effect upon a proper disposition, always subject to a later disclaimer.[1080] The presumption of acceptance applies even to donees who are infants or who lack the capacity to contract, as well as to the

---

1073. *London and County Banking Co Ltd v London and River Plate Bank* (1888) 21 QBD 535, 541.

1074. NEW ZEALAND: *Irvin v. Brookes* [1937] NZLR 73, 13 NZLJ 20 (SC).

1075. *Standing v Bowring* (1886) LR 31 Ch D 282, 288 (CA); see also *Siggers v Evans* (1855) 5 El & Bl 367, 3 CLR 1209.

1076. 20 Halsbury part 1 sub Gifts no. 51.

1077. Id.

1078. *In re Paradise Motor Co Ltd* [1968] 2 All ER 625 (CA).

1079. Brown § 7.14. See Georgia C Ann. § 44-5-81; *Winsor v. Powell*, 497 P.2d 292, 304 (Kan. 1972). According to the Restatement (Third), acceptance, though required, is normally presumed. Restatement (Third) of Property (Wills and Other Donative Transfers) § 6.1 b and comment i.

1080. Brown § 7.14.

donee of a gift delivered through an intermediary. It often applies even when the donee learns of the gift only after the donor's death.[1081] The presumption applies even if, as a consequence of the gift, the donee becomes liable for governmentally imposed costs, such as those for environmental cleanup or historical preservation,[1082] though it does not apply to gifts that are coupled with an obligation. "If the subject matter of the gift carries with it a liability of some kind, as when the transfer is part sale and part gift, or the donee is required to pay off a lien against the subject matter of the gift, the gift is not complete until the donee has accepted the gift and the attendant responsibilities."[1083] Moreover the presumption probably does not apply if the donee is aware of the gift but has hesitated or acted equivocally.[1084]

Courts are occasionally willing to presume acceptance of a gift coupled with an obligation. In one case, the gift was subject both to the donee's assumption of a mortgage on the property and the donee's agreement to convey other land back to the donor.[1085] Moreover, the donee did not learn of the gift, and therefore was unable to accept, until after the donor's death. Due to the gift's onerous nature, acceptance would normally have been required and would normally have been ineffective after the donor's death. The court however presumed acceptance. As Brown remarked, the donee, not the court, should decide whether the gift is onerous.[1086] The presumption of acceptance is designed to further the donor's aims and to assist a donee who is unaware of the gift.[1087] One line of American cases holds that the presumption does not apply when the donee actually knows of the gift and neither accepts nor repudiates.[1088]

1059. *Disclaimer.* Disclaimer of donative transfers is now governed in twelve states by the Uniform Disclaimer of Property Interests Act. Under this uniform act, a disclaimer of a property interest must be made in writing.[1089] There is no time limit. The only general bar to disclaimer is acceptance.[1090] A proper disclaimer will, in most cases, keep the property from the donee's creditors.

1081. *Halisey v. Howard,* 172 A.2d 379 (Conn. 1961); *Estate of Tardibone,* 94 N.Y.S.2d 724, 726 (Sur. Ct. 1949); *Scherer v. Hyland,* 380 A.2d 698, 702 (N.J. 1977).

1082. Restatement (Second) of Property (Donative Transfers) § 32.3 comment e (1992).

1083. Id. § 31.1 comment l (1992).

1084. Brown § 7.14 at 129.

1085. *Taylor v. Sanford,* 193 S.W. 661 (Tex. 1917).

1086. Brown § 7.14 note 13.

1087. Id. § 7.14.

1088. *Mahoney v. Martin,* 83 P. 982 (Kan. 1905).

1089. Uniform Disclaimer of Property Interests Act § 5 par. c. For a critique of the Act, see Hirsch.

1090. Uniform Disclaimer of Property Interests Act § 13.

d. Justification

1060. *Usually accepted.* The reason for the common law acceptance rules was stated long ago. "[T]here is a strong intendment of law, that for a man to take an estate it is for his benefit, and no man can be supposed to be unwilling to do that which is for his advantage."[1091] At least for non-onerous gifts, the position seems to have merit. Most purely beneficial gifts are accepted. Social custom suggests that gifts generally should not be refused. "No man ought to look a given horse in the mouth."[1092]

D. PERFECTION

1061. *Additional formalities.* Some legal systems distinguish between the formalities required to complete the gift as between the donor and the donee and those additional formalities necessary to perfect the gift as against third parties.

1. France and Belgium

1062. *General rule.* In French law, completion of the formalities prescribed for disposition and acceptance immediately transfers all rights in the property to the donee. Delivery of the property is not required (CC art. 938).[1093] However, perfection with regard to third parties often requires a further act of publicity.[1094] The publicity involved is generally the same as would be required if the transfer were not gratuitous. Most conveyances of rights in real property are not effective (*opposable*) against third parties unless they have been recorded.[1095] When movables are gifted by solemn act, delivery is required.[1096] Perfection of assignments requires either notification (*signification*) or acceptance in a formal act.[1097] Order paper must be endorsed, bearer paper delivered.[1098]

1063. *Special immovables.* Special rules apply to the recordation of some immovables when the transfer results from a gift. During the French ancien régime, all gifts, unless specially excepted, were subject to registration (*insinuation*) to

---

1091. *Thompson v Leach* (1690) 2 Vent 198, 203, 86 ER 391, 394 (KB), rev'd on other grounds, (1692) 2 Vent 208, 86 ER 397 (HL).
1092. Heywood 13; Apperson 229.
1093. Flour and Souleau no. 134.
1094. 5 Planiol and Ripert no. 462; Flour and Souleau no. 135.
1095. FRANCE: Decree of 4 Jan. 1955, arts. 28 no. 1 lit. a, 30 no. 1; CC art. 2426 par. 1 (privileges and mortgages); Marty, Raynaud, and Jestaz nos. 748, 757; BELGIUM: Law of 16 Dec. 1851 arts. 1, 82.
1096. CC art. 1141.
1097. CC art. 1690.
1098. 7 Planiol and Ripert nos. 1136–1138.

protect family and heirs.[1099] Under the Directory, an additional recordation requirement was imposed for conveyance of rights in real property capable of serving as security (*susceptibles d'hypothèques*).[1100] At that point gifts were subject to a double recordation requirement. The insinuation requirement from the Ordinance, which was still in force, required registration with the clerk of the local court.[1101] In addition, if the gift involved rights capable of serving as security, they were to be recorded in the mortgage office.[1102] The Code Napoleon, over Tronchet's objection, dropped the insinuation requirement as applied generally to all gifts but maintained the recordation requirement for property subject to mortgage (art. 939). The code did not generally require recordation of transfers of real property. Recording was first required by the Recording Act of 1855, which was redrafted in 1955. However, the Recording Acts have not superseded the code's special rules requiring recordation of gifts of property subject to mortgage.

1064. *Recordation.* In French law today, perfection of rights in property subject to mortgage requires recordation of the formal act containing the gift, of the donee's acceptance, and of the donee's notification to the donor (CC art. 939).[1103] Recording is to take place in the district where the property is located. Failure to record may be invoked by any person with an interest, except those charged with carrying out the recording and their successors, as well as the donor, the donee, and their heirs (CC art. 941).[1104] As a statutory matter, the category of third parties who may invoke the failure to record is much broader for gifts than for other transfers of real property.[1105] However, the case law does not unanimously adhere to the statutory distinction. While one chamber of the French Cassation Court has adopted the broad interpretation,[1106] two other chambers restrict the gift law provision to coincide with the rules governing the failure to record

---

1099. Supra no. 743. For the history of the registration requirement, see Bufnoir 76–79, 129–132.

1100. Law of 11 Brumaire VII art. 26. Rights capable of serving as security include full title, a usufruct, an emphyteusis (*emphytéose*), and surface rights (*superficie*). FRANCE: C Nap. art. 2118; BELGIUM: Law of 16 Dec. 1851 art. 45.

1101. Law of 22 Frimaire VII art. 72.

1102. 3 Mazeaud (-Picod) nos. 650, 722; 7 De Page no. 978.

1103. 7 De Page no. 980.

1104. Decree of 4 Jan. 1955, art. 30 par. 2; 3 Planiol and Ripert no. 660.

1105. Compare CC art. 941 with Decree of 4 Jan. 1955, art. 30 no. 1. Under the Recording Act, a failure to record may be invoked only by those who have acquired competing rights to the same property from the same transferor. The Recording Act confirms that CC art. 941 continues to govern the failure to record a gift transfer. Decree of 4 Jan. 1955 art. 30 no. 2.

1106. Civ.¹ 19 Oct. 1966, D.S. 1967, 77 note J. Mazeaud; see Marty, Raynaud, and Jestaz no. 783.

nongratuitous conveyances.[1107] Gifts of present property between spouses are subject to the recording requirement—as they were even when they were revocable.[1108] However, gifts of future property between spouses, because the property is not determinable at the time of the gift, need not be recorded.[1109]

1065. *Justification.* To De Page, these rigorous recording provisions, together with the broad definition of those who may invoke them, suggest a bias against gift giving.[1110] According to Marty and Raynaud, these provisions "are animated by a sentiment of hostility towards gifts and tend much less toward protecting third-party purchasers and more toward protecting the donor's family and creditors. For that reason the sanctions for a failure to record are so different."[1111] Other authors, however, find that the restrictions represent a proper balance between the interests of the donor's creditors and the interests of those who have benefited from the gratuitous transfer.[1112]

1066. *Belgian law.* Under Belgian mortgage law, all transfers of rights to real property, whether gratuitous or onerous, are perfected by recordation.[1113] Belgian scholars believe that these recording provisions tacitly abrogated the Civil Code's special recording regime for gifts.[1114] Gift transfers are now subject to general recording principles.[1115] In this regime, the failure to record can be invoked only by transferees in good faith.[1116]

2. Other Civilian Systems

1067. *General principles.* In other civilian systems, perfection of gift transfers is governed by general principles. In Italian law, for example, gifts are perfected in

---

1107. Soc. 17 Oct. 1958, D. 1959, 465 note Savatier; Civ.³ 17 June 1980, J.C.P. 1981 II 19584 note Dagot.

1108. 7 De Page no. 982.

1109. Véron 100.

1110. It must be admitted that, since Antiquity, gifts have not been favored. The legislator finds them suspect because they most often result in despoiling families or benefit outsiders who do not always owe these benefits to worthy motives. One of the procedures imagined to combat gifts was to subject them to publicity, in the hope that many a donor would change course when required to bring their dealings into the light of day.

7 De Page no. 978.

1111. Marty, Raynaud, and Jestaz no. 778.

1112. Four and Souleau no. 135 *in fine.*

1113. Law of 16 Dec. 1851 art. 1.

1114. 3 Baugniet and Genin bk. 6 no. 212; 7 De Page no. 979.

1115. 7 De Page nos. 978–986, 1047–1048.

1116. Law of 16 Dec. 1851 art. 1 par. 1; 3 Baugniet and Genin bk. 6 no. 212. A third party with actual notice is not in good faith. Civ. 19 Mar. 1965, *Pas.* 1965 I 761 and note 1.

the same manner as nongratuitous transfers—delivery for movables[1117] and recording for immovables[1118] and movables subject to registration.[1119]

3. Common Law

1068. *Rare cases.* The common law only rarely requires additional formalities to render a fully executed gift effective *ergo omnes*. The Virginia Code provides that a gift effectuated by deed, even a gift of movables, is not effective against third parties until it is recorded.[1120]

E. RENUNCIATION

1069. *France.* A donee may wish to renounce a gift acceptance that was made by notarial act. The French courts do not agree on the form required. In principle, French gift law imposes an *equal dignities* rule on renunciation (*renonciation*). It must be done in the same form as the acceptance.[1121] Because title to the gift property is transferred upon acceptance and notification, renunciation is actually a return gift and is generally effective only if completed in the required formalities.

1070. *Exceptions.* However, some renunciations are valid without formalities.[1122] Grimaldi has compared the renunciation of acceptance to the donor's renunciation of rights reserved in the gift act. Transfer restrictions or a life annuity benefiting the donor may be renounced by a simple signed writing.[1123] The code imposes no form on such renunciations, even though they operate a transfer (to the donee) without a counterpart. Some scholars argue that renunciation, a neutral act, constitutes an indirect gift that is exempt from form requirements. For that reason as well, the donee's renunciation should also be valid without form. To reconcile the different positions, Grimaldi has proposed a dual solution. For gifts concluded by notarial act, renunciation must be completed in the same form. For other gifts, a simple writing should suffice.[1124] However, Grimaldi's position has not yet found an echo in the case reports.

1117. CC art. 1155.
1118. CC arts. 2643, 2644.
1119. CC arts. 2683, 2684; Torrente (2006) 613 note 1.
1120. Virginia C Ann. § 55–96 par. A no. 1.
1121. Civ.[1] 7 June 2006, *Bull. civ.* I no. 289, *Rép. not. Defrén.* 2006 art. 38496 at 1838 obs. Bertrand Gelot, D. 2007, 2134 obs. Marc Nicod.
1122. Michel Grimaldi, obs. to Civ.[1] 3 Jan. 2006, *Rev. trim. dr. civ.* 2007, 613.
1123. Civ.[1] 20 Feb. 2007, D. 2007, 2134 obs. Marc Nicod.
1124. Michel Grimaldi, obs. to Civ.[1] 3 Jan. 2006, *Rev. trim. dr. civ.* 2007 at 614.

7. REVOCATION

1071. *Distinct principles.* This chapter examines two ideas central to the law of gifts, the *general* and the *special* principles of irrevocability. Despite the similar names, the two principles are unrelated. Nonetheless the two concepts are traditionally examined together. The reason seems to be that the use of similar terms to name different concepts creates confusion, and that confusion is best dispelled when they are contrasted with one another.

1072. *General principle.* As a general rule in modern legal systems, contracts and other legal acts may not be unilaterally revoked once they have been validly concluded. This general principle of irrevocability also applies to gifts.[1] Civilian legal systems recognize several exceptions to the general principle. In particular circumstances, they grant the donor the unilateral right to revoke an executed gift. Those exceptions are examined here.

In many systems revocation is permitted if the donee's conduct manifests serious ingratitude. Revocation may also be available if, after making the gift, the donor becomes impoverished. In Romanic legal systems, revocation is permitted upon the birth of a child. In fact, until very recently, the birth of a child in France revoked many gifts by operation of law. Finally, some gifts between spouses are revocable in French law. In the common law, gifts are not unilaterally revocable for these reasons. This chapter examines each of these exceptions to the general principle. The most common ground for the unilateral revocation of an executed gift, namely the failure of a condition, is not examined here. The failure of a condition in a gift involves many of the complex questions raised by the doctrine of conditions in contract law. There is no room to explore them here.

1073. *Special principle.* The special principle of irrevocability relates to a different problem, namely the requirements for a valid gift. In many systems, a purported gift is invalid if the donor reserves the right to revoke some or all of the gift. The special principle of irrevocability is special in the sense that it is specific to

---

1. FRANCE: "Generally inter vivos gifts are irrevocable from the moment of execution.— The donee who has been given possession can return it to the donor only by means of a new gift clothed in the proper formalities." 1 Pothier tit. 15 no. 97. UNITED STATES: "[A] gift which is absolute and made voluntarily with a full understanding of its effect cannot be revoked by the donor, either by his act alone or with the aid of a judicial tribunal." *Hill v. Warner, Berman & Spitz*, 484 A.2d 344, 350 (N.J. App. Div. 1984).

gift law. Though contract law also voids illusory contracts—those that are entirely subject to the will of one party—gift law is considerably more restrictive. The special principle of irrevocability is perhaps best be understood as an exception, or a set of exceptions, to the principle of freedom of contract. If the gift is deemed to be revocable, the gift either fails to come into existence or is held to be void. Both civil and common-law systems generally recognize this principle. The special principle, because it concerns validity, is examined first.

A. THE SPECIAL PRINCIPLE OF IRREVOCABILITY

1074. *Validity.* In many jurisdictions, a gift is valid only if it is irrevocable, which means that the donor does not have the ability to alter or revoke the gift at will. The matter is difficult because a gift may be considered revocable even if the donor has not expressly reserved the right to revoke.

1. France and Belgium

1075. *Donner et retenir.* In French law, the special principle of irrevocability is traditionally stated in terms of the maxim "To give and retain is not permitted" (*Donner et retenir ne vaut*).[2] The maxim's meaning has greatly evolved over time.

a. Evolution

1076. *Origins.* The origin of the maxim appears to be a late Roman text that considered a gift to be valid only if there was actual delivery.[3] Medieval jurists retained the rule. They believed that permissiveness regarding gift giving encouraged overreaching and fraud. They also believed that the maxim provided useful protection for the heirs. At the time, the customary forced share protected against disinheritance by will but did not impede the donor's ability to alienate by gift. Medieval jurists believed they could limit gift giving by validating gifts only when the donor was willing to part with possession before death.

1077. *Customary law.* The maxim *Donner et retenir* was introduced into many customary laws[4] and noted by Loysel.[5] The force of the rule was that no gift was

---

2. For the history of the maxim, see 3 Planiol nos. 2592–2597. See also 5 Planiol and Ripert no. 427; 8 De Page no. 548.

3. "And so, in order to prevent use of force and stealth, let delivery follow immediately upon the gift, when the neighbors have been summoned and all the witnesses by whose faith the delivery will be verified have been employed." Const. of Constantine [A.D. 316], in Cod. Th. 8, 12, 1.

4. Customs of Paris arts. 273–274, in 3 Dumoulin (1691) 24–27; 1 Pothier tit. 15 no. 18.

5. 2 Loysel no. 659 at 92.

valid if the donor retained possession. If the donor had not parted with possession before death, the gift was void and could be claimed by the heirs.

1078. *Change of meaning.* Two related developments caused the meaning of the maxim to change. First, consensualist theories began to weaken the reliance on contractual formalities, even before the revolution. In line with this development, the delivery requirement was replaced by simple confirmation in the gift document that seisin (*ensaisinement*) had been transferred (*tradition feinte*). The second development was a reaction to the first. Jurists who sought to limit the practice of gift giving were increasingly deprived of the dissuasive force of the mandatory transfer of possession. As a result, customary law reinterpreted the maxim. Under the revised reading, the maxim was understood to prevent donors from reserving the unilateral right to revoke the gift. Gift contracts were considered void if they contained either clauses directly permitting the donor to revoke or conditions or other terms permitting the same result to be accomplished indirectly.

1079. *D'Aguesseau.* According to d'Aguesseau, the true meaning of the maxim was that an inter vivos gift was valid only if the donee became the indisputable owner (*propriétaire incommutable*) of the gift property.[6] In his Ordinance of 1731, d'Aguesseau prohibited two indirect methods of revocation. First, the Ordinance invalidated the gift of property that did not belong to the donor at the moment of the gift. It also voided gifts of both present and future property, even as to the property the donor then possessed (art. 15). "[I]t would nonetheless be unjust for the donor to abuse freedom of contract to the point of canceling or diminishing the gift by means of subsequent transfers that would depend exclusively on the donor's discretion."[7] The second prohibition invalidated any gift by which the donor required the donee to pay expenses or debts other than those that existed at the time of the gift.[8] Otherwise, "by increasing debts at the donor's discretion, the donor may exhaust or even entirely cancel, and thus indirectly revoke, an act that could not be revoked directly."[9]

1080. *Civil Code.* This evolution is embodied in the Civil Code. To begin with, the triumph of consensualism caused the drafters to reject the original import of the maxim *Donner et retenir*. Title to property passes at the conclusion of the gift act (art. 938). Delivery, even a *tradition feinte*, is not required. Second, the code expressly codifies the special principle of irrevocability (art. 894). At the time the

---

6. D'Aguesseau, Letter no. 290 of 25 June 1731, in 9 d'Aguesseau 360 at 364.
7. D'Aguesseau, Letter no. 293 of 30 June 1731, in 9 d'Aguesseau 370 at 377 (to the Parlement of Toulouse).
8. Ordinance art. 16.
9. D'Aguesseau, Letter no. 290 of 25 June 1731, in 9 d'Aguesseau 360 at 364.

code was drafted, the principle had come to mean that a valid gift may not contain a clause permitting the donor to cancel or reduce the gift at will.[10]

b. Justifications

1081. *Pothier.* Pothier justified the prerevolutionary form of the rule as a means to protect the donor.

> It is easily apparent why our law has provided that both delivery (*tradition*) and irrevocability are required for a valid gift. The spirit of our French law tends to keep property in the family and pass it to the heirs .... [S]ince it would be impossible to prevent the exercise of the right individuals naturally possess to dispose of what belongs to them by making inter vivos gifts, our law has decided in this regard, while respecting this right, nonetheless to limit it by rendering its exercise more difficult. It is for this reason that the law provides that no one may validly make a gift unless, at the moment of doing so, the donor parts with the property and renounces forever the possibility of making use of it. In this way the natural attachment that individuals have for their possessions, and the distaste they have for losing their property, will dissuade them from making gifts.[11]

1082. *Contemporary justifications.* Four justifications are typically advanced in France today to justify the special principle of irrevocability.[12] First, a gift act that contains a clause permitting free revocability is essentially a testamentary transfer. It should not take effect without the protections accorded by successions law. However, it is difficult to see the force of this justification. In French law, wills may be made in either holograph or mystical form (arts. 970, 976), neither of which involves a substantive consultation with a notary.

Second, the special principle furthers gift law's goal of discouraging gift giving and protecting donors from sudden urges of generosity. However, in an expert examination of the foundation (*fondement*) of CC art. 931, Xavier Lagarde has noted that donor protection has been used indiscriminately to justify both revocability and irrevocability.[13] On the one hand, French scholars argue that the *irrevocability* requirement protects donor consent by compelling them to confront the actual consequences of their gifts. On the other hand, the *revocability* of gifts between spouses has always been justified as a means to protect donors from momentary excesses of generosity (by allowing them to rescind the

---

10. The principle was already present in the thinking of the National Convention. See Decree of 22 Ventôse II no. 16.

11. 8 Pothier, *Donations* no. 65.

12. 8 De Page no. 550.

13. Lagarde 28.

transfer when their emotions cool). Lagarde concluded that the irrevocability requirement can have nothing to do with protecting the donor.[14]

Third, easy revocability would limit the free circulation of property because, in some cases, the donor may be able to trace the gift into the hands of third parties. The statement is accurate. The disadvantage is clear. Nonetheless, this fact cannot serve to justify special irrevocability. French successions law generally permits gifts that exceed the disposable share to be recovered, at times even those that have found their way into the hands of third parties.[15]

Finally, the donor who may freely revoke, it is argued, may use the threat of revocation to pressure the donee.[16] This is a plausible justification. Though the gift is gratuitous, the donee still owes a duty of gratitude, and the bounds of that duty are difficult to determine. "It is important to remember that whoever owes nothing also owes everything."[17] If gifts were revocable, the donor might threaten the donee with rescission unless more gratitude were forthcoming. In other words, special irrevocability seems designed to prevent the donee from becoming the donor's servant. Though the thought is coherent, the broad prohibition seems a somewhat excessive means to achieve so speculative a goal.

c. Critique

1083. *Questionable value.* Planiol believed that special irrevocability had outlived its usefulness.[18] The rule was of value in the ancien régime, at a time when no other means was available to protect the family from the donor's excesses. Today, given the extensive protections anchored in successions law, the rule's only remaining effect is to protect donors from themselves, which is a goal of questionable value when directed at adults with full legal capacity. Other scholars have also suggested that the principle should be abrogated.[19] An additional difficulty with the principle is that those in the know can easily circumvent its prohibitions. "The truth is that, in many ways, special irrevocability has become a scarecrow: it doesn't bother the larger animals since, when necessary, they know how to avoid it."[20] Those who today support special irrevocability tend to recognize that it may be idiosyncratic to the particular cultural situation prevailing in countries of the French legal tradition. "It is essentially an *artificial* rule, related to what we have called the regulation of gratuitous transfers, and can only be

---

14. Lagarde 42–43.
15. CC art. 924-4; see C Nap. arts. 929–930.
16. For an elaboration of this argument, see Lagarde 42.
17. Id. 42.
18. 3 Planiol no. 2597.
19. Malaurie and Aynès no. 431.
20. Brenner 110.

justified, especially historically, by this goal. The traditional nature of our law being such, it is difficult to think it away completely."[21]

d. Construction

1084. *Substantive rule.* Special irrevocability is a substantive rule of French gift law. It governs all gifts, even those exempted from the form requirements, though those gifts between spouses that remain revocable and those made in a marriage settlement are exempt.[22] The Civil Code expressly mentions a number of clauses that violate the principle of irrevocability and therefore render a gift void. The field is replete with subtle distinctions.

i. Future Property

1085. *Specific prohibition.* As discussed above, the code specifically prohibits gifts of future property (*biens à venir;* CC art. 943).[23] The concern is that, if the property is not in the donor's patrimony at the moment of the gift, the donor might revoke the gift by refusing to procure it. If a gift contains both present and future property and the gift is divisible, only the gift of future property is void.[24] Irrevocability affects gifts of future property in another way as well. If the donor attempts to gift the same property more than once, the subsequent transfers even if secured, do not take priority over the first, even if unsecured. Any other result would violate the spirit of irrevocability. Subsequent donees become the donor's creditors in the order the gifts were made.[25]

ii. The Donor's Discretion

1086. *Will of the donor.* The principle of irrevocability also prohibits a gift that is made under a condition that depends solely on the donor's will (*condition potestative;* CC art. 944).[26] The code prohibits similar conditions in onerous transactions (CC art. 1174), but the gift law prohibition is broader. A *pure* condition of will (*condition purement potestative*)—"I agree to perform, if I then so desire"—is a condition precedent that renders any contract void. A *simple* condition of will (*condition simplement potestative*)—"I will sell you my house, if I decide

---

21. 8 De Page no. 550.

22. Id. no. 551. For the revocability of gifts of future property between spouses, see infra no. 1301.

23. Supra nos. 359–365; 8 De Page no. 237; 5 Planiol and Ripert no. 439.

24. Under the Ordinance of 1731, gifts containing both present and future property were void even as to the present property and even if the property had been delivered. Ordinance art. 15.

25. Req. 7 Mar. 1860, D. 1860 I 153; 5 Planiol and Ripert no. 442. For a forceful presentation of the view that the *subsequent* donee should prevail, see note to Req. 4 Mar. 1860 id. For priority questions with regard to the claims of creditors other than subsequent donees, see 5 Planiol and Ripert id.

26. 8 De Page nos. 314–316, 555; 5 Planiol and Ripert nos. 431–432.

to move"—is permissible in all but gratuitous acts. Moreover, onerous acts are valid if the pure condition is a condition subsequent, whereas gratuitous acts are void if they contain such conditions, whether precedent or subsequent.[27] The contractual si praemoriar clause, which returns the gift to the donor if the donee predeceases, is permissible.[28] It does not depend on the donor's will and therefore does not violate the principle of irrevocability.

1087. *Rules of interpretation.* The rules of interpretation are also altered when these conditions are contained in a gift. Normally, a condition contrary to law in a gift is treated as though it had not been written. The condition, not the gift, is void (CC art. 900). A gift subject to a discretionary condition, however, is void as violative of the principle of irrevocability. Thus, a gift conditioned on whether the donor embarks on a trip or enters into a certain transaction is void, as is a gift the employer gives to an employee under the condition that the employee is still in the donor's service at the donor's death. The case law sometimes does not apply the rule (and therefore validates the gift) when mixed conditions are involved. Mixed conditions are those involving the will of a third party, such as a gift conditioned on whether the donor marries.

iii. Payment of Debts

1088. *Present debts.* The donor may validly require the donee to pay certain of the donor's expenses and debts.[29] Following the Ordinance of 1731 (art. 16), however, the code distinguishes between debts in existence at the moment the gift is made (*dettes présentes*) and debts contracted thereafter (*dettes futures*; CC art. 945).[30] The requirement that the donee pay the donor's current debts does not violate the principle of irrevocability, even if all the donor's debts are included.

1089. *Future debts.* The rules governing debts not yet incurred are complex. If the debt is specified, such as the obligation to pay for the donor's funeral, the gift is valid. If the donor does not contract the specified debt, the gift is invalid in the amount the debt would have represented. If the donor requires the payment of unspecified debts, the gift is void. The gift is also void if the donor requires payment of any debts contracted up to a certain sum. The gift remains void even if the donor contracts no debts. If the donor requires payment of both current and future obligations, the gift is considered indivisible and void.

---

27. 7 Planiol and Ripert no. 1028.
28. CC arts. 951–952; 5 Planiol and Ripert nos. 448–461; 8 De Page nos. 565–571 bis.
29. A gift conditioned on the payment of expenses or debts is known as a *donation avec charges.*
30. 5 Planiol and Ripert nos. 435–437; 8 De Page no. 556.

iv. Right to Dispose

1090. *Reservation of right.* The Civil Code further voids gifts to the extent the donor reserves the right to dispose of the property (CC art. 946).[31] The sixteenth-century *Coutume de Paris* already prohibited such gifts on the ground that they permitted the donor to circumvent the traditio requirement. Following the Ordinance of 1731 (art. 16), property gifted under such a reservation passes to the heirs if the donor does not dispose of the property.

v. Usufruct

1091. *Present gift.* The French Code expressly confirms that two clauses frequently included in gift acts do not violate the principle of irrevocability. The first is the reservation of a usufruct (CC art. 949).[32] The principle extends to a usufruct of money as well as of other types of property. Thus, if a donor, by present gift, irrevocably obligates the donor's estate to pay a certain sum to the donee, the gift is not invalidated by the fact that it is not due until the donor's death. The courts have interpreted such a gift as the creation of a debt, valid when created and payable at a later date.[33] The courts reason that such a gift immediately enters the donee's patrimony and is therefore not contingent on whether a particular piece of property remains in the donor's estate at death.

1092. *Effective at death.* However, if the gift only grants to the donee the right to receive a certain amount from the estate, the gift is of future property and therefore generally invalid. Moreover, the donor's reservation until death of both a usufruct and the underlying property right (*nue-propriété*) violates the principle of irrevocability.[34]

1093. *Quasi-usufruct.* Some scholars have suggested that it does not violate the irrevocability principle for the donor to retain a quasi-usufruct in a gift of investment paper (*valeur mobilière*).[35] A quasi-usufruct is similar to a usufruct but concerns consumable property. A quasi-usufructuary has the right to consume or even alienate the property, subject to the duty to return either property of the same quantity and quality or equivalent value at the end of the term. The purpose of this type of gift is to permit the donor to continue to manage the property. The risk is that the property might be lost through unwise investment decisions. Irrevocability is not violated because the code specifically requires the donor or the donor's heirs to compensate for any loss (CC art. 950).

---

31. 5 Planiol and Ripert nos. 433–434; 8 De Page no. 557.
32. 5 Planiol and Ripert nos. 443–447; 8 De Page nos. 560–564 ter.
33. Civ. 30 Nov. 1937, S. 1938 I 241 note René Morel.
34. Civ. 6 July 1863, D. 1863 I 286, S. 1863 I 421.
35. Grimaldi and Roux.

vi. Right to Substitute

1094. *Equivalent value.* Though not mentioned in the Civil Code and rarely discussed in the literature, it seems that a gift of stock is valid even though the donor reserves the right to substitute a sum of money for the shares. As long as the two are of equal value, the gift granting the donor the option to choose (*obligation facultative*) seems not to violate the French principle of irrevocability, even when exercised after delivery.[36]

e. Exceptions Regarding Spouses and Marriage

1095. *Between spouses.* Gifts between spouses are expressly exempted from the special irrevocability restrictions (CC art. 947). Until 2005, gifts between spouses were fundamentally revocable.[37] Today, gifts of future property during marriage remain revocable, whereas gifts of present property are revocable only for the failure of a condition or for ingratitude.[38]

1096. *Marriage settlement.* The French Code also exempts gifts made in a marriage settlement, either between the fiancés or by third persons (art. 1086), as well as the type of gift known as the contractual designation of an heir (*institution contractuelle*).[39] The code specifically permits marriage settlements to include gifts subject to the donor's right to dispose (CC art. 1086).[40]

2. Italy

1097. *Eliminated.* The Italian Civil Code of 1865 followed French law and included the principle of irrevocability in its definition of the gift.[41] It also codified the same applications of the rule that are found in French law.[42] The legal definition contained in the current Italian Code, however, no longer makes irrevocability an essential characteristic of the gift (art. 769). The reform commission decided that the principle was one of the "relics of French customary law that do not correspond to any necessity, either practical or doctrinal."[43]

---

36. Grimaldi and Gentilhomme.

37. CC former art. 1096, abrogated by Law of 26 May 2004 art. 21 par. 1. The corresponding Belgian provision was abrogated by Law of 30 Apr. 1958 art. 7 sec. 1 and by Law of 14 May 1981 art. 29.

38. French CC art. 1096 pars. 1–2 (2005).

39. CC arts. 1082–1083, 1093.

40. Under the Ordinance of 1731, if the donor did not exercise the right to dispose included in a marriage settlement the presumption was that the donor wished to leave the property to the donee (art. 18). It was therefore included in the gift. During the revolution, the Convention sought to ensure equality in the distribution of estates. It therefore provided that the property subject to the reservation would become part of the estate. Law of 18 Pluviôse V art. 2. The Civil Code reinstated the rule from 1731. CC art. 1086.

41. CC art. 1050 (1865).

42. CC arts. 1064, 1066–1067, 1069 (1865).

43. Relazione della Commissione Reale 92, in 2 Pandolfelli et al. art. 316 at 361; Torrente (2006) 390–391.

a. Traces of Irrevocability

1098. *Preserved or modified.* Nonetheless, the principle of irrevocability has not vanished from Italian gift law. Though some of the principle's applications have been abandoned, others have been preserved or modified. As noted above, Italian law not only maintains the prohibition against gifts of future property, but also justifies the rule as a useful impediment to gift giving.[44] The current Italian Code does not prohibit gifts subject to the donor's total discretion (*condizione meramente potestativa*), though such gifts continue to be proscribed based on the prohibition against such conditions in all legal acts.[45] The ban on gifts conditioned on the payment of unspecified future debts of the donor has been completely abrogated.

1099. *Right to dispose.* Though the donor is prohibited from reserving the right to dispose of the entire gift or a considerable part of it, current Italian law permits the donor to reserve the right to dispose of "a few objects" (*qualche oggetto*; art. 790). The commentators suggest that this rule represents an attenuation of the irrevocability principle.[46] The right to dispose is considered intuitu personae[47] and thus cannot be exercised by the heirs, or, by doctrinal extension, the estate's creditors. In contrast to French law, if the right to dispose is not exercised, the gifted property remains with the donee. The donor may also reserve the right to demand a certain sum of money from the donee—inferior, of course, to the value of the gift.

1100. *Alternative gifts.* General principles of Italian contracts law permit parties to undertake alternative obligations. The code provides rules to resolve the difficulties when the choice is not made (CC art. 1287). The scholars have asked how those rules should be applied in the gift context, and particularly whether a donor may make an alternative gift, namely the gift of a choice between different gift objects.[48] If the choice is granted to the donee or a third party, there seems to be no problem. If the choice is left to the donor, the scholars differ about how the donor can be compelled to make the choice. The code provision determines who would make the choice if a party fails to choose, but some scholars believe that applying that rule to gifts would negate the personal and spontaneous quality of the gift. Because irrevocability is not a general prerequisite for a valid gift in Italian law, the authors do not discuss whether allowing the donor not to chose would violate special irrevocability.

---

44. CC art. 771 par. 1; see supra nos. 366–367.
45. CC art. 1355; Torrente (2006) 391. Nonetheless, the Italian Code expressly permits the donor to make the gift subject to a condition subsequent that the donee, or the donee and the donee's heirs, survive the donor (*condizione de riversibilità*). CC art. 791.
46. Cendon art. 790 comment. For the corresponding French rules, see supra no. 1090.
47. Capozzi no. 359 at 857.
48. Id. no. 350 at 828–830.

b. Justification

1101. *Principle rejected.* Italian treatise writers generally reject the irrevocability principle. "It defends no interest that merits protection in this matter."[49] Torrente sugested that the goal the principle seeks to achieve, donor protection, might be better served by permitting the donor to revoke in case of regret. According to Biondi, the rule resulted from a misinterpretation of the Roman texts. There was never a legal basis for it.[50] In Maroi's view, the principle of irrevocability is the legal reflection of the colloquial understanding of gift giving.[51] History, comparative law, folklore, and custom all teach that irrevocability is essential to gift giving and that revocation has always been strongly discouraged. Italian has several sayings to the same effect. *Cosa data è peggio che venduta; Donato e ripigliato è peggio che rubato; Chi dà e ritoglie, il diavolo lo raccoglie.*[52] As Maroi's critics have pointed out, however, the fact that irrevocability is immanent in the social notion of the gift does not mean that the law may not permit modification of social convention by contract.[53] It may sometimes be good policy to permit the donor to reserve the right to revoke. When a parent has gifted an ongoing enterprise to a child, for example, the parent may wish to retain the right to revoke if the donee turns out to be an inept manager.

3. Spain

1102. *No special rule.* Spanish law also has tended to abandon the principle of irrevocability. The concept is not mentioned in the statutory definition of the gift (art. 618). The Spanish Civil Code has maintained the prohibition against gifts of future property (art. 635), but, as discussed above, the doctrinal reinterpretation of the prohibition leaves little room for it to operate.[54] Spanish contracts law declares void any obligations that depend exclusively on the obligor's will (art. 1115). Thus, as in Italian law, there is no need for a special rule prohibiting the right to revoke a gift.

a. The Donor's Debts

1103. *Doctrinal construction.* The gift made under the condition that the donee pay the donor's debts has produced an elaborate doctrinal construction in Spanish law. The Civil Code provides simply that if a gift requires the donee to pay the donor's debts, and if those debts are not enumerated, the donee will be

---

49. Torrente (2006) 390.
50. Biondi no. 25 and note 3.
51. Maroi.
52. Torrente (2006) 393. "What is gifted is worse [more definite] than what is sold;" "It's worse to gift it and take it back than to steal it;" and "Whoever gives and takes away the Devil will take."
53. Torrente (2006) 393.
54. Supra nos. 368–369.

required to pay only those debts contracted prior to the gift (art. 642). The code thus seems to provide a default rule, leaving to the gift contract the amount and kind of debts to be paid.

In the spirit of the principle of irrevocability, however, the authors have not been willing to concede such unlimited freedom to the parties. Albaladejo García, one of the principal commentators, concluded that it would violate both the letter and the spirit of the code's general provisions for the donee to agree to pay (up to the amount of the gift) all debts the donor may contract.[55] Moreover, a donee should be required to pay the donor's debts only if they are individually identified in writing (CC art. 633 par. 1). To resolve the various conflicts, Albaladejo García argued that only debts contracted prior to the gift are exempt from the enumeration requirement. Future debts, as in French law, must be specified. If the future debts are not specified, the donee is not obligated to pay them. In contrast to French law, the gift remains valid.

b. The Right to Dispose

1104. *Doctrinal views.* Spanish law also permits the donor to reserve the right to dispose of "some of the gifted property" (*algunos de los bienes donados*), including a sum of money, that, according to the scholars, may not exceed the value of the gift (CC art. 639). Lacruz Berdejo reads the provision as an implicit abrogation of the French maxim *Donner et retenir ne vaut.*[56] He would permit the right to dispose to cover the entire gift.[57] The one high court decision that may be read to limit the donor's rights in this regard is generally distinguished.[58]

The authors conclude that the donee benefits, even by a revocable gift. Even if required to return the property, the donee retains interest and other fruits. Moreover, because the gift is a contract, there is no reason not to apply the code provisions that generously protect freedom of contract (CC art. 1255). Other Spanish authors, however, influenced by the restrictions imposed in other legal systems, only exceptionally would permit the donor to reserve the right to dispose of the entire gift.

4. Germany

1105. *Customary law.* German customary law considered a gift transfer to be binding only in the presence of a return gift.[59] As a result, all gifts were revocable

---

55. Paz-Ares Rodríguez (-Albaladejo García) arts. 642–643 no. IV (referring to CC art. 1256 (invalidating contracts that leave performance exclusively in the hands of one of the parties) and arts. 1273, 1447, 1449 (requiring that the object of a contract be determinable)).

56. 2 Lacruz Berdejo no. 514 note 7.

57. Paz-Ares Rodríguez (-Albaladejo García) art. 639 no. II.

58. STS Civ. 7 July 1978, RJ 2755.

59. Supra no. 36; Ogris col. 1382; Hannig 151.

until the return gift was made. Revocability could be eliminated only by disguising the gift as an onerous transaction, as by agreeing to some consideration, either actual or apparent. According to the traditional conception, a gift passed only a limited property interest, similar to the common law life estate. The donor had the right to recover the gift for any of a number of reasons, including if the donee proved ungrateful or transferred the gift object to a third party or if the donor had become impecunious and required the gift for maintenance.[60]

1106. *Right to revoke today.* German law does not today require a gift to be irrevocable. Both the case law and the commentators seem to agree that the donor may reserve the right to revoke the gift, or any part of it, at any time and at the donor's discretion.[61] As discussed above, gifts of future property are permitted in German law as long as some patrimonial right passes to the donee at the moment of the gift.[62] German law does not contain provisions specially regulating gifts requiring the donee to pay the donor's debts or gifts in which the donor has reserved the right to dispose of some or all of the gift property.

5. The Common Law

1107. *Basic rule.* A common English saying testifies to the universal aversion toward the revocation of gifts. "Give a thing and take a thing, to wear the devil's gold ring."[63] Yet as far as the law is concerned, there is little unity in the different systems about the legal principle of irrevocability. Because a gift is valid only if it effectively transfers title, the right to revoke, in certain circumstances, may prevent title from passing. In Bracton's view, if the donor intends for the gift property to revert to the donor when something is done or fails to be done, the transfer is not a gift.[64] Both Fleta and Britton suggested that the common law's delivery requirement is at least in part designed to prevent revocability.[65]

a. India

1108. *Donor's discretion.* Indian law permits the parties to condition a gift on the happening of any specified event that does not depend on the donor's will.[66]

---

60. Ogris col. 1383.
61. MünchKomm-BGB (-Musielak) § 2301 no. 22.
62. Supra nos. 301–302, 370.
63. Apperson 230.
64. 2 Bracton 50.
65. "To give, therefore, is to cause property to belong effectively to the recipient: otherwise the gift will be useless since it can be invalidated and revoked: for example, if the gift is made of property belonging to someone else." Fleta bk. 3 ch. 3 at 5; see Britton bk. 2 ch. 3 no. 1 at 220.
66. Indian Transfer of Property Act § 126.

If the parties agree that the gift is revocable at the donor's will, the gift is void.[67] If only part of the gift is revocable, only that part is void. According to the official illustration in the Transfer of Property Act, if a gift is given under the condition of complete revocability, title does not pass and the property continues to belong to the donor.[68]

Under Islamic law, the hiba requires the immediate transfer of absolute ownership. If a hiba is made with conditions or restrictions, the conditions are void and the gift is valid. Thus, if a donor makes a gift with an option of cancelling within three days, the gift is valid and the option void.[69]

b. England

1109. *Power of revocation.* The English rule, even at law, is that a donor may validly provide in the gift for a power of revocation.[70] However, if such a power is reserved, the transaction is not immediately effective as a gift[71] and may be deemed to be testamentary.[72]

c. United States

1110. *Law and equity.* In American law, irrevocability is regulated differently in law and equity.

1111. *At law.* At law, the irrevocability principle limits gift giving in two respects. First, if the donor, when making a parol gift, retains possession or does not consummate the gift, the courts hold that the donor has retained the right to revoke. The locus poenitentiae precludes the finding of a gift.[73] Second, American law generally considers a gift to be void if, in making the gift, the donor reserves a power of revocation.[74] In some American jurisdictions, however, the reservation of the power to revoke does not void the gift.[75]

1112. *Differing interpretations.* In some states, the principle of irrevocability is even more strictly interpreted than in civilian jurisdictions. A court may refuse to enforce a gift on revocability grounds even if the power of revocation involves a contingency beyond the donor's control. One court invalidated the gift of a lottery ticket when the donor stated that she might reclaim it if she was able to

---

67. Id.

68. Id. illus. b.

69. Fyzee 220–221.

70. 20 Halsbury part 1 sub Gifts no. 58.

71. *Xenos v Wickham* (1866) 2 HL 296, 323 (Cranworth J).

72. *Fletcher v Fletcher* (1844) 4 Hare 67, 79, 67 ER 564.

73. *Cartall v. St. Louis Union Trust Co.*, 153 S.W.2d 370, 375 (Mo. 1941).

74. *Edson v. Lucas*, 40 F.2d 398, 404 (8th Cir. 1930); *Butler v. Sherwood*, 186 N.Y.S. 712, 714–715 (Sup. Ct. 1921); Fellows (1988) 46 note 41.

75. *Eisenberg v. Finston*, 87 A.2d 448, 450 (N.J. App. Div. 1952). See also Gulliver and Tilson 20.

attend the lottery. As the court explained, "to be legally binding a gift must have no strings attached."[76] Other courts hold that the gift is valid if the donor does not revoke before death.[77] Moreover, as noted above, deposits into a joint bank account may operate a gift even if the donor has the right to withdraw the funds.[78] Because a power of revocation does not invalidate a declaration of trust, Garvey argues that it should also not void a gift.[79]

1113. *Equity.* Equity permits the settlor to reserve a power of revocation in the declaration of trust.[80] The beneficiary's right vests immediately subject to later divesting. This equitable rule has been criticized. The right to revoke, when coupled with the settlor's reservation of a life interest, is virtually indistinguishable from a testamentary transfer. "The realist may affirm that there is no practical difference between a declaration of trust or other transfer of rights which is not to become effective until a future event, say the death of the settlor, and one which, though presently declared, is subject to the uncontrolled power of the settlor to revoke."[81]

B. CIRCUMSTANCES PERMITTING REVOCATION

1114. *Unilateral.* In the common law, an executed gift generally may not be revoked.[82] In civilian jurisdictions, in contrast, a donor may unilaterally revoke a fully executed gift in a number of circumstances. The civilian right to revoke derives ultimately from Roman law. Roman jurists were suspicious of gift giving and favored revocation rights as a means to destabilize the institution.[83] In this same tradition, the Prussian General Law accorded the donor broad discretion to revoke. Gifts not made before a court could be revoked, apparently for any reason, for a period of six months following delivery.[84] Even after the six months had

---

76. *Watkins v. Hodge,* 101 S.E.2d 657, 658 (S.C. 1958).

77. *Lippold v. Lippold,* 83 N.W. 809 (Iowa 1900).

78. Supra no. 944.

79. Implicit in our institution of private ownership is the idea that the law should place no undue burden on the right of individuals to dispose of their wealth as they see fit. If we permit a man to gratuitously dispose of his entire interest in a piece of property, it is, as Professor Brown observed, "somewhat arbitrary to deny him the possibility of creating, through gift, limited and lesser interests."
Garvey 282 (quoting the second edition of Brown).

80. *Appeal of Dickerson,* 8 A. 64 (Pa. 1887); 1 Scott and Ascher § 8.2.1; Brown § 7.21; Restatement (Third) of Trusts § 63 par. 1.

81. Brown § 7.21.

82. INDIA: Transfer of Property Act § 126; ENGLAND: 20 Halsbury part 1 sub Gifts no. 58; UNITED STATES: *Plant v. Plant,* 609 S.W.2d 93 (Ark. App. 1980); Brown § 7.1.

83. Ourliac and Malafosse 456.

84. Gen. Law pt. 1 tit. 11 §§ 1063, 1069, 1089–1090 (1794).

elapsed, gifts could be revoked for a number of reasons, such as if they exceeded half of the donor's patrimony.[85]

1115. *Variation.* Grounds for revocation vary somewhat from jurisdiction to jurisdiction. French law provides for three cases—failure to fulfill the conditions under which the gift was made, ingratitude, and the birth of a child. Gifts of future property between spouses also remain revocable. Other jurisdictions permit an impoverished donor either to recover the gift or to sue the donee for support. The nature, procedure, and effects of revocation also vary depending on the legal system. Some legal systems do not characterize the recovery of a gift upon the failure of a condition as a case of revocation. German law constructs the action as a form of contractual rescission governed by restitution law.[86] Italian law considers the matter in terms of the consequences that ensue when a condition fails to occur.[87]

The circumstances permitting revocation that are examined here include ingratitude, impoverishment, the birth of a child, and the revocation of gifts between spouses.[88] Revocation rules are especially complex. This is one of the most challenging areas in gift law.

1. Ingratitude

1116. *Most frequent.* The most frequently codified circumstance permitting revocation involves the donee whose conduct demonstrates a serious lack of gratitude. Ingratitude also appears to have been the first legally recognized grounds for revocation.

a. Introduction

i. History

1117. *Freed slaves.* From the Roman Republic through the classical period, gifts were generally irrevocable.[89] As an exception, revocation was permitted with regard to gifts made to freed slaves by their former slaveholders. The gifts could be revoked *ad nutum*, regardless of how long the donees had been in possession.[90] It seems that the exception was later reformulated in terms of the special duty of gratitude (*obsequium*) that freed slaves owed their former masters. Early in Roman

---

85. Id. §§ 1091–1177.

86. CC § 527 par. 1.

87. CC arts. 1353 ff.

88. As already mentioned, revocation for failure of a condition is not discussed here. The discussion would require an examination of the complex notion of conditions in general contract law, a task that would greatly exceed the limits of this study.

89. 1 Kaser 604.

90. "Even after gifts have been perfected and delivered to a freed slave (*libertus*), they may all be revoked at the will of the patron, regardless how long the freed slave has been in possession as lawful owner." *Fragmenta vaticana* no. 272. See also 8 De Page no. 679.

history, the freed slave's ingratitude may have resulted in a return to servitude. That sanction had been abolished by the classical period,[91] though criminal punishment may still have been available.[92] A rescript from the time of Diocletian suggests that ingratitude became the basis for revocation about the time of the rise of Christianity.[93] One result of the new belief system was to increase the rights of former slaves and to limit the freedom of former masters by specifying the situations in which they could revoke.

1118. *Constantine.* In order to punish children who, after emancipation, acted toward their fathers with arrogance or cruelty (*superbe crudeliterque*), Constantine, in 330, permitted fathers to revoke not only gifts given to such children but also their emancipation. When emancipation was revoked, all of the child's property, including the father's gifts, returned to the father.[94] Under Constans, revocation of gifts was permitted when children were merely undutiful (*impios*).[95] The right to revoke was eventually extended to benefit the mother and other ancestors as well.[96]

1119. *Justinian.* Justinian extended the right to revoke yet further to include all donors, whether or not the donee was a relative.[97] At the same time, Justinian limited revocation for ingratitude to situations involving proof of serious misbehavior, including serious wrongs (*iniuriae atroces*), offenses against the person, nonperformance of an obligation voluntarily assumed, and fraud causing serious harm to the donor's patrimony. Revocation of remunerative gifts was not permitted. The right to revoke, considered a penal action (one of the *actiones vindictam spirantes*), did not pass to the donor's heirs.[98]

ii. Social Context

1120. *Gratitude.* In clan-based societies, gratitude probably is not an element of the gift transaction.[99] In contrast, in both early Roman law and German customary law, the donee could retain the gift only if there was reciprocation or counterservice, even if only on a moral level.[100] Today gratitude plays an important role in social relationships. The donee's ingratitude is thought to violate the social economy of gift giving. The task for the law is to determine how it should respond to a breach of the extra-legal norms that structure the giving of gifts.

---

91. De Francisci.
92. Kaser (1938) 128–133; Biondi no. 340; 3 Planiol no. 2638.
93. *Fragmenta vaticana* no. 275; Biondi no. 340.
94. *Fragmenta vaticana* no. 248.
95. Cod. Th. 8, 13, 2.
96. Cod. Th. 8, 13, 1, 3 and 8, 13, 1, 6.
97. C. 8, 55, 56, 10; Biondi no. 340.
98. Cod. Th. 8, 13, 1, 5; Biondi no. 341.
99. Wagner-Hasel 158 and note 61; Gaul 225.
100. Wagner-Hasel 151–155.

1121. *Common law and civil law.* The common law chooses to respect customary norms by leaving individuals to choose their donees, to reap the rewards, and to suffer the consequences of their choices. As a result, the common law is unable to remedy the inability of customary norms to enforce a return of property that seems normatively required. The civil law, on the contrary, recognizes the power of the normative structure in which gift giving is embedded and completes the logic of the system by facilitating recovery of a benefit that is thought to be unjustly retained. These differences are difficult to explain. They may be partially due to the differing relation to the Roman heritage, but there are numerous other factors as well. The civil law has always been more suspicious of gift giving than is the common law, and perhaps for that reason as well is more willing to permit revocation.

Several common-law scholars have sensed that some remedy should be provided for serious ingratitude. They recognize that revocation would require an investigation into states of mind and the weighing of imprecise and personal factors, a kind of inquiry that the common law usually seeks to avoid.[101] Nonetheless, they argue that the difficulty of drawing an appropriate line cannot excuse the law's failure to take action in egregious situations. Stoljar has suggested that the desired result can be achieved by recourse to traditional concepts. All that is necessary is to imply a condition that the donee must behave in a manner not incompatible with the gift.[102]

iii. Legal Nature

1122. *Disagreement.* There is no agreement among the various civilian systems concerning the legal nature of the revocation for ingratitude. Revocation is not an instance of avoidance. The grounds for revocation generally arise after execution of the gift and therefore do not cause a defect in consent.[103] It has been suggested that revocation is related to cancellation due to a defect in the cause.[104] Yet, at least in much of today's Romanic civil law, the concept of cause is generally believed to fulfill its function at the moment the contract is concluded or, at the latest, when the gift is executed.

1123. *France.* In French law, revocation for failure to fulfill a condition is based on the tacit right of cancellation that the code implies in all synallagmatic contracts (art. 1184). Revocation for ingratitude is not structured in this way. The obligation of gratitude is not a legal condition. It is rather derived from morality.

---

101. Stoljar 251–252; Eisenberg (1979) 17–18.

102. Stoljar id. The technical construction would be a resulting trust coupled with a presumption of advancement. Gross ingratitude would cause the presumption to fail. The property would then result back to the donor.

103. If the grounds arise before the gift is completed, the gift may sometimes be avoided for mistake.

104. Torrente (2006) 673–674.

Only extreme cases are sanctioned by the law. French authors have suggested that revocation for ingratitude is a sanction for the donee's extreme failure to fulfill the moral obligation of gratitude.[105] Yet, as has been pointed out by the Italian authors, the ungrateful donee has violated a moral or social norm, an essential element of the normative structure of gift giving, but has not failed to perform an element of a legal synallagma.[106]

1124. *Italy.* Italian scholars reject the penal conception of revocation for ingratitude. They also reject the idea of an implied agreement. It never occurs to most donors that the donee might act ungratefully. The Italian discussion has settled on a different view. Moral conscience demands that a donee who commits reprehensible acts must surrender the gift. The law finds it appropriate, in these circumstances, to bow to moral sentiment.[107] Revocation for ingratitude is thus an action sui generis designed to protect extra-patrimonial interests. It has patrimonial effect only to the extent necessary.[108] Biondi agreed that gift revocation is unique. "Faced with the inanity of the theories, in truth more verbal than substantial, it is vain to attempt to subsume revocation under some other type of inefficacy. Revocation cannot be subsumed. Rather it must be added as another ground for the inefficacy of a transaction, one with its own construction."[109]

1125. *Germany.* In German law, revocation for ingratitude is a statutorily regulated instance of frustration of purpose (*Wegfall der Geschäftsgrundlage*).[110] The idea is that this type of revocation may best be understood as a form of unjust enrichment. The donee has been enriched.[111] The question is whether it is unjust for the ungrateful donee to retain the benefit. The inquiry necessarily points outside the law to the social conception of justice and the degree of respect (*Pietätsverhältnis*) expected in the donee-donor relationship.[112] The focus is on the particular facts.

1126. *Variation in structure.* Though revocation for ingratitude is widely recognized in the civil law, each system has chosen a somewhat different structure for the action. The differences are not merely in terms of the legal definition of ingratitude. They also include the constraints placed on the action and its consequences, both between the parties and as against third parties.

---

105. 5 Planiol and Ripert no. 500.
106. Torrente (2006) 674.
107. Id. 677.
108. Id. 676
109. Biondi no. 334.
110. Staudinger (-Wimmer-Leonhardt) § 530 no. 2.
111. Enrichment is an element of the German notion of the gift. Supra nos. 331–332. However, if, by the time revocation is sought the gift has been dissipated, the restitution action may be unavailable. German CC § 818 par. 3.
112. Staudinger (-Wimmer-Leonhardt) § 530 no. 3.

b. The Notion of Ingratitude

1127. *Law or fact.* Some civil codes enumerate the acts that constitute actionable ingratitude. In others, ingratitude is a matter of fact to be determined at trial.

i. France and Belgium

1128. *Enumerated acts.* French customary law recognized the right of revocation in case of ingratitude and multiplied the circumstances in which it applied. It was not until the Civil Code that the legally cognizable grounds were limited to three specific wrongs (art. 955). Under the code, revocation is justified in the following cases: an attempt on the donor's life; serious cruelty, crimes, or insults (*sévices, délits, ou injures graves*); and a refusal to provide maintenance (*refus d'aliments*). Jean Patarin has recently suggested that these norms have remained stable over the centuries because "they continue to be well adapted to the aspirations and the perennial traits of human character."[113] The three cases are considered exclusive. The Louisiana Civil Code, uniquely for an American state, permits revocation for ingratitude and has adopted a similar definition.[114]

(A) ATTEMPT ON THE DONOR'S LIFE

1129. *Intent to kill.* An attempt on the donor's life permits revocation only if there is intent to kill. There is no requirement that the attempt succeed or that it be prosecuted by the criminal law.[115] There has apparently never been a successful revocation on this ground, either in French or in Belgian law.[116]

(B) SERIOUS WRONGS

1130. *Intentional acts. Cruelty, crimes, or insults* are intentional acts against the donor's person or property. The right to revoke does not depend on whether the act has been punished by the criminal law.[117]

1131. *Adultery.* The current view is that it is a question of fact whether adultery constitutes grounds for revocation.[118] Patarin suggests that, because adultery is no longer an imperative ground for divorce, it should not automatically permit revocation for ingratitude.[119] Brenner, on the other hand, argues that, because

---

113. Jean Patarin, obs. to Civ.¹ 14 Jan. 2003, *Rev. trim. dr. civ.* 2003, 530.

114. Louisiana CC art. 1560.

115. 5 Planiol and Ripert no. 503.

116. 8 De Page no. 659.

117. 5 Planiol and Ripert nos. 504–505; 8 De Page no. 660.

118. Civ.¹ 19 Mar. 1985, *Bull. civ.* I no. 99, *Rev. trim. dr. civ.* 1986, 626 obs. Jean Patarin.

119. Jean Patarin id. 627.

gifts are no longer freely revocable between spouses,[120] revocation for ingratitude should be expanded to include any severe breach of spousal duties.[121]

1132. *Crimes.* Whether a crime should permit revocation is determined from the context. If the relationship between donor and donee involves severe conflict, the theft of the donor's jewelry may not constitute sufficient provocation.[122] Even physical restraint may be insufficient. In a recent case, the donee and other children of the donor broke into the donor's home and held him on the sofa until he agreed to return a Mercedes that belonged to the family business. The Cassation Court affirmed the trial court's finding that, in the context of a family with a history of conflict, the events were not sufficiently serious to permit revocation.[123]

1133. *Insults.* An insult involves serious and intentional harm to honor or reputation. Though the code permits the revocation of a testamentary bequest for ingratitude even when the insults are posthumous (art. 1047), Pothier taught that gifts may be revoked only for insults that are made during the donor's lifetime.[124] That is also the majority view today.

(C) REFUSAL OF SUPPORT

1134. *Donor in need.* Should a donor become needy, the code provides an action for maintenance against close relatives (arts. 205–211). The donor's only recourse against a donee who is not a relative is to revoke the gift.[125] Because the code considers the refusal to provide support a form of ingratitude, revocation is available only if the refusal is illegitimate.[126] Revocation would be improper if maintenance is available from those who are legally obligated to provide it or if the donee does not have sufficient resources. When the donor seeks to revoke, the donee may prevent revocation by offering to provide support. The court considers the parties' respective resources when determining whether the offer is appropriate.[127] The donor may ask for assistance only if needy, and the donee

---

120. Infra nos. 1301–1313.

121. Brenner 105–106.

122. Civ.[1] 14 Jan. 2003, *Bull. civ.* I no. 5, *Rev. trim. dr. civ.* 2003, 530 obs. Jean Patarin. The court decided against revocation, partially due to the large disproportion between the value of the purloined jewelry and the much greater value of the real and personal property that had been given by gift.

123. Civ.[1] 16 June 1998, D. 1998 IR 178, *Rev. trim. dr. civ.* 1998, 965 obs. Jean Patarin.

124. 1 Pothier tit. 15 no. 111. Planiol and Ripert misread Pothier's position. Cf. 5 Planiol and Ripert no. 505 at 641. Pothier also believed that revocation was proper in the case of insults to members of the donor's immediate family. 1 Pothier tit. 15 no. 110.

125. Civ.[1] Dec. 1919, D.P. 1920 I 5 note Ripert.

126. 8 De Page no. 661.

127. Paris 15 Dec. 1955, D.S. 1956, 128, *Rev. trim. dr. civ.* 1956, 381 obs. Savatier.

must respond only to the value of the gift.[128] Revocation fails if the property has perished by accident or *force majeure,* though not if it has simply been dissipated.

1135. *Priority.* There has been some dispute among scholars as to whether a donee is liable for maintenance if other individuals owe maintenance under the code. Some authors suggest that the donee may be asked only after the other actions have failed. Others have argued that the donee should be asked first, or that the court should fix the order equitably. It is now believed that any refusal on the donee's part may permit revocation.

ii. Italy

1136. *Greater sensitivity.* The revocation provisions in the Italian Code of 1865 closely followed French law.[129] The drafters of the current Italian Code believed that both Roman and French law suffered from indeterminacy.[130] They believed the extensive enumeration of cases contained in the current Italian Code achieves "not only superior precision but also ... a larger number of cases permitting revocation, thereby demonstrating a greater sensitivity."[131]

1137. *Enumeration.* Numerous cases are specified (art. 801). The first four instances cross-reference the provision governing disqualification from inheritance (art. 463 nos. 1–3). Revocation is permitted if the donee voluntarily kills or attempts to kill either the donor, the donor's spouse, or any of the donor's descendents or ancestors, as long as there is neither justification nor excuse. A second ground arises when the donee does harm to any of these same individuals in a way that constitutes homicide under the criminal law (principally killing in a duel or an assisted suicide). Third, revocation is justified if the donee accuses any of the same persons of a crime punishable either by life imprisonment[132] or by imprisonment of not less than three years, provided the criminal law has declared the accusation libelous. The final case involves a donee who testifies against the same individuals, if a criminal court has judged that testimony to be false.

Three circumstances of ingratitude are exclusive to gift law. These involve a serious wrong (*ingiuria grave*) to the donor, serious harm fraudulently caused to the donor's patrimony, and, finally, the unjustifiable refusal of maintenance owed according to provisions of the Civil Code relating to maintenance obligations among relatives (art. 433) and after adoption (art. 436), but (for reasons to be explained below) *not* including the obligation of maintenance the donee

---

128. 5 Planiol and Ripert no. 506; 8 De Page no. 661.
129. Italian CC arts. 1078–1090 (1865).
130. Biondi no. 342.
131. Id.
132. Italy has abolished the death penalty.

owes to the donor (art. 437). In all cases, the circumstances must have occurred subsequent to the conclusion of the gift. If they occurred beforehand, they may constitute grounds for avoidance based on mistake concerning the qualities of the donee, the gift may amount to forgiveness, or the circumstances may be irrelevant.[133]

(A) HOMICIDE OR LIBEL

1138. *Homicide.* The voluntary killing of the donor's spouse permits revocation even if the victim is separated from the donor and is at fault for the separation. According to a somewhat older view, homicide of a descendent or ancestor does not include the killing of adopted parents or children,[134] but more recent revisions to Italian family law may have rendered this view obsolete.

1139. *Libel.* Criminal libel permits revocation only if it results in a conviction. If the statute of limitations has run on the crime, revocation is not permitted.[135]

(B) SERIOUS WRONGS

1140. *Discretion.* The concept of *serious wrongs* leaves significant discretion to the judge. Revocation is not contingent either on the commission of a crime or on a criminal conviction.[136] The revocation action provides a civil sanction independent of the criminal law.[137] Wrongs are sufficiently serious only when the donee makes a conscious and voluntary assault directly against the donor's moral patrimony. The law is designed to sanction a clear sentiment of antipathy toward the donor, an expression of ingratitude that is repugnant to the social conscience.[138] In one case, revocation was permitted when the donee termed the donor a whore and a delinquent and threatened to kill her.[139] In another case, the gift was not revoked when the donee, the donor's daughter, failed to apply herself to her studies, dropped out of school, became a drug addict and dealer, drove a car without having a driver's a license, and suffered bodily harm during the course of an accident.[140] Despite the gravity of the donee's acts, she did not act with animosity directly against the donor or the donor's patrimony.

Revocation can be permitted after a single serious offense, as long as *animus iniuriandi* is present. In one case, revocation was permitted when a son removed his parents from their home after the parents gifted the house to him with all of

---

133. Torrente (2006) 678.

134. Cian and Trabucchi art. 463 no. II par. 2.

135. Id. no. III.

136. Biondi no. 342.

137. Capozzi no. 357 par. f; note to Cass. 28 Aug. 1997 no. 8165, *Giur. it.* 1998 II 2059 at 2060–2061.

138. Capozzi id.

139. Cass. 28 Aug. 1997 no. 8165, *Giur. it.* 1998 II 2059.

140. Cass. 5 Nov. 1990 no. 10614, *Giur. it.* 1991 I 676.

their other property.[141] A sudden moment of anger or a scholarly criticism does not permit revocation. *Wrongs* include offenses against personal integrity and moral patrimony, such as the donor's reputation and honor.[142] A husband may revoke a gift given before marriage to a wife who has committed adultery,[143] but the wife's father may not. A risk of harm, even if serious, does not permit revocation unless it materializes. Falsely claiming that other obligors lack solvency does not permit revocation if the donor is not required to pay on the guarantee.[144] There is some doubt as to whether a posthumous offense to the donor's reputation permits revocation.[145] There is also doubt about whether a juridical person may revoke based on such wrongs.[146] The gravity of the prejudice to the donor's patrimony is to be judged by reference to the donor's wealth and other circumstances. A relatively modest harm does not justify revocation.[147]

(C) REFUSAL OF MAINTENANCE

1141. *Different obligations.* The Italian Civil Code of 1865 followed the French Code in permitting revocation when the donee refused the donor's request for maintenance.[148] Revocation was permitted when the donee refused to perform the legal obligation of maintenance between close relatives. On the basis of that provision, Italian scholars asked whether revocation was also permitted if the donee violated a maintenance obligation that arose in a different context—for example, if one was included in the gift contract or in a will.[149]

Under the current code, the donee, merely by accepting the gift, becomes primarily obligated, in case of need, to provide the donor with support (art. 437). Gifts made in contemplation of marriage and remunerative gifts are excepted, though indirect gifts are not. If the donee fails to perform this obligation, the donor may sue for maintenance, though the donee's liability is limited to the value of the gift that remains in the donee's patrimony (art. 438 par. 3). Moreover, if the donee assumes a maintenance obligation as part of a donatio sub modo or otherwise, the code permits cancellation of the contract and restitution.[150] These two cases are instances of revocation for the failure of a condition. They do *not* constitute instances of revocation for ingratitude.

---

141. App. Caltanissetta 27 Jan. 1941, *Rep. Foro it.* 1941 *Donazione* no. 49.
142. Torrente (2006) 681.
143. Trib. Cagliari 18 Jan. 1913, *Rep. Foro. it.* 1913 *Donazione* no. 32.
144. Balbi 89–90; Capozzi no. 357 par. f.
145. Biondi no. 342 (contra); Torrente (2006) 683 (pro).
146. Biondi id. (contra).
147. Cian and Trabucchi art. 801 no. 5; Biondi no. 342.
148. Italian CC art. 1081 (1865).
149. Biondi no. 342 par. c; Torrente (2006) 684–685.
150. CC arts. 793 par. 4, 1453.

The remedy of revocation for ingratitude is limited to the breach of a maintenance obligation that arises among close relatives under family law. It requires proof of all of the elements of that obligation, including the donor's destitution, the donee's ability to provide support, and the inability of the primary support obligors (arts. 438, 441).

iii. Spain

1142. *Specified acts.* The Spanish Civil Code enumerates three categories of ingratitude (art. 648): the commission of a crime (*algún delito*) against the person, honor, or property of the donor; pressing charges in regard to certain types of crimes, even if the charges are later proven to be true, unless the charges relate to a crime committed against the donee, the donee's spouse, or against children under the donee's control; and unjustifiably refusing the donor's request for maintenance. Additional grounds permit revocation for ingratitude of gifts given in contemplation of marriage.

(A) CRIMES

1143. *Types of crime.* For some Spanish authors, the term *delito* is a technical concept. In the criminal law, it is used in contrast to *misdemeanor* (*falta*) to designate a serious crime (similar to a felony).[151] Because revocation provides a sanction, it must be read literally.[152] Yet even those authors who understand the term in its penal law sense do not suggest that a conviction is necessary, and all agree that revocation may occur even if the donee is only an accomplice. Other authors argue that, in the revocation context, the term is not to be understood as a reference to the criminal law but rather is meant nontechnically to encompass all reprehensible acts intentionally committed.[153] The courts interpret the provision broadly to include not only acts punishable as a crime but also "socially reprehensible conduct that might be declared criminal even if it has never been formally proscribed."[154]

(B) PRESSING CHARGES

1144. *Charges necessary.* Because Spanish law imposes a general duty to report the commission of a crime, revocation is not permitted merely because the donee accuses the donor of a crime. A gift can be revoked only if the donee presses charges when charges are necessary for prosecution.

---

151. Diez-Picazo and Gullón 346.
152. 2 Lacruz Berdejo no. 507 par. c.
153. Paz-Ares Rodríguez (-Díaz Alabart) art. 648 no. I.
154. STS Civ. 27 Feb. 1995, RJ 2775.

(C) REFUSAL OF SUPPORT

1145. *Maintenance obligation.* According to the scholars, the provision permitting revocation for refusing maintenance creates a maintenance obligation on the part of the donee.[155] Revocation due to a refusal of support may be based on the maintenance obligation that arises from the fact of the gift as well as on any other maintenance obligation between the parties, whether it arises from a family relationship or from contract.[156] Revocation is limited to the amount of the gift, together with interest and fruits collected after the request. If there are several donees, the obligation is in proportion to the value of the gifts. Some authors argue that, if third parties are obligated to provide maintenance by code provision or contract, the donee's obligation is subsidiary.[157] Other scholars consider the donee's obligation to be primary because the gift represents resources that formerly belonged to the donor.[158]

(D) IN CONSIDERATION OF MARRIAGE

1146. *Expanded notion.* Gifts given in consideration of marriage are revocable for ingratitude (CC art. 1343 par. 1). In the case of gifts between fiancés, the notion of ingratitude is expanded to include any ground of disinheritance listed in the code, together with fault for the parties' legal separation or divorce (art. 1343 par. 3). Grounds for disinheritance include serious or repeated failure to fulfill conjugal duties, loss of parental authority (*patria potestad*) due to a failure to perform parental obligations, as well as the grounds for being declared unworthy to succeed, which include the abandonment of children, their introduction into prostitution, or making an attempt on the life of the donor or on one of the donor's relatives.[159]

iv. Germany

1147. *Two grounds.* German law codifies two grounds for recovery of gifts that, in Romanic systems, are related. One is revocation for gross ingratitude. The other is recovery upon the donor's impoverishment. In German law, the two grounds are conceptually distinct. Gross ingratitude is examined here, while the donor's impoverishment is discussed below.[160]

(A) DRAFTING HISTORY

1148. *Rejection of enumeration.* The first draft of the German Civil Code followed the traditional method of codification by enumerating the types of ungrateful

---

155. Paz-Ares Rodríguez (-Díaz Alabart) art. 648 no. III; Diez-Picazo and Gullón 347.
156. STS Civ. 28 July 1998, RJ 5809.
157. Paz-Ares Rodríguez (-Díaz Alabart) art. 648 no. I.
158. Diez-Picazo and Gullón 347.
159. CC art. 855, together with arts. 170, 756.
160. Infra nos. 1202–1203, 1207–1210, 1213.

conduct that permit revocation.[161] The circumstances included acts threatening the donor's life or liberty, intentional injuries, serious insults, and intentional and serious harm to the donor's patrimony. In the second commission, the minority continued to support a listing of the circumstances permitting revocation. They argued that it would be impossible to subsume all relevant circumstances under a unitary legal concept. The majority, however, following suggestions from local governments, decided to permit greater judicial discretion. The belief was that any enumeration would be both too broad and too narrow. The enumerated grounds should not in all circumstances lead to revocation. Moreover, no enumeration could encompass all cases of serious ingratitude that deserved to be sanctioned.[162]

The Zurich Civil Code had already attempted to avoid overspecification in the related area of the testator's right to exclude an heir from the reserve. Disinheritance was permitted "[w]hen [the heir] has abandoned the testator in distress, in disregard of the duty of affection, or has grossly disrespected the testator or has obstinately neglected him."[163] The German Civil Code now provides a similar general clause. Gifts may be revoked due to gross ingratitude (*wegen groben Undankes*) whenever the donee commits a serious misdeed (*schwere Verfehlung*) against the donor or one of the donor's close relatives (CC § 530 par. 1).

(B) DUTY OF RESPECT

1149. *Debt of gratitude.* The acceptance of a gift creates in the donee a duty of respect (*Pietätsverhältnis*)[164] and a debt of gratitude.[165] Though no legal action is available to enforce the donee's obligation, the law permits revocation when the donee's conduct significantly deviates from what morality requires.[166] The misconduct must be objectively serious, though it need not be illegal. Subjectively, the donee must have shown a "blameworthy attitude that reveals a lack of gratitude."[167] The circumstances of the case, including the relationship between the parties and any provocation on the donor's part, must also be taken into account.[168] Ingratitude is a question of fact. It is interpreted in light of current conditions and popular morality, and thus varies according to time and place.[169]

---

161. Entwurf § 449; see also Prussian Gen. Law pt. 1 tit. 11 §§ 1152–1156.
162. 2 Mugdan 756; *Material der Dresdener Kommission* § 515, in 2 von Kübel 76–79.
163. Zurich CC § 976 (1887).
164. Staudinger (-Wimmer-Leonhardt) § 530 no. 3.
165. MünchKomm-BGB (-Kollhosser) § 530 no. 1.
166. Id. § 530 nos. 1–2.
167. Id. § 530 no. 2.
168. Staudinger (-Wimmer-Leonhardt) § 530 no. 18.
169. Id. § 530 no. 17.

(C) INTERPRETATION

1150. *Examples.* Due to the broad wording of the code provision, German legal scholars have attempted to find guidance in examples provided in the legislative history and related code provisions,[170] particularly in the circumstances indicated in the first draft of the code[171] and in various provisions of successions law, including those governing the recovery of the forced share from a descendant (CC § 2333) and the rules relating to the unworthiness to inherit (CC § 2339). The relevant circumstances include attempts on the life of the testator or a close relative, intentional bodily injury, a serious crime against the testator or the testator's spouse, the breach of a maintenance obligation, an immoral lifestyle, or a wrongful act that prevents the testator from completing a valid will. Additionally, the case law has permitted revocation in cases of malicious prosecution, adultery, unfounded attempts to subject the donor to guardianship, and testimony against the donor when spousal immunity was available.[172]

(D) PERSONAL NATURE

1151. *Directed toward the donor.* Because ingratitude is a question of moral responsibility, the law intervenes only when the ungrateful conduct is directed toward the donor. Misbehavior toward the donor's close relatives permits revocation only if, because of the relationship, it breaches a duty owed to the donor. There is no vicarious liability for agents, employees, or representatives unless the donee directed the activity. If the donee has killed the donor with premeditation and without excuse or justification or has otherwise prevented the donor's revocation, the donor's heirs may revoke (CC § 530 par. 2). The dominant view is that the personal nature of moral responsibility prevents revocation for ingratitude when either the donor or the donee are legal persons.[173] Others believe that corporations and associations should be treated the same as natural persons in this regard.[174]

v. The Common Law

1152. *Revocation not permitted.* The common law does not permit revocation based on the donee's ingratitude. There are also no provisions permitting a donor to revoke a gift upon becoming destitute. However, the common law does not permit individuals to benefit from their wrongs.[175] In limited circumstances, the common law achieves results similar to a right of revocation. For example, the

170. Id. § 530 no. 9; MünchKomm-BGB (-Kollhosser) § 530 no. 3.
171. Entwurf § 449.
172. Palandt (-Weidenkaff) § 530 no. 7.
173. Staudinger (-Wimmer-Leonhardt) § 530 no. 30.
174. MünchKomm-BGB (-Kollhosser) § 530 no. 9.
175. *U.S. v. Kwasniewski*, 91 F.Supp. 847, 851 (D. Mich. 1950).

beneficiary of a life insurance policy who wrongfully kills the insured cannot recover under the policy.[176]

c. Regime of the Action

1153. *Variations.* The regime of the action, which involves the types of gifts that may be revoked, the proper plaintiffs and defendants, the possibility of renunciation (in this context, forgiveness), the limitations period, and the role of the courts, vary considerably among civilian jurisdictions.

i. France and Belgium

1154. *All types of gifts.* In French law, all types of gifts may be revoked for ingratitude, including remunerative, indirect, and disguised gifts and gifts given between fiancés and spouses.[177] Manual gifts are also revocable, though customary gifts are exempted.[178] Gifts given by third parties in consideration of marriage are also exempted (CC art. 959). Such gifts are designed to benefit the donee's family.[179]

(A) PROPER PARTIES

1155. *Strictly personal.* Roman law conceived of revocation for ingratitude as a penal sanction to a civil delict. As a result, neither the right nor the burden of the action passed to the heirs.[180] French law has adopted this Roman understanding.[181] Revocation for ingratitude in French law is strictly personal, both as to the donor and to the donee.[182] It is thought that only the donor may decide whether forgiveness or revocation is appropriate. Thus, the donor's heirs and assigns may generally not bring the action, nor may creditors of the donor (CC art. 1166) or of the donor's heirs.[183] The action for revocation is personal to the donee as well. By application of general prescription maxims, the action may not be pursued against the donee's heirs unless it was begun before the donee's death (art. 957 par. 2).[184]

---

176. Id.; *Calaway v. Southern Farm Bureau Life Ins. Co., Inc.*, 619 S.W.2d 301, 302 (Ark. App. 1981).

177. 8 De Page no. 663; Terré and Lequette no. 518.

178. Terré and Lequette no. 518 and note 2.

179. 5 Planiol and Ripert no. 501 and note 2.

180. Biondi no. 341.

181. 5 Planiol and Ripert no. 500.

182. Id. nos. 509–510; 8 De Page no. 666.

183. 5 Planiol and Ripert no. 511; 8 De Page no. 668.

184. "All actions prescribed by death or the passage of time are preserved once the case is begun." (*Omnes actiones quae morte aut tempore pereunt semel inclusae judicio salvae permanent.*) See 5 Planiol and Ripert no. 512; 8 De Page no. 670.

1156. *Exceptions.* The heirs receive their right to revoke by transmission from the donor. They succeed to any action the donor commenced or still had the right to commence, but they have no action of their own. The action may be pursued by the donor's heirs in two situations: if the donor had already commenced the action or if the donor died before the preclusion period had run (art. 957 par. 2).[185] If the donor dies before learning the grounds for revocation, the heirs may bring the action within a year from the date they should have learned of the ingratitude. The Belgian Cassation Court has decided that only those heirs may sue who continue the deceased's person, and not those who merely succeed to the deceased's property.[186] The holding is controverted in the Belgian discussion.

1157. *Assignment.* As a practical matter, the right to revoke is not generally assigned, though nothing in French law prevents the assignment.[187] Assignors would retain the right to forgive the transgression but would have to indemnify the assignee.

(B) FORGIVENESS

1158. *Express or implied.* The donor may not renounce the right to revoke in advance but may forgive the donee once the act of ingratitude has occurred.[188] The donor's forgiveness (*pardon*) constitutes a valid defense to the revocation action. Forgiveness may be either express or implied.[189] De Page argued that the donor should not be precluded from revoking the gift merely because the donor had the human goodness to forgive the donee.[190]

(C) LIMITATIONS PERIOD

1159. *One year.* The code presumes forgiveness if the revocation action is not commenced within a year from the date of the donee's misconduct or from the date the donor could have become aware of it (art. 957 par. 1). Because the one-year time limit can be neither interrupted nor suspended, it is a period of preclusion (*déchéance*) and not a limitations period. If the misdeeds constitute a crime, the preclusion period runs from the date of the conviction.[191] Once the year has passed, the presumption of forgiveness is irrebuttable, and the donor may no longer revoke for ingratitude, either by action or by defense.[192] However, the

185. 8 De Page no. 667.
186. Civ. 3 July 1941, *Pas.* 1941 I 273; 8 De Page no. 666 par. B.
187. 5 Planiol and Ripert no. 511; 8 De Page no. 669.
188. 5 Planiol and Ripert no. 509.
189. Req. 4 Jan. 1842, S. 1842 I 244; Lyon 14 Jan. 1870, D. 1876 V 396 *Révocation* no. 4.
190. 8 De Page no. 665 par. D.
191. Civ.¹ 22 Nov. 1977, D. 1978 IR 241 obs. D. Martin.
192. 5 Planiol and Ripert no. 508.

preclusion period does not run if the insults and injuries continue. In such a case forgiveness cannot be presumed.[193] Thus, if the adultery of the donee spouse continues until the donor's death, the heirs have a year following the death to sue for revocation.[194]

(D) ROLE OF THE COURTS

1160. *Court action.* Revocation for ingratitude generally requires court intervention. It does not take place by operation of law (*de plein droit*) unless the parties have so agreed (CC arts. 956–957).[195] Under insurance law, however, a life insurance policy is automatically rendered invalid with regard to a beneficiary who is convicted of intentionally causing the death of the insured. If the beneficiary has made an attempt on the insured's life, the beneficiary's rights may be revoked, even if they have already vested.[196]

ii. Italy

1161. *Principle.* In Italian law, revocation applies not only to gifts made by public act but also to atypical liberalities (CC art. 809). As in French law, even disguised gifts may be revoked after the simulation is proven.[197] Gifts of modest value, valid in Italian law if there is delivery (CC art. 783), are also generally considered to be subject to revocation for ingratitude.[198] Biondi, however, has argued that they should not be revocable.[199] They are more social in character than legal and thus operate outside the legislative scheme.

(A) EXEMPTIONS

1162. *Necessaries.* Gifts necessary for the donee's well-being are exempt. This includes whatever the donee needs for maintenance, education, health care, clothing, and marriage, as well as for the donee's trousseau or artistic instruction, to the extent they are not extraordinary given the donee's economic situation.[200]

1163. *Customary gifts.* Gratuitous transfers that are made on the occasion of services performed or in conformity with custom do not constitute gifts (CC art. 770 par. 2) and are therefore not subject to revocation.[201]

---

193. Paris 21 Mar. 2002, *Rev. trim. dr. civ.* 2003, 532 at 533 obs. Jean Patarin.

194. Civ.[1] 19 Mar. 1985, *Bull. civ.* I no. 99, *Rev. trim. dr. civ.* 1986, 626 obs. Jean Patarin.

195. 5 Planiol and Ripert no. 507.

196. Ins. C L132–24 pars. 1, 3.

197. Biondi no. 335.

198. Torrente (2006) 706; Biondi id. For gifts of modest value, see supra no. 762.

199. Biondi no. 337 at 1045–1047.

200. CC arts. 809 par. 2, 742.

201. CC art. 809 par. 2; Biondi no. 337.

1164. *In consideration of marriage.* Gifts made in consideration of a particular marriage (*donazioni obnuziali*) are also irrevocable (CC art. 805). This exception does not include gifts given between fiancés prior to marriage. Those are considered customary gifts and are irrevocable because they are not governed by gift law.[202]

1165. *Remunerative gifts.* Some remunerative gifts are also irrevocable (CC art. 805). Under the former Italian Code, only "purely remunerative" gifts (*donazioni puramente rimuneratorie*) were exempt from revocation.[203] The provision was understood to mean that gifts were irrevocable if they corresponded to the value of the donee's services. Because the current Italian Code has deleted the word *purely,* the authors generally believe that all remunerative gifts are irrevocable.[204] Nonetheless, Biondi argued that no alteration of the former rule was intended and that only special remuneration should be exempt from revocation, for only then does the gift represent a counterpart for the donee's services.[205]

1166. *Public entities.* The preliminary draft of the Italian Code explicitly provided that gifts given to public entities (*enti pubblici*) were irrevocable for ingratitude.[206] The provision was eliminated in the final version not to alter the result but rather because it seemed clear that any acts of ingratitude that the entity's representatives commit should not be attributed to the entity. Scholars explain the result as a consequence of the canon law notion that, for revocation purposes, a wrongful act by the entity's representatives is not attributed to the entity.[207] Gifts made to private legal persons, such as associations and partnerships, are subject to revocation, provided the wrongful act is directly related to the organization's purpose.[208]

(B) PROPER PARTIES

1167. *No longer personal.* The former Italian Code followed the French model, which, in the tradition of Roman law, considers revocation to be a penal sanction that is personal between donor and donee.[209] The current Italian Code departs from this model. It permits the donor's heirs to bring the action against the

---

202. Torrente (2006) 704; Biondi no. 337 par. a; CC art. 770 par. 2. For customary gifts in Italian law, see supra nos. 763–766.

203. Italian CC art. 1087 (1865).

204. Torrente (2006) 703–704.

205. Biondi no. 337.

206. Relazione della Commissione Reale 106, in 2 Pandolfelli et al. art. 352 at 402 (concerning the preliminary draft of art. 434). Public entities can be either commercial, like stock companies, or political, such as administrative bodies.

207. De Stefano no. 4.

208. Torrente (2006) 705–706.

209. Italian CC art. 1082 par. 2 (1865).

donee's heirs (CC art. 802 par. 1). However, one aspect of the personal quality of the action remains. It may not be brought by the donor's creditors.[210]

The code permits the action to be brought "one year from the date the donor gained knowledge of the facts." On this basis, Biondi argued that the donor's heirs may bring the action only if the donor was aware of the ingratitude.[211] There should be no revocation if the donor never suffered from the affront. Torrente suggested that the provision is erroneously formulated.[212] As a technical matter, if the donor never learned of the ingratitude, the heirs would seem to be permitted to revoke until the statute of limitations has run. The better rule is to permit the heirs to revoke, provided a year has not run since *they* learned of the facts.[213] Creditors are not subrogated to the action.[214]

(C) RENUNCIATION

1168. *Public policy.* The former Italian Code precluded renunciation in advance only for revocation due to the birth of a child.[215] The current code considers the right to revoke a matter of public policy (*ordine pubblico*) that also may not be renounced in advance in case of ingratitude (CC art. 806). Afterward the right may be renounced either by unilateral act or by agreement. Renunciation may also be implied.[216] Torrente argues that an expression of forgiveness should not imply renunciation. Otherwise, the donor would be required to maintain an artificial hostility toward the donee until revocation.[217] Instead, renunciation should result only from a declaration of will expressing the desire to respect the validity of the gift.

(D) LIMITATIONS

1169. *One year.* Similar to French law, the Italian Code provides that the action for revocation must be brought within a year from the date the donor gained knowledge (*è venuto a conoscenza*) of the facts permitting revocation (CC art. 802 par. 1). If the donee intentionally kills the donor or fraudulently prevents revocation, the year begins to run from the date the heirs receive notice of the wrongful act (CC art. 802 par. 2). The one-year period is considered a period of preclusion

---

210. "[T]he right to benefit from the power of revocation is completely personal because it is attributed to protect interests chiefly of a moral order. Its patrimonial effects are subordinate and indirect." Capozzi no. 357 par. d.

211. Biondi no. 343; see also Cian and Trabucchi art. 802 no. 2.

212. Torrente (2006) 686; see also Cendon art. 802 no. 2.

213. Torrente (2006) 687, 690.

214. Biondi no. 343.

215. Italian CC art. 1084 (1865).

216. Biondi no. 336.

217. Torrente (2006) 710.

(*decadenza*) and not limitation. It is tolled if the donee acknowledges the donor's right to revoke (CC art. 2966).[218]

1170. *Donor's knowledge.* Difficulty arises in determining when the donor may be said to have *knowledge* of the facts permitting revocation.[219] In the French Code, the preclusion period is stated in terms of when the donor "could have learned" of the facts. The Italian Code provision is phrased in terms of the donor's knowledge. The broader question is how the donor can be said to know that the donee acted wrongfully. In the case of a crime, a conviction would seem to be necessary. In other cases, such as harm fraudulently caused to the donor's patrimony or maintenance unjustifiably refused, the donor, paradoxically, may not learn the truth until the facts are revealed at trial on the revocation action.

(E) ROLE OF THE COURTS

1171. *Judicial action.* Revocation for ingratitude is always the result of a judicial decision.[220] It never occurs *ipso iure*.

iii. Spain

1172. *Types of gifts.* Though Spanish scholars continue to discuss whether customary presents (*liberalidades de uso*) should be considered gifts,[221] they are, in any case, irrevocable.[222] Lacruz Berdejo argued that remunerative gifts should also be irrevocable for ingratitude,[223] while Albaladejo García, arguing from a code provision, suggested that remunerative gifts should be revocable to the extent the value of the gift exceeds the value of the services rendered.[224]

1173. *Proper parties.* The action does not pass to the heirs if the donor, though able to do so, did not sue (CC art. 653 par. 1). The action may not be brought by creditors nor may it be brought by the donor's legal representative, unless, before losing the capacity to act, the donor declared the intention to revoke.[225] The action may not be brought against the donee's heirs, unless the action was commenced before the donee's death (CC art. 653 par. 2).

1174. *Renunciation.* The right to revoke may not be renounced in advance (CC art. 652 sent. 1).

1175. *Limitations.* The preclusion period is one year. According to the scholars, the code incorrectly labels it a limitations period. The period runs from

---

218. Id. 689.
219. Biondi no. 344.
220. Id. no. 338.
221. See Paz-Ares Rodríguez (-Albaladejo García) art. 618 no. I (not governed by gift law).
222. 2 Lacruz Berdejo no. 508.
223. 2 Lacruz Berdejo no. 510.
224. Paz-Ares Rodríguez (-Albaladejo García) art. 622 no. II, referring to CC art. 622.
225. Paz-Ares Rodríguez (-Díaz Alabart) art. 653 no. I.

the moment the donor learned of the facts and was able to bring the action (CC art. 652 sent. 2).[226]

1176. *Role of the courts.* Revocation for ingratitude occurs by judicial pronouncement.[227]

iv. Germany

1177. *All gifts revocable.* With the exception of gifts required by custom (*Pflicht- und Anstandsschenkungen*), German law permits all gifts to be revoked for ingratitude.[228] Even gifts required by custom may be revoked to the extent their value exceeds what is required by social convention.[229] If a customary gift is indivisible, it may be revoked in exchange for a less valuable gift that meets the requirements of custom.[230] In certain cases, the donee may be asked to make monetary reimbursement equivalent to the excess value.[231]

(A) PROPER PARTIES

1178. *Personal right.* The right to revoke is understood as a right to alter a legal relationship (*Gestaltungsrecht*). It therefore does not pass by inheritance or assignment or as security to creditors.[232] Once the donor has revoked, however, the right to recover the gift may pass by inheritance.[233] The heirs may revoke only when the donee has intentionally and wrongfully killed the donor or unlawfully prevented revocation (CC § 530 par. 2). This right may pass by inheritance.[234] The gift may only be revoked as against the donee. Recovery is not available after the donee's death (CC § 532 sent. 2) unless the gift was revoked before the donee died, in which case recovery may be pursued against the heirs.[235]

(B) RENUNCIATION

1179. *Basic rule.* The donor may not renounce the right to revoke in advance but may do so after the facts have become known (CC § 533). However, the right to revoke may be contractually replaced in advance with a damage claim.[236]

1180. *Distinguished from forgiveness.* Renunciation (*Verzicht*) and forgiveness (*Verzeihung*) constitute two separate grounds for preclusion. Renunciation is

---

226. Id. no. III.
227. 2 Lacruz Berdejo no. 507 par. d.
228. Jauernig (-Mansel) §§ 530–533 no. I.
229. Staudinger (-Wimmer-Leonhardt) § 531 no. 22.
230. BGH 13 Feb. 1963, MDR 1963, 575.
231. Staudinger (-Wimmer-Leonhardt) § 534 no. 15.
232. Id. § 530 no. 8.
233. Id. § 532 no. 27.
234. Staudinger (-Wimmer-Leonhardt) § 530 no. 26.
235. Id. § 532 no. 9.
236. BGH 17 Sept. 1971, *Betrieb* 1971, 2151, MDR 1972, 36.

a legal act (*Rechtsgeschäft*). It is effected by a unilateral declaration of intent that is effective upon receipt.[237] The right to revoke may be renounced by the donor's representatives or heirs.

Forgiveness also precludes revocation (CC § 532). Forgiveness is a purely factual matter.[238] It takes effect when it is manifested in externally perceptible conduct. Forgiveness effectively precludes revocation even if the donor was unaware of the right to revoke. The donee need not have learned of the donor's forgiveness. There is no requirement that it be communicated.[239] It is operative even if the donor remains troubled by the donee's act (*Vergeben aber nicht vergessen*). Though forgiveness, once expressed, cannot be retracted, the Supreme Court has decided that the expression of forgiveness may be insufficient in the circumstances to constitute a true release (*Erlaßvertrag*).[240]

(c) LIMITATIONS

1181. *One year.* As in other civilian jurisdictions, the gift must be revoked within a year from the date the donor learns the relevant facts (CC § 532). When the right is accorded to the heirs (CC § 530 par. 2), the year begins to run from the moment the heirs are aware both of their inheritance and of the donee's misconduct.[241] As in other systems, the one-year period is a preclusion and not a limitations period.

(d) ROLE OF THE COURT

1182. *No court intervention.* In contrast to other civilian systems, revocation for ingratitude does not require the court's intervention. It is rather the result of the donor's declaration of intent (*Willenserklärung*). The declaration need not be made in any particular form. It is unilateral and effective upon receipt (*formlos, einseitig, und empfangsbedürftig*).[242] The declaration is sufficient if made by filing a lawsuit or in a will, provided the will is read and communicated to the donee.

v. The Common Law

1183. *No revocation.* As indicated above, the common law does not permit a donor to revoke a gift for ingratitude.[243]

d. Effects

1184. *Variation.* The effects of revocation, both between the parties and as to third parties, vary significantly among civilian jurisdictions.

---

237. Staudinger (-Wimmer-Leonhardt) § 533 no. 2.
238. MünchKomm-BGB (-Kolhosser) § 532 no. 2.
239. Staudinger (-Wimmer-Leonhardt) § 532 no. 2.
240. RG 8 Oct. 1923, LZ 1924, 86.
241. MünchKomm-BGB (-Kollhosser) § 532 no. 4.
242. Id. § 531 no. 1.
243. Supra no. 1152.

i. France and Belgium

(A) BETWEEN THE PARTIES

1185. *Retroactive effect.* As between the parties, revocation in French law is retro-active to the date of the gift.[244] The gift property must be returned if it is still in the donee's possession. If not, the donee must indemnify the donor for the property's value at the moment the revocation action was commenced (CC art. 958 par. 2). The donee must also compensate the donor for the value of any mortgages or servitudes that third parties validly acquired in the property. Leases in the property are maintained. The donee owes no indemnity, provided the lease is not of abnormal length.[245] Fruits are due only from the date the action was filed. If fruits were to be repaid from the date of the gift, the donee could be ruined, the scholars argue, because years may have passed. Equity seems to require that the donor compensate the donee for any improvements made to the recovered property, while the donee must pay for any undue deterioration.

(B) THIRD PARTIES

1186. *No retroactive effect.* In principle French law does not provide for retroactive effect against third parties.[246] This is consistent with the French law conception of revocation for ingratitude as a penal sanction. Because the fault was committed by the donee, the effect of the sanction on others should be limited. Moreover, no one should be expected to foresee that another will commit a tort.[247] Thus, any dispositions validly constituted by the donee, including mortgages or other security interests, remain valid when the gift returns to the donor (CC art. 958 par. 1).

1187. *Real property.* If revocation were to operate entirely prospectively, the donee would be able to dispose of the property between notice and judgment. To prevent this type of disposition, revocation actions regarding real property must be recorded by a note in the margin of the public record.[248] If the action is not recorded, it may be dismissed. Upon a successful revocation, any transfer made after recordation is retroactively invalidated.

1188. *Movables.* A transferee of movables who acquires possession in good faith is protected against revocation by the normal rules applicable to good faith purchase (CC art. 2279). De Page argued that this protection also applies to transferees who know of the ingratitude, provided the revocation action has not been

---

244. 5 Planiol and Ripert no. 514; 8 De Page no. 674.
245. 8 De Page no. 677.
246. 5 Planiol and Ripert no. 513.
247. 1 Delvincourt 772 note 9 to page 246.
248. 5 Planiol and Ripert no. 513; Decree of 4 Jan. 1955 art. 28 no. 4 lit. c.

filed and recorded.[249] Thus, a good faith transferee who acquires after learning of the *ingratitude* is protected, but transfer to a party who knows of the *action* may be avoided as a fraud on creditors.[250] For incorporeal movables not governed by the rules of good faith purchase, the scholars do not agree as to whether revocation should have retroactive effect.

ii. Italy

(A) BETWEEN THE PARTIES

1189. *No retroactive effect.* Revocation does not return the parties to the *status quo ante.*[251] The judgment of revocation transfers title *ex nunc* to the donor and imposes on the donee the obligation to return the gift, if the gift still exists, together with the fruits, as of the date the action is commenced (CC art. 807 par. 1). If the donee has transferred title, the donee must return the value of the gift at the moment the complaint is filed, together with fruits as of the same date (CC art. 807 par. 2). If the donee has validly constituted property rights in the gift object, whether those that burden the property, such as servitudes, or suretyship rights, such as mortgages, the donor must be indemnified for the diminution in value (CC art. 808 par. 2).

1190. *Risk of loss.* Some scholars argue that the risk of loss does not pass to the donee until the action is commenced. If the gift object perishes before that time, even if the loss is due to the donee's act or negligence, the donee's obligation to return the gift is discharged, and no damages or monetary restitution is due. Before receiving notice of the action, the donee is considered owner of the property. The law imposes no duty of care on an owner—*qui suo iure utitur neminem ledit.*[252]

Other authors take the position that the donee is liable for the property's destruction even if it occurs before the action is commenced.[253] As for improvements made before commencement of the action, the donee is considered to be a possessor in good faith—the possession itself is in good faith, despite the ingratitude at the level of the obligation—and is therefore entitled to compensation (CC art. 1150). The donee is also entitled to expenses for the production of

---

249. 8 De Page no. 676. CC art. 958 par. 1 protects third parties who take from the donee before the revocation complaint is recorded. This protection of third-party rights is thought to extend the more limited protection available under CC art. 2279. Id.

250. CC art. 1167 par. 1; 5 Planiol and Ripert no. 513; 8 De Page no. 676 par. B.

251. Biondi no. 339.

252. "Those who use their rights cause no one harm." Id. no. 339; Torrente (2006) 712.

253. Torrente (2006) 712 note 93 (citing authors).

any fruits required to be returned to the donor—*fructus non intelleguntur nisi deductis impensis* (CC art. 1149).[254]

(B) THIRD PARTIES

1191. *No retroactive effect.* In general, revocation does not affect the rights third parties acquire in the gift object prior to the commencement of the action (CC art. 808). However, if the gift involves real property or movables subject to registration, the donor is required to record the complaint (CC art. 2652 no. 1). If the donor records, the third party prevails only if the transfer from the donee is recorded first. If the transfer takes place while the action is pending and neither party has recorded, any judgment of revocation invalidates the transfer unless the third party has acquired title by good faith purchase.[255] As far as movables are concerned, even incorporeal movables, revocation does not affect transfers made to third parties before the commencement of the action. If a donee makes a transfer after the action is commenced, it is invalidated if the donor is successful, unless the third party acquires title by good faith purchase.

iii. Spain

(A) BETWEEN THE PARTIES

1192. *Object of value.* The donee, upon revocation, must return the gift object, or, if the gift has been irrevocably transferred, its value (CC art. 645 par. 1). The value of the gift is determined as of the moment the gift was made.[256] If a security interest has been validly created in the property, the donor may pay off the creditor and claim reimbursement from the donee.[257] Fruits are due from the moment the action is commenced (CC art. 651 par. 1). The donee's liability for loss or deterioration of the property (CC art. 457) and the donee's right to reimbursement for expenses and improvements (CC art. 453) are the same as those of a possessor in good faith.[258] If the donee attempts to defraud the donor by transferring the gift during the period following the events but before the action is commenced, the donee is liable for harm caused.[259]

(B) THIRD PARTIES

1193. *Recording.* As far as third parties are concerned, property rights the donee transfers before the complaint for revocation is recorded in the Property Register remain valid, despite a subsequent judgment for revocation (CC art. 649 par. 1).

---

254. "Fruits may not be recovered unless expenses are deducted."
255. CCP art. 111 par. 4; Palazzo art. 808 no. 3.
256. CC arts. 645 par. 3, 650 par. 1.
257. CC arts. 645 par. 2, 650 par. 2.
258. Paz-Ares Rodríguez (-Díaz Alabart) art. 645 no. II par. 4.
259. 2 Lacruz Berdejo no. 101.

In contrast to French and Italian law, only transfers for value are maintained.[260] The code considers a gratuitous transfer to a third party to be equivalent to a fraudulent conveyance (CC art. 1297 par. 1). Any transfers made after recordation are voided by the judgment (CC art. 649 par. 2). Based on the code's reference to recordation, scholars argue that the reach of revocation depends on the knowledge of the third-party transferee. Once the claim is recorded, the third party has knowledge as a matter of law. The same result should follow if the transferee actually knows or should or could have known of the action, regardless whether the property is movable or immovable.[261]

iv. Germany

1194. *Restitution law.* In German law, restitutions principles govern the effects of revocation for ingratitude.[262] The revocation provisions explicitly refer to them.[263] The reference involves both facts and law (*Tatbestandsverweisung*), which means it incorporates both the elements of fact and the legal effect of the relevant restitutionary action. That action is the *condictio ob causam finitam,* because revocation causes the legal basis for the transaction to disappear after performance.[264]

(A) BETWEEN THE PARTIES

1195. *Legal basis.* Upon a valid declaration of revocation, the legal basis (*Rechtsgrund*) for the gift transfer is said to disappear.[265] The donee is obligated to return the gift or, if that is no longer possible, to reimburse the donor for its value (CC § 818 par. 2). The return is considered impossible if the gift has been transferred to a third party and also if improvements have significantly increased the value of real estate.[266] Value means the objective commercial market value at the moment title was transferred to the donee.[267]

1196. *Donee protection.* The donee's duty to return the gift or to reimburse the donor for the gift's value is discharged to the extent the donee, in good faith, is no longer enriched (CC § 818 par. 3). The donee is no longer enriched when the gift is lost or the donee transfers it to a third party, even as a gift.[268] The donee is also no longer enriched when the quid pro quo for which the donee exchanged

---

260. Paz-Ares Rodríguez (-Díaz Alabart) art. 645 nos. I–II.
261. Id. art. 645 no. II par. 2.
262. 2 Windscheid § 367.
263. CC § 531 par. 2.
264. CC § 812 par. 1 sent. 2 alt. 1.
265. MünchKomm-BGB (-Kollhosser) § 531 no. 4.
266. BGH 10 July 1981, NJW 1981, 2687; Jauernig (-Stadler) § 818 nos. 5 and 12.
267. Jauernig (-Stadler) § 818 nos. 5, 14, and 17.
268. Id. § 818 nos. 6 and 29 ff.

the gift property has proved to be worthless. Thus, the donor generally bears the risk that the donee will put the gift to disadvantageous use.[269]

1197. *Fruits.* The donee is required to surrender the fruits and other profits (*Nutzungen*) earned by the gift, as well as any substitute received for its destruction or damage (*Surrogate*; CC § 818 par. 1). Savigny argued that the donee loses the good faith necessary to retain fruits when the donee decides to act ungratefully. In contrast, Windscheid thought that the donee lacks good faith only from the moment the donor actually revokes.[270]

1198. *Increased responsibilities.* If the donor sues to recover the gift, special rules apply. From the pendency of the action (*Rechtshängigkeit*), the donee's responsibilities are determined by reference to the general principles of obligor liability.[271] Some authors suggest that the action is pending from the date of the act that justified revocation.[272] The donee is liable from that moment for any destruction or deterioration caused by the donee's fault.[273] If the gift object includes a sum of money, the donee owes interest at the legal rate.[274] The donee becomes liable not only for actual fruits or profits taken from the gift but also for the value of the fruits that could have been obtained by diligent management.[275] The donee's enrichment is reduced by expenses or improvements to the property.[276] In the case of the donatio sub modo, the donee's enrichment is also reduced to the extent the condition has been performed. In contrast to the right of revocation, the donor may assign the right to restitution from a declared revocation.[277]

(B) THIRD PARTIES

1199. *No tracing.* In principle, the donor cannot trace the gift into the hands of third parties.[278] An exception is made when the third party received the property without compensation (*unentgeltlich*),[279] which means by gift, bequest, loan without interest, or bailment without rental payments.[280] In such a case, the third

---

269. Schlechtriem 784.
270. 2 Windscheid § 367 note. 18. According to the Prussian General Law, good faith was lost at the moment of the ungrateful act. Gen. Law pt. I tit. II § 1167.
271. CC § 818 par. 4; Palandt (-Sprau) § 818 no. 51.
272. CC § 819 par. 1 (by analogy); MünchKomm-BGB (-Kollhosser) § 531 no. 5; for the contrary view see Staudinger (-Wimmer-Leonhardt) § 531 no. 15.
273. CC §§ 292 par. 1, 989.
274. CC §§ 291, 288 par. 1, 247.
275. CC §§ 292 par. 2, 987.
276. Staudinger (-Wimmer-Leonhardt) § 531 no. 11.
277. MünchKomm-BGB (-Kollhosser) § 531 no. 7.
278. Staudinger (-Wimmer-Leonhardt) § 531 no. 17.
279. CC § 822; BGH 3 Feb. 1989, BGHZ 106, 354.
280. Jauernig (-Teichmann) § 822 nos. 2 and 5.

party must turn over the gift object or its value, together with proceeds and fruits.

v. The Common Law

1200. *No revocation.* As noted above, the common law does not permit revocation of an executed gift due to the donee's ingratitude.[281]

2. The Donor's Impoverishment

1201. *Recovery of gift or support.* If, after making the gift, the donor becomes impoverished, some systems permit the donor to recover the gift, or some portion of it, or to request monetary support.

a. The Notion of Impoverishment

i. Germany

1202. *Support for themselves or others.* Donors who, after executing the gift, become unable to support their lifestyle or to fulfill their duties of support to relatives, spouses, or former spouses, may ask their donees to return the gift (*Rückforderung wegen Verarmung*; CC § 528). A related code provision, discussed above, permits donors to refrain from executing gift promises if they would thereby lose the ability to support themselves or their dependents.[282] The donor may not recover the gift if destitution was either intentional or resulted from gross negligence (CC § 529 par. 1). Moreover, sufficient net worth prevents the donor from taking advantage of the provision, even if the donor cannot meet obligations from income alone.[283]

A typical situation involves parents who make an inter vivos advancement of a portion of their estate, only to discover that rising costs prevent them from meeting their obligations.[284] Some scholars suggest that the development of social welfare in Germany requires an expansive interpretation of the recovery provision to reduce the burden destitute donors place on the state.[285]

1203. *Donee's alternatives.* Donees are not required to return the gift if doing so would prevent them from providing for their own support or supporting those to whom they owe maintenance (CC § 529 par. 2). A donee may avoid returning the gift by agreeing to pay support to the donor and to satisfy the donor's legal maintenance obligations. Once the donee has transformed the obligation in this fashion, the donee may not unilaterally satisfy the obligation by returning the gift.

---

281. Supra no. 1152.
282. Supra nos. 721–724.
283. Staudinger (-Wimmer-Leonhardt) § 528 no. 9.
284. MünchKomm-BGB (-Kollhosser) § 528 no. 2.
285. Id. § 528 no. 3.

Moreover, the maintenance obligation, once assumed, is not limited to the value of the gift.[286]

ii. Italy

1204. *Support obligation.* The Italian Code provides that the donee is responsible before all other obligors to provide the donor with support (CC art. 437). Only gifts in contemplation of marriage and remunerative gifts are excepted.

iii. Spain

1205. *Gift limitation.* The Spanish Civil Code does not specifically permit the donor to revoke upon becoming destitute. However, a related provision sets limits to the donor's generosity. The donor may gift all property presently in the donor's patrimony, provided the donor retains "what is necessary for the donor to live in a manner that corresponds to the donor's circumstances."[287] The code does not address what is to happen if, due to the gift, the donor's resources prove to be insufficient. Some scholars argue that the gift is void as to the portion of the gift required for the donor's maintenance.[288] The donor's action would be in avoidance. Other authors, however, argue that the gift is valid, subject to the donor's right to recover the gift or some portion of it.[289]

Whatever the basis of the action, it is agreed that donors may recover what is necessary for their own subsistence, as well as support for those for whom they are responsible.[290] The amount necessary to maintain the donor's lifestyle is a question of fact. The donor's heirs and creditors are not protected by this action. Thus, if the donor originally reserved sufficient resources, but, as a result of inadequate financial planning, subsequently becomes impoverished, the donor may not revoke the gift.[291] This right of recovery is related to the donor's right to revoke the gift for ingratitude if the donee refuses to provide the donor with maintenance.[292]

iv. The Common Law

1206. *No right to revoke.* The common law generally does not recognize the donor's right to revoke on the grounds of improvidence or impoverishment.[293]

---

286. MünchKomm-BGB (-Kollhosser) § 528 no. 21.

287. Spanish CC § 634; see supra no. 388.

288. Diez-Picazo and Gullón 339–340.

289. 2 Lacruz Berdejo no. 503 par. a.

290. Paz-Ares Rodríguez (-Albaladejo García) art. 634 no. I.

291. 2 Lacruz Berdejo no. 503 par. a.

292. CC art. 648 no. 3; see supra no. 1145. See generally Quiñonero Cervantes.

293. "A gift which is consistent with law will not be declared invalid merely because the court regards the donor's act as improvident. Even though the gift is considered as unreasonable, if otherwise lawful it may not be set aside." *Amado v. Aguirre*, 161 P.2d 117, 119 (Ariz. 1945). The Uniform Probate Code, followed by statutes in many states, provides

However, as Eisenberg has pointed out, the courts take the reasonableness of the gift into account when evaluating the donor's capacity.[294]

b. Regime

i. Germany

1207. *Types of gift.* With the exception of customary gifts (*Pflicht- und Anstandsschenkungen*), all gifts may be recovered if the donor becomes destitute.[295]

1208. *Proper parties.* In general, the right to recover the gift is personal to the donor. It does not pass to the donor's heirs and can be assigned or given for security only in limited circumstances.[296] However, the social insurance office (*Träger der Sozialhilfe*) has the right to recover a gift made by a donor who lacks sufficient assets for reasonable maintenance. The social insurance office is subrogated by operation of law to the donor's claim against the donee to the extent the office provides the donor with support.[297] The claim is generally not extinguished by the donor's death.[298] When the value of the gift substantially exceeds the support provided, the courts permit the donee to retain the gift as long as the social insurance office is compensated for its payments.[299] The social insurance office need not prove that the donor became needy as a result of the gift.[300] Instead, the courts look to whether the donor was in need of support when social insurance payments began.

1209. *Forgiveness.* Because recovery for impoverishment is not related to ingratitude in German law, forgiveness is not a factor, though, as discussed above, the donee's agreement to pay maintenance prevents recovery. The right to recover the gift may not be renounced in advance.[301]

1210. *Limitations.* Recovery is precluded if the donor becomes needy more than ten years after the gift was made (CC § 529 par. 1). If the donor becomes destitute before the ten years have elapsed, the donor can request the return of the gift even thereafter.[302]

---

that wills are generally not revoked by change in circumstances. Unif. Prob. C § 2-804 par. f. Though some commentators have suggested that changed circumstances should revoke will substitutes, apparently no American court has followed this suggestion. McGovern 23.

294. Eisenberg (1979) 17 note 55, referring to *Richmond v. First Nat'l Bank*, 179 N.W. 59, 60 (Iowa 1920).

295. Jauernig (-Mansel) § 528–529 no. 1.

296. Id. no. 2; see German CC § 400.

297. Soc. C [SGB] bk. 12 § 93 par. 1.

298. BGH 14 June 1995, BGHZ 96, 380, NJW 1995, 2287.

299. BGH 29 Mar. 1985, BGHZ 94, 141.

300. BGH 19 Oct. 2004, DNotZ 2005, 281.

301. Jauernig (-Mansel) § 529 no. 2.

302. Staudinger (-Wimmer-Leonhardt) § 529 no. 7.

ii. Spain

1211. *Proper parties.* In Spanish law, several parties may all sue to recover the portion of the gift necessary for the donor's maintenance.[303] These include the donor, those obligated to provide the donor with support, and those whom the donor must support.

1212. *Limitations.* The Spanish Civil Code does not specify the limitations period. Because necessaries are at stake, it is felt the term should not be too restrictive. A period of fifteen years has been suggested, which is the period the code provides for personal actions for which no term is specified.[304]

c. Effects

1213. *Germany.* In German law, the recovery action is governed by the rules of restitution.[305] However, in contrast to revocation for ingratitude, the reference to restitution incorporates merely the legal effect of restitution (*Rechtsfolgenverweisung*).[306] The restitution action concerns only that portion of the gift necessary to provide for the donor's obligations.[307]

1214. *Spain.* In Spanish law as well, it is sometimes not necessary to invalidate the entire gift act. The gift remains in effect until it is proven that the gift left the donor with insufficient resources.[308] Restitution involves either return of the gift or payment of a sum of money, depending on whether the donor requires the gifted property for maintenance.

3. The Birth of a Child

1215. *Romanic systems.* Romanic systems permit a donor to revoke an executed gift, even one made many years earlier, upon the birth of a child.

a. Introduction

i. History

1216. *Continuing evolution.* Revocation due to the birth of a child has been subject to widely varying formulations and justifications. Very recently it has once again found a place on the legislative agenda.

---

303. Paz-Ares Rodríguez (-Albaladejo García) art. 634 no. V.
304. CC art. 1964; Paz-Ares Rodríguez (-Albaladejo García) arts. 634 no. V, 654–656 no. VI.
305. CC §§ 528 par. 1 sent. 1.
306. MünchKomm-BGB (-Kollhosser) §§ 528 no. 7, 531 no. 4.
307. Staudinger (-Wimmer-Leonhardt) § 528 no. 17.
308. Dir. gen. Registros 17 April 1907, *Juris. civ.* 1907 no. 24.

(A) ORIGINS

(1) *Si unquam*

1217. *Master and freed slaves.* Revocation of a gift due to the birth of a child was unknown for much of Roman history.[309] By the fourth century, as noted above, the master's right to revoke gifts given to former slaves, which was previously unlimited, was restricted to cases of ingratitude.[310] In the Constitution *Si unquam* of 355, Constans and Constantinus granted slaveholders the additional right to revoke upon the birth of a first child.[311] The rule seemed to make sense in the particular circumstances. Justinian included the constitution in the *Codex* but did not extend it.[312]

1218. *Lombard law.* Lombard customary law, codified in 643 in the *Edictum Rothari*, applied revocation based on the birth of a child to all gifts.[313] Though the edict was written in Latin and the Lombards occupied much of Byzantine Italy at the time, the extent of Roman influence is uncertain.

(2) *Glossators*

1219. *Controversy.* The glossators engaged in ardent controversy regarding each word of Si unquam. They asked why, if gifts to a former slave were revoked upon the birth of a child, the same rule should not apply to gifts between friends or gifts to the church. Despite the clear limitation in the text, some scholars

---

309. Biondi no. 345.

310. Supra no. 1117.

311. "If ever a master, having no children, transfers all or any part of his property to his freedmen by gift and thereafter begets children, let all these gifts revert to the donor's authority and jurisdiction." (*Si unquam libertis patronus, filios non habens, bona omnia vel partem aliquam facultatum fuerit donatione largitus, et postea susceperit liberos, totum quidquid largitus fuerit revertatur in eiusdem donatoris arbitrio ac dictione mansurum.*) C. 8, 55, 8. See 2 Kaser 399.

312. Biondi seems to suggest that gifts given by former slaves to their former masters could also be revoked in case of the birth of a child. This seems to be a typographical error. I have found no authority for this suggestion in the texts. Cf. Biondi no. 345.

313. If anyone, either because of age or other infirmity, despairs of ever having children and therefore transfers his property to someone else (*res suas alii thingauerit*), and if afterwards it happens that he begets legitimate children, then the whole *thinx*, that is the gift which was made before the children were born, is broken (*rumpatur*) and the one or more legitimate sons who were born afterwards shall be the heirs of their father in all things. If, moreover, there were one or more legitimate daughters or one or more natural [illegitimate] sons born after the gift had been made, they shall have their rights, just as provided above, as if nothing had been given to anyone else. And he who was given the property shall have only such an amount as the near relatives or the king's fisc would have received if the property had not been transferred.

Edictus Rothari art. 171 in Drew 82, original in Beyerle 44–45.

contended that Justinian had intended to generalize, just as he had generalized revocation based on ingratitude. Other scholars disagreed. By the sixteenth century, the controversy had become so intense that the French humanist scholar André Tiraqueau devoted an extraordinary treatise to the questions surrounding revocation for the birth of a child, yet even after reviewing the authorities he was unable to establish a workable consensus.[314] There is today no doubt that the glossators, who were working before the discovery of the *Fragmenta vaticana,* were mistaken in assuming that Si unquam represented a general principle.[315] By then, however, this institution had grown roots in custom and practice.

In the end, the glossators concluded that revocation upon the birth of a child was actually a version of rescission based on the failure of a condition.[316] They suggested that donors without children would not make gifts if they believed they would have progeny in the future. The doctors engaged in further prolonged discussions concerning whether the revocation operated *ex tunc* to negate all intervening transfers or *ex nunc* with the effect of a new transfer.

1220. *Marriage contract.* Because revocation was based on the assumption that the donor had not expected children, a particularly interesting question arose concerning whether gifts made in the marriage contract were subject to revocation. Bartolus contended that, in case of doubt, the contemplation of children was not to be presumed—*in dubio non praesumitur quis cogitare de liberis.* Other scholars assumed the contrary, suggesting that everyone at marriage contemplates the possibility of procreation.[317] Numerous other problems remained, particularly whether gifts made in the marriage contract by other relatives would be exempt. At the beginning of the sixteenth century, it seemed that some gifts made in the marriage settlement may be subject to Si unquam.

(B) FRANCE

1221. *Centuries of discussion.* French law has wrestled with revocation due to the birth of a child *(survenance d'enfant)* for five hundred years. The most recent legislative revision has now greatly limited its reach.

(1) The Case of Charles Dumoulin

1222. *Gift to his brother.* The great French jurist Charles Dumoulin (1500–1566) was instrumental in formulating the version of the rule that eventually passed into the French Civil Code.[318] At the age of 31, Dumoulin renounced life as a lawyer after being unfairly criticized in court for his stuttering.[319] He decided

---

314. 6 Tiraqueau.
315. Aubépin 157.
316. Id. 162.
317. Id. 165.
318. The following is taken principally from Aubépin 169–190.
319. Hello 9.

instead to create for himself a monastic solitude and to produce a commentary on the *Coutume de Paris*. In order to avoid the distractions caused by his inheritance, Dumoulin gave his worldly possessions to his brother Ferry, who was also a lawyer at the Paris court.

Ferry married and included in his marriage settlement a considerable dower (*douaire*) for his wife, Marguerite Maillard. The dower was secured by a legal mortgage on all of Ferry's possessions. Dumoulin signed the marriage settlement to confirm the gift of his property to his brother. Ferry and Marguerite had children. Dumoulin himself later married, and a child was born of his marriage.[320] Impecunious, Dumoulin asked Ferry to return the gift. In the meantime, Marguerite had died, leaving Ferry and the children. Due to the dower, Ferry was unable to return the property he had received from his brother.[321] In 1547 Dumoulin invoked Si unquam and petitioned for rescission. The Parlement de Paris rejected his petition.

1223. *Appeal.* On appeal, Dumoulin raised two issues. First, he argued that Si unquam applied to gifts made in the marriage settlement. Second, he argued that the revocation took effect ex tunc and returned the property free of encumbrances. In the interim, Dumoulin had written a treatise on the complex matter and offered it to the court as a guide to resolving the dispute.[322]

There was no legal consensus about the first question. The authors agreed that remunerative and onerous gifts, which generally meant gifts subject to an obligation, were not revoked by the birth of a child.[323] Some authors argued that gifts given in the marriage settlement were always onerous, since the husband would have demanded a larger dowry and would have given his wife a larger dower without the gifts. Those who opposed this view argued that, since the donor received nothing in exchange, gifts in the marriage settlement could not be considered onerous.

Dumoulin distinguished gifts made in a marriage settlement into four categories: those made from one spouse to the other, those from a spouse to a third party, those made to a spouse from a third party who was obligated to provide a dowry, and those from a third party with no obligation either to provide a dowry

---

320. "[E]specially since I had been devoted to the pursuits of Philosophy, so much so that the unhappy bachlerhood I had chosen so I might reflect about public matters (*Reipublicae philosophandi causa*) was overtaken by my decision to marry (which I did, not out of desire or wealth, but rather to establish and maintain a family and renew the pursuits of my leisure ...)." 3 Dumoulin (1681) no. 84.

321. Hello 22–23.

322. 3 Dumoulin (1681), *Tractatus*. The version of the treatise contained in Dumoulin's collected works was revised after the decision to include paragraphs discussing the court's opinion. Id. nos. 85–86.

323. 1 Louet 502–503.

or to make a gift to the couple.[324] Dumoulin argued that appropriate rules should govern each situation. Following Bartolus, some scholars argued that gifts given by parents in the marriage settlement were onerous up to the amount of the child's reserve and simple as to the remainder.[325] Dumoulin assured the court that he had been under no obligation to make the gift and that he received nothing of benefit from the transaction (*non respiciens favorem aut utilitatem donantis*).[326] His gift was a simple gift and therefore subject to revocation.

Dumoulin's treatise did not discuss the second question because the regime of revocation had by then become clear. Si unquam operated as a matter of law (*de plein droit*) as soon as the donor manifested an intent to revoke. The revocation operated ex tunc, which meant that it resulted from a tacit condition subsequent. The property returned to the donor free of any encumbrances that had attached while in the donee's hands. Fruits were owed from the receipt of notice.

1224. *Decision.* In 1551, in perhaps the most celebrated decision in the history of gift law, the Parlement of Paris, the judges dressed in their red ceremonial robes, decided in Dumoulin's favor and revoked the gift.[327] Before the decision, Ferry had requested, and Dumoulin had agreed, that the property would continue to serve as subsidiary security for the dower of Ferry's deceased wife.[328] Following the parties' agreement the court affirmed the security interest that secured the dower. The opinion thus resolved two questions. First, Si unquam applied to a nononerous gift made in the marriage contract by a third party. Second, the revocation returned the property free of all charges created by the donee. Nonetheless, both questions remained controversial, partially because it was not

324. 3 Dumoulin (1681), *Tractatus* no. 1.
325. 1 Louet 503.
326. 3 Dumoulin (1681), *Tractatus* no. 75.
327. Paris 12 Apr. 1551, 3 Dumoulin 543. A summary of the case is found in 1 Louet 503–504 and 1 Ricard no. 608. For a similar case, see Papon 376–377 no. 20.
328. 3 Dumoulin (1681), *Tractatus* no. 86; Bretonnier 107. *Dower* was intended to provide support to the surviving wife and her minor children by protecting them against the heirs' claims to the husband's property. Dower arose from custom, but it could also be established in the marriage settlement (*douaire préfix*), as was Ferry's. Though the rules were complex, the dower in effect provided the wife and surviving children with a life estate (*usufruit*) in a portion (often a third, though in Paris it was half) of the husband's real property. The reversion was in the husband's heirs. Customs of Paris arts. 247–264, in 1 Dumoulin (1691) 430–460; Ourliac and Malafosse 250–252, 271–273; see also 2 Bracton 265. In 1551 Ferry's children were still minors. Presumably Ferry insisted that Dumoulin's property should secure the dower in case Ferry were to die while his children were still underage.

generally known that the brothers had privately agreed to maintain the security interest.[329]

(2) Ordinance of 1731

1225. *Resolution.* The Ordinance of 1731 settled all controversy. It provided that all gifts were revoked by operation of law upon the birth of a child (arts. 39–41). The confusion caused by the private agreement among the Dumoulin brothers was also resolved. The Ordinance affirmed that revocation returned the gift property to the donor free of all charges created by the donee. It further specified that the property would not be burdened, even subsidiarily, as security for the restitution of the dower or dowry of the donee's wife, even if the gift was made in contemplation of the donee's marriage, even if the gift was included in the marriage contract, and even if the donor, by making the gift, personally guaranteed the husband's obligations under the marriage settlement (art. 42).

(3) Civil Code

1226. *Convention.* After the National Convention prohibited the giving of gifts to direct descendants and then made the prohibition retroactive to 1789, the question arose whether gifts made before that date might still be revoked on the occasion of the birth of a child. Berlier, for the Convention, responded that the Convention's provisions confirmed only those prerevolutionary gifts that were legally valid. Those decrees "were not intended to invalidate the mechanisms permitted by prior law for the restoration of natural order."[330] In other words, the revolutionaries, who opposed using gift giving to prefer one child over another, considered revocation on the birth of a child to be mandated by natural law.

1227. *Drafting discussion.* The draft of the Civil Code of Year VIII (1800) eliminated the birth of a child as a ground for revocation.[331] Three years later, the abrogation came up for discussion before the Conseil d'État.[332] Jean-Jacques-Régis de Cambacérès, second consul, noted that the draft provision deviated from the Ordinance. Treilhard justified the revision on the ground that donors are able to foresee, at the moment they make the gift, that they might one day have progeny. Maleville, one of the two drafters from the south of France, the region of *droit écrit* loyal to the Roman tradition, countered that not only had this ground of revocation been included in the Ordinance of 1731, but also that the

---

329. 5 Planiol and Ripert no. 516; see also Ourliac and Malafosse 506. For an explanation of the confusion, see 1 Ricard nos. 652–658. For the differing views among the regional Parlements, see Bretonnier 107–108.

330. Law of 9 Fructidor II no. 18. See supra no. 3.

331. Tit. 9, art. 68, in 2 Fenet 285. See 3 Planiol no. 2658.

332. Discussion of art. 65 (19 Ventôse XI [10 Mar. 1803]), in 12 Fenet 374–376.

Ordinance provided that the ground could not be waived. "[O]ne must be a parent to be able to judge the power of parental love." Treilhard replied that the authority of the Ordinance, however strong, should not prevail over experience and reflection. Though the birth of a child might cause the donor to regret the gift, regret is not a ground for the avoidance of executed contracts. Cambacérès nonetheless insisted on including revocation upon the birth of a child in the code. He argued that it attaches as a tacit condition to all gifts. The law should not insist on binding a donor who, in youth, made an ill-considered gift. When the vote was taken, abrogation was rejected.

At that point the drafters realized that no alternative text had been prepared. Tronchet suggested that it would not be wise to resuscitate the former case law. Under those decisions, gifts were not just revocable but were automatically revoked by operation of law. Portalis responded that revocation was designed to benefit the newborn. Because infants cannot exercise the right themselves, revocation should take place as a matter of law. Cambacérès ruled that further discussion was unnecessary. Another vote was taken, and the relevant provisions from the Ordinance of 1731 (arts. 39–45) were inserted into the code (arts. 960–66). This is why the text of those Baroque-era provisions, including the passage designed to resolve the confusion caused by the decision in Dumoulin's case two and a half centuries earlier, appear still today, only somewhat revised, among the otherwise lapidary articles of the French Civil Code.

(c) CONTEMPORARY DEVELOPMENTS

1228. *Italy.* Revocation on the birth of a child was also included in the current Italian Code in 1942 (art. 803).

1229. *Belgium.* The provisions in the Belgian Civil Code governing revocation on the birth of a child were abrogated in 1987.[333]

1230. *France.* In 2006 a consensus was reached that, though birth of a child as a grounds for revocation may originally have been designed to protect the donor's intent, it had evolved into an impediment to the transfer of property and a cause of insecurity.[334] As a result, this grounds of revocation was radically restricted.[335]

ii. Justification

1231. *Substitution of motives.* The radical egalitarian justification for permitting a donor to revoke upon the birth of a child became inapplicable once privilege and hierarchy were reestablished. The modern discussion has been less successful at finding a coherent justification for the institution.

---

333. Law of 31 Mar. 1987 art. 77.
334. Forgeard et al. (2007) no. 357 at 218.
335. Law of 23 June 2006 art. 15, revising CC arts. 960–966.

(A) REVOLUTIONARY VIEWS

1232. *Natural order.* The French revolutionaries had strong opinions about the role of gift giving. As discussed above, they believed that the father, by means of his ability to give gifts, to make a will, and to designate an heir, exercised despotic control over his family.[336] Gift giving functioned in the family the way royal prerogatives operated in the larger context of the state. In contrast, the revolution recognized every individual's natural right to freedom and equality. Gift giving seemed an artficial and authoritarian mechanism that had to be abolished.

In its place, the revolutionaries sought to reestablish the natural order, *natural* in the sense that it respected the natural freedom of the individual. Upon the death of their parents, all children were to have equal rights to family property. Parents had no right to interfere with that natural inheritance, either by preferring one child in the will or by giving away property inter vivos. Théophile Berlier spoke for the Convention when he emphasized that the prohibition of gift giving returned society to the natural order that had been perverted by centuries of unjustified privilege.[337]

Berlier also specifically addressed the right to revoke due to the birth of a child, which, in his view, was another mechanism for the "return to natural order."[338] At the moment the French Civil Code was formulated, the drafters were attempting to reconcile their intellectual project—their belief that parents do not have the right to dispossess their children, either by will or by gift—with the powerful social institution of gift giving, which they had come to understand they could not abolish. Revocation on the birth of a child provided the linchpin needed to reconcile radical egalitarianism with social custom. As long as individuals have no descendants, they have considerable discretion with their property. However, when a child is born, the law intervenes to reinstate natural order. From this point of view, the revocation provisions are awesomely coherent.

(B) MODERN DISCUSSION

1233. *Party autonomy.* Once the revolution ended and the regime of privilege and hierarchy was restored, the foundation for Berlier's justification was removed. Nineteenth century French theorists looked elsewhere. Troplong, for example, followed Domat in concluding that revocation on the birth of a child is based on party autonomy.[339]

The true legal basis of this revocation is thus paternal affection, which suggests that a father, instead of giving away his patrimony and his own wealth,

---

336. Supra no. 2.
337. Supra no. 3.
338. Supra no. 1226.
339. 8 De Page no. 680; 5 Planiol and Ripert no. 516; see 1 Domat no. 944.

would have reserved it for his child, had he foreseen he would have one. The gift is at that point negated in its cause. The law presumes that every gift made by an individual without children is subordinated to a condition, foreseen and accepted by the donee, that the latter will return the gift object if children, who occupy a higher place in the donor's affection, are born to him. The law here speaks the language of paternal love. It looks after the children to be born. It preserves for the family father the means necessary to nourish, raise, and endow those who will be procreated by his union.[340]

The difficulty with the implied condition (*condition résolutoire tacite*) is that, as examined below, French law, until very recently, did not permit the donor to renounce revocation in advance or, for that matter, even after the the child's birth. The only remaining justification was based on social policy. For two centuries, the only coherent justification of the rule was that it served to protect the family.[341] "Since gifts are viewed with suspicion by the law, especially as far as the interest of the family is concerned, the Code provides for revocation as a matter of gift law."[342] In Italian law too, revocation rests on the irrebuttable presumption that the gift is subject to the condition that the donor will continue without descendents.[343] The presumption is not based on the donor's reputed intent (since prior renunciation is not effective), but rather on the superior interest of the family.

iii. Criticism

1234. *Frontal critique.* Even in a field as replete with inexplicable archaisms as is gift law, no provision has been subjected to more vehement criticism. *[Q]uo nihil dici potest absurdius,* Vinnius already protested.[344] Voet pointed out that, when gifts are made, donors prefer the donees to themselves and obviously also mean to prefer the donees to their children—*dum ordinata charitas incipit a se ipsa.*[345] De Page called this ground of revocation "a juridical monster" based on "deformed historical origins," "a veritable accumulation of rules derogating from basic principles," "the regrettable, but inevitable result of a legislative project that pursues the sad ambition of imposing, by brute force, a solution manifestly contrary to

---

340. 3 Troplong no. 1365.

341. 8 De Page no. 680; 5 Planiol and Ripert no. 516.

342. Planiol and Ripert id.

343. Capozzi no. 357 pars. a and g.

344. "Nothing can be said to be more absurd than the fact that the donor's descendants will be preferred to the donee, to whom dominion over the property has been transferred fully and completely and from whom it will now be snatched away and given to another." Vinnius bk. 2 ch. 32 at 1056.

345. "Ordinarily charity begins at home." 5 Voet bk. 39 tit. 5 no. 26.

common sense."³⁴⁶ Even the principal French treatise writers could not endorse it. "It remains to be seen whether gifts are acts so dangerous as to require measures of protection so particular."³⁴⁷

1235. *Italian discussion.* Criticism of the institution in the Italian discussion has been less vehement, largely because, in Italian law, revocation does not occur by operation of law but rather is left to the donor. Scholars argue that it is useful to provide the donor with the opportunity to reevaluate the appropriateness of a gift once the new child has arrived.³⁴⁸

iv. Inconsistencies

1236. *Anomalies.* In addition to a justification, the numerous anomalies also require explanation. It might be suspected, for example, that those legal systems that attempt to maintain some degree of parity between gifts and wills would provide the same rules to govern both.³⁴⁹ Yet in France until 2007, gifts were revoked by operation of law upon the birth of a child, though there was no similar provision with regard to wills—with regard to which, under certain circumstances, it would almost seem appropriate.³⁵⁰ In Italian law, in contrast, wills are revoked by operation of law when a child is born (CC art. 687 par. 1), whereas gifts are revoked at the donor's discretion (CC art. 803).

1237. *Reform suggestions.* De lege ferenda it was suggested that the interests of the child may be sufficiently protected by the action for reduction, which would return gifts that exceed the donor's disposable share.³⁵¹ The action for reduction returns the gift to the donor's estate, where it is available for distribution to the donor's children. Revocation, on the other hand, returns the gift to the donor, who may again dispose of it, even gratuitously. On the other hand, it has been argued that the action in reduction does not permit the donor to take account of the economic exigencies that arise during the donor's lifetime on account of having to care for a young child.³⁵²

b. Essential Elements

1238. *Negative and positive.* Revocation depends on the presence of two elements. As a negative matter, the donor must not have descendants when the gift is made. Positively, a child must be born to the donor. Each element gives rise to numerous difficulties.

---

346. 8 De Page nos. 678, 681.
347. 5 Planiol and Ripert no. 516.
348. Torrente (2006) 693–694.
349. Biondi no. 346.
350. 5 Planiol and Ripert nos. 721–722.
351. Balbi no. 35; 8 De Page no. 680.
352. Torrente (2006) 693.

i. France and Belgium

(A) NO CHILDREN OR DESCENDANTS

1239. *Basic rule.* The French Civil Code permits donors to revoke if they had no "children or descendants actually living at the moment of the gift" (CC art. 960). If any number of children or descendants are alive when the gift is made, even if the only living descendants are grandchildren or great-grandchildren, the gift is not revocable. One descendant is sufficient to prevent revocation, even if that descendant is the donee and a second child is born.[353] If the donor is uncertain about the existence of offspring, the revocation fails. The burden is on the donor to demonstrate that there are no living descendants.[354]

1240. *Nasciturus.* An unborn child is not considered a *descendant* for this purpose (CC art. 961). The adage *Infans conceptus iam pro nato habetur* only applies when it is in the interest of the child—*quoties de commodis eius agitur.*[355] The authors and the case law under the ancien régime were divided. D'Aguesseau permitted revocation despite the presence of a conceived but unborn child (Ordinance art. 40). Pothier thought the provision was mistaken. It seemed unreasonable to presume that the donor makes the gift on the assumption there will be no children when, in fact, the donor, or the donor's spouse, is pregnant.[356] Some distinguished between gifts made by the father and those made by the mother.[357] From the moment the mother becomes pregnant, she assumes parental responsibility while the father often does not. Others suggested that the pregnant mother is conscious of the difficulties, but neither father nor mother is aware of the pleasures of parenthood until the child is born. That is how Pothier ultimately justified the rule. "The reason for it is that the person whose child has not yet been born has not yet experienced the tenderness for children that nature inspires in their parents."[358]

---

353. 5 Planiol and Ripert no. 519; 8 De Page nos. 686–697.

354. Ricard would have extended the revocation to include several cases in which the donor had living descendants at the time of the gift. He would have permitted a father to revoke if he had such ungrateful children that he gave away property to spite them. Moreover, if a father had only daughters, Ricard would have permitted revocation on the birth of a son. 1 Ricard nos. 597–598.

355. "A conceived child is considered already to have been born ... when it is in the child's interest."

356. 8 Pothier, *Donations* no. 159.

357. Bretonnier III.

358. 8 Pothier, *Donations* no. 159. Pothier's justification fails to explain the full extent of the rule, since gifts made by those who have had children in the past but have lost them still benefit from the revocation. 1 Delvincourt 772 note 3 to page 247. Moreover, not all authors found family life as satisfying as did Pothier.

> And if someone objects that the donor has not yet tasted the sweetness of paternity, I would respond that the expectation, in this case, is more pleasing and is

1241. *Illegitimate children.* Before the reform of French family law in 1972, numerous distinctions were required between legitimate children, legitimated children, adopted children, and children born out of wedlock. The presence of legitimate children or those legitimated at the moment of the gift prevented revocation. The existence of children born out of wedlock did not prevent revocation. That was the case even if the child was later legitimated—an exception to the usual retroactive effect of legitimation.[359] However, the gift was held to be irrevocable if it was made to the illegitimate child itself. The gift was considered both an advancement of inheritance (*avancement d'hoirie*) and the performance of a natural obligation. The presence of adopted children also did not prevent revocation. Children born to putative parents were assimilated to legitimate children.

1242. *Reforms.* As a result of the reforms, the presence of a child born out of wedlock now prevents revocation as long as kinship has been legally established.[360] Children who have benefited from plenary adoption (*adoption plénière*) are equated with legitimate issue (CC art. 356). Children who are subject only to simple adoption (*adoption simple*) do not actually enter the donor's family (CC art. 364 par. 1) and probably do not prevent revocation.

(B) BIRTH OF A CHILD

1243. *Alive and viable.* Revocation is premised on "the birth of a legitimate child to the donor, even if posthumous or ... the legitimation of a natural child by a subsequent marriage, if it is born after the gift was made"(CC art. 960).[361] The child must be born alive and viable.[362] However, as long as the child lives for a short time after birth, the child's death does not reinstate the gift (CC art. 964). Voet argued that the revocation action, if not exercised, should die with the child.[363] Yet *de lege lata* the child's death is irrelevant. "This is one of the anomalies that abound in this matter, further proof that the law in question is purely arbitrary."[364] Birth revokes the gift even if the child is born after the donor's

---

> capable of producing a greater effect than is the actuality. The grief and nuisance brought on by the presence of children greatly reduces the pleasure that the natural impulse to reproduce our kind might lead us to expect.

1 Ricard no. 590.

359. Aix 11 Mar. 1874, D.P. 1875 II 28.

360. 4 Mazeaud (-Leveneur and Mazeaud-Leveneur) no. 1517; Hauser 1385–1388 (discussing the case of the child born out of wedlock before the gift was made and whose kinship is established thereafter).

361. Under the ancien régime, Ricard suggested that the unexpected return of a child assumed to have been lost should also permit revocation. 1 Ricard no. 596. The French Civil Code does not include the provision, though it is found in the Italian Code. Infra no. 1250.

362. 5 Planiol and Ripert no. 520; 8 De Page nos. 698–707.

363. 5 Voet bk. 39 tit. 5 no. 29.

364. 13 Laurent no. 61.

death. Thus, in the unlikely case that a gift is made after the death of an only son who leaves a pregnant wife, the subsequent birth of the grandchild revokes the gift.[365]

1244. *Illegitimate children.* Before the reform of French family law, gifts were revoked only by the birth of a legitimate child or the legitimation of an illegitimate child born *after* the gift.[366] The subsequent legitimation of a child born out of wedlock *before* the making of the gift did not effect revocation.[367] The thought was that an illegitimate child should not be treated more favorably than a legitimate child, whose birth permits revocation only if it occurs after the gift is made.[368] French law also wished to prevent the donor from revoking the gift by the voluntary act of marrying the child's parent. For the same reason, adoption did not revoke the gift. The birth of a child to a good faith putative marriage, however, operated revocation.[369]

1245. *Family law reforms.* After the family law reforms, numerous authors suggested that the code should be interpreted expansively in the spirit of equality among siblings.[370] They suggested that the establishment of kinship, after the gift, of a child born out of wedlock should provide grounds for revocation regardless when the child was born.[371] Since 2007, revocation is available upon the birth of any issue of the donor (*enfant issu du donateur*; CC art. 960). Before the recent reforms, it was also unclear whether adoption was to be analogized to the birth of a child. The scholars suggested that it is more important to assimilate the rights of a child adopted by plenary adoption to those of a legitimate child (CC art. 358) than it is to prevent donors from using adoption as a voluntary means to revoke.[372] Since 2007, plenary adoption permits revocation (art. 960 *in fine*).

ii. Italy

(A) NO CHILDREN OR DESCENDANTS

1246. *Basic rule.* Italian law provides that a donor may revoke if the donor "did not have, or was unaware of having, legitimate children or descendants at the time of the gift" (CC art. 803 par. 1). Legitimate children or descendants include those who have been legitimated at the time of the gift. It also includes children

---

365. Id. no. 63; 8 Pothier, *Donations* no. 163 and note 1 at 407 (note Bugnet).

366. C Nap. art. 960; 8 De Page no. 702; 5 Planiol and Ripert no. 520.

367. Trib. gr. inst. Saintes 7 May 1996, *Rev. trim. dr. civ.* 1998, 718 obs. Jean Patarin.

368. "Communication officieuse à la Section de législation du Tribunat" (10 Germinal XI [31 Mar. 1803]), in 12 Fenet 455.

369. 1 Delvincourt 774 note 8 to page 247.

370. Terré and Lequette no. 528 *in fine*.

371. 4 Mazeaud (-Leveneur and Mazeaud-Leveneur) no. 1517.

372. Id.; Hauser 1388–89.

of putative marriages, as long as one of the parents, not necessarily the donor, is in good faith.[373] Some authors, following the text of the Code, maintain that the existence of illegitimate children does not bar revocation, while others argue that the spirit of the reforms in Italian family law require that legitimate and illegitimate children be treated equally in all respects.[374]

The code precludes revocation if the donor, at the time of the gift, had acknowledged a child born out of wedlock. The code does not specifically address the question whether a gift to the acknowledged child could be revoked upon the birth of a legitimate child.[375] The answer depends on the purpose of the norm. The Cassation Court held that the purpose of revocation on the birth of a child is to protect family resources for the benefit of the children.[376] Gifts to nonmembers of the family are therefore revocable. However, regardless whether acknowledged children should be assimilated to legitimate children, the Court held that a measure designed to protect the family should not be used to shift resources from one family member to another. Both acknowledged and legitimate children will receive their proper forced share upon the donor's death. In contrast, Carpino would have allowed revocation. He argued that the purpose of revocation, following the text of the code, is not simply to protect the family, but rather to protect the legitimate family.[377]

1247. *Adopted children.* It was previously believed that the presence of adoptive children did not preclude revocation.[378] "The reason is obvious. The feelings and duties that exist with regard to one's own children are much more profound than those that exist with regard to adopted children. With the former there is a bond of blood that is missing with respect to the latter.... [T]he birth of one's own child may cause an upheaval in one's emotions and convictions."[379] Today, however, it is generally conceded that the presence of children adopted in accordance with the Italian Law on Adoption[380] or under the abrogated special adoption (*adozione speciale*) are equated with legitimate children for purposes of revocation, while the presence of those adopted either by ordinary adoption (*adozione ordinaria*)[381] or by affiliation (*affiliazione*)[382] does not preclude revocation.[383]

373. Biondi no. 347; CC art. 128.
374. For the argument that the provision should be interpreted in the spirit of the reforms, see Perego 10; Capozzi no. 357 par. g.
375. Cendon art. 803–804 no. 1.
376. Cass. 4 June 1965 no. 1112, *Foro it.* 1965 I 948, *Giur. it.* 1966 I (1) 78 note Biondi (not revocable).
377. Carpino.
378. Biondi no. 347.
379. Torrente (2006) 694.
380. Law of 4 May 1983.
381. CC arts. 291–314.
382. CC former arts. 400–413 (abrogated).
383. Cendon arts. 803–804 no. 1; Capozzi no. 357 par. g.

1248. *Nasciturus*. As in French law, the gift may be revoked in Italian law even if the donor's child had been conceived when the gift was made. Italian scholars justify the rule in language reminiscent of Pothier:

> [G]iven the complexity of our psyche, the donor cannot adequately evaluate the child's interest when the donor does not yet have children, when the donor has not yet experienced filial love with the devotion that it provokes and its transcendence over every other emotion. The complex basis of the rule is not extremely logical, but it is profoundly attached to concrete reality and to our psychological being. The interest of the child, which did not assume importance even when the child had already been conceived, but that operates with great power after its birth, justifies granting to the parents and their heirs the right to "retract" the gift.[384]

1249. *No longer alive*. If the donor's child has died or is legally presumed to be dead (CC art. 58), the donor may revoke.[385] In contrast to French law, the donor's uncertainty about whether the child is still alive is equated with the child's non-existence and suffices to permit revocation. There is no need to prove a *iusta causa erroris*. The official declaration of death or of absence, however, is not the equivalent of the child's death for revocation purposes.[386] Though these declarations have many of the same effects as death,[387] it is not death but rather the donor's belief that the child is no longer alive that permits revocation. The issue is judged as a question of fact from the donor's point of view.[388]

(B) BIRTH OF A CHILD

1250. *Basic rule*. The positive prerequisite for revocation is "the birth or the existence of a legitimate child or descendant of the donor" (CC art. 803). If a child who is absent or presumed dead returns to the family, Italian law permits the donor to revoke. The text of the Code does not permit revocation upon the birth of a child out of wedlock. In this respect as well, however, many Italian authors have argued that the birth of a child out of wedlock should have the same effect as the birth of a legitimate child.[389]

1251. *Adoption*. The Code does not specifically provide for the case of adoption. There was formerly some unwillingness to permit adoption to provide grounds for revocation, principally because adoption depends on the affirmative act of the donor.[390] Today there seems to be agreement that adoption according to the Law

---

384. Torrente (2006) 693–694.
385. Biondi no. 347.
386. Id.
387. CC arts. 49–57, 58–64.
388. Biondi no. 347.
389. Perego 11.
390. Torrente (2006) 696.

on Adoption is equivalent to birth and permits revocation, whereas affiliation, and probably also special adoption, do not.[391]

1252. *Acknowledgment.* Revocation is also permitted upon the acknowledgment of an illegitimate child. A judicial determination of paternity has the same effect as an acknowledgment.[392] Acknowledgment does not permit revocation if, at the time of the gift, the donor was aware of the child's existence.[393]

1253. *Two-year limit.* The code contained a proviso, now invalidated, that permitted revocation only if the acknowledgment came within two years after the gift was made.[394] The two-year limitation was designed to prevent the donor from using acknowledgment as a discretionary means to revoke the gift.[395] Critics of the limitation argued that it violated the Italian Constitution by discriminating in favor of legitimate children, whose birth permits revocation whenever they are born.[396] The wording of the two-year provision seemed to require interpretation. Was revocation permitted, for example, if an illegitimate child was acknowledged more than two years after the gift and later legitimated, either by subsequent marriage or by judicial decree?[397] According to one view, revocation continued to be possible, despite the running of the two-year period, due to the additional event of legitimation.[398] There was also disagreement among scholars as to whether the two-year limitation applied when paternity was judicially established.[399]

1254. *Unconstitutional.* The two-year limitation has now been ruled unconstitutional.[400]

iii. Spain

(A) NO CHILDREN OR DESCENDANTS

1255. *No distinction.* In the Spanish Code, as in French and Italian law, revocation due to the birth of a child is permitted only if the donor had no children or descendants at the time of the gift (CC art. 644). Since 1981, the code does not

---

391. Cendon arts. 803–804 no. 1; Capozzi no. 357 par. g.

392. CC art. 277 par. 1; Capozzi id.

393. CC art. 803 par. 1 sent. 2.

394. Id.

395. Biondi no. 347.

396. Cupis; Cendon arts. 803–804 no. 1. The relevant provision of the Italian Constitution is art. 30 par. 3.

397. CC arts. 280–290.

398. Biondi no. 347 *in fine*; Torrente (2006) 700.

399. Compare Torrente (2006) 699 and Biondi no. 347 (arguing that the limitation applied) with Rescigno (-Carnevali) 595 note 31 and Cian and Trabucchi art. 803 no. 7 (arguing that it did not).

400. C. Cost. 3 July 2000 no. 2500, *Foro it.* 2001 I 1099.

distinguish between legitimate children and those born out of wedlock. The existence of either one prevents revocation.[401] Moreover, a judicial recognition of paternity before the gift is made also prevents revocation.[402] Because adoption substitutes the new filiation for the adoptee's former family relationship,[403] the existence of an adopted child prior to the gift prevents revocation as well.

1256. *Nasciturus.* According to the dominant view, the fact that a child is conceived at the moment of the gift does not prevent revocation.[404] Other authors argue that there is no need to protect donors in this situation.[405]

1257. *Knowledge.* Some Spanish scholars have argued that the mere existence of a child should not be sufficient to prevent revocation. Revocation should be precluded only if the donor was aware of the child when making the gift.[406] The code does not expressly mention the question of knowledge. These authors suggest that the issue was omitted because, at the time the code was drafted, the most prevalent cases involved legitimate or legitimated children, children whose existence the donor could hardly have ignored. Other scholars suggest that, in the converse case, the donor's subjective viewpoint should not be determinative. If a child whom the donor believed to exist at the moment of the gift later turns out not to exist, these authors argue that, because revocation is designed to protect the new child, it should be permitted, despite the fact that, subjectively, the donor has little claim to protection.[407]

(B) BIRTH OF A CHILD

1258. *Basic rule.* The second prerequisite is the birth of a child, even one born posthumously (CC art. 644 no. 1). Since 1981, no distinction is made between legitimate and illegitimate children. The Spanish Civil Code also expressly permits revocation upon the discovery that a child whom the donor had presumed to be dead is actually alive (CC art. 644 no. 2). If the child was declared absent, the donor has the burden of proving that the donor believed that the child was dead.

iv. Germany and the Common Law

1259. *German tradition.* Under the Prussian General Law of 1794, a donor's obligations under a gift contract were excused if, before the property was delivered, a child was born to the donor's family or a child who had previously been

---

401. Paz-Ares Rodríguez (-Díaz Alabart) art. 644 no. II par. 1.
402. Id. art. 644 no. II par. 6.
403. CC arts. 108 par. 2, 178 par. 1.
404. Paz-Ares Rodríguez (-Díaz Alabart) art. 644 no. II par. 3.
405. 2 Lacruz Berdejo no. 507.
406. Id.
407. Paz-Ares Rodríguez (-Díaz Alabart) art. 644 no. II par. 6.

considered lost was found.[408] Once the property was delivered, the birth or discovery of the child did not permit revocation.[409] The Pandectists were willing to permit the donor to revoke those gifts the donor probably would not have made if the donor had thought about having children.[410]

1260. *Germany and Switzerland today.* Legal systems in the Germanic tradition, such as German and Swiss law, do not today permit the donor to revoke a gift on the birth of a child.

1261. *Common law.* At common law, under the principle *si sine liberis testator decesserit*, a will was often revoked if the testator subsequently married and a child was born of the marriage.[411] Some courts held that revocation was presumed but that the circumstances might rebut the presumption.[412] As a general rule, the donatio mortis causa was not treated as a will for these purposes,[413] though one court held that the same principle should apply.[414] Today, wills are not revoked on these grounds, though children not provided for in the will often receive a statutory share.[415] It seems, however, that no common law court revokes inter vivos gifts on the subsequent birth of a child, even when revocation might seem appropriate.[416]

c. Regime

i. France and Belgium

1262. *All gifts.* The French Code is unusually insistent on the basic principle. This revocation applies to "[a]ll gifts inter vivos ... of whatever value these gifts may be, and in whatever form they have been made, and even if they were mutual or remunerative, even those that have been made in consideration of marriage by others than the spouses to each other." (CC art. 960). Nonetheless, French scholars agree that gifts of modest value and customary presents are excluded.[417] The code's refusal to exempt gifts given in consideration of marriage, which are exempt from revocation for ingratitude, is considered highly unusual, largely

---

408. Gen. Law pt. 1 tit. 11 § 1140.

409. Id. § 1141.

410. 2 Windscheid § 367 *in fine* and note 22.

411. *Gay v. Gay*, 4 So. 42 (Ala. 1888); *Appeal of Goodsell*, 10 A. 557 (Conn. 1887); California Prob. C former § 71 (repealed 1983).

412. ENGLAND: *Stuart-Gordon and Others* (1899) 7 SLT 79.

413. *McCoy v. Shawnee Bldg. & Loan Ass'n*, 251 P. 194, 195–196 (Kan. 1926).

414. *Bloomer v. Bloomer*, 2 Bradf. 339 (N.Y. Sur. Ct. 1853).

415. Connecticut Gen. Stats. Ann. § 45a-257b.

416. *Oetting v. Sparks*, 143 N.E. 184 (Ohio 1924). In *Oetting*, the unmarried donor, who had made her next of kin the beneficiary under her life insurance policy, died in childbirth. The court held that the child could not claim the benefit due under the policy.

417. 5 Planiol and Ripert no. 577; 8 De Page no. 684 par. 4.

because the donee's family may depend on these gifts for financial planning.[418] The benefit of a life insurance policy, which, in French law, becomes irrevocable upon acceptance by the beneficiary,[419] is also subject to this revocation,[420] even when it has already been disbursed, though in Belgium only to the amount of the premiums paid.[421]

(A) GIFTS BETWEEN SPOUSES

1263. *Exception*. Gifts made by one spouse to the other, either in the marriage settlement or during marriage, are expressly excepted (CC art. 1096 par. 3).[422] Today, the exception is largely superfluous with regard to gifts of future property, which are, in any case, revocable at will.[423] Before 2007, the practical consequence was that, though gifts between spouses were revocable at the will of one of the spouses, they were not revoked by operation of law upon the birth of a child.[424] The exception now serves to prevent the insertion in a gift act between spouses of revocation due to the birth of a child.

1264. *Divorce*. A more difficult question arises when the couple is divorced without issue and one spouse later remarries and has children by a different spouse. Traditionally the courts refused to permit the new parent to revoke gifts given to the previous spouse.[425] It has been argued that logic would permit revocation. If the couple contemplated children when they exchanged gifts, they were thinking only of their own.[426] "The solution generally admitted [precluding revocation] must be understood as a timid reaction against a system that is overly rigid and, for that reason, objectionable to the law."[427]

The two situations differ dramatically from the child's point of view. A child born to both spouses will inherit from both spouses and therefore is unaffected by the revocation, whereas a child born to the donor and a different spouse is not

---

418. 8 De Page no. 683 at 791 note 2.

419. Ins. C L132-9 par. 1.

420. Req. 7 May 1919, D. 1921 I 131; 5 Planiol and Ripert no. 517 at 654 note 2. Some authors suggest that, since life insurance benefits not accepted by the beneficiary do not constitute gifts, they should not be revoked upon the birth of a child. See Coron and Lucet 692–693. For the circumstances under which a repurchasable joint life insurance policy may constitute a gift to the survivor, see Com. 28 June 2005, *Rép. not. Defrén.* 2006 art. 38326 at 244–247 obs. Frédéric Douet.

421. 8 De Page no. 683 at 791 note 3.

422. 5 Planiol and Ripert no. 518; 8 De Page no. 684.

423. CC art. 1096 par. 1; see infra nos. 1301–1313.

424. For the current law regarding revocability of gifts of future property between spouses, see infra nos. 1301–1313.

425. Civ. 11 May 1857, D.P. 1857 I 215.

426. 1 Delvincourt 773 note 6 to page 247.

427. 8 De Page no. 684 par. 2.

the donee's heir and is therefore cut off from the gift. On these grounds, the Court of Paris has permitted the revocation.[428]

1265. *Illusory exception.* Prior to 2007, the code provided a second exception to revocation for the birth of a child, namely gifts given by the couple's ancestors in consideration of marriage.[429] The exception was generally considered to be illusory.[430] By hypothesis the donor-ancestor had at least one living child, namely the donee. Thus revocation would not be permitted in any case. The exception was not contained in the Ordinance of 1731. It was introduced into the code to overrule a case law precedent that a gift given to a first child was revoked by the birth of a second.[431] The 2007 reforms abolished the exception.

(B) PROPER PARTIES

1266. *Any interested person.* Prior to the recent reforms, any interested person could ask the court to recognize the cancellation—the donor, the donor's heirs, and the donor's assigns or creditors (CC art. 1166). The donor's children could not act independently as long as the donor was alive.

1267. *Today.* Today, only the donor may request revocation (CC art. 966 sent. 2).

(C) RENUNCIATION

1268. *Previously, no renunciation.* Under the ancien régime, the authors and the case law agreed that, since revocation was designed to benefit the child, the donor should not be able to renounce the right to recover the gift.[432] Under the Code, prior to 2007, revocation was considered a matter of public policy. The donor could not renounce, either before or after the child was born.[433] Confirmation was also not possible thereafter. If the donor wished the donee to have the gift, the only means to that end was to execute a new gift of the same gift object in observance of the required formalities. The one means of confirming the gift was technically complex. If a third party guaranteed the donee against revocation, the guarantee, even after the gift was revoked, was valid as a conditional gift. If the third party then delegated the guarantor's duties to the donor, the donor might have abandoned all right to the gift object in the donee's hands in satisfaction of the guarantee.[434]

---

428. Paris 23 June 1986, J.C.P. 1987 II 20785 note Montredon.

429. "[B]y others except by ancestors of the couple." C Nap. art. 960 phrase 5.

430. 5 Planiol and Ripert no. 518; 8 De Page no. 684 par. 1.

431. 1 Delvincourt 773 note 7 to page 247.

432. Bretonnier 110–111.

433. CC art. 965; Paris 1 Apr. 1851, D. 1853 II 37.

434. Toulouse 24 Mar. 1866, D. 1866 II 73 note Mourlon, S. 1867 II 9, on appeal, Req. 19 Feb. 1868, D. 1868 I 174, S. 1868 I 109.

1269. *Today.* Beginning in 2007, the donor may renounce the right to revoke at any time, either before or after the child is born (CC art. 965).

(D) LIMITATIONS

1270. *Previously, no limitations.* Because the gift was originally revoked by operation of law, there was no limitations period. The prescription period never ran.[435] The limitations question arose only with regard to the donor's action for possession. The code provided that, as to all parties having a right in the gift object, whether the donee, the donee's heirs or assigns, or others in possession, the donor's action was open for thirty years (CC art. 966)—the longest period permissible in French law for personal actions. Only those who had become good faith purchasers of movables (CC art. 2279) were protected.

The statute began to run from the date of birth of the donor's last—*last,* not first—child, even if that child was born posthumously (CC art. 966). D'Aguesseau, who included this provision in the Ordinance of 1731, suggested that each child should have an equal right to profit from revocation.[436] Pothier, hard-pressed to justify the almost incomprehensible favor with which this type of revocation was treated, suggested that, with the birth of each new child, the donor obtained a new right to revoke. "[T]hat is why, if the right that arose with the birth of the first child is limited by the lapse of thirty years since run, there remains yet the right given by the birth of the last one."[437]

Pothier's explanation, though highly creative, stumbles over the fact that French law did not provide the donor with a "right to revoke." Instead, the gift was revoked by operation of law. The birth of further children did not create additional rights to revoke. The question was simply how long the donor should be permitted to leave the gift unclaimed. The code decided to extend the action beyond the thirty years that otherwise constitute the maximum available under French law. This extended period seemed to some illogical, since, once the child was born, the gift had been revoked and was no longer the donee's property.[438] Delvincourt explained that the rule was due to the great favor enjoyed by this grounds of revocation.[439]

After thirty years, when the statute of limitations finally ran, it was with extinctive, and not acquisitive, effect. The donee did not gain new title, as is created by adverse possession. Instead the donor's right to reclaim the gift was simply

---

435. 5 Planiol and Ripert no. 522; 8 De Page no. 682 par. 5.

436. D'Aguesseau, Letter no. 290 of 25 June 1731, in 9 d'Aguesseau 360 at 368.

437. 8 Pothier, *Donations* no. 173.

438. 5 Planiol and Ripert no. 522.

439. "In general, I think that it is wrong to search for a legal justification for the provisions of this article .... It is sufficient to note that the Legislator singularly favored this grounds of revocation, and that is why provisions were adopted that are difficult to reconcile with general principles of law." 1 Delvincourt 775 note 1 to page 248.

extinguished. The gift revived, as a gift, and remained subject to collation and revocation for ingratitude. A further effect of these rules was to eliminate the shortened limitations period for third parties in good faith possession of immovables, which the code sets, depending on the distance between the owner's residence and the property, at either ten or twenty years (CC art. 2265).[440]

1271. *Today.* Beginning in 2007, the revocation action prescribes after five years. The prescription period still begins to run, as it always has, from the birth, or adoption, of the *last* child (CC art. 966 sent. 1).

(E) ROLE OF THE COURTS

1272. *Previously, by operation of law.* Prior to 2007, the most extraordinary aspect of the regime was that revocation was a matter of public policy (*ordre public*). Gifts were revoked by operation of law (*de plein droit*), independently of the will of any of the parties.[441] No action was necessary. The revocation took effect even if it was not requested and even if the donee remained in possession (CC art. 962). If the donor sued to recover the gift, the role of the court was to recognize the cancellation and order restitution. Because revocation was a matter of public policy, it could be raised for the first time on appeal, or even before the Cassation Court.[442] For the same reason, revocation was not subject to the normal recordation requirements for actions and judgments.[443]

1273. *Child's death.* The gift was canceled by the child's birth, even if the child died before revocation was sought (CC art. 964).[444] Collateral heirs, or possibly another donee, were thus preferred to the original donee. "That is irrational."[445]

1274. *Now only by action.* The most dramatic change operated by the 2007 reforms was to eliminate the public policy nature of this revocation. It no longer takes effect by operation of law. Instead, the revocation is, in two regards, optional. First, it is only available if it is provided for in the gift act. Second, it must be requested (CC arts. 960). The scope of revocation has thus been greatly reduced.

---

440. Since revocation took place by operation of law, the donee lost title on the child's birth. Anyone who purchased from the donee was buying from a non-owner (*a non domino*). Theoretically, the abbreviated adverse possession should have applied. As Delvincourt noted, the longer presciption period was "due to the fact, as I mentioned, that this matter is extremely favored." Id.

441. CC former arts. 960, 963; 5 Planiol and Ripert no. 521; 8 De Page no. 709.

442. 5 Planiol and Ripert no. 521 at 660 note 1; Bordeaux 22 Mar. 1899, D. 1900 II 72.

443. Decree of 4 Jan. 1955, art. 30 par. 1 no. 4 ("unless the grounds reside in the law").

444. The authors and case law under the ancien régime were divided as to whether the gift could be recovered after the child's death. Bretonnier 109.

445. 8 De Page no. 682 par. 2.

ii. Italy

1275. *Basic rule.* In Italian law, revocation due to the birth of a child is available with regard to the same gifts as those subject to revocation for ingratitude.[446] Revocation does not take place by operation of law but, as with revocation for ingratitude, requires a judicial decision. Revocation cannot be renounced in advance but may be renounced thereafter.

(A) LIMITATIONS

1276. *Five years.* The preclusion period is five years (CC art. 804 par. 1). The period begins to run, as in French law, from the birth of the donor's last child or last legitimate descendant. If the ground for this revocation was the fact that the donor learned of the existence of a child or descendent, the preclusion period runs from the date the donor became aware of the facts. If the operative fact was the acknowledgment of a child born out of wedlock, the five years run from the date of acknowledgment. For a legitimated child, the period begins with the date of legitimation.[447] Because the action, once extinguished, is revived by each subsequent birth, the gift may become irrevocable only after the donor's death.[448] In contrast to French law, the donor may not bring or continue the action after the death of the child or descendant whose birth gave rise to the action (CC art. 804 par. 2).

(B) PROPER PARTIES

1277. *Transmissible.* The action for revocation may be brought by the donor or the donor's heirs and against the donee or the donee's heirs.[449] There is some discussion concerning why the action is transmissible. Biondi suggested that, because the action is patrimonial in nature, it can be exercised, by virtue of the succession, against the *donee's* heirs.[450] However, because the action involves the donor's discretion, it may not be brought by the donor's assigns or creditors. For Biondi, the question is whether the action may be brought by the *donor's* heirs. The code does not expressly so provide, as it does in the case of revocation for ingratitude.[451] Biondi would permit the donor's heirs to bring the action, provided the elements of the claim were already present at the donor's death.[452] Torrente would also permit the heirs to bring the action, but not because the

446. Supra nos. 1161–1166.
447. Biondi no. 349; Torrente (2006) 701–702.
448. Cendon arts. 803–804 no. 2.
449. Torrente (2006) 700–701.
450. Biondi no. 348.
451. CC art. 802 par. 2.
452. Biondi no. 348.

action, in its patrimonial character, passes to the heirs as a matter of successions law, but rather because the action is designed to protect the family's interests. When the donor dies, the heirs, who were, during the donor's lifetime, the indirect beneficiaries of the donor's right to revoke, benefit from it directly. The discretionary power to act to protect the family then passes directly to the heirs.[453]

iii. Spain

1278. *Types of gift.* The Spanish Civil Code provides that all gifts are revocable upon the birth of a child (art. 644). In contrast to French law, this includes gifts given by one spouse to the other and applies whether the child is their own or is extramarital.[454] However, despite the clear text of the code, customary presents (*liberalidades de uso*) and remunerative gifts are not subject to this revocation.[455]

1279. *Parties.* The code provides that, at the donor's death, the action passes to the donor's children and descendants (CC art. 646 par. 2). Because the action may only be brought by those the revocation is designed to protect, the heirs may not pursue the action if they are not children or other descendants. This remains the case even if the donor commenced the action before death.[456]

1280. *Renunciation.* The right to revoke may not be renounced in advance (CC art. 646 par. 2), though the gift may be confirmed after the child is born.[457]

1281. *Limitations.* The action is subject to preclusion—which, according to the scholars, the code has incorrectly labeled a prescription period—five years after the donor learns of the birth of the donor's last child or of the existence of a child presumed to be dead (CC art. 646 par. 1). The fact that the donor must be aware of the birth of the child extends the *dies a quo,* in the case of a child born out of wedlock, to the date paternity is judicially established. Before that moment, the father would not have standing to bring the action.[458] If the child dies before the action is commenced or even while the action is pending, the justification for the revocation disappears, and the action must be dismissed.[459]

1282. *Judicial pronouncement.* Though the Civil Code provides that gifts are "revocable by the mere fact" that a child is born to the donor or that the donor learns of its existence (art. 644), the dominant view among the scholars is that this

---

453. Torrente (2006) 675–676.
454. STS Civ. 22 June 1989, RJ 4772; Paz-Ares Rodríguez (-Díaz Alabart) art. 644 no. II par. 7.
455. 2 Lacruz Berdejo nos. 508, 510. See supra no. 1172.
456. Paz-Ares Rodríguez (-Díaz Alabart) art. 646 no. II par. 3.
457. Id. *in fine*; 2 Lacruz Berdejo no. 507 par. a.
458. Paz-Ares Rodríguez (-Díaz Alabart) art. 646 no. II par. 2.
459. Id.

revocation, like revocation for ingratitude, occurs by judicial pronouncement rather than by operation of law,[460] unless the parties agree otherwise.[461]

iv. Other Systems

1283. *Germany and the common law.* As indicated above, revocation due to the birth of a child is not permitted in German law and is also unknown in common-law jurisdictions.

d. Effects

i. France and Belgium

(A) BETWEEN THE PARTIES

1284. *Basic rule.* As between the parties, the donee must return what was received as part of the gift. If the gift is of life insurance benefits, the donee returns the amount of the premiums paid.[462] If the property has suffered deterioration due to the donee's fault, an indemnity is due, though not if the damage or loss was caused by force majeure. If the gift has been lost by the donee's fault or if the gift object is a movable and its transfer to a third party puts it beyond the reach of revocation, the donee must pay its value.[463] The value is determined as of the date of revocation.

1285. *Fruits.* Fruits are due only from the date the donee is notified of the facts that permit revocation (CC art. 962). If the fruits collected after that date have been consumed, the donee must make restitution of their value. Because the gift was revoked by operation of law at the moment of the child's birth, Pothier noticed that, logically, the donee had no right to collect fruits after that date and should have to surrender them.[464] Yet the donee is permitted to retain the fruits because good faith serves as valid title.[465] Moreover, the donor is not permitted to prove that the donee learned of the birth before notification. In contrast to the usual rules, the donee does not lose good faith merely by learning from a third party of the birth or legitimation of the child.[466]

1286. *After recovering the gift.* Upon recovering the gift object, the donor is free to do with it as the donor chooses. The donor may transfer it to a third party, even

---

460. Paz-Ares Rodríguez (-Díaz Alabart) art. 646 no. I; 2 Lacruz Berdejo no. 507 par. a.

461. 2 Lacruz Berdejo no. 507 note 20.

462. 5 Planiol and Ripert no. 523.

463. 8 De Page no. 711. As discussed below, real property can be traced into the hands of third parties. Thus there would usually be no loss requiring compensation.

464. 8 Pothier, *Donations* no. 168.

465. Id. no. 169; 1 Pothier tit. 15 no. 108.

466. CC art. 550 par. 2.

gratuitously, gift it back to the original donee, keep it, or sell it.[467] As has been pointed out, the justification for this revocation—that it should be available to serve as a financial resource for the new child's support—does not coincide with its legal effects.

(B) THIRD PARTIES

1287. *Retroactive effect*. Revocation due to the birth of a child has a retroactive effect so complete that it is otherwise unknown in French law. As the code itself makes clear, "Property and rights included in the gift that has been revoked return to the donor's patrimony, free of all burdens and mortgages created by the donee" (CC art. 963). Retroactivity remains after the 2007 reforms, though it was only justified by the public policy nature of the revocation and had been vehemently criticized.[468] In some cases, it made property given by gift revocable for thirty years,[469] no matter how many hands it had passed through. Yet, with regard to many types of gift—indirect and disguised gifts, for example—the gratuitous nature of the transaction was not revealed by the chain of title.

1288. *Augmented*. Moreover, the retroactive effect is occasionally augmented. When a gift of real property under a si praemoriar condition is made by a third party in the donee's marriage settlement, a mortgage is statutorily imposed on the gift property in the wife's favor to secure the donee's obligations regarding the restitution of the dowry and the settlement's other provisions (CC art. 952).[470] The code expressly provides that, when the gift is revoked due to the birth of a child, this mortgage is retroactively canceled (CC art. 963). Furthermore, even if the gift property was gifted to the state, the inalienability of public property does not prevent revocation.[471] If real property has been attached and resold by the donee's creditors, the donor's revocation retroactively cancels the judicial sale.[472] In the case of movables, however, third parties are protected.[473] Those who acquire the property in good faith—without knowledge of the facts that permit revocation—obtain title free of revocation (CC art. 2279).

1289. *Fruits*. A third party is deemed no longer to be in good faith and is liable to return the fruits from the date the donee receives the required notice (CC art. 962) of the facts giving rise to the revocation (CC art. 549). Transactions entered into while the donee managed the property (*actes d'administration*), including many types of lease, are not invalidated by the revocation, provided

---

467. 5 Planiol and Ripert no. 524.
468. 8 De Page no. 715.
469. Id. no. 716.
470. 5 Planiol and Ripert no. 460; 8 De Page no. 571 par. B no. 2 lit. b.
471. Paris 16 Apr. 1926, D. 1927 II 127.
472. 8 De Page no. 715.
473. Id. no. 716.

they do not, by their reduced price or excessive duration, demonstrate fraud.[474] Upon revocation, the donee must be indemnified for expenses that benefited the property. Under the general principles of restitution, necessary expenses are fully indemnified, useful expenses are reimbursed to the extent they benefit the property, and unnecessary or extravagant expenditures are not reimbursed.[475] If the donee has improved the property in good faith, restitution is due according to the lesser of the amount expended and the value of the benefit.[476] If the gift was coupled with an obligation and the donee has already performed, the donee must be compensated for the benefit conferred.[477]

1290. *Criticism.* The extent of retroactivity has been particularly subject to criticism. Prior to 2007, many gifts conveyed precarious title. "In the current system, *no gift is certain.* All gifts are subject to a condition subsequent that is *latent* and *permanent.* Reconcile that with the fundamental principle of the irrevocability of gifts!"[478] The only gifts that were reliable were those given by donors who had living children or other descendants at the moment the gift was given. "[R]evocation due to the birth of a child satisfies only *sentimentalism, legal romanticism* .... Illogical, and even arbitrary ... ? Without doubt; but, we already know, from multiple examples, that this is the clearest and most certain characteristic of the entire law of gratuitous transfers."[479]

1291. *Reforms.* The 2007 reforms provide greater certainty. Revocation due to the birth of a child is available only if provided for in the gift act.

ii. Other Systems

1292. *Italy.* In Italian law, revocation due to the birth of a child has the same effects as revocation for ingratitude (CC arts. 807–808).[480]

1293. *Spain.* Though the Spanish Code treats separately the effects of revocation for ingratitude and revocation for birth of a child,[481] the rules are similarly construed in the case law and the scholarly discussion.[482]

1294. *Germany and the common law.* German law, like the common law, does not permit revocation due to the birth of a child.

---

474. Id. no. 718.
475. Id. no. 719; 5 Planiol and Ripert nos. 523, 498.
476. 3 Planiol and Ripert nos. 267–268.
477. 8 De Page no. 714 par. 1.
478. Id. no. 681 par. 1 (emphasis in original).
479. Id. nos. 708, 710.
480. Supra nos. 1189–1191.
481. CC arts. 649–651 (ingratitude) and 645 (birth of a child).
482. Paz-Ares Rodríguez (-Díaz Alabart) art. 649 no. I.

4. Revocation between Spouses

1295. *Not prohibited.* Roman law prohibited gifts between spouses. The incapacity resulting from the prohibition was examined above.[483] The French Civil Code adopted that prohibition in the attenuated form of revocability, which meant that, until 2005, gifts between spouses were freely revocable until death.[484] Though this rule has now been modified, some gifts between spouses remain revocable. Moreover, the discussion concerning the nature and effects of revocability constitutes an important chapter in the comparative law of gifts. The rules relating to the return of gifts between spouses upon divorce are subject to different rules.[485]

a. Revocable at Will

1296. *Ad nutum.* Until the Civil Code revisions that took effect on 1 January 2005,[486] what distinguished gifts between spouses from other gifts in French law was that, by nature, they were freely revocable until the donor's death.[487] Moreover, the donor was not required to justify the decision to revoke (*ad nutum*).[488] The essential revocability of these gifts not only represented an exception to the special principle of irrevocability but also presented a unique exception to the general principle that contracts are binding on the parties.[489] Only customary gifts were excepted.[490]

1297. *Justification.* The justification for revocability between spouses was that "the donor may have been moved by an excessive passion, and may later regret the unreflected generosity,"[491] or, as De Page expressed the idea, "Gifts between spouses are essentially dangerous."[492] The scholars believed that revocability corresponded better to the particular situation of the married couple than the potential alternatives, such as an absolute incapacity to receive or the inalienability of certain property. They argued that it permitted gifts that naturally arose in this

---

483. Supra nos. 546–548.
484. CC former art. 1096 par. 1.
485. Schwenzer 69–78.
486. Infra nos. 1301–1313.
487. 5 Planiol and Ripert no. 758. Gifts between cohabitants are not governed by these rules and have always been irrevocable. Versailles 9 July 1992, J.C.P. éd. N 1994 II 89 note Pillebout.
488. 5 Planiol and Ripert no. 759.
489. CC art. 1134; Flour and Souleau no. 446.
490. 8 De Page no. 776. Customary gifts include only those that are made on certain occasions, conform to a particular usage, and do not exceed a certain sum. Civ.¹ 15 Oct. 1963, *Bull. civ.* I no. 347; Civ.¹ 19 Dec. 1979, D. 1981, 449 note Foulon-Piganiol. See supra no. 320.
491. 5 Planiol and Ripert no. 759.
492. 8 De Page no. 756.

context, while providing an easy means to remedy the consequences of undue influence and lack of reflection.[493]

1298. *Criticism.* Even from the perspective of French law, these justifications were defective. Gifts made in similar contexts—such as those between fiancés or cohabitants—continued to be (and still are) irrevocable. Notaries, when drafting a marriage settlement, traditionally informed the couple that it was wiser to make any gifts after the wedding—though the notary did not typically explain the reason for the advice.[494] Moreover, as one scholar trenchantly noted, there is a logical problem. Two contradictory principles in French law—the principle of special irrevocability and the principle of revocability between spouses—have been justified as means to the same end, namely the protection of the donor's consent.[495]

b. Types of Gifts

1299. *Indirect revocability permitted.* Because revocation was freely permitted, those provisions of French gift law designed to prevent indirect revocation did not apply to gifts between spouses (CC art. 947).[496] Thus, spouses could give to each other gifts of future goods, gifts subject to the donor's discretion, and gifts subject to the payment of the debts the donor may contract in the future, as well as gifts in which the donor reserved the right to dispose of part of the gift property (CC arts. 943–46).

1300. *Future property.* Notarial practice suggests that, during the course of marriage, aside from customary gifts, gifts between spouses principally involve gifts of future property. The gifts are intended to improve the successoral situation of the surviving spouse and often involve a life estate (*usufruit*) in the property that passes to the heirs.[497]

Some scholars concluded that a gift of future property between spouses was "absolutely worthless."[498] The gift conveyed no actual right to any property. Moreover, the expectation it raised could be revoked for any reason, or no reason at all, at any time prior to the donor's death. Though notaries informed their clients of this fact when the gift acts were executed, some spouses preferred the formal gift act even though a holographic will, unilaterally drawn, would have accomplished the same result. The authors suggested that spouses tend to attach greater certainty to two signatures before a notary than to one without witnesses.

---

493. 5 Planiol and Ripert no. 759.
494. Flour and Souleau no. 447.
495. Brenner 95.
496. 8 De Page no. 767.
497. Véron 99.
498. Flour and Souleau no. 460.

The authors further speculated that many spouses found it more difficult to revoke a gift made openly than one that was made in secret.[499]

c. Reform

1301. *Present and future property.* Effective in 2005, free revocability depends on whether the gift is of present or future property. Gifts of future property remain revocable throughout marriage (CC art. 1096 par. 1), whereas gifts of present property are revocable only for failure of a condition or ingratitude (CC art. 1096 par. 2). Neither type of gift is revocable due to the birth of a child (art. 1096 par. 3).[500] The gift may also contain a condition permitting revocation in case of divorce, unless the clause is used to prevent the divorce.[501]

1302. *Justification.* Many scholars and practitioners supported the reforms. The grounds for mistrust between spouses are no greater than in other relationships, and free revocability created great legal insecurity, both for the spouses themselves and for third parties. The revision was partially designed to favor donee spouses during divorce. If gifts between spouses remained freely revocable, a judicial decision confirming the gift in the hands of the donee would be meaningless.[502] On the other hand, Brenner has argued that, because gifts between spouses generally suppose the continuation of the marriage, free revocability was appropriate.[503] He suggests that the courts should now rigorously enforce clauses that permit revocation in case of divorce.[504]

1303. *Further revision.* In 2006 the provision was again revised to limit irrevocability to gifts of present property that "take effect during the course of the marriage."[505] The purpose of the revision was to permit revocation of present property that takes effect at the donor's death, such as clauses granting a usufruct to the surviving spouse.[506]

d. Form Requirements

1304. *Two types.* Revocation can be either express or tacit.[507]

i. Express Revocation

1305. *Notarial act or will.* Given that the code is silent as to the required form, a 1947 case, still good law, was especially rigorous with regard to express revocation.

---

499. Id.
500. CC art. 1096, as modified by Law of 26 May 2004 art. 21-I.
501. Civ.' 13 Dec. 2005, *Rép. not. Defrén.* 2006 art. 38396 obs. Nathalie Peterka.
502. Sauvage 1430–1431.
503. Brenner 96–97.
504. Id. 107–108.
505. CC art. 1096 par. 2 (2007).
506. Forgeard et al. (2007) no. 362 at 222.
507. Flour and Souleau no. 458.

It permitted revocation only if carried out in a notarial act or in a will, even if the gift itself had been given as a manual gift.[508]

1306. *Criticism.* The authors have criticized this rigor. If the purpose of a formal act is to allow a notary to enlighten the donor about the consequences of parting with property, it makes little sense to require a formality for revocation. "Though the solution is legally sound, it is nonetheless shocking to simple common sense."[509] Ripert concluded that the rule demonstrated that the Cassation Court, in light of more recent codifications that freely permit gifts between spouses, now disfavors revocation and seeks to maintain these gifts. Though neither the courts nor the scholars discuss the idea, a compelling justification is available. The form requirement for express revocation ensures that revocation was actually intended. Without it the courts would be required to parse random comments made in conversation between the spouses for evidence of an intent to revoke.

1307. *Belgian law.* No particular form is required for express revocation in Belgian law.[510]

ii. Tacit Revocation

1308. *More flexible.* Tacit revocation is more broadly permitted. It may be accomplished by any act that is incompatible with the continuation of the gift, such as a sale or a subsequent gift made to a third party. A tacit revocation may also be accomplished by any act that unequivocally indicates that the donor intends to revoke, including a decision to sue for divorce.[511] In one case, the court held that the gift was revoked after an examination of all of the facts, including the donor's decision to sue for divorce, even though, due to war, the suit could not be brought. The donor transferred the gift valuables to a friend just before deportation with instructions that, if the donor should not survive, the valuables were to be transferred to the donor's parents rather than returned to the other spouse.[512]

---

508. Civ. 1 July 1947, D. 1947, 501 note Georges Ripert (concerning a manual gift). One of the foundational laws of the notarial profession provides that revocations can be made by notarial act. Law of 21 June 1843 art. 2 par. 1.

509. Ripert id. 502.

510. 8 De Page no. 779.

511. Dean Ripert believed that the 1947 decision also places severe limits on the effectiveness of tacit revocation. Georges Ripert, note to Civ. 1 July 1947, D. 1947, 501 at 502. In his view, the decision suggests that a gift cannot be revoked implictly by the conclusion of a sales agreement unless the property is recovered from the donee and delivered to the buyer.

512. Civ.[1] 14 Dec. 1960, *Bull. civ.* I no. 545; Flour and Souleau no. 458.

e. Regime

1309. *Former regime.* The former regime presumably continues to govern the revocation of those gifts between spouses that remain revocable, namely gifts of future property.

1310. *Parties.* Revocation is personal to the donor and cannot be exercised by the donor's heirs or creditors. The donor can freely revoke until the donor's death. While some authors suggest that the gift remains valid even if the donee predeceases the donor, others argue the contrary.[513] In any case, if the donee predeceases the donor, the gift is revocable as against the donee's heirs.

1311. *Public policy.* The right to revoke gifts made to a spouse is a matter of public policy and cannot be relinquished by contract.[514] As a practical matter, most gifts made between spouses are mutual, each being conditioned on the donee's survival. Because the Code Napoleon considered free revocability essential, the code originally prohibited spouses from making mutual gifts in a single act so that reciprocity would not inhibit revocation.[515]

f. Effects

1312. *Previously.* Revocation of gifts of present property between spouses operated retroactively to revoke any title conveyed to third parties,[516] even if the property had already been seized or otherwise attached by creditors.[517] Because free revocability was mandated by law, recording the transfer did not interfere with the right to revoke.[518]

1313. *Today.* Only gifts of future property remain revocable between spouses. Revocation of such gifts has the same effect as the revocation of a testamentary bequest.[519] It provides grounds for resolution (*caducité*), which generally does not have retroactive effect.[520]

---

513. Compare 5 Planiol and Ripert no. 764, applying CC art. 1092 (donee's survival not required) with Véron 101.

514. 5 Planiol and Ripert no. 760.

515. C Nap. art. 1097; Véron 101. The provision prohibited certain transactions useful in successions law. As a result, the courts limited its application. It was amended in 1938 and finally abrogated in 1963. 5 Planiol and Repert no. 756.

516. 5 Planiol and Ripert no. 761.

517. 8 De Page no. 784.

518. Brenner 95.

519. Civ.' 20 Oct. 1992, *Bull. civ.* I no. 256.

520. Grimaldi no. 1605. For the retroactivity question, see 2 Ghestin no. 725.

8. THE PLACE OF THE GIFT

1314. *Placement difficulties.* One of the most intriguing challenges in the private law is to find an appropriate systematic placement for the law of gifts. Marcel Mauss noted that it would require recourse to a number of legal institutions to capture the various legal aspects of gift giving: ownership, possession, pledge, hiring out, purchase and sale, deposit, mandate, and bequest.[1] Savigny seems to have been the first to understand the extent of the difficulty, and his discussion remains one of the most insightful.[2] Yet neither his solution nor any other is completely convincing.

1315. *Contract.* The virtually unanimous view in the contemporary civil law is that the gift is a contract. That is both the established doctrinal interpretation of the older codifications—in France,[3] Belgium,[4] Spain,[5] Germany,[6] and Italy[7]—as well as the trend in recent code revision—in the Netherlands[8] and Quebec.[9] Many civilian systems, following the German approach, consider the gift to be a nominate contract and regulate it in the special part of obligations law.

1316. *Other views.* Common-law jurisdictions reject the contractual characterization. This is due in part to the consideration doctrine. A gift promise, unless relied on, is generally unenforceable. Yet the consideration doctrine is only part of the problem. Even without the consideration doctrine, the notion of contract that prevails in the common law would not admit the institution of the gift. Instead, gifts are generally examined from the standpoint of property law—usually as a chapter in treatises devoted to the law of personal property.[10] Other doctrinal currents anchor the gift in successions law, family law, and even the law of restitution. Each of these characterizations grasps something essential about the gift, though, in the end, none is capable of explaining the institution.

---

1. Mauss 24.
2. Savigny (1841) 1–18.
3. Bufnoir 6; 5 Planiol and Ripert no. 360.
4. 8 De Page no. 18.
5. STS Civ. 31 July 1999, RJ 6221; Paz-Ares Rodríguez (-Albaladejo García) art. 618 no. II.
6. MünchKomm-BGB (-Kollhosser) § 516 no. 9.
7. CC art. 769.
8. Asser 58.
9. Quebec CC art. 1806.
10. Infra no. 1348.

The gift has not been successfully subsumed under any of the categories of the private law.

1317. *Stakes.* It might seem that little turns on the characterization discussion. The norms are what they are, regardless of their theoretical framework. Moreover, there is no definitive answer to the characterization question, no sense in which it can finally be determined that the gift either is or is not a type of contract. Characterization serves instead as one of the law's internal control mechanisms, an aspect of its eternal quest to ensure that like cases are decided alike.

If the discussion has stakes, they involve the attitude that a legal system brings to gift giving. This study began with the assertion that law making is an exercise in imagination. The institution chosen as the gift's home address will influence how a system perceives the legal needs of this social practice. If the gift is placed in contract, the discussion will be phrased in terms of norms from the general law of contract. There will be a presumption that any difference has to be justified, and a further presumption that exceptions should be strictly interpreted. For the Romanic systems, which do not extend to gift giving the full freedom of contract that applies in contract law, a more rigorous contractual characterization might prove liberating. But even contract law is too restrictive. The contractual framework would be useful if the social practice of gift giving was in harmony with the market institutions that are traditionally governed by contract law. But since gift giving and the market are in many ways opposites, the contractual characterization can never fully accommodate gift giving. More importantly, contract law is not designed to favor and facilitate it. A different characterization would encourage legal systems to orient gift law toward validating gifts and gift promises that are made in the forms that have become usual in social practice.

A. HISTORY

1318. *Roman law.* In classical Roman law, gifts could be made through a number of different legal institutions. The donatio was neither a contract nor even a legal act (*acte juridique, Rechtsgeschäft*) but merely a cause for the transfer of property.[11] Constantine transformed the gift from cause to legal act, specifically to a mode of transfer of title. Justinian inaugurated the contractual characterization.[12] The glossators accepted Justinian's view and debated whether the gift contract was nominate or innominate.[13] Renaissance commentators returned to the classical Roman understanding. Reasoning from the example of the release of a debt, they

---

11. D'Ors § 119.
12. Zimmermann 480–481, 494–495; Michel nos. 468–483.
13. Bellomo 959–960.

held that the gift was not a contract but rather the cause of various transactions.[14] Cujas and the legal humanists were caught in the middle. They were drawn to classical Roman doctrine, yet they realized that the gift was increasingly constructed like a sale.[15]

1319. *Customary law.* In the ancien régime, French jurists did not think of the gift as a contract.[16] In their view, a transaction was a contract only if it created obligations. Because the gift transfer takes place immediately, any obligation disappears as it arises. Perhaps even more importantly, the jurists of the *coutumes* may have wished to protect the donee by assuring that acceptance does not give rise to obligations.

1320. *French Civil Code.* The government's original draft of the French Civil Code expressly characterized the gift as a contract.[17] For Bigot de Préameneu, one of the code's drafters, the contractual nature of the gift was an unproblematic assumption. "Following the principles adopted to this point, the gift being a contract, and for this reason taking effect only by virtue of the meeting of the minds between the donor and the donee, it is deemed not to have been concluded when the agreement does not take place during the donor's lifetime."[18] However, Napoleon had been present a month earlier when the Conseil d'État discussed the code's proposed definition of the gift. After considering the government draft, the First Consul explained that a contract differs from a gift. A contract imposes mutual obligations on the contracting parties.[19] A discussion ensued in which the drafters considered whether it was advisable for the code to include any definitions at all. If a definition was needed, Maleville suggested, the gift could be defined as an *acte* rather than a contract.[20] Maleville's suggestion was accepted without further discussion. When the code's provisions were assembled, the gift was placed together with the will between successions law and contract law. The code expressly distinguishes three separate mechanisms

---

14. Id. 960–962.
15. "I do not agree ... that a gift is perfected solely by consent (*nudo consensu*) and that an action arises solely from donative intent, because in the past a gift was not perfected without a transfer of possession, i.e. by mancipatio or traditio. Today, the gift is a contract (*contractus*). It is perfected by agreement (*pacto*) and does not require further action, so the gift contract is effective from the moment it is concluded." 4 Cujas, *Commentaria accuratissima in libros Quaestionum Summi inter Veteres Jurisconsulti Æmilij Papiniani* bk. 10 ad *l. pacta conventa* at 254E.
16. Lagarde 49.
17. Tit. 9 art. 2, in 2 Fenet 274.
18. Bigot de Préameneu, Discussion contribution (12 Ventôse XI [3 Mar. 1803]), in 12 Fenet 362.
19. Bonaparte, Discussion contribution (7 Pluviôse XI [27 Jan. 1803]), in 12 Fenet 261.
20. Maleville, Discussion contribution, id. 262.

for the transfer of title: intestate succession, the gratuitous transfer, and as the effect of the performance of an obligation (art. 711).

1321. *Pandectists.* The German Pandectist scholars were influenced by the classical Roman understanding and did not generally accept the contractual characterization. In 1906 Windscheid noted that a majority of German scholars agreed that the gift belonged in the general part of the law dealing with legal acts.[21] Because the gift can be realized by recourse to a multitude of institutions, the gift cannot be considered a particular legal act. It is rather a *general character* (*allgemeiner Charakter*) that different legal acts might assume. Windscheid himself placed the gift among the special contracts, but he conceded that he was not convinced by the placement. Perhaps only a fellow Pandectist could grasp Windscheid's own solution. "The perfectly correct placement for the gift would be in a part of the law that presents the concrete facts on which the patrimonial transfer depends as such, apart from whether or not it creates an obligation."[22]

B. GIFT AS CONTRACT

1322. *Questions.* In principle, the contractual foundation would seem ideal. It accords the parties great freedom to structure their transaction. Yet gift law in many systems fits the contractual model only to a limited extent. German law has pursued the contractual construction with conviction. In other contractual systems, however, the law has focused instead on protecting consent. The protective mission causes gift law to vary significantly from the rules that govern other contracts. The discussion must therefore begin by examining the extent to which gift law norms in each system coincide with contract law in the same system. A second question broadens the focus and asks whether gift law, regardless of its details, respects the principles that provide the foundation for contract law. A final question opens the discussion yet further to ask whether the contractual characterization accords with the common understanding that nonjurists have of gift giving.

1. Correspondence

1323. *Exceptions.* In the common law, gift and contract are governed by different norms. In the civilian systems examined here, despite the contractual characterization, the norms of gift law also vary from those of the typical contractual regime. Of course, a particular contractual institution can be crafted to suit its special needs without abandoning its contractual nature. The important question

---

21. 2 Windscheid § 365 note 18 at 549–551.
22. Id.

is whether the exceptions are so important as to suggest that contract may not offer an appropriate home for gift law.

a. The Common Law

1324. *Evolution.* In the early nineteenth century, New York's Chancellor Kent suggested that the executed gift should be considered a contract.[23] However, once the common law of contract explicitly recognized the consideration doctrine as a basic principle, it became clear that there can be no contract without a bargain.[24] By the early twentieth century the contractual characterization was abandoned.[25] The common law today does not consider the gift, even once accepted, to be a contract.[26]

1325. *Acceptance.* The consideration doctrine is only one obstacle to the contractual characterization. Another is the fact that the donee's consent is usually presumed.[27] For that reason, as Bridge suggested, "gift is far removed from contract in the common law tradition."[28]

1326. *Creation of obligation.* Another difficulty arises from the common law notion of contract. The common law now tends to consider the creation of obligation as the defining feature of contractual liability. Contract usually refers to legal obligations that arise in the context of promising.[29] The American Restatement (Second) defines a contract as a promise or set of promises for the breach of which the law gives a remedy, or the performance of which the law recognizes as a duty.[30] Both Corbin and Farnsworth suggested that transactions that are immediately consummated, such as a present exchange or a cash sale, are not contracts. In these transactions all obligations are fulfilled at the moment the contract is concluded.[31]

---

23. "[E]very gift which is made perfect by delivery, and every grant, are executed contracts; for they are founded on the mutual consent of the parties." 2 Kent 353–354.

24. 2 Schouler (1896) § 57 at 64.

25. Baron 190–191.

26. "A gift is in truth a one party transaction. It is true that the donee must assent to the gift; otherwise no title could pass. But he is a passive party. He is simply a willing vessel into which the donor pours his bounty. The parties never intended to contract." Abbot 619.

27. Supra no. 1052.

28. Bridge 98.

29. UNITED STATES: Restatement (Second) of Contracts § 1 comment b; Murray § 2. ENGLAND: Anson (2002) 1–2.

30. Restatement (Second) of Contracts § 1. A promise in turn is defined as a manifestation of intent to act or refrain from acting so as to indicate that a commitment has been made. Id. § 2.

31. Corbin (1952) § 4; Farnsworth (2004) § 1.1 at 4. In his revised edition of Corbin's treatise, Perillo distinguishes several different senses of the term *contract*, thereby nuancing Corbin's original claim. 2 Corbin (1995) § 1.3 at 10–12.

As a technical matter, Corbin and Farnsworth were mistaken. Delivery does not exhaust the obligations under these contracts. For example, warranty obligations survive. Both barter transactions and cash sales are therefore understood as contracts in American law.[32] In a larger sense, however, Corbin and Farnsworth were right. The common law thinks of contract in terms of unperformed obligations. Farnsworth suggested that a present gift, because it involves no promises and creates no obligations, is not a contract.[33] In contrast, when the parties attach obligations to the gift, and often even when they merely add a condition, the transaction tends to be thought of as a contract rather than as a gift.[34]

1327. *Ordinary language.* In this regard, the common law coincides with ordinary language. The fact that obligations generally do not arise from a gift is perhaps the principal reason why, in ordinary language, gifts are not considered to be contracts. When private citizens reflect about contracts, they tend to think in terms of what the law requires of them and of the rights they gain and lose from the transaction. Gifts are thought of differently. They suggest good will and indicate something about the closeness of the relationship. In normal speech, an act that produces legal obligations is not a gift.

b. Germany

1328. *Few variations.* Among civilian systems, German gift law most closely follows contract principles. General capacity rules govern gift capacity. The execution of the gift generally takes place in the same forms required for contractual transfers. Perhaps because German gift law does not require proof of a valid cause, such as donative intent, it tends not to impose special measures for the protection of consent. The chief variations include a special form requirement for gift promises and the possibility of revocation.

1329. *Donee's assent.* Nonetheless, even German law makes exceptions. One particularly revealing set of exceptions are those related to mutual assent. If the gift is made without the donee's assent, the donor may request the donee to manifest acceptance within a stated period. If the period expires without rejection, the gift is deemed accepted (CC § 516 par. 2). When a gift is made by means of a third-party beneficiary contract, the right vests immediately even without acceptance.[35] The current Dutch Civil Code, which, in its revised version, follows the German tradition, goes even further. If the offer of gift is made to a particular person, it is considered accepted if the donee, upon learning of it, does not immediately

---

32. UCC §§ 2-106 par. 1 (present sale), 2-304 par. 1 (barter).

33. Farnsworth (2004) § 1.1 note 6.

34. Supra no. 234.

35. "The [third party] receives the absolute (*unentziehbares*) right to enforce the promise directly from the contract even without knowledge of the transaction. Vesting is independent of acceptance." RG 25 Feb. 1915, RGZ 88, 137 at 139.

reject it (art. 7:175 par. 2). Of course, it is often reasonable to regard the donee's silence as assent. Nonetheless, there is no actual agreement. The donee, for many reasons, may not have wanted the gift, may not have learned of it in time to send a rejection, or may have considered the risk of insulting the donor too great. Thus, even the German construction of gift law, which is designed to follow contract as closely as possible, requires some flexibility in the area of mutual consent. These provisions suggest that consent may not play the same role in gift law as it does in contract.

1330. *Nontransactional gifts.* German law also recognizes as gifts a number of benefits that do not result from transactions and therefore do not require the donee's assent at all. These are nontransactional gifts, gifts without agreement.[36] As noted above, if the donor knowingly permits a prescription period to elapse, abandons a security interest, or constructs a home on the property of another, German law considers it to be a gift.[37] In other words, even German law recognizes gifts that do not easily fit the contractual model.

c. France and Belgium

1331. *Other extreme.* French law presents the opposite extreme. Very little of the structure of French gift law corresponds to related French contract provisions. This does not mean that the contractual characterization is mistaken. It serves rather to confirm the vision French law has of the gift. Gift giving is thought to pose such a risk to potential donors and their families that the contractual regime must be significantly altered to protect them.

1332. *Consent.* The principal similarity between French gift law and contract is the requirement of consent. French gift law rigorously protects that consent. As a result, virtually no gift giving takes place without agreement. Yet the manner in which that consent must be expressed differs markedly from the corresponding contractual rules. Under French contract law, the offeror is bound to the offer for the time reasonably necessary for the offeree to examine the offer and respond.[38] In gift law, in contrast, the donor's offer, even when made in a notarial act, does not bind the donor until the donee notifies acceptance.[39] French contract law presumes acceptance when the offer is made exclusively in the offeree's interest,[40] yet French gift law neither presumes acceptance, nor recognizes tacit acceptance or acceptance by silence, even if the gift is made without charge, except for those gifts that escape the notarial form requirements. In contract law, no form is required for acceptance, while in gift law acceptance is effective in

36. Supra no. 751.
37. Staudinger (-Wimmer-Leonhardt) § 516 no. 27.
38. 2 Ghestin no. 218.
39. 8 De Page no. 384. See supra no. 1039.
40. 2 Ghestin no. 298.

principle only if done by notarial act. In French contract law, acceptance of a contract concluded at a distance is effective upon dispatch,[41] while gift acceptance is effective only upon the donor's receipt of notification of acceptance. In contract, the offeree may validly accept the offer even after the offeror's death or incapacity,[42] but that is not the case in gift law.

1333. *Other differences.* With regard to capacity, conditions, and the effect on third parties, the differences proliferate. Most revealing perhaps are the elaborate norms governing revocation. The notion of revocation makes little sense in the contractual context. The institution of contract would be turned on its head if a contractual transfer could be revoked for ingratitude or upon the birth of a child.

d. Italy

1334. *Intermediate placement.* During the 1930s, the drafters of the current Italian Civil Code, well aware of the characterization difficulties, decided to make gift law a transition between successions law and contract.

> In fact, if it is true that the gift is configured exactly like a contract, it is also true that it constitutes a contract sui generis, whose construction presents noticeable deviations with regard to the normal regulation of contractual relations. Many rules concerning gifts, such as those concerning the capacity to give and to receive, concerning nullity for illicit motives or for mistake concerning motive ... cause the construction of the gift to differ significantly from other types of contracts ....[43]

Italian law establishes numerous differences between contract and gift.[44] In a typical contract, either of the parties may be the offeror. Only the donor may make the offer of a gift. As a result, an acceptance that varies from the offer of gift does not constitute a counter-offer. Instead, the donor must make a new disposition, and the donee must again accept. Pre-contractual liability, which is generally available for fault in the process of contracting (CC art. 1337), is not available when the negotiations concern a gift. As Perozzi noted, there is a further, technical difficulty. In general, unilateral gifts are difficult to construct as contracts.[45] Unilateral contracts include the renunciation or acquisition of an inheritance for the benefit of another, the loss of an easement by non-use, the loss of property by adverse possession, the intentional loss of a trial, and the payment of another's debt without the debtor's participation. All of these acts may

---

41. Id. no. 256-1.
42. Id. nos. 222–223.
43. *Relazione al Re* no. 143, in 2 Pandofelli et al. 361. For a historical survey of the different characterizations of the gift in Italian doctrine, see Piccinini.
44. Capozzi no. 332 par. a.
45. Perozzi 327–328.

be done as indirect gifts. If these transactions must be contracts to be gifts, the agreement must have preceded the act. But then the act constitutes the execution of a prior obligation and is no longer gratuitous.

2. The Essence of Contract

1335. *Three fundamentals.* Another approach to the characterization dilemma is to consider the extent to which the various gift laws incorporate three typical characteristic features of contract, namely obligation, mutual assent, and party autonomy.

a. Obligation

1336. *Required duties.* Some gift laws impose obligations on the parties. If the obligations are contractual, that might justify a contractual characterization for the entire institution. As regards the donor, the codes only rarely seem to impose obligations sounding in contract. The relevant code provisions are concerned more with exoneration than obligation.[46] The civil codes displace the liability without fault that typically characterizes contractual transactions and replace it with liability based on egregious behavior that is more readily associated with tort—intentional harm, gross negligence, and fraudulent concealment. In French law, the donor generally does not guarantee either good title or the condition of the goods.[47] Planiol suggested that it is tort law and not the gift that creates these obligations.[48] In those legal systems that consider a gift effective before possession has been transferred, title passes at the moment of the gift and the donor is obligated to transfer possession. In some systems this obligation is considered contractual.[49] To a common lawyer, however, an action to recover possession after title has passed has more the feel of replevin.[50]

The donee's obligations are of different types. Charges or conditions may be agreed upon as elements of the gift transaction. When obligations are based on agreement, contractual remedies are appropriate.[51] Otherwise the gift, as a unilateral contract, imposes no obligations on the donee.[52] Nonetheless, the codes do impose a duty of gratitude. The donee's duty of gratitude prohibits the donee from committing serious wrongs against the donor.[53] It also requires the gift to

---

46. German CC §§ 521–524; Italian CC arts. 789, 798; 5 Planiol and Ripert no. 465. For German law, see Grundmann 462–473.

47. 5 Planiol and Ripert no. 466; 8 De Page nos. 596–597.

48. 3 Planiol nos. 2580–2584.

49. ITALY: Torrente (2006) 614.

50. De Page suggested that two actions are available, both the action for delivery under the contract and the replevin action based on the property right (*revendication*). 8 De Page no. 595.

51. 3 Planiol no. 2587.

52. 8 De Page no. 601.

53. 5 Planiol and Ripert nos. 469–470; 8 De Page no. 610.

be returned, or assistance provided, if the donor becomes impoverished.[54] It may be doubted whether these obligations arise from the gift. The wrongs that permit revocation are generally so serious that they are also sanctioned by tort law, and often penal law as well. Because the obligation to provide maintenance is generally satisfied by returning as much of the gift as remains in the donee's patrimony, this duty may perhaps best be characterized as a statutory regulation of changed circumstance. Italian law concludes that a gift is a unilateral contract, which means a contract that imposes obligations only on one party.[55] Overall, the obligations the civil law imposes on parties to the gift do not seem particularly contractual in nature.

b. Agreement

1337. *Donee's agreement.* In the German discussion, the principal argument for the contractual characterization is that no one can compel another to accept a benefit. "Therein is found another expression of a general principle from the BGB, namely that no one must let something be foisted upon them against their will."[56] The idea is already mentioned in the Digest.[57] No gift is valid without the donee's consent. A gift requires agreement. Gift is therefore contract.[58]

Yet the German Code itself contradicts the idea. It mentions several situations in which one party is permitted to convey a benefit on another without the recipient's consent (CC § 517). These involve cases in which a party purposefully refuses to acquire a patrimonial benefit or renounces a right, an inheritance, or a bequest. If the code recognizes some cases in which individuals may find benefits thrust upon them without their assent, there is no general principle to require constructing a gift like a contract.

1338. *Agreement and contract.* Agreement and contract are not equivalent notions. Merely to demonstrate that a transaction, even a legally recognized transaction, is based on agreement does not always demonstrate that it is contractual. There are many agreements that contract does not govern. In the common law, the agreement between the settlor and the trustee is governed by trust law not contract. An agreement to transfer or cancel a bill of exchange is governed by the law of negotiable instruments. An agreement concerning divorce and the division of

---

54. GERMANY: See supra nos. 1149–1151.

55. Capozzi no. 331 par. e. The unilateral contract is defined in CC art. 1333.

56. MünchKomm-BGB (-Kollhosser) § 516 no. 11. See also Staudinger (-Wimmer-Leonhardt) § 516 no. 39. "The ratio more fully explained in the preparatory materials is simple: protection was needed against officious intermeddlers (*aufdringliche Freigiebigkeit*)." Haymann 103.

57. "No one can acquire a gratuitous transfer without wanting to." (*Non potest liberalitas nolenti adquiri.*) D. 39, 5, 19, 2.

58. "The gift, being a contract, requires the consent of the donee, who must accept the offer." 5 Planiol and Ripert no. 360.

marital property is governed by family law. Conversely, many aspects of contract do not involve mutual consent. Common carriers and innkeepers are not permitted to refuse service. Antidiscrimination laws prevent the refusal to contract. Even more importantly, courts often imply terms into contracts that have only a tenuous connection to mutual assent. In sum, it seems that the mere fact that a gift involves an agreement, even one that is legally recognized, is not sufficient to demonstrate that it is contractual.

c. Party Autonomy

1339. *Prohibitions.* Party autonomy is a fundamental principle of contract law.[59] Yet much of gift law violates the principle. To the extent it does, the contractual characterization may be inappropriate. A good example involves the failure to observe required formalities. In the daily practice of contracting, parties occasionally fail to observe legal requirements, such as the statute of frauds or the consideration doctrine. Their agreement is not then legally enforceable. Yet the parties are not prevented from completing the transaction. In a sale governed by the UCC, for example, an oral contract for the sale of goods worth more than $5,000 is not legally enforceable.[60] Nonetheless, the parties are free to perform.[61] Once the transaction has been performed, it cannot be avoided, either by the parties themselves or by third persons.

Much of civilian gift law contradicts this principle. When the parties to a gift transaction fail to comply with mandated formalities, many gift laws do not just refuse enforcement. They actually forbid the transaction. Should a donor give a gift without complying with French gift formalities, unless an exception applies, the gift may be avoided by anyone with an interest. It cannot be ratified or confirmed. A gift must be done in the law's formalities or it cannot be done at all. While the law of contract formation deprives certain promisees of a legal remedy, gift law prohibits the transaction entirely and even unravels executed gifts. These effects contradict the spirit of party autonomy that lies at the foundation of contract.

3. Social Custom

1340. *Social mores.* Extra-legal factors do not confirm the explanation of gift giving in terms of agreement or contract. To the extent social mores are examined— the practices governed by gift law may perhaps legitimately be examined in this context—the idea that a gift requires agreement does not seem plausible. When examined under the magnifying glass, the donee's acceptance is not a manifestation of assent. When well-informed individuals, whether merchants or private citizens, receive offers to contract, they know that the appropriate response is

---

59. 6 Planiol and Ripert nos. 14–21.
60. UCC § 2-201 par. 1.
61. UCC § 2-201 par. 3 lit. c.

either to accept or to reject. A gift, on the other hand, is a fait accompli. The acceptance most frequently is nothing but the donee's expression of gratitude. Everyone knows that, in most circumstances, it is not permitted to refuse a gift. When a gift arrives, what is expected is not careful deliberation but a thank-you note.

In a longer perspective, as Marcel Mauss noted long since, gifts are not individual events. They are elements in a social process based on the obligations to give, to receive, and to reciprocate. Our agreement to participate in these practices is not of the same type as our decisions about which goods and services to purchase in the marketplace. It resembles more our adherence to the social contract. We participate in many aspects of daily life not because we have engaged in a cost-benefit analysis and have decided that the advantages outweigh the disadvantages. Rather we do much of what we do because we have been brought up to understand what is expected of us. We vote, we participate in religious ritual, and we volunteer for charity because that is what members of our society do. The giving and receiving of gifts is another foundational social activity. From the point of view of social practice, it has little to do with the law's notion of freedom of contract.

Perozzi was clear about the consequences. "The gift is never a contract."[62]

C. OTHER LEGAL CHARACTERIZATIONS

1341. *Alternatives.* Once doubts arise about whether gift law can properly be subsumed under contract, it becomes useful to seek alternatives. Several have been suggested.

1. Succession Law

1342. *France.* The French Civil Code regulates gifts together with the last will and testament in a separate category that the code calls *dispositions à titre gratuit* and which are known to modern scholarship as gratuitous transfers (*libéralités*). The will and the gift are grouped together because they govern all recognized gratuitous dispositions of property. Gift law governs those that take place inter vivos, whereas successions law regulates transfers that take place causa mortis.

1343. *Gift and will.* Though Biondo Biondi agrees that gifts are properly considered contracts, he noted that, in numerous ways, the legal concept of the gift is closer to the last will and testament than it is to anything else in the law.[63] To begin with, the *fulcrum* of both institutions is the disposition rather than the agreement. The capacity rules for gift giving resemble more closely the capacity

---

62. Perozzi 330.
63. Biondi no. 46.

to dispose than the capacity to contract. Generally neither a gift nor a will can be accomplished by agents, and Italian law explicitly invalidates a grant of general authority to make such dispositions.[64] Both gifts and testamentary bequests to those with significant authority over the donor are suspect. Both gifts and bequests may be made to unborn children, and, in some cases, even to those not yet conceived. Gifts and bequests that are void cannot be ratified. Both institutions permit revocation, and on similar grounds. Both gifts and bequests are interpreted chiefly by reference to the donor's intent rather than to the common intent of the parties. Governmental authorizations were long required for gifts and bequests to some entities. None of these similarities is shared with contract.

Furthermore, it is often suggested that gift law and successions law share the same fundamental concern, namely the goal of protecting the heirs against the alienation of family resources.[65] In civilian jurisdictions, the law typically protects heirs by the institution of forced heirship,[66] which guarantees to the heirs a share of the decedent's estate.[67] If the decedent has made gratuitous transfers in excess of the disposable share, bequests are reduced, and, if that reduction proves insufficient, inter vivos gifts too are recalled. Gift law formalities are more rigorous in systems that recognize the forced share. Dawson suggested that their role is to protect the heirs by facilitating the tracing of inter vivos gifts.

1344. *Difficulties.* Nonetheless, neither the concept of gratuitous transfer nor the law of successions provides a completely successful foundation for the inter vivos gift. To begin with, the norms that govern gift giving differ from those governing the will as much as the two coincide. In other words, as a technical matter, the two institutions do not form a conceptual unit. Moreover, it is unlikely that *protection of the heirs,* or any other particular conception of the purpose of gift law, will be able to provide a successful legal foundation for the institution. As discussed above, the purpose of gift norms remains unclear. Furthermore, even a cursory examination suggests that gift law's principal concerns are unrelated to decedents' estates. Many gift capacity restrictions are designed to protect donors from undue influence, even donors such as minors and wards who are as yet unconcerned with their estates. Other capacity restrictions pursue social policy goals, such as to prevent conflicts of interest or the accumulation of mortmain. Whether gift promises are enforceable or left to the donor's discretion has little significance for the successoral reserve. Gift formalities would seem the principal aspect of gift law with a successoral function. Rigorous formalities

---

64. CC arts. 631 par. 1, 778 par. 1.

65. Dawson (1980) 224–225.

66. Id. 29–54, 231–236.

67. For the French *réserve légale,* see 4 Mazeaud (-Leveneur and Mazeaud-Leveneur) nos. 859–875; supra no. 134.

might be thought to document the gift for purposes of protecting the reserve. Yet many systems do not impose specific formalities on gift giving. And some systems that require formalities permit many gifts to be made without the collaboration of a notary. Of the grounds for revocation, only the birth of a child seems to suggest successoral concerns, yet revocation in this context is universally thought to provide resources for the family rather than for the heirs.

2. Family Law

1345. *Undue influence.* Hans Baade suggested that gift law should be considered an aspect of family law.[68] Many of the gifts the law regulates are made within the family context—gifts for the benefit of a nonworking spouse, advancements of inheritance, and gifts to facilitate family life for newlyweds. Donors often require protection in such situations. In the family context, emotion easily overwhelms reasoned judgment, and there is often an increased risk of undue influence.

1346. *Difficulties.* Yet despite the great amount of gift giving that takes place among relatives, much gift giving in modern society occurs outside the family context, including contributions to charitable institutions of all kinds, made not only by individuals but also by business associations. For many gifts, family law protections would be irrelevant and at times obstructive.

3. Property Law

1347. *Transfer of property.* A third alternative is suggested by the placement of the gift in the French Civil Code—in Book Three concerning "Different Manners by Which Title to Property Is Acquired." Many have suggested that the gift is principally a means of transferring title. Property law would therefore be the appropriate characterization. Justinian's Institutes made the same choice.[69] Philipp Heck also suggested placing gift law within the framework of property law.[70] Rubio, a Spanish author, considered the gift a gratuitous unilateral act, a disposition of property from one patrimony to another.[71] The role of acceptance in this context, Rubio suggested, is not to create a meeting of the minds but simply to permit the transfer to take place. Under this conception, the gift is most appropriately understood as a disposition of property, its peculiarity being merely that the disposition is made gratuitously. Perozzi reached the same result after concluding that the gift lacks a cause.[72] The donor's only goal is to transfer title. There is no additional element, such as the intent to receive something in exchange. The gift is simply an uncaused transfer of property.

---

68. Baade 188.
69. Inst. 2, 7.
70. Heck § 94 par. 3 lit. a.
71. Rubio; supra no. 1048. The position is shared by a number of leading Spanish authors. See Carrión 783–787 (citing to the relevant literature).
72. Perozzi 328–[3]29.

1348. *Common law.* The property law foundation is also widely accepted in the common law. The American Law Institute has placed its discussion of gift law in the Restatement of Property.[73] Because the conveyancing of real property by deed does not require consideration, few gift law questions arise in that context. The chief question in the common law of gifts is whether there has been sufficient delivery of personal property. As a result, gift law is discussed in the relatively few treatises on the law governing personal property.[74]

1349. *Difficulties.* Yet the property law foundation is also problematic. First, as Savigny pointed out, gifts can be made even though no title passes, as, for example, by the release of a debt. Moreover, though the property law characterization adequately reflects the nature of the common law of gifts, it is unable to account for the highly complex structures of protectionism erected in some civilian systems. Furthermore, when examined more closely, the benefits of the characterization disappear. There are a great many institutions in the law devoted to the transfer of property rights. Title can pass at the conclusion of a contract, by deed, by delivery, by sale at judicial execution, by adverse possession, by the creation of a trust, upon death, or by estoppel. Because each of these modes of transfer is conceptually different, little is gained by considering them as variations on the same theme.

4. Restitution Law

1350. *Gift as legal cause.* A final suggestion is that the gift represents a general feature of many different transactions and is best considered in the general part of obligations law. That was the Roman view. In classical Roman law, the gift was not understood as a type of transaction but rather as one possible cause.[75] Savigny accepted this view, as did most of the Pandectists at the turn of the last century.[76] The theory contends that the law's recognition of gratuitous transfers is designed to prevent legal interference with completed transactions. Every legal system, no matter how minimally it intervenes in gift giving, must establish criteria sufficient to prevent the donor from recovering a gift by *condictio*. Restitution provides space for gift giving by accepting animus donandi as a sufficient reason to bar the restitutionary action. Though the common law does not have a name for this concept, common-law courts recognize that a completed gift prevents

---

73. The equitable equivalent, the declaration of trust, is governed by trust law and discussed both in treatises on trust law and in those concerned with equity. Because the distinction between legal and equitable title is unique to the common law, neither trust nor equity would offer a useful comparative foundation for gift law.

74. Brown; Bridge; Crossley Vaines.

75. Zimmermann 490; Michel nos. 468–469.

76. Savigny (1841) 3, 8–9; 2 Windscheid § 365 note 18 at 549.

recovery.[77] In German law this concept is known as a legal cause (*Rechtsgrund*). According to Savigny's theory, the basic function of the law of gifts is to provide a Rechtsgrund for the gift transfer.

1351. *Advantages.* The restitutionary characterization acknowledges a function that gift law necessarily fulfills in all modern legal systems. It provides the legal explanation for why a donor who parts with property without receiving a quid pro quo is nonetheless unable to recover it from the donee. This characterization also points beyond the law by recognizing the equivalence of animus donandi and quid pro quo.

1352. *Difficulties.* Yet these advantages also carry with them intractable disadvantages. To begin with, it begs the greatly vexed question about the nature of restitution law. At one extreme, as in German law, it governs virtually all instances in which property is recovered, whereas, at the other, as in the common law, it can be said to exist chiefly as a set of contract remedies. Even more importantly, the restitutionary characterization fails to resolve the very question for which a structural placement is needed, namely the justification of the institution. Structural justifications in the law typically attempt to demonstrate the similarity between the institution in question and other recognized legal norms. The recognition of animus donandi as a sufficient Rechtsgrund does nothing but restate the question.

D. THE REACH OF THE LAW

1353. *The limits of law.* This brief survey suggests that it may prove impossible to find a traditional legal foundation for the law of gifts. Archi's remark about the Constantinian reforms applies as well to modern law. "[E]verytime a legislature has wanted to systematize the gift in its formal structure, all that is achieved is that the resulting legislative scheme, however ample, has never been able to encompass every variety of gift."[78] Gift giving seems to be beyond the reach of the conceptual framework of the market-oriented private law. To some extent, it is even beyond the reach of the law. The contrast with contract is again instructive. The law of contract operates largely as the legal form for market transactions. The modern economy could not function if the law provided no remedy for breach. In other words, the market is constituted by the law. Gift giving, in contrast, is constituted outside the law by the social and familial relationships that imply obligations to give, to receive, and to reciprocate. When the law intervenes

---

77. "A valid gift is one that enables the donee, if sued by the donor or, more commonly by the donor's estate, to defeat the replevy action and keep the chattel." McGowan 358. See also *Callwood v. Cruse,* 2006 WL 1120646 *4 (V.I. Super.)

78. Archi (1964) 949.

in this context, it is often to hinder, though the obstruction is frequently justified by the need to protect the parties. Each system decides for itself the extent of protection that is required. But whether the protective rationale is accepted, as in French law, or largely rejected, as in German law and the common law, the institutional framework of gift giving requires legal remedies only in rare instances, such as to protect justifiable reliance and to bar a restitution action.

1. Necessity and Freedom

1354. *Kantian vision.* It is probably due to Kant's influence that contract law—and the law of obligations in general—occupies pride of place in many systems of legal education. If freedom means obedience to the rules we give ourselves, the law of contract would seem to incarnate the realm of freedom. It is thus a tribute to gift law that so much effort has been devoted to finding a place for it in the exalted domain of party autonomy. The Kantian vision also explains much of the striving to make the gift promise binding. It is frequently suggested that those legal systems that permit a donor to be bound to a gift promise offer greater possibilities for the exercise of freedom than those that do not.

Nonetheless, gift giving, from the point of view of contract, often seems to represent an arbitrary surrender to passion and emotion. Once again Savigny saw this most clearly.

> The arbitrariness involved in gift giving, what is considered dangerous about it, is not so much a function of the (perhaps ill-considered) choice of donee, but results rather from the decision to make any gift at all. In other words, it results from the fact that donors arbitrarily surrender a portion of the patrimony that they were intended to consume and use to fulfill their goals.[79]

1355. *Change of perspective.* Everything changes when the perspectives are reversed. From the point of view of the gift, contract seems to represent the realm of necessity rather than the realm of freedom. Contract law is the structure of the marketplace. It is there we sell what we produce and buy what we need to survive—food, clothing, shelter, and transportation. Very few of us would paint a picture of the good life that is limited to activity in the market. What is important in life takes place beyond the bargaining that is required to obtain the necessities—or even the luxuries—of daily life.

The realm of freedom begins with the decision to employ talent, time, wealth, and emotional energy to make a contribution to something larger than ourselves. The law rarely becomes involved in those activities by which we choose to make a difference. It is not involved when we decide to pitch in at the grill during the daycare center picnic, show a foreign visitor around town, or coach the local Little League team. The law provides limits to prevent carelessness, as it does in

---

79. Savigny (1841) 19.

all human activity, but it is not constitutive of these activities. Gift giving partakes of the web of obligation that arises from social and familial relationships, but it is also an integral part of the realm of freedom. The law must take account of it chiefly because it alters property relations. Gift law occupies an uneasy position between gift giving and the rest of the law. Much of the doctrinal work has been devoted to creating the structures that permit the two to coexist.

2. De lege ferenda

1356. *Social change.* Modern life is experiencing a remarkable legalization in all aspects of social relations. Yet, at the same time, ever more time and resources are devoted to gratuitous activity. The realm of freedom will continue to increase in our lives. That evolution will need to be anchored in the law. Though predictions are always hazardous, it seems appropriate at the end of this panorama to venture a vision of how the law of gifts might evolve.

a. New Vision

1357. *Protective regime.* Legal regimes that protect donors by erecting obstacles to gift giving are now outmoded. Future codifications will abandon this approach. There will always be individuals who prey on the weak, but the wider availability of information and education will make this less of a problem. In any case, gifts will continue to be avoidable on the basis of a defect of will—mistake, fraud, duress, and undue influence. The church no longer threatens temporal power. Charitable giving today emerges from a sense of civic responsibility rather than a fear of eternal damnation. Though the potential influence of religious cults and other sects will continue to cause concern, these matters are more for the police than for the arcane structures of gift law. The heirs are better protected by the successoral institution of the forced share than they are by gift formalities, especially given the common availability of exceptions to the form requirements.

1358. *Favor donationis.* The protective regime will be replaced by *favor donationis,* a pro-gift bias. Gift law will no longer prevent or impede the customary practice of gift giving. Instead, the law will reconcile itself to the fact that gifts will continue to be given no matter what the law prescribes. The law will assume the role of accommodating and assisting social custom.

b. New Forms

1359. *Gift promises.* Simplified forms will be available to make gift promises binding, particularly those to charitable institutions. "If contract law exists to extend the potential reach of private action, rather than to protect individuals against the consequences of their own acts, gratuitous promises (seriously intended) should plainly be enforced."[80]

---

80. Kull 61.

In the common law, in particular, exceptions to the consideration doctrine will reach beyond detrimental reliance to permit the enforcement of all gift promises that are sincerely meant. When a donor seriously intends to make a legally enforceable promise, courts will enforce it.[81] A writing may be a helpful indication that the promise was meant to have legal consequences, but courts will enforce promises even in the absence of the required formality, no matter how simple that form may be. Gerhard Kegel long ago recommended restricting the reach of the concept of gift in order to limit the extent of the form requirement.[82] In practice, the courts in most systems now base their decisions on all of the facts and circumstances of the case. They should be permitted to do so explicitly.[83]

1360. *Facilitating formalities.* The pro-gift bias will transform gift formalities. They will no longer be required. Gifts not made in the legally available forms will not be void. Instead, the forms will become a safe harbor for those who are aware of them and wish to ensure that their gifts will be valid. A number of convenient alternative mechanisms will be available. Examples of this trend include the Uniform Transfers to Minors Act in the United States, the French rules that in practice permit gifts to be made by any of three broad exceptions to the notarial act, and the rules that govern anatomical gifts everywhere. The specifics will vary according to the kind of property involved. The goal will be to validate those gift transfers that are most common in ordinary social and familial relations. Once formalities facilitate rather than impede, there will be no need to restrict the domain of gift law. Gratuitous transactions of all types will be made using the new gift forms.[84]

---

81. "I cannot resist the conclusion that the [consideration] doctrine is a mere incumbrance. A scientific or logical theory of contract would in my opinion take as the test of contractual intention the answer to the overriding question whether there was a deliberate and serious intention, free from illegality, immorality, mistake, fraud or duress, to make a binding contract. That must be in each case a question of fact." Wright 1251.

82. "A mature legal system need not require a form for a gift promise .... It seems unnecessary to warn the promisor, and the possibility that the promisor did not intend the promise to be legally binding should no longer mandate a form requirement but should rather lead to an especially careful examination in each case of the promisor's intent to create a claim ...." Gerhard Kegel, note to BGH 3 Apr. 1952, JZ 1952, 657 at 657.

83. "Without fixating on enumerated factors, as we have met them in the doctrines of consideration and cause, we intuit (*erspüren*) whether a promise is meant to be legally binding or whether it is merely a courtesy beyond the reach of the law containing only empty social formulae." Zweigert (1964) 353.

84. This is the spirit of Lloyd's suggestion regarding gift promise formalities:

It is quite possible to make the informal promise in writing supported by evidence of the promisor's intention to create a legal obligation the sole test; applicable irrespective of the knowledge or want of knowledge of the promisor [of the effect of the seal]. But the formal device [the seal] should be available where the parties

1361. *Distinctions.* The new gift forms will be more relevant to some types of property than it will be to others. Transfers of real estate are generally surrounded by sufficient formality, such as the deed in the common law or agreement and recordation in German law. More will usually not be necessary. On the other hand, a gratuitous transfer of incorporeal movables will be legally recognized either if the available safe harbor formalities have been satisfied or if the court is satisfied that the evidence demonstrates donative intent.

1362. *Intent.* The legal recognition of a valid gift will henceforth depend on a finding of clear donative intent. There are two aspects of this intent. The donor must have intended, first, that the transfer was to be gratuitous, and, second, that the transfer was to operate immediately. A gift completed in the prescribed forms will satisfy this proof. Satisfying the traditional delivery requirement will also offer relevant evidence. If the forms have not been employed, the courts will evaluate all of the facts and the circumstances. The role of the courts will be to determine whether a gift was actually intended and made.

c. The End of Protection

1363. *Capacity.* Capacity rules will be simplified to coincide with the capacity rules for other legal acts. In particular, the restrictions on the donative capacity of corporate entities and other associations will be abolished. Entities with so much wealth should be allowed to exercise a social conscience. The prohibitions of gift giving within special relationships—doctor and patient, clergy and congregant—are today much better discussed in terms of the general law of undue influence.

1364. *Revocation.* The law will no longer intervene to revoke executed gifts. Some argue that the institution is already in decline.[85] Revocation for ingratitude is no longer needed. Tort law provides remedies for most civil wrongs. Revocation due to the birth of a child has been so roundly criticized that the latest French code revision greatly restricted it. Revocation for impoverishment will be unnecessary as social services become more widely available. The goal will instead be to guarantee the legal security of executed gifts.

d. Autonomous Institution

1365. *Separate characterization.* The law's relationship to gift giving will improve once the contractual characterization is abandoned. As long as the gift is understood as a nominate contract, those legal systems that focus on donative intent

---

have knowledge, to enable them to definitely fix their rights and obligations at the time the promise is made. The uncertainty inherent in the informal device should not be extended beyond what necessity requires.
Lloyd 36.
85. Note to Cass. 28 Aug. 1997 no. 8165, *Giur. it.* 1998 II 2059 note 2.

will assume that the role of gift law is to protect consent. Those systems will remain suspicious of individuals who give away something for nothing. Though those gift laws that do not require proof of donative intent, such as the German system, do not significantly interfere with gift giving, causal systems use the contractual characterization as grounds for interventionism.

Even more importantly, the contractual characterization prevents legal systems from understanding the societal role of the gift and from developing norms that reflect its nature. That is one of the reasons it is so difficult to create a gift law that facilitates gift giving. Once the gift is characterized as an independent institution, the law will be freed to focus on its specific needs. The gift will be understood as a social institution with legally relevant effects but that remains largely beyond the law's sphere of influence. Legislators will recognize that gift giving involves motivations and experiences that are best left to social practice rather than constrained by contractual forms. Instead of seeking to subjugate customary practice, legal norms will treat it as a respectable source of normativity. Benefits will emerge not only for the practice of gift giving, but also, and perhaps especially, for the law. In the future, there will be—as there should be—less gift law.

3. Incommensurable Fields

1366. *Unique.* The law and the giving of gifts are largely incommensurable fields of human activity. Nonetheless, because the transfer of property is common to both domains, legal systems have had to acknowledge gift giving, though some have attempted to protect individuals from it. The protective measures imposed by some gift laws are unique in the history of legal regulation. Because gift giving is unique, it probably will never be possible to provide a convincing foundation for the norms that govern it within the general structure of the private law. Yet much can be learned from the incompatibility. The attempts to reconcile the demands of the law with those of the practice of gift giving have produced an intricate and instructive tapestry of comparative law, one that includes some of the most fascinating constructions ever imagined by the legal mind.

BIBLIOGRAPHY

The bibliography is divided into three sections. The first lists the secondary sources referenced in the notes by scholarly specialty and jurisdiction. Included are monographs, treatises, code commentaries, and journal articles. The second section gathers the same sources together in a single listing by author's name. The final section, arranged by jurisdiction, lists national and state statutes and regulations, together with uniform laws, model laws, and restatements.

1. SECONDARY SOURCES BY TOPIC AND COUNTRY

General

Apperson, G. L. 1993. *The Wordsworth Dictionary of Proverbs*. Ware: Wordsworth.

Baldwin, Neil. 1988. *Man Ray: American Artist*. New York: C. N. Potter.

Bataille, Georges. 1988. *The Accursed Share: An Essay on General Economy*, vol. 1: Consumption. Trans. Robert Hurley. New York: Zone.

Benveniste, Emile. 1973. *Indo-European Language and Society*. Miami linguistics series, no. 12. Ed. Jean Lallot. Trans. Elizabeth Palmer. Coral Gables, FL: University of Miami Press.

Bettelheim, Bruno. 1976. *The Uses of Enchantment: The Meaning and Importance of Fairy Tales*. New York: Knopf.

Bride's Book of Etiquette. 2003. New York: Perigee.

Foster, Stephen C. 1988. Configurations of Freedom. In *Perpetual Motif: The Art of Man Ray*, ed. Merry A. Foresta, 233–271. Washington DC: National Museum of American Art, Smithsonian Institution.

Henry, O. 1953. The Gift of the Magi. In *The Complete Works of O. Henry* 1: 7–11. Garden City, NY: Doubleday.

Heywood, John. 1906. *A Dialogue of the Effectual Proverbs in the English Tongue Concerning Marriage* [1562, 1566]. Ed. John Stephen Farmer. London: Gibbings.

Lempert, Robert J., Steven W. Popper, and Steven C. Bankes. 2003. *Shaping the Next One Hundred Years: New Methods for Quantitative, Long-Term Policy Analysis*. Santa Monica: RAND.

Lipson, D. Herbert. 2008. Off the Cuff. *Philadelphia Magazine*, August.

Mandeville, Bernard. 1997. *The Fable of the Bees and Other Writings*. Ed. E. J. Hundert. Indianapolis: Hackett Pub.

Martial. 1943. *Epigrams*. Trans. Walter C. A. Ker. Loeb Classical Library. Cambridge: Harvard University Press.

Nunberg, Geoffrey. 1990. Testimony before the State Legislature on California Proposition 63. In *Perspectives on Official English: The Campaign for English as the*

Official Language of the USA, ed. Karen L. Adams and Daniel T. Brink, 121–124. Contributions to the sociology of language, 57. Berlin: Mouton de Gruyter.

Reinhardt, Thomas. 2000. *Jenseits der Schrift: Dialogische Anthropologie nach der Postmoderne*. Frankfurt am Main: IKO, Verlag für Interkulturelle Kommunikation.

Schiffman, Harold F. 1996. *Linguistic Culture and Language Policy*. The Politics of Language. London: Routledge.

Shore, William H. 1999. *The Cathedral Within: Transforming Your Life by Giving Something Back*. New York: Random House.

Tatar, Maria. 1992. *Off With Their Heads! Fairy Tales and the Culture of Childhood*. Princeton: Princeton University Press.

Trần Ngọc Thêm. 2006. *Recherche sur l'identité de la culture vietnamienne*. Trans. Pham Xuân and Phan Thế Hồng. Hanoi: Editions Thế Giói.

Veblen, Thorstein. 1994. *The Theory of the Leisure Class*. Penguin twentieth-century classics. New York: Penguin Books.

Veyne, Paul. 1988. *Did the Greeks Believe in Their Myths? An Essay on the Constitutive Imagination*. Chicago: University of Chicago Press.

Wellek, René. 1963. The Crisis of Comparative Literature. In René Wellek, *Concepts of Criticism*, ed. Stephen G. Nichols, Jr., 282–295. New Haven: Yale University Press.

General Gift

Arnsperger, Christian. 2000. Gift giving Practice and Noncontextual Habitus: How (not) to Be Fooled by Mauss. In Vandevelde ed. 71–92.

Cheal, David. 1988. *The Gift Economy*. London: Routledge.

Godbout, Jacques, and Alain Caillé. 1998. *The World of the Gift*. Trans. Donald Winkler. Montreal: McGill-Queen's University Press.

Gregory, C. A. 1982. *Gifts and Commodities*. London: Academic Press.

Grimm, Jakob. 1965. Über Schenken und Geben. In Jakob Grimm, *Kleinere Schriften: Abhandlungen zur Mythologie und Sittenkunde* 2: 173–210. Hildesheim: Georg Olms.

Hyde, Lewis. 1983. *The Gift: Imagination and the Erotic Life of Property*. New York: Vintage Books.

Ohnuma, Reiko. 1998. The Gift of the Body and the Gift of Dharma. *History of Religions* 37: 323–359.

Osteen, Mark, ed. 2002. *The Question of the Gift: Essays across Disciplines*. Routledge Studies in Anthropology, 2. London: Routledge.

Regan, Tom. 1983. *The Case for Animal Rights*. Berkeley: University of California Press.

Schrift, Alan D., ed. 1997. *The Logic of the Gift: Toward an Ethic of Generosity*. New York: Routledge.

Starobinski, Jean. 1997. *Largesse*. Chicago: University of Chicago Press.

Strom, Stephanie. 2008. Helmsley, Dogs' Best Friend, Left Them up to $8 Billion. *New York Times*, 2 July, sec. A.

Symposium. 1991. Donner, reçevoir, et rendre—l'autre paradigm. *Revue du Mauss* no. 11.

Symposium. 1991a. Le don perdu et retrouvé. *Revue du Mauss* no. 12.

Titmuss, Richard M. 1971. *The Gift Relationship: From Human Blood to Social Policy*. New York: Pantheon Books.

Vandevelde, Anatoon, ed. 2000. *Gifts and Interests*. Leuven: Peeters.

Philosophy

Derrida, Jacques. 1992. *Given Time. I, Counterfeit Money*. Trans. Peggy Kamuf. Chicago: University of Chicago Press.

Derrida, Jacques. 1995. *The Gift of Death*. Religion and postmodernism. Chicago: University of Chicago Press.

Emerson, Ralph Waldo. 1988. Gifts [1844]. In *Essays by Ralph Waldo Emerson: first and second series complete in one volume* 374–379. New York: Perennial Library.

Heidegger, Martin. 1996. *Being and Time: A Translation of Sein und Zeit*. SUNY series in contemporary continental philosophy. Trans. Joan Stambaugh. Albany, NY: State University of New York Press.

Kemp, Peter. 1982. Death and Gift. *Journal of the American Academy of Religion* 50: 459–471.

Marion, Jean-Luc. 2002. *Being Given: Toward a Phenomenology of Givenness*. Cultural Memory in the Present. Trans. Jeffrey L. Kosky. Stanford, CA: Stanford University Press.

Ricoeur, Paul. 1971. The Model of the Text: Meaningful Action Considered as a Text. *Social Research* 38: 529–62.

Rousseau, Jean-Jacques. 1979. *Reveries of the Solitary Walker* [1782]. Trans. Peter France. Penguin Classics. Harmondsworth: Penguin Books.

Schroeder, Jeanne L. 1999. Pandora's Amphora: The Ambiguity of Gifts. *UCLA Law Review* 46: 815–904.

Shapiro, Gary. 1997. The Metaphysics of Presents: Nietzsche's Gift, the Debt to Emerson, Heidegger's Values. In Schrift ed. 274–291.

Voltaire. 1901. *A Philosophical Dictionary* [1764]. In *The Works of Voltaire; A Contemporary Version*, ed. John Morley, vols. 5–14. Trans. William F. Fleming. Paris: Done by the craftsmen of the St. Hubert Guild [E.R. DuMont].

Social Science Methodology

Ackerknecht, Erwin H. 1954. On the Comparative Method in Anthropology. In Spencer ed. 117–125.

Boas, Franz. 1896. The Limitations of the Comparative Method of Anthropology. *Science* 4: 901–908.

Camic, Charles. 1986. The Return of the Functionalists. Review of *Neofunctionalism*, by Jeffrey C. Alexander. *Contemporary Sociology* 15: 692–695.

Colson, Elizabeth. 1975. Review of *The Interpretation of Cultures*, by Clifford Geertz. *Contemporary Sociology* 4: 637–638.

Davis, Kingsley. 1959. The Myth of Functional Analysis as a Special Method in Sociology and Anthropology. *American Sociological Review* 24: 757–772.

Durkheim, Emile. 1982. *The Rules of Sociological Method*. Ed. Steven Lukes. Trans. W. D. Halls. New York: Free Press.

Geertz, Clifford. 1973. *The Interpretation of Cultures: Selected Essays*. New York: Basic Books.

Geertz, Clifford. 1973a. The Cerebral Savage: On the Work of Claude Lévi-Strauss. In Geertz 1973: 345–359.

Geertz, Clifford. 1973b. Deep Play: Notes on the Balinese Cockfight. In Geertz 1973: 412–453.

Geertz, Clifford. 1973c. The Impact of the Concept of Culture on the Concept of Man. In Geertz 1973: 33–54.

Geertz, Clifford. 1973d. Religion As a Cultural System. In Geertz 1973: 87–125.

Geertz, Clifford. 1973e. Thick Description: Toward an Interpretive Theory of Culture. In Geertz 1973: 3–30.

Geertz, Clifford. 1983. *Local Knowledge: Further Essays in Interpretive Anthropology.* New York: Basic Books.

Geertz, Clifford. 1983a. Blurred Genres: The Refiguration of Social Thought. In Geertz 1983: 19–35.

Geertz, Clifford. 1983b. Introduction. In Geertz 1983: 3–16.

Geertz, Clifford. 1983c. Local Knowledge: Fact and Law in Comparative Perspective. In Geertz 1983: 167–234.

Goldschmidt, Walter Rochs. 1966. *Comparative Functionalism: An Essay in Anthropological Theory.* Berkeley: University of California Press.

Greenblatt, Stephen. 1997. The Touch of the Real. *Representations* 59: 14–29.

Gregg, Dorothy, and Elgin Williams. 1948. The Dismal Science of Functionalism. *American Anthropologist* 50: 594–611.

Handler, Richard. 1991. An Interview with Clifford Geertz. *Current Anthropology* 32: 603–613.

Harris, Marvin. 1976. History and Significance of the Emic/Etic Distinction. *Annual Review of Anthropology* 5: 329–50.

Haupt, Heinz-Gerhard, and Jürgen Kocka. 1996. Historischer Vergleich: Methoden, Aufgaben, Probleme. Eine Einleitung. In *Geschichte und Vergleich: Ansätze und Ergebnisse international vergleichender Geschichtsschreibung,* ed. Heinz-Gerhard Haupt and Jürgen Kocka, 9–45. Frankfurt: Campus.

Hunt, Lynn Avery. 1989. Introduction: History, Culture, and Text. In *The New Cultural History,* ed. Lynn Avery Hunt, 1–22. Studies on the History of Society and Culture, 6. Berkeley: University of California Press.

Kallen, Horace M. 1937. Functionalism. In *Encyclopaedia of the Social Sciences,* ed. Edwin Robert Anderson Seligman and Alvin Saunders Johnson, 5: 523–526. New York: Macmillan Co.

Kuhn, Thomas S. 1970. *The Structure of Scientific Revolutions.* Chicago: University of Chicago Press.

Lijphart, Arend. 1971. Comparative Politics and the Comparative Method. *American Political Science Review* 65: 682–693.

Malinowski, Bronislaw. 1937. Culture. In *Encyclopaedia of the Social Sciences,* ed. Edwin Robert Anderson Seligman and Alvin Saunders Johnson, 3: 621–646. New York: Macmillan Co.

Malinowski, Bronislaw. 1939. The Group and the Individual in Functional Analysis. *American Journal of Sociology* 46: 938–964.

Malinowski, Bronislaw. 1944. *A Scientific Theory of Culture and Other Essays.* Chapel Hill: University of North Carolina Press.

Merton, Robert King. 1968. Manifest and Latent Functions. In Robert King Merton, *Social Theory and Social Structure* 73–138. Enlarged ed. New York: Free Press.

Mills, David. 2000. Review of *Arguments with Ethnography: Comparative Approaches to History, Politics and Religion,* by Ioan M. Lewis. *Bulletin of the School of Oriental and African Studies* 63: 326–27.

Radcliffe-Brown, A. R. 1935a. On the Concept of Function in Social Science. *American Anthropologist* 37: 394–402.

Radcliffe-Brown, A. R. 1935b. Patrilineal and Matrilineal Succession. *Iowa Law Review* 20: 286–303.

Radcliffe-Brown, A. R. 1940. On Social Structure. *Journal of the Royal Anthropological Institute* 70: 1–12.

Radcliffe-Brown, A. R. 1949. Functionalism: A Protest. *American Anthropologist* 51: 320–323.

Radcliffe-Brown, A. R. 1951. The Comparative Method in Social Anthropology. *Journal of the Royal Anthropological Institute* 81: 15–22.

Rosaldo, Renato I., Jr. 1997. A Note on Geertz as a Cultural Essayist. *Representations* 59: 30–34.

Roseberry, William. 1982. Balinese Cockfights and the Seduction of Anthropology. *Social Research* 49: 1013–1028.

Rothacker, Erich. 1947. *Logik und Systematik der Geisteswissenschaften*. Bonn: H. Bouvier.

Schneider, Mark A. 1987. Culture-as-Text in the Work of Clifford Geertz. *Theory and Society* 16: 809–839.

Sewell, William H., Jr. 1997. Geertz, Cultural Systems, and History: From Synchrony to Transformation. *Representations* 59: 35–55.

Shankman, Paul. 1984. The Thick and the Thin: On the Interpretive Theoretical Program of Clifford Geertz [and Comments and Reply]. *Current Anthropology* 25: 261–280.

Sjoberg, Gideon. 1955. The Comparative Method in the Social Sciences. *Philosophy of Science* 22: 106–117.

Spencer, Robert F., ed. 1954. *Method and Perspective in Anthropology: Papers in Honor of Wilson D. Wallis*. Minneapolis: University of Minnesota Press.

Swidler, Ann. 1996. Geertz's Ambiguous Legacy. *Contemporary Sociology* 25: 299–302.

Turner, Jonathan H., and Alexandra R. Maryanski. 1988. Is "Neofunctionalism" Really Functional? *Sociological Theory* 6: 110–121.

Winch, Peter. 2008. *The Idea of a Social Science and Its Relation to Philosophy* [1958]. Routledge Classics. London: Routledge.

Anthropology

Beidelman, T. O. 1989. Agonistic Exchange: Homeric Reciprocity and the Heritage of Simmel and Mauss. *Cultural Anthropology* 4: 227–259.

Benedict, Ruth. 1959. *Patterns of Culture* [1934]. Boston: Houghton Mifflin.

Carrier, James. 1991. Gifts, Commodities, and Social Relations: A Maussian View of Exchange. *Sociological Forum* 6: 119–136.

Gaul, Wilhelm. 1914. Das Geschenk nach Form und Inhalt im besonderen untersucht an afrikanischen Völkern. *Archiv für Anthropologie* 13: 223–279.

Godelier, Maurice. 1999. *The Enigma of the Gift*. Trans. Nora Scott. [Chicago]: University of Chicago Press.

Greene, John Patrick. 2002. French Encounters with Material Culture of the South Pacific. *Eighteenth-Century Life* 26: 225–245.

James, Wendy, and N. J. Allen, ed. 1998. *Marcel Mauss: A Centenary Tribute*. Methodology and history in anthropology, vol. 1. New York: Berghahn Books.

Karsenti, Bruno. 1998. The Maussian Shift: A Second Foundation for Sociology in France? In James and Allen ed. 71–82.

Lévi-Strauss, Claude. 1969. *The Elementary Structures of Kinship*. Trans. James Harle Bell and John Richard von Sturmer. Boston: Beacon Press.

Lévi-Strauss, Claude. 1987. *Introduction to the Work of Marcel Mauss*. Trans. Felicity Baker. London: Routledge & Kegan Paul.

Lévi-Strauss, Claude. 1992. *Tristes tropiques*. New York: Penguin Books.

Malinowski, Bronislaw. 1964. *Argonauts of the Western Pacific* [1922]. London: G. Routledge & Sons.

Malinowski, Bronislaw. 1989. *Crime and Custom in Savage Society* [1926]. Totowa, NJ: Rowman & Littlefield.

Mauss, Marcel. 1990. *The Gift: The form and reason for exchange in archaic societies* [1924]. Trans. W. D. Halls. London: Routledge.

Mauss, Marcel. 1997. "Gift, Gift" [1924]. In Schrift ed. 28–32.

Miller, William Ian. 2007. Is a Gift Forever? *Representations* 100: 13–22.

Morgan, Lewis Henry. 1877. *Ancient Society: or, Researches in the line of human progress from savagery, through barbarism to civilization*. New York: Henry Holt.

Parry, Jonathan. 1986. The Gift, the Indian Gift, and the "Indian Gift." *Man* 21: 453–473.

Pétursdóttir, Þóra. 2007. *"Deyr Fé, Deyja Frændr": Re-animating mortuary remains from Viking Age Iceland*. MA-Thesis in Archaeology. [Tromsø, Norway]: Faculty of Social Sciences: University of Tromsø.

Radcliffe-Brown, A. R. 1948. *The Andaman Islanders* [1922]. Glencoe, IL: Free Press.

Raheja, Gloria Goodwin. 1988. *The Poison in the Gift: Ritual, Prestation, and the Dominant Caste in a North Indian Village*. Chicago: University of Chicago Press.

Sahlins, Marshall David. 1972. *Stone Age Economics*. Chicago: Aldine-Atherton.

Strathern, Andrew. 1983. The Kula in Comparative Perspective. In *The Kula: New Perspectives on Massim Exchange*, ed. Jerry W. Leach and Edmund Leach, 73–88. Cambridge: Cambridge University Press.

Weiner, Annette B. 1992. *Inalienable Possessions: The Paradox of Keeping-While-Giving*. Berkeley: University of California Press.

Potlatch

Barnett, H. G. 1938. The Nature of the Potlatch. *American Anthropologist* 40: 349–358.

Boas, Franz. 1966. *Kwakiutl Ethnography*. Ed. Helen Codere. Chicago: University of Chicago Press.

Carpenter, Carole Henderson. 1981. Sacred, Precious Things: Repatriation of Potlatch Art. *artmagazine* 12: 64–70.

Codere, Helen. 1950. *Fighting with Property: A Study of Kwakiutl Potlatching and Warfare, 1792–1930*. New York: J. J. Augustin.

Cole, Douglas, and Ira Chaikin. 1990. *An Iron Hand upon the People: The Law against the Potlatch on the Northwest Coast*. Vancouver: Douglas & McIntyre.

Halliday, William May. 1935. *Potlatch and Totem, and the Recollections of an Indian Agent*. London: J. M. Dent & Sons Ltd.

Harring, Sidney L. 1998. *White Man's Law: Native People in Nineteenth-Century Canadian Jurisprudence*. Toronto: Osgoode Society for Canadian Legal History by University of Toronto Press.

Indian Claims Commission. 2004. *Annual Report 2003–04*. [Ottawa]: [Minister of Public Works and Government Services Canada].

Loo, Tina. 1992. Dan Cramer's Potlatch: Law as Coercion, Symbol, and Rhetoric in British Columbia, 1884–1951. *Canadian Historical Review* 73: 125–165.

Orans, Martin. 1975. Domesticating the Functional Dragon: An Analysis of Piddocke's Potlatch. *American Anthropologist* 77: 312–328.

Piddocke, Stuart. 1965. The Potlatch System of the Southern Kwakiutl: A New Perspective. *Southwestern Journal of Anthropology* 21: 244–264.

Rosman, Abraham, and Paula G. Rubel. 1971. *Feasting with Mine Enemy: Rank and Exchange Among Northwest Coast Societies*. New York: Columbia University Press.

Rosman, Abraham, and Paula G. Rubel. 1972. The Potlatch: A Structural Analysis. *American Anthropologist* 74: 658–671.

Snyder, Sally. 1975. Quest for the Sacred in Northern Puget Sound: An Interpretation of Potlatch. *Ethnology* 14: 149–61.

Sociology

Befu, Harumi. 1968. Gift Giving in a Modernizing Japan. *Monumenta Nipponica* 23: 445–456.

Bendix, Reinhard. 1977. *Max Weber: An Intellectual Portrait*. Berkeley: University of California Press.

Berking, Helmuth. 1999. *Sociology of Giving*. London: Sage.

Bourdieu, Pierre. 1990. *The Logic of Practice*. Trans. Richard Nice. Stanford, CA: Stanford University Press.

Bourdieu, Pierre. 1997. Marginalia—Some Additional Notes on the Gift. In Schrift ed. 231–241.

Camerer, Colin. 1988. Gifts as Economic Signals and Social Symbols. *American Journal of Sociology* 94: S180–S214 (Supplement).

Caplow, Theodore. 1984. Rule Enforcement without Visible Means: Christmas Gift Giving in Middletown. *American Journal of Sociology* 89: 1306–1323.

Carrier, James. 1990. Gifts in a World of Commodities: The Ideology of the Perfect Gift in American Society. *Social Analysis* 24: 19–37.

Di Leonardo, Micaela. 1987. The Female World of Cards and Holidays: Women, Families, and the Work of Kinship. *Signs* 12: 440–453.

Jhering, Rudolf von. 1889. *Das Trinkgeld*. 3rd ed. Braunschweig: G. Westermann.

Margolis, Diane Rothbard. 1984. *Gifts, Commodities and the Tribute Factor: A Feminist Reformation of Sociological Theory*. Wellesley, MA: Wellesley College, Center for Research on Women.

Schwartz, Barry. 1967. The Social Psychology of the Gift. *American Journal of Sociology* 73: 1–11.

Silber, Ilana F. 1995. Gift Giving in the Great Traditions: The Case of Donations to Monasteries in the Medieval West. *Archives européenes de sociologie* 36: 209–243.

Silber, Ilana F. 1998. Modern Philanthropy: Reassessing the Viability of a Maussian Perspective. In James and Allen ed. 134–150.

Silber, Ilana F. 2000. Beyond Purity and Danger: Gift-Giving in the Monotheistic Religions. In Vandevelde ed. 115–132.

Weber, Max. 1978. *Economy and Society: An Outline of Interpretive Sociology*. Ed. Guenther Roth and Claus Wittich. Berkeley: University of California Press.

Zelizer, Viviana A. Rotman. 1994. *The Social Meaning of Money*. New York: Basic Books.

Economics

Andreoni, James. 1989. Giving with Impure Altruism: Applications to Charity and Ricardian Equivalence. *Journal of Political Economy* 97: 1447–1458.

Arrow, Kenneth J. 1972. Gifts and Exchanges. *Philosophy & Public Affairs* 1: 343–362.

Becker, Gary S. 1974. A Theory of Social Interactions. *Journal of Political Economy* 82: 1063–1093.

Davis, J. 1972. Gifts and the U.K. Economy. *Man* 7: 408–429.

Hochman, Harold M., and James D. Rogers. 1969. Pareto Optimal Redistribution. *American Economic Review* 59: 542–557.

Klundert, Theo van de, and Jeroen van de Ven. 1999. On the Viability of Gift Exchange in a Market Environment. [Tilburg: Tilburg University]. http://www.appropriate-economics.org/materials/giftexchangemarketenvironment.pdf.

Posner, Eric. 1997. Altruism, Status, and Trust in the Law of Gifts and Gratuitous Transfers. *Wisconsin Law Review* 1997: 567–609.

Posner, Richard A. 1977. Gratuitous Promises in Economics and Law. *Journal of Legal Studies* 6: 411–426.

Posner, Richard A. 2007. *Economic Analysis of Law.* 7th ed. Austin, TX: Wolters Kluwer for Aspen Publishers.

Sen, Amartya K. 1977. Rational Fools: A Critique of the Behavioral Foundations of Economic Theory. *Philosophy & Public Affairs* 6: 317–344.

Shavell, Steven. 1991. An Economic Analysis of Altruism and Deferred Gifts. *Journal of Legal Studies* 20: 401–421.

Solnick, Sara J., and David Hemenway. 1996. The Deadweight Loss of Christmas: Comment. *American Economic Review* 86: 1299–1305.

Ven, Jeroen van de. 2000. The Economics of the Gift. [Tilburg: Tilburg University]. http://papers.ssrn.com/sol3/papers.cfm?abstract_id=244683.

Ven, Jeroen van de. 2002. The Demand for Social Approval and Status as a Motivation to Give. *Journal of Institutional and Theoretical Economics* 158: 464–482.

Waldfogel, Joel. 1993. The Deadweight Loss of Christmas. *American Economic Review* 83: 1328–1336.

Waldfogel, Joel. 1996. The Deadweight Loss of Christmas: Reply. *American Economic Review* 86: 1306–1308.

Webley, Paul, and Richenda Wilson. 1989. Social Relationships and the Unacceptability of Money as a Gift. *Journal of Social Psychology* 129: 85–91.

General History

Algazi, Gadi. 2003. Introduction: Doing Things with Gifts. In Algazi, Groebner, and Jussen, ed. 9–27.

Algazi, Gadi, Valentin Groebner, and Bernhard Jussen, ed. 2003. *Negotiating the Gift: Pre-Modern Figurations of Exchange.* Veröffentlichungen des Max-Planck-Instituts für Geschichte, 188. Göttingen: Vanderhoeck & Ruprecht.

Anchel, Robert. 1910. Hérault de Séchelles, Marie Jean. *Encyclopædia Britannica* 13: 333. 11th ed. New York: Encyclopædia Britannica.

Bernier, Georges. 1995. *Hérault de Séchelles: biographie.* Paris: Julliard.

Carlyle, Thomas. 2002. *The French Revolution: A History* [1837]. The Modern Library classics. New York: Modern Library.

Coe, Sophie D., and Michael D. Coe. 2003. *The True History of Chocolate.* London: Thames & Hudson.

Cohen, Esther, and Mayke De Jong, ed. 2001. *Medieval Transformations: Texts, Power, and Gifts in Context.* Cultures, beliefs, and traditions, vol. 11. Leiden: Brill.

Curta, Florin. 2006. Merovingian and Carolingian Gift Giving. *Speculum* 81: 671–699.

Dard, Émile. 1907. *Un épicurien sous la terreur, Hérault de Séchelles (1759–1794): D'après des Documents inédits.* Paris: Perrin et cie.

Darnton, Robert. 1985. *The Great Cat Massacre and Other Episodes in French Cultural History.* New York: Vintage Books.

Davis, Natalie Zemon. 2000. *The Gift in Sixteenth-Century France*. The Curti Lectures. Madison: University of Wisconsin Press.

Desan, Suzanne. 2004. *The Family on Trial in Revolutionary France*. Studies on the history of society and culture, 51. Berkeley: University of California Press.

Donlan, Walter. 1989. The Unequal Exchange between Glaucus and Diomedes in Light of the Homeric Gift-Economy. *Phoenix* 43: 1–15.

Duby, Georges. 1968. *Rural Economy and Country Life in the Medieval West*. Columbia: University of South Carolina Press.

Finley, M. I. 1979. *The World of Odysseus*. 2nd ed. New York: Penguin.

Geary, Patrick J. 2003. Gift Exchange and Social Science Modeling: The Limitations of a Construct. In Algazi, Groebner, and Jussen, ed. 129–140.

Groebner, Valentin. 2001. Accountancies and *Arcana*: Registering the Gift in Late Medieval Cities. In Cohen and De Jong ed. 219–243.

Grønbech, Wilhelm Peter. 1954. Gabentausch. In Wilhelm Peter Grønbech, *Kultur und Religion der Germanen* 2: 55–77. 5th ed. Darmstadt: Wissenschaftliche Buchgemeinschaft.

Gurevich, A. Ya. 1968. Wealth and Gift-Bestowal among the Ancient Scandinavians. *Scandinavica* 7: 126–138.

Hannig, Jürgen. 1986. Ars donandi. Zur Ökonomie des Schenkens im früheren Mittelalter. *Geschichte in Wissenschaft und Unterricht* 37: 149–162.

Harbsmeier, Michael. 2003. Gifts and Discoveries: Gift Exchange in Early Modern Narratives of Exploration and Discovery. In Algazi, Groebner, and Jussen, ed. 381–410.

Hirschbiegel, Jan. 2003. *Étrennes: Untersuchungen zum höfischen Geschenkverkehr im spätmittelalterlichen Frankreich der Zeit König Karls VI. (1380–1422)*. Pariser historische Studien, vol. 60. München: Oldenbourg.

Hunt, Lynn Avery. 1984. *Politics, Culture, and Class in the French Revolution*. Studies on the History of Society and Culture, 1. Berkeley: University of California Press.

Jones, Peter. 1985. *Politics and Rural Society: The Southern Massif Central, c. 1750–1880*. Cambridge: Cambridge University Press.

Kulischer, Iosif. M. 1976. *Allgemeine Wirtschaftsgeschichte des Mittelalters und der Neuzeit* [1928], vol. 1. Darmstadt: Wissenschaftliche Buchgesellschaft.

Labaree, Benjamin Woods. 1964. *The Boston Tea Party*. New York: Oxford University Press.

Le Roy Ladurie, Emmanuel. 1976. Family Structures and Inheritance Customs in Sixteenth-Century France. In *Family and Inheritance: Rural Society in Western Europe, 1200–1800*, ed. Jack Goody, Joan Thirsk, and E. P. Thompson, 37–70. Cambridge: Cambridge University Press.

Marais, Jean-Luc. 1999. *Histoire du don en France de 1800 à 1939: Dons et legs charitables, pieux et philanthropiques*. Rennes: Presses universitaires de Rennes.

Monnier, Francis. 1860. *Le Chancelier d'Aguesseau, sa conduite et ses idées politiques et son influence sur le mouvement des esprits pendant la première moitié du XVIIIᵉ siècle. Avec des documents nouveaux et plusieurs ouvrages inédits du chancelier*. Paris: Didier.

Moxham, Roy. 2003. *Tea: Addiction, Exploitation and Empire*. London: Constable.

Panckoucke, Charles Joseph, and Thuau-Grandville. 1789–. *Gazette nationale, ou, Le moniteur universel*. Paris: Chez H. Agasse, Libraire.

Schama, Simon. 1990. *Citizens: A Chronicle of the French Revolution*. New York: Vintage Books.

Schmoller, Gustav. 1875. *Strassburg zur Zeit der Zunftkämpfe und die Reform seiner Verfassung und Verwaltung im XV. Jahrhundert.* Quellen und Forschungen zur Sprach- und Culturgeschichte der Germanischen Völker, 11. Strassburg: Karl J. Trübner.

Storez, Isabelle. 1996. *Le chancelier Henri François d'Aguesseau (1668–1751): monarchiste et libéral.* Paris: Publisud.

Wagner-Hasel, Beate. 2000. *Der Stoff der Gaben: Kultur und Politik des Schenkens und Tauschens im archaischen Griechenland.* Campus historische Studien, vol. 28. Frankfurt: Campus.

Wagner-Hasel, Beate. 2003. Egoistic Exchange and Altruistic Gift: On the Roots of Marcel Mauss's Theory of the Gift. In Algazi, Groebner, and Jussen, ed. 141–171.

Weber-Kellermann, Ingeborg. 1968. Über den Brauch des Schenkens: Ein Beitrag zur Geschichte der Kinderbescherung. In *Volksüberlieferung: Festschrift für Kurt Ranke zur Vollendung des 60. Lebensjahres,* ed. Fritz Harkot, Karel Constant Peeters, and Robert Wildhaber, 1–8. Göttingen: O. Schwartz.

White, Stephen D. 1988. *Custom, Kinship, and Gifts to Saints: The laudatio parentum in Western France, 1050–1150.* Studies in legal history. Chapel Hill: University of North Carolina Press.

Wood, Ian. 2000. The Exchange of Gifts Among the Late Antique Aristocracy. In *El Disco de Teodosio,* ed. Martín Almagro Gorbea, 301–314. Madrid: Real Academia de la Historia.

Legal History

Adam, William. 1840. *The Law and Custom of Slavery in British India: In a Series of Letters to Thomas Fowell Buxton, Esq.* Boston: Weeks, Jordan, & Co.

Bellomo, Manlio. 1964. Donazione (diritto intermedio). In *Enciclopedia del diritto* 13: 955–965. [Milano]: Giuffrè.

Beyerle, Franz. 1962. *Leges Langobardorum, 643–866.* Germanenrechte, n. F.: Westgermanisches Recht, [9]. 2nd ed. Witzenhausen: Deutschrechtlicher Instituts-Verlag.

Byrnes, William H., IV. 2005. Ancient Roman Munificence: The Development of the Practice and Law of Charity. *Rutgers Law Review* 57: 1043–1110.

Drew, Katherine Fischer. 1973. *The Lombard Laws.* Sources of medieval history. Philadelphia: University of Pennsylvania Press.

Hyland, Richard. 1994. *Pacta Sunt Servanda:* A Meditation. *Virginia Journal of International Law* 34: 405–433.

Irnerius. 1894. *Summa codicis des Irnerius mit einer Einleitung.* Ed. Hermann Fitting. Berlin: Guttentag.

Jones, Gareth H. 1969. *History of the Law of Charity, 1532–1827.* Cambridge studies in English legal history. London: Cambridge University Press.

Ourliac, Paul, and Jehan de Malafosse. 1968. *Histoire du droit privé,* vol. 3. Paris: Presses universitaires de France.

Pappenheim, Max. 1933. Über die Rechtsnatur der altgermanischen Schenkung. *Zeitschrift der Savigny-Stiftung für Rechtsgeschichte (Germanistische Abteilung)* 53: 35–88.

Placentinus, Petrus. 1962. *Placentini Summa Codicis: accessit proemium quod in Moguntina editione desiderabatur* [1536]. Ed. Francesco Calasso.Torino: Bottega d'Erasmo.

Raban, Sandra. 1974. Mortmain in Medieval England. *Past and Present* 62: 3–26.

Scovazzi, Marco. 1958. La donazione nel diritto germanico. *Rivista di storia del diritto italiano* 31: 247–267.

Traer, James F. 1980. *Marriage and the Family in Eighteenth-Century France*. Ithaca, NY: Cornell University Press.

Vinnius, Arnoldus. 1840. *Arnoldi Vinnii jc. Selectarum juris quaestionum libri duo nunc primum eiusdem auctoris commentario in Institutiones Justinianeas conjunctim edicti, quibus multa commentarii loca illustrantur, ac intricatissimae juris materiae nondum ventilatae, omnibus legum Romanorum candidatis ultilissimae, dilucide enodantur.* 9th ed. Florentiae: apud Josephum Celli.

Voet, Johannes. 1827–1828. *Commentariorum ad Pandectas libri quinquaginta, in quibus praeter romani juris principia ac controversias illustriores jus etiam hodiernum, et praecipuae fori quaestiones excutiuntur.* Bassani: suis typis Remondini edidit.

Yver, Jean. 1966. *Égalité entre héritiers et exclusion des enfants dotés: Essai de géographie coutumière.* Paris: Sirey.

Roman Law

Amelotti, Mario. 1964. Donazione: donazione mortis causa—diritto romano. In *Enciclopedia del diritto* 13: 1000–1002. [Milano]: Giuffrè.

Archi, Gian Gualberto. 1958. L'evoluzione della donazione nell'epoca postclassica. *Revue internationale des droits de l'antiquité* 5: 391–426.

Archi, Gian Gualberto. 1964. Donazione (diritto romano). In *Enciclopedia del diritto* 13: 930–955. [Milano]: Giuffrè.

Ascoli, Alfredo. 1894. Sulla legge Cincia. *Bulletino dell'Istituto di diritto romano* 6: 173–228.

Baltrusch, Ernst. 1989. *Regimen morum: Die Reglementierung des Privatlebens der Senatoren und Ritter in der römischen Republik und frühen Kaiserzeit.* Vestigia, vol. 41. München: C.H. Beck.

Buckland, W. W. 2007. *A Text-Book of Roman Law from Augustus to Justinian.* Ed. Peter Stein. 3rd ed. Cambridge: Cambridge University Press.

Casavola, Franco. 1960. *Lex Cincia: Contributo alla storia delle origini della donazione romana.* Pubblicazioni della Facoltà giuridica dell'Università di Napoli, 44. Napoli: Jovene.

Corbett, Percy Ellwood. 1969. *The Roman Law of Marriage.* Oxford: Clarendon Press.

De Francisci, P. 1926. La revocatio in servitutem del liberto ingrato. In *Mélanges de droit romain dédiés à Georges Cornil*, ed. Paul Collinet and Fernand de Vissher 1: 295–323. Gand: Vanderpoorten & Co.

Dupont, Clémence. 1962. Les donations dans les constitutions de Constantin. *Revue internationale des droits de l'antiquité* 9: 291–324.

Girard, Paul Frédéric. 1924. *Manuel élémentaire de droit romain.* 7th ed. Paris: Rousseau et cie.

Kaser, Max. 1938. Die Geschichte der Patronatsgewalt über Freigelassene. *Zeitschrift der Savigny-Stiftung für Rechtsgeschichte (Romanistische Abteilung)* 58: 88–135.

Kaser, Max. 1971–1975. *Das römische Privatrecht.* Handbuch der Altertumswissenschaft, dept. 10 tome 3 vol. 3. 2nd ed. München: Beck.

Lévy, Jean-Philippe. 1949. Essai sur la promesse de donation en droit romain. *Revue internationale des droits de l'antiquité* 3: 91–136.

Michel, Jacques Henri. 1962. *Gratuité en droit romain*. Études d'histoire et d'ethnologie juridiques. Bruxelles: Université Libre de Bruxelles, Institut de Sociologie.

Mommsen, Theodor, Paul Krueger, and Alan Watson. 1985. *The Digest of Justinian* [Latin text with English translation]. Philadelphia: University of Pennsylvania Press.

Nicholas, Barry. 1962. *An Introduction to Roman law*. Clarendon law series. Oxford: Clarendon Press.

Ors, Alvaro d'. [1973]. *Derecho privado romano*. Pamplona: Ediciones Universidad de Navarra.

Sadashige, Jacqui. 2002. Catullus and the Gift of Sentiment in Republican Rome. In Osteen ed. 149–171.

Sandars, Thomas Collett. 1970. *The Institutes of Justinian with English Introduction, Translation, and Notes* [1922]. Westport, CT: Greenwood Press.

Savigny, Friedrich Carl von. 1841. *System des heutigen Römischen Rechts*, vol. 4. Berlin: Veit und Comp.

Savigny, Friedrich Carl von. 1850. Ueber die *lex Cincia de donis et muneribus* und deren spätere Umbildungen [1818]. In Friedrich Carl von Savigny, *Vermischte Schriften* 1: 315–385. Berlin: Veit und Comp.

Watson, Alan. 1968. *The Law of Property in the Later Roman Republic*. Oxford: Clarendon Press.

Zimmermann, Reinhard. 1990. *The Law of Obligations: Roman Foundations of the Civilian Tradition*. Cape Town: Juta.

Canon Law

Ansegius, Saint. 1996. *Die Kapitulariensammlung des Ansegius*. Monumenta Germaniae historica, tome 1. Ed. Gerhard Schmitz. Hannover: Hahnsche Buchhandlung.

De Stefano, Antonio. 1964. Donazione: diritto canonico. In *Enciclopedia del diritto* 13: [996]–1000. [Milano]: Giuffrè.

Henricus de Segusio, Cardinal Hostiensis. 1581. *In Primum Decretalium librum Commentaria*. Venetiis: Apud Ivntas.

Comparative Law Methodology

Constantinesco, Léontin-Jean. *Traité de droit comparé*. Paris: Librairie générale de droit et de jurisprudence.
  Tome 1: *Introduction au droit comparé*. 1972.
  Tome 2: *La méthode comparative*. 1974.
  Tome 3: *La science des droits comparés*. 1983.

Dannemann, Gerhard. 2006. Comparative Law: Study of Similarities or Differences? In Reimann and Zimmermann ed. 383–419.

David, René, and John E. C. Brierley. 1985. *Major Legal Systems in the World Today: An Introduction to the Comparative Study of Law*. 3rd ed. London: Stevens & Sons.

Frankenberg, Günter. 1985. Critical Comparisons: Re-thinking Comparative Law. *Harvard International Law Journal* 26: 411–455.

Glenn, H. Patrick. 2006. Comparative Legal Families and Comparative Legal Traditions. In Reimann and Zimmermann ed. 421–440.

Husa, Jaakko. 2003. Farewell to Functionalism or Methodological Tolerance? *Rabels Zeitschrift für ausländisches und internationales Privatrecht* [RabelsZ] 77: 419–447.

Hyland, Richard. 1996. Comparative Law. In *A Companion to Philosophy of Law and Legal Theory*, ed. Dennis M. Patterson, 184–99. Blackwell Companions to Philosophy, 7. Cambridge, MA: Blackwell Publishers.

Hyland, Richard. 2007. Evening in Lisbon. In *Festschrift für Claus-Wilhelm Canaris zum 70. Geburtstag*, ed. Andreas Heldrich, Jürgen Prölss, and Ingo Koller, 2: 1135–1154. München: Beck.

Kötz, Hein. 1990. Rechtsvergleichung und Rechtsdogmatik. *Rabels Zeitschrift für ausländisches und internationales Privatrecht* [RabelsZ] 54: 203–216.

Kötz, Hein. 1998. Abschied von der Rechtskreislehre? *Zeitschrift für europäisches Privatrecht* 6: 493–505.

Legrand, Pierre. 1995. Comparative Legal Studies and Commitment to Theory. *Modern Law Review* 58: 262–273.

Michaels, Ralf. 2006. The Functional Method of Comparative Law. In Reimann and Zimmermann ed. 339–382.

Mincke, Wolfgang. 1984. Eine vergleichende Rechtswissenschaft. *Zeitschrift für vergleichende Rechtswissenschaft* 83: 315–328.

Reimann, Mathias, and Reinhard Zimmermann, ed. 2006. *The Oxford Handbook of Comparative Law*. Oxford: Oxford University Press.

Zweigert, Konrad, and Hein Kötz. 1998. *An Introduction to Comparative Law*. Trans. Tony Weir. 3rd ed. Oxford: Clarendon Press.

Comparative Law

Abadie, Alberto, and Sebastien Gay. 2006. The Impact of Presumed Consent Legislation on Cadaveric Organ Donation: A Cross-Country Study. *Journal of Health Economics* 25: 599–620.

Baade, Hans. 1980. Donations Reconsidered. Review of *Gifts and Promises*, by John Philip Dawson. *Texas Law Review* 59: 179–190.

Boele-Woelki, Katharina, and Angelika Fuchs, ed. 2003. *Legal Recognition of Same-Sex Couples in Europe*. European family law series, 1. Antwerp: Intersentia.

Comment. 1951. Assignment by Check—A Comparative Study. *Yale Law Journal* 60: 1007–1025.

Dawson, John Philip. 1961. *Negotiorum Gestio:* The Altruistic Intermeddler. *Harvard Law Review* 74: 817–65, 1073–1129.

Dawson, John Philip. 1980. *Gifts and Promises: Continental and American Law Compared.* Storrs lectures on jurisprudence, 1978. New Haven: Yale University Press.

Des concubinages: Droit interne, droit international, droit comparé: Études offertes à Jacqueline Rubellin-Devichi. 2002. Paris: Litec.

Fratcher, William Franklin. 1973. Trust. In *International Encyclopedia of Comparative Law*, vol. 6, ed. Athanassios N. Yiannopoulos, ch. 11. Tübingen: J.C.B. Mohr (Paul Siebeck).

Gordley, James. 1997. Contract in Pre-Commercial Societies and in Western History. In *International Encyclopedia of Comparative Law*, vol. 7, ed. Arthur T. vonMehren, ch. 11. Tübingen: J.C.B. Mohr (Paul Siebeck).

Gorla, Gino. 1954. *Il contratto. Problemi fondamentali trattati con il metodo comparativo e casistico.* Milano: Giuffrè.

Gutmann, Thomas, and Ulrich Schroth. 2002. *Organlebendspende in Europa: Rechtliche Regelungsmodelle, ethische Diskussion und praktische Dynamik.* MedR Schriftenreihe Medizinrecht. Berlin: Springer.

Haymann, Franz. 1905. *Die Schenkung unter einer Auflage nach römischem und deutschem bürgerlichem Recht.* Berlin: F. Vahlen.

Hyland, Richard. 2004. The American Experience: Restatements, the UCC, Uniform Laws, and Transnational Coordination. In *Towards a European Civil Code*, ed. A.S. Hartkamp and E. H. Hondius, 59–75. 3rd ed. Nijmegen: Ars Aequi Libri.

International Association of Legal Science. 1973–. *International Encyclopedia of Comparative Law*. Tübingen: J.C.B. Mohr (Paul Siebeck).

Kessler, Friedrich. 1954. Einige Betrachtungen zur Lehre von der Consideration. In *Festschrift für Ernst Rabel*, ed. Hans Dölle, Max Rheinstein, and Konrad Zweigert, 1: 251–276. Tübingen: Mohr.

Lorenz, Werner. 1969. Entgeltliche und unentgeltliche Geschäfte: Eine vergleichende Betrachtung des deutschen und des anglo-amerikanischen Rechts. In *Ius privatum gentium: Festschrift für Max Rheinstein zum 70. Geburtstag am 5. Juli 1969*, ed. Ernst von Caemmerer, Soia Mentschikoff, and Konrad Zweigert, 2: 547–568. Tübingen: Mohr (Siebeck).

Lorenzen, Ernest G. 1928. The Negotiorum Gestio in Roman and Modern Civil Law. *Cornell Law Quarterly* 13: 190–210.

Mäntysaari, Petri. 1998. *Mängelhaftung beim Kauf von Gesellschaftsanteilen: Eine vergleichende Untersuchung zum deutschen, finnischen und schwedischen Recht*. Helsingfors: Hanken, Swedish School of Economics and Business Administration.

Mitchell, Léonie M. 1928. The British Conception of Negotiable Instruments *v.* the French. *Journal of Comparative Legislation and International Law* 10: 237–247.

Noonan, John Thomas, Jr. 1984. *Bribes*. New York: MacMillan.

Schlechtriem, Peter. 2000. *Restitution und Bereicherungsausgleich in Europa: eine rechtsvergleichende Darstellung*. Tübingen: Mohr Siebeck.

Schwenzer, Ingeborg H. 1997. Restitution of Benefits in Family Relationships. In *International Encyclopedia of Comparative Law*, vol. 10, ed. Peter Schlechtriem, ch. 12. Tübingen: J.C.B. Mohr (Paul Siebeck).

Sheehan, Duncan. 2006. Negotiorum Gestio: A Civilian Concept in the Common Law? *International & Comparative Law Quarterly* 55: 253–279.

Siebert, Wolfgang. 1927–1938. Schenkung. In *Rechtsvergleichendes Handwörterbuch für das Zivil- und Handelsrecht des In- und Auslandes*, ed. Franz Schlegelberger, 6: 144–159. Berlin: F. Vahlen.

Stern, Walter. 1965. Consideration and Gift. *International & Comparative Law Quarterly* 14: 675–684.

Von Mehren, Arthur Taylor. 1959. Civil-Law Analogues to Consideration: An Exercise in Comparative Analysis. *Harvard Law Review* 72: 1009–1078.

Weir, Tony. 1975. The Common Law System. In *International Encyclopedia of Comparative Law*, vol. 2, ed. René David. Structure and the Divisions of the Law, ch. 2, 77–114. Tübingen: J.C.B. Mohr (Paul Siebeck).

Wintemute, Robert, and Mads Tønnesson Andenæs, ed. 2001. *Legal Recognition of Same-Sex Partnerships: A Study of National, European, and International Law*. Oxford: Hart Publishing.

Zweigert, Konrad. 1964. Seriositätsindizien: Rechtsvergleichende Bemerkungen zur Scheidung verbindlicher Geschäfte von unverbindlichen. *Juristenzeitung* [JZ] 19: 349–354.

Argentina

Llerena, Baldormero. 1931. *Concordancias y comentarios del Código civil argentino*. 3rd ed. Buenos Aires: Librería y editorial "La Facultad," J. Roldán y c.a.

Belgium

Baugniet, Jean, and Alfred Genin. *Répertoire notarial*. Bruxelles: F. Larcier.
    Tome 3, bk. 6: *Les libéralités: Dispositions générales*. Ed. Jean Sace. 1993.
De Page, Henri. *Traité élémentaire de droit civil belge: principes, doctrine, jurisprudence*.
    Bruxelles: Bruylant.
    Tome 1: *Introduction; théorie générale des droits et des lois; les personnes; la famille*.
        3rd ed. 1962.
    Tome 2: *Les incapables; les obligations*. 3rd ed. 1964.
    Tome 7, vol. 2: *De la transmission des droits réels immobiliers; de la prescription*.
        Ed. René Dekkers. 1943.
    Tome 8, vol. 1: *Les libéralités (généralités); les donations*. 2nd ed. 1962.
De Page, Philippe. 1992. La cause immorale et l'union libre. In De Page and
    De Valkeneer ed. 163–179.
De Page, Philippe, and Roland De Valkeneer, ed. 1992. *L'Union libre: Actes du colloque
    tenu à l'Université Libre de Bruxelles le 16 octobre 1992*. Collection de la Faculté de droit
    de l'Université libre de Bruxelles. Bruxelles: Bruylant.
De Schutter, Olivier, and Anne Weyembergh. 2001. "Statutory Cohabitation" Under
    Belgian Law: A Step Towards Same-Sex Marriage? In Wintemute and Andenæs ed.
    465–474.
Laurent, François. 1878. *Principes de droit civil français*. 3rd ed. Bruxelles: Bruylant-
    Christophe & Cie.

Canada

Commentaires du ministre de la Justice: le Code civil du Québec: un mouvement de société.
    1993. [Quebec:] Government du Québec, Ministère de la justice.
Venne, Sharon Helen. 1981. *Indian Acts and Amendments 1868–1975: An Indexed
    Collection*. [Saskatoon]: University of Saskatchewan, Native Law Centre.

France

Aguesseau, Henri François d'. 1776. *Oeuvres de M. le chancelier d'Aguesseau*. Paris:
    Libraires associés.
Arrighi, Jean-Pierre. 1980. Le don manuel par chèque. *Recueil Dalloz* [D.] 1980
    Chronique 165–170.
Ascencio, Paule. 1975. L'annulation des donations immorales entre concubins: Cause ou
    notion de condition résolutoire. *Revue trimestrielle de droit civil* 73: 248–263.
Aubépin, [H]. 1855. De l'influence de Dumoulin sur certains points du droit civil. *Revue
    critique de législation et de jurisprudence* 7: 145–190.
Aubry, Charles, and Charles Rau. 1875. *Cours de droit civil français d'après la méthode de
    Zachariae*. 4th ed. Paris: Marchal et Billard.
Aubry, Charles, and Charles Rau. 1954. *Droit civil français*, vol. 10. Ed. Paul Esmein.
    6th ed. Paris: Librairies Techniques.
Barrière, Louis-Augustin. 2002. Penser le(s) concubinage(s): La doctrine française et le
    concubinage depuis le Code civil. In *Des concubinages* 143–181.
Baudry-Lacantinerie, G. 1905. *Traité théorique et pratique de droit civil: Des donations entre
    vifs et des testaments*. 3rd ed. Paris: L. Larose et L. Tenin.
Bayart, M. 1953. D'Aguesseau, économiste. In *Le Chancelier Henri-François d'Aguesseau*
    94–102.

Beaubrun, Marcel. 2004. Quelques observations sur une offre de loi dénommée "Des libéralités," *Répertoire du notariat Defrénois* art. 38039.

Beudant, Léon Charles Anatole, Robert Beudant, and Paul Lerebours-Pigeonnière. 1934–1953. *Cours de droit civil français.* 2nd ed. Paris: Rousseau & Cie.

Blaise, Henry. 1965. La formation au XIXe siècle de la jurisprudence sur les donations déguisées. In *Mélanges offerts à René Savatier* 89–114. Paris: Dalloz.

Borrillo, Daniel. 2001. The *"Pacte Civil de Solidarité"* in France: Midway Between Marriage and Cohabitation. In Wintemute and Andenæs ed. 475–492.

Boujeka, Augustin. 2003. Des libéralités par chèque. *Recueil Dalloz* [D.] 2003: 2712–2715.

Bourjon, François. 1770. *Le droit commun de France, et la Coutume de Paris réduits en principes, tirés des loix, des ordonnances, des arrêts, des jurisconsultes & des auteurs, & mis dans l'ordre d'un commentaire complet & méthodique sur cette coutume: contenant, dans cet ordre, les usages du Châtelet sur les liquidations, les comptes, les partages, les substitutions, les dîmes, & toutes autres matières.* New ed. Paris: Grange.

Brault, Jean-Claude. 1998. L'intention libérale dans les relations familiales. *Répertoire du notariat Defrénois* art. 36900.

Brenner, Claude. 2005. Brèves observations sur la révocation des donations entre époux après la loi du 26 mai 2004 relative au divorce. *Répertoire du notariat Defrénois* art. 38084.

Bretonnier, Barthélemy Joseph. 1783. *Recueil par ordre alphabétique, des principales questions de droit, qui se jugent diversement dans les différents Tribunaux du Royaume. Avec des Réflexions pour concilier la diversité de la Jurisprudence, & la rendre uniforme dans tous les Tribunaux.* Ed. Boucher d'Argis. 5th ed. Paris: Chez Le Boucher.

Brissaud, Jean. 1968. *A History of French Private Law* [1912]. The Continental Legal History Series, vol. 3. Trans. Rapelje Howell. South Hackensack, NJ: Rothman Reprints.

Bufnoir, Claude. 1924. *Propriété et contrat: Théorie des Modes d'acquisition des droits réels et des Sources des Obligations.* Ed. Etienne Bartin. 2nd ed. Paris: Rousseau.

Carbonnier, Jean. 1953. L'importance de D'Aguesseau pour son temps et pour le notre. In *Le Chancelier Henri-François d'Aguesseau* 36–41.

Carbonnier, Jean. *Droit civil.* Paris: Presses universitaires de France.
Vol. 1: *Introduction, Les personnes.* 13th ed. 1980.
Vol. 3: *Les biens.* 10th ed. 1980.
Vol. 4: *Les obligations.* 10th ed. 1979.

Carbonnier, Jean. 1983. *Flexible droit: Textes pour une sociologie du droit sans rigueur.* 5th ed. Paris: Librairie générale de droit et de jurisprudence.

Carette, A. A. [1843]. *Lois annotées, ou, Lois, décrets, ordonnances, avis du Conseil d'État, etc.: avec notes historiques, de concordance et de jurisprudence. 1789–1830.* Paris: Administration du Recueil général des lois et des arrêts.

Carette, A.-A., and L.-M. Devilleneuve. 1854. *Lois annotées, ou, Lois, décrets, ordonnances, avis du Conseil d'État, etc., avec notes historiques, de concordance et de jurisprudence.* 2nd series, 1831–1848. Paris: Administration du Recueil général des lois et des arrêts.

Champeaux, Jean. 1931. *Étude sur la notion juridique de l'acte à titre gratuit en droit civil français.* Mâcon: Buguet-Comptour.

Le Chancelier Henri-François d'Aguesseau, Limoges 1668–Fresnes 1751; journées d'étude tenues à Limoges à l'occasion du bicentenaire de sa mort (Octobre 1951). 1953. Limoges: Librairie Desvilles.

Coron, Denis, and Frédéric Lucet. 2000. Assurance-vie, union libre et révocation pour survenance d'enfant. *Répertoire du notariat Defrénois* art. 37183.

Cujas, Jacques. 1722. *Jacobi Cujacij J.C. præstantissimi Opera omnia in decem tomos distributa. Quibus continentur tam Priora, sive quæ ipse superstes edi curavit; quam Posteriora, sive que post obitum ejus edita sunt.* Ed. Charles Annibale Fabrot. Neapoli: Typis ac Sumptibus Michaelis Alysii Mutio.

Dagot, Michel. 1971. Réflexions sur l'article 1099-1 du Code civil (l'acquisition d'un bien par un époux au moyen de deniers donnés par l'autre à cette fin). *Semaine juridique* [J.C.P.] 1971 II 2397.

Dagot, Michel. 2000. Des donations non solennelles. *Semaine juridique* [J.C.P.] 2000 I 248.

Delvincourt, Claude Etienne. 1813. *Cours de Code Napoléon: Ouvrage divisé en deux Parties, dont la première contient la Troisième Édition des INSTITUTES DE DROIT CIVIL FRANÇAIS, du même Auteur, revue et corrigée par lui; et la seconde, les Notes et Explications sur lesdites Institutes.* Paris: P. Gueffier.

Dementhon, Henri. 1964. *Traité du domaine de l'état.* 6th ed. Paris: Dalloz.

Devilleneuve, L. M., and P. Gilbert. 1851. *Jurisprudence du XIXᴱ siècle, ou Table générale alphabétique et chronologique du Recueil général des lois et des arrêts (1791 à 1850)*, vol. 2. Paris: Administration du recueil.

Domat, Jean. 1850. *The Civil Law in Its Natural Order.* Ed. Luther S. Cushing. Trans. William Strahan. Boston: Charles C. Little and James Brown.

Dumoulin, Charles. 1681. *Caroli Molinæi Franciæ et Germaniæ celeberrimi jurisconsulti, et in Supremo Parisiorum Senatu antiqui advocati, Omnia quæ extant opera, ex variis librorum apothecis, in quibus latebant, nunc primùm eruta, & simul typis commissa, permultisque mendis, quibus sensim scatebant, ad exemplaria tùm ab Authore recognita, tùm à Viris Doctissimis, Jurisque Peritissimis inter legendum notata, & quàm fieri potuit diligentissimè purgata.* Ed. François Pinsson and Julien Brodeau. New ed. Parisiis: In Officina P. Rocolet.

Tome 3: *Tractatus duo analytici, Prior, de Donationibus factis vel confirmatis in contractu matrimonii; Posterior, de inofficiosis Testamentis, Donationibus & Dotibus, ejusdem Aucthoris Franciæ & Germaniæ Jureconsulti, & in supremo Parisiorum Senatu antiqui Advocati Juris praxisque consultissimi*, 513–543.

Dumoulin, Charles. 1691. *Coutumes de la prevosté et vicomté de Paris.* Ed. J. Tournet, Jacques Joly, and Charles Labbé. Paris: Chez Guillaume Cavelier.

Dupeyroux, Jean Jacques. 1955. *Contribution à la théorie générale de l'acte à titre gratuit.* Paris: Librairie générale de droit et de jurisprudence.

Duvergier, Jean Baptiste. 1834–1838. *Collection complète des Lois, Décrets, Ordonnances, Réglemens, Avis du Conseil-d'État, publiée sur les éditions officielles du Louvre; de l'Imprimerie nationale, par Baudouin; et du Bulletin des Lois; De 1788 à 1830 inclusivement, par ordre chronologique, Continuée depuis 1830.* 2nd ed. Paris: A. Guyot et Scribe.

Esmein, Paul. 1953. *Cours de droit civil. Licence 3me année, 1953–1954.* Paris: Cours de droit.

Fenet, P. A. 1968. *Recueil complet des travaux préparatoires du Code civil: suivi d'une édition de ce code, à laquelle sont ajoutés les lois, décrets et ordonnances formant le complément de la législation civile de la France, et où se trouvent indiqués, sous chaque article séparément, tous les passages du recueil qui s'y rattachent* [1827]. Osnabrück: Otto Zeller.

Flour, Jacques, and Jean Luc Aubert. 1975. *Les obligations*, vol. 1. Collection U. Paris: A. Colin.

Flour, Jacques, and Henri Souleau. 1982. *Les libéralités*. Collection U. Paris: A Colin.

Forgeard, Marie-Cécile, Richard Crône, and Bertrand Gelot. 2002. *La réforme des successions: Loi du 3 décembre 2001, commentaire & formules*. Paris: Defrénois.

Forgeard, Marie-Cécile, Richard Crône, and Bertrand Gelot. 2007. *Le nouveau droit des successions et des libéralités: Loi du 23 juin 2006, commentaires et formules*. Paris: Defrénois.

Garat, Dominique Joseph. 1785. Aux Auteurs du Journal. *Journal de Paris*, no. 219, 7 August.

Ghestin, Jacques. *Traité de droit civil*. Paris: Librairie générale de droit et de jurisprudence.

    Vol. 1: *Introduction générale*. Ed. Jacques Ghestin and Gilles Goubeaux. 3rd ed. 1990.

    Vol. 2: *Les obligations: Le contrat: formation*. Ed. Jacques Ghestin. 2nd ed. 1988.

Gobert, Michelle. 1957. *Essai sur le rôle de l'obligation naturelle*. [Paris]: Sirey.

Grenouilleau, J. B. 1977. Commentaire de la loi no. 76-1181 du 22 décembre 1976 relative aux prélèvements d'organes. *Recueil Dalloz* [D.] 1977 Chronique 213–220.

Grimaldi, Michel. 2000. *Droit civil: Libéralités, Partages d'ascendants*. Paris: Litec.

Grimaldi, Michel, and Rémy Gentilhomme. 1999. La donation de titres sociaux assortie d'une faculté conventionnelle de modification unilatérale de l'objet donné. *Répertoire du notariat Defrénois* art. 36932.

Grimaldi, Michel, and Jean-François Roux. 1994. La donation de valeurs mobilières avec réserve de quasi-usufruit. *Répertoire du notariat Defrénois* art. 35677.

Hamel, Joseph. 1920. *La notion de cause dans les libéralités: étude de la jurisprudence française et recherche d'une définition*. Paris: Recueil Sirey.

Harsin, Paul. 1928. *Les doctrines monétaires et financières en France du XVIe au XVIIIe siècles*. Paris: F. Alcan.

Hauser, Jean. 2001. Révocation des donations pour survenance d'enfants: Quelles donations et quels enfants? *Répertoire du notariat Defrénois* art. 37437.

Hello, Charles Guillaume. 1839. *Essai sur la vie et les ouvrages de Dumoulin*. Paris: Bureau de la Revue de législation et de jurisprudence.

Hiez, David. 2003. *Étude critique de la notion de patrimoine en droit privé actuel*. Bibliothèque de droit privé, tome 399. Paris: L.G.D.J.

Huet-Weiller, Danièle. 1981. "L'union libre" (La cohabitation sans mariage). *American Journal of Comparative Law*. 29: 247–277.

Isambert, François André, and Athanase Jean Léger Jourdan. 1821–1830. *Recueil général des anciennes lois françaises, depuis l'an 420 jusqu'à la révolution de 1789: contenant la notice des principaux monumens des Mérovingiens, des Carlovingiens et des Capétiens, et le texte des ordonnances, édits, déclarations, lettres-patentes, réglemens, arrêts du Conseil, etc., de la troisième race, qui ne sont pas abrogés, ou qui peuvent servir, soit à l'interprétation, soit à l'histoire du droit public et privé, avec notes de concordance, table chronologique et table générale analytique et alphabétique des matières*. Paris: Berlin-Le-Prieur.

Josserand, Louis. 1930. Sur la nature juridique des donations entre époux lorsqu'elles portent sur des biens à venir. *Dalloz Hebdomadaire* [D.H.] 1930 Chronique 21–24.

Josserand, Louis. 1936. Le déclin du titre gratuit et sa transformation. In Louis Josserand, *Évolutions et actualités: conférences de droit civil* 135–158. Paris: Recueil Sirey.

Lagarde, Xavier. 1997. Réflexions sur le fondement de l'article 931 du code civil. *Revue trimestrielle de droit civil* 96: 25–51.

Le Guidec, Raymond. 2002. Le Pacs et la transmission des biens entre concubins. In *Des concubinages* 133–142.

Libchaber, Rémy. 2000. Pour une redéfinition de la donation indirecte. *Répertoire du notariat Defrénois* art. 37273.

Locré, J. G. 1827. *La Législation civile, commerciale et criminelle de la France, ou Commentaire et complément des Codes français.* Paris: Treuttel Würtz.

Louet, Georges. 1693. *Recueil de plusieurs notables arrests du Parlement de Paris, pris de memoires de Monsieur Maistre Georges Loüet, Conseiller du Roy au mesme Parlement.* Paris: Chez Denys Thierry, Jean Guignard.

Loysel, Antoine. 1846. *Institutes coutumières.* Ed. Eusèbe de Laurière, André-Marie-Jean-Jacques Dupin, and Edouard Laboulaye. New ed. Paris: Videcoq.

Malaurie, Philippe. 2006. Libéralités, bonnes mœurs et relations adultères. *Répertoire du notariat Defrénois* art. 38305.

Malaurie, Philippe. 2007. La réforme de la protection juridique des majeurs. *Répertoire du notariat Defrénois* art. 38569.

Malaurie, Philippe, and Laurent Aynès. 1998. *Cours de droit civil: Les successions, les libéralités.* 4th ed. Paris: Éditions Cujas.

Marty, Gabriel, Pierre Raynaud, and Philippe Jestaz. 1987. *Droit civil: Les sûretés, la publicité foncière.* 2nd ed. Paris: Sirey.

Mavidal, Jérôme, and Emile Laurent. 1969. *Archives parlementaires de 1787 à 1860: Recueil complet des débats législatifs & politiques des Chambres françaises.* 1st series. Nendeln/Liechtenstein: Kraus Reprint.

Mazeaud, Henri, Léon Mazeaud, and Jean Mazeaud. *Leçons de droit civil.* Paris: Montchrestien.
    Tome 1: *Introduction à l'etude du droit*, vol. 1. Ed. François Chabas. 10th ed. 1991.
    Tome 2: *Obligations: théorie générale*, vol. 1. Ed. François Chabas. 9th ed. 1998.
    Tome 3: *Sûretés, publicité foncière*, vol. 1. Ed. Yves Picod. 7th ed. 1999.
    Tome 4: *Successions, libéralités*, vol. 2. Ed. Laurent Leveneur and Sabine Mazeaud-Leveneur. 5th ed. 1999.

Mazzoni, Cosimo Marco. 2004. Le don, c'est le drame: Le don anonyme et le don despotique. *Revue trimestrielle de droit civil* 2004: 701–712.

Méau-Lautour, Huguette. 1985. *La donation déguisée en droit civil français: Contribution à la théorie générale de la donation.* Bibliothèque de droit privé, tome 184. Paris: Librairie générale de droit et de jurisprudence.

Merlin, Philippe Antoine. 1820. *Recueil alphabétique des questions de droit qui se présentent le plus fréquemment dans les tribunaux; Ouvrage dans lequel sont fondus et classés la plupart des plaidoyers et réquisitoires de l'auteur, avec le texte des arrêts de la Cour de cassation qui s'en sont ensuivis*, vol. 2. Paris: Garnery.

Merlin, Philippe Antoine. 1825. *Répertoire universel et raisonné de jurisprudence.* 5th ed. Bruxelles: H. Tarlier.

Montredon, Jean-François. 1989. *La désolennisation des libéralités.* Bibliothèque de droit privé, tome 209. Paris: Librairie générale de droit et de jurisprudence.

Najjar, Ibrahim. 2003. Prix "sous-évalué" et intention libérale. *Recueil Dalloz* [D.] 2003: 2591.

Papon, Jean. 1568. *Nouvelle et cinquième édition dv Recveil d'arrests notables des cours sovveraines de France.* Lyon: Iean de Tovrnes.

Peterka, Nathalie. 2001. *Les dons manuels.* Paris: Librairie générale de droit et de jurisprudence.

Piedelièvre, Alain. 2004. L'aménagement des libéralités entre époux par la loi du 26 mai 2004. *Recueil Dalloz* [D.] 2004: 2512–2516.

Planiol, Marcel. 1928–32. *Traité élémentaire de droit civil, conforme au programme officiel des facultés de droit.* 11th ed. Paris: Librairie générale de droit & de jurisprudence.

Planiol, Marcel, and Georges Ripert, *Traité pratique de droit civil français.* 2nd ed. Paris: Librairie générale de droit et de jurisprudence.

    Tome 3: *Les biens.* Ed. Maurice Picard. 1952.

    Tome 4: *Successions.* Ed. Jacques Maury and Henri Vialleton. 1956.

    Tome 5: *Donations et testaments.* Ed. André Trasbot and Yvon Loussourarn. 1957.

    Tome 6: *Obligations,* pt. 1. Ed. Paul Esmein. 1952.

    Tome 7: *Obligations,* pt. 2. Ed. Paul Esmein, Jean Radouant, and Gabriel Gabolde. 1954.

    Tome 8: *Les régimes matrimoniaux,* pt. 1. Ed. Jean Boulanger. 1957.

    Tome 10: *Contrats civils,* pt. 1. Ed. Joseph Hamel (sales); François Givord and André Tunc (loan for use). 1956.

Pothier, Robert Joseph. 1845. *Œuvres de Pothier annotées et mises en corrélation avec le Code civil et la législation actuelle.* Ed. M. Bugnet. Paris: Cosse.

    Tome 1: *Coutume d'Orléans.*

    Tome 3: *Vente,* 1–258.

    Tome 8: *Traité des donations entre-vifs,* 347–453.

Pradel, Jean. 1996. *Droit pénal,* vol. 1. 11th ed. Paris: Editions Cujas.

Regnault, Henri. 1929. *Les ordonnances civiles du Chancelier Daguesseau: Les donations et l'Ordonnance de 1731.* Paris: Recueil Sirey.

Ricard, Jean-Marie. 1783. *Traité des donations entre-vifs et testamentaires.* Ed. Antoine Bergier. Riom: M. Dégoutte.

Ripert, Georges. 1949. *La règle morale dans les obligations civiles.* 4th ed. Paris: Librairie générale de droit et de jurisprudence.

Ripert, Georges, and Jean Boulanger. 1956–1959. *Traité de droit civil d'après le traité de Planiol.* Paris: Librairie générale de droit et de jurisprudence.

Sahlins, Peter. 2004. *Unnaturally French: Foreign Citizens in the Old Regime and After.* Ithaca, NY: Cornell University Press.

Sauvage, François. 2004. Des conséquences du divorce sur les libéralités entre époux et les avantages matrimoniaux. *Répertoire du notariat Defrénois* art. 38038.

Souleau, Henri. 1991. *Les successions.* Collection U. 3rd ed. Paris: A. Colin.

Terré, François, and Yves Lequette. 1997. *Droit civil: Les successions, Les libéralités.* Paris: Dalloz.

Terrien, Guillaume. 1578. *Commentaires du droict ciuil, tant public que priué, obserué au pays & Duché de Normandie.* 2nd ed. Paris: Chez Iacques du Puys.

Tiraqueau, André. 1588. *Andreae Tiraqvelli regii in cvria Parisiensi Senatoris dignissimi, Opera omnia, quae hactenus extant, septem tomis distincta.* Venetijs: apud Ioannem Baptistam Somaschum.

    Tome 6: *Commentariorum in l. Si vnquàm, C. de reuocandis donationibus.*

Tracol, Xavier. 2003. The Pacte civil de solidarité (Pacs). In Boele-Woelki and Fuchs ed. 68–83.

Troplong, Raymond-Théodore. 1855. *Des donations entre-vifs et des testaments: ou Commentaire du titre II du livre III du code Napoléon.* Droit civil expliqué. Paris: C. Hingray.

Véron, Michel. 1965. La donation de biens à venir entre époux au cours du mariage et la loi du 6 novembre 1963. *Recueil Dalloz* [D.] 1965 Chronique 99.

Viatte, Jean. 1974. Des restrictions à la capacité de recevoir des enfants adultérins: Historique de l'art. 908 du Code civil. *Gazette du Palais* [*Gaz. Pal.*] 1974 II Chronique 828–830.

Viollet, Paul. 1905. *Histoire du droit civil français, accompagnée de notions de droit canonique et d'indications bibliographiques.* 3rd ed. Paris: Larose et Tenin.

Germany

Alternativkommentar. 1979. *Kommentar zum Bürgerlichen Gesetzbuch: in sechs Bänden,* vol. 3. Ed. Wolfgang Däubler and Gert Brüggemeier. Neuwied: Luchterhand.
§§ 516–534. Ed. Wolfgang Däubler.

Baumbach, Adolf, and Wolfgang Hefermehl. 1993. *Wechselgesetz und Scheckgesetz: mit Nebengesetzen und einer Einführung in das Wertpapierrecht.* 18th ed. München: C.H. Beck.

Burckhard, Hugo. 1899. *Zum Begriff der Schenkung.* Erlangen: Palm & Enke.

Entwurf eines bürgerlichen Gesetzbuches für das Deutsche Reich: Erste Lesung. 1888. Berlin: Guttentag.

Fikentscher, Wolfgang. 1992. *Schuldrecht.* 8th ed. Berlin: de Gruyter.

Fleischer, Holger. 2001. Unternehmensspenden und Leitungsermessen des Vorstands im Aktienrecht. *Die Aktiengesellschaft* [AG] 46: 171–181.

Forkel, Hans. 1974. Verfügungen über Teile des menschlichen Körpers. *Juristenzeitung* [JZ] 29: 593–599.

Grundmann. Stefan. 1998. Zur Dogmatik der unentgeltlichen Rechtsgeschäfte. *Archiv fuer die civilistische Praxis* [AcP] 198: 457–488.

Gutmann, Thomas. 2006. *Für ein neues Transplantationsgesetz: Eine Bestandsaufnahme des Novellierungsbedarfs im Recht der Transplantationsmedizin.* MedR Schriftenreihe Medizinrecht. Berlin: Springer.

Heck, Philipp. 1929. *Grundriß des Schuldrechts.* Tübingen: J.C.B. Mohr (P. Siebeck).

Höfling, Wolfram, and Stephan Rixen. 1996. *Verfassungsfragen der Transplantationsmedizin: Hirntodkriterium und Transplantationsgesetz in der Diskussion.* Tübingen: Mohr.

Hüffer, Uwe. 2008. *Aktiengesetz.* Beck'sche Kurz-Kommentare, vol. 53. 8th ed. München: C.H. Beck.

Jauernig, Othmar. 2004. *Bürgerliches Gesetzbuch.* 11th ed. München: C.H. Beck.
§§ 1–240. Ed. Othmar Jauernig.
§§ 311–311c. Ed. Astrid Stadler.
§§ 433–480. Ed. Christian Berger.
§§ 488–534. Ed. Heinz-Peter Mansel.
§§ 809–822. Ed. Astrid Stadler.
§§ 854–1296. Ed. Othmar Jauernig.
§§ 1922–2385. Ed. Rolf Stürner.

Kessler, Manfred Heinz. 1995. Die Leitungsmacht des Vorstandes einer Aktiengesellschaft (II). *Die Aktiengesellschaft* [AG] 40: 120–132.

Kieckebusch, Joachim. 1928. Schenkung. In *Handwörterbuch der Rechtswissenschaft,* ed. Fritz Stier-Somolo and Alexander Elster, 5: 282–288. Berlin: Walter de Gruyter.

Kind, Sandra. 2000. Darf der Vorstand einer AG Spenden an politische Parteien vergeben? *Neue Zeitschrift für Gesellschaftsrecht* [NZG] 3: 567–73.

Kölner Kommentar zum Aktiengesetz: §§ 76–117 AktG und Mitbestimmung im Aufsichtsrat. 1996. Ed. Carsten Peter Claussen and Wolfgang Zöllner. 2nd ed. Köln: Heymann.
§§ 76–117. Ed. Hans-Joachim Mertens.

Kommentar zum Gesetz betreffend die Gesellschaften mit beschränkter Haftung (GmbH-Gesetz). 2002. Ed. Lutz Michalski and Gerhard Dannecker. München: C.H. Beck.
§ 43. Ed. Ulrich Haas.

Kübel, Franz Friedrich Philipp von. 1980. *Recht der Schuldverhältnisse.* Berlin: de Gruyter.

Larenz, Karl. 1986. *Lehrbuch des Schuldrechts,* vol. 2, pt. 1. 13th ed. München: C.H. Beck.

Lutter, Marcus, and Walter Bayer. 2004. *GmbH-Gesetz: Kommentar.* 16th ed. Köln: O. Schmidt.

Motive zu dem Entwurfe eines Bürgerlichen Gesetzbuches für das Deutsche Reich. 1888. Berlin: J. Guttentag (D. Collin).

Mugdan, B. 1899. *Die gesammten Materialien zum Bürgerlichen Gesetzbuch für das deutsche Reich.* Berlin: Decker.

Müller-Freienfels, Wolfram. 1968. Zur Rechtsprechung beim sog. "Mätressen-Testament." *Juristenzeitung* [JZ] 23: 441–449.

Münchener Kommentar zum Aktiengesetz (AktG). 2004. Ed. Otto A. Altenburger and Bruno Kropff. 2nd ed. München: Beck.
§§ 76–94. Ed. Wolfgang Hefermehl and Gerald Spindler.

Münchener Kommentar zum Bürgerlichen Gesetzbuch (BGB). Ed. Kurt Rebmann, Franz-Jürgen Säcker, and Roland Rixecker. München: Beck.
§§ 21–89. Ed. Dieter Reuter. 5th ed. 2006.
§§ 134–138. Ed. Theo Mayer-Maly and Christian Armbrüster. 4th ed. 2001.
§§ 284–312. Ed. Reinhold Thode. 4th ed. 2001.
§§ 328–345. Ed. Peter Gottwald. 4th ed. 2003.
§§ 387–397. Ed. Martin Schlüter. 4th ed. 2003.
§§ 398–413. Ed. Günther H. Roth. 4th ed. 2003.
§§ 414–419. Ed. Wernhard Möschel. 4th ed. 2003.
§§ 516–534. Ed. Helmut Kollhosser. 4th ed. 2004.
§§ 705–740. Ed. Peter Ulmer. 4th ed. 2004.
§§ 1773–1921. Ed. Dieter Schwab. 4th ed. 2002.
§§ 2274–2302. Ed. Hans-Joachim Musielak. 4th ed. 2004.

Nehlsen-von Stryk, Karin. 1987. Unentgeltliches schuldrechtliches Wohnrecht. Zur Abgrenzungsproblematik von Leihe und Schenkung. *Archiv fuer die civilistische Praxis* [AcP] 187: 552–602.

Nickel, Lars Christoph, Angelika Schmidt-Preisigke, and Helmut Sengler. 2001. *Transplantationsgesetz: Kommentar.* Kohlhammer Krankenhaus. Stuttgart: Kohlhammer.

Ogris, Werner. 1990. Schenkung. In *Handwörterbuch zur deutschen Rechtsgeschichte* [HRG], ed. Adalbert Erler and Ekkehard Kaufmann, col. 1382–1384. [Berlin]: Erich Schmidt.

Palandt, Otto. 2006. *Bürgerliches Gesetzbuch.* 65th ed. München: C.H. Beck.
§§ 311b–432. Ed. Christian Grüneberg.
§§ 516–606. Ed. Walter Weidenkaff.
§§ 631–853. Ed. Hartwig Sprau.

Schmidt, Karsten. 2002. *Gesellschaftsrecht.* 4th ed. Köln: C. Heymanns.

Schroth, Ulrich. 2005. *Transplantationsgesetz: Kommentar*. München: Beck.
  Einleitung nos. I–II. Ed. Peter König.
  §§ 3–4. Ed. Ulrich Schroth.
Schütz, Wilhelm. 1964. Schenkweise Sicherheiten. *Juristische Rundschau* [JR] 1964:
  453–454.
Slapnicar, Klaus. 1983. Unentgeltliches Wohnen nach geltendem Recht ist Leihe,
  nicht Schenkung—Dogmengeschichtliches zu BGHZ 82, 354. *Juristenzeitung* [JZ]
  38: 325–331.
Staudingers Kommentar zum Bürgerlichen Gesetzbuch: mit Einführungsgesetz und
  Nebengesetzen. Ed. Reinhard Bork, Norbert Habermann, Julius Staudinger, Christian
  Bar, and Karl-Dieter Albrecht. 13th ed. Berlin: Sellier-de Gruyter.
  §§ I–14. Ed. Norbert Habermann, Heinrich Honsell, and Günter Weick. 2004.
  §§ 90–103. Ed. Joachim Jickeli and Malte Stieper. 2004.
  §§ 134–163. Ed. Rolf Sack. 2003.
  §§ 164–181. Ed. Eberhard Schilken. 2004.
  §§ 328–361b. Ed. Rainer Jagmann, Dagmar Kaiser, and Volker Rieble. 2001.
  §§ 516–534. Ed. Susanne Wimmer-Leonhardt. 2005.
Windscheid, Bernhard. 1906. *Lehrbuch des Pandektenrechts*. Ed. Theodor Kipp. 9th ed.
  Frankfurt a.M.: Rütten & Loening.
Zöllner, Wolfgang. 1982. *Wertpapierrecht: Ein Studienbuch*. Juristische Kurz-Lehrbücher.
  München: Beck.

India

Derrett, J. Duncan M. 1963. *Introduction to Modern Hindu Law*. [Bombay]: Indian
  Branch, Oxford University Press.
Fyzee, Asaf Ali Asghar. 1974. *Outlines of Muhammadan Law*. Delhi: Oxford University
  Press.
Gour, Hari Singh. 1990. *Sir Hari Singh Gour's Law of Transfer: being commentaries on the*
  Transfer of Property Act, 1882, vol. 2. Ed. M. H. Beg and S. K. Verma. Allahabad: Law
  Publishers.
Keith, A. Berriedale. 1925. The Personality of an Idol. *Journal of Comparative Legislation*
  8: 255–257.
Mulla, Dinshah Fardunji. 1985. *Mulla on the Transfer of Property Act, 1882.* Ed.
  H. R. Khanna and P. M. Bakshi. 7th ed. Bombay: N.M. Tripathi.
Nair, M. Krishan. 1978. *The Law of Contracts*. 4th ed. Bombay: Orient Longman.
Patra, Atul Chandra. 1966. *The Indian Contract Act, 1872*. London: Asia Pub. House.
Ramachandran, V. G. 1983. *The Law of Contract in India: A Comparative Study,* vol. 2.
  2nd ed. Lucknow: Eastern Book Co.
Row, T. V. Sanjiva. 1991. *Sanjiva Row's Contracts and law relating to tenders, buildings and*
  engineering contracts, vol. 2. Ed. Raghbirtal Bhagatram Sethi and Gyanendra Kumar.
  9th ed. Allahabad [India]: Law Publishers.

Italy

Angeloni, Franco. 1994. *Liberalità e solidarietà: Contributo allo studio del volontariato*.
  Le monografie di Contratto e impresa, 34. Padova: CEDAM.
Ascoli, Alfredo. 1935. *Trattato delle donazioni*. 2nd ed. Milano: Società editrice
  libraria.

Balbi, Giovanni. 1964. *La donazione.* [Milano]: Vallardi.

Biondi, Biondo. 1961. *Le donazioni.* Trattato di diritto civile italiano, vol. 12, tome 4. Torino: Unione tipografico-editrice torinese.

Capozzi, Guido. 2002. *Successioni e donazioni,* tome 2. 2nd ed. Milano: Giuffrè.

Carnevali, Ugo. 1974. Liberalità (atti di). In *Enciclopedia del diritto* 24: 214–224. [Milano]: Giuffrè.

Carnevali, Ugo. 1989. Donazione: Diritto civile. In *Enciclopedia giuridica,* vol. 12. Roma: Istituto della Enciclopedia Italiana.

Carpino, Brunetto. 1968. Revoca della donazione al figlio naturale riconosciuto per sopravvenienza di figli legittimi. *Rivista trimestrale di diritto e procedura civile* 22: 800–806.

Casulli, Vincenzo Rodolfo. 1964. Donazione (diritto civile). In *Enciclopedia del diritto* 13: 966–992. [Milano]: Giuffrè.

Casulli, Vincenzo Rodolfo. 1964a. Donazione: donazione mortis causa—diritto civile. In *Enciclopedia del diritto* 13: 1002–1005. [Milano]: Giuffrè.

Cataudella, Antonio. 1970. Considerazioni in tema di donazione liberatoria. *Rivista trimestrale di diritto e procedura civile* 24: 757–767.

Cendon, Paolo. 1991. *Commentario al Codice civile.* Torino: UTET.

Cian, Giorgio, and Alberto Trabucchi. 1992. *Commentario breve al codice civile.* Brevaria iuris, 1. 4th ed. Padova: CEDAM.

Cupis, Adriano de. 1989. Sulla revocazione della donazione per riconoscimento di un figlio naturale. *Rivista di diritto civile* 1989 II 275–278.

Manenti, Carlo. 1911. Sul concetto di donazione. *Rivista di diritto civile* 1911: 328–389.

Maroi, Fulvio. 1956. Una sopravvivenza arcaica: l'irrevocabilità della donazione. In Fulvio Maroi, *Scritti giuridici* 1: 549–561. Pubblicazioni della Facoltà di giurisprudenza dell'Università di Roma, 1–2. Milano: A. Giuffrè.

Lavori preparatori per la riforma del codice civile. Osservazioni e proposte sul progetto del Libro terzo; successioni e donazioni. 1937. Roma.

Moscati, Enrico. 1979. Obbligazioni naturali. In *Enciclopedia del diritto* 29: 353–383. [Milano]: Giuffrè.

Oppo, Giorgio. 1947. *Adempimento e liberalità.* Milano: Giuffrè.

Palazzo, Antonio. 2000. *Le donazioni.* Il Codice civile, artt. 769–809. 2nd ed. Milano: Giuffrè.

Pandolfelli, Gaetano, Gaetano Scarpello, Marion Stella Richter, and Gastone Dallari. *Codice civile: Illustrato con i lavori preparatori e disposizioni de attuazione e transitorie.* Milano: Giuffrè.
[Vol. 2:] Libro delle successioni per causa di morte e delle donazioni. 1939.
[Vol. 4:] Libro delle obbligazioni. 1942.

Perozzi, Silvio. 1897. Intorno alla donazione. Review of *Il concetto della donazione nel diritto romano con richiami al codice civile italiano,* by Alfredo Ascoli. *Archivio giuridico* 58: 313–344, 527–553.

Perego, Enrico. 1980. La revocazione delle disposizioni testamentarie e della donazione per sopravvenienza di figli e la riforma del diritto di famiglia. *Giurisprudenza italiana* [*Giur. it.*] 1980 IV 8–11.

Piccinini, Silvia. 1992. Profili della donazione dal Codice 1865 ad oggi. *Rivista di diritto civile* 1992 II 173–198.

Rescigno, Pietro. *Trattato di diritto privato.* 2nd ed. Torino: UTET.
Vol. 6, tome 2: *Successioni, "Le Donazioni."* Ed. Ugo Carnevali. 2000.

Richter, Giorgio Stella. 2003. La donazione nella famiglia di fatto. *Rivista di diritto civile* 2003 II 143–161.

Sacco, Rodolfo. 1993. *Il contratto*. Trattato di diritto civile. Ed. Giorgio De Nova. Torino: UTET.

Torrente, Andrea. 1956. *La donazione*. Trattato di diritto civile e commerciale, vol. 22. Milano: Giuffrè.

Torrente, Andrea. 2006. *La donazione*. Trattato di diritto civile e commerciale, vol. 22. Ed. Ugo Carnevali and Andrea Mora. 2nd ed. Milano: Giuffrè.

Torrente, Andrea, and Piero Schlesinger. 1981. *Manuale di diritto privato*. Manuali giuridici, 1. 11th ed. Milano: A. Giuffrè.

Netherlands

Asser, Carel. 1997. *Verbintenissenrecht*, pt. 4–II. Algemene leer der overeenkomsten. Ed. Arthur Severijn Hartkamp. Deventer: Tjeenk Willink.

Spain

Álvarez Lata, Natalia. 1998. Parejas de Hecho: Perspectiva Jurisprudencial. *Derecho Privado y Constitución* 1998 (12): 7–68.

Carrión Olmos, Salvador. 1996. Algunas consideraciones sobre la naturaleza de la donación (con especial referencia a la mecánica traslativa de aquélla). *Actualidad civil* 1996: 775–794.

Casanovas i Mussons, Anna. 2003. La dualidad de funciones de la aceptación de la donación: Los artículos 623 y 629 del Código civil. In *Estudios jurídicos en homenaje al profesor Luis Díez-Picazo*, ed. Antonio Cabanillas Sánchez, 2: 1611–1628. Madrid: Thomson/Civitas.

Castro, Federico de. 1953. La simulación y el requisito de la donación de cosa inmueble: Sentencia de 23 de junio de 1953. *Anuario de derecho civil* 6: 1003–1016.

Díaz Alabart, Silvia. 1980. La nulidad de las donaciones de inmuebles simuladas bajo compraventa. *Revista de derecho privado* 64: 1101–1123.

Díez Pastor, José Luis. 1952. La donación al no concebido. *Anales de la Academia Matritense del Notariado* 6: 111–164.

Díez Picazo, Luis, and Antonio Gullón Ballesteros. 1989. *Sistema de derecho civil*, vol. 2. 6th ed. Madrid: Editorial Tecnos.

García García, José Manuel. 1998. Breves notas en defensa de la donación como negocio jurídico adquisitivo del dominio. *Revista jurídica de Catalunya* 97: 273–279.

Gullón Ballesteros, Antonio. 1968. *Curso de Derecho civil: Contratos en especial, responsabilidad extracontractual*. Madrid: Editorial Tecnos.

Lacruz Berdejo, José Luis. *Elementos de derecho civil*.
    Tome 2: *Derecho de obligaciones*, vol. 3. Ed. Agustín Luna Serrano and Jésus Delgado Echeverría. 2nd ed. 1986. Barcelona: Librería Bosch.
    Tome 4: *Derecho de familia*. Ed. Joaquín Rams Albesa. 2nd ed. 2005. Madrid: Dykinson.

Lalaguna, Enrique. 1964. Los artículos 623 y 629 del código civil y la naturaleza de la donación. *Revista de derecho privado* 48: 275–99.

Manresa y Navarro, José María. 1969. *Comentarios al Código civil español*, vol. 9. Ed. Francisco de Cárdenas, Santiago Chamorro Piñero, and Francisco Bonet Ramón. 6th ed. Madrid: Instituto editorial Reus, Centro de enseñanza y publicaciones, s.a.

Martín Casals, Miquel. 2003. Same-Sex Partnerships in the Legislation of Spanish Autonomous Communities. In Boele-Woelki and Fuchs ed. 54–67.

Martínez Velencoso, Luz María. 2002. Validez de la donación de inmueble encubierta en escritura pública de compraventa: Comentario a la STS de 1 febrero 2002 (RJ 2002, 2098). *Revista de derecho patrimonial* 9: 205–215.

Ortega Pardo, Gregorio José. 1949. Donaciones indirectas. *Anuario de derecho civil* 2: 918–980.

Paz-Ares Rodríguez, Cándido. 1991. *Comentario del Código civil.* Madrid: Secretaría General Técnica, Centro de Publicaciones.

    Arts. 218–221. Ed. José Javier Hualde Sánchez.

    Arts. 618–643. Ed. Manuel Albaladejo García.

    Arts. 644–646. Ed. Silvia Díaz Alabart.

    Arts. 648–653. Ed. Silvia Díaz Alabart.

    Arts. 654–656. Ed. Manuel Albaladejo García.

    Arts. 752–762. Ed. Silvia Díaz Alabart.

    Arts. 1274–1277. Ed. Manuel Amorós Guardiola.

    Arts. 1315–1324. Ed. María José Herrero García.

Quiñonero Cervantes, Enrique. 1990. *La protección del interés del donante (Estudio de los artículos 634 y 648-3° del Código civil).* Murcia: Universidad de Murcia.

Rubio Torrano, Enrique. 1981. Los artículos 623 y 629 del Código Civil: Apuntes para otra explicación. *Revista crítica de derecho inmobiliario* 57: 351–73.

Vallet de Goytisolo, Juan B. 1978. *Estudios sobre Donaciones.* Madrid: Montecorvo.

Vallet de Goytisolo, Juan B. 1978a. Notas acerca de las donaciones indirectas. In Vallet de Goytisolo 1978: 293–301.

Vallet de Goytisolo, Juan B. 1978b. Las donaciones de bienes inmuebles disimuladas según la jurisprudencia del tribunal supremo. In Vallet de Goytisolo 1978: 591–681.

United Kingdom

Anson, William Reynell. 1901. Assignment of Choses in Action. *Law Quarterly Review* 17: 90–94.

Anson, William Reynell. 2002. *Anson's Law of Contract.* Ed. J. Beatson. 28th ed. Oxford: Oxford University Press.

Atiyah, P. S. 1986. *Essays on Contract.* Oxford: Clarendon Press.

Barlow, A. C. H. 1956. Gift *inter vivos* of a Chose in Possession by Delivery of a Key. *Modern Law Review* 19: 394–404.

Blackstone, William. 1979. *Commentaries on the Laws of England* [1765–1769]. Chicago: University of Chicago Press.

Bracton, Henry de. 1968. *On the Laws and Customs of England.* Ed. George E. Woodbine. Trans. Samuel E. Thorne. Cambridge: Published in association with the Selden Society by the Belknap Press of Harvard University Press.

Bridge, Michael G. 2002. *Personal Property Law.* Clarendon law series. 3rd ed. Oxford: Oxford University Press.

Britton. 1865. Ed. Francis Morgan Nichols. Oxford: Clarendon Press.

Bromley, P. M., and N. V. Lowe. 1992. *Family Law.* 8th ed. London: Butterworths.

Chitty, Joseph. 2004. *Chitty on Contracts.* The common law library. Ed. H. G. Beale. 29th ed. London: Sweet & Maxwell.

Coke, Edward. 1797. *The Third Part of the Institutes of the Laws of England: Concerning High Treason, and Other Pleas of the Crown and Criminal Causes.* London: E. and R. Brooke.

Coke, Edward. 1809. *The First Part of the Institutes of the Laws of England; or, A Commentary upon Littleton: Not the Name of the Author only, but of the Law itself.*

Ed. Francis Hargrave and Charles Butler. 16th ed. London: Printed by L. Hansard & Sons for E. Brooke.

Comment. 1849. On the Doctrine of Nudum Pactum in the English Law. *Law Review and Quarterly Journal of British and Foreign Jurisprudence* 10: 56–70.

Costigan, George P. 1911. Gifts *Inter Vivos* of Choses in Action. *Law Quarterly Review* 27: 326–40.

Crossley Vaines, James. 1967. *Personal Property*. 4th ed. London: Butterworths.

Fleta. 1972. Ed. and trans. H. G. Richardson and G. O. Sayles, vol. 3, bks. 3–4. London: Selden Society.

Glanvill, Ranulf de. 1965. *The treatise on the laws and customs of the realm of England commonly called Glanvill*. Medieval texts. Ed. and trans. G. D. G. Hall. London: Nelson.

Gray, Kevin J., and Susan Francis Gray. 2003. *Land Law*. Butterworths core text series. 3rd ed. London: LexisNexis.

Hall, J. C. 1959. Gift of Part of a Debt. *Cambridge Law Journal* 1959: 99–119.

Halsbury, Hardinge Stanley Giffard. *Halsbury's Laws of England*. Ed. Quintin Hogg Hailsham of St. Marylebone. 4th ed. (reissue). London: Butterworths.

Vol. 5 pt. 3 sub Children and Young Persons. 2001.

Vol. 6 sub Choses in Action. 2003.

Vol. 9 pt. 1 sub Contract. 1998.

Vol. 20 pt. 1 sub Gifts. 2004.

Vol. 48 sub Trusts. 2007.

Hart, H. L. A. 1948. The Ascription of Responsibility and Rights. *Proceedings of the Aristotelian Society* 49: 171–194.

Jaconelli, Joseph. 2006. Problems in the Rule in *Strong v Bird*. *Conveyancer and Property Lawyer* 2006: 432–50.

Jenks, Edward. 1900. Consideration and the Assignment of Choses in Action. *Law Quarterly Review* 16: 241–48.

Keeton, G.W. 1935. Is Consideration Necessary for Equitable Assignments of Choses in Action? *Bell Yard: Journal of the Law Society's School of Law* 15: 10–17.

Law Revision Committee. 1937. *Sixth Interim Report (Statute of Frauds and the Doctrine of Consideration)*. Cmd 5449. London: H.M. Stationery Off.

Lord, Hazel D. 2001. Husband and Wife: English Marriage Law from 1750: A Bibliographic Essay. *Southern California Review of Law and Women's Studies* 11: 1–89.

Maitland, Frederic William. 1886. The Mystery of Seisin. *Law Quarterly Review* 2: 481–496.

Maitland, Frederic William. 1949. *Equity: A Course of Lectures*. Ed. A. H. Chaytor, W. J. Whittaker, and John Brunyate. 2nd ed. Cambridge: University Press.

Megarry, Robert E. 1943. Consideration and Equitable Assignments of Legal Choses in Action. *Law Quarterly Review* 59: 58–62.

Megarry, Robert, and William Wade. 1984. *The Law of Real Property*. 5th ed. London: Stevens.

Oakley, A. J. 2008. *Parker and Mellows: The Modern Law of Trusts*. 9th ed. London: Sweet & Maxwell.

Palmer, Francis Beaufort. 1992. *Palmer's Company Law*. Ed. Geoffrey Morse. 25th ed. London: Sweet & Maxwell.

Parkinson, J. E. 1993. *Corporate Power and Responsibility: Issues in the Theory of Company Law*. Oxford: Clarendon Press.

Plucknett, Theodore Frank Thomas. 1956. *A Concise History of the Common Law.* 5th ed. Boston: Little, Brown.

Pollock, Frederick. 1890. Gifts of Chattels Without Delivery. *Law Quarterly Review* 6: 446–451.

Probert, Rebecca. 2004. *Sutton v Mishcon de Reya and Gawor & Co* — Cohabitation contracts and Swedish sex slaves. *Child and Family Law Quarterly* 16: 453–464.

Stoljar, Samuel. 1956. A Rationale of Gifts and Favours. *Modern Law Review* 19: 237–254.

Thomas, Geraint W., and Alastair Hudson. 2004. *The Law of Trusts.* Oxford: Oxford University Press.

Treitel, G. H. 2007. *The Law of Contract.* Ed. Edwin Peel. 12th ed. London: Sweet & Maxwell.

Wright, Robert Alderson (Baron). 1936. Ought the Doctrine of Consideration to be Abolished from the Common Law? *Harvard Law Review* 49: 1225–1253.

United States of America

Abbot, Edwin H., Jr. 1910. Mistake of Fact as a Ground for Affirmative Equitable Relief. *Harvard Law Review* 23: 608–26.

Am.Jur.2d. *American Jurisprudence; a Modern Comprehensive Text Statement of American Law, State and Federal.* 2nd ed. St. Paul, MN: West Group.
Vol. 23 sub Deeds. 2002.
Vol. 38 sub Gifts. 1999.
Vol. 41 sub Husband and Wife. 2005.
Vol. 42 sub Infants. 2000.

Arensberg, Charles C. 1947. Seals and the Uniform Written Obligations Act. *Temple Law Quarterly* 21: 122–133.

Baron, Jane B. 1989. Gifts, Bargains, and Form. *Indiana Law Journal* 64: 155–203.

Bishop, Joel Prentiss. 1873. *Commentaries on the Law of Statutory Crimes: embracing the general principles of interpretation of statutes; particular principles applicable in criminal cases; leading doctrines of the common law of crimes, and discussions of the specific statutory offenses, as to both law and procedure.* Boston: Little, Brown, and Co.

Bogert, George Gleason, and George Taylor Bogert. 1979. *The Law of Trusts and Trustees: A Treatise Covering the Law Relating to Trusts and Allied Subjects Affecting Trust Creation and Administration: with forms.* St. Paul, MN: West.
Cum. Supp. Ed. Amy Morris Hess. 2008.

Book Note. 1978. Review of *The Ages of American Law*, by Grant Gilmore. *Harvard Law Review* 91: 906–908.

Brennan, Troyen A., et al. 2006. Health Industry Practices That Create Conflicts of Interest: A Policy Proposal for Academic Medical Centers. *Journal of the American Medical Association* 295: 429–433.

Brown, Ray Andrews. 1975. *The Law of Personal Property.* Ed. Walter B. Rauschenbush. 3rd ed. Chicago: Callaghan.

Bruton, Paul W. 1930. The Requirement of Delivery as Applied to Gifts of Choses in Action. *Yale Law Journal* 39: 837–860.

Bryant, Taimie L. 2008. Sacrificing the Sacrifice of Animals: Legal Personhood for Animals, the Status of Animals as Property, and the Presumed Primacy of Humans. *Rutgers Law Journal* 39: 247–330.

Bucklin, Leonard H. 2002. Woe Unto Those Who Request Consent: Ethical and Legal Considerations in Rejecting a Deceased's Anatomical Gift Because There Is No Consent by the Survivors. *North Dakota Law Review* 78: 323–354.

C.J.S. *Corpus Juris Secundum: A Complete Restatement of the Entire American Law as Developed by All Reported Cases.* St. Paul, MN: Thomson/West.
Vol. 38A sub Gifts. 1996.
Vol. 41 sub Husband and Wife. 1996.

Comment. 1852. Gifts in View of Death. *American Law Register* 1: 1–10.

Corbin, Arthur L. 1952. *Corbin on Contracts.* One Volume Edition. St. Paul, MN: West Publishing Co.

Corbin, Arthur L. *Corbin on Contracts.* Rev. ed.
Vol. 2: *Formation of Contracts.* Ed. Joseph M. Perillo and Helen Hadjiyannakis Bender. 1995. St. Paul, MN: West Publishing Co.
Vol. 9: *Third Party Beneficiaries, Assignments, Joint and Several Contracts.* Ed. John E. Murray, Jr. 2007. Newark, NJ: LexisNexis.

Curtis, Arthur R. 1939. Effect of Uniform Stock Transfer Act Upon Gratuitous Transfer of Corporate Shares by Written Assignment. *Yale Law Journal* 48: 897–902.

Danzig, Richard. 1977. The Death of Contract and the Life of the Profession: Observations on the Intellectual State of Legal Academia. *Stanford Law Review* 29: 1125–1134.

Dawson, John Philip. 1983. Legal Realism and Legal Scholarship. *Journal of Legal Education* 33: 406–411.

Dickinson, Edwin D. 1921. Gratuitous Partial Assignments. *Yale Law Journal* 31: 1–14.

Eisenberg, Melvin. 1979. Donative Promises. *University of Chicago Law Review* 47: 1–33.

Eisenberg, Melvin. 1997. The World of Contract and the World of Gift. *California Law Review* 85: 821–866.

Farnsworth, E. Allan. 1995. Promises to Make Gifts. *American Journal of Comparative Law* 43: 359–378.

Farnsworth, E. Allan. 2004. *Contracts.* 4th ed. New York: Aspen Publishers.

Feinman, Jay. 1992. The Last Promissory Estoppel Article. *Fordham Law Review* 61: 303–316.

Fellows, Mary Louise. 1986. The Slayer Rule: Not Solely a Matter of Equity. *Iowa Law Review* 71: 489–555.

Fellows, Mary Louise. 1988. Donative Promises Redux. In *Property Law and Legal Education: Essays in Honor of John E. Cribbet*, ed. Peter Hay and Michael H. Hoeflich, 27–52. Urbana: University of Illinois Press.

Fletcher, William Meade. *Cyclopedia of the Law of Private Corporations.* Rev. ed. Chicago: Callaghan.
Vol. 1A. Ed. Carla A. Jones and Britta M. Larsen. 2002.
Vol. 6A. Ed. Publisher's staff. 2005.

Frazier, Barbara. 2001. "But I Can't Marry You": Who Is Entitled to the Engagement Ring When the Conditional Performance Falls Short of the Altar? *Journal of the American Academy of Matrimonial Lawyers* 17: 419–439.

Fuller, Lon. 1941. Consideration and Form. *Columbia Law Review* 41: 799–824.

Fuller, Lon. 1958. Positivism and Fidelity to Law—A Reply to Professor Hart. *Harvard Law Review* 71: 630–672.

G., G. S. 1926. Gift of savings deposit by delivery of pass book. *American Law Reports* [A.L.R.] 40: 1249–1263.

Garvey, John L. 1966. Revocable Gifts of Personal Property: A Possible Will Substitute. *Catholic University Law Review* 16: 119–157, 256–282.

Gilmore, Grant. 1974. *The Death of Contract*. Columbus, OH: Ohio State University Press.

Gilmore, Grant. 1977. *The Ages of American Law*. Storrs lectures on jurisprudence, 1974. New Haven: Yale University Press.

Glassman, Adam D. 2004. I Do! or Do I? A Practical Guide to Love, Courtship, and Heartbreak in New York—or—Who Gets the Ring Back Following a Broken Engagement? *Buffalo Women's Law Journal* 12: 47–99.

Goetz, Charles J., and Robert E. Scott. 1980. Enforcing Promises: An Examination of the Basis of Contract. *Yale Law Journal* 89: 1261–1322.

Gordley, James. 1995. Enforcing Promises. *California Law Review* 82: 547–614.

Graves, Charles A. 1896. Gifts of Personalty. *Virginia Law Register* 1: 871–894.

Gulliver, Ashbel G., and Catherine J. Tilson. 1941. Classification of Gratuitous Transfers. *Yale Law Journal* 51: 1–39.

H., R. E. 1933. Gift of savings deposit by delivery of pass book. *American Law Reports* [A.L.R.] 84: 558–566.

Hart, Henry Melvin, and Albert M. Sacks. 1994. *The Legal Process: Basic Problems in the Making and Application of Law*. Ed. William N. Eskridge and Philip P. Frickey. Westbury, NY: Foundation Press.

Havighurst, Harold C. 1936. Gifts of Bank Deposits. *North Carolina Law Review* 14: 129–159.

Hillman, Robert A. 1995. The Triumph of Gilmore's *The Death of Contract*. *Northwestern University Law Review* 90: 32–48.

Hines, N. William. 1970. Personal Property Joint Tenancies: More Law, Fact, and Fancy. *Minnesota Law Review* 54: 509–583.

Hirsch, Adam J. 2001. Revisions in Need of Revising: The Uniform Disclaimer of Property Interests Act. *Florida State University Law Review* 29: 109–187.

Holmes, Oliver Wendell. 1963. *The Common Law* [1881]. Ed. Mark DeWolfe Howe. Boston: Little, Brown.

Horowitz, Morton J. 1977. *The Transformation of American Law, 1780–1860*. Cambridge: Harvard University Press.

Jerry, Robert H. 2002. *Understanding Insurance Law*. 3rd ed. Newark, NJ: LexisNexis.

Kent, James. 1826–1830. *Commentaries on American Law*. New York: O. Halsted.

Kessler, Friedrich, and Grant Gilmore. 1970. *Contracts: Cases and Materials*. 2nd ed. Boston: Little, Brown.

Kreitner, Roy. 2001. The Gift Beyond the Grave: Revisiting the Question of Consideration. *Columbia Law Review* 101: 1876–1957.

Kull, Andrew. 1992. Reconsidering Gratuitous Promises. *Journal of Legal Studies* 21: 39–65.

Labatt, C. B. 1895. The Inconsistencies of the Laws of Gifts. *American Law Review* 29: 361–372.

LeFevre, E. 1954. Gift or other voluntary transfer by husband as fraud on wife. *American Law Reports, 2nd series* [A.L.R.2d] 49: 521–615.

Leslie, Melanie B. 1999. Enforcing Family Promises: Reliance, Reciprocity, and Relational Contract. *North Carolina Law Review* 77: 551–636.

Llewellyn, Karl N. 1941. On the Complexity of Consideration: A Foreword. *Columbia Law Review* 41: 777–782.

Llewellyn, Karl N. 2008. *The Bramble Bush* [1930]. New York: Oxford University Press.

Lloyd, William J. 1946. Consideration and the Seal in New York—An Unsatisfactory Legislative Program. *Columbia Law Review* 46: 1–36.

McClanahan, W. S. 1982. *Community Property Law in the United States*. Rochester, NY: Lawyers Co-operative.

McGovern, William M., Jr. 1972. The Payable on Death Account and Other Will Substitutes. *Northwestern Law Review* 67: 7–41.

McGowan, Chad A. 1996. Special Delivery: Does the Postman Have to Ring at All—The Current State of the Delivery Requirement for Valid Gifts. *Real Property, Probate and Trust Journal* 31: 357–391.

MacNeil, Ian R., and David Campbell. 2001. *The Relational Theory of Contract: Selected Works of Ian MacNeil*. Modern legal studies. London: Sweet & Maxwell.

Mechem, Philip. 1925. Gifts of Corporation Shares. *Illinois Law Review* 20: 9–30.

Mechem, Philip. 1926–1927. The Requirement of Delivery in Gifts of Chattels and of Choses in Action Evidenced by Commercial Instruments. *Illinois Law Review* 21: 341–374, 457–487, 568–609.

Murray, John Edward. 2001. *Murray on Contracts*. Newark, NJ: LexisNexis.

National Conference of Commissioners on Uniform State Laws. 1925. *Handbook of the National Conference of Commissioners on Uniform State Laws and Proceedings of the Thirty-fifth Annual Meeting*.

Note. 1924. Joint Savings-Bank Deposits and Rights of Survivorship Therein. *Harvard Law Review* 38: 243–245.

Note. 1926. Real Property—Gifts Causa Mortis of Land. *Yale Law Journal* 35: 511–512.

Note. 1929. The Uniform Written Obligations Act. *Columbia Law Review* 29: 206–209.

Note. 1939. Methods of Circumventing the Civil Disabilities of Convicts. *Yale Law Journal* 48: 912–916.

Note. 1956. Recent Legislation to Facilitate Gifts of Securities to Minors. *Harvard Law Review* 69: 1479–1490.

Page, William Herbert. 1920. *The Law of Contracts*. 2nd ed. Cincinnati: W.H. Anderson Co.

Pomeroy, John Norton. 1905. *A Treatise on Equity Jurisprudence, as Administered in the United States of America; Adapted for All the States, and to the Union of Legal and Equitable Remedies under the Reformed Procedure*. San Francisco: Bancroft-Whitney.

Pound, Roscoe. Consideration in Equity. In *Legal Essays in Honor of John H. Wigmore*. *Illinois Law Review* 13: 667–692.

Radin, Max. 1930. Statutory Interpretation. *Harvard Law Review* 43: 863–885.

Rundell, Oliver S. 1918. Gifts of *Choses* in Action. *Yale Law Journal* 27: 643–655.

Scott, Austin Wakeman, and William Franklin Fratcher. 1987. *The Law of Trusts*. 4th ed. Boston: Little, Brown.

Scott, Austin Wakeman, William Franklin Fratcher, and Mark L. Ascher [Scott and Ascher]. 2006. *Scott and Ascher on Trusts*. 5th ed. New York, NY: Aspen Publishers.

Schouler, James. 1886. Oral Wills and Death-Bed Gifts. *Law Quarterly Review* 2: 444–452.

Schouler, James. 1896. *A Treatise on the Law of Personal Property*. 3rd ed. Boston: Little, Brown.

Shattuck, Warren L. 1937. Gratuitous Promises—A New Writ? *Michigan Law Review* 35: 908–945.

Spivey, Gary D. 1972. Creation of Joint Savings Account or Savings Certificate as Gift to Survivor. *American Law Reports*, 3rd series [A.L.R.3d] 43: 971–1061.

Steele, Sherman. 1926. The Uniform Written Obligations Act—A Criticism. *Illinois Law Review* 21: 185–190.

Stone, Harlan F. 1920. Delivery in Gifts of Personal Property. *Columbia Law Review* 20: 196–201.

Sykes, Edward I. 1935–1938. Consideration in Equitable Assignments of Choses in Action. *Res Judicatae* 1: 125–129.

Symposium. 1995. Reconsidering Grant Gilmore's *The Death of Contract*. *Northwestern University Law Review* 90: 1–266.

Symposium. 1997. Corporate Philanthropy: Law, Culture, Education and Politics. *New York Law School Law Review* 41: 753–1328.

Teeven, Kevin M. 1998. *Promises on Prior Obligations at Common Law*. Contributions in legal studies, no. 85. Westport, Conn: Greenwood Press.

Tellier, L. S. 1948. Opening savings account in sole name of another, without complete surrender of passbook, as a gift. *American Law Reports*, 2nd series [A.L.R.2d] 1: 538–547.

Temple, Judson L. 1974. Gifts Effected by Written Instrument: *Faith Lutheran Retirement Home v. Veis*. *Montana Law Review* 35: 132–143.

Thompson on Real Property. 2001. Ed. David A. Thomas. 2nd ed. Newark, NJ: LexisNexis.

Thornton, W. W. 1893. *A Treatise on the Law Relating to Gifts and Advancement*. Philadelphia: T. & J.W. Johnson.

Toobin, Jeffrey. 2008. Rich Bitch: The legal battle over trust funds for pets. *New Yorker*, 29 Sept.

Truog, Robert D. 2005. The Ethics of Organ Donation by Living Donors. *New England Journal of Medicine* 353: 444–446.

Tushnet, Rebecca. 1998. Rules of Engagement. *Yale Law Journal* 107: 2583–2618.

Unger, Roberto Mangabeira. 1986. *The Critical Legal Studies Movement*. Cambridge: Harvard University Press.

White, Byron F. 1950. Recovery of Engagement Gifts: California Civil Code Section 1590. *California Law Review* 38: 529–534.

Williston, Samuel. 1930. Gifts of Rights under Contracts in Writing by Delivery of the Writing. *Yale Law Journal* 40: 1–16.

Williston, Samuel. 2008. *A Treatise on the Law of Contracts*. Ed. Richard A. Lord. 4th ed. Eagan, MN: Thomson/West.

Yorio, Edward, and Steve Thel. 1991. The Promissory Basis of Section 90. *Yale Law Journal* 101: 111–167.

Zinman, Seth D. 1994. Judging Gift Rules by Their Wrappings—Towards a Clearer Articulation of Federal Employee Gift-Acceptance Rules. *Catholic University Law Review* 44: 141–204.

2. SECONDARY SOURCES BY AUTHOR

Abadie, Alberto, and Sebastien Gay. 2006. The Impact of Presumed Consent Legislation on Cadaveric Organ Donation: A Cross-Country Study. *Journal of Health Economics* 25: 599–620.

Abbot, Edwin H., Jr. 1910. Mistake of Fact as a Ground for Affirmative Equitable Relief. *Harvard Law Review* 23: 608–26.

Ackerknecht, Erwin H. 1954. On the Comparative Method in Anthropology. In Spencer ed. 117–125.

Adam, William. 1840. *The Law and Custom of Slavery in British India: In a Series of Letters to Thomas Fowell Buxton, Esq.* Boston: Weeks, Jordan, & Co.

Aguesseau, Henri François d'. 1776. *Oeuvres de M. le chancelier d'Aguesseau.* Paris: Libraires associés.

Algazi, Gadi. 2003. *Introduction: Doing Things with Gifts.* In Algazi, Groebner, and Jussen, ed. 9–27.

Algazi, Gadi, Valentin Groebner, and Bernhard Jussen, ed. 2003. *Negotiating the Gift: Pre-Modern Figurations of Exchange.* Veröffentlichungen des Max-Planck-Instituts für Geschichte, 188. Göttingen: Vanderhoeck & Ruprecht.

Alternativkommentar. 1979. *Kommentar zum Bürgerlichen Gesetzbuch: in sechs Bänden,* vol. 3. Ed. Wolfgang Däubler and Gert Brüggemeier. Neuwied: Luchterhand. §§ 516–534. Ed. Wolfgang Däubler.

Álvarez Lata, Natalia. 1998. Parejas de Hecho: Perspectiva Jurisprudencial. *Derecho Privado y Constitución* 1998 (12): 7–68.

Am.Jur.2d. *American Jurisprudence; a Modern Comprehensive Text Statement of American Law, State and Federal.* 2nd ed. St. Paul, MN: West Group.
  Vol. 23 sub Deeds. 2002.
  Vol. 38 sub Gifts. 1999.
  Vol. 41 sub Husband and Wife. 2005.
  Vol. 42 sub Infants. 2000.

Amelotti, Mario. 1964. Donazione: donazione mortis causa—diritto romano. In *Enciclopedia del diritto* 13: 1000–1002. [Milano]: Giuffrè.

Anchel, Robert. 1910. Hérault de Séchelles, Marie Jean. *Encyclopædia Britannica* 13: 333. 11th ed. New York: Encyclopædia Britannica.

Andreoni, James. 1989. Giving with Impure Altruism: Applications to Charity and Ricardian Equivalence. *Journal of Political Economy* 97: 1447–1458.

Angeloni, Franco. 1994. *Liberalità e solidarietà: Contributo allo studio del volontariato.* Le monografie di Contratto e impresa, 34. Padova: CEDAM.

Ansegius, Saint. 1996. *Die Kapitulariensammlung des Ansegius.* Monumenta Germaniae historica, tome 1. Ed. Gerhard Schmitz. Hannover: Hahnsche Buchhandlung.

Anson, William Reynell. 1901. Assignment of Choses in Action. *Law Quarterly Review* 17: 90–94.

Anson, William Reynell. 2002. *Anson's Law of Contract.* Ed. J. Beatson. 28th ed. Oxford: Oxford University Press.

Apperson, G. L. 1993. *The Wordsworth Dictionary of Proverbs.* Ware: Wordsworth.

Archi, Gian Gualberto. 1958. L'evoluzione della donazione nell'epoca postclassica. *Revue internationale des droits de l'antiquité* 5: 391–426.

Archi, Gian Gualberto. 1964. Donazione (diritto romano). In *Enciclopedia del diritto* 13: 930–955. [Milano]: Giuffrè.

Arensberg, Charles C. 1947. Seals and the Uniform Written Obligations Act. *Temple Law Quarterly* 21: 122–133.

Arnsperger, Christian. 2000. Gift giving Practice and Noncontextual Habitus: How (not) to Be Fooled by Mauss. In Vandevelde ed. 71–92.

Arrighi, Jean-Pierre. 1980. Le don manuel par chèque. *Recueil Dalloz* [D.] 1980 Chronique 165–170.

Arrow, Kenneth J. 1972. Gifts and Exchanges. *Philosophy & Public Affairs* 1: 343–362.

Ascencio, Paule. 1975. L'annulation des donations immorales entre concubins: Cause ou notion de condition résolutoire. *Revue trimestrielle de droit civil* 73: 248–263.

Ascoli, Alfredo. 1894. Sulla legge Cincia. *Bulletino dell'Istituto di diritto romano* 6: 173–228.

Ascoli, Alfredo. 1935. *Trattato delle donazioni*. 2nd ed. Milano: Società editrice libraria.

Asser, Carel. 1997. *Verbintenissenrecht*, pt. 4–II. Algemene leer der overeenkomsten. Ed. Arthur Severijn Hartkamp. Deventer: Tjeenk Willink.

Atiyah, P. S. 1986. *Essays on Contract*. Oxford: Clarendon Press.

Aubépin, [H]. 1855. De l'influence de Dumoulin sur certains points du droit civil. *Revue critique de législation et de jurisprudence* 7: 145–190.

Aubry, Charles, and Charles Rau. 1875. *Cours de droit civil français d'après la méthode de Zachariae*. 4th ed. Paris: Marchal et Billard.

Aubry, Charles, and Charles Rau. 1954. *Droit civil français*, vol. 10. Ed. Paul Esmein. 6th ed. Paris: Librairies Techniques.

Baade, Hans. 1980. Donations Reconsidered. Review of *Gifts and Promises*, by John Philip Dawson. *Texas Law Review* 59: 179–190.

Balbi, Giovanni. 1964. *La donazione*. [Milano]: Vallardi.

Baldwin, Neil. 1988. *Man Ray: American Artist*. New York: C. N. Potter.

Baltrusch, Ernst. 1989. *Regimen morum: Die Reglementierung des Privatlebens der Senatoren und Ritter in der römischen Republik und frühen Kaiserzeit*. Vestigia, vol. 41. München: C.H. Beck.

Barlow, A. C. H. 1956. Gift *inter vivos* of a Chose in Possession by Delivery of a Key. *Modern Law Review* 19: 394–404.

Barnett, H. G. 1938. The Nature of the Potlatch. *American Anthropologist* 40: 349–358.

Baron, Jane B. 1989. Gifts, Bargains, and Form. *Indiana Law Journal* 64: 155–203.

Barrière, Louis-Augustin. 2002. Penser le(s) concubinage(s): La doctrine française et le concubinage depuis le Code civil. In *Des concubinages* 143–181.

Bataille, Georges. 1988. *The Accursed Share: An Essay on General Economy*, vol. 1: Consumption. Trans. Robert Hurley. New York: Zone.

Baudry-Lacantinerie, G. 1905. *Traité théorique et pratique de droit civil: Des donations entre vifs et des testaments*. 3rd ed. Paris: L. Larose et L. Tenin.

Baugniet, Jean, and Alfred Genin. *Répertoire notarial*. Bruxelles: F. Larcier. Tome 3, bk. 6: *Les libéralités: Dispositions générales*. Ed. Jean Sace. 1993.

Baumbach, Adolf, and Wolfgang Hefermehl. 1993. *Wechselgesetz und Scheckgesetz: mit Nebengesetzen und einer Einführung in das Wertpapierrecht*. 18th ed. München: C.H. Beck.

Bayart, M. 1953. D'Aguesseau, économiste. In *Le Chancelier Henri-François d'Aguesseau* 94–102.

Beaubrun, Marcel. 2004. Quelques observations sur une offre de loi dénommée "Des libéralités," *Répertoire du notariat Defrénois* art. 38039.

Becker, Gary S. 1974. A Theory of Social Interactions. *Journal of Political Economy* 82: 1063–1093.

Befu, Harumi. 1968. Gift Giving in a Modernizing Japan. *Monumenta Nipponica* 23: 445–456.

Beidelman, T. O. 1989. Agonistic Exchange: Homeric Reciprocity and the Heritage of Simmel and Mauss. *Cultural Anthropology* 4: 227–259.

Bellomo, Manlio. 1964. Donazione (diritto intermedio). In *Enciclopedia del diritto* 13: 955–965. [Milano]: Giuffrè.

Bendix, Reinhard. 1977. *Max Weber: An Intellectual Portrait*. Berkeley: University of California Press.

Benedict, Ruth. 1959. *Patterns of Culture* [1934]. Boston: Houghton Mifflin.

Benveniste, Emile. 1973. *Indo-European Language and Society*. Miami linguistics series, no. 12. Ed. Jean Lallot. Trans. Elizabeth Palmer. Coral Gables, FL: University of Miami Press.

Berking, Helmuth. 1999. *Sociology of Giving*. London: Sage.

Bernier, Georges. 1995. *Hérault de Séchelles: biographie*. Paris: Julliard.

Bettelheim, Bruno. 1976. *The Uses of Enchantment: The Meaning and Importance of Fairy Tales*. New York: Knopf.

Beudant, Léon Charles Anatole, Robert Beudant, and Paul Lerebours-Pigeonnière. 1934–1953. *Cours de droit civil français*. 2nd ed. Paris: Rousseau & Cie.

Beyerle, Franz. 1962. *Leges Langobardorum, 643–866*. Germanenrechte, n. F.: Westgermanisches Recht, [9]. 2nd ed. Witzenhausen: Deutschrechtlicher Instituts-Verlag.

Biondi, Biondo. 1961. *Le donazioni*. Trattato di diritto civile italiano, vol. 12, tome 4. Torino: Unione tipografpico-editrice torinese.

Bishop, Joel Prentiss. 1873. *Commentaries on the Law of Statutory Crimes: embracing the general principles of interpretation of statutes; particular principles applicable in criminal cases; leading doctrines of the common law of crimes, and discussions of the specific statutory offenses, as to both law and procedure*. Boston: Little, Brown, and Co.

Blackstone, William. 1979. *Commentaries on the Laws of England* [1765–1769]. Chicago: University of Chicago Press.

Blaise, Henry. 1965. La formation au XIXe siècle de la jurisprudence sur les donations déguisées. In *Mélanges offerts à René Savatier* 89–114. Paris: Dalloz.

Boas, Franz. 1896. The Limitations of the Comparative Method of Anthropology. *Science* 4: 901–908.

Boas, Franz. 1966. *Kwakiutl Ethnography*. Ed. Helen Codere. Chicago: University of Chicago Press.

Boele-Woelki, Katharina, and Angelika Fuchs, ed. 2003. *Legal Recognition of Same-Sex Couples in Europe*. European family law series, 1. Antwerp: Intersentia.

Bogert, George Gleason, and George Taylor Bogert. 1979. *The Law of Trusts and Trustees: A Treatise Covering the Law Relating to Trusts and Allied Subjects Affecting Trust Creation and Administration: with forms*. St. Paul, MN: West.
Cum. Supp. Ed. Amy Morris Hess. 2008.

Book Note. 1978. Review of *The Ages of American Law*, by Grant Gilmore. *Harvard Law Review* 91: 906–908.

Borrillo, Daniel. 2001. The *"Pacte Civil de Solidarité"* in France: Midway Between Marriage and Cohabitation. In Wintemute and Andenæs ed. 475–492.

Boujeka, Augustin. 2003. Des libéralités par chèque. *Recueil Dalloz* [D.] 2003: 2712–2715.

Bourdieu, Pierre. 1990. *The Logic of Practice*. Trans. Richard Nice. Stanford, CA: Stanford University Press.

Bourdieu, Pierre. 1997. Marginalia—Some Additional Notes on the Gift. In Schrift ed. 231–241.

Bourjon, François. 1770. *Le droit commun de France, et la Coutume de Paris réduits en principes, tirés des loix, des ordonnances, des arrêts, des jurisconsultes & des auteurs, & mis dans l'ordre d'un commentaire complet & méthodique sur cette coutume: contenant, dans cet ordre, les usages du Châtelet sur les liquidations, les comptes, les partages, les substitutions, les dîmes, & toutes autres matières*. New ed. Paris: Grange.

Bracton, Henry de. 1968. *On the Laws and Customs of England*. Ed. George E. Woodbine. Trans. Samuel E. Thorne. Cambridge: Published in association with the Selden Society by the Belknap Press of Harvard University Press.

Brault, Jean-Claude. 1998. L'intention libérale dans les relations familiales. *Répertoire du notariat Defrénois* art. 36900.

Brennan, Troyen A., et al. 2006. Health Industry Practices That Create Conflicts of Interest: A Policy Proposal for Academic Medical Centers. *Journal of the American Medical Association* 295: 429–433.

Brenner, Claude. 2005. Brèves observations sur la révocation des donations entre époux après la loi du 26 mai 2004 relative au divorce. *Répertoire du notariat Defrénois* art. 38084.

Bretonnier, Barthélemy Joseph. 1783. *Recueil par ordre alphabétique, des principales questions de droit, qui se jugent diversement dans les différents Tribunaux du Royaume. Avec des Réflexions pour concilier la diversité de la Jurisprudence, & la rendre uniforme dans tous les Tribunaux.* Ed. Boucher d'Argis. 5th ed. Paris: Chez Le Boucher.

Bride's Book of Etiquette. 2003. New York: Perigee.

Bridge, Michael G. 2002. *Personal Property Law.* Clarendon law series. 3rd ed. Oxford: Oxford University Press.

Brissaud, Jean. 1968. *A History of French Private Law* [1912]. The Continental Legal History Series, vol. 3. Trans. Rapelje Howell. South Hackensack, NJ: Rothman Reprints.

Britton. 1865. Ed. Francis Morgan Nichols. Oxford: Clarendon Press.

Bromley, P. M., and N. V. Lowe. 1992. *Family Law.* 8th ed. London: Butterworths.

Brown, Ray Andrews. 1975. *The Law of Personal Property.* Ed. Walter B. Rauschenbush. 3rd ed. Chicago: Callaghan.

Bruton, Paul W. 1930. The Requirement of Delivery as Applied to Gifts of Choses in Action. *Yale Law Journal* 39: 837–860.

Bryant, Taimie L. 2008. Sacrificing the Sacrifice of Animals: Legal Personhood for Animals, the Status of Animals as Property, and the Presumed Primacy of Humans. *Rutgers Law Journal* 39: 247–330.

Buckland, W. W. 2007. *A Text-Book of Roman Law from Augustus to Justinian.* Ed. Peter Stein. 3rd ed. Cambridge: Cambridge University Press.

Bucklin, Leonard H. 2002. Woe Unto Those Who Request Consent: Ethical and Legal Considerations in Rejecting a Deceased's Anatomical Gift Because There Is No Consent by the Survivors. *North Dakota Law Review* 78: 323–354.

Bufnoir, Claude. 1924. *Propriété et contrat: Théorie des Modes d'acquisition des droits réels et des Sources des Obligations.* Ed. Etienne Bartin. 2nd ed. Paris: Rousseau.

Burckhard, Hugo. 1899. *Zum Begriff der Schenkung.* Erlangen: Palm & Enke.

Byrnes, William H., IV. 2005. Ancient Roman Munificence: The Development of the Practice and Law of Charity. *Rutgers Law Review* 57: 1043–1110.

C.J.S. *Corpus Juris Secundum: A Complete Restatement of the Entire American Law as Developed by All Reported Cases.* St. Paul, MN: Thomson/West.
Vol. 38A sub Gifts. 1996.
Vol. 41 sub Husband and Wife. 1996.

Camerer, Colin. 1988. Gifts as Economic Signals and Social Symbols. *American Journal of Sociology* 94: S180–S214 (Supplement).

Camic, Charles. 1986. The Return of the Functionalists. Review of *Neofunctionalism*, by Jeffrey C. Alexander. *Contemporary Sociology* 15: 692–695.

Caplow, Theodore. 1984. Rule Enforcement without Visible Means: Christmas Gift Giving in Middletown. *American Journal of Sociology* 89: 1306–1323.

Capozzi, Guido. 2002. *Successioni e donazioni*, tome 2. 2nd ed. Milano: Giuffrè.

Carbonnier, Jean. 1953. L'importance de D'Aguesseau pour son temps et pour le notre. In *Le Chancelier Henri-François d'Aguesseau* 36–41.

Carbonnier, Jean. *Droit civil.* Paris: Presses universitaires de France.

Vol. 1: *Introduction, Les personnes.* 13th ed. 1980.

Vol. 3: *Les biens.* 10th ed. 1980.

Vol. 4: *Les obligations.* 10th ed. 1979.

Carbonnier, Jean. 1983. *Flexible droit: Textes pour une sociologie du droit sans rigueur.* 5th ed. Paris: Librairie générale de droit et de jurisprudence.

Carette, A. A. [1843]. *Lois annotées, ou, Lois, décrets, ordonnances, avis du Conseil d'État, etc.: avec notes historiques, de concordance et de jurisprudence. 1789–1830.* Paris: Administration du Recueil général des lois et des arrêts.

Carette, A.-A., and L.-M. Devilleneuve. 1854. *Lois annotées, ou, Lois, décrets, ordonnances, avis du Conseil d'État, etc., avec notes historiques, de concordance et de jurisprudence.* 2nd series, 1831–1848. Paris: Administration du Recueil général des lois et des arrêts.

Carlyle, Thomas. 2002. *The French Revolution: A History* [1837]. The Modern Library classics. New York: Modern Library.

Carnevali, Ugo. 1974. Liberalità (atti di). In *Enciclopedia del diritto* 24: 214–224. [Milano]: Giuffrè.

Carnevali, Ugo. 1989. Donazione: Diritto civile. In *Enciclopedia giuridica,* vol. 12. Roma: Istituto della Enciclopedia Italiana.

Carpenter, Carole Henderson. 1981. Sacred, Precious Things: Repatriation of Potlatch Art. *artmagazine* 12: 64–70.

Carpino, Brunetto. 1968. Revoca della donazione al figlio naturale riconosciuto per sopravvenienza di figli legittimi. *Rivista trimestrale di diritto e procedura civile* 22: 800–806.

Carrier, James. 1990. Gifts in a World of Commodities: The Ideology of the Perfect Gift in American Society. *Social Analysis* 24: 19–37.

Carrier, James. 1991. Gifts, Commodities, and Social Relations: A Maussian View of Exchange. *Sociological Forum* 6: 119–136.

Carrión Olmos, Salvador. 1996. Algunas consideraciones sobre la naturaleza de la donación (con especial referencia a la mecánica traslativa de aquélla). *Actualidad civil* 1996: 775–794.

Casanovas i Mussons, Anna. 2003. La dualidad de funciones de la aceptación de la donación: Los artículos 623 y 629 del Código civil. In *Estudios jurídicos en homenaje al profesor Luis Díez-Picazo,* ed. Antonio Cabanillas Sánchez, 2: 1611–1628. Madrid: Thomson/Civitas.

Casavola, Franco. 1960. *Lex Cincia: Contributo alla storia delle origini della donazione romana.* Pubblicazioni della Facoltà giuridica dell'Università di Napoli, 44. Napoli: Jovene.

Castro, Federico de. 1953. La simulación y el requisito de la donación de cosa inmueble: Sentencia de 23 de junio de 1953. *Anuario de derecho civil* 6: 1003–1016.

Casulli, Vincenzo Rodolfo. 1964. Donazione (diritto civile). In *Enciclopedia del diritto* 13: 966–992. [Milano]: Giuffrè.

Casulli, Vincenzo Rodolfo. 1964a. Donazione: donazione mortis causa—diritto civile. In *Enciclopedia del diritto* 13: 1002–1005. [Milano]: Giuffrè.

Cataudella, Antonio. 1970. Considerazioni in tema di donazione liberatoria. *Rivista trimestrale di diritto e procedura civile* 24: 757–767.

Cendon, Paolo. 1991. *Commentario al Codice civile.* Torino: UTET.

Champeaux, Jean. 1931. *Étude sur la notion juridique de l'acte à titre gratuit en droit civil français*. Mâcon: Buguet-Comptour.

Cheal, David. 1988. *The Gift Economy*. London: Routledge.

Le Chancelier Henri-François d'Aguesseau, Limoges 1668–Fresnes 1751; journées d'étude tenues à Limoges à l'occasion du bicentenaire de sa mort (Octobre 1951). 1953. Limoges: Librairie Desvilles.

Chitty, Joseph. 2004. *Chitty on Contracts*. The common law library. Ed. H. G. Beale. 29th ed. London: Sweet & Maxwell.

Cian, Giorgio, and Alberto Trabucchi. 1992. *Commentario breve al codice civile*. Brevaria iuris, I. 4th ed. Padova: CEDAM.

Codere, Helen. 1950. *Fighting with Property: A Study of Kwakiutl Potlatching and Warfare, 1792–1930*. New York: J. J. Augustin.

Coe, Sophie D., and Michael D. Coe. 2003. *The True History of Chocolate*. London: Thames & Hudson.

Cohen, Esther, and Mayke De Jong, ed. 2001. *Medieval Transformations: Texts, Power, and Gifts in Context*. Cultures, beliefs, and traditions, vol. II. Leiden: Brill.

Coke, Edward. 1797. *The Third Part of the Institutes of the Laws of England: Concerning High Treason, and Other Pleas of the Crown and Criminal Causes*. London: E. and R. Brooke.

Coke, Edward. 1809. *The First Part of the Institutes of the Laws of England; or, A Commentary upon Littleton: Not the Name of the Author only, but of the Law itself*. Ed. Francis Hargrave and Charles Butler. 16th ed. London: Printed by L. Hansard & Sons for E. Brooke.

Cole, Douglas, and Ira Chaikin. 1990. *An Iron Hand upon the People: The Law against the Potlatch on the Northwest Coast*. Vancouver: Douglas & McIntyre.

Colson, Elizabeth. 1975. Review of *The Interpretation of Cultures*, by Clifford Geertz. *Contemporary Sociology* 4: 637–638.

Comment. 1849. On the Doctrine of Nudum Pactum in the English Law. *Law Review and Quarterly Journal of British and Foreign Jurisprudence* 10: 56–70.

Comment. 1852. Gifts in View of Death. *American Law Register* 1: 1–10.

Comment. 1951. Assignment by Check—A Comparative Study. *Yale Law Journal* 60: 1007–1025.

Commentaires du ministre de la Justice: le Code civil du Québec: un mouvement de société. 1993. [Quebec:] Government du Québec, Ministère de la justice.

Constantinesco, Léontin-Jean. *Traité de droit comparé*. Paris: Librairie générale de droit et de jurisprudence.
    Tome 1: *Introduction au droit comparé*. 1972.
    Tome 2: *La méthode comparative*. 1974.
    Tome 3: *La science des droits comparés*. 1983.

Corbett, Percy Ellwood. 1969. *The Roman Law of Marriage*. Oxford: Clarendon Press.

Corbin, Arthur L. 1952. *Corbin on Contracts*. One Volume Edition. St. Paul, MN: West Publishing Co.

Corbin, Arthur L. *Corbin on Contracts*. Rev. ed.
    Vol. 2: *Formation of Contracts*. Ed. Joseph M. Perillo and Helen Hadjiyannakis Bender. 1995. St. Paul, MN: West Publishing Co.
    Vol. 9: *Third Party Beneficiaries, Assignments, Joint and Several Contracts*. Ed. John E. Murray, Jr. 2007. Newark, NJ: LexisNexis.

Coron, Denis, and Frédéric Lucet. 2000. Assurance-vie, union libre et révocation pour survenance d'enfant. *Répertoire du notariat Defrénois* art. 37183.

Costigan, George P. 1911. Gifts *Inter Vivos* of *Choses* in Action. *Law Quarterly Review* 27: 326–40.

Crossley Vaines, James. 1967. *Personal Property.* 4th ed. London: Butterworths.

Cujas, Jacques. 1722. *Jacobi Cujacij J.C. præstantissimi Opera omnia in decem tomos distributa. Quibus continentur tam Priora, sive quæ ipse superstes edi curavit; quam Posteriora, sive que post obitum ejus edita sunt.* Ed. Charles Annibale Fabrot. Neapoli: Typis ac Sumptibus Michaelis Alysii Mutio.

Cupis, Adriano de. 1989. Sulla revocazione della donazione per riconoscimento di un figlio naturale. *Rivista di diritto civile* 1989 II 275–278.

Curta, Florin. 2006. Merovingian and Carolingian Gift Giving. *Speculum* 81: 671–699.

Curtis, Arthur R. 1939. Effect of Uniform Stock Transfer Act Upon Gratuitous Transfer of Corporate Shares by Written Assignment. *Yale Law Journal* 48: 897–902.

Dagot, Michel. 1971. Réflexions sur l'article 1099-1 du Code civil (l'acquisition d'un bien par un époux au moyen de deniers donnés par l'autre à cette fin). *Semaine juridique* [J.C.P.] 1971 II 2397.

Dagot, Michel. 2000. Des donations non solennelles. *Semaine juridique* [J.C.P.] 2000 I 248.

Dannemann, Gerhard. 2006. Comparative Law: Study of Similarities or Differences? In Reimann and Zimmermann ed. 383–419.

Danzig, Richard. 1977. The Death of Contract and the Life of the Profession: Observations on the Intellectual State of Legal Academia. *Stanford Law Review* 29: 1125–1134.

Dard, Émile. 1907. *Un épicurien sous la terreur, Hérault de Séchelles (1759–1794): D'après des Documents inédits.* Paris: Perrin et cie.

Darnton, Robert. 1985. *The Great Cat Massacre and Other Episodes in French Cultural History.* New York: Vintage Books.

David, René, and John E. C. Brierley. 1985. *Major Legal Systems in the World Today: An Introduction to the Comparative Study of Law.* 3rd ed. London: Stevens & Sons.

Davis, J. 1972. Gifts and the U.K. Economy. *Man* 7: 408–429.

Davis, Kingsley. 1959. The Myth of Functional Analysis as a Special Method in Sociology and Anthropology. *American Sociological Review* 24: 757–772.

Davis, Natalie Zemon. 2000. *The Gift in Sixteenth-Century France.* The Curti Lectures. Madison: University of Wisconsin Press.

Dawson, John Philip. 1961. *Negotiorum Gestio:* The Altruistic Intermeddler. *Harvard Law Review* 74: 817–65, 1073–1129.

Dawson, John Philip. 1980. *Gifts and Promises: Continental and American Law Compared.* Storrs lectures on jurisprudence, 1978. New Haven: Yale University Press.

Dawson, John Philip. 1983. Legal Realism and Legal Scholarship. *Journal of Legal Education* 33: 406–411.

De Francisci, P. 1926. La revocatio in servitutem del liberto ingrato. In *Mélanges de droit romain dédiés à Georges Cornil,* ed. Paul Collinet and Fernand de Vissher 1: 295–323. Gand: Vanderpoorten & Co.

De Page, Henri. *Traité élémentaire de droit civil belge: principes, doctrine, jurisprudence.* Bruxelles: Bruylant.

    Tome 1: *Introduction; théorie générale des droits et des lois; les personnes; la famille.* 3rd ed. 1962.

Tome 2: *Les incapables; les obligations.* 3rd ed. 1964.

Tome 7, vol. 2: *De la transmission des droits réels immobiliers; de la prescription.* Ed. René Dekkers. 1943.

Tome 8, vol. 1: *Les libéralités (généralités); les donations.* 2nd ed. 1962.

De Page, Philippe. 1992. La cause immorale et l'union libre. In De Page and De Valkeneer ed. 163–179.

De Page, Philippe, and Roland De Valkeneer, ed. 1992. *L'Union libre: Actes du colloque tenu à l'Université Libre de Bruxelles le 16 octobre 1992.* Collection de la Faculté de droit de l'Université libre de Bruxelles. Bruxelles: Bruylant.

De Schutter, Olivier, and Anne Weyembergh. 2001. "Statutory Cohabitation" Under Belgian Law: A Step Towards Same-Sex Marriage? In Wintemute and Andenæs ed. 465–474.

De Stefano, Antonio. 1964. Donazione: diritto canonico. In *Enciclopedia del diritto* 13: [996]–1000. [Milano]: Giuffrè.

Delvincourt, Claude Etienne. 1813. *Cours de Code Napoléon: Ouvrage divisé en deux Parties, dont la première contient la Troisième Édition des INSTITUTES DE DROIT CIVIL FRANÇAIS, du même Auteur, revue et corrigée par lui; et la seconde, les Notes et Explications sur lesdites Institutes.* Paris: P. Gueffier.

Dementhon, Henri. 1964. *Traité du domaine de l'état.* 6th ed. Paris: Dalloz.

Derrett, J. Duncan M. 1963. *Introduction to Modern Hindu Law.* [Bombay]: Indian Branch, Oxford University Press.

Derrida, Jacques. 1992. *Given Time. I, Counterfeit Money.* Trans. Peggy Kamuf. Chicago: University of Chicago Press.

Derrida, Jacques. 1995. *The Gift of Death.* Religion and postmodernism. Chicago: University of Chicago Press.

Des concubinages: Droit interne, droit international, droit comparé: Études offertes à Jacqueline Rubellin-Devichi. 2002. Paris: Litec.

Desan, Suzanne. 2004. *The Family on Trial in Revolutionary France.* Studies on the history of society and culture, 51. Berkeley: University of California Press.

Devilleneuve, L. M., and P. Gilbert. 1851. *Jurisprudence du XIXE siècle, ou Table générale alphabétique et chronologique du Recueil général des lois et des arrêts (1791 à 1850),* vol. 2. Paris: Administration du recueil.

Di Leonardo, Micaela. 1987. The Female World of Cards and Holidays: Women, Families, and the Work of Kinship. *Signs* 12: 440–453.

Díaz Alabart, Silvia. 1980. La nulidad de las donaciones de inmuebles simuladas bajo compraventa. *Revista de derecho privado* 64: 1101–1123.

Dickinson, Edwin D. 1921. Gratuitous Partial Assignments. *Yale Law Journal* 31: 1–14.

Díez Pastor, José Luis. 1952. La donación al no concebido. *Anales de la Academia Matritense del Notariado* 6: 111–164.

Díez Picazo, Luis, and Antonio Gullón Ballesteros. 1989. *Sistema de derecho civil,* vol. 2. 6th ed. Madrid: Editorial Tecnos.

Domat, Jean. 1850. *The Civil Law in Its Natural Order.* Ed. Luther S. Cushing. Trans. William Strahan. Boston: Charles C. Little and James Brown.

Donlan, Walter. 1989. The Unequal Exchange between Glaucus and Diomedes in Light of the Homeric Gift-Economy. *Phoenix* 43: 1–15.

Drew, Katherine Fischer. 1973. *The Lombard Laws.* Sources of medieval history. Philadelphia: University of Pennsylvania Press.

Duby, Georges. 1968. *Rural Economy and Country Life in the Medieval West.* Columbia: University of South Carolina Press.

Dumoulin, Charles. 1681. *Caroli Molinæi Franciæ et Germaniæ celeberrimi jurisconsulti, et in Supremo Parisiorum Senatu antiqui advocati, Omnia quæ extant opera, ex variis librorum apothecis, in quibus latebant, nunc primùm eruta, & simul typis commissa, permultisque mendis, quibus sensim scatebant, ad exemplaria tùm ab Authore recognita, tùm à Viris Doctissimis, Jurisque Peritissimis inter legendum notata, & quàm fieri potuit diligentissimè purgata.* Ed. François Pinsson and Julien Brodeau. New ed. Parisiis: In Officina P. Rocolet.

    Tome 3: *Tractatus duo analytici, Prior, de Donationibus factis vel confirmatis in contractu matrimonii; Posterior, de inofficiosis Testamentis, Donationibus & Dotibus, ejusdem Aucthoris Franciæ & Germaniæ Jureconsulti, & in supremo Parisiorum Senatu antiqui Advocati Juris praxisque consultissimi, 513–543.*

Dumoulin, Charles. 1691. *Coutumes de la prevosté et vicomté de Paris.* Ed. J. Tournet, Jacques Joly, and Charles Labbé. Paris: Chez Guillaume Cavelier.

Dupeyroux, Jean Jacques. 1955. *Contribution à la théorie générale de l'acte à titre gratuit.* Paris: Librairie générale de droit et de jurisprudence.

Dupont, Clémence. 1962. Les donations dans les constitutions de Constantin. *Revue internationale des droits de l'antiquité* 9: 291–324.

Durkheim, Emile. 1982. *The Rules of Sociological Method.* Ed. Steven Lukes. Trans. W. D. Halls. New York: Free Press.

Duvergier, Jean Baptiste. 1834–1838. *Collection complète des Lois, Décrets, Ordonnances, Réglemens, Avis du Conseil-d'État, publiée sur les éditions officielles du Louvre; de l'Imprimerie nationale, par Baudouin; et du Bulletin des Lois; De 1788 à 1830 inclusivement, par ordre chronologique, Continuée depuis 1830.* 2nd ed. Paris: A. Guyot et Scribe.

Eisenberg, Melvin. 1979. Donative Promises. *University of Chicago Law Review* 47: 1–33.

Eisenberg, Melvin. 1997. The World of Contract and the World of Gift. *California Law Review* 85: 821–866.

Emerson, Ralph Waldo. 1988. Gifts [1844]. In *Essays by Ralph Waldo Emerson: first and second series complete in one volume* 374–379. New York: Perennial Library.

Entwurf eines bürgerlichen Gesetzbuches für das Deutsche Reich: Erste Lesung. 1888. Berlin: Guttentag.

Esmein, Paul. 1953. *Cours de droit civil. Licence 3me année, 1953–1954.* Paris: Cours de droit.

Farnsworth, E. Allan. 1995. Promises to Make Gifts. *American Journal of Comparative Law* 43: 359–378.

Farnsworth, E. Allan. 2004. *Contracts.* 4th ed. New York: Aspen Publishers.

Feinman, Jay. 1992. The Last Promissory Estoppel Article. *Fordham Law Review* 61: 303–316.

Fellows, Mary Louise. 1986. The Slayer Rule: Not Solely a Matter of Equity. *Iowa Law Review* 71: 489–555.

Fellows, Mary Louise. 1988. Donative Promises Redux. In *Property Law and Legal Education: Essays in Honor of John E. Cribbet,* ed. Peter Hay and Michael H. Hoeflich, 27–52. Urbana: University of Illinois Press.

Fenet, P. A. 1968. *Recueil complet des travaux préparatoires du Code civil: suivi d'une édition de ce code, à laquelle sont ajoutés les lois, décrets et ordonnances formant le complément de la législation civile de la France, et où se trouvent indiqués, sous chaque article séparément, tous les passages du recueil qui s'y rattachent* [1827]. Osnabrück: Otto Zeller.

Fikentscher, Wolfgang. 1992. *Schuldrecht.* 8th ed. Berlin: de Gruyter.

Finley, M. I. 1979. *The World of Odysseus.* 2nd ed. New York: Penguin.

Fleischer, Holger. 2001. Unternehmensspenden und Leitungsermessen des Vorstands im Aktienrecht. *Die Aktiengesellschaft* [AG] 46: 171–181.

Fleta. 1972. Ed. and trans. H. G. Richardson and G. O. Sayles, vol. 3, bks. 3–4. London: Selden Society.

Fletcher, William Meade. *Cyclopedia of the Law of Private Corporations.* Rev. ed. Chicago: Callaghan.

Vol. 1A. Ed. Carla A. Jones and Britta M. Larsen. 2002.

Vol. 6A. Ed. Publisher's staff. 2005.

Flour, Jacques, and Jean Luc Aubert. 1975. *Les obligations*, vol. 1. Collection U. Paris: A. Colin.

Flour, Jacques, and Henri Souleau. 1982. *Les libéralités.* Collection U. Paris: A Colin.

Forgeard, Marie-Cécile, Richard Crône, and Bertrand Gelot. 2002. *La réforme des successions: Loi du 3 décembre 2001, commentaire & formules.* Paris: Defrénois.

Forgeard, Marie-Cécile, Richard Crône, and Bertrand Gelot. 2007. *Le nouveau droit des successions et des libéralités: Loi du 23 juin 2006, commentaires et formules.* Paris: Defrénois.

Forkel, Hans. 1974. Verfügungen über Teile des menschlichen Körpers. *Juristenzeitung* [JZ] 29: 593–599.

Foster, Stephen C. 1988. Configurations of Freedom. In *Perpetual Motif: The Art of Man Ray*, ed. Merry A. Foresta, 233–271. Washington DC: National Museum of American Art, Smithsonian Institution.

Frankenberg, Günter. 1985. Critical Comparisons: Re-thinking Comparative Law. *Harvard International Law Journal* 26: 411–455.

Fratcher, William Franklin. 1973. Trust. In *International Encyclopedia of Comparative Law*, vol. 6, ed. Athanassios N. Yiannopoulos, ch. 11. Tübingen: J.C.B. Mohr (Paul Siebeck).

Frazier, Barbara. 2001. "But I Can't Marry You": Who Is Entitled to the Engagement Ring When the Conditional Performance Falls Short of the Altar? *Journal of the American Academy of Matrimonial Lawyers* 17: 419–439.

Fuller, Lon. 1941. Consideration and Form. *Columbia Law Review* 41: 799–824.

Fuller, Lon. 1958. Positivism and Fidelity to Law—A Reply to Professor Hart. *Harvard Law Review* 71: 630–672.

Fyzee, Asaf Ali Asghar. 1974. *Outlines of Muhammadan Law.* Delhi: Oxford University Press.

G., G. S. 1926. Gift of savings deposit by delivery of pass book. *American Law Reports* [A.L.R.] 40: 1249–1263.

Garat, Dominique Joseph. 1785. Aux Auteurs du Journal. *Journal de Paris*, no. 219, 7 August.

García García, José Manuel. 1998. Breves notas en defensa de la donación como negocio jurídico adquisitivo del dominio. *Revista jurídica de Catalunya* 97: 273–279.

Garvey, John L. 1966. Revocable Gifts of Personal Property: A Possible Will Substitute. *Catholic University Law Review* 16: 119–157, 256–282.

Gaul, Wilhelm. 1914. Das Geschenk nach Form und Inhalt im besonderen untersucht an afrikanischen Völkern. *Archiv für Anthropologie* 13: 223–279.

Geary, Patrick J. 2003. Gift Exchange and Social Science Modeling: The Limitations of a Construct. In Algazi, Groebner, and Jussen, ed. 129–140.

Geertz, Clifford. 1973. *The Interpretation of Cultures: Selected Essays.* New York: Basic Books.

Geertz, Clifford. 1973a. The Cerebral Savage: On the Work of Claude Lévi-Strauss.
    In Geertz 1973: 345–359.
Geertz, Clifford. 1973b. Deep Play: Notes on the Balinese Cockfight. In Geertz 1973:
    412–453.
Geertz, Clifford. 1973c. The Impact of the Concept of Culture on the Concept of Man.
    In Geertz 1973: 33–54.
Geertz, Clifford. 1973d. Religion As a Cultural System. In Geertz 1973: 87–125.
Geertz, Clifford. 1973e. Thick Description: Toward an Interpretive Theory of Culture.
    In Geertz 1973: 3–30.
Geertz, Clifford. 1983. Local Knowledge: Further Essays in Interpretive Anthropology.
    New York: Basic Books.
Geertz, Clifford. 1983a. Blurred Genres: The Refiguration of Social Thought. In Geertz
    1983: 19–35.
Geertz, Clifford. 1983b. Introduction. In Geertz 1983: 3–16.
Geertz, Clifford. 1983c. Local Knowledge: Fact and Law in Comparative Perspective.
    In Geertz 1983: 167–234.
Ghestin, Jacques. Traité de droit civil. Paris: Librairie générale de droit et de
    jurisprudence.
    Vol. 1: Introduction générale. Ed. Jacques Ghestin and Gilles Goubeaux. 3rd
        ed. 1990.
    Vol. 2: Les obligations: Le contrat: formation. Ed. Jacques Ghestin. 2nd ed. 1988.
Gilmore, Grant. 1974. The Death of Contract. Columbus, OH: Ohio State University
    Press.
Gilmore, Grant. 1977. The Ages of American Law. Storrs lectures on jurisprudence, 1974.
    New Haven: Yale University Press.
Girard, Paul Frédéric. 1924. Manuel élémentaire de droit romain. 7th ed. Paris: Rousseau
    et cie.
Glanvill, Ranulf de. 1965. The treatise on the laws and customs of the realm of England
    commonly called Glanvill. Medieval texts. Ed. and trans. G. D. G. Hall. London:
    Nelson.
Glassman, Adam D. 2004. I Do! or Do I? A Practical Guide to Love, Courtship, and
    Heartbreak in New York—or—Who Gets the Ring Back Following a Broken
    Engagement? Buffalo Women's Law Journal 12: 47–99.
Glenn, H. Patrick. 2006. Comparative Legal Families and Comparative Legal Traditions.
    In Reimann and Zimmermann ed. 421–440.
Gobert, Michelle. 1957. Essai sur le rôle de l'obligation naturelle. [Paris]: Sirey.
Godbout, Jacques, and Alain Caillé. 1998. The World of the Gift. Trans. Donald Winkler.
    Montreal: McGill-Queen's University Press.
Godelier, Maurice. 1999. The Enigma of the Gift. Trans. Nora Scott. [Chicago]: University
    of Chicago Press.
Goetz, Charles J., and Robert E. Scott. 1980. Enforcing Promises: An Examination of the
    Basis of Contract. Yale Law Journal 89: 1261–1322.
Goldschmidt, Walter Rochs. 1966. Comparative Functionalism: An Essay in
    Anthropological Theory. Berkeley: University of California Press.
Gordley, James. 1995. Enforcing Promises. California Law Review 82: 547–614.
Gordley, James. 1997. Contract in Pre-Commercial Societies and in Western History. In
    International Encyclopedia of Comparative Law, vol. 7, ed. Arthur T. vonMehren, ch. 11.
    Tübingen: J.C.B. Mohr (Paul Sicbeck).

Gorla, Gino. 1954. *Il contratto. Problemi fondamentali trattati con il metodo comparativo e casistico*. Milano: Giuffrè.

Gour, Hari Singh. 1990. *Sir Hari Singh Gour's Law of Transfer: being commentaries on the Transfer of Property Act, 1882*, vol. 2. Ed. M. H. Beg and S. K. Verma. Allahabad: Law Publishers.

Graves, Charles A. 1896. Gifts of Personalty. *Virginia Law Register* 1: 871–894.

Gray, Kevin J., and Susan Francis Gray. 2003. *Land Law*. Butterworths core text series. 3rd ed. London: LexisNexis.

Greenblatt, Stephen. 1997. The Touch of the Real. *Representations* 59: 14–29.

Greene, John Patrick. 2002. French Encounters with Material Culture of the South Pacific. *Eighteenth-Century Life* 26: 225–245.

Gregg, Dorothy, and Elgin Williams. 1948. The Dismal Science of Functionalism. *American Anthropologist* 50: 594–611.

Gregory, C. A. 1982. *Gifts and Commodities*. London: Academic Press.

Grenouilleau, J. B. 1977. Commentaire de la loi no. 76-1181 du 22 décembre 1976 relative aux prélèvements d'organes. *Recueil Dalloz* [D.] 1977 Chronique 213–220.

Grimaldi, Michel. 2000. *Droit civil: Libéralités, Partages d'ascendants*. Paris: Litec.

Grimaldi, Michel, and Rémy Gentilhomme. 1999. La donation de titres sociaux assortie d'une faculté conventionnelle de modification unilatérale de l'objet donné. *Répertoire du notariat Defrénois* art. 36932.

Grimaldi, Michel, and Jean-François Roux. 1994. La donation de valeurs mobilières avec réserve de quasi-usufruit. *Répertoire du notariat Defrénois* art. 35677.

Grimm, Jakob. 1965. Über Schenken und Geben. In Jakob Grimm, *Kleinere Schriften: Abhandlungen zur Mythologie und Sittenkunde* 2: 173–210. Hildesheim: Georg Olms.

Groebner, Valentin. 2001. Accountancies and *Arcana*: Registering the Gift in Late Medieval Cities. In Cohen and De Jong ed. 219–243.

Grønbech, Wilhelm Peter. 1954. Gabentausch. In Wilhelm Peter Grønbech, *Kultur und Religion der Germanen* 2: 55–77. 5th ed. Darmstadt: Wissenschaftliche Buchgemeinschaft.

Grundmann. Stefan. 1998. Zur Dogmatik der unentgeltlichen Rechtsgeschäfte. *Archiv fuer die civilistische Praxis* [AcP] 198: 457–488.

Gulliver, Ashbel G., and Catherine J. Tilson. 1941. Classification of Gratuitous Transfers. *Yale Law Journal* 51: 1–39.

Gullón Ballesteros, Antonio. 1968. *Curso de Derecho civil: Contratos en especial, responsabilidad extracontractual*. Madrid: Editorial Tecnos.

Gurevich, A. Ya. 1968. Wealth and Gift-Bestowal among the Ancient Scandinavians. *Scandinavica* 7: 126–138.

Gutmann, Thomas. 2006. *Für ein neues Transplantationsgesetz: Eine Bestandsaufnahme des Novellierungsbedarfs im Recht der Transplantationsmedizin*. MedR Schriftenreihe Medizinrecht. Berlin: Springer.

Gutmann, Thomas, and Ulrich Schroth. 2002. *Organlebendspende in Europa: Rechtliche Regelungsmodelle, ethische Diskussion und praktische Dynamik*. MedR Schriftenreihe Medizinrecht. Berlin: Springer.

H., R. E. 1933. Gift of savings deposit by delivery of pass book. *American Law Reports* [A.L.R.] 84: 558–566.

Hall, J. C. 1959. Gift of Part of a Debt. *Cambridge Law Journal* 1959: 99–119.

Halliday, William May. 1935. *Potlatch and Totem, and the Recollections of an Indian Agent*. London: J. M. Dent & Sons Ltd.

Halsbury, Hardinge Stanley Giffard. *Halsbury's Laws of England.* Ed. Quintin Hogg
    Hailsham of St. Marylebone. 4th ed. (reissue). London: Butterworths.
    Vol. 5 pt. 3 sub Children and Young Persons. 2001.
    Vol. 6 sub Choses in Action. 2003.
    Vol. 9 pt. 1 sub Contract. 1998.
    Vol. 20 pt. 1 sub Gifts. 2004.
    Vol. 48 sub Trusts. 2007.
Hamel, Joseph. 1920. *La notion de cause dans les libéralités: étude de la jurisprudence
    française et recherche d'une définition.* Paris: Recueil Sirey.
Handler, Richard. 1991. An Interview with Clifford Geertz. *Current Anthropology* 32:
    603–613.
Hannig, Jürgen. 1986. Ars donandi. Zur Ökonomie des Schenkens im früheren
    Mittelalter. *Geschichte in Wissenschaft und Unterricht* 37: 149–162.
Harbsmeier, Michael. 2003. Gifts and Discoveries: Gift Exchange in Early Modern
    Narratives of Exploration and Discovery. In Algazi, Groebner, and Jussen, ed.
    381–410.
Harring, Sidney L. 1998. *White Man's Law: Native People in Nineteenth-Century Canadian
    Jurisprudence.* Toronto: Osgoode Society for Canadian Legal History by University of
    Toronto Press.
Harris, Marvin. 1976. History and Significance of the Emic/Etic Distinction. *Annual
    Review of Anthropology* 5: 329–50.
Harsin, Paul. 1928. *Les doctrines monétaires et financières en France du XVIe au XVIIIe
    siècles.* Paris: F. Alcan.
Hart, H. L. A. 1948. The Ascription of Responsibility and Rights. *Proceedings of the
    Aristotelian Society* 49: 171–194.
Hart, Henry Melvin, and Albert M. Sacks. 1994. *The Legal Process: Basic Problems in the
    Making and Application of Law.* Ed. William N. Eskridge and Philip P. Frickey.
    Westbury, NY: Foundation Press.
Haupt, Heinz-Gerhard, and Jürgen Kocka. 1996. Historischer Vergleich: Methoden,
    Aufgaben, Probleme. Eine Einleitung. In *Geschichte und Vergleich: Ansätze und
    Ergebnisse international vergleichender Geschichtsschreibung,* ed. Heinz-Gerhard Haupt
    and Jürgen Kocka, 9–45. Frankfurt: Campus.
Hauser, Jean. 2001. Révocation des donations pour survenance d'enfants: Quelles
    donations et quels enfants? *Répertoire du notariat Defrénois* art. 37437.
Havighurst, Harold C. 1936. Gifts of Bank Deposits. *North Carolina Law Review*
    14: 129–159.
Haymann, Franz. 1905. *Die Schenkung unter einer Auflage nach römischem und deutschem
    bürgerlichem Recht.* Berlin: F. Vahlen.
Heck, Philipp. 1929. *Grundriß des Schuldrechts.* Tübingen: J.C.B. Mohr
    (P. Siebeck).
Heidegger, Martin. 1996. *Being and Time: A Translation of Sein und Zeit.* SUNY series in
    contemporary continental philosophy. Trans. Joan Stambaugh. Albany, NY: State
    University of New York Press.
Hello, Charles Guillaume. 1839. *Essai sur la vie et les ouvrages de Dumoulin.* Paris: Bureau
    de la Revue de législation et de jurisprudence.
Henricus de Segusio, Cardinal Hostiensis. 1581. *In Primum Decretalium librum
    Commentaria.* Venetiis: Apud Ivntas.
Henry, O. 1953. The Gift of the Magi. In *The Complete Works of O. Henry* 1: 7–11. Garden
    City, NY: Doubleday.

Heywood, John. 1906. *A Dialogue of the Effectual Proverbs in the English Tongue Concerning Marriage* [1562, 1566]. Ed. John Stephen Farmer. London: Gibbings.

Hiez, David. 2003. *Étude critique de la notion de patrimoine en droit privé actuel.* Bibliothèque de droit privé, tome 399. Paris: L.G.D.J.

Hillman, Robert A. 1995. The Triumph of Gilmore's *The Death of Contract. Northwestern University Law Review* 90: 32–48.

Hines, N. William. 1970. Personal Property Joint Tenancies: More Law, Fact, and Fancy. *Minnesota Law Review* 54: 509–583.

Hirsch, Adam J. 2001. Revisions in Need of Revising: The Uniform Disclaimer of Property Interests Act. *Florida State University Law Review* 29: 109–187.

Hirschbiegel, Jan. 2003. *Étrennes: Untersuchungen zum höfischen Geschenkverkehr im spätmittelalterlichen Frankreich der Zeit König Karls VI. (1380–1422).* Pariser historische Studien, vol. 60. München: Oldenbourg.

Hochman, Harold M., and James D. Rogers. 1969. Pareto Optimal Redistribution. *American Economic Review* 59: 542–557.

Höfling, Wolfram, and Stephan Rixen. 1996. *Verfassungsfragen der Transplantationsmedizin: Hirntodkriterium und Transplantationsgesetz in der Diskussion.* Tübingen: Mohr.

Holmes, Oliver Wendell. 1963. *The Common Law* [1881]. Ed. Mark DeWolfe Howe. Boston: Little, Brown.

Horowitz, Morton J. 1977. *The Transformation of American Law, 1780–1860.* Cambridge: Harvard University Press.

Huet-Weiller, Danièle. 1981. "L'union libre" (La cohabitation sans mariage). *American Journal of Comparative Law.* 29: 247–277.

Hüffer, Uwe. 2008. *Aktiengesetz.* Beck'sche Kurz-Kommentare, vol. 53. 8th ed. München: C.H. Beck.

Hunt, Lynn Avery. 1984. *Politics, Culture, and Class in the French Revolution.* Studies on the History of Society and Culture, 1. Berkeley: University of California Press.

Hunt, Lynn Avery. 1989. Introduction: History, Culture, and Text. In *The New Cultural History,* ed. Lynn Avery Hunt, 1–22. Studies on the History of Society and Culture, 6. Berkeley: University of California Press.

Husa, Jaakko. 2003. Farewell to Functionalism or Methodological Tolerance? *Rabels Zeitschrift für ausländisches und internationales Privatrecht* [RabelsZ] 77: 419–447.

Hyde, Lewis. 1983. *The Gift: Imagination and the Erotic Life of Property.* New York: Vintage Books.

Hyland, Richard. 1994. *Pacta Sunt Servanda:* A Meditation. *Virginia Journal of International Law* 34: 405–433.

Hyland, Richard. 1996. Comparative Law. In *A Companion to Philosophy of Law and Legal Theory,* ed. Dennis M. Patterson, 184–99. Blackwell Companions to Philosophy, 7. Cambridge, MA: Blackwell Publishers.

Hyland, Richard. 2004. The American Experience: Restatements, the UCC, Uniform Laws, and Transnational Coordination. In *Towards a European Civil Code,* ed. A. S. Hartkamp and E. H. Hondius, 59–75. 3rd ed. Nijmegen: Ars Aequi Libri.

Hyland, Richard. 2007. Evening in Lisbon. In *Festschrift für Claus-Wilhelm Canaris zum 70. Geburtstag,* ed. Andreas Heldrich, Jürgen Prölss, and Ingo Koller, 2: 1135–1154. München: Beck.

Indian Claims Commission. 2004. *Annual Report 2003–04.* [Ottawa]: [Minister of Public Works and Government Services Canada].

International Association of Legal Science. 1973–. *International Encyclopedia of Comparative Law*. Tübingen: J.C.B. Mohr (Paul Siebeck).

Irnerius. 1894. *Summa codicis des Irnerius mit einer Einleitung*. Ed. Hermann Fitting. Berlin: Guttentag.

Isambert, François André, and Athanase Jean Léger Jourdan. 1821–1830. *Recueil général des anciennes lois françaises, depuis l'an 420 jusqu'à la révolution de 1789: contenant la notice des principaux monumens des Mérovingiens, des Carlovingiens et des Capétians, et le texte des ordonnances, édits, déclarations, lettres-patentes, réglemens, arrêts du Conseil, etc., de la troisième race, qui ne sont pas abrogés, ou qui peuvent servir, soit à l'interprétation, soit à l'histoire du droit public et privé, avec notes de concordance, table chronologique et table générale analytique et alphabétique des matières*. Paris: Berlin-Le-Prieur.

Jaconelli, Joseph. 2006. Problems in the Rule in *Strong v Bird*. Conveyancer and Property Lawyer 2006: 432–450.

James, Wendy, and N. J. Allen, ed. 1998. *Marcel Mauss: A Centenary Tribute*. Methodology and history in anthropology, vol. 1. New York: Berghahn Books.

Jauernig, Othmar. 2004. *Bürgerliches Gesetzbuch*. 11th ed. München: C.H. Beck.
　§§ 1–240. Ed. Othmar Jauernig.
　§§ 311–311c. Ed. Astrid Stadler.
　§§ 433–480. Ed. Christian Berger.
　§§ 488–534. Ed. Heinz-Peter Mansel.
　§§ 809–822. Ed. Astrid Stadler.
　§§ 854–1296. Ed. Othmar Jauernig.
　§§ 1922–2385. Ed. Rolf Stürner.

Jenks, Edward. 1900. Consideration and the Assignment of Choses in Action. *Law Quarterly Review* 16: 241–248.

Jerry, Robert H. 2002. *Understanding Insurance Law*. 3rd ed. Newark, NJ: LexisNexis.

Jhering, Rudolf von. 1889. *Das Trinkgeld*. 3rd ed. Braunschweig: G. Westermann.

Jones, Gareth H. 1969. *History of the Law of Charity, 1532–1827*. Cambridge studies in English legal history. London: Cambridge University Press.

Jones, Peter. 1985. *Politics and Rural Society: The Southern Massif Central, c. 1750–1880*. Cambridge: Cambridge University Press.

Josserand, Louis. 1930. Sur la nature juridique des donations entre époux lorsqu'elles portent sur des biens à venir. *Dalloz Hebdomadaire* [D.H.] 1930 Chronique 21–24.

Josserand, Louis. 1936. Le déclin du titre gratuit et sa transformation. In Louis Josserand, *Évolutions et actualités: conférences de droit civil* 135–158. Paris: Recueil Sirey.

Kallen, Horace M. 1937. Functionalism. In *Encyclopaedia of the Social Sciences*, ed. Edwin Robert Anderson Seligman and Alvin Saunders Johnson, 5: 523–526. New York: Macmillan Co.

Karsenti, Bruno. 1998. The Maussian Shift: A Second Foundation for Sociology in France? In James and Allen ed. 71–82.

Kaser, Max. 1938. Die Geschichte der Patronatsgewalt über Freigelassene. *Zeitschrift der Savigny-Stiftung für Rechtsgeschichte (Romanistische Abteilung)* 58: 88–135.

Kaser, Max. 1971–1975. *Das römische Privatrecht*. Handbuch der Altertumswissenschaft, dept. 10 tome 3 vol. 3. 2nd ed. München: Beck.

Keeton, G.W. 1935. Is Consideration Necessary for Equitable Assignments of Choses in Action? *Bell Yard: Journal of the Law Society's School of Law* 15: 10–17.

Keith, A. Berriedale. 1925. The Personality of an Idol. *Journal of Comparative Legislation* 8: 255–257.

Kemp, Peter. 1982. Death and Gift. *Journal of the American Academy of Religion* 50: 459–471.

Kent, James. 1826–1830. *Commentaries on American Law.* New York: O. Halsted.

Kessler, Friedrich. 1954. Einige Betrachtungen zur Lehre von der Consideration. In *Festschrift für Ernst Rabel*, ed. Hans Dölle, Max Rheinstein, and Konrad Zweigert, 1: 251–276. Tübingen: Mohr.

Kessler, Friedrich, and Grant Gilmore. 1970. *Contracts: Cases and Materials.* 2nd ed. Boston: Little, Brown.

Kessler, Manfred Heinz. 1995. Die Leitungsmacht des Vorstandes einer Aktiengesellschaft (II). *Die Aktiengesellschaft* [AG] 40: 120–132.

Kieckebusch, Joachim. 1928. Schenkung. In *Handwörterbuch der Rechtswissenschaft*, ed. Fritz Stier-Somolo and Alexander Elster, 5: 282–288. Berlin: Walter de Gruyter.

Kind, Sandra. 2000. Darf der Vorstand einer AG Spenden an politische Parteien vergeben? *Neue Zeitschrift für Gesellschaftsrecht* [NZG] 3: 567–73.

Klundert, Theo van de, and Jeroen van de Ven. 1999. On the Viability of Gift Exchange in a Market Environment. [Tilburg: Tilburg University]. http://www.appropriate-economics.org/materials/giftexchangemarketenvironment.pdf.

Kölner Kommentar zum Aktiengesetz: §§ 76–117 AktG und Mitbestimmung im Aufsichtsrat. 1996. Ed. Carsten Peter Claussen and Wolfgang Zöllner. 2nd ed. Köln: Heymann. §§ 76–117. Ed. Hans-Joachim Mertens.

Kommentar zum Gesetz betreffend die Gesellschaften mit beschränkter Haftung (GmbH-Gesetz). 2002. Ed. Lutz Michalski and Gerhard Dannecker. München: C.H. Beck. § 43. Ed. Ulrich Haas.

Kötz, Hein. 1990. Rechtsvergleichung und Rechtsdogmatik. *Rabels Zeitschrift für ausländisches und internationales Privatrecht* [RabelsZ] 54: 203–216.

Kötz, Hein. 1998. Abschied von der Rechtskreislehre? *Zeitschrift für europäisches Privatrecht* 6: 493–505.

Kreitner, Roy. 2001. The Gift Beyond the Grave: Revisiting the Question of Consideration. *Columbia Law Review* 101: 1876–1957.

Kübel, Franz Friedrich Philipp von. 1980. *Recht der Schuldverhältnisse.* Berlin: de Gruyter.

Kuhn, Thomas S. 1970. *The Structure of Scientific Revolutions.* Chicago: University of Chicago Press.

Kulischer, Iosif. M. 1976. *Allgemeine Wirtschaftsgeschichte des Mittelalters und der Neuzeit* [1928], vol. 1. Darmstadt: Wissenschaftliche Buchgesellschaft.

Kull, Andrew. 1992. Reconsidering Gratuitous Promises. *Journal of Legal Studies* 21: 39–65.

Labaree, Benjamin Woods. 1964. *The Boston Tea Party.* New York: Oxford University Press.

Labatt, C. B. 1895. The Inconsistencies of the Laws of Gifts. *American Law Review* 29: 361–372.

Lacruz Berdejo, José Luis. *Elementos de derecho civil.*
Tome 2: *Derecho de obligaciones*, vol. 3. Ed. Agustín Luna Serrano and Jésus Delgado Echeverría. 2nd ed. 1986. Barcelona: Librería Bosch.
Tome 4: *Derecho de familia.* Ed. Joaquín Rams Albesa. 2nd ed. 2005. Madrid: Dykinson.

Lagarde, Xavier. 1997. Réflexions sur le fondement de l'article 931 du code civil. *Revue trimestrielle de droit civil* 96: 25–51.

Lalaguna, Enrique. 1964. Los artículos 623 y 629 del código civil y la naturaleza de la donación. *Revista de derecho privado* 48: 275–99.

Larenz, Karl. 1986. *Lehrbuch des Schuldrechts*, vol. 2, pt. 1. 13th ed. München: C.H. Beck.

Laurent, François. 1878. *Principes de droit civil français*. 3rd ed. Bruxelles: Bruylant-Christophe & Cie.

Lavori preparatori per la riforma del codice civile. Osservazioni e proposte sul progetto del Libro terzo; successioni e donazioni. 1937. Roma.

Law Revision Committee. 1937. *Sixth Interim Report (Statute of Frauds and the Doctrine of Consideration).* Cmd 5449. London: H.M. Stationery Off.

Le Guidec, Raymond. 2002. Le Pacs et la transmission des biens entre concubins. In *Des concubinages* 133–142.

Le Roy Ladurie, Emmanuel. 1976. Family Structures and Inheritance Customs in Sixteenth-Century France. In *Family and Inheritance: Rural Society in Western Europe, 1200–1800*, ed. Jack Goody, Joan Thirsk, and E. P. Thompson, 37–70. Cambridge: Cambridge University Press.

LeFevre, E. 1954. Gift or other voluntary transfer by husband as fraud on wife. *American Law Reports*, 2nd series [A.L.R.2d] 49: 521–615.

Legrand, Pierre. 1995. Comparative Legal Studies and Commitment to Theory. *Modern Law Review* 58: 262–273.

Lempert, Robert J., Steven W. Popper, and Steven C. Bankes. 2003. *Shaping the Next One Hundred Years: New Methods for Quantitative, Long-Term Policy Analysis.* Santa Monica: RAND.

Leslie, Melanie B. 1999. Enforcing Family Promises: Reliance, Reciprocity, and Relational Contract. *North Carolina Law Review* 77: 551–636.

Lévi-Strauss, Claude. 1969. *The Elementary Structures of Kinship.* Trans. James Harle Bell and John Richard von Sturmer. Boston: Beacon Press.

Lévi-Strauss, Claude. 1987. *Introduction to the Work of Marcel Mauss.* Trans. Felicity Baker. London: Routledge & Kegan Paul.

Lévi-Strauss, Claude. 1992. *Tristes tropiques.* New York: Penguin Books.

Lévy, Jean-Philippe. 1949. Essai sur la promesse de donation en droit romain. *Revue internationale des droits de l'antiquité* 3: 91–136.

Libchaber, Rémy. 2000. Pour une redéfinition de la donation indirecte. *Répertoire du notariat Defrénois* art. 37273.

Lijphart, Arend. 1971. Comparative Politics and the Comparative Method. *American Political Science Review* 65: 682–693.

Lipson, D. Herbert. 2008. Off the Cuff. *Philadelphia Magazine*, August.

Llerena, Baldormero. 1931. *Concordancias y comentarios del Código civil argentino.* 3rd ed. Buenos Aires: Librería y editorial "La Facultad," J. Roldán y c.a.

Llewellyn, Karl N. 1941. On the Complexity of Consideration: A Foreword. *Columbia Law Review* 41: 777–782.

Llewellyn, Karl N. 2008. *The Bramble Bush* [1930]. New York: Oxford University Press.

Lloyd, William J. 1946. Consideration and the Seal in New York—An Unsatisfactory Legislative Program. *Columbia Law Review* 46: 1–36.

Locré, J. G. 1827. *La Législation civile, commerciale et criminelle de la France, ou Commentaire et complément des Codes français.* Paris: Treuttel Würtz.

Loo, Tina. 1992. Dan Cramer's Potlatch: Law as Coercion, Symbol, and Rhetoric in British Columbia, 1884–1951. *Canadian Historical Review* 73: 125–165.

Lord, Hazel D. 2001. Husband and Wife: English Marriage Law from 1750: A Bibliographic Essay. *Southern California Review of Law and Women's Studies* 11: 1–89.

Lorenz, Werner. 1969. Entgeltliche und unentgeltliche Geschäfte: Eine vergleichende Betrachtung des deutschen und des anglo-amerikanischen Rechts. In *Ius privatum gentium: Festschrift für Max Rheinstein zum 70. Geburtstag am 5. Juli 1969*, ed. Ernst von Caemmerer, Soia Mentschikoff, and Konrad Zweigert, 2: 547–568. Tübingen: Mohr (Siebeck).

Lorenzen, Ernest G. 1928. The Negotiorum Gestio in Roman and Modern Civil Law. *Cornell Law Quarterly* 13: 190–210.

Louet, Georges. 1693. *Recueil de plusieurs notables arrests du Parlement de Paris, pris de memoires de Monsieur Maistre Georges Loüet, Conseiller du Roy au mesme Parlement*. Paris: Chez Denys Thierry, Jean Guignard.

Loysel, Antoine. 1846. *Institutes coutumières*. Ed. Eusèbe de Laurière, André-Marie-Jean-Jacques Dupin, and Edouard Laboulaye. New ed. Paris: Videcoq.

Lutter, Marcus, and Walter Bayer. 2004. *GmbH-Gesetz: Kommentar*. 16th ed. Köln: O. Schmidt.

MacNeil, Ian R., and David Campbell. 2001. *The Relational Theory of Contract: Selected Works of Ian MacNeil*. Modern legal studies. London: Sweet & Maxwell.

Maitland, Frederic William. 1886. The Mystery of Seisin. *Law Quarterly Review* 2: 481–496.

Maitland, Frederic William. 1949. *Equity: A Course of Lectures*. Ed. A. H. Chaytor, W. J. Whittaker, and John Brunyate. 2nd ed. Cambridge: University Press.

Malaurie, Philippe. 2006. Libéralités, bonnes mœurs et relations adultères. *Répertoire du notariat Defrénois* art. 38305.

Malaurie, Philippe. 2007. La réforme de la protection juridique des majeurs. *Répertoire du notariat Defrénois* art. 38569.

Malaurie, Philippe, and Laurent Aynès. 1998. *Cours de droit civil: Les successions, les libéralités*. 4th ed. Paris: Éditions Cujas.

Malinowski, Bronislaw. 1937. Culture. In *Encyclopaedia of the Social Sciences*, ed. Edwin Robert Anderson Seligman and Alvin Saunders Johnson, 3: 621–646. New York: Macmillan Co.

Malinowski, Bronislaw. 1939. The Group and the Individual in Functional Analysis. *American Journal of Sociology* 46: 938–964.

Malinowski, Bronislaw. 1944. *A Scientific Theory of Culture and Other Essays*. Chapel Hill: University of North Carolina Press.

Malinowski, Bronislaw. 1964. *Argonauts of the Western Pacific* [1922]. London: G. Routledge & Sons.

Malinowski, Bronislaw. 1989. *Crime and Custom in Savage Society* [1926]. Totowa, NJ: Rowman & Littlefield.

Mandeville, Bernard. 1997. *The Fable of the Bees and Other Writings*. Ed. E. J. Hundert. Indianapolis: Hackett Pub.

Manenti, Carlo. 1911. Sul concetto di donazione. *Rivista di diritto civile* 1911: 328–389.

Manresa y Navarro, José María. 1969. *Comentarios al Código civil español*, vol. 9. Ed. Francisco de Cárdenas, Santiago Chamorro Piñero, and Francisco Bonet Ramón. 6th ed. Madrid: Instituto editorial Reus, Centro de enseñanza y publicaciones, s.a.

Mäntysaari, Petri. 1998. *Mängelhaftung beim Kauf von Gesellschaftsanteilen: Eine vergleichende Untersuchung zum deutschen, finnischen und schwedischen Recht*. Helsingfors: Hanken, Swedish School of Economics and Business Administration.

Marais, Jean-Luc. 1999. *Histoire du don en France de 1800 à 1939: Dons et legs charitables, pieux et philanthropiques.* Rennes: Presses universitaires de Rennes.

Margolis, Diane Rothbard. 1984. *Gifts, Commodities and the Tribute Factor: A Feminist Reformation of Sociological Theory.* Wellesley, MA: Wellesley College, Center for Research on Women.

Marion, Jean-Luc. 2002. *Being Given: Toward a Phenomenology of Givenness.* Cultural Memory in the Present. Trans. Jeffrey L. Kosky. Stanford, CA: Stanford University Press.

Maroi, Fulvio. 1956. Una sopravvivenza arcaica: l'irrevocabilità della donazione. In Fulvio Maroi, *Scritti giuridici* 1: 549–561. Pubblicazioni della Facoltà di giurisprudenza dell'Università di Roma, 1–2. Milano: A. Giuffrè.

Martial. 1943. *Epigrams.* Trans. Walter C. A. Ker. Loeb Classical Library. Cambridge: Harvard University Press.

Martín Casals, Miquel. 2003. Same-Sex Partnerships in the Legislation of Spanish Autonomous Communities. In Boele-Woelki and Fuchs ed. 54–67.

Martínez Velencoso, Luz María. 2002. Validez de la donación de inmueble encubierta en escritura pública de compraventa: Comentario a la STS de 1 febrero 2002 (RJ 2002, 2098). *Revista de derecho patrimonial* 9: 205–215.

Marty, Gabriel, Pierre Raynaud, and Philippe Jestaz. 1987. *Droit civil: Les sûretés, la publicité foncière.* 2nd ed. Paris: Sirey.

Mauss, Marcel. 1990. *The Gift: The form and reason for exchange in archaic societies* [1924]. Trans. W. D. Halls. London: Routledge.

Mauss, Marcel. 1997. "Gift, Gift" [1924]. In Schrift ed. 28–32.

Mavidal, Jérôme, and Emile Laurent. 1969. *Archives parlementaires de 1787 à 1860: Recueil complet des débats législatifs & politiques des Chambres françaises.* 1st series. Nendeln/Liechtenstein: Kraus Reprint.

Mazeaud, Henri, Léon Mazeaud, and Jean Mazeaud. *Leçons de droit civil.* Paris: Montchrestien.

Tome 1: *Introduction à l'etude du droit*, vol. 1. Ed. François Chabas. 10th ed. 1991.

Tome 2: *Obligations: théorie générale*, vol. 1. Ed. François Chabas. 9th ed. 1998.

Tome 3: *Sûretés, publicité foncière*, vol. 1. Ed. Yves Picod. 7th ed. 1999.

Tome 4: *Successions, libéralités*, vol. 2. Ed. Laurent Leveneur and Sabine Mazeaud-Leveneur. 5th ed. 1999.

Mazzoni, Cosimo Marco. 2004. Le don, c'est le drame: Le don anonyme et le don despotique. *Revue trimestrielle de droit civil* 2004: 701–712.

McClanahan, W. S. 1982. *Community Property Law in the United States.* Rochester, NY: Lawyers Co-operative.

McGovern, William M., Jr. 1972. The Payable on Death Account and Other Will Substitutes. *Northwestern Law Review* 67: 7–41.

McGowan, Chad A. 1996. Special Delivery: Does the Postman Have to Ring at All—The Current State of the Delivery Requirement for Valid Gifts. *Real Property, Probate and Trust Journal* 31: 357–391.

Méau-Lautour, Huguette. 1985. *La donation déguisée en droit civil français: Contribution à la théorie générale de la donation.* Bibliothèque de droit privé, tome 184. Paris: Librairie générale de droit et de jurisprudence.

Mechem, Philip. 1925. Gifts of Corporation Shares. *Illinois Law Review* 20: 9–30.

Mechem, Philip. 1926–1927. The Requirement of Delivery in Gifts of Chattels and of Choses in Action Evidenced by Commercial Instruments. *Illinois Law Review* 21: 341–374, 457–487, 568–609.

Megarry, Robert E. 1943. Consideration and Equitable Assignments of Legal Choses in Action. *Law Quarterly Review* 59: 58–62.

Megarry, Robert, and William Wade. 1984. *The Law of Real Property*. 5th ed. London: Stevens.

Merlin, Philippe Antoine. 1820. *Recueil alphabétique des questions de droit qui se présentent le plus fréquemment dans les tribunaux; Ouvrage dans lequel sont fondus et classés la plupart des plaidoyers et réquisitoires de l'auteur, avec le texte des arrêts de la Cour de cassation qui s'en sont ensuivis*, vol. 2. Paris: Garnery.

Merlin, Philippe Antoine. 1825. *Répertoire universel et raisonné de jurisprudence*. 5th ed. Bruxelles: H. Tarlier.

Merton, Robert King. 1968. Manifest and Latent Functions. In Robert King Merton, *Social Theory and Social Structure* 73–138. Enlarged ed. New York: Free Press.

Michaels, Ralf. 2006. The Functional Method of Comparative Law. In Reimann and Zimmermann ed. 339–382.

Michel, Jacques Henri. 1962. *Gratuité en droit romain*. Études d'histoire et d'ethnologie juridiques. Bruxelles: Université Libre de Bruxelles, Institut de Sociologie.

Miller, William Ian. 2007. Is a Gift Forever? *Representations* 100: 13–22.

Mills, David. 2000. Review of *Arguments with Ethnography: Comparative Approaches to History, Politics and Religion*, by Ioan M. Lewis. *Bulletin of the School of Oriental and African Studies* 63: 326–327.

Mincke, Wolfgang. 1984. Eine vergleichende Rechtswissenschaft. *Zeitschrift für vergleichende Rechtswissenschaft* 83: 315–328.

Mitchell, Léonie M. 1928. The British Conception of Negotiable Instruments *v.* the French. *Journal of Comparative Legislation and International Law* 10: 237–247.

Mommsen, Theodor, Paul Krueger, and Alan Watson. 1985. *The Digest of Justinian* [Latin text with English translation]. Philadelphia: University of Pennsylvania Press.

Monnier, Francis. 1860. *Le Chancelier d'Aguesseau, sa conduite et ses idées politiques et son influence sur le mouvement des esprits pendant la première moitié du XVIIIᵉ siècle. Avec des documents nouveaux et plusieurs ouvrages inédits du chancelier*. Paris: Didier.

Montredon, Jean-François. 1989. *La désolennisation des libéralités*. Bibliothèque de droit privé, tome 209. Paris: Librairie générale de droit et de jurisprudence.

Morgan, Lewis Henry. 1877. *Ancient Society: or, Researches in the line of human progress from savagery, through barbarism to civilization*. New York: Henry Holt.

Moscati, Enrico. 1979. Obbligazioni naturali. In *Enciclopedia del diritto* 29: 353–383. [Milano]: Giuffrè.

Motive zu dem Entwurfe eines Bürgerlichen Gesetzbuches für das Deutsche Reich. 1888. Berlin: J. Guttentag (D. Collin).

Moxham, Roy. 2003. *Tea: Addiction, Exploitation and Empire*. London: Constable.

Mugdan, B. 1899. *Die gesammten Materialien zum Bürgerlichen Gesetzbuch für das deutsche Reich*. Berlin: Decker.

Mulla, Dinshah Fardunji. 1985. *Mulla on the Transfer of Property Act, 1882*. Ed. H. R. Khanna and P. M. Bakshi. 7th ed. Bombay: N.M. Tripathi.

Müller-Freienfels, Wolfram. 1968. Zur Rechtsprechung beim sog. "Mätressen-Testament." *Juristenzeitung* [JZ] 23: 441–449.

Münchener Kommentar zum Aktiengesetz (AktG). 2004. Ed. Otto A. Altenburger and Bruno Kropff. 2nd ed. München: Beck.

§§ 76–94. Ed. Wolfgang Hefermehl and Gerald Spindler.

Münchener Kommentar zum Bürgerlichen Gesetzbuch (BGB). Ed. Kurt Rebmann,
Franz-Jürgen Säcker, and Roland Rixecker. München: Beck.
 §§ 21–89. Ed. Dieter Reuter. 5th ed. 2006.
 §§ 134–138. Ed. Theo Mayer-Maly and Christian Armbrüster. 4th ed. 2001.
 §§ 284–312. Ed. Reinhold Thode. 4th ed. 2001.
 §§ 328–345. Ed. Peter Gottwald. 4th ed. 2003.
 §§ 387–397. Ed. Martin Schlüter. 4th ed. 2003.
 §§ 398–413. Ed. Günther H. Roth. 4th ed. 2003.
 §§ 414–419. Ed. Wernhard Möschel. 4th ed. 2003.
 §§ 516–534. Ed. Helmut Kollhosser. 4th ed. 2004.
 §§ 705–740. Ed. Peter Ulmer. 4th ed. 2004.
 §§ 1773–1921. Ed. Dieter Schwab. 4th ed. 2002.
 §§ 2274–2302. Ed. Hans-Joachim Musielak. 4th ed. 2004.
Murray, John Edward. 2001. *Murray on Contracts.* Newark, NJ: LexisNexis.
Nair, M. Krishan. 1978. *The Law of Contracts.* 4th ed. Bombay: Orient Longman.
Najjar, Ibrahim. 2003. Prix "sous-évalué" et intention libérale. *Recueil Dalloz* [D.]
 2003: 2591.
National Conference of Commissioners on Uniform State Laws. 1925. *Handbook of the
 National Conference of Commissioners on Uniform State Laws and Proceedings of the
 Thirty-fifth Annual Meeting.*
Nehlsen-von Stryk, Karin. 1987. Unentgeltliches schuldrechtliches Wohnrecht. Zur
 Abgrenzungsproblematik von Leihe und Schenkung. *Archiv fuer die civilistische Praxis*
 [AcP] 187: 552–602.
Nicholas, Barry. 1962. *An Introduction to Roman law.* Clarendon law series. Oxford:
 Clarendon Press.
Nickel, Lars Christoph, Angelika Schmidt-Preisigke, and Helmut Sengler. 2001.
 Transplantationsgesetz: Kommentar. Kohlhammer Krankenhaus. Stuttgart:
 Kohlhammer.
Noonan, John Thomas, Jr. 1984. *Bribes.* New York: MacMillan.
Note. 1924. Joint Savings-Bank Deposits and Rights of Survivorship Therein. *Harvard
 Law Review* 38: 243–245.
Note. 1926. Real Property—Gifts Causa Mortis of Land. *Yale Law Journal* 35: 511–512.
Note. 1929. The Uniform Written Obligations Act. *Columbia Law Review* 29:
 206–209.
Note. 1939. Methods of Circumventing the Civil Disabilities of Convicts. *Yale Law
 Journal* 48: 912–916.
Note. 1956. Recent Legislation to Facilitate Gifts of Securities to Minors. *Harvard Law
 Review* 69: 1479–1490.
Nunberg, Geoffrey. 1990. Testimony before the State Legislature on California
 Proposition 63. In *Perspectives on Official English: The Campaign for English as the
 Official Language of the USA,* ed. Karen L. Adams and Daniel T. Brink, 121–124.
 Contributions to the sociology of language, 57. Berlin: Mouton de Gruyter.
Oakley, A. J. 2008. *Parker and Mellows: The Modern Law of Trusts.* 9th ed. London:
 Sweet & Maxwell.
Ogris, Werner. 1990. Schenkung. In *Handwörterbuch zur deutschen Rechtsgeschichte*
 [HRG], ed. Adalbert Erler and Ekkehard Kaufmann, col. 1382–1384. [Berlin]: Erich
 Schmidt.
Ohnuma, Reiko. 1998. The Gift of the Body and the Gift of Dharma. *History of Religions*
 37: 323–359.

Oppo, Giorgio. 1947. *Adempimento e liberalità*. Milano: Giuffrè.

Orans, Martin. 1975. Domesticating the Functional Dragon: An Analysis of Piddocke's Potlatch. *American Anthropologist* 77: 312–328.

Ors, Alvaro d'. [1973]. *Derecho privado romano*. Pamplona: Ediciones Universidad de Navarra.

Ortega Pardo, Gregorio José. 1949. Donaciones indirectas. *Anuario de derecho civil* 2: 918–980.

Osteen, Mark, ed. 2002. *The Question of the Gift: Essays across Disciplines*. Routledge Studies in Anthropology, 2. London: Routledge.

Ourliac, Paul, and Jehan de Malafosse. 1968. *Histoire du droit privé*, vol. 3. Paris: Presses universitaires de France.

Page, William Herbert. 1920. *The Law of Contracts*. 2nd ed. Cincinnati: W.H. Anderson Co.

Palandt, Otto. 2006. *Bürgerliches Gesetzbuch*. 65th ed. München: C.H. Beck.
　§§ 311b–432. Ed. Christian Grüneberg.
　§§ 516–606. Ed. Walter Weidenkaff.
　§§ 631–853. Ed. Hartwig Sprau.

Palazzo, Antonio. 2000. *Le donazioni*. Il Codice civile, artt. 769–809. 2nd ed. Milano: Giuffrè.

Palmer, Francis Beaufort. 1992. *Palmer's Company Law*. Ed. Geoffrey Morse. 25th ed. London: Sweet & Maxwell.

Panckoucke, Charles Joseph, and Thuau-Grandville. 1789–. *Gazette nationale, ou, Le moniteur universel*. Paris: Chez H. Agasse, Libraire.

Pandolfelli, Gaetano, Gaetano Scarpello, Marion Stella Richter, and Gastone Dallari. *Codice civile: Illustrato con i lavori preparatori e disposizioni de attuazione e transitorie*. Milano: Giuffrè.
　[Vol. 2:] Libro delle successioni per causa di morte e delle donazioni. 1939.
　[Vol. 4:] Libro delle obbligazioni. 1942.

Papon, Jean. 1568. *Nouvelle et cinquième édition dv Recveil d'arrests notables des cours sovveraines de France*. Lyon: Iean de Tovrnes.

Pappenheim, Max. 1933. Über die Rechtsnatur der altgermanischen Schenkung. *Zeitschrift der Savigny-Stiftung für Rechtsgeschichte (Germanistische Abteilung)* 53: 35–88.

Parkinson, J. E. 1993. *Corporate Power and Responsibility: Issues in the Theory of Company Law*. Oxford: Clarendon Press.

Parry, Jonathan. 1986. The Gift, the Indian Gift, and the "Indian Gift." *Man* 21: 453–473.

Patra, Atul Chandra. 1966. *The Indian Contract Act, 1872*. London: Asia Pub. House.

Paz-Ares Rodríguez, Cándido. 1991. *Comentario del Código civil*. Madrid: Secretaría General Técnica, Centro de Publicaciones.
　Arts. 218–221. Ed. José Javier Hualde Sánchez.
　Arts. 618–643. Ed. Manuel Albaladejo García.
　Arts. 644–646. Ed. Silvia Díaz Alabart.
　Arts. 648–653. Ed. Silvia Díaz Alabart.
　Arts. 654–656. Ed. Manuel Albaladejo García.
　Arts. 752–762. Ed. Silvia Díaz Alabart.
　Arts. 1274–1277. Ed. Manuel Amorós Guardiola.
　Arts. 1315–1324. Ed. María José Herrero García.

Perego, Enrico. 1980. La revocazione delle disposizioni testamentarie e della donazione per sopravvenienza di figli e la riforma del diritto di famiglia. *Giurisprudenza italiana* [*Giur. it.*] 1980 IV 8–11.

Perozzi, Silvio. 1897. Intorno alla donazione. Review of *Il concetto della donazione nel diritto romano con richiami al codice civile italiano*, by Alfredo Ascoli. *Archivio giuridico* 58: 313–344, 527–553.

Peterka, Nathalie. 2001. *Les dons manuels*. Paris: Librairie générale de droit et de jurisprudence.

Pétursdóttir, Þóra. 2007. *"Deyr Fé, Deyja Frændr": Re-animating mortuary remains from Viking Age Iceland*. MA-Thesis in Archaeology. [Tromsø, Norway]: Faculty of Social Sciences: University of Tromsø.

Piccinini, Silvia. 1992. Profili della donazione dal Codice 1865 ad oggi. *Rivista di diritto civile* 1992 II 173–198.

Piddocke, Stuart. 1965. The Potlatch System of the Southern Kwakiutl: A New Perspective. *Southwestern Journal of Anthropology* 21: 244–264.

Piedelièvre, Alain. 2004. L'aménagement des libéralités entre époux par la loi du 26 mai 2004. *Recueil Dalloz* [D.] 2004: 2512–2516.

Placentinus, Petrus. 1962. *Placentini Summa Codicis: accessit proemium quod in Moguntina editione desiderabatur* [1536]. Ed. Francesco Calasso.Torino: Bottega d'Erasmo.

Planiol, Marcel. 1928–32. *Traité élémentaire de droit civil, conforme au programme officiel des facultés de droit*. 11th ed. Paris: Librairie générale de droit & de jurisprudence.

Planiol, Marcel, and Georges Ripert, *Traité pratique de droit civil français*. 2nd ed. Paris: Librairie générale de droit et de jurisprudence.

Tome 3: *Les biens*. Ed. Maurice Picard. 1952.

Tome 4: *Successions*. Ed. Jacques Maury and Henri Vialleton. 1956.

Tome 5: *Donations et testaments*. Ed. André Trasbot and Yvon Loussouarn. 1957.

Tome 6: *Obligations*, pt. 1. Ed. Paul Esmein. 1952.

Tome 7: *Obligations*, pt. 2. Ed. Paul Esmein, Jean Radouant, and Gabriel Gabolde. 1954.

Tome 8: *Les régimes matrimoniaux*, pt. 1. Ed. Jean Boulanger. 1957.

Tome 10: *Contrats civils*, pt. 1. Ed. Joseph Hamel (sales); François Givord and André Tunc (loan for use). 1956.

Plucknett, Theodore Frank Thomas. 1956. *A Concise History of the Common Law*. 5th ed. Boston: Little, Brown.

Pollock, Frederick. 1890. Gifts of Chattels Without Delivery. *Law Quarterly Review* 6: 446–451.

Pomeroy, John Norton. 1905. *A Treatise on Equity Jurisprudence, as Administered in the United States of America; Adapted for All the States, and to the Union of Legal and Equitable Remedies under the Reformed Procedure*. San Francisco: Bancroft-Whitney.

Posner, Eric. 1997. Altruism, Status, and Trust in the Law of Gifts and Gratuitous Transfers. *Wisconsin Law Review* 1997: 567–609.

Posner, Richard A. 1977. Gratuitous Promises in Economics and Law. *Journal of Legal Studies* 6: 411–426.

Posner, Richard A. 2007. *Economic Analysis of Law*. 7th ed. Austin, TX: Wolters Kluwer for Aspen Publishers.

Pothier, Robert Joseph. 1845. *Œuvres de Pothier annotées et mises en corrélation avec le Code civil et la législation actuelle*. Ed. M. Bugnet. Paris: Cosse.

Tome 1: *Coutume d'Orléans*.

Tome 3: *Vente*, 1–258

Tome 8: *Traité des donations entre-vifs*, 347–453.

Pound, Roscoe. Consideration in Equity. In *Legal Essays in Honor of John H. Wigmore*. *Illinois Law Review* 13: 667–692.

Pradel, Jean. 1996. *Droit pénal*, vol. 1. 11th ed. Paris: Editions Cujas.

Probert, Rebecca. 2004. *Sutton v Mishcon de Reya and Gawor & Co* — Cohabitation contracts and Swedish sex slaves. *Child and Family Law Quarterly* 16: 453–464.

Quiñonero Cervantes, Enrique. 1990. *La protección del interés del donante (Estudio de los artículos 634 y 648-3° del Código civil)*. Murcia: Universidad de Murcia.

Raban, Sandra. 1974. Mortmain in Medieval England. *Past and Present* 62: 3–26.

Radcliffe-Brown, A. R. 1935a. On the Concept of Function in Social Science. *American Anthropologist* 37: 394–402.

Radcliffe-Brown, A. R. 1935b. Patrilineal and Matrilineal Succession. *Iowa Law Review* 20: 286–303.

Radcliffe-Brown, A. R. 1940. On Social Structure. *Journal of the Royal Anthropological Institute* 70: 1–12.

Radcliffe-Brown, A. R. 1948. *The Andaman Islanders* [1922]. Glencoe, IL: Free Press.

Radcliffe-Brown, A. R. 1949. Functionalism: A Protest. *American Anthropologist* 51: 320–323.

Radcliffe-Brown, A. R. 1951. The Comparative Method in Social Anthropology. *Journal of the Royal Anthropological Institute* 81: 15–22.

Radin, Max. 1930. Statutory Interpretation. *Harvard Law Review* 43: 863–885.

Raheja, Gloria Goodwin. 1988. *The Poison in the Gift: Ritual, Prestation, and the Dominant Caste in a North Indian Village*. Chicago: University of Chicago Press.

Ramachandran, V. G. 1983. *The Law of Contract in India: A Comparative Study*, vol. 2. 2nd ed. Lucknow: Eastern Book Co.

Regan, Tom. 1983. *The Case for Animal Rights*. Berkeley: University of California Press.

Regnault, Henri. 1929. *Les ordonnances civiles du Chancelier Daguesseau: Les donations et l'Ordonnance de 1731*. Paris: Recueil Sirey.

Reimann, Mathias, and Reinhard Zimmermann, ed. 2006. *The Oxford Handbook of Comparative Law*. Oxford: Oxford University Press.

Reinhardt, Thomas. 2000. *Jenseits der Schrift: Dialogische Anthropologie nach der Postmoderne*. Frankfurt am Main: IKO, Verlag für Interkulturelle Kommunikation.

Rescigno, Pietro. *Trattato di diritto privato*. 2nd ed. Torino: UTET.
Vol. 6, tome 2: *Successioni, "Le Donazioni."* Ed. Ugo Carnevali. 2000.

Ricard, Jean-Marie. 1783. *Traité des donations entre-vifs et testamentaire*. Ed. Antoine Bergier. Riom: M. Dégoutte.

Richter, Giorgio Stella. 2003. *La donazione nella famiglia di fatto. Rivista di diritto civile* 2003 II 143–161.

Ricoeur, Paul. 1971. The Model of the Text: Meaningful Action Considered as a Text. *Social Research* 38: 529–62.

Ripert, Georges. 1949. *La règle morale dans les obligations civiles*. 4th ed. Paris: Librairie générale de droit et de jurisprudence.

Ripert, Georges, and Jean Boulanger. 1956–1959. *Traité de droit civil d'après le traité de Planiol*. Paris: Librairie générale de droit et de jurisprudence.

Rosaldo, Renato I., Jr. 1997. A Note on Geertz as a Cultural Essayist. *Representations* 59: 30–34.

Roseberry, William. 1982. Balinese Cockfights and the Seduction of Anthropology. *Social Research* 49: 1013–1028.

Rosman, Abraham, and Paula G. Rubel. 1971. *Feasting with Mine Enemy: Rank and Exchange Among Northwest Coast Societies*. New York: Columbia University Press.

Rosman, Abraham, and Paula G. Rubel. 1972. The Potlatch: A Structural Analysis. *American Anthropologist* 74: 658–671.

Rothacker, Erich. 1947. *Logik und Systematik der Geisteswissenschaften.* Bonn: H. Bouvier.

Rousseau, Jean-Jacques. 1979. *Reveries of the Solitary Walker* [1782]. Trans. Peter France. Penguin Classics. Harmondsworth: Penguin Books.

Row, T. V. Sanjiva. 1991. *Sanjiva Row's Contracts and law relating to tenders, buildings and engineering contracts,* vol. 2. Ed. Raghbirtal Bhagatram Sethi and Gyanendra Kumar. 9th ed. Allahabad [India]: Law Publishers.

Rubio Torrano, Enrique. 1981. Los artículos 623 y 629 del Código Civil: Apuntes para otra explicación. *Revista crítica de derecho inmobiliario* 57: 351–73.

Rundell, Oliver S. 1918. Gifts of *Choses* in Action. *Yale Law Journal* 27: 643–655.

Sacco, Rodolfo. 1993. *Il contratto.* Trattato di diritto civile. Ed. Giorgio De Nova. Torino: UTET.

Sadashige, Jacqui. 2002. Catullus and the Gift of Sentiment in Republican Rome. In Osteen ed. 149–171.

Sahlins, Marshall David. 1972. *Stone Age Economics.* Chicago: Aldine-Atherton.

Sahlins, Peter. 2004. *Unnaturally French: Foreign Citizens in the Old Regime and After.* Ithaca, NY: Cornell University Press.

Sandars, Thomas Collett. 1970. *The Institutes of Justinian with English Introduction, Translation, and Notes* [1922]. Westport, CT: Greenwood Press.

Sauvage, François. 2004. Des conséquences du divorce sur les libéralités entre époux et les avantages matrimoniaux. *Répertoire du notariat Defrénois* art. 38038.

Savigny, Friedrich Carl von. 1841. *System des heutigen Römischen Rechts,* vol. 4. Berlin: Veit und Comp.

Savigny, Friedrich Carl von. 1850. Ueber die *lex Cincia de donis et muneribus* und deren spätere Umbildungen [1818]. In Friedrich Carl von Savigny, *Vermischte Schriften* 1: 315–385. Berlin: Veit und Comp.

Schama, Simon. 1990. *Citizens: A Chronicle of the French Revolution.* New York: Vintage Books.

Schiffman, Harold F. 1996. *Linguistic Culture and Language Policy.* The Politics of Language. London: Routledge.

Schlechtriem, Peter. 2000. *Restitution und Bereicherungsausgleich in Europa: eine rechtsvergleichende Darstellung.* Tübingen: Mohr Siebeck.

Schmidt, Karsten. 2002. *Gesellschaftsrecht.* 4th ed. Köln: C. Heymanns.

Schmoller, Gustav. 1875. *Strassburg zur Zeit der Zunftkämpfe und die Reform seiner Verfassung und Verwaltung im XV. Jahrhundert.* Quellen und Forschungen zur Sprach- und Culturgeschichte der Germanischen Völker, 11. Strassburg: Karl J. Trübner.

Schneider, Mark A. 1987. Culture-as-Text in the Work of Clifford Geertz. *Theory and Society* 16: 809–839.

Schouler, James. 1886. Oral Wills and Death-Bed Gifts. *Law Quarterly Review* 2: 444–452.

Schouler, James. 1896. *A Treatise on the Law of Personal Property.* 3rd ed. Boston: Little, Brown.

Schrift, Alan D., ed. 1997. *The Logic of the Gift: Toward an Ethic of Generosity.* New York: Routledge.

Schroeder, Jeanne L. 1999. Pandora's Amphora: The Ambiguity of Gifts. *UCLA Law Review* 46: 815–904.

Schroth, Ulrich. 2005. *Transplantationsgesetz: Kommentar.* München: Beck. Einleitung nos. 1–11. Ed. Peter König. §§ 3–4. Ed. Ulrich Schroth.

Schütz, Wilhelm. 1964. Schenkweise Sicherheiten. *Juristische Rundschau* [JR] 1964: 453–454.

Schwartz, Barry. 1967. The Social Psychology of the Gift. *American Journal of Sociology* 73: 1–11.

Schwenzer, Ingeborg H. 1997. Restitution of Benefits in Family Relationships. In *International Encyclopedia of Comparative Law*, vol. 10, ed. Peter Schlechtriem, ch. 12. Tübingen: J.C.B. Mohr (Paul Siebeck).

Scott, Austin Wakeman, and William Franklin Fratcher. 1987. *The Law of Trusts*. 4th ed. Boston: Little, Brown.

Scott, Austin Wakeman, William Franklin Fratcher, and Mark L. Ascher [Scott and Ascher]. 2006. *Scott and Ascher on Trusts*. 5th ed. New York, NY: Aspen Publishers.

Scovazzi, Marco. 1958. La donazione nel diritto germanico. *Rivista di storia del diritto italiano* 31: 247–267.

Sen, Amartya K. 1977. Rational Fools: A Critique of the Behavioral Foundations of Economic Theory. *Philosophy & Public Affairs* 6: 317–344.

Sewell, William H., Jr. 1997. Geertz, Cultural Systems, and History: From Synchrony to Transformation. *Representations* 59: 35–55.

Shankman, Paul. 1984. The Thick and the Thin: On the Interpretive Theoretical Program of Clifford Geertz [and Comments and Reply]. *Current Anthropology* 25: 261–280.

Shapiro, Gary. 1997. The Metaphysics of Presents: Nietzsche's Gift, the Debt to Emerson, Heidegger's Values. In Schrift ed. 274–291.

Shattuck, Warren L. 1937. Gratuitous Promises—A New Writ? *Michigan Law Review* 35: 908–945.

Shavell, Steven. 1991. An Economic Analysis of Altruism and Deferred Gifts. *Journal of Legal Studies* 20: 401–421.

Sheehan, Duncan. 2006. Negotiorum Gestio: A Civilian Concept in the Common Law? *International & Comparative Law Quarterly* 55: 253–279.

Shore, William H. 1999. *The Cathedral Within: Transforming Your Life by Giving Something Back*. New York: Random House.

Siebert, Wolfgang. 1927–1938. Schenkung. In *Rechtsvergleichendes Handwörterbuch für das Zivil- und Handelsrecht des In- und Auslandes*, ed. Franz Schlegelberger, 6: 144–159. Berlin: F. Vahlen.

Silber, Ilana F. 1995. Gift Giving in the Great Traditions: The Case of Donations to Monasteries in the Medieval West. *Archives européenes de sociologie* 36: 209–243.

Silber, Ilana F. 1998. Modern Philanthropy: Reassessing the Viability of a Maussian Perspective. In James and Allen ed. 134–150.

Silber, Ilana F. 2000. Beyond Purity and Danger: Gift-Giving in the Monotheistic Religions. In Vandevelde ed. 115–132.

Sjoberg, Gideon. 1955. The Comparative Method in the Social Sciences. *Philosophy of Science* 22: 106–117.

Slapnicar, Klaus. 1983. Unentgeltliches Wohnen nach geltendem Recht ist Leihe, nicht Schenkung—Dogmengeschichtliches zu BGHZ 82, 354. *Juristenzeitung* [JZ] 38: 325–331.

Snyder, Sally. 1975. Quest for the Sacred in Northern Puget Sound: An Interpretation of Potlatch. *Ethnology* 14: 149–61.

Solnick, Sara J., and David Hemenway. 1996. The Deadweight Loss of Christmas: Comment. *American Economic Review* 86: 1299–1305.

Souleau, Henri. 1991. *Les successions*. Collection U. 3rd ed. Paris: A. Colin.

Spencer, Robert F., ed. 1954. *Method and Perspective in Anthropology: Papers in Honor of Wilson D. Wallis.* Minneapolis: University of Minnesota Press.

Spivey, Gary D. 1972. Creation of Joint Savings Account or Savings Certificate as Gift to Survivor. *American Law Reports,* 3rd series [A.L.R.3d] 43: 971–1061.

Starobinski, Jean. 1997. *Largesse.* Chicago: University of Chicago Press.

Staudingers Kommentar zum Bürgerlichen Gesetzbuch: mit Einführungsgesetz und Nebengesetzen. Ed. Reinhard Bork, Norbert Habermann, Julius Staudinger, Christian Bar, and Karl-Dieter Albrecht. 13th ed. Berlin: Sellier-de Gruyter.

    §§ 1–14. Ed. Norbert Habermann, Heinrich Honsell, and Günter Weick. 2004.

    §§ 90–103. Ed. Joachim Jickeli and Malte Stieper. 2004.

    §§ 134–163. Ed. Rolf Sack. 2003.

    §§ 164–181. Ed. Eberhard Schilken. 2004.

    §§ 328–361b. Ed. Rainer Jagmann, Dagmar Kaiser, and Volker Rieble. 2001.

    §§ 516–534. Ed. Susanne Wimmer-Leonhardt. 2005.

Steele, Sherman. 1926. The Uniform Written Obligations Act—A Criticism. *Illinois Law Review* 21: 185–190.

Stern, Walter. 1965. Consideration and Gift. *International & Comparative Law Quarterly* 14: 675–684.

Stoljar, Samuel. 1956. A Rationale of Gifts and Favours. *Modern Law Review* 19: 237–254.

Stone, Harlan F. 1920. Delivery in Gifts of Personal Property. *Columbia Law Review* 20: 196–201.

Storez, Isabelle. 1996. *Le chancelier Henri François d'Aguesseau (1668–1751): monarchiste et libéral.* Paris: Publisud.

Strathern, Andrew. 1983. The Kula in Comparative Perspective. In *The Kula: New Perspectives on Massim Exchange,* ed. Jerry W. Leach and Edmund Leach, 73–88. Cambridge: Cambridge University Press.

Strom, Stephanie. 2008. Helmsley, Dogs' Best Friend, Left Them up to $8 Billion. *New York Times,* 2 July, sec. A.

Swidler, Ann. 1996. Geertz's Ambiguous Legacy. *Contemporary Sociology* 25: 299–302.

Sykes, Edward I. 1935–1938. Consideration in Equitable Assignments of Choses in Action. *Res Judicatae* 1: 125–129.

Symposium. 1991. Donner, recevoir, et rendre—l'autre paradigm. *Revue du Mauss* no. 11.

Symposium. 1991a. Le don perdu et retrouvé. *Revue du Mauss* no. 12.

Symposium. 1995. Reconsidering Grant Gilmore's *The Death of Contract. Northwestern University Law Review* 90: 1–266.

Symposium. 1997. Corporate Philanthropy: Law, Culture, Education and Politics. *New York Law School Law Review* 41: 753–1328.

Tatar, Maria. 1992. *Off With Their Heads! Fairy Tales and the Culture of Childhood.* Princeton: Princeton University Press.

Teeven, Kevin M. 1998. *Promises on Prior Obligations at Common Law.* Contributions in legal studies, no. 85. Westport, Conn: Greenwood Press.

Tellier, L. S. 1948. Opening savings account in sole name of another, without complete surrender of passbook, as a gift. *American Law Reports,* 2nd series [A.L.R.2d] 1: 538–547.

Temple, Judson L. 1974. Gifts Effected by Written Instrument: *Faith Lutheran Retirement Home v. Veis. Montana Law Review* 35: 132–143.

Terré, François, and Yves Lequette. 1997. *Droit civil: Les successions, Les libéralités*. Paris: Dalloz.

Terrien, Guillaume. 1578. *Commentaires du droict ciuil, tant public que priué, obserué au pays & Duché de Normandie*. 2nd ed. Paris: Chez Iacques du Puys.

Thomas, Geraint W., and Alastair Hudson. 2004. *The Law of Trusts*. Oxford: Oxford University Press.

Thompson on Real Property. 2001. Ed. David A. Thomas. 2nd ed. Newark, NJ: LexisNexis.

Thornton, W. W. 1893. *A Treatise on the Law Relating to Gifts and Advancement*. Philadelphia: T. & J.W. Johnson.

Tiraqueau, André. 1588. *Andreae Tiraqvelli regii in cvria Parisiensi Senatoris dignissimi, Opera omnia, quae hactenus extant, septem tomis distincta*. Venetijs: apud Ioannem Baptistam Somaschum.

Tome 6: *Commentariorum in l. Si vnquàm, C. de reuocandis donationibus*.

Titmuss, Richard M. 1971. *The Gift Relationship: From Human Blood to Social Policy*. New York: Pantheon Books.

Toobin, Jeffrey. 2008. Rich Bitch: The legal battle over trust funds for pets. *New Yorker*, 29 Sept.

Torrente, Andrea. 1956. *La donazione*. Trattato di diritto civile e commerciale, vol. 22. Milano: Giuffrè.

Torrente, Andrea. 2006. *La donazione*. Trattato di diritto civile e commerciale, vol. 22. Ed. Ugo Carnevali and Andrea Mora. 2nd ed. Milano: Giuffrè.

Torrente, Andrea, and Piero Schlesinger. 1981. *Manuale di diritto privato*. Manuali giuridici, 1. 11th ed. Milano: A. Giuffrè.

Tracol, Xavier. 2003. The Pacte civil de solidarité (Pacs). In Boele-Woelki and Fuchs ed. 68–83.

Traer, James F. 1980. *Marriage and the Family in Eighteenth-Century France*. Ithaca, NY: Cornell University Press.

Trần Ngọc Thêm. 2006. *Recherche sur l'identité de la culture vietnamienne*. Trans. Pham Xuân and Phan Thế Hồng. Hanoi: Editions Thế Giói.

Treitel, G. H. 2007. *The Law of Contract*. Ed. Edwin Peel. 12th ed. London: Sweet & Maxwell.

Troplong, Raymond-Théodore. 1855. *Des donations entre-vifs et des testaments: ou Commentaire du titre II du livre III du code Napoléon*. Droit civil expliqué. Paris: C. Hingray.

Truog, Robert D. 2005. The Ethics of Organ Donation by Living Donors. *New England Journal of Medicine* 353: 444–446.

Turner, Jonathan H., and Alexandra R. Maryanski. 1988. Is "Neofunctionalism" Really Functional? *Sociological Theory* 6: 110–121.

Tushnet, Rebecca. 1998. Rules of Engagement. *Yale Law Journal* 107: 2583–2618.

Unger, Roberto Mangabeira. 1986. *The Critical Legal Studies Movement*. Cambridge: Harvard University Press.

Vallet de Goytisolo, Juan B. 1978. *Estudios sobre Donaciones*. Madrid: Montecorvo.

Vallet de Goytisolo, Juan B. 1978a. Notas acerca de las donaciones indirectas. In Vallet de Goytisolo 1978: 293–301.

Vallet de Goytisolo, Juan B. 1978b. Las donaciones de bienes inmuebles disimuladas según la jurisprudencia del tribunal supremo. In Vallet de Goytisolo 1978: 591–681.

Vandevelde, Anatoon, ed. 2000. *Gifts and Interests*. Leuven: Peeters.

Veblen, Thorstein. 1994. *The Theory of the Leisure Class*. Penguin twentieth-century classics. New York: Penguin Books.

Ven, Jeroen van de. 2000. The Economics of the Gift. [Tilburg: Tilburg University]. http://papers.ssrn.com/sol3/papers.cfm?abstract_id=244683.

Ven, Jeroen van de. 2002. The Demand for Social Approval and Status as a Motivation to Give. *Journal of Institutional and Theoretical Economics* 158: 464–482.

Venne, Sharon Helen. 1981. *Indian Acts and Amendments 1868–1975: An Indexed Collection*. [Saskatoon]: University of Saskatchewan, Native Law Centre.

Véron, Michel. 1965. La donation de biens à venir entre époux au cours du mariage et la loi du 6 novembre 1963. *Recueil Dalloz* [D.] 1965 Chronique 99.

Veyne, Paul. 1988. *Did the Greeks Believe in Their Myths? An Essay on the Constitutive Imagination*. Chicago: University of Chicago Press.

Viatte, Jean. 1974. Des restrictions à la capacité de reçevoir des enfants adultérins: Historique de l'art. 908 du Code civil. *Gazette du Palais* [*Gaz. Pal.*] 1974 II Chronique 828–830.

Vinnius, Arnoldus. 1840. *Arnoldi Vinnii jc. Selectarum juris quaestionum libri duo nunc primum eiusdem auctoris commentario in Institutiones Justinianeas conjunctim edicti, quibus multa commentarii loca illustrantur, ac intricatissimae juris materiae nondum ventilatae, omnibus legum Romanorum candidatis utilissimae, dilucide enodantur.* 9th ed. Florentiae: apud Josephum Celli.

Viollet, Paul. 1905. *Histoire du droit civil français, accompagnée de notions de droit canonique et d'indications bibliographiques.* 3rd ed. Paris: Larose et Tenin.

Voet, Johannes. 1827–1828. *Commentariorum ad Pandectas libri quinquaginta, in quibus praeter romani juris principia ac controversias illustriores jus etiam hodiernum, et praecipuae fori quaestiones excutiuntur.* Bassani: suis typis Remondini edidit.

Voltaire. 1901. *A Philosophical Dictionary* [1764]. In *The Works of Voltaire; A Contemporary Version*, ed. John Morley, vols. 5–14. Trans. William F. Fleming. Paris: Done by the craftsmen of the St. Hubert Guild [E.R. DuMont].

Von Mehren, Arthur Taylor. 1959. Civil-Law Analogues to Consideration: An Exercise in Comparative Analysis. *Harvard Law Review* 72: 1009–1078.

Wagner-Hasel, Beate. 2000. *Der Stoff der Gaben: Kultur und Politik des Schenkens und Tauschens im archaischen Griechenland.* Campus historische Studien, vol. 28. Frankfurt: Campus.

Wagner-Hasel, Beate. 2003. Egoistic Exchange and Altruistic Gift: On the Roots of Marcel Mauss's Theory of the Gift. In Algazi, Groebner, and Jussen, ed. 141–171.

Waldfogel, Joel. 1993. The Deadweight Loss of Christmas. *American Economic Review* 83: 1328–1336.

Waldfogel, Joel. 1996. The Deadweight Loss of Christmas: Reply. *American Economic Review* 86: 1306–1308.

Watson, Alan. 1968. *The Law of Property in the Later Roman Republic.* Oxford: Clarendon Press.

Weber, Max. 1978. *Economy and Society: An Outline of Interpretive Sociology.* Ed. Guenther Roth and Claus Wittich. Berkeley: University of California Press.

Weber-Kellermann, Ingeborg. 1968. Über den Brauch des Schenkens: Ein Beitrag zur Geschichte der Kinderbescherung. In *Volksüberlieferung: Festschrift für Kurt Ranke zur Vollendung des 60. Lebensjahres*, ed. Fritz Harkot, Karel Constant Peeters, and Robert Wildhaber, 1–8. Göttingen: O. Schwartz.

Webley, Paul, and Richenda Wilson. 1989. Social Relationships and the Unacceptability of Money as a Gift. *Journal of Social Psychology* 129: 85–91.

Weiner, Annette B. 1992. *Inalienable Possessions: The Paradox of Keeping-While-Giving.* Berkeley: University of California Press.

Weir, Tony. 1975. The Common Law System. In *International Encyclopedia of Comparative Law*, vol. 2, ed. René David. Structure and the Divisions of the Law, ch. 2, 77–114. Tübingen: J.C.B. Mohr (Paul Siebeck).

Wellek, René. 1963. The Crisis of Comparative Literature. In René Wellek, *Concepts of Criticism*, ed. Stephen G. Nichols, Jr., 282–295. New Haven: Yale University Press.

White, Byron F. 1950. Recovery of Engagement Gifts: California Civil Code Section 1590. *California Law Review* 38: 529–534.

White, Stephen D. 1988. *Custom, Kinship, and Gifts to Saints: The laudatio parentum in Western France, 1050–1150*. Studies in legal history. Chapel Hill: University of North Carolina Press.

Williston, Samuel. 1930. Gifts of Rights under Contracts in Writing by Delivery of the Writing. *Yale Law Journal* 40: 1–16.

Williston, Samuel. 2008. *A Treatise on the Law of Contracts*. Ed. Richard A. Lord. 4th ed. Eagan, MN: Thomson/West.

Winch, Peter. 2008. *The Idea of a Social Science and Its Relation to Philosophy* [1958]. Routledge Classics. London: Routledge.

Windscheid, Bernhard. 1906. *Lehrbuch des Pandektenrechts*. Ed. Theodor Kipp. 9th ed. Frankfurt a.M.: Rütten & Loening.

Wintemute, Robert, and Mads Tønnesson Andenæs, ed. 2001. *Legal Recognition of Same-Sex Partnerships: A Study of National, European, and International Law*. Oxford: Hart Publishing.

Wood, Ian. 2000. The Exchange of Gifts Among the Late Antique Aristocracy. In *El Disco de Teodosio*, ed. Martín Almagro Gorbea, 301–314. Madrid: Real Academia de la Historia.

Wright, Robert Alderson (Baron). 1936. Ought the Doctrine of Consideration to be Abolished from the Common Law? *Harvard Law Review* 49: 1225–1253.

Yorio, Edward, and Steve Thel. 1991. The Promissory Basis of Section 90. *Yale Law Journal* 101: 111–167.

Yver, Jean. 1966. *Égalité entre héritiers et exclusion des enfants dotés: Essai de géographie coutumière*. Paris: Sirey.

Zelizer, Viviana A. Rotman. 1994. *The Social Meaning of Money*. New York: Basic Books.

Zimmermann, Reinhard. 1990. *The Law of Obligations: Roman Foundations of the Civilian Tradition*. Cape Town: Juta.

Zinman, Seth D. 1994. Judging Gift Rules by Their Wrappings—Towards a Clearer Articulation of Federal Employee Gift-Acceptance Rules. *Catholic University Law Review* 44: 141–204.

Zöllner, Wolfgang. 1982. *Wertpapierrecht: Ein Studienbuch*. Juristische Kurz-Lehrbücher. München: Beck.

Zweigert, Konrad. 1964. Seriositätsindizien: Rechtsvergleichende Bemerkungen zur Scheidung verbindlicher Geschäfte von unverbindlichen. *Juristenzeitung* [JZ] 19: 349–354.

Zweigert, Konrad, and Hein Kötz. 1998. *An Introduction to Comparative Law*. Trans. Tony Weir. 3rd ed. Oxford: Clarendon Press.

3. STATUTORY AND RELATED MATERIAL

Entries are arranged in reverse chronological order by jurisdiction. Code provisions are not listed.

European Law

Council of Bars and Law Societies of Europe. 2006. Code of Conduct for European Lawyers.

Belgium

Law reforming divorce (*réformant le divorce*) of 27 Apr. 2007. *Moniteur belge*, 7 June 2007.

Law modifying the law of 13 June 1986 concerning the removal and transplantation of organs (*modifiant la loi du 13 juin 1986 sur le prélèvement et la transplantation d'organes*) of 25 Feb. 2007. *Moniteur belge*, 13 Apr. 2007.

Law abrogating legal interdiction (*supprimant l'interdiction légale*) of 22 Nov. 2004. *Moniteur belge*, 9 Dec. 2004.

Program-law (*Loi-programme*) of 22 Dec. 2003. *Moniteur belge*, 31 Dec. 2003.

Law establishing legal cohabitation (*instaurant la cohabitation légale*) of 23 Nov. 1998. *Moniteur belge*, 12 Jan. 1999.

Law abrogating Penal Code arts. 387 and 390 concerning adultery (*abrogeant les articles 387 et 390 du Code pénal en matière d'adultère*) of 20 May 1987. *Moniteur belge*, 12 June 1987.

Law modifying various legal norms regarding filiation (*modifiant diverses dispositions légales relatives à la filiation*) of 31 Mar. 1987. *Moniteur belge*, 27 May 1987.

Order organizing the manner for expressing the intent of the donor or of the persons mentioned in art. 10, § 2, of the law of 13 June 1986 concerning the removal and transplantation of organs (*Arrêté royal organisant le mode d'expression de la volonté du donneur ou des personnnes visées à l'article 10, § 2, de la loi du 13 juin 1986 sur le prélèvement et la transplantation d'organes*) of 30 Oct. 1986. *Moniteur belge*, 14 Feb. 1987.

Order organizing the manner of expressing consent to the removal of organs and tissue from living persons (*Arrêté royal organisant le mode d'expression du consentement au prélèvement d'organes et de tissus sur des personnes vivantes*) of 30 Oct. 1986. *Moniteur belge*, 14 Feb. 1987.

Law concerning the removal and transplantation of organs (*sur le prélèvement et la transplantation d'organes*) of 13 June 1986. *Moniteur belge*, 14 Feb. 1987.

Law modifying successoral rights of the surviving spouse (*modifiant les droits successoraux du conjoint survivant*) of 14 May 1981. *Moniteur belge*, 27 May 1981.

Law concerning the respective rights and duties of spouses and matrimonial property (*relative aux droits et devoirs respectifs des époux et aux régimes matrimoniaux*) of 14 July 1976. *Moniteur belge*, 18 Sept. 1976.

Law concerning the respective rights and duties of spouses (*relative aux droits et devoirs respectifs des époux*) of 30 April 1958. *Moniteur belge*, 10 May 1958.

Law extending to all civil persons the benefit of the provisional acceptance of inter vivos gratuitous transfers (*portant extension à toutes les personnes civiles du bénéfice de l'acceptation provisoire des libéralités faites par actes entre vifs*) of 12 July 1931. *Moniteur belge*, 15 July 1931.

Law according civil personality to charitable associations and establishments of public benefit (*accordant la personnalité civile aux associations sans but lucrative et aux établissements d'utilité publique*) of 27 June 1921. *Moniteur belge*, 1 July 1921.

Law establishing conditional release and conditional conviction in the criminal law (*établissant la libération conditionnelle et les condamnations conditionnelles dans le système pénal*) of 31 May 1888. *Moniteur belge*, 3 June 1888.

Law concerning foundations in favor of education or for the benefit of scholarship students (*relative aux fondations en faveur de l'enseignement ou au profit des boursiers*) of 19 Dec.1864. *Moniteur belge*, 24 Dec. 1864.

Law of mortgages (*Loi hypothécaire*) of 16 Dec. 1851. *Moniteur belge*, 22 Dec. 1851.

Law abrogating the law of 20 May 1837 regarding international reciprocity in matters of successions and gifts, replacing arts. 726 and 912 of the civil code (*qui abroge la loi du 20 mai 1837 relative à la réciprocité internationale en matière de successions et de donations, qui remplace les articles 726 et 912 du code civil*) of 27 Apr. 1865. *Moniteur belge*, 28 Apr. 1865.

France

Law no. 2007-308 promulgating reform of legal protection for adult incompetents (*portant réforme de la protection juridique des majeurs*) of 5 Mar. 2007. *Journal officiel*, 7 Mar., p. 4325.

Law no. 2006-728 promulgating reforms to successions and gratuitous transfers (*portant réforme des successions et des libéralités*) of 24 June 2006. *Journal officiel*, 24 June, p. 9513.

Order no. 2005-856 concerning simplification of the regime of gratuitous transfers made to associations, foundations, and congregations, of certain administrative declarations required by associations, and modification of the obligations of associations and foundations concerning their annual financial statements (*portant simplification du régime des libéralités consenties aux associations, fondations et congrégations, de certaines déclarations administratives incombant aux associations, et modification des obligations des associations et fondations relatives à leurs comptes annuels*) of 28 July 2005. *Journal officiel*, 29 July, p. 12350.

Law no. 2004-439 concerning divorce (*relative au divorce*) of 26 May 2004. *Journal officiel*, 27 May, p. 9319.

Decree no. 2002-449 concerning simplification of the administrative procedure applicable to bequests in favor of the state, the departments, the communes and of their establishments and the associations, foundations, and congregations and to control transfers by associations or foundations recognized to be of public utility (*portant simplification de la procédure administrative applicable aux legs en faveur de l'État, des départements, des communes et de leurs établissements et des associations, fondations et congrégations et au contrôle des actes de disposition des associations ou fondations reconnues d'utilité publique*) of 2 Apr. 2002. *Journal officiel*, 4 Apr., p. 5912.

Law no. 2002-305 concerning parental authority (*relative à l'autorité parentale*) of 4 Mar. 2002. *Journal officiel*, 5 Mar., p. 4161.

Law no. 2001-1135 concerning the rights of the surviving spouse and of children of adulterous relationships and modernizing various norms of successions law (*relative aux droits du conjoint survivant et des enfants adultérins et modernissant diverses dispositions de droit successoral*) of 3 Dec. 2001. *Journal officiel*, 4 Dec., p. 19279.

Law no. 2001-504 intended to reinforce the prevention and repression of sectarian movements that violate human rights and fundamental freedoms (*tendant à renforcer la prévention et la répression des mouvements sectaires portant atteinte aux droits de l'homme et aux libertés fondamentales*) of 12 June 2001. *Journal officiel*, 13 June, p. 9337.

Law no. 99-944 concerning the Civil Solidarity Pact (*relative au pacte civil de solidarité*) of 15 Nov. 1999. *Journal officiel*, 16 Nov., p. 16959.

Law no. 89-475 concerning the care provided for consideration by individuals in their homes to the aged or disabled adults (*relative à l'accueil par des particuliers, à leur domicile, à titre onéreux, de personnes âgées ou handicapées adultes*) of 10 July 1989. *Journal officiel*, 12 July, p. 8761.

Law no. 87-571 concerning the development of patronage in the arts (*sur le developpement du mécénat*) of 23 July 1987. *Journal officiel*, 24 July, p. 8255.

Law no. 79-1181 concerning the removal of human organs (*relative aux prélèvements d'organes*) of 22 Dec. 1976. *Journal officiel*, 23 Dec., p. 7365.

Law no. 72-3 concerning filiation (*sur la filiation*) of 3 January 1972. *Journal officiel*, 5 Jan., p. 145.

Law no. 66-1012 modifying art. 1007 of the civil code regarding the handwritten will and art. 9 of the law of 25 Ventôse of Year XI containing the organization of the public notary (*modifiant l'article 1007 du code civil relatif au testament olographe et l'article 9 de la loi du 25 ventôse an XI contenant organization du notariat*) of 28 Dec. 1966. *Journal officiel*, 29 Dec., p. 11626.

Decree no. 66-388 concerning the supervision of associations, foundations, and congregations (*relatif à la tutelle administrative des associations, fondations et congregations*) of 13 June 1966. *Journal officiel*, 17 June, p. 4870.

Decree no. 55-22 reforming the real property recording acts (*portant réforme de la publicité foncière*) of 4 Jan. 1955. *Journal officiel*, 7 Jan., p. 346.

Law modifying arts. 4 and 5 of the law of 24 May 1825 concerning female congregations (*tendant à modifier les art. 4 et 5 de la loi du 24 mai 1825 sur les congregations de femmes*) of 30 May 1941. *Journal officiel*, 5 June.

Law modifying the texts of the civil code concerning the capacity of married women (*portant modification des texts du code civil relatifs à la capacité de la femme mariée*) of 18 Feb. 1938. *Journal officiel*, 19 Feb.

Law no. 40484 concerning the contract of association (*relative au contrat d'association*) of 1 July 1901. *Journal officiel*, 2 July.

Law no. 39559 concerning the administrative supervision of gifts and bequests (*sur la tutelle administrative en matière de dons et legs*) of 4–6 Feb. 1901. *Journal officiel*, 6 Feb.

Law no. 14,221 concerning municipal organization (*sur l'organisation municipale*) of 5–6 Apr. 1884. *Journal officiel*, 6 Apr.

Law no. 10,713 concerning the form of notarial acts (*sur la forme des actes notariés*) of 21 June 1843. *Bulletin des lois*, no. 1015.

Law no. 921 concerning the authorization and legal existence of congregations and religious communities of women (*relative à l'autorisation et à l'existence légale des Congrégations et Communautés religieuses de femmes*) of 24 May 1825. *Bulletin des lois*, no. 40.

Laws and Decrees Promulgated during the French Revolution

Law providing for the organization of the profession of the notary (*contenant organisation du notariat*) of 25 Ventôse XI [16 Mar. 1803]. In Duvergier 14: 16–39.

Law concerning gratuitous transfers done by inter vivos act or last will and testament (*concernant les libéralités par actes entre-vifs ou de dernière volonté*) of 4 Germinal VIII [25 Mar. 1800]. In Duvergier 12: 169–170.

Law concerning recording (*sur l'enregistrement*) of 22 Frimaire VII [12 Dec. 1798]. In Duvergier 11: 90–135.

Law regarding the regime of mortgages (*sur le régime hypothécaire*) of 11 Brumaire VII [1 Nov. 1798]. In Duvergier 11: 12–27.

Law concerning successions (*relative aux successions*) of 18 Pluviôse V [6 Feb. 1797].
In Duvergier 9: 275-278.

Decree concerning the abrogation of the retroactive effect of the laws [decrees] of 5 and
12 Brumaire and 17 Nivôse of Year II regarding successions, gifts, etc. (*relatif à
l'abolition de l'effect retroactif des lois des 5 et 12 brumaire et du 17 nivose an 2, concernant
les successions, donations, etc.*) of 3 Vendémiaire IV [25 Sept. 1795]. In Duvergier
8: 289.

Decree providing that the terms of the decrees of 5 Brumaire and 17 Nivôse concerning
successions will take effect only from the date of their promulgation (*portant que les
dispositions de ceux des 5 brumaire et 17 nivose sur les successions, n'auront d'effet que du
jour de leur promulgation*) of 9 Fructidor III [26 Aug. 1795]. In Duvergier 8: 246.

Decree suspending all actions based on the retroactive effect of the Law [Decree] of 17
Nivôse concerning successions (*qui suspend toute action intentée d'après l'effet rétroactif
de la loi du 17 nivôse sur les successions*) of 5 Floréal III [24 Apr. 1795]. In Duvergier
8: 94.

Law concerning various questions related to gifts, successions, and substitutions (*sur
diverses questions relatives aux donations, successions et substitutions*) of 9 Fructidor II
[26 Aug. 1794]. In Duvergier 7: 255-260.

Decree providing that there are no grounds for reconsideration of various questions
related to the Decree of last 17 Nivôse (*portant qu'il n'y a pas lieu à délibérer sur diverses
questions relatives au décret du 17 Nivôse dernier*) of 22 Ventôse II [12 Mar. 1794].
In Duvergier 7: 97–105.

Decree relating to gifts and successions (*relatif aux donations et successions*) of 17–21
Nivôse II [6–10 Jan. 1794]. In Duvergier 6: 373–384.

Decree concerning gifts, pensions, and bequests made since 14 July 1789 (*relatif aux
dons, pensions et legs faits depuis le 14 juillet 1789*) of 5–7 Frimaire II [25–27 Nov. 1793].
In Duvergier 6: 303.

Decree containing several provisions concerning civil acts and contracts (*contenant
plusieurs dispositions relatives aux actes et contrats civils*) of 5 Brumaire II [26 Oct. 1793].
In Duvergier 6: 256–257.

Decree concerning the punishment of émigrés (*concernant les peines portées contre les
émigrés*) of 28 Mar.–5 Apr. 1793. In Duvergier 5: 218–228.

Decree abolishing the power to make gratuitous transfers to direct descendants (*qui
abolit la faculté de tester en ligne directe*) of 7–11 Mar. 1793. In Duvergier 5: 185.

Decree requiring a report concerning equality in the distribution of decedents' estates
(*pour faire un rapport concernant l'égalité des partages dans les successions*) of
5 Mar. 1793. In Duvergier 5: 182.

Decree abolishing entailment (*qui abolit les substitutions*) of 14–15 Nov. 1792. In
Duvergier 5: 44–45.

Decree concerning feudal privileges (*relatif aux droits féodaux*) of 25 Aug. 1792.
In Duvergier 4: 355–358.

Decree concerning the abolition of various signorial rights, notably those that were
previously attached to signorial justice and the means of redeeming rights deemed
redeemable (*concernant l'abolition de plusieurs droits seigneuriaux, notamment de ceux
qui étaient ci-devant annexés à la justice seigneuriale, et le mode de rachat de ceux qui ont
été déclarés rachetables*) of 13–20 Apr. 1791. In Duvergier 2: 295–302.

Decree concerning the distribution of intestate estates (*relatif au partage des successions ab
intestat*) of 8–15 Apr. 1791. In Duvergier 2: 287–288.

Decree concerning abolition of the right of escheat, of the right of confiscation, and elimination of the procedures related to these rights (*portant abolition du droit d'aubaine, de détraction, et extinction des procédures relatives à ces droits*) of 6–18 Aug. 1790. In Duvergier 1: 272–273.

Decree concerning the capacity of members of religious communities who have left their institutions to inherit to the exclusion of the taxing authority and to dispose of their property, and concerning the rights and obligations of such members who will live together (*sur la capacité des religieux sortis du cloître, pour hériter à l'exclusion du fisc et pour disposer de leurs biens, et sur la jouissance et les obligations des religieux qui vivront en commun*) of 19–26 Mar. 1790. In Duvergier 1: 125.

Decree concerning feudal privilege (*relatif aux droits féodaux*) of 15–28 Mar. 1790. In Duvergier 1: 114–121.

Decree declaring the successoral incapacity of members of religious communities who have left their institutions (*qui déclare incapables de successions les religieux sortis de leurs maisons*) of 20 Feb.–26 Mar. 1790. In Duvergier 1: 101.

LAWS AND ORDINANCES OF THE ANCIEN RÉGIME

Ordinance concerning gifts (*sur les donations*) of 1731. In Isambert and Jourdan no. 415, 21: 343–354.

Ordinance concerning the complaints of the estates assembled in Paris in 1614, and of the assembly of notables held in Rouen and Paris in 1617 and 1626 (*sur les plaintes des états assemblés à Paris en 1614, et de l'assemblée des notables réunis à Rouen et à Paris, en 1617 et 1626*) [Code Michaud] of 1629. In Isambert and Jourdan no. 162, 16: 225–342.

Edict concerning festivals and banquets (*des festins & banquets*) of 1563. In Terrien 151–152.

Ordinance [of Moulins] concerning legal reform (*sur la réforme de la justice*) of 1566. In Isambert and Jourdan no. 110, 14: 189–212.

Ordinance [of Villers-Cotterêts] concerning acts of justice (*sur le fait de la justice*) of 1539. In Isambert and Jourdan no. 188, 12: 600–40.

Germany

Law concerning the regulation of the legal status of provincial officials (*Gesetz zur Regelung des Statusrechts der Beamtinnen und Beamten in den Ländern—Beamtenstatusgesetz* [BeamtStG]) of 17 June 2008. *Bundesgesetzblatt* I 1010.

Social Code XII—Public assistance (*Sozialgesetzbuch XII—Sozialhilfe*) of 27 Dec. 2003. *Bundesgesetzblatt* I 3022.

Law concerning federal officials (*Bundesbeamtengesetz* [BBG]) of 31 Mar. 1999. *Bundesgesetzblatt* I 675.

Law governing blood transfusions (*Gesetz zur Regelung des Transfusionswesens—Transfusionsgesetz* [TFG]) of 1 July 1998. *Bundesgesetzblatt* I 1752.

Law concerning the donation, removal, and transfer of organs (*Gesetz über die Spende, Entnahme und Übertragung von Organen—Transplantationsgesetz* [TPG]) of 5 Nov. 1997. *Bundesgesetzblatt* I 2631.

Law concerning judges in Germany (*Deutsches Richtergesetz*) of 19 April 1972. *Bundesgesetzblatt* I 713.

Federal law concerning lawyers (*Bundesrechtsanwaltsordnung* [BRAO]) of 1 Aug. 1959. *Bundesgesetzblatt* I 565.

Framework law for the unification of the law governing civil servants (*Rahmengesetz zur Vereinheitlichung des Beamtenrechts* [BRRG]) of 1 July 1957. *Bundesgesetzblatt* I 667.

India

Transplantation of Human Organs Act (LIXF of 1992).
Hindu Succession Act (XXX of 1956).
Transfer of Property Act (IV of 1882).
Contract Act (IX of 1872).

Israel

Gift Law 5728-1968. *Laws of the State of Israel* [LSI] 22: 113.

Italy

Law no. 192, modifying art. 13 of Law no. 127 of 15 May 1997 and art. 473 of the civil code (*Modifica dell'articulo 13 della legge 15 maggio 1997, n. 127, e dell'articulo 473 del codice civile*) of 22 June 2000. *Gazzetta Ufficiale*, 12 July, no. 161.

Decree concerning the removal and transplantation of organs and tissue, implementing limitations periods relating to the declaration of intent regarding the gift of organs for the purpose of transplant (*Disposizione in materia de prelievi e di trapianti di organi e di tessuti, attuativo delle prescrizioni relative alla dichiarazione di volontà dei cittadini sulla donazione di organi a scopo di trapianto*) of 8 Apr. 2000. *Gazzetta Ufficiale*, 15 Apr., no. 89.

Law no. 91 concerning the removal and transplantation of organs and tissue (*Disposizioni in materia di prelievi e di trapianti di organi e di tessuti*) of 1 Apr. 1999. *Gazzetta Ufficiale*, 15 Apr., no. 87.

Law no. 127 concerning urgent measures for the simplification of administrative action and of decision and inspection procedures (*Misure urgenti per lo snellimento dell'attività amministrativa e dei procedimenti di decisione e di controllo*) of 15 May 1997. *Gazzetta Ufficiale*, 17 May, no. 113.

Law no. 301 concerning the removal and grafting of corneas (*Norme in materia di prelievi ed innesti di cornea*) of 12 Aug. 1993. *Gazzetta Ufficiale*, 17 Aug., no. 192.

Law no. 184 concerning adoption and the foster care of minors (*Disciplina dell'adozione e dell'affidamento dei minori*) of 4 May 1983. *Gazzetta Ufficiale*, 17 May, no. 133 special issue.

Law no. 151 on the reform of family law (*Riforma del diritto di famiglia*) of 19 May 1975. *Gazzetta Ufficiale*, 23 May, no. 135 special edition.

Law no. 458 concerning kidney transplant among living persons (*Trapianto del rene tra persone viventi*) of 26 June 1967. *Gazzetta Ufficiale*, 27 June, no. 160 special edition.

Decree no. 267 concerning the regime of bankruptcy, agreements among creditors, estate administration, and mandatory liquidation (*Disciplina del fallimento, del concordato preventivo, dell'amministrazione controllata e della liquidazione coatta amministrativa*) of 16 Mar. 1942. *Gazzetta Ufficiale*, 6 Apr., no. 81.

Law no. 848 concerning ecclesiastical entities and also concerning the civil administration of patrimonies intended for religious purposes (*Disposizioni sugli Enti ecclesiastici e sulle Amministrazioni civili dei patrimoni destinati a fini di culto*) of 27 May 1929. *Gazzetta Ufficiale*, 8 June, no. 133.

Law no. 89 concerning the organization of the public notary and of notarial archives (*Sull'ordinamento del notariato e degli archivi notarili*) of 16 Feb. 1913. *Gazzetta Ufficiale*, 7 Mar., no. 55.

Nepal

Law no. 19 on Gifts and Donations (*Dan Bakas Ko*) of 1963, Muluki Ain (Legal Code) Part III, p. 156.

Spain

Law no. 10 concerning the fourth book of the Civil Code of Catalonia relating to successions law (*del libro cuarto del Código civil de Cataluña, relativo a las sucesiones*) of 10 July 2008. *Boletín Oficial del Estado*, 7 Aug. 2008, no. 190.

Decree no. 2070 regulating the removal and clinical use of human organs and territorial coordination with regard to the donation and transplantation of organs and tissue (*Regula las actividades de obtención y utilización clínica de órganos humanos y la coordinación territorial en materia de donación y trasplante de órganos y tejidos*) of 30 Dec. 1999. *Boletín Oficial del Estado*, 4 Jan. 2000, no. 3.

Law no. 11 modifying the Civil Code in matters of filiation, parental authority, and the economic regime of marriage (*Modificación del Código Civil en materia de filiación, patria potestad y régimen económico del matrimonio*) of 13 May 1981. *Boletín Oficial del Estado*, 19 May, no. 119.

Law no. 30 concerning organ removal and transplantation (*Extracción y trasplante de órganos*) of 27 Oct. 1979. *Boletín Oficial del Estado*, 6 Nov., no. 266.

Law concerning the organization of the public notary (*para el arreglo del Notariado*) of 28 May 1862. *Gaceta de Madrid*, 29 May.

REGIONAL LAWS

ARAGON: Law no. 2 concerning the marital property regime and widowhood (*de Régimen Económico Matrimonial y Viudedad*) of 12 Feb. 2003. *Boletín Oficial del Estado*, 13 Mar., no. 62.

United Kingdom

The Human Tissue Act 2004 (Persons who Lack Capacity to Consent and Transplants), Regulations 2006, no. 1659.

Civil Partnership Act 2004, c. 33.

Human Tissue Act 2004, c. 30.

Human Fertilisation and Embryology Act 1990, c. 37.

Law of Property (Miscellaneous Provisions) Act 1989, c. 34.

Family Law Reform Act 1987, c. 42.

Companies Act 1985, c. 6.

Mental Health Act 1983, c. 20.

Law Reform (Miscellaneous Provisions) Act 1970, c. 33.

Stock Transfer Act 1963, c. 18.

Charities Act 1960, c. 58.

Law Reform (Married Women and Tortfeasors) Act 1935, c. 30.

Law of Property Act 1925, c. 20.

Mortmain and Charitable Uses Act 1891, c. 73.

Bills of Sale Act 1878, c. 31.
Supreme Court of Judicature Act 1873, c. 66.
Policies of Assurance Act 1867, c. 144.
Companies Clauses Consolidation Act 1845, c. 16.
East India Company Act 1781, c. 70.
Mortmain Act (Act to restrain the Disposition of Lands) 1736, c. 36.
Statute of Frauds 1677, c. 3.
Statute of Westminster (*Quia emptores*) 1290.
Statute of Mortmain (*de viris religiosis*) 1279.
Magna Carta (9 Hen. III) 1225.

United States of America

FEDERAL LEGISLATION

Banks and Banking, U.S.C.A. title 12 (1994).
National Organ Transplant Act, U.S.C.A. title 42 (1984).
The Congress, U.S.C.A. title 2 (1993).
Revenue Act 1935, Pub. L. No. 74-407, 49 Stat. 1014.

UNIFORM LAWS

Uniform Power of Attorney Act 2006, www.law.upenn.edu/bll/archives/ulc/
    dpoaa/2008_final.htm.
Uniform Anatomical Gift Act 2006, revised 2008, www.anatomicalgiftact.org/
    DesktopDefault.aspx?tabindex=1&tabid=63.
Uniform Probate Code 2004, amended 2008, www.nccusl.org, or www.law.upenn.edu/
    bll/ulc/upc/final2005.htm.
Uniform Parentage Act 2000, revised 2002, 9B *Uniform Laws Annotated* [U.L.A.]
    4 (Cum. Ann. Pocket Pt. 2005).
Uniform Disclaimer of Property Interests 1999, amended 2002 and 2006, 8A U.L.A.
    159 (2003).
Uniform Nonprobate Transfers on Death Act 1989, 8B U.L.A. 57, 79 (2001).
Uniform Multiple-Person Accounts Act 1989, 8B U.L.A. 7, 19–22 (2001).
Uniform Anatomical Gift Act 1987, 8A U.L.A. 3 (2003).
Uniform Fraudulent Transfer Act 1984, 7A U.L.A., Pt. II, 266 (1999).
Uniform Marital Property Act 1983, 9A U.L.A., Pt. I, 103 (1998).
Uniform Transfers to Minors Act 1983, 8C U.L.A. 1 (2001).
Uniform Durable Power of Attorney Act 1979, 8A U.L.A. 233 (2003).
Uniform Anatomical Gift Act 1968, 8A U.L.A. 69 (2003).
Uniform Gifts to Minors Act 1966, 8A U.L.A. 420 (1993), 9B U.L.A. 25 (Cum. Ann.
    Pocket Pt. 2005).
Uniform Gifts to Minors Act 1956, 8A U.L.A. 420 (1993).
Uniform Stock Transfer Act 1909, 6 U.L.A. 1 (1922).

MODEL ACTS AND MODEL RULES

ABA Model Rules of Professional Conduct 1983 (Chicago 2003).
Revised Model Business Corporation Act 1984 (Englewood Cliffs 1994).
ABA Model Code of Professional Responsibility 1969 (Chicago 1982).
Model Business Corporation Act Annotated (2d ed. 1971).
Model Written Obligations Act 1925, 9C U.L.A. 378 (1957).

RESTATEMENTS AND PRINCIPLES

Restatement of the Law (Third) of Property (Wills and Other Donative Transfers) (2003).
Restatement of the Law (Third) of Trusts (2003).
Principles of the Law of Family Dissolution: Analysis and Recommendations (2002).
Restatement (Third) of the Law Governing Lawyers (2000).
Principles of Corporate Governance 1992 (1994).
Restatement of the Law (Second) of Property (Donative Transfers) (1992).
Restatement of the Law (Second) of Contracts (1981).
Restatement of the Law (Second) of Trusts (1959).
Restatement of the Law of Restitution (1937).
Restatement of the Law of Property (Future Interests) (1936).
Restatement of the Law of Contracts (1932).

STATE LAW

CALIFORNIA: California Canons of Judicial Ethics 2005, www.courtinfo.ca.gov/rules/
appendix/appdiv2.pdf.
DELAWARE: General Corporation Law, Delaware Code Ann., tit. 8, vol. 4 (2001).
FLORIDA: Domestic Relations, West's Florida Stats. Ann., tit. 43, vol. 21A (2005).
ILLINOIS: Illinois Trust and Payable on Death Accounts Act 1991, West's Smith-Hurd Ill.
Compiled Stats. Ann., Chap. 205 (1991), amended by Public Act 92-285 § 5 (2002);
Illinois Code of Professional Responsibility, 107 Ill.2d 604, 645 (1987); Illinois Code
of Judicial Conduct, 107 Ill.2d 232, 272–73 (1987); Probate Act 1975, West's Smith-
Hurd Ill. Compiled Stats. Ann., Chap. 755 (1992).
INDIANA: Probate, Burns Indiana Stats. Ann., tit. 29 (2000).
KANSAS: Legislature, Kansas Stats. Ann., chap. 46, vol. 3B (2000).
MICHIGAN: Student Athletes and the Receipt of Money Act of 1988, Michigan Stats. Ann.
§ 600.2968 (West 2004); Revised Judicature Act 1961, Michigan Compiled Laws
Ann., chap. 600 (2000).
MISSISSIPPI: Regulation of Trade, Commerce and Investments, West's Ann. Mississippi
Code, tit. 75, vol. 25 (1999).
NEW MEXICO: Trials, West's New Mexico Stats. Ann., chap. 38, vol. 12 (2003).
NEW YORK: Banking Law, McKinney's Consolidated Laws of New York Ann., chap. 2, bk.
4 (2001).
PENNSYLVANIA: Statute of Frauds, Purdon's Pennsylvania Stats. and Consolidated Stats.
Ann., tit. 33 (1997); Canons of Judicial Ethics, 425 Pa. xxiii (1965).

INDEX

Numbers refer to paragraphs, not pages.

A

acceptance of gifts, 1034–1060, 1337
  common law, 1052–1059
    England, 1056–1057
    India, 1053–1055
    presumptions, 1052, 1325
    United States, 1058–1059
  Constantine, constitution on, 738
  France and Belgium, 1035–1042, 1332
    associations, authorization for, 511
    exceptions to express acceptance, 1041
    express acceptance, 1037
    gifts to unborn children, 444
    notification of, 1038, 1042
    renunciation of, 1069–1070
    when effective, 1039
  Germany, 1049–1051, 1329, 1337
  Italy, 1043–1045
    associations, authorization for, 520–521
    gifts to unborn children, 454
  Spain, 1046–1048
acknowledgment of a debt, as a gift
  France, 329
    as indirect gift, 675, 835
  Germany
    form requirement, 665
adopted children, revocation upon the birth of a child
  France and Belgium, 1241, 1242
  Italy, 1247, 1251
  Spain, 1255
adulterous relationships, gifts to children of, 531–536, 537, 558–560, 637
adultery
  cohabitation and, 558–562, 566, 568, 573, 574–575, 581–582

  revocation for ingratitude, 1131, 1140, 1150, 1159
  testamentary bequests and (Germany), 574
adult incompetents
  capacity to give, 404–410
    civil law, 406
    common law, 405
    durable power of attorney, 410
    England, 405, 407
    France, 407
    Germany, 406, 407, 410
    gifts by the ward, 407
    gifts by the guardian, 408
    Italy, 406, 407
    role of the courts, 409
    United States, 405, 407
  customary gifts (Italy), 766
Aeneid, 33
agonistic gift exchange, 16, 37
Aguesseau, Henri François d', 2, 44.
  See also Ordinance of 1731 (France)
  drafting the Ordinance of 1731, 292, 444
  on gifts of all the donor's property, 387
  on gifts to legal persons, 503
  on the inventory requirement, 778
  on manual gifts, 780, 785, 795
  on the meaning of *Donner et retenir*, 1079
  on the notarial act, 743, 774
Albaladejo García, Manuel
  on gifts of future property, 369
  on gifts of movables, 848, 849
  on gifts of rights, 850
  on irrevocability, 1103
  on the revocation of remunerative gifts, 1172

Numbers refer to paragraphs, not pages.

Numbers refer to paragraphs, not pages.

Numbers refer to paragraphs, not pages.

Numbers refer to paragraphs, not pages.

Numbers refer to paragraphs, not pages.

Numbers refer to paragraphs, not pages.

Numbers refer to paragraphs, not pages.

Numbers refer to paragraphs, not pages.

Numbers refer to paragraphs, not pages.

Numbers refer to paragraphs, not pages.

Numbers refer to paragraphs, not pages.

Numbers refer to paragraphs, not pages.

Numbers refer to paragraphs, not pages.

Numbers refer to paragraphs, not pages.

Numbers refer to paragraphs, not pages.